Personality Theories
A Comparative Analysis

Personality Theories

A Comparative Analysis

Fifth Edition

Salvatore R. Maddi

Professor of Psychology in Social Ecology
University of California, Irvine

BROOKS/COLE PUBLISHING COMPANY
Pacific Grove, California

I⟨T⟩P ™ The trademark ITP is used under license.

Sponsoring editor: *Paul E. O'Connell*
Project editor: *Jane Lightell*
Production manager: *Stephen K. Emry*
Cover Design: *Maureen McCutcheon*
Compositor: *Weimer Typesetting Co., Inc.*
Printer: *Arcata Graphics/Kingsport*

Library of Congress Cataloging-in-Publication Data

Maddi, Salvatore R.
    Personality theories : a comparative analysis / Salvatore, R.
Maddi.—5th ed.
    p.   cm.
    Bibliography
    Includes index.
    ISBN 0-534-10696-X
    Former ISBN 0-256-03245-9
    1. Personality.   I. Title.
BF698.M237 1989
155.2—dc19   88-1607

Printed in the United States of America
10 9 8 7 6 5 4

Preface

I am so pleased that this book has been useful enough to enter its fifth edition. Over the years, many students and teachers have gone out of their way to tell me of its value for them. This has affirmed for me the utility of a comparative analysis of personality approaches. You will find the main features of this analysis still there: Once explicated, theories are compared and contrasted in order to illuminate the overall models of human behavior they express, and then rational and empirical efforts are made to resolve the issues separating these models. The overall aim of this analysis is to help people think through the most promising views of personality.

Despite the persistence of a comparative analytic approach, this edition includes many changes. The chapters on personality research methods and on assessment and psychotherapy are wholly new. They add the concreteness of procedure and application to what was a more abstract emphasis on theory before. The other changes involve extensive updating of theoretical and research sections. Overall, the fifth edition is a more complete and current comparison of personality approaches than were the earlier versions.

These days the trend in teaching personality is away from theories and toward research findings. In various ways we are told that the comprehensive personality theories are too vague and interpretive—the leftovers of a previous, prescientific age in psychology. We are also told that the findings of personality research, however fragmentary and simplified they may be, are the only sound basis for teaching. The end result of this trend is courses that emphasize seemingly unrelated topics overly defined by the research designs and assessment methods employed, with the whole person quite lost from view. This amounts to throwing the baby out with the bath water.

From its very beginning, this book was intended as an alternative to uncritical theoretical emphases, on the one hand, and fragmentary research emphases on the other. I still maintain that it is not only possible but also profitable to wed theory and research, and that a ready mechanism for this is comparative analysis. In this approach, research becomes theory-relevant and theory becomes rigorous and empirically sound. The person emerges clearly and the requirements of science are served.

My book takes existing comprehensive theories of personality as a starting point, not out of any undue reverence for the past, but because these seminal views would only be reinvented soon if they were to be discarded. In any event, my emphasis is less on them as individual bodies of thought to be preserved as such than it is on the underlying models of personality that they reveal. Although the three models that emerge may not be exhaustive, they are generic enough to have withstood the test of time. The issues separating these models provide an integrative structure for our notoriously fragmented personality field. And when efforts are mounted to resolve these issues by reason and research, a future of changing, ever-improving personality knowledge is approached.

In some circles, previous editions of this book gained the reputation of being difficult for undergraduates to understand. This was certainly not my intent. The organization of the book into clearly marked sections and subsections facilitates varied organizations and uses—some things can be emphasized and others omitted. Care is taken to indicate why material is included and placed where it is. Readers are encouraged to bring their own experience to bear in appreciating theoretical points. The overall thrust of approaches that lends organization to the parts is elaborated. Most important, readers are treated to a frame of reference concerning the parts of a personality theory, the models for human behavior that pertain, and the relevance of personality research. Over the years I have talked with many undergraduate students who have used my book. Their message is that although the vocabulary and information to which they are exposed is demanding, they find themselves learning so much that is becomes exciting. Rather than engage in the dry task of memorizing facts, they master principles from which they can derive the necessary knowledge. Through the conversational style of the book, they feel in dialogue with me even if someone else is teaching the course. Many report that what they learned stayed with them and informed their functioning even much later. That so many readers took the trouble to contact me is very gratifying.

So I encourage you not to turn away from this book because it may appear formidable. Give it a chance, as others have to their benefit. You should also know that the fifth edition has been simplified for style and vocabulary. I guess that on growing older, I cherish ease and directness of communication more than before.

The fifth edition could not have been prepared without the diligent work of my secretary, Beverly McKinney, that master of the word processor. I also thank my editor, Paul O'Connell, who kept me working, and my colleagues Carol Whalen and Wendy Goldberg for valuable editorial and factual help. I also owe a great debt to my students over the years for their enthusiasm and criticism, which has improved this book with each edition.

Salvatore R. Maddi

Contents

List of Figures and Tables

CHAPTER 1

Personality and Personology

The many available books on personality fall into two main categories: benevolent eclecticism and partisan zealotry. A book written from the standpoint of *benevolent eclecticism* tends to include many theories of personality, each given relatively equal space. When the book is good, you are made to understand why the theorist felt compelled to make the stated assumptions. Theory follows theory neatly in the discussion, with little concern for the possible incompatibilities organized between the two covers. An air of humility permeates the whole endeavor. The writer does not claim to be worthy of resolving the differences of opinion and assumption existing among the theorists. He or she justifies the presentation by saying that it is valuable just to present the various theories in demonstrating the richness of the field and that the existing differences of opinion are currently beyond our meager power to resolve by reason or experiment. Sometimes we are even given the pious assurance that someday, in a glorious future of comprehensive knowledge, it will be clear which theory is best. At other times the writer doubts that any particular theory will emerge victorious, as if theorizing were no more than a perpetual game, engaged in primarily as a stimulant.

In the benevolently eclectic approach, it is assumed that all theorists are entitled to be heard and appreciated simply because they theorize. Sometimes in such books there is even a place—usually a final, short chapter—in which a bit of attention is given to cataloging the similarities and differences among the various theories. But the aim here is to ensure that the reader will grasp the essential meaning of each theory, not to provide springboards to further analysis. When empirical research is included in such books, it only illustrates individual theories; it does not bear on the crucial differences among them. Good examples of benevolent eclecticism are *Introduction to Theories of Personality* by Hall and Lindzey (1985) and *Personality: Theory, Assessment and Research* by Pervin (1970). Most books in which an editor brings together the writings of many authors also fall into this category.

The book written with *partisan zealotry* contrasts sharply with what I have just described. By intent, such books express one—and only one—approach to personality. The topics considered, research presented, and conclusions reached are all predictable from the assumptions of the approach. The writer sometimes adopts a polemical style aimed at persuading the reader that the writer's viewpoint is best. Other viewpoints are either badly slighted or included only to be criticized. When such books are done well, they provide the reader with a vivid account of a theory. When done poorly, they are ludicrously one-sided, misinterpreting other theories or willfully insulating the reader against any possibility of recognizing another point of view. Some representative examples are *Personality: Dynamics and Development* by Sarnoff (1962), *Pattern and Growth in Personality* by Allport (1961), and *Personality: A Behavioral Analysis* by Lundin (1974).

It has become more common in recent years for personality textbooks to appear nontheoretical. They emphasize research and present conclusions in terms of facts rather than assumptions. In such books, comprehensive theories are abhorred on the grounds that they are subscientific or merely speculative. Actually, it is not possible to do research without having some theory in mind. Given this widely accepted conclusion among scientists, it seems better to make one's theory explicit than to pretend that no theorizing has occurred.

Once one perceives the implicit theorizing in seemingly nontheoretical personality textbooks, they will generally fall into either the benevolent eclecticism or partisan zealotry camps. Those that show benevolent eclecticism may try to fit various research themes together with little concern for possible incompatibilities. Because these research themes are listed as "examples" of work being done, they need not be compared and contrasted. And partisan textbooks that avoid theoretical elaboration are no less zealous because their underlying assumptions are implicit.

It is surprising that so many of the available books on personality fall into one of these two categories, because there is another clear possibility having obvious value. This third type of book transcends the limitations of benevolent eclecticism and partisan zealotry while showing some similarity to each. From benevolent eclecticism, it borrows the breadth and balance necessary for considering many theories of personality; from partisan zealotry, it borrows the conviction that some theories are better than others. The overall aim of this third kind of book, which I call *comparative analysis,* is to uncover the similarities and differences among many existing approaches to personality as a starting point for determining which type of approach is the most fruitful. Such comparison helps clarify the issues separating the various types of theorizing. Once these issues are posed, rational and empirical analyses can be conducted to determine which types of theorizing are best. In such a book, the purpose of including research is to help delineate the important issues separating the various approaches. Comparative analysis should be comprehensive, orderly, and evaluative in searching for improved understanding. This book is an example of this approach.

Several books that have appeared since this one was first offered in 1968 seem to have adopted a comparative analytic stance. An example is Liebert and Spiegler (1982). Such books usually consider several general approaches or categories of theorizing and also include research results. These certainly are characteristics of comparative analysis. But what is missing is a method of systematic comparison and contrast of approaches to bring out issues that are then resolved through research. Instead, such books have the more limited aim of giving examples of personality approaches and research. On close scrutiny, this approach tends more toward benevolent eclecticism than toward rigorous comparative analysis.

Benevolent eclecticism and partisan zealotry are useful orientations in the initial stage of the development of a field. People having partisan zeal ensure that the hard work of formulating, refining, selling, and defending particular viewpoints gets done. It is probably only through the loyalty and commitment of its supporters that a particular approach eventually gets a proper hearing. Benevolent eclectics, on the other hand, help keep people's minds open, leaving them free to accept or reject the zealots' arguments. In addition, benevolent eclecticism allows the difficult, heavily intuitive work of theory formulation to go forward without being prematurely hampered by hard-headed, cynical evaluation.

But once a number of coherent theories are available, neither benevolent eclecticism nor partisan zealotry will spur much further development of the field. The zealots will merely continue trusting in, advocating, and seeking rational and empirical demonstrations of their particular theories. The benevolent eclectics will stand aside, casting a blessing on all the bustling, partisan activity taking place. No one will try to determine the relative value of the various existing approaches. Succeeding generations of workers will duplicate their predecessors, with slight increases in sophistication. But there will be no sweeping changes, no dramatic advances unless an attitude of comparative analysis develops.

If there is enough interest in systematic inquiry into the relative merits of different forms of theorizing, people in the field can conjoin their efforts rather than dissipate their energy in competitive, partisan disputes. This conjoining of efforts produces an intermediate stage in the development of the field, leading toward the end of determining the really worthwhile theories. When, armed with really trustworthy and effective theories, the field enters a fully mature stage of development, its knowledge is applied in a way that significantly changes and improves the process of living.

It seems to me that the personality field is in an unnecessarily prolonged infancy. We have had a set of reasonably coherent theories for some time now. Occasionally a new one comes along, but it usually seems more of a rephrasing or elaboration of an earlier theory than a departure from it. More and more personality research gets done each year; yet we have made little progress toward weeding out some theories as empirically unworkable. This lack of progress is partly due to research that is partisan rather than directed squarely at the issues separating the various types of theorizing. Although researchers typically insist that the existing personality theories are irrelevant to their work, it is, of course, impossible to do personality research without being guided by a personality theory. The fragmentation of theory and research produced by supposedly atheoretical research is at present a serious impediment to progress in the personality field. I fear that the retarded development of an attitude of comparative analysis is beginning to produce stagnation in this area. It is in the interest of helping to eradicate this problem that I write this book.

WHAT PERSONOLOGISTS DO

In our private lives, none of us seriously doubts that personality exists. Indeed, we routinely take our own and others' personalities into account in day-to-day decisions and activities. But once we try to specify the nature of personality in some precise way, it seems to evaporate before our eyes, leaving us frustrated and uncertain. This has even happened to some psychologists, leading them to seriously contend that personality does not exist. Such a contention seems to me as unfounded as personality is elusive. We must expect the elucidation of personality to be difficult, for it is, after all, the most ubiquitous and human thing about us. We cannot gain much understanding of it by studying subhuman organisms, and our ability to accurately observe other humans is limited by the need to filter all observations through our own personalities. But personality is here to stay, so I suggest that we simply accept the difficulty of our task and plunge right in.

To understand what personality is, we could start by reviewing the available definitions; indeed, Allport (1937) did just this. But I think we would gain little by proceeding in this fashion, for there are myriad definitions, each quite detailed and complex. We would be lost in a maze of words that could have but little impact. I suggest instead that we look in a general way at what people in the personality field do. The implications of their activities will give us an overall, vivid idea of the nature of personality.

The statements I am about to make may not apply equally to the activities of every person in the personality field. Unless you grant me the leeway of searching for commonalities among most, but not necessarily all, of the workers in the field, we will get nowhere. After all, there are no statistics or explicit data we can use—indeed, it is difficult even to be sure just who is in the field and who is not. So we must approach our task in a rather general way.

Let us start by adopting a name for the kind of person we will be describing. Following Murray (1938), let us call him or her a *personologist:* someone who is expert in the study and understanding of the consistent patterns of thoughts, feelings, and actions people demonstrate. Many psychologists and psychiatrists indisputably can be called personologists. Their work involves any or all of four activities: psychotherapy, assessment, research, and theorizing. *Psychotherapy* involves sensitively listening to and interacting with people toward the goal of ameliorating their problems. In *assessment,* the personologist uses techniques such as personality or skills tests in order to pinpoint a person's problems or capabilities, either for the person's own information or for someone else, such as a prospective employer. In psychotherapy and assessment, the personologist is interested mainly in clients' specific needs. In *research,* he or she typically is more concerned with general knowledge. The research may require people to perform certain tasks in order to determine similarities and differences in their behavior, both within themselves and with respect to one another. Personality *theorizing* tends to come out of the personologist's experiences in these activities; it brings these experiences to bear on the perceived nature of people in general. With this brief introduction, let us focus more concretely on how the personologist habitually functions.

First, we can observe that *the personologist tends to study groups of people or, if only a few individuals are studied, the concern is with how representative they are of people in general.* Occasionally the personologist studies only one person for his or her own sake, as does the biographer. Sometimes the reason is that the person is extraordinary (say, Abraham Lincoln). Other times it is the task of psychotherapy or assessment that leads the personologist to focus on one person. Nonetheless, he or she engages in such study of an individual in order to subsequently compare and contrast that person with others. This is because an important interest of the personologist is the *commonalities among persons.* Indeed, in research a technical requirement is that the observed group be representative of people in general. The personologist approaches the task of understanding people with the systematic, orderly thoroughness of the scientist rather than the impressionistic anecdotalism of the fiction writer. The personologist, however, need not shun the imaginativeness of his or her humanist neighbor merely because of an insistence on systematic sampling.

Despite this deeply ingrained interest in commonalities, the personologist also expends great effort in the *attempt to identify and classify differences among people.* There is no basic incompatibility between the search for commonalities and the search for differences, though individual personologists frequently show preference for one or the other. Whereas the search for commonalities proceeds at an abstract, interpretive level, the quest for differences involves a concrete, face-value analysis of observable behavior. Personologists engaged in assessment are especially sensitive to individual differences. Such differences are tapped by the personality tests so often taken on entrance to college or for job evaluation purposes. The personologist's overall aim is a classification of styles of being, with the similarities and differences among the categories within the classification clearly specified. The personologist's interest is much like the chemist's concern with the periodic table of elements.

The personologist is not alone in identifying and classifying the similarities and differences that exist among people. Social and biological scientists study them as well, but they tend to be interested in those similarities and differences produced by pressures in the external environment or biological factors of the internal environment. Thus, a sociologist is concerned with such things as the similarities in voting behavior within a certain socioeconomic class or the differences in such behavior traceable to differences in socioeconomic class. Further, the sociologist may study the behavioral similarities of all people playing the social role of father and the differences between their behavior and that of persons not playing this role. In contrast, a neurophysiologist might be concerned with the similarities among people under the effects of a tranquilizer and the differences between them and people under the effects of alcohol. Of all the biological and social scientists interested in similarities and differences in people's behavior, *the personologist is unusual in not restricting interest to behavior easily traceable to the social and biological pressures of the moment.* This is not to say that the personologist is necessarily uninterested in behavior that reflects social or biological pressures. But beyond this, the personologist's interest is particularly peaked when it becomes apparent that not everyone in the same socioeconomic class votes the same way, that not all fathers act similarly in that role, and that there is a wide range of mentation in people under the effects of alcohol. In other words, one thing the personologist looks for is *evidence of differences among people when the biological and social pressures seem the same.* The personologist is also intrigued *when the same behavior is observed even though the biological and social pressures differ.* Still another way of saying all this is that the personologist is especially interested in *individuality.*

A philosopher or theologian might share the personologist's special interest in behavior not easily explained in social or biological terms but would tend to consider such behavior as spiritual, inspired by God, or expressive of free will. In contrast, the personologist attributes such behavior to the psychological characteristics and tendencies the person has brought to the immediate situation. These characteristics and tendencies constitute personality. Personality may well have developed out of early family experiences, but in itself it becomes a cause of behavior. For the personologist, people's behavior is influenced not only by the momentary social and biological pressures but by their personalities as well. The personologist is not against admitting that social and biological pressures affect behavior, but he or she does think that exclusive emphasis on these factors oversimplifies the understanding of living. Personality should be recognized as an integral part of behavioral processes, without recourse to any mysterious notions of the supernatural or free will. Among social and biological scientists, then, *the personologist believes most deeply in the complexity of life.*

But it is not just transitory similarities and differences among people that intrigue the personologist. Implicit in the notion of personality as a structured entity that influences behavior is the *emphasis on characteristics of behavior that show continuity in time.* If personality changes at all, it changes slowly. Therefore, if personality influences behavior, the direction and intensity of the influence ought to persist, producing behavior that is continuous and regular. If the sexual instinct is part of personality, for example, sexually relevant behavior—say, flirtation or dating—ought to be a stable aspect of the person's life. The personologist is interested not only in the repetition of certain behaviors but in sequences of functionally related behaviors occurring over time. This emphasis on recurrent behavior clearly is one reason why personologists like to study people through prolonged contacts such as psychotherapy. By repeated observation, the personologist sees personality more completely and accurately. Even when there is only one observation possible, he or she typically uses some test of personality that has been specially developed to detect just those aspects of the person's behavior most likely to persist. An important gauge of the adequacy of the test is its stability, or the likelihood that it will yield the same information on a person at two different points in time.

Actually, it is possible to pinpoint the kind of behavior studied by the personologist even further. He or she is not interested in every aspect of the commonalities and differences in people's functioning that show continuity in time. Within this extensive category of functioning, *the personologist tends to restrict attention to behaviors that seem to have psychological importance*. This amounts to a focus on thoughts, feelings, and actions, leaving to the biological scientist such continuous aspects of functioning as acetylcholine cycle and blood pressure. The personologist is not even interested in such discrete phenomena as a muscle contraction or the time necessary for an eye to adjust to an increase of light, unless they are part of some larger unit of functioning with apparent psychological significance in the sense of some ready relationship to the major goals and directions of the person's life. Thus, the personologist is much more at home discussing such behaviors as studying for an examination or writing a love letter than with such behaviors as accurately discriminating between two tones or even increasing one's heart rate. Personologists are generally quite willing to grant that the psychological functioning they study has a physiological substrate, but they typically do not place primary importance on physiological study and explanation.

One definite implication of the personologist's emphasis on understanding thoughts, feelings, and actions is that *subhuman organisms are not very useful to study*. It is simply too indirect and risky to try to understand jealousy, for example, by seeking to specify its precise, unique physiological substrate so that it can be studied in a subhuman organism that cannot tell you what it feels. The study of thoughts and feelings requires complex communication through a rich language. In this sense, the proper study of the human being is the human being.

Other social scientists also concern themselves with thoughts, feelings, and actions rather than more microscopic or fragmentary aspects of functioning. But the personologist tends to study thoughts, feelings, and actions more comprehensively. The economist is interested in economic behavior, the sociologist in behavior that affects or reflects the social system, and the political scientist in political behavior. In contrast, *the personologist is interested in all rather than only some of the psychological behavior that shows continuity in time*. It is often said that the personologist is concerned with the whole person, and this is reasonably accurate when qualified by the previously discussed restriction to psychological behaviors with continuity in time. The characteristics and tendencies called *personality* have comprehensive effects on thoughts, feelings, and actions. Hence, behavior must be studied widely. More than any other social scientist and psychologist, personologists seek integrated knowledge of the human being. They are interested in the economic, social, and political behaviors emphasized by other social scientists. They are also interested in the processes of learning, perception, memory, development, and so forth on which other kinds of psychologists focus. They aim to integrate all these bits of knowledge into an overall account of people's functioning.

Finally, a perusal of the theorizing and research that personologists conduct makes it clear that *personologists are primarily interested in the adult human being*. Many believe implicitly that personality does not jell until some time after childhood and, hence, its effects are clearly and consistently apparent only after maturity. To be sure, it is common for personologists to explain present personality on the basis of learning experiences in early life. But investigation into early life experiences is invariably aimed at understanding adult functioning. Indeed, some personologists do not even elaborate on the developmental process, finding it sufficient to simply assume that it has taken place. By and large, the personologist is interested primarily in the fruit of development—a settled personality that exerts a pervasive influence on present and future behavior. Hence, the common subjects of observation, research, and psychotherapy tend to be adults.

WHAT PERSONALITY IS

At this point, we can make a statement about the overall nature of personality that will be meaningful in terms of the kinds of things personologists do: *Personality is a stable set of tendencies and characteristics that determine those commonalities and differences in people's psychological behavior (thoughts, feelings, and actions) that have continuity in time and that may not be easily understood as the sole result of the social and biological pressures of the moment.*

The only part of this statement that may need elaboration is the reference to "tendencies and characteristics." *Tendencies* are the processes that determine directionality in thoughts, feelings, and actions. They exist in the service of goals or functions. *Characteristics* are static personality structures used to explain not the movement toward goals or the achievement of functions but the fact and content of goals or requirements. They are also used to explain thoughts, feelings, and actions that seem less directional than repetitive in nature. An example of a tendency might be the attempt to achieve perfection in living, whereas related characteristics would be the ideals, such as beauty or generosity, that define perfection. We will have much more to say about characteristics and tendencies later; for the moment, we need only a general sense of what they mean.

THE PERSONOLOGIST'S THREE KINDS OF KNOWLEDGE

Because psychology claims to be a science, one might think that all of the personologist's theoretical statements follow from research. Research is either exploratory or confirmatory. Exploratory research involves *systematic observation* of behavior in a reasonably large group of persons chosen as representative of people in general, with the aim of stating hypotheses on the nature and purpose of the behavior. These hypotheses are then tested as to their empirical truth or falsity in confirmatory research that is carefully designed for relevancy. Confirmed hypotheses represent *empirical knowledge,* which can be characterized as public, precise, and systematic.

It is important to emphasize that personality theories are not based solely—or even primarily—on empirical knowledge, whatever claims to scientific validity the field may mount. To my mind, this state of affairs is neither surprising nor disadvantageous. It is not surprising because the personality field is still in an early stage of development. When set alongside the richness and complexity of people and their lives, the empirical knowledge available to the personologist is scanty and sometimes so partisan as to be severely limited in generality. Thus, it is little wonder that personality theories are not based completely on empirical knowledge. Far from being disadvantageous, the inclusion in personality theories of statements not firmly based in research is a potentially fruitful procedure at this early stage in the field's development. The leeway this procedure grants permits the theorist to consider the full complexity of the human being. It is true that the theorist risks being wrong, but when the empirical development of the field catches up, he or she will find that out soon enough—and there is also the possibility that the theorist will have been right.

To some what I have said may sound heretical, but to me it hardly seems unusual. After all, theory in any field is virtually never restricted to statements based on empirical knowledge alone. In addition, the nonempirical statements do represent two other definite kinds of knowledge: those based on the processes of intuition and reason. To appreciate intuition, recall the times you have been seized by an inarticulate, private, and emotional, though vivid, immediate, and compelling, sense of the meaning of what is happening. The substance of these hunches constitutes *intuitive knowledge.* In contrast, there have been times when you carefully and calmly thought through the meaning, parts, and implications of things and arrived at your conclusions through deduction from a set of assumptions. In this case you are dealing with *rational knowledge,* which is reflective, explicit, logical, analytical, precise, and intellective. Intuitive and rational knowledge are not arbitrary and mysterious things. They emanate from your own experience and the exercise of your own mind and may therefore contain useful clues to what is true.

Intuitive knowledge, operated on by reason, may become rational knowledge. Further, both intuitive and rational knowledge may merge with empirical knowledge when the appropriate research is done. But none of this changes the fact that at any time you may be functioning with a conglomerate of intuitive, rational, and empirical knowledge. So too may a personologist's theories embody such a mixture. And if further justification for the inclusion of intuitive and rational knowledge in a theory of personality were needed, I would point to other respectable endeavors in which these kinds of knowledge were paramount and empiricism considered relatively unimportant. The artist in exercising imagination and the theologian in building faith are dealing primarily with intuitive knowledge while reason is clearly the hallmark of the mathematician and the philosopher.

Each of the three modes of knowing can serve as a check on the others. Something that seems sensible on the basis of reasoning may so rankle the intuition as to suggest limitations in the rational assumptions being made. Something that seems clear empirically may turn contradictory when viewed rationally, and this may alert us to an unrecognized and erroneous interpretation of data. Our insistent intuitive idea may be less convincing when it proves illogical on detailed analysis. In the early stages of a field such as personology, there is no royal road to truth; rather, there are three intertwining roads, all of which should be traversed to better assail the secrets of the terrain.

Whether or not you find my attempt to justify the use of all three modes of knowing convincing, you should recognize that they are indeed used by personality theorists. Inevitably the initial stages of theory formulation are, as in any creative act, intuitive in nature. The theorist makes decisions as to where to start and what assumptions to emphasize on grounds that are by no means exclusively rational or empirical. One has a hunch and follows it up. One feels comfortable with a particular view of life and so celebrates it in theory. Sometimes one realizes the intuitive bases of one's theorizing and sometimes not. To be sure, the intuitive early stage of theory construction gives way to a stage in which rationality is uppermost. But this does not change the fact that the theorist begins with largely intuitive knowledge. Because of this, theories bear the stamp of intuition even when they have been developed to a respectable degree of rationality.

But however intuitive the initial theorizing may have been, the personologist accepts the task of formulating explicit views in terms of a series of assumptions justified by common experience. From these assumptions, the major theoretical propositions of the theory will be deduced. Sometimes you will be asked to accept these propositions as necessary, inexorable conclusions following from the assumptions. Although it is uncommon to find personologists arguing the unequivocal truth of their propositions in a manner indicating sole reliance on the rational mode of knowing, their obvious investment in those propositions and occasional disdain for empirical evidence suggest a strong commitment to reason.

Sometimes the personologist is more of an empiricist than this. Certainly he or she believes in the standard that nothing that cannot be supported by some kind of empirical evidence deserves inclusion in a theory of personality. In addition, many theorists actively formulate empirically testable hypotheses stemming from their assumptions. Some even conduct the empirical tests themselves rather than leave that task to other personologists. But among psychologists, the personologist is hardly insistent on denying intuition and rejecting any assumptions supported only by reason. To the contrary, the personologist will tolerate intuitive and rational knowledge in theorizing, while accepting the necessity of relying on empiricism whenever in doubt. This catholicity and lack of skepticism have not earned the personologist respect among psychologists, but they have permitted a vigor of conceptualization and a willingness to tackle complex problems.

In reading the chapters that follow, it will benefit you to remain alert to these three kinds of knowledge. Try to see their impact on each theorist and theory in terms of your own sense of intuition, reason, and empiricism. In this way you will be not merely a passive bystander but someone who is developing views on what is valuable in the personality field. It is admittedly difficult to analyze a theory intuitively, for intuition is not really an evaluative process. The two best things you can do are to have a global intuitive reaction to a theory and to try to recognize when the theorist's formulations are primarily intuitive. Usually I will help you by suggesting, at the outset of a discussion of a theory, some basis in your own experience for intuitively understanding its essence. In addition, I will comment whenever a particular stance taken by a theorist is clearly and deeply intuitive or temperamental in character. Of course, much more detailed analysis of theory can be done rationally and empirically. As you can see from the chapter titles, the major analyses I will attempt involve reason and empiricism. In discussing rational analysis, I will try to alert you to the logical consistencies or inconsistencies in theories, the explicit or implicit status of their assumptions and propositions, and the conclusions that are presumed to require no empirical test. In discussing empirical analysis, I will try to evaluate theories on the basis of relevant research that permits some testing of predictions.

THE CORE AND PERIPHERY OF PERSONALITY

Before you go on to the other chapters of this book, you should know something about their organization and what prompted it. The major organizational principle apparent in Chapters 3 through 11 is the basic distinction between the core and periphery of personality. It is common for personality theories to make two kinds of statements. The first refers to what I call the *core of personality*. It delineates the things that are common to all people and discloses the inherent attributes of human beings. These common features do not change in the course of living, and they exert an extensive, pervasive influence on behavior. But theorists also tend to make statements about more concrete attributes of personality that are readily observed in behavior. These attributes delineate what I call the *periphery of personality*. They are generally learned rather than inherent, and each has a relatively circumscribed influence on behavior. They are used by the theorist mainly to explain differences among people.

Theories of personality typically have both core and peripheral statements, and this seems sensible insofar as the personologist is interested in the commonalities and differences among people. In core theorizing, the personologist makes a major statement about the overall directionality, purpose, and function of human life. This statement takes the form of postulating one or perhaps two *core tendencies,* such as the assumption that all behavior constitutes an attempt to actualize one's inherent potentialities. Core theorizing also includes *core characteristics,* or the personality structures implied in the core tendency. In the example of the actualizing tendency, the core characteristics might be such inherent potentialities as sexuality or aggressiveness.

It is at the peripheral level that the theorist makes a major statement concerning the concrete styles of life that differ from person to person. One way the theorist does this is by postulating a number of *peripheral characteristics,* which relate only to some part of behavior. For example, the need for achievement is a peripheral characteristic referring only to competitive behavior in a context permitting success and failure. It does not refer to love, cooperation, or anything else and therefore can be used to understand only some of the observable behavior.

The function of peripheral characteristics is to permit the understanding of differences among people. One can say that Mr. Oliver has a need for achievement whereas Mr. Sterling has the trait of obstinacy. One can also say that Mr. Oliver has a higher need for achievement than does Mr. Sterling. Theorists differ in the number of peripheral characteristics they postulate; the higher the number, the greater the concern shown for individual differences. Peripheral characteristics are the smallest, most homogeneous explanatory elements the theorist believes are possible. Many people use the term *trait* for what I am describing. I avoid that term, however, because some theories of personality consider traits to be only one of a number of different kinds of peripheral characteristics.

The *type* is a larger, more general concept that is also commonly employed in peripheral theorizing. Each type comprises a number of peripheral characteristics, organized into larger units that relate to commonly encountered ways of life. Sometimes a personologist will offer a *typology,* or comprehensive classification of types. It is an exhaustive statement of the different styles of life that are possible. Typically, one or more types are designated as ideal ways of life, whereas the others are considered nonideal. The nonideal types are believed to be either predispositions to psychopathology or actual kinds of psychopathology.

The link between the core and periphery of personality is covered in the *developmental statement.* In the beginning, the core tendency and characteristics are expressed in interaction with other persons (e.g., family, strangers) and social institutions (e.g., laws, schools). The resulting experience—reward, punishment, knowledge—congeals into peripheral characteristics and types. One's personality type is generally considered to be a function of the particular kind of family setting in which one matured. The best developmental conditions lead to the ideal personality types, while less adequate conditions supposedly culminate in the nonideal personality types.

It may seem extremely arbitrary to call one style of life ideal and others nonideal. Actually, this kind of common evaluation is no more arbitrary than anything else in personality theorizing. A type is considered ideal because it, among all possibilities, most fully expresses the core tendency and characteristics. In other words, the personologist says that the best lifestyle is the one that most fulfills the overall purpose of human life as articulated in a particular theory.

The basic parts of a personality theory are depicted in Figure 1–1. As the circles get bigger, the units become more general, more fundamental to the core tendency. The dotted arrows indicate several possible lines of development. The one actually occurring depends on the kinds of experience the person encounters in the process of expressing his or her core tendency. I have filled in one arrow to show that it is typical for personality theories to specify an ideal course of development leading to an ideal peripheral personality (e.g., if the core tendency is to actualize inherent potentialities, ideal development takes place when parents foster and encourage the child, and all this culminates in a self-actualized peripheral personality).

As mentioned earlier, personality theories arise from personologists' activities of doing research, assessing persons, and helping them in psychotherapy. But conversely, the theory also influences these activities. When you assess a person's personality, you are of necessity working with a particular typology and its component peripheral characteristics. The personality theory is useful here because it permits pinpointing of differences among persons—of the especially "Johnian" quality of John, as Allport used to say. When you

FIGURE 1–1   Schematic Representation of the Parts of a Personality Theory

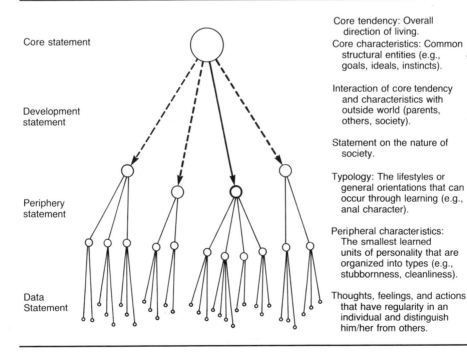

Core statement

Development statement

Periphery statement

Data Statement

Core tendency: Overall direction of living.
Core characteristics: Common structural entities (e.g., goals, ideals, instincts).

Interaction of core tendency and characteristics with outside world (parents, others, society).

Statement on the nature of society.

Typology: The lifestyles or general orientations that can occur through learning (e.g., anal character).

Peripheral characteristics: The smallest learned units of personality that are organized into types (e.g., stubbornness, cleanliness).

Thoughts, feelings, and actions that have regularity in an individual and distinguish him/her from others.

attempt to do psychotherapy, you must decide on the basis of your view of human nature (core of personality) and the particular peripheral personality confronting you (is it ideal or not?) what changes need to be implemented. Looked at in this way, psychotherapy is a special case of development (needed client change through interaction with the therapist), so the therapist's view of development is also involved. And, as I shall contend throughout the book, research in the personality area should also address, in precise fashion, the theories available to us. Thus, theory helps shape all of the personologist's activities.

SELECTION OF THEORISTS FOR INCLUSION IN THIS BOOK

A book that attempts comparative analysis in the personality area is only as strong as the approaches it includes are comprehensive and representative. I have tried to keep this in mind in selecting theories for discussion. I have included not only theories popular in psychiatry (e.g., Freud, ego psychology) and psychology (e.g., Rogers, Murray) but theories that are not especially popular (e.g., Rank, Angyal). You will find both theories postulated some time ago (e.g., Adler, Allport) and some that are recent (e.g., Fiske & Maddi, Bakan). There are theories that stress the core (e.g., Rogers, Maslow) and others that emphasize the periphery (e.g., McClelland, Erikson). Some stress emotional phenomena (e.g., Freud, Rogers), while others focus on intellective phenomena (e.g., Kelly, existentialism). There are theories that emanate from the practice of psychotherapy (e.g., Adler, Jung) and those that reflect the academic and research pursuits of the university setting (e.g., White, Allport). I have included not only those that are reasonably comprehensive (e.g., Fromm, Freud) but those that are incomplete (e.g., White, Angyal). There are even positions (e.g., behaviorism, social learning theory) that have ambiguous status as personality theories, though they are quite important in contemporary psychology. I have also tried to mention recent psychotherapies (e.g., transactional analysis, gestalt therapy) in which the personality implications are incompletely developed.

If personologists will have any quarrel with my choice of theories, it is likely to involve the absence of Lewin, Sheldon, Sullivan, and Horney. I have omitted them because their thinking no longer seems to have great direct impact on the personality field. Few personologists would consider themselves followers of these theorists. In an older theory, this state of affairs signifies a decline in importance. But Lewin—and, to some extent, the others—have influenced personologists whose own theories are currently more influential. It seemed sufficient to include these later theories in the book. Finally, while I have excluded Horney, I have included many variants on the psychoanalytic theme.

Although I cannot claim to have included all theories of personality, I have covered quite a few and taken pains to ensure that my sampling accurately reflects the field. I have not excluded any that would dramatically change the conclusions reached throughout this book. Interestingly, I found all these theories to express only three basic models for personality theorizing. To be sure, each model has two versions and some variants. Nonetheless, the basic ways of theorizing about personality are apparently few.

COVERAGE OF THEORY, RESEARCH, ASSESSMENT, AND THERAPY

Among the four functions of the personologist, *theorizing* and doing *research* mainly produce new knowledge, whereas *assessment* and *psychotherapy* chiefly apply knowledge that is already available. As such, theorizing and research are intellective or speculative activities, while assessment and therapy are practical activities. By mentioning this difference, I do not mean to imply that one kind of activity is more or less important or grand than another. Actually, the four activities form a meaningful whole. Theorizing has an integrative function, because whether explicit or implicit it determines what and how research, assessment, and therapy get done. Research is important because it is especially suited, through the collection of systematic and relevant empirical observations, to testing the validity of existing theory and contributing new information that can shape further theorizing. Assessment and psychotherapy are important primarily because they serve the needs of persons with disabled personalities. But assessment and psychotherapy can also help in evaluating theory and contributing new observations that can influence future theorizing. The four functions are organically related to one another—indeed, some personologists engage in all of them. The most common orientation for a personologist is to engage in at least two functions, and it is rare to find one isolated in a single function.

Although this book emphasizes personological theory and research, it by no means excludes assessment and therapy from consideration. As mentioned above, the decision to emphasize theory stems from its integrative function. If you understand a personologist's theory, you have a ready basis for appreciating why and how he or she does research, assessment, and therapy. Therefore, an emphasis on theory is a sound introduction to personology. The corollary emphasis on research is important because the comparative analytical approach taken here requires considerable attention to the evaluation and testing of existing theory. Because of the importance of theorizing and research to the aims of this book, I will attempt to cover both areas of personology in depth.

I cannot claim the same breadth of coverage of assessment and therapy. These are complex, specialized activities that require more emphasis than would be possible in this book and in a single personality course. There are a craft and many component skills involved in assessment and therapy that take considerable time and effort to explicate, teach, and acquire. But in the chapters that follow, I discuss the theorizing behind the assessment and therapy practices deriving from the various theories of personality. I do this partly because all four functions of the personologist are an integral whole, partly in order to give a vivid sense of the similarities and differences among the various theories, and partly to provide a bridge to other books and courses on the practice of assessment and therapy.

By and large, discussions of assessment and therapy occur alongside explications of theory in the following pages. In this fashion, you can get an organic sense of how the practical activities of the personologist issue from the intellective activities. The research sections are separated in order to permit a focus on evaluation of theories. Having research discussions follow theoretical ones is logical, and will allow you to use this book in a flexible way that would be impossible if the two were run together.

CHAPTER 2
Methods in Personality Study

Before we embark on our journey through personality theorizing and research, let us consider the various ways in which information about personality can be obtained. As you will see, there are various formalized methods of inquiry that are used in research to test personality theories in a systematic way. Application of these methods helps generate what I called *empirical knowledge* in the previous chapter. But these methods are not just the researcher's inventions; rather, we all use aspects of them informally and unself-consciously in our everyday lives as we try to make sense out of our experience. This contributes to our intuitive knowledge, as mentioned in Chapter 1. To gain rational knowledge, personologists apply these inquiry methods more systematically and deliberately when theorizing about personality.

Because the inquiry methods we will cover are often used informally as well as formally, I will alert you to their basis in commonsense, everyday living. But I will also help you to see what is involved as they become the systematic procedures of the personality researcher. It is not my aim here to make you technically proficient in the research use of these methods. Instead, I want to prepare you for critically understanding the theorizing and research you will be reading about in subsequent chapters.

COVARIATION—OR WHAT GOES WITH WHAT

An important task of the personologist is to determine which aspects of thoughts, feelings, and actions fit together and which are separate from one another. Do people who think critically of others also act competitively toward them? Do people who feel unhappy act shy and think others dislike them? Human behavior is complicated, and the variety of combinations of human thoughts, feelings, and actions is mind-boggling. The whole area of inquiry into these combinations is little understood.

When we get to know someone, we intuitively try to figure out which of their characteristics go together. We express what we have learned through this process when we describe that person to ourselves or to others. Harry dresses well, always seems to know what to say, keeps up not only with his studies but with current events; but he is always alone, and no one seems to feel close to him. Sarah laughs too loudly, doesn't seem to listen to others, cries easily, gets good grades only if she likes the teacher; but she will sit up all night with a friend who is in trouble, and she dreams of being married and having lots of kids. By noting these things, we are observing correspondences, or *covariations,* and trying to see overall patterns.

Personality theorists start in much the same way. Their curiosity about people leads them to observe behavioral covariations in them. When the theorist considers which of these correspondences in behavior are common, the peripheral characteristics (see Chapter 1) of the theory are born. These smallest aspects of personality that can be conceptualized are intended to refer to differences among persons. Because the theorist tries to make his or her intuitions regarding behavior very explicit and systematic by formulating definitions and complete descriptions, the resulting peripheral characteristics may be termed *rational knowledge.* This peripheral statement in a personality theory is a more systematic version of what we all do out of common sense in trying to understand the people we meet.

Another important task of the personologist concerns how covarying characteristics cluster together to form patterns. The question of patterns is simply a more complex version of the question of covariation. Two characteristics may covary, or be related, at which point they begin to define a pattern, or cluster. Observing that persons who are neat also tend to be punctual establishes covariation. When the observation extends not only to neatness and punctuality but also to stubbornness, a sense of justice, and a tendency to feel guilty, one is identifying a pattern in the clustering of several characteristics. Discerning pattern is even more complex and difficult than establishing covariation.

Technique for Measuring Covariation

Research Method: Correlation.   In order to do research on the peripheral characteristics of personality theory, it is necessary to have some way of empirically evaluating which characteristics go together. This is done through statistical procedures that measure *correlation.*

We can calculate a correlation if we can measure two or more peripheral characteristics in the same group of subjects (when persons are studied in research, they are called *subjects*). The measurement must be quantitative; that is, numbers ordered as to intensity must result from the measurement.

The quantification may be gross, as in the case in which we note the simple presence or absence of some characteristic. For example, we may have a test that tells us whether or not undergraduate subjects are neurotic. It may also indicate whether they have grown up in broken or intact homes. Because we have measured both dichotomous (either/or) characteristics in the same group of subjects, we can formulate the so-called *contingency table* illustrated in Table 2–1. It is called a contingency table because each of the four cells tells us something about how a subject's score on one characteristic is contingent on or relates to the other characteristic.

TABLE 2–1   Contingency Table Relating Broken versus Intact Homes and Neurotic versus Normal Undergraduate Subjects: Positive Relationship

	Broken home	Intact home
Neurotic undergraduates	20	5
Normal undergraduates	5	20

The numbers in the cells are, of course, fictitious. But whatever numbers would actually result in such a study, we could calculate the likelihood that there was a meaningful empirical relationship between the two characteristics. The statistic commonly used on data of the sort shown in Table 2–1 is the *chi-square*. It gets larger as the difference between the cells in the table increases.

The numbers used in Table 2–1 show that the two pairs of diagonal cells differ appreciably. This pattern of results is called a *positive* relationship, indicating that the presence of one characteristic is associated with the presence of the other. In other words, neurotic subjects tend to come from broken homes. The reversed pattern of results, shown in Table 2–2, would be called a *negative* relationship, because the presence of one characteristic is contingent on the absence of the other. In other words, neurotic subjects come from homes in which there was no upheaval. In both tables, the calculated estimate of significance would be reported as $p < .001$. This means that the probability (p) of the observed pattern of results happening just by chance is less than 1 in 1,000 times. We would be justified in thinking of this result as meaningful; because it would happen again and again, it must be real.

TABLE 2–2   Contingency Table Relating Broken versus Intact Homes and Neurotic versus Normal Undergraduate Subjects: Negative Relationship

	Broken home	Intact home
Neurotic undergraduates	5	20
Normal undergraduates	20	5

Frequently in personality research, one or both of the characteristics being studied are quantified at more subtle levels than just presence or absence. Suppose we could measure how much neuroticism subjects show rather than considering this an all-or-nothing phenomenon. If the other characteristic were still dichotomous, as in broken versus intact home, the statistic to calculate would be the so-called *point biserial correlation*. Once again we could test the likelihood that the pattern of results obtained might have occurred merely by chance.

The most common situation in personality research occurs when both characteristics can be measured at several levels. Suppose our theory tells us that persons who are stubborn also tend to be neat (as you will see in Chapter 7, Freud's theory actually says something like this). Suppose further that we use questionnaires in which persons' answers to questions permit us to give them a numerical score of 0 to 10 on stubbornness and on neatness. Then we would be able to construct a contingency table with cells arranged 10 by 10. Figure 2–1 is an example of such a table; for convenience, points representing each subject's score on both characteristics at once take the place of cells.

The pattern of scores shown in Figure 2–1 seems to define a line sloping from the lower left to the upper right of the table. This is, once again, a *positive* relationship (the greater the stubbornness, the greater the neatness). The opposite pattern would reveal a *negative* relationship (the greater the stubbornness, the less the neatness). Whatever the pattern, the closer the points come to defining a line, the stronger is the relationship. Figure 2–2 shows what an absence of relationship would look like.

The statistic commonly used to test for the strength of relationship is the *Pearson product-moment correlation*. It can range from + 1.00 (maximum positive relationship) through 0 to − 1.00 (maximum negative relationship). Certain kinds of data require other statistics, such as the *rank order correlation* (used to determine whether a person's rank on one variable predicts his or her rank on the other). For all of these statistics, it is possible to estimate the likelihood that the observed relationship occurred merely by chance.

By now, you can appreciate how correlational methods provide a powerful basis for evaluating the accuracy and importance of rational or intuitive knowledge. If there is no empirical correlation between two characteristics, you may want to reconsider your pet notions and systematic theories to the contrary. Even if there is a definite empirical relationship (i.e., it is not likely to have occurred by chance) but a weak one (e.g., + 0.25, or − 0.25), you may want to rethink them.

Correlational methods arise from the same attempts to observe and understand human behavior that we engage in throughout our everyday lives and that personality theorists employ when they build their conceptualizations. The difference is that correlational methods transform these intuitive and rational modes of operation into the systematic, quantitative efforts we call *empirical*.

FIGURE 2–1   Contingency Table Relating Stubbornness and Neatness:
Positive Relationship

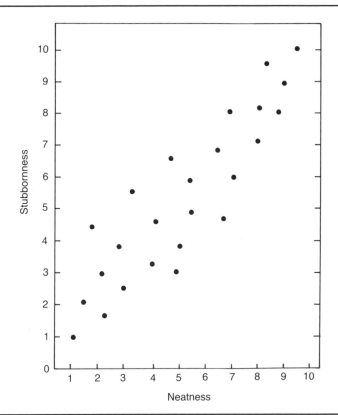

Research Method: Factor Analysis.   In addition to correlational methods, which relate individual characteristics, there is a statistical method for the empirical study of clusters of characteristics. It is called *factor analysis* and is based on a complex computation related to the simpler correlation already discussed. Factors can be extracted from the distribution of subjects' scores on the various characteristics.

The factor analysis procedure aims to identify the smallest number of factors needed to describe the ways in which several characteristics covary. The higher the correlations shared by some subgroup of characteristics under study, the greater the likelihood that it will define a factor. Factor analysis can also determine whether it is more accurate to describe the identified factors as correlated or uncorrelated. Because the analysis explores this question through geometric means, correlated factors are called *oblique* (i.e., the lines

FIGURE 2–2   Contingency Table Relating Stubbornness and Neatness: No
Relationship.

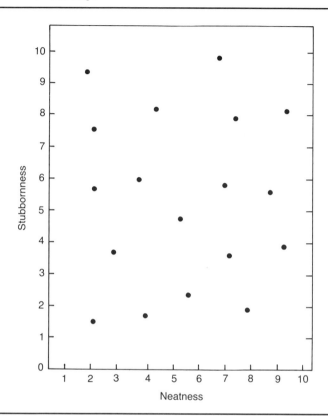

representing factors intersect at oblique angles). Uncorrelated factors are
called *orthogonal* (i.e., the lines representing them intersect at right angles).

The major use of factor analysis in psychology has been to explore the
covariation patterns among the characteristics that have been measured. Ideally, these characteristics have been selected for some specific theoretical
reason, but in any case the factor analysis will identify the existing clusters.

Perhaps the most important use of factor analysis in personology is as an
empirical check on some theoretical formulation about clustering. For example, in the Freudian view of the periphery of personality, the anal character
type is neat, punctual, stubborn, and competitive, whereas the oral character
type is suggestible, cooperative, passive, and dependent. If we were able
to measure these eight characteristics on a sample of subjects, we could employ factor analysis to see whether there were two empirically identifiable

factors and whether each was defined by the theoretically appropriate four characteristics.

We will discuss this use of factor analysis in more detail in Chapter 11. For the moment, it is enough for you to recognize that the rational knowledge arrived at by theorizing can be checked by the empirical knowledge emerging from factor analytic studies. Empirical factors correspond with the "types" in the peripheral statement of personality theories.

CAUSALITY—OR WHAT INFLUENCES WHAT

When a personality theorist considers neatness, punctuality, stubbornness, and competitiveness to occur together and to define the anal character type, there is little causal influence involved. It is not that neatness causes punctuality and so forth, nor that having an anal character type causes neatness; rather, having the characteristics of neatness and so on simply defines an anal character type. In personality theories, peripheral statements taken by themselves do not imply cause and effect.

Causal influence in personology usually arises when the developmental and core statements interact to influence the peripheral statement. Let me oversimplify to make an example: Freud theorized that all youngsters express their sex instinct (core statement), and if their parents respond too punitively during the oral or anal stages of maturation (developmental statement), the emerging personality type (peripheral statement) will be oral or anal, respectively. Without the sex instinct there would be no character types. But you cannot understand how the types come about just by the core idea that we all have a sex instinct. The parental reactions in the various stages of development are an essential ingredient in causing the types. Separately, the sex instinct and the patterned, parental reactions are each *necessary but not sufficient* conditions for the types. Together, the sex instinct and the parental reactions form the *necessary and sufficient* conditions for understanding the types.

Something similar to this rational knowledge occurs when, at a more intuitive level, we try to understand how people got to be the way they appear. Earlier we observed Harry's and Sarah's particular and different styles. When we wonder how Harry came to be lonely and Sarah to be quick to laugh or cry, we are raising a causal question that implies core and developmental assumptions. These assumptions may not be psychoanalytic at all. We may think, for example, that Harry and Sarah must have been rewarded by their parents (a developmental assumption) when they expressed, respectively, inborn needs for success and intimacy (a core assumption). It is natural, once we have noticed patterns of behavioral covariation, to wonder how they came into being and to develop such assumptions. When personologists devise core and developmental formulations, they are doing more systematically (at a rational level of knowledge) what most of us do frequently at an intuitive level.

Techniques for Measuring Causality

Research Method: The Experiment. The classic empirical procedure for testing causal theorizing is the *experiment*. As shown in Table 2–3, the experimental design calls for at least one group of subjects (called the *experimental group*), which is exposed to the supposed necessary and sufficient conditions (called the *treatment*) for the effect or result we are interested in understanding, and another group (called the *control group*) in which these conditions do not occur. It is important that the only difference between the groups concerns the supposed necessary and sufficient conditions. If the effect or results under study appear in the experimental group and not in the control group (or at least appear more strongly in the former than in the latter), that constitutes empirical evidence to support the causal theorizing.

The inference that it is the condition or treatment that caused the effect is supported by three crucial features of experiments. First, the effect must be seen (or seen most readily) only when the condition is present. Second, the condition or treatment must precede the effect. Finally, if it is apparent that the experimental and control groups differed in no respect other than the condition or treatment, it is reasonable to conclude that the condition caused the effect.

Imagine testing by experiment the Freudian causal theorizing mentioned in simplified form earlier. We might take infants shortly after birth and assign them at random to one of three groups. Let us call them the oral experimental, anal experimental, and control groups. As the theory assumes that all persons have a sex drive (core statement), we need not worry about differences across groups in this attribute. Assignment of infants to groups at random means that each infant has the same probability as the others of being assigned to each group. We can achieve random assignment by some chance procedure, such as throwing dice, or we can use the tables of random numbers especially constructed for this purpose. Random assignment is important because it increases the likelihood that there will be no other differences (say in age or sex) between the groups except for the treatment.

To fulfill the experimental design, we would have the parents in the oral experimental group punish the sexual behaviors of their children during the first year of life (which Freud identifies as the *oral stage*) and the anal experimental group parents do so during the second year (identified by Freud as the

TABLE 2–3 Experimental Design

Groups	Treatment	Expected Effect
Experimental	Applied	Present
Control	Not applied	Absent

anal stage). The parents in the control group would not punish the sexual behaviors of their youngsters during either the first or second years of life.

For Freud's theory of development to be supported empirically, the subjects in the oral experimental group would subsequently have to show predominance of the oral character type and the subjects in the anal experimental group predominance of the anal character type. The control group subjects must show predominance of neither character type. So we need some quantitative measurement of orality and anality with which to compare the three groups. The results can be evaluated by a statistical test called *analysis of variance,* which determines the probability that the difference among the averages occurred by chance. Another statistic called the t-*test* can be used to achieve the same purpose.

Note from this example that there can be more than one experimental group in an experiment As well as more than one control group. What guides us in all this is the logic of the theoretical formulation being tested and the importance of ruling out alternative explanations of findings. Because Freud's formulation differentiates the causal conditions of oral and anal character types, it made sense to include two relevant experimental groups. Had it seemed cogent to us that perhaps orality and anality are produced not by parental punishment but by the very fact of having been reared by our natural parents, we might have added a second control group to check on this alternative explanation. Such a control group would have involved youngsters reared by persons other than their natural parents. If they showed less orality and anality than the other groups, our explanation would have been empirically supported.

I hope you have noticed the absurdity surrounding our extended example of an experiment! It is simply not practical to try to get parents to punish or not punish their children or have them reared by others just to satisfy our research requirements. Even if it were feasible, it would be unethical to play with the lives of youngsters in this way. Although the experiment is on paper a powerful technique for testing theoretical formulations, it is often not directly usable in the personality area. Of course, experiments that water down the causal formulations of personality theory are more feasible to do, but inference from their results is accordingly difficult and uncertain.

Research Method: The Natural Experiment.   Fortunately, there is a better way to test causal formulations. Called the *natural experiment,* it capitalizes on the fact that things often happen naturally that for reasons of practicality and propriety could not be made to happen by intent. Careful study of these events can fulfill an experimental design that otherwise would be unfeasible.

To test the Freudian formulation with a natural experiment, we could work through hospital maternity wards to get information about the birth of infants. We could get their parents' permission to study (but not interfere with) family interaction patterns. By observing these patterns periodically during the first and second years of the youngsters' lives, we could judge which of them were punished during the first year, which during the second year, and which in neither year and assign them to the oral experimental, anal experimental, and control groups, respectively. We might even find some newborns given up for adoption if we wanted to fill out that second control group of those not raised by their natural parents. In this way, we would come very close to fulfilling our experimental design!

To go all the way, however, we would have to worry about whether the naturally constructed groups differed in any important ways besides punishment versus no punishment. For instance, if the control group contained more females than the other two groups, the results, even if they appeared to support Freudian theory, might really be only reflecting some unsuspected tendency of males to develop more orality and anality than females. This alternative explanation is plausible because, in our natural experiment, punishment/no punishment is *confounded* in our research design with maleness/femaleness, and it is difficult to know which variable is responsible for the result.

Fortunately, there is a statistical procedure for correcting this design fault of confounding. It involves a quantitative way of deleting the effect of the confounding variable. Employing this procedure turns an analysis of variance into an *analysis of covariance* (the term signifying that covarying or confounding variables have been statistically controlled).

The natural experiment is a powerful empirical technique in personology. It is generally more useful than the contrived experiment. When needed attention is paid to possible confounding factors, natural experiments are a valuable way to empirically test the causal formulations of personality theorizing.

To Summarize

Now you have had an introduction to the major methods of inquiry in personology. There are empirical techniques that are best for understanding covariation and patterning. Other techniques work best where causal inference is involved. Although these are rather technical, they have their origins in the commonsense ways in which we all try to understand one another, whether intuitively as ordinary folk or rationally in systematic personality theorizing. But now it is time to change gears.

PERSONALITY DATA

Thus far, we have focused on how to analyze personality data by such means as correlations and factor analysis. In doing so, we have assumed we already have the data to be analyzed. Now let us consider how the data are generated in the first place. What do we measure when we want information about personality? One answer to this question concerns the sources of personality data and another the techniques of measurement.

Sources of Personality Data

There are three main sources of personality data: (1) the person's self-report, (2) the report about the person by those who know him or her, and (3) the judgment made about the person by an expert. The data obtained from these three sources may or may not agree. This does not mean that one source is more right or wrong than the others: rather, you must choose the data sources most appropriate to what you want to know.

If you want to know what people think about themselves, it is appropriate to obtain self-report. If they say "I am intelligent," or "I'm capable of hard work," or even "I don't know who I am or what I want," you may learn something relevant. Notice that all these statements are interpretations the person makes about himself or herself. The conclusion "I am intelligent" is reached by ruling out possible alternatives such as "I am so persistent that I appear more intelligent than I really am" or "It is the stupidity of the others around me that makes me look more intelligent than I really am."

In contrast, if you want to know what others think of a person, it makes sense to ask them. Depending on your purpose, you might ask the person's friends, parents, lovers, or teachers, but you probably would not ask a complete stranger. If others say "John is a nasty, unpredictable, untrustworthy person" or "Mary is always so helpful and supportive," you learn something relevant to personality. Once again these statements are interpretations of the person, but this time made by others. The same John described so unsympathetically by his associates might appear to himself merely frightened, overwhelmed, and desperately in need of friends. Who is right? Perhaps both sides! Clinical psychologists certainly know that it is not uncommon for frightened and desperate people to act in ways that are unpredictable and troublesome to others. This is the kind of pattern that led the great sociologist Erving Goffman to define paranoia as acting so suspiciously as to force others to be unsupportive—a kind of self-fulfilling prophecy.

The final source of personality data is experts. If you want to determine whether a person shows particular, concrete peripheral characteristics as explicated by a certain theory of personality, you might want a specialist in that theory to render a judgment. The raw material or observations for the judgment might be the very same ones the person and relevant others would scrutinize in reaching their interpretations. But the interpretation reached by the expert presumably would be more sophisticated with regard to the personality theory. To a Freudian expert, John might appear to be an anal character type. Of course, if the expert is right, this does not mean that John and the others must be wrong. All could be right! Each interpretation is made from a different standpoint and for a different purpose.

It might seem as if the basic source of data is expert judgment. After all, the expert makes relevant, sophisticated appraisals that refer explicitly to personality theories. But you should recognize that expert judgments are not made in a vacuum; they are based on observations, often among which are self-reports or evaluations by others. Thus, all three sources of data are useful in personology.

Expert judgment may also be claimed as most basic because it is usually more explicit and less intuitive than self-report and others' reports. We all reflect intuitively on ourselves and on others without strictly adhering to any full-fledged personality theory. In contrast, the expert is much more likely to organize observations explicitly to explicate a particular theory of personality. What is involved here is rational as opposed to intuitive knowledge (see Chapter 1).

To clarify the claim in favor of the experts, let us return to the previous example of John, who feels frightened and desperate whereas others see him as nasty and untrustworthy. The expert judgment that he is an anal character type is possible because Freudian theory assumes that ordinary people are not fully aware of what is really true about themselves and others. So the reports of John himself and of those around him are regarded as relevant but imperfect; they reveal their true meaning only through the interpretation of experts.

The limitation on this claim that expert judgment is the most basic source of data is the direct counterassumption made in some personality theories. The theory of Carl Rogers, for example, assumes that the expert can never know any person as well as that person knows himself or herself. The Rogerian expert would accept a person's self-report as the basic data on personality.

Each of the three sources of personality data can be useful. We need to be alert to our specific purposes and underlying theories in collecting personality data. These will help us decide which sources of data to emphasize.

Techniques for Measuring Generated Data

In attempting to grasp personality measurement techniques, it is helpful to distinguish those that generate the human behavior to be studied from those that apply to human behaviors that take place naturally. Among the former techniques are the *interview,* the *questionnaire,* and the *performance task.*

Research Method: The Interview.   The *interview* is a verbal interaction in which a researcher obtains information relevant to a specific research aim from a subject. Usually the interaction is face to face; sometimes it may be conducted by other means, such as the telephone. Interview formats range from unstructured to structured.

In an unstructured interview, the researcher presents broad questions or topics (e.g., "How would you describe yourself?" or "What are your opinions about politics?") and the subject is free to answer in any manner he or she wishes. Unstructured interview formats permit the researcher to follow whatever comes up in response to the broad questions and go wherever it may lead, as long as it is relevant to the research aim. In following up, the researcher may ask questions not part of the original set or contribute his or her own observations in a conversational manner.

In a very structured interview, the researcher's questions are set in advance and are less global. Even follow-up is structured in the sense that the so-called *probes* (additional questions) are specified in advance. Structured interviews try to get the same sort of information from every subject. A portion of a structured interview format appears in Table 2–4. As you can see, the

TABLE 2–4   Part of a Structured Interview Format on Parental Attitudes toward Teenagers

Questions	Probes (to be asked only if the question does not elicit the needed information)
Section 1: Demographic Facts	
1. What is your name?	1. None
2. How old are you?	2. None
3. How many children do you have and what are their ages?	3. None
4. What is your current marital status?	4. How many times have you been married? Did your marriage(s) end in divorce or some other way?
Section 2: General Attitudes	
1. What do you think it's like being a teenager today?	1. Is it different from in your day? Is it easy? or hard?
2. What are the best and worst things about being a teenager today?	2. Can you think of any other things?
3. What would you do to help teenagers grow up well?	3. Anything else you can think of?
4. If you had a teenager, would you impose rules of conduct?	4. Would you let the teenager go his or her own way?
5. If so, what would those rules be? List them in order of importance	5. Anything else you can think of?
Section 3: Personal Information	
1. How do you get along with your own teenager(s)?	1. Can you say more about what it's like when you are together?
2. Do you generally agree on what your teenager(s) should be doing or not doing?	2. Say more, please. Is there anything else you can remember?
3. Are you satisfied or frustrated with your teenager(s)?	3. Please say more.

researchers devising such a sequence of questions have a clear initial idea of what information they want from the subject.

Usually interviews are planned so that the most general, easiest, and least intimate questions come first. In the example in Table 2–4, the strategy behind asking for factual details first is that they should be easiest and least threatening for subjects. Such questions help subjects get into the process of responding. Notice also that following the factual items, questions go from general to specific. The hope is that because subjects are relatively unconstrained at first, they will disclose what is really on their minds. The more specific later questions are designed to ensure that certain crucial information is obtained from all subjects in case they have not volunteered it already. As you can see, the most intimate questions appear last. It is assumed that by that time, subjects have become sufficiently familiar with being interviewed and trust the interviewer enough to perhaps divulge personal, potentially embarrassing information that they might otherwise withhold. Of course, this strategy is not always successful.

Research Method: The Questionnaire. The *questionnaire* is a set of questions or statements, the responses to which are designed to yield information relevant to the research aim. Interviews and questionnaires are similar; questionnaires can also be designed as unstructured or structured. One major difference between the two is that with the questionnaire, the researcher need not interact with the subject in order for data to be generated. Hence, questionnaires can be administered to groups of subjects, sent through the mail, or put on computer diskettes. Generating data by questionnaire techniques is less labor intensive for the researcher. It can also preserve subjects' anonymity as they may not even have to identify themselves and may never actually be seen.

Unstructured questionnaires include broad questions that give the subject leeway in responding. Examples might include "List your best friends of this year, and describe each of them in your own words" or "Describe yourself in your own words, indicating which are your most important attributes." In these unstructured questions, subjects can choose to write a lot or a little, and they may approach the questions in a variety of ways.

Structured questionnaires use less global questions and do not permit elaborate, open-ended responses from subjects. An example of part of a structured questionnaire appears in Table 2–5. Notice that in this case subjects respond only by indicating whether they agree or disagree with each item. These are so-called *true-false* items. Another format for responding is the *rating-scale* item. The questions appearing in Table 2–5 would be transformed into rating-scale items if the subject were asked to pick the appropriate number, with 0, 1, 2, and 3 standing for "not at all true," "a little true," "somewhat true," and "completely true," respectively. Whatever the form of response required, structured questionnaires are calculated to equalize the elaborateness of the answers to every question from every subject.

Two other common forms of questionnaire items are the forced-choice and the checklist. In the forced-choice format, questions or attitudinal statements

TABLE 2-5   Part of a True-False Questionnaire on Parental Attitudes toward Teenagers

Question	Response (Circle one)	
1. Teenagers tend not to understand their parents' problems.	T	F
2. Teenagers are very generous with their friends.	T	F
3. By the teenage years, youngsters are good company for their parents.	T	F
4. Cruelty characterizes the relationships of teenagers.	T	F
5. Teenagers drink too much.	T	F
6. Most teenagers do not use drugs.	T	F
7. Sometimes I can't understand how teenagers avoid disasters.	T	F
8. With a little help from their parents, teenagers get along just fine.	T	F
9. Teenagers try very hard to grow up.	T	F
10. I wish I were a teenager again.	T	F

are paired and the subject is asked which of the two seems more relevant or accurate. Examples of such item pairs are given in Table 2–6. Each statement is paired with each of the other statements. This makes it possible to rank order the judged acceptability of all statements for all subjects.

TABLE 2–6   Part of a Forced-Choice Questionnaire on Beliefs Concerning Personal Control

Instructions: Circle the item number in each pair of items that best expresses your opinion.

1. If you try hard, you can usually reach your goals.
2. Those who get ahead are just lucky.

1. The best things in life come your way when you least expect them.
2. If you try hard, you can usually reach your goals.

1. Those who get ahead are just lucky.
2. Through learning, you can increase your competence.

1. If you try hard, you can usually reach your goals.
2. The best things in life come your way when you least expect them.

1. Through learning, you can increase your competence.
2. Those who get ahead are just lucky.

1. The best things in life come your way when you least expect them.
2. Through learning, you can increase your competence.

1. Through learning, you can increase your competence.
2. If you try hard, you can usually reach your goals.

1. Those who get ahead are just lucky.
2. The best things in life come your way when you least expect them.

The *checklist* typically includes simple statements or even single words, and subjects check those that are relevant. Although checklist items are usually not themselves questions, the assumptions behind the test imply questions. You can see this in the items in Table 2–7, all of which can be transformed into questions by prefixing them with "Did you experience" and following them with "in the last year?"

Psychologists who develop questionnaires are very concerned that they avoid various so-called *response biases* to which subjects may fall prey. An important bias is *image maintenance,* or the tendency of subjects to present themselves in a favorable (rather than accurate) light through their responses. To avoid this, questionnaire developers sometimes try to word items to hide their real intent or to make each choice appear equally favorable or even neutral. This is done so that the subject's score will reflect the hoped-for content rather than image maintenance. Other biases are *acquiescence* (the general tendency to agree with statements) and *negativism* (the tendency to disagree with same). A way to minimize response biases is to word half of the questionnaire items positively and the other half negatively. Questionnaire item construction has become very technical; for now it is sufficient that you be aware of some of the major response biases that can interfere with obtaining sound research data.

Interviews versus questionnaires.   There are advantages and disadvantages to interviews and questionnaires. Going into some of these will help you understand the research you will be reading in later chapters. Basically, inter-

TABLE 2–7   Part of a Checklist on Recent Life Events

Instructions: Please indicate whether the events listed in the left-hand column happened to you in the last year. Do this by putting a check mark in the second or third column if the event happened within 6 months or between 6 and 12 months of today's date. If the event happened in both 6-month periods, check both columns.

	Time from Today's Date	
Events	*0–6 Months*	*6–12 Months*
Death of a loved one		
You leave home for college		
Birth of a sibling		
Your parents divorce		
A parent remarries		
A serious financial reversal		
Personal bankruptcy		
You fail a course		
You fall in love		
A friend leaves town		

views have the advantage of giving subjects more freedom to express themselves, because they can respond in their own way to questions. In contrast, questionnaires require brief, unelaborated answers from subjects. Subjects feel more manipulated by questionnaires.

Response freedom in interviews can also be a disadvantage. Using an interview, the researcher cannot be sure of obtaining comparable information from each subject. One subject may elaborate on a topic that another does not even address. This makes it difficult to arrive at a quantitative score for each subject on all the variables under study. In contrast, questionnaires aim at such quantification, which is one of their strengths.

We might, of course, wonder whether this quantification from questionnaires is valid, as subjects are somewhat forced into the mold shaped by the set of questions used and the lack of response elaboration permitted. For example, suppose I force you to answer only "yes" or "no" to the question "Do you have a lot of trouble studying?" You might end up saying "yes" even though you would have wanted to explain that although sometimes you are unable to study, at other times you have no trouble doing so. And it may all depend on whether or not you feel in love with someone at the time. In an interview, you might have been able to express this complexity. But then the interviewer would have had to struggle with how to make your statement comparable with that of another interviewee who did not mention such complexity. Did this other subject fail to elaborate out of a wish not to get into all that or because for him or her there is no complexity surrounding studying?

No doubt a major reason why questionnaires are used so much in personality research is their already mentioned efficiency. One researcher can collect data on large groups of subjects, and these groups need not even meet together (if the mail is used). Added to this efficiency factor is the ease of questionnaire quantification produced by subject responses that are unelaborated and comparable across the group studied.

By comparison, interviews are labor intensive and often yield complex responses that are difficult to quantify and compare across subjects. But interviews yield richer, more complete, less manipulated or contrived expressions from subjects. This means that interviews are better used when the research aim is exploratory—that is, when the researcher is not sure what data are most important and needs to see just what subjects may or may not have to say about certain topics. Questionnaires are better used when the research aim is less exploratory than concerned with testing some settled hypotheses. This means that the researcher knows what data are important and is not concerned with extraneous things that subjects may say.

Research Method: The Performance Task.   In the *performance task,* the researcher has subjects perform an activity and judges their performance with regard to some research aim. You may think that both interviews and questionnaires should qualify as performance tasks; after all, answering questions qualifies as a task. But interviews and questionnaires differ in an important way from the performance task as defined here in that they require subjects to reflect on and judge their own behavior before giving a response. For example, if I ask you "Are you too aggressive?" you must, in order to respond, remember past thoughts, feelings, and actions and judge not only whether you express aggression but whether that aggression is too intense. In contrast, a performance task might put you in a group of people with the instruction that everyone get to know one another. The researcher would observe what you say and do, reaching his or her own conclusion as to whether you are too aggressive. The most important feature of performance tasks is that the subject's response is not a self-evaluation but some relevant performance that the researcher will judge.

Psychologists have been very ingenious in devising performance tasks that can elicit from subjects the kinds of thoughts, feelings, and actions that are relevant to research aims. Sometimes the performance tasks are highly staged; in the *lost-letter* technique, for example, a subject is led to find a stamped letter on the ground, and the research question is whether he or she will mail it or open it. Of course, the researcher is hidden somewhere watching the ensuing drama, forming judgments about the subject's honesty and social responsibility.

Sometimes performance tasks are less staged. In the extreme, for example, the researcher may merely follow the subject around during some period of daily activity. This relatively unstructured approach has the advantage of showing the whole range of the subject's actions. Like all unstructured techniques, however, the resulting observations may not be comparable with those of other subjects, and quantification may be difficult. Again, unstructured approaches are best when the research aim is exploratory. If the researcher is more sure of the observations needed to fulfill the research aim, structured performance tasks are preferable for ease of quantification and comparability across the group of subjects.

Whether structured or unstructured, performance tasks are important when the research aim is best served by expert judgment, as previously discussed. If, for example, your personality theory considers the real motives for actions to be unconscious (as in Freud's approach), you might be better off observing subjects' behavior in relevant tasks and forming your own judgments as to their motives than by asking them in interviews or questionnaires why they do things.

A particular form of performance test that has been important in personology is the *projective test*. In this kind of test, ambiguous stimuli are presented to the subject, whose task is to determine the meaning of what is perceived. As there are no right or wrong answers, the act of fantasy through which meaning is attributed involves a projection onto the stimuli of the subject's personality. The subject may or may not realize what he or she is revealing. What makes projective tests a performance task is that the subject's responses are evaluated by the researcher in order to determine what is being revealed.

A famous example of a projective test is Murray's (1943) *Thematic Apperception Test*. It is composed of a set of ambiguous pictures of people about each of which the respondent is supposed to compose a story with a beginning, middle, and end that indicates what is going on. You can imagine what a difference it would make in interpreting what a subject is like if the composed story were about hatching a murder plot as opposed to discussing an anticipated vacation! The requirement of composing entire stories makes it quite likely that subjects will reveal things they may not have intended to disclose or may not even have realized in themselves. Because they are thematic and, typically, interpersonal, the fantasies expressed on this test are rich in material with which the expert can interpret personality.

Another example of a projective test is the *Rorschach Test* (Rorschach, 1942). This is a set of ten inkblots, and the subject is asked to imagine all the things each one might look like. Figure 2–3 shows the kind of inkblot that might be used. Once again the meaning of the responses "It's an avenging eagle swooping down on us sinners" and "It's a warm, fuzzy fur rug to snuggle into" is very different in personality implications. The procedures for scoring test responses have become very complex and technical. There are not only several competing scoring systems but several forms of the test itself. There is no need to delve into these complexities here.

The Psychotherapy Session.   Some data collection contexts are complex combinations of interview, questionnaire, and performance task. A good example is the *psychotherapy session*. It is contrived in the sense that it is not a naturally occurring relationship. Although it involves considerable intimacy (the client reveals innermost thoughts, feelings, and actions), the relationship is one-sided (the therapist does not reveal these things). It involves a contract for service (the client pays the therapist for services rendered), although an unusual one (the correspondence between service and pay is often intangible

FIGURE 2–3   Inkblots

and complex). Further, this contrived situation we call *psychotherapy* typically includes aspects of the interview and the performance task and perhaps even questionnaires and other verbal tests. But it is not devised primarily for research aims. Instead, it serves treatment goals, and that may sometimes jeopardize the needs of research.

I include the psychotherapy session as a research method because it is frequently used for collection of personality data. These data may include not only the therapist/researcher's expert judgments but also the client/subject's self-evaluations and actions in performance tasks. These self-evaluations and actions may correspond with or contradict the expert judgments.

As described here, the psychotherapy session may seem too complex to be useful as a measurement technique. Its major advantage, however, is that as sessions accumulate, the researcher (and perhaps the subject) usually becomes increasingly sure of the evaluation. Client/subjects typically reveal themselves in therapy because they want to facilitate the process of treatment and they want to come to trust their therapists. When researchers do one-time interview or questionnaire administrations, subjects may well withhold important information and present themselves in the best light. After all, subjects interviewed or given a questionnaire typically have no relationship with the researcher sufficient to build trust. So why should they reveal all without being sure of how it will be used?

Simple performance tasks might seem to circumvent this tendency toward image maintenance because they do not require the subject's self-evaluations. But notice that it is typical in performance tasks for there to also be no continuing relationship between the researcher and the subject. Thus, subjects might be reticent to behave in a completely open fashion in many performance tasks, taking care to reveal only behaviors that will put them in a favorable light. So the researcher may not have all the observations needed to reach sound expert judgments. It would appear that the psychotherapy session, however complex, is worth struggling with in the attempt to reach meaningful empirical knowledge.

Reliability

As discussed in Chapter 1, *personality* refers to characteristics that have continuity over time and across situations. Thus, the measures we use to chart these characteristics must show them to be internally consistent and stable. Only then will we be sure that we have measured with *reliability*.

It is possible to determine the *internal consistency* of a questionnaire by looking at those several items considered conceptually relevant to each personality characteristic studied. For example, a measure of ego strength might include such questions as "Do you wake up in the morning full of energy to face the day?" "Are you usually afraid to meet new people?" and "Do you often doubt the value of what you are doing?" To these, the highest score on ego strength would be responses of "yes," "no," and "no," respectively. Other patterns are possible. You can study the internal consistency of such a set of questions by calculating the likelihood of a consistent pattern of answers in a sample of subjects. The most efficient statistic for doing this is *coefficient alpha*. The higher it is, the greater the consistency of the measure.

Stability of a measure is determined by repeating it one or more times on the same subjects under similar circumstances. The time between administrations of the measure is usually long enough so that subjects cannot merely remember and thus repeat what they said last time and not so long that one could legitimately expect subjects' personalities to have changed. For periods of, say, two weeks or a month, the higher the correlation between subjects' scores on both administrations, the greater the stability of the measure.

Techniques for Measuring Natural Data

Natural data are not generated by the researcher. They include anything people do in going through their days (and nights), and much of this can be relevant to such broad research interests as personology defines. In empirical research, it is useful to have some record of natural data that can be returned to again and again when measuring personality characteristics.

Written documents are a typical kind of record of natural data used by researchers. These can include anything from a record of business transactions to a diary. Needless to say, some written records are richer and more revealing than others and are therefore more highly valued in research. Other kinds of records can also be valuable. Video- or audiotapes of ongoing experiences are increasingly important resources in research.

The documents may include statements about the subjects made by themselves or by others. Further, the documents may chronicle subjects' thoughts, feelings, and actions in a way that does not emphasize self-reflection. But, of course, none of these statements or chronicles have been made for research purposes. An additional important feature of natural documents is that they are not restricted to present-day activities. The researcher can study subjects' remote pasts if documents are available.

Research Method: Content Analysis.   The major procedure for turning documented natural data into measured personality characteristics is *content analysis*. In this approach, the researcher develops criteria for determining how the kind of natural data at hand can express the characteristic under study. For example, if the relevant characteristic is gregariousness and the data are a subject's diaries, the researcher can list, through the record of real and imagined events, all the ways the subject expresses interest in being with others. These can include not only concrete instances of meeting with others but also dreams of having been with them and waking-state feelings of loneliness (as these are all things that might well be included in diaries).

The researcher could be content with a global judgment of the degree of the subject's preoccupation with others or could push for more precise quantification. To do the latter, it would be necessary to specify what constitutes an instance of gregariousness. In a written record like a diary, an instance might be a verbal unit, such as a sentence or a paragraph. Or it might be some more functional unit (however long or short), such as the recording of an episode. Whatever the criterion of an instance, its specification is very important because it permits the researcher to count. The more instances of real or wished-for social interaction, the greater the gregariousness of the subject.

Interscorer Agreement. Frequently, content analysis involves the researcher in interpretation of what he or she is observing. Sometimes the meaning appears clear. For example, the diary statement "I spent the whole evening wishing for a friend—or even just an acquaintance—to talk to or be with" clearly expresses gregariousness. But does the statement "I spent the whole evening feeling restless, as if something not entirely clear to me was missing" express gregariousness? Some researchers might think so, whereas others might not. Who would be right? It could be hard to determine, because researchers using the same scoring criteria may differ in opinion as to what they are perceiving.

The only safe procedure is to determine how much two or more scorers agree and not be satisfied until the agreement is high. It has become standard practice among researchers to demonstrate inter scorer agreement whenever it is content analysis that has generated personality data.

Research Method: Psychobiography.   Of late, a particular approach to content analysis has become popular in personology. It uses as many documents, past and present, as can be amassed and aims to understand the holistic pattern of an individual life. It is, therefore, aptly called *psychobiography* (Runyan, 1982). As the word indicates, this is a biography with a distinctly psychological slant (rather than political, for example). In addition to its expressly psychological task, psychobiography aims to be as systematic as possible. Toward this aim, psychobiographers do a lot of content analysis of documents and interviewing of the subject when possible.

In general, psychobiographies focus on persons who are somehow remarkable—eminent, famous, or talented—to discern the universal personality and social forces that produced them. In helping us understand these, the psychobiographer teaches us all about living.

One weakness of psychobiographies is that interscorer agreement on content analyses is almost never studied. The overall psychobiographical task is complex, in-depth understanding of an entire life. And the data are often difficult to obtain—perhaps documents buried in archives or rushed interviews with the eminent. It is understandable (if unfortunate), therefore, that psychobiographers work alone. Needless to say, when you work alone, you tend not to evaluate interscorer agreement.

To Summarize

In obtaining personality data, the researcher must decide whether to use existing materials or to generate data. We make similar decisions in our everyday efforts to understand one another: In learning about people, we can observe their natural comings and goings or we can ask them questions. Researchers try to make similar decisions in a conscious, systematic way. Their efforts have led to an extensive technology for generating and evaluating personality data. Now, before we shift from an appreciation of this technology to the personality theories, there is a final matter to ponder.

THE SUBJECTS STUDIED

Thus far, in considering personality research we have focused on how personality data are generated and analyzed. A word should be added here on the choice of subjects to study. Perhaps it goes without saying that human beings are the natural subjects of personality research. But this may bear noting in a field—psychology—that often uses lower animals as subjects. To use lower animals in personality research is such an indirect approach to what we want to understand (patterns of thoughts, feelings, and actions) and presents such grave measurement problems (can we be sure of an animal's thoughts and feelings?) as to be virtually useless.

But which humans should we study? The young or old, the rich or poor, males or females, normals or psychotics, Christians or Jews? Certainly we should not fall into choosing a sample of subjects merely because they are available. A typical failing is that of using college sophomores as subjects because both they and the researchers tend to be at universities, even though the research aim is not limited to adolescents. However interesting they may be, college students are developmentally different from children, adults, and the aged, and it is therefore difficult to generalize findings concerning them to other age groups.

Nor should psychotherapy clients be used as subjects without careful consideration. After all, persons seek psychotherapy when they are in trouble, when they have failed to live satisfyingly. Is it appropriate, then, to generalize what is learned through psychotherapy sessions to people who have not sought such treatment? Once again we see that in selecting subjects it is important to keep in mind a sense of their appropriateness to the research aims.

A FINAL WORD

In this consideration of the subjects and how data are generated and analyzed, I have tried to accomplish several things. One is to show how the methods used to produce empirical tests of personality theories emanate from (though refine upon) the commonsense ways we all use to try to understand ourselves and others. Another is to express how using personality methods involves interrelated research decisions about whom to study, how to observe them, and how to analyze what is being observed so that empirical conclusions can be reached.

Some of the chapters that follow (notably 6, 10, 11, 12, and 13) emphasize research. If you keep in mind what you have learned here as you read them, you may be helped to appreciate and evaluate the many avenues of personality research.

CHAPTER 3
The Core of Personality:
Conflict Model

By now the groundwork for our consideration of actual theories of personality has been laid. We know that the personologist's theorizing stems from an interest in identifying and understanding the ways in which people are similar to and different from one another. The identification of differences among people forms the basis for theorizing about the periphery of personality, with its emphasis on personality types. The identification of similarities among people is the basis for theorizing about the core of personality, with its emphasis on the characteristics and tendencies that define human nature and are constantly expressed in living.

In this and the next three chapters, I will present many personologists' views on the core of personality. In considering the core of personality, one asks the question "What are the basic attributes and long-time directions of the human being?" Core tendencies and characteristics are, by nature, very general. Thus, one would expect to see their influence not in any isolated segment of behavior but in the overall pattern of functioning.

When I first began thinking about personality viewpoints, I tended to classify them in some conventional fashion such as whether they emphasize thought processes (cognitive), defenses (dynamic), or peripheral characteristics (such as traits), much as in Mischel's (1981) recent book. But no such classifications seemed to capture the essential pattern or overall meaning behind any of the theories concerning the nature of human life. After many false starts and reconsiderations, I have arrived at three broad, workable categories of theorizing. Their essential meaning is captured by calling them the *conflict model,* the *fulfillment model,* and the *consistency model.*

In the *conflict model,* it is assumed that the person is continuously and inevitably caught in the clash between two great forces that are defined in content to be continually acting, necessarily opposed, and unchangeable. According to this model, life must be a compromise, which at best involves a dynamic balance of the two forces and at worst a foredoomed attempt to deny the existence of one of them. There are two versions of the conflict model. In the *psychosocial version,* the source of one force is within the individual and the source of the other in groups or societies. In the *intrapsychic version,* both forces arise from within the person regardless of his or her status as an individual or a social entity.

In contrast, the *fulfillment model* assumes only one great force and locates it within the individual. Life is seen as the progressively greater expression of this force. Although conflict is possible, it is neither necessary nor continuous. Indeed, when it occurs, it represents an unfortunate failure in living rather than an unavoidable condition. Like the conflict model, the fulfillment model has two versions. In the *actualization version,* the great force takes the form of a genetic blueprint that determines the person's special capabilities. One lives richly by actualizing that which is potential at birth. The *perfection version,* on the other hand, does not emphasize genetically determined capabilities so much as ideas of what is fine, excellent, and meaningful in life. The force constitutes striving toward these ideals of perfection regardless of whether that entails expressing one's own genetic capabilities or inferiorities. In both forms of the fulfillment model, the content of the great force is set and specifiable.

The *consistency model* places little emphasis on great forces, whether single or dual or in conflict or not; rather, it emphasizes the formative influence of feedback from the external world on the individual. Feedback that is consistent with what was expected or what has been customary produces no change. But inconsistency between the feedback and the expectation or custom creates discomfort and the pressure to alleviate it. Life is understood as the extended attempt to maintain consistency. Whereas the conflict of the conflict model is continuous, unavoidable, set in content, and controllable but not eradicable, the inconsistency of the consistency model is avoidable and variable in content. In contrast to the fulfillment model, the consistency model assumes no predetermined capabilities or ideals as guides to living. The consistency model also has two versions. The *cognitive dissonance version* emphasizes the thought categories in which inconsistency can arise. There may be inconsistency between two thoughts or between an expectation and a perception of what actually happens. In contrast, the *activation version* emphasizes consistency or inconsistency between the customary degree of bodily tension or activation and that which actually exists at a given time.

In introducing these three models and their versions, I have not tried to convince you of their meaningfulness and utility in ordering the existing theories of personality. I believe that when we confront actual theories and analyze their similarities and differences, we will find most of them to be clear examples of a single version of a model. Further, I believe you will find the theories less distorted than illuminated by the process of ordering them under these models and versions. But I could be wrong. Certainly you will find a few theories that are not pure expressions of a model. How many such variants can one tolerate before beginning to question the classification scheme? I have found them to be tolerably few, but you may not. At the very least, I feel sure that using the classificatory system in reading the following pages will stimulate your own thinking about the nature of existing personality theories. The personality field is so chaotic at present that all classificatory, organizational attempts are to be welcomed.

CONFLICT MODEL: PSYCHOSOCIAL VERSION

In discussing the conflict model, we shall first consider the *psychosocial version,* which assumes two great and opposing forces, one of which is inherent in the individual and the other in groups or societies. The major example of this kind of theory is that of Freud, and we will discuss it first. Then we will consider the theories of Murray and ego psychology. These are similar to Freud's, but they back away somewhat from Freud's notion that conflict is continual. For Murray and the ego psychologists a part of life remains free of conflict. While their theories drift away from the pure psychosocial conflict model, they remain sufficiently close to be considered a variant.

Freud's Position

Sigmund Freud (born in Moravia, 1856; died in London, 1939) looms as such a giant to both his advocates and opponents, that it is difficult to see him objectively even in our time. Nonetheless, we must try. Freud was deeply committed to his work, family, friends, colleagues, and principles. From youth he showed the brilliant intelligence, tenacity, and independence that marked him for greatness and the social rejection that frequently accompanies this. A physician who strayed far from the orthodox medical emphasis on physical causes of disease, Freud promulgated views that seemed the devil's work to most of his colleagues. For most of his life, Freud was considered a fanatic obsessed with sex, and he was denied recognition by the medical community. In defense, Freud drew his circle of admirers even closer around him, insisting on their loyalty to his theoretical principles. It is not surprising that Freud's views would have been rejected even though they resulted directly from his observations of patients, for they constituted a kind of intellectual indictment of his age, with its stuffy, sterile, Victorian values.

From the beginning, Freud and his inner circle emphasized the mental causation of certain maladies and set about developing a therapy for the mind rather than the body. Both on his own and through this group, Freud has had an immense influence on personology. So intense was the interaction between the members of the inner circle—mainly young, energetic, ambitious physicians—and their visionary though somewhat paternalistic leader that sparks occasionally flew. Here and there a member of this extraordinary group would leave or be expelled. It is a tribute to Freud's intellectual impact on them that these outcasts typically went on to develop influential theories of their own that reflected a psychoanalytic parentage.

Freud's theoretical legacy is complex. He wrote a great deal, changed his mind often, and left many loose ends where he could not decide among theoretical alternatives. Further, he has been copiously interpreted by allies and enemies alike, as well as by revisionists interested primarily in using him as a respectable basis for their own thoughts. I have adopted a selective strategy that focuses on Freud himself and on his main ideas rather than on side statements and exploratory forays, however intriguing they may be.

Freud views the core tendency of living as the *tendency to maximize instinctual gratification while minimizing punishment and guilt.* You would do well to reflect for a moment on the commonsense meaning of this idea. Think of the last time you wanted to do something selfish and were worried about being hurt if you did or felt immoral for having had the wish in the first place. If your wish was strong enough, you could not resolve your conflict by simply saying to yourself that you would not carry it out. And if you resolved the conflict by acting on only the part of your wish that would not incur punishment from others or guilt from within, you had an intuitive, if homey, basis in personal experience for understanding what Freud meant.

Of course, Freud had in mind a more precise, formal concept of conflict than can be completely comprehended from looking at simple experiences of this type. As we will see later, some of Freud's ideas cannot be borne out by introspective analysis. In any event, when looked at from a formal, theoretical point of view, Freud's basic tendency of living includes a position on (1) the instincts, (2) the sources of punishment and guilt, and (3) the mechanism of defense whereby instincts are satisfied while punishment and guilt are avoided.

The Instincts.   Freud postulates a number of instincts that are common to all human beings as an inherent, unchanging aspect of human nature. In our terminology, Freud's instincts are core characteristics of personality. Although he discusses three types of instinct, all of them have the same general form, differing only in content. All instincts have a *source,* a type of *energy* or driving force, an *aim,* and an *object.*

Components of an Instinct.   The *source* of an instinct is invariably rooted in the biological character of the organism—in the very process of metabolism itself. Freud (1925b) says:

> By the source of an instinct is meant the somatic process which occurs in an organ or part of the body and whose stimulus is represented in mental life by an instinct. We do not know whether this process is regularly of a chemical nature or whether it may also correspond to the release of other, e.g., mechanical forces. The study of the sources of instincts lies outside the scope of psychology. (p.66)

Thus, the instinct is not the bodily process itself but the mental representation of it. Freud makes it clear that psychic manifestations, such as thoughts, wishes, and even emotions, are expressive of and dependent on bodily activities and processes. This is why many personologists have dubbed Freud's theory *biological* rather than *psychological.* But while his emphasis is biological, Freud certainly considers the instincts influential through their grip on mental life.

What type of *energy* or *driving force* characterizes instincts? Having accepted that the source of an instinct is the somatic and metabolic processes of organisms, we may inquire how this bodily message is interpreted by the mind. Freud invariably considers the message to concern a state of biological deprivation. The energy of an instinct is rooted in such bodily deprivation states as "dryness of the mucous membrane of the pharynx or an irritation of the mucous membrane of the stomach . . ." (Freud, 1925b, p. 61). Thus, the source and energy of instincts originate from within the organism itself. Freud can say "when a strong light falls on the eye, it is not an instinctual stimulus . . . " (1925b, p. 61) because such stimulation is not achieved through processes internal and intrinsic to the organism as a functioning biological system. By referring to such processes as dryness of mucous membranes, Freud establishes that the bodily messages to the mind are not only internal but also expressive of the organism's biological requirements. An instinct is a sign that the organism lacks something it needs, that it is in a state of deprivation. Such deprivation states are experienced as *tension,* or pressure. Freud (1925) writes, "By the pressure . . . of an instinct we understand its motor factor, the amount of force or the measure of the demand for work which it represents. The characteristic of exercising pressure is common to all instincts; it is in fact their very essence" (p. 65).

Freud uses the distinction between stimulation entering the nervous system from the outside world and the internal stimulation of instincts to make another important point. In contrast to external stimulation, instinctual stimulation is constant. The amount of instinctual tension, pressure, or energy is above zero because such tension is a biological requirement of a functioning organism. An organism metabolizing normally will have such frequent need for food, water, and the like that parching or irritation of mucous membranes will almost always be taking place in one part of the body or another. Thus, Freud (1925) writes:

> An instinct . . . never operates as a force giving a *momentary* impact but always as a constant one. Moreover, since it impinges not from without but from within the organism, no flight can avail against it. A better term for an instinctual stimulus is a "need." What does away with a need is a "satisfaction." This can be attained only by an appropriate . . . alteration of the internal source of stimulation. (p. 62)

The tension of deprivation states will always be with the person, and that means that the instincts will always exert an influence on the person's living.

Thus far, we have established that instincts have their source in bodily processes and are driven by the tension and pressure of biological deprivation. From this, we can guess what Freud considers the overall *aim* of instincts to be: "The aim . . . of an instinct is in every instance satisfaction, which can only be obtained by removing the state of stimulation at the source of the instinct" (1925b, p. 65). In other words, the aim of all instincts is to reduce the tension of biological deprivation. The ideal state, never reached because of the continuing nature of instinctual demands, is the bliss of quiescence, which is probably most closely approximated in deep sleep.

The final general attribute of the instinct is its *object,* by which Freud means the thing or things, usually in the external world but possibly within the person, that serves to satisfy or ease the tension of deprivation:

> The object . . . of an instinct is the thing in regard to which or through which the instinct is able to achieve its aim. It is what is most variable about an instinct and is not originally connected with it, but becomes assigned to it only in consequence of being peculiarly fitted to make satisfaction possible. (1925b. p. 65)

There is typically more than one thing or event that can ease the tension of an instinct. One or another of these objects may become especially important depending on one's particular learning experiences. But it is possible to specify the range of potential satisfiers of a given instinct because they are implied in the instinct's definition. For example, only edible things qualify as objects for the hunger need. When a person recognizes an object as an important satisfier, that process is called *cathexis,* defined as the investment of an object with instinctual energy.

You may be wondering what instincts have to do with mental life. Though basically biological, instincts have important psychic implications. While the terminology for various attributes of instincts is not vividly mental, mental terms are appropriate as long as one keeps in mind that Freud postulates the body and the mind to be closely interconnected. The psychic or mental expression of the source and object of the instinct is a *wish.* A wish for food, for example, expresses the metabolic requirements for nutrients in molar psychological terms. The psychic or mental expression of the tension and aim of the instinct is *uncomfortable emotions.* According to Freud, wishes and associated emotions accurately express biological requirements through the close interconnection between the brain (the presumed physiological locus of wishes and emotions) and the soma and viscera (the presumed source of biological requirements), mediated by the autonomic or involuntary nervous system and the endocrine system. Recognize that Freud attributes a major and unchanging portion of mental life, entailing wishes and associated uncomfortable emotions, to the biological requirements of the organism. Recognize further that he gives this portion of mentation a huge role in determining the person's life.

Content of an Instinct.   Now that we have a sense of the general form of the instinct concept as developed in psychoanalytic theory, we can profitably consider the content of the instincts postulated by Freud. There are three kinds of instinct present in everyone. All are subsumed under the concept of the *id,* a summary term for all the instincts postulated by Freud. The term "*id*" could easily have been translated from the Latin as "*it,*" which would have more accurately conveyed Freud's belief that instincts are experienced as foreign rather than as part of ourselves. In the terminology of this book, the id is a core characteristic of personality, as the three groups of instincts arrayed within it were assumed by Freud to be common to everyone.

Throughout his career as a personologist, Freud argued for the existence of a group of instincts that function to preserve biological life. These *self-*

preservation or *life instincts* (Freud, 1925b) include those for *food, water,* and *air*. Their source is in *anabolism,* or the aspect of metabolism that entails growth. The energy of these instincts comes from the discomfort and tension associated with irritated mucous membranes in the gastrointestinal and respiratory tracts. The instinctual aim is to reduce tension and discomfort by obtaining objects, such as food or water, that can ease the membrane irritation.

Although the life instincts are obviously basic, Freud gave them much less attention than he did the *sexual instinct,* which was also an integral part of his theorizing from the very beginning. This instinct originates in the metabolic process in those parts of the body differentiated for sexual reproduction in the broadest sense. This includes not only the genitalia per se but the secondary sexual areas, such as the breasts, and the orifices, such as the mouth and anus, that can participate in sexual arousal. The energy of the sexual instinct, which Freud called *libido,* comes from the sensitivity, irritation, or tension in these various organs when they are deprived of sexual expression. Obviously, the overall aim of the instinct is release of this tension through intercourse, orgasm, and ejaculation. And the most comprehensive object or goal for this instinct is intercourse with an attractive person of the opposite sex. Any other possible aims and objects, such as kissing, fondling of breasts, genitalia, and anus, stimulation of the mouth and anus through activities related to eating and eliminating, masturbation with orgasm, intercourse with an unattractive person, and homosexual relations, are considered only partial by Freud and therefore capable of producing only partial gratification of the instinct.

When such partial aims and objects are more important to the person than the comprehensive ones, the reason may be simply developmental immaturity. The sexual instinct is considered to be much slower to mature than the other instincts. For a youngster, primary gratification through oral stimulation or masturbation is quite appropriate to the prepubescent developmental stage. But if an adult favors partial aims and objects, the explanation points toward faulty development and psychopathology.

Freud's notions of comprehensive and partial objects has led some critics to think his theory very middle class, in that it seems to designate human sexual processes only for procreation and not for pleasure. This is not a valid criticism, for Freud well understood the function of the pleasurable "partial" sexual activities to be that of setting the stage for vigorous intercourse and orgasm and contributing to one's overall sexual satisfaction. He meant the sexual instinct to cover far more areas of the body and types of activities and pleasures than is associated with a "conventional" view of sex. It is only when one or another of the partial goals becomes primary for an adult that he would worry.

Freud's distinction between the sexual instinct and the previously mentioned life instincts seems to imply that the former does not have a survival function. But this is not entirely true. Although the sexual instinct does not ensure the individual's survival by providing the impetus for obtaining needed nutrients and raw materials for metabolism (as do the life instincts), it does ensure survival of the species by providing the impetus for procreation. And

Freud certainly recognizes that survival of the species is ultimately important to survival of individuals. Nonetheless, it must be said that although the sexual instinct, like all instincts, is rooted in biological requirements, these requirements are not immediately relevant to the survival of the individual having the instinct. That the sexual instinct expresses a biological requirement can be shown by the painfully high levels of tension and discomfort that ensue from enforced sexual continence. But this requirement does not have a strong, obvious effect on individual survival; some people, such as priests and nuns, live in fairly complete sexual abstinence without taking many years off their lives (as far as anyone knows). It is true that once you define sexuality as broadly as Freud does, you can believe that even celibates can achieve some partial gratification of their sexual instinct, and it may be just this that permits them to survive. It is also true that Freud would expect the conditions of celibacy to lead to certain symptoms, albeit subtle, of psychological malady. In any case, the sexual instinct is rooted in biological requirements that do not affect the individual's immediate survival. After all, in the case of the life instincts, if you abstained from food or water for very long, there would be no need to search for subtle symptoms—you would die!

The disproportionate attention Freud gave to the sexual instinct certainly cannot be understood as a function of its greater importance for survival than needs for food, water, and the like. It received so much attention because it seemed a much greater contributor to conflict than life instincts. And in a theory such as Freud's, conflict forms and shapes the person's life. One reason why the sexual instinct was seen as the major source of conflict is that it matures so slowly and has so many parts that can be satisfied in so many ways. In contrast, the life instincts are simple, needing little maturation and capable of being satisfied in only a few ways. The sexual instinct can be more affected by what one learns in early life than can the life instincts. As we shall see in the following section, Freud's views on society's reactions to expressions of the sexual instinct clearly explain why conflict arises from early influences.

During the latter part of his career, Freud began to be convinced that there is yet a third kind of instinct and that it functions as an antagonist to the life instincts. The aim of this *death instinct* is the biological death of the person. It is so extraordinary to assume that a basic tendency of the organism is to push toward death that consideration of Freud's reasons for doing this are clearly in order. Freud began theorizing in terms of the death instinct when he was well along in his life. Not only could he note the physiological and psychological changes going on within him as he aged; he had also reached the age at which it is increasingly common to find those around us dying. Further, there was his own jaw cancer, which, though contained by treatment, must have brought the possibility of his death to the center of his attention during his last years. It is clear that Freud had a strong dread of death during this period (Bakan, 1966).

It is fashionable these days to consider death as rendering life meaningless in rational terms, because death, though the only absolute thing in existence, is itself unpredictable. Ours is also a time in which even hard sciences, such as physics, are abandoning the attempt to attribute causes to every observable event. But in Freud's time, many scientists believed in a strong form of the deterministic hypothesis; in other words, they expected to be able to discover a cause for every event. Freud gave evidence very early in his career of the strength of his own belief in this when he took such phenomena as dreams and slips of the tongue to be important events with causes, a point of view then uncommon in medical circles. Such a strong believer in determinism would naturally take death to be a phenomenon with a rational, specifiable cause, especially when his or her own life circumstances conspired to render death personally salient.

In searching for a rational cause of death, Freud could not have been content with a purely physiological theory of the breakdown, fatigue, or rigidification of body systems. He was too committed to assuming a psychological component to biological processes for the physiological view to have seemed sufficient. Freud had to assume a psychological—indeed, motivational—cause of death that also reflected a profound biological truth in order to remain consistent with his previous theorizing.

Consistency and personal concern were not, of course, the only reasons for Freud's theory of the death instinct. This assumption provided a rational way of understanding death not only as a natural concomitant of aging but as a result of decision making, as in murder and suicide. War could be understood as mass expression of the death instinct. In this regard it is not surprising that Freud's major interest in the death instinct developed following World War I. He explained even acts of aggression toward oneself and others as being partial or disguised expressions of the tendency toward death. Like the life instincts, the death instinct had its source in the biological process of metabolism. Even in the individual cell, along with the anabolic processes, which determine its birth and growth, are the catabolic processes, which determine its decay and eventual death.

Freud never developed the idea of the death instinct as completely as he did that of the life instincts. If the somatic source of the death instinct is catabolism, its aim is presumably the reduction of tension arising from the biological necessity of decay. It is not clear, however, that any such tension reduction really occurs. Nowhere do we find detailed discussions of energy associated with the death instinct that would parallel libido theory. Further, while a few objects for the death instinct can be specified, Freud's writings lack comprehensive discussions of such matters. Finally, the notion of the death instinct is not embedded in a developmental theory as are the life and sexual instincts.

As if there were not enough difficulties, there is an additional, logistical problem created by Freud's assumption that the life instincts are actively opposed by a death instinct. To make the theory consistent, it is necessary to specify the precise nature of the relationship between the two antagonistic forces. Freud's rudimentary statements concerning the relationship are not theoretically satisfactory. He felt that in the normal course of events the life instincts are stronger than the death instinct, but late in life the tide turns. In some disordered personalities of any age, the death instinct can be more powerful than the life instinct. It is also possible for the death instinct to be stronger at certain times in a person's life, such as periods of sleep and self-condemnation. In statements such as these, Freud is doing no more than making observations and describing them in terms of the two notions of death and life instincts. His approach seems arbitrary and inconsistent. Such difficulties have led many psychologists to be particularly skeptical of the concept of the death instinct. According to them, everything that Freud can account for with the concept can also be explained as aggression resulting from frustration in the attempt to satisfy the life and sexual instincts, a position with which Freud himself would have agreed until the latter part of his life. But to other intellectuals (e.g., Brown, 1959), the concept of the death instinct has been very intriguing.

In concluding this section on instincts, I would like to emphasize a crucial point that you must grasp fully if you are to understand Freud's position. The wishes and emotions of the id are deeply self-centered—indeed, selfish—in nature. They express the person's basic, unadulterated, biological nature. They have no social refinements. The id wants what it wants when it wants it, without regard for what other people may need, prefer, or insist on. Looked at as an individual, the human being is basically selfish and uncivilized, according to Freud. As you will see in the next section, it is this inherent selfishness that makes conflict inevitable.

You should also recognize that the instincts, as they exist in the id, are hopelessly ineffective in the external world. What good does it do to have wishes and emotions expressing your biological necessities unless you know how to reach what you want and have the capability to carry out that knowledge? Very little or no good is Freud's answer. On the basis of the id alone, you would be able to satisfy instincts only through wish-fulfilling fantasy (called *primary process* thought)—and fantasy would not help much when what you need is real bread. Luckily, the infant ordinarily is tended by parents until it has learned to fend for itself. It must learn which of the appropriate objects of its instincts are available in the environment, where they are likely to be, and what instrumental behaviors are likely to obtain them. In all this learning, it must express selectivity, accuracy, memory, and self-correction. In a word, it must act intelligently. In Freud's terms, the infant must develop an *ego* (the Latin word for *self*).

At birth, the infant's entire mind is composed of id wishes and emotions. But as experience accumulates, part of the mind differentiates from the id and becomes ego. In large measure, the ego is the part of the mind comprising the thought and perceptual processes involved in recognition, remembrance, and action relevant to satisfying instincts (called *secondary process* thought). It is important to recognize that this great function of the ego is to aid in satisfying instincts in the external world. In bringing about satisfaction, the ego has the advantage of control over the voluntary nervous system and musculature. The ego and its component processes, being common to all persons, should be considered core characteristics of personality along with the id and its components.

Freud has done a very interesting thing in this theorizing: He has made the mind a bridge from the metabolic requirements of the body to the intelligent actions and interactions monitored by mental life. The metabolic processes produce the wishes and discomforts of the id, and the ego comes into being in order to guide the intelligence and the muscles of the body in efficiently serving the metabolic processes. With the advent of the ego, the attempt to achieve biological necessities becomes not only selfish but effective. Freud calls this *pleasure principle functioning* to indicate both its selfish and its biologically satisfying quality. In early life, the human being engages solely in pleasure principle functioning. As you may have surmised, the part of Freud's core statement concerning maximization of instinctual gratification refers to pleasure principle functioning. But then society rears its head. . . .

The Sources of Punishment and Guilt. The key to understanding Freud's view of the sources of punishment and guilt is that he believes the instincts to be not simply self-centered but necessarily antagonistic to the principles of orderly, civilized living. The instincts aim only for the reduction of tension due to metabolic requirements. Such requirements are, after all, characteristic of individual organisms alone. According to Freud, if everyone were to act out their natural, uninhibited instinctual demands—that is, function at the level of pleasure principle alone—the world would be an unimaginably horrendous place. In the process of grabbing what you want when you wanted it, you inevitably would encounter others who wanted the same thing at the same time or who would be disadvantaged by your gain. You would have to compete with them or vanquish their defense. You would fight violently, without regard for the restrained and orderly manners of civilization, and to the victor would go the spoils of instinctual gratification.

No one can be sure of victory always. But accepting that you may be unable to satisfy your instincts is anathema to the selfish id. Because people must live together, pleasure principle functioning leads to the risk of failure in obtaining precisely that which defines it. And, of course, a world in which people keep to themselves, living as hermits, is implausible. Actually, Freud's position makes such isolation impossible, as it would lead to frustration of at least one instinct—that for sex—which requires the social interaction of intercourse.

The best that aggregates of persons, or societies, can do is aim for cooperation and order so as to maximize gratification for all. This pressure toward the common good, which in Freud's terms means equalizing the possibilities of instinctual gratification for all society members, is the second great force in our terminology. Social living requires rules and regulations for conduct which cut into pleasure principle functioning in the sense of uninhibited, unfettered pursuit of instinctual delights. But rules and regulations are the most effective measures for ensuring a predictable maximum of instinctual gratification for all. Freud assumes that the aims of the individual are selfish whereas those of society are for the common good. If people must function in groups, the seemingly paradoxical development of civilized behavior in those persons who have no naturally generous, altruistic interest toward others is inevitable. Because individuals and society are seen as having antagonistic aims, the one selfish and the other communal, Freud's theory is classified here as an example of the psychosocial conflict model.

Freud derives the importance of civilization from a position that takes selfish natural human characteristics as a starting point for understanding life through simply accepting the fact that persons must live in close interaction with one another. He expresses this view in vivid, parable form in his book *Totem and Taboo* (1952), a story of the beginning of civilization. At the start, there are a father and mother and their many sons. True to the sexual instincts of the phallic stage of psychosexual development (to be discussed in Chapter 7), the sons wish to murder the father in order to sexually possess the mother. Being pleasure principle creatures, they actually carry out this instinctual wish. But once the father is out of the way, they find themselves thwarted in their selfish desires by the ensuing competition among them and thereby come to realize the futility of having committed murder. So the most direct route to instinctual gratification—pleasure principle functioning—turns out to be ineffective in the long run because all the sons unfortunately want the same goal. Finally, the sons band together and adopt a set of rules designed to avoid future difficulties by restricting the expression of instincts to those forms not damaging to the group as a whole. This, in the parable, is the beginning of civilization, with its emphasis on reverence toward the dead father (totem) and the taboo on incest, coupled with the institutionalization of marriage. Together these taboos and sanctions ensure as much satisfaction of the sexual instinct for each member of society as is possible without inordinate risk of battle over and deprivation of sexual objects.

We are now in a position to consider the matters of punishment and guilt. These have their source in the communal requirements of society. When people transgress the rules and regulations of civilization, they are punished by the society's representatives. Young people are common transgressors, because they function at the level of the pleasure principle, not yet having learned the rules and regulations governing adult life. Parents are common punishers, acting in the role of societal representatives, because they are around the youngsters most often. Such punishments as physical damage, psychological humiliation, and withdrawal of love are all effective, according to Freudians, because they increase tension in the organism. Even though the increase in tension is caused by an external action of punishment, its discomforting organismic effects are considered similar to those caused by instinctual deprivation. Tension is tension, and whenever it is present the person must try to decrease it in some way. As society is greater and more powerful than individuals, the latter's method of avoiding punishment, especially when they are youngsters and relatively powerless, is to curb instinctual expression so as not to brook retaliation. Punishment comes from outside the person and expresses the societal requirements of communal living. Although expressive of the same requirements, guilt comes from within the person. In order to understand this, you must keep in mind that children grow up under the influence of their parents, who are in large part representatives of society with the assigned task of teaching children to accept the rules and regulations that will render them civilized adults. Certainly parents punish children for unbridled instinctual expression and, as a pattern of accumulated punishments emerges, children learn something of the nature of the rules. In addition, the parents supplement this dawning knowledge with verbal instruction. Over time, the combination of the two techniques leads children to internalize the rules. Once these exist in their memory, they can feel guilt. From then on, they can realize for themselves when some wish transgresses the common good and can feel morally culpable even if they do not act on it. A portion of the mind hitherto devoted to ego processes becomes differentiated, or set apart, for the purpose of representing the rules and regulations of society in terms of the abstract ideas of good/bad and right/wrong. Freud's name for this set of ideas is the *superego*. Because its presence and, to some extent, its contents are common to all persons in the same society, it constitutes a core characteristic of personality in our terminology. As the internal counterpart of earlier punishments, guilt is assumed to have the same effect of raising organismic tension, which must then be reduced. Guilt, like the society it mirrors, is powerful enough to lead persons to inhibit their instincts in an attempt to avoid punishment. Instincts can be expressed only insofar as guilt is kept to a minimum.

We now have all the elements for understanding Freud's core tendency of personality. Persons attempt to maximize instinctual gratification while minimizing punishment and guilt because that is the best they can do in decreasing tension given the basically antagonistic nature of the individual and society. With the accumulation of punishment and the development of the superego, the ego takes on its second major function. Recall that the first function of the ego is to provide the cognitive and actional structure for effective satisfaction of instincts in the external world. The second ego function is to translate instinctual demands into actions consistent with superego demands. The ego, therefore, is the architect of the core tendency, which Freud calls *reality principle functioning*. Reality principle functioning takes into account not only instinctual demands but the equally inexorable—and, unfortunately, opposed—demands of society. In reality principle functioning, people choose only socially acceptable forms and routines of instinctual functioning. The young man will not sleep with his mother; instead, he will find another girl, who is sexually attached to no one, and marry her. Hungry persons will not steal bread; rather, they will get jobs and earn the money to pay bakers for the time they have had to spend away from their own instinctual gratification.

Perhaps because of his early biological training in medicine, Freud always considered it important to determine where the energy or fuel for particular organismic functions came from. According to him, the instincts get their energy from their metabolic sources and the ego and superego share the energy of the instincts. This is not really as strange as it might seem, for the ego and superego make possible maximum instinct gratification.

We are now in a position to reflect knowledgeably on why Freud emphasized the sexual instinct much more than the life and death instincts. Actually, the death instinct was a concept from his later life, and he was so uncertain about it that its relative lack of emphasis seems understandable. But the difference in emphasis on the sexual and life instincts requires further comment, as both instincts were basic parts of his theorizing virtually from the beginning. Clearly the sexual instinct received the lion's share of attention because Freud believed it to be surrounded with much more psychosocial conflict than the life instincts. The life instincts have an immediately obvious role in maintaining biological survival, and they can rise to intense levels after just a short period of deprivation. But although unbridled expression of the life instincts will conflict with societal requirements, these instincts are so obviously important that all societies provide institutionalized bases for satisfying them regularly and rapidly lest they become too strong. So, three meals a day, with one or two snacks thrown in, are common in our society, and water and other liquids are more or less continually available.

Insofar as the life instincts are readily satisfied, they are not a chronic source of intense conflict. Not so with the sexual instinct. To be sure, we have the institution of marriage, which can provide the socially sanctioned basis for frequent sexual gratification. But what of the person who is not married or the child who has only rudimentary ways of repressing the sexual instinct? Society has no concrete way of planning for such people's sexual needs. They may indeed find sexual gratification, but generally not in a socially sanctioned and respectable way. When an unmarried person has sex without "attachment," he or she may be frowned on. When children masturbate, it is imagined that they will damage themselves through such "monstrous activity." Even if such attitudes are diminishing these days, it is still clear that Western society has provided less extensive and effective institutional means for the satisfaction of the sexual instinct than for the life instincts. This situation, according to Freud, surrounds the sexual instinct with conflict. Freud emphasized the sexual instinct so much that he defined personality development in terms of it. His well-known oral, anal, phallic, latency, and genital stages are called psychosexual stages of development. And with the biological maturing of the sexual instinct at puberty, the personality jells, changing little thenceforward.

Defense.   Freud's core theorizing involves not only a position on the nature of the instincts and the sources of punishment and guilt but also a position on the mechanism that maximizes instinct gratification while minimizing punishment and guilt. This mechanism is contained in the concept of *defense*. If you fully express your instincts in action, you will be punished by other people. If you fully recognize your instincts, you will experience guilt even without acting on them. The instincts are inexorable forces pushing for expression. This is the major conflict of life, and it is eased somewhat through the process of defense.

The way in which defenses are aroused is simple enough. Whenever an instinct becomes strong enough to be a potential source of conflict, an alarm reaction occurs in the form of anxiety. Anxiety is a diffuse feeling—somewhat lacking in specific content—of discomfort and impending disaster. This anxiety reaction represents the anticipation of punishment and guilt based on remembrance of past punishment and guilt, and it triggers the defensive process. Defense eases the conflict between the demands of instincts and society by striking a compromise between them. The defense limits personal awareness and expression in action of the instinct to only that part or form of it that is acceptable to other people and to one's internalized standards. Hence, one's actions become acceptable both to society and to oneself, and one avoids punishment and guilt. For example, if a son's real instinctual wish is to possess his mother sexually, the defensive form of his wish may be the desire to stay close to her, nurture her, and keep her from harm. The defensive wish and actions are not only acceptable to others and to his own superego; they also permit partial instinctual gratification through closeness to mother and through keeping her for himself.

Defensive processes are aroused more frequently than one might think. To Freud's way of thinking, defense is a ubiquitous thing, because instincts (which are inherently antisocial) are never at zero intensity and, hence, conflict between instinctual and societal aims—which is the basis for defense—is never absent. As all behavior is motivated by or infused with instincts, so is all behavior, to a Freudian, defensive!

This conclusion has extraordinary implications. If all behavior is defensive, people are unaware of their true wishes, feelings, and aims. These true instinctual elements are represented in the mind, but as mental content inaccessible to awareness. The paradoxical ring of this position has been the source of many attacks on Freudian thinking, which we shall consider further in Chapter 6. If all behavior is defensive, whatever mental content we are aware of is no more than epiphenomenal, or a pale shadow of the truth. Thus, wishing to remain close to and nurture mother might very well be part of what one would feel if one really wanted to possess her sexually, but one would never infer the presence of the latter wish from the former.

The defenses function to keep repressed desires out of consciousness more or less indefinitely. Thus, the truth about oneself is perhaps permanently inaccessible. To say that all behavior is defensive has much more alarming implications than does considering only some behavior defensive. If, as Freud believed, the truth about oneself is ordinarily unavailable, how can learning, or any real change in personality, take place? Leaving aside for a moment the possibility of change through psychoanalysis—the form of psychotherapy associated with the Freudian position—we should discard as useless some of our most cherished ideas about rationality as the basis for living and educating. If logical thinking and debate cannot even have the real truth to work on, how can such processes possibly produce any meaningful result? An eminent anti-Freudian personologist, Gordon W. Allport (1955), puts the problem this way:

> Up to now the "behavioral sciences," including psychology, have not provided us with a picture of man capable of creating or living in a democracy. These sciences in large part have imitated the billiard ball model of physics, now of course outmoded. They have delivered into our hands a psychology of an organism pushed by drives and molded by environmental circumstance. . . . But the theory of democracy requires also that man possess a measure of rationality, a portion of freedom, a generic conscience, propriate ideals, and unique value. We cannot defend the ballot box or liberal education, nor advocate free discussion and democratic institutions, unless man has the potential capacity to profit therefrom. (p. 100)

Because all behavior, according to Freud, is not only motivated but defensive, we are forced, in his frame of reference, to accept a view of humans as controlled by forces from within and pressures from without and, furthermore, as ignorant of that damning fact!

You may think that especially in this last phrase I am being unfair to Freud by making him seem overly pessimistic and deterministic. After all, does he not really mean that since we use defensive processes to ease conflict, we especially need to recognize that our conscious beliefs about ourselves are not necessarily the whole truth? If he does, there is really no incompatibility between the Socratic injunction to "know thyself" and the Freudian view. Is Freud not merely emphasizing how important it is to plumb the full depths of our minds? Freud's use of free association can be seen as proof that he believed one could circumvent the inhibition of consciousness produced by defense. Although modern-day psychoanalytic thinkers have added to Freud's position in such a manner as to make this "know thyself" interpretation plausible, I think it distorts what Freud himself meant.

Most people find this interpretation of Freud compelling because it presents humans as fallible but also perfectible, a position deeply rooted in Western thought and religion. But even if you think you know yourself rather well through introspection and experience, even if you think you have seen your own foibles, defensive operations, and bedrock instincts, Freud would not have accepted your self-knowledge as valid unless, perhaps, you had been in psychoanalysis for many years. He would have seen your beliefs concerning the nature of your defensive operations and real wishes as defensive in themselves! You cannot know the real truth about yourself simply because you have the pious goal of being honest and working hard at it.

You cannot get behind your own defenses because the defensive process itself is outside of awareness. If your defenses operated consciously, they would not be effective at all. You would know that you were constantly lying to yourself and to the world. A consciously operating process of defense would not insulate you from guilt, though it could be successful in avoiding punishment. Indeed, we all employ techniques for hiding our conscious intent from others when we think they will find it unacceptable. While these are somewhat analogous to what Freud meant by defenses, they fall short of the important meaning of that concept—for the defense is a way of lying to yourself as well as other people.

You can lie to yourself effectively only if you do not realize you are doing so. Defense operates unconsciously, and you cannot penetrate defensive processes to obtain real truth simply by an earnest attempt to do so. Unless you have had the very unusual experience of a momentary breakdown of a defense, you have no basis in personal experience for fully understanding the theory of defense. Freud would not be impressed by your personal account of your own defensive operations and underlying instinctual desires. He would see it as symptomatic of a deeply ingrained structure of unconscious defenses.

There are times when defenses break down and a glimpse of the real truth ensues. These occur when the person is in psychoanalysis or is severely debilitated through psychological or physical stress. The breakdown in defense is accompanied by acute guilt and anxiety—the feeling that life is about to end terribly—indeed, *should* end for someone so worthless. One cannot stay in such a state for very long and still maintain integrity and organization. If defenses are not reinstituted, madness or catastrophe will result regardless of whether the source of breakdown was debilitation or psychotherapy. I choose such strong words because Freud felt he was talking about matters of life and death. It is a tribute to the success of defensive processes that such starkness is rarely experienced fully.

If defenses, once breached, must be reinstated in order to avoid catastrophic disintegration of personality, not even psychoanalysis can or should try to remove all the defenses. But then what did Freud mean when he characterized the goal of psychotherapy with the dramatic axiom "Where id was there shall ego be" (1933, p. 112)? In trying to understand this statement, we must be clear on the nature of id and ego. The id is the mental representation, in the form of wishes and feelings, of selfish instincts whose source lies in somatic and metabolic processes. By themselves, instincts are relatively ineffective in the world; instincts do not include knowledge of the instrumentalities governing the actions that ensure gratification, nor do they include knowledge of the necessity of avoiding open conflict with other people. The ego is constituted largely of knowledge of the instrumentalities effective in instinct gratification and of techniques of conforming to the inescapable requirements of society. The ego ensures a maximum of instinct gratification and a minimum of trouble through the processes of perception, memory, and judgment and their relation to the voluntary nervous system, guided throughout by the knowledge mentioned above. The most important part of the ego is the defenses. It is largely the defensive processes that permit effective operation of the only successful tendency of life—reality principle functioning.

Freud's statement "Where id was there shall ego be" is often interpreted to mean that in psychoanalysis, unconscious mentation is made conscious, and defenses are removed in favor of a more open basis for experiencing. However, this does not appear to be accurate. While the id is largely unconscious, it is not true that the ego is largely conscious. Remember that the defenses, which are themselves unconscious, represent the lion's share of the ego, according to Freud. Furthermore, a large part of the id is unconscious only because of the action of the ego's defensive processes. So the notion of replacing id with ego is not very likely to mean making the unconscious conscious. The id has a permanent place in the Freudian psyche; he considered it a natural human endowment. What did he mean, then, by his famous statement, with all its figurativeness and fuzziness? As you may have guessed from my description of id and ego in the previous paragraphs, I think Freud meant that pleasure principle functioning so characteristic of the id in isolation and so ineffective in the world, must give way to reality principle functioning, if psychotherapy is to be judged successful. Reality principle functioning, you will remember, is what we have been calling Freud's core tendency of living.

Lacan (Mehlman, 1972), a contemporary French psychoanalyst, essentially agrees with my interpretation of Freud's famous statement. Reconsidering the original German *"Wo es war, soll ich werden,"* Lacan asserts that the translation could well have been "Where id (or it) was, there must ego (or I) arrive at." This definitely implies that the goal of psychotherapy is less to increase consciousness than to heighten instinctual gratification brought about by rendering the ego an instrument of the id.

So far, we have focused on defensiveness as a general mechanism for striking a compromise between the demands of instincts and those of society. Actually, Freud's theory of personality details more different kinds of defense than any other theory. His daughter Anna Freud (1946) lists such examples of defense as *repression, regression, reaction formation, denial, projection,* and *sublimation*. While we will not discuss these different kinds of defense until Chapter 7, on the peripheral characteristics of personality, it is important to recognize here that one crucial distinction among defenses is the degree to which they distort the underlying instincts. The more successful the psychosexual development has been, the more the person's functioning is characterized by defenses, such as sublimation, that minimally distort instinctual reality. Developmental failings, produced by fixations (or arrested growth), are defined partially by the existence of grossly distortive defenses, such as projection.

But even the highest form of functioning, bespeaking exemplary development, is characterized by defensiveness, because the true antisocial nature of the instincts must be hidden from oneself and the world. Freud (1938) takes this so far as to assert that well (not poorly) developed adults, in falling in love, unconsciously choose partners who resemble their opposite-sex parents. Expressing this love fulfills unconscious incestuous fantasies. This instinctual truth is hidden by that most sophisticated defensive operation, *sublimation*.

The most accurate description of the goal of psychoanalysis, if the position is to have logical consistency, is as the substitution, for defenses that heavily distort truth, of defenses that more closely approximate it. But as there is no alternative to defensive behavior, there is always at least some distortion of truth and, hence, unconsciousness of some of the most basic things about oneself. Freud's theory of personality is probably the most pessimistic in existence.

A word more will enhance understanding of the dimensions of this pessimism. Freud discusses development in terms of the biological maturation of the sexual instinct and delineates the five well-known stages called *oral, anal, phallic, latency,* and *genital.* In each stage, a mental state accompanies the biological state. Fixations at any of these stages except the last are thought to result in adult personalities or *character types* that embody the mental defenses and traits characteristic of that stage. We will discuss these matters much more fully later. For the moment, it is enough to realize that the first three—and most crucial—stages of psychosexual development cover roughly the first five years of life. The phallic stage, incorporating as it does the famous Oedipal struggle, is believed to be followed by a period of biological dormancy. This latency period, unelaborated on by Freud, persists until the advent of puberty. Puberty opens the genital stage, which continues until death. The extraordinary discrepancy between the attention given the earliest childhood years and the rest of life indicates that for Freud nothing of real developmental importance happens after age five. The outlines of personality are essentially fixed by then, with the rest of life being a repetition of the early patterns. To be sure, the person becomes more complex with age, but nothing basic really changes.

Persons familiar with Freud may contend that his pessimism is more characteristic of his earlier works. But there is also evidence of pessimism in the later works, in which the death instinct is formulated for the first time (Freud, 1922a) and the inevitability of defensiveness is reasserted (e.g., Freud, 1922b). In the latter work, Freud suggests that the effect of World War I was to strip away the comforting repression of the death instinct in which all humans were engaging. Had Freud been leaning toward a new-found optimism, he could have argued at this point that such a new level of consciousness would spur psychological development. Instead, he predicted that people's consciousness of their own viciousness would prove too much to bear, leading to a renewal of defensiveness. Some would revert to a primitive defense—projection—and imagine that there really were enemies out there, from whom they must protect themselves (through aggression, of course). Others would take a more sophisticated route by seeming to accept death as the outcome of aggression but rejecting it at a deeper level. Through rationalizations such as the belief in an afterlife or the contention that we achieve immortality in our works and our children, the stark reality of the death instinct is blunted. One way or another, we defend against awareness of the instinctual truth because we cannot bear it. If he changed as he aged, Freud probably became more rather than less pessimistic.

Murray's Position

Like Freud, Henry A. Murray (born in New York City, 1893) has lived a complex, cosmopolitan life. He began his career as a physician. Throughout his early professional years as a physiologist and surgeon, Murray demonstrated a profound interest in psychic considerations by conducting serious psychological studies of his colleagues and patients. Eventually his psychological interests, fired by the psychoanalyst Jung, the study of philosophy, and his own intense life, got the better of him. Having decided on a serious commitment to personology—a word that he coined—Murray was appointed director of the Harvard Psychological Clinic by Morton Prince. The years he gave to this role, which ended with the advent of World War II, constituted an extremely active, exciting, and productive period in the life of the Clinic. Much as Freud had done before him, Murray gathered together an extraordinary group of young and capable psychologists, who worked in close collaboration on the development of a theory of personality. But the source of evidence for this theory was not psychotherapy with disturbed people so much as systematic research on the lives of the articulate, gifted undergraduates at Harvard University. The aspects of Murray's theory stemming from this source relate to the periphery of personality and will be discussed in Chapter 7. This theorizing on the peripheral has had a tremendous impact on personology, both directly through Murray and his colleagues, many of whom are extraordinary figures in the field, and indirectly through its effect on the testing movement.

But the core considerations in Murray's theory that we will discuss here are distinctly psychoanalytic. At the same time that Murray was heading the Harvard Psychological Clinic, he was being trained as a psychoanalyst (by members of Freud's inner circle) and finally became a charter member of the Boston Psychoanalytic Society. His work as a psychotherapist for disturbed people expressed the side of him that was a committed Freudian.

As you may have surmised, Murray's position is frustratingly heterogeneous. Though rich and fertile, his thinking is also disturbingly eclectic—so much so that it is difficult to know whether to classify his view as a conflict position. In statements about the core of personality that are most relevant to such classification, Murray is quite similar to Freud. But there is a great deal more to Murray, whose heterogeneous theorizing reflects the nature of his life. In the early days of World War II Murray established and directed the first extensive, systematic assessment unit for the Office of Strategic Services. For his work he was awarded the Legion of Merit in 1946. Over the years, Murray has made a strong commitment to the study of literature, ranking as an expert on the work of Herman Melville. And, far from restricting himself to the biological emphasis of Freudianism, Murray has branched out into the study of anthropology and sociology for their relevance to the understanding of humans. (For additional information on Murray's life as it relates to his theorizing, see Maddi and Costa [1972]).

For Murray (1938), Freud's conceptualization of the core tendency of life will do quite well: *The person tries to maximize instinctual gratification while minimizing punishment and guilt.* Like Freud, Murray talks in terms of the core characteristics of id, ego, and superego. Murray too considers the id to be the part of personality that contributes energy and direction for behavior. In short, the id summarizes the person's motivation. In discussing motivation more precisely, Murray uses the language of life and sexual instincts and gives an important place to considerations of psychosexual development. The superego is for him, as for Freud, a cultural implant, learned through the punishment and approval of parents, that functions to inhibit the socially destructive expression of instincts. So, on the one hand, we see the emphasis on instincts as self-interested nature; on the other, we see social living as requiring some relinquishment of complete instinctual gratification. Society protects itself by punishing antisocial actions. Since punishment is painful, individuals avoid antisocial actions and the resulting social punishment or superego-induced guilt, thus maximizing instinctual gratification. In the carrying out of this core tendency, the ego has the role of mediating between the poles of the conflict through the use of the voluntary nervous system and musculature in planning, ordering, and defensive processes. In all this, Murray and Freud are in close agreement: Conflict is inevitable, and life must therefore be, at best, a compromise that minimizes the conflict or at least makes it bearable. For this reason, I have called Murray a *conflict theorist*.

But there are differences in emphasis between Freud and Murray in conceptualizing the core of personality. In Murray's approach, all these differences occur in the direction of decreasing the inevitability of conflict. Murray believes that while the id certainly contains the familiar selfish instincts, it also includes other motivational tendencies, such as the needs for love and achievement, that are less clearly inconsistent with social living. These basic motivational tendencies are inherent to the organism rather than secondary motivations derived from the selfish instincts through learning and the operation of defenses, as they would by for Freud. So the notion of replacing id with ego is not likely to mean making unconscious things become conscious. Clearly the needs for love and achievement are not inconsistent with civilized living— indeed, they promote it. If they are inherent, humans, in their most natural state, are not temperamentally incapable of communal living. Hence, Murray's view of the id, compared with Freud's, is less in keeping with a conflict position.

Turning to the superego, we find that here too Murray has elaborated on and eclecticized Freud's view. For Murray, the superego is not only the taboos and sanctions instilled by parents when a child is at a tender, cognitively uncritical age; it is also a sophisticated set of principles and ideals for living based on considerable personal experience with many people and life contexts. Even great literature is a contributor to superego development according to Murray. The superego grows in individuality and sophistication throughout life rather than remaining, as Freud contends, the unshakable vestige of early trials and tribulations. In Murray's view, superego does not necessarily oppose the id; as the id is not completely selfish, neither is the superego completely in the service of the needs of others. So in his treatment of superego, Murray's modifications of Freud decrease the inevitability of conflict in living.

While conflict and its minimization remain essential to understanding the core of personality in Murray's theory, Murray does include functioning that is not conflict defined. He has also elaborated the idea of ego beyond what Freud had in mind. In classical Freud, the role of the ego is essentially limited to carrying out the core tendency of maximizing instinctual gratification while minimizing punishment and guilt. Going beyond this, Murray (Murray & Kluckhohn, 1956, p. 26) elaborates ego functions that relate to the expression of socially acceptable id tendencies. Whereas Freud stresses defensive operations as the substance of the ego and as the primary basis for resolving conflicts, Murray stresses cognitive and actional procedures for planning and executing behaviors in the absence of conflict. These procedures include such things as *rational thought* and *accurate perception* (Maddi, 1963; Maddi & Costa, 1972). As Maddi (1963, p. 194) points out, Murray even goes so far as to assume, somewhat implicitly, that the ego has an inborn basis separate from that of the id. He does this by attributing ego functioning in part to the natural requirement of the nervous system for information.

These modifications of Freud's thinking have a number of general effects well worthy of note. For one, consciousness—true, accurate representation of experience in awareness—is not only logically possible but extremely important in Murray's position. Each person is some conglomerate of consciousness and unconsciousness, the former expressing conflict-free aspects of personality and the latter defensive resolutions of conflict. Another departure from Freud is that for Murray motivational tendencies do not necessarily aim for tension reduction. Murray (Murray & Kluckhohn, 1956, pp. 36–37) contends that the absence of tension is less rewarding than the process of getting from higher to lower states of tension. People may actually increase their tension to heighten their pleasure when tension is subsequently decreased. Once again we find Murray unwilling to accept the most extreme form of classical Freudian thinking.

Actually, when we focus on his modifications of Freud, Murray looks not unlike some of the theorists discussed in the chapters on the fulfillment model. But in his core theorizing, Murray is still basically a conflict theorist. His treatment of development also follows Freud's lead rather closely. There are modifications here, too, but they do not remove the emphasis on conflict. Murray (1938) identifies what he calls *complexes,* which essentially are groups of traits and styles that result from fixations at one or another of the Freudian stages of development. To be sure, Murray does add to Freud's developmental formulation. At the younger end, for example, Murray describes the *claustral complex,* a group of traits characteristic of the intrauterine stage of life. He also identifies a *urethral stage,* which falls between the oral and anal stages. In sum, Murray's view of complexes as the result of fixations in psychosexual development, as well as his other, previously mentioned views, suggests that he is in the conflict camp.

All things considered, it may be best to consider Murray's position as a variant on the pure conflict theory. Though conflict and its minimization still remain the most basic considerations, Murray postulates an aspect of ego functioning that is independent of the id and, hence, potentially free of conflict.

Ego Psychology

Murray is certainly one of the first theorists of general psychoanalytic persuasion to embrace the possibility that some proportion of functioning, however small, might not be concerned with conflict and its minimization. This possibility has found its most characteristic expression in the writings of Hartmann, Kris, and Loewenstein (1947), who developed the notion of a *conflict-free ego sphere*. They argued that some of the ego's functions are carried out with energy not derived from the id. In other words, the ego has some functions that are not in the service of instinct gratification and the avoidance of pain. The authors go so far as to assume that the ego does not emerge out of the inborn id at all; rather, both ego and id have their origin in inherited predispositions and have their own independent sources of development. At least the part of the ego that does not deal with conflict has its own inborn source of energy with which to carry out its functions. The conflict-free portion of the ego has different objectives than the id's. It includes such functions (much like those Murray has stressed) as rational thought processes, accurate perceptual processes, and muscular coordination, which the person uses to accomplish intellectual and social objectives that are not psychosexual in nature. Some writers, such as Hendrick (1943), have even assumed the existence of ego instincts, such as *to master*. The source of the mastery instinct is in the environmental challenge to function effectively, and its aim is to reduce the tension resulting from this challenge. Though somewhat different from Murray's idea of the need for information, which influences ego functioning, the mastery instinct similarly provides a logical theoretical justification for assuming an inborn ego.

The innate bases of ego autonomy are called *primary,* to distinguish them from *secondary* bases, which are rooted in experience. In an authoritative statement, Rapaport (1958) says:

> We no longer assume that the ego arises from the id, but rather that the ego and the id both arise by differentiation from a common undifferentiated matrix, in which the apparatuses that differentiate into the ego's means of orientation, or reality-testing, and of action, are already present. These, termed *apparatuses of primary autonomy,* serve drive gratification and enter conflict as independent ego factors. They are the memory apparatus, the motor apparatus, the perceptual apparatuses, and the threshold apparatuses (including the drive- and affect-discharge thresholds). They are evolutionary givens which, by virtue of their

long history of selection and modification, have become the primary guarantees of the organism's "fitting in" with (adaptedness to) its environment. In other words, the primary guarantees of the ego's autonomy from the id seem to be the very apparatuses which guarantee the organism's adaptedness to the environment.

The *apparatuses of secondary autonomy* arise either from instinctual modes and vicissitudes, as these become "estranged" from their instinctual sources, or from defensive structures formed in the process of conflict-solution, as these undergo a "change of function" and become apparatuses serving adaptation. In other words, the apparatuses of secondary autonomy are not "innate" but arise from "experience." Thus this secondary guarantee of ego autonomy also involves reality relations. While it is obvious that without relationships to a real external environment we would be solipsistic beings, a long detour was necessary before we could see clearly that the autonomy of the ego from the id—our safeguard against solipsism—is guaranteed by these innate and acquired apparatuses which keep us attuned to our environment.

The "change of function" by which initially instinctual and defensive considerations become autonomous remains a mystery. Rapaport somehow links the process with adaptation to the demands of external reality. From these ambiguities and the emphasis on the necessity of guarantees, it would seem that ego autonomy is precarious at best.

The newer brand of psychoanalytic thinking represented by Rapaport and Hartmann is called *ego psychology*. It is professed by contemporary psychoanalytic thinkers, many of whom trace their intellectual lineage directly to Freud or members of his inner circle. Ego psychology currently is very popular, because to many personologists it seems to improve on Freud's cramped view of life in a way that preserves his basic insights. Ego psychologists are fond of pointing out that Freud must have held a rudimentary form of their position because he spoke of the life instincts as ego-preservative (Freud, 1925b). Be this as it may, there is overwhelming emphasis in Freud on the ego as derived from the id and as striking the conflict-induced compromise of reality principle functioning. Anyone who finds ego psychology a worthwhile elaboration of Freud's thinking must face the implications of assuming an inborn ego and a conflict-free ego sphere. Ego psychology is no mere extension of Freud; rather, it represents a radical break with psychoanalytic tradition.

It is surely a radical change in psychoanalytic theory to decide that not all but only some behavior is defensive and that not all but only some behavior is expressive of selfish instincts. Fixations and psychosexual stages are no longer adequately descriptive of development. The decrease in the overwhelming importance of the early years as developmental stages is particularly notable in the work of ego psychologist Erikson (1950). I will detail his view of development in Chapter 7; for now, note that he describes eight developmental stages covering personality changes throughout the whole life span. As you know, Freud considered fewer developmental stages and saw personality as being relatively well set by puberty. To this ego psychology adds a belief in the human capacity to be rational and logical in reaching decisions and solving problems. As you will see in the next chapter, further modifications of psychoanalytic theory in the direction of decreasing the pervasiveness and significance of conflict and defense result in what I have come to call the *fulfillment model*. Ego psychology presents a view of humanity that is considerably more optimistic than that offered by Freud: It takes a step in the direction of affirming the possibility of fulfillment in human life.

Certainly Murray and the ego psychologists have radically changed psychoanalytic thought. And even though the changes may render that body of thinking more satisfying to contemporary personologists, they undoubtedly cloud some of the most appealing aspects of the classical Freudian approach. When the ego comprised only the mechanisms of defense with which conflict could be reduced, the id was still the only inherent aspect of personality. And the id, of course, could be justified on biological grounds. The sexual instinct in particular was tied to physiological processes, and the psychosexual stages of development were thought to follow the organism's biological development. But can clearly biological bases of the instincts or drives be attributed to the conflict-free portion of the ego? Further if one also considers the modifications of the id suggested by Murray, whereby motivations other than the survival, sex, and death instincts are considered inherent to the person, the id loses virtually all of its original meaning. It is only the wish to preserve the name *id* that underlies Murray's usage, for in his way of thinking id and motivation in its most general sense are one and the same. The modifications of Freudian theory by Murray and the ego psychologists should be taken seriously. They constitute a shift in thinking and are more than just logical extensions of Freud's theories.

As you can imagine, I am reticent to abstract from the ego psychology literature, which is heterogeneous enough to border on amorphousness, any definite statement of a core tendency. Since ego psychologists see themselves as being basically in the Freudian camp, they can be considered as sharing Freud's core tendency. But it is important to remember that they, like Murray, postulate some instincts that are not irrevocably opposed to society.

The Object-Relations Position

Psychoanalytic theory refers to persons other than oneself as objects. This oddly impersonal usage is understandable in Freud, who regarded interpersonal relations in the early years as being somewhat predetermined by instinctual demands and by the inevitable conflict between the child and its parents. Also, he regarded the interpersonal relations of adult years as transference phenomena, shadowy reflections of earlier unresolved conflicts. Originally, Freud believed that the only reason other persons can become at all important is that instinctual energy—libido—is projected outward by a gratification-hungry id onto whoever can facilitate that gratification. This process is supposed to happen unconsciously, and any ensuing love or regard for objects amounts to a narcissism, or self-love, called *primary* or *basic* (Freud, 1927). Thus, although Freud talked a great deal about interpersonal relations, his theory rendered persons other than oneself as surprisingly uninfluential except as stereotypic objects of one's instincts.

Object-relations theory grew as a corrective attempt to invest interpersonal relations with a more significant role in personality development. Its general message is that the value of others and the course and effect of interactions with them are not a programmed, automatic outcome of instinctual considerations. Personality can be shaped in many different directions depending on the specifics of interpersonal encounters.

The early work on object relations was done by Melanie Klein (1948) and the founders of ego psychology, notably Hartmann. But this movement has never been a tightly unified enterprise. Modell (1977), for example, is the most conciliatory toward instinct theory, arguing that Freud (1927) had the kernels of object-relations theory in his views of *secondary narcissism,* which is a process whereby the ego identifies with the objects originally invested with value (cathected) by the id in order to be loved itself. Fairbairn (1954), on the other hand, calls for a radical break with Freud. Kernberg (1976) and Bowlby (1969) are somewhere in the middle.

There is really nothing in object-relations theory concrete and uncontroversial enough to serve as a core statement. But if there were, it would probably emphasize the *tendency to develop a self.* The self is regarded as a composite of units, each an image deriving from significant interpersonal relations. Some units concern *self-image* (what you think of and expect from yourself), others *object images* (what you think of and expect from other people), and still others *affect dispositions* (tendencies toward emotional states that reflect how you felt during interpersonal relations). For Kernberg (1976), the driving force behind interpersonal relations is still instinctual energy, or *libido,* and hence self-development occurs parallel to the character development based on psychosexual stages discussed by Freud. Thus, self units can be considered as influencing the content of ego and superego. But for Fairbairn (1954), instincts have receded into the background, as "libido is a function of the ego and the ego is fundamentally object seeking." Object-relations theory can still be classified as a variant on the psychosocial conflict model, because Kernberg's position is the more common with theorists of this stripe. But if Fairbairn's thinking prevailed, we would be dealing with a frankly fulfillment position.

There is perhaps more agreement among these theorists on the developmental stages of the self. The first stage is one of normal *autism,* a primary undifferentiated state covering the first months of life. If development is ideal, autism gives way to a normal state of *symbiosis,* in which there is confusion of self and object in the child's mind because neither is perceived as independent of the other. This stage lasts two to seven months, after which it gives way to a *differentiation state,* in which self and object are clearly separate. Under continuing ideal development, the differentiation stage shifts at about two years of age into an *integration stage,* in which the self- and object representations, perceived as independent, are fit into relationship with each other. If all goes well, the child should enter the Oedipal conflict with stable differentiated and integrated self and object representations, all of which get consolidated, through dealing with that conflict, into the ego and superego of adult life.

The task of development is not only differentiation and integration but also the emergence of a sense of identity. In the earliest stages, the child vacillates between ways of thinking and being, expressing first one self unit and then another. This instability is characteristic of the phenomenon of *splitting* (Kernberg, 1976), a defensive attempt to deal with being overwhelmed by more potent adults. The next step in identity development involves *introjection,* literal incorporation of objects into the mind. Later in development comes the less primitive process of *identification,* in which objects have influence but need not be "swallowed whole." Through the gradual increase in identifications, the stable differentiations and integrations that mark mature identity take place. It is unclear just how much reliance object-relations theorists wish to place on defensiveness in the developmental process. Splitting is clearly a defense, which, like all others, distorts reality. Introjection and identification are also considered defenses by Freudians, and the object-relations theorists do not clearly contradict this usage. Indeed, Kernberg suggests that in order for development to be sound, the splitting defense characteristic of earliest mental life must be replaced by the more mature defense of repression. For all their emphasis on how interpersonal relations can influence persons in myriad ways, object-relations theorists are not quite ready to say that ideal functioning is devoid of defenses. This is further evidence that they currently are still best classified as psychosocial conflict theorists.

The object-relations position does not as yet include a catalogue of types or styles of adult living. Ideal functioning, however, clearly involves deep and stable relations with others, tolerance of ambivalence toward loved objects, capacity for tolerating guilt and separateness and for working through crises of depression, an integrated self-concept, and correspondence between behavior patterns and self-concept (Kernberg, 1976). These positive attributes are more likely to occur when the interpersonal relations between children and their parents are characterized by love, support, and respect but also a lack of parental overindulgence. Object-relations theorists also specify pathologies of self development (to be discussed in Chapter 7).

Beyond Ego Psychology: Narcissism and Transactional Analysis

Two recent theoretical developments within the psychoanalytic movement may go beyond even the transformations brought about by ego psychology: the *self-psychology* of Heinz Kohut (1971, 1977) and the *transactional analysis* of Eric Berne (1964). Originally psychoanalysts, both personologists have asserted that their positions improve on the conflict emphasis of Freud without being incompatible with it. But they make very different assumptions from those of their great ancestor. The positions of Kohut and Berne are attracting attention and should therefore be mentioned here, even though they are still quite fragmentary and evolving as personality theories.

It is difficult to specify a core tendency, or life purpose, for Kohut's position, because to date it has been devoted almost completely to conceptualizing psychopathological states. Nonetheless, there are some implications in the statements about pathology that are important for human nature and ideal development. Kohut assumes that the human is characterized from birth not only by the Freudian tendency to maximize instinctual gratification while minimizing punishment and guilt but also by the tendency to *enhance and order functioning through the experience of self*. The well-developed self has a consciously appreciated sense of who and what one is that lends meaning and direction to behavior.

Although the self is not present at birth, it begins to form in earliest childhood as the result of the expression of two core characteristics and parental reactions to them. The core characteristics, considered as basic as the Freudian instincts, are the *need to be mirrored* and the *need to idealize*. The first need refers to children's wishes to have their expressions and products recognized, approved of, and admired. The most important mirroring person in children's lives is the mother. It is also necessary for children to idealize and hence identify with others more capable than themselves. The most important figure for idealization is the father. The mirroring and idealizing needs underlie later *ambitions* and *goals,* respectively.

When mother mirrors her child, and father permits himself to be idealized, the developmental condition necessary for vigorous selfhood is present. In this condition, a *nuclear* self will emerge, probably during the second year of life. This nuclear self is defined as *bipolar,* including archaic nuclear ambitions (deriving from having been mirrored) on the one hand and archaic nuclear goals (deriving from having idealized) on the other. Kohut describes a "tension arc" between these two poles as stimulating the expression (and hence development) of the child's rudimentary skills and talents. In this fashion, a good beginning has been made toward a productive and creative maturity, characterized by a stable and secure sense of self that integrates and renders coherent the various facets of life experience.

But if mother fails to mirror generously or father removes himself as an object of idealization, the child's self development will be damaged. The child may grow to adulthood feeling inadequate and apathetic. Also, talents and skills will have been insufficiently developed. These immaturities are depicted as *narcissistic personality* or *behavior disorders*. Kohut believes that schizophrenia and borderline psychotic states are also well understood as indications of faulty self-development.

Kohut's theorizing seems very far from Freud's and raises the question of the relationship between the two positions. The psychosexual conflicts of traditional Freudian theory do take place, according to Kohut, but so does self-development. At the oral, anal, phallic, and latency stages of psychosexual development, a drama is being enacted that concerns the expression of mirroring and idealizing needs and parental reactions to them. Kohut believes that at each stage the child must receive the optimal blend of sexual gratification and frustration if fixation and developmental problems are to be avoided. But this optimal blend must also include sufficient opportunities for mirroring and idealization, or development can also be jeopardized.

In most of his statements, Kohut appears to fit into ego psychology. He accepts the Freudian emphasis on inevitable conflict between individual and society, child and parents, and id and superego. But he regards the equally important self development as being separate from the instincts and, if development has been good, potentially free of conflicts or defensive operations. Looked at this way, Kohut's position has something of the same internal implausibility of other ego psychologies: How can the person be at the same time in constant, inevitable conflict and conflict free?

Sometimes Kohut seems to resolve this difficulty by pushing Freudian assumptions even further into the background and moving still closer to a fulfillment (rather than conflict) mode of theorizing. For example, Kohut (1977) suggests that (1) the nuclear self is reasonably well formed *before* the supposedly all-important Oedipal situation occurs; (2) the conflict and pain of the Oedipal situation may be not inevitable but the result of having an insufficiently developed self with which to interact with parents; and (3) present-day society breeds disorders of the self more than the neuroses emphasized by Freud. However careful he is to credit Freud, Kohut may be leaving behind ego psychology and the conflict model.

Something similar may be taking place for Eric Berne (1964), who formulated *transactional analysis,* a popular contemporary psychotherapy. A Freudian psychoanalyst by training, Berne began by emphasizing what he called *structural analysis,* the underlying assumption of which is that in every person there are three ego (or mental) states: namely the child, the parent, and the adult. The *child* state involves an unsocialized appreciation and expression of physiological processes. The *parent* state is an internalized representation of taboos and sanctions learned through interaction with one's parents. The *adult* state emphasizes rational, unevaluative, problem-solving thought. Given all this, it is mystifying to find that Berne disavows the obvious parallel between his three ego states and the Freudian id, superego, and ego. He has two grounds for this disavowal. One is that child, adult, and parent states are phenomenological, or readily apparent in personal experience, whereas id, ego, and superego are merely "theoretical constructs." Needless to say, Freudians would not agree with this portrayal of their approach as abstract. The second ground for disavowal is that transactional analysis supposedly makes little use of the concept of the unconscious. But Berne does speak of *exclusion,* which indicates the denial and inhibition of entire ego states, and *contamination,* or the intermixing of two ego states without awareness of what has happened. Exclusion is too close to repression or denial and unconsciousness to be entirely convincing. But Berne deemphasizes this concept, and in that sense transactional analysis appears to be much like other ego psychologies.

In his psychotherapeutic work, Berne and his followers have moved further and further away from the original Freudian roots. Although structural analysis of the child, adult, and parent in us is still practiced, much additional elaboration has taken place. At the core level, it is assumed that there are not only biological survival drives but (and even more important) psychological needs called *stroke hunger, structure hunger, excitement hunger, recognition hunger,* and *leadership hunger. Stroke hunger* basically involves a soothing sort of physical contact, though in adulthood many persons get by with pale shadows of contact, such as simple attention. *Structure hunger* is evidenced when people invest their lives with meaning; it refers specifically to the activities selected to fill up the time. *Excitement hunger* is the wish not to be bored. *Recognition* and *leadership hunger* describes the person's basic need for social approval and influence. These drives and needs are core characteristics, that is, unlearned goals present in all human beings. Although Berne does not explicitly state a core tendency, he implies that *persons strive for socially satisfying and meaningful lives.* Something resembling the Freudian instincts and their gratification still exists, but it increasingly takes a back seat, with social and psychological matters gaining greater emphasis. Berne's discussions of these latter issues hardly assume necessary, inevitable conflict. As transactional analysis evolves, it becomes less of a conflict theory and more of a fulfillment theory.

The rest of Berne's position concerns the periphery of personality, or that which aids in understanding individual differences. As such, it will be discussed in Chapter 7. Suffice it to say here that out of the interaction with its parents and the broader society, the child develops a *life script,* which is a plan that organizes energies and directions. Associated with this is a *life position,* or a set of learned assumptions people make about whether they and others with whom they interact are acceptable, or "OK." From this emphasis on whether "I'm OK and you're OK" develop other aspects of lifestyle useful in understanding characteristic patterns of interaction. These patterns are governed by the games that people play. These games involve *gimmicks, discounting,* and *rackets,* all learned techniques with which people attempt to reach the goals of their life scripts. Although transactional analysis shares with the Freudian approach a propensity to ferret out the "basest" aspects of human nature—as you can perhaps tell from the concepts it employs—those same concepts show just how far the position has departed from its Freudian origin.

CONFLICT MODEL: INTRAPSYCHIC VERSION

Thus far, we have discussed theories that exemplify the psychosocial type of conflict model. Here the inevitable conflict arises from two great forces, one of which has its source in the individual and the other in the group. The core tendency of this type expresses the necessity for compromise between the requirements of individuals and those of groups. Social aims are internalized at some point in a person's development, following which both great opposing forces are represented in the mind. In contrast, the *intrapsychic version* of the conflict model starts with the assumption that the opposing forces that render conflict inevitable are inherent parts of the person. The conflict starts and remains within the psyche, and it does not depend on whether one lives for oneself alone or in the company of others. Although the theories we will consider in this section are clearly examples of the conflict model, they are discriminably different in some of their implications from those considered in the previous section. As we will see in more detail later, one important difference between the two conflict positions is that the intrapsychic type relies much less heavily on the concept of defensiveness than does the psychosocial type.

Rank's Position

Otto Rank (born in Vienna, 1884; died in New York, 1939) started out as a member of Freud's inner circle and for many years was respected by that group as a brilliant nonmedical contributor to the psychoanalytic movement. Although he did practice psychotherapy, Rank spent much of his intellectual energy applying his view to the understanding of phenomena other than psychopathology. In addition to his own writing, Rank founded or edited three influential European journals on psychoanalysis. The fact that he was not a physician and that his training was in philosophy, psychology, history, and art was a welcomed stimulus to Freud and the other psychoanalysts. But as Rank became increasingly invested in certain heretical ideas, his relations with the psychoanalytic circle were strained past the breaking point. Today the prevailing version of Rank's thinking seems very different from Freud's position, though there are unquestionable similarities in form. It is perhaps unfortunate for the psychoanalytic movement that Rank left the inner circle, for they lost his stimulating influence. As we review his theory, it will become clear that he had many thoughts that have since flowered in personology.

The core tendency in Rank's (1929, 1945) theory is easily stated and clearly establishes the position as a pure expression of the intrapsychic conflict model. According to him, all functioning is expressive of the *tendency to minimize the fear of life while at the same time minimizing the fear of death.* To a Rankian, the terms *life* and *death* have a special meaning that you should understand before you attempt to relate this core tendency to your own personal experience. In this view, life is equivalent to the process of separation and individualization whereas death is the opposite, namely, union, fusion, and dependency. Thus, the core tendency concerns the opposing fears that you will be a unique (lonely) individual or, conversely, that you will be fused with (undifferentiated from) other people. Many of you have experienced this opposition in deciding whether or not to leave home to go to college. When you thought you should leave home, you experienced, in the prospect of separation from people familiar and dear to you, the fear of life. When you thought you might stay at home, you experienced, in the prospect of failing to grow and develop further, the fear of death. To go away with no plan for continuing your relationship to those left behind would minimize your fear of death but intensify your fear of life. Conversely, to stay behind with no plan for extending and broadening your personal development would minimize your fear of life but intensify your fear of death. You may have minimized both fears by deciding to go to a college close by so that you can continue to live at home or by leaving to go to school determined to write and visit home frequently.

According to Rank, life is essentially a series of situations in which you are called on either to achieve greater separation and individuality or, renouncing that possibility, to regress to the old and familiar. And from his statement of core tendency, it is clear that even the best solution in such situations will be a compromise, the two fears involved being unavoidably opposed. But as we shall see, there is much more than this to Rank's position.

Nature and Bases of the Two Fears.   The two fears— of life and of death— are experienced as uncomfortable tension states, much as in the anxiety concept stressed by other conflict theorists. Rank prefers the term *fear* because it implies a definite object, whereas anxiety is a more diffuse state, although the two are similar in their bodily effects. The person's overall aim can be characterized as tension reduction. In this Rank is similar to the other conflict theorists, but he differs when he discusses origins of the two fears.

Although Rank might agree with Freud that each person possesses certain biological instincts, such as those for food, water, and sex, he would not consider them of special importance for understanding personality, for they do not provide the intrinsic basis for conflict. Much more important is the inexorable tendency for living things to separate and individuate. The very act of launching forth on life, the act of birth, is a profound separation of the neonate from its mother's body. Rank (1929) believes that being born is a deeply traumatic experience because one must relinquish the warm, relatively constant environment of the womb, in which one's needs are automatically met, for the more variable, potentially harsher world outside, in which for the first time one experiences the discomfort of needs insufficiently and tardily served.

Early in his career, Rank considered the birth trauma the most significant event in life. Later on, though he still gave it a primary position, he came to consider it only the first in a long series of separation experiences that are as inevitable as life itself. The separations are caused by biological, psychological, and social developments that are indistinguishable from life. Typically the second major separation occurs upon weaning, when the child must face the tragedy of relinquishing mother's fecund breast and the warm, protected place at her side. This separation is rapidly followed by the even greater decrease in contact with mother precipitated by the maturation of locomotor processes. Other common separation experiences are going to school, becoming individuated enough to render meaningless and anachronistic the friendships and attachments of an early age, and leaving home to strike out on one's own. For Rank, to be alive is to be faced with a continual series of separations through which one becomes a unique psychological, social, and biological person. Living is a fearsome process because it inevitably entails separations, which simultaneously precipitate uncertainty as to what will happen, require one to assume greater and greater responsibility for oneself, and render one ever more alone and lonely.

If separation and individuation arouse so much fear, why not avoid them completely? According to Rank, to avoid them completely would be to repudiate life and could be accomplished only by killing oneself. But this is no solution at all. Individuation is an integral, normal part of being alive. The fact that life is an inevitable process of separation is also the basis of the fear of death. To avoid separation and individuation in any way, such as refusing to develop or merging mindlessly with other people and things, so blatantly violates the nature of life, according to Rank, that it engenders the fear of obliteration. So the person is caught between two poles of a conflict that is inherent in being alive. Anything done to reduce the fear of living will increase the fear of dying, and vice versa. The only way to achieve a workable existence, therefore, is to strike a compromise that will balance, or hold to a minimum, both opposing forces. In this emphasis on compromise, one sees that Rank's is a true conflict theory even though it is of the intrapsychic rather than psychosocial type.

The existentialists, as you will see in Chapter 4, take a position that appears similar to Rank's. In the existential view, life is also a continual experience of choice between climbing the ladder of individuation, which involves separation, or refusing to do so. But, in contrast to Rank, the existentialists advocate achieving individuation, regardless of the toll. They do not endorse the compromise considered ideal by Rank, who stops short of damning the individual to social isolation.

The Will as a Force in Life.   The other important core characteristic in Rank's theory is the *will*. The will is somewhat logically analogous to Freud's ego in the notion that there is some aspect of personality that has an overall organizing function, that integrates all separate experiences into a composite sense of total being. Both concepts refer to a process of development considered necessary and unavoidable. Children inevitably will develop an ego according to Freud and a will according to Rank. Finally, both concepts are deeply implicated in the theorist's explanations of how the core tendency gets carried out. For Freud, the ego is a set of mainly unconscious defensive strategies for ensuring maximum instinctual gratification with minimum punishment and guilt. In contrast, Rank's concept of will refers to an organized sense of who and what you are that in its most vigorously developed form is not defensive and aids in minimizing the life and death fears. In contrast to Freud's ego, however, Rank's will *consciously* implements the compromise solution to conflict.

The will begins to develop some time following birth, when experience has accumulated in such a manner that children realize there is a difference between themselves and other people or things. Upon this recognition, the will begins to be an active force whereby children come to experience their own selves as a reality. The will first emerges as *counterwill;* in other words, children learn that they can say no to adults and to their own impulses. This is already a signal achievement. It is the beginning of a conscious integration of the person as a unit distinct from anything else. According to Rank, counterwill is wholesomely rooted in the basic tendency of life toward separation and individuation. But, as you can imagine, it has the effect of shattering union between children and their parents—and union is necessary in order to minimize the fear of life. Rank theorizes that the expression of counterwill leads to *guilt* because of the incompatibility of such a negative manifestation of will with the equally necessary pursuit of union. Thus, the child may hit its mother and then feel guilty when the mother frowns. Rank believes that the highest form of living involves a more mature expression of will than that seen in counterwill with its attendant guilt over forced separation.

The isolation and separation forced by expression of counterwill can be overcome by parental love of children. Ideally, parents are aware of and accept counterwill as a lovable part of their children's efforts to establish themselves as independent beings. Such parents will continue to support their children, and soon counterwill will begin to give way to a more mature expression of will. This mature will incorporates both a sense of the person's separateness and uniqueness and the ties to other people and things. In the words of Munroe (1955),

> Ideally, the beloved and loving sexual partner supplies the full mutuality of relationship whereby their own will is accepted in and through the "other" and becomes a positive, constructive force. The own will does not arouse guilt because it is loved by the other. The mature person loves himself in the other, and the other in himself. Awareness of difference, of partialization, enriches the new sense of union. This union is not the effortless bliss of the womb, but a constantly renewed creation. (p. 584)

Clearly the mature will provides the basis for successfully expressing the core tendency of minimizing fear of both life and death. The will eases fear of death by providing recognition of the separate parts of the person and of his or her difference from others. It eases fear of life by providing recognition of the organization of the parts of the person into a dynamic totality and by encouraging a sense of common cause with mutual respect for other people. Only when both functions of the will operate simultaneously are both fears minimized.

The will is not always so vigorously and completely developed because of certain limitations in the parent-child relationship. These will be covered in the section of this theory discussed in Chapter 7 on peripheral characteristics of personality. For now, note that Rank does not explicitly rely on the concept of defense, even though his is a conflict theory that makes even the most successful life a compromise. Clearly the most ideal, vigorous development of will has little defensiveness about it. The truth of one's real nature is not distorted due to its incompatibility with society. This differs greatly from the position of the pure psychosocial conflict theorist, to whom even the highest form of life is defensive in character. The intrapsychic version of the conflict model generally puts less emphasis on defensiveness than does the psychosocial version.

Angyal and Bakan.   Andras Angyal (1941, 1951, 1965) and David Bakan (1966, 1968, 1971) have independently developed positions that are very similar to each other and to the position of Rank. Although Angyal and Bakan do not cover all aspects of personality in their theorizing, they share with Rank many characteristics of intrapsychic conflict approach.

For Angyal, the core tendency is the *attempt to maximize both the expression of autonomy and the expression of homonomy* (or surrender). Similarly, Bakan's core tendency is the *attempt to maximize both the expression of agency and the expression of communion.* The core characteristics of personality for Angyal are *autonomy* and *homonomy*; for Bakan they are *agency* and *communion*. All four concepts refer simultaneously to pressure on the person to function in a certain way or direction and to the stable aspects of personality that result from such functioning.

Autonomy and agency are similar in that they signify functioning that leads to separation from other people and from the physical environment and to separation of parts of oneself from one another. They also refer to the stable fruits of such functioning, namely, differentiation of personality and independence in relation to other people and things. Whereas the concept of autonomy tends to emphasize aloofness and the concept of agency manipulativeness, the differences between them are less important than the similarities. They also share a kinship with Rank's concept of the fear of death (leading as it does to separation and individuation).

Homonomy (surrender) and communion are similar in that they emphasize functioning that leads toward relatedness with others and with the physical environment. Both also underlie the integration of the parts of oneself into a unified whole. Homonomy and communion also signify the stable fruits of such functioning, namely, a network of intimate relationships (with lovers, children, friends), an embeddedness in social institutions larger than oneself (e.g., having a profession, religious affiliation, political commitment), and a sense of physical belonging (to a home, geographical area). While the concept of homonomy implies more passivity (surrender) than does the more instrumental communion, this difference is less important than the similarities. As you can see, these concepts cover ground similar to that of Rank's idea of the fear of life (leading as it does to union).

The simultaneous processes of differentiation and integration, considered by Angyal and Bakan to be the most constructive solution to the problem of the two opposing forces, is also emphasized by Rank. The process, called *psychological growth* by fulfillment theorists (for whom it is a common emphasis), seems terribly optimistic for the conflict model. Clearly intrapsychic conflict theorists see the highest form of living as a process of development rather than the set, defensive state for which pure psychosocial conflict theorists argue. The process of simultaneous differentiation and integration smacks neither of reality distortion nor of screening some things out of consciousness. Indeed, so optimistic do Rank, Angyal, and Bakan seem concerning the most constructive form of living that one may well question whether it represents a compromise at all. But simultaneous differentiation and integration do represent a compromise—the best that can be arranged given the underlying background of two constant, intense, unchangeable forces pulling in opposite directions. The bedrock assumption of all conflict theories, be they intrapsychic or psychosocial, is that the person is a house forever divided!

Thus far, I have only discussed the highest form of living according to Bakan, Angyal, and Rank. They also discuss less constructive ways of functioning. These constitute failures to establish compromises that balance the two opposing forces. Instead, a disproportionate or even overwhelming amount of one of the two forces is expressed. In describing the ways in which the person falls short of achieving a workable compromise between the two forces, Rank says that the danger of renouncing the tendency toward union involves the suffering of neurosis, whereas renouncing the tendency toward separation can lead to the banality of adjustment. Angyal and Bakan emphasize only the danger of denying union. Indeed, the entire range of psychological and physical maladies, from alienation to cancer, are traced by Bakan (1966, 1968) to the expression of agency unmitigated by the mellowing effects of communion.

Gestalt Psychotherapy

Frederick Perls (1969a, 1969b, 1969c) has developed a popular position called *Gestalt psychotherapy*. Primarily a therapy, this position nonetheless includes some assumptions about personality. Although these assumptions are hardly fixed and represent a complex amalgam of different theoretical emphases, the main thrust appears to fit the intrapsychic conflict model. The theorizing includes formulations similar in content to those of Rank, Angyal, and Bakan.

In this complex and unfolding position, the universe is seen as a continuous flow of energy and matter. The human is part of this flow but is uniquely predisposed to comprehend what is going on. In attempting to comprehend, the human breaks down the universal continuum into bits and pieces that are labeled and treated as separate entities. In this fashion are born the notions of different persons, things, events, times, places, parts of a person, and much else. By playing with these bits conceptually, the human finds relationships among them and, in that sense, discovers processes. A *process,* according to Perls, is two bits and a happening. It is in the depiction of happenings that the basically intrapsychic nature of the theorizing is apparent. A *happening* is the simultaneous attraction and repulsion, described as a "tendency-to-merge-with" and an "urge-to-remain-differentiated-from," that characterizes all relationships between bits. The term *gestalt* refers to the whole formed of two or more bits related by the dynamic tension of their inevitable opposition. Clearly this is a conflict position.

What makes Gestalt psychotherapy an intrapsychic form of the conflict model is the origin in the human mind of not only the bits constituting comprehensible experience but their oppositional relationships. Relationships between bits do end (e.g., two friends may no longer see each other, or the tension between going to work and relaxing at the beach may be resolved), which may suggest that the position is not really expressive of the conflict model. But it should be recognized that as soon as the two bits cease to oppose each other in a relationship, each enters a relationship of opposition with other existing bits. The overriding fact of human existence is conflict fashioned out of human imaginativeness in the attempt to comprehend the universe.

Like Rank and the other intrapsychic conflict theorists, Perls believes that vigorous consciousness is possible. Defenses and the resulting decreased levels of awareness can occur in human beings, but these do not characterize the highest forms of development. In this belief, Perls clearly differs from Freud. He depicts vigorous awareness as that which flows between the two opposing bits. The opposition stimulates keen awareness, and the sense of understanding involved in that awareness is of the inevitability of conflict. When, in an adult, awareness is minimal or takes the form of a sense of unity rather than opposition, there has been a disturbance of consciousness. Appreciation of opposition not only constitutes vigorous awareness; it paves the way for creativity as well. Although creativity involves changing meaning through altering relationships between bits, it does not have the implication of conflict resolution so much as shifts in oppositions. Pulling these threads together, we can hazard a core statement for Perls: *Humans strive to comprehend life by identifying bits of experience and construing them in relationships of simultaneous attraction and repulsion.*

It may seem odd that Perls emphasizes the perception of conflict as the main thrust of activity. But you should recognize just how pervasive he thinks this kind of perception is. For example, a person's sense of something external that is called "reality" is, for Perls, nothing more than the projection of human imaginativeness. The definition of self as contrasted from but also somehow involved with this external reality is to be understood as an expression of the core tendency to construe bits of experience as being simultaneously attracted and repulsed. Awareness is born out of contrast: the present with the past or future, oneself with others, good with bad. Without conflict, there is no understanding. And without a doubt, the conflict is of an intrapsychic sort.

As for core characteristics, Perls offers three phases, or modes of thinking: the social, the psychophysical, and the spiritual. Although they develop sequentially, they are also present as potentialities at birth and throughout adult life.

The developmentally earliest is the *social phase,* so named because the child requires interaction with others for survival. During this phase, the child begins to develop an awareness of others as they fulfill and frustrate physical needs and comfort.

Next comes the *psychophysical phase,* which encompasses most of life. Here, the person becomes self-aware, which sharpens the social awareness that has already been going on; indeed, most of the construing of bits and relationships takes place here. Also emerging during this phase is personality, which comprises the self, self-image, and being. *Being* is the biological organism as construed by the mind. As such, being entails a greedy, growing composite of organically rooted processes and the activity involved. The *self,* or awareness of one's dimensions and purposes as distinct from others and from nature, emerges through experiences of conflict between being and the external world. The self is defined mainly in terms of one's interests and pleasures. *Self-image* reflects one's developing views of what one should want and be and results from incorporating the views of others. Being, self, and self-image, all figments of the person's imagination, are constantly in conflict.

Finally, some persons develop beyond the psychophysical phase into a *spiritual phase,* characterized by an intuitive (rather than concretely sensory) apprehension of meanings beyond being, self, and self-image.

These phases are intangible and cosmic in meaning. Nevertheless, they involve the simultaneous attraction and repulsion of bits of experience.

Perls also has a position on development. The progressions from one phase to another and from being to self and self-image within the psychophysical stage are hastened by two types of reactions from others: acknowledgment and approbation. *Acknowledgment* is recognition by others of the person and his or her actions. It has a positive and approving implication, as in Kohut's mirroring. The child plays and calls to its parents, "Watch me!" Through acknowledgment by others, the person develops self-awareness and self-appreciation. But the criticality involved in self-image is learned through *approval* (and, presumably, disapproval) from others. Developmentally speaking, both acknowledgment and approval occur inevitably, consolidating the tendency to perceive bits of experiences as simultaneously attractive (acknowledgment) and repulsive (approval). In reacting to the child with acknowledgment and approval, the parents themselves participate in this ubiquitous cycle of attraction and repulsion.

As will be elaborated further in Chapter 7, Perls offers no typology. But he does suggest that under certain circumstances the normal process of construing bits and relationships and then continually reconstruing is interrupted or fixed. The result of this interruption is poetically termed a *blister,* that is, a fixed pattern of traits constituting the person's character. Although Perls is by no means clear about blisters, several points are apparent. First, blisters are no more expressions of conflict than is the more normal flow of experience. Second, blisters result from external social pressures that halt the normal process whereby bits form new conflictual relationships with each other. Finally, blisters form the symptoms to be worked out in psychotherapy, the aim of which is not to resolve conflict but to restore the flow in which conflictual relationships begin and end and are supplanted by new ones. This aim is expressed in the technique of confronting the client with a reaction that contrasts or conflicts with his or her words or actions.

Rank, Bakan, and Angyal have emphasized the perils of denial of inevitable intrapsychic conflict (by defending against one great force or the other). Though he employs a similar type of theorizing, Perls has put the emphasis in psychopathology on the fixing of a conflict rather than its denial. In the following section, we can see both approaches.

Jung's Position

Carl Gustav Jung (born in Kessewil, on Lake Constance in Switzerland, 1875; died in Kusnacht, Switzerland, 1961) has provided a theory of such complexity and uniqueness as to be unlike anything else in the personality field. This does not imply its unequivocal soundness, however, for it is checkered with ambiguities and inconsistencies. Nonetheless, by any calculation Jung is a major figure in personology and an influential thinker of our century. Perhaps because of the influence of his father, a clergyman, Jung first thought to study philosophy and archaeology. But supposedly a dream convinced him to study medicine and science.

His early interest in psychiatry was spurred by Eugen Bleuler and Pierre Janet. Jung was very impressed with Freud's first great book, *The Interpretation of Dreams* (1900), and by 1906 a regular correspondence had sprung up between them. Jung became a member of Freud's inner circle. Their mutual admiration was great, and Freud regarded Jung as his successor; indeed, Jung became the first president of the International Psychoanalytic Association in 1910. But soon after, the relationship between Freud and Jung became fraught with theoretical and personal disagreements, and in 1917 Jung resigned his presidency of and membership in that organization. Freud and Jung never saw each other again, even though both have written interpretations of their relationship and differences (e.g., Freud, 1925, 1957; Jung, 1961). After the break, Jung went on to develop his own approach, which he called *analytic psychol-*

ogy. Once again we have evidence of the excellence of Freud that attracted other strong, creative persons—and once again evidence that such persons do not get along easily.

As its name suggests, Jung's approach retains much of its Freudian parentage. This is most apparent in its form, which emphasizes the importance of dreams as expressions of the unconscious and of the integration of biological and mental phenomena. But the differences between Freudian and Jungian theory are much more important than the similarities. Generally stated, the main differences entail, on Jung's part, a de-emphasis of sexuality coupled with a greater emphasis on spirituality (in both its mystical and religious senses) and focus on cultural universals in human experience rather than individual idiosyncrasies. It is these differences above all that won Jung a small but devoted following and underlie a groundswell of current interest in his theorizing. Jung seems to speak of our spiritual bankruptcy by enabling us to feel grounded in the past and future of humankind rather than limited to our own insignificant life circumstances.

It is no simple matter to state Jung's core tendency in a few words. His is probably the most complex personality theory that exists. We will see how he tends to use concepts in a way different from the common meaning established in much of the personological literature. We will also experience the inevitable indefiniteness associated with his mysticism! But one thing will emerge clearly: For Jung, life, behavior, and psyche reek with conflict. At great risk of oversimplification, I venture to say that the overall directionality in his theory is the *tendency toward attainment of selfhood*. It is less simple than we might think to arrive at some intuitive understanding of what Jung means here. For him, the self is definitely not a conscious sense of what one is or could be, as is commonly thought in personology. Instead, it is the totality of all the conflicting characteristics of personality. Perhaps the best way to grasp his meaning is to visualize the self as a hub of a wheel, with the spokes describing the force or tension of opposing personality characteristics. To attain selfhood is to have balanced off all the conflicting polarities. Sometimes selfhood is seen as a conflict-free state, but more often it seems a balance among opposing forces (Jung, 1953b). In any event, complete selfhood is considered an ideal that is virtually impossible to attain.

Core Characteristics.   There are several core characteristics underlying Jung's theory and, as you shall see, they tend to oppose one another. Of particular importance is the *ego,* which for Jung is the conscious mind directing the business of everyday living. It comprises complex combinations of conscious perceptions, thoughts, memories, and feelings, which lead to a sense of one's identity and continuity. In defining the ego as completely conscious, Jung deviates from Freud, for whom the ego is at least partly unconscious. The unconscious part, you will recall, is the defenses. Although Jung does assume defensiveness, he emphasizes it less than does Freud and does not localize its processes in the ego.

For Jung, unconscious processes are always in opposition to conscious ones. This opposition is inevitable and even helpful, as will become apparent in the discussion that follows. For now, we need only note the distinction Jung makes between the personal unconscious and the collective unconscious.

The *personal unconscious* is very similar to what Freud meant by unconscious and preconscious material. It consists of experiences that were once conscious and either have been defensively forced out of awareness because of their threatening nature, as in Freud's unconscious, or are merely no longer within the focus of attention as in Freud's preconscious. For Jung, the preconscious material can become conscious by a shift in focus of attention, and the unconscious material can become conscious by a relaxation of defenses. He believed in a true alternative to defensiveness, in which material defended against can once again gain accurate, complete consciousness. In contrast, Freud believed that our awareness never reflects more than a pale shadow of truth.

The *collective unconscious,* which reflects not individual experience but the accumulated experience of the human species, is Jung's most striking, unique, and controversial concept. According to Jung, all of the events that have occured over the eons of human history make their contribution to the life of each contemporary person in the form of a "species memory." Humans have suffered dilemmas, fought to the death, loved successfully and in vain, reared their young or abandoned them, sought nutriments and starved, experienced the power of nature, and so forth since the beginning of time. Their fears, joys, triumphs, tragedies, beliefs, problem solutions—in short, the sum of knowledge they have gained—have not been lost. New generations of children are not blank slates who cannot know anything of importance unless they learn it themselves. Rather, the accumulated culture of humankind is lodged in the psyche at birth, in the form of a collective unconscious. In fact, Jung even implies that he believes prehuman and subhuman history to have made some contribution to the collective unconscious as well!

To be sure, this collective knowledge is unconscious—indeed, it cannot, in contrast to the experience constituting the personal unconscious, become conscious through redirection of attention or relaxation of defenses. The collective unconscious was never conscious in the history of an individual and, hence, can never become so, no matter how hard people (or our therapists) may try. But the collective unconscious does have an enormous influence on behavior as well as an indirect effect on consciousness most clearly seen in such events as the déjà vu experience and the sense of the uncanny.

Jung probably arrived at his view of the collective unconscious out of a fascination with primitive mentality, art, and religion, to say nothing of dreams. He came to believe that the difference between primitive and modern mentality is not in degree of rationality but in the assumptions made about the nature of the world. Modern persons assume that all events "have a natural and perceptible cause" (Jung, 1933a, p. 130), this being one of our principal dogmas. Jung contends that this assumption is *actually* borne out only about half the time but we shrug off this disturbing fact by references to "chance." But "Primitive man expects more of an explanation. What we call chance is to him arbitrary power," says Jung (1933a, p. 132), who does not find such thinking especially strange. He encourages us to see this primitive belief in the context out of which it emerged, at the same time indicating its hold on him with an engaging account of personal experience in the jungle (1933a):

> In the Kitoshi region south of Mount Elgo, I went for an excursion into the Kabras forest. There, in the thick grass, I nearly stepped on a puff-adder, and only managed to jump away in time. In the afternoon my companion returned from a hunt, deathly pale and trembling in every limb. He had almost been bitten by a seven-foot mamba which darted at his back from a termite hill. Without a doubt he would have been killed had he not been able at the last moment to wound the animal with a shot. At nine o'clock that night our camp was attacked by a pack of ravenous hyenas which had surprised and mauled a man in his sleep the day before. In spite of the fire they swarmed into the hut of our cook who fled screaming over the stockade. Thenceforth there were no accidents throughout the whole of our journey. Such a day gave our Negroes food for thought. For us it was a simple multiplication of accidents, but for them the inevitable fulfillment of an omen that had occurred upon the first day of our journey into the wilds. It so happened that we had fallen, car, bridge, and all, into a stream we were trying to cross. Our boys had exchanged glances on that occasion as if to say: "Well, that's a fine start." To cap the climax a tropical thunderstorm blew up and soaked us so thoroughly that I was prostrated with fever for several days. On the evening of the day when my friend had had such a narrow escape out hunting, I could not help saying to him as we white men sat looking at one another: "It seems to me as if trouble had begun still further back. Do you remember the dream you told me in Zurich just before we left?" At that time he had had a very impressive nightmare. He dreamed that he was hunting in Africa, and was suddenly attacked by a huge mamba, so that he woke up with a cry of terror. The dream had greatly disturbed him, and he now confessed to the thought that it had portended the death of one of us. He had of course assumed that I was to die, because we always hope it is the "other fellow." But it was he who later fell ill of a severe malarial fever that brought him to the edge of the grave.
>
> To read of such a conversation in a corner of the world where there are no snakes and no malaria-bearing mosquitoes means very little. One must imagine the velvety blue of a tropical night, the overhanging black masses of gigantic trees standing in a virgin forest, the mysterious voices of the nocturnal spaces, a lonely fire with loaded rifles stacked beside it, mosquito-nets, boiled swamp-water to drink, and above all the conviction expressed by an old Afrikaner who knew what he was saying: "This isn't man's country—it's God's country." There man is not king; it is rather nature—the animals, plants, and microbes. Given the mood that goes with the place, one understands how it is that we found a dawning significance in things that anywhere else would provoke a smile. That is the world of unrestrained, capricious powers with which primitive man has to deal day by day. The extraordinary event is no joke to him. He draws his

own conclusions. "It is not a good place"—"The day is unfavorable"—and who knows what dangers he avoids by following such warnings.
     Magic is the science of the jungle. (pp. 138–140)

Jung is saying that in contexts not under human control thoughts of evil omens, spirits, and bewitchment are universal psychic expressions, not just the illogical bent of primitive mentality. Modern persons also become superstitious when confronting the real capriciousness of nature, from which they are usually protected.
     Then Jung goes on to ask himself whether this suspiciousness to which persons are prone might be an accurate response to external, supernatural forces, be they gods or devils:

Shall we, for the moment at least, venture the hypothesis that the primitive belief in arbitrary powers is justified by the facts and not merely from a psychological point of view? The question is nothing less than this: does the psyche in general—that is, the spirit, or the unconscious—arise in us; or is the psyche, in the early stages of consciousness, actually outside us in the form of arbitrary powers with intentions of their own, and does it gradually come to take its place within us in the course of psychic development? (pp.146-147)

It is to Jung's credit that he had the courage to actually pose this question for himself, to consider the real possibility of a supernatural order, however antithetical to science that would be. After considerable struggle, he seems to have rejected a supernatural order in favor of the collective unconscious, which, though panindividual, need not imply anything different in kind from mentality.
     Jung takes a step on the way to assuming a collective unconscious rather than a supernatural order when he decides that such phenomena as superstitiousness and sense of the uncanny are essentially elaborated projections. These phenomena occur in primitives somewhat more frequently than in moderns "because of the undifferentiated state of [the primitive's] mind and his consequent inability to criticize himself" (Jung, 1933a, pp. 142–143). Any proneness to superstitious belief that moderns retain is due to accumulated memory of the past superstitious beliefs of the human species. While such beliefs are usually activated by some unpredictability or strangeness in the environment, their cause is nonetheless the collective unconscious.
     In a sense, then, Jung contends that we are one with our ancestors. In us live the battles they fought, the fears they experienced, the loves they nurtured. The doctrine of inheritance of acquired characteristics seems to be what Jung had in mind, even though it is in ill repute these days. According to Jung (1933a):

Not only the religious teacher, but the pedagogue as well, assumes that it is possible to implant in the human psyche something that was not previously there. The power of suggestion and influence is a fact; even the most modern behaviorism expects far-reaching results from this quarter. The idea of a complicated building-up of the psyche is expressed in primitive form in many widespread beliefs—for instance, possession, the incarnation of ancestral spirits, the immigration of souls, and so forth. When someone sneezes, we still say: "God bless you," and mean by it: "I hope your new soul will do no harm." When in the course of our own development we grow out of many-sided contradictions and achieve a unified personality, we experience something like a complicated growing-together of the psyche. Since the human body is built up by inheritance out of a number of Mendelian units, it does not seem altogether out of the question that the human psyche is similarly put together. (p.148)

But it is unclear whether Jung means the collective unconscious to be literally the accumulated specific experiences that our ancestors happen to have had or something less concrete. He does refer to recurring themes, problems, and preoccupations in the collective unconscious, suggesting that there is something universal about it that reflects the human condition more comprehensively than the mere specifics of actual experience. This quality of universality in the collective unconscious is most clearly seen in Jung's explanation of art and the artist (1933a). He is critical of Freud here, on the basis of overspecificity:

> Freud thought that he had found a key in his procedure of deriving the work of art from the personal experiences of the artist. It is true that certain possibilities lay in this direction, for it is conceivable that a work of art, no less than a neurosis, might be traced back to those knots in psychic life that we call the complexes. . . . Freud takes the neurosis as a substitute for a direct means of gratification. He therefore regrets it as something inappropriate—a mistake, a dodge, an excuse, a voluntary blindness. . . . And a work of art is brought into questionable proximity with the neurosis when it is taken as something which can be analyzed in terms of the poet's repressions. . . . No objection can be raised if it is admitted that this approach amounts to nothing more than the elucidation of those personal determinants without which a work of art is unthinkable. But should the claim be made that such an analysis accounts for the work of art itself, then a categorical denial is called for. (pp. 167–168)

This statement makes two things clear. First, a work of art is not to be understood simply as expressive of what Jung calls the *personal unconscious*—those once conscious experiences that have been defended against. Secondly, the collective unconscious, which also figures in the work of art, is probably not just the history of our ancestors' personal unconsciousness. The tone of universality that Jung intends (1933a) is clearly expressed in statements such as:

> What is essential in a work of art is that it should rise far above the realm of personal life and speak from the spirit and heart of the poet as man to the spirit and heart of mankind. The personal aspect is a limitation—and even a sin—in the realm of art. . . . The artist is not a person endowed with free will who seeks his own ends, but one who allows art to realize its purposes through him. As a human being he may have moods and a will and personal aims, but as an artist he is a "man" in a higher sense—he is "collective man"—one who carries and shapes the unconscious, psychic life of mankind. (p.168)

What Jung means is that the work of art issues not from the artist's particular experiences or even talents but from the collective unconscious to which he or she has become especially sensitive. In this sense, the collective unconscious must refer to the age-old considerations that form life, not merely the chronology of each individual ancestor's experiences.

As an aside, let me mention that Jung has an influence in a still-raging battle over the proper stance in art criticism. These days, many art critics adopt an approach that analyzes a work in order to clarify the particular facets of the artist's personality that have found expression. This is a somewhat Freudian school of criticism, and it has gained considerable force. There are, however, both traditionalists and a new wave in art criticism that favor an approach that searches for the universality in each creation, regardless of the artist's personal life. These critics are, according to Jung, on the right track. I should also mention that most artists would favor Jung's view, having long resented what they perceive as an overconcretization and devaluation of their art by the Freudian emphasis on creativity as expressive of personal neurosis, or at least idiosyncrasy. To generalize beyond art, it seems clear that Jung gives more importance to the collective unconscious than to the personal unconscious. For him, though the personal unconscious is the stuff of neurosis, the collective unconscious permits a valuable identification with what is universal and eternal.

Thus far, I have mentioned only general conceptions about the nature of the collective unconscious and some of the observations underlying Jung's assumption of it. It is now time to indicate the content of this highly complicated but intriguing concept. The content takes the form of *archetypes,* which are also, though less frequently, called *dominants, imagoes, primordial images,* and *mythological images* (Jung, 1953a). An archetype is a universal form, or predisposition to characteristic thoughts and feelings. Although the archetype is by nature unconscious and incapable of becoming conscious, it tends to create images or visions that correspond to aspects of conscious experience. Thus, the mother archetype in all of us produces a vague, intuitive image of a nurturant, loving, accepting force, which we then project onto our actual mothers. An archetype is an inherited, generic form of something that determines in part how we perceive our experiences. From time immemorial persons have experienced mothers, and their experiences have been homogeneous enough to have permanently emblazoned upon the psyche the essence of mother. Our experience of actual mother is, then, a conglomerate of the generic idea of mother and the particular characteristics our real mothers happen to have. These two sources of experience may or may not match well—indeed, it is unlikely that they will match completely, even in the best of circumstances, and hence conflict between archetypes (collective unconscious) and conscious experience (ego) is to be expected. There may well also be conflict between archetypes and the personal unconscious, since the latter is formed out of concrete and troublesome personal experience, while the former expresses essences.

But the matter is even more complicated than I have indicated. For Jung (1959b), the archetypes do not have content in any concrete sense but only form:

> Again and again I encounter the mistaken notion that an archetype is determined in regard to its content, in other words, that it is a kind of unconscious idea (if such an expression be permissible). It is necessary to point out once more that archetypes are not determined as regards their content, but only as regards their form and then only to a limited degree. A primordial image is determined as to its content only when it has become conscious and is therefore filled out with the material of conscious experience. Its form, however, as I have explained elsewhere, might perhaps be compared to the axial system of a crystal, which, as it were, preforms the crystalline structure in the mother liquid, although it has no material existence of its own. (p.79)

Once you have grasped this emphasis on archetypes as forms or essences, you can understand why they can never become conscious; it is not that they are defended against; rather, they are only prototypes or possibilities. In addition, this definition in terms of forms makes it clearer why an archetype can, according to Jung, express itself in such a wide range of content. Hence, the mother archetype can express itself in "the Church, university, city or country, heaven, earth, the worlds, the sea or any still waters, matter even, the underworld and the moon" (Jung, 1959b, p. 81). Of course, any actual human being can function as a symbol of an archetype. As you can imagine, it must be very difficult to determine when one is dealing with archetypal experience versus individual experience and, in the case of the former, which archetypes are involved. Jung offers no help beyond recognizing the difficulty and indicating the need for comprehensive, deeply intuitive observation done by persons who are not only sensitive to what they hear and see but also steeped in the world's cultures and history.

Agreeing with Freud, Jung proposes that the most fertile ground for information about the unconscious in general is imaginative productions, such as works of art and dreams. Indeed, Jung seems to have invented the free-association test, in which the person is presented with various words to which he or she must respond with the first thought that comes to mind. But by now you can anticipate Jung's disagreement with Freud, which is consistent across all imaginative productions. According to Jung, Freud overlooks the collective unconscious, focusing exclusively on the personal unconscious. The end result is overly concrete explanations. To illustrate this, Jung (1959b) criticizes Freud's interpretation of Leonardo da Vinci's famous painting of St. Anne and the Virgin with the Christ child. Freud concluded that the painting expressed Leonardo's wish to recapture the two mothers he had actually had (apparently he was born to one mother and wet-nursed by another). For Freud, the painting expresses repressed personal experiences only. Jung insists, however, that the theme of two mothers is very common in art, myth, and fantasy. Think, says Jung, of the myth of Heracles, born of a human mother and unwittingly adopted by the goddess Hera. Also, it is common for children to fantasize that their parents are not really their true ones. Relevant too is the widespread practice of providing godparents to supplement the blood parents. Not all this could have been promulgated by persons who had actually experienced two mothers in childhood; rather, the theme of dual parentage is based, according to Jung, on something so universal as to alert us to the presence of an archetype. Leonardo was in the grips of this archetype, rather than playing out some strictly personal drama.

Another aspect of Freud's excessive concreteness, Jung says, is the use of biological rather than spiritual explanations for fantasies. Dreams provide Freud with the occasion to trace the vicissitudes of sex and death instincts, structured as biological imperatives. But, says Jung (1933a), it is nonsensical to assume that something concretely biological can be symbolically represented in fantasy:

> It is well known that the Freudian school operates with hard and fast sexual "symbols"; but these are just what I would call signs, for they are made to stand for sexuality, and this is supposed to be something definitive. As a matter of fact, Freud's concept of sexuality is thoroughly elastic, and so vague that it can be made to include almost anything. . . . Instead of taking the dogmatic stand that rests upon the illusion that we know something because we have a familiar word for it, I prefer to regard the symbol as the announcement of something unknown, hard to recognize and not to be fully determined. Take, for instance, the so-called phallic symbols, which are supposed to stand for the *membrum virile* and nothing more. . . . As was customary throughout antiquity, primitive people today make a free use of phallic symbols, yet it never occurs to them to confuse the phallus, as a ritualistic symbol, with the *actual* penis. They always take the phallus to mean the creative *mana,* the power of healing and fertility, "that which is unusually potent". . . . Its equivalents in mythology and in dreams are the bull, the ass, the pomegranate, the *yoni,* the he-goat, the lightning, the horse's hoof, the dance, the magical cohabitation in the furrow, and the menstrual fluid, to mention only a few of many. That which underlies all of these images—and sexuality itself—is an archetypal content that is hard to grasp, and that finds its best psychological expression in the primitive *mana* symbol. (pp. 21–22)

In sharp contradiction to Freud, Jung is actually suggesting that it is essences or archetypes that are at the heart of the unconscious and that even sexuality derives its importance from the archetype expressed in it. Jung simply does not believe that human biology (instincts, drives, metabolism) has much to do with psychic life and its hold on behavior.

This is not to say that sexuality and animal urges are unimportant for Jung; rather, he sees them as deriving not from biological imperatives but from an archetype, the *shadow,* that has evolved through time so far as to warrant being treated as a core characteristic of personality. The shadow consists of essentialistic forms of the animal instincts humans inherited from lower forms of life (Jung, 1959c). As such, it typifies the animal possibility of human nature.

It often expresses itself in thoughts and behaviors of a socially unacceptable sort. These may be either hidden from public view, remaining in the ego, or actually defended against, becoming part of the personal unconscious. The shadow is also responsible for the human conception of original sin and, when projected outward, becomes the devil or even some concrete enemy. But the shadow is not all bad. It lends vitality and passion to life. Strange as it may seem, Jung believes that it is actually the shadow, which is an essence and not a biological necessity, that underlies the sexual and death wishes that figure so centrally in the Freudian view. This suggests that by endorsing the Freudian view we may actually be defining our lives along lines that are needlessly and excessively animalistic.

There are several other archetypes that, like the shadow, have evolved far enough to be considered core characteristics that form life. Especially intriguing are the *anima* and the *animus* (Jung, 1953b, 1959a). These are the archetypes providing a basis for bisexuality. Certainly it is known that at the biological level, the male and female secrete both male and female sex hormones, not just the one appropriate to their dominant sex. But even if this were not true, Jung would want to postulate an archetypal basis for bisexuality, because he considers it so apparent once one adopts the purview of anthropology, history, and art rather than some narrower, culture-bound approach. Present in both biological sexes, the feminine archetype is *anima* and the masculine archetype is *animus*. These archetypes are based on the accumulated experience of man with woman and vice versa. Jung feels that the whole nature of each biological sex presupposes the other. The (mental) archetypes underlie the manifestation in each biological sex of characteristics of the other (e.g., sensitivity in a man, aggressiveness in a woman) and determine the attractiveness of the opposite biological sex. Through these archetypes, each biological sex can appreciate and understand the role of its opposite. But if in any concrete instance anima or animus is projected onto someone of the opposite sex without sufficient regard for his or her real character, misunderstandings and conflict will result. Perhaps a biological male will try to find his idealized image of a woman (anima) in an actual biological female he knows. If after projecting his anima onto her he realizes the inevitable discrepancies between ideals and actualities, he may suffer bitter disappointment and never know why. Once again we perceive the ready potential for conflict between the archetypes of the collective unconscious and the actualities of experience.

Another important archetype is the *persona* (Jung, 1953b), which is the mask that persons adopt in response to the demands of social convention and tradition as well as their own archetypal needs. The purpose of the persona is to make a good impression both on others and on oneself. Presumably this archetype has developed out of the accumulated experience of human beings with the need to assume social roles in order to facilitate interaction. In fulfilling the persona archetype by developing a "public" personality, one can defend against unacceptable thoughts and feelings (thereby swelling the personal unconscious) or remain conscious of putting one's best foot forward (which involves the ego). The latter route leads to a sense of alienation from others, because one is conscious of tricking them; the former involves the alienation from self inherent in the personal unconscious.

There are several other archetypes, though no definitive list is available. Jung and his associates have described the archetypes of the *old wise man, God,* the *child,* the *hero, magic, power, birth, rebirth,* and *death* in addition to those already covered. One more, that of *unity* (which underlies the *self*) is of great importance, but discussion of it will be delayed until a more appropriate point.

Intrapsychic Conflict and Selfhood.   There is little question but that Jung's position exemplifies the conflict model. Polarization, the opposition of elements, is basic to understanding how his theory conceptualizes life. According to Jung, all that is human—indeed, everything in the universe—exists, changes, and thrives due to conflict and opposition. It is more difficult to determine whether his view is essentially of the psychosocial or intrapsychic conflict type. Let us examine his concepts further with a view toward settling this matter.

The existence of a personal unconscious certainly indicates that what appears to be psychosocial conflict exists. Some conscious thoughts and impulses are threatening and hence pushed out of awareness by defenses. As in Freud, the threat is of punishment or guilt, those twin pains deriving originally from the individual's opposition to society. It is certainly true that the unacceptable thoughts and impulses need not always be sexual or aggressive for Jung, but this does not really shift the form of conflict involved.

There are two considerations, however, that cast doubt on the possibility that Jung's is a psychosocial form of conflict theory. First, it is not clear that the conflict between individual and social pressures is inevitable. After all, Jung makes very little of the personal unconscious, relying for most of his explanations on the collective unconscious. In addition, the ego represents true, accurate consciousness, not the half-truth of rationalization. A full-bodied psychosocial conflict theory cannot postulate a true, accurate consciousness, because the conflict between individual and society is inevitable and the individual—always the weaker—must engage in the distortion of defensiveness. Jung makes it clear that defenses can be relaxed and, therefore, the personal unconscious can become conscious. Because it is possible, in his view, to have a distortion-free consciousness, his is probably best not considered a psychosocial conflict theory.

The second reason against a psychosocial conflict classification is even more compelling. Recall that in Freud the individual's contribution to the psychosocial conflict is considered to be a biological selfishness that is as somatic and real as metabolism itself. In contrast, biology is incidental to Jung's view of conflict. It is vital to recognize that the shadow, or locus of animalistic thoughts and impulses, is an archetype, not a biological imperative. This essence of animalism is part of the collective unconscious, which is a mental phenomenon that expresses essential forms of functioning based on the experiential past of humankind. Thoughts and impulses that are sufficiently selfish to clash with the common good are, therefore, more recapitulations of past mental experience than biological imperatives. Even if it be said that in the beginning—the first time in history that an individual clashed with others— a biological imperative was operating (and it is not certain that Jung would agree), this would not change the fact that all modern persons inherit a mental (not biological) predisposition to think and act selfishly because their ancestors have done so.

These may seem like excessively subtle distinctions, but bear with me. I am trying to show that for Jung there is basically no causation of any human importance that is other than mental. Jung sometimes refers to mental life as *spirit* (1933a, pp. 171–195), in contrast to *matter,* which is everything else of a physical nature, animal, vegetable, or mineral. In extolling the nonbiological nature of mentality, Jung says:

> But people who are not above the general level of consciousness have not yet discovered that it is . . . presumptuous and fantastic for us to assume that matter produces spirit; that apes give rise to human beings; that from the harmonious interplay of the drives of hunger, love, and power Kant's *Critique of Pure Reason* should have arisen; that the brain-cells manufacture thoughts, and that all this could not possibly be other than it is. (p. 176)

What a far cry this is from Freud! And notice how the final phrase suggests that once you make mentality your primary explanatory principle, nothing is impossible anymore. The limits on change are only the limits of imagination.

With such a psyche-centered view, one inevitably must come to question whether apparently causal considerations such as societal pressures (taboos and sanctions) are anything more than figments of the imagination. It seems quite clear that Jung (1933a) intends us to believe that since societal pressures must be perceived before they can be acknowledged as such, they have the status of psychic rather than social realities:

> Without a doubt psychic happenings constitute our only, immediate experience. . . . My sense impressions, for all that they force upon me a world of impenetrable objects occupying space, are psychic images, and these alone are my immediate experience, for they alone are the immediate objects of my consciousness. . . . All our knowledge is conditioned by the psyche which, because it alone is immediate, is superlatively real. Here there is a reality to which the psychologist can appeal—namely, psychic reality. . . . If I change my concept of reality in such a way as to admit that all psychic happenings are real—and no other use of the concept is valid—this puts an end to the conflict of matter and mind as contradictory explanatory principles. (pp. 189–190)

In the final sentence, Jung makes it perfectly clear that what may have appeared as a psychosocial conflict—the contradiction of mind by the "matter" of presumed social imperatives—is really no more than an intrapsychic conflict. If society seems opposed to the individual, it is because it is perceived that way, not because that is its unchangeable real nature. If more documentation were needed, there is Jung's dramatic statement in which he indicates the prepotency of the psyche: "In that one moment in which I came to know, the world sprang into being; without that moment it would never have been." (1959b, p. 96)

The basically intrapsychic nature of Jung's conflict theory is apparent in the way he uses it to understand persons and phenomena. There is conflict between a person's conscious perception of his or her sexuality and the presence of both anima and animus, between persona, other archetypes, and consciousness—indeed, among any and all of the core characteristics postulated. Intrapsychic conflict is the basic fact of life. But conflict, though inevitable, is not merely painful, something to be defended against. On the contrary, the opposition of elements in the psyche provides energy, as we shall see in the next section, and stimulates growth. It is not surprising, therefore, to find Jung (1933a) extolling the unconscious:

> It is well known that the Freudian school presents the unconscious in a thoroughly depreciatory light, just as also it looks on primitive man as little better than a wild beast. . . . Have the horrors of the World War really not opened our eyes? Are we still unable to see that man's conscious mind is even more devilish and perverse than the unconscious? . . . The unconscious is not a demonic monster, but a thing of nature that is perfectly neutral as far as moral sense, aesthetic sense and intellectual judgement go. It is dangerous only when our conscious attitude becomes hopelessly false. And this danger grows in the measure that we practice repressions. . . . That which my critic feared—I mean the overwhelming of consciousness by the unconscious—is most likely to occur when the unconscious is excluded from life by repressions, or is misunderstood and depreciated. (pp. 16–17)

To remain open to emanations from the collective unconscious is to stand on the shoulders of all who have gone before. And to permit the personal unconscious to become conscious again is to recapture the richness of one's particular past. In contrast to psychosocial conflict positions, intrapsychic ones see conflict as valuable and not to be defended against just because it is inevitable.

Indeed, the ideal, according to Jung, is for persons to actively concern themselves with unconscious as well as conscious experiences and to try to fit the two into a dynamic balance. The tension, pain, and difficulty involved are not to be avoided, for they are the stuff of life itself. Actually, Jung (1953b) postulated an archetype called the *self* in formalizing this ideal:

> If we picture the conscious mind with the ego as its centre, as being opposed to the unconscious, and if we now add to our mental picture the process of assimilating the unconscious, we can think of this assimilation as a kind of approximation of conscious and unconscious, where the centre of the total personality no longer coincides with the ego, but with a point midway between the conscious and unconscious. This would be the point of a new equilibrium, a new centering of the total personality, a virtual centre which, on account of its focal position between conscious and unconscious, ensures for the personality a new and more solid foundation. (p. 219)

Clearly, in pursuing selfhood one does not eliminate conflict (the conscious and unconscious remain opposed) so much as set the two conflicting poles of personality into juxtaposition and communication. In contrast to common personological usage, Jung defines the self as a conglomerate of conscious and unconscious experience.

Energy Concepts.   We now have covered the core characteristics involved in the core tendency of attempting to attain selfhood. But Jung also postulates several energy principles that are intrinsic to this core tendency. The energy involved in the psychological activities of thinking, feeling, and acting is called *psychic energy* (Jung, 1960a). Its sources are ambiguous. Sometimes Jung states that it derives from the very conflict of core characteristics already mentioned; sometimes, in more Freudian fashion, he considers it to be based on such biological processes as metabolism. In any event, the amount of psychic energy invested in thoughts, feelings, and actions as elements of personality is called the *value* of those elements. Value is essentially a measure of element intensity and is related to Freud's notion of cathexis.

We are now in a position to appreciate Jung's two main energy principles, which are psychological versions of the first and second laws of thermodynamics. The *principle of equivalence* (Jung, 1960a) states that if the value of any element of personality increases or decreases, this shift will be compensated for by an opposite shift in another element. For example, if a person loses interest in someone or an activity, someone else or another activity will increase in attractiveness. Applied to broader elements of personality, this principle indicates that if energy is removed from the ego, for example, it will be reinvested elsewhere, perhaps in the personal unconscious or the persona. The person who becomes concerned with internal experience does so at the expense of attention to external experience, and vice versa.

The *principle of entropy* (Jung, 1960a), in its psychological form, states that the distribution of energy in the psyche seeks an equilibrium, or balance. Thus, if two beliefs are of unequal value or strength, the general tendency will be for the stronger belief to become weaker and the weaker stronger. As to broad elements of personality, if the ego is, for example, stronger (more relied on in everyday life) than the shadow, the tendency over time will be for them to come closer together in value.

These two energy principles constitute the essential dynamics of the core tendency of seeking selfhood. Indeed, according to Jung, the ideal state—in which the total energy is evenly distributed (the ultimate outcome of the two energy principles) throughout the various elements of personality—is selfhood. In that state, consciousness and unconsciousness have equal energy, as does any particular thought, feeling, or action and the others. Do not misunderstand this state of balance for a conflict-free situation. That conflict would still underlie psychic functioning even if selfhood were attained is shown by the emphasis on equilibrium. Each element has the same value as the others. The elements have not, however, lost their identity, and the balance is a dynamic one based on the tension of opposition.

In postulating the principles of equivalence and entropy, Jung is emphasizing the psyche as a closed system, unaffected by input from external sources. It is only in such a system that decreases in the energy of one element would produce compensatory increases in the energy of another and there would be a general tendency toward a balance of energies. But Jung (1960a) does not believe that the psyche is a completely closed system. There are inputs of energy from somatic processes such as metabolism and from the outside world in such forms as punishment and encouragement. These external inputs are regular and inevitable enough to render it impossible, in Jung's view, for one to ever attain complete selfhood. Complete selfhood is, in this sense, an ideal to be striven for but never completed. Perhaps its unattainability is fortunate, because when perfect entropy is reached in a system, that system will run down and stop, there being no further possibility of the energy differentials that lead to movement. Perhaps we have discovered a basis for rapport between Jung and the later Freud, who came to believe—paradoxically—that the goal of all life is death.

In this discussion, we have considered three bases for interaction among elements of personality, namely, opposition, compensation, and dynamic balance. These are all consistent with the intrapsychic conflict model. But Jung (1960a) intimates a fourth: unity. On the face of it, this suggests that there is an alternative in this system to conflict. Along these lines, Jung proposes a *transcendent function,* whose aim is to integrate personality elements into an overall whole. This transcendent function, which seems to be less another energy principle than a dynamic rather than static picture of the self, inclines the person toward a unification of the opposing trends within the personality. Other forces, such as the defensiveness associated with the personal unconscious, may oppose the transcendent function, but it will tend to work toward unification anyway. If nothing else, it will be expressed at the unconscious level in the desire for wholeness that Jung claims is seen in many dreams and myths.

But what sense of unity can a theory so steeped in intrapsychic conflict as a fact of life possibly have? The answer is a paradoxical or mystical sense. In order to appreciate Jung's ideas on unity, you must recognize his belief that opposites attract and that the opposite of every truth is also true. The metaphor he adopts for this paradoxical unity is the *mandala,* or *circle,* which appears in Sanskrit writings and in many religions. If opposing polarities, such as consciousness versus unconsciousness, can be represented as a straight line whose ends race off in opposite directions, the mandala image transforms the straight line into a perfect circle. In this case, the ends at the same time race apart but also toward each other. In Jung's thinking, the mandala symbol is closely allied to the self and to the entropy principle.

The problem with the mandala metaphor is that it really does not aptly describe polarities and oppositions. One does not resolve the conflict inherent in a *defined* opposition by suddenly deciding to bend a straight line into a circle, because this only contradicts the defined opposition. Jung is working with a paradoxical sense of unity. Perhaps he even recognized this, for he believed that the transcendent function could not completely triumph, as self-hood could not really be attained.

Selfhood is not possible in the final analysis because the principle of entropy requires a closed system to culminate in equilibrium and Jung adamantly believes that the psyche is not really a closed system. That Jung talks about unity at all rather than just compensation, opposition, and dynamic balance reflects the extraordinary complexity of his theorizing and his lack of concern for mere inconsistencies in his thinking. He may also have been holding out the possibility that the human will evolve, at some future time, into a being described better in fulfillment than in conflict terms. This evolutionary possibility is not inconsistent with his emphasis on the collective unconscious as the content of the human's past experiences. For the moment, however, we would do well to conclude that on balance Jung's views are of the intrapsychic conflict type.

Developmental Considerations.   Once we turn to development, the optimism of Jung's position, in contrast to its Freudian ancestry, becomes apparent. Jung believes that individuals are constantly trying to grow and occasionally meeting with some success in their efforts. The story of personality development hardly ends with childhood, as far as he is concerned. Indeed, as intimated above, the human species is also constantly evolving more differentiated and conscious forms of existence. In this regard, the collective unconscious provides a basis whereby all modern persons stand on the shoulders of their predecessors and are therefore able to see a little further than they could.

More specifically, Jung (1960c) believed that in the earliest years psychic energy is invested primarily in activities necessary for physical survival. Jung considers sexuality per se to start becoming important somewhere around the age of five (the time of Freud's Oedipal conflict). Adolescence is basically an amplification of these early beginnings. Early adulthood involves employing these activities in more broad and complex commitments, such as to a vocation, a family, and a community. Although Jung does not postulate hard and fast developmental stages, his position thus far is similar to Freud's.

The big contrast with Freud, however, occurs in conceptualization of the latter half of life. Jung's position here is an important contribution that various subsequent personologists have taken up. He believes that a radical change takes place in persons when they reach the late thirties and early forties. Biological and social interests, activities, and orientations to the external, material world recede, to be replaced by an inward-turning spirituality. Wisdom and patience take the place of physical and mental assertiveness. The person becomes more religious, cultural, philosophical, and intuitive. In the ideal case, the strident emphasis on consciousness of the early years is tempered by an acceptance of unconscious experience (e.g., intuitions, mysteries) and an assimilation of it into everyday life. But if the transition is not well navigated, the end result is spiritual bankruptcy and a hellish end of life. Jung (1933a) feels that modern persons especially have difficulty making this transition because traditional and religious values have deteriorated in the face of industrialization without being replaced by any other ideological justification for spirituality. In this, he agrees with existential psychology.

Jung used many different concepts to articulate his views on development. He contrasted *causality* with *teleology* in order to lend philosophical sophistication to his optimism. According to the teleological viewpoint, human personality can be comprehended in terms of future goals. Causality, in contrast, explains the present in terms of the past. Jung felt both were necessary for complete understanding, and he criticized Freud for considering only causality. Similar in form is his distinction between *progression* and *regression*. Jung does not mean these as defenses in any strict sense; rather, he wanted to emphasize the forward thrust of development as progression and the shrinking to a safe past as regression. Although both occur in any person's life, progression is more a sign of growth than is regression. In special instances, however, regression may involve a beneficial tapping of the well of the unconscious. Another, similar distinction concerns *sublimation* and *repression,* processes that, once again, are reminiscent of defenses but somehow less concrete and specific than in Freud. In sublimation, psychic energy is transferred from primitive, instinctual, undifferentiated processes to more cultural, spiritual, complex processes. For example, when energy is withdrawn from sexual activity and given to religious activity, sublimation is said to have occurred. But when discharge of energy is blocked by some internal or external obstacle, repression takes place. The energy is then transferred to the personal unconscious, blocking development. Although the thinking is too complicated to recount here, note that Jung felt that underlying the processes of sublimation/repression, and progression/regression are the energy principles of equivalence and entropy.

Another way Jung discusses development is as psychological growth, or the progessively increasing tendency toward differentiation and integration. The basis for differentiation is inherent in the conflicting nature of core characteristics. Integration is expressive of the self archetype and the transcendent function. The shift in adulthood from material to spiritual concerns is part and parcel of the tendency to attain selfhood and integration. Apparently Jung (1960b) was willing to carry his notions of spirituality to extremes quite uncommon in a scientist. Late in life, he postulated the *principle of synchronicity,* which is intended to be an explanation of the contiguous or simultaneous occurrence of events that, though not causes of one another, indicate some commonality in the collective unconscious. With this principle, Jung intended to take seriously such disputed phenomena as telepathy and clairvoyance. For him, simultaneous events, such as thinking of a long-lost friend and having that person arrive unexpectedly or awakening with the fear that someone has been hurt only to find out later that this has indeed occurred, express the principle of synchronicity. This principle does not cause the simultaneous events; instead, it indicates the multiple expressions of archetypes. An archetype can express itself in someone's thoughts (e.g., you remember a long-lost friend)

and in the occurrence of an external event (e.g., the friend arrives unexpectedly). With the addition of the principle of synchronicity, Jung has evolved the
notion of collective unconscious into something very close to a universal force
that does not even depend on the existence of individual psyches for expression. With this principle, he is at his most mystical.

It is extremely difficult to approach evaluation of Jung's position. If the
usual procedures of scientific, analytical thought were to be applied, the position could be easily faulted. For example, the principle of synchronicity is
actually not an explanation at all but a description of an observed relationship.
All Jung is saying is that two events occurring together do so because sometimes seemingly disparate events occur together. If he were to contend more—
namely, that archetypes actively precipitate seemingly disparate though simultaneous events—archetypes essentially would constitute the very supernatural
order Jung has also decried. Similarly, the assumption of a transcendent function seems to contradict the principles of equivalence and entropy and the
other assumptions concerning the inevitability of conflict.

But I have the nagging feeling that by tackling Jung's theory with the tools
of logic we are missing what there is of value in it. Let us conclude that the
theory is full of logical inconsistencies and ambiguities and try nonetheless to
capture its intent. In doing this, we will emerge with an emphasis on mind or
spirit as the architect of life. Jung is much more humanistic than Freud and
others who have given important roles to biological and social forces in the
determination of behavior. In this regard, the collective unconscious and its
archetypes can be considered the inherent structure of mind. It is this inherent
structure that sets limits on human freedom of imagination and action, not the
body or society. No doubt it is this extreme spirituality that underlies Jung's
appeal today.

CHAPTER 4

The Core of Personality: Fulfillment Model

We have just considered some personality theories that conceptualize the core of personality as reflecting the ongoing conflict between two irrevocably opposed forces. In the conflict model, life is always seen as a compromise, the purpose of which is to minimize the conflict. But the conflict is always potentially large and debilitating and, hence, the compromise has an uncertain quality.

The theories we will consider in this chapter conceptualize the core of personality quite differently. They typically assume only one basic force in the human. Therefore, life is considered not a compromise but the process of the unfolding of the one force. I call the position exemplified by these theories the *fulfillment model*. There are two versions of the fulfillment model, the difference between them being the nature of the postulated force. If the force is the tendency to express to an ever greater degree the capabilities, potentialities, or talents based in one's genetic constitution, we are dealing with the actualization version. In the perfection version, the force is the tendency to strive for what will make life ideal or complete, perhaps even by compensating for functional or genetic weak spots. The actualization version is humanistic, whereas the perfection version is idealistic.

FULFILLMENT MODEL: ACTUALIZATION VERSION

In considering the *actualization version,* I will first discuss the theory of Rogers and examine its basis in the work of Goldstein. Then I will turn to the other actualization theorist, Maslow. Although Maslow's position is similar in many important ways to that of Rogers, Maslow postulates not one but two forces within the person. The two forces, however, are not conceived in such a fashion that they would necessarily oppose each other, and, even if they were, one force is considered much less important than the other. Maslow's theory clearly is an actualization version of the fulfillment model, but its postulation of two different forces within the person prompts me to consider it a variant of that model.

Rogers's Position

Carl R. Rogers (born in the suburbs of Chicago, 1902; died in La Jolla, California, 1987) differed from many psychotherapists in holding a Ph.D. rather than a medical degree and in his Protestant background. He apparently considered the strict religious background of his early life to be heavily restricting and burdensome. Early in life, Rogers was interested primarily in the biological and physical sciences. After graduation from college, however, his concerns shifted sufficiently to prompt him to enter the Union Theological Seminary in New York City. Perhaps this shift indicated an attempt to work through his feelings concerning his earlier background; the seminary he entered is well known for its liberality. Before long, Rogers transferred to Columbia University, where he was influenced by the humanistic philosophy of John Dewey and first encountered clinical psychology. In his initial clinical work he was exposed to a strongly Freudian view, which even then was not convincing to him because it denied the importance of people's conscious views of themselves. Rogers worked for several years at the Rochester Guidance Center, of which he became director. In the context of colleagues of heterogeneous personological convictions and stimulated by the daily practice of psychotherapy, Rogers began to formulate his own position. The person whose work touched him most at this time was Otto Rank, who by then had broken with Freud due to espousal of the position discussed in Chapter 3.

On leaving his clinical post, Rogers entered university life, taking on the role of teacher and researcher. During his association with the University of Chicago, he was elected president of the American Psychological Association (1946–1947). With his increasing attention to developing a theory of personality and psychotherapy—an inevitable effect of entering university life—Rogers became increasingly influenced by theorists who stressed the importance of one's self-view as a determinant of behavior, among them Goldstein, Maslow, Angyal, and Sullivan. Next came several years at the University of Wisconsin, where Rogers interacted with psychiatrists and worked with severely disturbed clients. Rogers continued his theorizing at the Center for Studies of the Person, an organization in La Jolla, California, dedicated to the investigation of not only interpersonal relations but broader social issues such as war and peace.

Although there are a number of theorists similar to Rogers, his position is the most comprehensive, developed, and psychological of its type. It is, therefore, a good way of introducing you to that kind of thinking. Rogers (1959) is very clear about the core of personality. For him, *the core tendency of humans is to actualize their potentialities*. This means that there is a pressure in people that leads them in the direction of becoming whatever it is in their inherited nature to be. It is difficult for people to appreciate this actualizing tendency on the intuitive ground of their own experience. Certainly we have all had the experience of wanting or feeling impelled to accomplish something. But these experiences are usually at a level too concrete to be directly relevant to the actualizing tendency as stated. We usually experience ourselves as wanting to get good grades, to learn to dance well, or to be imaginative rather than in the more abstract sense of acting in concert with our inherent nature. The somewhat concrete experiences mentioned may not be irrelevant, of course, since what the actualizing tendency will lead to in persons' functioning will depend on the content of their inherent potentialities. For example, if being imaginative is an inherent potentiality, wanting to be imaginative will certainly qualify as one expression of the actualizing tendency. And in our search for some intuitive basis for understanding Rogers's position, we should not overlook the strong possibility that at least some people seem to sometimes have personal experience of an urging to express themselves—somehow and in something—that is difficult to talk about because it is so formless and abstract. Perhaps such occasional experiences are direct representations of the actualizing tendency.

Keeping in mind the questions raised by our attempt to find a basis in our personal experience for understanding Rogers, let us now turn to a more formal approach to his theory. Once we assume an actualizing tendency as the basic directionality of the person, we raise consideration of (1) the content of the inherent potentialities, (2) the nature of the actualizing tendency itself, and (3) the manner in which the inherent potentialities and the actualizing tendency interact in the process of living.

The Inherent Potentialities of Human Beings.   About the only statement Rogers makes concerning the nature of the inherent potentialities is aimed at differentiating his position from that of Freud. According to Rogers, all of the human's potentialities are in the service of the maintenance and enhancement of life. Hence, one will not find anything such as a death instinct if Rogers is right. For Rogers death occurs accidentally, as the end result of biological breakdown with no primarily psychological significance, or through a decision on the person's part, which is usually a sign of psychological maladjustment rather than something true to human nature. Actually, I am being much more explicit concerning the view of death in this theory than Rogers ever was, though I believe what I have said fits the spirit of his thinking.

But discounting the concept of the death instinct, Freud and Rogers might seem less far apart. Freud would find congenial the notion that inherent potentialities (he would call them *instincts*) function to maintain and enhance life. Actually, there is a world of difference between the two theorists, and it has to do with their views on the relationship of the person to society. Recall that for Freud the person emerges as selfish and competitive in the pursuit of life. Society is viewed as necessarily in conflict with individuals, as the requirements of corporate living are antithetical to the most direct expression of instincts. In contrast, Rogers assumes that what is consistent with the maintenance and enhancement of individuals' lives is also consistent with the maintenance and enhancement of the lives of the people around them. For Rogers, there is nothing in human nature that, if accurately and straightforwardly expressed, would obviate the possibility of community by being seriously destructive to other people. While Rogers does not assume that it is part of human nature to be communal, he does indicate that persons, in their least corrupted form, will be so appreciative of themselves and vigorous in their living as to be capable of deep appreciation of others as well. Although persons do not need community in some imperative way, their nature is such that if they are not maladjusted they can delight in other people.

You may wonder at this point how Rogers would address the seemingly plausible reasons why Freud assumed human nature to be antithetical to social living. What about all the ways in which one person hurts another? Would not mutual destructiveness increase if society's rules and regulations were relaxed? Is it not merely pie in the sky to think people are pure deep down? Rogers would answer out of irrepressible optimism. He would point out that more countries are at peace than at war, that world wars are still more unusual than world peace, that societies with many complex laws and taboos do not have less crime than more lax societies, that the overwhelming majority of people abhor death as something foreign to them, and that infants show very little behavior indicating socially destructive tendencies. In other words, Rogers would not find Freud's reasons for believing the human to be selfish and potentially destructive compelling. To be sure, one can observe selfishness and destructiveness, but the question then becomes that of deciding what such observations really say about human nature. At one level, Rogers is saying that such observations are random enough to be best considered expressions of distortions of true human nature rather than, as in Freud, direct expressions of that nature.

At another level, Rogers has more positive reasons for his view on the constructive nature of the human. These reasons come from observations of people in social contexts ranging all the way from psychotherapy to international diplomacy. One observation is that misunderstandings and suspiciousness lead to antagonism and even competition among people. When the misunderstandings are spoken to directly, suspiciousness decreases and antagonistic, competitive behaviors give way to cooperative and appreciative ways of being. This is not to say that people will always agree among themselves; rather, it means that if there is no misunderstanding, the remaining disagreements will be honest and mutually respected. Another observation is that when persons feel hopeless and unworthy, they will disregard others and in many ways treat them poorly. But when they begin to accept themselves, they will also gain in appreciation and acceptance of others. They can appreciate and accept not only the ways in which others resemble them but—and probably more important—the ways in which they differ. These kinds of observations incline Rogers to the belief that the human's true nature—its inherent potentialities—is consistent with the maintenance and enhancement not only of the person's own living but of social living as well. It is only when the inherent potentialities suffer distorted expression due to maladjustment that behavior destructive to oneself and others is found.

The most important thing about the above observations for the theoretical difference between Freud and Rogers is that Rogers contends that behavior destructive to others always occurs along with behavior destructive to oneself. Rogers believes that if Freud were right, one would characteristically see behavior constructive to oneself taking place as the other side of the coin of behavior destructive to others, at least when society is least vigilant. Rogers finds little evidence of this.

Of course, the weakness in Rogers's observations is that they do not occur outside of the regulatory function of society and hence, while they are reasonably compelling, they are not definitive. In attempting to find observations uncontaminated by social pressure, one could go to infants or subhuman organisms. Unfortunately, infants are not good sources of information because they are so undeveloped that one might erroneously decide they are basically selfish, confusing maturational primitivity with lack of interest in the welfare of others. Even at that, Rogers contends there is little in children's behavior to show they are self-seeking at the expense of other people. But anyone awakened to the wail of youngsters in the middle of the night is justified, it seems to me, in not finding Rogers's contention completely convincing. While Rogers surely would agree that these children were preoccupied with their own needs at that point, he would ask whether the observation was really sufficient to justify the extreme conclusion that human nature is basically incompatible with community—and, in truth, the observation is insufficient.

This state of nondefinitive information prompts turning to the lower animals. Rogers has indeed done this and, as you will see later, this is thoroughly appropriate logically, for the actualizing tendency is not restricted to humans or even subhumans; rather, it applies to all living things, vegetable and animal. At one point, Rogers (1961, pp. 177–178) asks that we consider the lion, certainly a worthy and reasonably representative member of the animal world. Presumably the lion is unencumbered by societal restrictions in any Freudian sense. While this certainly can be disputed, I suppose it is more or less true. The lion, it turns out, is rather benign, having intercourse mainly with its mate and only occasionally with other lions, caring for its young in a rather loving way until they are old enough to go out into the world, and killing only when hungry or in defense of self and family. Here there is no gratuitous evil, nor any evidence of self-interest that is truly incompatible with the interests of others. The similarity between the life of the lion and that of the human is not accidental, according to Rogers. If the human expressed its natural potentialities, it would live a reasonably ordered, constructive, even moral life without needing to be held in check by society.

At this point, I must call a halt to this controversy over the compatibility of human nature with community, for it cannot be settled easily. Certainly, someone holding Freud's view could find in the animal world organisms that murder at random (rather than in self-defense), such as the wolverine or the weasel, or could focus on the severe limitation to the possibility of self-actualization inflicted by the lion on its prey. And so the argument goes. It will suffice for the present to recognize that the fulfillment model exemplified by Rogers is a serious and worthy alternative to the psychosocial conflict model.

Having appreciated the view that the inherent potentialities function to maintain and enhance life, we are in a position to inquire further as to their precise content. Extraordinary as it is, Rogers is almost mute on this matter! About the most insight one can gain through careful reading of Rogers is that he is thinking in terms of some sort of genetic blueprint, to which substance is added as life progresses. But the precise outlines of the blueprint are a mystery. Does it have to do with such biological considerations as the size and tonus of muscles, the excellence of brain structures and organization, and the rapidity of metabolic functioning? Does it concern more psychological considerations, such as the need to master or to be imaginative or gregarious? Rogers gives virtually no guidance. Another question that goes unanswered is whether—and if so, how—people differ in their inherent potentialities. As we will see, when considering the peripheral level of personality, it is very useful in a theory of this type to be able to postulate such individual differences. In truth, one gets the sense that Rogers agrees, but nowhere is he explicit enough to inspire certainty.

Surely it would be difficult to make a list of things that constitute a genetic blueprint from a personologist's point of view. This undoubtedly is part of the reason why Rogers is mute. But there is a reason beyond this difficulty, for Rogers is an intelligent, perceptive person who has shown no prior reticence to tackle and solve difficult problems. I think that the basic reason for Rogers's muteness is that making a list of inherent attributes would violate his intuitive sense of human freedom. He so vividly sees life as a changing, shifting, unfolding, unpredictable, vibrant thing that to theorize about some set list of characteristics would amount to shackling something wild and free.

A word about the history of this theory will make the above more convincing. Rogers's first and abiding interest has been in psychotherapy, in helping people beset by problems of living to find the bases for a more adequate, meaningful existence. He quickly broke away from orthodox theories and techniques of psychotherapy, such as the psychoanalytic approach, and for a period of time was known in psychology as an antitheoretical practitioner. He did not rush to develop a theory of psychotherapy because he was so deeply enmeshed in helping people that he cared little whether he had conceptual clarity as long as what was happening was beneficial. And it seemed to be. After a time, when his therapeutic experience had accumulated, he began to develop a theory about how successful therapeutic outcomes could be understood.

His theory of personality was an even later outgrowth of his theory of psychotherapy. And here lies the crux of my point. In psychotherapy, it is very helpful—for client and therapist alike—to believe in a view of the organism as unlimited in what it can become. It is helpful because you are already dealing with a client who is terribly limited by self-destructive symptom patterns and has lost conviction about becoming anyone worthwhile. In such a situation, it is necessary to hold out a view of life that is extreme enough in its opposition to the client's view to be able to serve as the needed corrective. Once it is believed, the client can draw tremendous strength from the Rogerian emphasis on freedom, a strength that will help to mobilize the persistence and energy needed to change deeply entrenched and destructive life patterns. Rogers's emphasis on unlimited possibilities in life has been so valuable in psychotherapy that it is not surprising that he would have retained it in his theory of personality.

But a theory of personality is not a theory of psychotherapy. In a theory of personality, you are not starting with an already disordered person; rather, when you make statements about core tendencies and characteristics, you are talking about the true nature of humans. While we may admire Rogers's temperamental unwillingness to set limits to life's possibilities, we should also recognize that the model of personality theory he has adopted sets up the logical requirement of precision concerning the genetic blueprint that would make his position complete enough to be usable. Without doubt, in being mute on the substantive characteristics of the genetic blueprint once having assumed its existence, Rogers is doing what in Freud's position would amount to considering instincts to be important determinants of action without saying what they are. All the richness of understanding contributed by Freud's view that there are life, sexual, and death instincts would, of course, be lost.

It might seem that in view of the obvious difficulty of theorizing in advance on the content of inherent potentialities, one is justified in looking at the actual behavior of particular persons and inferring from that what must be their potentialities. Certainly this inductive approach is one important way in which theories get built. But we must recognize that while such a strategy is useful in theory construction, it is totally unacceptable except on this temporary basis. It behooves the theorist employing such a strategy to recognize it as simply an expedient that limits the theory's usefulness. Unless such a cautionary stance is adopted, the theorist will fall into the logically unacceptable dilemma of circular reasoning. In Rogers's case, the dilemma would go as follows. He would propose that inherent potentialities determine all behavior while advocating using any and all observed behavior to discover the inherent potentialities. The circularity in this position involves defining what is to do the explaining in terms of what is to be explained. With such an approach, the theorist can never be proven wrong—nor proven right. Acceptance of such a circular position can occur only on the basis of faith (a kind of intuitive knowledge). It is necessary to be able to define a person's inherent potentialities by some logical or empirical means independent of the behavior they explain. Only then will it be possible to determine the soundness of Rogers's position. Until then, the lack of specificity as to the content of inherent potentialities will remain a dangerously seductive elastic clause.

The Actualizing Tendency. I have already pointed out that the actualizing tendency is the organism's push to become what its inherent potentialities suit it to be, these potentialities aiming toward the maintenance and enhancement of life. In taking a closer look at the actualizing tendency, the first thing to note is its organismic—actually, biological—rather than psychological na-

ture. It is rooted in the physiological processes of the entire body. It is a way
of talking about the tendency of organic matter to develop and multiply. In this,
the actualizing tendency is more like Freud's life and sexual instincts than his
death instinct. But the actualizing tendency is much broader than the life and
sex instincts per se. It certainly includes such things as food and water requirements, but only as a special case of the much more general characteristic of
living matter to develop along the lines of its function. So when a fetus develops
from a fertilized egg, when muscle and skin tissue differentiate, when secondary sex characteristics appear, when there is hormonal instigation of an inflammatory reaction in the case of injury to the body, we see the working of the
actualizing tendency as fully as in the more obvious case of intentional actions.
I say this because Rogers has made it quite clear that the actualizing tendency
is characteristic not only of human beings and animals but of all living things.
Waxing poetic, he makes this point clearly at the beginning of a paper (1963):

> During a vacation weekend some months ago I was standing on a headland
> overlooking one of the rugged coves which dot the coastline of northern Cali-
> fornia. Several large rock outcroppings were at the mouth of the cove, and these
> received the full force of the great Pacific combers which, beating upon them,
> broke into mountains of spray before surging into the cliff-lined shore. As I
> watched the waves breaking over these large rocks in the distance, I noticed
> with surprise what appeared to be tiny palm trees on the rocks, no more than
> two or three feet high, taking the pounding of the breakers. Through my binoc-
> ulars I saw that these were some type of seaweed, with a slender "trunk"
> topped off with a head of leaves. As one examined a specimen in the interval
> between the waves it seemed clear that this fragile, erect, top-heavy plant would
> be utterly crushed and broken by the next breaker. When the wave crunched
> down upon it, the trunk bent almost flat, the leaves were whipped into a straight
> line by the torrent of the water, yet the moment the wave had passed, here was
> the plant again, erect, tough, resilient. It seemed incredible that it was able to
> take this incessant pounding hour after hour, day after night, week after week,
> perhaps, for all I know, year after year, and all the time nourishing itself, ex-
> tending its domain, reproducing itself; in short, maintaining and enhancing
> itself in this process which, in our shorthand, we call growth. Here in this
> palmlike seaweed was the tenacity of life, the forward thrust of life, the ability
> to push into an incredibly hostile environment and not only hold its own, but to
> adapt, develop, become itself. (pp. 1–2)

The actualizing tendency is the biological pressure to fulfill the genetic
blueprint whatever the difficulty created by the environment. The above passage also indicates that the actualizing tendency does not aim at tension reduction as do the core tendencies of conflict theorists. The life and development
of the seaweed, as described by Rogers, is simply not to be understood as the
pursuit of comfort and quiescence. If the actualizing tendency is to be characterized in tension terms at all, it must involve tension *increase* rather than
reduction. Certainly the expression of "tenacity of life" and "forward thrust of
life" and such extraordinary phenomena as "to push into an incredibly hostile
environment" would precipitate increased rather than decreased organismic

tension. Satisfaction of the actualizing tendency is to be understood in terms of fulfillment of a grand design rather than of ease and comfort. As you will see, all the fulfillment positions involve tension increase, in sharp contrast to the conflict positions, all of which involved tension decrease in one form or another.

While the actualizing tendency is common to all living matter, it is not surprising that some of the expressions it takes in the human being, according to Rogers, would be unlikely at the subhuman level. Like all living things, the human shows the basic organismic or biological form of the actualizing tendency, whose aim is to express the inherent potentialities. But the human also shows rather distinctly psychological forms of the actualizing tendency. The most important of these is the *tendency toward self-actualization* (Rogers, 1959, p. 196). This differs from the actualizing tendency in that it involves the *self*. For Rogers, the self is

> . . . the organized, consistent conceptual gestalt composed of perceptions of the characteristics of the "I" or "me" and the perceptions of the relationships of the "I" or "me" to others and to various aspects of life, together with the values attached to these perceptions. It is a gestalt which is available to awareness though not necessarily in awareness. (p. 200)

Thus, the self-actualization tendency is the pressure to behave and develop—experience oneself—consistently with one's conscious view of what one is. As you will see in the following, Rogers's concept of self is similar to Rank's will.

The self-concept presumably is a peculiarly human manifestation. To understand how it comes into being, we must consider two additional offshoots of the actualizing tendency in the human being: the need for positive regard and the need for positive self-regard (Rogers, 1959, pp. 108–109). Both are considered secondary or learned needs, commonly developed in early infancy, that represent specialized expressions of the overall actualizing tendency. The *need for positive regard* refers to the person's satisfaction at receiving the approval of others and frustration at receiving disapproval. The *need for positive self-regard* is a more internalized version of this—in other words, it refers to personal satisfaction at approving and dissatisfaction at disapproving of oneself. Because persons have a need for positive regard, they are sensitive to, or can be affected by, the attitudes toward them of the significant people in their lives. In the process of gaining approval and disapproval from others, persons develop a conscious sense of who they are, called a *self-concept*. Along with this, they develop a need for positive self-regard, which ensures that the tendency toward self-actualization will take the form of favoring behavior and development that are consistent with the self-concept. The person is unlikely to persist in functioning incompatibly with the self-concept because this would frustrate the need for positive self-regard.

To summarize in the terminology of this book, Rogers considers the core tendencies of personality to be (1) the inherent attempt of the organism to actualize or develop all of its capacities in ways that will serve to maintain and enhance life and (2) the attempt to actualize the self-concept, which is a psychological manifestation of (1). The needs for positive regard and positive self-regard are secondary or learned offshoots of these core tendencies, explicating the motivational mechanism whereby the actualization of self-concept is attempted. The characteristics at the core of personality are (1) the inherent potentialities, which define the ways in which the actualizing tendency will be expressed, and (2) the self-concept, which defines the ways in which the self-actualizing tendency will be expressed. These tendencies and characteristics are at the core of personality because they are common to all persons and have a pervasive influence on living.

The Way to Actualization of Potentialities.   It is crucial to an understanding of maximal fulfillment to recognize that while the inherent potentialities are genetically determined, the self-concept is socially determined. This makes it possible to imagine discrepancies between these two sets of core characteristics; one's sense of who and what one is may deviate from what one's organismic potentialities actually suit one to be. But in order for this kind of discrepancy to exist, people must have been failed by society. Although society often fails the person in this way, it does not have to do so. Society is not inevitably antagonistic to the individual, as it is assumed to be by Freud and the psychosocial conflict theorists.

Rogers (1961, pp. 31-48) has a good deal to say about the nature of society's failure. He calls it *conditional positive regard*. What he means is the situation in which only some but not all of your actions, thoughts, and feelings are approved of and supported by the significant people in your life. Thus, as you develop a self-concept, the fact that what other people think of you is important will lead you to see yourself only in terms of those of your actions, thoughts, and feelings that have received approval and support. Your self-concept will be based on what Rogers calls *conditions of worth,* that is, standards for discerning what is valuable and what not valuable about yourself. Conditions of worth as a concept serve much the same logical function as does the superego in Freud's theory. Both concepts represent something implanted by society that serves as an ethical monitor of your functioning.

The existence of conditions of worth in the self-concept brings into operation a defensiveness similar to that postulated by Freud. Once you have conditions of worth, some of the thoughts, feelings, and actions in which you could well engage will make you feel unworthy or guilty; hence, a process of defense is set in motion. As in Freud, the defense is activated when the person receives some small cue, in the form of *anxiety,* that unworthy behavior is about to occur. Rogers details two general kinds of defenses: *denial* and *distortion*. His approach thus falls short of Freud's elaborate list of defenses. Discussion of these matters will be deferred until Chapter 8.

Although there is much similarity between Rogers and Freud in the notion of societal implants concerning ethical functioning and defensive operations to shield the person from the pain of feeling unworthy and to aid in bending behavior to moral standards, there is a critical difference as well. For Freud defensive operations lead to the most successful life, whereas for Rogers they result in a crippling restriction on living. This difference follows from other differences in the positions. For Freud, the conflict between individual and society is inevitable because the individual is by nature unsuited for community, even though social living is obviously necessary to the broader matters of survival of the species and development of culture. In contrast, for Rogers, though there is often conflict between individual and society—witness conditional positive regard as a reaction to expressions of inherent potentialities—the conflict is not at all inevitable. There is no necessary incompatibility between individual and society, because there is nothing in the individual's genetic blueprint that obviates community. While for Freud the good life involves expression of your true nature only within the necessary limitations of other people's rights, for Rogers the good life involves nothing less than maximal expression of your true nature. Conditions of worth and defensive processes are considered crippling because they lead to a rejection of thoughts, feelings, or actions that truly express inherent potentialities, a state called *incongruence*. In other words, once conditions of worth and defense exist, it is impossible to fully actualize your potentialities. You cannot become all that you could be. You will have lost out on part of your genetic birthright.

How can these dire consequences be avoided? You must be lucky enough to have experienced as a youngster *unconditional positive regard* (Rogers, 1961, pp. 31-48) from the significant people in your environment. The major Rogerian developmental statement concerns the existence of this unconditional positive regard, meaning that these significant people value and respect you as a person and, therefore, support and accept your behavior even if they disagree with it. Rogers does not literally mean that every possible action must be approved regardless of the consequences to yourself and others. Obviously a young child must be restrained if it tries to run into the path of a moving truck. But if the child is to experience a continuance of positive regard despite the restraint, it must be clear from the adult's way of restraining that there is no diminution of respect and general approval. If the child is beaten or told it is bad for wanting to run across the street, it is not being positively regarded. If, in contrast, the child is simply held back and told in words appropriate to its age level that running across the street is dangerous, it is still being respected as a human being. In conceptualizing unconditional positive regard, Rogers emphasizes an atmosphere of valuing and loving more than an absence of all constraints. There are obviously a whole host of things that the child must learn about the world in order to effectively negotiate its complexities. But these things can be learned in an atmosphere fostering either self-acceptance or self-denial, and this makes all the difference for Rogers.

If you grow up in an atmosphere of unconditional positive regard, you develop no conditions of worth and no defensiveness. Your self-concept is broader and deeper, including a much larger proportion of the thoughts, feelings, and actions that express your inherent potentialities. In addition, your self-concept is more flexible and changing. This is because new thoughts, feelings, and actions brought about by the continual unfolding of the actualizing tendency can be consciously appreciated (there being no defense) and incorporated into the self-concept (there being no limiting conditions of worth). The state in which the self-concept embraces more or less all of your potentialities is called *congruence,* which signifies that the self-concept has not shriveled to only part of what you are and can be. The state of flexibility in which new experiences can occur and be consciously appreciated is called *openness to experience,* meaning that no watering down through defenses is taking place.

Thus, for Rogers the way to actualize your potentialities in the fullest manner is to possess a self-concept that does not include conditions of worth and, therefore, precipitates no defenses. It follows from this that you will (1) respect and value all manifestations of yourself, (2) be conscious of virtually all there is to know about yourself, and (3) be flexible and open to new experience. In this way, the work of becoming what it is in your nature to be can go forward undisturbed. You will be what Rogers calls a *fully functioning person.* And, as indicated earlier, far from being self-interestedly antisocial, as would be expected in the Freudian view of a person without defenses, you will value, appreciate, enjoy, and approve of other people because you value, appreciate, enjoy, and approve of yourself.

Rogers and Goldstein.   Many of the concepts found in Rogers and other actualization theorists can be traced to the position of Kurt Goldstein (1963). A physiologist interested in how people adjust to brain damage, Goldstein offers less a theory of personality than a theory of the organism. Nonetheless, it will be helpful to understanding Rogers's views to note their similarity to and difference from Goldstein.

Like Rogers, Goldstein assumes that the core characteristics of personality are the inherent potentialities and the core tendency is the push toward realization in the actual living of these inherent potentialities. Furthermore, both theorists agree that the core tendency and characteristics ensure the maintenance and enhancement of life and are not in any necessary way incompatible with community. Although both theorists assume a basic push in the person toward realizing potentialities, Rogers calls this the actualizing tendency whereas Goldstein calls it the *self-actualizing tendency.* Rogers saves the latter term for the push to realize one's subjective sense of who one is, preferring the former term to refer to a more organismic, biological process of development. Goldstein can agree to the organismic, biological nature of the basic push to realize one's potentialities and still call this a self-actualizing tendency because he does not have a psychological sense of the concept of self. For Goldstein, the self is virtually the same as the organism. Nowhere in Goldstein's theory is there recourse to the importance of a phenomenal self-concept.

This means that Goldstein gives no formal theoretical role to such matters as conditions of worth and attempts to become in actual behavior what you think you should be. He also gives no formal theoretical role to conflict due to expressions of the actualizing tendency threatening to, or actually falling outside of, the limits set by conditions of worth. And hence he assigns no formal theoretical role to defense, at least as a mechanism for avoiding psychologically determined anxiety and guilt. There is also no role in Goldstein's thinking for offshoots of the basic push to actualize potentialities that could be considered the need for positive regard and the need for positive self-regard. As you can see, Goldstein's theory is much simpler than that of Rogers. It also cannot explain as much. Strictly speaking, Goldstein cannot consider such phenomena as guilt, unconscious cognitions, and acting in terms of one's aspirations.

Generally speaking, Goldstein stays away from the kinds of phenomena mentioned above. Actually, the only one of the three that receives significant attention is unconscious cognition, and the point of view Goldstein takes is that there is no such thing in Freud's sense. For the unconscious—in the sense of cognitions in the mind but actively barred from consciousness—Goldstein substitutes the view that cognitions not actually at the center of attention at the moment may remain in the mind in unsalient form. But whenever the situation the person faces warrants it, the unsalient cognitions can be called to the center of attention.

As is typical of all fulfillment theorists, Goldstein fails to see society as having requirements that not only must be served if civilization is to survive but are also in opposition to basic human nature. For Goldstein, as for Rogers, the external environment serves two functions for the person. First, it provides contexts, even tasks, to be performed in the enactment of fulfillment. Second, the environment can interfere with normal, vigorous actualization of potentialities. As would be expected from his minimally psychological viewpoint, Goldstein offers no complicated or detailed account of development through interaction with society and the physical world, but what he does provide is consistent with the fulfillment position. The self-actualization tendency will lead to the fulfillment of the genetic blueprint unless normal social support and freedom from physical danger are lacking. If there is danger, or actual damage to the person, catastrophic anxiety will result. *Catastrophic anxiety* is the fear of coming to an end, or being overwhelmed, or disintegrating. Catastrophic anxiety leads to a diversion of self-actualization pressure away from the vigorous pursuit of life enhancement to the equally valuable but more conservative pursuit of life maintenance. In this case, the person does not grow so much as survive. Although the life maintenance reaction to catastrophic anxiety may sound less remarkable than the growth taking place in its absence, it should be clearly recognized that for Goldstein the one is as much an expression of the self-actualization tendency as is the other. They differ only in that one is the best that can be done with an injured organism while the other involves no such limitation.

Note that Rogers's theory parallels Goldstein's at a more psychological level. In Rogers, functioning defensively because of conditions of worth amounts to the maintenance of life. For life to be enhanced rather than merely maintained, there must be freedom from defensiveness due to an absence of conditions of worth. Conditions of worth in Rogers's theory are psychological entities analogous to physical injury in Goldstein's theory. Another way of viewing this is that threat to the person from the outside takes a social form for Rogers more than for Goldstein, though neither believes threat to be inevitable. The counterpart in Rogers for Goldstein's emphasis on physical injury to the organism is psychological injury in the form of conditions of worth. As a physically damaged organism orients itself toward maintenance rather than life enhancement, so does the psychologically damaged organism considered by Rogers, through the action of defensive processes.

I wish to make a final point about the inherent potentialities. On this matter, we find both theorists agreeing on something like a genetic blueprint. Although neither Goldstein nor Rogers really specifies the content of the blueprint, Goldstein does suggest a technique whereby one can diagnose the inherent potentialities from the behavior one observes. It is Goldstein's belief that specifically in a person's preferences and in what he or she does well, one can see evidence of the underlying genetic blueprint. You should recognize that this is only a mere beginning toward the goal of content specification, for as a theoretician you can say nothing about that content which is general and prior to concrete observations. You must have a person in front of you to observe so that you can diagnose his or her preferences and competencies. Having done so, you can speculate about that person's inherent potentialities. Such speculation will not necessarily tell you anything valid about the next person's potentialities. Nonetheless, Goldstein's technique of diagnosis is a step forward in precision if it can be used in a manner that avoids complete circularity of reasoning. If you can assume that only some of any person's behavior will express his or her preferences and competencies, you can say that only those behaviors clarify the nature of potentialities. Behavior that does not express preferences and competencies is to be understood in some other way. Because Goldstein's position focuses on only some behavior, it avoids the circularity inherent in saying that all behavior expresses potentialities and it is potentialities that produce behavior.

Maslow's Position

The second actualization position we will discuss is that of Abraham Maslow (born in New York City, 1908; died in La Jolla, California, 1970). Maslow received his Ph. D. in 1934. Throughout his career he concentrated on research, teaching, and writing. The observations he used in theorizing tended to stem from research on normal and creative people rather than from psychopathology and psychotherapy. An abiding concern of Maslow's was the betterment of society and the individual life. After serving at a number of universities, Maslow became chair of the Department of Psychology at Brandeis University in 1961. This distinguished personologist was elected president of the American Psychological Association. By the time of his death, he had emerged as a popular leader of humanistic trends in our society.

Maslow developed his position slowly over many years and was responsive to and influenced by the work of like-minded personologists such as Allport and Rogers. For three reasons, I have included discussion of his view here even though he is in strong agreement on many points with Rogers. First, on some very important matters he is more detailed and complete than is Rogers. Second—paradoxically enough—his discursive, highly eclectic approach to theorizing and writing renders his position ambiguous at the same time that he is willing to tackle problems others have avoided. Thus, there are both good and bad practices to be learned from Maslow by the student of personology. Third, Maslow's position is a variant of the fulfillment model. For Maslow, fulfillment is the most important, but not the only, directionality in the person. In view of the complexity introduced by this fact, the ensuing discussion will be broken down into three broad topics: (1) the core tendencies of personality, (2) the core characteristics of personality, and (3) the way to fulfillment.

The Core Tendencies of Personality.   Maslow (1962, 1967, 1969) agrees with Rogers and Goldstein in imputing to the person as a core tendency the *push toward actualization of inherent potentialities*. Although Maslow seems to recognize the importance of self-concept in much of his writing, he does not explicitly give it the significance and type of role that we find in Rogers. For Maslow, actualization of inherent potentialities virtually ensures development of a self-concept and, while he associates mental illness with faulty actualization, he does not attribute the cause of the faultiness to a restricting self-concept. It seems to me that Maslow's position lies somewhere between those of Rogers and Goldstein—to wit, Maslow names the push toward realizing one's potentialities the *self-actualizing tendency* and appears to emphasize the physiological organism at some times and the phenomenal self at others.

Now to what makes Maslow's theory a variant of the fulfillment model. He (Maslow, 1955, 1962) recognizes another tendency, common to all persons and therefore part of the core of personality, that does not have the same connotations of fulfillment inherent in the actualizing tendency. Although he never quite puts it this way, this other tendency is the *push to satisfy needs ensuring physical and psychological survival*. The model appropriate to this tendency is that of needing help rather than pursuing fulfillment.

The survival tendency appears prior to, or is prepotent over, the actualization tendency in that a certain modicum of satisfaction of the former is necessary before the person can engage in vigorous expression of the latter. But this is not to say that the survival tendency is more important than the actualization tendency in any other way. The survival tendency can only maintain life; it cannot enhance it. Only the actualization tendency can lead to a rich and deeply meaningful life. Thus, although both survival and actualization tendencies are clearly part of the core of personality, the special importance

Maslow gives to the latter makes his position a fulfillment theory, albeit a variant on that theme. His position is not in the conflict tradition, because the survival and actualization tendencies are not conceptualized as antagonistic to each other. It is true that if the survival tendency does not achieve a measure of satisfaction, the actualization tendency will not be vigorously expressed. However, this is not the same as saying that one tendency inhibits or counteracts the other.

Maslow makes some lucid statements concerning the concrete nature of the actualizing tendency (1962):

> It is necessary to understand that capacities, organs, and organ systems press to function and express themselves and to be used and exercised, and that such use is satisfying and disuse irritating. . . . In the normal development of the normal child, it is now known that *most* of the time, if he is given a really free choice, he will choose what is good for his growth. This he does because it tastes good, feels good, gives pleasure or *delight*.

Maslow makes the concept of actualizing tendency more concrete and tangible by pinpointing its physiological sources and their psychological concomitants. The *physiological source* is the tendency of somatic components of the organism to function according to their design. The *psychological concomitant* is the person's tendency to make choices that are satisfying. When the person uses satisfaction as a guide, choices will be made that are consistent with the proper functioning of his or her somatic components because using these components according to their design will cause satisfaction. Note the similarity between this position and the Freudian one in which bodily requirements (e.g., for food or sex) are represented in mental life in such a fashion that decisions and actions suit them. But once you consider the concrete content of organismic requirements, the similarity ends. Maslow's position clearly indicates that the person does not actualize potentialities out of any sense of destiny or any self-conscious desire to function well. Indeed, the person who truly actualizes potentialities experiences nothing grander than a general sense of well-being. Actualization theorists tend to distrust self-conscious attempts to do well.

When we try to more fully describe Maslow's ideas about the relationship of the two basic tendencies in the core of personality, we encounter ambiguities. The survival tendency is stronger than—takes precedence over—the actualizing tendency. The actualizing tendency is strong and vigorous only when the survival tendency has been satisfied. This relationship is certainly meant to hold developmentally—the major task of childhood is to satisfy the survival tendency, though once this is accomplished, the actualizing tendency increases in saliency—but it can also be applied at any point in life. For example, a person who has achieved vigorous expression of the actualizing tendency might, through environmental circumstances, find survival threatened anew and revert temporarily or even chronically to expressions of the survival tendency. Interestingly, Machiavelli might have subscribed to a similar viewpoint, for he believed that refined, civilized, cultured persons are that way only because they live in an environment devoid of personal threat and that once threatened they will be much meaner in appearance and easier to control. But Machiavelli believed that this showed the greater importance of the survival tendency, whereas Maslow feels that the survival tendency is important only because it sets the stage for the actualizing tendency. Both beliefs are logically possible, and Maslow's choice exemplifies his irrepressible optimism.

Maslow's decision to cast the survival and actualizing tendencies in motivational terms has been popular with actualization theorists in general. According to Maslow (1955), the actualization tendency is growth motivation whereas the survival tendency is deprivation motivation. *Deprivation motivation* refers to urges to strive for goal states, the absence of which cause pain and discomfort. The aim of deprivation motivation is to decrease the organismic tension built up through deficit states that represent deviations from homeostatic balance (the self-regulating nature of the organism). Organismic survival requires nutritional substances; hence, when food has not been ingested for awhile, visceral organ activity produces a rising tension level, experienced psychologically as hunger, that precipitates instrumental actions designed to reach the goal state. The goal state is satiation, which is considered the normal, homeostatic state, characterized as tensionless. This is an old model for motivation that achieved its definitive modern statement in the writings of the physiologist Walter B. Cannon. Note that it is the model subscribed to by Freud and the other conflict theorists.

In contrasting deprivation motivation with growth motivation, Maslow may have been taking another cue from Cannon (1929), who said that once the homeostatic needs are satisfied, the "priceless unessentials of life" can be sought. In any event, *growth motivation,* which Maslow claims has been inadequately recognized in the past, refers to urges to enrich living and to enlarge experience because to do so increases one's delight at being alive. Growth motivation does not involve the repairing of deficits so much as the expansion of horizons. The goal states of growth motivation, if they exist at all, are very general in nature. Growth motivation does not start with sharp discomfort that must be eased, and its aim is less the reduction of tension than its actual increase. Satisfaction has to do with realization of capabilities or ideals through a process whereby the organism becomes more complex, differentiated, and potent. This enlargement of the organism seems to require, if anything, that satisfaction go hand in hand with tension increase.

Unfortunately, growth motivation as an idea is logically inconsistent. It assumes that there exists a kind of motivation that does not involve striving toward something that is lacking. But the motivation construct is such that in order to define a motive, you must specify a goal state that is to be achieved and the course of action instrumental to reaching it (Peters, 1958; Maddi & Costa, 1972). A motive without a specifiable goal state would not be a motive at all. And once you define a goal, you are of necessity assuming that the person having the motive is in a deprived state until he or she reaches it. In a logical sense, then, there is no way to define a motive that does not follow the so-called deprivation model. I think Maslow is reaching for a valuable distinction among kinds of tendencies, but it is poorly stated by the terms *deprivation motivation* and *growth motivation*.

I am by no means suggesting the abandonment of the concept of actualizing tendency; rather, what is at issue is its status as a motive. In this regard, I have tried to convince you that if Maslow and the others wish to consider the actualizing tendency as a motive, it must conform to a deprivation model because that is appropriate to the logic of the motivation construct. The actualizing tendency as motive must refer to a goal state that is valued but not yet achieved (and that is where the deprivation comes in) and to the actions instrumental to its achievement. But I should also make it clear that the actualizing tendency need not be considered a motive simply because it exerts a causal influence on behavior. A theorist could decide to consider it an organismic tendency, much like metabolism or maturation, that does not engage the person's intelligence and decision-making capabilities. Since such a model does not imply purpose in a psychological sense (Peters, 1958), the language of motivation is irrelevant. Indeed, Maslow could easily give up the motivational model for the actualizing tendency, for he has said "Maturity, or self-actualization, from the (motivational) point of view, means to transcend the deficiency needs. This state can be described then as meta-motivated, or unmotivated" (Maslow, 1962).

Although it would seem that Maslow recognizes the value of casting the actualizing tendency in nonmotivational terms, the disconcerting inconsistency and ambiguity of his writing are well exemplified by the appearance of the above quote directly following the point in the article at which the idea of self-actualization as growth motivation has been developed! It is as if Maslow, in thinking in terms of the intuitively apparent difference between a tendency to actualize one's capabilities and a tendency to satisfy one's survival needs, and in recognizing the inherently motivational nature of the latter, could not resist the symmetry produced by generalizing the motivational model to the actualizing tendency as well. Although such generalization may have seemed neat to him at first, on reflection the very kind of logical difficulty I pointed out must have arisen to plague him, leading to contradictory statements in the same breath. In Chapter 10, I will show how core tendencies, such as that of actualizing one's potentialities, can be considered forces that produce directionality in living without being cast in motivational terms.

The Core Characteristics of Personality.   Now let us consider the core characteristics of personality that correspond to the two core tendencies. In the case of the tendency to satisfy physical and psychological survival needs, Maslow lists *physiogical needs, safety needs, needs for belongingness* and *love,* and *esteem needs*. The first two on the list are the more physiological and less psychological. But even the last two, though heavily psychological, are more relevant to survival, or the repairing of deficits, than to the fulfillment of one's potentialities. Notice that the intent is a hierarchical organization. In other words, when the physiological needs are satisfied, the safety needs become salient and can be attended to; when the physiological and safety needs are both satisfied, the needs for belongingness and love become salient and can be attended to; and so forth.

Maslow also specifies the core characteristics relevant to the actualizing tendency. We should greet such specification with special interest, as we have already noted that most actualization positions suffer from the weakness of being mute concerning the content of inherent potentialities. In this company, Maslow is a worthy exception, but he misses the laurel wreath through being confusing once again. I will try, however, to piece together the essence of his position concerning the inherent potentialities.

One relevant kind of information comes in Maslow's discussions of the hierarchy of needs mentioned above. Actually, Maslow lists two additional needs that stand higher than those already discussed: the *need for self-actualization,* followed by the *need for cognitive understanding.* His manner of identifying these two needs in the hierarchy suggests not only that they are independent of each other but that the need for cognitive understanding is an even higher expression of human nature than is self-actualization. But he cannot really mean this, because his position would then become fraught with contradictions and incompletions. So, taking all he says into account, it seems to me most likely that these two needs refer to different aspects of the inherent potentialities that unfold due to the action of the actualizing tendency. The need for cognitive understanding could be considered a psychological reflection of the inherent function of the nervous system, namely, the processing of information. A number of other theorists considered in this volume (e.g., Murray, Rogers, White, Allport) would also find such an assumption useful. Actually, this kind of view has certainly crept into psychology and finds direct expression even in two theorists in the Rogerian tradition: Butler and Rice (1963) develop the notion that self-actualization occurs as a result of the nervous system's hunger for stimulation. But to return to the main theme, if the inherent potentialities referred to as "need for self-actualization" and "need for cognitive understanding" do indeed represent expressions of the actualizing tendency, the former must be inaccurately labeled, as can be seen by its redundancy. Let us delve further into Maslow's writing to see whether we can discover the proper label for this content.

Of particular relevance are the statements he makes about human nature. At the outset, he emphasizes that people are both similar to and different from one another (Maslow, 1962). Then, in agreement with Rogers and Goldstein, he says, "This inner nature, as much as we know of it so far, is definitely not 'evil,' but is either what we adults in our culture call 'good,' or else it is neutral. The most accurate way to express this is to say that it is 'prior to good and evil'." Now we come to statements that purport to provide even more concrete specification of the content of human nature. According to Maslow (1962),

> We have, each one of us, an essential inner nature which is intrinsic, given, "natural" and usually, very resistant to change. . . . I include in this inner nature instinctoid needs, capacities, talents, anatomical equipment, physiological balances, prenatal and natal injuries, and traumata to the neonatus. Whether defense and coping mechanisms, "style of life," and other characterological traits, all shaped in the first few years of life, should be included, is still a matter for discussion. I would say "yes" and proceed on the assumption that this raw material very quickly starts growing into a self as it meets the world outside and begins to have transactions with it.

You may experience an initial flush of enthusiasm at first reading this statement, but I ask you to reflect on it for a moment. To me, the statement teaches us little because it is too omnibus. As a specification of the inherent potentialities relevant to the actualizing tendency, it is really no advantage over muteness. As a statement of all that is in human nature—that is, the inherent potentialities plus the deficiency needs—it might be helpful if we were told what things went in which of the two categories. Indeed, it is not clear that this is even the right track to follow, for Maslow includes such things as defenses and coping mechanisms. In his own terms, these things are not even clearly innate, rather than learned, and yet they occur in a statement of the human's "inner nature."

There are a few other relevant statements in the same article that we could note here, but they are equally discursive and confusing. At one point, Maslow indicates that because humans have evolved away from strong instincts, it is hard for them to know and experience their inner nature. The same seems to be true for the theorist regarding the inherent potentialities! I conclude that Maslow's attempt to specify the content of these potentialities is, because of its omnibus and loose nature, no more useful than the absence of such statements on the part of other actualization theorists.

The Way to Fulfillment.   The conditions under which fulfillment occurs are very similar for both Maslow and Rogers, although there are some superficial differences in terminology. According to Maslow, satisfaction of the survival tendency is all that is necessary to ensure that self-actualization will occur. While the existence of the survival tendency guarantees that persons will seek the goal states that are prerequisites to self-actualization, whether they will be successful really hinges on the nature of their physical and social environment. This is true when persons are young because they are not developed enough to be independent of the assistance of others and when they are adult because if their environment lacks the basis for physical and psychological survival, no amount of effort will result in success. But if the survival needs, both physical and psychological, are assuaged, the naturally unfolding process of fulfillment will be ensured by the existence of the actualizing tendency and inherent potentialities. When you recognize that satisfaction of the deficiency needs requires that the person be loved, respected, and accepted, along with receiving the stuff with which to assuage physiological want and be kept out of harm's way, it becomes clear that Maslow is in essential agreement with Rogers. The difference between them is that the actualizing tendency incorporates both the maintenance and the enhancement of life for Rogers whereas it incorporates only enhancement for Maslow, with maintenance being the function of the survival tendency. As far as I can tell, however, this difference does not lead to much discrepancy in the views of individual and society that each holds.

The two theorists are also in essential agreement on what the person achieving self-actualization would be like. Rogers speaks of the fully functioning person as characterized by congruence between sense of self and organismic qualities, love of self and others, openness to experience, and fairly continual change in living. Maslow uses slightly different words, such as *creative living, peak experiences, unselfish love,* and *unbiased understanding*, but, in point of fact, means very much the same things.

In closing this discussion of Maslow's position, I would like to call your attention to the general implications of the view that survival needs must be met before vigorous actualization of potentialities can occur. Clearly this means that the person must be nurtured, loved, and respected in order to amount to anything. As charmingly humanistic as this viewpoint is, I think it can be seriously criticized. There are countless examples of people who have been significantly creative despite early lives that included little nurturance, love, and respect. From the contemporary scene, James Baldwin is certainly an example. It is hard to imagine a developmental environment more destructive than his. Assailed on all fronts by psychological, social, and economic deprivation to the point of inhumanity, he still emerged as a productive, creative writer and critic. To carry this criticism further, let me point out that one implication of Maslow's position is that when survival needs are frustrated at any point in time—not simply in childhood—there ought to be a concomitant temporary decrease in vigorous self-actualization. But, as I have pointed out elsewhere (Maddi, 1965), there are many contradictory examples to be found in the lives of great persons:

> We should keep in mind that John Bunyan began *Pilgrim's Progress* in the humiliating and rigidly regulated environment of a prison, and that Christ developed and preached his new ideas in a societal context that had become oppressively structured, to say nothing of the dangers he encountered. The blossoming of creativity during the Renaissance used to be attributed to the newly found wonder of leisure time, of time in which to contemplate and imagine. But it is now recognized that the Renaissance was an era of tremendous upheaval, chaos, and strife, in which flourished not only creativity, but also vice and intrigue of wondrous variety. Far from being free and permissive, it was an environment in which the artist and scientist had to scramble to get and keep the indulgence and protection of a patron, and hope that the patron would remain more powerful than his enemies for a while at least. And if further evidence were needed . . . I could turn to the concentration camp. Even in this environment so bent on psychological and physical destruction . . . some people could still think and observe creatively enough to develop the kernels of new

philosophies of life, later to be written about in such books as *The Informed Heart* and *From Death Camp to Existentialism. . . .* And picture Galileo as he prayed on his knees by the side of the bed at night that he might gain God's aid in finding the inspiration for a creative idea to be converted into money to placate his creditors. Toulouse-Lautrec and many others were in rather constant physical pain as they expressed their creativity. I hardly need mention that Van Gogh created under the pressure of a fantastic assortment of torments. Finally, in *A Moveable Feast,* Hemingway specifically blames the atrophy of his creativity on his transition from a poor artist, who frequently went hungry and cold, to a pampered associate of the rich, for whom life had become easy and placid.

Is it really clear that when survival needs are unsatisfied, self-actualization will be curtailed?

Maslow might have responded to this criticism by saying that his position is accurate in general regardless of the fact that one can point to exceptions, as in the examples above. For most people, he might argue, the realization of potentialities requires the prior satisfaction of survival needs. Presumably there will always be a few people who are so extraordinary that their lives will be creative whether or not they are nurtured. Maslow might want to suggest that these people could have been even greater had their survival needs achieved more satisfaction. This is a plausible, but by no means devastating retort to my criticism. We shall not attempt to solve the disagreement here; it is enough that you be aware of it.

FULFILLMENT MODEL: PERFECTION VERSION

In the actualization version of the fulfillment model, persons are conceptualized as trying to become what their inherent potentialities actually suit them to be. If the person has the genes pertaining to high intelligence, fulfillment will involve a life characterized by frequent intellectual endeavor. Fulfillment follows the course determined by something like a genetic blueprint. The *perfection version* of the fulfillment model is quite different: Its fulfillment follows the course determined by ideals and values concerning the good life. These ideals and values need not mirror the person's inherent or genetically determined capabilities—indeed, perfection theorists frequently stress the person's attempt to overcome real or imagined inferiorities. The perfection version is an expression of idealism, whereas the actualization version is an expression of humanism.

The purest example of the perfection version is the word of Alfred Adler, although Robert W. White's recent writings are clearly in the same genre. Gordon Allport and Erich Fromm emerge as primarily perfection theorists, but with some tendencies toward the actualization position as well. Finally, existential psychology emerges as a surprisingly valid example of the class.

Adler's Position

Alfred Adler (born in Vienna, 1870; died in Scotland, 1937) received his M.D. in 1895 and practiced general medicine early in his career. Soon, however, he shifted to psychiatry and became a charter member of the Vienna Psychoanalytic Society. Ironically, as Adler came to serve as president of that august group, the ideas he was developing seemed so heretical that he was severely criticized and denounced, whereupon he resigned his office and membership. He then formed his own group, known as Individual Psychology, which became quite active. Following World War I, in which he served as an army physician, Adler expressed his commitment to public service by establishing the first child guidance clinics in connection with the Viennese school system. In 1935 Adler came to the United States, where he taught his point of view at the Long Island College of Medicine and continued to be a prolific and forceful writer.

Although there is a clear thread of continuity running through Adler's writings at various stages in his life, there is also considerable evolution. I shall therefore emphasize his final views but attempt to give some sense of how he got there as well.

The core tendency of personality for Adler can be simply stated: It is the *striving toward superiority or perfection* (Adler, 1927, 1930; Ansbacher & Ansbacher, 1956). Superficially, this core tendency seems similar to that of the actualization theorists, but it is actually quite different. If you had to refer the actualizing tendency to your own intuitive experience, you would do so by remembering when you had a vivid sense of who and what you were and attempted to function consistently with that. But when you think of striving toward superiority or perfection, you inevitably are led to remember those times when you were dissatisfied with your talents or capabilities as you saw them and actively tried to transcend them to a higher level of functioning.

Sources of Striving toward Perfection.   It would be well to start this section with a greater sense of Adler's thinking concerning his postulated core tendency of personality. Although originally part of Freud's inner circle, Adler became convinced early in his professional life that aggressive urges are more important in life than are sexual ones. He elaborated on this conviction by identifying as the basic drive in humans the now famous *will to power* with its implications of competition and advantage. At this middle stage in his thinking, Adler clearly emphasized self-interest and Machiavellianism as the wellsprings of life. But as he grew older and attempted to find greater compatibility between his theoretical view of humans and his personal commitment to public service, he shifted his emphasis of the core tendency from power to superiority or perfection. The goal of the striving toward perfection is not social distinction or a position of power; rather, it is the full realization of the ideal life. In describing the striving toward perfection, Adler (1930) says:

> I began to see clearly in every psychological phenomenon the striving for supe-
> riority. It runs parallel to physical growth and is an intrinsic necessity of life
> itself. It lies at the root of all solutions of life's problems and is manifested in
> the way in which we meet these problems. All our functions follow its direction.
> They strive for conquest, security, increase, either in the right or in the wrong
> direction. The impetus from minus to plus never ends. The urge from below to
> above never ceases. Whatever premises all our philosophers and psychologists
> dream of—self-preservation, pleasure principle, equalization—all these are but
> vague representations, attempts to express the great upward drive. (p. 398)

It may sound to you as if Adler means something very like the actualizing
tendency, with its emphasis on inherent potentialities. However, this is not the
case. Adler draws the analogy to physical growth only to dramatize his belief
in the inevitability and ubiquitousness of the tendency toward perfection.
Achieving perfection, however, is not a matter of expressing potentialities so
much as a matter of struggling for completion. Adler's emphasis is clearly seen
in his concept of *fictional finalism,* which expresses the goal of the core tendency. The word *finalism* refers merely to striving for an end or goal state. The
word *fictional* is crucial in that it indicates that what the person is striving to
reach is an ideal, or fiction. Ideals are not potentialities rooted in the genetic
blueprint. The most abstract and general ideal is that of perfection, which is
the core characteristic associated with the core tendency. In Chapter 8, on
peripheral personality, we shall discuss the more concrete fictional finalisms
that develop as a function of one or another of the developmental courses
outlined by Adlerians.

Another important aspect of the core tendency reflected in the above
passage is that, in tension terms, Adler presumes that all people strive toward
increases rather than decreases of tension. The references to attempting to be
superior, to physical growth, and to a great upward drive that goes from minus
to plus all strongly suggest increases in complexity, effort, and energy. Clearly
Adler does not see the person as striving for peace, quiet, and tension reduction. In this emphasis on tension increase we see that the perfection version of
the fulfillment model is similar to the actualization version.

But these two versions differ in an important way. In the actualization
version, it is enough to be unencumbered by a destructive society. The core
tendency will express itself spontaneously, because it is based on a genetic
blueprint. In contrast, the perfection version requires that the person work
hard to make a reality of what is only a vague possibility at birth. Striving for
perfection will occur only if persons have high ideals and discipline themselves
accordingly. Witness Adler's (1964) words on the matter:

> The high degree of cooperation and social culture which man needs for his very
> existence demands spontaneous social effort, and the dominant purpose of
> education is to evoke it. Social feeling is not inborn; but it is an innate poten-
> tiality which has to be consciously developed. (p. 31)

Although he is speaking here mainly of the part of perfection striving that involves trying to perfect one's society as well, Adler gives the same emphasis to more individualistic efforts to better oneself.

At this point, we must pursue the question of the content of the core tendency in much the same manner as we did with Rogers and Maslow. You will remember that Rogers assumed inherent potentialities to be the core characteristics of personality but then neglected to specify their content. Maslow attempted such specification, but he was so scattered, amorphous, and confusing that he shed little light on the problem. Essentially, neither theorist gives us enough formal theoretical basis for determining what the assumed inherent potentialities are so that we can avoid the circular position of deciding that everything that persons have already done must have stemmed from some potentiality of theirs. A position as circular as this cannot be put to empirical test and, hence, cannot achieve the status of acceptable empirical knowledge. Content specification is no less important for Adler simply because his core characteristics are ideals, or fictional finalisms, rather than potentialities.

What has Adler to say about the content of his core characteristics? First, he indicates that the striving toward perfection is innate, and that it may manifest itself in myriad ways. Going on from there, Adler offers a number of ideas concerning the precise sources of "the great upward drive." These ideas are *organ inferiority, feelings of inferiority,* and *compensation,* which in their most general forms should be considered core characteristics of personality. Early in his career, when Adler was still concerned with medicine, he developed the notion of organ inferiority as an explanation of the localization of illness in one part of the body rather than another. The notion is simply that the body breaks down at its weak spots, which are caused by peculiarities of either heredity or development (Adler, 1917). As Adler became more psychological in orientation, he developed the notion that people attempt to compensate for organ inferiorities and that this compensatory effort has important implications for their living. The compensatory effort can be directed at the organ inferiority itself—as in the case of Demosthenes, who stuttered as a child and became, through striving, one of the world's greatest orators—or at the strengthening of related though different organs, as in the case of the blind person who develops extraordinary auditory sensitivity.

As Adler's psychological sophistication deepened, he shifted emphasis from organ inferiority to *feelings* of inferiority, whether they arise from actual physical handicaps or from subjectively felt psychological and social disabilities. Such feelings arise from incompleteness or imperfection in any sphere of life (Adler, 1931). Indeed, an important and valuable sense of inferiority is that which comes from the contemplation of complete perfection. Says Adler (1956, p. 23): "In comparison with unattainable ideal perfection, the individual is continually filled by an inferiority feeling and motivated by it." For Adler, feelings of inferiority are the subjectively appreciated aspect of the striving for perfection. As such, feelings of inferiority are not only constructive forces in living; they are a ready basis for diagnosing the lines along which the core tendency of personality will be expressed in any given person. While Adler has not provided us with a complete catalogue of specific ways in which the striving toward perfection can manifest itself in all people, he has given us a sign for identifying its specific manifestations that will always be consistent with his theoretical meaning. The identification of inferiority feelings does not depend on achieved superiority. Indeed, feelings of inferiority normally precede attempts to achieve perfection and, hence, can be determined independently of the attempts and also used as predictors of them. Adler's formulation of the fulfillment position has avoided the circularity found in the actualization positions of Rogers and Maslow. Adler is very similar to Goldstein in postulating a technique for diagnosing the content directions that the core tendency will take. I submit that Adler's emphasis on feelings of inferiority is as true to the perfection position as Goldstein's emphasis on preference is true to the actualization position.

Adler's emphasis on feelings of inferiority and Goldstein's on preferences dramatize the basic difference between the perfection and actualization versions of the fulfillment model. Actualization positions assume that the core tendency acts along the lines of real, usually innate organismic potentialities. If a person had a strong inclination toward wrestling, for example, actualization theories would assume wrestling to express some inherent potentialities, perhaps strength, resilience, and suppleness of skeletal musculature. But Adler would not reach the same conclusion. For Adler, it is feelings of inferiority that would lead to strong inclinations toward wrestling. And feelings of inferiority might as easily stem from characteristics of skeletal musculature opposite to those mentioned above. Feelings of inferiority might also develop from having been beaten in wrestling or some other physical combat. Thus, for Adler, though the tendency to strive toward perfection is itself innate, the directions in which it leads the person are expressive of idealizations of life. Indeed, the most likely directions are those in which inherent potentialities are meager. The aim of striving toward perfection carries the definite connotation of overcoming any limitations in potentialities that may exist in the person. To hazard an analogy from the game of bridge, actualization theorists tend to see fulfillment as the result of playing your long suit, whereas Adler tends to see fulfillment as the result of playing your short suit capably enough to make it as effective as your long suit.

So, in determining the lines along which the perfection tendency will find expression, the content of feelings of inferiority is of diagnostic importance. The other aspect of Adler's position relevant to determining the content expressive of the perfection tendency is the assumption that the human is both an individual and a social being. In the realm of individual living, humans will strive for perfection of themselves; in the realm of group living, they will strive for the perfection of society. The individualistic and social expressions are simply different facets of the same tendency to strive for perfection. Agreeing with the actualization theorists, Adler sees person and society as essentially compatible (Adler, 1939).

It is interesting to note that the assumption that fulfillment requires constructive social as well as individual functioning occurs late in Adler's thinking. In breaking with Freud, Adler shifted emphasis in the content of the core tendency from sexuality to aggressiveness. But during the early and middle portions of his career, Adler did not explicitly reject the Freudian model of the individual as inevitably in conflict with society. Adler's "will to power" clearly viewed social interaction as "dog-eat-dog" in character. But paradoxically enough, Adler held the private, extratheoretical belief that constructive social living is valuable and rewarding. Perhaps it was this belief that pried him loose over the years from the conflict aspects of the Freudian model—for certainly, in Adler's final position, both individual and social sides of persons are inherent, and there is no antagonism between them.

The Results of Expressing the Perfection Tendency.   This concluding section on Adler will be brief, as the relevant concepts are actually more appropriately considered at the periphery of personality. But just to round out the picture of Adler's theory, you should note that the expression of the perfection tendency over time results in the formation of a *style of life,* or a pattern of characteristics determined by both feelings of inferiority and attempts at compensation. But the style of life is not the same as these feelings and compensations; rather, it is the habits and traits resulting from them. Like the character type concept of psychoanalytic theory, the style of life concept accounts for differences among people and is therefore a peripheral characteristic of personality.

Styles of life can be grouped broadly as either constructive or destructive. As to development, it is the *family atmosphere* during the early years that leads to constructive or destructive styles of life. If your parents respect and encourage you, a constructive style will develop. A destructive style will result from parental disrespect and abandonment. Constructive styles, which are the highest form of living, are defined in terms of cooperation and generous interaction with people in the process of striving for perfection. Destructive styles are defined in terms of competitiveness and jealousy toward others in the striving for perfection. In neither constructive nor destructive styles of life is there much formal emphasis on the concept of defense; it is even less important in Adler's theory than in the actualization positions of Rogers and Maslow. Another important influence on life style is *family constellation,* notably involving birth order. This will be discussed in Chapter 8.

Adler offers a related concept, the *creative self,* which, though it has been popular among certain personologists, is nonetheless quite vague. It seems to cover the same ground as style of life but has more of a connotation of free will on the part of the person. If this concept indicates no more than an emphasis on the person as an active influence on life, then that is a common idea among fulfillment theorists. But the creative self also suggests a truly mystical process whereby behavior bearing no historical relationship to prior behavior or development can occur. This temperamental disposition to view persons as free links Adler with Rogers, as well as other fulfillment theorists yet to be discussed.

White's Position

Robert W. White (born 1904) received his Ph.D. in history and government in 1937. At the outset of his career he taught in these fields, but he quickly shifted his interests to personology. White was part of the extraordinary group of psychologists gathered together by Murray at the Harvard Psychological Clinic. While teaching at Harvard, White began to formulate his views concerning psychopathology and personality, drawing his observations from the psychotherapeutic interaction and from research. From 1957 to 1962, he served as chair of the influential Department of Social Relations at Harvard.

White's position is properly classed with Adler's, the differences between them being less important than the similarities. Although White's view constitutes the beginning of what may well become a complete theory of personality, at the moment it is somewhat incomplete. White (1959) talks about the core tendency in two ways: as the *attempt to produce effects through one's actions (effectance motivation)* and the *attempt to achieve competence in one's functioning (competence motivation)*. It is not entirely clear what he means the relationship between these two tendencies to be. But most of White's writings (1959, 1960, 1963) suggest that effectance motivation is to be considered an early form of the later competence motivation. Effectance motivation can be seen in the young child who delights in the sound produced when it accidentally drops a rattle on the floor and quickly learns to drop it regularly. And what even greater pleasure if the child can produce the additional effect of having an adult retrieve the rattle each time it is dropped! White sees exploratory behavior and play as ways in which the young child can experience itself as a potent influence in the world. In attempting to encourage readers to take effectance motivation seriously, White (1960) cites evidence indicating that by the end of the first year of life, the typical child is playing six or more hours a day. This amount of time actually exceeds the working day of many adults—at a stage in the child's life usually considered expressive of oral forms of sexuality or of dependency!

On the grounds of its generality, White (1959) concludes that effectance motivation must be at least as important as other tendencies that may exist in the child. It may even have a biological basis in the nervous systems requirement for stimulation and information. White suggests that the human nervous system must have developed, through a process of natural selection, into a unit functioning to process information or stimulus input. If this is so, effectance motivation might well serve the basic biological purpose of keeping the nervous system supplied with a continuous stream of stimulus input. One definite accompaniment of such a view is the notion that White's core tendency, looked at from the viewpoint of biological energy, is best considered as being in the service of tension increase rather than tension decrease. In this, White is in accord with other fulfillment theorists and in opposition to conflict theorists.

As the child grows, the mere attempt to have an effect on the world naturally shades into the attempt to deal with life's tasks in a competent manner. The transition is produced by the fact that the expression of effectance motivation leads the child to become experienced and knowledgeable and to grow in *actual competence* and the *sense of competence*. The shift in core tendency from effectance to competence motivation is certainly functional because, as the child ages, it is assigned an ever increasing number of tasks by society. The child must walk alone, feed and dress itself, go to school, meet and interact with people outside the family, get good grades, choose a life's work and pursue it, establish a family, and so forth. In order to achieve fulfillment in life, persons must seek competence and have some measure of success in this search.

White is not specific in detailing the core characteristics associated with the tendency to strive toward competence. The fragmentary nature of his theory at this early stage of its development certainly makes unequivocal classification difficult. Nonetheless, I have little doubt that it is a perfection version of the fulfillment model. To be sure, the tendencies toward competence and effectance are innate. But this alone does not constitute an actualization position. Recall that Adler also assumes that the striving toward perfection is innate. It is also true that White sometimes implies that he would recognize certain inherent potentialities and that people might be assumed to differ in the nature of their endowment with such potentialities. I grant you that this begins to sound like an actualization position. But we must keep in mind that White chose to name the mature form of his core tendency in terms of competence. The denotations and connotations of the word *competence* are much more in line with a perfection than an actualization position. If you are driven to be competent, you will strive hardest when you perceive some evidence or possibility of incompetence, even though that incompetence might be expressive of some meager inherent potentiality. In striving for competence, you are hardly likely to just do what you prefer, because you have in mind some conception of what it means to be competent. White's theory is much more in the idealistic mold of perfection positions than in the humanistic mold of actualization positions.

Allport's Position

Gordon W. Allport (born in Indiana, 1897; died in Cambridge, Massachusetts, 1967) received a Ph.D. in psychology in 1922. In addition to psychology, he studied philosophy and taught sociology, showing from the start the kinds of ethical and social concerns that were to mark his personality theorizing. He was an extremely literate man, interested in what was going on in many fields neighboring his own. During a long and prolific career, Allport received many honors, including election to the presidency of the American Psychological Association and several other psychological organizations. In addition, for twelve years he was editor of the influential *Journal of Abnormal and Social Psychology*. Allport never practiced psychotherapy and did not see the data of that context as relevant to personality theorizing. More pertinent for him were observations of excellent, capable, and gifted people.

Over the course of a long career, Allport wrote extensively on personality, social psychology, religion, and ethics. In all these fields, his views showed steady evolution. This evolutionary change, coupled with the diversity of his concerns, makes summary of his views difficult. As with Freud, I will have to stress those of Allport's statements that are most recent and those that were most consistently made. But even with adopting such a strategy, it is much more difficult than with Freud to formulate Allport's view of the core tendency of personality. In the earliest expression of his position, Allport emphasized traits and other peripheral characteristics of personality more than core considerations. But since those days, he evolved concepts more naturally relevant to the understanding of basic, lifelong directions. Nonetheless, it is difficult to point to any specific core tendency. At times, Allport seems to assume an actualizing tendency, though he does not make such an assumption explicitly. And yet, he also seems to believe that competence motivation and similar notions are important. In thinking all this over for some time, I have come to the firm conclusion that when Allport refers to such concepts as self-actualization and competence motivation, he gives them the status of examples of the kind of view of humans he has in mind. None of them is to be taken as the core tendency itself in any precise fashion. Allport's view of the core tendency is meant to be more general than these examples.

It seems to me that in the most accurate rendition of his thinking, the core tendency is *functioning in a manner expressive of the self*. He has a technical name for the self—*proprium;* hence, the core tendency may be called *propriate functioning* (Allport, 1955). As he considers life a developmental process, whose lines are largely determined by the self, or proprium, his viewpoint is properly regarded as a fulfillment position. As I will show later, although he incorporates elements of the actualization version, his theory is best considered an example of the perfection version. But first I should point out that there is an additional core tendency in Allport's system. As in Maslow, it is the *tendency to satisfy biological survival needs*. This tendency is clearly meant to be different, though not incompatible with, propriate functioning. In addition, Allport definitely sees satisfying biological needs as less important in determining the value and meaning of life than is the heavily psychological propriate functioning. Hence, Allport's theory is a variant of the fulfillment position in much the same way as is Maslow's actualization viewpoint. Like all variants of the fulfillment position, Allport's theory assumes that one core tendency—propriate functioning—is in the service of the highest development of the person, whereas the other core tendency—satisfaction of biological needs—merely ensures the person's physical survival. Indeed, Allport (1955) calls the tendency toward biological survival by the disparaging name *opportunistic functioning*.

Just to start you thinking along the lines of Allport's meaning, let me suggest a basis in common personal experience for intuitive understanding of propriate functioning. Recall the last time you wanted to do something or become some particular way because you felt that it would express the most important things about yourself. Such ideals are an important part of the self, according to Allport. If the wish to reach the ideals was strong enough, you very likely also experienced ample energy and determination for working toward them. Such personally relevant striving is also part of the self for Allport. Finally, you may have been aware at the time of the deep way in which the ideals and striving came out of the most personal (and possibly unexpressed) sense of who and what you are. Such functioning impels the person toward the future, according to Allport, whereas opportunistic functioning is experienced as little more than the placation of internal biological forces that are tangential to the important things in life.

Specific Propriate and Opportunistic Functions.   Since Allport (1955, 1961) says so little about the opportunistic functions, it will be easiest to consider them first. He is somewhat willing to accept whatever biological needs other psychologists and physiologists have uncovered, such as those for food, water, air, and the avoidance of pain. If there is any definitive attribute of the class of needs indicating opportunistic functioning, it is that they aim toward the reduction of physiological tension. Allport considers such functioning opportunistic because when release of tension and discomfort takes place, the actions aimed at removing the tension are not determined by such psychological considerations as values and principles. However useful such functioning may be in ensuring physical survival, it is opportunistic because, in Allport's view, it does not reflect psychological meaning (see Maddi, 1963; Maddi & Costa, 1972).

Allport's (1955, 1961) stance makes it abundantly clear that the important thing in life is propriate functioning. It is the *self* that defines the lines along which life is meaningfully led, and the self has little to do with questions of biological survival. One can die physically all the while one is leading a meaningful life—indeed, many of the martyrs did just this. The meaningfulness of life is a psychological consideration, and one cannot derive the psychological level of understanding from the biological one. In this position, Allport is completely opposed to Freud and other instinct theorists. And, as you will have begun to see, his view of propriate functioning is not even as organismically or biologically based as is the core tendency of actualization theorists. His is basically a perfection position.

As you can imagine from his emphasis as presented above, Allport has a great deal to say about the content of propriate functioning (core characteristics). Of all the theorists who consider the self important, Allport is distinguished in his detailed elaboration of just what he takes that aspect of personality to include. Allport feels that such detailed specification of the contents of self is important not only because your readers can thereby be more sure of what you mean but more specifically because the concept of self was the source of so much misunderstanding and bitterness among psychologists in previous years. To many, the concept of self has seemed to be nothing more than a slightly dressed-up version of the old notion of soul, with its attendant implications of divine implantation and independence of the mortal laws governing organismic functioning. Allport's heroic attempt to specify precisely what comprises the self is not simply an effort for clarity. It is also an expression of the view that this concept need not be mysterious or supernatural; rather, it is a collection of executive functions, clearly within the purview of psychology.

For Allport, the first step in specifying the content of self is to assume that it includes only those aspects of experience that seem essential, warm, and of central importance to the person. Thus, his definition of self is phenomenological, that is, follows what the individual personally believes to be significant. The second step is to detail a set of functions of the self that are common to all sound adults. In what was perhaps a too extreme attempt to demonstrate the unmysterious nature of the self, Allport (1955, pp. 41–56) first considered the proprium to be a set of ongoing functions with no underlying structure. More recently, however, he seemed ready to recognize that function necessarily implies structure even though his emphasis was still on function (Allport, 1961, pp. 110–138). In any event, the functions of the proprium are *sense of body, self-identity, self-esteem, self-extension, rational coping, self-image,* and *propriate striving.*

You can easily demonstrate the pervasiveness and importance of your *sense of body,* even though it is usually automatic and outside the focus of attention, by performing a little exercise suggested by Allport. Think of spitting saliva into a glass and then drinking it down. You are likely to feel revolted, even though you swallow the saliva in your mouth all the time. The saliva in your mouth is part of your sense of body, whereas the same saliva outside the confines of your body becomes a foreign thing. In less striking fashion, pain, injuries, and the like can make you aware of the sense of body that is always operating on the fringe of attention. Allport contends that bodily sense is a factor in the life decisions that you reach, though in truth it is the most rudimentary of the propriate functions.

Whereas you have a sense of your body primarily through kinesthetic, proprioceptive, and tactual cues, the propriate function of *self-identity* is the set of ideas you use to define yourself. You may conceive yourself as a lawyer, a generous person, or a great lover, but whatever the set of ideas about yourself, the ones that self-identity comprises are those that are most central and important to you.

Self-esteem, another propriate function, is closely related to self-identity. Self-esteem defines the bases on which you feel worthwhile. These bases will be ideas of self, much like those that comprise self-identity, with the added feature of giving more precise guidelines for living. If you have a certain self-identity, you will try to function consistently with it. But functioning inconsistently with your self-identity will not necessarily be a source of pain. Once you begin to have ideas about yourself that are tied to your worthiness, however, you will have much fewer degrees of freedom for your behavior.

By including *self-extension* in the propriate functions, Allport gives recognition to the importance of things, people, and events that are actually different from yourself but that you nonetheless define as central to your existence. It is as if you extend yourself, or at least your definition of self, so as to include other aspects of the world. Thus, for a particular male, his car, wife, daughter, and stamp collection may, for all intents and purposes, be parts of his self. This means that he sees them as really indistinguishable from himself, governed by the same laws and sharing the same fate. So a dent to the fender of his car is in some sense as painful as would be a disfigurement of his own face; his daughter's failing grade in school injures his own self-esteem; and his wife's unfaithfulness has the same effect as if he had betrayed his own principles.

By including *rational coping* as a propriate function, Allport means to indicate the centrality for the person of thinking about and dealing with problems and tasks in a reasoned, logical way. Allport is contending that people actually define themselves as rational beings and that this aspect of self-definition is very important to understanding the kinds of lives they lead. If you defined yourself as irrational, you would indeed be a very different and, for Allport, opportunistic person.

For Allport, the propriate functions, or core characteristics of personality, do not operate independently; rather, they intermingle, producing a life expressive of the core tendency of personality, called *propriate functioning.* As you can tell from the core characteristics, propriate functioning involves the capacity to work hard for what you want, with what you want defined by a set of values and principles, and by a less abstract, though pervasive sense of who you are, all of this guided by a deep commitment to rationality. Thus, propriate functioning is *proactive, future oriented* and *psychological.*

In calling propriate functioning *proactive,* Allport means to contrast it with *reactive* functioning, which to him is opportunistic. In distinguishing proactive behavior, Allport (see Maddi, 1963; Maddi & Costa, 1972) makes the point that psychology has a painfully ready tendency to deal only with behavior that is a response to some external environmental pressure. Even the fact that behavior goes by the technical name of *response* for psychologists indicates that they believe life to be a reaction to influences external to the person. For

Allport, reactive behavior is the least important thing to understand about the functioning of sound adult human beings. For such people, only behavior having the purpose of satisfying the requirement of biological survival is reactive in nature. Such opportunistic functioning is determined by the organism's biological needs in conjunction with the features of the external environment that are either frustrating or satisfying those needs. The person exercises little flexibility or individuality in opportunistic functioning. In contrast, functioning in a manner expressive of the proprium, or self, is proactive because it influences the external environment rather than being influenced by it. When you are expressing your own sense of who you are, your behavior shows choice, flexibility, and individuality—for, after all, your sense of self is not tied to simple, inexorable biological considerations that differ little from what characterizes lower animals. The proprium is developed out of the rich store of psychological experience coming through imagination, judgment, social interaction, and familiarity with human culture and history. To label behavior caused by propriate aspirations and convictions *reactive* is to miss the extraordinary degree to which humans can be forces influencing their own destiny.

In calling propriate functioning *future oriented,* Allport means to contrast it with opportunistic functioning in yet another way. Opportunistic functioning is governed by unchanging biological needs and, hence, is characterized by the development of habits. If you are hungry, you learn the most efficient ways to obtain food from the environment around you; then, every time you are hungry, you react in the same way that proved efficient before. Opportunistic functioning is *past oriented* in the sense that it involves the operation of long-standing habits that have proven fruitful in ensuring biological survival. Each time a biological need is aroused, the person is faced with the task of diminishing a state of tension in order to get back to a relatively tensionless state. According to Allport, propriate functioning is wholly different from this. The goals of propriate functioning involve bringing about states that have no precise precedent in the person. Think of aspirations, and recognize that they attempt to bring persons to an existential state they have never experienced before, at least for themselves. The fact that propriate functioning relies so heavily on imagination as a guide to action means that the person will not be functioning habitually and in keeping with what has happened in the past. In addition, propriate functioning will not be an attempt to return to a past state of lack of tension. Indeed, it will very likely bring tension increase, as the proprium does not necessarily complement the biological needs. So a person driven by the propriate ambition to express something in a poem may work long into the night, caring little for the mounting tension of lack of food and physical fatigue. The point here is that propriate functioning is aimed at future, previously unexperienced states, in contrast to opportunistic functioning, which aims to reestablish the "good old days."

We need say little more concerning why Allport classifies propriate functioning as psychological in nature. Opportunistic functioning is underlain by the organism's biological givens. In contrast, propriate functioning has much more to do with ideas, feelings, introspections, and other considerations more properly considered at the psychological rather than biological level of experience. This is not to say that there is no physiological substrate for mentation and emotion. But propriate functioning is not understood very well until one adopts the viewpoint that ideas and feelings are genuine and important determinants of behavior, which are very likely to differ from determinants expressing biological survival. In this emphasis on the difference between the psychological and biological aspects of life, Allport comes close to being a conflict rather than fulfillment theorist. But I think his position is more appropriately considered a variant of the fulfillment position, because opportunistic functioning can complement, as well as oppose, propriate functioning and because it is considered as playing a negligible role in the life of the sound adult.

Among fulfillment theorists, Allport is unique in the explicitness with which he specifies the content of core characteristics. You will remember that actualization theorists gave us little with which to know what is contained in people's inherent capabilities, and Adler did only slightly better in providing us with a diagnostic aid—feelings of inferiority—with which to identify the particular directions the push toward perfection was taking in concrete instances. Allport goes still further with his specification of the content of the propriate functions. Having his statements, we may expect (if the theory is correct) to find a sense of body, self-identity, self-esteem, rational coping, self-extension, and propriate striving in all people. To be sure, these core characteristics may take somewhat different shape in different people as a function of differences in previous experience and even genetic constitution. Nonetheless Allport has been much more explicit and precise concerning the directions life will take than have been other fulfillment theorists.

Certainly it must be said that the kind of life—proactive, future oriented, or psychological—ensuing from expression of the propriate functions is much the same as that envisioned by other actualization and perfection theorists. These theorists are also similar in their emphasis on the self and introspection as factors that determine life directions. But if we strain to discern the essential spirit of these theories, keeping in mind the possibility of error due to the insufficient precision of most of them, we arrive at certain differences in emphasis. Of the propriate functions, only the sense of body seems rooted in the organism's inherent nature. The other propriate functions bear little necessary relation to inherent potentialities. Add to this Allport's stress on aspirations (*self-image*) and working hard to reach them (*propriate striving*), and it becomes clear that his position is closer to those of the perfection theorists Adler and White than to the actualization theorists. Of course, Allport's position is diametrically opposed to Freud's. The propriate functions are noninstinctual, conscious, rational processes whereby life is led in an ever changing way that shows proaction, future orientation, and choice. In contrast, Freud sees unconscious, inexorable, unchanging, biological instincts as the only real determinant of life.

A final point needs to be made here. Fulfillment theorists generally stress individuality. Recall that I even suggested that the vagueness of content in the core characteristics seen in actualization theorists and the emphasis on free will in Adler are partly due to reticence to infringe on the assumed freedom to be an individual. Now of all fulfillment theorists, Allport traditionally has been the most ardent supporter of the doctrine of individuality. Indeed, he said early in his career (Allport, 1937) that due to each person's uniqueness, the concepts used to describe him or her cannot be employed with anyone else. While he more recently adopted a less severe version of this position (Allport, 1962), he still emphasized individuality to an extraordinary degree. (In Chapter 8, you will see this emphasis more clearly.) Actually, Allport has been severely criticized by many other psychologists for having such an extreme notion on individuality that no generalizations from person to person seem possible. But with the publication of his notion of the proprium, Allport clearly took a long step away from his previous position. Whether this was because he was criticized is immaterial. What you should recognize is that the propriate functions appear in all persons and, therefore, define the commonality among them.

Developmental Course of Propriate and Opportunistic Functions. Allport (1955) believes that at the beginning of life the person is mainly a biological organism, with the psychological dimension of life developing gradually. Initially, then, human functioning is primarily opportunistic, with all the indications of reactivity and past orientation. Infants have little personality; their opportunistic behavior is determined by ongoing chemical processes and environmental pressures. At first, infants can express discomfort only in rather reflexive ways when strong viscerogenic drives exist, and they function solely according to the principle of tension reduction. During this early period, infants are extremely dependent on others, particularly their mothers, for nurturance and affection.

For Allport (1955), what the child's future life will be like depends substantially on whether or not nurturance and affection are given. If they are, the preconditions for the development of a gradually more differentiated and personally integrated lifestyle or personality are met. With enough security, the kernels of selfhood begin to develop near the end of the first year of life. The first signs of consciousness take the form of recognizable experience of the body (bodily sense). The second and third years see the beginnings of self-identity and then self-image. From age six to twelve, the rational coping qualities of the proprium become apparent. In adolescence, propriate striving is in increasing evidence. Although the various propriate functions begin their development at different ages, they all act interdependently by the time adulthood is reached.

As the propriate functions are ever more richly and vigorously expressed, they lead to the development of a gradually increasing set of peripheral personality characteristics. Allport calls these peripheral characteristics *personal dispositions*, or concrete, readily expressed, and consistently observed traits such as gregariousness or honesty. We will consider personal dispositions in Chapter 8; for now, recognize that as the proprium develops, undifferentiated, reactive, opportunistic behavior aimed at reducing tension caused by survival needs recedes in importance, being replaced by propriate functioning, which involves increases in tension, is proactive, and leads to increasing subtlety and awareness.

According to Allport (1961), the infant begins as a relatively undifferentiated organism, reacting more or less as a totality. As the proprium develops, the person becomes more and more differentiated through the accrual of an increasing number of personal dispositions. With still more experience and development, differentiated parts are continually integrated. In short, Allport sees development as the simultaneous increase in psychological differentiation and integration. He calls this *psychological growth* (see Maddi, 1963; Maddi & Costa, 1972). The differentiation is seen in the diversity of personal dispositions, a matter to be discussed later. The integration is seen in what Allport calls *psychological maturity,* whose aspects suggest that it is the structural or stable resultant of a history of expression of the propriate functions. The aspects of maturity are (1) specific, enduring extensions of self, (2) dependable techniques (such as tolerance) for warm relating to others, (3) stable emotional security or self-acceptance, (4) habits of realistic perception, (5) skills and problem centeredness, (6) established self-objectification in the form of insight and humor, and (7) a unifying philosophy of life, including a particular value orientation, differentiated religious sentiment, and personalized conscience. The more vigorous the expression of propriate functions, the greater the likelihood of developing all aspects of psychological maturity in adulthood. These aspects can serve an integrative function in the personality because, as you can see, they deal with general questions relating to the meaning and value of life—questions that concern every person. These characteristics of maturity permit organization of the personal dispositions, which are, of course, much more concrete, habitual orientations toward life. Clearly, for Allport, psychological maturity is a state characterized by tension-increasing, perfection-oriented behavior. Such behavior is not defensive, according to Allport (1955). In these emphases, he is very much like the other fulfillment theorists.

The preceding paragraphs depict the course of development that unfolds when the infant's early dependency has been warmly met. But if succorance and affection are not readily available, the child may react with signs of insecurity, initially including aggression and demandingness and later jealousy and egotism. Vigorous development of propriate functioning will be jeopardized, the individual remaining relatively undifferentiated and deficient in integrative characteristics of maturity. Tension reduction will remain an important aim. Such an adult will show evidence of defensiveness, with attendant lack of awareness of self. Allport would consider such a person mentally ill, though he is not interested enough in the matter to give it any further consideration.

In the specification of the developmental course of propriate and opportunistic functions, Allport is once again more explicit and complete than other fulfillment theorists. And once again, if I am not mistaken, he is closer in spirit to the perfection than the actualization theorists. The actualization theorists would probably be uneasy with Allport's strong emphasis on a stable structure of the self in the form of values, principles, and conscience, which serves an integrative function by ordering and rendering meaningful more concrete experiences. In contrast, actualization theorists see the self-concept as a flexible entity, as continually changing, and as much less vividly conscious. Allport's view of psychological maturity might seem to actualization theorists to stand in the way of real openness to experience.

Fromm's Position

Erich Fromm (born in Frankfurt, Germany, 1900; died in New York, 1980) studied psychology and sociology in his college years. He obtained a Ph.D. from the University of Heidelberg in 1922, after which he received training in psychoanalysis in Munich and Berlin. In 1933, he came to the United States as a lecturer at the Chicago Psychoanalytic Institute and subsequently entered private practice in New York City. Still later in his career, he taught at a number of universities and institutes in this country, finally leaving to head the Mexican Psychoanalytic Institute in Mexico City. In recent years, Fromm not only continued to write but also trained many students in his psychotherapeutic techniques and theorizing.

Fromm's intriguing viewpoint includes elements of the conflict model and of both the actualization and perfection versions of the fulfillment model. As you can see from his location in this chapter, I believe the perfection aspects of his position to be paramount.

To begin, Fromm (1947) distinguishes between *animal nature* and *human nature*. Animal nature is roughly defined by biochemical and psychological bases and mechanisms for physical survival. While the human certainly has an animal nature, it is the only organism possessing a human nature as well. This fact has, according to Fromm, rendered the human's animal nature its least important part. Even without my discussing the specific content of human nature you should recognize the similarity among Fromm, Allport, and Maslow. Fromm is especially close to Allport, for both de-emphasize the importance of animal nature or opportunistic functioning in the human in favor of human nature or propriate functioning. Indeed, the only really accurate rendition of a core tendency for Fromm would be the *attempt to fulfill one's human nature*. Implied in his theory may be another core tendency concerning the satisfaction of one's animal nature, but nowhere does Fromm emphasize this.

Even when persons shrink from vigorous expression of human nature, they are best characterized in Fromm's terms as avoiding humanness rather than embracing creatureness. Human beings can never really become creatures simply because they happen to possess biological survival needs. Obviously it is because of this emphasis on pursuing one's human nature that I have classed Fromm as a fulfillment theorist (although he assumes an animal as well as human nature). It is not without uneasiness that I do this, for in at least one place in his writings (Fromm, 1947, p. 41), he specifically suggests that it is the antagonism between the person's human and animal natures that provides the impetus to development and living. This is clearly a conflict statement. But it is a rare occurrence in his writings, which generally stress the pursuit of humanness to an intense degree and barely acknowledge the fact of the person's animal nature.

In order to understand Fromm's position more fully and determine whether it is properly considered an actualization or perfection version of the fulfillment model, we must scrutinize the proposed content of human nature. Fortunately, Fromm has a good deal to say about what human nature entails and in this achieves a degree of theoretical precision like that of Allport and superior to that of the actualization theorists. Fromm (1947) starts by saying that organisms whose nature is primarily animal are one with the world of nature. There is no sharp separation among themselves, other organisms, and the environment around them. They have no experience of separateness.

But human nature is unique under the sun, and it therefore leads to extraordinary potentialities and problems. Perhaps the most basic characteristic of human nature is the ability to know itself and the things that differ from it. Once an organism is endowed with such knowledge, it is inevitably separate from nature and other organisms. Looked at positively, this separateness is freedom; looked at negatively, it is alienation (Fromm, 1941). The freedom and independence stemming from the person's human nature can lead to great heights of creative accomplishment. Fear of the loneliness and isolation involved in acting on human nature often leads persons to forgo their birthright of freedom.

Humans can never function as if their nature were solely animal, but they can approach this debasement by shrinking from the freedom that would come through acting vigorously on their human nature. This shrinking is not straightforward acting on an animal nature; hence, it is never as satisfactory as the simple life of animals, and it is clearly inferior to the vigorous expression of humanness. Shrinking from freedom amounts to social conformity and what Allport would call *reactive behavior* on the individual level. It is a defensive way of life, though Fromm does not discuss defense in any systematic manner. In contrast, acting on one's human nature leads to productiveness and a nondefensive way of life. Fromm's emphasis on freedom, productiveness, individuality, and lack of defense as expressions of the highest form of living are thoroughly consistent with other fulfillment theories. Conflict theorists like Freud also stress productiveness in the highest form of living. You may wonder, therefore, whether Fromm is really making a fulfillment statement. He is, because for him productiveness is not cast in the light of adjustment to society, as it is in conflict theories. A productive person would be adjusted to society, according to Fromm (1955), only if the society were constructive or sane. If it were not, the productive person would not choose to be maladjusted—only conformists, shrinking from their human nature, would adjust.

True to the fulfillment model, Fromm does not assume a basic antagonism between individual and society. He stresses that human nature will achieve expression in the ways that are effective and possible given the existing societal and cultural climate. As in other fulfillment positions, Fromm believes that when human nature is pervertedly expressed (in the shrinking from freedom leading to conformity and reactivity), the blame is society's. Authoritarian, dictatorial, monolithic, punitive societies increase the likelihood that their members will fall short of vigorous humanness. But society need not be coercive; hence, when it is, Fromm (1955) is quick to condemn it as pathological.

Fromm is often considered a social psychological theorist by personologists of psychoanalytic persuasion. In a way, this is a mistake. Actually, Freud more than Fromm emphasizes society's importance by assuming it to be a force that cannot be avoided, transcended, or changed. Fromm, like all fulfillment theorists, gives primary importance to the full expression of the individual and cares little for adjustment to society. The only sense in which it is reasonable to consider Fromm a social psychological theorist is that he has been a consistent critic of past and contemporary societies, setting himself the task of clarifying how pathological societies pervert human nature. In this, he is similar to, though perhaps more systematic than, other fulfillment theorists.

Fromm has concretely specified the content of human nature. The core characteristics associated with the core tendency are the needs for relatedness, transcendence, rootedness, identity, and frame of reference. The *need for relatedness* stems from the stark fact that the person, in becoming human, has been torn from the animal's primary union with nature. In place of this unthinking, simple merging with nature, the human must use reason and imagination to create relations with nature and other people. The most satisfying relationships are those based on productive love, which always implies mutuality, generosity, and respect. The *need for transcendence* is the motivational basis for proactive functioning. It is the urge to become a productive individual rather than a mere creature. The *need for rootedness* apparently is very similar to the need for relatedness. Fromm says that it is part of human nature to seek roots in the world, and that the most satisfying roots are those based on a feeling of brotherhood with others. The person's *need for personal identity* is similar to the need for transcendence in that both lead toward individuality. In striving for an identity, the most satisfying procedure is to rely on one's talents and productive capabilities. Failing that, identity of a less satisfying sort can be achieved through identification with other people or ideas. Finally, there is the *need for a frame of reference,* a stable and consistent way of perceiving and comprehending the world. Once one gets down to this level of concreteness concerning the content of human nature, the tension-increasing nature of its pursuit becomes apparent. So again Fromm emerges as a fulfillment theorist.

The similarities between Fromm's needs and Allport's propriate functions should not have escaped your attention. The need for transcendence is like propriate striving, the need for rootedness is like self-extension, the need for personal identity is like self-identity and self-esteem, and the need for a frame of reference is like the rational coping out of which develops a philosophy of life. The similarities in content between the core characteristics in these two positions is one piece of evidence that inclines me to believe that Fromm's position is best considered a perfection rather than actualization theory. The human, according to Fromm, seems to be striving toward an ideal conceptualization of the perfect life rather than merely expressing inherent capabilities in an unself-conscious fashion. To be sure, perfection is defined in terms of what human nature could be. But for any given person, human nature is not merely the sum total of particular strengths and weaknesses; it is more universal than that. Fromm believes that it is within the person's power to achieve perfection, but the path is not simply that of expressing inherited weaknesses. This emphasis is clearly seen in Fromm's (1956) book *The Art of Loving,* which includes a set of exercises for becoming capable in loving. In contrast, actualization theorists are likely to believe that adequate loving and such obviously constructive things come quite naturally to the undefensive person. Fromm seems more a perfection theorist because he believes that conscious effort toward achieving an ideal is necessary in order to realize meaningful fulfillment.

Existential Psychology

There has been a sharply increased interest of late in existentialism. This interest has shown itself over a broad spectrum of society, including not only personologists and psychotherapists but professionals of every sort, political activists, members of the clergy, students, and the person on the street. This has happened even though the body of thought commonly labeled *existentialism* is extremely amorphous, shifting in emphases from country to country, continent to continent, and even theorist to theorist. It seems to me that much of existential thought really constitutes a set of attitudes for living, a manifesto more than a systematic theory of personality. On these grounds, existentialism could have been omitted from this book. But because of its unique and influential position, it has a rightful place here.

I have selected the threads in existential thought that are rigorous and most relevant to personality theory. Thus, what follows concerns not the theorizing of any one person but a plurality. I shall refer little to the philosophical founders of existentialism, Kierkegaard and Heidegger, favoring instead those of their followers who have attempted to translate their thinking into statements about personality. Foremost among these are the Europeans: Ludwig Binswanger (born in Kreuzlingen, Switzerland, 1881; died in Kreuzlingen,

1966), Medard Boss (born in St. Gallen, Switzerland, 1903; has resided in Zurich for most of his life), and Victor Frankl (born in Vienna, 1905, where he still lives). Major figures who have worked in the United States are Rollo May (born in New York City, 1909), and Paul Tillich (born in Starzeddel, Kreis Guben, Prussia, 1886; died in Chicago, 1965). But it will also be necessary to refer to work by other existential psychologists.

Binswanger, Boss, and Frankl all knew Freud and were heavily influenced by his thinking early in their careers. But the major intellectual influences on them were Kierkegaard and Heidegger. It is not inaccurate to characterize Binswanger, Boss, and Frankl as having attempted to translate Heidegger's philosophical stance into a workable approach to psychotherapy. All physicians, Binswanger served for many years as chief medical director (a post his father held before him) of the Bellevue Sanatorium in Kreuzlingen, Boss was professor in the University of Zurich medical school as well as director of the institute of Daseinsanalytic Therapy, and Frankl is currently professor in the University of Vienna medical school and director of the Neurological Polyclinic there. Tillich was a theologian, an interpreter of Christianity in our modern times of spiritual emptiness. He taught at such prominent schools as Harvard University and the University of Chicago, creating an enormous effect on modern religious theory, to say nothing of psychology. May served as a training therapist at a distinguished center for psychotherapy, the William Alanson White Institute in New York City.

It is no easy feat to state a core tendency for existential psychology in a few words. Not only is there the difficulty of many different voices, all using slightly different words; there is also the complication that the words are often poetic, metaphoric, sometimes seeming to have polemic, emotional intent rather than intellectual precision. What is clear, however, is the emphasis on being genuine, honest, and true and on making decisions and shouldering responsibility for them. All in all, an apt phrasing of the core tendency might be *to achieve authentic being.* The word *being,* or *existence,* or the German *Dasein* is pregnant with meaning for the existentialist. It does not refer to some passive creatureness, though it partially includes this. Instead, it signifies the special quality of existing that is characteristic of humans, a quality that heavily involves mentality, intelligence, and awareness. The adjective *authentic* is meant to carry some of these connotations and also to indicate the emphasis of existential psychology on honesty, a stance difficult to manage due to the inherently frightening and demanding nature of life. More often than not, according to existentialists, people shrink from authenticity.

In order to gain a relevant, albeit oversimplified intuition concerning the meaning of achieving authentic being, search your memory for times when you understood and accepted yourself most, when you were aware of your vanities, sentimentalities, follies, and weaknesses, yet were somehow able to assert the importance of your life. You could anticipate with vigor your future experiences even though you could not entirely predict or control them, and this frightened you. As you will see, the main emphases of existential psychology are expressed in such experiences.

Core Characteristics.   My attempt to render the existential viewpoint as systematic theory may violate existentialists' sensibilities as to what is important. They are steeped in the phenomenological approach, namely, the attempt to understand in no terms other than immediate, vividly appreciated, but unanalyzed sensory experience. In a sense, what I have been calling *intuitive understanding* is considered by many existentialists as the only important psychological knowledge. Once you commit yourself to a phenomenological approach, it logically follows that you will consider one person's reality to differ from that of neighbors, for each person is likely to perceive things differently. Thus, the existentialist's aversion to formal, abstract theorizing is twopronged. Abstraction is the antithesis of intuitive truth, and the latter varies in any case from person to person.

This antitheoretical stance seems strongest among European existentialists. For example, Hall and Lindzey (1970) quote a personal communication from Boss:

> I can only hope that existential psychology will never develop into a theory in its modern meaning of the natural sciences. All that existential psychology can contribute to psychology is to teach the scientists to remain with the experienced and experienceable facts and phenomena, to let these phenomena tell the scientists their meaning and their references, and so do the encountered objects justice—in short, becoming more "objective" again. (p. 580)

Let me post a conundrum that may help here. Is that object I am sitting on a mass of relatively slow-moving atomic particles, a construction of shaped and polished woods having low brittleness and therefore able to carry weight, or a chair? Of course, it is all three, and any existentialist would agree. But in human terms, the existentialist would hasten to add, it is a chair, nothing else— except, perhaps, colors and textures readily perceived with the senses. To talk of atomic particles, and even of brittleness, is to theorize in the manner of the natural sciences.

Presumably Boss would accept theorizing in some human fashion. But once you have called a chair a chair, about all you can do without becoming abstract and analytical is recognize that chairs may differ in shape and colors. Boss and other European existentialists seem to accept a natural limitation on theorizing in order for it to remain true to the human experience of things. American existentialists are less sure, being somewhat more willing to theorize about antecedents to the phenomenal experience (e.g., what learning experiences condition perceptions?). Yet the Europeans are not quite consistent, for if they were it would be impossible to define core characteristics of personality, and it is they who have gone furthest in formulating them. As you will see, although these core characteristics strictly adhere to phenomenological givens, they imply capabilities of the human organism. As such, a statement on human nature can be derived from them, a statement that, like all others, is abstract and essentialistic. Although the vivid appreciation of immediate sensory experience is all the more important because it is so often excluded from a role in everyday life, Boss seems to be fighting a losing battle by insisting that existentialism avoid formalization. Formalization does inevitably mean abstracting, but without it the transition from mere attitudes to working theories probably could not be made.

Being-in-the-world (Binswanger, 1963; Boss, 1963) is a basic core characteristic intended to emphasize the unity of person and environment. The emphasis is not merely one of interaction between the person and his or her environment; rather, person and environment are essentially one and the same. This is because both being and world are human creations, so interdependent as to be inseparable. Of course, the human body and the things in our environment have physical reality—shape, size, weight. But these physical properties are irrelevant for existentialists. When they speak of being, they emphasize the sum total of intuitive sensory experiences combined with memories, fantasies, and anticipations. When they speak of world, they emphasize the environment persons create for themselves through exercising the capacities producing being and the expression of that being in action. Both being and world are intensely personal. Being is mentality considering our individual selves, and world is mentality considering our surroundings.

In order to understand a person's existence, one must appreciate the manner in which being and world merge. In explicating being-in-the-world, May (1958) says:

> *World is the structure of meaningful relationships in which a person exists and in the design of which he participates.* Thus world includes the past events which condition my existence and all the vast variety of deterministic influences which operate upon me. But it is these *as I relate to them*, am aware of them, carry them with me, molding, inevitably forming, building them in every minute of relating. For to be aware of one's world means at the same time to be designing it. (pp. 59–60)*

It is instructive to contemplate May's (1958) words concerning being, for they are complementary to those about world, and also imply something about human nature:

> The full meaning of the term "human being" will be clearer if the reader will keep in mind that "being" is a participle, a verb form implying that someone is in the process of *being something*. It is unfortunate that, when used as a general noun in English, the term "being" connotes a static substance, and when used as a particular noun such as *a* being, it is usually assumed to refer to an entity, say, such as a soldier to be counted as a unit. Rather "being" should be understood, when used as a general noun, to mean *potentia,* the source of potentiality; "being" is the potentiality by which the acorn becomes the oak or each of us becomes what he truly is. And when used in a particular sense such as *a* human being, it always has the dynamic connotation of someone in process, the

---

person being something. Perhaps, therefore, *becoming* connotes more accurately the meaning of the term in this country. We can understand another human being only as we see what he is moving toward, what he is becoming; and we can know ourselves only as we "project our *potentia* in action." The significant tense for human beings is thus the *future*—that is to say, the critical question is what I am pointing toward, becoming, what I will be in the immediate future.

Thus, being in the human sense is not given once and for all. It does not unfold automatically as the oak tree does from the acorn. For an intrinsic and inseparable element in being human is self-consciousness. Man . . . is the particular being who has to be aware of himself, be responsible for himself, if he is to become himself. He also is that particular being who knows that at some future moment he will not be; he is the being who is always in a dialectical relation with non-being, death. And he not only knows he will sometime not be, but he can, in his own choices, slough off and forfeit his being. (pp. 41–42)

This passage clearly identifies self or being as process rather than as some static, unchanging content and in that sense is reminiscent of the actualization fulfillment model as epitomized in Rogers. But the crucial difference is that the process of becoming May describes is not a natural one in the sense of being easy or linking humans with lower animals. May could never, as did Rogers, give as an example of becoming a seaweed growing and flourishing though pounded incessantly by waves. Seaweeds do not have mentality or self-consciousness and therefore never choose. For May and other existentialists, being is so essentially a matter of choice that humans can even choose against it by committing suicide—by precipitating nonbeing. When May and other existentialists refer to fulfilling one's potentialities, they mean something closer to Fromm and other perfection fulfillment theorists than to the actualization fulfillment position. Achieving one's potentialities involves, for May, a painful and continual process of soul searching and decision making in the face of doubt and loneliness. This is more a matter of striving to do the best one can than indulging a genetic birthright. Much of what follows will lend additional evidence for this interpretation.

But what are these potentialities that are expressed in the process of authentic being? Like actualization fulfillment theorists, existentialists are far from clear on this matter. Such theorizing probably would be too abstract and essentialistic for their phenomenologically conditioned tastes. But there are some clues available. One is that these potentialities are expressed in a process rather than in something irrevocably fixed. The biggest clue involves the distinctions made among three broad modes of being-in-the-world: *Umwelt*, *Mitwelt*, and *Eigenwelt* (Binswanger, 1963; Boss, 1963; Frankl, 1960; May, 1958). *Umwelt* literally means *the world around you*, but it connotes the biological and physical world. *Mitwelt*, or *with-world*, refers to the world of persons, of one's fellow humans. *Eigenwelt* means *own-world*, and refers to the internal dialogue of relationship to oneself. It is important to recognize that all three modes assume the operation of mind—awareness. So the *Umwelt* is not some objective consideration of the biological and physical characteristics determining a person's relationship to the surrounding world; rather, it concerns *one's construal* of the biological and physical tie between oneself and the world. So too with the *Mitwelt,* which refers to one's perceptions of and orientations toward one's interactions with others and with social institutions. It is hardly necessary to point out this operation of self-consciousness in the case of the *Eigenwelt,* for it cannot be defined at all unless it includes a consciousness that can consider itself an object.

It is best to interpret these three modes of being as general frames of reference. In any being-in-the world, there will have to be some general orientation to biological, social, and personal experiences. But the precise nature of these three orientations can shift considerably and differ from person to person. An example of the difficulties ensuing from a narrower interpretation of the three modes, which ascribes to them some content considered necessary because of their biological, social, and personal nature, can be found in Keen's recent (1970) explication of existential thought. He presents the three modes of being as being-in-the-world, being-for-others, and being-for-oneself. For him, being-in-the-world involves natural, unreflective experiencing, being-for-others adopts external, social criteria for functioning, and being-for-oneself involves self-conscious reflection on one's existence. Although these distinctions seem similar to those presented earlier, they are quite different in their emphases. Being-for-others has the negative connotation of someone who is subjugated to convention that is not the defining characteristic of *Mitwelt.* One's *Mitwelt* may involve conventionality, but it might also concern intimacy and even an unconventional social commitment. In Keen's concepts, there is an implied antagonism between being-in-the-world and being-for-oneself in that the former is easy and natural and the latter incessantly introspective. Small wonder that Keen seems to favor being-in-the-world as the mode of existence that leads to the good life. This, of course, leads to an inconsistency in spirit, for his being-for-oneself carries the major possibility for the considered, rational life so important to existentialists and is clearly more uniquely human than is his being-in-the-world. Yet it is the latter that is considered more advantageous.

It is closer to the original meaning of Binswanger and Boss, who are primarily responsible for the three modes of being, to consider *Umwelt, Mitwelt,* and *Eigenwelt* as referring to biological, social, and personal experiencing, leaving aside for additional consideration what is good and bad about the person's commitment in each mode. From this position, it is possible to discern a meaning for the human potentialities to which May refers. Following Frankl's (1960) lead, Maddi (1967, 1970) assumes that human nature comprises biological, social, and psychological needs. The biological needs include those for food, water, and air and refer to functions that must be expressed if the person is to survive physically. The social needs include those for contact and communication, the frustration of which leads to intense loneliness and loss of sense of self. The psychological needs are considered to be for symbolization (or classification), imagination, and judgment. Although the three sets of needs are reminiscent of Maslow's biological, security, and cognitive-understanding (or self-actualization) needs, Maddi does not propose them as being organized into a hierarchy.

Of the three sets of needs, the psychological ones most closely characterize the existential emphasis. The process of symbolizing or classifying involves abstracting from the specifics of an experience that which is general enough to be compared with other experiences. When you symbolize, the end results are categories with which to recognize and order experiences. Because you will be unable to recognize an experience for which you have no category, it can be said that the more categories that exist in your cognitive mass, the greater will be the meaningfulness of experience for you. Imagining involves combining and recombining categories, memories, and ideas in a manner that does not require input from the external world. According to Maddi, the aim of imagining is change, in the sense that the imagined state is invariably thought of as more interesting or advantageous than present actualities. With every change that takes place (whether in thought or in action), the amount of information available increases. Thus, meaning, in the sense of amount of information, is greater the more active the imagination. Finally, judgment involves evaluating experience in a manner that leads to considering it either good or bad (moral judgment) or pleasant or unpleasant (preferential judgment). The values and preferences resulting from the judgmental process also increase meaning by giving one a personal basis for orienting oneself to experience.

What Maddi is saying is that the human needs to symbolize, imagine, and judge in order to feel satisfied and avoid frustration because that is the nature of the organism. One argument he offers (Maddi, 1970) for assuming psychological needs to be core characteristics is the universality of symbolization, imagination, and judgment. Once you recognize that words are symbols, it becomes apparent that thought and communication, if not perception as well, would be impossible without symbolization. That every society ever studied has a mythology suggests the universality of imagining on a grand scale. And Osgood (1962) indicates that the tendency to make evaluations is universal in all the societies and culture areas that he studied. A supplementary argument based on evolutionary theory can be formulated (Maddi, 1970). After all, the human mind is the ultimate wonder of evolution, winning for its owner a preeminent place among the creatures even though the human is physically puny and frail. The strength of that mind is that it can take in, order, evaluate, and anticipate vast amounts of information and hence act effectively. Once such a marvelous nervous system evolved, it could hardly lie fallow. Its requirement is that it perform the operations for which it was designed. Some research (e.g., Riesen, 1961) indicates that neural structures must be used in infancy if they are to develop normally. The human needs to symbolize, imagine, and judge because that is what the central nervous system is designed to do. And since symbolizing, imagining, and judging all create meaning, it would seem that the search for meaning is an inherent, unlearned aspect of human nature.

Let us now return to all three sets of core characteristics, namely, the biological, social, and psychological needs. The mere existence of neither biological nor social needs differentiates the human from lower animals. Biological needs reflect metabolic requirements and, in their most straightforward sense, leave little room for taste and subtlety. Cooked meat tastes better and is more digestible than raw meat, but in the absence of the wherewithal to cook, raw meat undoubtedly will be eaten. Although it may be much nicer and more hygienic to eliminate in a modern toilet, the pants will be fouled sooner than the biological organism will be damaged. Insofar as our biological needs do not differ from those of lower animals, there is no basis in them for decorum, subtlety, and taste.

So too with social needs, which would also seem to exist in lower animals, to judge from the prevalence in even relatively primitive species of a rudimentary social structure involving simple social roles. Social needs seem to be most straightforwardly met by engaging in a wide range of interactions with people. Talking with service personnel, colleagues, acquaintances, and friends, dating, going to and having parties, dinners, and lunch meetings are ways to communicate and have contact. Even simply watching people go by or having them around as background fulfills some needs, as is attested to by the ubiquitous sidewalk café in Europe. All these things satisfy the social needs by increasing the number and variety of people interacted with. But another way to meet these needs is to work in depth toward increasing the richness of a few intense relationships. This way involves intimacy and love in that you come to feel that some other person or persons are very important to you and you to them. You do not wish to keep your mutual experience just on the surface but prefer to go progressively deeper, creating new levels of experience all the while.

Working from Maddi's rendition of human nature, let us return to the *Umwelt* (biological experience), *Mitwelt* (social experience), and *Eigenwelt* (personal experience) emphasized by Binswanger and Boss. Maddi has argued that the more vigorous the expression of psychological needs (symbolization, imagination, and judgment), the more will the *Umwelt* include taste and subtlety, the *Mitwelt* intimacy and love, and the *Eigenwelt* complexity and individuality. This is because intense symbolization, imagination, and judgment will result in many categories with which to classify experience, many ideas about change, and many values and preferences. Also, the larger the number of these cognitions, the more unusual they will be. This individuality is one criterion for an ideal personality according to existentialists (Binswanger, 1963; Boss, 1963; Frankl, 1960; Maddi, 1970; May, 1958). But you should note that uniqueness is characterized by individualism, not by stony isolation from people. Indeed, vigorous expression of psychological needs is considered encouragement toward intimacy and love rather than toward more superficial forms of socializing.

Once it is assumed that human nature includes biological, social, and psychological needs, it is natural to consider the ideal to be vigorous expression of all three. When this happens, there is a tendency for *Umwelt, Mitwelt,* and *Eigenwelt* to merge, producing a unitary whole. This unitary quality will be apparent not only at any given point in time but also in the manner in which present experience is tied to the past and the anticipated future. Spatial and temporal unity occur because the vigorous expression of symbolization, imagination, and judgment tends to order, interpret, and influence biological and social expressions. This unitary quality of being-in-the-world is another existentialist criterion for an ideal personality (Binswanger, 1963; Boss, 1963; Frankl, 1960; Keen, 1970; Maddi, 1970; May, 1958).

Vigorous expression of psychological needs lends humanness to the human being. Actually, it is impossible for a person to fail entirely to express psychological needs, because they are rooted in the very nature of the central nervous system. But this does not mean that everyone expresses them as vigorously as possible. Maddi (1967, 1970) believes that through developmental failures some persons learn to make only rudimentary use of symbolization, imagination, and judgment. These persons have only a few categories for recognition, ideas about change, and values and preferences. In addition, the contents of these cognitions are common, stereotyped, and conventional. Such conforming persons resemble lower animals as much as is possible in humans; their *Eigenwelt* are simple and conventional, and their *Umwelt* and *Mitwelt* show a relative absence of taste, subtlety, intimacy, and love. In addition, *Umwelt, Mitwelt,* and *Eigenwelt* are fragmented rather than unified. These people's sense of the present will not be tied to past or future. Though they may feel nagging dissatisfaction with their lives, they will be unable to pull themselves up by their mental bootstraps. Their personalities will be nonideal.

Existential Dynamics.   The heart of the existential position is its view of directionality in living. Basic to an understanding of what is concretely involved in the core tendency of striving for authentic being is the assumption that everything in life is a situation requiring decision or choice. As there is no alternative envisaged to decision making, every moment in life expresses *intentionality* (Boss, 1963; Keen, 1970). Freud too believed that all behavior is motivated, but whereas to him motivation is largely unconscious, to existentialists it is largely conscious. Indeed, it is persons' propensity for consciousness that necessitates their formulating their lives as a series of decisions or choices. The human is by nature intelligent—a symbolizing, imagining, and judging organism—and therefore cannot avoid decisions, however much he or she might wish for some easier path.

As there is no alternative to decision making for the human, life will be led to the fullest by recognizing and accepting this fact. In order to properly recognize the necessity of continual decision making, it is useful to practice vigorous symbolization, imagination, and judgment, because this will ensure a complex and sophisticated cognitive mass. And rich expression of those psychological processes is certainly an aid in actually making decisions, for such expression underlies the ability to pose problems, consider alternatives and possible outcomes, and then enact plans. Life is a series of decisions whether or not one recognizes it. But life is best led by preparation for and commitment to the decisions that one must face.

In the decision-making process, emotions play an overshadowing role. A decision, whatever its content, always takes the form of posing one alternative that pushes the person into the future, the unknown, the unpredictable and another alternative that pulls the person into the past, the status quo, the familiar. While choosing the future is an attractive prospect because of the challenge and growth possibilities it offers, it is uncharted and therefore anxiety provoking. And while choosing the past is an attractive prospect because it is comfortable and relaxing, it involves sacrificing the possibility of development and brings with it the guilt of missed opportunity. Existentialists speak of this anxiety and guilt as *ontological* (e.g., May, 1958), or an inevitable part of being. This formulation is reminiscent of Rank, who emphasizes the inherent opposition of fear of life and fear of death. But whereas intrapsychic conflict theorists advocate a compromise that minimizes both fears, existentialists do nothing of the kind. What is ideal for existentialists is to choose the future and accept ontological anxiety as an unfortunate concomitant of authentic being (Binswanger, 1963; Boss, 1963; Frankl, 1960; Kobasa & Maddi, 1977; May, 1958).

Of course, it is impossible to grow to adulthood without having shrunk from some chances to push forward into one's future. Thus, there will be in any person some accumulated ontological guilt. And like the anxiety, this guilt must be accepted for it is a genuine expression of the life one has led. One cannot alleviate this guilt by resolving not to be so hard on oneself, because this would amount to a falsification of the reality of one's life. Such a falsification would corrupt one's being-in-the-world through the denial that by certain choices one has inevitably limited other opportunities. To falsify—to deny ontological guilt—is to forfeit attainment of authentic being (Kobasa & Maddi, 1977).

But merely accepting ontological guilt is not enough. One must also arrange to minimize it by choosing often on the side of realizing future possibilities. One must find some way of persisting in the face of ontological anxiety. Persisting does not mean denying the really frightening nature of moving toward the unknown. To deny ontological anxiety, all the while appearing to choose the future, is to make a pseudo-choice and to jeopardize attainment of authentic being through lying to oneself (Binswanger, 1963; Boss, 1963; Frankl, 1960; May, 1958; Tillich, 1952). Indeed, much of what existentialists mean by the necessity of taking responsibility for your own life is precisely this recognition of the hazards of choosing the future and choosing it nonetheless. You must recognize that through your own commitments you may end in tragedy in order to win the possibility of triumphing (Kobasa & Maddi, 1977). And this is not to say that you will triumph if you choose the future—you will win only the possibility of doing so. In the emphasis on remaining aware of ontological anxiety and guilt and choosing to optimize the former and minimize the latter in order to realize one's possibilities, we see vividly why existential psychology is a perfection fulfillment rather than intrapsychic conflict position. Although existentialism conceives of an inherent conflict between anxiety and guilt, it does not advocate a compromise designed to minimize both. It assumes that only through persisting in the face of anxiety can one win through a full realization of the potentialities for being.

Before considering the important question of how one can manage to persist in the face of ontological anxiety, we would do well to consider further the precise nature of this emotion. Tillich (1952) has identified three forms of ontological anxiety, namely, fear over human finitude, fear over the necessity of action in the absence of knowledge of outcomes, and fear of meaninglessness. In the first, the emphasis is on the sheer terror over the fact, presumably known to humans alone, that they will die, perhaps when they least expect it. The second recognizes that one tries to make decisions in order to achieve goals one cherishes. But there is no guarantee that a successful outcome will occur, and if one realizes that the decisions are one's own (and presumably could have been made differently had one only known), this is very frightening. The third fear concerns the ultimate question of what existence is worth if one can shape it and has the responsibility to do so but may die or end up losing all one wanted. This contemplation raises the awful suspicion that life is meaningless—a very disconcerting experience indeed! To these fears, Bugental (1965) adds a fourth: the fear of isolation. This refers to the recognition that is part and parcel of consciousness that since you make your own decisions, you may be rejected by all and end up completely alone.

In the face of all this, how comforting it would seem to reject individuality and personal initiative in favor of convention and tradition! If you do not take chances, if you let others be your guide, if you agree at all costs, if you give up these foolish fantasies that life could be better than it is, if you stop trying to reflect on your experience in the vain attempt to understand, if you accept rather than judge, you will not have to face the anxieties mentioned above. You can have a nice, solid, respectable, happy life. Right? Not at all, according to the existentialists. If you abnegate the birthright of individuality contained in the psychological needs, you will gain comfort only in the short run—if that. You will become conventional and banal, showing little taste and complexity and relating to others in only superficial ways. You will have to avoid using your own wits not only in order to remain conventional but to keep alive the incredible lie you have perpetrated on yourself (Keen, 1970). Worse still, yours will be an inauthentic being not only in the eyes of serious persons but in your own. You are, after all, a human being and cannot avoid self-scrutiny entirely, no matter how hard you try. Here and there a stray thought of beauty, a daydream of love, the observation of persons who seem truly themselves, will haunt you. As life goes on and the lie's inevitable effect of halting development and enthusiasm for life persists, you will wonder why conventional success and approval do so little to lift your spirits. You will be in the grips of severe ontological guilt. This is what provoked Thoreau to exclaim that "most men lead lives of quiet desperation" and Kierkegaard to warn of "the sickness unto death."

You cannot defend successfully against the necessity of self-reliant decision making, according to the existentialists. If you try, all that will happen is that ontological anxiety and guilt, those natural concomitants of living, will get transformed into neurotic, inauthentic forms of themselves. *Neurotic anxiety* heavily involves shame, taking the form of fear that you and others will know how frightened you are (Keen, 1970). Because you deny that ontological anxiety is a natural part of living, you try to hide it. But even worse is what happens to ontological guilt that when accepted takes the form of dissatisfaction because of specific things you did or did not do that stifled opportunities. *Neurotic guilt* is much more devastating, taking the form of condemnation of one's entire being rather than only particular acts. There is some hope of rectifying particular acts but little of reclaiming a being comprehensively rejected (Keen, 1970; May, 1958). Suicide is, in the existentialist view, a frequent response to massive neurotic guilt.

Avoidance of decision making and growth causes dreadful psychopathology; ontological anxiety, honestly faced, is also gravely painful. How can the human hope to face it and have a satisfying life? An early existential answer (Kierkegaard, 1954) was *faith in God,* who made the human mind a godlike thing. This position contends that through the exercise of intelligence in decision making, one draws closer to a unity with God after death. For many modern-day existentialists, faith in God will not be convincing as a basis for persisting in the face of ontological anxiety. A particularly pessimistic contemporary position (Camus, 1955) considers a full appreciation of the *absurdity* of life (in which people search for meaning when there is none to be found) the only viable basis for living. More compelling, it seems to me, is the equally modern view that what people need is *courage* (Tillich, 1952), or recognition of their true power and dignity among living things. In a sense, the courage to persist is the other side of the coin of ontological anxiety. There is a sense of power in recognizing that it is precisely because humans are so beautifully intelligent as to be able to fashion life rather than be fashioned by it that they *can* experience anxiety. Anxiety may seem a bearable burden in exchange for the power to create one's own meaning through symbolizing, imagining, judging, and the actions following therefrom.

This emphasis on ontological anxiety as a sign of freedom and power is why Tillich (1952) considers doubt to be the "god above God." Frankl (1960) gives powerful expression to the idea that ontological anxiety or doubt is actually a sign of ideal functioning:

> Challenging the meaning of life can . . . never be taken as a manifestation of morbidity or abnormality; it is rather the truest expression of the state of being human, the mark of the most human nature in man. For we can easily imagine highly developed animals or insects—say bees or ants—which in many aspects of their social organization are actually superior to man. But we can never imagine any such creature raising the question of the meaning of its own exis-

tence, and thus challenging that existence. It is reserved for man alone to find his very existence questionable, to experience the whole dubiousness of being. More than such faculties as power of speech, conceptual thinking, or walking erect, this factor of doubting the significance of his own existence is what sets man apart from animal. (p. 30)

Nothing so centrally part of human nature as ontological anxiety could ever be defined as psychopathological. And there is considerable dignity in confronting this anxiety, for to do so is to reach a high point of humanity. Only when you have clearly seen the abyss and jumped into it with no assurance of survival can you call yourself a human being. Then, if you survive, shall you be called hero, for you will have created your own life.

Freedom and Necessity.   A theme running throughout existential theorizing is that through vigorous symbolization, imagination, and judgment one can achieve freedom. Through mental activity, one is supposed to create a world. Yet there seem to be limits on this freedom, to judge from Existentialists' frequent reference to the necessities or givens of life. These givens are variously called *facticity* (Sartre, 1956) and the *ground* or *thrownness* of existence (Binswanger, 1958). Just what is necessity and what possibility?

Perhaps as much as any personological position, existentialism shows respect for necessities or givens. The major, unassailable given, after all, is that each person will die. Nonbeing is an inherent part of being. But there are other givens. If you are born a woman, menses and the childbearing function are givens. And there are particular social situations in which necessity abounds. Frankl (1960) is especially eloquent in this regard when he talks of being forcibly imprisoned in a concentration camp during World War II. Perhaps it will surprise you to find existential psychologists advocating acceptance of givens. For example, Binswanger (1958, p. 340) says, "The more stubbornly the human being opposes his being-thrown into existence . . . the more strongly this thrownness gains in influence." The end result of this is debilitating in "that a person does not stand autonomously in his world, that he blocks himself off from the ground of his existence, that he does not take his existence upon himself but trusts himself to alien powers, that he makes alien powers 'responsible' for his fate instead of himself" (Binswanger, 1963, p. 290). In other words, accepting the limits set on the possibilities of your existence by certain imposed biological and social forces enables you to be more authentic because you do not have to lie to yourself. The value of accepting givens is the same as accepting ontological anxiety and guilt as inherent aspects of living. It is only by remaining honest that one has any chance at all of pursuing those possibilities that are available. Accepting your inability to influence certain things makes you more aware of what you can influence, paradoxical though that may seem at first blush.

This is not to say that existential psychologists advocate passive acquiescence to social and biological forces. Actually, Frankl (1960) believes that those persons who could not survive the concentration camps succumbed either because they considered themselves completely and unalterably trapped or because they denied that they were incarcerated at all. But those who survived did so through a frank acceptance that some portion of their existence was not under their control and a continual exploration, through symbolizing, imagining, and judging, of what freedom or maneuvering space was left to them. The first value of this approach is that they discovered some portion of freedom and therefore could retain some sense of human dignity. The second value is that as they set their wits to work constructively on the matter, they carved out more freedom than they initially would have imagined and than was available to others less fortunate. But recognize that their fortunateness was self-determined by their own courage to face straightforwardly a horrendous imposition on freedom in spite of the pain of such honesty. It was their persistence in being authentic in the face of suffering that permitted them to use their wits to gain greater freedom. Thus, one accepts a necessity in order to more clearly explore the possibilities of freedom left. In this, one often discovers that the necessity is smaller and less important than initially thought.

But according to existentialists, there are very few *actual* necessities beyond some biological factors. Most of us never experience forced incarceration. Much more debilitating than failing to accept an actual necessity is construing things that are actually only possibilities as necessities (Maddi, 1988). Persons unhappy in their jobs or their marriages may complain that they cannot make any changes. Perhaps they feel they could not get another job or that responsibilities as husband and wife preclude dissolving the marriage. It would not be unusual in such a situation to hear an existential psychotherapist questioning whether there really are no other jobs and no other ways of fulfilling obligations. The persons in this example have construed particular life commitments, which were freely made and can be freely changed, as necessities. This confusion of possibilities as necessities is at the heart of psychopathology, according to existentialists (Binswanger, 1963; Boss, 1963; Keen, 1970; Maddi, 1987). Typically, when persons draw this conclusion they want to abdicate personal responsibility, blaming failures on a destructive society they can do nothing about. They want to roll over and die and be pitied for it. They lack the courage that would permit authentic being, choosing to lie to themselves and others instead.

Existential psychology is definitely a perfection fulfillment position. There is little sympathy in the existential position for the act of treating possibilities as necessities; persons are considered to have the wherewithal to exercise greater freedom if they would only try. Some positions exemplifying the conflict model would be much more sympathetic to the failure to attempt some wanted goal, because the conflict model is built on compromise. For the existentialist, the guilt one feels on staying in a marriage against one's will is *true* or ontological guilt. An existential psychotherapist would not try to remove the guilt so much as amplify the experience of it in order to force the person to recognize the portion of freedom surrendered unnecessarily. In contrast, a classical Freudian psychotherapist might try to help the person decrease guilt on the grounds that it was only due to an overly harsh superego blocking a workable compromise between necessary individual and social pressures. Similarly, an intrapsychic conflict therapist might find the cause of the person's guilt in an overbearing autonomy and encourage its diminution to pave the way for a compromise expressing more communion. Even an actualization fulfillment therapist might be skeptical that the guilt pointed toward a beneficial direction of movement on the grounds that it is feelings of well-being that augur personal fulfillment. This therapist too might try to decrease the guilt.

We are now in a position to understand more fully what the existential psychologist means by *freedom*. It is not some mysterious free will, undetermined in any way by past experience, constituting something virtually supernatural and not to be understood. Rather, as Gendlin (1965–1966) makes clear, it is the process of using one's wits—symbolization, imagination, and judgment—to construct possibilities. In discussing freedom, Gendlin (1965–1966) says,

> An oversimplified existentialism would have it that you can choose yourself to be any way you wish. You simply leap out of your situation and your past. This would be a flat denial of all our sufferings and failing attempts to be a certain way just by wishing we were. That is not what existentialism means at all. But, then, what is choice and freedom? Sartre, discussing the example of a cafe waiter, points out that "cafe waiter" is, of course, only a role. The living man fills the role, rather than being defined by it. But, says Sartre, that does not mean that he can just simply choose to be a diplomat instead. There is "facticity," the situation and conditions about us which we cannot arbitrarily wave away. We must "surpass" situations in our interpreting them and acting in them; we cannot just choose them to be different. There is no such magic freedom as simply choosing ourselves to be other than what we are. Without difficult, sensitive steps, we do not become free of the constraints we are under.
>
> The same may be said about a man's past, his upbringing, his learnings. The past is surpassed in the present, but this is no arbitrary anything-you-please. The same relationship between a given (facticity) and a movement (freedom, surpassing) holds here . . . the given does not have in it what we later make of it; and yet, what we make of it is related to what was given, must follow from it in certain ways, and just some ways fit. How I can surpass my past is not logically or analytically deducible from it. Surpassing is living action; but not just any arbitrary action brings the felt response of authentic surpassing. It is hard to devise such a mode of action, and we often fail to do so.

What we construct through symbolization, imagination, and judgment is freedom in the sense that the end result changes us and it is not strictly deducible in advance from a knowledge of our past. It represents a new frame of reference and format for action that we worked at creating, that we rendered consistent with our past, and that we can truly believe. We worked hard; we were not breathed on mysteriously by God. This achievement of freedom is properly called *transcendence,* and though its specific content in any case would be very difficult to predict in advance, the process of thought that renders it likely is predictably common in some persons and uncommon in others. This is the story of development, which we will take up in Chapter 8.

Suggested in Gendlin's (1965–66) position on freedom is a full-blown sense of life as a series of decisions. As he makes clear, the alternatives in any decisional situation are as much posed by the person as they are given:

> Another error committed when [the person's mental process of] explication is left out is to view choice as between already given alternatives. This is not existentialism but a bad misunderstanding of it. . . . Situations are all in terms of what we may do, not do, suffer, avoid, succeed in, or miss. A situation is never pure facticity. . . . The facticity of . . . posed alternatives is not to be accepted as though the binding facts I now see were ultimate; but neither can we simply wave away the facts. We don't always succeed in explicating new alternatives so well that we combine all we desire in one, while avoiding all that we wish to avoid. But free choice is not the choice between the two, bad, given alternatives. Free choice necessitates the creation of new alternatives which make stepping stones of what were obstacles. (pp. 135–136)

Thus, the involvement of symbolization, imagination, and judgment in the very posing of alternatives is also a part of transcendence, which turns what seemed given into a possibility capable of change.

This discussion permits pinpointing of the existential position on defensiveness. Although existentialists do assume defensiveness, they mean something quite different from the usual meaning of repressing from consciousness that which is socially unacceptable. The occasion for defensiveness, according to existentialists, is cowardice in the face of ontological anxiety (this is virtually the same as the inability to believe in one's own power of intelligence). The end result is the distortion resident in neurotic anxiety and guilt and the confusion of possibilities with necessities. One has evaded the real cognitive work involved in achieving transcendence as opposed to hiding one's antisocial tendencies from scrutiny, as in the Freudian explanation.

Concluding Remarks.   At this time, existential psychology is hardly a unitary body of theory free of ambiguities and disagreements. What I have tried to do is select those parts of various theorists' approaches that seem to fit together into something approaching a coherent position. It is premature to indulge in a rigorous analysis of the strengths and weaknesses of this tentative formulation. At the moment, it seems best to absorb the main existentialist emphasis presented here and to gain a sense of its similarities to and differences from other personological positions.

Rational-Emotive Therapy

Albert Ellis (1962) has been developing a psychotherapy since the 1950s that appears to fall within the perfection version of the fulfillment model. To date, this approach must be regarded as fragmentary in its formulations concerning personality, lacking a well-developed, internally consistent core and developmental and peripheral statements. But its current popularity prompts me to include at least some mention of it here.

Ellis appears to assume two core tendencies. One innate direction of persons is *to think irrationally and harm themselves;* the other is *to gain understanding of their folly and train themselves to change their self-destructive ways.* Although this dual statement suggests a conflict position because the core tendencies seem to contradict to each other, it is actually a fulfillment statement. After all, the second tendency corrects the first. In other words, the ideal life does not involve a compromise between the two core tendencies so much as a counteraction of the first by the second; through discipline, one comes to live rationally despite one's initial proclivity toward irrationality. In the fulfillment mode this clearly is a perfection emphasis, in which one must rise above one's weaknesses to attain the good life.

The developmental statement in this theory is restricted to the assertion that interaction with parents and other adults typically intensifies the innate tendency of youngsters to be irrational and self-destructive. Thus, most people fail to learn to live rationally. When they do, rationality typically comes in adulthood or even later, and it necessitates considerable effort and even therapeutic help. This theory has little or no peripheral statement whereby one can understand persisting individual differences in any systematic way.

Being basically a psychotherapy, Ellis's position most heavily emphasizes how the irrational and self-destructive tendency expresses itself. Basically, the process involves irrational interpretation of events. Whenever an event is less than perfect for people, their tendency to be irrational and self-destructive leads them to exaggerate. The event is not merely unfortunate—it is unbearable. People are not merely unsatisfied—they are worthless. Then, shocked by their views of life as terrible and of themselves as incapable, they engage in yet another cycle of magical thinking from which they emerge as disgusting and in need of punishment. This cycle intensifies. The aim of the constructive core tendency is to cut into all this irrationality. Through hard and consistent effort not to exaggerate, persons can come to see events and themselves more realistically. According to Ellis, this entails perceiving negative events as unfortunate but bearable and oneself as having experienced a reversal but not being damaged in the ability to correct this in the future. With such insistence, obsessive spirals of self-destructive thought do not get underway.

Rational-emotive psychotherapy attempts to strengthen the constructive, rational core tendency by direct assault on the irrational, destructive core tendency. It is a confrontation therapy in which the therapist battles the client's negative views of self and world through a combination of contradicting these views with evidence and insisting that the negative views be changed. There is no encouragement of transference, as in psychoanalytic therapies, nor is there the unconditional positive regard of actualization therapies. Ellis assumes that the client is wrong about how he or she has construed experience and needs to be shaken out of depression and self-pity with debate and exhortation. The therapy emphasizes the present and future rather than the past.

Rational-emotive therapy is a bona fide, if brutal, expression of the perfection fulfillment approach. Although it places relatively more emphasis on self-destructiveness, it leaves no doubt that rationality and constructive living are possible and preferable. Like other perfection fulfillment positions, this one emphasizes how persons attribute meaning to experience and thereby construct their worlds. This attributive process is considered much more important as a determinant of behavior than the genetic blueprints of the actualization theorists and the instincts of the psychoanalysts. Even the psychotherapeutic techniques offered by Ellis fit well into the perfection fulfillment approach, emphasizing as they do confrontation and the present. Although reminiscent of the existential approach, rational-emotive therapy deviates from this view in various ways. Perhaps the basic theoretical difference is that rational-emotive therapy assumes that there is indeed a true reality that will be seen the same way by all persons who manage to be rational. In contrast, existential psychology proposes that each person constructs his or her own reality and that operating rationally does not amount to becoming the same as everyone else who does so. This difference shows up not only in various theoretical formulations in the theories but in the therapies as well. Although existential therapy is also a confrontation approach, it is better prepared to identify individual differences as rational and constructive. Perhaps this difference aids us in understanding why rational-emotive therapy has not yet developed a clear peripheral statement, as such statements emphasize individual differences.

CHAPTER 5

The Core of Personality: Consistency Model

In its version of the core tendency of personality, the consistency model emphasizes the importance of the information the person gets from interacting with the external world. The model assumes that people will develop personalities that increase the likelihood of their getting the kind of information that is best for them. The personality is determined much more by the feedback from interaction with the world than it is by the human's inherent attributes.

In comparison with consistency theories, both fulfillment and conflict theories put much greater emphasis on an inherent nature as a component of personality that determines life's course. According to fulfillment theories, life is an unfolding of the human's inherent nature. And even when conflict theories stress society as an important force in living, they assume that personality is in large measure an expression of the human's inherent characteristics. For both fulfillment and conflict theories, personality is far more influenced by the attributes the human brings into the world than is the case for consistency positions.

To be sure, consistency positions make some minimal assumptions about what is inherent in humans, but they are much more concerned with the compatibility among aspects of the content of personality than with the nature of that content. For consistency theorists, such content is largely learned and represents the history of feedback resulting from interacting with the world. Certainly feedback influences the content of personality along the lines of the assumed core tendencies of personality, and these core tendencies are inherent in human nature, but one cannot specify what particular content will result. As you will see, the implications of this kind of position are very different from those of fulfillment and conflict positions.

CONSISTENCY MODEL: COGNITIVE DISSONANCE VERSION

There are two basic versions of the consistency model. In the first, which I call the *cognitive dissonance version* , the important elements in the determination of consistency are cognitions. The cognitions may be thoughts, expectations, attitudes, opinions, or even perceptions. Discrepancies or consistencies among cognitive elements may occur either within or across these categories. There may be agreement or disagreement between two thoughts, between a thought and a perception, and so forth. All cognitive dissonance versions of the consistency model assume that discrepancies among cognitive elements produce an emotional state that provides the energy and direction for behavior.

In the pure form of this position, exemplified by the theory of Kelly, both large and small discrepancies bring discomfort, anxiety, and tension. These emotional reactions in turn produce behavior aimed at reducing the discrepancy and ensuring that it will not recur. After exploring Kelly's position we will examine its similarity to Festinger's. Finally, we will discuss McClelland, whose point of view is properly classed as a variant on the cognitive dissonance version of the consistency model. For McClelland, only large discrepancies result in emotional discomfort and avoidance, whereas small discrepancies are actually thought to result in pleasurable emotion and approach behavior.

Kelly's Position

George A. Kelly (born 1905; died 1967) received his Ph.D. in psychology from the University of Iowa after having studied both in the United States and England. He spent his career in university settings, where he combined teaching with student counseling. For a number of years he was director of the Psychological Clinic at Ohio State University, and he held a professorship at Brandeis University at the time of his death. Although Kelly did not publish as much as some other personologists, he influenced many students over the years, some of whom have remained avidly loyal to his views. These views have also aroused considerable attention, particularly in England, where philosophers and psychologists have joined in their praise and criticism. Typically Kelly is lauded for emphasizing how persons create their own lives through construing experience (and are therefore free). He is criticized for not having recognized allies in existentialism and phenomenology whose stimulation could have led to greater specification of his theory.

Although Kelly developed his position over a period of many years, it was not presented in the literature until recently. This is partly the reason why it is not too well known among psychologists. Also, Kelly's approach has a distinctly intellectual or mentalistic ring, and it is therefore somewhat at a disadvantage in a field long dominated by views of the human as emotional and instinctual. Actually, Kelly's position deserves a hearing precisely because it is so different from prevailing views, and because it is relatively complete and carefully wrought.

The core tendency of personality from Kelly's (1955) point of view is easily stated: It is *the human's continual attempt to predict and control the events of experience.* Kelly bases his model for the human not on the biological organism or on the frame of reference of happiness and unhappiness but on the scientific pursuit of truth. Truth is not necessarily what pleases or satisfies our immediate desires and needs; rather, it is what convinces us of its inexorable reality. The scientific pursuit of truth is the empirical procedure of formulating hypotheses and testing them out in the tangible world of actual experience. Depending on whether a hypothesis is supported by facts or events, the scientist retains it or discards it regardless of its appeal. Kelly deeply believed that it is as scientists that people approach the task of living. The only important difference between real scientists and people in general is that scientists are more self-conscious and precise about the methods and procedures employed, which are in other ways the same as the latter's.

In arguing for the centrality for living of the scientific model, Kelly (1955) says:

> It is customary to say that *the scientist's ultimate aim is to predict and control.* This is a summary statement that psychologists frequently like to quote in characterizing their own aspirations. Yet, curiously enough, psychologists rarely credit the human subjects in their experiments with having similar aspirations. It is as though the psychologist were saying to himself, "I, being a *psychologist,* and therefore a *scientist,* am performing this experiment in order to improve the prediction and control of certain human phenomena; but my subject, being merely a human organism, is obviously propelled by inexorable drives welling up within him, or else he is in gluttonous pursuit of sustenance and shelter."(p.5)

If both psychologists and their subjects are capable and intelligent humans, and the psychologists attempt to predict and control, why should not their subjects be making the same attempt? It is only naïveté that leads to any other conclusion.

Kelly could well bolster this logical argument with an empirical one. Psychologists who do personality research are very sensitive to the possibility that their measurement operations will be contaminated by the subject's wish to appear in a socially desirable and appropriate light. It seems that virtually any time a psychologist gives subjects a set of questions to answer about themselves, they will try to answer in ways that will make them look good or give the psychologist what is wanted. It is also clear that subjects are terribly interested in the measurement's purpose and in the outcome of their participation in the research. A personologist naive enough not to recognize that subjects are very interested in predicting what the experiment is about and controlling what is made of their performance will very likely fail in the research efforts. If the personologist apparently succeeds, it will be only by having been unintentionally clever enough to use the subject's attempts to predict and control for his or her own ends. The most sophisticated approach to this problem of measurement is to construct tests that employ techniques for canceling out the effects of subjects' trying to determine the goals of the research and responding in a socially desirable manner (e.g., Edwards, 1957; Jackson & Messick, 1958).

If you have ever been a subject in a psychological experiment, you may intuitively understand Kelly's insistence on the importance of the attempt to predict and control one's experience. Perhaps you can remember wondering what was going to be done to you and what was the point of the research. Perhaps you asked questions or watched closely to try to find out what was going on. Failing this, perhaps you aimed to make a particular impact on the experiment rather than leave the matter undefined. You may not have trusted the psychologist's account of why your participation was needed. All of these possibilities exemplify the disrupting effect of uncertainty and the attempt to achieve certainty.

We could even agree with Kelly on the importance of being able to predict and control and still remain unconvinced that he has clarified the human condition. But he actually has a great deal more to say about personality, as we shall see through focusing on the (1) development, (2) use, and (3) change of constructs and construct systems.

Development of Constructs and Construct Systems.   According to Kelly, the person's first step in attempting to predict and control experience is to engage in the construing of events. Early in life, before much construing has taken place, experience is made up of a seemingly random and continuous flow of events. For Kelly, events have an actual existence separate from the person, but they do not achieve importance for understanding personality until the person construes them. The process of *construing* classes certain events together with others that are considered similar and contrasts them with others that are considered different.

In the initial stages of construing, you begin to focus on certain general features of the random events flowing by until you recognize what you consider to be repetitions, or replications, of events. Because you have abstracted what for you is the essence of a particular event, you can identify a repetition of that event in the future. You have transcended the literal event and achieved abstract representation of its essence. It is only through such a process of generalization and abstraction that the events of one's experience can become meaningful and orderly. Without active attempts to construe, it would not be possible to find the world a familiar place and to form expectations about what will happen next. Kelly is very clear in his belief that since construing is an interpretive process, not a mere description of literal reality, it will be done differently by different people. Of the many possible ways of classifying events according to similarities and differences, all are plausible.

However, Kelly fails to explain why people construe along particular lines. To say that certain core characteristics of personality, or inherent capabilities, influence the direction of construing would not be in the spirit of the consistency model, which emphasizes environmental feedback as mostly determining personality content. If Kelly dealt with the question of why different persons construe along different lines, he probably would have to do so in terms of their various histories of environmental experience. He would say that you construe either along the lines that have been taught to you by significant others or along those that are a natural outgrowth of your own world of experience. That Kelly has been reticent to develop his theory along these lines should be kept in mind, as we will encounter other reticences that can be construed in a particular way.

In any event, the result of the process of construing is the construct. A core characteristic of personality, the *construct* is a dichotomous idea or abstraction, such as good-bad or chromatic-achromatic. Constructs are categories of thought that grow out of the interpretations we place on events and, as we shall see in the next section, serve the purpose of helping us to anticipate future events. In considering the construct to be dichotomous, Kelly deeply believes that he is mirroring the nature of common thought. In order to develop a construct at all, he believes, you must have noted a minimum of two events that seem similar to each other and different from a third. The process of perceiving similarity is deeply entwined with the process of perceiving difference. Whenever you claim that two things—say, wood and metal—are similar, perhaps in being hard, you are also implying that they are different from soft things such as water. The existence of hard things requires that there also be soft things to serve as contrasts. In a more general sense, whatever we perceive contrasts with something other than itself. Thus, Kelly feels that constructs are inherently dichotomous in nature. This is not changed for him by the fact that a person may seem to be using only one pole of a construct. If a person is, for example, talking only in terms of the goodness of people with no reference to badness, this merely means that the badness pole of the goodness-badness construct is implicit. It does not mean that it is nonexistent. There are no unipolar constructs.

Here is an example of a construct and how it is formed. Imagine that you have no constructs in the area of heterosexual relationships. You do, however, have a basic tendency to predict and control the events of your experience. In the normal course of events, you will find yourself in the company of people of the opposite sex, and your urge to predict and control your experience will find expression in attempting to understand and interpret these encounters. You will look for similarities and differences in the encounters on which to base abstraction that will render the encounters meaningful and predictable.

Consider three encounters with people of the opposite sex. The first and third may leave you enthusiastic and joyous, while the second may threaten and disturb you. You could develop the idea, or construct, of *satisfying-dissatisfying* as a relevant dimension of heterosexual relationship. The first and third encounters may also involve people who are excitable, imaginative, inconsistent, and unusual and the second someone who is orderly, even-tempered, pragmatic, and acquiescent. On the basis of these observations, you could develop the construct of *creative-banal*. The first and second encounters might involve people who get good grades, have no trouble finishing papers, and make tangible contributions to other people's lives, whereas the third might involve a person who shuns evaluations, does not complete courses, and does nothing for other people. On the basis of these observations, you could formulate the construct of *productive-nonproductive* as yet another relevant dimension of heterosexual relationship. These are only a few of the many possible constructs that could be catalogued here.

In the course of experiencing events a person will develop many constructs, because events are numerous and multifaceted enough to stimulate many separate interpretive conclusions. But rather than remaining separate, the many constructs a person develops tend to become organized into a hierarchical *construct system*, in which constructs are either superordinate or subordinate to one another. There are two kinds of relationships among constructs. First, "a construct may be superordinate to another because each pole of the subordinate construct forms a part of the context for the two poles of the superordinate" (Sechrest, 1963, p. 214). In our extended example, the construct *satisfying-dissatisfying* would be superordinate to the construct *creative-banal* if people who are creative are satisfying and people who are banal are dissatisfying and if things other than creativity and banality contribute to their satisfying or dissatisfying nature. In other words, creativity-banality is parallel but subordinate to satisfying-dissatisfying because of the lesser generality of the former construct.

In order to illustrate the second kind of subordinate relationship, I will have to extend our already extended example. But first, recall that the construct *productive-nonproductive* was formed on the basis of similarity between the first and second encounters, with the third being different. Regardless of whether that construct is more or less general than the other two, it remains independent of them and cannot be organized in the same hierarchy with them. Productivity-nonproductivity has nothing to do with whether the person will be considered creative or banal or whether interaction with him or her will be satisfying or dissatisfying. This is because productivity-nonproductivity is a construct that was formed on the basis of different groupings of event attributes than the other two constructs. Observations such as this led Kelly to theorize that although constructs tend to be organized into systems, some constructs will be so independent of, or incompatible with, one another that they will exist either alone or as part of separate (and possibly competing) construct systems.

To illustrate this second type of hierarchical relationship, let us add a fourth encounter with someone of the opposite sex to our example and assume that the experience relates to the creative pole of the creative-banal construct. Thus, the first, third, and fourth encounters are with creative people, whereas the second is with a banal person. Let us assume further that there are characteristics of the first and fourth encounters that suggest generosity, while the third encounter suggests stinginess and the second is neutral with regard to these two considerations. The resulting construct, *generosity-stinginess,* has a hitherto undiscussed type of relationship with creative-banal. Regardless of which is the more general and, hence, higher in the hierarchy, the entire generosity-stinginess construct fits into the creative pole of the creative-banal construct, because all the creative people in the example are either generous or stingy. It is meaningless to consider the generosity or stinginess of the banal people. Note that in both types of hierarchical relationship, the constructs to which a given construct is superordinate or subordinate is a matter of relative generality.

Kelly does not theorize about the lines along which construing will take place, even though he could do so within the framework of a consistency position by focusing on environmental determinants of construing. Nowhere in Kelly's writing is there a list or typology of likely constructs. Kelly does not describe the kinds of constructs one can expect to find in persons with particular histories of environmental interaction. However, he does indicate an explicit, effective procedure for discerning the content of constructs that exist in any person whom you may confront. In other words, you can determine what a person's constructs contain once you are faced with him or her, even though as a theorist you could not have predicted them in advance of the actual confrontation. Thus, while Kelly's theory cannot be completely predictive—a puzzling fault in a position that takes the scientific model as the measure of the human—it is moderately usable in that you can at least describe people once you encounter them (T. Mischel, 1964; Holland, 1970). The procedure for determining a person's constructs is called the *Role Repertory Test* or *Grid* (Kelly, 1955; Bannister & Mair, 1968), and it is thoroughly consistent with the theory. Briefly, it involves having people identify the significant people in their lives (e.g., mother, father, best high school teacher) and then judging their similarities and differences through considering them in all possible combinations of three. The judgment requires that two of the three people in each combination be specified as similar in some way and different from the third. Then, by analyzing and summarizing all the dichotomous judgments made by the person you are testing, you can determine the number and content of the constructs composing his or her system. It is quite an ingenious test!

Although Kelly does not precisely specify the construct content likely in people with particular histories, he does conceptualize certain general attributes of constructs that help to render his position concrete and usable. For example, he thinks it is important to know whether a construct is permeable and preemptive (Kelly, 1955, pp. 156–157). If a construct is *permeable,* hitherto unencountered events can be subsumed within it, whereas an impermeable construct can be used to understand only those events that went into its original formulation. A *preemptive* construct is one that renders the events it subsumes unavailable for subsumption within other constructs. These characteristics of constructs seem relevant to how flexible and adaptable the person is likely to be.

The Use of Constructs and Construct Systems.   Thus far in examining how persons go about attempting to predict and control the events of their experience, we have seen that they develop constructs organized into one or more hierarchical systems. Constructs are interpretations of events arrived at through what amounts to a process of inductive reasoning. A construct system is essentially a theory of the world of experience or of subportions of it. All this is quite consistent with the model of the human as scientist, as is the use to which constructs and construct systems are put, according to Kelly. Once the scientist develops, through inductive reasoning, a theory concerning the significance of observed events, he or she will use that theory in a deductive fashion to anticipate and influence events that have not yet occurred. These deductive processes will lead to the formulation of hypotheses or predictions and to attempts to test them by manipulation or control of the environment.

The most ambiguous and fragmentary part of Kelly's position is the matter of how constructs and construct systems are used in anticipation and action (Holland, 1970). To understand this, it is first necessary to recognize that events achieve significance for the person only when they are subsumed within constructs. Kelly says that the constructs and construct systems that you have right now will determine the importance of future events for you. Constructs are useful in attempts to predict and control the future in that they give you a tangible basis for expecting the kinds of events that are likely to occur and for interpreting their meaning. For example, if you have the construct system mentioned earlier, you will look forward to a new heterosexual encounter with the expectation that it will be satisfying or dissatisfying, creative or banal, productive or nonproductive, and characterized by generosity or stinginess. You will not expect it to involve anything more or less in the way of possibilities. The higher a construct concerning heterosexual encounter is on the hierarchy, the more it will determine expectation. Thus, if satisfying-dissatisfying is the most general of these constructs, you will expect it to apply unequivocally to the imminent encounter, whereas you may be less certain of the applicability of some less general construct such as productive-nonproductive.

So the first way in which construct systems are relevant to prediction and control is that they provide you with a set of expectations about future experience. But the only predictions you can make solely on the basis of a set of hierarchically organized constructs are very general: All you can say is that the forthcoming heterosexual encounter will be satisfying *or* dissatisfying, creative *or* banal, and so forth. You cannot expect it to definitely be one or the other. The decision as to which pole of the relevant construct to favor in forming expectations is a terribly important matter for Kelly's theory if it is to permit precise understanding of people's attempts to predict and control.

When people favor one pole of a construct over the other in anticipating the future, they are making what Kelly (1955, pp. 64-68) calls the *elaborative choice*. What determines this choice? It is not that one pole has turned out to be more accurate in the past, though such an actuarial basis is certainly plausible for Kelly's kind of theory. Instead, he says that "A person chooses for himself that alternative in a dichotomized construct through which he anticipates the greater possibility for extension and definition of his system" (Kelly, 1955, p. 64). This statement seems quite consistent with the core tendency of prediction and control. If your aim in life is prediction and control, you must strive to perfect the construct system on which the success of your aim depends. But there are really two strategies whereby one can succeed in predicting events. One is to develop a construct system that works well for a given set of events and restrict yourself to experiencing just those events. The other is to develop a construct system so comprehensive and valid that no restriction of experiential possibilities is necessary because virtually any event can be accurately anticipated.

Kelly recognizes both strategies in his notion of elaborative choice. The adventurous strategy is to favor the pole of the construct that is likely to expand the construct system. The conservative strategy is to favor the pole of the construct that is likely to lead to maintenance or protection of the construct system in its present form. The conservative choice leads to constricted certainty, whereas the adventurous choice leads to broadened understanding.

Although Kelly provides descriptive terminology for recognizing conservative and adventurous choices, he does not say why or when one kind of choice takes precedence over the other. This is a severe drawback in the position, as it is the elaborative choice that determines the anticipations so directly expressive of the human's core tendency. In recognizing this drawback, Sechrest (1963), a student of Kelly who has written interpretively on the position, says:

> There is probably in the [elaborative choice] an implicit assumption of some alternating extension and consolidation of the construction system. When the person feels secure and capable of anticipating events correctly, he will make choices that offer possibilities of extending his system, even at the risk of being wrong, but then a period of consolidation will follow in which he will make choices that reduce exposure to error but are confirmative.(p. 221)

Although this is an ingenious extension of the theory, there is little direct evidence for it in Kelly's writings. For the present, we will have to make do with a theory that, while descriptively complete, falls short of explaining the use of conservative and adventurous choices in arriving at predictions.

This drawback needs to be understood along with the other two mentioned earlier. Kelly fails to specify the lines along which construing takes place, the actual content of the ensuing constructs, and, finally, the bases upon which constructs are used in adventurous or conservative ways. When theorists in the conflict and fulfillment traditions are confronted with the explanation of such directional behaviors, they tend to assume the determining influence of instincts, inherent potentialities, emotions, emotional conflicts, or motives. It is understandable that Kelly would not have recourse to such possibilities, as his is a consistency position that not only stresses the learned nature of personality but also is billed as being free of hedonic and motivational assumptions. What the human is trying to do, according to Kelly, is predict and control, not express some inner nature or set of needs or delight in pleasure. But his disavowal of fulfillment and conflict assumptions does not solve his problem as set forth above. He must find a basis for rendering his position more complete and predictive that is also consistent with his kind of approach. But I am not sure Kelly would agree to the need for theoretical additions. He is so insistent on the individual's freedom of choice in life that he may actually be temperamentally unwilling to infringe on his idealistic stance by theorizing about life as a precisely determined thing. Recall that I also suggested this of Rogers, Adler, and Allport. These theorists, though in different theoretical traditions, have been vociferous, uncompromising exponents of freedom of choice in living.

Thus far in the discussion of the use of constructs and construct systems in the prediction and control of experience, we have focused on anticipations or expectations rather than on actions. With regard to anticipation processes, we have seen that Kelly provides a partial basis for understanding how they result and what their content will be. They come about as a natural concomitant of the constructs that come to mind whenever one is faced with the possibility of certain kinds of events, and their content involves the favored poles of the relevant constructs. Kelly's position is only partial because we are not told why certain directions of construing are chosen instead of others or why and when particular poles will be favored.

Turning to the determination of action, we find that Kelly's position is even more sketchy and ambiguous than it is with regard to anticipation. In agreement with this criticism, Sechrest (1963) says:

> [The notion of elaborative choice] is the most directly related to the prediction of overt behavior, but, as will be seen, there are serious problems in moving from an individual's construct system to his behavior in any particular situation . . . . If [the elaborative choice] provides the essential link between the construction system and observable behavior, the nature of the link has not been precisely described. One gets the impression that the predictions to be made from [the elaborative choice] are not at all exact. (pp. 219–220)

In general, Kelly does not really discuss action, presumably subsuming it under anticipation broadly conceived (cf. Landfield, 1976; Mancuso, 1976; Sechrest, 1977). This indicates that insofar as one wanted to focus on action per se, one would imagine Kelly's position to be that action is complementary to, or an extension of, expectation. So if your constructs lead you to expect that a forthcoming heterosexual encounter will be creative, you presumably should act in a fashion consistent with that. But what this means more concretely remains a mystery in Kelly's position. We can speculate on what action complementary to anticipation might be and say, for example, that if you are expecting an interaction to be creative, you might act on it in terms of what creativity means to you. Perhaps you would be sensitive, free associational, and unevaluative in the things you said and did in the interaction.

As you can imagine, if people act in a way complementary to their expectations and then succeed, this strongly supports the idea that their construct system is valid. If your construct system leads to expecting a creative encounter and you therefore act effectively in a creative manner, you are much more likely to conclude that you were right in your expectation than you would be had you acted in some other way. It is not at all clear, however, that the scientist model for the human leads to the view that action should be complementary to expectation. When scientists have hypotheses, they set about testing them. Testing involves actions designed to show not only whether a hypothesis is true but—more important—whether it is false. Scientists essentially try to disprove their hypotheses, and only if they are unsuccessful in this will they accept the hypotheses as valid. We would expect Kelly, generalizing from the scientific model, to take the view that persons would not act to complement their expectations so much as to rigorously test them.

To be sure, this strategy of testing would require a rather cold-blooded attitude toward life, but such an attitude seems to be an integral part of Kelly's basic assumptions. If your aim in life is to anticipate experience accurately, you must spend all your time testing your expectations so that your construct system will closely conform to reality. Kelly's position leads one to conceptualize actions as primarily hypothesis testing in nature.

What would hypothesis-testing action look like? Kelly gives no help whatsoever in this. But working in the spirit of his approach, we could take a stab at answering the question. If the construct you deemed relevant to an imminent heterosexual encounter is *productive-nonproductive* and you have made the elaborative choice of expectation that the encounter will be productive rather than nonproductive, hypothesis-testing action would involve acting in such a way as to keep the poles of productiveness and nonproductiveness in balance. In any event, hypothesis-testing action would not involve attempts to stimulate just productiveness or just nonproductiveness in the encounter. To encourage experience relevant to only one pole of the construct would be to jeopardize any possibility of determining whether the expectation based on elaborative choice was really accurate.

In trying to talk specifically about hypothesis-testing action, I exceed the formal theoretical apparatus provided by Kelly, who seems rather unconcerned about action as a category of human functioning separate from mentation. This is a serious limitation for some personologists who believe that if Kelly were to elaborate his theory to give action a more important status, the purity of the approach, with its singular concern with anticipation as the core tendency, would be lost. Seeing this purity as a drawback, Bruner (1956) asks if it is really true that the attempt to avoid the disruptive surprise associated with inaccurate prediction is the only force directing life. In specific criticism of the maintenance and expansion of the construct system as a whole as the only basis for decisions, Bruner says, "I rather suspect that when some people get angry or inspired or in love, they couldn't care less about their 'system as a whole.'" Later in the same book review, Bruner further criticizes Kelly's unwillingness to acknowledge that emotions have a determining influence on anticipation and actions:

> The book fails signally, I think, in dealing convincingly with the human passions. There was a strategy in Freud's choice of Moses or Michelangelo or Little Hans. If it is true that Freud was too often the victim of the dramatic instance,

it is also true that with the same coin he paid his way to an understanding of the depths and heights of *la condition humaine*. By comparison, the young men and women of Professor Kelly's clinical examples are worried about their dates, their studies, and their conformity. If Freud's clinical world is a grotesque of *fin de siècle* Vienna, Kelly's is a gloss of the post-adolescent peer group of Columbus, Ohio, who are indeed in the process of constructing their worlds. Which is more "real"? I have no idea. I wish Professor Kelly would treat more "most religious men in the most religious moments," or even just Nijinsky or Gabriel d'Annunzio.

Bruner suggests that even if many young college men and women can be well understood by assuming that they are trying to develop construct systems with which to successfully predict events, this is not necessarily true of everyone. Even if only a few people are more ruled by their passions than the Columbus college students—and certainly if the emotions have some influence for many people—Bruner's criticism needs to be taken seriously.

Kelly would probably argue that if one's constructs have emotional content (e.g., angry-happy, anxious-calm, joyous-sad), one's functioning will be governed by emotional considerations. Passionate persons are so because the constructs they have developed to deal with experience are of an emotional nature. But even such persons would be seen by Kelly as using these emotional constructs in the attempt to anticipate experience accurately by an orderly application and elaboration of their construct systems. Bruner suspects, however, that persons in the grips of passions may abandon their construct systems and their interest in accurately anticipating experience. The dispute between Kelly and Bruner is a basic one and will not be easily solved. Perhaps a step toward resolving it would involve consideration of when emotions have a disruptive effect and when a mobilizing or organizing effect.

The Change of Constructs.   In concluding discussion of Kelly's position, I wish to focus on how constructs change. Some points raised here will help you gain more comprehensive understanding of the position and may also make some of my interpretations to this point more convincing.

Essentially, constructs change when they lead to anticipations that turn out to be inaccurate. For Kelly, the major task of life is to predict events accurately. Constructs are the bases on which anticipation and action occur. It follows from this that constructs are useful only when they permit accurate prediction of events. When they do not, constructs are changed and the new predictions are then tested. Thus, a person's construct system represents the results up to that time of a process of rational trial and error in the development of what amounts to a theory of the world of experience. It is the emphasis on congruence between this theory as a predictive system and the real world of events that puts Kelly's position in the consistency mold.

When there is lack of consistency—in other words, when expectations are not confirmed by events—the person experiences *anxiety*. Kelly's (1955, p. 495) definition of anxiety as "the awareness that the events with which one is confronted lie outside the range of convenience of his construct system" is unusual in personology. In this definition, the content of expectations and events is really irrelevant to the arousal of anxiety. It is the lack of fit between expectations and events—inconsistency—that leads to the uncomfortable feeling we know as anxiety.

You should not imagine, as some serious students of construct theory have done (e.g., Sechrest, 1963), that Kelly sees anxiety as the result of only significant or large discrepancies between events and anticipations. Kelly (1955), in quotes such as the following, clearly establishes that any and all inaccuracies of prediction, no matter how small or seemingly unimportant, precipitate anxiety:

> From the standpoint of the psychology of personal constructs, anxiety, per se, is not to be classified as either good or bad. It represents the awareness that one's construction system does not apply to the events at hand. It is, therefore, a preconsideration for making revisions . . . . Our definition of anxiety also covers the little confusions and puzzles of everyday living. The sum of a column of numbers does not check. Anxiety! We add it up again, it still does not check. More anxiety! We add it up another way. Good adjustment. Ah, there was our error! (pp. 498–499)

It is statements such as this that led Bruner (1956) to characterize Kelly's core tendency as the avoidance of disruptive surprises. It is amply clear that with Kelly we are dealing with a tension reduction view. Anxiety is a tension state, and it must be minimized. Note that the anxiety of disconfirmation of expectations is the springboard for construct system change. Even if the anticipation expresses the adventurous form of the elaborative choice, anxiety will result as long as the ensuing events differ from those anticipated.

While Kelly's emphasis on the discomfort of unexpected events makes sense on the surface, consider its implications further. There is little in the theory that would help us gain understanding of boredom, which clearly is also a state of discomfort. How humdrum life would be if the goal involved in Kelly's core tendency of personality were actually achieved!

Oddly, Kelly does seem to recognize that complete anticipational accuracy—the aim of his core tendency—would involve unpleasant boredom. He suggests that persons will like best areas of experience that are complicated enough to yield small discrepancies between anticipations and occurrences but are basically predictable enough not to cause whole construct systems to be called into question (Kelly, 1955, p. 735). Such areas of experience, he intimates, will stimulate adventurous rather than conservative choices. However sensible this position may seem from a descriptive point of view, it is hardly in the main thrust of a theory that so heavily emphasizes accuracy in all of one's anticipations—"the little confusions and puzzles of everyday living" as well as the large crises.

Construct system change is clearly based on the discrepancy between anticipation and occurrence. Anticipatory error leads to anxiety, which is uncomfortable enough to precipitate construct system change and, hence, to cause new anticipations to be tested for their accuracy. There are no immutable instincts, defenses, or unconscious determinants of functioning to interfere with the trial-and-error process whereby one tries to see the world accurately. The only aspects of the theory that could interfere with the straightforwardness of the trial-and-error process are guilt and hostility, and they stand out like sore thumbs amidst the rest. *Hostility,* according to Kelly (1955, p. 533), is the "continued effort to extort validational evidence in favor of a type of social prediction which has already been recognized as a failure." *Guilt* is defined as "the awareness of dislodgement of the self from one's core role structure"(Kelly, 1955, p. 533). These two concepts are unnatural to the theory not because it is particularly difficult to see the meaning intended but because there is no additional theoretical structure within which to embed them. They are swimming upstream, as it were, against the current formed by an otherwise consistent theoretical structure in which constructs are readily changed when they do not permit accurate anticipation. Nowhere in the theory aside from the notion of hostility is there any way of expecting that the person will maintain a construct in the face of evidence of its invalidity. And nowhere in the theory aside from the notion of guilt is there any particular emphasis on the self (which for Kelly is just another construct) as having a status somehow independent of the construct system. It is as if in these two notions Kelly were making concessions to ways of thinking about humans that are more natural to other theories that adopt a model of living as an irrational and defensive process. Despite what I have just said here, it is interesting to note that the concepts of hostility and self have captured the interest of some personologists (e.g., Bannister & Fransella, 1971) influenced by Kelly.

Kelly and Festinger.   Leon Festinger and a number of other social psychologists have developed a consistency position closely related to Kelly's. But as Festinger is concerned mainly with social psychological phenomena such as attitude change, his views will not be considered in any detail here. The basic principle of Festinger's (1958) position is that *whenever cognitive dissonance exists, the person will employ procedures for reducing it.* This position, like Kelly's, takes *cognitions* to be the elements relevant to consistency. In Festinger's position, cognitions can be beliefs, attitudes, ideas, or perceptions. For example, a state of inconsistency or dissonance might exist when the idea of yourself as a fair person is confronted with the perception of yourself as acting in a discriminatory fashion. While many dissonances will involve the ethical domain, this need not be so. Indeed, any expectation that is disconfirmed by one's perception of events constitutes dissonance, regardless of whether the expectation and perception involve you, someone else, or the inanimate world. Kelly and Festinger agree on the consequences of dissonance or disconfirmed expectations as anxiety, or at least some generalized emotional discomfort and tension, that serves as the mainspring for change aimed at avoiding that which caused the tension. But here there is an important difference in emphasis between the positions of Festinger and Kelly.

You will recall that Kelly emphasizes a rational procedure of trial and error in changing constructs so that they eventually provide an accurate basis for predicting events. In contrast, Festinger's emphasis is not so exclusively on rationality and on fitting cognition to the actual dimensions of a real world of events. Instead, Festinger contends that the person will change one or the other of the cognitions involved in the dissonance, or the nature of the relationship between them, without regard for the niceties of the real world. According to Festinger, people are as likely to distort reality as anything else in their attempt to avoid dissonance. In this emphasis on the irrational, Festinger is much closer to Freud than to Kelly. For Freud, you will recall, defenses are procedures whereby reality is distorted so that anxiety over conflict will not be felt. If there is a difference between Freud and Festinger in techniques for avoiding anxiety, it is that the content of conflict for Freud is invariably sexual and moral, whereas Festinger casts his net more widely than this. Some other personologists, such as Rogers, who also have use for a notion of defense as a distortion of reality but do not especially restrict the content of underlying conflict, may therefore come even closer than Freud to Festinger.

An example may help to dramatize the flavor of irrationality in Festinger's version of the consistency model. Suppose you believe that a man whom you respect and love very much is actually immortal—a god. This is one cognition. But suppose also that you see him die what is clearly a mortal's death on the cross. This second cognition is dissonant with the first and precipitates anxiety. The anxiety results not because you lost a loved one but because you are in turmoil as to what to believe. Therefore, in order to remove the anxiety you have to decrease the dissonance. You may well do this by developing a third cognition that says that he did not really die but simply left earthly life. Armed with this belief, you even have the basis for rejoicing. And, in order to protect yourself from the possibility of anxiety in the future—for, after all, the perception of the death on the cross is rather vivid—you proselytize. If you can convince others of your new, dissonance-reducing belief, you can believe it more unequivocally yourself. Kelly's position would have been in agreement with this example until the point of dissonance reduction, at which he would be more likely to predict change in the original belief of immortality as the most realistic procedure.

Festinger has developed his theory for the purpose of understanding attitude change rather than personality. It is understandable, therefore, that he offers little that could clarify core characteristics and peripheral aspects of personality. For this reason, we need go no further into his point of view. It will suffice to record the substantial agreement in basic assumptions between Kelly and Festinger. In Festinger's position, as in Kelly's, we find a point of view within which one would not emphasize boredom as a significantly unpleasant human experience.

McClelland's Position

David C. McClelland (born in New York City, 1917) received a Ph.D. in psychology from Yale University in 1941. The son of a Protestant minister who later became a college president, McClelland has spent his career teaching and doing research on personality in university settings. He showed his leadership capacity and interest in public service by serving as chair of the Department of Psychology at Wesleyan University and as deputy director of the Behavioral Sciences Division of the Ford Foundation. Following these posts, he became head of the Center for Research in Personality and then chair of the Department of Social Relations at Harvard University. Deeply influenced by Murray and by the broad social science emphasis at Harvard, McClelland spent the early part of his career developing and testing his theory of personality and recently has been investigating its social applications in underdeveloped societies throughout the world. Now at the Center for Applied Social Science at Boston University, he is investigating the physiological implications of various psychological motives.

For McClelland, as for Kelly and Festinger, the consistency or discrepancy between expectations and events is basic to the understanding of behavior. But whereas Kelly and Festinger find all inconsistency to result in unpleasant feelings and avoidance, McClelland considers this outcome to occur only when the degree of inconsistency is large. For him, small discrepancies between expectations and events are more properly considered as resulting in pleasant feelings and approach behavior. His position, a variant of the consistency model, is that the core tendency of personality is *to minimize large discrepancies between expectation and occurrence while maximizing small discrepancies*.

In finding an intuitive basis in your own experience for understanding McClelland's position, you would do well to think of times of uncertainty and times of boredom. In all of our lives, there are times when our sheer inability to determine what will happen next and related inability to know clearly what is happening now are a source of threat and discomfort. Also, there are times when everything is so predictable and clear that we wish something novel and unpredictable would happen. The introspective fact that people sometimes want to increase predictability and sometimes decrease it was the starting point for McClelland's theorizing. As indicated in the core tendency, he believes that people crave small degrees of unpredictability and avoid large degrees of it. I can imagine that at least for some of you, the introspective evidence for this position is not readily available. Because of this, it will be useful now to go on to a more rational analysis of the position, returning later to a point of correspondence between reason and intuition.

The Core Characteristics Associated with the Core Tendency. For McClelland (McClelland, Atkinson, Clark, & Lowell, 1953), certain core characteristics are present at birth and others develop through learning. The innate core characteristics underlie the core tendency, while the learned ones do not. But let me be less abstract. By virtue of being born, the person has the ability to experience pleasant feelings, or *positive affect,* and unpleasant feelings, or *negative affect.* McClelland is not concerned with distinctions between particular emotions, such as love and joy in the positive class or anger and fear in the negative class. The two broad classes suffice for his theoretical purposes, and although he does not say so, one forms the impression that he may even assume that the innate apparatus for the experience of affect is simple and undifferentiated enough to permit only two affective states, which though amorphous and imprecise, clearly differ as to whether they are pleasant or unpleasant. Another assumption, closely related to that of an innate basis for experiencing positive and negative affect, is that people find the latter affective state obnoxious enough to avoid and the former attractive enough to seek. There is nothing, however, in the innate tendency to avoid negative affect and seek positive affect to explain the particular techniques for avoiding and seeking what we may observe in a person. These techniques are a matter of learning.

Having assumed an innate basis for feeling positive and negative affect, McClelland needs to tell us what it is that can trigger one reaction versus the other. As his core tendency would indicate, he gives this role to the match between expectancies and occurrences. An *expectancy* is a cognitive unit, or thought, that refers to what you imagine will be the content and timing of events in the future. Clearly the expectancy is similar to the construct of Kelly and the cognition of Festinger. McClelland recognizes, as do they, events as real aspects of the world, though they must be appreciated by persons in order to have any significance for their living. Like Kelly and Festinger, McClelland assumes that expectancies are formed on the basis of past experience and that different people may well form different expectancies owing to peculiarities of their background. McClelland suggests that the mechanism whereby expectancies are learned is contiguity. In other words, if the events in a given set occur in the same sequence often enough, you will abstract from your experience the expectation that the same thing will happen in the future. So whenever you encounter the first of this series of events, you will have a definite idea of what is coming next. For McClelland, there need be no reward at the end of the series, such as the proverbial pot at the end of the rainbow, in order for you to learn the sequence. You learn it simply because it is there and is repeated in your experience a sufficient number of times. This idea of learning without reinforcement is similar in emphasis to Kelly, though for both theorists it is important to know whether an expectancy that is learned turns out to be accurate in order to understand when it is retained, discarded, or changed.

In this regard, we have seen that for Kelly any degree of inaccuracy of expectation leads to anxiety and pressure to discard and change the expectation. Not so for McClelland. Only large discrepancies between expectation and occurrence have those consequences. In contrast, small discrepancies lead to positive affect and the retaining of the expectation. It is this emphasis that makes McClelland's approach a variant of the consistency model.

McClelland's emphasis on quantifying the match or mismatch between expectation and event, though intriguing, raises the question of the manner in which quantification is to be done, for a number of possibilities present themselves. McClelland himself is apparently undecided—even concerning the demarcation point between large and small discrepancies—undoubtedly out of a sense of the complexity of the problem. Perhaps the most obvious way of quantifying the agreement between expectation and occurrence would be to determine the number of elements or parts of the expectation, the number of elements or parts of the corresponding event, and then calculate the proportion of elements that agreed. This technique, for all its ponderousness, would be useful for at least fairly complex expectancies. Expectancies referring to propositional speech would be good examples. The sentence "A rose is a rose is a rose" is striking because it is an occurrence discrepant from expectations concerning sequence of types of words in intelligible speech. In attempting to identify elements for purposes of quantifying degree of discrepancy, one might use parts of speech as elements.

But here we encounter a vexing problem. Not all parts of speech are equally important—indeed, in almost all instances of naturally occurring sequences of events, some of the events will be more significant to the person than others. Perhaps, then, another and more meaningful way to quantify the degree of discrepancy between expectation and occurrence is to order elements of expectation and occurrence by their importance. One could then say that the greater the importance of the event inaccurately predicted, the larger the discrepancy between expectation and occurrence.

I am afraid we will not be able to solve the problem of quantification here. The problem is important and has not been overcome as yet. A theory that cannot tell you how to distinguish between small and large discrepancies when they supposedly have drastically different effects is severely handicapped in its ability to provide believable explanations of phenomena. But even so, it is not without utility, as I will show in the next chapter. For the moment, I have tried to alert you to the value of attempts to develop the theory in such fashion that it can, at some future time, provide consistent, workable bases for quantification.

Influence of the Core Tendency on Personality Development. McClelland's theory differs in two important ways from the consistency positions already considered. The first—the emphasis on moderate rather than total anticipational accuracy as the ultimate goal of living—has already been mentioned. The second is the emphasis McClelland puts on action in addition to the more purely cognitive-affective considerations of consistency. These two emphases in McClelland's thinking are usefully considered together in attempting to understand the way in which expression of the core tendency leads to personality development.

I have already indicated that positions such as Kelly's cannot logically consider boredom to be an important factor in life. McClelland has made moderate anticipational accuracy the ideal because of the belief that complete accuracy over any significant period of time would be too monotonous and boring for comfort. If you consider boredom to be an unpleasant state, you have an intuitive basis for understanding McClelland's position, however strange it may sound initially. In sum, McClelland's position grants a hardiness and vivacity to the human that is not really found in other consistency positions. For McClelland, as for other consistency theorists, the greater the discrepancy between expectation and occurrence, the more intense is the organismic tension. But his position is not a simple tension reduction view, as are the others. Instead, McClelland considers the moderate tension associated with moderate anticipational inaccuracy to be ideal. Not only too much but too little tension is avoided. This is the first consistency position we have encountered that explicitly takes this stance.

Of all the consistency positions, McClelland's is the most oriented toward explaining action. Kelly's theory considers actions as mere extensions of anticipations. While this is perhaps understandable in a position that stresses total accuracy of prediction as the ultimate goal of life, there is still a critical problem created by the collapse of the distinction between anticipation and action, because then it is no longer logically possible to consider action strategies aimed at providing tests of anticipations.

The difference of opinion hinges on the fact that while Kelly makes the achievement of total accuracy the real aim of life, McClelland considers accuracy of anticipation as the basis for the development of personality characteristics that are not particularly in the service of accurate anticipation. For example, in Kelly's theory constructs, which are the elements of personality, are formed, used, and changed for the single purpose of ensuring better and better prediction. In McClelland's theory, the expectation is only one element of personality. The other major element is the *motive* (McClelland, 1951). But while the nature and content of motives certainly reflect the person's history of anticipational accuracy and inaccuracy, the purpose of motives is not primarily to make correct predictions. Motives are influencers of action in the direction of specific goals, but they have little direct relationship to considerations of accuracy.

This point will become clearer if I trace for you the manner in which expression of the core tendency leads to the development of motives. Remember that the positive affect associated with moderate inaccuracy and the negative affect associated with great inaccuracy lead, respectively, to approach and avoidance actions. When persons have experienced a small discrepancy between expectation and occurrence, they bring themselves closer to the area of experience involved; if the discrepancy is large, they avoid it. Let us consider two common areas of experience: affiliation with people and achievement in work.

Suppose that a child's most frequent experience in the affiliative domain is to have its expectations greatly violated because of parents who are complex, inconsistent, and unpredictable. Assume that the child is young enough to be impressionable and unable to choose associates easily. Its predominant affective tone in interpersonal relationships will be unpleasant. If this condition goes on for any length of time, the child will develop an enduring orientation (or motive) to avoid people. Every time the possibility of interaction arises, the memory of painful emotional consequences will also arise, leading the child to avoid others. But what you must see is that the goal of the motive is avoidance of interaction, not the achievement of total accuracy of prediction!

Now consider the area of work achievement. Suppose our youngster's most frequent experience in this area is that of having expectations violated only slightly by occurrences. The child's expectations will not be so greatly disconfirmed as to cause discouragement and not so completely accurate as to bring boredom and indifference. Instead, the youngster will come to regard working as a source of mild and pleasant surprises. This kind of accumulation of experience can be brought about by parents (McClelland *et al.* 1953, p. 62) who watch the child carefully enough to know when it has mastered some task it is working on and who are sensible enough to then give it another task that is a little but not completely outside of its capabilities. Under such conditions, the youngster will learn an enduring orientation (or motive) to strive for success (or achievement) in work. Again the goal of the motive is to approach or seek work, not to try for total accuracy of prediction!

I should point out that if the parents in the affiliation example were more like the parents in the work example, a motive to approach interaction would have been learned. Similarly, if the parents in the work example were more like those in the affiliation example, a motive to avoid work would result. In every area of experience an approach motive and an avoidance motive are possible, according to McClelland. But we will pursue this further in Chapter 9, as motives are actually peripheral characteristics of personality in his thinking, their main usefulness being in understanding individual differences.

In closing, I should make it clear that the absence of reference to the concept of defense in this section is not an oversight. Like Kelly's position, McClelland's gives no role to this concept. Even avoidance actions and motives are not, strictly speaking, defensive in the sense of debarring mental content from awareness.

CONSISTENCY MODEL: ACTIVATION VERSION

The cognitive dissonance version of the consistency model considers the match or mismatch among cognitive elements, typically expectations and perceptions of events. In contrast, the version of the consistency model to be discussed here considers the match or mismatch between customary and actual levels of activation or tension. As in all consistency positions, content is relatively unimportant. The theory of Fiske and Maddi is virtually the only activation position that has relevance for personality.

Fiske and Maddi's Position

Donald W. Fiske (born in Massachusetts, 1916), after an early education at Harvard, received his Ph.D. in psychology from the University of Michigan in 1948. In a career of teaching and research in university settings, his major interests have been measurement of personality variables and understanding the conditions under which human behavior shows variability. At Harvard and in the Office of Strategic Services during World War II, Fiske came under the influence of Murray, Allport, and White. Fiske has been president of the Midwestern Psychological Association and chair of the Department of Psychology at the University of Chicago.

Salvatore R. Maddi (born in New York City, 1933), received his Ph.D. in psychology from Harvard in 1960. During his time at Harvard, he was fortunate enough to have as teachers Allport, Bakan, McClelland, Murray, and White. In a career emphasizing teaching and research in the university setting, Maddi's predominant interests have been in the need for variety, personality change, creativity, and stress-related disorders. His views on existential psychology, his other theoretical commitment, were covered in Chapter 4. Maddi's collaboration with Fiske began in 1960 and over the years produced the position described here. Maddi has been director of the Clinical Training Program and the Undergraduate Psychology Program in the Department of Psychology at the University of Chicago and Director of the Program in Social Ecology at the University of California, Irvine.

Activation theory is a contemporary development in psychology that has arisen from several subfields of the discipline. Understandably enough given its complexity, the personality field has been among the last and least affected by activation theorizing. But Fiske and Maddi (1961; Maddi & Propst, 1971) offer a version of activation theory that is not only more systematic and complete than most but also is quite relevant to personality. In the cognitive dissonance version of consistency theory, the emphasis is on the discrepancy or match between two cognitive elements, usually an expectation or belief on the one hand and a perception of some event on the other. In the activation theory offered by Fiske and Maddi, discrepancy is also the major determinant of behavior. However, the discrepancy is not between two cognitive elements but between the level of activation to which persons are accustomed and the level of activation they actually have at a given moment. Discrepancies between the customary and actual levels of activation always produce behavior whose aim is to reduce them. Therefore, Fiske and Maddi's position exemplifies the pure consistency model.

Let me plunge into discussion of the position by stating its core tendency, which is that *persons will attempt to maintain the level of activation to which they are accustomed (that is characteristic of them)*. To understand the meaning of this core tendency, recognize that *activation* refers to your level of excitement, or alertness, or energy. Try to remember times when what was going on excited you more or less than usual or required more or less alertness and energy than customary. If you found the situation either too exciting or too dull and tried to do something about it, or found the alertness and energy demands too great or too slight and tried to do something about them, you have within yourself a basis for intuitive understanding of the core tendency offered by Fiske and Maddi. Actually, some of you may have difficulty recognizing the relevance of your own experience without additional, detailed consideration of the position. I think this is because the position is rather new and unfamiliar and because the psychological import of the concept of activation is not immediately apparent. Let us hasten, therefore, to more detailed study of the position.

Customary and Actual Levels of Activation. According to Fiske and Maddi (1961, p. 14), activation is a neuropsychological concept, referring on the psychological side to the common core of meaning in such terms as alertness, attentiveness, tension, and subjective excitement and on the neural side to the state of excitation in a postulated center of the brain. It is clear that on the psychological side, Fiske and Maddi are concerned with a general quality of organismic excitation similar to what so many other theorists we have considered refer to as tension. Fiske and Maddi attempt to make this view more plausible by exploring its neural substrate. On the neural side, they suggest that the reticular formation, a large subcortical area of the brain, is the focus of activation. In this, they are following much precedent (e.g., Jasper, 1958; O'Leary & Coben, 1958; Samuels, 1959) and attempting to integrate psychological and physiological levels of theorizing.

Having offered a rough definition of activation, Fiske and Maddi turn to the determinants of this state of excitation. They postulate three dimensions and three sources of stimulation, subsuming all these activation-influencing characteristics under the term *impact*. The three dimensions of stimulation are intensity, meaningfulness, and variation. *Intensity,* defined in terms of physical energy, is an obvious attribute of stimulation. A loud noise is more intense than a soft noise. *Meaningfulness* requires more clarification. Generally speaking, any stimulus, in order to be recognized as such, has to have meaning. However, Fiske and Maddi use meaningfulness in a more restricted sense. They refer primarily to the significance of a stimulus for the experiencing organism. For example, the word "vase" has less meaningfulness for most people than do the words "fire" or "love." In considering *variation,* Fiske and Maddi make a number of points. First, variation refers to a state in which the current stimulus differs from that which preceded it—differs in either intensity, meaningfulness, or both. So one aspect is *change.* Another aspect of variation is *novelty,* or the state in which the current stimulus is unusual—infrequent in the person's total experience—regardless of how much it differs from the stimulus immediately preceding it. The final aspect of variation is *unexpectedness,* or the state in which the current stimulus deviates from what the person had come to expect regardless of whether it constitutes a change or is unusual in an overall sense.

Talking about the dimensions of stimulation that can influence activation prompts consideration of the sources of stimulation, if for no other reason than completeness. The three sources stipulated by Fiske and Maddi are exteroceptive, interoceptive, and cortical. *Exteroceptive* stimulation involves chemical, electrical, or mechanical excitation of the sense organs that are sensitive to events in the external world. In contrast, *interoceptive* stimulation refers to such excitation of the sense organs that are sensitive to events within the body.

These two sources of stimulation are already well known and require no justification. But it is unusual to consider *cortical* stimulation. Most psychologists who consider physiological events in the cortex tend to see them as reflecting stimulation from other places in the body or from the outside world. What Fiske and Maddi are suggesting is that the cortex itself be considered one of the actual sources of stimulation. They are on logically sound ground in so doing, as the brain locus of activation is considered to be a subcortical center. That they are possibly on sound anatomical and physiological ground is suggested by the recent discovery that the cortex not only receives but sends nerve fibers to the reticular formation, which, as you will recall, is the implicated subcortical center. Hebb (1955) has suggested that the fibers sent to the reticular formation by the cortex may constitute the physiological substrate for understanding "the immediate drive properties of cognitive processes."

Fiske and Maddi make activation level a direct function of impact. Impact is, in turn, some direct function of the moment-to-moment intensity, meaningfulness, and variation of stimulation from interoceptive, exteroceptive, and cortical sources. Activation, impact, and the dimensions and sources of impact, being common to all persons, are core characteristics of personality.

Thus far, the theorizing of Fiske and Maddi may seem too complex and removed from phenomena of psychological significance to be useful to the personologist. But bear with me, for the psychological significance of their position will soon emerge. As for complexity, you should recognize the possibility that the kind of completeness Fiske and Maddi aim for may not only require such complexity but may be quite useful in fostering understanding. Perhaps you have noticed, for example, that the discrepancy between expectation and occurrence stressed by McClelland and Kelly is represented as merely one aspect of variation by Fiske and Maddi. The other theorists make unexpectedness the basic determinant of tension or anxiety, terms that differ little in meaning from activation as used by Fiske and Maddi. But once you are introduced to Fiske and Maddi's broad definition of stimulus characteristics producing impact, you are likely to begin wondering whether the other theorists have not oversimplified their thinking concerning the determinants of tension.

Having considered *actual level of activation,* which is given at any moment in time by the total impact of stimulation, we can turn to the *customary level of activation.* Fiske and Maddi assume that the levels of activation a person experiences over the course of many days tend to be fairly similar. After all, the regularities and continuities of living should result in day-to-day similarities in the intensity, meaningfulness, and variation of stimulation from the various sources. Over time, the person should come to experience a particular level of activation as normal, that is, usual for a particular part of the day. These customary levels of activation can be roughly measured by averaging the actual activation curves for a person over a period of some days. Such measurement was performed by Kleitman (1939), who found a regularity called the *cycle of existence,* with a single major rise and fall during the waking period. After waking, higher organisms typically show an increasing degree of alertness, then a relatively long period with a gradual rise and later a gradual decline and, finally, a sharper decline toward drowsiness and return to the sleeping state. A number of physiological variables, such as heart rate and body temperature, follow the same course (Kleitman & Ramsaroop, 1948; Sidis, 1908). Fiske and Maddi assume that the curve described as the cycle of existence is the curve of customary level of activation. Whatever differences in shape the customary level of activation may take from person to person, everyone possesses it. Thus, it is a core characteristic of personality, as is the previously discussed actual level of activation.

Once one has postulated an actual and a customary level of activation, it is almost natural to consider the match or mismatch between them to be important. And this is just what Fiske and Maddi do. Their core tendency refers to the person's attempt to maintain actual activation at the level customary for that time of the day. If actual activation deviates from customary level, *impact-modifying behavior* is instituted. Two kinds of deviation are possible. When actual activation level is above that which is customary, *impact-decreasing behavior* occurs; when actual activation level is below that which is customary, *impact-increasing behavior* results. Note that impact-decreasing behavior must involve attempts to decrease the intensity, meaningfulness, or variation of stimulation from interoceptive, exteroceptive, or cortical sources and that impact-increasing behavior does the opposite.

Fiske and Maddi are classed as consistency theorists because they consider the overall directionality of living to be the search for a match between actual and customary levels of activation. In clarifying why people show the core tendency, Fiske and Maddi (1961) assume that the coincidence of actual and customary levels of activation is experienced as a state of well-being, whereas discrepancies between them lead to increasing degrees of negative affect the larger they get. It is to avoid the discomfort of negative affect that people attempt to reduce discrepancies between actual and customary levels of activation. Success in this attempt is experienced as positive affect.

Fiske and Maddi's theory is a pure consistency position, because the ideal state is a complete absence of discrepancy between actual and customary levels of activation. There is no notion, as in McClelland's variant position, that a small degree of discrepancy is a positive thing. But the idea that positions such as Kelly's are limited because they do not give importance to avoidance of boredom is incorporated by Fiske and Maddi. They theorize that the customary level of activation can be undershot as well as overshot by actual activation. When it is undershot, the person will actively seek out stimulation of greater variation, meaningfulness, and intensity. In part, this means he or she will seek out unexpected events. This property of Fiske and Maddi's position is associated with two others that deserve mention. The first is that Fiske and Maddi do not make tension reduction the aim of all functioning, as do the other pure consistency theorists. Although theirs is a pure consistency position, Fiske and Maddi agree with McClelland that some of the person's functioning aims to reduce tension or activation whereas some aims to increase it. They also assume that everyday life situations involve some variation (change, novelty, unexpectedness) as well as some intensity and meaningfulness. In other words, some more than minimal degree of variation is assumed to be normal. This assumption is implicit in the notion that the customary level of activation is indeed high enough at all times during the day that it can be undershot by the actual level of activation. To Fiske and Maddi, the assumption in other pure consistency positions that an absence of unexpectedness is the ideal situation seems inconsistent with everyday life. Fiske and Maddi agree with McClelland that the human being would be bored in a situation of total certainty and predictability because its impact would be too low to produce activation that came up to customary levels.

Fiske and Maddi's theory is a good example of what is called a *homeostatic position*. In other words, whenever there is a deviation from some type of norm—in this case, customary level of activation—there is an attempt, which gets stronger the greater the deviation, to return to the norm. In psychology, all tension reduction theories tend to be considered homeostatic. Thus, the theories of Freud, Angyal, Bakan, Rank, Kelly, and Festinger are considered homeostatic positions, although it strikes me that these theories are really only half of the homeostatic model because the norm they assume is a minimum state. This means that the norm can only be exceeded and not undershot because it is a state of least excitation. Fiske and Maddi's theory seems, by comparison with the others, a true homeostatic position in that the norm is some quantity greater than minimum and less than maximum. Once a theory such as Fiske and Maddi's is established, the partial inapplicability to the other theories of the concept of homeostasis becomes apparent.

Many concepts have been mentioned in the preceding pages, and perhaps it would be well to close this subsection by summarizing them in the terminology of the core of personality. The tendency of persons to maintain the level of activation that is characteristic or customary for them is the core tendency of personality. There are no differences across people in this tendency, which infuses all of living. There are a number of core characteristics of personality associated with this core tendency. They are actual level of activation, customary level of activation, discrepancy between the two, impact-increasing behavior, and impact-decreasing behavior. These concepts bear the same invariant relationships to one another in all people. To be sure, there are many sources of individual differences—customary levels of activation may vary, for example, and there may be many different strategies for increasing or decreasing impact—but these are matters for discussion in Chapter 9 on the periphery of personality.

Formation of the Characteristic Curve of Activation. Fiske and Maddi do not consider the customary curve of activation to be present at birth; rather, it is probably formed out of experience. To be sure, they suggest the possibility that genetic considerations, presently not well understood, may predispose the person to a customary curve of activation having a particular shape and height. But the accumulated experience of particular levels of activation at specific times of the day is considered the major formative influence on the characteristic curve of activation. Thus, the first important influence of the environment for the person is as the major determinant of the characteristic curve of activation. This determination takes place sometime during childhood, though Fiske and Maddi are quite vague on this. In a way their vagueness is not very surprising, for we have seen that the consistency model gives little attention to the content of experience and of inherent nature. In Kelly and McClelland, it is the fact of discrepancy between expectation and occurrence, not the content of the discrepancy, that influences behavior. For Fiske and Maddi, it is the impact of early stimulation, not its content, that has a formative influence. Once you de-emphasize the importance of stimulus content and of inherent nature, you have little logical impetus to develop elaborate theories of stages of development during which the content of one's wishes and the content of reactions from significant others are important.

But Fiske and Maddi do believe that as experience accumulates, as the stimulation patterns of successive days recur again and again, the characteristic curve of activation begins to solidify. Once set, this curve changes little under ordinary circumstances. This is because of the nature of the effects on personality and experience of the impetus to maintain activation at the characteristic level.

At this point, it is essential to distinguish between *correction* for discrepancies between actual and characteristic levels of activation that really occur and *anticipatory attempts* to ensure that such discrepancies will not occur (Maddi & Propst, 1971). I will discuss anticipatory functioning now, as it is basic to understanding why the characteristic curve of activation does not change once solidified, and defer consideration of correctional functioning until Chapter 9. As experience accumulates, the person learns certain habitual ways of functioning that help preclude large discrepancies between actual and characteristic levels of activation. These ways of influencing the impact of present and future intensity, meaningfulness, and variation of stimulation from interoceptive, exteroceptive, and cortical sources form a large part of the peripheral personality. If peripheral personality is a successful expression of core tendency, the conditions under which the characteristic curve of activation would change are not encountered. The person's range of experience and activities is selected and maintained in order to yield degrees of impact at various times during the day that result in actual levels of activation that would match characteristic levels. If anything, the longer the person lives, the more deeply entrenched will be his or her characteristic curve of activation. Only if the person were forced to be in prolonged circumstances of unusual impact levels—for example, the battlefield—would there be conditions of stimulation likely to shift the characteristic curve of activation.

Anticipational and Correctional Attempts to Maintain Consistency.   It may seem to you that Fiske and Maddi, like Freud, consider personality as remaining essentially static after childhood, but this is not the case. Although the customary curve of activation is believed to remain roughly the same under ordinary circumstances, behavior and personality processes expressing the anticipatory function of the core tendency must actually change in order for this curve to remain steady. This may seem paradoxical, but it is really very simple and understandable. One function of the anticipatory processes is to ensure that future levels of activation will not fall below characteristic ones. However, any stimulation, regardless of its initial effect, will lose impact as it is prolonged. We adapt to stimulation that has appreciable duration. A sound that initially seems loud becomes overlooked if it continues long enough. Something initially meaningful becomes ordinary as time goes on. Variation is especially short-lived, for any novel or unexpected stimulus loses so much impact after a while that it may become boring. A great deal of research testifies to the conclusion that the initial impact of stimulation decreases as its experience is prolonged (see Fiske & Maddi, 1961).

What this means is that as persons live longer and longer, they must continually shift their anticipatory strategies for ensuring that future levels of activation will not be too low for comfort. In action, persons must constantly broaden their range of activities and interests. In thought and feeling, they must become more and more subtle and differentiated in order to increase the impact of future stimulation. A Jackson Pollack painting might have a low level of impact for you because it seems nothing more than a smear of colors, repetitive at best. But if you increase the subtlety of your cognitive and affective processes, you will be much more sensitive to the same painting on seeing it in the future. Then it may have great impact, for you will perceive the many strands of paint built up layer upon layer and the subtle differences among various parts of the canvas. Whether or not we agree on Jackson Pollack, I think you can see what is meant by ever increasing cognitive and emotional differentiation as a basis for ensuring that activation will not fall too low in the future. To try to see the universe in a grain of sand is to make a cognitive, affective elaboration of experience in order to offset its natural tendency to lose impact when prolonged or reexperienced.

But in order to properly maintain characteristic activation, the person must also develop anticipatory strategies to ensure that future impact will not be higher than the characteristic level. This is especially necessary in order to balance off the possible, though unintended side effects of anticipatory attempts to keep activation from falling below the characteristic level. When you try to ensure this by becoming more cognitively, affectively, and actionally differentiated, you cannot precisely predict where the thing will end. If you are forever intensifying your search for new and more meaningful and intense experiences, you are increasing the likelihood of precipitating a crisis in which your ability to keep what happens to you within manageable limits will be threatened. You might unwittingly precipitate a state of impact so great as to result in an uncomfortably high level of activation. To be sure, if this were to happen, then according to the theory you would scramble to correct the high level of activation. But it is inefficient to wait until activation is already too high before acting, just as it is inefficient to rely on correction of levels of activation that are already too low.

Progressively greater cognitive, affective, and actional differentiation is the anticipatory technique for keeping up activation, but what is the technique for keeping activation low enough? Maddi and Propst (1963) indicate that the strategy for ensuring that future levels of activation will not be too high is the progressive increase in principles and techniques for integrating the elements of cognition, affect, and action differentiated in order to ensure that activation will not be too low. The essence of integration is the organization of the differentiated elements into broad categories of function or significance. Integrative processes permit you to see how some experience is similar in meaning and intensity to other experiences, regardless of how it may differ in terms of the more concrete analysis expressive of differentiation processes. There is no conflict between the processes of differentiation and integration. No matter how sensitive you become to our Jackson Pollack painting on the basis of differentiation processes, you can also place it in the overall scheme of his work, the work of contemporaries, and the history of art through exercise of integrative processes. Integrative processes function to ensure that activation levels experienced in the future will not be wildly high without blanketing out the sensitivity of experiencing needed to avoid drastically low activation levels.

Actually, as you can tell, the picture of personality offered is one in which there is continual change through the life span, this change being in the service of ensuring a minimum of discrepancy between actual and customary levels of activation. The change involves progressively greater differentiation and integration, or what we have encountered before as psychological growth. With varying emphasis, this notion appears in actualization and perfection versions of the fulfillment model. It is not particularly characteristic of psychosocial conflict theories, but it does play some role in intrapsychic conflict theories. Fiske and Maddi's position seems advantageous, because it explains psychological growth rather than simply assuming it.

Now it is possible to return to correctional rather than anticipatory processes in order to understand their special significance. First, it is obvious that a correction for discrepancy between actual and characteristic levels of activation is necessary only when anticipatory processes have failed. For the adult, correctional attempts have the quality of emergency maneuvers (Maddi & Propst, 1971). Simply put, Maddi and Propst believe that impact-decreasing behavior aimed at reducing an actual level of activation that is already higher than characteristic operates to distort reality in the sense of screening out stimuli. They see impact-increasing behavior aimed at augmenting an actual level of activation that is already lower than characteristic to be equally distorting of reality but to involve the kind of distortion that adds something to the stimulation that is not really there. These sensitizing and desensitizing aspects of correctional behavior come close to one aspect of the traditional meaning of *defense*. But we must be careful to recognize that Maddi and Propst do not mean to imply the active debarring from awareness of impulses and wishes that form a real but dangerous part of the person. They merely assume a mechanism for exaggerating or underestimating the real impact of stimulation. In this, they come closer than any other consistency theorists to emphasizing a concept of defense.

In summary, Fiske and Maddi's position is a consistency theory that focuses on discrepancy between actual and customary activation rather than accuracy of prediction. As worded, it is broad enough to subsume other consistency positions having this latter focus. Fiske and Maddi conceptualize behavior and personality as oriented partly toward tension reduction and partly toward tension increase. In this, their approach resembles McClelland's, though theirs is a pure rather than variant consistency position. Fiske and Maddi, like other consistency theorists, are eclectic with regard to content in that their conceptualization of humans and society includes little that is necessary and immutable. They believe that the essential features of the core of personality remain fixed but peripheral personality changes continually throughout life to satisfy the requirements of the core tendency. This continual change is in the direction of simultaneous increases in differentiation and integration, or psychological growth.

CHAPTER 6

Rational and Empirical Analyses
of Core Considerations

The previous chapters covered the theorizing of a goodly number of personologists. Yet only three basic models for personality theorizing have emerged. These models characterize the person's inmost processes in terms of conflict, fulfillment, or consistency. Of course, some variants on the models exist, and each model has two discernible versions. Further, every personologist lends his or her own special emphases and verbal nuances. Nonetheless, it is very significant that there are so few ways of conceptualizing the overall directionality and universal features of life.

In Chapters 3–5, I focused on distinguishing among the various theories that exemplify each of the three models. In this chapter, I will emphasize some conclusions about the essential nature of the models. Following that, I will pinpoint some issues regarding the core of personality raised by the similarities and differences among the models. These matters constitute the rational analysis mentioned in the title of this chapter. Then, I will conduct the empirical analysis promised in the chapter title by discussing the results of systematic research that bear on the issues. This will constitute a beginning for the arduous but necessary task of determining the strengths and weaknesses inherent in the three models.

ESSENTIAL FEATURES OF THE THREE MODELS

The Conflict Model

Everything essential to the conflict model can be understood once one grasps the idea that in this view the human is inextricably caught up in the opposition of two great forces. In the intrapsychic version of the conflict position, exemplified by the theories of Rank, Angyal, Bakan, and Jung, great forces originate within the person. Although it may not be immediately apparent, Jung's position also stresses two great forces: the individualistic, worldly, practical activities of the ego (or conscious mind) and the universal, communal, mysterious intuitions of the collective unconscious. In the psychosocial version of the conflict model, one of the forces is inherent in the person and the other is inherent in society. The theories of Freud, Murray, and the ego psychologists make this kind of conflict assumption. In all conflict theories, conflict is experienced as an uncomfortable state of tension and anxiety. The overall aim of life, therefore, is to reduce tension and anxiety as much as possible by minimizing conflict.

In all versions of the conflict model, life is, at best, a compromise. This view is inevitable once one assumes an inherent and unavoidable conflict at the core of personality. The compromise cannot take the form of erasing one of the two great forces, for both forces are inherent and basic even if one of them does not originate in the person. Therefore, psychological sickness or maladjustment is usually defined by conflict theorists as the attempt to live as if only one of the two forces existed. Such an attempt must be considered a failure, if the logic of the conflict model is to be served. In Rank's theory, excessive placation of the death fear leads to neurotic isolation, whereas excessive placation of the life fear leads to herd conformity. In the theories of Freud and Murray, unmitigated expression of instincts, the force inherent in the person, is defined as psychopathy and leads in the direction of destruction of self and others, whereas unmitigated expression of the force inherent in society, in the form of superego, leads to the excessive, unrealistic, punitive guilt and defensiveness that create neurosis. Clearly, then, the attempt to live as if there were only one rather than two great forces is unworkable.

What will work is a compromise in which balance between the opposing forces is achieved. Thus, the concrete patterns of living must always express both forces at the same time in order for the life to be effective. While it is certainly possible within the limits of the conflict model to imagine a workable compromise in which one force occasionally will gain ascendancy over the other, these occurrences must be superimposed on an underlying dynamic balance between the forces. In Rank's terms, one must minimize both the fear of life and the fear of death. Jung dignifies the achieved balance between ego and the collective unconscious with the term *selfhood*. For Freud, Murray, and the ego psychologists, the highest purpose of life is to gain a maximum degree of instinct gratification with a minimum degree of punishment and guilt. Here too we see the notion of a balancing of the two great forces, in the form of id and superego requirements. With a conflict model, the best that can be achieved in life is the compromise of balance.

But more must be said about the versions of the conflict model that assume one force to be inherent in the person and the other inherent in society. Since the forces must be opposing in order for conflict to ensue, this version usually defines the human as an individual with selfish aims, and society in terms of the corporate good. Because society is made up of other intelligent beings, the individual's selfishness can be detected and severely punished and he or she can be made to feel ashamed and guilty. This means that one of the two forces—that inherent in society—has the power to detect and thwart the other, individualistic force. But the individualistic force has no similar power. Therefore, if a compromise involving balance is to be achieved, the individualistic force must have some protection with which to offset the detecting and thwarting power of the societal force. If there were no such protection, the person would have to renounce human nature, and this would obviate a compromise.

What I am trying to show is that the logic of the psychosocial version of the conflict model readily leads to the concept of defense as a continuous, necessary process in successful living. It is defensiveness that offsets the special detecting and thwarting power of the societal force. In attempting to avoid the punishment and guilt they would suffer due to their selfish instincts, persons institute defenses that have the dual purpose of shielding them from recognition of selfishness and of encouraging instinctual expression in ways that are relatively innocuous from the standpoint of society. Freud's theory, of course, is the prime example of this kind of position. Recall that he even dubs unmitigated expression of instincts *pleasure principle* functioning and attempting to maximize instinctual gratification while minimizing punishment and guilt *reality principle* functioning.

So, whenever you encounter a conflict position in which one force is inherent in the person and the other in society, you can expect, if the position is logically consistent, that the concept of defense will be preeminent in the achievement of a compromise of balance, which is the healthiest state. The distinction in such positions between mental health and mental illness is not made in terms of whether or not defenses exist, for there are always defenses. Instead, the distinction is made in terms of whether the defenses promote the effective compromise of balance or the ineffective denial of one of the two opposing forces.

Turning for comparison to the version of conflict theory that assumes both opposing forces to be inherent in the person, we do not find the emphasis on defense found in the psychosocial version discussed above. Because both forces originate in the person, there is no special problem of one force detecting and thwarting the other. Hence, there is no logical necessity for the more vulnerable force to be supplemented by some concept that serves a protective function. It is not surprising to me that Rank, Angyal, and Bakan have not emphasized the concept of defense in their theorizing, even though one could say with some truth that their theories are not as completely developed as those of the psychosocial theorists. In this context, Jung's emphasis on eliminating the personal unconscious and accepting the collective unconscious becomes understandable. In point of fact, the intrapsychic theorists do not need a protective concept, and therefore, their view of a compromise of balance does not emphasize defensiveness.

In the psychosocial position, involving as it does such emphasis on compromise and defense, the highest or healthiest form of living is defined primarily in terms of the person's adjustment to the socially determined corporate good. Such a position inevitably involves defining the highest form of living in terms of dependability, considerateness, responsibility, generosity, morality, and conformity. Indeed, one finds this emphasis on what might be called "good citizenship" in the theories of Freud and the other psychosocial theorists. A little of this emphasis is also found in the intrapsychic theorists. That the intrapsychic version of the conflict model places less emphasis on adjustment to the pressures of society in its definition of the healthiest state is to be understood in terms of its relatively low reliance on the concept of defense coupled with its assumption that both opposing forces originate within the person.

Another concomitant of the conflict model's emphasis on compromise and defense is the view that the personality is rather completely set in its general outlines by the time childhood is over. The rest of life can be reasonably well characterized as a filling out and elaboration of the patterns established early in life. Whatever change in personality takes place during adulthood is more a matter of degree than of kind. And indeed, stability of personality is a more salient fact for conflict theorists than is personality change. Once again, what I have just said is more true for the psychosocial than the intrapsychic versions of the model, because the former more clearly emphasizes defense.

An additional word on the content of the two forces in conflict theories is in order. All versions of the conflict model tend to stress one force as individualistic and the other as communal regardless of whether or not both forces are seen as rising from the organism itself. Death fear is a tendency toward independence and uniqueness, whereas life fear is a tendency toward dependence and similarity with others. For Jung, the ego is a mainly individualistic thing whereas the collective unconscious is that which relates one to humankind. While there is perhaps no strict logical necessity that the two opposing forces of a conflict theory stress individualistic and communal content, they nonetheless do so.

The Fulfillment Model

In order to understand the fulfillment model, you must realize that it assumes only one great force in living rather than the two that conflict theories postulate. Although fulfillment positions sometimes conceptualize a way in which the person can get into conflict, conflict is not inevitable or basic. Hence, the fulfillment theories do not see life as necessarily a compromise; rather, they see it as the unfolding of the one great force, with the most successful living involving the most vigorous expression of it. In the fulfillment model, the more vigorous the expression of the force, the greater the experience of tension. Tension is not intimately associated with anxiety, however, as it is in the conflict model. Although fulfillment positions do not, strictly speaking, assume that the person aims at the increase of tension per se, such increases are an integral part of expressing the great force and are not, in any case, avoided.

One version of the fulfillment model emphasizes the realization of one's inherent capabilities. Here you will recognize the actualization theories of Rogers and Maslow. Adler, White, Allport, Fromm, and the existential psychologists define another version of the fulfillment model that stresses the perfection of life through striving toward ideals. Rather than considering individually unique potentialities, as would actualization theorists, perfection theorists stress the capabilities of the human species. This can be seen in Fromm's emphasis on human nature and in Adler's and White's emphasis on mastery and compensation for initial inferiorities.

Turning to a more concrete consideration of the content of the great force, we find fulfillment theorists in agreement that it is heavily psychological in nature. It is oriented less toward mere survival through use of capabilities than toward the enhancement of living, above and beyond survival, that can come through perfection or the expression of capabilities. Many fulfillment theorists, such as Maslow, Allport, Fromm, and the existentialists, actually separate the human's animal nature from its human nature. The pursuit of animal nature, which leads to survival, is relatively unimportant alongside the pursuit of human nature. Although the great force tends to be identified with human nature alone, there are exceptions among fulfillment theorists. Rogers is the only personologist in this group who makes little distinction between animal and human nature, preferring to consider the great force to be that which underlies both enhancement and survival.

Although the great force of the fulfillment theorists tends to be individualistic in nature, it is not antisocial like it is in the conflict theories. Fulfillment theorists generally see no particular difference between successful individual living and successful group living. If persons are vigorously expressing the great force, their lives with themselves and with others will be rich, varied, and satisfying. Adler's is perhaps the most formal statement of this emphasis in that he specifies both mastery and social interest as facets of the core tendency of personality. As fulfillment theorists see no difference between the requirements of individual living and those of group living, they do not conceptualize any inevitability of conflict here.

But as existentialism makes especially clear, conventionality is not the most constructive social commitment. Probably because of this, conflict can arise between the person and the social context. Fulfillment theorists who have elaborated on this matter—notably Rogers, Maslow, Fromm, and existential psychologists—make it clear that such conflict is due to a society that has become inhuman and punitive. Only when it is thwarted by society can expression of the great force lead to conflict. Although fulfillment theorists are generally somewhat vague about how society can become inhuman and punitive, they do tend to stress, with Rogers, significant people in the person's life who are too crabbed to accept him or her completely and lovingly and suggest, with Fromm, the roots of such difficulties in the economic, political, and cultural milieu.

It is this kind of conflict, according to fulfillment theorists, that jeopardizes vigorous expression of the great force, eventuating in an unnecessarily trivial, conforming, unsatisfying life. Mental illness is defined by fulfillment theorists as the attempt to live as if the great force did not exist in order to avoid conflict between it and a societal context. As you can see, this inhibiting definition is similar in fulfillment and conflict theory. The difference, of course, is that in fulfillment theory there is only one great force that can be denied and hence, only one class of illness, whereas conflict theory conceptualizes two great forces that can be denied and thus two ways of becoming ill. Interestingly, some fulfillment theorists, in considering the conflict between the person and an inhuman social context, have recourse to the concept of defense. This is most notably true of Rogers, but it appears in Maslow, Fromm, Allport, and existential psychology as well. In some ways, the concept of defense used works similarly to that of psychoanalytic theory. In talking of a punitive, inhuman society, fulfillment theorists postulate an intelligent force bent on detecting and thwarting part or all of the great force. Persons can be punished and made to feel guilt. Therefore, they protect themselves by instituting defensive processes such that they (1) do not see the parts of the great force that would make them fear retribution and (2) channel expression of the great force along socially innocuous paths.

Although the concept of defense works in the same manner as and is similar in purpose to that in conflict theory, we must recognize a very important difference. For fulfillment theorists, conflict is not inevitable and the highest form of living is not a compromise. Thus, defense has a logical function in their thinking only if, and when, conflict actually develops. Even if conflict is found to develop fairly often, fulfillment theorists have no reason to define defensiveness as part of the highest state of being, or mental health. This is the major significance of the difference between fulfillment and conflict positions. It means that the fulfillment model defines the highest form of living in terms of transcendence of society rather than conformity to it. Emphasis in ideal living is on imaginativeness, spontaneity, individuality, self-reliance, openness to experience, and an unflinching knowledge of the inmost recesses of oneself. This emphasis contrasts sharply with that on good citizenship found in the conflict model.

When they consider the entire life span, fulfillment theorists think in terms of a fairly continual developmental process in which personality changes throughout childhood, adolescence, and adulthood. The changes are generally considered as indicating progressively greater differentiation and integration, or psychological growth, at least when conflict and defense do not interfere. This emphasis on personality change in the direction of growth is very understandable considering the fulfillment theorists' assumption of only one great force that normally leads persons to attempt to realize their capabilities or perfect themselves. Continual personality change is as logically a part of fulfillment theory as is the conflict model's emphasis on personality stability following the childhood years.

The Consistency Model

In order to appreciate the meaning of the consistency model, we must recognize that it does not stress the importance of the specific content of personality and inherent forces; rather, it considers the importance of the congruence, compatibility, or fit among various aspects of personality or elements of content. In the cognitive dissonance version of the model, these elements of content are cognitive in nature. For Kelly, one such cognitive element is the construct, or hypothesis, and the other is the perception of actual occurrences. McClelland's emphasis is very similar in that one kind of element is the expectation and the other the perception of events. Regardless of their differences, all these theories agree that one element deals primarily with ideas or expectations about what the world and you are like whereas the other primarily concerns observations or perceptions on what the world and you seem to actually be doing. In contrast, the version of the consistency model exemplified by Fiske and Maddi concerns itself with the match between the level of excitation or tension that is customary for the person and that which he or she is actually experiencing at some point in time. The activation version is nonetheless similar to the cognitive dissonance version in stressing past experience as a basis for coming to grips with what is happening now and in considering any content as important as any other.

In its pure form, the cognitive dissonance version of the consistency model is strictly a tension-reduction viewpoint. Its major message is that inconsistency or incompatibility between a given idea or expectancy and a certain observation is an intensely uncomfortable state of high tension and anxiety—so uncomfortable that in the attempt to avoid incompatibilities and thereby reduce tension, the whole story of life is contained. For Kelly, the entire personality is either the result of attempts to avoid and resolve incompatibilities or the expression of unresolved incompatibilities. Once you get to McClelland's variant of the cognitive dissonance position, however, you find a viewpoint that agrees with the purer theories only for large incompatibilities and considers small incompatibilities to be actually pleasant and therefore sought after. Incompatibilities are still characterized as tension states, but it is no longer assumed that all degrees of tension are unpleasant. McClelland's position amounts to a portrayal of the person as seeking small increments in tension but avoiding large increments. Concerning tension, the activation version of the consistency model is more similar to McClelland than to Kelly. Activation is characterized as tension, but the person is not portrayed as uniformly minimizing tension. When the tension level is higher than customary it will be reduced, but when it is lower than customary it will be increased. The person finds tension of a too meager degree as unpleasant as tension of a too intense degree.

According to the consistency model, the only attributes of the person considered both inherent and important for understanding personality are (1) the bases for reacting emotionally to incompatibilities and (2) the broad techniques whereby unpleasant emotional experiences can be terminated. But the content of thoughts and perceptions are learned, as is the customary level of activation. Unlike conflict and fulfillment theories, consistency theories offer no definition of great forces in terms of concrete, immutable content. This eclecticism with regard to the likely content of personality is the major reason why consistency theories stress individual uniqueness and the peripheral rather than core level of personality.

Because they do not stress conflict in which one of the two opposing forces has the power to detect and thwart the other, consistency theories should have no need for the concept of defense. And lo and behold, they do not use it! In Kelly's view, when a construct fails to accurately predict an observed occurrence, the construct is modified to make it potentially more predictive of the world of events. This process of modification is properly considered rational trial and error. McClelland believes that the person straightforwardly approaches those domains of experience that typically have yielded small degrees of unexpectedness and avoids those that typically have yielded great degrees of unexpectedness. Actually, McClelland and Kelly explicitly indicate that the concept of defense is unnecessary. This emphasis is even more extreme than in fulfillment theory, which, though it does not make defense constant, recognizes its importance under certain circumstances of living.

In contrast, Fiske and Maddi tend somewhat toward the conceptualization of defensiveness. They refer to the person's attempts to correct for situations in which a discrepancy between actual and customary activation has already taken place. Such correction is achieved by manufacturing or denying stimulus impact according to whether the activation level needs to be raised or lowered. Such corrections distort the real impact of the stimulation. But Fiske and Maddi do not explicitly use the concept of defense and do not refer in their notion of correction to any inhibition of real parts of human nature to avoid conflict with society. All in all, it seems reasonable to conclude that the concept of defense is not very important in the consistency model.

In considering the person's entire life span, the consistency model, like the fulfillment model, portrays personality as changing fairly continuously. This emphasis on change seems understandable in a position that does not emphasize conflict, defense, or inherent personality characteristics with their immutable content. Personality change should occur as a concomitant of the natural process of encountering different events in the world of experience. If there is any difference between the fulfillment and consistency models regarding the nature of personality change, it is that the former emphasizes patterned change in the form of ever increasing differentiation and integration, or psychological growth, more than does the latter. But this distinction comes very close to splitting hairs. After all, psychological growth is a notion implicit in Kelly's thinking and of explicit importance in the theorizing of Fiske and Maddi, who actually provide an explanation for it rather than merely assuming it as do most of the fulfillment theorists.

SOME ISSUES RAISED BY THE THREE MODELS

As we have seen, conflict, fulfillment, and consistency models differ in a number of ways, some very abstract. Conflict theory, for example, assumes that the person and society basically aim at different things, while fulfillment theory assumes that the goals of the person and society are compatible. Such abstract differences raise issues that are difficult to resolve, certainly in terms of empirical evidence and even in terms of rational argumentation. From my point of view, the most fruitful inquiry that can be conducted with such abstract characteristics is that of determining whether each position has logical consistency. Thus, if a theory makes the assumption that the person and society are antagonistic, it is only logical to also assume that life is, at best, a compromise. To see life otherwise would be inconsistent with the assumption of inevitable conflict.

I tried to consider the internal logic of the three models and to determine, in some rudimentary way, how well certain theories exemplifying the models conform to that logic. This is a very difficult task, partly because the particular theories are sometimes incompletely explicit and metaphorically stated. Nonetheless, it seems reasonably clear to me that most conflict, fulfillment, and consistency theories show reasonable logical consistency. But even more important, the essential features of these models, aside from any particular theories that fall within them, are quite consistent. These three models, then, emerge as serious descriptions of the core of personality.

But is there anything more we can do toward deciding which of the models, or their features, are most fruitful for understanding personality? Certainly. Although further consideration of the very abstract issues raised by their differences is not likely to be useful, it seems to me that there are some slightly more concrete issues deducible from these differences that may well bear further exploration here. The issues I have in mind refer more directly to empirical considerations. Hence, there is much to learn from addressing these issues. As you will see, some of them involve only differences between two of the models and others agreement of two of the models and disagreement with the third.

First Issue: Is the Concept of Defense Tenable?

Both conflict and fulfillment positions use the concept of defense, whereas consistency positions ordinarily do not consider the concept necessary. The concept of defense has also come in for considerable criticism from psychologists who are not personologists and from philosophers, mainly on the grounds that it seems too implausible. Therefore, this first issue is very important in our attempt to determine the most fruitful directions in which to theorize about human personality.

We should approach discussion of this issue by first ensuring that we are in agreement concerning the meaning of the concept of defense. According to all theorists who use the concept, a defense is a technique for avoiding the anxiety that would be aroused by recognizing that there existed in you some thought or action that would lead to punishment, guilt, or feelings of unworthiness. The bases of punishment, guilt, and feelings of unworthiness, according to most such theorists, are in conflictful parent-child relationships, the conflict resulting either because the aims of the person and the society are inevitably incompatible or because these aims have become incompatible through society's failure. The defense is instituted virtually at the same time as the arousal of anxiety, and therefore little anxiety is actually experienced if the defense is effective. Once instituted, the defense tends to persist because the underlying conflict also persists.

The successful defense avoids anxiety by distorting or denying to awareness the underlying conflict. It does so by blocking recognition of the thoughts or actions that would bring the person into difficulty with society or its internalized form in the conscience. This blocking of recognition is an active process, not merely the absence of awareness through inattention or habit. Indeed, the person would be unable to become aware of the thoughts or actions even if he or she tried or were pushed by others. The underlying conflict would have to be resolved or at least accepted before any awareness could occur.

As you can see, any theory of defense is a complicated thing. It includes a conceptualization of both conflict and unconscious mental content. An additional complication is the fact that theorists who use the concept of defense generally recognize different kinds of defensive operations. The smallest number of defenses is found in Rogers's theory, which considers only out-and-out denial and then less extreme distortion. The largest number is found in psychoanalytic thinking, which includes such examples as repression, projection, denial, reaction formation, intellectualization, undoing, and sublimation. In psychoanalytic theory, each of these defenses has different effects on living, though all have the general purpose of warding off anxiety by rendering conflicts unconscious.

The development and popularity of the concept of defense came about through the observations of personologists interested primarily in psychopathological states. By and large, these observations represent unsystematic empirical evidence in the form of insight-provoking cases. Summarizing them would be a useful way to attain a precise, sharp appreciation of the issue concerning the tenability of the concept of defense. Many of the most compelling of these observations were made by Freud and his early collaborator (Breuer & Freud, 1936) in their study of hysterical women. These women had symptoms—paralysis or anesthesia of the hands, blindness, incessant aches, inability to speak—most peculiar for people who seemed free of physical defects. Their symptoms often were nonsensical from a physiological point of view. For example, an inability to feel in the hands—the so-called *glove anesthesia*—would be almost impossible to come by on the basis of injury to the nervous system (Freud, 1893). The nerve groupings in a hand make it much more likely to lose feeling in one side or the other than in the whole hand. Further, injury to the nerve tracts in the arm or shoulder would produce more widespread defects than in the hand alone. In addition, when both hands are rendered devoid of sensation, whatever strange injury took place in one arm or shoulder would have also had to occur in the other—a most unlikely prospect! One could think that damage to the central nervous system was the cause, but again such damage would have more widespread effects than on the hands alone. As a further example of the physiological nonsense of hysterical symptoms, it was observed that paralyses in these people were not associated with progressive deterioration of muscular tonus even though the muscles were apparently unused. These weird phenomena inclined many physicians of that time to the belief that the apparent absence of physical injury was due not to their own limited diagnostic capability but to the nonphysical basis of the symptoms.

In an urgent attempt to learn more about this disorder, Freud and Breuer began hypnotizing their patients in the hope of overcoming the symptoms. Picture their amazement when it became apparent that hysterical symptoms are lost in the hypnotized state! Glove anesthesias, paralyses, blindness—all were removed only to return soon after termination of the hypnotic state. This was the definitive observation of the nonphysical basis of hysterical symptoms. So as to learn more about what these hysterical women were like, Freud and Breuer began asking them questions and encouraging them to say whatever was in their minds. Two things were clearly established. First, these people were not particularly disturbed by their symptoms, however bizarre they were. One would think that such extreme symptoms in the absence of apparent cause would move anyone to anxiety. But instead the women showed what Charcot had already dubbed the *sublime indifference of the hysteric*. Second, the women understood and remembered less about themselves than did people free of such symptoms. Often friends were more helpful in relating the patient's past than she herself. In addition, the patients showed little curiosity about and awareness of what was happening to them and to the world around them. They were intellectually uncritical to an inordinate degree. But when pushed to remember specific events from childhood through the combined effects of saying whatever came into their heads and having their utterances interpreted by the physician, they often became extremely anxious. And lo and behold, as confrontations accumulated, the anxieties diminished—as well as the symptoms—all the while that it became progressively easier for them to remember past events.

These observations led Freud and Breuer to an explanation of hysteria stressing the concept of defense. For them, hysteria is clearly caused psychologically rather than physically. The immediate cause is a mechanism of defense—repression—that has the effect of blocking action and thought. What actions and thoughts? Obviously ones that could be anxiety provoking. What would they be? Obviously ones that would bring retaliation from society or make the person feel guilty. So the deeper cause is conflict, which, because of its ability to arouse anxiety, leads to defense. But since the actions and thoughts defended against are important and basic, they cannot be rendered nonexistent through defense; they must find some sort of expression. The symptoms are their distorted expression. From here, it was only a hop, skip, and jump to the identification of other defenses and conflicts as underlying other psychopathological states. The extraordinarily powerful model of defense was launched. Later personologists interested in psychopathology have in some cases elaborated and in others simplified the theory of defense, but they have left it essentially unchanged. When that theory is found it will invariably involve conflict, leading to anxiety, responded to with defense, which takes the form of denying the conflict to awareness in order to avoid the anxiety.

The tenability of the concept of defense is questioned most insistently by philosophers to whom the concept seems preposterous. If there is an active process whereby conflicts are held out of awareness, there must be some part of the person that can perceive reality and decide what the rest of the person shall and shall not be permitted to know. On the face of it, this idea of a person within a person seems nonsensical to critics of the concept of defense. In the following discussion, we shall consider a number of specific criticisms of attempts to empirically demonstrate the action of defenses. You should recognize that every one of these specific criticisms follows from the general stance that theorizing about persons within persons is foolish. Note that the person-within-a-person criticism refers not to the existence of different parts of the organism—a fact easy enough to accept—but to the attribution of characteristics of the whole organism, such as intelligence and choice, to the separate parts. So the part of the organism that does the defending as well as the part affected by the defense is considered intelligent, perceptive, and capable of choice. This leads critics of the concept of defense to say that the notion amounts to merely talking about one organism as if it were two. But since it obviously is not two organisms, defense is a nonsensical concept regardless of its dramatic appeal.

Clearly the organism is only one. Hence, if the concept of defense necessitated treatment of the organism as two, it would be rather untenable on rational grounds. But the question to be asked at this point is whether it would be possible to translate the extremely figurative language used by defense theorists into terms less implicative of persons within persons. Surely Freud did far too much talking about superegos *fighting* ids and egos *siding with* or *deceiving* one or the other. Such words properly characterize relations among people and, when used to describe relations among parts of the same person, are at best analogical and at worst illogical. It may be possible, however, to describe the relations among parts of personality in terms that capture the essential import of defense while avoiding nonsense. If so, this will amount to demonstrating the analogical status of current statements concerning defense through translating them into statements that describe the techniques whereby consciousness is denied in terms consistent with the known capabilities of single organisms.

But before any attempt at such translation is made, it must be clear that empirical evidence suggests that a concept of defense is useful to invoke. Certainly the anecdotal observations I mentioned earlier are partial evidence—but *only* partial, as they have not been made systematically. What I mean is that the psychotherapists making the observations did so only on people who came to them as patients and, by and large, did not require even that observations of defense be made on all or at least a large proportion of the subjects. Psychotherapists have been known to make conclusions on the basis of striking observations of as few as one or two patients. However exciting these conclusions may be, they may not apply to people in general even though it is typical to assume that they do. In addition, psychotherapists' conclusions are often too interpretive for disinterested psychological observers to accept. The bases on which the interpretations have been made are sometimes unstated, raising questions concerning the consistency and objectivity with which they have been applied. Such a state of affairs requires that there be a body of more rigorously systematic empirical observations before it is agreed that there is evidence suggesting the action of something like a defense.

Fortunately, over the past thirty or so years a large number of research studies on the existence and operation of defenses have been done. It is impossible to cover them all here, but I can refer you to a number of able reviews (Allport, 1955; Chabot, 1973; Erdelyi, 1974; Eriksen, 1963; Holmes, 1974; MacKinnon & Dukes, 1962; Sears, 1944). Here I will discuss some of the more representative and instructive of these studies. Most often the research effort has been devoted to investigations of repression or denial, a type of defense relevant to all theories incorporating this concept. Some attention has also been given to projection and regression, methods of defense that are more specific to psychoanalytic theory.

The bulk of the studies reviewed in this chapter concern the general form of defensiveness that might be called *repression*. This process is important not only in psychoanalytic theory but in many other positions. The studies concern defensiveness effects on perception and memory. Consideration of research on the specific, highly differentiated defenses associated most exclusively with Freud's position is deferred until Chapter 11, where it is more appropriate. But before turning to repression, let us consider two studies on *regression* that suggest an important point about how and on whom studies of defensiveness should be done.

The first study concerning regression is often cited but is not very useful. Mowrer (1940) used small numbers of rats in an experiment involving electric shock. One group of rats was permitted to learn by trial and error that the shock through the grilled floor on which they stood could be turned off by pressing a foot pedal. Another group was given shocks for an approximately equal amount of time but had no pedal to press. Eventually, the latter group learned to avoid shock by sitting up on their hind legs. Once this behavior was firmly instilled, a foot pedal was inserted and the rats were permitted to learn to use it. From this point on, both groups were frustrated by receiving a shock whenever they pressed this foot pedal; in other words, when they tried to turn off the floor shock they got a shock from what had been the instrument of salvation. The rats that originally had learned to avoid shock by standing on their hind legs almost immediately regressed to that habit, while the other rats persisted in pushing the pedal.

What is wrong with this experiment as a demonstration of regression? The major problem is that it does not take into account the fact that regression is a notion inextricably embedded in a broader theoretical framework. For psychoanalysts, regression involves going from a latter stage of psychosexual development to an earlier one, in a partial or more complete sense, this movement being a function of fixation and frustration. By *fixation,* Freud means the overly strong attachment to a particular stage of psychosexual development; by *frustration,* he means the prevention of instinctual gratification in whatever stage the person is in. When frustration becomes strong, retreat to a previous, fixated psychosexual stage may take place. This is called regression. Now it is possible, I suppose, that rats undergo a rudimentary form of psychosexual development; at least, their mating behavior improves with practice. But even if this were considered as qualifying the rat as an organism on which to test the concept of regression, Mowrer clearly has made no test because standing up or pushing a pedal to avoid shock really does not bear sensibly on psychosexual development. This experiment has nothing to do with the concept of regression even though it may be regarded as having demonstrated that a newly learned habit may be relinquished, when no longer effective, for a previously learned one. One thing is clear: If defensiveness is to be studied in subhuman organisms, they must at least have some form of psychosexual development and the specific behaviors studied must be convincing analogues of the human behaviors on which psychoanalytic theory focuses (cf. Hunt, 1964). As these criteria are essentially unreached in animal studies, they are thus far of little utility for testing psychoanalytic notions of defense.

You might be thinking that if regression were divested of its psychoanalytic parentage, Mowrer's demonstration would be positive evidence. But even without considering psychosexual stages of development, the concept of defense requires some active process of debarring from consciousness in order to reduce anxiety. In regression, this debarring is effected through returning to some earlier state of being. If rats are to be proper organisms for study they must have consciousness, for only then will debarring from consciousness constitute a useful procedure of defense. Many psychologists might be willing to assume that rats or some even higher animals have consciousness. But even if consciousness analogous to what can be obtained in humans through self-report exists in animals, its methodological inaccessibility is a formidable barrier. Consciousness may or may not exist in an animal, and if it does it may or may not provide sensible analogies to the human conflict, guilt, and anxiety considered to be the springboards of defense. Even with an emancipated concept of regression, it becomes clear that the study of subhuman organisms is so imprecise as to be of marginal utility. The same is true for the study of other defenses, as all require an organism whose consciousness can be scrutinized.

Somewhat more convincing is a well-known study of regression by Barker, Dembo, and Lewin (1941). They used 30 preschool children as subjects, turning them loose in a free play situation. All were above average in intelligence. The children were encouraged to play alone with some toys for a half hour. The next day they were brought back but this time played first with some much more desirable toys. After the first fifteen minutes, the investigator returned the children to the other end of the room without explanation and permitted them to play with the original, less attractive toys for a half hour. During this half hour, the desirable toys were in full view but unavailable. Barker et al. reasoned that if regression is a reality, the frustration involved in giving up the desirable toys would lead to more destructive play with the less desirable toys than the children had shown on the first day of play. The investigators tried to establish age norms for constructiveness of play to see whether any decrease in this characteristic could indeed be thought to represent becoming more childish. Their result clearly showed that the expected destructiveness occurs.

This study incorporates one important element of the regression notion, namely, that it is a process of primitivization—of becoming more childish. But the study is not particularly relevant to the psychoanalytic notion of regression, because there was little concern with the specifics of psychosexual development. The results might be used, however, to support a concept of regression emancipated from psychoanalytic theory. The only fly in the ointment—which will crop up constantly in the following discussion—is that there is no way of knowing if the primitivization shown really occurred without conscious awareness, as it would have had to in order to be a bona fide expression of defense. This shortcoming might have been avoided, as the subjects were humans and not rats, and therefore could have been questioned.

We are now ready to traverse the terrain of repression research. Remember that the concept of defense contains the notion that something mental of an unpleasant nature is being denied awareness. It is important, therefore, to employ human subjects and attempt to determine whether the defensive process, though measurable by the experimenter, is really unavailable to the subject's awareness.

The defense mechanism of repression involves debarring from awareness any sensation, perception, thought, or action that would conflict with values and principles instilled in you by society and has the immediate function of avoiding the anxiety that would accompany awareness of the conflict. The meaning of the concept of repression in psychoanalytic theory is much the same as in other theories of defense, except that in psychoanalytic theory the personal contribution to the conflict invariably can be traced to the life, sexual, or death instincts. In considering research studies of repression, we will be working at the heart of the issue of the tenability of the concept of defense, as repression is ubiquitously recognized in theories of defense and is considered the basic defense even in psychoanalytic theory. Indeed, Freud first used the concept of repression before hitting on that of defense and switched his primary emphasis to the latter only when it became clear to him that there are additional, more elaborate techniques than repression for avoiding consciousness.

It is fortunate that repression comes so close to the heart of the concept of defense, for there have been many relevant studies. Indeed, such studies, dubbed the "new look" in perception, attracted intense interest in the 1950s and have continued until recently (Erdelyi, 1974). The basic issue of the tenability of the concept of defense waxed hot in the form of specific research controversies during this exciting time in personology. Certainly there were studies of repression before the 1950s, but they tended to involve memory of action more than perception and therefore were less striking than the "new look" work. Let us turn to the more perceptual work before considering the memory work.

The notion that people can be especially defensive or especially vigilant in their perception of things as a function of aspects of personality such as needs and values was introduced in a series of articles by Bruner and Postman (1947a, 1947b) and Postman, Bruner, and McGinnies (1948). All of these experiments used the tachistoscope, a device that presents visual stimuli for controllable and very brief lengths of time. Generally speaking, the tachistoscopic procedure involves presenting the stimulus for too short a time to permit recognition and then gradually increasing the duration of subsequent presentations. Subjects are to say what they think the stimulus is after each exposure, with the important data being the length of exposure that accompanies correct perception. Stimuli that have different content or have been presented under varying conditions may have different exposure lengths associated with correct perception. Recognizing this is basic to understanding the notions of perceptual vigilance and defense. Indeed, the existence of a group of stimuli that required shorter or longer exposure times for correct perception than did the general run of stimuli led these investigators to invoke these two ideas.

Bruner and Postman (1947a) found that those stimuli associated with experimentally produced anxiety had faster recognition times than did stimuli not associated with anxiety. In developing the notion of perceptual vigilance, these investigators suggested that stimuli of special importance to the person are enhanced in perception and recognized sooner. The other studies concerned the concept of perceptual defense. In the first of these (Bruner & Postman, 1947b), a word association task was initially administered. Subjects varied, of course, in the speed with which they could think of an associate to the words the experimenter presented. Then these words were presented to the subjects again, only this time tachistoscopically.

Bruner and Postman found that for some subjects words that involved long association times—this presumably indicating emotional disturbance—required much longer tachistoscopic exposures for recognition than did words with medium or short association times. They dubbed this lengthened recognition time *perceptual defense* and likened it to repression, whereby anxiety-provoking stimuli are defended against in perception or prevented from coming to awareness. But Bruner and Postman also found that in certain other subjects long-association-time words had lower tachistoscopic recognition time, again suggesting the relevance of the notion of perceptual vigilance.

The Postman, Bruner, and McGinnies (1948) study supplements the other two in suggesting that values as well as anxiety and underlying emotional disturbance can affect perception. They chose words for tachistoscopic presentation that represented six broad value areas (e.g., religion, economics, aesthetics) and sought to determine beforehand their subjects' commitment to these value areas through the use of a relevant standard psychological test.

Sure enough, they found a relationship between the intensity of subjects' commitment to each value area and the speed with which they recognized tachistoscopically presented words relevant to those areas. Subjects with an intense commitment to theoretical values, for example, had faster recognition times for words from this value area and slower recognition times for words from value areas to which they had minimal commitment. The concepts of perceptual vigilance and defense again were used to explain the results.

Although these three studies have more or less bearing on the concept of repression, it was not until the subsequent study of McGinnies (1949) that the relevance of this kind of research became unquestionably clear. McGinnies selected a group of socially taboo words, such as *whore, bitch, belly,* and *Kotex,* and a group of neutral, acceptable words for tachistoscopic presentation to college student subjects. All the while that his subjects were trying to tell him what they saw in the tachistoscope, McGinnies was also measuring their galvanic skin responses. The galvanic skin response is essentially an index of the electrical conductivity of the skin, which rises in a very sensitive way when sweating increases. Such increases in sweating generally have been considered indicative of emotional arousal, or anxiety.

McGinnies obtained striking results. Not only did the taboo words require longer tachistoscopic exposure for correct recognition; subjects also showed increases in sweating on the tachistoscopic exposures of the taboo words that were too brief to permit visual recognition. No comparable increase in sweating prior to conscious recognition occurred with neutral words. These findings are detailed in Table 6–1, where the measures of sweating appear in the first two columns and those of recognition time in the last two. The higher recognition time for taboo words was considered a manifestation of perceptual defense. The greater sweating accompanying prerecognition trials with taboo words was considered an indication not only of the active nature of defensive processes but of an unconscious detection or manifestation of anxiety elicited by the words.

Extraordinary as the results of this study may seem, they are just what you would expect from the action of the defense mechanisms, of repression or denial. If some percepts are to be debarred from consciousness, some part of the organism must be able to detect them and rule them out. The findings concerning increased sweating suggest that there is some kind of organismic response to taboo words and that this incipient emotional response is part of the process of denial to awareness. McGinnies's choice of taboo words was also appropriate, reflecting as they did psychosexual matters unsuitable for polite discussion and thought.

Lest we conclude prematurely that there is clear empirical evidence favoring the existence of the repressive defense, we should recognize that no sooner had McGinnies's results appeared than they were resoundingly attacked. The specific criticisms reflected the general disbelief that the concept of defense is tenable because it seems to require theorizing about a person within a person. Howes and Solomon (1950) voiced the criticism in a strong and capable manner.

TABLE 6–1   Summary of the Raw Data and Statistical Tests for All Observers with Respect to Both Galvanic Skin Response and Thresholds of Recognition for Neutral and Critical Stimulus Words

Observer	Mean Microammeter Readings during Prerecognition Exposures		Mean Thresholds of Recognition	
	Neutral Words	Critical Words	Neutral Words	Critical Words
1	37.80	40.46	.055	.184
2	40.96	41.53	.044	.094
3	39.31	42.06	.054	.080
4	38.34	40.80	.103	.126
5	41.48	43.76	.040	.064
6	41.41	47.08	.070	.130
7	40.75	39.94	.057	.104
8	39.98	42.85	.063	.076
9	39.44	42.68	.059	.130
10	40.02	42.71	.049	.223
11	39.88	41.55	.046	.077
12	41.27	44.02	.057	.091
13	40.56	41.37	.033	.037
14	40.19	41.42	.034	.054
15	40.85	40.63	.046	.056
16	40.83	41.84	.036	.046
	Mean diff. = 1.98 $t = 5.10\ P < .01$		Mean diff. = .045 $t = 3.96\ P < .01$	

SOURCE: "Emotionality and Perceptual Defense" by E. McGinnies, 1949, *Psychological Review, 56.*

The first criticism was that subjects might well have known in a conscious way the content of the taboo words for some trials before they felt certain enough of their knowledge to voice it. After all, if you were in their position and saw what looked like "Kotex," you might not have wanted to risk saying that to an adult and an authority—the experimenter—unless you were absolutely sure you were right. But maybe you started sweating as soon as you first thought the word was "Kotex." As you can see, this is a serious criticism. If it is true, all that is meant by the finding concerning longer tachistoscopic times for taboo words is that people decide which of their thoughts and perceptions to express so as to avoid unnecessary embarrassment. There is nothing here of defense in the sense of an unconsciously operating process actively debarring certain percepts from awareness.

The second criticism made by Howes and Solomon concerned the fact that the taboo and neutral words McGinnies used differed markedly in their familiarity or frequency of past occurrence in the subjects' experience. By consulting the listing of the frequency with which major words appear in written usage prepared by Thorndike and Lorge (1944), Howes and Solomon determined that McGinnies's taboo words appear with much lower frequency than his neutral words. This led to the criticism that the different tachistoscopic lengths required for the perception of words was a function of the frequency with which those words had been experienced in the past rather than of any involvement with defensive operations. This criticism is general enough to apply to the three experiments described above as well as this one. These two psychologists really put their teeth into the criticism when they demonstrated in further studies (Howes & Solomon, 1951; Solomon & Howes, 1951) that tachistoscopic exposure lengths for word recognition could be predicted from the Thorndike-Lorge tables of word frequency.

Even though the frequency criticism has obvious cogency and some empirical support, there is the rankling thought that it is really not as devastating as it might seem at first. After all, if you are interested in the frequency with which persons have experienced a word in the past, you must take into account not only instances coming their way from some external source, e.g., books, speeches, other people, but also occurrences resulting from their own imaginations and thought processes. Once you recognize this fact, the engaging simplicity of the explanation Solomon and Howes put forth is largely lost. Not only does their frequency explanation become extraordinarily more complex; it is not clear that it is even testable anymore. What is a comprehensive measure of frequency of experience of a word in the past? Certainly the Thorndike-Lorge listings cannot be used, since they reflect rather formal, written usage for public consumption—the kind of usage found in magazines and newspapers. Especially when you are interested in the frequency of experience of taboo words, you cannot possibly trust the Thorndike-Lorge word lists. Such lists certainly underestimate frequency of exposure to such words, especially when you take into account the person's own thoughts and fantasies alongside verbal interactions with others that are informal and private in nature. So what could the relationship between Thorndike-Lorge word frequency and tachistoscopic recognition time found by Solomon and Howes (1951) and Howes and Solomon (1951) possibly mean?

Fortunately, psychologists such as Eriksen (1963) have scrutinized the data of these two studies and partially answered this question. It turns out that "practically all of the relationship can be traced to a difference between words having zero or very low frequencies in the Thorndike-Lorge counts and words having high frequency" (Eriksen, 1963, p. 40). For words in the frequency range of 10 to 3,000 occurrences per million in the above count, there is virtually no relationship between frequency of occurrence and tachistoscopic recognition time! This useful bit of information means that the frequency criticism of Solomon and Howes is cogent only when one works with words having especially high or low frequencies of occurrence in formal, public usage. This more accurate version of the criticism hardly destroys the findings of Bruner and Postman (1947a, 1947b), Postman, Bruner, and McGinnies (1948), and McGinnies (1949). Following his reanalysis of the findings of Solomon and Howes (1951) and Howes and Solomon (1951), Eriksen (1963) concludes that "we may note that the empirical relationship between frequency of past occurrence and recognition threshold has been amply demonstrated, although the magnitude of this relationship has undoubtedly been considerably overestimated."

We can now return to the other criticism made by Solomon and Howes, namely, that the relatively long exposure times associated with taboo words reflect merely a conscious decision on the subjects' part not to risk embarrassment should they have been wrong in thinking the words improper. This criticism is completely sound from the viewpoint of reason when leveled at the McGinnies experiment but has considerably less relevance to the other experiments because they employed not taboo words but anxiety-provoking or value-related ones. It should not have been embarrassing for subjects to report such words, even if they turned out to be wrong. Nonetheless, it is the McGinnies experiment that comes closest to a demonstration of the defense mechanism of repression as it is normally used in theories of defense.

There is no logical counterargument to the Solomon and Howes criticism, but there is one empirical study that escapes the criticism while still bearing on repression. In this study, McCleary and Lazarus (1949) used nonsense syllables for stimuli in place of meaningful words. For half of the nonsense syllables, an unpleasant, anxiety-provoking effect was established by accompanying a one-second exposure of the syllable with an electric shock. Through a series of such exposures, they produced the effect of increased sweating, measured by the galvanic skin response, every time one of the syllables associated with electric shock appeared. After this conditioning had been established, all of the syllables, including the half that had not been associated with shock, were presented at tachistoscopic speeds ranging from extremely brief up to the approximate time required for accurate perception by most people. As in the McGinnies experiment, the galvanic skin response was recorded on each tachistoscopic trial, along with the subjects' verbal report of what they saw. In the tachistoscopic part of the experiment, no electric shock was used. As you can see, the experiment's design was the same as that of McGinnies except that nonsense syllables were used in place of taboo words, with some of the syllables rendered anxiety provoking by the pretachistoscopic pairing with electric shock. Thus, one cannot say with any cogency either that the shocked versus nonshocked nonsense syllables had been more frequent in the subjects' past experience or that they were socially unacceptable and therefore the source of potential embarrassment. McCleary and Lazarus's study successfully avoids both criticisms made by Solomon and Howes.

We should, therefore, be especially interested in the results in order that we may consider the empirical tenability of the concept of defense. Now let us first consider the trials in which the subjects' verbal reports were wrong. In these trials, McCleary and Lazarus (1949) found that sweating was greater for the previously shocked syllables than for those unaccompanied by shock. They conclude that "at tachistoscopic exposure speeds too rapid for conscious discrimination . . . the subject is still capable of responding in a discriminatory way." They suggested the term *subception* for this apparently autonomic form of perception. Clearly these results support the part of the theory of defense that involves a keen sensitivity on the part of some aspect of the organism to potentially threatening perceptions that permits them to be guarded against. But this experiment does not show that the previously shocked syllables required longer tachistoscopic exposure times for accurate perception than did the nonshocked syllables—indeed, the opposite result was obtained, something more consistent with the idea of perceptual vigilance than perceptual defense! Taken as a whole, this study only partially supports the repressive aspect of defense. Perhaps this state of affairs can be traced to what was lost in the process of developing a design that could circumvent the criticism of Solomon and Howes. While the shocked nonsense syllables undoubtedly were unpleasant stimuli, it is not at all clear—or likely—that they articulated in any deep way the kinds of intense underlying conflict that all defense theorists agree should provoke defenses. The McCleary and Lazarus study presents, as laboratory experiments frequently must, a pale shadow of life. Once this is appreciated, it may seem surprising that even the subception part of defensiveness could be demonstrated.

Another approach to circumventing the criticisms of Solomon and Howes is exemplified in a study by Cowen and Beier (1954). They decided to retain taboo and neutral words as the stimuli, increasing the likelihood of engaging more deep-seated conflicts than could be done with the technique of McCleary and Lazarus. Instead of tachistoscopic presentation, these investigators achieved a similar effect by using blurred typewritten copies of the words arranged into booklets. The arrangement was such that successive pages went from very blurred to very clear for each word. The important datum was the number of pages that had to be turned before the word was correctly identified.

In order to avoid the criticism involving word familiarity, Cowen and Beier correlated number of pages turned for correct identification with the frequency of occurrence listed for the word by Thorndike and Lorge. They found the correlation to be zero for the words they used. In order to avoid the criticisms involving embarrassment at verbalizing taboo words, they had half the subjects report to an experimenter of the same sex and the other half to one of the opposite sex. In addition, all experimenters read the entire list of words to be used, including the taboo ones, to the subjects before the experiment began. Cowen and Beier reasoned that the combination of these two procedures should decrease the embarrassment factor to the point where it could not be invoked in the explanation of findings. In addition, they demonstrated that there were no important differences in the results they obtained between experimenter-subject pairs of same and opposite sex.

The main result of this study was that the taboo words indeed required more page turns for correct identification than did the neutral words. These results corroborate those of McGinnies in the context of a design that at least comes close to avoiding the criticisms of Solomon and Howes. Considering these results along with those of McCleary and Lazarus, whose study also avoids the criticisms, the empirical case for the existence of a repressive defense is reasonably sound. One could still say of the Cowen and Beier study that there was some remaining embarrassment, even though the experimenter had alerted subjects as to the nature of the words they would see, but this comes much closer to hairsplitting than it did in the McGinnies study.

Blum (1955) tried another approach to avoid the criticisms leveled at the initial perceptual defense studies. He used as stimulus materials pictures taken from his Blacky Test (Blum, 1949), which show a young dog in various interactions with two older dogs (its parents). As is described more fully in Chapter 11, the interactions were chosen to exemplify facets of parent-child relationships considered important in psychoanalytic theory. Blum presented a slide with four of these pictures tachistoscopically to subjects, who had to say which picture was in each of the four positions. All subjects knew the eleven Blacky pictures well but did not know that in reality it was the same four pictures being presented on each of the forty-eight trials (the pictures were rotated so that they appeared in each position the same number of times over the trials). After the experiment, all subjects said that they were unable to recognize any of the pictures and for them the experiment was a kind of guessing game.

On the basis of other information, it was determined that some subjects actually had conflicts relating to some of the pictures and no conflicts relating to others. Blum reasoned that there should be fewer identifications of conflict-laden pictures than of nonconflictual pictures. But you should recognize that since subjects thought all eleven Blacky pictures would appear, though only four actually did, they might well have identified pictures that were not presented. Blum argued that there should be no difference in frequency of calling conflictual and nonconflictual pictures that were not presented. This is because the perceptual defense notion requires that a threatening stimulus actually occur, else there is no special reason for defensiveness. The results were as expected. For actually presented pictures, the means on calling conflictual and nonconflictual pictures were 9.42 and 17.12, respectively; for pictures not presented, the mean calls were 15.20 and 16.69, respectively. It is especially interesting that among highly conflictual pictures, those not actually presented were called by subjects much more than were those presented.

Bootzin and Natsoulas (1965) performed a similar experiment that had some additional refinements and utilized a combination of threatening and nonthreatening stimuli on each trial. Suffice it to say that their results also justified the interpretation of a defensive process. While it is not entirely clear in this or Blum's study whether the defense takes place in the perceptual process itself or somewhere between perception and the subject's verbal response (see Natsoulas, 1965), there seems to be defensiveness of some kind.

Having concluded that there is at least some empirical support for the concept of repression, we should now turn to the vexing problem posed by the findings that suggest a process of perceptual vigilance. Thus far, we have observed in passing that some subjects seem to be particularly sensitive rather than insensitive to words that refer to their dominant inherent values and to words and nonsense syllables that are anxiety provoking. It is important for us to decide what meaning to attribute to perceptual vigilance, as it seems to exist, for better or for worse, alongside perceptual defense. But before pursuing the matter further, let me introduce you to an important related body of research concerning the effects of repression on memory rather than on perception.

Research interest in the effects of repression on memory actually predates concern with its effects on perception. Rosenzweig and Mason (1934) clearly did the first study in this tradition. As subjects they used forty children and gave each child the task of solving a series of jigsaw puzzles, with a prize for the child who did best. The experimenters had arranged things beforehand so that each child was permitted to finish half of the tasks assigned to him or her but was interrupted in working on the other half. The interruptions were carried out in such a manner that the children thought they were failing at those tasks. After forty-five minutes of puzzle solving followed by a free interval of one minute, subjects were asked to name the picture puzzles they remembered having worked on. Of the forty children, sixteen remembered more completed than "failed" tasks, thirteen recalled fewer completed than "failed" tasks, nine recalled an equal number of both, and two recalled no tasks. At best, only sixteen of the forty subjects could be thought of as remembering according to a theory of repression. Thirteen subjects seemed particularly sensitive to their failures, which should have been anxiety provoking. In these two groups, we have phenomenon analogous to perceptual defense and perceptual vigilance. The subjects who were especially good at recalling their failures should not be considered more accurate than those who could remember only their successes; rather, it is the nine subjects who remembered an equal number of completed and failed tasks whose mental functioning was most accurate to reality. The same holds true for subjects showing perceptual defense and vigilance, though the data are not as clear as in Rosenzweig and Mason. When persons need more exposures in order to recognize some of a group of stimuli, they are being selectively insensitive and, therefore, inaccurate to reality. When they need fewer exposures, they are being selectively sensitive, which is also a form of inaccuracy to reality. Only people who are neither vigilant nor defensive have perceptual processes accurate to reality. Although such people undoubtedly exist in the perception studies described earlier, they have not been singled out for analysis in the way they were by Rosenzweig and Mason.

Thinking that the number of subjects showing repression could be increased over what it was in Rosenzweig and Mason's study by arousing a sense of pride in accomplishment, Rosenzweig (1933, 1943) designed another experiment. He presented the same kind of puzzles to one group of adult subjects as an "intelligence test" and to another group in an informal manner emphasizing the test itself rather than individual performance. The first groups should have had their pride aroused, whereas the second group should not have had their self-esteem threatened. Then, as in the original study, each subject completed half the puzzles and "failed" the other half. Under the pride-arousing condition, 17 subjects remembered more finished tasks, eight more unfinished tasks, and five both equally. Under the less stressful condition, only seven subjects remembered more finished tasks while nineteen remembered more unfinished tasks and four showed no difference between the two. The findings clearly show that the greater the threat to self-esteem, the stronger are repressive tendencies. But it is still true that in this study some subjects seemed especially sensitive to their failures and some showed neither sensitivity nor insensitivity. I should point out that it has been typical to criticize these studies for using the interrupted-task technique (e.g., Sears, 1950), because when there is no special threat to self-esteem and interruption is not structured by the experimenter as failure, the technique is widely known to lead to a preponderant tendency to recall the interrupted rather than completed tasks (see Zeigarnik, 1927). The criticism states that it is unwise to try to demonstrate repression, requiring as it does the opposite recall, on such a procedure. From my point of view, this is not a sensible criticism. Special sensitivity to uncompleted tasks has never been convincingly explained and remains an intriguing phenomenon because it suggests defensiveness in its inaccurate rendition of reality and is analogous to the phenomenon of perceptual vigilance.

In another study, MacKinnon and Dukes (1962) attempted to arouse guilt in their subjects, reasoning that this procedure would initiate defensive reactions. Each of the ninety-three subjects was left alone, though secretly observed by the experimenter through a one-way vision screen, to work on a series of tasks so difficult as to be impossible to solve for practically all people. The subjects were given a booklet containing the answers to all problems. They were told they could not look at the answers while working the problems. MacKinnon and Dukes argued that repression could be expected to occur only in subjects who violated the prohibition—43 percent of the group—and then only if they felt guilty about their violations.

When subsequently asked to recall the problems they had worked on, violators (most of whom showed no signs of guilt) remembered most often the problems whose solutions they had seen and least often those whose solutions they had not. A small, atypical group of subjects, who had violated the prohibition and gave signs of guilt in behavior and verbal report, tended to recall problems whose solutions they had looked up less well than they did other problems. These results are particularly interesting, because they suggest that one can expect a defensive reaction only when some conflict has actually been created for the person.

Several other studies have employed a different procedure to investigate the effects of repression on memory. Zeller (1950) first constructed experimental and control groups out of pretested subjects so that there were no group differences in number of trials necessary to learn a set of neutral verbal materials (nonsense syllables). Then the groups were given a psychomotor test rigged so that the control subjects would perform well and have an enjoyable experience while the experimental subjects would perform badly and feel threatened. Following this, all subjects had to relearn the originally neutral materials. It was interpreted as a sign of repression (instituted in the face of threat and generalizing to the associated verbal materials) that experimental subjects required more trials to relearn than did the control subjects. The final procedure involved explaining the rigging of success and failure on the psychomotor task to the experimental subjects and then retesting for speed of relearning. The effect of the debriefing should have been to remove the threat and, hence, the occasion for repression. Consistent with this, the experimental and control groups were no longer different in learning speed. This last finding suggests what Freud meant in "the return of the repressed": If that which has been repressed is still in the mind, it should be recoverable when defensiveness is no longer necessary. Zeller (1951) also demonstrated these effects when the behavior scrutinized for signs of repression is free-recall rather than number of trials to relearn. By now there have been several independent reports of similar findings (e.g., Flavell, 1955; Penn, 1964).

Predictably, criticisms have arisen from researchers convinced that an explanation alternative to that of repression is best. Aborn's (1953) findings suggest that when subjects in the kind of situation used by Zeller are given special instructions to attend to the material to be learned, there is no difference in performance between those who are threatened and those who are not. This simple instruction to remain alert should not have been effective if repression was indeed operating, because defenses are supposed to operate unconsciously. In a similar assault on the repression interpretation, D'Zurilla (1965) showed that in the kind of situation Zeller used, the threatened subjects reported thinking about the psychomotor task more than did the nonthreatened subjects. D'Zurriila argued that if the slower learning of the threatened subjects was indeed due to repression, they should have thought about the materials less, not more.

Holmes and Schallow (1969) tried to provide direct evidence that an interference interpretation is at least as cogent as that involving repression. To a procedure similar to that of Zeller, they added a group that experienced interference (the task they were performing was interrupted at 30 second intervals by portions of a movie). As shown in Figure 6–1, both this group and the more usual threatened group recalled the materials previously learned less well than the control group which was neither threatened nor interrupted. Following debriefing, there were no recall differences among the three groups. Holmes and Schallow believe that not only interruption but also threat is best interpreted as an interference rather than defensiveness phenomenon (cf. Holmes, 1974). It is equally plausible, however, that recall can be worsened in several ways, including interference and repression. In a way, it is surprising that results should emerge from experiments such as these that are at all supportive

FIGURE 6–1   Mean Number of Words Recalled on Test 1, Before Experimental Manipulation; Test 2, After Experimental Manipulation; and Test 3, After Debriefing.

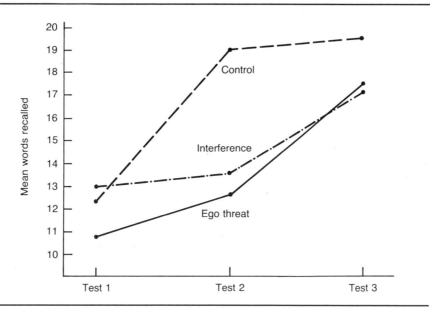

SOURCE: "Reduced Recall After Ego Threat: Repression or Response Competition?" by D. S. Holmes and J. R. Schallow, 1969, *Journal of Personality and Social Psychology, 13*.

of the defensiveness hypothesis, because the conditions of threat are really not such extreme assaults upon the person as those that have provoked personality theorists to their hypotheses about repression.

A flaw in the preceding studies concerning recall and relearning is that only repression was studied. Although repression is admittedly the basic defense, there are others which might even have the effect of especially sensitizing the person. Truax (1957) has reported an experiment of special importance because it took this problem into account. Using a personality test, he selected subjects high and low in the tendency to repress, reasoning that only the former would respond to threat by decreased recall and slow relearning. Truax introduced another procedural improvement in this research tradition by associating threat with only some of the stimulus materials to be learned and exposing all subjects to all stimuli. Thus, subjects served as their own controls. His findings are consistent with the defensiveness theory in that subjects prone to repression indeed recalled and relearned the threatening stimuli less well than the nonthreatening stimuli. If anything, subjects not prone to repression did better on threatening than nonthreatening stimuli. Although this study lends formidable support for the existence of defensiveness, controversy still abounds. Tudor and Holmes (1973) have reported a similar study using recall for completed and uncompleted tasks under stress and nonstress conditions. They did not find that subjects prone to repression recalled fewer incompletions under stress, as one might expect from the standpoint of repression. But their findings are severely complicated by differences in the original learning of completed and uncompleted tasks.

As is so often the case in research, a number of ground-breaking studies must be done in order for the methodological and substantive problems in the area to become clear. Research on defensiveness is no exception to this process. The maturing of defensiveness research is clearly seen in the work of personologists such as Eriksen who have joined together emphases on perception and memory in the context of a more sophisticated version of defense theory than earlier investigators employed. Eriksen (1963) points out

> . . . that the clinical concept of repression is more sophisticated than to assume that all people or even a majority of people automatically repress any sexual or aggressive ideation, or that all anxiety-arousing thoughts or feelings are repressed. Instead, repression is a defense mechanism used sometimes by some people to handle anxiety-arousing thoughts or feelings whose anxiety-provoking nature is a function of the individual's own unique past experience. Thus one would not expect a great deal of communality among people in terms of the kind of stimuli that should lead to repression. Furthermore, theories of personality dynamics also recognize that there are other types of defense mechanisms. Repression is not the only way individuals defend against ego-threatening stimulation.
>
> Intellectualization, reaction formation, and projection are defensive mechanisms that one might expect actually to lead to a sensitization for a stimulus related to the conflict. In the instance of reaction formation, the person manifesting this defense seems to be particularly alert to finding and stamping out the evil that he denies in himself. Similarly, in the case of projection, those manifesting this defense are considered to be hyper-alert to detecting the presence of the defended-against impulse in others. Intellectualization frequently leads to a considerable preoccupation with the subject matter of the unacceptable impulse.
>
> These differences in defensive mechanisms would be expected to have different perceptual concomitants. In the case of repression or denial one might expect a tendency for the subject to manifest avoidance or higher duration thresholds for stimuli related to the sources of conflict. On the other hand, those manifesting defenses of intellectualization, reaction formation or projection might be expected to show a lower duration threshold for anxiety-related stimuli. (pp. 42–43)

There are two things of great importance in this passage. The first is that perceptual vigilance may reflect the sensitizing defenses, such as reaction formation and intellectualization, whereas perceptual defense reflects the desensitizing defenses, such as repression and denial. I would suggest, further, that sensitization and desensitization effects on memory, in the form of recall for failed or completed tasks, also reflect these two kinds of defensive process. The second important point is that research concerning the effects of defense on perception should include independent information on the kinds of defenses the subject generally tends to use, so that one can predict precisely what kinds of perceptual effects one will find. It seems to me that this point is well taken in the study of defensive effects on memory and other aspects of cognition.

Eriksen has done a number of studies guided by these criteria. In the first, he (Eriksen, 1951a) used hospitalized mental patients who were selected on the basis of their having conflicts in specified need areas and their likelihood of manifesting desensitizing defensive operations. The degree of emotional disturbance in the three need areas of aggression, homosexuality, and succorance was assessed through use of a modified word association technique. Disturbance scores on this test were then related to the subjects' tachistoscopic recognition times for pictures, some of which related to the three need areas and some of which did not. Patients whose word associations showed significant disturbance in a need area were found to require longer exposure intervals for recognition of the corresponding need-related pictures than for recognition of neutral pictures. The correlations describing this effect are shown in the first three rows of the final three columns in Table 6–2. In another, similar study, Eriksen (1951b) found that emotional stimuli did not necessarily lead to high tachistoscopic recognition times. Subjects who showed extensive, overtly aggressive behavior and who expressed aggressive content in composing stories about pictures were found to have lower recognition times for tachistoscopically presented pictures having aggressive content.

Lazarus, Eriksen, and Fonda (1951) pinpointed the meaning of the opposing trends found in the above two studies. Psychiatric outpatients were used as subjects and classified on the basis of their therapeutic interviews and other clinical tests as either sensitizers or repressers depending on whether they characteristically responded to anxiety in terms of intellectualization as a defense or tended to avoid and deny thoughts and ideas related to the conflicts.

TABLE 6–2   Intercorrelation of the Word Association and Perceptual Recognition Scores for the Three Need Areas*

Score	Word Association			Perceptual Recognition		
	Agg.	*Suc.*	*Homo.*	*Agg.*	*Suc.*	*Homo.*
Word association						
Aggression	.636	.582		.417	.435	.216
Succorance		.282		−.281	.611	.180
Homosexuality				−.101	.264	.314
Perceptual recognition						
Aggression					.352	.180
Succorance						.060

*Eta is used as the measure of relationship. Evaluated via the F test, an eta of .415 is significant at the .95 level.

SOURCE: "Perceptual Defense as a Function of Unacceptable Needs" by C.W. Eriksen, 1951, *Journal of Abnormal and Social Psychology, 46.*

TABLE 6–3   Comparison of Intellectualizers and Repressers on Perceptual Recognition and Sentence Completion Test

Auditory Perceptual Recognition	Repressers (N = 12)		Intellectualizers (N = 13)		
	Mean	S.D.	Mean	S.D.	t
Sex*	− .25	1.18	+ 1.60	1.48	3.32
Hostility*	− 1.10	1.32	+ .30	1.25	2.67
Neutral*	5.27	1.59	6.17	1.59	1.36
Sentence completion test					
Sex	6.20	1.39	9.10	4.52	2.02
Hostility	5.50	1.70	8.00	4.31	1.77

Note: For a one-tailed test, *t* values of 1.71 and 2.50 are significant at the .05 and the .01 levels, respectively.
*Using adjusted sense-perceived scores (that is, subtracting neutral score from score on critical materials—sex and hostility, respectively; if less critical material was correctly perceived than neutral, score would be minus).

SOURCE: "Personality Dynamics in Auditory Perceptual Recognition" by R.S. Lazarus, C. W. Eriksen, and C. P. Fonda, 1951, *Journal of Personality, 19.*

The results, as shown in Table 6–3, indicated that the sensitizers tended to give freely aggressive and sexual endings to a sentence completion test whereas the repressers tended to block or distort into innocuous forms sentence completion items that normally would suggest either aggressive or sexual content. Further, when performance on the sentence completion test was compared with auditory perception of hostile and sexual sentences heard against a noise background, the sensitizers were superior to the repressers in recognition of the emotional content.

Eriksen (1952) also did a study relating the effects of repression on perception and on memory. He put a group of college freshmen through a series of tasks, half of which they were permitted to finish and half of which involved interruption, in much the manner of Rosenzweig's work. The tasks were structured as measures of intelligence and the interruptions as failures. As we would expect on the basis of Rosenzweig's work, the subjects showed wide differences in preponderance of recall of completed or interrupted tasks. The two groups were then administered a word association test, and in a subsequent testing session their tachistoscopic exposure times for correct recognition of long-, medium-, and short-association-time words were determined. As shown in Table 6–4, the subjects who recalled successfully completed tasks on the memory study showed higher tachistoscopic exposure times for correct recognition of long-association-time words, whereas subjects who recalled their failures on the memory study showed no significant relationship between recognition times and association times. Once you get to a study that is this sophisticated, concerns itself with the related effects of a defensive process on

TABLE 6–4   Correlations between Association Times and Recognition Thresholds for the Success-Recall and Failure-Recall Groups Where Recognition Thresholds Have Been Corrected for Total Group Performance

Subjects	Success-Recall		Subjects	Failure-Recall	
	r	z		r	z
A	.49	.54	a	.02	.02
B	.46	.50	b	.11	.11
C	.24	.25	c	.05	.05
D	.29	.30	d	.21	.21
E	.43	.46	e	.04	.04
F	.30	.31	f	.00	.00
G	.29	.30	g	−.13	−.13
	.38			.04	

Mean z score:
Combined
   variance
   estimate: .012

$t = 5.73$ $p < .001$

SOURCE: "Defense Against Ego-Threat in Memory and Perception" by C. W. Eriksen, 1952, *Journal of Abnormal and Social Psychology*, 47.

more than one cognitive function, and considers more than one kind of defensive process, the types of criticisms that seemed so weighty when leveled at the perceptual studies of Postman, Bruner, and McGinnies virtually lose all significance. There are by now numerous other studies like this one, but we will not review them all. We will, however, consider two more research themes because they exemplify the gradual broadening, deepening, and enrichment that has taken place in defensiveness research.

In the first theme, Eriksen and his associates (Eriksen, 1954; Eriksen & Brown, 1956; Eriksen & Davids, 1955) successfully related the difference between sensitizing and repressing to the difference between hysterical and psychasthenic tendencies as measured by a respected test of psychopathological tendencies, the Minnesota Multiphasic Personality Inventory. In current psychoanalytic conceptions of neurosis, the defense mechanism of repression is predominantly associated with hysteria while that of intellectualization is considered characteristic of the obsessive-compulsive or psychasthenic neurosis. Eriksen found that subjects scoring high on the hysteria scale tended to recall successfully completed tasks on the memory test following task performance, whereas subjects scoring high on the psychasthenia scale tended to recall failed tasks. More recently, Cook (1985) reported that repressers showed more sweating (measured by electrical skin conductance) while giving a videotaped talk about themselves, even though they were conscious of less distress, than did sensitizers.

As part of this theme, it is now common to measure a repressive-defensive style involving subjective report of low anxiety along with strong signs of image maintenance or responding in a socially desirable fashion (Weinberger, Schwartz, & Davidson, 1979). Such repressive-defensive subjects show greater physiological arousal in stressful tasks (Qualls, 1983) and have fewer memories of their activities (Davis & Schwartz, 1986) than do subjects low in image-maintenance, whether they are high or low in reported anxiety. There is much support in this kind of research for the notion of defense.

In the second research theme, Gur and Sackeim (1979; Sackeim & Gur, 1978, 1979) have meticulously investigated a particular kind of self-deception, namely, the misidentification of one's own voice when it is played back as one of a series of voices all reading the same passage. They argue that in order for such misidentification to qualify as true defensive self-deception, it must be shown that subjects (1) simultaneously hold two contradictory beliefs about what voice they are hearing, (2) are unaware or unconscious of one of the beliefs, and (3) have a motivational commitment to keep that belief unconscious.

In surprisingly ingenious and precise research, Gur and Sackeim were able to find evidence for all three criteria of self-deception. First, in findings reminiscent of the "subception" mentioned earlier, they showed that subjects whose verbal report misidentified the voices to which they were listening showed in their sweating changes (galvanic skin response) that they discriminated their own voices from others at the physiological level. Thus, these subjects appeared to hold two contradictory beliefs at the same time. That they were unaware of one of these beliefs (second criterion) was shown by post-experimental interviews in which they gave no sign of realizing that they had misidentified voices and by a complex assessment of presence or absence of a well-known, telltale galvanic skin response change that normally occurs in response to the voice following one's own. It appears, therefore, that the subjects were not aware of having one of the contradictory beliefs. The final, or motivational, criterion was approached in two ways. In one study, it was shown that questionnaire respondents who indicated a tendency toward self-deception failed to correctly identify their own voices more often than did those with high self-esteem. In an attempt to demonstrate the causal status of motivational tendencies, Gur and Sackeim did another study in which they found that by increasing or decreasing subjects' self-esteem by making them think they were exceptional or poor in intelligence, they could increase or decrease their subsequent tendency to misidentify their own voices. Through a combination of these two studies, it seems plausible to conclude that the tendency to misidentify voices is indeed defensive and not due just to inattention.

The Gur and Sackeim studies are too complicated to be presented in detail here, but they emerge as a model for this area, despite some recent controversy

(Douglas & Gibbins, 1983; Sackeim & Gur, 1985; Gibbins & Douglas, 1985). Along with the work on repressive and sensitizing styles, these studies represent formidable evidence for the tenability of the concept of defense.

The studies cited demonstrate empirical support for the existence of human defensive reactions that extend across learning, perceptual, and memory processes. Other research in defensiveness adds little new to what we have already considered. To be sure, there seem to be at least two broad categories of defensiveness, namely, desensitization and sensitization. And certainly there are many loose ends, some of which will prove relevant to issues I will pose later. But with regard to the present issue of whether a concept of defense is tenable, we clearly must conclude that there are systematic empirical findings that recommend the concept to us. Happily enough, the systematic studies concur with the anecdotal clinical observations with which we began discussion of the issue. By way of more precise summary, the operation of defenses has been shown both when certain stimuli were rendered anxiety-provoking through experimental manipulation and when stimuli were chosen so as to be likely to engage common conflicts permeating the subjects' lives. The effects of sensitizing and desensitizing defenses have been shown on perception of stimuli exposed for brief periods of time and on memory of activities engaged in previously. In some of the most recent studies, these two kinds of effect have been shown to occur together and in a manner consistent with the implications of different kinds of defenses for psychopathological tendencies.

Although we can now say with some authority that there is evidence supporting the notion of defense as an explanatory concept, we are still left with the nagging criticism, underlying this whole issue, of the nonsensical nature of theorizing that assumes a person within a person. It is time to grapple with this criticism now that it is clear that there is rigorously scientific evidence recommending the concept of defense to us. As I suggested earlier, if it is possible to suggest a basis on which the overly figurative language that incessantly surrounds the concept of defense can be translated into language descriptive of known capabilities of single organisms, the person-within-a-person criticism will lose considerable force. I believe that recent physiological and cognitive experimentation and theorizing make this translation possible and propose to discuss this matter now. Much of what I will say follows the brilliant start made by Bruner (1957b) in his introduction of the concept of *gating*. To set the orientation from which the idea of gating emerges, Bruner quotes from the physiologist Adrian (1954), who was knighted for his excellence:

> The operations of the brain stem seem to be related to particular fields of sensory information which vary from moment to moment with the shifts of our attention. The signals from the sense organs must be treated differently when we attend to them and when we do not, and if we could decide how and where the divergencies arise, we should be nearer to understanding how the level of consciousness is reached. The question is whether the afferent messages that evoke sensations are allowed at all times to reach the cerebral cortex or are sometimes blocked at a lower level. Clearly we can reduce the inflow from the

sense organs as we do by closing the eyes and relaxing the muscles when we wish to sleep and it is quite probable that the sensitivity of some of the sense organs can be directly influenced by the central nervous system. But even in deep sleep or coma there is no reason to believe that sensory messages no longer reach the central nervous system. At some stage therefore on their passage to consciousness the messages meet with barriers that are sometimes open and sometimes closed. Where are these barriers, in the cortex, the brain stem, or elsewhere? (pp. 238–239)

How far this statement goes beyond the old notion of the nervous system involving little more than stimulation of a sense organ, conduction of that stimulation to the sensory area of the cortex, translation into an action message in the motor cortex, and transmission from there peripherally to the muscles! Adrian is clearly positing central nervous system control of stimulation coming into the organism. Such control, dubbed *gating* by Bruner, would, if discovered, render the psychological concept of defense much more plausible. In the possibility of central nervous system control of peripheral stimulation lies the basis for translating the concept of defense into the kind of sensible terms that will obviate the person-within-a-person criticism.

There is even some empirical evidence to support the notion of gating. Hernandez-Peon, Scherrer, and Jouvet (1956) did a physiological experiment on cats in which they arranged to obtain a recording of the electrical discharge, called *potential,* in the nerve cells just past the auditory sense organ, called the *cochlear nucleus,* on the way toward the brain. They arranged their apparatus such that whenever they sounded a click in a cat's ear, they could determine the intensity and rate of electrical impulses in those nerves immediately central to the sense organ. After recording enough to determine the normal level of electrical activity as a response to the sounds, Hernandez-Peon et al. introduced three kinds of nonauditory distractors. While being exposed to the click, cats were shown two mice in a bell jar, were given fish odors to smell, or were shocked on the forepaw,—that is, visual, olfactory, and somatic distractors were employed. Strange and marvelous to tell, electrical activity in the nerves just central to the cochlear nucleus were markedly reduced under all three conditions over what it had been without the distractors! Presumably, messages being transmitted to the brain over one sensory channel entered into some central nervous system process whereby stimulation reaching another sense organ was not transmitted beyond that organ. Even without knowing more about this mysterious process, we can recognize that it clearly indicates the tenability of the concept of defense at the physiological level of analysis. The nervous system apparently can do what seemed so nonsensical to many psychologists and philosophers.

Hernandez-Peon and his associates have given evidence suggesting a physiological basis for desensitizing defenses at least in the auditory perceptual system. The work of other investigators (e.g., Galambos, Sheatz, & Vernier, 1956; Granit, 1955) suggests the generality of this phenomenon beyond the auditory modality and also gives evidence of a similar physiological mechanism for the sensitizing defenses. One of the clearest demonstrations of the latter—again in the auditory modality—occurs in Galambos et al. (1956). They utilized a recording procedure and experimental design similar to that of Hernandez-Peon et al., except that they made the click presented at the cat's ear a signal for subsequent shock. Once the cats had learned the click's signal value, the presentation of the click without the shock was enough to produce a greater burst of electrical activity from the nerve cells central to the cochlear nucleus than occurred in control animals for which the click did not function as a shock signal. It is as if the learning process involved a tuning of the auditory system to be more sensitive to clicks than normally.

More complete and precise evidence that the central nervous system tunes or detunes peripheral sensory systems is provided by Galambos (1956) in an ingenious study. Arranging recording apparatus in a fashion similar to that in his previous study and that of Hernandez-Peon et al., Galambos also stimulated the superior olivary nucleus of his cats (the superior olivary nucleus is a major subcortical center of the brain for the auditory system). He found that whenever he stimulated this nucleus, the electrical activity occurring just central to the cochlear nucleus in response to the clicks presented at the ear was markedly reduced. What Galambos did was produce the effect found by Hernandez-Peon et al. by stimulating a brain center directly rather than by providing stimulation in a nonauditory sensory modality. These results are an important link in the chain demonstrating central nervous system control of peripheral sensitivity.

Although some of the research findings mentioned here have proven difficult to replicate, some additional research and theorizing have suggested the existence of a gating mechanism for pain (Clark & Hunt, 1971; Melzack & Wall, 1968), a sensation that has for so long resisted explanation. It is also compelling that effects have been found in humans that may be macroscopic counterparts to physiological gating. For example, visual perception experiments show that subjects' pupils expand and contract in diameter partly as a function of their attitudes and needs (Hess, 1965) and these changes in pupil size may alter perceivers' sensitivity to external stimuli (Hutt & Anderson, 1967).

The kind of evidence provided by the studies in this section clearly is relevant to the effects of defenses on perception but not immediately so to other effects of defenses. Nevertheless, I encourage you to recognize that there are sensory systems other than the traditional, obvious ones having to do with stimulation reaching the organism from the outside world. There are sensory systems that alert the organism to its internal world, such as the kinesthetic and proprioceptive systems. It is certainly possible that such systems are also tuned by the central nervous system; if so, there is ample basis for more widespread effects of defense than on exteroceptive perception alone. Although evidence for interoceptive tuning is absent at this point, I submit that the revolutionary step has already been taken in such work as Galambos and Hernandez-Peon and in the theorizing of Adrian, Bruner, and Melzack and Wall.

Perhaps exteroceptive and interoceptive sensory stimulation entering the central nervous system is comparable to a template or model of stimulation existing in the memory. This template or model could well be affected by the past history of reward and punishment encountered in dealing with other people. When incoming stimulation and the template match well, no gating occurs. But when they do not match, the discrepancy may constitute the physiological concomitant of conflict and anxiety. The mismatch may instigate some control process that sensitizes or desensitizes some or all exteroceptive and interoceptive sensory modalities such that only the stimulation that matches the template would be permitted to pass on to the brain. Stimulation not permitted to pass on would then be unconscious, because it was literally not in the brain even though it existed at the level of the sense organs.

This position is quite consistent with the views on selective attention developing in the field of cognitive psychology. According to Erdelyi (1974), processing of stimulation by humans involves a great deal of central nervous system control of peripheral stimulation. It is theorized that stimulus input is first stored in the nervous system as raw, or uncoded, data. These raw data images fade rapidly, however, as they are too numerous for the storage capacities of the central nervous system. Therefore, they must be encoded, or reduced by a categorizing process (such as grouping by perceived similarities and differences), so that they can be retained for a longer period in short-term storage. This encoding process is controlled by the contents of long-term memory, such as the person's wishes, values, expectancies, and defensive requirements. According to Erdelyi, input stored as raw data is not yet conscious but can have such effects as arousing defensive operations. Only when input has entered short-term storage does it become conscious; note, however, that it will already have been transformed into something acceptable. Finally, input from short-term storage can undergo further alteration and become part of long-term memory, where it will, in turn, have a controlling effect on subsequent input. In the attempt to understand how persons can utilize the enormous flood of stimulation they experience without becoming overwhelmed, cognitive psychologists have provided personologists with a view of mental life quite consistent with theories of defensiveness.

As you can see, the person-within-a-person criticism recedes in cogency once theorizing such as that of Erdelyi (and the research that stands behind it) is available. Now we can talk in more descriptive and less figurative terms of raw-data storage, short-term storage, and long-term memory and delineate how matches and mismatches among the contents of these units can trigger defenses and the transformation of stimulus input. It seems to me that all this renders the concept of defense more plausible than its critics would have admitted some years ago. For the moment, I am ready to conclude that it is tenable.

This conclusion has an obvious bearing on the three models of personality we have been considering. Clearly it is not a black mark against a model that includes, or even relies on, the concept of defense. The empirical evidence showing the existence of sensitizing and desensitizing behaviors actually favors the models that specifically employ the concept of defense. On this basis, the conflict and fulfillment models, in all their versions, seem fruitful. The consistency model seems less so, for the concept of defense is not a logically integral part of it. This is least true as a criticism of the activation version of the consistency model exemplified by the theory of Fiske and Maddi. In their discussion of corrections for discrepancies between customary and actual levels of activation that literally have taken place, Fiske and Maddi stress behavior that has the characteristics of the sensitizing and desensitizing processes supported by the research we have considered.

Second Issue: Is All Behavior Defensive?

Having encountered empirical support for the belief that defensive behavior occurs, we must now consider whether all or only some behavior is defensive in character. There is an issue involved here, because the pure form of the psychosocial conflict model would assume that all behavior is defensive whereas most other models assume this of only some behavior. Actually, the cognitive dissonance version of the consistency model gives no explicit role to defense. Most of the anecdotal and empirical evidence relevant to this issue has already been discussed in the previous section. Of particular importance is research permitting one to see whether there is behavior that does not distort reality in a context entailing pressure toward distortion.

Meager though the findings are, I have pointed out that each time a study was designed and analyzed such that it was possible to note not only desensitization and sensitization but normal or accurate sensitivity, some subjects fell into this last category. This result is most clear in the experiments on memory, and it has persisted through all experimental attempts to increase the likelihood of defense through pressuring subjects. Apparently some people do function nondefensively at least some of the time. It will do no good to say that this shows merely that the experiment was successful only for some people—that only some had their anxieties aroused and conflicts engaged. This very statement recognizes that some people function without defensiveness at least some of the time!

Although similar evidence from perceptual studies is harder to come by, there is some. For example, in their study of self-deception Gur and Sackeim (1979) found that some subjects were always accurate (where inaccuracy signifies defensiveness) in the task of identifying their own voices and those of others presented in a series. But most perception investigators have not been particularly interested in the proportion of their subjects who perceived accurately—that is, not in an unsensitive or hypersensitive fashion; hence, they have not analyzed their data so as to make this information available. But a perusal of their findings clearly shows two things: There are marked differences in perceptual speed among the subjects in a typical study, and the average differences in time necessary for perception of critical as opposed to neutral words typically are quite small. These two kinds of results strongly suggest that the proportion of subjects perceiving accurately might well be sizable.

In my judgment, the evidence, though not extensive, supports the contention that some people do not appear to appreciably distort reality, even when pressured and threatened. Therefore, we have an empirical basis for resolving the issue posed earlier in favor of the position that some but not all behavior is defensive. This conclusion has far-reaching implications, particularly that the pure conflict model of the psychosocial type is limited in usefulness for understanding personality. You will recall that this kind of model employs a concept of defense because it postulates an individual with essentially selfish concerns and a society with antithetical concerns and the capability of ferreting out and punishing selfishness. The concept of defense is used in such theories to account for the whole orientation of a person's life whereby he or she can avoid punishment and guilt while still protecting some small basis for self-satisfaction. The asserted ubiquitousness of defensiveness in this model is called into question by our empirical analysis. But the usefulness of the intrapsychic version of the conflict model is not challenged, for this version recognizes the existence of defensive behavior without assuming that all behavior is defensive. The same is true of the variant on the psychosocial version of the conflict model exemplified by Murray and the ego psychologists. This position assumes an inherent basis for functioning without conflict and, therefore, without defense. The conflict theory that fares worst on the basis of our conclusion concerning the second issue is that of Freud.

As you can see, the fulfillment model is completely supported by our conclusion. This is because the model conceptualizes conflict, anxiety, and defense as possible but not inevitable outcomes of living. In all versions and variants of this model, defense occurs but is not ubiquitous. As already suggested in concluding discussion of the first issue, the cognitive dissonance version of the consistency model is called into question by the empirical evidence indicating the existence of defensive behavior. But the activation version of this model, exemplified by the theory of Fiske and Maddi, was considered tenable. The conclusion reached here reinforces the tenability of this position, because the position certainly does not make correctional (quasi-defensive) behaviors ubiquitous; they occur only when anticipational behaviors have failed. Anticipational behaviors might well fail in laboratory situations, in which one cannot completely select one's experiences.

Third Issue: Is the Highest Form of Living Adaptive or Transcendent?

You will recall that according to the pure psychosocial version of the conflict model, the highest form of living is that which involves adaptation to the imperatives of society. Clearly this position is related to the assumption of ubiquitous conflict between individual and society, with defensiveness being the individual's only protection. According to this position, maturity involves such traits as dependability, generosity, loyalty, respect for others and society, steady productivity, and evenness of mood. Immature behaviors involve impulsivity, rebelliousness, disrespect for others and social institutions, and general unpredictability. In sharp contrast, the fulfillment model considers repetitive, conforming, unimaginative behavior to be defensive and immature. This is consistent with the position's devaluation of social adjustment as a goal of life. Transcendence of social conventions (which are not considered imperatives) is virtually necessary for vigorous, mature living. Understandably enough, maturity is characterized by the fulfillment model as nondefensive and free of psychosocial conflict. Other versions and variants of the conflict model fall somewhere between the two extremes I have drawn. The consistency model is not characterizable on this third issue.

Although the third issue can be precisely pinpointed, it is not clear to me that it can really be settled by empirical analysis. Certainly we can well expect to find evidence in people of both adaptive and transcendent behaviors. Which type is better will inevitably be a matter of opinion. A conflict theorist can assert with cogency that someone showing good citizenship is an excellent person. A fulfillment theorist can wax equally eloquent on someone whose artistic inclination leads him or her to function outside of social conventions. In order for empirical analysis to resolve this issue in a definitive manner, both conflict and fulfillment theorists would have to agree on the admirability of one discernible kind of person. Then a consideration of the behavioral traits of this kind of person might clarify whether he or she seems primarily adaptational or transcendent. Perhaps the closest we can come to such agreement is with the creative person. Creative people currently are celebrated in our culture as having achieved a pinnacle of living. They are lauded, envied, emulated, and supported by government grants. Both conflict and fulfillment theorists would consider them admirable people. We must be just a bit careful, however, for some people still harbor suspicion that the creative person is really unsavory, dangerous, and lazy. In addition, if you asked people to identify the creative members of their group, there might well be considerable disagreement. Nonetheless, studying the behavioral traits of creative people is probably as close as we can come to an empirical basis for resolving the third issue.

Although there are a number of recent studies of creative people, none is so carefully done and comprehensive as that of MacKinnon (1965; Hall & MacKinnon, 1969). Having decided to concentrate on architects, MacKinnon asked eminent administrators and educators in that field to nominate the most creative members of the profession. By pooling the information thus obtained, he was able to select a sample of architects who were generally agreed on as being creative. By comparison with a control group of randomly selected architects, the creative group included a great many prizewinners and leaders. Although it is not entirely clear what the measure of creativity means in this study, it is not likely to be far from the current emphases of psychologists. It is rather generally agreed now that the creative act produces something both novel and significant and that the creative person is someone who produces creative acts consistently (Bruner, 1962b; Jackson & Messick, 1965; Taylor & Getzels, 1975).

MacKinnon's creative architects were compared with the control group on many tests of personality. One of the most overwhelmingly clear findings of this study is that the creative architects were more transcendent than the control group. They described themselves as being rather uninterested in socializing, unconcerned about their popularity with and acceptance by others, unusual and idiosyncratic in their habits and beliefs, and more concerned with quality than acceptability or quantity in their work. Although they considered themselves able to be intimate with friends, they cared little for social amenities. In addition, they did not seem overly concerned with their self-preoccupation and their disdain for the social system. Lest you doubt whether these self-descriptions bear any relationship to the way other people saw these creative architects, let me assure you that they do. On the basis of personal contact with them over a period of some days, MacKinnon's staff of psychologists found the creative architects to be much as they described themselves. The creative architects were less predictable, repetitive, and conforming but more imaginative, intense, and original than the control architects. Corroboration of the transcendent qualities mentioned thus far was also obtained from the creative architects life histories. All in all, they were not adapting to social institutions so much as changing them or else functioning outside of them.

Albeit on a less comprehensive scale, many other studies of creativity support the findings reviewed above. For example, Cross, Cattell, and Butcher (1967) compared sixty-three visual artists and twenty-eight craft students with a matched control group on scores derived from the 16 Personality Factor Questionnaire (devised by Cattell and Stice, 1957). Statistically significant differences in average scores were found on twelve of the sixteen factors, with the craft students typically falling between the artists and the control subjects. Especially salient features of the artists' personalities were assertiveness (or dominance), self-sufficiency, personal integration, casualness, Bohemian tendencies, and low superego strength. In addition to these transcendent qualities, they were high in suspiciousness, proneness to guilt, tension, and emotional instability. This hint of inconsistency was also found by Barron (1963), who summarized ten years of research as indicating the presence in artistically creative persons of spirituality and a belief in self-renewal but also the possibility of personal conflict. Recently, Helson and Crutchfield (1970) and Helson

(1973a; 1973b; 1977) reported that creative mathematicians and writers are more unconventional, assertive, and independent than their less creative counterparts.

Perhaps the intimation of difficulty in relating to others is a somewhat natural sequel of the transcendent orientation present in creative persons. In this regard, Schaefer (1969), like so many other investigators, found creative adolescents (and, for that matter, adults) to show tolerance for ambiguity, impulsivity, craving for novelty, autonomy, and self-assertiveness. The theme of unconventionality was carried through by Getzels and Csikszentmihalyi (1976), who found their creative art students especially good at posing problems (rather than accepting problems as structured for them by others).

There is little point in chronicling the other studies of creativity (see Razik, 1965; Stein, 1968), for all are in essential agreement on the transcendent quality of the phenomenon. Even historical research into the lives of persons remembered as having been greatly creative (e.g., Maddi, 1965) testify to the transcendent nature of their lives. There is a streak of what might almost be called selfishness in great persons. Most of them have deeply believed in their own greatness. Even Freud, the arch–conflict theorist, seems to have had such a belief (Jones, 1955). Studies of living persons identified as creative support this conclusion (e.g., Taylor, 1963). These various sources of evidence incline me to the conclusion that the highest form of functioning is transcendent rather than adaptive.

This conclusion clearly favors the fulfillment model over the conflict model in its psychosocial version. Not especially hurt by the findings are the intrapsychic versions of the conflict and consistency models. In classical Freudian thinking, which is the prototype of psychosocial conflict theory, there was no convincing explanation of creativity. Creativity tended to be seen as somewhat akin to madness. In madness, the person is as close to lacking defenses as it is possible to be, according to classical psychoanalytic thinking. In this state, functioning is chaotic, destructive, and riddled with anxiety. Instincts are fairly directly expressed, to the detriment of the person and others in the surroundings. Creativity is considered less violent and psychopathological but somehow on the same continuum. The creative act was accounted for as an instinctual expression over which the person has little control. Clearly this attempt to explain creativity is untenable in light of the findings of studies such as those reviewed here. It was only with the advent of ego psychology that personologists who found themselves temperamentally in the psychoanalytic camp could explain creativity in a manner that made it distinguishable from madness. But this explanation requires the addition to the psychosocial conflict model of aspects of a fulfillment model. The result is really a new theory, as I pointed out in Chapter 3.

The ego psychology explanation of creativity involves *regression in the service of the ego* (Kris, 1952). In this context, regression, or the retreat to an earlier level of development, is not an unavoidable, unrecognized attempt to avoid anxiety. Instead, it is a consciously precipitated return to a more childish state in order to find inspiration through momentarily relinquishing the very socialization that is considered so valuable in everyday life. So while regression in the service of the ego retains the reality-distorting element of defensiveness, there is nothing defensive about its conscious operation and subjection to self-control. The ego psychology explanation of creativity comes as close to the fulfillment model as it can while retaining something of the conflict model; creativity is not properly considered defensive, even though it involves some relinquishment of social realities.

There is very little by way of systematic empirical evidence for or against this psychoanalytic view. One relevant study, however, is that of Gray (1969), who aimed at determining the relationship between a measure of regression in the service of the ego and a measure of creativity in a sample of 100 male undergraduates. Although he initially found a positive correlation between the two, the correlation was essentially removed by his correcting for the effects of sheer productivity of responses. This suggests that the presumed relationship between creativity and regression in the service of the ego is really a reflection of the more general variable of productivity.

Fourth Issue: Is Cognitive Dissonance Invariably Unpleasant and Avoided?

The pure cognitive dissonance version of the consistency model makes any degree and kind of discrepancy among expectancies, thoughts, and perceptions the source of emotional discomfort and attempts at avoidance. It is true that here and there in Kelly's writings one can find a suggestion that small discrepancies may be interesting as long as no construct is threatened with disconfirmation. But the overwhelming thrust of this theory is on the value of consistency. Even Kelly's dimensions of transition reflecting reactions to some sort of discrepancy are all negative emotions (e.g., anxiety, hostility). Obviously this position is very sensible. To perceive something different from what one thought or expected is to have been wrong—and who can rest easy with that? To think one way and perceive yourself as acting another way is to be dishonest, cowardly, or inept, none of which is acceptable. To harbor two discrepant thoughts or beliefs at the same time is to be confused—and who wants that? The principle is the same whether the inconsistency is small or large, important or unimportant.

The issue of whether this position is accurate is raised from a number of sectors of psychology. Within the cognitive dissonance model itself we have the variant position, exemplified by McClelland, which contends that only large discrepancies are unpleasant and avoided whereas small discrepancies are actually pleasurable and sought after. Moreover, in the activation version of the consistency model, exemplified by the theory of Fiske and Maddi, there is the view that cognitive dissonance, in the degree required for maintenance of customary levels of activation, will be pleasant and pursued. Somewhat complete disagreement with the pure cognitive dissonance version of the consistency model has been shown by an increasing number of psychologists who believe that variety has significant positive value for the organism.

In addition, the fulfillment model does not agree with the cognitive dissonance model in any proper sense. If cognitive consistency stood in the way of fulfillment, for fulfillment theorists consistency would be actually unpleasant. In this, fulfillment theorists would agree with Emerson (1940) in his crackling line from the essay on self-reliance, "A foolish consistency is the hobgoblin of little minds." In fulfillment theory, there is the sense that cognitive consistency usually means the person's conformity with an external, societal definition of life. To be consistent often is to give up fulfillment. The disagreement of fulfillment theorists would not depend on how large the cognitive dissonance was, as in the case of McClelland and Fiske and Maddi, but on the content of the inconsistency.

Superficially, the conflict model would seem to agree rather closely with the cognitive dissonance version of the consistency model. After all, conflict is the incompatibility between two opposing forces. But you must keep in mind that in conflict theory it is not *any* discrepancy that is important but only discrepancies between the two forces considered to be basic to the person. So at the very least, conflict theory is much narrower in its specificity to particular content than is cognitive dissonance theory. But the difference does not end here. You should also recognize that it is possible to imagine a discrepancy that, because it involves no conflict between the two opposing forces, would not necessarily be considered unpleasant and to be avoided by a conflict theorist. It is only when discrepancy is synonymous with conflict that conflict theory would agree with cognitive dissonance theory. Thus, like fulfillment theory, conflict theory would be at issue with cognitive dissonance theory only in the case of certain matters of content.

We are now ready to turn to empirical evidence bearing on the issue. Surprisingly, Kelly's theory, the most comprehensive example of the pure cognitive dissonance version of the consistency model—has generated no systematic research relevant to determining whether dissonance is invariably unpleasant and avoided. Happily, however, study upon study has come out of Festinger's position, which, though not a theory of personality, is certainly in agreement with Kelly's on the issue before us. We will now consider important and representative examples of this body of research, along with criticisms that have been raised. Following this, we will examine systematic research representing the opposing point of view—that of variety theory—along with relevant criticism. Finally, we will find some basis for resolving the issue.

Research attempting to demonstrate the avoidance of cognitive dissonance aroused considerable enthusiasm in the past. I think the reason for the enthusiasm is clear. Festinger and his various associates presented in a persuasive, impassioned, and committed way a scheme for understanding social and individual change that was at the same time extraordinarily simple but comprehensive. In addition, they argued their position not in the arid arena of pure thought but in the rich, complex context of important life events. And when

they did experiments, they focused on results that,though predicted by dissonance theory, would not have been predicted from more familiar and obvious
frames of reference.

I would like to start our review of the research in this tradition by quoting
at length from an article by Festinger (1958) that shows not only dramatic
forcefulness of exposition but emphasis on significant life events. The episode
described is from a naturalistic or observational piece of research:

> Another intriguing example of the reduction of dissonance in a startling manner
> comes from a study I did together with Riecken and Schachter. . . . of a group
> of people who predicted that, on a given date, a catastrophic flood would over-
> whelm most of the world. This prediction of the catastrophic flood had been
> given to the people in direct communications from the gods and was an integral
> part of their religious beliefs. When the predicted date arrived and passed there
> was considerable dissonance established in these people. They continued to
> believe in their gods and in the validity of the communications from them, and
> at the same time they knew that the prediction of the flood had been wrong. We
> observed the movement as participants for approximately two months preced-
> ing and one month after this unequivocal disproof of part of their belief. The
> point of the study was, of course, to observe how they would react to the
> dissonance. Let me give you a few of the details of the disproof and how they
> reacted to it.
>
> For some time it had been clear to the people in the group that those who
> were chosen were to be picked up by flying saucers before the cataclysm oc-
> curred. Some of the believers, these mainly college students, were advised to
> go home and wait individually for the flying saucer that would arrive for each of
> them. This was reasonable and plausible, since the date of the cataclysm hap-
> pened to occur during an academic holiday. Most of the group, including the
> most central and most heavily committed members, gathered together in the
> home of the woman who received the message from the gods to wait together
> for the arrival of the saucer. For these latter, disproof of the prediction, in the
> form of evidence that the messages were not valid, began to occur four days
> before the predicted event was to take place. A message informed them that a
> saucer would land in the back yard of the house at 4:00 p.m. to pick up the
> members of the group. With coat in hand they waited, but no saucer came. A
> later message told them there had been a delay—the saucer would arrive at
> midnight. Midst absolute secrecy (the neighbors and press must not know) they
> waited outdoors on a cold and snowy night for over an hour, but still no saucer
> came. At about 3:00 a.m. they gave up, interpreting the events of that night as a
> test, a drill, and a rehearsal for the real pickup which would still soon take
> place.
>
> Tensely, they waited for the final orders to come through—for the messages
> which would tell them the time, place, and procedure for the actual pickup.
> Finally, on the day before the cataclysm was to strike, the messages came. At
> midnight a man would come to the door of the house and take them to the place
> where the flying saucer would be parked. More messages came that day, one
> after another, instructing them in the passwords that would be necessary in
> order to board the saucer, in preparatory procedures such as removal of metal
> from clothing, removal of personal identification, maintaining silence at certain

times, and the like. The day was spent by the group in preparation and rehearsal of the necessary procedures and, when midnight came, the group sat waiting in readiness. But no knock came at the door, no one came to lead them to the flying saucer.

From midnight to five o'clock in the morning the group sat there struggling to understand what had happened, struggling to find some explanation that would enable them to recover somewhat from the shattering realization that they would not be picked up by a flying saucer and that consequently the flood itself would not occur as predicted. It is doubtful that anyone alone, without the support of the others, could have withstood the impact of this disproof of the prediction. Indeed, those members of the group who had gone to their homes to wait alone, alone in the sense that they did not have other believers with them, did not withstand it. Almost all of them became skeptics afterward. In other words, without easily obtainable social support to begin reducing the dissonance, the dissonance was sufficient to cause the belief to be discarded in spite of the commitment to it. But the members of the group who had gathered together in the home of the woman who received the messages could, and did, provide social support for one another. They kept reassuring one another of the validity of the messages and that some explanation would be found.

At fifteen minutes before five o'clock that morning an explanation was found that was at least temporarily satisfactory. A message arrived from God which, in effect, said that He had saved the world and stayed the flood because of this group and the light and strength this group had spread throughout the world that night.

The behavior of these people from that moment onwards presented a revealing contrast to their previous behavior. These people who had been disinterested in publicity and even avoided it, became avid publicity seekers. For four successive days, finding a new reason each day, they invited the press into the house, gave lengthy interviews, and attempted to attract the public to their ideas. The first day they called the newspapers and news services, informed them of the fact that the world had been saved and invited them to come and get interviews. The second day, a ban on having photographs taken was lifted, and the newspapers were once more called to inform them of the fact and to invite them to come to the house and take pictures. On the third day they once more called the press to inform them that on the next afternoon they would gather on their front lawn singing and that it was possible a space man would visit them at that time. What is more, the general public was specifically invited to come and watch. And on the fourth day, newspapermen and about two hundred people came to watch the group singing on their front lawn. There were almost no lengths to which these people would not go to attract publicity and potential believers in the validity of the messages. If, indeed, more and more converts could be found, more and more people who believed in the messages and the things the messages said, then the dissonance between their belief and the knowledge that the messages had not been correct could be reduced. (pp. 74–76)

Dramatic as this episode is, it cannot be considered a completely convincing demonstration of the principle of cognitive dissonance reduction. There are just too many other possibly important factors. The situation, like most naturally occurring ones, involves so many overlapping factors that it only ambiguously demonstrates the sole importance of any one of them. Controlled and systematic laboratory research is needed to supplement naturalistic observation. Festinger clearly agrees, for in the very next paragraph he says:

> These examples, while they do illustrate attempts to reduce dissonance in rather surprising directions, still leave much to be desired. One would also like to be able to show that such dissonance-reduction phenomena do occur under controlled laboratory conditions and that the magnitude of the effect does depend upon the magnitude of the dissonance which exists. (p.76)

Festinger then goes on to describe an experiment (Festinger & Carlsmith, 1959) that aimed at such precise demonstration of the avoidance of inconsistency. Subjects were told they were participating in a study of measures of performance, whereas in reality they were made to do a boring, repetitive task for one hour. At the end of that time, the subjects were given a false explanation of the purpose of the experiment: that it concerned the effects of expectation on task performance. Some subjects were then asked if they would stay on and take the place of the research assistant for a few minutes, as he was away for the day. They would have to deceive the next incoming subject that the task to be performed—actually the same boring one the deceiving subject had just finished—was quite interesting and enjoyable. For supposedly taking the research assistant's place, subjects in one group were given $1 each and those in the other $20 each. Some subjects refused to be hired, but the others went along with the deception. A control group of subjects was not asked to take part in any deception. At the end of the study, all subjects—deceiving and control—were seen by an interviewer, who supposedly was part of the psychology department's program of evaluating its members' experiments. During the interview, subjects were asked to rate the experiment along four dimensions. These ratings actually constituted the data of the study. The averages based on them are shown in Table 6–5. Three dimensions showed no significant differences between the $1, $20, and control groups. But there were significant differences in ratings of enjoyment of the experiment. These ratings had been done on a scale from -5 (dull), through zero (neutral) to $+5$ (enjoyable). The control group rated the experiment as just a little on the dull side, the $1 group thought it was somewhat enjoyable, and the $20 group was neutral. The small difference between the control and $20 groups was not significant.

Festinger and Carlsmith find these results quite supportive of the hypothesis that people tend to reduce cognitive dissonance. They reason that whereas both the $1 and $20 groups had dissonance due to the inconsistency between their perception of the task as boring and their perception of themselves as publicly extolling its enjoyability, the dissonance is actually much less for the $20 group. This is because those subjects could at least tell themselves that they were being well paid to lie while the poor $1 subjects did not even have enough financial recompense for their deception. Therefore, it is understandable, according to the experimenters, that the $1 group actually reported most

TABLE 6–5   Average Ratings on Interview Questions for Each Condition

| | Experimental Condition | | |
| | Control (N = 20) | One Dollar (N = 20) | Twenty Dollars (N = 20) |
Question on Interview			
How enjoyable tasks were (rated from −5 to +5)	−.45	+1.35	−.05
How much they learned (rated from 0 to 10)	3.08	2.80	3.15
Scientific importance (rated from 0 to 10)	5.60	6.45	5.18
Participate in similar exp. (rated from −5 to +5)	−.62	+1.20	−.25

SOURCE: "Cognitive Consequences of Forced Compliance" by L. Festinger and J. M. Carlsmith, 1959, *Journal of Abnormal and Social Psychology, 58.*

enjoyment of the task in retrospect, since this shift in their opinion of the task would constitute a reduction of dissonance. Note how ingenious this experiment really was. Common sense and reinforcement theory would predict that the $20 group, not the $1 group, would subsequently report the greatest enjoyment, as they got the most out of their participation and lied no more severely than did the $1 group. The results obtained are not only consistent with the resolution of inconsistency—they are quite surprising.

Many criticisms have been directed at this and similar experiments. But before considering them, let us assume that the results do mean what Festinger and Carlsmith conclude. But even if that were so, there is no evidence to indicate that small inconsistencies lead to avoidance behavior. The difference between the control and $20 groups in rated enjoyment of the task is nonexistent from a statistical point of view. There is only evidence that large inconsistencies, as experienced by the $1 group, may lead to attempts to reduce them by concluding that the task must have been enjoyable. So, from the viewpoint of the issue we are discussing, we should probably conclude no more than that there is evidence that large inconsistencies are unpleasant and avoided.

But the criticism leveled at this and similar experiments has been strong and compelling, raising doubt as to whether the results show anything at all about reactions to dissonance. The major critics of dissonance reduction research have been Chapanis and Chapanis (1964), and I shall rely heavily on their analyses.

First of all they wonder how much the experiment was successful in arousing dissonance at all. In this study, the experience of dissonance hinges on the repetitive task really being experienced as boring when being performed. And yet, the control group, who did this task but was not asked to deceive subsequent subjects, rated it as only slightly boring, as very little different from neutral (see the entry corresponding to the first row and column of Table 6–5). Either the task was not really as monotonous as the experimenters thought or the general instructions initially given subjects about studying the effects of expectation on performance were sufficient to interest them in participating to the point where the monotonous nature of the task was not the single, or even most important, factor in their enjoyment. So Chapanis and Chapanis conclude that the experiment does not permit us to check whether discrepant cognitions of any real magnitude were in fact produced.

An even more serious criticism involves the difference in plausibility between the $20 and $1 remuneration for acting as research assistants. At that time, $20 was a lot of money for an undergraduate, even when it represented a whole day's pay. When offered for something that must have been less than 30 minutes' work, it is difficult to imagine a student accepting the money without becoming wary and alert to possible tricks. In fact, more than 16 percent of the original subjects in the $20 group had to be discarded because they voiced suspicions or refused to be hired! Under such circumstances, Chapanis and Chapanis conclude, it seems likely that those who were retained might have hedged or been evasive about their evaluation of the experiment because they were generally apprehensive about its nature and purpose. And, of course, the average enjoyment rating of neutral, representing as it does the middle point of a dimension running from unenjoyable to enjoyable, is a very ambiguous result in that it could well represent the canceling out of a number of opposing trends within the group. In any event, while the $1 remuneration seems plausible enough, the same cannot be said for the $20 one. Chapanis and Chapanis conclude correctly that it is therefore impossible to rule out alternative explanations of the results to that offered by Festinger and Carlsmith.

A cogent alternative has actually been offered by Rosenberg (1965) in a study that attempts to correct some of the pitfalls of a study very much like Festinger and Carlsmith's. This study was conducted by Cohen and reported by Brehm and Cohen (1962). Its general design was similar to that of Festinger and Carlsmith except that it included four degrees of remuneration rather than two. The prediction was that the greater the remuneration, the smaller the dissonance reduction, where such reduction could be seen as a change in original attitude. The subjects were Yale undergraduates, and the study was conducted immediately following a campus riot that had been quelled by police. The experimenter, appearing at randomly chosen dormitory rooms, ascertained through inquiry that the subject's disapproved of the police actions. Then the subjects were asked to write an essay in support of the police actions, the justification being that the experimenter was interested in obtaining examples of arguments that could be supportive. The subjects were also told that they would receive a certain amount of pay for writing the essay against their own position; one group was offered $.50, another $1, another $5, and another $10. After writing the counterattitudinal essay, the subjects were asked to fill out a questionnaire concerning their real reactions to the police action on the grounds that

Now that you have looked at some of the reasons for the actions of the New Haven police, we would like to get some of your reactions to the issue: *you may possibly want to look at the situation in the light of this*. So, would you please fill out this questionnaire.

A control group was given this final attitude questionnaire but was not required to write the essay and received no remuneration.

Cohen found that the $5 and $10 groups did not differ significantly from the control group in expressed attitude toward the New Haven police. But the subjects in the $.50 group were less negative toward the police than the $1 subjects, who in turn were less than the $10 subjects. In addition, both the $.50 and $1 groups significantly differed from the control group. As you can see, the results seem to bear out the original prediction rather well. But Rosenberg (1965) suggests the importance in the explanation of the results of *evaluation apprehension* and general *annoyance toward the experimenter* in following up the suspiciousness hypothesis of Chapanis and Chapanis. Rosenberg writes that his point of view

> would suggest that in this study, as in others of similar design, the low-dissonance (high reward) subjects would be more likely to suspect that the experimenter had some unrevealed purpose. The gross discrepancy between spending a few minutes writing an essay and the large sum offered, the fact that this large sum had not yet been delivered by the time the subject was handed the attitude questionnaire, the fact that he was virtually invited to show that he had become more positive toward the New Haven police: all these could have served to engender suspicion and thus to arouse evaluation apprehension and negative affect toward the experimenter. Either or both of these motivating states could probably be most efficiently reduced by the subject to show anything but fairly strong disapproval of the New Haven police; for the subject who had come to believe that his autonomy in the face of a monetary lure was being assessed, remaining "anti-police" would demonstrate that he *had* autonomy; for the subject who perceived an indirect and disingenuous attempt to change his attitude and felt some reactive anger, holding fast to his original attitude could appear to be a relevant way of frustrating the experimenter. Furthermore, with each *step* of increase in reward we could expect an increase in the proportion of subjects who had been brought to a motivating level of evaluation apprehension or affect arousal.

Rosenberg then performed his own experiment in an attempt to correct the problem he had found in previous studies. The general way to improve on previous designs would be to make the collection of attitude information following performance of the task that is supposed to create dissonance as separate from the rest of the study as possible. Rosenberg accomplished this in two ways. First, he created a believable situation in which the final attitude information was collected by experimenters other than those who had conducted the earlier part of the study. Second, subjects were paid for their performance in the first part of the study before they progressed to the latter part. The first method clearly was an improvement on Cohen's procedure, in which the same person collected all data. It is true that Festinger and Carlsmith used different experimenters to administer the task and collect the enjoyment data, but their design was such that a suspicious subject might well have perceived a connection between the two. In contrast, Rosenberg developed an elaborate but believable rationale for the independence of the part of the experiment designed to arouse dissonance. The two parts were not only conducted by different people but involved different buildings and different institutional affiliations. Therefore, it is unlikely that any forthcoming results such as those of Cohen and of Festinger and Carlsmith could be explained by the effects of fear of evaluation and anger toward the experimenter as easily as by dissonance reduction attempts.

But with this improved design, Rosenberg obtained results directly opposite to those expected by dissonance theory. As shown by the averages (M) reported in Table 6–6, he found that the greater the reward, the greater the attitude change in the direction of the essay the subject had been asked to write away from his original attitude. In other words, the more money the subject got for writing an essay discrepant with his views, the more doing so would change his attitudes. This result is more obvious than that predicted by dissonance theory and throws the previous results of Festinger and Carlsmith and of Cohen into serious doubt.

The question concerning the studies just discussed is whether they demonstrate the effects of attempts to reduce dissonance or of the guardedness and resentment resulting from the subject's incredulity. There is another group of studies by the dissonance experimenters that have been criticized by

TABLE 6–6   Group Means and Differences among Groups on Attitude toward the Rose Bowl Ban

Group	M	\$.50	\$1	\$.50 and \$1	\$5
			Group Differences*		
Control	1.45	$z = 1.97$, $p < .03$	$z = 1.80$, $p < .04$	$z = 2.31$, $p < .015$	$z = 3.93$, $p < .0001$
\$.50	2.24		$z = .11$		$z = 1.77$, $p < .04$
\$1	2.32				$z = 1.81$, $p < .04$
\$.50 and \$1	2.28				$z = 2.11$, $p < .02$
\$5	3.24				

Note: Overall difference among groups as assessed by Kruskal-Wallis test: $H = 17.89$, $p < .001$.
*Tested by Mann-Whitney z, one-tailed.

SOURCE: "When Dissonance Fails: On Eliminating Evaluation Apprehension from Attitude Measurement" by M. J. Rosenberg, 1965, *Journal of Personality and Social Psychology, 1*.

Chapanis and Chapanis in a different though related manner. Let us take one study (Aronson & Mills, 1959) from this group as an example. College women volunteered to participate in a series of group discussions on the psychology of sex. In a preparticipation interview, some of the women were told they would have to pass an embarrassment test to see if they were tough enough to stand the group discussion. Women in the severe-embarrassment group had to read out loud in the presence of the male experimenter some vivid descriptions of sexual activity and a list of obscene sex words. Women in the mild-embarrassment group read some bland sexual material. All females in the study were told they had successfully passed the embarrassment test. After this, each subject listened to a recording of a group discussion that they were told was a spontaneous discussion of the type they might be in, but in reality was carefully planned and staged by the experimenters as a dull and banal discussion of the sexual behavior of animals. Finally, the design called for a control group that only listened to the simulated group discussion and had taken no embarrassment test previously. All groups then rated the tape-recorded discussion, its participants, and their own interest in future discussions. The results showed that the ratings of the severe-embarrassment group were, on the average, somewhat more favorable than those of the other two groups. Aronson and Mills believe these results show that the more painful the initiation, the more the subjects subsequently liked the group. In successfully passing the severe-embarrassment test, the females in that group had undergone a painful experience in order to gain the right to be part of the subsequent group discussions, which, however, turned out to be so dull that they must have realized the initiation procedure was not worth it. This produced dissonance, which was reduced by reevaluating the group discussion as more interesting than it really was.

In criticizing this experiment and the conclusions reached, Chapanis and Chapanis (1964) say:

> All this may be so, but in order to accept the author's explanation we must be sure the girls really did hold these discrepant cognitions, and no others. We have to be sure, for instance, that they felt no relief when they found the group discussion banal instead of embarrassing, that success in passing a difficult test (the embarrassment test) did not alter their evaluation of the task, that the sexual material did not evoke any vicarious pleasure or expectation of pleasure in the future, and that the group discussion was so dull that the girls would have regretted participating. There is no way of checking directly on the first three conditions, although other experimental evidence suggests that their effect is not negligible. However, to check on the fourth factor we have the data from the control group showing that the group discussion was, in fact, more interesting than not (it received an average rating of 10 on a 0–15 scale). It is, therefore, difficult to believe that the girls regretted participating. To sum up, since the design of this experiment does not exclude the possibility that pleasurable cognitions were introduced by the sequence of events, and since, in addition, the existence of "painful" cognitions was not demonstrated, we cannot accept the author's interpretation without serious reservations.

These critics continue by suggesting that if there is anything to the notion that severity of initiation increased liking of the group, it lies in the feeling of successful accomplishment: "The more severe the test, the stronger is the pleasurable feeling of success in overcoming the obstacle. There is no need to postulate a drive due to dissonance if a *pleasure principle* can account for the results quite successfully." Chapanis and Chapanis point out that the problems with the Aronson and Mills study crop up in other dissonance studies as well.

The technical term for the problem pinpointed above is *confounding of variables*. In other words, the results could have been produced by either attempts to reduce dissonance or the behavioral effects of some sort of relief. The two variables overlap, or are confounded by the experimental design. Obviously the principal aim of any experiment is to avoid confounding. In natural situations, confounding often occurs, but the whole purpose of the experiment is to improve on nature in the sense of holding constant or neutralizing all possible factors save one. That one is made artificially stronger or weaker in the experimental group so that by comparing the effects in this group with the behavior of a control group, one can assess the causal influences of the single factor. What Chapanis and Chapanis are saying in all of their criticisms is that the experiments performed by the dissonance investigators fail in one way or another because of the confounding of two or more factors.

The criticism of confounding is leveled at even more studies in the dissonance tradition than presented thus far. In one dramatic instance, Chapanis and Chapanis discuss an experiment reported by Aronson (1961) in which an attempt was made to pit dissonance theory against reinforcement theory. Reinforcement theory says that stimuli associated with reward gain in attractiveness, whereas dissonance theory indicates that stimuli not associated with reward may actually gain in attractiveness if one has had to expend effort in attempting to attain them. What looks like an ingenious design with which to test this proposition Chapanis and Chapanis demolish by making it crystal clear that there is confounding of effort expended with the rate at which reward is obtained. As a result, no unambiguous conclusions can be drawn as to the effect of effort on the attractiveness of stimuli worked for. Similar confounding of factors is pointed out in other studies as well.

To make matters worse, once the catalogue of criticisms due to faulty experimental design is exhausted, one finds a whole additional catalog of controversial treatments of data. Chapanis and Chapanis point out that it is a regular occurrence in dissonance research to discard subjects from the analysis of results after the way they performed is already known to the experimenter. This is a severe criticism, as such a procedure undermines the whole idea of scientific objectivity. As Chapanis and Chapanis point out, one can always find a rationalization for excluding subjects that leads to finding support for one's hypothesis. Hence, exclusion should always take place before the data have been scrutinized. Not only have there been frequent instances of violation of this rule; the grounds given for exclusion of subjects often have been unconvincing to disinterested observers. Brehm and Cohen (1959), for example, indicate that "[subjects] who failed to choose the alternative initially marked as most liked, were excluded because they gave unreliable or invalid ratings." There is no further explanation of what the investigators might have meant! Using the study of Cohen, Brehm, and Fleming (1958) as an example, Chapanis and Chapanis point out how the reasons given for exclusion of subjects are often self-contradictory. In a study by Ehrlich, Guttman, Schonbach, and Mills (1957), one reason or another was given to justify excluding what amounted to 82 percent of the original sample! When such a large proportion of a sample is discarded, it is virtually impossible to know what the results really mean and certainly impossible to know to whom any conclusions reached could possibly apply. In other studies in which the proportion of subjects excluded was lower, it nonetheless was often true that the proportions excluded from different groups (e.g., high dissonance, low dissonance, control) differed. Chapanis and Chapanis are correct in concluding that some undetermined proportion of dissonance studies may be reporting as fact statistically significant differences among groups that are no more than artifacts due to exclusion of subjects!

Even worse than exclusion of subjects in the manner described above is the kind of reallocation of subjects from one group to another that is found in the study by Raven and Fishbein (1961). These investigators took subjects who did not conform to their predictions and instead of rejecting them—which would have been questionable enough—actually shifted them from the experimental group to the control group. As Chapanis and Chapanis conclude, "rejection of cases is poor procedure, but reallocation of [subjects] from experimental to control group, across the independent variable, violates the whole concept of controlled experimentation."

Continuing in their demolition of dissonance research, Chapanis and Chapanis point out that in some studies, the number of subjects who refused to participate once informed that they would have to deceive others or write something they did not believe was sufficiently large that not taking them into account in reaching conclusions led to misunderstandings. If persons refuse to participate, they are actually showing themselves to be unexplainable on the grounds of dissonance theory; yet the conclusions reached offer no guidance as to what sector of the population may be properly understood on the basis of the results of the studies. Following this, Chapanis and Chapanis close their review with a section on inadequate procedures for the statistical analysis of results, once again implicating many of the studies performed in the dissonance tradition.

What can we conclude about this body of research billed as having demonstrated that cognitive dissonance is always unpleasant and avoided? One thing to note is that investigators in this area have been so concerned with showing how their predictions differ from those of other more familiar and competitive theories and also with applying their dissonance formulation to complex, important social events that they have been led to experimental designs involving elaborate instructions and intricate relationships between subject and experimenter. Such complex designs are almost bound to confound certain variables and require discarding of some subjects. But in dissonance research, there is so much confounding and discarding that it is simply impossible to be sure that results clarify the effects of dissonance alone.

Now it may be that the problems of confounding and discarding can be corrected. Albeit with less enthusiasm and zeal, perhaps simpler, more believable designs could be arranged that would better permit testing of dissonance theory. Even so, we would have to conclude that until such research is done, the case for dissonance as being always unpleasant and avoided has not been made. But the situation may be even worse than that. Chapanis and Chapanis (1964) seem to think that dissonance theory is such a whopping oversimplification that confounding of variables and exclusion of subjects are inevitable! The concluding statement of their review is:

> The magical appeal of Festinger's theory arises from its extreme simplicity both in formulation and in application. But in our review we have seen that this simplicity was generally deceptive; in point of fact it often concealed a large number of confounded variables. Clearly much can be done to untangle this confounding of variables by careful experimental design. Nonetheless, there may still remain another problem more fundamental than this. In general, a cognitive dissonance interpretation of a social situation means that the relevant social factors can be condensed into two simple statements. To be sure, Festinger does not say formally that a dissonance theory interpretation works only for two discrepant statements; but it is precisely because in practice he does so limit it that the theory has had so much acceptance. Which brings us now to the crux of the matter: *is it really possible to reduce the essentials of a complex social situation to just two phrases?* Reluctantly we must say "no." To condense most complex social situations into two, and only two, simple dissonant statements represents so great a level of abstraction that the model no longer bears any reasonable resemblance to reality. Indeed the experimenter is left thereby with such emasculated predictors that he must perforce resort to a multiplicity of ad hoc hypotheses to account for unexpected findings. We see then that the most attractive feature of cognitive dissonance theory, its simplicity, is in actual fact a self-defeating limitation. (pp. 20–21)

All this was not sufficient to end what apparently has been an extraordinary interest in and commitment to dissonance theory. Silverman (1964) rises to its defense by insisting that Chapanis and Chapanis had shown only that their alternative explanations of research findings in the area were possible, not persuasive. In addition, he asserts that the exclusion of subjects was done without knowledge of results and was therefore sound. But Silverman seems to be missing the point, which is made as soon as alternative explanations are plausible and when the exclusion of subjects is so rampant that it is difficult to know what population the results represent. When this kind of situation occurs, it can be fairly said that the theory in question has not been proven. Although dissonance research continued to be done, and believed in, as attested to by the appearance of no less than a handbook (Abelson, Aronson,

McGuire, Newcomb, Rosenberg, & Tannenbaum, 1969) and several novel studies (e.g., Cooper & Goethals, 1974; Cooper & Scalise, 1974) on the subject matter, it was clearly dwindling.

But with virtually every accumulation of studies in one or another topic relevant to dissonance theory, another review of the literature appeared asserting the actual lack of support for the theory once one dug below the surface. Elms (1967) argued that although it is quite true that reinforcement (or incentive) theory and dissonance theory often provide opposite predictions of phenomena, it is the former, not the latter, that seems the more supported by research. He reinterpreted studies that initially appeared to support dissonance theory as actually supporting incentive theory and also reported several studies that are difficult to construe in any other way than as supporting incentive theory. Among the latter are the studies of Janis and Gilmore (1965) and Elms and Janis (1965) concerning role playing. In both, student subjects were asked to role play counterattitudinally in return for an either high or low monetary reward. Some subjects were led to believe that the sponsor of the role playing was a positively regarded organization, whereas others thought it was a negatively regarded organization. Subjects were given varying amounts of money as an incentive for role playing, and attitude measures were taken immediately following the experiment. Janis and Gilmore found that subjects who believed that the organization was a positive one showed significantly more positive attitudes about counterattitudinal role playing than did subjects who believed the organization was a negative one. Similarly, Elms and Janis found that in the positive-sponsorship situation, highly rewarded subjects showed greater positive attitude change than those receiving low reward and in the negative-sponsorship situation, low-reward subjects showed an insignificant trend toward more positive attitude change than did highly rewarded subjects. These studies, reminiscent of Rosenberg's (1965), are quite inconsistent with dissonance theory. In an attempt to contend that the Elms and Janis study was an unfair test of dissonance theory, Brehm (1965) omits reference to the positive-sponsorship situation, which provides, of course, the major refutation of the position.

As if dissonance theory were not beleaguered enough, Rhine (1967) raised serious problems about its ability to account for findings in the area of information selectivity. He asserted that failure to confirm hypotheses about information selectivity would be a serious blow to dissonance theory, for Festinger (1957, p. 3) has said; "When dissonance is present, in addition to trying to reduce it, *the person will actively avoid situations and information* which would likely increase the dissonance" (italics mine). A main difficulty with available research on information selectivity, according to Rhine, is that it is not really relevant to the test of dissonance hypotheses. The degree to which information is avoided or sought will be a U-shaped function of amount of dissonance by a complicated set of assumptions presented by Festinger (1957, p. 130). Any study that attempts to test predictions stemming from this U-shaped curve must include at least three levels of dissonance, preferably quite different in intensity. Yet the available studies involve no more than two levels. In addition, it is important for proper empirical testing of the predictions to be able to separate seeking information from avoiding it. Once again Rhine (1967) demonstrates how available research has failed to permit such separation. He even suggests how this design limitation could be overcome with the proper control groups. In any event, Rhine concludes that the dissonance explanation of information selectivity has not been proven and even suggests the plausibility of a curiosity explanation:

> Consider, for example, Adams' (1961) study of mothers who favored environment over heredity as an explanation of children's behavior. He found that mothers hearing a talk supporting heredity were more interested in getting further information about the heredity-environment issue than those hearing a talk supporting their environment bias. This was interpreted by Adams to mean that dissonance leads to information seeking. If hearing the opposite side of the issue arouses more curiosity than hearing support for a view one already accepts, then the finding could be explained by curiosity instead of dissonance. Curiosity motivation is rarely, if ever, ruled out in selectivity research. If there is any problem from which curiosity should be considered a possible explanation, it is one in which information seeking is a critical dependent variable. Controlling curiosity is particularly imperative when instructions for determining seeking behavior often explicitly request ratings or rankings in terms of interest in the information.

And, of course, if curiosity might explain even some forms of information seeking, it becomes very difficult to contend, as our issue states, that cognitive dissonance is invariably unpleasant and avoided.

Actually, when a position such as dissonance theory has attracted so many devoted researchers and generated so many studies but is still open to the charge of not having been proven, it is reasonable to surmise that something is seriously wrong. Either the theory is so ambiguous as to be unprovable or it is more wrong than right, however much we try to stave off this conclusion with ingenious explanations and counterexplanations. It is beginning to seem as if empirical support for dissonance theory requires very delicately staged experimental situations and carefully primed subjects. At least, there are studies done in naturalistic rather than contrived settings that do not support the theory. For example, Petersen and Hergenhahn (1968) hypothesized that their elementary school subjects, when presented with evidence that they had done more poorly on an academic task than their self-images would tolerate, would consequently make some sort of effort to reduce this dissonance. But there was no difference in this regard between this group and a group whose members' academic performances matched their self-appraisals.

The research considered thus far focuses on presumed attempts to reduce dissonance. Also relevant to our issue would be the sheer demonstration that dissonance is invariably unpleasant (regardless of whether one then tries to reduce it). There is, however, remarkably little information concerning verbalizations or other direct measures of emotional response in the dissonance research literature. Kiesler and Pallak (1976) reviewed studies with the aim of determining whether dissonance is "arousing" and had to reach extremely tentative conclusions because the evidence they found was almost invariably indirect. The trouble with indirect evidence is that it must be interpreted a lot and, as we have seen, there has been all too much interpretation associated with dissonance research already. Kiesler and Pallak do suggest that dissonance manipulations may be arousing or motivating for subjects but strongly hedge their conclusion. Even at that, however, there is no way of knowing whether "arousal" was an invariably unpleasant experience; after all, pleasant emotions are also "arousing." Once again we must conclude that the case for discrepancies between expectation and occurrence as invariably unpleasant and avoided simply has not been proven.

The next step in considering the issue would seem to be consideration of the body of data accumulated to demonstrate that change, novelty, and complexity of stimulation are desired and sought after. If these data are convincing, it can at least be said that cognitive dissonance cannot always be unpleasant and avoided. This is true because variety almost of necessity is also dissonance, since such aspects of it as novelty and unexpectedness must be defined as some experimental difference between some set of beliefs or expectancies on the one hand and some set of event perceptions on the other. Variety research essentially makes three points—that variety is (1) necessary for effective development and adult functioning, (2) sought after, and (3) pleasant, at least in moderate degree. Fiske and Maddi (1961) have brought together research from various corners of psychology and physiology in support of these three points; therefore, the discussion that follows leans heavily on their formulations. But other psychologists (e.g., Berlyne, 1960; Duffy, 1963) have also provided able reviews of an extensive body of research.

The references to data obtained on subhuman organisms in the following pages may strike you as inconsistent with my previous unwillingness to consider such data concerning defensiveness. Actually, there is no inconsistency. Animal data were ruled out of contention for the study of defensiveness largely because such study heavily concerns mentation, which is methodologically inaccessible in organisms below humans. But two of the three conclusions concerning variety mentioned in the previous paragraph need not rely primarily or even heavily on the scrutiny of mentation. Subhuman organisms can well be studied in determining whether variety is necessary for effective development and adult functioning and whether it is sought after, because these questions can be convincingly resolved by observed action and performance. Of course, it is much more difficult to determine whether variety is pleasant without having available mentation in the form of verbal report. Hence, you will see that the data I review with regard to this question are gleaned exclusively from the human level.

I will not spend much time on the conclusion that variety is necessary for effective development and adult functioning, as it is not as directly relevant to the issue confronting us as are the other two points. Suffice it to say that the studies relevant to this conclusion generally proceed by reducing the variation and intensity of stimulation impinging on the organism and then observing the effects of doing so at either the physiological or behavioral level. Whether the study concerns development or adult functioning depends on the subjects' ages. In studies of young monkeys deprived of variation and intensity of stimulation from infancy, Riesen (1961) has shown subsequent deficits at both the physiological level, in cellular abnormalities of the retina and optic nerve, and the behavioral level, in lack of coordination of actions. Paralleling these behavioral findings at the human level are the studies of Ribble and Spitz (in Thompson & Schaefer, 1961) comparing infants reared in orphanages with infants reared at home or in prison with their mothers. The children reared in the orphanage were retarded in walking, talking, smiling, and crawling and generally were more apathetic, unemotional, and subdued than were the other infants. In addition, the orphanage children were more susceptible to diseases and showed a higher death rate. Although Ribble and Spitz stress the ambiguous concept of "mothering" in attempting to explain their results, other psychologists, such as Yarrow (1961), argue cogently for the importance of a marked reduction in the intensity and variety of stimulation from what it would have been in a more usual environment. The studies of Ribble and Spitz were so imperfectly performed from a methodological point of view that I would not even mention them here except that they show such a striking parallel with Riesen's work on monkeys. More recently, Harlow and others (e.g., Griffin & Harlow, 1966; Harlow, Harlow, Dodsworth, & Arling, 1966) reported results of very carefully planned studies of monkeys that build upon the start made by Riesen. Harlow found that rearing infant monkeys in the absence of intense and varying stimuli leads to adults that are incapable of copulating, are afraid of other monkeys and living things, and appear very disturbed emotionally. The monkeys do not seem able to learn to overcome these deficits. If more evidence of the generality of such effects were needed, there are similar studies involving other species (e.g., Konrad & Bagshaw, 1970; Lessac & Solomon, 1969). Apparently beagles and cats also showed behavioral deficits at adulthood after having been deprived of stimulation in childhood. There is strong evidence at the animal level, and suggestive evidence at the human level, that variety is necessary for normal development.

The research concerning the need for variety in order to function as a normal adult has been done largely under the well-known label of *sensory deprivation*. To make a long story short, a number of studies (see Fiske, 1961) suggest that markedly decreasing the variation and intensity of stimulation available to adult humans leads, in time, to a number of signs of disordered functioning. They include such symptoms as the inability to concentrate, intense feelings of emotional discomfort, and bizarre mentation reminiscent of hallucinations and delusions. Some of the deficits persist for a little while after the sensory deprivation has been terminated. This is not to say that such strong and disturbing results occur in all subjects or even in all studies done so far. Fuerst and Zubek (1968), for example, report mild or, in some instances, no impairment to their male subjects on cognitive tests administered following three days of either darkness and silence or unpatterned light and white noise. But the battery of tests was also administered prior to sensory isolation, and there was a relationship between pre- and postexperimental scores. This and other studies suggest that individual differences and the specifics of the experimental situation have as yet an only partially understood role in the effects of deprivation of stimulation. Nonetheless, these studies of adults, along with the already mentioned studies on infants, suggest that variety is necessary for normal development and functioning.

The second conclusion I mentioned before is that variety is sought after, rather than avoided, as cognitive dissonance positions would predict. Many of the most important studies supporting this point have been done at the subhuman level. There have been so many of these studies that it is not necessary, let alone possible, to review them all here. It is more important to grasp the import of the body of research than to know each and every study.

The research essentially involves two kinds of experiments. One kind concerns habituation to a particular environment followed by a change in or addition to it and observation of the effects of doing so. A straightforward example is Berlyne's (1955) study in which rats were permitted to become familiar with a rectangular cage with a little alcove at one end. After familiarization had taken place, a series of objects were added to the environment by placing them in the alcove. The rats' reaction to the objects was what interested Berlyne. He found that the various objects produced exploratory behavior, such as sniffing, licking, and touching. These findings are typical for such studies; whenever you change or add to an already familiar environment, you get an increase in exploratory behavior. This conclusion applies at the human level also (Maddi, 1961a), even though there are fewer studies there than at the animal level.

The second kind of study demonstrating that variety is sought after involves putting subjects in an environment that is arranged such that they must choose which portion of it to experience. (They cannot experience it all at any one time.) Subsequent to the first choice, he is put into the environment again and permitted to choose the portion to experience next. Typical of such studies is that of Dennis (1939), who put rats into a maze shaped like the letter T. In running through the maze, the rats had to turn either right or left when they reached the bar of the T. In this study, as in many similar ones (see Dember, 1961), it was found that after choosing either the right or left arm of the T, the rats ran to the opposite arm when returned to the beginning of the maze. This phenomenon has been called *spontaneous alternation*. It suggests that variety is sought after for, on the second try, the subject chooses to experience that part of the environment not experienced on the first try. There is by now ample evidence that spontaneous alternation also occurs at the human level (e.g., Schultz, 1964).

The major criticism leveled at this body of research concerns whether it really shows that variety is sought after or some other explanation of exploratory behavior and spontaneous alternation is more adequate. This general criticism takes a number of concrete forms. For example, spontaneous alternation has been attributed by some psychologists to such causes as satiation for the particular muscular movements made in turning one way rather than the other (reactive inhibition) and satiation for the stimuli in the part of the maze first seen (stimulus satiation). Both of these explanations are meant to be alternatives to that concerning variety as an attractive stimulus.

Dember (1956) did an experiment that demonstrates conclusively that the variety explanation is better. It is an ingenious experiment and deserves our attention. This investigator also used a T maze but modified it in two ways. One involved installing glass doors at the intersection of the stem and the arms of the T such that the rats could look into both arms but enter neither. The other involved painting one arm of the T black, and the other white. Thus, on the first try in the maze the rats saw both white and black portions that they could not actually enter. For the second try, the investigator made two changes: He removed the glass doors, making it possible to enter the arms of the T, and he changed one of the arms from black to white, thereby rendering both arms the same color. Proponents of reactive inhibition, as an explanation of spontaneous alternation, would not expect any difference in the frequency with which the two arms were entered on this second try, because, since no arms were entered on the first try, there would have been no opportunity for the muscular movements involved in turning right or left to become satiated and therefore subsequently avoided. Similarly, proponents of stimulus satiation would not expect differential frequency of entrance into the two arms, because on the second try both are the same color and, since that color was represented on the first try, there should be no difference in the satiating nature of the two arms. But proponents of the position that variety is sought after would clearly predict that on the second try rats would enter the arm whose color was changed from what it had been on the first try. In a resounding demonstration of the greater utility of one explanation over others, Dember found that seventeen out of twenty rats entered the changed arm on the second try! This experiment was so incisively designed that in one fell swoop reactive inhibition and stimulus satiation were demolished as possible explanations of spontaneous alternation.

But there is another, alternative explanation of spontaneous alternation and exploratory behavior that has not been demolished by Dember's experiment. This explanation, offered by Berlyne (1957, 1960), holds that variety is certainly approached, not because it is pleasant, desired, or needed but because it increases conflict and uncertainty and thereby is unpleasant enough to instigate the attempt to gain greater familiarity with the source of the variety in hope of decreasing uncertainty and conflict. In exploring a new aspect of the environment, or in alternating spontaneously, the organism is trying to obtain the information with which to render old and familiar—and therefore unthreatening—that which is novel. Clearly this position would also have predicted entrance into the changed arm of the T in Dember's experiment and, hence, is a viable competitor to the position that variety is sought after because it is attractive and interesting. As long as Berlyne's position can explain the research results thus far mentioned, as well as that which claims variety to be attractive, we cannot conclude that there is empirical support for the contention that variety is not always unpleasant and avoided.

Although Berlyne's position is ingenious, it is unlikely to be true, because it destroys the distinction between approaching a stimulus and avoiding it. If novelty were indeed threatening, Berlyne could as easily have predicted that it would be run from as that it would be pursued. Yet, running from and pursuing novelty are very different things, not convincingly understood as merely alternative ways of achieving the same end. On logical grounds, Berlyne's position seems weak.

Empirical research also suggests the faultiness of demolishing the distinction between approach and avoidance. Welker (1959) put rats into a large rectangular box that was well lit and included different kinds of objects. Off to one side of the rectangle was a small, dark, empty alcove. His rats darted about frantically until they found the alcove and then took shelter in it. After a while, they forayed forth from the alcove, with their movements in the larger rectangle now calmer and more deliberate. There is a clear observational distinction between the behavior in the large rectangle before entering the alcove and after leaving it. The early behavior seems like avoidance, while the latter seems like approach. If this distinction is important, we must take seriously the inability of a position such as Berlyne's to account for it. He would have to call both the early and the later behavior *exploratory* and explain them in the same fashion, namely, as attempts to decrease the conflict produced by novelty. More recently, Berlyne (1967) seems to have given up his earlier position, in part on the basis of observations of the sort reported by Welker. In acknowledging that interest in novelty may occur because it is pleasing, Berlyne (1967) says:

> There has been much talk of the human craving for excitement and stimulation. . . . Experiments on exploratory behavior . . . and play . . . show that higher animals often find access to stimulation gratifying and that properties known to raise arousal—such as novelty, surprisingness, complexity—may enhance the reward value of exteroceptive stimuli.(p.29)

Then Berlyne actually goes on to marshal evidence against his former view of the aversive effects of variety through its enhancement of conflict!

Of particular relevance to the argument that variety is attractive are two studies by Maddi and Andrews (1966) that measured the degree to which variety is sought after by the novelty of stories composed about pictures. As the pictures were rather unstructured, permitting a wide range of stories, it can be fairly said that people who produce novel stories are actually creating their own variety. That story novelty may well indicate seeking of variety and nothing else is suggested by the absence of relationship between it and such other general characteristics as intelligence, social class, productivity, the needs for achievement, affiliation, and power, and the tendency to respond in a socially desirable fashion (Maddi & Andrews, 1966; Maddi, Propst, & Feldinger, 1965).

Also included in the Maddi and Andrews studies are self-descriptions concerning the attractiveness of variety. These self-descriptions took the form of indicating whether one liked or disliked certain statements, such as "I move my furniture around frequently" and "I often vary my activities." These statements were organized into standard scales from a number of personality tests, such as the Need for Change Scale of the Activities Index (Stern, 1958). As you can see in Table 6–7, Maddi and Andrews found evidence in both studies that the greater the tendency to seek variety, the greater the preference for and attractiveness of variety.

Csikszentmihalyi (1975) has also reported an interlocking set of studies of relevance here. When questioned closely, his subjects reported liking best situations in which their capabilities were slightly less than the difficulty of the task. Not only were such situations reported as most engrossing; other observations of performance made by this investigator confirmed that subjects indeed became most involved in them, losing track of self and time. Looked at from our present perspective, these situations must have involved perceived discrepancies, uncertainties, and novelty.

It would seem very difficult to maintain the view that variety seeking occurs out of its discomforting and threatening nature in the face of results such as those obtained by Maddi and Andrews and by Csikszentmihalyi. Apparently it is precisely those people who like variety most who expend effort in seeking it. Also, people in general seem to regard situations involving novelty as most engrossing and worthwhile.

TABLE 6–7   Product-Moment Correlations between Novelty of Productions and Variables Reflecting Preferences for Variety

	Novelty of Productions
Study I ($N = 78$)	
16 PF Factor H (Timid-adventurous)[*]	− .02
16 PF Factor I (Touch-sensitive)	.33[†]
16 PF Factor Q (Conservative-experimenting)	.28[‡]
Study II ($N = 56$)	
AI *n* Change scale	.25[§]
AI *n* Play scale	.18
AI Impulsivity scale	.27[‖]

[*]The terms listed are recommended by Cattel for identifying the poles of the factors. The list term is for the low end of the factor.
[†]Probability is less than .005 by one-tailed test.
[‡]Probability is less than .01 by one-tailed test.
[§]Probability is less than .05 by one-tailed test.
[‖]Probability is less than .025 by one-tailed test.

SOURCE: Adapted from "The Need for Variety in Fantasy and Self-description" by S.R. Maddi and S. Andrews, 1966, *Journal of Personality, 34.*

Another study by Maddi (1961c) concerns the nature of the emotional reaction to different degrees of variety. It is a very important study for reaching a conclusion concerning the issue we have been discussing. Subjects were given a booklet and instructed to perform two tasks simultaneously. Whenever they were given a signal, they were to write down a prediction as to whether the next page of the booklet would contain a number or the beginning of a sentence. After predicting, they turned the page, were again given the signal to predict, again turned the page, and so forth. Thus, the first task was to predict what would take place. In the course of the experiment the subjects got fairly immediate feedback on the accuracy or inaccuracy of their predictions. Whenever the page they turned to showed the beginning of a sentence, they were supposed to finish the sentence in whatever manner they wished. Thus, the second task was to complete sentences.

Subjects in the experimental group experienced a regular pattern of stimuli as follows. Each group of three successive pages of the booklet, starting from the first, showed the pattern of number, number, sentence beginning. This pattern recurred eight times without interruption. From the subjects' predictions, it was possible to obtain the percentage of accurate predictions within each pattern of number, number, sentence beginning. As you might expect, the average percentage of accuracy increased from a low of 26 to a high of 95 during the eight pattern repetitions. Now the sentence completions made by the subjects at the end of each pattern were used as a measure of affective tone, or the degree to which the subjects were having pleasant or unpleasant feelings. Each sentence completion was scored on a five-point scale according to whether it showed strongly positive affect (5), mildly positive affect (4), neutral affect (3), mildly negative affect (2), or strongly negative affect (1), and mean affect scores associated with each pattern repetition were computed. As shown in Figure 6–2, Maddi found that in the experimental group affect was initially negative or unpleasant but, as the pattern was repeated, rose to a peak of positive or pleasant affect and then became negative once more. Interestingly, the greatest intensity of positive affect occurred on the third-pattern repetition, during which the subjects were inaccurate on 33 percent of their predictions. While inaccuracy of prediction decreased from 76 to 33 percent during the first three pattern repetitions, affective tone went from negative to positive. And while inaccuracy of prediction decreased from 33 to 6 percent during the last five pattern repetitions, affective tone went from positive to negative.

Let us linger over the meaning of these results. The percentage of inaccuracy provides a precise index of the degree to which a discrepancy exists between what is expected and what actually occurs. Therefore, if theorists who stress the unpleasant nature of unexpectedness and dissonance, such as Kelly and Festinger, were right, Maddi should have obtained results indicating that as the percentage of accuracy increased negative affect gave way to positive affect. Berlyne should have expected the same thing, as inaccuracy in this case defines what is unexpected and therefore novel. It becomes terribly important,

FIGURE 6–2   Mean Affect Scores as Function of Number of Series Experienced

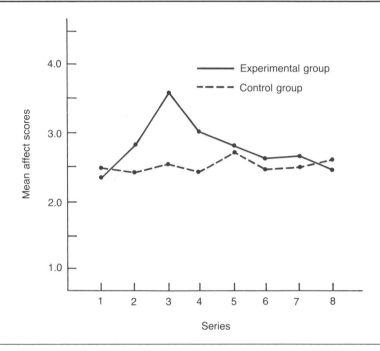

SOURCE: Adapted from "Affective Tone during Environmental Regularity and Change" by S. R. Maddi, 1961, *Journal of Abnormal and Social Psychology, 62*.

once you have recognized this, that Maddi's results show the peak of positive affect when prediction is still 33 percent inaccurate, and that further decreases in inaccuracy are associated with progressively greater negative affect. These results favor the position that mild variety—call it unexpectedness, dissonance, or discrepancy—is a pleasant experience. Taking all of Maddi's results into account, the most comprehensive conclusion to draw is that small degrees of variety are pleasant and large degrees unpleasant.

Maddi reports two other findings from this study that generally support the interpretation just offered. The first finding involves the relationship between prediction and affect when the pattern of numbers and sentence beginnings were changed after the eight repetitions. Some subjects in the experimental group experienced a large change in pattern and others a small change, these effects being confirmed by the amount of increase in predictional inaccuracy. As shown in Figure 6–3, the subjects of the experimental group experiencing the small change showed a striking increase in positive affect even though they were actually becoming more inaccurate than they had been during the pattern repetitions. In contrast, the experimental group subjects experiencing the large change did not show a spurt in positive affect and, of course, were becoming greatly inaccurate. The final finding of this study con-

FIGURE 6–3   Mean Difference Scores Associated with Treatments 0, 1, and 2

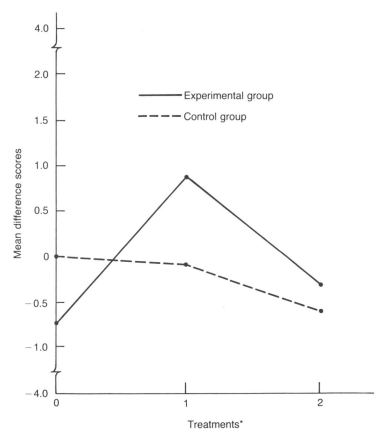

*The treatments represent, respectively, 0, 1, and 2 degrees of change in order of events for the prediction and no-prediction groups.

SOURCE: Adapted from "Affective Tone during Environmental Regularity and Change" by S. R. Maddi, 1961, *Journal of Abnormal and Social Psychology, 62.*

cerns a control group, whose subjects also received numbers and words on the pages of the booklet but found them arranged in a random and therefore unpredictable order. Figures 6–2 and 6–3 show results for this group that are entirely different from those already presented. Affect for the control group generally was negative throughout the experiment.

To tie together the various threads of discussion concerning the third issue, we can say that there is empirical support for the conclusion that cognitive dissonance is not invariably unpleasant and avoided.

The evidence seems to be accumulating that moderate degrees of unexpectedness and novelty are approached and found pleasant, whereas larger and smaller degrees are unpleasant and avoided (e.g., Berlyne, 1960; Dorfman, 1965; Maddi, 1961b; Munsinger & Kessen, 1964; Vitz, 1966). In addition, some evidence (e.g., Maddi & Andrews, 1966) indicates that persons may differ in the range of variety they consider pleasant. In light of all this, it is strange to find some psychologists still holding to the belief that variety is attractive in all degrees (e.g., Nunnally, 1971) or not at all (e.g., Zajonc, 1968). By now, there is enough known in variety research to suggest that Nunnally's conclusion is based on his having designed experiments that did not sample subjects' reactions over a wide enough range of variety to obtain avoidance as well as approach tendencies (see Maddi, 1971). But Zajonc's argument is more elaborate and bears very directly on the issue under discussion here.

In his spirited monograph, Zajonc (1968) reviews many linguistic studies and reports several experiments done by him and his students to the effect that mere exposure to (familiarity with) stimuli increases their attractiveness. First he collected many correlational studies in which the judged value of words was found to covary with their frequency of usage. Impressive though this array of studies may seem it must be recognized that correlations do not permit the inference of causality. Although Zajonc construes the studies as showing that the more a word is used, the more it takes on positive emotional tone, he also could have concluded the very opposite. Indeed, it makes more sense to consider the studies as showing that it is the positively toned words that get used most. Otherwise, one would be in the odd position of contending that even a word like "friendly" had a negative charge when first entering the language (because it was unfamiliar) and became positive only through use. At that point, the prefixed word "unfriendly" must have been devised in order to offset the positive drift due to increased familiarity. This is not a very plausible position on the creation of language, though Zajonc subscribes to it.

Perhaps the difficulty here is that Zajonc is stretching for a complete explanation of the affective charge of stimuli with only one of the several factors that are important. At some level, familiarity is a factor that can contribute to positive affective charge—but so is meaning. After all, words have meaning in addition to familiarity. The positive affective charge of a word like "friendly" derives as much, if not more, from its agreeable meaning (in the form of connotations and remembrances of fellowship) as from its frequency of occurrence. Zajonc does report some experiments, rather than correlational studies, using meaningful stimuli. As I would have expected, he obtained much weaker, even inconsistent results when he tried experimentally to increase the positivity of meaningful stimuli by presenting them often.

Most of Zajonc's reported experiments utilize meaningless stimuli (nonsense syllables, "Chinese" ideographs) that are presented at varying frequencies to subjects with the expectation that those presented most will be most attractive. In general, he has obtained results supporting this expectation. But the research reviewed earlier suggests that Zajonc should have obtained a U-shaped curve, in which the stimuli presented with intermediate frequency would be most attractive and those presented less or more frequently less attractive. Perhaps the difficulty with Zajonc's procedure is similar to Nunnally's. Zajonc may not have employed a sufficiently large number of repetitions to render the initially meaningless stimuli monotonous and therefore unattractive. This is possible even though he did use up to twenty-five exposures of some stimuli. After all, in each experiment many meaningless stimuli were presented, all with different frequencies of occurrence and in an essentially unpredictable order. Amidst all this uncertainty, twenty-five repetitions may have been just enough to render a stimulus moderately familiar and therefore positive in affective charge.

Finally, in an attempt to round out his position, Zajonc assumes that exploratory behavior results from conflict and negative affect over an unfamiliar stimulus, much in the manner of early Berlyne (1960). Most of the evidence he marshals for this view shows that unfamiliar stimuli increase reaction time and galvanic skin response. But these are certainly indirect measures of negative affective charge, the precise meaning of which is hard to determine. The most direct measures are verbal statements, but he reports such data in only one study done by a student of his (Harrison, 1967). In this study, different samples of subjects were used to measure the intensity of exploratory behavior and the preference value evoked by a set of stimuli. A substantial negative correlation was found between exploration and preference, but it is quite possible that this study ran afoul of individual differences. In Harrison's exploratory condition, the subjects who explored intensely might have expressed preference for the novel stimuli had they been asked; in the other condition, the subjects who disliked the stimuli might not have explored them if permitted to. Such a state of affairs could have produced the obtained correlation for reasons opposite to those Zajonc assumed. The Maddi and Andrews (1966) study mentioned earlier is a better source of information on the relationship between exploration and preference, as both were measured on the same subjects.

Recent research influenced by Zajonc has yielded results consistent with my remarks. Hill (1978) reviews this body of research as indicating that as exposure to stimuli is prolonged, preference initially increases, then decreases. Apparently the research tradition of "mere exposure" is merging with the earlier work of novelty theorists.

The upshot of all this is to render the pure cognitive dissonance version of the consistency model rather untenable, insisting as it does that all degrees of inconsistency are unpleasant for and avoided by all people. Our discussion clearly favors the variant position represented by the theory of McClelland and the activation version of the consistency model. As I indicated before, this issue does not have trenchant implications for the question of whether conflict and fulfillment models are more or less tenable than consistency models. Conflict and fulfillment models sometimes agree with consistency models and sometimes do not, indicating that for the former, questions of consistency and inconsistency are not the basic ones. More basic for them are considerations of the content involved in consistencies and inconsistencies.

Fifth Issue: Is All Behavior in the Service of Tension Reduction?

You will recall that the conflict model and the cognitive dissonance version of the consistency model consider the aim of all functioning to be reduction in tension. Thus, supporters of these models would answer the above question affirmatively. But supporters of all other models would give a flatly negative answer. If fulfillment theorists were at all willing to describe functioning in terms of orientation toward tension, they would say that people aim toward tension increase in the major part of their living and only incidentally at tension decrease. Fiske and Maddi, exemplifying the activation version of the consistency model, actively assume that the person seeks both increases and decreases in tension depending on specified circumstances. Let us pursue an empirical answer to this fifth issue, for clearly it is one that has powerful consequences for determining the most fruitful way to conceptualize personality.

Most of the research bearing directly on tension dispositions is at the subhuman level. Once again, though I considered empirical study of subhuman organisms virtually useless in clarifying questions concerning the concept of defense, I do not feel similarly regarding the concept of tension. Tension, after all, seems to involve excitation of the nervous system and is rarely defined as a mental state. Clearly the concept of tension can be applied to human and subhuman alike, without changing the meaning intended for it by the personologist. Therefore, it should not trouble us that we shall have to rely heavily on empirical studies of animals in order to reach a conclusion concerning the fifth issue.

Of clear relevance for our purposes is the extensive literature on learning done in the tradition of behaviorism. Many behaviorists have assumed that all behavior has the primary goal of reducing tension, and they have provided many empirical demonstrations of this point of view. According to the behaviorist, learning is the establishment of a bond between a particular stimulus and a particular response (S-R bond) such that the organism gives the response whenever the stimulus is presented to it. This learned link between stimulus and response becomes established when the response brings about a decrease in the level of tension existing in the organism. This decrease in tension is called a *reward* or *reinforcement*. For example, if the stimulus is a T maze, seen by the rat from the vantage point of the starting box in the stem of the T, and if the rat has a high tension state produced by having been deprived of food for many hours, running down the stem of the maze and turning into the right-hand arm—which contains food that the rat is permitted to eat and thereby reduce the tension of hunger—constitutes learning. The next time the rat is put into the maze in a hungry state, it will turn right because the reward of having eaten, or having reduced tension there, will lead it to try the same behavior again. This type of result actually has been shown in hundreds of experiments (see Hilgard, 1956). A wide range of deprivation states have been used (e.g., food, water, and sexual deprivation), all with the same overall result: If the organism experiencing a high tension state can reduce that state by giving a particular response when faced with a certain stimulus, it will learn to do that, whereas an organism lacking a high tension state (i.e., satiated for the major needs) will learn no such link between stimulus and response.

Although most of the studies have involved rats in a maze, a wide range of other organisms and stimulus contexts have been used. A number of studies even achieved the refinement of demonstrating that the speed and accuracy of learning rises with increases in tension level. Until a few years ago, the literature on learning yielded the firm, secure conclusion that decreases in tension are so valuable to the organism that it will orient its behavior toward bringing them about. Certainly the import of these studies for our issue supports the contention that all behavior is concerned with tension reduction.

Unassailable though the above body of findings has seemed, a few dissonant studies gradually appeared. Some of these studies concerned what came to be called *latent learning*. It was discovered (see Hilgard, 1956) that if rats were left in a maze for some period of time during which they were not in any particularly high tension state and had no opportunity to reduce tension states in any event, they would subsequently behave as if they had learned a good deal about the maze. When introduced into the maze on a later occasion with a high state of tension and the possibility of reducing that state by performing a particular response, they would learn that response more quickly than rats that had not received the earlier opportunity to explore the maze under tensionless conditions. So apparently learning can take place without the occurrence of decrease in tension.

Another set of dissonant studies concerned the phenomenon of spontaneous alternation, discussed under the fourth issue. In these studies, it became perfectly clear that even had a rat filled with tension been able to reduce that tension by making a particular turn in a maze, it would quite likely turn the opposite way on the next trial (see Dember, 1961). The previously mentioned tendency of an organism to give the response previously associated with tension reduction turns out to be an average tendency. In other words, over a set of trials the organism will give the response associated with tension reduction more than any other response. But if you look at the sequence of responses given during the set of trials, you will also see a tendency to alternate responses, even though this means accepting that tension reduction will not occur as often as the situation makes possible. On the basis of such findings, it would seem that not all behavior is in the service of tension reduction.

The final group of dissonant studies (e.g., Freeman, 1933, 1938, 1940; Yerkes & Dodson, 1908) challenged the conclusion that the greater the tension state, the more rapid and accurate the learning when giving the learned response ensures the experience of tension decrease. These studies employed tasks or contexts for learning that were more difficult than the admittedly rudimentary T maze. The striking conclusion was reached that for complex learning tasks there is a level of tension beyond which learning becomes inaccurate and inefficient. In other words, moderate tension states lead to better learning than do intense ones when the task is complex. This is so even though learning involves giving the response that leads to tension reduction. It would seem that the neat relationship between amount of tension reduction and speed of learning described earlier is true only in rudimentary learning situations.

While these dissonant studies were still only a trickle, behaviorists tried to shore up their brave conclusion concerning the necessity of tension reduction for learning to take place. Latent learning was considered an anomaly, difficult to understand, and not even clearly something to be called "learning." Surely, the behaviorist argued, one would not want to make any sweeping revisions in such a heavily supported conclusion on the basis of a mere handful of studies whose meaning everyone agreed was unclear. By calling the findings of these few studies *latent* learning, the behaviorist was able to put them in a category separate from the main body of learning studies and thereby forget about them. Concerning spontaneous alternation, the behaviorist hit on a formulation that rendered the findings consistent with the emphasis on tension reduction: that along with the usually considered biological survival needs, there is a need to explore, or manipulate. This manipulo-exploratory need can, like the others, contribute to the organism's level of tension. Spontaneous alternation is, then, the best strategy for the rat to employ in order to bring about the greatest overall reduction of tension through satisfying not only the biological survival need heightened by experimental manipulation but the need to explore as well. The upshot of this interpretation is that one can still conclude that all learning occurs in the context of tension reduction. Finally, the behaviorist attempted to account for the findings of studies utilizing complex learning tasks by suggesting that the effect of very high tension states in such situations is to render the organism unable to search out all the relevant information with which to learn, so insistent is its search for the wherewithal for tension reduction. Fallible though an organism thus conceived is, it still can be presumed to orient all its behavior toward tension reduction.

Even with such ingenious and spirited interpretations of the dissonant studies, it soon became apparent that the behaviorist's position was inadequate. The dissonant studies went from a trickle to a torrent and, for a while, seemed to be done simply for the fun of demonstrating once again the inadequacy of the behaviorist's position. As the dissonant studies reached torrential proportions, the underlying unity of their meaning became apparent: Not all learning requires tension reduction, nor is all behavior in the service of tension reduction. In a brilliant speech voicing these conclusions, Harlow (1953) articulated what has become the modern view. He began by giving rational arguments against the behaviorist's position:

> There are logical reasons why a drive-reduction theory of learning, a theory which emphasizes the role of internal, physiological-state motivation, is entirely untenable, as a motivational theory of learning. The internal drives are cyclical and operate, certainly at any effective level of intensity, for only a brief fraction of any organism's waking life. The classical hunger drive physiologically defined ceases almost as soon as food—or nonfood—is ingested. This, as far as we know,

is the only case in which a single swallow portends anything of importance. The temporal brevity of operation of the internal drive states obviously offers a minimal opportunity for conditioning and a maximal opportunity for extinction. The human being, at least in the continental United States, may go for days or even years without ever experiencing true hunger or thirst.

Harlow is suggesting that the situation of strong tension is not common enough in most people's lives to take it as the starting point for a motivational theory of learning. Not enough of the person's time can be considered as being spent in attempting to decrease high tension states. Much of the empirical evidence providing general support for these conclusions came from Harlow's laboratory (Harlow, 1959; Harlow, Harlow, & Meyer, 1950), in which studies of manipulatory behavior in primates had been taking place. It became apparent that primates are terribly intrigued by puzzles that they can manipulate and will learn to solve them in the absence of biological drive reduction. Indeed, introducing food as a reward for solving a puzzle once it already has been experienced has the effect of increasing the errors made in solution attempts. In another dramatic study, whose major findings are shown in Figure 6–4, Butler and Alexander (1955) reported that monkeys will learn to open the door to their opaque aluminum cage merely in order to gain the opportunity to gaze out on the activity in the laboratory and monkey colony. To judge

FIGURE 6–4   Main Response Duration and Mean Number of Responses as a Function of Days

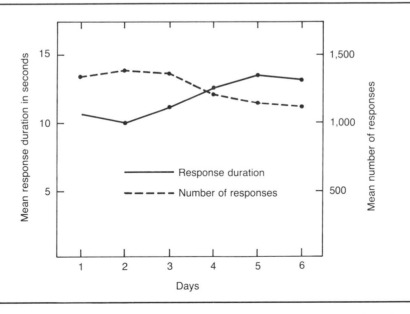

SOURCE: "Daily Patterns of Visual Exploratory Behavior in the Monkey" by R. A. Butler and H. M. Alexander, *Journal of Comparative Physiological Psychology, 48.*

from Figure 6–4, the monkeys hardly lost interest in observing the laboratory, though the activity may well have increased rather than decreased tension.

Summarizing these studies, Harlow (1953) says:

> Observations and experiments on monkeys convinced us that there was as much evidence to indicate that a strong drive inhibits learning as to indicate that it facilitates learning. It was the speaker's feeling that monkeys learned more efficiently if they were given food before testing, and as a result, the speaker routinely fed his subjects before every training session. The rhesus monkey is equipped with enormous cheek pouches, and consequently many subjects would begin the educational process with a rich store of incentives crammed into the buccal cavity. When the monkey made a correct response, it would add a raisin to the buccal storehouse and swallow a little previously munched food. Following an incorrect response, the monkey would also swallow a little stored food. Thus, both correct and incorrect responses invariably resulted in S-R theory drive reduction. It is obvious that under these conditions the monkey cannot learn, but the present speaker developed an understandable skepticism of this hypothesis when the monkeys stubbornly persisted in learning, learning rapidly, and learning problems of great complexity. Because food was continuously available in the monkey's mouth, an explanation in terms of differential fractional anticipatory goal responses did not appear attractive. It would seem that the Lord was simply unaware of drive-reduction learning theory when he created, or permitted the gradual evolution of the rhesus monkey.

Obviously Harlow does not mean that the rhesus monkey is a single exception to the law that learning is mediated by tension reduction. Indeed, he goes on in the speech to cite evidence similar to the above concerning other primates, including humans, and even rodents. One of the most striking studies mentioned is that of Sheffield and Roby (1950), in which learning in rats was shown without biological drive reduction. Hungry rats learned to choose the arm in a T maze that led to water sweetened with saccharine, a nonnutritive substance, over the arm leading to plain water. The major results of this study are shown in Figure 6–5, which indicates that as days went by the rats made more choices leading to the saccharine solution; they ran faster and drank more. Harlow (1953) concludes:

> It may be stated unequivocally that, regardless of any relationship that may be found for other animals, there are no data indicating that intensity of drive state and the presumably correlated amount of drive reduction are positively related to learning efficiency in primates.
>
> In point of fact there is no reason to believe that the rodentological data will prove to differ significantly from those of monkey, chimpanzee, and man.

If such important behavior as that involved in learning is to some degree independent of tension reduction, we are justified in concluding that not all functioning is in its service.

Harlow actually goes further than this to suggest that some behavior in learning situations brings about increases rather than decreases in tension.

FIGURE 6–5 Acquisition in a T Maze with Saccharine Solution (1.30 Grams per Liter) as Reward

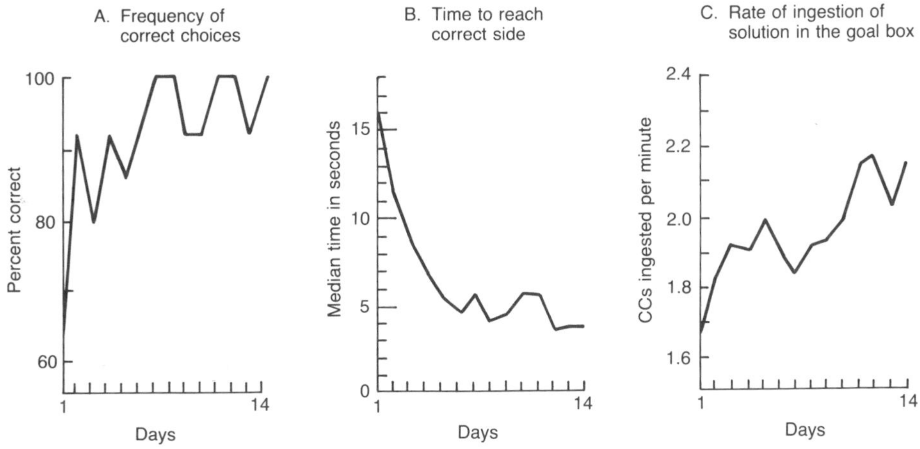
A. Frequency of correct choices
Percent correct
100
80
60
1
14
Days
B. Time to reach correct side
Median time in seconds
15
10
5
0
1
14
Days
C. Rate of ingestion of solution in the goal box
CCs ingested per minute
2.4
2.2
2.0
1.8
1.6
1
14
Days

SOURCE: "Reward Value of a Non-Nutrient Sweet Taste" by F. D. Sheffield and T. B. Roby, *Journal of Comparative and Physiological Psychology, 42.*

Such increases, if not intended, are at least tolerated. Harlow (1953) cites some evidence for this from studies conducted in his laboratory and also includes one striking ancedote:

> Twenty years ago at the Gilas Park Zoo, in Madison, we observed an adult orangutan given two blocks of wood, one with a round hole, one with a square hole, and two plungers, one round and one square. Intellectual curiosity alone led it to work on these tasks often for many minutes at a time, and to solve the problem of inserting the round plunger in both sides. The orangutan never solved the problem of inserting the square peg into the round hole, but inasmuch as it passed away with perforated ulcers a month after the problem was presented, we can honestly say that it died trying. And in defense of this orangutan, let it be stated that it died working on more complex problems than are investigated by most present-day theorists.

The suggestion made here is that once you study learning tasks of sufficient complexity to resemble the actual life experiences of organisms (T mazes clearly fall short of this), you find evidence on every side of behavior that bears little discernible relationship to any aim to reduce tension. Indeed, perhaps intriguing problems that spark the organism's curiosity lead to persistent behavior that has the effect of raising tension, even to dangerous levels. Anyone who has become excited and stimulated at a party or by an intellectual task to such a degree that he or she stayed up long into the night and expended lots of energy, without the slightest thought for the next day, knows what Harlow means. Some of the most interesting behaviors definitely seem to arouse rather than decrease tension.

In the years since Harlow made his speech, more systematic studies concerning the possibility of tension increase as an aim have been done. Most of these studies have already been mentioned in discussion of the fourth issue. Perhaps the single most convincing body of work on the intent to increase tension is that involving sensory deprivation (cf. Fiske, 1961). As I already mentioned, these studies show that when you deprive persons of the usual levels of sensory stimulation, they go to sleep (a sign of low tension level) and when they awaken experience great discomfort and an intense wish for stimulation. It is even possible that the hallucinatory mentation mentioned by investigators in this field is the organism's attempt to manufacture stimulation and tension. Certainly it has been clearly shown that the presentation of even the most banal stimulation (e.g., a recording of instructions) is greeted by subjects with enthusiasm and relief. Subjects will keep requesting such banal stimulation and, when all else fails, leave the experiment in intense discomfort. It is not hard to conclude from such evidence that some behavior is in the service of tension increase. Also supporting this conclusion are the studies of Dember (1956) and Eisenberger, Myers, Sanders, and Shanab (1970) indicating that spontaneous alternation involves a positive interest in stimulus change, and Maddi and Andrews (1966), indicating that the people who most produce novelty are also the most interested in it. These studies are relevant because novelty and change undoubtedly are tension-increasing occurrences.

These compelling findings have led some behaviorists to abandon their position. Consider Berlyne (1960), who initially developed an ingenious behavioristic argument in which studies such as the above would be explained as special cases of the attempt to reduce tension, strange as that may sound. Berlyne postulates that in the absence of external stimulation the organism actually becomes very tense due to spontaneously occurring internal stimulation. Subsequent attempts to increase external stimulation should therefore be understood as attempts to decrease the overall level of tension. Presumably external stimulation has some inhibiting effects on spontaneous internal stimulation.

You should first recognize what an extraordinarily complicated explanation this is. Sometimes external stimulation is talked about as if it increased tension, as when the laboratory rat is shocked and recoils in pain, and sometimes it is considered as decreasing tension, as when the sensorily deprived subject is permitted to hear the instructions. An explanation of this type rises or falls on the forcefulness of its treatment of whatever internal conditions are invoked to account for the two opposite effects of external stimulation. Even if there were not this theoretical difficulty, the notion that external stimulation actually decreases overall tension cannot adequately cover all the data. It must be remembered that it is typical of subjects in sensory deprivation experiments to fall asleep and to remain groggy, lethargic, and unable to think even after awakening. None of this sounds like a high state of tension. And are the ulcers that killed Harlow's monkey to be understood as the result of tension decreases stemming from working on puzzles?

With the all too rare commitment to empirical knowledge of the true scientist, Berlyne (1967) subsequently modified his position such that tension increase along with tension decrease is now recognized as rewarding. Although he still believed that boredom may be a high tension state, he did admit to a lack of experimental evidence for this view and went on to define classes of reinforcers that function because they increase tension. The first is ecological stimuli, which presumably have been important for survival and adaptation and therefore are rewarding even though they increase tension. In this regard, Berlyne noted studies that have obtained introspective reports of pleasure accompanying painful sensations produced by pricks, pressures, and pinches. Another class of rewarding tension increasers are novel, complex, and surprising stimuli (called *collative properties* by Berlyne). The research evidence here already has been covered in discussion of the fourth issue. Berlyne also noted that particularly in the area of verbal learning increases in tension seem to be facilitative. Some studies have shown that the higher the level of arousal during learning, the greater the probability of long-term recall, though the smaller the probability of short-term recall. In other studies, even immediate recall has been improved by the application of various arousal-raising treatments during learning, such as white noise, tones, induced muscular tension, and physical exercise. In trying to explain these findings, Berlyne (1967) says:

> We must therefore seek an alternative account of the effects of arousal on verbal learning. The one that emerges is . . . that verbal responses will be reinforced most effectively when arousal is at an intermediate level. Tests held some time after training—preferably 24 hours or more—give the surest measures of reinforcement. Immediate and short-term recall must depend on an interaction between the reinforcing effect of arousal and the effect of arousal on performance. We can expect these two effects to follow different inverted U-shaped functions. (p. 69)

Berlyne seems to be saying that moderate levels of arousal (or tension) are rewarding whereas lower or higher levels are not. In some experimental settings it may seem as if only tension reduction is rewarding and in other settings just the opposite. In reality, the difficulty is that the settings "reveal only one portion of the non-monotonic [U-shaped] curve" (Berlyne, 1967, p. 69). In the years since Berlyne's statement, little has happened to provoke any change in conclusion. Apparently agreement has been reached that tension increase is important to organisms, and empirical attention has settled on comparing the various theories to account for this phenomenon (see Eisenberger, 1972).

We are reaching the conclusion that not all behavior is oriented toward tension reduction and that some behavior may even be directed at tension increase. This outcome of exploring the fifth issue tends to favor the fulfillment model and the activation version of the consistency model. Not so supported are the conflict model and the cognitive dissonance version of the consistency model.

Sixth Issue: Does Personality Show Radical Change after the Childhood Years Have Passed?

Consistency and fulfillment positions are on one side of this issue and conflict positions are, by and large, on the other. According to the pure psychosocial conflict model, there should be no radical change in personality once there is solidification of the defensive patterns established to avoid the anxiety that reflects underlying conflict. As these patterns are considered set by the time childhood has passed, conflict positions would not expect adulthood, or even adolescence, to be a time of radical personality change. What I have just said does not apply as much to the intrapsychic version of the conflict model, as it emphasizes the concept of defense only in nonideal functioning. But absence of radical change after childhood is clearly assumed by pure psychosocial conflict theorists such as Freud. In this theory, it is even typical to name the patterns of peripheral characteristics, or personality types, in terms of the early childhood stages of psychosexual development. In considering adolescence and adulthood as constituting only one developmental stage, Freud vividly shows his emphasis on the essentially unchanging nature of adult personality. Any changes taking place beyond puberty are not basic or radical. In contrast, fulfillment positions see personality as a rather continually changing thing, with no sharp difference in changeability between childhood, adolescence, and adulthood. This emphasis on fluidity is most apparent in Rogers and the other actualization theorists, who do not consider even the self-concept to be particularly stable. But the emphasis is also strong in some perfection theorists, such as the existential psychologists, who see life as a series of changes toward ever increasing individuality. Perfection theorists tend to emphasize personality change in the direction of psychological growth, or simultaneously increasing differentiation and integration. Consistency positions also assume rather continual change in personality, having little recourse to a concept of defense. The cognitive dissonance version of the consistency model attributes to the person the frequent changes in personality that occur in the attempt to minimize the discrepancy between expectations and perceived occurrences. Finally, the activation version of this model emphasizes the concept of psychological growth.

You may have noticed that I stated the issue in such a way that what is of interest is the occurrence of radical change in personality. It was necessary to do this because no sensible theorists, regardless of the model of theorizing adopted, would dispute that certain unextraordinary changes in degree take place during adolescence and adulthood. If, say, a person with the kind of personality called *anal* by Freudians was stubborn in childhood and became a bit less or more so in adulthood, no one would consider this theoretically disconcerting. In a literal sense, change would have occurred, but no special difficulty for the conflict model would have been created thereby. Radical changes in personality are a different matter. If a person's personality type shifted from oral in childhood to phallic in adulthood, we would have a situation unexpected by Freudians. The only way Freudians could explain such a radical change in adulthood would be to postulate the intervention of an unusual and potent life context, such as psychotherapy or catastrophe. If radical change in personality can be shown in the absence of such extraordinary occurrences, the psychosocial conflict model will not have been confirmed. Thus, in order to pinpoint the issue such that it will really separate the various models, it is necessary to restrict ourselves to conditions or contexts that can be considered more natural and usual than participating in psychotherapy. These more natural conditions include such things as getting married, having children, going to college, changing jobs, and moving to a new location.

You should note that my depiction of the psychosocial conflict position is least accurate for ego psychology. The major ego psychologist, Erikson, does, after all, emphasize eight developmental ages stretching across the entire life span. And in his recent popular account, Levinson (1978) argues within a generally ego-psychological framework for such adulthood changes as the "mid-life crisis." But do not conclude that the Freudian emphasis on stability during adolescence and adulthood is a thing of the past. Recently Litz (1976), an authoritative Freudian, wrote a book ostensibly about development throughout life that devotes barely 70 of 615 pages to adulthood years. Most of the book is about the first few years of life. Theorists influenced by psychosocial conflict thinking, be they identifiable as ego psychologists or pure Freudians, generally tend to disbelieve in radical change following the childhood years.

On the face of it, the study of personality change is most effectively done by testing the same group of people at the beginning and at the end of the period of time under consideration—the so-called *longitudinal* study (see Chapter 2). Although this is the most appropriate kind of study, there are obvious difficulties associated with having to wait long periods of time in order to obtain data. After the initial testing, subjects may move to dozens of locations, no longer be willing to participate, or even die. Such difficulties have held down the number of longitudinal studies attempted. Fortunately, there are by now several such studies with reasonably careful data collection procedures, and they will be emphasized in what follows.

In earlier years, the difficulties inherent in longitudinal studies provoked investigators to rely instead on the so-called *cross-sectional* study. In cross-sectional studies, a number of groups of subjects are employed with each group differing in age. Groups are tested only once, and the differences among them are attributed to the effects of the span of years separating their ages. Obviously this kind of study has the advantage of taking very little time and effort by comparison with the longitudinal study. But the cross-sectional study is also more risky, because it must be assumed that the various groups were similar in personality during the period of time ending with the age of the youngest group. Usually there is no way to check this assumption. But suppose the span of years separating the adolescent and adult groups is large, say, thirty years. In thirty years' time, it is rather likely that child-rearing practices would have changed enough to make it risky to assume similarity of childhood personality for all groups. And if the groups differed in personality during childhood, it may be no more than this fact that the investigator is observing and erroneously attributing to the effects of moving through adolescence. Because of these problems, I will not rely on cross-sectional studies, though they will be mentioned as suggestive.

Turning to relevant longitudinal studies, we encounter an early effort by Tuddenham (1959) that is instructive. He interviewed seventy-two males and females first during their adolescence and again in their early or middle adulthood. The interview material was rated for fifty-three personality variables, some fairly descriptive and some inferential. Correlations between subjects' earlier and later scores generally were positive but quite low, the average being only .27 for males and .24 for females. These correlations are so low that one really could not effectively predict what a person would be like in young adulthood from his or her scores in early adolescence. But there are two problems in interpreting these findings as indicating personality change. Unfortunately, pairs of raters did not always agree strongly, and the pair of raters working on the interview data for the first testing was different from the pair working on the second testing. These two methodological problems could have produced the apparent lack of personality stability.

The college years are a ready source of information about personality change following childhood. Although most such studies have been cross-sectional, a few have been longitudinal in design. Among these, the report by Freedman and Bereiter (1963) is notable not only for its carefulness but also because it extends even beyond the college years. Their subjects were females from the classes of 1954, 1955, and 1956 at Vassar College, numbering seventy-eight, seventy-four, and seventy-nine, respectively. These subjects had taken the Vassar Attitude Inventory (VAI), the Minnesota Multiphasic Personality Inventory (MMPI), and the California Personality Inventory (CPI) as freshmen, again as seniors, and finally three to four years after graduation. There was evidence of systematic and important change during the college years, the nature of which was confirmed by other studies (e.g., Sanford, 1962). On the VAI, the subjects seemed to have become, as seniors, less ethnocentric and authoritarian while becoming more expressive of impulses and rebellious independence. Changes in scores on the MMPI and CPI indicated a shift toward psychopathology and away from conventional adjustment. But three to four years after graduation, these general trends had more or less been reversed. At the final testing, repression and suppression of impulses had increased on the VAI, scores on the psychopathology scales of the MMPI had decreased, and the picture obtained from the CPI was in the direction of conventional adjustment. Although the changes demonstrated in this study were not especially large, they did tend to reverse direction and are therefore striking.

All the studies mentioned thus far used test-retest agreement on the same measures as a procedure for determining the degree of personality stability or change. A few longitudinal studies, however, employed a more global, interpretive criterion of stability based on the determination of analogous rather than literally similar behaviors at the different ages considered. These studies worked at a genotypical (underlying) level, whereas the others employed a phenotypical (obvious) level of analysis, to borrow a distinction from biology. Whether or not the genotypical approach is really more appropriate, you should recognize that it renders observation of change less likely due to the abstract, interpretive level at which observation takes place.

In one genotypical study, Anderson (1960) tested all children in a Minnesota county who were enrolled in school from grades four to twelve, and then retested them five to seven years later, by which time some of them were in their twenties. He concluded that of the measures of intelligence and personality obtained at the first testing, only the former play an important role in predicting later adjustment. In spite of an approach unsuited to focusing on literal changes in behavior, Anderson reports that personality variables do not seem to be patterned by age.

In a major genotypical study, Kagan and Moss (1962) inclined to just the opposite conclusion. Twenty-one males and females were rated on a set of personality variables at four intervals during their childhoods and again during their twenties. Correlations were computed between certain childhood behaviors and their theoretically analogous adult behaviors. These results are presented in Figure 6–6, which also indicates the kinds of behaviors considered. Kagan and Moss (1962) concluded that

> Many of the behaviors exhibited by the child aged six to ten, and a few during the age period three to six, were moderately good predictors of theoretically related behaviors during early childhood. Passive withdrawal from stressful situations, dependency on family, ease-of-anger arousal, involvement in intellectual mastery, social interaction anxiety, sex-role identification, and pattern of sexual behavior in adulthood were each related to reasonably analogous behavioral dispositions during the early school years . . . . These results offer strong support for the generalization that aspects of adult personality begin to take form during early childhood.(pp. 266–268)

Actually, this seems to me rather unconvincing as a conclusion based on the findings in Figure 6–6. Even with an approach weighted toward the discovery of personality stability, we find that five of the seven correlations shown for males and all seven for females are below .50. The average correlation is about .41 for males and .31 for females. To my mind, these findings show that there is more change than stability in personality, even when one adopts a genotypical approach!

FIGURE 6–6   Summary of Relations between Selected Child Behaviors (Six to
Ten Years of Age) and Theoretically Similar Adult Behaviors

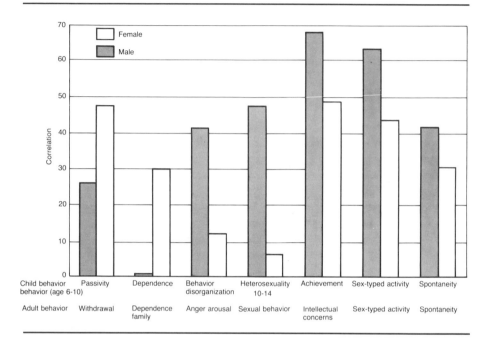

SOURCE: *Birth to Maturity: A Study in Psychological Development* by J. Kagan and H. A. Moss, 1962, New
York: Wiley.

Following their brave conclusions, Kagan and Moss (1962) made statements more consistent with the amount of change they observed, for example:

> Not all of the childhood reactions displayed long-term continuity. Compulsivity
> and irrational fears during childhood were not predictive of similar responses
> during adulthood. Moreover, task persistence and excessive irritability during
> the first three years of life showed no relation to phenotypically similar behav-
> iors during later childhood. (p. 269)

In another statement, Kagan and Moss (1962) gave what seems to me the crux
of the matter:

> However, the degree of continuity of these response classes was intimately
> dependent upon its congruence with traditional standards for sex-role charac-
> teristics. The differential stability of passivity, dependency, aggression, and
> sexuality for males and females emphasizes the importance of cultural roles in
> determining both behavioral change and stability. (p. 268)

Indeed, with results showing more change than stability, it would seem wise to
conclude that whatever stability exists from childhood to adulthood occurs
along the lines of sex-role definitions important to culture. When some aspect

of personality is not intimately connected with what is defined as a sex role, it may well change enough in adulthood to be virtually unpredictable from childhood personality.

In a recent study of large scope, Block (1971) collected follow-up data in adulthood from subjects who had been extensively tested by other investigators during childhood and adolescence. The variety of data available included interviews, teacher and peer reports, self-reports, and several structured personality tests. Genotypical data concerning stability or change in personality were derived from these protocols by ratings made by several psychologists. Mean correlations for the 171 subjects between junior high school and senior high school ages were .77 and .75 for males and females, respectively. Between senior high school and adulthood, they were .56 and .54 for males and females, respectively. But the range of correlations was so great as to indicate that a number of subjects had changed a good deal though some remained much the same. Block identified six female and five male types that differed not only in personality content but in degree of change from childhood to adulthood. Some of these types changed too much to be consistent with the contention that personality remains rather stable once the childhood years are past. Block's unusual approach of isolating types partly on the basis of changeability has provided findings that clearly bear on the issue under discussion.

Recently Bachman, O'Malley, and Johnston (1978) reported a longitudinal study using a sample of 16,000 subjects chosen so as to be representative of the U.S. population. The subjects were first tested when in high school and then followed for eight years, during which the investigators examined the impact of such events as college, marriage, unemployment, childbearing and military service on attitudes, self-esteem, aggression, and various other behaviors. Bachman et al. conclude that these events had relatively little effect and that "the dominant picture that emerges from this research is not change but stability." Once again we are faced with a problem of interpretation. The test-retest correlations reported in this study rarely exceeded the range of .40 to .50. Hence, one might have chosen to emphasize change over stability, as such correlations do not provide an adequate basis for predicting behavior over the eight-year period.

Shifting our attention to the latter half of life—from young adulthood through middle adulthood to old age—we find very few longitudinal studies to go by. There is the report by Terman and Oden (1959) following up on a group of gifted, extraordinary children studied years before who had since reached their forties. Originally each child selected for study was in the top 1 percent of the population in intelligence quotient (IQ). The data on personality have not been systematically analyzed, but in general it appears that the superior child has become the superior adult. Although there is evidence of stability here, one must be careful in generalizing from this study both because it deals with such an unusual group of people and because its major concern is with intelligence rather than personality.

In another study, Kelly (1955) tested 300 engaged couples first when they were in their twenties and again when they were in their forties. After correcting his correlations for attenuation, Kelly concluded that individual consistency was highest in the areas of values and vocational interests (correlations of approximately .50) and lowest with regard to self-ratings and other personality variables (correlations of approximately .30). Kelly points out that "our findings indicate that significant changes in human personality may continue to occur during the years of adulthood." This conclusion is even more likely to be accurate when one realizes that the correlations of approximately .30 and .50 are only estimates of what would have been found had the measures employed been more adequate. Actually, Kelly's obtained correlations must have been lower than the figures mentioned here. In a recent study, Haan and Dey (1974) obtained a picture of great change in their longitudinal study of personality in the period from adolescence to later adulthood. Their findings indicate that adulthood is a time of major reorganization in personality.

All in all, the studies reviewed to this point show so much evidence of change that many experts in human development (e.g., Neugarten, 1964; Stevenson, 1957) have concluded against stability during the adulthood years. For example, Neugarten (1964) says:

> Whether the studies are test-retest or antecedent-consequent [notypical] in design . . . the general picture with regard to consistency of adult personality can be summarized by saying that measures taken at long time intervals tend to produce statistically reliable, but relatively low, correlations . . . . The indication is that while there is continuity of personality measurable by present techniques, the larger proportion of the variance in the measures used (in the final testing) remains unaccounted for. Making allowances for the fallibility of measures with regard to reliability, the implication is that there is at least as much change as there is stability.

But Costa and McCrae (1977, 1978) dispute this conclusion on the basis of new findings. On a sample of adult males studied over a ten-year interval, they found that the genotypical variables of anxiety, extroversion-introversion, and neuroticism showed stability correlations ranging from .58 to .84. The individual questionnaire scales (from the 16 Personality Factor Questionnaire) on which these genotypical analyses were based showed lower stability correlations—from .44 to .63. In addition, Costa, McCrae, and Arenberg (1980) have reported another longitudinal study in which 460 males were tested three times over a 12-year period with the Guilford-Zimmerman Temperament Survey. Some of their results appear in Table 6–8, which shows strong evidence for stability over twelve years in the various traits measured. The stability is evident across young, middle, and old subsamples. This, other recent work by Costa and McCrae, and a study by Conley (1984) suggest that the adult years are ones of relative stability for some aspects of personality. But as the longitudinal studies mentioned earlier indicate there seems to be evidence for per-

TABLE 6–8 Twelve-Year Retest Coefficients for Guilford-Zimmerman
Temperament Survey Scales in Different Age Groups

Scales	Total Age 20–76	Young Age 20–44	Middle Age 45–59	Old Age 60–76
General activity	.77 (192)	.77 (60)	.83 (93)	.78 (39)
Restraint	.72 (193)	.61 (62)	.74 (94)	.76 (37)
Ascendance	.83 (194)	.85 (62)	.85 (95)	.77 (37)
Sociability	.74 (182)	.64 (62)*	.81 (88)	.66 (32)
Emotional stability	.70 (203)	.63 (68)	.76 (96)	.71 (39)
Objectivity	.69 (191)	.66 (64)	.76 (87)	.59 (40)
Friendliness	.74 (193)	.74 (64)†	.68 (88)‡	.87 (41)
Thoughtfulness	.73 (199)	.78 (64)	.71 (94)	.71 (41)
Personal relations	.68 (188)	.70 (62)	.64 (89)	.73 (37)
Masculinity	.72 (200)	.73 (66)	.71 (94)	.70 (40)
Mean stability	.73	.72	.75	.73

Note: *N*s given in parentheses. All correlations significant at $p < .001$.
*Difference between Young and Middle significant at $p < .05$.
†Difference between Young and Old significant at $p < .05$.
‡Difference between Middle and Old significant at $p < .01$.

SOURCE: Adapted from "Enduring Dispositions in Adult Males" by P. T. Costa, Jr., R. R. McCrae, and D. Arenberg, 1980, *Journal of Personality and Social Psychology*.

sonality change in the transition from childhood to adolescence and from adolescence to adulthood.

Before concluding this review, let me alert you to a body of research that, though relevant, is sometimes overlooked because it does not come out of the questionnaire tradition. I refer to the series of studies by Witkin and his associates (Witkin, Dyk, Faterson, Goodenough, & Karp, 1962; Witkin, Lewis, Hertzman, Machover, Meissner, & Wapner, 1954) on *psychological differentiation,* which they define as the "degree of articulation of experience of the world; degree of articulation of experience of self, reflected particularly in the nature of the body concept and extent of development of a sense of separate identity; and extent of development of specialized, structured controls and defenses" (Witkin et al., 1962, p. 16). The two things emphasized in this definition are the number of aspects or parts to the personality and the separateness of persons from the world around them. These emphases square quite well with discussions of differentiation reviewed in previous chapters of this book. Witkin et al. (1962) also refer to *integration,* indicating its function in binding together and organizing the parts of personality discriminated from one another by differentiation. They present the intriguing point of view that integrative processes will determine the nature of the adjustment and degree of effectiveness that characterize the person whereas differentiation bears little relationship to such matters. But they conduct no research on integrative processes.

In measuring psychological differentiation, Witkin and his associates heavily rely on a number of ingenious tests of the ability to be analytical in perceptual situations. Analytical perception ability is considered an indicant of psychological differentiation, because it involves a separateness of self and body from the outside world and a sensitivity to the parts of things in general. In the Embedded Figures Test, the person is presented with a series of complex geometrical figures. The speed and accuracy with which he or she can detect previously seen simple figures that have been hidden within the complex ones is taken as a measure of psychological differentiation. In order to detect the embedded simple figure, the person must be able to analyze the complex figure into its component parts. The Rod and Frame Test presents the person with a rod surrounded by a square frame as the only visible things in a darkened room. The person is asked to adjust the rod to the upright position, which is complicated by the frame's tilt a certain number of degrees to either the left or the right. The average accuracy of rod adjustment to the upright position over a series of trials is taken as another measure of psychological differentiation. According to Witkin et al., accurate adjustment of the rod requires that the person disregard the cues provided by the surrounding frame and instead use kinesthetic and proprioceptive cues stemming from his or her body. Finally, in the Body Adjustment Test, the person sits in a seat placed within an experimental room. Both seat and room can be tilted by the experimenter. The person's task is to adjust his or her seated body to the upright position from a starting point at which the chair is tilted to either the right or the left and the room is tilted in the same or opposite direction. Once again the accuracy with which the body is adjusted to the upright position is taken as a measure of psychological differentiation because in order to be successful, one must overlook visual cues from the external environment and rely on the awareness of kinesthetic and proprioceptive cues signaling the positioning of one's body. Scores on these three tests intercorrelate moderately and show adequate reliability (Witkin et al., 1962, p. 40).

Although these investigators have concentrated on their perceptual tests, they have also employed more cognitive measures involving persons composing stories about vague pictures (Thematic Apperception Test), indicating what inkblots look like to them (Rorschach Test), and drawing pictures of themselves and others (Draw-A-Person Test). In all these tasks, the aim is to detect aspects of psychological differentiation such as articulateness of experience and articulateness of body image. What is by now a large body of empirical evidence (Witkin et al., 1954; Witkin et al., 1962) indicates that these nonperceptual measures correlate with the perceptual ones such that it is sensible to consider them all as mirroring some facet of the overall characteristic of psychological differentiation. Those of you who are familiar with Witkin's earlier (1954) emphasis on the concepts of *field dependence* and *field independence* should note the fact that he (Witkin et al., 1962) shifted from these concepts to that of psychological differentiation largely on the basis of the empirical association between the original perceptual measures and the cognitive ones just mentioned.

Having given you some background on Witkin's work, I can now describe the longitudinal studies relevant to determining what happens to the level of psychological differentiation during the life span. Witkin et al. (1962, pp. 374-377) report two studies of special relevance. One involved a group of twenty-six males and twenty-seven females, studied first at age eight and again at age thirteen. The second group consisted of thirty males and thirty females studied at ages ten, fourteen, seventeen. With regard to the perceptual measures of psychological differentiation, the same trend was observed in both studies. In the words of the investigators (Witkin et al., 1962, p. 374), "The ability to determine the position of the body apart from the tilted room, to perceive the position of a rod independently of the tilted frame, to pick out a simple figure obscured by a complex design, tends to improve, on the whole, until about the age of 17." Thereafter, the rate of increase in psychological differentiation decreases and, for females, may actually reverse slightly in direction. A parallel finding was obtained concerning articulateness of body concept as measured in the figure drawings made by the subjects. Witkin et al. (1962, p. 376) conclude that "Children who showed a relatively articulated body concept at 10 showed it 7 years later as well, even though the drawings at the two ages gave evidence of a general change toward more sophisticated representation of the human body." Also reported (Witkin et al., 1962) are other studies concerning the period from infancy to age nine and the college years. The picture that emerges from all these studies is essentially the same: Psychological differentiation shows a rapid increase from infancy through about the middle of adolescence and a more gradual increase from that point on into young adulthood. In addition, the early differences among people in degree of psychological differentiation are maintained all the while everyone is increasing in that characteristic. Certainly there is clear evidence that differentiation continues to occur beyond the childhood years.

One last observation from these studies bears on the more general question of whether radical changes in personality occur following childhood. In connection with the attempt to study changes in body concept between the ages of ten and seventeen, Witkin et al. (1962) had occasion to consider not only articulateness but content of figure drawings, concluding that there were:

1. Vast changes in kinds of interests . . . which resulted in marked differences in content of drawings by the same child.
2. Marked decrease in drawing features suggestive of disturbance or pathology.
3. Changes in main conflict areas. Thus, the large and varied changes that occur in this period of life are reflected in the drawings; some of the changes are in content aspects of personality, others refer to nature of integration, still others to extent of differentiation.

Witkin believes that along with the gradual increases in differentiation (and presumably integration, though he does not study that) there occur radical shifts in the content (including conflicts) of personality.

But there is one study (Schwartz & Carp, 1967) that suggests a peak in psychological differentiation (measured by both the Rod and Frame and Embedded Figures tests) at about age twenty-five, and a gradual decline thereafter. If this finding holds up, we will be observing a phenomenon similiar to that in the previously mentioned questionnaire studies. It may well be that personality changes from childhood through young adulthood but remains relatively stable from that point on.

The cross-sectional studies available generally favor the conclusion that radical change in personality takes place beyond the childhood years. As such, these studies agree with the longitudinal studies that consider the period from childhood to young adulthood and differ with those that cover the adulthood years. But cross-sectional studies are, in any event, less definitive than longitudinal ones and therefore will not be elaborated on here.

It is time to draw our consideration of the sixth issue to a close. There seems clear evidence for radical change in personality in the years immediately following childhood and some (though more equivocal) evidence for the ensuing years. In a recent review, Rutter (1984) concluded that the weight of evidence is against personality theories that posit an invariant set of developmental stages and a fixating effect of certain early experiences on later development. One intriguing notion gaining force of late (e.g., Moss & Kuypers, 1974; Neugarten, 1980) is that while there may not be the regular stages (e.g., intimacy versus isolation, mid-life crisis) previously thought to punctuate adulthood and, hence, no correspondingly regular changes in behavior, there may be considerable individual variability as to how much change occurs and at what age it takes place. All in all, the findings do not support the pure psychosocial version of the conflict model. But there is general support for the other models insofar as they would predict substantial personality change in the years from childhood to young adulthood. These models do tend to predict that change will continue throughout adulthood, however, and some recent findings suggest that this may not occur.

CONCLUDING REMARKS

We have come a long, long way in Chapters 3, 4, 5, and 6 and are finally in a position to put together what we have learned. In considering the first two issues posed in this chapter, we have formed an empirical basis for concluding that the concept of defense is tenable and that some, but not all, behavior is defensive. These conclusions support all bases for core-level theorizing except the pure psychosocial version of the conflict model, which assumes all behavior to be defensive. In pursuing the third issue, we reached the tentative conclusion that the highest form of functioning is transcendent rather than adaptive. This conclusion supports the fulfillment model, is contrary to the conflict model (at least in its psychosocial version), and fails to have any special significance for the consistency model. But we should give little weight to this conclusion, as it is no stronger than our assumption that fulfillment and conflict theorists alike would designate the creative person as the clearest embodiment of the highest form of functioning. Considering the fourth issue taught us that only large discrepancies from expectation (or dissonances) are unpleasant and avoided whereas small discrepancies are actually pleasant and sought after. This conclusion actively favors two forms of the consistency model and activation and variant cognitive dissonance versions but does not support the pure cognitive dissonance version of that model. The other models are not actively touched by this conclusion. We resolved the fifth issue by concluding that while some behavior aims at tension reduction, other behavior aims at tension increase. Favored are the activation and variant cognitive dissonance versions of the consistency model and the fulfillment model in general. Contradicted are the pure cognitive dissonance version of the consistency model and all forms of the conflict model except, perhaps, the variant of its psychosocial version. On investigating the sixth issue, it became apparent that there are radical shifts in the content of personality during the period from childhood to young adulthood. All in all, the fulfillment and consistency models are favored and the conflict model is not.

Merely by totaling the number of times a model has been supported or contradicted by our empirical analysis leads us to interesting and surprisingly clear overall conclusions. The only models that were never contradicted are both versions of the fulfillment model and the activation version of the consistency model. The only models that were never supported are the pure psychosocial versions of the conflict model and the pure cognitive dissonance version of the consistency model. The other models fall in between these two extremes but are more frequently contradicted than supported.

It is interesting that the models most supported by our empirical analysis are also not at all logically incompatible. Although one could certainly adopt either version of the fulfillment model or the activation version of the consistency model, one could also combine them without being logically inconsistent. In combining them, one would be assuming both a tendency to actualize potentialities of perfect living and a tendency to minimize discrepancies between customary and actual levels of activation. That both assumptions could be harmoniously included in the same theory is suggested by their shared basic compatibility in the fundamental questions regarding defensiveness, tension reduction and increase, and personality change. Though compatible, I believe they stress different aspects of behavior and, hence, their combination might result in an even more comprehensive personality theory. But at the moment, this is only speculation.

Lest you embrace these overall conclusions too completely, I must remind you that we have not yet considered the statements at the peripheral level of personality made by the various models. Perhaps one of the models that falls between the extremes of support and disconfirmation with regard to core considerations will actually do a better job at the peripheral level than any other model. We must evaluate peripheral-level statements before attaining a comprehensive basis for judging the relative value of the models.

CHAPTER 7

The Periphery of Personality: Conflict Model

Statements about the core of personality depict the tendencies and characteristics that are present in all persons at all times and that influence the overall directionality of life. In contrast, each peripheral aspect of personality is learned, present in some rather than all people, and specific rather than general in its effect on behavior. Peripheral concepts of personality are the ones that relate most clearly, immediately, and obviously to the behavior constituting data (or that which is to be explained). The ideal theory of personality would include both core and peripheral statements. The core statements are important for understanding how people share a common psychological nature. The peripheral statements are important for understanding their behavioral or stylistic differences.

You should keep in mind as you read this chapter that there are two general kinds of peripheral characteristics. In Chapter 1, they were called *peripheral characteristics* and *types*. The peripheral characteristic is the smallest, most homogeneous unit of personality considered feasible by the theorist. It is what is used to explain the behavioral regularities observed in individuals. For example, a theorist may attribute the behaviors of calling people on the telephone, going to many parties, joining clubs, and talking a lot to the trait of gregariousness. Gregariousness would constitute a peripheral characteristic of personality if it were considered something learned and not present equally in all persons.

Personologists often have used the term *trait* for what I am calling a *peripheral characteristic*. I have avoided such usage because, as you will see, some theorists postulate homogeneous particles of personality whose content is inconsistent with the connotations of the term *trait*. Typically theorists will postulate a number of peripheral characteristics, each of which can be present or absent in the personality of any given person. But when theorists employ the concept of type, they essentially group together sets of concrete peripheral characteristics, thus forming larger, less homogeneous units that more vividly describe the styles of living observed in people. The function of the type concept is to get at the "Johnian" quality of John.

In this chapter, we will consider the peripheral statements included in the various theories covered in previous chapters. Some of the theorists make an explicit distinction between periphery and core, whereas others either leave it to us to make the distinction or concentrate so much on the core that it is hard to determine what, if anything, they have to say about the periphery. In addition, among the theorists who actually consider the periphery, some emphasize the type concept and some the peripheral characteristics.

CONFLICT MODEL: PSYCHOSOCIAL VERSION

Freud's Position

It is wise to consider Freud first, for his viewpoint provides a good example of the distinction between the core and periphery of personality. Freud assumed that all persons have the same set of instincts concerning survival, sexuality, and death. Clearly this is an assumption involving the core of personality, for it is inconceivable, in his theory, that one person would have only survival and sex instincts but not the death instinct and another only the death instinct or only the sex instinct. All persons have all instincts, and these forces exert a continual, general influence on all functioning. For Freud, then, the *id* or repository of the instincts is clearly part of the core of personality.

The parts of the personality called *ego* and *superego* should also be considered part of the core, though the reasons for this are not as obvious as in the case of the id. Although it has become fashionable in some psychoanalytic circles to talk of people with more or less ego and superego, it nonetheless remains true that no one can be considered as without ego or superego. The absence of ego is theoretically impossible, because the ego comes into being by virtue of the existence of the id and the consequent necessity of satisfying instincts through interaction with the world. Without an ego, there would be no chance of consistent gratification and therefore no chance of physical and psychological survival. Similarly, it is theoretically impossible to conceive of a person without a superego, because that part of personality is born out of the conflict between the person and the world, a conflict as inevitable as selfish instincts that cannot be gratified independently of other people and things. It is the requirements of society that determine the superego—and, for Freud, individual life is inconceivable without the existence of society.

But to say that the ego and superego are core characteristics of personality along with the id is to mask an important difference between the first two and the last. In *content,* the id is the same for all persons, but this is not true for the ego and superego. For Freud, the ego consists of defenses and their concrete expressions in traits or consistencies of everyday functioning. In his theory it is true that all persons are defensive, but they are not defensive in the same way. Psychoanalysts have distinguished a number of different defenses and theorized about the developmental conditions determining their appearance in a particular person. In specifying the kinds of defenses that can be used, Freudians are making statements about the periphery of personality. This is even more obvious when they begin detailing the concrete habits expressive of the various defenses, as we will see in a moment. Each defense is learned and specific either to a particular person or to a part of a person's behavior. Something quite similar is true for the superego: While present in all persons, its contents may vary according to the quirks of one's parents. Consequently, the taboos and sanctions recognized in one person may differ somewhat from those of the next. In considering the content of both ego and superego, we are dealing with the periphery of personality. The basic reason for this is that the content of ego and superego, in contrast to that of the id, is largely determined by the kinds of people and things encountered in the external environment.

Actually, the Freudian position on the periphery of personality is most vividly contained in the classification of *character types*. This can be clearly seen in Fenichel (1945), who says:

> Character, as the habitual mode of bringing into harmony the tasks presented by internal demands and by the external world, is necessarily a function of the constant, organized, and integrating part of the personality which is the ego; indeed, ego was defined as that part of the organism that handles the communication between the instinctual demands and the external world. The question of character would thus be the question of when and how the ego acquires the qualities by which it habitually adjusts itself to the demands of instinctual drives and of the external world, and later also of the superego . . . . The term character stresses the habitual form of a given reaction, its relative constancy. (p. 467)

Later Fenichel indicates that character is the content not only of the ego but of the superego:

> The latest complication in the structure of the ego, the erection of the superego, is also decisive in forming the habitual patterns of character. What an individual considers good or bad is characteristic for him; likewise, whether or not he takes the commands of his conscience seriously, and whether he obeys his conscience or tries to rebel against it. (p. 468)

In these two quotes, it is clear that character is a learned pattern of fairly consistent ways of functioning, which varies somewhat from person to person. In order to undercut the terribly abstract terminology Fenichel uses, I encourage you to recognize that character is the most obvious psychological thing about a person—what you would say if someone asked you to describe a friend.

Actually, it is possible to be more concrete, even in the structure of psychoanalytic terminology. A *character type* is a group of traits that expresses (1) particular underlying defenses, (2) a particular underlying conflict, (3) a particular response on the part of others to an underlying conflict, or (4) any combination of these. A *trait*, it turns out, can be primarily a pattern of thought, feeling or action or some combination of these. In our terms, traits are peripheral characteristics. Before we discuss the content of particular character types, note that the character type is learned and represents the results of the interaction between the child, who is selfishly striving for instinctual gratification, and the society, in the form of parents whose task is to uphold the common good. We will find that not only in this theory but in all others the periphery is the fruit of earlier attempts to express the core tendency in a particular social and cultural context.

Character types are the product of development; hence, it is fitting that they bear the names of the various psychosexual stages, reflecting as they do the Freudian position on development. The major stages of psychosexual development are the *oral, anal, phallic, latency,* and *genital.* Each stage has a particular concrete form of sexual instinct and arouses a specific range of reactions from parents. This amounts to saying that each stage is defined by a particular concrete version of the general conflict between the sexual instinct and society. It should not be surprising, then, that each stage has its own typical defenses, as the various defenses are differentially effective against different forms of conflict. And, as you will see, each stage but one has a particular character type associated with it. The concrete forms of the sexual instinct associated with the various stages of psychosexual development are summarized in their names. As you can see, there is an anatomical location designated in each name except that for the latency stage. Even conservative psychoanalytic thinkers are beginning to believe that the latency stage is not a true inherent aspect of the sexual instinct but a culturally determined period of developmental quiescence. The dubious status of the latency stage is reflected in the absence of an associated character type. Therefore, we will not concern ourselves with the latency period.

It should not have escaped your notice that the psychosexual stages refer exclusively to the sexual instinct. But what about the survival and death instincts? Are there developmental stages and character types associated with them as well? There are no developmental stages, and while some psychoanalysts have attempted to designate relevant character types, they are not widely accepted and are often fragmentary and confusing. The general state of affairs reflects the overwhelming importance, in Freudian thinking, of the sexual instinct. It is not at all inappropriate to say that the Freudian theory of personality hinges on sexuality as the basic human nature.

The oral, anal, phallic, and genital stages of development roughly cover, respectively, the first year of life, the second year, the third through fifth years, and the years from puberty onward. Obviously one must go through the first three stages in order to reach the fourth. If the first three stages are successfully traversed, genitality is vigorous and full. But if any of the developmental experiences in one or more of the three pregenital stages is destructive, that stage or stages will have a lingering effect on later behavior. It is in order to indicate this lingering effect on the adult that three of the character types are named *oral, anal,* and *phallic* and, of course, the fourth character type *genital.* The fourth represents psychological maturity, whereas the other three represent different qualities of immaturity. Each of the pregenital stages entails a particular form of childish sexual wish and impulse. To ensure successful progress through that stage, the child must receive from parents and the world enough gratification to not feel hopelessly deprived and frustrated but not so much that it becomes too pleasant to remain in that particular phase of immaturity. If there is either too much frustration or too much indulgence, the child becomes *fixated,* or stuck, at that particular level of development. This means that in adulthood the person will show traits—thoughts, emotions, actions—characteristic of the particular conflict, defenses, and parental reactions defining that pregenital stage.

Now we are in a position to examine the content of the various psychosexual stages of development. At the beginning we find the *oral stage,* in which the anatomical location of the sexual instinct is the mouth. According to Freud, the development of the nervous system proceeds from the brain downward and outward, ensuring that the mouth region will be the first body orifice suited to the experience of pleasure and pain. Of course, the survival instincts for food and water also ensure that the mouth will be an important region in the organism's experience. But Freud's emphasis is more on the mouth as a tactually and gustatorily erotic area. In other words, the child is presumed to crave and enjoy stimulation of the mouth region through touch, taste, and use of muscle. The craving and enjoyment are early forms of what will finally become mature sexuality in the genital stage.

In order to understand the *oral character type,* you must recognize that the oral form of sexual instinct leads to actions and fantasies involved in *taking* and *receiving* and that the conflicts salient at the oral stage therefore are those precipitated by these selfish activities (Fenichel, 1945, pp. 488–492). Freudians consider taking and receiving as being generalizations of the mouth activities during the first year of life. Receiving is the generalization of the earliest, passive (*oral incorporative*) situation, in which the mouth is pleasurably stimulated by people and things in the process of being fed and caressed. Taking is the generalization of the slightly later, somewhat less passive (*oral aggressive*) situation, in which children contrive to gain oral satisfaction through sucking, putting things in their mouths, chewing, biting, and even vocalizing.

There is, of course, an inevitable conflict between the child's unmitigated, selfish wish to receive and take and the parents' own needs and duties, which do not permit unlimited time and attention to their offspring. The best that can happen is that the parents will provide a modicum of instinctual satisfaction for their child. If they fall short of this modicum by severely punishing the child for its needs to receive and take or by simply not having enough nurturance within them to make any difference, the inevitable conflict will be greatly intensified. This intensification will require the child to develop especially strong and pervasive defenses, the employment of which is tantamount to a fixation, or arresting of growth. Once such defenses are instituted, change and development are impaired. The parents can also exceed the modicum of oral gratification by trying to be more nurturant than is consistent with their own needs and duties. This deviation from the ideal also will intensify the inevitable conflict, because the nurturance will be only superficially satisfying, carrying with it such resentment and having so many strings attached as to be counterfeit. Again the child will be frustrated and in pain and will have to institute defenses of such intensity and pervasiveness as to constitute fixation.

Now that we have described how conflict is intensified, leading to oral fixation, it would be theoretically satisfying to be able to compose an exhaustive list of defenses and traits that constitute the oral character. Unfortunately, however, psychoanalytic thinking is not that neat, although Abraham (1927a, 1927b) and Glover (1925, 1926, 1928) have made some beginnings. One can interpret their remarks as indicating that some traits recurring frequently in the oral character are *optimism-pessimism, gullibility-suspiciousnes, manipulativeness-passivity, admiration-envy,* and *cockiness-self-belittlement.* It is common for Freudians to think in terms of traits having two opposing extremes—so-called *bipolar traits*—either poles of which indicates fixation. It is tempting to think that one pole of the dimension expresses the fixation due to overindulgence (e.g., optimism) and the other the fixation of deprivation (e.g., pessimism). But it is difficult to determine how consistent such usage is with Freudian intent, as some Freudians suggest that people vacillate from one pole of a dimension to the other (e.g., now optimistic, now pessimistic). In any event, the bipolar traits refer fairly directly to attitudes, initiated in the course of interacting with parents, concerning whether the world is a satisfying or depriving place and whether one is capable of helping oneself to achieve satisfaction. Optimism, pessimism, gullibility, suspiciousness, and admiration are unrealistic estimates of the likelihood of being nurtured by other people. In manipulativeness and passivity, we see unconstructive tendencies to wrest satisfaction from the world or to lie back and wait until it falls into one's mouth. Cockiness indicates an unrealistically affluent sense of one's own resources, whereas envy and self-belittlement suggest quite the opposite. The unrealistic quality of all these extremes indicates their defensive nature.

Having described some traits of the oral character and having indicated their unrealistic nature, it would be theoretically satisfying to be able to list the defenses typical of the oral stage that find expression in these traits. But, as before, I must say that psychoanalytic thinking is not that neat, though a few beginnings have been made. The defenses most often mentioned as part of the oral character are projection, denial, and introjection. *Projection* is the process of being unaware of wishes, feelings, and impulses in oneself that might provoke punishment and guilt and simultaneously misperceiving other people as having these same wishes, feelings, and impulses. *Denial* is the simpler process of being unaware of the presence of things, people, or events in the external world that could arouse anxiety by either provoking selfish instincts or signaling impending punishment. *Introjection* is the process of incorporating another person—virtually becoming that person—in order to avoid either that person's threatening nature or the potential danger in one's own instincts. All three defenses are rather unsophisticated and quite debilitating in that they grossly distort reality. Denial is the main determinant of optimism and pessimism, which involve attention to only some aspects of the world. Gullibility can also be attributed to the action of denial. Although denial may have some function in suspicion, it is more clearly an expression of projection in that one attributes to others all those nasty manipulative and stingy tendencies that one fails to see in oneself. Manipulativeness and overgenerosity most likely express introjection, or the incorporation of overindulgent parents. The other traits can be explained as expressions of almost any of the three defenses.

Happily we can be even more theoretically precise concerning the anal stage and character than was true above. The *anal stage* is marked by the shift in anatomical location of the sexual instinct from the mouth to the anal orifice. This shift is brought about, according to Freud, by the joint impact of nervous system development to the point where voluntary control of the anal sphincters is possible and of intensified parental attempts to encourage excretory continence in the child. The child, for the first time, experiences the pleasurable and painful stimulation associated with eliminating and retaining feces and begins to experiment with manipulating this stimulation through consciously eliminating and retaining.

To fully apprehend the *anal character type,* you should recognize that the anal form of the sexual instinct includes actions and fantasies involved in *giving* and *withholding,* which are generalizations of the anal activities during the second year of life. *Giving (anal expulsiveness)* is the generalization of the voluntarily controlled voiding of the bowels. *Withholding (anal retentiveness)* is the generalization of the voluntary decision not to void the bowels. Both activities are inherently pleasurable but also bring children into inevitable conflict with their parents, who require that the giving and withholding be done according to schedule and propriety. Again the best that can happen is that the parents will permit a modicum of anal gratification while still upholding the socially important rules of cleanliness and hygiene. If the parents are too punitive and disgusted at the child's messing or, conversely, too indulgent for the child's own social and hygienic good and for their own proprieties, the conflict inevitably will intensify. Like oral overindulgence, anal overindulgence is really counterfeit. With the intensification of conflict comes the extreme and pervasive defenses that constitute fixation. This arresting of growth means that the adult personality will be anal in nature.

The traits and defenses of the anal character have been fairly precisely specified by both Freud (1925a, 1925c, 1925d, 1925e) and others (e.g., Abraham, 1927c; Fenichel, 1945, pp. 278–284; Glover, 1926). Among the traits are *stinginess-overgenerosity, constrictedness-expansiveness, stubbornness-acquiescence, orderliness-messiness, rigid punctuality-tardiness, meticulousness-dirtiness,* and *precision-vagueness.* These traits express in thought process, interaction, and the general conduct of life various concrete forms of the impulses to give and withhold and the conflicts surrounding them that are characteristic of the anal stage of psychosexual development. As in the oral character, these anal traits show an unrealistic orientation at both poles. Further, this unrealistic orientation is a sign of the defensive nature of the traits.

The defenses considered characteristic of the anal stage and character type are intellectualization, reaction formation, isolation, and undoing. In *intellectualization,* the person loses consciousness of the real, instinctual significance of wishes and actions and substitutes a false reason that is more socially acceptable but really amounts to mere rationalizations. *Reaction formation* is the process of losing awareness of one's true wishes and impulses and substituting awareness of the directly opposite ones. In *isolation,* the connecting link normally present between the cognitive and affective components of wishes and impulses is severed so that while a semblance of the true nature of the wishes and impulses remains in consciousness, they no longer seem the source of unpleasant emotions such as anxiety. *Undoing* is a defense whereby certain thoughts and actions cancel out or atone for anxiety-provoking thoughts and actions.

While it is impossible to explicate precisely and exhaustively just how these defenses give rise to the traits of the anal character, some discussion along these lines is possible. Reaction formation leads to the renunciation of such socially unacceptable qualities as messiness, tardiness, and stinginess and the assertion of oneself as quite the opposite: as meticulously clean, painstakingly punctual, and incredibly generous. This defense leads to the saintly qualities displayed by the anal character. Through the intellectualization defense, these saintly qualities, plus such characteristics as precision and stubbornness, are strengthened in their status as part of the self. The reliance on isolation, as well as the other defenses, permits glaring examples of the opposite of the saintly qualities—for example, messiness and dirtiness—to be clearly shown in the person's behavior without discomfort or anxiety. Finally, the action of undoing is seen not only in such direct characteristics as orderliness, implying symmetry and organization, but indirectly in the sometimes rapid shift from one pole to the other of the various traits mentioned above. One can avoid intense discomfort at an act of messiness if one can quickly atone for it with an extraordinary act of orderliness.

For vividness, I will close discussion of the anal character type with a striking description from the psychoanalytic literature (Rado, 1959):

> A rough sketch . . . would depict him as highly opinionated and proud of his superior intelligence, avowed rationality, keen sense of reality, and "unswerving integrity." He may indeed be an honest man, but he may also turn out to be a sanctimonious hypocrite. He is the ultimate perfectionist. While very sensitive to his own hurt, he may, at the same time, be destructively critical, spiteful, vindictive and given to bitter irony and to bearing grudges in trivial matters. Or, on the contrary, he may be overcautious, bent on avoiding any possibility of conflict. His "common sense" militates against what he views as fancies of the imagination; he is a "man of facts," not of fancies. He smiles condescendingly at people who are fascinated by mysticism, including "the unconscious" and dreams, but let him undergo some psychoanalytic treatment of the classical type, and he will switch to attributing oracular significance to slips of the tongue

or pen. As a "man of reason" he cannot admit even to himself that he is super-stitious. His interest in fine arts is slight or pretended; his true admiration is reserved for mathematics, the exact sciences, technology, and the new world of electronic computing machines. In contrast to the expressional, so-called hys-terical type, he rarely has artistic gifts and conspicuously lacks genuine charm and grace. His amatory interests are laden with ulterior motivations and pre-tense. (p. 326)

This lucid, if somewhat impressionistic, description makes it perfectly clear what a person with the kind of traits and defenses mentioned earlier would be likely to encounter. The extremes of behavior depicted and the pejorative language employed clearly indicate the presumed unconstructive, immature nature of the anal character.

Now let us consider the *phallic stage,* which is the last of the so-called pregenital, or immature, stages of psychosexual development. This stage pre-sumably is brought about by the shift in anatomical location of the sexual instinct from the anus to the genitalia, though how this can be explained in terms of nervous system development when the two regions are so close to each other remains one of the many obscurities in psychoanalytic thinking. Recognizing, then, that the anatomical basis for distinguishing an anal from a phallic stage is virtually absent, let us nonetheless consider a more general psychosocial basis for the distinction.

By the time children have reached the third year of life, they begin to explore their bodies more systematically and are also more alert to the bodies of others. That the genitalia become a major source of pleasure and pain for the first time is an assumption based on the observed increase in self-manipu-lation, or masturbation, in the manipulation and exploration of the genitalia of other boys and girls, and in the initiation of fantasies that have a frankly heterosexual quality. Children talk of marrying the opposite-sexed parent and displacing the same-sexed parent. They talk of being a father or a mother. The phallic stage is the time of the well-known *Oedipal conflict,* a concept of over-whelming importance in Freudian theory.

The key to understanding the *phallic character type* is recognition that this final pregenital form of the sexual instinct involves thoughts and actions con-cerning *the body as a frankly sexual thing* and *interaction between people as sexual* in nature. If the child's unabashed craving for genital stimulation and for genitalized contact with parents and others is severely frustrated out of the parents' own embarrassment, fears, and secret fantasies, the child will experi-ence intense conflict. Children will also experience intense conflict if their cravings seem to be overindulged, for the encouragement to replace the same-sexed parent in the opposite-sexed parent's affections inevitably runs afoul of the societal taboo against incest. Fixation is the result of both deprivation and overindulgence of craving for genital stimulation and genitalized relationships.

As in the case of the oral and anal stages, some conflict is inevitable in the phallic stage, even if the parents give a modicum of satisfaction to the child.

The inevitability of conflict is seen in the fact that although children must obtain enough gratification of genital cravings to develop a sense of themselves as worthwhile sexual beings, they must also give up selfish interest in the opposite-sexed parent as the object of their sexuality. As they give up interest in the opposite-sexed parent, they begin to long to be adults (Freudians talk of this as a specialized part of the superego called the *ego-ideal*). But when the inevitable conflict is intensified by over- or underindulgence, children will experience anxiety in the form of concern not only that they will lose the affections of the opposite-sexed parent but that the same-sexed parent will retaliate for the competition by damaging the child's genitalia. Both the latter fear, so-called *castration anxiety,* and the former fear, so-called *separation anxiety,* play an extraordinarily important role in Freudian thinking. Freud meant them very literally, although it has been common among later psychoanalysts to generalize their meaning.

The traits and defensive patterns of the phallic character have been described in detail by Reich (1931, 1933) and others (e.g., Abraham, 1927d). Among the traits are *vanity–self-hatred, pride-humility, blind courage–timidity, brashness-bashfulness, gregariousness-isolation, stylishness-plainness, flirtatiousness–avoidance of heterosexuality, chastity-promiscuity,* and *gaiety-sadness. These traits are present in some degree in people with the phallic character and represent either the genital craving directly or its curtailment due to fear of separation or castration. Some of the trait poles, such as blind courage and promiscuity, represent acting on the cravings in the face of the above-mentioned fears. In general, the major defense underlying the phallic traits is repression,* or unawareness of one's own instinctual wishes and actions in order to avoid anxiety. While the superficiality involved in the poles of some phallic traits may well be understandable as the result of massive repression, it is quite difficult to imagine how the complex traits mentioned above could all result from that one defense mechanism. But you should recognize that once persons have progressed to the phallic stage of development, they also have available to them the defenses of the earlier stages through which they have already gone. Similarly, people in the anal stage have the defenses more typical of the oral stage available to them. There is no difficulty at all in understanding how the traits of the phallic character come about if they can be considered expressive of not only repression but also other defenses. Still, the content of the phallic or, for that matter, the anal and oral traits is defined by the type of psychosexual conflict dominant during that stage of development.

Thus, a concrete description of persons with a phallic character would go something like this. They are preoccupied with their own beauty and extraordinariness, needing constant recognition of such by others to feel comfortable. If they get this support and appreciation, they may well be delightful, interesting, provocative, spontaneous, and dramatic. If they are not greatly appreciated and sought after, they may slip into black thoughts of worthlessness, ugliness, and incompetence, appearing to be a pale shadow of their former selves. In general, they seek the company of people of the opposite sex, enjoy enticing them and receiving their appreciation, but they shy away from vigorous, deep, committed sexual relationships. In the male, the phallic character is either effeminate or masculine in an obvious and inflexible way. The phallic character in a female renders her an exaggeration of femininity—a "southern belle," if you will. She may be chaste or promiscuous, but, if the latter, will nonetheless give the impression of naïveté, childishness, and inner purity.

Oral, anal, and phallic characters are not to be considered psychopathological (mentally ill), although they do represent immaturity and carry the seeds of psychopathology. But in order for psychopathology to ensue, the person must encounter severe environmental stress that breaks down the pregenital character structure. It is true that the nature of the pregenital character is considered a determinant of the nature of the psychopathological state. The breakdown of the oral character frequently leads to schizophrenia, and the breakdown of the anal character leads to obsessive-compulsive neurosis. Breakdown of the phallic character often leads to hysteria in women and homosexuality or perversion in men. These considerations do not contradict the fact that character types are not psychopathological states, even though the pregenital types represent developmental immaturities.

All this brings us to the *genital stage* and *genital character,* which represent the pinnacle of development and maturity, according to Freudians. Although the genital stage is considered a true psychosexual stage, it is not easily distinguished from the others on the basis of anatomical location of the sexual instinct, the relevant location being the same as for the phallic stage. But Freudians do point to the complete physical maturation of the sexual system such that orgasm, ejaculation, and pregnancy become possible. Indeed, orgasm is considered to be the hallmark of satisfaction. But orgasm is combined with the erotic pleasures of the pregenital stages, yielding full adult expression of the sexual instinct. Although reaching the genital stage with no existing fixations at lower stages of development is the ideal condition, according to Freudians, this does not mean that genital functioning is free of conflict and nondefensive in nature. The person must still subscribe to societal sanctions and taboos in expressing the sexual instinct, and hence there is implied conflict. But the conflict is minimal, and it can be resolved by that at once more mature and least rigidifying of defensive processes, sublimation. *Sublimation* involves changing the object of the sexual instinct to be more socially acceptable than the original or most obvious one but in no other way disrupting or blocking its expression. Of all the defenses, sublimation involves the least damming up of the libido, or energy, that is straining for expression. So instead of pursuing mother, as the boy is wont to do in the phallic stage, he pursues other females outside of the family and in so doing accepts society's set of responsibilities and rules concerning heterosexual relationships. That all love is for Freud (1938) essentially "on the rebound" (the child having to give up its original attraction to the opposite-sexed parent) demonstrates once again the compromise nature of even ideal personality.

Although sublimation is clearly the defense associated with the genital character, it is difficult to specify any list of relevant traits. This is because trait names of the genital character might sound too much like others already mentioned as pregenital to effectively convey what Freudians mean, which is that genital persons are fully potent and capable in whatever they do. They are fully socialized and adjusted, yet do not suffer greatly from this. They are courageous without the driven recklessness of the phallic character. They are satisfied with self without the overweening pride and vanity of the phallic character. They love heterosexually without the alarming neediness and dependence of the oral character. They work diligently and effectively without the compulsivity and competitiveness of the anal character. They are altruistic and generous without the cloying saintliness of the anal character. In short, they maximize instinctual gratification while minimizing punishment and guilt.

As I have said many times before, one cannot help but be struck by the extraordinary emphasis Freud gives to sexuality. Nowhere is this more apparent than in the treatment of the character types, or peripheral characteristics of personality. It becomes perfectly clear that even the obvious differences among people are determined by various facets of the sexual instinct and attendant conflicts. Freudian thinking often has been criticized for its single-minded sexual emphasis. Although the criticism seem cogent, we must recognize that they have been made by modern persons, in societies grossly different from that in which Freud worked at the turn of the twentieth century. In his day, it was generally not conceded that sexuality plays an important, natural part in living. The sexual act was for reproduction, not pleasure, and partial expressions of sexuality and sexual interest before physiological adulthood were not regarded as natural at all. Officially it was an extraordinarily pristine atmosphere, one in which Freudian thinking must have been a much needed if explosive correction. In order to give you the full impact of this arid thinking lest you doubt the picture I have painted, I will quote from an authoritative book entitled *Maiden, Wife, and Mother: How to Attain Health, Beauty, Happiness.* This handbook is by Mary R. Melendy (1901), who was both an M.D. and a Ph.D. with seven or eight distinguished titles to her credit. In a chapter on being a good mother to boys, Melendy writes:

> Teach him that these [sexual] organs are given as a sacred trust, that in maturer years he may be the means of giving life to those who shall live forever.
>
> Impress upon him that if these organs are abused, or if they are put to any use besides that for which God made them—and He did not intend they should be used at all until man is fully grown—they will bring disease and ruin upon those who abuse and disobey those laws which God has made to govern them.
>
> If he has ever learned to handle his sexual organs, or to touch them in any way except to keep them clean, teach him not to do it again. If he does, he will not grow up happy, healthy, and strong.
>
> Teach him that when he handles or excites the sexual organs, all parts of the body suffer, because they are connected by nerves that run throughout the

system. This is why it is called "self-abuse." The whole body is abused when this part of the body is handled or excited in any manner whatever.

Teach them to shun all children who indulge in this loathsome habit, or all children who talk about these things. The sin is terrible, and is, in fact, worse than lying or stealing! For although these are wicked and will ruin their soul, yet this habit of self-abuse will ruin both soul and body.

If the sexual organs are handled it brings too much blood to these parts, and this produces a diseased condition; it also causes disease in other organs of the body, because they are left with a less amount of blood than they ought to have. The sexual organs, too, are very closely connected with the spine and the brain by means of the nerves, and if they are handled, or if you keep thinking about them, these nerves get excited and become exhausted, and this makes the back ache, the brain heavy and the whole body weak.

It lays the foundation for consumption, paralysis and heart disease. It weakens the memory, makes a boy careless, negligent and listless.

It even makes many lose their minds; others, when grown, commit suicide.

How often mothers see their little boys handling themselves, and let it pass, because they think the boys will outgrow the habit, and do not realize the strong hold it has upon them! I say to you, who love your boys—"Watch!"

Don't think it does no harm to your boy because he does not suffer now, for the effects of this vice come on so slowly that the victim is often very near death before you realize that he has done himself harm.

The boy with no knowledge of the consequences, and with no one to warn him, finds momentary pleasure in its practice, and so contracts a habit which grows on him, undermining his health, poisoning his mind, arresting his development, and laying the foundation for future misery.

Do not read this book and forget it, for it contains earnest and living truths. Do not let false modesty stand in your way, but from this time on keep this thought in mind—"the saving of your boy." Follow its teachings and you will bless God as long as you live. Read it to your neighbors, who, like yourself, have growing boys, and urge them, for the sake of humanity, to heed its advice.

Right here I want to relate a fact that came under my observation. In our immediate neighborhood lived an intelligent, good and sensible couple. They had a boy about five years of age who was growing fretful, pale and puny. After trying all other remedies to restore him to vigor of body and mind, they journeyed from place to place hoping to leave the offending cause behind.

I had often suggested to the mother that "self-abuse" might be the cause, but no, she would not have it so, and said, "You must be mistaken, as he has inherited no such tendencies nor has he been taught it by playmates—we have guarded him carefully."

Finally, however, she took up a medical book and made a study of it and, after much thought, said, "I cannot believe it, yet it describes Charlie's case exactly. I will watch."

To her surprise, she found notwithstanding all her convictions to the contrary, that Charles was a victim to this loathsome habit.

On going to his bed, after he had gone to sleep, she found his hands still upon the organ, just as they were when he fell asleep. She watched this carefully for a few days, then took him in her confidence and told him of the dreadful evil effects. Finding the habit so firmly fixed, she feared that telling him, at his age, what effect it would have upon his future would not eradicate the evil as soon as she hoped so, after studying the case for a time, she hit upon the following remedy. Although unscientific, literally speaking, it had the desired effect. Feeling that something must be done to stop, and stop at once, the awful habit, she said, "Did you know, Charles, that if you keep up this habit of 'self-abuse' that a brown spot will come on your abdomen, light brown at first, and grow darker each week until it eats a sore right into your system, and if it keeps on, will eventually kill you?"

After Charlie had gone to sleep, and finding his hands again on the sexual organs, to prove to him the truth of her argument, she took a bottle of "Iodine" and, with the cork, put on the abdomen a quantity sufficient to give it a light brown color, and about the size of a pea. Next night, in bathing him, she discovered the spot, and said, "Look! Already it has come!" The boy cried out in very fear, and promised not to repeat it again.

The next night the mother put on a second application which made the spot darker and a trifle sore. Charlie watched the spot as he would a reptile that was lurking about to do its deadly work—and the mother was never again obliged to use the "Iodine."

This harrowing excerpt is not untypical of the state of educated and sophisticated thought at the turn of the century. If Freud is right, how exacerbated would have been Charlie's Oedipal conflict! And, of course, one can find accounts in the same book concerning the evils of "self-abuse" in girls: a moralistic, punitive attitude concerning bowel training and a depriving, rigidly regulated approach to early feeding. It was on this scene that Freud arrived to preach the naturalness of pregenital sexual cravings and actions and the evils of excessive punitiveness and deprivation on the part of parents. Perhaps it is no wonder that his theory is so preoccupied with sexuality when the period in which he lived had so denied eroticism. But our time and Freud's time differ. We have learned the lessons Freud taught. We accept and act constructively toward pregenital and genital sexuality to a degree that would have gladdened his heart. Indeed, we have changed so much that Freud's emphasis on sexuality seems to almost sidetrack us from the most important concerns of contemporary life.

Freud's emphasis on sexuality has seemed so extreme that many personologists have contended that he used sex as nothing more than a metaphor for pleasure seeking. This interpretation clearly does no justice to Freud's intent, for he is very explicit about his emphasis on sexuality per se. After all, he chose to distinguish the sexual instinct from other pleasure-oriented instincts, and he named all of the developmental stages psychosexual, not psychopleasurable. If further evidence of his intent were needed, one could point to his having disbarred certain psychoanalysts from his inner circle because they watered down the literal sexual message of his theory, thereby rendering it more palatable to nonbelievers (Jones, 1955). Substituting pleasure seeking for literal sexuality may make Freud's formulations seem more modern, but it does not illuminate his real intent.

Murray's Position

Murray's major peripheral characteristic is the *need*. Needs are motivational in nature; that is, they are tendencies to move in the direction of goals. Unlike the Freudian instincts, which are also motivational in nature, needs are largely learned, and they involve goals and actions more concrete and close to everyday life than do instincts. Given this concrete quality of goal definition, it should not surprise you to know that Murray postulates a large number of needs. Murray has in mind such needs as those for affiliation, achievement, power, succorance, and play. Even when Murray mentions the need for sex, it is clear that he is referring to the narrow meaning that most people would endorse, namely, the attempt to achieve the goal of intercourse. Indeed, Murray's concept of needs is functionally closer to the Freudian concept of trait than to that of instinct. Different needs may be represented in different people; hence, need analysis is useful in pinpointing individuality.

Since needs stand at the same level of personality analysis as do the Freudian traits, we might expect Murray to provide a scheme whereby needs are organized into psychologically meaningful patterns, such as the Freudian character types. Sure enough, Murray does talk of the oral, anal, phallic, and genital types we have already discussed and even adds to these the claustral and urethral types (Murray, 1938). The *claustral type,* or, as Murray prefers to call it, *claustral complex,* stems from fixation during intrauterine life and refers to a set of characteristics amounting to amorphousness and extreme passivity. The *urethral type,* or *urethral complex,* also talked about by some theorists more closely associated with Freud, involves fixation during the time when urinating actively and passively is a great source of pleasure (between oral and anal stages) and refers to competitiveness, ambition, self-worship, and feelings of omnipotence. But nowhere in Murray's writings is it clear that he intends to use the six complexes or types as categories for subsuming or classifying the various needs he has delineated.

As you will recall, Murray, being basically a psychoanalytic thinker, also uses the concepts of id, ego, and superego. These three aspects of personality exist in all persons and, hence, should be considered part of the core of personality. But, as you will also recall, Murray has changed the meaning of all three concepts from that favored by Freud. Even more than in Freud, the contents of superego and ego may differ from person to person and thus are for Murray, peripheral aspects of personality. In contrast to Freud, Murray finds the id to also vary in content from person to person. For Murray, the id is not one unchanging set of instincts but the repository of any and all motivations, presumably even the needs mentioned above. Hence, in Murray the id contents are also peripheral aspects of personality. But if the contents of id, ego, and superego are peripheral, what are the characteristics of the core? Core characteristics become, for Murray, very abstract and contentless. They are the incessant motivatedness of persons and their equally incessant attempts to reach their goals within the restrictions of the environment and of their own values and principles.

These conclusions suggest that Murray's needs might be considered the content characteristics of the id, whereas, you will recall, Freudian traits are considered content characteristics of the ego. But needs are not innate, according to Murray, and hence do not fit neatly into the meaning of the id, which meaning he at least partially endorses. Needs are too motivational in character to be considered the content of the superego. This leaves the ego, but the fit is no better here, as he (Murray & Kluckhohn, 1956, p. 26) assumes the ego to be constituted of an elaborate set of functions. These functions are really *abilities* in the perceptual, apperceptual, intellectual, and affective realms of experience. To complicate matters even further, although his emphasis would seem to imply that the ego is to be considered a set of abilities rather than the specific, learned, habitual styles of coping that constitute needs, Murray does, at one point in his writing (Murray & Kluckhohn, 1956, p. 31), suggest in true psychoanalytic fashion that the general system of learned needs may well be part of the ego.

Elsewhere I have discussed these complications and ambiguities at greater length than is possible here (Maddi, 1963). For present purposes, it is enough to recognize that the question of the nature of the relationship between core and peripheral characteristics of personality is an important consideration in understanding a theory fully and that Murray has not yet achieved a clear statement of his view of this relationship. A reasonable lead, which does not seem inconsistent with his general intent, would be to consider learned needs as being personality units that are formed out of the interaction between the core tendency of maximizing instinctual gratification while minimizing punishment and guilt and the specific environmental contexts encountered in living. The learned needs would then exist as a more changeable, less central, though more immediately expressed layer of personality. In such a scheme id, ego, and superego would differ from needs and indeed would play, along with environmental contexts, a causal role in the development of needs. Adopting such a scheme would also be useful to more traditional psychoanalytic thinking, for the subsuming of traits into the ego is a dubious theoretical step given the otherwise consistent emphasis on the ego as a set of abilities or functions. The emphasis on ego as functions actually is as strong in psychoanalytic thinking as it is in Murray, regardless of the fact that Murray does not see all of these functions as defensive. If Freudians adopted this suggestion, character types would be considered a peripheral layer of personality that is more immediately expressed and more changeable than is the core level.

Actually, Murray's major contribution to personology has been his taxonomy of needs and his extensive and continuing attempts to collect systematic empirical evidence bearing on it. He is quite rare in his emphasis on the careful delineation and study of peripheral characteristics. It is worth our while, therefore, to dwell longer on the concept of need and its measurement. According to Murray (1938), the *need* is

> a construct (a convenient fiction or hypothetical concept) which stands for a force . . . in the brain region, a force which organizes perception, apperception, intellection, conation and action in such a way as to transform in a certain direction an existing, unsatisfying situation. A need is sometimes provoked directly by internal processes of a certain kind . . . but, more frequently (when in a state of readiness) by the occurrence of one of a few commonly effective press. (pp. 123–124)

Needs affect functioning by producing perceptions, interpretations, feelings, and actions that are equivalent in meaning or purpose. In order to diagnose a particular need as present in a person, one must observe equivalences of meaning in his or her (1) initiating or reacting inner state, (2) perception of the external situation, (3) imagined goal or aim, (4) directionality of concomitant movements and words, and (5) produced effect, if any (Murray, 1954, pp. 456–463). Take as an example the need for affiliation. The inner state may be those specific cognitive and affective conditions best described as *loneliness*. This loneliness may be initiating in that it exists regardless of whether or not the actual environmental circumstances are so affiliatively depriving. Or it may be reacting in the sense that it must be aroused by affiliatively depriving circumstances. Regardless of whether or not the circumstances actually are depriving, the person must perceive them as such. The person must have as an imaginary goal a state of close and warm interaction with people. In addition, his or her plans, activities, and statements about what to do ought to show a consistent direction leading to closer contact with people. Finally, any effects that follow from the actions must be those consistent with the goals and aims. When all these things are present, one can be sure that the person has a need for affiliation. In general, needs are not perceived as steady states: they are aroused by real or imagined deprivation. When aroused, they exist as tension states leading to instrumental behavior, which, if successful, brings about the goal state. Experience of the goal state brings satiation and a reduction in tension. A necessary concomitant of choosing the need construct as the basic peripheral characteristic is an emphasis on the waxing and waning of directional behaviors.

Over the years, Murray has experimented with a number of apparently overlapping classifications of types and qualities of needs. But unlike the Freudian character types, Murray's classificatory schemes do not tie groups of needs together into consistent and recognizable kinds of people. Instead, Murray's aim is to provide schemes for understanding the various kinds of needs that are possible. One of his classifications takes into account the degree to which the person's aim in activity is intrinsic or extrinsic to the form of that activity. This leads to the distinction between activity needs and effect needs.

Activity needs, or tendencies to "engage in a certain kind of activity for its own sake" (Murray, 1954, p. 445), are subdivided into *process needs,* involving action, for the sheer pleasure to be derived from the exercise of available capabilities, and *mode needs,* which are satisfied by the excellence of activity rather than its mere occurrence (Murray, 1954, p. 446). It is significant that Murray is one of the few personologists to make a concrete attempt to conceptualize activity that occurs for its own sake. In contrast, *effect needs* are marked by attempts to bring about a particular desired effect or goal that is extrinsic to the activity undertaken, which serves a purely instrumental purpose (Murray & Kluckhohn, 1956, p. 15).

Another classificatory attempt seems to emphasize the origin of the need and, hence, the particular direction of activity that it imposes. In this attempt, viscerogenic, mental, and sociorelational needs are distinguished (Murray, 1954, pp. 445–452; Murray & Kluckhohn, 1956, pp. 13–21). The well-known *viscerogenic needs* (e.g., need for food) stem from tissue requirements and have very specific, easily recognizable goals. The *mental needs* are usually overlooked; they stem from the fact that "the human mind is inherently a transforming, creating, and representing organ; its function is to make symbols for things, to combine and recombine these symbols incessantly, and communicate the most interesting of these combinations in a variety of languages, discursive (referential, scientific) and expressive (emotive, artistic)" (Murray & Kluckhohn, 1956, p. 16). As the viscera have certain requirements, so does the mind, and both sets of requirements stem from human nature. Mental needs do not have very specific goal states. *Sociorelational needs* arise from the inherently social nature of humans (Murray, 1959, pp. 45–57) and include such specific dispositions as the *need for roleship*—the need "to become and to remain an accepted and respected, differentiated and integrated part of a congenial, functioning group, the collective purposes of which are congruent with the individual's ideas" (Murray, 1954, pp. 451–452). As described, the need for roleship seems to imply particular learning produced by the individual's experiences against the ever present background of his or her inherent sociorelational nature.

If you think that Murray's idea of the core of personality presented in Chapter 3 is simpler and more psychoanalytic in flavor than the view of human nature implied in his need classifications, you are right. It is as if Murray transcended the narrow, sexually oriented conflict model precisely when he turned to describing and organizing people's needs at the level of their everyday behavior. Murray has never actually come to terms with the implication of his having departed from the Freudian model. This has lead to the rather chaotic quality of Murray's writings when looked at from the viewpoint of formal personality theory. Assuming, in describing sociorelational needs, that human nature is inherently gregarious contradicts the Freudian conflict model. Yet nowhere does Murray discuss this complication. His is a mind in transition, resulting in theoretical writings that seem fragmentary though provocative and intriguing. We will see a similar problem in the so-called ego psychologists.

Another discussion of need classification (Murray, 1954, pp. 445–452) includes two additional types of needs that presumably cut across the mental, viscerogenic, and sociorelational and seem to emphasize approach and avoidance tendencies. These are *creative needs,* which aim at the construction of new and useful thoughts and objects, and *negative needs,* which aim at the avoidance or termination of unpleasant, noxious conditions. Finally, Murray's earliest and most famous taxonomy (Murray, 1938, pp. 152–226) distinguishes what are primarily effect needs of a mental, viscerogenic, and sociogenic variety on the basis of a much more fine-grained consideration of goals. These needs appear in Table 7–1. Associated with them are distinctions among

TABLE 7–1   List of Needs for Murray

Need	*Definition*
n Abasement	To submit passively to external force. To accept injury, blame, criticism, punishment. To surrender. To become resigned to fate. To admit inferiority, error, wrongdoing, or defeat. To confess and atone. To blame, belittle, or mutilate the self. To seek and enjoy pain, punishment, illness, and misfortune.
n Achievement	To accomplish something difficult. To master, manipulate, or organize physical objects, human beings, or ideas. To do this as rapidly and as independently as possible. To overcome obstacles and attain a high standard. To excel oneself. To rival and surpass others. To increase self-regard by the successful exercise of talent.
n Affiliation	To draw near and enjoyably cooperate or reciprocate with an allied other (another who resembles the subject or who likes the subject). To please and win affection of a cathected object. To adhere and remain loyal to a friend.
n Aggression	To overcome opposition forcefully. To fight. To revenge an injury. To attack, injure, or kill another. To oppose forcefully or punish another.
n Autonomy	To get free, shake off restraint, break out of confinement. To resist coercion and restriction. To avoid or quit activities prescribed by domineering authorities. To be independent and free to act according to impulse. To be unattached, irresponsible. To defy convention.
n Counteraction	To master or make up for a failure by restriving. To obliterate a humiliation by resumed action. To overcome weaknesses, to repress fear. To efface a dishonor by action. To search for obstacles and difficulties to overcome. To maintain self-respect and pride on a high level.
n Defendance	To defend the self against assault, criticism, and blame. To conceal or justify a misdeed, failure, or humiliation. To vindicate the ego.

TABLE 7–1   *(concluded)*

Need	*Definition*
n Deference	To admire and support a superior. To praise, honor, or eulogize. To yield eagerly to the influence of an allied other. To emulate an exemplar. To conform to custom.
n Dominance	To control one's human environment. To influence or direct the behavior of others by suggestion, seduction, persuasion, or command. To dissuade, restrain, or prohibit.
n Exhibition	To make an impression. To be seen and heard. To excite, amaze, fascinate, entertain, shock, intrigue, amuse, or entice others.
n Harm avoidance	To avoid pain, physical injury, illness, and death. To escape from a dangerous situation. To take precautionary measures.
n Infavoidance	To avoid humiliation. To quit embarrassing situations or to avoid conditions which may lead to belittlement: the scorn, derision, or indifference of others. To refrain from action because of the fear of failure.
n Nurturance	To give sympathy and gratify the needs of a helpless object; an infant or any object that is weak, disabled, tired, inexperienced, infirm, defeated, humiliated, lonely, dejected, sick, mentally confused. To assist an object in danger. To feed, help, support, console, protect, comfort, nurse, heal.
n Order	To put things in order. To achieve cleanliness, arrangement, organization, balance, neatness, tidiness, and precision.
n Play	To act for "fun" without further purpose. To like to laugh and make jokes. To seek enjoyable relaxation of stress. To participate in games, sports, dancing, drinking parties, cards.
n Rejection	To separate oneself from a negatively cathected object. To exclude, abandon, expel, or remain indifferent to an inferior object. To snub or jilt an object.
n Sentience	To seek and enjoy sensuous impressions.
n Sex	To form and further an erotic relationship. To have sexual intercourse.
n Succorance	To have one's needs gratified by the sympathetic aid of an allied object. To be nursed, supported, sustained, surrounded, protected, loved, advised, guided, indulged, forgiven, consoled. To remain close to a devoted protector. To always have a supporter.
n Understanding	To ask or answer general questions. To be interested in theory. To speculate, formulate, analyze, and generalize.

SOURCE: *Explorations in Personality*, edited by H. A. Murray. Copyright 1938 by Oxford University Press, Inc. Revised 1966 by H. A. Murray. Reprinted by permission.

certain qualities that they may possess. Needs can be proactive or reactive, diffuse or focal, latent or overt, conscious or unconscious (Murray, 1938, pp. 111–115; 1954, pp. 447–450).

I have gone into this degree of detail concerning these various schemes to point out that Murray's writings yield a bewildering array of overlapping classifications of needs. It is difficult to come by any one authoritative classification, and Murray has not addressed the relationships among the available schemes in sufficient detail to make his thinking clear. While his shifting distinctions and the resulting ambiguities probably represent the difficulty of conceptualizing human complexities, they also stem from the extreme heterogeneity of functioning subsumed by the need concept. As you must have noted before as we discussed the example of need for affiliation, each need can be manifested in many internal and external ways, and Murray wishes to consider a great number of needs. It is not surprising that they overlap. Also, reasoning from behavioral observations to a great number and variety of needs, as Murray has done, precipitates a large and heterogeneous mass of assumed organismic requirements. No wonder that finding a basis for clarifying needs that will keep them reasonably distinct in theory and in practice is difficult! Given the inherent heterogeneity of his need concept, Murray may be attempting a fineness of distinction too great for classificatory neatness and clarity.

Such overrefinement of a basically heterogeneous concept could make for considerable difficulty in using or applying need analysis. If so, this would be a great problem in verifying the theory, as peripheral concepts of personality are the ones that should relate most clearly, immediately, and obviously to the behavior that constitutes data. Murray (1938) was the guiding light in a massive attempt to find empirical evidence for the existence of his long list of needs. This research project was a pioneering effort, involving many personologists in the intensive observation and testing of fifty college students. Murray and his collaborators provided detailed operational descriptions for each need. But one is not reassured on reading these descriptions, for there seems too much overlap among the needs, and it is very difficult to make fine distinctions among them. This difficulty is bound to be compounded in the typical research situation, in which the investigator finds available only some rather than all of the possible manifestations of needs. It is understandable, then, that in this major attempt to employ Murray's list of needs, it was necessary to reach the diagnosis of particular needs by majority vote of a group of skilled investigators after considerable debate concerning their observations. This hardly bespeaks objectivity, and I would implicate the inherent heterogeneity of the need concept as the main culprit.

Perhaps because of this problem, Murray (1954, pp. 463–464) has moved in the direction of substituting the *value-vector* concept for the need. The *vector* principle refers to the nature of the directionality shown by behavior (e.g., rejection, acquisition, construction); the *value* principle refers to the ideals that are important to people (e.g., knowledge, beauty, authority). A value-vector matrix is compiled in diagnosing what each person believes is worthwhile and the particular ways in which he or she moves to make those beliefs an actuality. At this early stage in its use, the value-vector system seems to involve less heterogeneity and fewer organismic assumptions than does the need system. The values and vectors currently listed are simple and few enough to permit agreement among investigators on their identification.

Until the value-vector system is further developed, the need concept must be considered the major peripheral characteristic in Murray's theory. The need is by its nature something that waxes and wanes, that is strong during deprivation and weak under satiating conditions. Thus, the concept is best suited to the explanation of behavior that also increases and decreases rather than remaining steady. But much of the person's behavior is steady and repetitive. In attempting to account for such behavior, Murray has recourse to the concept of *need-integrate* (Murray, 1938, pp. 109–110), which refers to the stable habits and attitudes that develop out of the previous expression of needs. In its implied stability, the need-integrate is more analogous to the trait concept used by other theorists than to the need concept. Unfortunately, Murray neither considers the possible content of major need-integrates nor elaborates on the concept in other ways that would alert us to its intended use.

Murray also details the various environmental events, called *press*, that can, by occurring in childhood, influence the strength with which needs develop (Murray, 1938, pp. 291–292). A list of these press is shown in Table 7–2. Once a need has been learned, press may trigger the need, which exists as a predisposition for certain actions. But the pressure referred to in the press concept can be either objectively real or only subjectively perceived. The subjectively experienced pressure is called *beta* press and is to be distinguished from the objective pressure, or *alpha* press (Murray 1938, pp. 115–123).

These considerations have led Murray to posit an interactional unit, the *thema,* or combination of a need and a press, as basic for the personologist. But Murray is unclear as to whether the press component of the thema refers to individuals' own perceptions of the situational forces acting on them or to objective forces themselves. If it is the beta (subjective) press that is intended, this suggests a belief on Murray's part that the internal factors governing people's perception must be accepted if behavior is to be understood. But it may well be the alpha (objective) press that is intended, because, as the need and need-integrate concepts already include certain influences on perception, the beta press would seem to be superfluous as a component of the thema. If the alpha press is intended, Murray seems to be calling for analysis and clarification of the objective demand characteristics of situations that force the person's behavior.

However intriguing the concepts of value-vector, need-integrate, and press may be, they are so unelaborated as to lead me to conclude that we must simply accept the need concept as the one we can work with and await future theoretical developments. In closing, I should point out that Murray has also made some suggestions as to how needs may be related to one another. He includes discussion of the *unity-thema* (Murray, 1938, pp. 604–605), a need-press combination that is very pervasive because it is formed in early life. He also offers the concepts of *prepotency* (Murray, 1938, p. 452), which refers to

TABLE 7–2   Press Relevant in Childhood

1. p Family insupport	5. p Rejection, unconcern and scorn
a. Cultural discord	6. p Rival, competing contemporary
b. Family discord	7. p Birth of sibling
c. Capricious discipline	8. p Aggression
d. Parental separation	*a.* Maltreatment by elder male,
e. Absence of parent: father, mother	elder female
f. Parental illness: father, mother	*b.* Maltreatment by contemporaries
g. Death of parent: father, mother	*c.* Quarrelsome contemporaries
h. Inferior parent: father, mother	9. p Dominance, coercion, and
i. Dissimilar parent: father, mother	prohibition
j. Poverty	*a.* Discipline
k. Unsettled home	*b.* Religious training
2. p Danger or misfortune	10. p Nurturance, indulgence
a. Physical insupport, height	11. p Succorance, demands for
b. Water	tenderness
c. Aloneness, darkness	12. p Deference, praise, recognition
d. Inclement weather, lightning	13. p Affiliation, friendships
e. Fire	14. p Sex
f. Accident	*a.* Exposure
g. Animal	*b.* Seduction; homosexual,
3. p Lack or loss	heterosexual
a. Of nourishment	*c.* Parental intercourse
b. Of possessions	15. p Deception or betrayal
c. Of companions	16. p Inferiority
d. Of variety	*a.* Physical
4. p Retention, withholding objects	*b.* Social
	c. Intellectual

SOURCE: *Explorations in Personality*, edited by H. A. Murray. Copyright 1938 by Oxford University Press, Inc. Revised 1966 by H. A. Murray. Reprinted by permission.

the degree to which a need takes precedence over others when it is aroused, and *subsidiation* (Murray, 1938, pp. 86–88), which indicates that less potent needs can actually become instrumental to the satisfaction of more potent ones. To indicate that any particular behavior may express a number of needs at the same time, Murray (1938, p. 86) offers the notion of *fusion*. Murray is clearly toying with hierarchical organization of needs, but he really has done little more in this regard than point the way toward future theoretical development.

Erikson's Position

The ego psychologist's position on the periphery of personality is, of course, similar to Freud's. Any deviation from Freud is in the direction of seeing life as a series of developmental stages that continue into adulthood.

The position of ego psychology is most clearly seen in the theorizing of Eric H. Erikson.

Erikson delineates eight stages of human development, each with a particular pattern of traits, or peripheral characteristics, associated with fixation at that stage. The first four stages are closely related to the Freudian oral, anal, phallic, and latency periods, though Erikson clearly is more interested in their psychosocial significance than in their biological nature. This emphasis permits him to include the latency period as significant for adult functioning even though this period does not have a strong biological justification. And then, instead of one genital period, extending from puberty to death, Erikson delineates four more developmental stages that bear no relationship whatever to biological considerations of sexual instinct and libido. In Erikson, the Freudian emphasis on biological sexuality has been almost completely lost except for those psychosexual conflicts surrounding feeling, eliminating, and such. As to be expected from the discussion in Chapter 3 on ego psychology as a variant of the conflict model, Erikson's position is a peculiar, though intriguing, conglomerate of Freud and something more like a fulfillment position.

According to Erickson, the first ("oral") developmental stage involves the bases for *general trust* or *basic mistrust*. In this stage, children are more helpless than they will ever be again and other people must nurture, protect, and reassure them. If these needs are filled, children will look on the world and their participation in it with a generally trustful attitude; if severely deprived, they will be distrustful. In later years, their trusting or distrusting will make an extraordinary difference in the nature of their lives. By trust and basic distrust, Erikson implies a group of traits similar to a character type, though not detailed specifically. In this lack of detailing—characteristic of all the trait groups deriving from his eight stages—Erikson unfortunately falls short in his theorizing about the periphery of personality. One cannot easily proceed from Erikson's statements to the concrete behavior of people, not knowing clearly what to look for to determine trust or distrust in a person's character. In any event, he does provide interesting descriptions of the overall emphasis of his position, such as in the following (Erikson, 1950):

> The firm establishment of enduring patterns for the solution of the nuclear conflict of basic trust versus basic mistrust in mere existence is the first task of the ego, and thus first of all a task for maternal care. But let it be said here that the amount of trust derived from earliest infantile experience does not seem to depend on absolute quantities of food or demonstrations of love, but rather on the quality of the maternal relationship. Mothers, I think, create a sense of trust in their children by that kind of administration which in its quality combines sensitive care of the baby's individual needs and a firm sense of personal trustworthiness within the trusted framework of their culture's life style. This forms the basis in the child for a sense of being "all right," of being oneself, and of becoming what other people trust one will become. . . . Parents must not only have certain ways of guiding by prohibition and permission; they must also be able to represent to the child a deep, an almost somatic conviction that there is a meaning to what they are doing. (pp. 221–222)

In this vivid description of the ways in which parents help the child to progress through the first stage successfully to develop trust or fail the child by precipitating a fixation and subsequent distrust, Erikson makes it clear how far he has shifted from Freud's original emphasis in the direction of psychosocial rather than biological forces. The above quote emphasizes a loving mother-child relationship that transcends the physical in its deep, human meaningfulness.

The first stage of development lasts, like Freud's oral period, for roughly the first year of life. Then we come to the second stage, which coincides with Freud's anal stage of the second year of life. Although Erikson (1950, p. 222) clearly intends this coincidence, saying "Anal muscular maturation sets the stage for experimentation with two simultaneous sets of social modalities; holding on and letting go," his emphasis is again on the social rather than biological implications of the stage. According to Erikson, successful passage through this second stage leads to later traits showing *autonomy,* whereas fixation leads to later expressions of *shame and doubt.* In explaining how this comes about, Erikson starts by emphasizing that his is still basically a conflict position:

> As is the case with all of these modalities, their basic conflicts can lead in the end to either hostile or benign expectations and attitudes. Thus to hold on can become a destructive and cruel retaining or restraining, and it can become a pattern of care: to have and to hold. To let go, too, can turn into an inimical letting loose of destructive forces, or it can become a relaxed "to let pass" and "to let be." (p. 222)

For Erikson, the crucial development of this second stage is the psychosocial ability to make a choice for oneself. The child can choose to hold on or let go, the bowel movement being a particularly vivid example of this, but no longer the basic definitive characteristic of the stage. Continuing, Erikson (1950) says,

> If denied the gradual and well-guided experience of the autonomy of free choice . . . the child will turn against himself all his urge to discriminate and to manipulate. He will overmanipulate himself, he will develop a precocious conscience. Instead of taking possession of things in order to test them by purposeful repetition, he will become obsessed by his own repetitiveness. By such obsessiveness, of course, he then learns to repossess the environment and to gain power by stubborn and minute control, where he could not find large-scale mutual regulation. (p. 222)

Here we see the similarity in character traits attributed by Erikson and Freud to the second stage of development.

Erikson then clarifies why he thinks this second stage leaves the person with either autonomy or shame and doubt. If the social environment encourages children to stand on their own feet, yet protects them against meaningless and arbitrary experiences of shame and doubt resulting from excessive, unthinking punishment for attempts to exercise their own decision-making powers, the seeds of later autonomy will be sown. But when children encounter a lot of punishment, which can easily happen at a time when their fledgling decision-making powers are unreliable, the seeds of later attitudes of shame and doubt will be sown. Erikson thinks that shame is rage, felt at being punished for trying to be autonomous, turned inward against the self—it is not the punishers who are wrong, it is you, because you are inept and unworthy. This sense of shame goes hand in hand with self-doubt. Instead of learning to rely on a gradually maturing decision-making prowess, severely punished children doubt their own ability to function competently and independently. As adults, they are constantly in doubt, scurrying to hide themselves lest they feel shamed by the scrutiny of others.

Erikson's third stage, much like the Freudian phallic stage, roughly covers the years from three through five. True to his psychosocial emphasis, Erikson sees successful outcome of this third stage in traits expressing *initiative* and *responsibility* and unsuccessful outcome in *guilty functioning*. Following his own words (Erikson, 1959), we find that this stage of infantile genitality adds to the inventory of basic social modalities

> that of "making," first in the sense of "being on the make." There is no simpler, stronger word to match the social modalities previously enumerated. The word suggests pleasure in attack and conquest. In the boy, the emphasis remains on the phallic-intrusive modes; in the girl it turns to modes of "catching" in more aggressive forms of snatching and "bitchy" possessiveness, or in the milder form of making oneself attractive and endearing.
>
> The danger of this stage is a sense of guilt over the goals contemplated and the acts initiated in one's exuberant enjoyment of new locomotor and mental power; acts of aggressive manipulation and coercion which go far beyond the executive capacity of organism and mind and therefore call for an energetic halt on one's contemplated initiative. (pp. 224–225)

As in Freud, we find here that the natural object of children's initiative is the opposite-sexed parent, whom they wish to capture and possess. Children, of course, must inevitably fail. If the child's parents have loved and helped him or her enough, however, the child will learn by the failure to "turn from an exclusive, pregenital attachment to his parents to the slow process of becoming a parent, a carrier of tradition" (Erikson, 1959, p. 225). The basis for adult initiative and responsibility will have been achieved. But if the failure is exaggerated by unnecessary punitiveness, the child will experience considerable resignation and guilt, experiences that will form the basis in later life for acquiescence, feelings of unworthiness, and even irresponsibility.

Next comes Erikson's view of the latency stage, eventful in development even if somewhat devoid of special biological significance. Erikson's (1950) own words are particularly worth quoting here:

> Before the child, psychologically already a rudimentary parent, can become a biological parent, he must begin to be a worker and potential provider. With the oncoming latency period, the normally advanced child forgets, or rather sublimates the necessity to "make" people by direct attack or to become papa and mama in a hurry; he now learns to win recognition by producing things. He has

mastered the ambulatory field and the organ modes. He has experienced a sense of finality regarding the fact that there is no workable future within the womb of his family, and thus becomes ready to apply himself to given skills and tasks, which go far beyond the mere playful expression of his organ modes or the pleasure in the function of his limbs. He develops industry—i.e., he adjusts himself to the inorganic laws of the tool world. He can become an eager and absorbed unit of a productive situation. To bring a productive situation to completion is an aim which gradually supersedes the whims and wishes of his autonomous organism.

His danger, at this stage, lies in a sense of inadequacy and inferiority. If he despairs of his tools and skills or of his status among his tool partners . . . he abandons hope for the ability to identify early with others who apply themselves to the same general section of the tool world. (pp. 226–227)

According to Erikson, the successful completion of the latency stage leads to the traits expressing *industry,* whereas unsuccessful completion leads to the traits expressing *inferiority*.

In our discussion of the four stages thus far, we have seen much that is similar to Freud, though there is far more emphasis on their psychosocial significance. In addition, Erikson has the advantage over other psychoanalytic thinkers of being more explicit than they. For this reason, and because of his representative status among ego psychologists, I would certainly be justified in devoting considerable attention to him. But there is an even more important reason for scrutinizing his theorizing: He breaks up the period of adulthood into several segments and gives them the status of real developmental stages. In the general sphere of psychoanalytic thinking, it would not have been possible to achieve this view of developmental stages in adulthood without dropping Freud's heavy emphasis on the organism's anatomy and physiology. Many people initially favorable to Freudian thinking have broken away from it because of the short shrift it gives to adulthood. Murray was among these, for in explaining the reasons for the course his career has taken, he said that he found Freud good as far as he went but that he did not go far enough to fulfill the allegory, to record "the heroic adult and his tragic end" (Murray, 1959, p. 13). But Murray did not go so far as to advance the story of adult development himself. In contrast Erickson, in reserving four of his eight stages for the years following puberty, certainly has tried to improve on Freud.

For Erikson, each new stage inherits the legacy of past stages. Weak points in character contributed by earlier fixations will influence—indeed, jeopardize—successful development in the current stage. This characteristic of Erikson's theorizing is evident in his description of the latency period quoted above. It is necessary to keep this in mind when considering the four remaining stages.

The fifth stage is that in which *identity* or *role diffusion* occurs. Successful development leads to the bases of a clear adult identity, whereas unsuccessful development leads to a scattered, fragmentary, diffuse, shifting sense of who one is. In Erikson's (1950) words;

> With the establishment of a good relationship to the world of skills and tools, and with the advent of sexual maturity, childhood proper comes to an end. Youth begins. But in puberty and adolescence all sameness and continuities relied on earlier are questioned again because of a rapidity of body growth which equals that of early childhood and because of the entirely new addition of physical genital maturity. The growing . . . youths . . . are now primarily concerned with what they appear to be in the eyes of others compared with what they feel they are, and with the question of how to connect the roles and skills cultivated earlier with the occupational prototypes of the day.
>
> The integration now taking place in the form of ego identity is more than the sum of the childhood identifications. It is the accrued experience of the ego's ability to integrate these identifications with the vicissitudes of the libido, with the aptitudes developed out of endowment, and with the opportunities offered in social roles. The sense of ego identity, then, is the accrued confidence that the inner sameness and continuity are matched by the sameness and continuity of one's meaning for others, as evidenced in the tangible promise of a "career." (pp. 227–228)

According to Erikson, the task of settling on an identity is so hard and so fraught with anxiety that youngsters often overidentify, for protection, with the heroes of cliques and crowds to the point of apparent loss of identity. Much of youthful "falling in love" also can be understood in this fashion. Such overidentifying is to be expected, but if the task of finding an identity is too fraught with conflict due to lack of proper environmental support and understanding, the youngster may remain in this condition. When he or she is older, this identity problem will show up as role diffusion.

In the sixth stage, which begins certainly by the time adolescence ends, society expects the person to leave parents and other more protective societal institutions, such as school, and begin to function as a mature and able adult. According to Erikson, in order to reap the rewards available during this stage, persons must direct their functioning toward *intimacy*. If there is any inevitable conflict in this stage so undominated by parents and pregenital, pleasure principle functioning, it is brought about by the tremendous difficulty in achieving intimacy in complex, impersonal societies. With this stage and subsequent ones, Erikson has, like other ego psychologists, transcended the pure conflict model, for the inevitability of conflict based on societal complexity seems quite questionable. In any event, should persons fail to achieve intimacy, they will slip into *isolation*. As before, persons approach this sixth stage with the legacy of earlier development. The more successfully they have traversed earlier developmental stages, the greater the likelihood that they will achieve intimacy.

Erikson's idea of intimacy is an elaboration of Freud's sage remark that one aspect of normalcy is the ability to love. Erikson (1950, pp. 230–231) lists the concrete capabilities that this implies as "(1) mutuality of orgasm, (2) with a loved partner, (3) of the other sex, (4) with whom one is able and willing to regulate the cycles of work, procreation, and recreation, (5) so as to secure for the offspring, too, a satisfactory development." As you can see, the characteristic of achieving intimacy would be very similar to what other psychoanalytic thinkers describe in the genital character type. But in order to have the chance to achieve intimacy, persons must offer themselves freely in situations that require a minimum of self-protection, situations such as sexual union and close friendship. If previous development has been unsuccessful, persons may be unwilling to risk the pain attendant on momentary failures in the search for intimacy. In that case, they will shrink into a deep sense of isolation and consequent self-absorption.

As adulthood progresses, the seventh stage of development opens. The particular focus of this stage is *generativity* versus *stagnation*. Interestingly, Erikson (1950, p. 231) calls this a *nuclear conflict,* although it is still not clear in the terms used in Chapter 3 that the conflict is inevitable. Be that as it may, let us recognize that Erikson (1950) means by generativity

> primarily the interest in establishing and guiding the next generation or whatever in a given case may become the absorbing object of a parental kind of responsibility. Where this enrichment fails, a regression from generativity to an obsessive need for pseudo intimacy, punctuated by moments of mutual repulsion, takes place, often with a pervading sense . . . of individual stagnation and interpersonal impoverishment. (p. 231)

Generativity and stagnation certainly are included in the intimacy or isolation of the sixth stage, but Erikson singles out this seventh stage because he feels that questions of generativity or stagnation gradually became more important as adulthood progresses.

The final stage of development is not clearly associated with any particular time in the life span, but one may presume it to be something that begins around the period of middle age or perhaps a bit later. It is the stage in which persons achieve *ego integrity* if they have developed successfully and *despair* if unsuccessfully. Once again the most direct way to Erikson's meanings is through his own words (1950):

> Only he who in some way has taken care of things and people and has adapted himself to the triumphs and disappointments adherent to being, by necessity, the originator of others and the generator of things and ideas—only he may gradually grow the fruit of these seven stages. I know no better word for it than ego integrity. Lacking a clear definition, I shall point to a few constituents of this stage of mind. It is the ego's accrued assurance of its proclivity for order and meaning. It is a post-narcissistic love of the human ego—not of the self—as an experience which conveys some world order and spiritual sense, no matter how dearly paid for. It is the acceptance of one's one and only life cycle as something that had to be and that, by necessity, permitted of no substitutions: it thus means a new, a different love of one's parents. . . . Although aware of the relativity of all the various life cycles which have given meaning to human striving, the possessor of integrity is ready to defend the dignity of his own life style against all physical and economic threats. For he knows that an individual life is the accidental coincidence of but one life cycle with but one segment of history; and that for him all human integrity stands or falls with the one style of integrity of which he partakes . . . . Before this final solution, death loses its sting.

> The lack or loss of this accrued ego integration is signified by fear of death; the one and only life cycle is not accepted as the ultimate of life. Despair expresses the feeling that the time is short, too short for the attempt to start another life and to try out alternate roads to integrity. Disgust hides despair. (pp. 231–232)

Although his precise meaning is perhaps a little obscured by the dramatic intent of his writing, Erikson does provide some basis for our understanding the traits or peripheral characteristics of people with integrity or despair. In this final stage we clearly see a definite shift in the person's concerns from what will happen in the future to what has already happened.

This brings to a close our discussion of Erickson's eight stages of development. To have theorized about them is to have taken on a formidable task, as you must realize by now. Certainly Erikson's figurativeness and ambiguities must be regarded in the light of the enormity of the task. And actually, we can piece together a fairly clear typology of character. We have the person of integrity, who has such characteristics as an overall sense of what his or her life is about, who accepts that life, who does not fear death, and who is not typically in despair. These are all characteristics that could be measured, though Erikson comes nowhere near providing us with precise definitions of them. Such a person would also show the characteristics of successful development associated with the previous seven stages. The person who has failed the achievement of integrity would show the characteristics of one or more developmental failures in the previous stages.

Continuing for a moment down the scale of development, we could say that a person who has achieved generativity shows a strong interest in public affairs, especially as they have influenced the future of the world, and a strong commitment to rearing children. If the person showed these kinds of characteristics and was too young for the stage of integrity versus despair to be relevant, we would expect to find the additional characteristics associated with successful development at earlier stages. But if the person was old enough for the eighth stage, he or she would show, in addition to generativity, either integrity or despair. If despair, we would expect, along with generativity, some attributes of developmental failure at earlier stages; if integrity, we would probably see only the attributes of earlier developmental success. To complete this scheme, if the person showed the opposite of generativity—stagnation—we would expect additional attributes signifying earlier developmental failures. When the person reached the age of the eighth stage of development, despair would be more likely than integrity.

It probably is not necessary for me to take this statement of typology further. You can see by now that Erikson's position permits some reasonably clear statements to be made about the characteristics one can find in people as a result of their developmental past. Indeed, you should also be able to see that the various types of peripheral personality patterns can be related to one another in the sense that one can predict—on knowing, let us say, that someone has achieved generativity—the nature of his or her future and past development. This is a sign that the various character types are integrated into Erikson's theory rather than simply representing descriptions of his observations of people. While his position has an unfinished quality, there being many loose ends, it is certainly a brave beginning.

The Object-Relations Position

Being concerned primarily with psychopathology and its treatment, the object-relations theorists do not have a complete peripheral statement. But they do specify some attributes of mature or ideal self-identity. These are deep and stable relations with others, tolerance of ambivalence toward loved objects, capacity for tolerating guilt and separation and for working through crises of depression, an integrated self-concept, and correspondence between behavior patterns and the self-concept (Kernberg, 1976). Mature self-identity presumably results from parental support that is loving without being overindulgent. It is unclear to what degree mature self-identity is considered defensive, as various object-relations theorists stand on different sides of this question.

Three levels of pathology in self-identity are discussed, though they cannot be given much attention here. At the least pathological level is a well-integrated but severe and punitive superego, a well-integrated ego, and overly inhibitory or phobic character defenses sometimes coupled with reaction formations. Social adaptation is not severely impaired, and there can be fairly deep, stable relations with persons. Guilt and mourning are also possible. Into this level would fit much of what Freudians consider to be anal and phallic character types plus their associated neuroses.

The next higher level of self-identity pathology involves an even more punitive superego and a less integrated ego. Social adaptation is still fairly adequate, though the operation of more primitive defenses of an oral nature and a tendency toward splitting (emotional and behavioral instability) are present. In this category would fit what the Freudians regard as oral, passive-aggressive, and narcissistic character types.

The highest level of self-identity pathology involves considerable disintegration of ego and superego and socially maladaptive, ineffective behavior. As superego integration is minimal, criminality and other forms of social deviance are common. Accompanying this is the relative inability to experience guilt. Reliance on the extremely primitive defense of splitting lends a chaotic, disintegrated quality to behavior. In Freudian terms, this level includes the borderline and frankly psychotic states.

Kohut's Position

Kohut (1971) has offered a typology that deviates considerably from the Freudian view. To be sure, the definitions and descriptions are less precise than we would like, but they do give a flavor of things to come at this early stage of psychoanalytic self-theorizing.

The ideal type is the *autonomous self,* characterized by self-esteem and self-confidence. Because of this security, the person is not excessively dependent on others or a mere replica of the parents. Developmentally, the ideal situation is for the child to have its core needs—to be mirrored and to idealize—satisfied in interaction with the parents (see Chapter 3). In this, it is less important how the parents *resolve* to interact than what they *are*—in other words, it is as models that they affect their child. If the parents are at peace with their own needs to shine and succeed, their child's exhibitionism will be accepted and responded to. Parental tranquility and pride of accomplishment will calm the child and encourage the development of its own goals. But true to the Freudian beginnings, Kohut believes that there must be some frustration, otherwise the child may become passive, complacent, and a mere shadow of the parents. It is argued that even the best of parents are sometimes too preoccupied to mirror and encourage idealization well. These minor and transitory ruptures in the parent-child relationship will stimulate the child to develop a sense of self and strive for autonomy.

When the child is not so fortunate as to have mirroring and idealizing needs well satisfied, one or another of the nonideal personality types will result. These types are classified as *narcissistic personality disorders* and *narcissistic behavior disorders*. In Kohut's usage, *personality* refers to generalized attitudes, ways of thinking, or cognitive styles, whereas *behavior* refers to actions of a habitual nature. It is easy to be confused by the term *disorders*. Apparently, it is meant to include not only frankly psychopathological states but states within the normal range that, though deviations from the ideal, are livable and common.

Grouped as narcissistic personality disorders are the understimulated self, the fragmented self, the overstimulated self, and the overburdened self. Persons showing the *understimulated self* lack vitality, experience themselves as boring and apathetic, and are experienced that way by others. The understimulated self results from prolonged lack of responsiveness on the parents' part toward their child. Persons who have been thus understimulated will do anything to create excitement to ward off the feeling of deadness that otherwise would overtake them. In childhood, such attempts to create excitement include head-banging and compulsive masturbation. In adolescence, one observes daredevil activities. In adulthood, there is likely to be promiscuity and perversion in the sexual sphere and gambling, substance abuse, and hypersociability in the nonsexual sphere.

Persons with the *fragmented self* are extremely vulnerable to setbacks or reversals, responding with a sharp decrease in self-esteem, disorganization, and an anxious loss of a sense of continuity of the self in time and space. This fragmentation may even be observed in mode of dress and gait. Kohut discusses this type resulting from the same deprivation of parental responsiveness to the child as in the case of the understimulated self. Perhaps some shade of difference in the developmental formulation is intended, as it would seem logical to consider fragmentation to stem from erratic parental responsiveness rather than a more general lack of response.

Persons with an *overstimulated self* are subject to being flooded by unrealistic fantasies of greatness that produce tension and anxiety and, hence, they will try to avoid situations in which they could become the center of attention. They will often shy away from creative activities because of the fear of destruction by losing a sense of autonomy. According to Kohut, the developmental problem leading to the overstimulated self is excessive responsiveness of the parents through an overindulgence of the child's mirroring and idealizing needs. Thus, the child grows into adulthood with a grandiosity that is uncontrollable and frightening.

Very similar is the *overburdened self,* which involves perceptions of the external world as hostile and reactions to insignificant stimuli as attacks or frustrations. This attitude of irritability and suspiciousness flares up in response to specific slights and disappears quickly when the offense has passed. The developmental difficulty in this case is a frustration of the idealizing need more than of the mirroring need. In short, the child has not been provided with the opportunity to identify with the calmness of an apparently omnipotent parent, presumably because this parent is uncomfortable in the realm of accomplishment. Thus, the child has to do too much for itself in the area of goal setting and grows into an easily overburdened adulthood.

While the types mentioned above stress patterns of thought that are only sometimes expressed clearly in action, the narcissistic behavior disorders considered next can be seen primarily in actions. They are the mirror-hungry personality, the ideal-hungry personality, and the alter ego–hungry personality. The *mirror-hungry personality* is famished for admiration and appreciation, feeling an inner sense of worthlessness deriving from parental frustration of the need to be admired and appreciated. Consequently, the mirror-hungry personality leads persons to display themselves incessantly. Such persons generally flit from relationship to relationship and performance to performance, in an insatiable attempt to get attention.

Persons with the *ideal-hungry personality* are forever in search of others whom they can admire for their prestige, power, beauty, intelligence, or moral stature. They feel worthwhile only as long as they can look up to someone because it was specifically in the area of the idealizing need that they were frustrated in childhood. As adults, their craving cannot really be satisfied, stemming as it does from early frustrations, and sooner or later each person they admire comes to appear less than perfect. So the search for someone to idealize continues.

Persons with the *alter ego–hungry personality* can experience a sense of self as real and acceptable only when they relate to others who slavishly conform to their opinions, values, and ways. The developmental lack in this case is presumably due to frustration of both mirroring and idealizing needs. Once again the void cannot be filled, and the alter ego–hungry person discovers that the other is not himself or herself and consequently feels estranged. These persons commonly engage in a restless search for one alter ego after another.

For Kohut, all the types discussed to this point are within the normal range. There is no difference among them in degree of childhood frustration of self-needs (to be mirrored and to idealize). All have had too much frustration of ideal self-development. The content differences in the types are considered to be the result of particular patterns of early frustration, though it is by no means true that these patterns have thus far been clearly and precisely delineated. Kohut does mention some types he regards as frankly pathological, suggesting that they result from self-need frustrations that are more intense and complete than what we have already discussed. These pathological types are beyond the scope of this book and will therefore only be mentioned. They are the *merger-hungry personality* (in whom other persons literally function as the self-structure that is absent), the *contact-shunning personality* (who must avoid others because the need for them is so intense), and various borderline and schizophrenic states that Kohut suggests are better understood in terms of "self psychology" than traditional psychoanalytic theorizing.

According to Kohut (1977), self disorders cannot be treated by traditional psychoanalytic therapy, in which the therapist alternates between being a "blank screen" and making telling interpretations. Such therapy is successful only when the client is able to project emotions for others onto the therapist in the process called *transference*. But persons with self disorders cannot project emotions consistently because they are too personally preoccupied, even when they seem to be relating to others, and hence must be approached differently. They must be mirrored (appreciated, respected) and permitted to idealize the therapist (hence, the therapist must let himself or herself be known rather than remain shadowy) in the hope that by filling the void they experienced in childhood, sound self-development will be stimulated. Kohut's therapy seems a combination of the Rogerian emphasis on unconditional positive regard (mirroring) and the existential emphasis on providing the client with models (idealizing). As such, a great break with psychoanalytic techniques has occurred.

Berne's Position

Although Berne's (1964) theorizing is concerned primarily with understanding constructive and destructive aspects of social interaction, in the process of explicating these many implicit and explicit assumptions concerning personality, types emerge. At the moment, the writings of transactional analysts represent a conglomerate of views, and there is no definitive personality typology. Consequently, the best I can do is indicate some of the conceptual features presumably present in all types regardless of their content and give you some examples of particular types that have been delineated.

Early experience is important in that it leads to the development of a *life script*, or a plan (typically not conscious) that organizes energies and directions. As such, the life script qualifies as a personality type. It is learned not only out of direct interaction with parents but through other cultural influences (e.g., fairy tales, movie heroes). All life scripts include a *life position*, which comprises learned assumptions about the acceptability of self and others. There are four basic life positions: "I'm OK and you're OK," "I'm OK and you're not OK," "I'm not OK but you're OK," and "Neither you nor I are OK." The particular life position persons learn and the specific content contributed by the life script combine to make certain *games* likely for them.

Games (Berne, 1964) are "a series of ulterior transactions leading progressively to a well-defined climax; a set of operations with a gimmick." As such, a *gimmick* is an unexpected twist. It, along with such other interactional characteristics as *discounting* (a procedure of persuading persons that they are not OK) and *rackets* (chronic emotions used manipulatively, such as anger or guilt) are learned techniques whereby persons attempt to reach the goals of their life scripts. Both games and life scripts involve various configurations of the three ego states (Child, Adult, Parent) present in all persons. Thus, one life script (and the games to which it leads) may have Parent predominating and Child suppressed, and so forth.

It is an inherent characteristic of transactional analysis that the life scripts, or personality types, merge with the games people play. For example, the *Alcoholic* is talked about both as a life script and as a part in a game. Similarly, the *Rescuer* and the *Dummy*, who are usually found playing the Alcoholic game along with the Alcoholic, are also life scripts. Other life scripts and associated games described are *Debtor, Kick Me, Frigid Woman, Cavalier, Homely Sage,* and *Look How Hard I've Tried*. Various suggestions have been made for classifying these life scripts, such as *Get-On-With-It* and *Get-Nowhere-With-It* scripts.

By and large, the scripts and games have the ring of obvious, recognizable foibles and in that sense need little further description here. In addition, there is just too much flux in transactional analysis these days to justify much more detailing. It should be noted, however, that Berne's therapy also constitutes a break with traditional psychoanalysis. The therapy is done in groups, both large or small, and takes the form of disclosure by the therapist through direct confrontation of the games engaged in by the group members. Then, of course, the group members also are free to comment on the manipulative attempts they employ on one another. In that it has some concern for understanding unconscious phenomena, transactional analysis somewhat resembles psychoanalysis. However, its techniques and goals are far more similar to those of Gestalt psychotherapy and other so-called confrontation approaches.

CONFLICT MODEL: INTRAPSYCHIC VERSION

Rank's Position

Rank's position on the periphery of personality seems both lucid and simple, as it is based on the logical possibilities presented by his core-level assumptions. The key to understanding Rank's statement of personality types is the simple recognition that once you postulate one force leading toward individuation and another toward unity, three possibilities for stable patterns of functioning emerge. These patterns can express individuality to the exclusion of unity, unity to the exclusion of individuality, or a blend of the two. Logically, there are no other possibilities. Concretely, these are the only possibilities on which Rank focuses.

Let us approach discussion of the personality types with a word about development. Birth disrupts the primitive unity of embryo and mother. From birth onward, there are many other separations between persons and their environment, separations as inevitable as life itself. Through these enforced separations, persons become more and more differentiated. The pressure toward unity can no longer take the primitive form of merging with the world but must involve complex and subtle integrations of the parts of the person and of the person with other things and people. As they grow in this sort of experience, children come to know their own selves as a totality. From this point onward, the active form of the self, called *will* by Rank, is a serious force in the shaping of life. Essentially the will involves a sense of what one wants to accomplish and who one is in the context of the rest of the world.

The will has its beginning, according to Rank, as *counterwill*. As children come to learn that they can say no to adults and to their own impulses, they feel a sense of personal identity stemming from counterwill. Although immature, the expression of counterwill is an important accomplishment, as it presages, in normal development, the conscious, satisfying, active integration of person with world that for Rank constitutes maturity. Munroe (1955) provides an especially clear discussion of the counterwill:

> The counter-will, developed *against* the parents and later representatives of external forces, against the "other" or "others," is thus wholesomely rooted in the basic human striving toward life and individualization. By itself, however, it tends to destroy the *union* which is equally necessary to the human spirit. Assertion of the counter-will, therefore, tends to arouse feelings of "guilt." The profound distress implicit in the effort to be one's own self at the expense of the previous sense of union and support Rank calls *ethical* guilt. He contrasts this almost universal and potentially creative problem with *moralistic* guilt, which arises when one has committed an act disapproved by one's society or one's own socially developed code of behavior. Ethical guilt goes deeper. It may arise with *any* expression of the own will—and also with any compliance which, for the person, has involved an abrogation of such willing, even though correct from a moralistic standpoint. Ethical guilt, if I understand Rank aright, is his term for the tension between two poles of human experience—separation and union. . . . Resolution of this guilt becomes, for Rank, the human ideal and the goal of psychotherapy. (pp. 585-586)

Ethical guilt can be resolved only through the achievement of simultaneous differentiation and integration, or psychological growth. Psychological growth is encouraged in the early years by a love relationship between child and parent. This relationship must, of course, include in its definition the child's need for succorance and support, even when it is expressing counterwill against the parents. Ideally the parents accept the child's counterwill as a lovable part of its effort to establish its own self as an independent being. At the same time, the parents must assume responsibility for nurturing the child and teaching it the realities of the external world. If the child receives this kind of care, it will progress from the expression of counterwill to the expression of mature will, or selfhood.

The ensuing personality type, called the *artist,* is the Rankian ideal. Rank does not use the term *artist* in its conventional meaning. Many painters, writers, and the like definitely would not be artists by his definition. The artist is the person who has accepted both the fear of life and the fear of death, both the inevitable pressure toward individuation and the unavoidable longing for union, and achieved an integration of the two. The artist's personal will expresses both differentiation and integration. Munroe (1955) gives something of the flavor of Rank's thinking on this type:

> We have seen that this [psychological growth] requires an acceptance by the individual of his personal will as valuable—an acceptance begun in the counterwill. But this personal will cannot become truly constructive until it is accepted by another person. Until the person can feel that his own will is *right* (i.e., not guilty), until he can feel that it is accepted by "others," he cannot fully resolve the problem of separation with its counterpart of union. Rank's artist . . . does not stand alone on a pinnacle of individual worth. On the contrary "he who loseth his life shall find it." The act of separation is not enough, no matter how heroically accomplished. Neither is sacrifice of the self, whether it takes the form of heroic altruism and self-immolation or the unthinking compromise of the average man. These are the poles of experience, neither of which can fully express the human ideal. Rank's choice of the term *artist* for the human ideal is an attempt to convey a sense of creative integration as the highest goal of man. (pp. 585–586)

Rank has described what he means articulately enough to suggest some of the relevant peripheral characteristics. For example, the artist type certainly would include people who showed a high degree of differentiation and integration in their thoughts, feelings, and actions. In addition, they would show intimacy with and commitment to other people without slavish loyalties or undue concern for social proprieties. In their work, they would be productive in the direction of unusualness but also usefulness. In short, they would show many of the signs of transcendence associated with the ideal personality as characterized by the fulfillment model. But that Rank's position is still in the conflict tradition is indicated by his insistence that persons cannot live ideally unless their way is acceptable to at least some other people.

One of the remaining two personality types is called the *neurotic person,* who expresses the tendency toward separation to the exclusion of the tendency toward union. Like artists, neurotics have committed themselves to the pain of separation from the herd but have not won through to the artist's constructive integrations with the world. Instead of expressing mature will or selfhood, neurotics seem fixated at the level of counterwill. In other words, they act either against people or completely separately from them. In addition, though their personalities show much differentiation, they are weak on integrating principles. Their sense of separateness is likely to be ridden by hostility and moralistic rather than ethical guilt. Here there is a clue to the developmental handicap that culminates in the neurotic type. The handicap has to do with the child having been made to feel wrong and unworthy at the time when the negativism implied in counterwill was actually normal, with the result that the child overcompensated by strongly embracing counterwill as a defensive self-justification. In adulthood, neurotics continue to show counterwill as the only sign of their own selfhood. Again some of the peripheral characteristics embodying the neurotic personality type can be discerned: The neurotic would be hostile, negative, arrogant, isolationistic, critical of others, highly guilty, and so forth.

The final personality type is that of the *average person,* or someone who expresses the tendency toward union to the exclusion of the tendency toward individuation. Although the neurotic is, in Rank's mind, clearly inferior to the artist, the average person is inferior to both. Average persons are the most inferior because they have never seriously entertained the possibility of their own individuality. They act as if the right to individuality, guaranteed by the trauma of birth, were not there at all. Munroe (1955) once again provides a vivid description of what Rank had in mind:

> Every child develops something of a counter-will through the ordinary pains and frustrations of post-uterine existence. Many children, however, soon find it possible to so identify their own will with that of their parents as to avoid much of the guilt of separation and the pain of developing their own will further. Adaptation to the will of the parents and later to the dictates of a wider society is the keynote of these characters. Where there is no effort toward individuation, there is also no conflict about conformance. The person's life may be hard or dull, but as long as the person takes its external conditions for granted, so long as they seem really part of himself, he is spared the inner distress of guilt. Rank does not refer here to people who consciously conform for the sake of expediency. The average man is the man who naturally conforms to his society because he has never thought of doing anything else. His relations with his society are reminiscent of the symbiotic relationships between person and environment which prevailed in the womb. They represent the first and easiest solution to the problem set by birth. This essentially adaptive individual has a relatively harmonious relationship to his society, but only because he has never truly differentiated his own will from the significant surroundings. He is the prey of social change as victim or executioner. His truths are illusory and his virtues may vanish overnight if the social configuration to which he belongs shifts its values. (p. 585)

The average person would be characterized by such concrete peripheral characteristics as conformity, dependability, superficiality, suggestibility, and lack of dissatisfaction. The emphasis in this type is on adaptation. The developmental handicap involves an overwhelmingly negative response to the first expressions of counterwill that led the child to embrace for dear life the precise ways of its parents and the broader society.

This concludes my presentation of the personality types described by Rank. Intriguing and immediately identifiable in our own experience as they are, I urge you to realize that in Rank's position, there are only three kinds of people you can describe. This number cannot really be increased by considering mixed types, for the types offered largely exclude one another. One cannot be both artistic and average or even artistic and neurotic. You should carefully consider whether three personality types are enough to describe the full range of ways of life. We shall return to this point in Chapter 11.

Perls's Position

Although Perls offers no typology, he does theorize about how the general flow and change of human behavior, which he regards as ideal, can be interrupted or fixed. This fixity constitutes something like character structure or personality types. You will recall that for Perls experience is the continual process of identifying bits of the ongoing flux and construing relationships of simultaneous attraction and repulsion among them. The conflict involved in this construing is resolved when the relationship among the bits ends, but it is immediately replaced by the conflict that occurs when these bits enter into relationship with other bits. The ideal person would be continually changing and thus indescribable in terms of personality types.

When the ongoing process of experience is interrupted, a so-called *blister,* or fixed pattern of traits, is created. Although Perls is not very detailed concerning blisters, some points are clear. Blisters express no more conflict than does the uninterrupted process of experience; rather, in a blister the conflict is static, or unchanging, because the relationship among bits continues instead of giving way to new relationships. It is clear that this fixity of conflict is somehow a function of external pressures, but there is little systematic discussion of such matters available. The final point you should keep in mind is that blisters form the symptoms to be dealt with in psychotherapy. In this, Perls aims not to resolve conflict but to restore the flow in which relationships of conflict begin and end and are supplanted by new ones. Psychotherapy almost always takes place in groups and involves confronting clients with interpretations that contrast with what they say, do, or believe. The sense of contrast and conflict underlying the personality theory also permeates the psychotherapeutic technique.

Jung's Position

Jung (1933b) offers an ingenious conceptualization of personality types that is in some ways consistent and in others inconsistent with the rest of his thinking. The main distinction he makes is between the attitudes of *introversion* and *extroversion:*

> The two types are essentially different, presenting so striking a contrast, that their existence, even to the uninitiated in psychological matters, becomes an

obvious fact, when once attention has been drawn to it. Who does not know those taciturn, impenetrable, often shy natures, who form such a vivid contrast to those other open, sociable, serene maybe, or at least friendly and accessible characters, who are on good terms with all the world, or, even when disagreeing with it, still hold a relation to it by which they and it are mutually affected. (p. 412)

At the observational level, extroverted persons are concerned with the external world of things and people, whereas introverted persons focus on the internal world of their own ruminations. This useful observational distinction has been adopted by many psychologists and laypersons.

It is important to understand how Jung uses the distinction between introversion and extroversion not only in readily observed differences among people but in deeper elements of psychic life. In this regard, you should note that everyone, according to Jung, is capable of being both introverted and extroverted, even though these actually are opposite tendencies. This assumption is quite consistent with the intrapsychic conflict model—the personality is composed of intrinsically opposed elements. As the person grows to adulthood, one of the attitudes comes to be dominant so that observationally he or she is either introverted or extroverted. This assumption implies that an attitude becomes dominant through some process of learning, though Jung does not specify what it is. It is mainly because we are dealing with a learned basis whereby persons differ from one another that the introversion-extroversion distinction is considered part of the periphery rather than core of personality.

Once an attitude becomes dominant, the person seems to be somewhat ruled by it. This does not mean, however, that the opposing attitude has no effect at all. The nondominant attitude does not evaporate but becomes unconscious. As part of the personal unconscious, the nondominant attitude exerts a subtle effect, expressed in unexpected inconsistencies of behavior and vague longings to be other than what one seems. Thus, persons in whom introversion is dominant generally will be ruminative, reflective, and concerned with their own inner worlds, but they nonetheless will experience a nagging wish to break out of their own minds into the world of action and interchange with others and will actually make occasional gross and unexpected forays into extroverted behavior. Another sign of the potency of repressed extroversion in persons may be that they will find overtly extroverted persons strangely attractive though different. Thus, when Jung speaks of an introverted person, he means someone in whom introversion is dominant and conscious and in whom extroversion is nondominant and unconscious but nonetheless present. For the extroverted person, the opposite is true.

In developing his typology, Jung (1933b) adds four additional distinctions that he calls *functional modes*. These modes, which constitute general styles of experiencing, are thinking, feeling, sensing, and intuiting. Thinking and feeling are grouped together as *rational* in that they involve value judgments. The valuation in the *thinking* mode involves classifying separate ideas or observations under general concepts and organizing these concepts systematically to determine meaning. In the *feeling* mode, the evaluation lies in determining whether an idea or observation is liked or disliked. However strange it may seem to consider feeling a rational function, Jung does this because feeling, as he defines it, shares with thinking the capacity to order and organize experience. Feeling does this by enabling the person to determine preferences.

In contrast, sensing and intuiting do not lead to establishment of order and involve no value judgments. Therefore, they are considered *irrational* functions, though Jung does not mean this classification in any disparaging way. In *sensing,* one simply experiences the presence and qualities of things in an unevaluative, open way. *Intuiting* involves apprehending the essential characteristics of something in a manner that is immediately unreflective. Whereas sensing involves literal recognition, intuiting means grasping latent, underlying, or future possibilities.

As with introversion-extroversion, everyone has the capability for thinking, feeling, sensing, and intuiting, though typically one function becomes dominant through learning. According to Jung, the two rational functions oppose each other as do the two irrational functions. Thus, if one of the rational functions achieves dominance, the other is relegated to the personal unconscious, there to exert a subtle, underground influence on experiencing. Further, the two irrational functions are subordinated to the dominant rational function with the role of assisting it. Needless to say, the same sort of relationships hold if it is one of the irrational functions that achieves dominance. For example, if thinking is dominant, feeling is unrecognized by the person, though it manifests itself in wishes and dreams, in occasional lapses into strong emotions, and in the attractiveness of persons in whom feeling is dominant. The functions of sensing and intuiting are conscious and active but in the service of the thinking function. The person might well accumulate a wide range of sensations in order to operate on them with thought processes, and his or her intuitions might serve to initiate more systematic thought. With this example, you should be able to puzzle through the other combinations.

Jung (1933b) combines the introversion-extroversion distinction with the thinking-feeling and sensing-intuiting distinctions in arriving at what he calls *psychological types*. The types are *introversive-rational, introversive-irrational, extroversive-rational,* and *extroversive-irrational*. Of course, each type involving rational functions is further subdivided according to whether thinking or feeling is dominant, and each type involving irrational functions is broken down into sensing or intuitive dominance. This makes a total of eight basic personality types.

Although Jung is explicit in his typology, he offers no systematic list of peripheral characteristics to go along with it. From his descriptions of the personality types one can derive some notions as to concrete peripheral characteristics, but it is difficult to be absolutely sure. Presumably, thinking introverts believe theories and not facts are important, and they have a vague dread of the opposite sex. The latter occurs because sexual expression is in general both extroverted and concerned with feeling, and the thinking introvert has repressed these tendencies. The feeling introvert has a deep sense of God, freedom, immortality, and other values but can be mischievously cruel because not only extroversion but thinking has been repressed. Sensing introverts tend to be guided by what happens to them, with no operation of judgment, especially in regard to themselves. Finally, intuiting introverts discern possibilities and pursue them without regard for themselves and others but cannot understand why they are undervalued by others. The latter is true because of the repression of not only extroversion but also sensing, which produces persons who are insensitive to what is going on around them.

Turning to the extroverted types, there is the thinking extrovert, whose ideas are banal and dull and for whom the end justifies the means. These characteristics are understandable in someone who represses introversive tendencies and, due to repression of feeling, lacks a sense of what is proper and worthwhile. The feeling extrovert displays extravagant though unbelievable feelings and, though enjoying excellent rapport with others, hurts them with tactlessness. The disadvantage for this type stems from the de-emphasis on logical and problem-solving thought inherent in repression of thinking and introversion. In the sensing extrovert, one finds a thoroughly realistic person who nonetheless is rather slavishly bound to specifics and facts. This person never seems to get beyond the surface of things due to the repression of intuiting and introversion. Finally, the intuiting extrovert always seizes new things with enthusiasm but is apt to become involved with unsuitable persons of the opposite sex. Though capable of discerning possibilities, the intuiting extrovert, by having repressed sensing and introversion, is rendered somewhat unable to judge the results of his or her enthusiasms.

In each personality type, there are strengths according to what is dominant and conscious and weaknessness due to what is nondominant and repressed. None of these types can be considered ideal or even relatively better than the others, according to Jung. Instead, Jung considers the attainment of selfhood to be ideal. This process involves growing out of one's personality type, as it were, so that none of one's human capabilities is submerged and unconscious. In attaining selfhood, thinking introverts would have to become conscious of their feelings and extroversion capabilities and integrate these into their everyday lives. They would, at the point of success, have no personality type at all. They would have fulfilled all their capabilities. In selfhood, one attains a universal personality, in which the personal unconscious has shrunk to zero and life's actions are a joint function of the ego and the collective unconscious.

Jung's statements on peripheral characteristics of personality are consistent with his core statements in that both express the intrapsychic model, as indicated earlier. But there is an inconsistency between core and periphery due to Jung's failure to tell us how the personality types develop out of interactions between core and society. Clearly the types are learned. But it is not so clear how they develop as a function of one's experiences. Certainly, to define the personality type in Jungian terms is to simultaneously make a statement about at least some of the content of the personal unconscious and ego. What is dominant in a type is represented in the ego as conscious experience, and what is nondominant in the personal unconscious as repressions. It is harder to know how the collective unconscious feeds into the personality types. One also misses reference to parent-child interactions in a manner that could help systematize ideas on the development of personality types.

Jung does say that personality types develop early in life and are the major basis for behavior throughout young adulthood. But by the time the early forties are reached, there is a general shift in personality toward introspection and rumination. This is the time when the transition may be made from a personality type to selfhood. If the transition is not made, general despair and hopelessness may attend later adulthood. In order to successfully make the transition, persons must become more conscious of their personal unconscious and be attuned to the emanations into consciousness of the collective unconscious. What this will mean in content terms is more or less determined by the personality type; thinking introverts will have to become sensitive to their feelings and extroversive tendencies, and so forth. In addition, one must accept and value the collective unconscious. This means, among other things, accepting experiences of the uncanny, of things beyond individual control. It also means identifying with humankind and all living things in an uncritical, appreciative way. This part of Jung's view of the ideal is not very different from Zen Buddhism. In psychotherapy, Jung has ingenious ways of aiding persons in the transition from specific personality types to selfhood. These include spending time and effort at fantasy and imaginative activities, such as painting and daydreaming.

CHAPTER 8

The Periphery of Personality: Fulfillment Model

At the core level, the differences between conflict and fulfillment models are readily apparent. By comparing the content of the last chapter with that of this one, it will be possible to determine to what degree the two models differ in conceptualizing the most tangible aspects of personality.

FULFILLMENT MODEL: ACTUALIZATION VERSION

Rogers's Position

As I implied earlier, a good heuristic device for detecting the parts of a personality theory that are peripheral in nature is to try to spot the points at which statements about the differences among people occur. In Rogers's theory, only one broad distinction among ways of living is made, this leading to the separation of people into two general types. In core-level terminology, these types comprise the people in whom the actualizing tendency is vigorously expressed, leading to the enhancement and enrichment of living, as opposed to the people in whom the actualizing tendency is protectively and defensively expressed, leading to the mere maintenance of living. Someone falling into the first type would be called a *fully functioning person;* someone falling into the second type would be considered *maladjusted* (Rogers, 1959). Of course, Rogers does not really believe that all people fall neatly into one type or the other; rather, there are degrees to which people resemble one or the other extreme.

If Rogers went no further in his theorizing, all one would be able to say about persons is that they are either fully functioning or maladjusted. But fortunately, Rogers has elaborated on the meaning of this core-level distinction in peripheral-level terms. He (Rogers, 1961, pp. 183–196) delineated a set of peripheral characteristics pertaining to people who are fully functioning, thus giving this type the kind of specificity indispensable in actually describing people. The first of these characteristics is *openness to experience,* intended to signify the polar opposite of *defensiveness*. According to Rogers (1961), in a person open to experience

> every stimulus—whether originating within the organism or in the environ-ment—would be freely relayed through the nervous system without being dis-torted by any defensive mechanism. There would be no need of the mechanism of "subception" whereby the organism is forewarned of any experience threat-ening to the self . . . . Thus, one aspect of this process which I am naming "the good life" appears to be a movement away from the pole of defensiveness toward the pole of openness to experience. The individual is becoming more able to listen to himself, to experience what is going on within himself. He is more open to his feelings of fear and discouragement and pain. He is also more open to his feelings of courage and tenderness, and awe. He is free to live his feelings subjectively, as they exist in him, and also free to be aware of these feelings. (pp. 187–188)

Actually, on studying this statement it becomes clear that openness to experi-ence is probably a group of peripheral characteristics rather than only one. If you think in the most concrete terms of how you would expect persons who are open to experience to be, you will recognize that a number of characteris-tics are involved. At the least, we can say that people open to experience would be *emotional,* showing both positive and negative affects, and *reflective,* show-ing a richness of information about themselves. These clearly are peripheral characteristics because they would be used to describe only part of any per-son's behavior and to typify differences among people. Breaking down complex and heterogeneous concepts such as openness to experience into their com-ponent parts can only render peripheral-level theorizing more useful, as at the peripheral level you are, of course, concerned with understanding people on the most concrete levels.

Rogers's next characteristic of the fully functioning person, which he calls *existential living,* is even more clearly a set of interrelated characteristics. Existential living involves the nebulous quality of living fully at each and every moment. The subjective experience of doing so is that each moment is new and different from the preceding one. In elaborating on this existential quality, Rogers (1961) says:

> One way of expressing the fluidity which is present in such existential living is to say that the self and personality emerge *from* experience, rather than expe-rience being translated or twisted to fit preconceived self-structure. It means that one becomes a participant in and observer of the ongoing process of or-ganismic experience, rather than being in control of it.
>
> Such living in the moment means an absence of rigidity, of tight organization, of the imposition of structure on experience. It means instead a maximum of adaptability, a discovery of structure *in* experience, a flowing, changing organi-zation of self and personality. (pp. 188–189)

Among the peripheral characteristics discernible in Rogers's notion of existen-tial living are *flexibility, adaptability, spontaneity,* and *inductive thinking.*

Another characteristic of the fully functioning person is what Rogers calls *organismic trusting*. The meaning of this concept is not immediately apparent; therefore, I will quote from Rogers's description (1961):

> The person who is fully open to his experience would have access to all of the available data in the situation, on which to base his behavior; the social demands, his own complex and possibly conflicting needs, his memories of similar situations, his perception of the uniqueness of this situation, etc., etc. The data would be very complex indeed. But he could permit his total organism, his consciousness participating, to consider each stimulus, need, and demand, its relative intensity and importance, and out of this complex weighing and balancing, discover that course of action which would come closest to satisfying all his needs in the situation. An analogy which might come close to a description would be to compare this person to a giant electronic computing machine. Since he is open to his experience, all of the data from his sense impressions, from his memory, from previous learning, from visceral and internal states is fed into the machine. The machine takes all of these multitudinous pulls and forces which are fed in as data, and quickly computes the course of action which would be the most economical vector of need satisfaction in this existential situation. This is the behavior of our hypothetical person.
>
>   The defects which in most of us make this process untrustworthy are the inclusion of information which does *not* belong to this present situation, or the exclusion of information which *does*. (p. 190)*

Apparently Rogers has in mind the ability to let a decision come to you rather than trying to force it into existence and to trust the decision as a worthy format for action even if its bases are not completely, unassailably apparent. This characteristic amounts to trusting your organism, of which, you will recognize, your consciousness is only one part.

There are two final characteristics, which are actually implied in those already discussed. The first is *experiential freedom,* the sense that one is free to choose among alternative courses of action. Rogers does not really assume free will here in the old, philosophical sense. All he means is that fully functioning persons experience themselves as choosing freely regardless of the sad fact that their actions may indeed be determined by their past experiences. The fully functioning person has the marvelous, exuberant feeling of personal power that comes with believing that anything is possible and what happens really depends on him or her. The final characteristic is *creativity,* or the penchant for producing new and effective thoughts, actions, and things. You can see that if people have available to them all of their organismic capabilities and experience and also are flexible, they are quite likely to be consistent producers of new and useful entities.

Put all these qualities together and you have the fully functioning person—actualization theory's true gift to the human race. The composite picture is one of great richness, as is so clearly seen in these words (Rogers, 1961):

> One last implication I should like to mention is that this process of living in the good life involves a wider range, a greater richness, than the constricted living in which most of us find ourselves. To be a part of this process means that one is involved in the frequently frightening and frequently satisfying experience of a more sensitive living, with greater range, greater variety, greater richness. It seems to me that clients who have moved significantly in therapy live more intimately with their feelings of pain, but also more vividly with their feelings of ecstasy; that anger is more clearly felt, but so also is love; that fear is an experience they know more deeply, but so is courage. And the reason they can thus live fully in a wider range is that they have this underlying confidence in themselves as trustworthy instruments for encountering life.
>
> I believe it will have become evident why, for me, adjectives such as happy, contented, blissful, enjoyable, do not seem quite appropriate to any general description of this process I have called the good life, even though the person in this process would experience each one of these feelings at appropriate times. But the adjectives which seem more generally fitting are adjectives such as enriching, exciting, rewarding, challenging, meaningful. This process of the good life is not, I am convinced, a life for the faint-hearted. It involves the stretching and growing of becoming more and more of one's potentialities. (pp. 195–196)

There is a clear difference in emphasis on what is ideal in living between Rogers and psychosocial conflict thinkers such as Freud. I trust the difference will not have escaped your attention. The psychoanalytic ideal is one of responsibility, capability, commitment, effectiveness, and adaptation to social "realities," whereas the Rogerian ideal stresses experiential richness, range of living, flexibility, spontaneity, immediacy, and change. This difference, which emerges clearly when one reaches the level of peripheral characteristics of personality, is traceable primarily to the fact that psychoanalytic theory is a psychosocial conflict position and Rogerian theory a fulfillment position. The emphasis in the former is on compromise and defense and in the latter on expressing potentialities. That Rogers (1977) does not regard acceptance of social institutions and conventions as guides for adequate living is shown in his recent writings on the power of individuals to effect radical social reform.

Having covered the peripheral characteristics defining one of the two great Rogerian types, it remains to discuss the other. This is quite easily done, as the other, maladjusted type, which emphasizes maintaining rather than enhancing living, is nothing more than the opposite of the fully functioning personality. Persons in this maintaining mode are *defensive* rather than open to experience, *live according to a preconceived plan* rather than existentially, and *disregard their organism* rather than trust it. More or less as a consequence of these things, they feel *manipulated* rather than free and are *common* and *conforming* rather than creative. These characteristics of the maladjusted person all follow from the existence of *conditions of worth*, which, as mentioned in Chapter 4, are the kind of sanctions learned from significant others in the person's life. Because these others respected only some of the person's potentialities, he or she in turn was led to the same pattern of differential or partial self-acceptance and respect. Conditions of worth, like Freud's superego, are the basis for defense.

However engaging and true to your own experience these two personality types may be, I encourage you to recognize that they are only two. Also, there is no basis in Rogers's writing for considering various combinations of the set of peripheral characteristics that constitute fully functioning or maladjusted types. You have no formal theoretical justification for expecting, let us say, that one person might be high in openness to experience while being low in existential living, for being high in one brings with it the expectation that the other will be strongly represented as well. Although Rogers is fairly concrete concerning the peripheral level of personality, it is nonetheless true that his theory permits you to say only two kinds of things about people. This is particularly surprising because Rogers shows such humanistic emphasis on individuality. This interest in the many different ways in which people can live is shown in passages such as this (Rogers, 1963):

> Perhaps it should be stressed that these generalizations regarding the direction of the [actualization] process in which [people] are engaged exist in a context of enormously diverse specific behaviors, with different meanings for different individuals. Thus, progress toward maturity for one means developing sufficient autonomy to divorce himself from an unsuitable marriage partner; in another it means living more constructively with the partner he has. For one student it means working hard to obtain better grades; for another it means a lessened compulsiveness and a willingness to accept poorer grades. So we must recognize that the generalizations about this process of change are abstractions drawn from a very complex diversified picture. (p. 9)

This passage, in which Rogers discusses how clients come closer to the fully functioning life, sounds fine until you scrutinize it. On reflection, it becomes apparent that any behavior—some act or its opposite—can express full functioning. As we recognized before, such a position is too elastic for easy testing. One cannot determine whether it is true or false. In my opinion, the difficulty stems from Rogers's obvious interest in a comprehensive understanding of living that inevitably means taking seriously such concrete behavior patterns as leaving or staying in a marriage, even though he gives only the formal theoretical apparatus with which to make a few general distinctions. The difficulty can be traced to Rogers's position being first and foremost a theory of psychotherapy and only secondarily a theory of personality. It is certainly appropriate for a theory of psychotherapy to concern itself with only two basic things—maladjustment and the fullest utilization of potentialities. But once you theorize about personality, you take on the task of understanding all there is about a person that has any regularity. This inevitably leads you to consider many specific differences among people—too many for proper understanding by a theory that recognizes only two personality types. I do not for a moment deny that Rogerian theory can be developed so as to be more comprehensive, making it theoretically possible, for example, to understand why full functioning would take the form of leaving a marriage for one person and staying for another. I am simply saying that such development, though needed, has not as yet been accomplished. In contrast, Erikson's position permits many more distinctions among personality types than does Rogers's. My criticism of Rogers applies with only slightly less force to Rank, who postulates merely three personality types.

In concluding, I wish to point out that Rogers's theory, like the others, makes personality types and peripheral characteristics a function of the interaction between core tendencies and environmental encounters—in other words, development. For Rogers, if the core tendency of actualizing potentialities is met with unconditional positive regard from significant others, the person will show the peripheral characteristics of the fully functioning type. In contrast, if the core tendency is met with conditional positive regard, conditions of worth and the other signs of maladjustment will ensue. But unlike those found in Freud and Erikson, the Rogerian personality types do not refer to particular periods of life. Rogerian theory does not utilize the idea of stages of development.

Maslow's Position

Although Maslow, the other actualization theorist, names many peripheral characteristics in his discussion of personality, he is not at all systematic about delineating of personality types. He names characteristics more for illustration than to provide a set, dependable scheme whereby one can identify and understand various patterns of living. In this Maslow's writing is particularly deceptive, because it is so rich in vivid, illustrative references to courageousness, humor, spontaneity, and the like.

The only personality type with which Maslow concerns himself sufficiently to describe in the concrete terms necessary at the peripheral level of analysis is that which bespeaks complete psychological maturity. In core terms, these are people who have fully actualized themselves through vigorous expression of potentialities, search for knowledge, and interest in beauty. Maslow (1955) informally collected information about such a group of persons for the purpose of better understanding their peripheral characteristics. Among the persons he included in his group were Lincoln, Jefferson, Walt Whitman, Thoreau, Beethoven, Eleanor Roosevelt, Einstein, and some of his own friends and acquaintances! The common features, or traits, of these people turn out to be (1) *realistic orientation,* (2) *acceptance* of self, others, and natural world, (3) *spontaneity,* (4) *task orientation* rather than self-preoccupation, (5) *sense of privacy,* (6) *independence,* (7) vivid *appreciativeness,* (8) *spirituality* that is not necessarily religious in a formal sense, (9) sense of *identity with humankind,*

(10) feelings of *intimacy* with a few loved ones, (11) *democratic values,* (12) recognition of the *difference between means and ends,* (13) *humor* that is philosophical rather than hostile, (14) *creativeness,* and (15) *nonconformism.* Although this list is long and heterogeneous enough to escape easy integration into an organized picture of personality, it certainly is consistent with Maslow's general emphasis and is similar in many respects to Rogers's description of the fully functioning person. We can certainly take these fifteen characteristics as the starting point for delineating of the mature personality type according to actualization theorists, even though a number of the designations would require additional elaboration and definition in order to be really useful in describing people.

Maslow presents little else that can pass as a personality type; his preoccupation is with fostering the growth of a humanistic psychology. If you recall his notion of hierarchy of needs (Chapter 4), however, you will see that the possibility of fixation at some developmental point below full self-actualization is implicit in his position, with the resultant logical capability of describing different immature personality types. Although Maslow himself does not explore these implications of his position, we should note that there could be personality types oriented toward the satisfaction of (1) physiological needs, (2) safety needs, (3) needs for belongingness, and (4) needs for esteem. The potentiality for a typology of personality at the peripheral level of analysis is greater in Maslow than in Rogers, though Maslow has done little to implement a concrete basis for understanding different ways of life.

FULFILLMENT MODEL: PERFECTION VERSION

Adler's Position

Adler's viewpoint on the periphery of personality is carried in his concept of *style of life* (Ansbacher & Ansbacher, 1956; Ansbacher, 1967). Your style of life (or type) is the pattern of interrelated peripheral characteristics that find regular expression in you and that determine your individuality. The rudiments of style of life are established by five years of age, and there is no basic change thereafter except on the occasion of such special intervention as psychotherapy. Adler clearly specifies the relationship between periphery and core of personality (Ansbacher & Ansbacher, 1956) when he indicates that a person's style of life is the concrete result of the course taken by the core tendency of striving for perfection in the context of existing and imagined inferiorities and the particular family situation involved. Real and imagined inferiorities stem primarily from *organ weaknesses* and the specifics of *family constellation* (Dreikurs, 1963). The idea of organ weakness is clear enough, I suppose, regardless of the ticklish problem of diagnosis. An organ weakness can be anything from overly small hands to a heart with leaky valves.

By *family constellation,* Adlerians generally mean the person's status with regard to his or her siblings. Adler (Ansbacher & Ansbacher, 1956) emphasizes the roles of oldest child, second child, youngest child, and only child. In brief, the oldest child must be "dethroned," that is, give up the position of undisputed attention and affection when another sibling is born. Because of this, the oldest child cannot escape some feelings of resentment and hatred toward siblings and parents. The second child is in a more advantageous position. It never received undisputed attention and, hence, does not feel bereft at the birth of a younger sibling. The presence of an older sibling, or *pacemaker* (Ansbacher & Ansbacher, 1956, p. 379), is a challenge to develop rapidly. The youngest child has many pacemakers to goad development and never has the experience of losing attention to a "successor." Whereas the oldest child reveres the past and views siblings with alarm and the second child accepts the realities of sharing attention, the youngest child can concentrate on catching up to elders, feeling secure in the affection lavished on it by everyone in the family. The other family constellation Adler discusses is that in which all siblings are of the same sex, in which case there is a special problem of sexual identity.

Birth order partially determines the network of inferiorities felt in a family, which is complicated by the presence of real inferiorities with a basis in organ weaknesses. By the interaction of these inferiority feelings, a complex set of rivalries and alliances is formed. For example, an oldest child with strong intellectual capabilities may arouse rivalry in a younger child, which might be expressed in direct intellectual competition or in avoidance of the intellectual domain in favor of areas less dominated by the older child. Or a youngest child, indulged in and helped by everyone else in the family, may respond to the pacemaking function of older siblings by excelling beyond them all (Ansbacher & Ansbacher, 1956, p. 381).

Persons' sense of their inferiorities and their means of circumventing or transcending them are expressive of the core tendency of striving for superiority. But there is more to it than this. The style of life will evolve from the content of real and imagined inferiorities and from the manner in which they are transcended or circumvented. This manner of dealing with inferiorities will be greatly influenced by the *family atmosphere,* or general values, attitudes, and action patterns of family members, notably parents. If the atmosphere established by the parents is one of cooperation, mutual trust, respect, help, and understanding, the child will be encouraged to express its attempt to overcome inferiorities in a manner that is constructive for it and for others. In such an atmosphere, an oldest child, for example, will respond to being dethroned not with disobedience and criticality but with an attempt to nurture and develop the younger sibling. But if the family atmosphere is one of competition and distrust, neglect, or even pampering the child will be destructive in trying to overcome inferiorities (Ansbacher & Ansbacher, 1956, pp. 369–375). Whether the child will be active or passive in these attempts will be influenced by whether the family atmosphere involves encouragement to give and initiate as well as to receive. Thus, the two distinctions out of which Adlerians have formulated a typology of style of life are *constructiveness-destructiveness* and *activeness-passiveness.*

Perhaps this sounds as if family atmosphere provides a complete account-ing of the constructiveness-destructiveness and activeness-passiveness of styles of life. While this is indeed the position that makes most sense in the framework of Adlerian thought, I must point out that some eminent Adlerians (e.g., Dreikurs, 1963) make this only part of the story, with the rest involving free will. According to them, persons have free choice, uninfluenced by past experience, over the nature of their orientation toward inferiorities. Dreikurs (1963) says:

> This asserts the child's ability to decide what to do with an obstacle he encoun-ters, although such a decision does not take place on the conscious level, for the child may not have developed more than a rudimentary verbal capacity when such a decision is required. Adler's contention of such freedom of choice was—and still is—incomprehensible to most students of psychology. They want to know what induces one child to give up, another to compensate, and still another to overcompensate. They cannot believe there is nothing that "makes" a child do it; that it is his own conclusion, his own response, his own evaluation of the situation which is influential. It is a creative act, which in itself is a phenomenon that our deterministically oriented contemporaries find difficult to comprehend. (p. 247)

If "creative acts" refer to something godlike, something that has no anteced-ents in past experience or personality itself, Dreikurs surely has left the scien-tific fold. But if "creative acts" can themselves be explained as the end results of a particular pattern of past experience, there is little problem except the confusion fostered by using words such as *free will*. I have assumed that Dreikurs really means this latter view and that his confusing terminology can be traced to a zealous attempt to convince readers that the child indeed has a structure and a substance. I make this assumption on the basis of statements by Adler (1964) such as the following, which seem inconsistent with unmiti-gated free will:

> No soul develops in freedom. Each one is in mental, emotional and nutritional dependence upon his immediate environment on the earth and in the cosmos, yet so far independent that he must take up these relations seriously: he must answer them as the questions of life. (p. 36)

If it is the freeing effect of an exercised consciousness that is meant, family atmosphere is the only concept necessary for explaining the means by which the child will strive for superiority.

As you can surmise from preceding discussions, four types of peripheral personality, or life style, have been suggested by Adlerians: the *active-con-structive, passive-constructive, active-destructive,* and *passive-destructive* styles. These styles are established in childhood, and it is assumed that they change little thereafter.

The constructive-destructive distinction refers mainly to the direction of social interest, while the active-passive distinction tends to concern the more individualistic implications of striving for perfection. Actually, Adler (1964) considers the active-constructive style as epitomizing mental health:

It is almost impossible to exaggerate the value of an increase in social feeling. The mind improves, for intelligence is a communal function. The feeling of worth and value is heightened, giving courage and an optimistic view, and there is a sense of acquiescence in the common advantages and drawbacks of our lot. The individual feels at home in life and feels his existence to be worthwhile just so far as he is useful to others and is overcoming common instead of private feelings of inferiority. Not only the ethical nature, but the right attitude in aesthetics, the best understanding of the beautiful and the ugly will always be founded upon the truest social feeling. (p. 79)

This passage emphasizes the importance of a cooperative connection with others and society, even so far as to say that the healthiest form of inferiority feelings is that which links one with the failings of all people. In the following passage, Adler (1964) emphasizes the active, or more individualistic, aspects of healthy living:

Courage, an optimistic attitude, common sense, and feeling of being at home upon the crust of the earth, will enable [the healthy person] to face advantages and disadvantages with equal firmness. His goal of superiority will be identified with ideas of serving the human race and of overcoming its difficulties with his creative power. (pp. 47–48)

The passive-destructive style is considered as epitomizing psychopathology, as you may have imagined. But in order to understand the intended emphasis, you should recognize that passivity need not involve inertia, or doing nothing. It can—and usually does—involve a concerted unwillingness to solve one's problems and assume one's responsibilities. Instead, other people are blamed. With this in mind, Adler's (1964) words are illuminating:

In the investigation of a neurotic style of life we must always suspect an opponent, and note who suffers most because of the patient's condition. Usually this is a member of the family, and sometimes a person of the other sex, though there are cases in which the illness is an attack upon society as a whole. There is always this element of concealed accusation in neurosis, the patient feeling as though he were deprived of his *right*—i.e., of the center of attention—and wanting to fix the responsibility and blame upon someone. By such hidden vengeance and accusation, by excluding social activity whilst fighting against persons and rules, the problem-child and the neurotic find some relief from their dissatisfaction. (p. 81)

Of the remaining two styles, the passive-constructive should be more healthy than the active-destructive. This is because the constructive-destructive dimension (having to do with social interest) is somewhat more important than activeness-passiveness in determining what is ideal. But here we meet an ambiguity, signaled by the absence of descriptions in the Adlerian literature of the passive-constructive style. Probably this style does not really exist in Adlerians' minds, because even the activeness-passiveness dimension is bound up with considerations of social interest and constructiveness is not really thought of in passive terms.

For further clarification, it would be useful to focus more concretely on how these four (or are they three?) styles are actually concretized in specific behavioral terms. Here there is not too much to go on, as concrete behaviors expressive of lifestyles are regarded by Adlerians as varying widely. Each of these styles comprises a set of goals or finalisms that are arbitrary and subjective and are therefore considered fictional. Despite the striking nature of the term *fictional finalism,* it seems that here Adlerians are simply stressing the motivational character of the attributes that constitute styles of life.

Dreikurs (1963) has specified the fictional finalisms associated with the four lifestyles mentioned above. But it should be kept in mind that Dreikurs originally was attempting to explicate ways in which children could misbehave; hence, the lifestyles he details have little to do with constructiveness. But he has attempted to generalize his position such that we can consider it as having some relevance to constructiveness without too much risk of distortion. The four goals he considers are (1) the attainment of *attention* and *service,* (2) the *abolition →* abrogation of *power,* (3) the achievement of *revenge,* and (4) the bid to be *left alone.* Actually, only the first kind of goal applies to the two constructive styles of life, which involve cooperation and respect for others as well as for self. Hence, considerations of power, revenge, and isolation are irrelevant. The hallmark of the active-constructive style of life is *ambitiousness,* or orientation toward success, whereas that of the passive-constructive style is *charm,* or receiving special attention for what one is rather than for what one does. As implied above, all four kinds of goals are relevant in the case of the two destructive or competitive and distrustful styles. In the active-destructive style, the attention-getting goal takes the form of being a *nuisance,* whereas the power, revenge, and isolation goals take the forms of *rebelliousness, viciousness,* and *denigration,* respectively. The attention-getting, power, revenge, and isolation goals in the passive-destructive style take the concrete forms of *laziness, stubbornness, passive aggression,* and *despair,* respectively.

Let us consider how the organ inferiority mentioned earlier, overly small hands, might be dealt with in each of the four styles of life. The person with an active-constructive style of life might try to overcome smallness of hands in a direct, uncompromising, and socially useful fashion. Possessing musical talent and interest, the person might attempt to be a concert pianist in spite of small hands, relying on dexterity and practice to achieve excellence. The organ inferiority would be overcome by ambitiousness and success. In contrast, the passive-constructive person might beautify the small hands in some manner so that the very things that were inferior to begin with would now become the object of admiration. Superiority would have been achieved through charm. The active-destructive person might be a nuisance by nagging people to remember the handicap and seek power, revenge, and denigration by manipulating people with normal hands to feel guilty and irresponsible for being so well endowed and self-satisfied. Finally, the passive-destructive person might show laziness through not working because of the handicap and indicate stubbornness, passive aggression, and despair by refusing charity and other attempts to help.

Although my examples involve actual organ inferiority, the same kind of thinking takes place in imagined, or psychologically determined, inferiorities. I also ask you to note something mentioned previously. It is the constructive-destructive distinction that carries the major implications for mental health and illness for Adlerians. The two destructive orientations are psychopathological, whereas the two constructive ones are healthy. If the attempt to attain superiority is engaged in at the expense of others, it is pathological; if it proceeds in cooperation with other people, it is healthy.

Dreikurs (1963) originally developed his typology for use with children and adolescents, though it could readily be applied to adults as well. Another attempt at a typology by an Adlerian, Mosak (1971), is frankly concerned with adults and should be mentioned here. Unfortunately, Mosak devotes little attention to how the types he identifies fit into the Adlerian dimensions of constructiveness-destructiveness and activity-passivity. Mosak (1971) mentions (1) the *getters,* who exploit and manipulate life and others by actively or passively putting them into their service; (2) the *drivers,* whose overconscientiousness and dedication to their goals rarely permit them to rest; (3) the *controllers,* who either wish to control life or ensure that it will not control them; (4) the *good persons,* who prefer to live by higher moral standards than their contemporaries; (5) the *victims,* who always lose; (6) the *martyrs,* who attain nobility through "dying" for causes or principles; (7) the *babies,* who find their place in life through charm, cuteness, and exploitation of others; and (8) the *excitement seekers,* who despise routine and revel in commotion. Several other types mentioned are less easy to outline. One disconcerting feature of Mosak's typology is that it seems to refer rather exclusively to negatively toned styles. It is therefore unclear how he stands on ideal personality.

Although Adlerian attempts at typology do not seem developed enough to be objectively applied and studied, a theoretical start certainly has been made. The goals discussed, especially by Dreikurs, generally are the kind one would expect given the overall emphasis of the Adlerian position on the painfulness of inferiority and the striving to overcome it. And certainly the attributes of everyday life considered by this theory are somewhat different—and therefore especially interesting—from the well-known ones addressed by Freudians and Rogerians.

Incidentally, although Adler's position makes of the periphery of personality something that is established through learning during the first few years of life, it does not, in contrast to Freud, distinguish personality types on the basis of developmental stages. Rather than stages, Adler uses family constellation, inferiorities, and family atmosphere as the bases of distinguishing types. This is consistent with Adler's holistic or global emphasis, in which the fine discrimination of the second year of life from the third or fourth would seem unfruitful. For Adler, such things as family atmosphere would be unlikely to change enough to allow one to attribute particular forms of adult personality to developments during brief periods of early childhood.

White's Position

White gives us no more than a sketch of the lines along which he might develop a position on the periphery of personality. These key concepts are *competence* versus *incompetence* and *sense of competence* versus *shame*. In the normal course of events, expression of the core tendency—the need to have an effect on the world—leads, through practice of capabilities to actual competence and also to the subjective experience of a sense of competence. But if parents thwart and punish expressions of effectance motivation—the attempt to produce effects through one's actions—actual incompetence and the subjective experience of shame will result. White (1960) makes a neat distinction between shame and guilt: Shame is the experience of shortcoming or failure to reach a valued goal through lack of ability; guilt implies touching or transgressing a moral boundary. Shame is connected with incompetence. In contrast, guilt does not imply that one is unable to do something; it signifies that one has done or is thinking of doing something within one's power that is forbidden. Guilt is connected with conscience, not competence. In any event, if White were to develop the implications of his position for the peripheral level of personality, he undoubtedly would offer a typology of people based on their specific competencies and incompetencies and on the contents of their shame and sense of competence.

Actually, the overall form such a classification would take may be inferred from White's (1960) great sympathy for Erikson's version of ego psychology. Erkison's view of the eight stages of the human, discussed earlier in this chapter, is for White a very discerning developmental picture of the periphery of personality. Where White disagrees with Erikson is on the centrality of the psychosocial conflict model proposed by Freud. According to White, Erikson fails to recognize that most aspects of the character types and developmental stages he considers are better understood by a competence model than by a conflict model. Although Erikson certainly has, like other ego psychologists, championed a view of the ego as independent of the id rather than merely an extension of it, for White he is still too wedded to his early psychoanalytic beginnings.

In order to communicate his view, White (1960) provides an excellent discussion of the psychosexual stages of development in which he tries to show that the conflict model, though clearly relevant to some of the things going on in development, is inadequate to explain most of the modes of functioning, or character traits, detailed by Erikson. Concerning the anal stage, White says:

The bowel training model is wrong, I think, in two ways. First, it concerns a function that is governed by the autonomic nervous system, that never comes under direct voluntary control, and that does not carry the experience of initiative that goes with voluntary action. The child may be proud when he can meet parental expectations, but it will be pride in meeting a somewhat mysterious demand by a somewhat mysterious process of habit formation, not the pride of mastering things directly by trial and by effort expended, as when one learns to throw or to bat a ball. Second, it is a situation in which cultural requirements inevitably prevail. Every child is bowel trained. This is a far greater victory for authority than generally prevails elsewhere; in other matters the child preserves more freedom to resist, plead, cajole, and force compromises on his surrounding adults. In short, the bowel training model all but eliminates the initiative and versatility on the child's part that is the essential aspect of any true autonomy. The best outcome of the bowel training problem is that the child will come to will the inevitable. (pp. 118–119)

White points to what he considers a mismatch between Erikson's emphasis on autonomy as the result of successful completion of the anal stage and his choice, along with Freud, of the bowel-training situation as the major vehicle whereby autonomy can be learned.

Similarly, White (1960) points out the difficulty in considering the Oedipal conflict of the phallic stage prototypic for initiative:

And it seems to me that the Oedipal prototype falls short as a general model for the phallic stage in just the way toilet training failed for the anal stage. Once again Freud selected as his central image a hopeless situation, one where defeat for the child is inevitable. The child must learn to renounce the whole Oedipal wish, just as he must learn to renounce any thought of not being bowel trained. I submit the idea that if these were the true and determinative models it would be quite a problem to explain the survival of any sense of initiative. These models help us to understand why we have shame and guilt, but they do not give us much reason to suppose that we could emerge with autonomy and initiative. The competence model is not so harsh, though it certainly is not intended to gloss over the tragic features of childhood. (p. 125)

White follows through on his sense of the logical mismatch between Erikson's view of development and the Freudian conflict position by incorporating the genital stage into the general criticism presented above. According to Freudians, the sexual act—and, more specifically, the orgasm—is the prototype of maturity or genitality. But while the orgasm is logically well suited to serve as the prototype for love in a more general sense, it is not at all well suited for understanding work. Working and loving can be used as summary terms for most of what Erikson and other psychoanalytic thinkers typify as successful adult living. Love, like the orgasm, involves intense, sporadic, and impulsive emotions, thoughts, and actions. But working is quite the opposite in its emphasis upon stability, persistence, and self-control. For White, the competence model is much more appropriate for understanding the many aspects of adult functioning that have to do with work and productivity than is the Freudian conflict position.

The thrust of White's remarks is that while the Freudian position is not exactly irrelevant to what is happening in development, it is not nearly as central as has been supposed. White accepts Erikson's chronology and classification of character traits or types, but he finds them more naturally suited to an explanatory model that is of the fulfillment rather than conflict type and that stresses effectance motivation and competence rather than sexuality per se. Although he cannot make the kind of basic criticism of orality as prototypic of the first year of life that he did concerning the anal, phallic, and genital stages, White nonetheless has accumulated many observations of behavior during the first year that are not readily understood in oral terms. He (White, 1960) says:

> Somehow the image has gotten into our minds that the infant's time [during the first year] is divided between eating and sleeping. Peter Wolff (1959) is now showing that this is not true even for newborn infants, who show distinct forerunners of what will later become playful exploratory activity. Gesell notes that at four weeks there is apt to be a waking time in the later afternoon during which visual experience begins to be accumulated. At 16 weeks this period may last for half an hour, and the times increase steadily up to one year, when Gesell's typical "behavior day" shows an hour of play before breakfast, two hours before lunch, an hour's carriage ride and another hour of social play during the afternoon, and perhaps still another hour before being put to bed. At the age of 12 months the child is already putting in a six-hour day of play, not to mention the overtime that occurs during meals and the bath. (pp. 110–111)

Clearly there is a lot of activity during the first year of life that is difficult to understand as oral or even as a generalization from an oral prototype. And then, of course, White makes hay with the latency stage, a time that psychoanalysts have never pretended to be able to understand in terms of their sexual conflict position. White finds the name latency a complete misnomer, for the period is one of intense activity relative to social and work competence.

In his criticisms of the Freudian conflict position as an explanation of Eriksonian character types, White implies a developmental theory of effectance motivation and a specific set of social consequences of this development. During the first year of life, children do not act as an integrated unit, displaying instead rudimentary, discrete examples of effectance motivation. The rudimentary nature of children's capacities at this time is shown in the involvement of hands, mouths, and voices in the attempt to produce effects in the world and in the easy distractability that gives their attempts a playful, unimportant appearance. Actually, these attempts are very important, for by the end of their first year children gain some of their later basis for competence in interacting with the inanimate and social worlds. According to White, it is the physical maturation enabling walking and the cognitive maturation enabling development of a sense of oneself as an organized entity that mark the next developmental stage. In this stage, effectance motivation is expressed in a more concerted, organized, persistent way, building on the competencies gained during the first stage and expanding to include locomotion.

In the social domain, children experience themselves as much more of a force than previously. The battle of the toilet is one result of this, but it is only an example, rather than a prototype, of a more general negativism that is to be understood as the beginning of assertiveness. Continuing, White suggests that what is called the phallic stage and initiated, according to psychoanalytic thinkers, by genital eroticism is really a stage of development marked by great increases in three spheres of competence: locomotion, language, and imagination. Locomotion reaches the point of being a serviceable tool rather than a difficult stunt. Language likewise reaches a state in which it can support wider understanding and social exchange. Imagination marks the point where children can first maintain the fantasy of an imaginary companion. They also begin to cast themselves in adult roles. White believes that this growth in competence leads to intrinsic emotional and interpersonal crises that have little to do with sexuality. He (White, 1960) argues:

> Perhaps the best way to make this clear is to imagine for the moment a child in the phallic stage who is normal in every way except that no increase in genital sensitivity takes place. This child would still make locomotor, linguistic, and imaginative progress, would become interested in being like adults, would make comparisons as to size, would be competitive and subject to defeats and humiliations, would be curious, ask endless questions and encounter rebuffs, would have had dreams and guilt feelings over imagined assertive or aggressive actions, would learn about sex roles, would struggle to understand his relation to other family members, and might very well ask about marrying one of the parents. All of these things arise inescapably from progress in the growth of competence. They all have important emotional consequences. In all these situations there is a chance to maintain and strengthen a sense of initiative; in all there is also a chance that the environment will act so as to impose a burden of guilt. (pp. 124–125)

According to White, by the time children have reached the latency period they have progressed in competence and in the maturation of the organism to the point where they are no longer satisfied with exploration, play, and make-believe. In line with their interest in being adults, children need to feel useful and to be able to make things and deal with things that have significance in the adult world. And, of course, they go from this state to that called genital, in which they really begin to assume the roles and responsibilities of an adult.

In closing this section on White, it is important that you recognize his endorsement of the developmental stages and character types suggested by Erikson and his spirited argument that they are more naturally derived from a fulfillment model stressing effectance and competence than from a conflict model stressing sexuality and compromise. Although Adler and White have similar views of the core of personality, White has a more elaborate, differentiated view of the periphery of personality.

Allport's Position

Allport, like Murray, has given considerable attention to the problem of determining the best way to conceptualize peripheral characteristics. But reaching a rather different conclusion than Murray, Allport has chosen for his major peripheral characteristic something resembling a trait or grouping of habits. Originally he (Allport, 1937) called his concept the *personal trait* but later renamed it the *personal disposition* (Allport, 1961, p. 273), defined as "a generalized neuropsychic structure (peculiar to the individual), with the capacity to render many stimuli functionally equivalent, and to initiate and guide consistent (equivalent) forms of adaptive and stylistic behavior." I will compare the personal disposition to Murray's need concept, as Murray is the other personologist considered thus far who takes the concrete implications of his peripheral concepts seriously enough to offer careful definitions and detailed descriptions.

First let us consider the presumed effects of personal dispositions on the person's functioning. Allport indicates that the personal disposition operates by producing equivalence in function and meaning among perceptions, interpretations, feelings, and actions not necessarily equivalent in the natural world. In discussing this influence, Allport (1961, p. 322) develops the following example. While Russians, college professors, liberals, peace organizations, and antisegregationists may seem different to many observers, to a person with the personal disposition *fear of communism,* all of these stimulus configurations may be equivalent in their perceived "communist" properties. Such a personal disposition would also engender response sequences that are equivalent in their function of reducing the perceived threat of communism. The person might advocate war with the Russians, be suspicious of teachers, vote for extreme right-wing persons and policies, join the Ku Klux Klan, and so forth. Stimulus and response equivalences are identified on the basis of perceived meanings and related coping behaviors rather than on any necessarily obvious similarities. Although similar to the personal disposition in some respects, the need concept stresses to a greater degree the directional organization of behavior, with a sequence of acts that are instrumental to reaching a goal, followed by acts that involve consummation of the goal.

Another way of stating this difference between the personal disposition and the need concept is to say that the latter is more motivational than the former. For the need, the equivalences of functioning produced are closely tied to the goal the person is trying to achieve, to what might be called the "why" of behavior. Hence, need-produced behavior shows waxing and waning corresponding to whether the need is aroused or satisfied. In contrast, the personal disposition, like other trait concepts, is a steady, unvarying entity, exerting a continuous influence on functioning. There is little waxing and waning because, properly speaking, there is no goal to be striven for and reached. The personal disposition concept seems to give a larger place to the "what" and "how" of behavior than does the need concept. But care must be taken not to conclude that Allport is uninterested in motivation. Actually, he (Allport, 1961, p. 370) considers all personal dispositions as having greater or less intention included within them, calling them *dynamic* and *stylistic,* respectively (pp. 222–223). All in all, dynamic personal dispositions are reminiscent of needs, whereas stylistic dispositions may be somewhat like Murray's need-integrates (see Chapter 7).

The next difference concerns the disposition of tension. The need functions according to some variety of the tension reduction principle, virtually by logical necessity, whereas most personal dispositions are considered as not having tension reduction as an aim. This difference is not to be construed as indicating that Allport's concept must lack motivational significance, however, as for him motivation is, in its most important or propriate sense, somewhat synonymous with conscious intent rather than a tension state (Allport 1961, pp. 222–225).

Having covered some of the implications of the personal disposition concept, we can now turn to an emphasis of overwhelming importance for Allport. He believes that each personal disposition is unique to the person being studied. Actually, Allport (1961, p. 349) includes in his peripheral theorizing the less important concept of *common trait* to account for the similarities attributable to possession of a common human nature and a common culture. But the common trait, though an admissible and useful concept, is for him an abstraction arrived at by generalizing across people, and hence it necessarily misses the actual dispositions of each person to some degree. The real personality is considered as emerging only when personal dispositions are assessed, and this requires intensive study of a person's past, present, and anticipated future functioning through the use of such techniques as the case history and content analysis of personal documents (Allport, 1961, pp. 367–369; Allport, 1962). Allport (Allport & Odbert, 1936) has been unwilling to narrow the number of dispositions any further than the combinations that would be possible using the 18,000 or so common trait names in the English language.

Given the emphasis on uniqueness, it is not at all surprising that Allport nowhere offers any list of usual personal dispositions. The closest he comes to specifying the typical content of personal dispositions is to suggest two bases for classifying them. One classification (Allport, 1961, p. 365) involves the pervasiveness and consistency with which personal dispositions influence functioning. Distinctions are made among cardinal, central, and secondary dispositions. *Cardinal dispositions,* if they exist in a personality, will set the entire pattern of a person's life. *Central dispositions,* possessed by virtually all people, are significant stabilizing features of functioning. *Secondary dispositions* produce relatively transient organization. The other classificatory principle is less clear and bears some resemblance to that just described. It refers to the degree to which a disposition is at the core of a person's being (Allport,

1961, p. 264). Application of this principle leads to the Lewinian distinction between the *genotypical* and *phenotypical* disposition. The latter, though it involves some regularity in responses, is less a reflection of the essential nature of personality that lies behind the responses than is the former. But Allport's discussion is sketchy, and it is not entirely clear what difference there is between genotypical and cardinal dispositions on the one hand and phenotypical and central dispositions on the other. You should also recognize that what little attempt Allport has made to organize or categorize personal dispositions is not for purposes of delineating types or styles of living. This absence of emphasis on types may also be due to his extreme position on uniqueness.

If one person's personal dispositions may be entirely different from others' how can you make lists of dispositions and organize them into types? And yet, while Allport is being true to the logic of his assumption concerning uniqueness in not offering lists of dispositions and a typology, he certainly has delivered into our hands a viewpoint on the periphery of personality that is very difficult to employ in any concrete way. About all Allport really gives us to go on in using his position is the notion that dispositions can be identified by the fact that they produce stimulus and response equivalences. But this is hardly enough. Human functioning is sufficiently complex so that without the benefit of more concrete guidelines, stimulus and response equivalences can be found at many different levels and in many different ways. Each investigator is thrown completely on his or her own artistry in each diagnosis of a disposition. An investigator cannot derive much assistance from others' diagnoses or even from his or her own prior diagnoses. And one certainly cannot predict in advance of observation what any person's dispositions will be like. Nor can one be entirely sure that one is even using the personal disposition concept in the manner Allport intended.

But Allport, like Murray, must at least be given credit for having carefully delineated the nature, if not the content, of his peripheral characteristic and having attempted to describe the manner in which it influences functioning. Such theoretical care concerning peripheral characteristics is a valuable commodity on the personological scene. It is the kind of care that could lead to viewpoints so well developed and specified as to make their use and empirical testing really possible. But unfortunately, Allport's theoretical efforts have fallen short of this goal of usability and empirical testability because of his extreme emphasis on the uniqueness of personal dispositions. Certainly, then, we should carefully consider the reasons for his heavy emphasis in attempting to determine whether it is really necessary. But I shall defer this consideration until Chapter 10.

What remains for discussion here is the nature of the relationship between personal dispositions (the periphery of personality) and propriate functions (the core of personality). Allport virtually has never discussed this relationship directly, so I shall have to piece together what seem like relevant implications.

In his earliest statement of the proprium, Allport (1955, pp. 41–56) makes it quite clear that it comprises general, pervasive functions or capabilities that are common to all humans and have little in the way of structure or fixed content. If this is so, personal dispositions clearly are not to be considered part of the proprium per se, representing as they do structural bases for lumping together certain stimuli and responses in a manner particular to one person alone. But later Allport (1961, pp. 110–138) leaves one uncertain as to whether or not the proprium includes structural considerations. If it does, cardinal and genotypical dispositions, which are so general, might actually be included as part of the core of personality. But this is not likely to be Allport's true intent, for he also seems to suggest that personality structure is formed out of the interaction between propriate functions and environmental contexts.

A much more likely and useful position would be to consider that the propriate functions, which comprise the core tendencies and characteristics, are not themselves combinations of dispositions but the major forces precipitating and combining with the person's life experiences to form dispositions. For example, *propriate striving* would refer to the universal propensity for phenomenally important intentioning or, more simply, for working hard to reach goals that seem personally significant. Because of propriate striving, it would be possible to develop cardinal and central dispositions with dynamic properties. Cardinal—and, for that matter, even genotypical—dispositions would not, then, stand at the core of personality; rather, they would be the most general and pervasive of a person's dispositions. No matter how general and pervasive, however, dispositions would be peripheral by comparison with propriate functions. In this manner, cardinal and genotypical dispositions could be put to their intended use of pinpointing individuality, because if considered part of the periphery they would not have to be common to all persons.

A personality theory is a changing, growing thing, and it may well be that Allport was moving in the direction I have suggested above. He was perhaps attempting to conceptualize components of personality that seem to be sets of personal dispositions that reflect the qualities of propriate functioning. Examples of this type of unit are his characteristics of maturity (Allport, 1961, pp. 275–307), such as specific, enduring *extension of the self*, techniques for *warm relating to others* (such as tolerance), stable *emotional security* or self-acceptance, habits of *realistic perception, skills* and *problem centeredness,* established *self-objectification* in the form of *insight* and *humor,* and a unifying *philosophy of life* that includes particular *value orientations,* differentiated *religious sentiment,* and a generic, *personalized conscience.* If I see his movement accurately, Allport, in describing the characteristics of maturing, was breaking out of the trap of overemphasis on uniqueness. The end result of doing so might have been a classification of personality types achieved along content lines and reflecting the concrete ramifications in behavior of the core tendency of propriate functioning.

As personal dispositions are clearly learned, it is important to ask how this learning takes place. First, you must recognize that personal dispositions are expressive of propriate functioning, if for no other reason than that they describe individuality. But initially the infant's functioning is opportunistic rather than propriate. Opportunistic functioning is regulated by, and in the service of, needs of a biological nature. At this level of functioning infants have little freedom of choice, reacting to pressures rather than being themselves a force in the world. If children receive the support, love, and nourishment they need at this early stage, they will begin to develop the kernels of selfhood. This means that there will be a shift from opportunistic to propriate functioning and, as you know (see Chapter 4), propriate functioning is proactive rather than reactive, being regulated by the person's own psychological goals, values, and principles—the stuff of personal dispositions.

Probably early opportunistic striving provides the basis for what later becomes personal dispositions. Allport suggests that the original opportunistic strivings are expressed in certain patterns of action that come into being because they are useful in satisfying these strivings. But once the person has matured a bit and been sufficiently nurtured and supported by other people, opportunistic goals recede in importance because they can be satisfied readily and their existence is not a source of anxiety. The instrumental action patterns do not necessarily atrophy, however, even though they are no longer needed since the opportunistic goals are less important. Some of the action patterns become *functionally autonomous* (Allport, 1961, p. 229) of their origins and continue to exist as personal dispositions. The action patterns that continue to exist in this fashion are probably those that best articulate with the general propriate functions, which, you may recall, include such things as self-identity and self-extension.

In his famous phrase, *functional autonomy,* Allport wished to convey his belief that action patterns, including values, opinions, and goals, are not limited in importance simply because they may have started out in the service of some biological need that is no longer central. But Allport often has been criticized for vagueness in delineating the concept of functional autonomy: How does it work? What are its implications? What is the organismic basis for such an idea? Allport recently has attempted to clarify and specify the concept somewhat. He suggests that propriate functional autonomy comes about because the presumed energy potential the human possesses exceeds that contributed by survival needs, and hence there is an ongoing tendency to utilize this excess by increasing competence and pressing toward a unification of life (Allport, 1961, pp. 249–253).

Allport's thinking concerning specific mechanisms whereby functional autonomy takes place remains somewhat vague, and thus provides a number of bases for controversy. He has not circumvented the repeated criticism that functional autonomy is more of an assertion than an explanation, although he (Allport, 1961) does suggest that an extremely critical reception indicates an already closed mind to his concept, which, he says,

> is merely a way of stating that men's motives change and grow in the course of life, because it is the nature of man that they should do so. Only theorists wedded to a reactive, homeostatic, quasi-closed model of man find difficulty in agreeing. (pp. 252–253).

Fromm's Position

Fromm is one of the most sophisticated and perhaps the most complete of the personologists on the nature of the periphery of personality. His concrete peripheral characteristic is the *character trait*, and he has described *orientations* or character types that comprise sets of interrelated traits. Profoundly influenced by Freud, Fromm (1947) tends to compare and contrast his own view with that of the conflict theorist:

> The theory presented . . . follows Freud's characterology in essential points: in the assumption that character traits underlie behavior and must be inferred from it; that they constitute forces which, though powerful, the person may be entirely unconscious of. It follows Freud also in the assumption that the fundamental entity in characters is not the single character trait but the total character organization from which a number of single character traits follow. These character traits are to be understood as a syndrome which results from a particular organization or, as I shall call it, orientation of character. (p. 57)

You may recognize that not only Fromm and Freud but also Adler and Erikson are in rather explicit agreement on the assumptions stated so clearly above. In addition, such personologists as White, Murray, and Allport would probably agree, though their emphases on particular traits or needs rather than on types lead to some uncertainty. The note in the above quote that sounds new to our discussion is the recognition that there is a difference between a character trait and the behavior it is used to explain. As I will argue in Chapter 10, it is important for personologists to recognize this, because doing so will lead them to focus on what are the data, after all, that they want to explain. Any theorist should take this matter seriously, but the personologist often does not. Fromm makes clear what must be true for all personologists, namely, that the peripheral characteristic of personality is an explanatory concept—something the theorist devised—rather than a mere description of the observational facts.

Now to the content of Fromm's position on the periphery of personality. His character types are four *nonproductive orientations* and one *productive orientation*. In the nonproductive classification, there are the *receptive, exploitative, hoarding,* and *marketing orientations*. In Fromm's (1947) words, the person with a receptive orientation

> feels "the source of all good" to be outside, and he believes that the only way to get what he wants—be it something material, be it affection, love, knowledge, pleasure—is to receive it from that outside source. In this orientation the problem of love is almost exclusively that of "being loved" and not that of loving. Such people tend to be indiscriminate in the choice of their love objects, because being loved by anybody is such an overwhelming experience for them that they "fall for" anybody who gives them love or what looks like love . . . . Their orientation is the same in the sphere of thinking: if intelligent, they make the best listeners, since their orientation is one of receiving, not of producing, ideas . . . . They show a particular kind of loyalty, at the bottom of which is the

gratitude for the hand that feeds them and the fear of ever losing it . . . . It is difficult for them to say "no," and they are easily caught between conflicting loyalties and promises. . . .

They are dependent not only on authorities for knowledge and help but on people in general for any kind of support. . . . This receptive type has great fondness for food and drink. These persons tend to overcome anxiety and depression by eating and drinking . . . . By and large, the outlook of people in this receptive orientation is optimistic and friendly; they have a certain confidence in life and its gifts, but they become anxious and distraught when their "source of supply" is threatened. (pp. 62–63)

Fromm has added to this vivid description a concrete list of the traits comprising the receptive orientation. These traits have a positive and negative pole, that is, they sound more admirable at one pole than at the other. Fromm includes both poles because he feels that the more deeply your personality reflects the nonproductive, receptive type, the better will the negative poles of the traits describe your behavior. But if the receptive orientation is mitigated by some degree of a more productive orientation, the positive poles of the traits will be more accurate. I will return to this point after we have viewed all the orientations. For the moment, we should focus on the list of traits, which is as follows (Fromm, 1947, p. 114):

Receptive Orientation	
Positive Aspect	*Negative Aspect*
Accepting	Passive, without initiative
Responsive	Opinionless, characterless
Devoted	Submissive
Modest	Without pride
Charming	Parasitical
Adaptable	Unprincipled
Socially adjusted	Servile, without self-confidence
Idealistic	Unrealistic
Sensitive	Cowardly
Polite	Spineless
Optimistic	Wishful thinking
Trusting	Gullible
Tender	Sentimental

You probably can imagine what Fromm means by the *exploitative orientation*. He describes it this way (Fromm, 1947):

The exploitative orientation, like the receptive, has as its basic premise the feeling that the source of all good is outside, that whatever one wants to get must be sought there, and that one cannot produce anything oneself. The difference between the two, however, is that the exploitative type does not expect to receive things from others as gifts, but to take them away from others by force or cunning. . . . In the realm of love and affection these people tend to grab and steal. They feel attracted only to people whom they can take away from somebody else. . . . We find the same attitude with regard to thinking and intellectual pursuits. Such people will tend not to produce ideas but to steal them. . . . They use and exploit anybody and anything from whom or from which they can squeeze something. . . . This orientation seems to be symbolized by the biting mouth which is often a prominent feature in such people. (pp. 64–65)

A list of character traits is also included for the exploitative orientation (Fromm, 1947, p. 115):

Exploitative Orientation

Positive Aspect	*Negative Aspect*
Active	Exploitative
Able to take initiative	Aggressive
Able to make claims	Egocentric
Proud	Conceited
Impulsive	Rash
Self-confident	Arrogant
Captivating	Seducing

The third nonproductive style of life is the *hoarding orientation*. Once again Fromm (1947) vividly describes this orientation:

While the receptive and exploitative types are similar inasmuch as both expect to get things from the outside world, the hoarding orientation is essentially different. This orientation makes people have little faith in anything new they might get from the outside world; their security is based upon hoarding and saving, while spending is felt to be a threat. They have surrounded themselves, as it were, by a protective wall, and their main aim is to bring as much as possible into this fortified position and to let as little as possible out of it. Their miserliness refers to money and material things as well as to feelings and thoughts. Love is essentially a possession: they do not give love but try to get it by possessing the "beloved. . . ." Their sentimentality makes the past appear as golden; they hold on to it and indulge in the memories of bygone feelings and experiences. . . . One can recognize these people too by facial expression and gestures. Theirs is the tight-lipped mouth; their gestures are characteristic of their withdrawal attitude. . . . Another characteristic element in this attitude is pedantic orderliness. The hoarder will be orderly with things, thoughts, or feelings, but again, as with memory, his orderliness is sterile and rigid. . . . His compulsive cleanliness is another expression of his need to undo contact with the outside world. (pp. 65–66)

The list of character traits comprising the hoarding orientation is as follows (Fromm, 1947, p. 115):

Hoarding Orientation	
Positive Aspect	*Negative Aspect*
Practical	Unimaginative
Economical	Stingy
Careful	Suspicious
Reserved	Cold
Patient	Lethargic
Cautious	Anxious
Steadfast, tenacious	Stubborn
Imperturbable	Indolent
Composed under stress	Inert
Orderly	Pedantic
Methodical	Obsessional
Loyal	Possessive

It should not have escaped your attention that the three orientations described thus far are similar in some ways to Freudian character types. Both the receptive and exploitative orientations are reminiscent of the oral character type. And indeed, if one follows some psychoanalytic thinkers, such as Abraham (1927a, 1927b), who distinguish between oral-incorporative and oral-aggressive character types, the fit becomes even closer. Oral-incorporativeness resembles the receptive orientation, and oral-aggressiveness seems like the exploitative orientation. In addition, the hoarding orientation is quite reminiscent of the anal character type.

These similarities should not surprise you, for Fromm started out as a psychoanalytic thinker, though he gradually developed a very different view. The existence in his theory of the first three orientations indicates that Fromm found some Freudian statements concerning the periphery of personality to be warranted. But, as you will see next, he does include some orientations that have no counterpart in psychoanalytic thinking. If you add to this the fact that Fromm is very different from Freud at the core level of personality, you will see that it is a mistake to consider Fromm a neo-Freudian thinker. Even though he admits the value of some of Freud's statements concerning character types, Fromm explains their development on grounds that have nothing to do with psychosexuality.

I will consider Fromm's developmental views in a moment, but for now, let us return to a consideration of the remaining orientations.

The final nonproductive style of life is the *marketing orientation,* and in delineating it, Fromm expresses much of his originality as a personality theorist. Fromm (1947) takes the modern marketplace as the model for this orientation, which involves the person's being reduced to a commodity:

> The modern market is no longer a meeting place but a mechanism characterized by abstract and impersonal demand. One produces for this market, not for a known circle of customers; its verdict is based on laws of supply and demand; and it determines whether the commodity can be sold and at what price . . . . The character orientation which is rooted in the experience of oneself as a commodity and of one's value as exchange value I call the marketing orientation.
>
> In our time the marketing orientation has been growing rapidly, together with the development of a new market that is a phenomenon of the last decades—the "personality market." . . . The principle of evaluation is the same on both the personality and the commodity market: on the one, personalities are offered for sale; on the other, commodities. Value in both cases is their exchange value, for which use value is a necessary but not a sufficient condition . . . . However, if we ask what the respective weight of skill and personality as a condition for success is, we find that only in exceptional cases is success predominantly the result of skill and of certain other human qualities like honesty, decency, and integrity. Although the proportion between skill and human qualities on the one hand and "personality" on the other hand as prerequisites for success varies, the "personality factor" always plays a decisive role. Success depends largely on how well a person sells himself on the market, how well he gets his personality across, how nice a "package" he is; whether he is "cheerful," "sound," "aggressive," "reliable," "ambitious"; furthermore what his family background is, what club he belongs to, and whether he knows the right people . . . . Like the handbag, one has to be in fashion on the personality market, and in order to be in fashion one has to know what kind of personality is most in demand . . . . Since modern man experiences himself both as the seller and as the commodity to be sold on the market, his self-esteem depends on conditions beyond his control. If he is "successful," he is valuable; if he is not, he is worthless. The degree of insecurity which results from this orientation can hardly be overestimated. If one feels that one's value is not constituted primarily by the human qualities one possesses, but by one's success on a competitive market with ever-changing conditions, one's self-esteem is bound to be shaky and in constant need of confirmation by others. Hence one is driven to strive relentlessly for success, and any setback is a severe threat to one's self-esteem; helplessness, insecurity, and inferiority feelings are the result. If the vicissitudes of the market are the judges of one's value, the sense of dignity and pride is destroyed. (pp. 68–72)

The marketing orientation underlies the problem of alienation that has been so vivid in the minds of contemporary social critics, sociologists, and personologists. This orientation is clearly different from anything Freud considered, and yet seems quite valid in contemporary life. The character traits comprising the marketing orientation are as follows (Fromm, 1947, p. 116):

Marketing Orientation

Positive Aspect	Negative Aspect
Purposeful	Opportunistic
Able to change	Inconsistent
Youthful	Childish
Forward-looking	Without a future or a past
Open-minded	Without principle and values
Social	Unable to be alone
Experimenting	Aimless
Undogmatic	Relativistic
Efficient	Overactive
Curious	Tactless
Intelligent	Intellectualistic
Adaptable	Undiscriminating
Tolerant	Indifferent
Witty	Silly
Generous	Wasteful

Having discussed the four nonproductive orientations, we now come to what Fromm considers to be the ideal character type—the productive orientation. As you will see, the productive orientation bears similarity to the Freudian genital character—and to the fully functioning or self-actualizing personalities of Rogers and Maslow, as well as to the active-constructive style of life of the Adlerians—and the mature personality according to Allport. Once again I will let Fromm (1947) speak for himself in describing the *productive orientation:*

> In discussing the *productive character* I venture beyond critical analysis and inquire into the nature of the fully developed character that is the aim of human development and simultaneously the ideal of humanistic ethics. . . . The "productive orientation" of personality refers to a fundamental attitude, a *mode of relatedness* in all realms of human experience. It covers mental, emotional, and sensory responses to others, to oneself, and to things. Productiveness is man's ability to use his powers and to realize the potentialities inherent in him. If we say *he* must use *his* powers we imply that he must be free and not dependent on someone who controls his powers. We imply, furthermore, that he is guided by reason, since he can make use of his powers only if he knows what they are, how to use them, and what to use them for. Productiveness means that he experiences himself as the embodiment of his powers and as the "actor"; that he feels himself one with his powers and at the same time that they are not marked and alienated from him . . . . Productiveness is man's realization of the potentialities characteristic of him, the use of his *powers.* . . . How is man related to the world when he uses his powers productively?. . . . The world outside oneself can be experienced in two ways: reproductively by perceiving actuality in the same fashion as a film makes a literal record of things photo-

graphed . . . and *generatively* by conceiving it, by enlivening and recreating this new material through the spontaneous activity of one's own mental and emotional powers . . . . Human existence is characterized by the fact that man is alone and separated from the world; not being able to stand the separation, he is impelled to seek for relatedness and oneness. There are many ways in which he can realize this need, but only one in which he, as a unique entity, remains intact; only one in which his own powers unfold in the very process of being related. It is the paradox of human existence that man must simultaneously seek for closeness and for independence; for oneness with others and at the same time for the preservation of his uniqueness and particularity. As we have shown, the answer to this paradox—and to the moral problem of man—is *productiveness.*

One can be productively related to the world by acting and by comprehending. Man *produces things,* and in the process of creation he exercises his powers over matter. Man *comprehends the world,* mentally and emotionally, through love and through reason. His power of reason enables him to penetrate through the surface and grasp the essence of his object by getting into active relation with it. His power of love enables him to break through the wall which separates him from another person and to comprehend him. Although love and reason are only two different forms of comprehending the world and although neither is possible without the other, they are expressions of different powers, that of emotion and that of thinking, and hence must be discussed separately. (pp. 83–97)

Fromm lists no set traits that compose the productive orientation. This is partly because he feels that the truly productive person would not be predictable enough to be pinned down to fixed traits. By productiveness, after all, he mean's not sticking to a job or acting in a repetitive way but something more like creativity and transcendence. But there are certainly some traits, such as imaginativeness, that one could list for the productive orientation, so the reason of unpredictability cannot be sufficient to explain why Fromm chooses not to offer a list of traits. The rest of the reason lies in the relationship he suggests between the productive and nonproductive orientations. According to Fromm, it is very unlikely that anyone would show a completely developed productive orientation. In this Fromm is much like Rogers, who indicates that the fully functioning person is an ideal characterization of life, not actually achieved in toto by anyone. What one normally finds, according to Fromm, is some combination of productive and nonproductive orientations. This is why Fromm bothered to include positive along with negative poles for the traits composing the nonproductive orientations. The more the productive orientation is combined with the nonproductive one, the more accurate will be the positive poles of the traits composing the nonproductive orientation. Thus, the positive aspects of the traits listed under nonproductive orientations can be used to characterize the productive qualities of a person's style of life.

As I mentioned in introducing the discussion of the productivity orientation, it bears resemblance to the ideal peripheral personality of a number of other theorists. Now you can probably see what I meant. The emphasis on actualizing one's capabilities and being creative is similar to Rogers and Maslow. The emphasis on concrete productions and the orientation toward perfection are similar to White and Adler. The emphasis on reason and love is similar to Allport's discussion of psychological maturity. And, although the quotes I selected do not play it up, there is similarity to Freud in the fact that mature sexuality, in the sense of orgasm and progeny, are also considered productive. That Fromm's views are similar not only to other fulfillment theorists but to some conflict theorists reflects at the peripheral level the classificatory problem we had with him at the core level (see Chapter 4). Although Fromm is primarily a fulfillment theorist, he incorporates elements of the conflict emphasis as well.

Before leaving Fromm, we should consider his view of development, or the way in which the various orientations can come about through the interaction between the core tendency and the environments in which it is expressed. As I indicated before, Fromm's view of development is very different from Freud's. First, the core tendency is different. For Fromm, a person's life is basically an attempt to realize human nature, which includes, you will remember, such needs as those for relatedness, transcendence, and identity. Psychosexuality plays a small part in all this. The second divergence from Freud is in the nature of the parent-child interaction that is considered important in understanding the resultant peripheral personality types. For Fromm, the three important types of interaction are *symbiotic relatedness, withdrawal-destructiveness,* and *love* (Fromm, 1947, pp. 107–108). In the symbiotic situation,

> the person is related to others but loses or never attains his independence; he avoids the danger of aloneness by becoming part of another person, either by being "swallowed" by that person or by "swallowing" him.

Being swallowed by parents, as it were, leads to the masochistic patterns of behavior culminating in the receptive orientation. This whole pattern is encouraged by parents who render the child dependent on them but in the specially violating way that entails laying oneself bare to be used by others in one's search for satisfaction. But if the reverse situation occurs—if the parents abnegate authority to the child by catering to its every whim and encouraging it to use them—the resulting pattern will be more like sadism. This sadism in the child will culminate in the exploitative orientation, expressing as it does dependence on others for purposes of violating them.

The symbiotic relationship is one of closeness to and intimacy with the other person, though at the expense of freedom and integrity. In contrast, the withdrawal-destructiveness type of parent-child relationship is characterized by *distance*. According to Fromm (1947):

> In the phenomenon here described, withdrawal becomes the main form of relatedness to others, a negative relatedness, as it were. Its emotional equivalent is the feeling of indifference toward others, often accompanied by a compensatory feeling of self-inflation. (pp. 109–110)

This withdrawal pattern, which will culminate in the marketing orientation, is encouraged by parents who are destructive toward the child. In other words, they will not simply frustrate its needs but will attempt to subjugate and destroy it. In the face of such an onslaught, the child will cope with the sense of powerlessness by retreating and becoming indifferent. But the destructiveness that engenders withdrawal need not be on the parents' part. Indeed, if the parents are indifferent and withdrawn from the child, it may well develop the pattern of destructiveness, which, according to Fromm (1947, p. 110) is the active form of withdrawal. The resulting pattern of assertiveness will culminate in the hoarding orientation.

As you undoubtedly have anticipated, when the parent-child relationship is one of love, with all its implications of mutual respect, support, and appreciation, children will develop in the direction of productive orientation. Loved by their parents, children will love themselves and will have no reason not to love others.

It is as members of their culture that parents affect their children, and hence one may expect each of the various orientations to be prominent under a particular set of cultural conditions. Fromm feels that the receptive, exploitative, and hoarding orientations were especially characteristic of the eighteenth and nineteenth centuries, though they are by no means absent now. He dates their prominence thusly because they require a form of society in which one group has an institutionalized right to exploit another group. Since the exploited group has no power to change, or any idea of changing its situation, it will tend to look up to its masters as its providers—hence the receptive orientation. The societal model for the exploitative character goes back to piratical and feudal ancestors and goes forward from there to the robber barons of the ninteenth century who exploited the continent's natural resources. "The hoarding orientation," according to Fromm (1947, p. 81), "existed side by side with the exploitative orientation in the eighteenth and nineteenth centuries. The hoarding type was conservative, less interested in ruthless acquisition than in methodical economic pursuits, based on sound principles and on the preservation of what had been acquired." Fromm associates the hoarding orientation with the Protestant ethic. But the marketing orientation has reached a position of predominance only in the twentieth century, with its emphasis on the modern marketplace and its materialistic, superficial values. And, as you might expect, the societal model consistent with the productive orientation has not yet emerged on the world scene, according to Fromm. It is describable, however, and would, in a phrase, suit the human needs of persons rather than the economic needs of the marketplace. It would be a truly *sane* society (Fromm, 1955).

It is with some disquietude that I conclude this discussion of Fromm's position on the periphery of personality. Of the theorists thus far covered, he has been by far the most explicit and complete concerning traits and orientations. No one else has endeavored to actually list the traits that constitute the character types he wishes to consider. While it is true that Murray and Allport have given more care to the delineation and definition of their peripheral characteristics of need and personal disposition, Fromm surpasses them in organizing traits into types. One has the feeling that someone could easily provide precise definitions for the traits he employs. All this pleases me greatly about Fromm. It should be possible to determine the empirical fruitfulness of Fromm's position, because he has gone a long way toward the theoretical formalism necessary for making a position really usable. But for all this, I find myself disappointed that I am not particularly enlightened or convinced by his account of development. Sometimes he suggests that children will develop in manners opposite to the ways they have been treated by their parents. This is seen in the notion that parents who "swallow up" their offspring will produce children who ask the world to swallow them. But at other times, he suggests that children will develop in a manner similar to that of the parents or of the society that they represent. This seems implicit in such notions as that the existence in society of a downtrodden class was necessary as a model for the receptive orientation. But if you were a member of this downtrodden class, would you, according to Fromm, swallow up your children or encourage them to swallow you? Common sense suggests the latter, and yet knowledge that classes tend to perpetuate themselves indicates the former. Fromm himself seems unable to decide. I do not want to make too much of this criticism, as the difficulty can, after all, be resolved. It is a matter for future theoretical effort. All in all, I commend Fromm's position to you as an excellent example of peripheral theorizing, regardless of whether or not it turns out to be supported by empirical evidence.

Existential Psychology

Although there are implications in existential thought that could lead to a position on peripheral personality, existentialists differ as to whether such theorizing is worthwhile. Binswanger (1963) and Boss (1963), at one extreme, say very little that is explicit, systematic, or formal about development, types, and peripheral characteristics. To be sure, their discussions of authentic as opposed to inauthentic being definitely imply two general styles of operating. But nowhere do they explicate these implications, probably believing, with the actualization fulfillment theorists, that to do so would be inconsistent with their overall emphasis on freedom. Less extreme is Keen (1970), who, though not offering a position on peripheral personality per se, does indicate something of the form development takes in early life. At the other extreme are Kobasa and Maddi (1977; Maddi, 1967, 1970), who elaborate on two main personality types and several transitional types, all complete with a developmental history linking core to periphery. What follows will be based largely on the writings of Keen, Kobasa, and Maddi, but you are cautioned to recognize that though they believe themselves to be working in the spirit of existentialism, there are others in that tradition who would disagree.

As you will recall from Chapter 4, existential psychologists emphasize the difference between facing ontological anxiety and guilt squarely and lying to yourself. When you lie, you act as if life were not a series of decisions that you have the responsibility for making, relying instead on the erroneous belief that certain forces acting on you constitute necessities. But if you remain honest or authentic, you realize that these forces are actually only possibilities that you can choose to be affected by or to transcend. This process of creating your own life heavily involves the use of mental powers in what Gendlin (1965–1966) calls the *explication of experience* and Bugental (1976) the *search for identity*. The two main personality types Kobasa and Maddi (1977) propose essentially state the differences between authentic and inauthentic being as styles or habitual predispositions, though their terminology is sometimes a little different from that above.

At the core level, Kobasa and Maddi (1977) postulate the presence of biological, social, and psychological needs, considering this consistent with the conceptualization in existential theorizing of *Umwelt, Mitwelt,* and *Eigenwelt* (see Chapter 4). It is the psychological needs—for symbolizing, imagining, and judging—that carry that uniqueness of the human being, both as a species and as an individual. The more you symbolize, imagine, and judge, the greater and more unusual will be your storehouse of (1) categories with which to recognize, (2) ideas about desired change, and (3) values and preferences. But since biological and social needs are also parts of human nature, the best life will be that which vigorously expresses all three sets of needs.

The personality type that expresses inauthentic being comes about when the psychological needs have been defended against. Such persons make minimal use of symbolization, imagination, and judgment, which means that their thoughts are few, gross, and stereotyped. They do express biological and social needs but show the simplest, least subtle forms of them due to the relative absence of psychological expression. Maddi (1970) considers this personality type as showing biological and social reductionism, and labels it *conformism.* Why it is conformism is apparent in the self-definition (sense of identity) and the world view it entails. The conformist's *sense of identity* is as nothing more than a player of social roles and an embodiment of creature needs. The difficulty is not that persons are not these two things but that what they are in addition finds little representation in the conformist's self-definition.

Let us focus on social reductionism for a moment. If your *Mitwelt* (construed social world) is such that you view yourself as nothing more than a player of social roles, you are, in effect, accepting the idea that the social system is a terribly potent force in living, with institutions and laws that transcend individuals and have lives of their own. This inclines you to the belief that the current content and form of the social system is its necessary and unchangeable nature and that individuals have no choice but to conform to its pressures. In the long run, conforming to social system pressures even comes to appear morally worthwhile. You develop the conviction that it is the social system as currently constituted that protects everyone against chaos;

therefore, we all ought to do our share to support its institutions, however restricting they may be. The way to give this support is to play adequately the social roles given to you as a responsibility of citizenship.

There are parallel implications in biological reductionism. If your *Umwelt* (construed biological and physical world) is such that you view yourself as nothing more than an embodiment of creature needs, for you such needs as those for food and water are terribly important and real forces in living. Physical survival seems unquestionably of paramount importance, and hence the degree to which biological needs are satisfied is taken as the hallmark of adequate living. It becomes difficult to imagine justifying deprivation of these needs under any circumstances. Any alternative to direct, immediate, and constant expression of these needs—if an alternative could be construed as possible—would be unwise, because it would violate all that is important.

If your *Umwelt* and *Mitwelt* are characterized by biological and social reductionism, you must necessarily feel powerless in the face of social pressures from outside and biological pressures from inside. Creatureness and social roles seem like givens, like causal factors independent of your puny power to influence them. You will not experience life as a series of decisions willingly made. Indeed, you would never seriously reject a social role or change it. You would never think to question just how important physical survival is. Soon you will become your social roles and biological needs—there being no longer any act of consciousness worth speaking of to mark the fact that your identity is not the only one possible. There will be little basis for raising abstract questions about the nature of existence.

The generalization of your conformist identity into a world view potentiates your difficulties on a grand scale. This *world view* is based on pragmatism and materialism. The pragmatism comes primarily from viewing not only yourself but everyone else as having to play the assigned social roles. The only relevant question becomes how good the people are in enacting these roles. Materialism comes primarily from the belief that not only you but others are no more than embodiments of biological needs. This leads to coveting not only the goods that are objects of the needs (e.g., clothes to make one attractive) but the processes instrumental to obtaining them (e.g., making money). The pursuit of material things is elevated to the status of a natural process.

With this self-definition and world view, it is easy to see how the conformist would often be in conflict. The conflict is inherent in the likelihood that social roles and creature needs will lead in different, if not incompatible, directions. While social roles become institutionalized along the lines of what is socially acceptable, biological needs are defined in terms of animalistic urges, without regard for propriety. The only consciousness of self that conformists ever feel consistently has to do with their inability to satisfy both aspects of their identity with the same set of actions. They will try to assuage biological and social pressures at different times or in different places, keeping possible incompatibilities from the eyes of others and from direct confrontation in their own awareness. Their being-in-the-world will be fragmentary, disunified, a pastiche of bits and pieces.

The conformist's relationships with others are contractual rather than intimate. If you and everyone else are considered bound by certain rules of social interaction and in need of certain material goods for satisfaction and survival, relationships will tend to be based on the economic grounds of who is getting what from whom, when, and for how much. Conformists will not be willing to just let an interaction go in whatever direction that develops, nor will they be willing to continue or terminate it on the basis of how interesting or stimulating it is. Instead, they will want it structured in advance, and it will have to be clear all along what is in it for them in terms of social status or material advance. And once they get what they want, there will be no further reason for contact. Bonds of affection, loyalty, camaraderie, and love will not tend to develop in any meaningful sense. The conformist's relations will tend to be rather cold-blooded, even though the absence from them of intimacy and spontaneity will leave a nagging sense of loneliness and disappointment.

However unappetizing conformism seems, Maddi (1967, 1970) regards it not as frank psychopathology but as predisposition to psychopathology. Conformism is too common and livable to be regarded as sickness, though it has its own characteristic sufferings and limitations. The main disadvantage of conformism, according to Maddi, is that it renders the person vulnerable to certain stresses, whose occurrence can precipitate existential sickness. The stresses are those that can disrupt being-in-the-world by disconfirming one's self-definition as a player of social roles and an embodiment of biological needs. The three such stresses Maddi (1967, 1970) lists are the threat of imminent death, gross disruption of the social order, and repeated confrontation with the limitations on deep and comprehensive experiencing produced by conformism. The first of these has its disconfirming effect by demonstrating human finitude to someone who has, in stressing the paramount importance of physical survival, forgotten that he or she will die. The second disconfirms the belief in society as absolute to someone who has assumed it cannot change. The third is a direct disconfirmation of the conformist's being-in-the-world, usually occasioned by the strenuous objections of someone who is suffering because of his or her superficiality. The sickness resulting from such disconfirmations is called *existential* because in all its forms it reveals a breakdown in the ability to consider life meaningful and worthwhile (Maddi, 1967, 1970).

As you might expect, the personality type epitomizing authentic being is the opposite of conformism. In this ideal type, there is vigorous expression of psychological needs along with biological and social needs. This leads to biological and social experiencing showing considerable taste, subtlety, intimacy, and love due to the humanizing, organizing effects of symbolization, imagination, and judgment. This personality type is called *individualism* because the vigorous expression of psychological needs involves an extensive and unusual set of ideas about self and world (Maddi, 1967, 1970; Kobasa & Maddi, 1977).

True to what has been said, individualists define themselves (*sense of identity*) as persons with a mental life through which they can understand and influence their social and biological experience and urges. Although they recognize and accept social and biological pressures, they do not feel powerless in the face of them and experience considerable room to maneuver in the process of finding just the right life for themselves. They believe they are capable of choice and have freedom, though they are not so naïve as to think that there are no constraints on them, no necessities. They question whether things that seem constraints really are recalcitrant to influence.

Understandably, in their *world view* individualists see society as the creation of persons and as properly in their service. They believe humans to be unique among living things because their extraordinary mental powers make it possible for them to be masters of their own fates. Certainly the individualist will be realistic enough to recognize that social systems are not always responsive to their publics and that persons often act as if they believe themselves no different from the apes. But he or she will consider such social systems and such persons to be less than ideal, to have fallen short of what it is within human power to achieve. The value of this judgment is that it provides the individualist with a format for action. As an individualist, one may decide to withdraw from such inhuman societies and persons. Alternatively, one may try to convince the people that they are wrong and influence the social system through political action.

This ideal personality type is called the *individualist* with no connotations of a steely aloofness or indifference to others. Individualists are so designated because their actions and thoughts are relatively uncommon and expressive of psychological, rather than social or biological, needs. Actually, they will relate to others more deeply than will the conformist. They will substitute intimacy for contract. Just because their lives will be frequently changing and unfolding should not suggest lack of discipline or persistence. Do not be misled by the emphasis on subtlety, taste, intimacy, and love. More than anyone else, individualists will have standards, know what they want, and be willing and able to pursue their desires with rigor and self-reliance. They can even perform unpleasant tasks gracefully if these are definitely related to reaching the desired goals. And they will show the courage, born of a belief in their own power and dignity, to face ontological anxiety.

Certainly individualists sound like fine persons. But beyond this attractiveness, their value inheres in not being vulnerable to stress. Neither the threat of imminent death nor gross disruption of the social order would disconfirm the self-definition of individualists. The accumulated sense of superficiality in living would simply not occur and so would never be a problem. All in all, their being-in-the-world would be very hardy indeed (Maddi & Kobasa, 1984).

Like Rogers and Maslow, Maddi has postulated only two personality types, even though his general position emphasizes individuality so much that one would expect more types to be proposed. To be sure, the individualist type embodies the emphasis on individuality (with its implication of heterogeneity in behavior), but it must still be considered a drawback that the formal theorizing permits only two kinds of people to be distinguished. Probably there are several subtypes of individualist and conformist that can be distinguished. Perhaps one route would be to subdivide the conformist type according to whether biological or social needs are paramount in expression. And perhaps the individualist type could be subdivided into those who are primarily symbolizers, imaginers, or judgers. This separation of mental styles is a bit reminiscent of Jung's peripheral theorizing. Another drawback of Maddi's peripheral statement is that although types are proposed, there is no formal consideration of peripheral characteristics. Several are implied and perhaps could be more explicitly stated in the future.

As is common among existential psychologists, Maddi (1967, 1970) was at first quite sketchy about development. Existentialists generally assume that being-in-the-world is learned, but they do not take you beyond this truism to precise consideration of just how a particular style, as opposed to some other, develops. Fortunately, however, both Keen (1970) and Kobasa and Maddi (1977) have now taken the plunge into developmental theorizing. As it is the simpler of the two, Keen's account will be considered first.

Keen (1970) presents four developmental stages, which, though not tied to Maddi's personality types, are quite consistent with the general existential emphasis. The first stage is *fusion,* in which the distinction between subject and object has not been made by the child. The second stage is *separation,* which begins at the point during the first year when the child experiences itself as different from the rest. In the third stage, or *satellization,* "the child's experience of subjectness and objectness reverse themselves" (Keen, 1970, p. 41), and the child falls into orbit around the parents. Where it had been the triumphant center of gravity in the separation stage, the child must give ground to the superior judgment and power of adults, which amounts to emphasizing what Keen calls *being-for-others.* But in return, the child gains considerable security. And here Keen makes the interesting point, reminiscent of the Freudian position on how parents can avoid instilling fixations, that to stimulate the child's being-in-the-world, it is useful to apply mild punishment. While severe punishment renders the child unwilling to explore possibilities and lack of punishment does not allow possibilities to be recognized, mild punishment actually broadens the child's sense of alternatives and decreases acceptance of parentally endorsed options. The final stage then emerges as *similarity,* in which by age seven or so the child is beginning to assess accurately the degree to which it and the others (parents, siblings, peers) are alike and different.

This, of course, is the sound developmental path, culminating in authentic being or an individualistic style. But the major developmental hazards are pressures that lead the child toward lying. Although Keen is clear about how lying to others and oneself jeopardizes authentic being, he is unfortunately ambiguous about what brings this lying about. Presumably it is anything in parents and other significant adults that will interfere with the ideal developmental course mentioned above. The most serious interference, according to Keen, is too severe or insufficient punishment during the satellization stage such that the child never emerges from dependence on the wishes and beliefs of others. In delineating how authenticity comes about, Kobasa and Maddi (1977) distinguish between early and later development. In the former state, children are dependent on their parents and therefore quite impressionable, whereas the latter state involves development by self-initiation. When conditions are ideal, what differentiates early from later development is the emergence in the early period of *courage,* or what Kobasa and Maddi (Kobasa, 1979; Maddi & Kobasa, 1984) now call *hardiness.* If the conditions for development are faulty, hardiness will never be really learned and the self-initiation marking later development will be jeopardized.

There are several ways in which parents can instill hardiness in their children. They can (1) expose children to a richness and diversity of experience, (2) freely impose limits based on their own sense of what is meaningful in life, (3) love and respect their children as budding individuals, and (4) teach the value of vigorous symbolization, imagination, and judgment directly and by example. The role of the first activity is obvious: The greater the range and diversity of experience to which children are exposed, the more likely they will be to symbolize, imagine, and judge richly and complexly. This reaction on the children's part is all the more likely if parents are communicating the importance of construing richly and complexly. As indicated in the fourth point above, this communication can be made by parents as models when they are vigorously symbolizing, imagining, and judging in their own lives. The communication can be more didactic as well, even to the point of providing children with homey exercises. The imposition of limits mentioned above may appear out of place alongside the other seemingly more permissive techniques, but you should recognize that this emphasis is one reason why existential psychology is a perfection and not an actualization position. When the limits express the parents' sincere views on what makes life meaningful and worthwhile, when these do not therefore show spite or insecurity, and when they are applied with obvious love, they can be developmentally useful. Their usefulness is twofold: They provide an occasion to learn about *facticity* (unchangeable givens, you will recall), and they encourage energetic use of symbolization, imagination, and judgment in the attempt to circumvent the limits. All of these developmental conditions need to be enacted with love and respect for children as immature persons struggling to become individuals. It is not just any old love and respect that will work; rather, it must be tied to support of decision-making initiatives. In other words, the parents must show their affection by truly helping their children to become independent of them. Kobasa and Maddi (1977; Maddi & Kobasa, 1984) suggest that the best way to do this is to structure situations so that children will be encouraged to always reach just beyond their grasp. In this fashion, the children will not be lulled into prolonged dependency. But it is also necessary to shield children from failure in tasks that are obviously too demanding.

To the degree that these various developmental conditions are met in the early years, children will develop the beginnings of courage. In this sense, *courage* refers to a willingness to make decisions for the future (the unknown) and take responsibility for the outcomes. Persons are aided in this by the secure belief that if outcomes are unsatisfactory, they can exercise symbolization, imagination, and judgment in corrective decision making. If you believe that your life is partly of your own making, you can accept reversals because you can change them, too. Once this sense of courage or hardiness emerges, early development comes to an end. Kobasa and Maddi do not specify an age for this but seem to presume a time during adolescence for most persons, if later development occurs at all.

There are two developmental stages postulated for later development before the ultimate ideal of authenticity is reached. The first is called the *aesthetic orientation,* which takes place as soon as the person emerges from the bosom of the family. In a wider world with a freshly developed sense of freedom and self-reliance, persons with a good start are likely to become self-indulgent. They may use their decision-making powers for pleasure, reveling in the moment, exploiting others and the environment, and making no lasting commitments. This orientation is not merely passivity and dependency but the first (and therefore perhaps understandably misguided) attempt at independent functioning made by persons whose early developmental experiences have been beneficial. The self-indulgence of aestheticism comes about because their early child-rearing experiences, though necessary and beneficial, nonetheless have been strenuous. These children have had to strive and to assume responsibility, so they become hedonistic at the first opportunity.

Although aesthetically oriented persons derive pleasure through hedonism for a while, sooner or later they experience failure. All parties end at some point, and their enjoyment value does not outlive them. Relationships entered into with little commitment or discrimination also end quickly and are soon forgotten. What at first seemed like wonderful freedom becomes emptiness. Persons whose early development has instilled courage or hardiness in them will finally learn from these failures. Painfully, such persons realize that the trouble with self-centered aestheticism is that it involves living in the present only, as if the past and future were unimportant. Without commitment and planning, it is too easy to end up in loneliness and emptiness. The recognition dawns that aestheticism amounts to being controlled by others—whoever has the next party, the next person to fall in love with, some new political cause by which to be carried away. The aesthetic lifestyle that promised such independence is only a trap.

Having learned this, the person in the grips of self-determined development proceeds to the next phase—the *idealistic orientation.* The attempt now is to incorporate the future and the past into the present by making decisions as if current commitments and values have always been and always will be the same. Now when such persons love, they love forever. When they engage in political behavior, it is with the undying belief that lofty principles can actually be embodied in particular persons and particular events. In their zeal to correct their former errors, they fail to recognize that persons, situations, and emotional commitments change and that the relationship between ideals and practical occurrences is problematic.

Because persons with the idealistic orientation act as if they have complete control over events that in reality are too complex to be fully controlled by any individual, they inevitably encounter failure experiences. A love vowed eternally ends all the more painfully because its end was unexpected. Event after event forces recognition that complex social phenomena involve shifting loyalties, vested interests, and even accidental factors beyond one's control. Once again, failures spur development. With the deepening of insight on the limited control persons have over events and others, the idealistic orientation comes to an end and the period of *authentic being* begins. To the characteristics of individuality delineated by Maddi (1967, 1970), Kobasa and Maddi (1977) add a sense of the importance of integrating past, present, and future and an acceptance of the imperfect control that persons have over events and others. It is not clear, once again, what age is involved in the transition from idealism to authenticity. Although this undoubtedly is because the rate of self-initiated development differs for different persons, Kobasa and Maddi seem to imply a transition no earlier than middle adulthood.

Clearly persons who have developed courage are able to learn by failure. This is because they are not so overwhelmed by it that they must shrink defensively from its implications. A sharp contrast is drawn with persons whose developmental experiences have been inconsistent with the emergence of courage or hardiness. To see what these debilitating experiences would be, you need only consider the opposite of the four parental stances mentioned earlier. When persons do not develop hardiness, they remain in a prolonged period of early development, as it were. In other words, they remain dependent and passive even though they are advancing in years. They may even appear to have experiences reminiscent of aestheticism and idealism. But they are rather unable to learn by failing, since failure is so debilitating that it is never frankly confronted. They muddle through life, not engaged in any true developmental trajectory. As described earlier, they are conformists.

Ellis's Position

There is really nothing to say here regarding rational-emotive therapy. It simply has no peripheral statement. Positions that are primarily therapies and only secondarily personality theories de-emphasize typologies. As Ellis's approach is almost exclusively a therapy, it is in this sense not surprising that it overlooks styles of functioning. But what is surprising is that an approach so concerned with understanding human behavior could fail to provide an important part of the conceptual apparatus for doing so, whatever its main emphasis.

CHAPTER 9

The Periphery of Personality: Consistency Model

It became clear in Chapter 5 that at the core level of personality the consistency model does not emphasize content. Thus, rather than specifying an inherent human nature, it focuses on the interaction of persons with their environments. What remains to be determined is the model's disposition toward content at the periphery of personality. Interestingly, we shall see that of the three theories considered here, one fails to specify the content of peripheral characteristics, another is quite eclectic, and the third considers the kind of content that could well be learned in the pursuit of consistency.

CONSISTENCY MODEL: COGNITIVE DISSONANCE VERSION

Kelly's Position

Kelly's basic unit of personality is the *personal construct*. Personal constructs are organized into *construction systems,* which compose the personality. As you will recall from Chapter 5, Kelly offers the general definition of the construct as a dichotomous idea or abstraction. He also gives some notion of the basically hierarchical manner in which constructs are organized into systems. Constructs lie at the core of personality, for they do not differentiate one person from another. In order to have a position on the periphery of personality, Kelly could have tended to specify the content for sets of personal constructs defining the commonly encountered construction systems. Nowhere does he do this. Like Allport, Kelly is adamant on the uniqueness of people and the attendant uselessness of attempting to specify what they may be like in advance of actually encountering them. Each person is so different from the next, in Kelly's view, that the most a theorist can do is provide a consistent set of notions about the common units of personality and how they are organized. To presume that these units and organizations have typical content is to do violence to human uniqueness. Indeed, if Allport's recent specification of the contents of psychological maturity does indicate, as I have suggested, the first step in the development of a typology of character, he actually is less extreme in his insistence on individuality than is Kelly.

The closest Kelly comes to a position on the periphery of personality can be seen in two aspects of his theorizing: (1) the specification of different types of constructs in terms of their logical and functional properties and (2) the specification of techniques for identifying the content of persons' constructs once you have them concretely before you. As to the first point, many of the different types of constructs were mentioned in Chapter 5. You will recall the distinctions among such things as *constellatory, propositional,* and *preemptive constructs.* In addition, Kelly (1955, pp. 532–533) suggests that constructs can be *preverbal* (having no consistent word symbols to represent them), *comprehensive* (subsuming a wide variety of events), *incidental* (subsuming a narrow variety of events), *superordinate* (including other constructs as one of their elements), *subordinate* (being included as an element of other constructs), *tight* (leading to unvarying predictions), or *loose* (leading to varying predictions while maintaining their identity). Further, Kelly (1955, p. 533) specifies what he calls *dimensions of transition,* which refer to change in constructs or their organization over time. Among these dimensions of transition are some familiar emotions, such as *anxiety* (the awareness that the events that confront one lie outside the predictive potentialities of one's construction system) and *aggressiveness* (the active elaboration of one's perceptual field). There are also some dimensions of transition that refer more to the successive use of different types of constructs than to emotional states. An example is the *creativity cycle,* in which one starts with loosened constructions and terminates with tightened ones. In all this, Kelly clearly is trying to deal with a number of content considerations usually considered important by personologists. It is hard to avoid the feeling, however sympathetic one may be to Kelly's kind of theory, that these matters are given short shrift. Is creativity simply the process of starting with loose constructs, which lead to diverse predictions, and ending with tight constructs, which lead to specific predictions? Is anxiety nothing more than the awareness that you have encountered something you do not understand? Kelly's position is spirited and ingenious, but it tells only part of the story of personality, leaving the drama of peripheral characteristics undisclosed.

The other point at which Kelly comes closest to explicating the periphery is in his specification of the manner of assessing construct content. We already covered part of this in Chapter 5, where it is made clear that the Role Repertory Test is the most definitive manner of determining the content of the person's constructs. Not only will this test disclose content; it will also give information on how the various existing constructs are organized in the person's construction system. In addition to all this, Kelly (1955, pp. 452–485) also offers guidelines for assessment based on less definitive information than that available in the Role Repertory Test. Such information typically is found in interviews, but personal documents, such as diaries, can also be used in assessment. Interviews and personal documents can be useful if the personologist remains sensitive to what the person is actually saying and is credulous concerning it. Kelly believes that through the adoption of attitudes of credulity and perceptual literalness, the personologist can discover the constructs a person uses and the way in which they will influence perception of similarities and differences among events. But you can imagine how hard the identification of such regularities would be as soon as you deal with human experiences of any degree of complexity. Indeed, when Kelly (1955, pp. 319–359; 1962) tries to show how this kind of assessment actually gets done, you are left with a sense that the statements made about constructs are only among those that could be made rather than being definitive. In addition, it is hardly convincing that the statements about constructs permit insight into the essential features of the person's character or style of life. It is hard to avoid the conclusion that Kelly's position would be more meaningful if he offered some inklings as to typical character types.

McClelland's Position

McClelland, like Allport and Murray, concerns himself extensively with precise definition of peripheral characteristics. He does not just toss off concepts such as trait or style, leaving their real meanings to be discerned by others. His concern with the proper, clear definitions of the concrete units of personality that differentiate one person from another bespeaks special emphasis on the periphery. Unlike the other theorists thus far considered, McClelland assumes not one but three kinds of peripheral characteristics: *motive, trait,* and *schemata.* Each characteristic has a separate definition, process of development, and type of effect on functioning.

Let us turn first to a consideration of the motive concept, as it is the most important of the three in McClelland's thinking and follows most naturally from his conceptualization of the core of personality. McClelland (1951, p. 466) defines a *motive* as "a strong affective association, characterized by an anticipatory goal reaction and based on past association of certain cues with pleasure or pain." Surprisingly, the essential meaning of this rather opaque statement is very straightforward. What McClelland means is that whenever some cue arouses in you the anticipation of some change in state that will increase either pleasure or pain, you have a motive. Anything from a ringing doorbell to a rapidly beating heart can serve as a cue as long as it constitutes a signal that some change in state is imminent. Stimuli become cues on the basis of past experience. The anticipated change in state also comes out of past experience and may have specific content ranging from the expectation that you will be successful to the expectation that you will enter into close contact with other people. Finally, the anticipated change in state must be associated with the expectation of an increase in either positive or negative affect if one is to properly invoke the motive concept for what is happening. To paraphrase, then, a motive is a state of mind aroused by some stimulus situation that signals an imminent change that will be either pleasant or unpleasant. McClelland assumes that persons will act on their motives so as to bring about the anticipated pleasure or avoid the anticipated displeasure, as the case may be. When the anticipated change in state includes a positive affect, it is considered an *approach motive* in that the person tries to turn the anticipation into a reality. In contrast, the anticipated change in state that includes negative affect is an *avoidance motive* in that the person works to keep the anticipation from becoming a reality.

This division into two broad classes is the first step McClelland takes in specifying the content of people's motives. The second step essentially is that of endorsing Murray's extensive list of needs, which includes the needs for nurturance, compliance, and so forth. Of the needs on this list, McClelland has focused on three—the needs for achievement, affiliation, and power. In relating this list to the distinction between approach and avoidance motives, McClelland seems to postulate an approach and an avoidance version of each need. The avoidance version of the need for achievement is called *fear of failure,* which indicates reacting to a cue that a competitive situation exists by anticipating failure. The attendant negative affect leads to attempts to avoid the situation. In contrast, the approach version of the need for achievement involves reacting to a cue about a competitive situation with anticipation of success and attendant positive affect and attempting to thrust oneself actively into the fray. Although McClelland's meaning is clear, he often slips into the confusing position of calling this approach version of the need for achievement nothing other than the need for achievement. It would be much less confusing to call it something like *hope for success,* as does one of his associates of McClelland (Atkinson, 1957) and thereby preserve a verbal basis for distinguishing approach and avoidance versions of a common motivational characteristic. In any event, McClelland presumes that there are also approach and avoidance versions of other needs.

There are two additional considerations to be discussed in regard to motives: their effect on behavior and their process of development. As to effects on behavior, it is presumed that the arousal of motives increases the amount and intensity of behavior. This effect is observable not only in overt actions but in thought processes (McClelland, 1951, p. 482). When there is a task to be addressed, increased motivation leads to increased output on the task. Another general effect of motives is achievement of interrelatedness among diverse aspects of the person's behavior (McClelland, 1951, pp. 485–486). Motivation is believed to organize responses and introduce trends into behavior, producing orientation and direction. According to McClelland, it is this capacity of the motive concept to make sense out of varied responses that distinguishes it from other explanatory concepts of personality and makes it so useful. The final effect of motivation is that of sensitization (McClelland, 1951, pp. 488–489). People in a state of motivation seem more sensitive to some kinds of environmental cues than to others. There seems to be a lowering of perceptual, if not sensory, thresholds to the specific kinds of stimulation relevant to the motive.

Although McClelland assumes that the effects of increase, interrelation, and sensitization of behavior take place in the case of both approach and avoidance motives, there are subtle differences traceable to these two motivation classes. Thus, though both approach and avoidance motives lead to in- ←1 creases in the amount of behavior, approach motives do so by augmenting of effective, efficient behaviors, whereas avoidance motives do so by producing ineffective, obsessive behaviors. In imagination, for example, approach motives lead to anticipation of the satisfaction of success and concern with how best to plan for adequate task performance. In contrast, avoidance motives would lead to imagination obsessed with the obstacles to reaching the goal and unrealistic thoughts of magical satisfaction. To carry through our analysis, although both kinds of motive would lead to behavioral interrelatedness, approach motives ←2 would lead to organizations focused on effective instrumental actions and achievable goals, whereas avoidance motives would produce organizations stressing passive expressions of need and frustration. Finally, in producing ←3 sensitization, approach motives would highlight cues associated with challenge and satisfaction, whereas avoidance motives would highlight cues associated with threat and dissatisfaction. So approach and avoidance motives can be considered as having similar gross effects on behavior, with clear and distinct differences in behavioral effects at a more subtle level of analysis.

We can now turn to the process whereby McClelland believes motives develop. In considering this, it will be possible to see the relationship between core and peripheral levels of personality in his theory. You will recall that the core tendency according to McClelland is the maximization of small discrepancies and the minimization of large discrepancies between expectation and occurrence. Small discrepancies result in positive affect and large discrepancies in negative affect. In McClelland's view, in a particular domain of living characterized by small discrepancies people will come to learn an approach motive, whereas in a domain characterized by large discrepancies they will learn an avoidance motive. If the domain yields little in the way of any discrepancy—if it is completely predictable—persons will come to be indifferent to it altogether. Now that I have said this, it should begin to become apparent to you why McClelland defines motivation as he does. In simple terms, what McClelland means is that if you have enough pleasant emotional experiences in a certain area of functioning then you will learn to expect pleasant experiences each time you approach a relevant situation involving that area. In contrast, if you have had sufficient unpleasant experiences in that area, you will learn to expect unpleasant experiences whenever some cue is present and, therefore, attempt to avoid the situation.

In order to dramatize McClelland's meaning, I will quote from his account of the development of the achievement motive (McClelland, Atkinson, Clark, & Lowell, 1953):

> A concrete example involving the development of the achievement motive may help explain its implications in practice. Suppose a child is given a new toy car for Christmas to play with. Initially, unless he has had other toy cars, his expectations . . . as to what it will do are nonexistent, and he can derive little or no positive or negative affect from manipulating it until such expectations

are developed. Gradually, if he plays with it (as he will be encouraged to by his parents in our culture), he will develop certain expectations of varying probabilities which will be confirmed or not confirmed. Unless the nonconfirmations are too many (which may happen if the toy is too complex), he should be able to build up reasonably certain expectations as to what it will do *and confirm them*. In short, he gets pleasure from playing with the car. But what happens then? Why doesn't he continue playing with it the rest of his life? The fact is, of course, that his expectations become certainties, confirmation becomes 100 per cent, and we say that he loses interest or gets bored with the car; he should get bored or satiated, according to the theory, since the discrepancies from certainty are no longer sufficient to yield pleasure. However, pleasure can be reintroduced into the situation, as any parent knows, by buying a somewhat more complex car, by making the old car do somewhat different things, or perhaps by letting the old car alone for six months until the expectations about it have changed (e.g., decrease in probability). So, if a child is to continue to get pleasure from achievement situations like manipulating toy cars, he must continually work with more and more complex objects or situations permitting mastery, since, if he works long enough at any particular level of mastery, his expectations and their confirmation will become certain and he will get bored. (p.62)

Here McClelland clearly is talking about the approach version of the achievement motive. One would certainly expect that after this kind of early experience each time the person recognized a cue indicating the existence of a mastery situation, he or she would experience a sense of challenge, and the anticipation that reaching the goal of mastery would lead to emotional satisfaction.

McClelland et al. (1953) also describe the development of an avoidance version of the achievement motive:

> In the second place, there are limits placed on the development of *n* achievement by the negative affect which results from too large discrepancies between expectations and events. Thus Johnny may develop expectations as to what a model airplane or a solved arithmetic problem looks like, but he may be unable to confirm these expectations at all, or only very partially. The result is negative affect, and cues associated with these activities may be expected to evoke avoidance motives. To develop an achievement approach motive, parents or circumstances must contrive to provide opportunities for mastery which, because they are just beyond the child's present knowledge, will provide continuing pleasure. If the opportunities are too limited, boredom should result and the child should develop no interest in achievement (and have a low *n* achievement score when he grows up). If the opportunities are well beyond his capabilities, negative affect should result and he may develop an avoidance motive as far as achievement is concerned. (p. 65)

After an early history of large discrepancies between expectation and experience in mastery situations, the person would learn an avoidance version of the achievement motive. This would mean that each time you recognized a cue that a mastery situation existed, you would experience threat and the anticipation of failure.

The core tendency concerning discrepancy size and its relation to affective experience refers, of course, to any area of functioning, not only that concerning achievement. Therefore, persons can learn approach or avoidance versions of many different motives depending on the specific experiences they encounter in the world. As you can see from the above quotes, in McClelland's theory parents serve the very important role of influencing, if not determining, the degree of discrepancy characterizing the various areas of functioning over at least the period of time when the child is relatively dependent. McClelland indicates that most motives are learned in childhood, though he does not provide very specific periods for the learning of particular motives. There is little sign in his writing regarding stages of development—and indeed, the postulation of stages generally requires more emphasis on inherent attributes and capabilities than is present in consistency theories. McClelland et al. (1953, pp. 68–74) do detail the basis in development for different degrees of a motive, but such detail is beyond my purpose here. Nonetheless, it should be clear by now that this theory is the most detailed and precise of those we have considered concerning peripheral characteristics.

In theorizing about the power motive, McClelland recently (1975) has suggested that development is not complete once approach or avoidance goals have been established for an area through early experience. At least in the case of the power motive, there are four transformations; intake, autonomy, assertion, and generativity. The intake phase presumably covers the learning of the motive, as already discussed. The autonomy phase encompasses the gradual independence of the motive from the conditions under which it was learned. In the assertion phase, an even more insistent attempt to reach the goals at any cost takes place. But in the generativity phase, feedback obtained in the course of acting from a motive results in a more socialized, less rapacious form of the motive that is consistent with the well-being of others and the social system. At the moment, it is not clear whether this intriguing emphasis on changes in a motive after its establishment is intended to apply to motives other than that for power.

Recently Atkinson and Raynor (1975) have modified and extended McClelland's theorizing. Their first step was to conceptualize motives as even more cognitive than originally proposed and to incorporate expectancies (of what goes with what in the environment) and incentives (the value of outcomes) into the formulation whereby one attempts to predict behavior (Atkinson & Birch, 1970). Their second step was to structure the problem for a motive construct as the explanation of changes in the ongoing stream of human action rather than the more mundane reference to single, concrete behaviors. This leads to a view of human action as a series of linked episodes perceived by the actor as extending into the future. Motivation for an immediate task is to be understood as dependent on how it is related to future events and opportunities in the opinion of the person involved. For example, studying in order to get a good grade on an exam reaches beyond the exam if it is perceived as a step toward passing the course, getting a job, and establishing a career. All the perceived future outcomes must be taken into account in assessing the motivation to study for the exam. Atkinson and Raynor provide complicated formulae for prediction attempts. This theoretical step moves McClelland's original formulation further in the direction of a comprehensive basis for understanding action and gives it an existential flavor through showing its impact on the decision-making process. Needless to say, the notion that motives explain behavioral changes rather than repetitions is retained.

Before we turn from McClelland's motive concept to his views concerning the other two peripheral characteristics, I would like to introduce you to his unorthodox position concerning the biological drives, such as those for food and water. It is best to use his (McClelland, et al., 1953) own words here:

> Now according to our theory, how could we explain the fact that the longer an animal is deprived of food the more motivated he appears to become? Since most psychologists have been accustomed to thinking of biological need states as the primary sources of motivation, this is a very important question for us to discuss. In the first place, it is clear that in terms of our theory food deprivation does not produce a motive the first time it occurs. The lack of food in a baby rat or a baby human being will doubtless result in diffuse bodily changes of various sorts, but these do not constitute a motive until they are paired with a subsequent change in affect. More specifically, if the organism is to survive, the cues subsequent to food deprivation must always be associated with eating, and eating results in two types of affective change—pleasurable taste sensations, and relief from internal visceral tensions. Thus internal (or external) cues resulting from food deprivation are associated very early and very regularly in all individuals with positive affective change, and thus they become capable of arousing the hunger *motive* with great dependability. (pp. 81–84)

McClelland goes on to an explanation of why the motive gets stronger as food deprivation increases. We need not go into this. It will suffice to recognize that for McClelland there are no motives at birth, even though there are physiological needs that can render the organism uncomfortable in a diffuse way. A motive involves a concrete, tangible set of goals and actions instrumental to reaching them. Hence, a motive must be learned on the basis of relevant experience. One can speak of motives in regard to physiological needs only when they have, through learning, come to be represented psychologically as anticipations, goals, and instrumentalities. This kind of learning is mediated for McClelland by affective experience, and that is tied to discrepancies between expectations and experiences. For all these reasons, biological needs cannot be considered the basic building block of personality for McClelland.

Remaining to be discussed are the other two peripheral characteristics, traits and schemata. After presenting an extensive and excellent analysis of what other personologists have meant by the term *trait*, McClelland (1951, p. 216) concludes that it should be defined as "the learned tendency of an individual to react as he has reacted more or less successfully in the past in similar situations when similarly motivated." In other words, when persons are faced with what they perceive to be the same situation with the same variety and intensity of motivation that they have encountered in the past, they tend to perform the type of response that previously satisfied the demands of the situation and motivation.

By McClelland's definitions, a trait and a motive are actually very different. A motive is a set of anticipations that take the concrete form of goals and emotional involvement and a commitment to whatever course of action is likely, given the nature of the existing situation, to lead to the fulfillment of those anticipations. Responses expressive of the need for achievement, for example, very likely will differ considerably over time, as the situations in which this motive will be aroused may differ widely in their characteristics. A motive leads to consistency of intent but not necessarily of actual responses.

In contrast, a trait is no more than a collection of habits that have nothing of the goal-directedness of the motive. The trait of expansiveness, for example, leads you to act expansively every time a situation that is similar to the ones in which you learned to be expansive comes up. According to McClelland, a trait is learned because a certain style of functioning is rewarded consistently in a particular kind of situation. But this is not the same as saying that the trait has motivational properties. Perhaps people laughed and listened to you whenever you happened to be expansive in their presence, and so now you have the habit or trait of expansiveness in social situations. For McClelland, if your expansiveness has the status of a trait you will act this way in social situations because you are used to doing so and with no act of consciousness or intent. If, however, expansiveness had the status of a motive in you, or was part of an instrumental course of action leading to a goal, you might be expansive in a social situation on the basis of intent to act that way rather than simply because it felt natural and familiar to you. A motive can often lead you to do unfamiliar, untried things, whereas a trait can never have this function.

In his definitions of motive and trait, McClelland celebrates a distinction so clear in our own experience that it amazes me that virtually no other personologist has made it in any precise way. Generally speaking, those who rely on the concept of trait include in it both intentional and habitual behaviors, as do those who tend to rely only on the concept of need. According to McClelland, however, both concepts are needed because of clear differences between intentional and habitual functioning. The trait concept can explain response repetition, whereas the motive concept can explain sequentially arranged series of responses, in which each response is actually different. I think that Murray, in distinguishing needs and need-integrates, and Allport, in distinguishing dynamic and stylistic traits, were recognizing what McClelland makes explicit.

McClelland sees reason for yet another distinction, for which he employs the concept of *schema*. Unfortunately, he offers no concise definition of the schema (plural: *schemata*), but he definitely means it to be a unit of cognition or mentation. Actually, it is a symbolization of past experience—it stands for the past experience rather than being it and is inevitably a simplification (McClelland, 1951, p. 254). Words and language generally are good examples of schemata. But obviously McClelland means to emphasize not just any schemata that may exist but those that characterize the particular person you are trying to understand. For this, it would be much more important to know the person's effective vocabulary, for example, than it would be to know the full range of words available in the language.

Examples of schemata recognized by McClelland (1951, pp. 239–282) are ideas, values, and social roles. Whereas motives are learned on the basis of the typical degree of discrepancy between expectations and occurrences and traits are learned on the basis of the acts that are consistently rewarded, the learning of schemata is more directly representative of cultural transmission. The particular peculiarities of parents and significant others strongly affect motive and trait learning. In contrast, such things as ideas, values, and social roles are determined in the main by the nature of the culture in which the person exists. Ideas, values, and social roles often are communicated rather directly, in verbal terms, with the units of communication being social institutions, such as family, school, and church, rather than individuals per se. McClelland believes that schemata have a general, pervasive influence on the processes of perception, memory, and thinking. Obviously the possibilities you can imagine, the observables that will be salient enough for you to notice, the things you will remember, and even the thoughts you can have will be limited and influenced by the set of ideas, values, and social roles you have internalized.

Although the identification of three distinct classes of peripheral characteristics may strike you as a breath of fresh air at this point, following all the fuzziness we have encountered in previously considered theories, it is probably not entirely clear that motives, traits, and schemata are really that different. Perhaps we can get greater insight into McClelland's meaning if we consider the nature of the presumed relationship among these three entities, for related they surely must be. But such consideration is difficult, for most of McClelland's discourse on the matter is scattered throughout his writing and not summarized in any one place. Nonetheless, we should make an attempt.

You will recall that a motive has as its primary characteristic *intent* and can be described as a directional force. In contrast, a trait is primarily an habitual basis for performing as one performed before in a similar situation. Finally, a schema is primarily a cognitive unit referring to some aspect of the shared definitions whereby people in the same society live. The schema is not intentional in any strict sense, though ideas, values, and roles often include prescriptions for action.

With this as an introduction, let us take a concrete example from the achievement domain and follow through some of the distinctions we can make. Recall that the definition of a motive involves the arousal of an intention by a cue. The perception of aspects of the environment as cues to the presence of an achievement or success-failure situation requires the presence of achievement schemata in the form of ideas concerning achievement. But one could certainly have such achievement schemata without also possessing an achievement motive. If one had no such motive, one would be able to recognize the existence of an achievement situation and simply not participate in it. But if the achievement motive were also present, one would get involved in the sense of attempting to bring about success or avoid failure. So the trigger for the achievement motive is the achievement schemata. The content of these schemata can influence where and when the achievement motive is displayed, though the vigor and imaginativeness of attempts to reach success or avoid failure are clearly determined by the intensity of the motive itself. The eventual effectiveness of attempts to reach success or avoid failure is a function of achievement traits. Such traits are habits of persistence and are not, strictly speaking, a product of motive intensity or existence of achievement schemata. They are separate entities in themselves. Such a trait as persistence could be in the service of an achievement need, as in this example, but it could function quite separately from that need as well. If we generalized from this extended example in the hope of arriving at some preliminary statement of the differences and interrelation among McClelland's three peripheral concepts, we would come to something like this: Schemata form the general frame of reference for living and determine the concrete possibilities available for each life; motives are the basis for personal rather than culturally shared intentions and determine the content and intensity of directional activity; traits form the style of a person's functioning and determine the routine, habitual behaviors.

The discussion thus far should have given you some abstract sense of what McClelland means by traits, schemata, and motives. He becomes concrete in detailing the contents of these three kinds of characteristics. But before turning to that, I would like to point out a problem concerning the relationship of the core and peripheral levels of personality in McClelland's theory. As traits, schemata, and motives clearly are at the peripheral level of personality, they should be presented as formed out of the interaction of the core tendency with the external world. But the core tendency as described by McClelland is really relevant only to the development of motives. Traits and schemata seem to be formed in some way other than as the result of maximizing small discrepancies between expectations and occurrences while minimizing large discrepancies. McClelland's statements about the learning of traits and schemata suggest other assumptions about the core of personality that go beyond that mentioned above. But he is not explicit about this. There is little for us to do at the moment but live with the confusion resulting from the inconsistency between his core and peripheral statements. I suggest that we consider the usefulness for understanding observable behavior not only of motives but of traits and schemata, even though the latter two concepts currently exist as disinherited from the core.

Having recognized this confusion, we can turn to consideration of the content of motives, traits, and schemata. For motives, McClelland adopts the list offered by Murray (1938), which includes such things as the needs for achievement, affiliation, power, succorance, and change. There are forty such needs, which are fairly concrete and mirror people's commonsense, everyday concerns. If you asked people what motivated them, they very likely would say that they wanted achievement, affiliation, power, and so forth. McClelland offers no particular list of traits, being inclined to accept whatever habits other psychologists may think are important. So there is no specification of content for traits as precise as that for motives. Finally, McClelland suggests two kinds of content for schemata. The first refers to ideas and values and constitutes an endorsement of the classification offered by Spranger (1928). That classification includes ideas and values concerning economic, aesthetic, social, political, religious, and purely theoretical realms of life. The second refers to social roles, and here McClelland endorses the classification offered by Linton (1945). This classification breaks down roles into those involving age, sex, family position, occupation, and association group membership. Different behavior is expected from people of various roles and ages. Fathers, sons, sisters, brothers, aunts, and cousins differ from one another, as do lawyers from laborers or liberals, Methodists, and Boy Scouts from one another. McClelland analyzes the content of roles as culturally patterned sets of traits. Indeed, McClelland's (1951, p. 293) definition of role is as "a cluster of traits (or pattern of behavior) which serves as the culturally normal or modal solution to recurrent, usually social problems peculiar to a particular status or position in society." Although roles are clusters of traits, the role characteristic is something that expresses a rather universalistic social problem and cultural solution. In contrast, traits that are not parts of roles are learned on the basis of experience peculiar to the family environment in which a person is reared, and they express no cultural or societal universal. Actually, it seems to me that roles must also include motives insofar as the regular and recurrent accomplishment of certain goals is necessary for validating one's occupancy of a culturally defined position. I will discuss this implication of the schema concept in the next chapter.

One of the most striking things about the content McClelland gives to his motive, trait, and schema concepts is its eclecticism. In this, he exemplifies the point made in Chapter 5 that consistency theories tend to be eclectic with regard to personality content. This tendency stems from minimal assumptions concerning the content and inevitability of inherent human attributes. As I have already indicated, his theory includes two peripheral concepts—schemata and traits—that are not even derived from the one core tendency he offers. And now we see that the content attributed to the three peripheral characteristics does not stem from the overall fabric of his theory. Instead, McClelland has culled from the available psychological, anthropological, and sociological literature the lists that seem most complete and least tied to any particular theoretical assumptions. This is clear evidence of the eclectic emphasis of consistency theories. So eclectic is his theorizing concerning content that McClelland does not even consider whether the implications of the lists endorsed for schemata, traits, and motives are consistent. I mean to suggest not that they are inconsistent but that the question of consistency is not important to him.

Actually, McClelland's theory is, in terms of precision concerning peripheral characteristics, virtually a model for the personologist. Not only has he provided careful definitions of his three concepts—definitions that at least attempt to clarify the similarities and differences among them—but has offered guidelines for measuring their content. The technical way of putting this is that McClelland has offered *operational definitions* to supplement his theoretical definitions. Operational definitions tell you what operations you must perform in order to determine the existence and intensity of what you want to know about. An operational definition of body temperature, for example, is the mercury level on the calibrated scale of a thermometer. Of all the personologists considered thus far, McClelland and Murray are alone in having attempted this at once tedious, difficult, and indispensable step in theorizing. Without operational definitions of peripheral characteristics, you, as the user of the theory, can never be sure whether what you are working with is what the theorist intended in his or her lofty, abstract writing.

I cannot hope to give a detailed accounting of the actual nature of the operational definitions here, but some examples should give you the flavor of what has been offered. Since a motive involves so much intent to reach a currently absent goal, it is only reasonable that one not measure it under conditions in which the environment is so structured and familiar as to call up old, habitual ways of doing things or in which the socially proper things to do are so clear that only those ways of functioning will be elicited. The attempt to be socially appropriate is based on behavior determined by schemata, and habitual behavior is determined by traits. Motives refer more to very personal desires. It is therefore thoroughly understandable that McClelland would specify fantasy as the raw material in which to search for motives. In order to elicit fantasy in some sort of standardized way, he specifies a set of ambiguous pictures of people to be presented to subjects with instructions to compose stories about what has happened, is happening, and will happen. The pictures are ambiguous enough and the task sufficiently unusual that one may be reasonably sure that neither traits nor schemata will be major determinants of behavior. The stories are then scored for the presence or absence of motives.

Take the need for achievement as an example. The operational definition of this need is *competition with a standard of excellence,* with the approach form of it stressing hope for success and the avoidance form stressing fear of failure. So when scoring the approach form, one looks for aspects of the story indicating the concrete wish to succeed, anticipation of success, the overcoming of obstacles to success, and positive affect in connection with statements of competition with a standard of excellence. In contrast, when scoring the avoidance form, one looks for the concrete wish to avoid failure, worry about failure, specification of seemingly insurmountable obstacles to success, and negative affect in connection with statements of competition with a standard of excellence. McClelland et al. (1953) have formalized what I have said in terms of scoring rules for imaginative stories.

If one were interested not in the need for achievement but in schemata concerning achievement that might exist in the person, one would, on the basis of what I mentioned earlier, stress what the person says in describing himself or herself when the situation is publicly defined as relevant to achievement. McClelland suggests the operational format of a set of achievement-related questions that persons answer as true or false of themselves. McClelland is perfectly willing to have schemata measured by any standard questionnaire concerning values, such as the Allport-Vernon-Lindzey (1951) test called *A Study of Values*. This test attempts to measure Spranger's value orientations on the basis of true-false questions. You can by now predict what McClelland would specify as the operations with which to measure achievement traits. He would put persons into familiar situations and observe the pervasiveness of such behaviors as persistence. He would not ask persons whether they are persistent, or scrutinize their fantasy, so much as actually watch them perform in familiar, achievement-related situations, such as studying for tests.

One final matter should be touched. You will recall that many personologists organize the peripheral characteristics they specify into personality types. Like Allport and Murray, McClelland has not gone far in this direction. The concrete traits, schemata, and motives he specifies remain more or less separate from one another. He has told us how to measure them, so we could do just that and let their interrelationships emerge from our empirical work. But there certainly is little theoretical specification of probable interrelationships. This too is very understandable in a consistency theorist, who would have little reason for predicting one organization of peripheral characteristics as more likely than another. About as far as McClelland (1961) has gone in specifying personality types is to summarize in theoretical terms the empirical fruits of a large-scale research attempt to determine the influence of achievement motives, and, to a lesser extent, achievement traits and schemata, on the behavior of people taken as individuals and as members of a society. We will discuss his research in Chapter 11 and, hence, need not go further here.

CONSISTENCY MODEL: ACTIVATION VERSION

Maddi's Position

Elaborating on the core theorizing he and Fiske have offered, Maddi and his students have developed a view of the periphery of personality, including an emphasis on both peripheral characteristics and their organization into personality types. Although the activation view of the periphery of personality has an unfinished quality, it should be kept in mind that it is a very recent development within personology. The fortunate aspect of its recency of development is that it has been possible to profit from the earlier theoretical efforts of other personologists. In order to understand the derivation of peripheral characteristics and personality types from the core aspects of activation theory, you must keep in mind three basic kinds of similarity and difference among people (Maddi & Propst, 1971), to be discussed in the following paragraphs.

The first consideration is the characteristic curve of activation. Here the core statement of similarity among people is that they all have such a curve which takes the general shape of Kleitman's cycle of existence (see Chapter 5). In other words, activation customarily rises sharply after waking, then increases more gradually to some point in the middle of the day, then begins to decline gradually, and finally declines more rapidly as sleep approaches. But Maddi and Propst (1971) hold out the possibility that there are differences among people concerning the sharpness of rise and fall and the point during the day at which the shift from rising to falling takes place. Individual differences in the shape of the customary curve of activation may well help in explaining of so-called night people and day people. Surely we have all encountered people who are most alert and effective early in the morning or late at night, with the middle of the day being somewhat indifferently placed between the two extremes. People who have an unusually high early morning or late night characteristic level of activation should, by comparison with more usual people, show more intense, impact-increasing behavior in the early morning or late evening, respectively. Unfortunately, Maddi and Propst do not follow up on this intriguing suggestion. Made in passing, their suggestion represents one of the only references by personologists considered in this book to the possible importance of differences among people in the patterning of activities during a single day.

The second basic consideration of similarity and difference among people involves the average height of a person's characteristic curve of activation. The core statement is that everybody has a characteristic curve of activation that varies over some range of values between zero and an absolute maximum. But the statement of individual differences, leading to a position on the periphery of personality, is that the range of values covered by any person's activation curve need not be the same as that for another person. These differences can be pinpointed by comparing the averages of each person's range of characteristic activation values over the course of several days. This brings us to the basic distinction offered by Maddi and Propst (1971) in developing a typology of peripheral personality: the distinction between *high-activation* and *low-activation* people. At the most obvious level, this distinction refers to the assumption that the average of the characteristic curve of activation is higher for some people than for others. But if you recall the discussion of Fiske and Maddi's position from Chapter 5, you will recognize that this distinction must subsume many points of difference between these two kinds of people. High-activation people spend the major part of their time and effort pursuing stimulus impact in order to keep their actual activation levels from falling too low; low-activation people spend most of their time and effort avoiding impact so as to keep their actual activation level from getting too high. In order to obtain a more concrete understanding of the peripheral personalities of these two kinds of people, we must consider the third basic kind of similarity and difference among people.

This third consideration involves the anticipatory and correctional techniques used for maintaining actual activation at the characteristic level. At the core level, it is assumed that all people are similar in that they employ anticipational and correctional techniques for increasing or decreasing stimulus impact in a manner consistent with the shared necessity of minimizing discrepancies between actual and customary levels of activation. But the theory also provides a basis for understanding individual differences in these anticipational and correctional techniques by explicating the many contributors to impact. You may recall that impact is considered a joint function of the intensity, meaningfulness, and variety of stimulation from interoceptive, cortical, and exteroceptive sources (see Chapter 5). Impact, of course, determines the actual activation level. Maddi and Propst (1971) have outlined some of the implications of the definition of impact for differences among people in peripheral personality. First, a person may favor or find salient one of the three attributes of stimulation (i.e., intensity, meaningfulness, variety) in his or her anticipational and correctional strategies. The high- and low-activation personality types are each subdivided into three parts reflecting this distinction concerning preference for particular stimulus attributes. High-activation people who favor intensity, meaningfulness, or variety are considered as having an *approach motive* for *intensity, meaningfulness,* or *variety,* respectively. Low-activation people for whom intensity, meaningfulness, or variety is most salient are thought to have an *avoidance motive* for *intensity, meaningfulness,* or *variety,* respectively. The terms *approach* and *avoidance motivation* are used in much the same manner as in McClelland's position, with the approach motives often called *needs* and the avoidance motives *fears.*

At this point, it should be clear that Maddi and Propst offer a typology of peripheral personality that includes three high- and three low-activation types, with the three subdivisions of each major type bearing content resemblances. So, for example, *high-activation-need-for-meaningfulness* persons would spend most of their time and effort in instrumental behavior aimed at the goal of increasing the meaningfulness of their experience, with this concrete directionality having the overall function of keeping their actual activation levels from falling too low. Just the opposite would be true for *low-activation-fear-of-meaningfulness* persons. Orientations toward particular stimulus attributes are considered motivational because it is these attributes that can actually augment or diminish impact. The three approach and three avoidance motives represent peripheral characteristics in the terminology of this book.

In order to gain further understanding of the activation position on peripheral personality, it is necessary to introduce additional distinctions. One has to do with the favored source of stimulation. Here Maddi, Propst, and Feldinger (1965) collapse the three distinctions offered by Fiske and Maddi (1961) into two—the internal and the external. As the distinction between cortical and interoceptive sources postulated by Fiske and Maddi undoubtedly will be quite hard to make in practice, the simplification suggested by Maddi et al. (1965) seems reasonable. In any event, it is considered important to know whether the person is oriented toward internal or external sources of stimulation. This distinction recognizes that one way of regulating impact is to look to sources of stimulation essentially outside the body (anything from thunderclaps or scenery to music or other people) and another way is to turn within the organism (focusing on anything from thoughts or daydreams to pains or dizziness). The former orientation is called the *external trait* and the latter the *internal trait,* with the term *trait* used in the manner of McClelland to emphasize habitual rather than motivational behavior. In finding internal or external stimulation salient, the person is not necessarily raising or lowering impact. The distinction being made is similar to Jung's regarding introversion-extroversion. It is only when persons begin to manipulate stimulation, be it external or internal, by pursuing or avoiding intensity, meaningfulness, or variety that they show the goal-directedness of motivation. The external and internal traits are simply habits of emphasis and, of course, represent peripheral characteristics in our terminology. The distinction as to salient source of stimulation must be made within each of the six personality types already mentioned, raising the overall number of kinds of people considered to twelve.

As if this were not complicated enough, Maddi, Charlens, Maddi, and Smith (1962) offer yet another distinction that must be taken into account in understanding the activation position on peripheral personality: the distinction between the *active* and the *passive trait.* The emphasis here is much the same as in Allport's distinction between proactive and reactive functioning. Persons with the active trait have the habit of initiative, such that they influence the external and even internal stimulus environment, whereas persons with the passive trait are habitually indolent, permitting themselves to be influenced by internal and external stimuli over which they have no subjective control. The activeness-passiveness distinction is especially important in understanding differences among people in the proportion of their time spent in anticipational as opposed to frankly correctional behaviors. Active persons will anticipate their activation requirements well, because they are self-reliant and initiating. We should expect to see in such persons the fruits of anticipational functioning. As I will elaborate later, these fruits include such things as psychological differentiation and integration. In contrast, passive persons will not anticipate their activation requirements well, and they frequently will be in the position of having to correct for actual activation levels that already have become too high or fallen too low. There will be a "last-ditch-stand" quality to the passive person that Maddi and Propst (1971) suggest involves distorting reality. Although the activeness-passiveness distinction is not firmly attached to the rest of activation theory, Maddi et al. (1962) seem to consider it important, and hence we should too, recognizing that it represents an inconsistency in theorizing. We noted a similar inconsistency in McClelland's peripheral theorizing, and we can give this one the same interpretation. Consistency theorists de-emphasize core assumptions involving specified content to such a degree that they tend to be eclectic at the peripheral level. Nonetheless, the distinction as to activeness/passiveness must be made within each of the twelve personality types we already have, making a staggering total of twenty-four in all!

Lest you rush to criticize activation theory too harshly for postulating such a large number of personality types, let me make several points. First, some theorists, such as Allport and Kelly, apparently are willing to entertain an unlimited number of personality types, such is their emphasis on individuality. Infinity surely is a larger value than twenty-four. Furthermore, some theorists, such as McClelland, Murray, and Erikson, may end up with quite a sizable number of personality types when their peripheral-level theorizing becomes complete and explicit enough for us to entertain a count. After all, Murray and McClelland have postulated a huge number of peripheral characteristics, and Erikson has only sketched out a typology, not bothering to consider the subtypes implicit in his theorizing. In this context, activation theory can at least say that the twenty-four types it proposes are all that are likely given the nature and number of its core-level assumptions. And this brings us to a final point, which is that the actual number of types considered important by activation theorists may well dwindle as time goes on. After all, the theory has rarely been used in practice, and there has been little opportunity for the relevant empirical evidence to ride herd on the play of reason.

My presentation of the activation typology has been very abstract, and I would not be surprised to find it lacking in vividness for you. Let me therefore try to describe the types a little more fully. In this description, you will also gain insight into the kinds of behavior the peripheral characteristics and typology are meant to explain. Most of the description that follows will indeed concern the kinds of observable phenomena that activation theorists feel it is important to explain.

High-activation persons with active and external traits will be "go-getters," seeking out challenges to meet in the physical and social environments. They will be energetic and voracious in their appetites. Interested in a wide range of concrete, tangible events and things, they will be hard to keep up with. Although they will not be especially hampered by pressures toward conformity, they will tend to be insistent on facts, not fancies. They will spend little time in rumination or daydreaming. They will be straightforward and not complex and subtle so much as extensively committed and enthusiastic. They will want to encounter people and things rather continuously. If they also have a high need for meaningfulness, they will be pursuers of causes and problems—statespeople, businesspeople, or journalists rather than scholars. But if they have a high need for intensity, they may pursue action and tumult per se, being athletes, or soldiers, or bon vivants. And if they have a high need for variety, they will show curiosity about causes and mechanisms governing persons and things, being adventurers, explorers, or world travelers.

Now let us switch to high-activation persons in whom the active trait occurs with the internal rather than external trait. They will show little outward evidence of the pursuit of impact. Perhaps the most one would notice externally is a wealth of knowledge and similar fruits of an active orientation toward internal processes. They will be thinkers and daydreamers, responding to the challenges posed by the limitations of mind and body with little regard for the tangible affairs of the outside world. They will be subtle and complex, showing depth and considerable cognitive and emotional differentiation. They will not be especially social, though they may have some close, intimate friends. In general, they will not be interested in the obvious, surface manifestations of people and things. If they also have a high need for meaningfulness, they will lead the life of the mind, engaging in scholarly, ruminatory, philosophical pursuits. If instead they have a high need for intensity, they will pursue sensations and emotions, perhaps as poets and lovers. Should they have a high need for variety, however, they will strive for novelty and originality in some sort of creative or imaginative endeavor.

By way of sharp contrast, let us turn to the personality types involving low activation. Low-activation persons with active and external traits will be the eternal conservationists, bent on heading off social and physical disorganization and conflict through negotiation, control, and integrative attempts. They will tend to be conformists and advocates of stability at any cost. Though reasonably energetic, they will tend to be simple in their tastes and involvements. If they also have a high fear of meaningfulness, they will express their organizational and integrational interest in a manner involving the simplification of problems and the avoidance of ambiguities. Should they have a high fear of intensity instead, they will tend to exert a dampening effect on vigorous, potentially disorganized external conditions, perhaps becoming efficiency experts. If they have a high fear of variety, they will seek to force routine on the environment, preferring the familiar and the predictable to the new.

Persons low in activation with a combination of active and internal traits will be somewhat different. They too will be conservationists, but with special emphasis on their own organisms. In other words, they will be advocates of the golden mean, taking care to avoid excesses and indulgences of any kind. They will avoid putting any kind of strain on persons, be it a pleasant or unpleasant experience. Their personalities will be simple, uncomplex, devoid of inconsistencies—in short, integrated and dependable. If they have a high fear of meaningfulness, they will show a notable absence of detailed and diverse thoughts and daydreams, tending instead toward stable and recurring cognitive themes with the function of rendering any given experience similar to what has gone before. If they have a high fear of intensity, they will have an ascetic emphasis about them, naturally avoiding sensation for its own sake. And if they have a high fear of variety, they will force themselves to function consistently and stably, giving a picture of dependability and constancy devoid of flamboyance.

Thus far, we have considered the personality types that include the active trait. As you can see, the various types differ depending on considerations other than activeness. There is even the implication that the high-activation types are more extraordinary and interesting people than the low-activation types. Certainly the high-activation types are at least more vivid and describable. But the essential difference between high- and low-activation types is not that between the ideal and non ideal forms of living, which correspond more closely with the distinction between active and passive traits. All personality types involving the active trait are rich in anticipational techniques. This means that they provide a successful basis for selecting the kinds of experiences that will minimize discrepancies between actual and customary levels of activation. As people falling into these types therefore do not experience discrepancies often, they feel reasonably satisfied with their lives, experience little frustration and negative affect, and are, in truth, effective in their own ways. You may like the high-activation types better, feeling them to be more interesting and important, but they are no different in their ability to fulfill their view of the good life than are the low-activation types. In contrast, the personality types that include the passive trait are somewhat chronically frustrated and ineffective. It is these types, to be described next, that activation theorists consider nonideal.

High-activation persons with external and passive traits will have the standards, attitudes, and goals of their counterparts with the active trait but will not have available to them the action habits with which to consistently bring about their own satisfaction. To be sure, they will profess an interest in challenges, voraciousness of appetite, and a wide range of interests. But they will do little about all this. They will have the same emphasis on concrete, tangible, external realities as their more action-oriented counterparts. But they will have few anticipational techniques for avoiding situations wherein their actual levels of activation will be lower than is characteristic for them. About the only anticipational technique they will have is the passive one of preferring situations that have been associated with high impact in the past. But they will have no concrete way of bringing about these preferred situations, depending instead on their "natural" occurrence. They will be dilettantes or consumers rather than producers of impact. With regularity, they will be in the uncomfortable position of correcting for an actual level of activation that is already too low. The emergency nature of this position will contribute to their behavior its defensive or distortional quality (see Chapter 5). Depending on whether they also have a high need for meaningfulness, intensity, or variety, the distortional corrections will take the form of artificially augmenting the meaning, intensity, or variety of what is happening in the environment. Something banal may be seen as pregnant with meaning, something simple as complex, and something monotonous as subtly new. Such distortions may sometimes involve gross, paranoid suspiciousness toward other people and the imputation of human or even supernatural attributes to the inanimate environment.

Next are the high-activation persons with internal and passive traits. These persons too will profess many of the interests and activities expressed by their more action-oriented counterparts but without carrying through on what they profess. Their personalities will not show the degree of differentiation and complexity one would expect from hearing them talk. Nor will they actually spend much time in true exploratory and imaginative thought. They will be bored, uninvolved, and dissatisfied and frequently faced with the emergency task of correcting for actual activation levels that have fallen too low.

The particular way in which they distort the reality of their internal stimulation in order to bring about the correction will, as usual, be understandable in terms of whether the need for meaningfulness, intensity, or variety is strongest in them. Because the distortion involves internal more than external stimulation, the end result of the process may even include such phenomena as hallucinations and delusions.

Let us turn to the types that involve low activation. When persons combine low activation with external and passive traits, they will sound like conservationists but somehow will be unable to protect themselves from high impact through controlling and ordering the social and physical environments. In their simplicity and ineptitude, they frequently will be swamped by stimulation that leads to excessively high levels of activation. Rather than interact actively with the environment in order to bend it to their impact requirements, they will renounce it. Their best protection from the regular experience of excessive activation will be to shrink from the world, becoming hermits, tramps, or even schizophrenics. Of course, the quality of the withdrawal from the world will be influenced by whether it is meaningfulness, intensity, or variety that they especially fear.

Finally, we come to the personality type that includes low activation and both internal and passive traits. Once again such persons would appear to be much like their more active counterparts. They will advocate the golden mean and deplore excesses of any kind. Their personalities will indeed be simple and uncomplex. But they will not be especially effective in anticipating the imminent possibility of excessive impact and, hence, will find themselves faced with the need to reduce it fairly regularly. Being oriented toward internal sources of stimulation, they will tend to employ what are usually called the *desensitizing* or *repressive* defenses. In this fashion, they will render ineffective the organismic sources of impact. The particular defenses employed can be at least partially understood on the basis of whether the fear of meaningfulness, intensity, or variety is especially strong in them.

Hopefully, this brief description has lent some vividness to the personality typology offered by activation theory. There is little more to say except to note that some developmental assumptions definitely have been made in arriving at this typology. It has been assumed that the characteristic curve of activation becomes solidified early in life, after which time it changes little. Also, some learned basis has been assumed for the activeness-passiveness and external-internal traits, as well as for the needs for or fears of meaningfulness, intensity, and variety. None of these assumptions are sufficiently detailed in developmental hypotheses by this as yet incomplete personality theory. Some rudimentary developmental statements concerning the characteristic curve of activation were reviewed in Chapter 5, and Maddi (1961b) has offered some suggestions concerning how high and low needs for variety may be learned. Nothing more is available.

It seems clear now that activation theory somewhat differs in emphasis from most kinds of personality theory (although, of course, it is closest to other consistency theories). While activation theory can claim to address some phenomena (e.g., activity level, boredom) not emphasized elsewhere, it might well have difficulty explaining phenomena that are easy for other approaches. For example, it is not immediately apparent how activation theory would explain such universally accepted human events as guilt and self-condemnation.

CHAPTER 10
Rational Analysis of Peripheral Considerations

In the preceding three chapters, we reviewed many points of view on the periphery of personality. It is now time to consider the similarities and differences among these views so that we can better appreciate the essential features of what personologists consider to be people's concrete ways of living. An understanding of these essential features will be useful in approaching the empirical analysis in Chapter 11, the aim of which is to identify the kinds of peripheral assumptions that seem most fruitful in the light of available evidence.

The first section of this chapter will compare, contrast, and analyze the various kinds of peripheral characteristics that appear in peripheral theorizing. The next section will attempt similar discussion of the conceptualizations of personality types. These two sections will not be organized around the three models of personality, as the formal issues arising from different peripheral conceptualizations are somewhat independent of the models involved. However, bear with these sections, even if they seem a bit disorganized, for certain fairly definite conclusions are reached in the end. The final section of this chapter analyzes the content of peripheral statements by comparing and contrasting the particular theories as expressions of the three models.

THE VARIOUS KINDS OF
PERIPHERAL CHARACTERISTICS

In beginning our discussion of the peripheral characteristics that have been postulated, I will focus on their nature and function. Despite the many differences in terminology and emphasis that we encounter in the peripheral theories, only three basic kinds of peripheral characteristics seem to emerge. One kind concerns goals and instrumental strategies, another concerns unselfconscious habits of performance, and the third concerns ideas, values, and principles of thought. Examples of the first, or motivational, unit are the *need* (Murray), *motive* (McClelland, Maddi), *dynamic disposition* (Allport), *fictional finalism* (Adler), and *defense* (Freud). If it seems strange to list defense with the others, recognize that defenses have the goal of avoiding anxiety and in this are not very dissimilar to avoidance motives. The major example of the kind of peripheral characteristic involving unself-conscious habits of performance is the *trait* as used by McClelland, Maddi, Adler, Fromm, and Freud. Also relevant, however, are the *need-integrate* (Murray) and *stylistic disposition* (Allport). Finally, the kind of peripheral characteristic emphasizing principles of thought is exemplified by the *schema* (McClelland), *personal construct* (Kelly), *sense of identity* (existential psychologists), and perhaps *condition of worth* (Rogers). Jung's functional *modes* also seem to emphasize thought, though they may be too broad for consideration as peripheral characteristics.

Not only are there basically just three kinds of peripheral characteristics, but, interestingly enough, none of them seems more pervasive in one of the models for personality theorizing than in the others. Some explicit form of motivational concept and an explicitly cognitive concept appear in examples of the conflict, fulfillment, and consistency models. The trait concept is by all odds the most popular, and it appears in the theories that exemplify all three models. Actually, the trait concept is sometimes so broadly defined as to include a cognitive or motivational emphasis along with a habit focus. It can hardly be said that the nature and function of the peripheral characteristics appearing in a theory follow in any precise fashion from the personality model they represent.

Probably the major factor in a theorist's decision as to the form and nature of the peripheral characteristics to be employed is a sense of what will be necessary in order to explain the behavioral phenomena that seem important. After all, the models seem broad enough in their logical possibilities to permit any and all of the three kinds of peripheral characteristic. The models may well influence the kind of content emphasized at the periphery of personality, but I will not discuss this possibility until later. For the moment, let us delve further into the tie I have suggested between the kinds of peripheral characteristics one employs and the behavioral phenomena one feels it is important to explain.

Motives and Traits

The most common distinction among kinds of peripheral characteristics is that between motivation and habit. Of the personologists, McClelland is the most insistent on this distinction, defining motive and trait as being mutually exclusive. Maddi is in complete agreement, having adopted McClelland's usage. Although Adler does not discuss the matter at any length, he must be in essential agreement, as he distinguishes sharply between the fictional finalisms (motives) and the traits that make up character. Murray, with his distinction between needs and need-integrates, and Allport, who distinguishes between dynamic and stylistic dispositions, show substantial similarity to McClelland. But they hardly agree with him completely, being unwilling to define motivational and habit concepts in a mutually exclusive fashion. Although it may not seem so at first, Freud also offers a basis for the distinction, in postulating not only traits but the more motivational defenses as components of character types. Clearly he does not separate the two completely, as defenses are at a high level of generality and tend to subsume, or at least foster the learning of, traits.

To be sure, the remaining personologists who engage in peripheral theorizing to any degree do not offer an explicit basis for distinguishing between motives and traits. But it is difficult to determine whether this is so because the theorists actively consider drawing such a distinction a mistake or simply because they are relatively unconcerned about the precision and completeness of peripheral theorizing. Working in terms of the overall spirit of the theorizing, I would surmise that Erikson, Rank, and Fromm would not be against the distinction in principle. After all, they tend to rely on an extremely broad and flexible definition of the trait in their peripheral theorizing all the while they are describing the person in strongly motivational terms. It is more difficult to say how the few remaining personologists would react to the possibility of distinguishing between motives and traits. Only Rogers (1963) has gone on record as suggesting opposition to the distinction, asserting that the motive concept is unnecessary in what we would call peripheral theorizing.

Taking all the positions into account, it seems clear that the distinction between motive and trait is important in the peripheral theorizing of at least half, if not a majority, of the personologists we are considering. Those who are most explicit in drawing this distinction make it clear that they do so because of the conviction that there are two different classes of behavior to be observed in people. So different do these classes of behavior seem that it appears natural and appropriate to explain them through different kinds of peripheral characteristics. You will recall from the discussion of McClelland's peripheral theorizing that the two classes of observed behavior are called *directional* and *repetitive*. Let us dwell further on the distinction between these classes in order to clarify the personologist's bases for employing the motive and trait concepts.

Repetitive behavior is very simple. Whenever a situation comes up that is similar to what you have experienced before, you will tend to repeat old behaviors automatically without having to make a decision about it. Indeed, you may well have no awareness of these old behaviors. Such habitual behavior is mechanical and not expressive of the intellect; you may not even notice yourself manifesting it. A great deal of behavior is of this sort. One person may have a particularly characteristic choice of words or voicepitch in social situations; another may have an especially aggressive way of driving a car; another may dress according to a certain color scheme; another may be expansive when confronted with people of the opposite sex. If you pointed out these behaviors to the people exhibiting them, they might well be surprised, perhaps even to the point of doubting the veracity of your observations. And if you asked them to decide their personal goals, they would not include expansiveness, particular choice of words, and so forth.

Goal-directed behavior is as different as it can be from the stylistic behavior just described. Obviously in goal-directed behavior you have an explicit goal, something that can be put into words and toward which you work. The task of reaching the goal requires you to be ingenious in finding and performing just those instrumental acts that will be successful in your environment. If you have the goal of feeding yourself because you are hungry and you are in the environment of a modern American home, the most successful instrumental acts probably will be those involved in finding and searching the refrigerator and pantry. But if you have the same goal and find yourself in the environment of a forest, you will employ the instrumental acts of trying to find a stream where there might be fish to be caught, or of stalking land game, or of searching out edible vegetation. Which of these possibilities you carried out and in what order would likely be determined by the particular characteristics of the forest as presented to you. Although the goal in the home and forest examples is the same, the directional behavior aimed at reaching the goal differs because it must be suited to the characteristics of the environment. If it were pointed out to you what kinds of actions you were observed doing, you would hardly be surprised. Indeed, you would explain that you were doing those things in order to try to gain food in the particular circumstances you had encountered. The obviously different actions in the two examples are rendered functionally equivalent by the existence in you of the same goal of getting food. Goal-directed behavior thus appears to be intelligent rather than mechanical in nature. What this means is that people pursuing goals must assess the nature of the environment, make decisions as to the best strategy in a manner that will enable them to change their minds if they encounter additional information originally unavailable. There is too much self-consciousness and decision making in this kind of behavior to consider it mechanical. It involves the operation of intellect.

Although the distinction we are discussing seems clear, I can imagine some psychologists saying that it really cannot be drawn in practice, for behavior has a unitary quality. From the standpoint of this holistic position, the distinction mentioned above is a false one, however rational it may sound, because all aspects of behavior are so interdependent as to be inseparable. I do not find this argument convincing. If the opposition is to any separation of behaviors into classes, then the holistic position borders on an evasion of the psychologist's difficult but unavoidable task of deciding what he or she is supposed to explain. To say that all behavior is to be explained and not classify it into various categories is to structure the explanatory task in a manner that must lead to failure. To avoid classification would be like physicists asserting that their task is to explain the universe without being willing to discuss the various physical entities that compose it.

But the holistic argument might be directed against the particular distinction between repetitive and directional behaviors rather than against all possible distinctions. To be sure, the decision as to whether one was observing repetitive or directional behavior would be difficult to make in practice. But it pays to have an open mind and to explore the distinction further, especially because so many personologists seem to have adopted some form of it. How could we structure observation so as to enter into the spirit of the distinction?

Certainly, if you permit yourself to do no more than observe the overt behavior of a person in some unspecified situation, it may well be unclear whether what you are observing is behavior that repeats old habits or behavior that is directed toward future goals. But nobody advocating the distinction between repetitive and directional behaviors would be so naïve. In order to try to distinguish between these two categories of behavior, you would first have to observe the person repeatedly over a wide range of situations. To discern repetitive behavior, you would look for recurrences that did not seem to be parts of sequences and that seemed tied to the repetition of situations. To discern directional behavior, you would look for discrete actions that seemed to bear sequential relationship to one another and that were not restricted in occurrence to repetitive situations. The identification of sequences of action would be greatly facilitated by the person's verbal statements concerning his or her personal goals. Such statements certainly would be obtained by anyone wanting to distinguish between repetitive from directional behaviors. If you accept the importance of distinguishing repetitive and directional behaviors, it will seem natural and appropriate to explain the former with some sort of habit or trait concept and the latter with some type of motive concept.

To the Rescue of the Concept of Motivation

One definite implication of adopting some form of the motive and trait concepts in peripheral theorizing is that not all behavior is motivated! All behavior can be considered caused, for the trait is as much a cause of mechanical, repetitive behavior as the motive is of intellective, directional behavior. Nonetheless, a trait is not a motive. Some personologists have difficulty accepting a theoretical formulation that suggests that not all behavior is motivated. Invariably these are personologists who have attributed motivational significance to their postulated core tendencies. Certainly, if the core tendency is motivational, by virtue of the fact that it is considered to infuse all functioning there cannot be some functioning that is without motivation. Some theorists who attribute motivational properties to their core tendency, such as Rogers and Maslow, do not make an explicit distinction between motive and trait at the peripheral level. As they do not assume a basically nonmotivational entity at the periphery, there is no inconsistency between their core and peripheral theorizing. But other theorists who tend to attribute motivational significance to their core tendency, such as Freud, also fall into the logical dilemma of using the trait concept in discussing the periphery. Fortunately, I think there is a simple way out of this dilemma that does little or no violence to the real intent of the various personality theories and may at the same time render more clear and precise the nature of the motivation concept.

Greater clarity and precision in the use of the motivation concept would certainly make it more intellectually appealing to many psychologists. We have reached the bewildering point at which virtually any sort of behavior will be called *motivated* by some psychologist. Birds flying, bees buzzing, ladies sweating, babies playing, monkeys solving problems, rats hoarding, cockroaches crawling, and people sleeping will all be described in a diverse array of motivational terms. So loosely is the concept used and so huge are the differences of opinion from psychologist to psychologist that it would not be surprising to find people turning away from motivational explanations altogether. A trend in that direction may well be underway, to judge from the fact that a number of eminent psychologists (e.g., Kelly, 1955; Skinner, 1950) can gather followings for approaches to understanding behavior that profess to exclude the motivation concept.

But as most personologists consider the motivation concept too valuable to abandon, it seems wise to work toward clarity and precision in its use. The distinction drawn between motive and trait, which involves restriction of the relevance of the motivation concept to identifiably directional behaviors, seems a step toward clarity and precision. This view, apparently based on the intent of many personologists, is very close to that of Peters (1958), who, in an excellent logical analysis of the motivation concept, concludes that it is best suited to explaining behavior that involves the existence of a personal goal and strategies instrumental to achieving it. Recently Kagan (1972) and Dember (1974) have adopted similar views. As anything that can properly be called a personal goal will really be rather concrete and specific, it seems to me that the motivation concept is most appropriately applied at the peripheral level of personality. A core tendency is simply too general and universalistic to achieve representation in the person's mind as a goal and attendant instrumental strategies.

There is a logical dilemma in assuming all behavior to be motivated at the same time that one of the concepts you employ at the peripheral level is essentially nonmotivational. The way out is to deny motivational significance to your core tendency. This path recommends itself to us because it would encourage clarity and precision in the use of the motivation concept. But before adopting this solution, we must consider what would be lost by divesting core tendencies of motivational significance. The major reason why some personologists attribute motivational significance to core tendencies is that they wish to emphasize that these tendencies are meant to describe requirements of the organism and overall directionalities that are so basic as to be common to all people. I am prepared to grant that if core tendencies did not refer to these basic requirements and directionalities, they would not be fulfilling their intended theoretical purpose. The question is whether they can fulfill this purpose without being accorded motivational status. If we can find an affirmative answer to this question, we can accept the solution to the above dilemma.

In pursuing the answer to the question, we should consider the core tendencies, as postulated by personologists, that do not seem heavily invested with motivational import. McClelland's theorizing is a good example. According to him, it is common to all persons to experience negative affect when the discrepancy between expectation and occurrence is large and positive affect when it is small. Negative affect leads to avoidance behavior and positive affect to approach behavior. As we would expect of any proper core statement, the positive and negative affects disclose certain organismic requirements and the approach and avoidance behaviors indicate directionality. But in neither affect nor behavioral adjustment to it is there evidence of proaction or intellect. There is little choice, decision making, or flexibility (at least before considerable learning has occurred); rather, the approach and avoidance behaviors are automatic, almost reflexive organismic adjustments to comfort and discomfort. Such behavior is more like a tropism than anything else. Something happens and you are drawn to it, something else happens and you are repelled by it. There are no personal goals, instrumental strategies, choices, or manipulation of the environment and, hence, no motivational significance.

In McClelland's theorizing, the core tendency is the core tendency, not a motivation. Or, if you prefer another name, the core tendency could be referred to as a *drive,* once again distinguishing it from a motive. Actually, the distinction between *drive* and *motive* is often made in the psychological literature. A drive is more biological and/or mechanical and less self-conscious and/or intellective than a motive. Drive-induced behavior may lead to experiences through which motives are learned, but what is learned may bear little concrete relationship to the underlying drive. Thus, the drive to approach small and avoid large discrepancies between expectation and occurrence may lead to a strong achievement motive. But it is only when the concrete standards (goal) of excellence and competitive strategies for attaining them are present in the person's mind that McClelland will talk in motivational terms.

Maddi's activation theorizing agrees in this respect with McClelland's. The core tendency to maintain activation at the characteristic level is not motivational because it merely represents the organism's requirements and whatever automatic adjustments to them are available. Maddi attributes motivational significance only to the goal-oriented, intellective attempt to either increase or decrease the variety, meaningfulness, or intensity of stimulation. It is certainly true that in pursuing any of these motives activation level may well change in the direction of the organism's requirements. But the person's intent still is not precisely that of producing such activation changes.

From considering the theorizing of McClelland and Maddi, we have learned that it is possible to postulate a core tendency that expresses organismic requirements and overall directions without being motivational at the same time. In order to do this, you must couch your core tendency in terms of mechanical, reactive, driven behaviors existing prior to learning. Motives clearly emerge as learned units comprising goals and proactive, intellective behaviors that, though very likely consistent with the organismic requirements, do not express them directly. Let us try to apply these principles to other personality theories in order to determine what is gained and what is lost.

The principles fit Rogers's theory easily. He describes his actualizing tendency in terms that indicate it to be the organism's natural, inherent requirement to develop along the lines of its potentialities. The process of actualization involves no conscious intent, awareness, or decision. Actualization goes on simply because it is an expression of the organism's nature. Indeed, attempts to use the intellect and be proactive about the business of actualization usually misfire and are regarded with skepticism by Rogers. This is as clear a nonmotivational statement of core tendency as there is in the personological literature.

In spite of this, Rogers often refers to the actualizing tendency as a *motive*. As you may recall from Chapter 4, Rogers imputes the actualizing tendency not only to humans or animals but to all other living things. I quoted Rogers in that chapter as referring to a giant seaweed actualizing itself all the while it is being buffeted by the surf. Poetically forceful as this example is, it makes it perfectly clear that Rogers cannot mean to consider the actualizing tendency to be motivational and still be convincing on logical grounds. If the actualizing tendency is a motive, we would have to agree that seaweed assumes its size, shape, color, and other attributes because it intends to do so! This clearly cannot be. Seaweed becomes what it becomes because it is equipped with a genetic blueprint and is programmed to actualize it. No choice or manipulation of the environment is involved. What is operating are organismic requirements and drives, not motives. Similarly, when Rogers applies this same actualizing tendency to humans, it is not a motive.

My analysis does not doom Rogers to go forever without a concept of motivation. He could, if he so desired, develop a motivational concept at the peripheral level of personality that emphasized learned goals and instrumental strategies. This peripheral motivation might even be structured as the development through learning of more psychological forms of the actualizing tendency. Perhaps Rogers's *need for positive regard* and *need for positive self-regard* are where motivation should be considered to inhere. For that matter, even a concept such as need for achievement might be considered the concrete, peripheral result of expressing the actualizing tendency when an existing inherent potentiality happened to find best expression competitively and the environment supported competition. I cannot help but note that this kind of development of and emphasis on the peripheral level of personality would be welcome in Rogers's theory, which currently has very little to say in this regard. Unfortunately, Rogers (1963) has clearly stated a disbelief in the value of theorizing about specific motives in the manner of McClelland. This disbelief simply does not change the fact, however, that Rogers's imputation of motivational significance to the actualizing tendency itself seems rather poetical and inconsistent with the most precise use of the motivation concept.

Other personologists, such as Adler, Freud, Erikson, White, Fromm, and the existentialists, also tend to attribute motivational significance to their core tendencies, but they describe them in ways that indicate more proaction and intellect than does Rogers. It may seem at first as if these theorists have adhered to the canons of clarity and precision concerning the motivation concept that I advocated earlier and still have found a way to apply it at the core level. If this is really true, we should simply accept that personologists can, with equal logical rigor, assume that all or only some behavior is motivated. But I for one still find it difficult to endorse attributing motivational characteristics to core tendencies, because organismic requirements exist at such a high level of generality as to be unconvincing as personal goals. Let me express my meaning gradually by considering a few of the personologists just mentioned.

Adler, for example, sees the tendency toward perfection as underlying all functioning and as being motivational in nature. He does not impute this "great upward drive," as he puts it, to plants and animals, and he does describe it in terms that indicate the existence of personal goals and concern with appropriate instrumentalities. Out of a sense of inferiority, the person will develop a compensatory goal and then organize his or her energies and attention toward attaining it. All this certainly sounds like an admissible motivational explanation of directional, proactive behavior. But let us look more closely at the personal goal. This will take the form of what Adler calls a *fictional finalism*. A fictional finalism might be wanting to be beautiful, charming, famous, respected, intelligent, or generous but not very likely wanting to be perfect. In other words, the actual goal a person has will be more specific, limited, and peculiar to him or her than is the universalistic core tendency. It is in the fictional finalism and associated strategies of instrumental action that motivation inheres. The overall core tendency toward perfection, while it provides an explanation of the directional commonality of all persons, is not properly understood as a motive, for it is probably too ubiquitous to achieve direct representation in the mind as a personal goal. This kind of core tendency, though more unique to organisms that can have personal goals than is that of Rogers, is still better considered an organismic requirement than a motive. In Adler the motives are the fictional finalism, which are, of course, at the peripheral level of personality.

As I indicated earlier, something that the organism requires can very well be called a *drive* and the attempt to satisfy that need a *motive*. So we can even agree with Adler's designation of his core tendency as a drive if we are careful to recognize that drive and motive differ in their implications. In Adler, drive (tendency toward perfection) translates into motive (fictional finalism) through learning and development. It may sound to you as if I have done little more than change some words around and insist on a rigor of usage that borders on intellectual preciosity. I do not think this is true. Recognize that once we accept that Adler's core tendency may be an organismic drive but not a motive and that motivation is a peripheral consideration, it becomes possible to believe that not all behavior is motivated without giving up a belief in Adlerian theory. Indeed, one can even recognize, in addition to fictional finalisms, peripheral characteristics that are not motivational in nature without doing rational damage to the theory. And certainly Adlerians seem to want to include in the style of life traits, such as charmingness, that explain repetitive behavior. Accepting my analysis means that you need not defend the inclusion of traits in the periphery of personality all the while you are trying to cast your core tendency in motivational terms, with the disconcerting result of a logical requirement that all behavior be motivated.

The conclusions reached above can also be applied to the other personologists. Allport apparently does not consider his core tendency toward psychological maturity to be motivational, and that is a good thing. It is unlikely that this tendency would actually achieve representation in the mind as a personal goal. More likely, one would have much more concrete goals, such as becoming a good physician, father, friend, or lover. These personal goals might well represent the results of the core tendency, but they are themselves peripheral manifestations. They are reasonable examples of what Allport might call *dynamic traits*. In Maslow's case, it can also be said that the core tendency of self-actualization is unlikely to appear as a personal goal in people. Much more likely is the appearance of more concrete goals. Fromm's core tendency of attempting to express human nature is another case in point. Fromm does break down this general tendency into a number of parts, such as the need for rootedness. And it is more likely that these relatively concrete aspects of the core tendency would achieve mental representation as personal goals. But probably one must become even more concrete before the kinds of things that are commonly considered goals are encountered. So too with White's point of view. It is unlikely that people do all the things they do because they are imbued with the single motivation to be competent. All the things they do may well add up to a tendency toward competence in the theorist's mind, but this is a different thing. Similarly, the existentialist's emphasis on authentic being also is probably too broad and encompassing to be motivational, though the particular decisions that one faces in life could well be. With regard to all these theories, it can be said that the core tendency is most clearly considered not a motive but an organismic requirement or even drive. This permits saving the motivation construct for the kind of concrete, goal-oriented behavior found at the periphery of personality. And this means that such theories could then easily incorporate the possibility that not all behavior is motivated.

Let us turn now to the psychoanalytic thinkers, Freud, Murray, and Erikson, whose shared position we can treat in much the same manner as we have the theorists already considered. The core tendency of maximizing instinctual gratification while minimizing punishment and guilt is probably at too high a level of generality to achieve concrete representation as goal states and attendant instrumentalities. Happily, however, psychoanalytic theory provides a built-in basis for more specificity concerning the locus of motivation. Let us consider the instinctive (pleasure principle) and defensive (reality principle) parts of the core tendency separately.

The instincts not only have their source in and derive their energy from organismic requirements; they also have aims and objects. Indeed, the major psychic or mental significance of the instincts is in the form of objects and the wish to obtain them. Psychoanalytic thinkers use the term *object* in much the same manner as we use the term *goal* or *goal state*. Generally speaking, people learn to recognize and pursue those relevant objects available in their environment. This is not so different from saying that people learn personal goals and attendant instrumental strategies. Psychoanalytic thinkers would come most of the way toward adopting the motivational view we are considering in this section by using the term *motivation* to refer only to the objects and possibly the aims of the instincts, leaving their source and energy to be accounted for as organismic requirements and drives.

A matching concretization and restriction of imputed motivational significance would also be helpful concerning the defensive part of the core tendency. It is unlikely that the abstract, ubiquitous attempt to avoid all punishment and guilt registers in the mind as a personal goal. But it is very likely that people have specific avoidance goals that lead them to shun the very situations expressive of the specific objects and aims of their instincts. Such a goal might be to avoid being hit by mother (when the instinctual object and aim of stealing money, let us say, is aroused). The specific defense instituted to realize the avoidance goal can, in our terminology, be considered an instrumental strategy. Interestingly, although Freud considers the defenses as operating unconsciously, he describes them in the terminology of intellect and choice (Peters, 1958). All in all, specific avoidance goals and attendant defensive instrumentalities clearly can be considered motivational.

In this section I have tried to sketch how, with little loss in explanatory power, the various personality theories could be adjusted where and when necessary to permit a use of the motivation concept that is clear, precise, consistent, and readily acceptable from the standpoint of reason. This usage involves considering core tendencies and characteristics as representing organismic drives and requirements, saving the motivation concept to apply to the peripheral level, with its personal goals and intellective strategies for reaching them. Of all the theories, only the psychoanalytic one appears to lose much of its original impact, which depended so much on the notion of unconscious motivation. What does this new use of the motivation concept do to the unconscious contents of the mind?

The Problem of the Unconscious

Perhaps some of you have become rather disconcerted on reading the last few pages. It must be clear that in stressing personal goals as the hallmark of motivation, I am taking the position that nothing that cannot easily register in a person's awareness as something he or she wants really has motivational significance. I seem to be embracing a phenomenology of motivation. What the person professes wanting is what we, as personologists, would have to agree is wanted. This must seem to do violence to those of you who believe in unconscious motivation, for that position requires, by definition, that there be some goals toward which persons work of which they will be unaware. Even if you cannot imagine me to be enough of a Freudian to be disturbed by your discomfort, you have read Chapter 6, in which I presented a strong empirical case for the existence of defense at least in some people and in which I tried to translate defense theory into something more palatable to reason. Therefore, I must have some belief in the existence of unconscious processes. You could conclude that I am just being inconsistent in also taking the position described in the last few pages. Let me hasten to indicate that this is not the case.

In my position on motivation, it is necessary that the personal goal have been conscious only at one time. If this condition is met, you can be sure that you are dealing with a genuine personal goal rather than some goal merely imputed to the person by the personologist. But the personal goal, though conscious at first, need not stay that way. If it precipitates personal conflict (e.g., I really want to hug Mother, but if I do, Father will get angry and punish me), it may well be defended against and, hence, drop out of consciousness. My position can well accept the possibility that a personal goal that is defended against because it precipitates a personal conflict will continue to affect behavior even though no longer available to awareness. The behavior thus affected will still show decision making and instrumental sequences of acts, though these might be a little less organized by virtue of the absence of conscious appreciation of the goal that is being pursued. What my position excludes is the possibility that what I am calling *organismic requirements* are unconscious motives. Recognize that this possibility is excluded only because I believe such organismic requirements to be too general, ubiquitous, and universal to ever achieve mental representation as personal goals, not because I do not believe in unconscious motivation. If something was never a personal goal, it can hardly be defended against.

Actually, I think my position is very close to Freud's real intent, granting the existence of some semantic differences and some confusions. Freud concerns himself mainly with unconscious motives that would, in his estimation, have been conscious except for the action of defenses. These unconscious motives seem close to what I am talking about. But Freud also makes occasional, and to my mind uneasy, reference to a part of the unconscious that had never been, and could never be, conscious. He thought this might be the collective or racial unconscious emphasized by Jung. Freud was not always sure it really existed in the mind as, of course, the unconscious should in his view. I think I know what Freud was getting at. Might he not have been recognizing, however tentatively and imperfectly, that the most universal and general organismic requirements do not achieve mental representation as goals even though they exert a broad influence on behavior? In any event, I think my position on motivation does not do great violence to the notion of unconscious motivation in psychoanalytic thinking. And certainly it must do even less damage to other personality theories that utilize the concept of defense, for they are much less specific concerning the necessary content of conflicts than is psychoanalytic theory.

But you must recognize that even as acceptance of my position makes motivation a peripheral characteristic, therefore leading to the conclusion that not all behavior is motivated, so too does it lead to the notion that not all behavior has a component of unconscious motivation. Primarily behaviors stemming from a personal goal that has been forced from awareness by defenses can be considered unconsciously motivated. This conclusion accords nicely with the discussion of defensiveness in Chapter 6, which found that not all behavior is defensive. But accepting this conclusion will require a shift in thinking on the part of some people of psychoanalytic inclination who believe that all behavior is at least partially determined by unconscious motivation. Perhaps it will help to recognize that all behavior might well be influenced in a very general way by the organismic requirement of maximizing instinctual gratification while minimizing punishment and guilt, even though the precise explanation of the particular aspects of behavior you see now or at another time will be achieved primarily with peripheral constructs that will only sometimes involve unconscious motivation. Actually, what I am suggesting accords well with Freud's original intent in theorizing, which was to find an explanation for the oddities and paradoxes of behavior.

As Peters (1958) points out, Freud wanted to explain slips of the tongue, dreams, and hypnotic dissociation, and this clearly colored his development of the notion of unconscious motivation. In other words, Freud developed the concept of unconscious motivation to explain those things that people did, or omitted doing, for which they had no adequate explanation themselves. These things clearly were not accidental, as some theorists thought at the time, for the people to whom they happened were displeased by their inability to understand, and the occurrences were so directional and predictable that they seemed motivated. Peters (1958) makes a very good point here. Had Freud been convinced by people's own explanations of these oddities of behavior, he would never have developed the notion of unconscious motivation. Peters generalizes from this to say that it is only when the explanations persons give for their behavior do not convince us that we should look to the possibility of unconscious motivation. This is what Freud would have done and what we should do too.

Thus, imagine that we see a young man suddenly stop in the process of walking down the street, veer, and cross to the other side. If we ask him why he did this and he says that he spied a tobacconist's shop on the other side of the street and went toward it because he needed tobacco, there is nothing to stop us from being convinced. The behavior was directional and appropriate to a personal goal of which the person was aware (i.e., to get tobacco). There is no call here for invoking the concept of unconscious motivation. There is no oddity. But suppose everything else was the same save that the young man ran rather than walked across the street. If he gave the same explanation as above, we would still be left wondering why he ran. If there were no cars around, and if the store was not about to close, running would have been an oddity. If the man could tell us nothing more than that he wanted tobacco, we might well suspect that his actions were at least partly influenced by unconscious motivation.

It seems to me that my position on motivation has the advantage, in consideration of unconscious motivation, of getting us back to the kind of thing Freud had in mind. Unconscious motivation is an explanatory construct that should be employed only when it seems relevant, that is, when persons' own accounts of goals are unconvincing as explanations of their behavior. This use of the concept of unconscious motivation is more defensible from the viewpoint of reason than is that which makes all behavior somehow an expression of unconscious motivation. The latter approach seems understandable to me only if theorists have some investment in second-guessing people or in convincing them that theorists know people better than people know themselves, or in rendering people pessimistic and distrustful concerning themselves and others.

Jung's case is complicated by his assumption of both a personal and a collective unconscious. The personal unconscious formed by the action of defenses can be handled, as in Freud, as a special case of motivation. But, according to the position I have been developing, the collective unconscious, having never been conscious at all, does not qualify as motivation. Do not be troubled by this, for it is not even clear that Jung meant the collective unconscious to be motivational in the precise sense of determining directional as opposed to repetitive behaviors. The collective unconscious emphasizes thought structures—typical ways of posing problems and seeking solutions—that are especially common for the human species. Only the derivatives of these essences or archetypes ever even become concrete enough to achieve or affect consciousness, according to Jung. It does not seem likely that he would have objected to considering the archetypes as expressing organismic requirements, saving the term *motivation* for the learned goals and aims that develop in persons as the result of complex interactions between themselves and the environment.

Schemata

Thus far, I have taken the position that it is sensible for a peripheral theory of personality to include two types of explanatory construct—motive and trait. In doing so, I have closely followed McClelland. But what of his schema concept? Is this too a useful ingredient in peripheral-level theorizing? You will recall that I advocated including both motive and trait concepts because they seemed useful in explaining two different categories of observable behavior—directional and repetitive. If we feel that classifying all behavior as either directional or repetitive is sufficiently comprehensive and differentiated to do little violence to the meaning of behavior, we will find little cause to advocate a schema concept. After all, what would it explain then? But should we feel that this dual classification of behavior is so gross that it violates our sense of what is happening in our own lives and those of the people around us, we will find additional classificatory categories helpful. Perhaps then the schema concept will seem a welcome explanatory device.

With this in mind, let us examine the schema concept more closely. McClelland defines schemata as cognitive maps or units, primarily taking the concrete form of values and social roles. In addition, he feels that schemata represent a shared cultural, rather than personal, level of experience. What he had in mind was distinguishing between behavior that involves the pursuit of personal goals and behavior that involves the pursuit or upholding of societal goals—for, after all, what are values and social roles but mutually agreed-on standards for behavior in aggregations of people? McClelland is actually suggesting that the motive construct be used to explain behavior directed at attainment of personal goals and the schema concept to explain behavior directed at attaining or maintaining societal goals. When persons act in order to be socially appropriate or moral, they are being determined by the sense of social roles and values they have incorporated from their culture. When they act in order to reach a goal that refers to their own advancement or satisfaction, they are being determined by their motives. And when they act in an automatic, unreflective manner, they are being determined by their traits.

What are the implications of this discussion of schemata for our classification of behavior as directional or repetitive? Essentially, schema-determined behavior is directional in nature. It exhibits the same qualities of intelligent functioning found in motivated behavior, namely, decision making and flexible tuning of instrumental actions to the particular characteristics of the environment that is encountered. But the goal worked toward will be one agreed on by the members of the relevant society as being important and worthwhile in relations among people. The goal of a motive is not defined by consensus, nor does it necessarily regulate group behavior.

Schema-determined behavior is not repetitive in nature. In order to see this, take generosity as an example. People may act generously without intending to—in other words, in an automatic, repetitive way—or may actively and self-consciously attempt to act generously. In the first instance, we would be observing the *trait* of generosity and in the second the *schema* of generosity. It would be possible for someone actively trying to be generous to have the *motive* of generosity, but only in a culture that did not make generosity a value or a role. If you can recognize the possibility of analyzing behavior into two broad categories called *repetitive* and *directional,* with the directional category subdivided into that which is associated with personal goals and that with societal goals, you can conclude that it is useful to include in theories of the periphery of personality the concepts of trait, motive, and schema.

Theories of the periphery that employ only one concept, or even two, are not as likely to be clear, precise, and comprehensive as are those that employ all three. This is especially true when the theory specifically restricts the consideration of behavioral categories to fewer than these three. So when Kelly's consistency theory employs only cognitive explanatory constructs and construes behavior as if it were little more than mental activity, we may be left with a feeling of incompletion because not all that is important in behavior is considered. Actually, however, many theories of personality contain the rudiments of the triadic characterization of the periphery that I have been advocating. In psychoanalytic theories, such as those of Freud, Erikson, and Murray, there is not only an id but a superego. The content of the superego is essentially social goals. The process of satisfying id and placating superego could well lead the theorist to incorporate both motive and schema concepts at the peripheral level. And yet, interestingly enough, two out of three of these psychoanalytic theories employ only the concept of trait, which is the least predictable of the three from the core assumption of existence of id and superego! But in looking at the list of things these theorists call *traits,* it is easy to imagine reclassifying them as either traits, motives, or schemata. This reclassificational possibility exists in other theories as well, notably those of Fromm, Maslow, and Rogers. Finally, the universalistic social emphases of Adler and Jung suggest that their peripheral positions, if developed further, might find utility in the schema concept. The existentialists would seem to be a dissenting voice, for though they emphasize cognition, they also stress the individualistic use of it.

THE PERIPHERAL CONCEPT OF TYPE

Until this point, we have concentrated on the peripheral characteristics. These are the supposedly indivisible, and therefore basic, building blocks of peripheral theories of personality. But by themselves they are too concrete to give much sense of the actual flavor of a person's life. They are the trees in the forest, and although a careful study of individual trees will yield much understanding of the nature of trees, it will not by itself clarify the overall dimensions of the forest to any great extent. Lest we lose the forest for the trees, let us turn our attention to another kind of concept relevant to peripheral-level theorizing. This concept occurs at a higher level of generality and has the function of subsuming and grouping together the peripheral characteristics into meaningful patterns. An analogous concept in chemistry would be compounds, which represent the meaningful combination of elements into more complex units.

For Freud, Fromm, Maddi, Rank, and Jung, this more complex, organizational characteristic is *character* or *personality type.* Adler gets at the same thing when he offers the concepts of *style of life.* So does Murray in his concept of *complex,* though he fails, for some mysterious reason, to formally subsume his more concrete concept, *need,* under this more general one. The other personologists do not really offer an organizational concept. In some cases— notably Rogers, Maslow, and existential psychology—the distinctions made among types of people are too few to require such a concept. These positions only distinguish between people succeeding and failing in vigorous expression of the core tendency. These theorists need do no more, therefore, than name these two kinds of people in terms of the content of their personalities. Thus, Rogers talks of the *fully functioning* and the *maladjusted* person, and Maslow, though less terminologically consistent, is similar in emphasis, while Maddi considers *individualism* and *conformism.*

Other personologists, such as Allport and Kelly, are so insistent on the importance of individuality that they not only fail to offer type concepts but also avoid designating the possible contents of peripheral characteristics. These are related omissions, for organizing the peripheral characteristics into types must be done largely along content lines; hence, in order to offer a type concept, the theorist must be committed to specifying the common content of personality. Allport, more than Kelly, provides a possible basis for theoretical development leading to delineation of the content of peripheral traits in his nicely detailed propriate functions. Thus, one might explore the theoretical yield of considering some people as showing peripheral characteristics indicating a personality type that stresses *rational coping,* or *propriate striving,* and so on.

Finally, there are personologists—notably McClelland—whose omission of a type concept is more difficult to understand. McClelland certainly specifies both kind and content of his peripheral characteristics and in so doing indicates a fine-grained interest in comprehensiveness. But he does very little in terms of organizing these peripheral characteristics into types. Perhaps this omission stems from his deep eclecticism concerning personality content. Since McClelland derives the content of his motive, trait, and schema concepts from the work of many different people, it is difficult to put it all together into meaningful patterns. And, of course, his core tendency is relatively content-less, so no help can be sought from that quarter.

It should be quite clear from this summary that the type concept provides no particular basis for distinguishing among conflict, fulfillment, and consistency positions. This is not surprising, since we already have seen that the kinds of peripheral characteristics are not specific to the three models and types are combinations of these characteristics. It does not even seem that the omission of the type concept is specific to one or two models, as this occurs in examples of all three.

We have encountered three reasons why personologists, in their peripheral level theorizing, omit reference to coherent patterns of concrete characteristics for which the type concept is appropriate. The reason in McClelland's case does not really represent a theoretical conviction obviating specification of types as much as it is a consequence of his eclecticism with regard to personality content. McClelland would never argue that the concept of personality type is unworthwhile. Indeed, his own work on personality factors leading to economic development (McClelland, 1961), in which he seems to be developing a type of personality involving achievement traits, motives, and schemata, indicates that he has nothing against the notion of types. He simply is in the position of having little formal theoretical basis for postulating them.

But the other two reasons for avoiding the type concept are backed by more ideological commitment. In one of these two cases (e.g., Rogers, Maslow, and existentialism), we find that only two kinds of persons are considered important enough to specify in content terms, rendering elaboration of a type concept superfluous. One cannot criticize a theorist for failing to be superfluous. But one can question whether considering only two kinds of people is really being complete. Such theorists seem to believe that the only important thing to know about persons is whether they are actualizing themselves or becoming authentic. I hope that if this book has convinced you of anything, it is that such theorizing is not complete enough to do justice to the complexity of life.

The other ideologically bolstered reason for omission of the type concept is the general emphasis on individuality. We will talk more about the problem of individuality in a moment, but for now you should realize the severe limitations on a theory imposed by its dedication to the proposition that all persons are unique. You will have noticed that the theories of Allport and Kelly could not even be discussed in any detail in this chapter, so unspecific are they concerning the peripheral level of personality. The same extreme emphasis on individuality is found in some existential psychologists. These positions really can only be used to understand data you already have in hand. They provide little or no basis for predicting what kinds of people you are likely to encounter. As such, they do not improve much on common sense.

The Problem of Individuality

Personologists differ in the degree to which they stress individuality. Those who tend to believe that people are similar enough to be understood adequately by grouping them into a small number of types include Freud, Rank, Adler, Fromm, Jung, and Maddi. Another group of personologists substantially agree with this position, though they have less to say about types. These personologists are best described as believing that there is some small set of dimensions or variables that can be profitably applied to all persons from the viewpoint of understanding. Included in this group would be Erikson, White, and McClelland. In contrast to the personologists already mentioned, there is a group that is rather militant concerning individuality. Regardless of whether or not their theories do justice to their beliefs, these personologists have a steadfast ideological commitment to the idea that people are more different from one another than they are similar. Included in this group are Rogers, Maslow, Allport, Kelly, and the existentialists.

It will be instructive to consider the point of view of the most ideologically committed and verbally forceful of the individualists, Gordon Allport. For him (Allport, 1955, p. 22), "each person is an idiom unto himself, an apparent violation of the syntax of the species." In explicating this position, Allport (1955, p. 22) focuses on the apparently limitless range of potential behavior available to the human by virtue of a big brain and a relative absence of instincts and ventures the opinion (1955, p. 23) "that all of the animals of the world are psychologically less distinct from one another than one man is from other men." All this is strong medicine that could kill the patient—psychology—already feverishly struggling for general laws that psychologists believe would make its scientific status indisputable. To anyone engaged in this struggle, Allport's position must seem cruel heresy, and hence further consideration of it is in order.

Allport (1937, p. 4) argues that the major task of personology is to understand and predict the individual case rather than the contrived average case. Concepts and relationships aimed at predicting the average case are called *nomothetic*. A concept such as McClelland's need for achievement would be considered nomothetic by Allport because of the belief that many people can be given a score on need for achievement. According to Allport, it is only by distorting each person's behavior somewhat that the concept of need for achievement can be applied. The distortion is invariably considered as involving the disregarding of important qualitative differences among people in favor of describing them all in similar, average terms. Now if nomothetic concepts and laws, derived from and applicable to the data on aggregates of people, were completely adequate for predicting each individual case, there would be little purpose in Allport's championing of the inviolability of individuality. In practice, however, perfect prediction and understanding using nomothetic concepts and laws are never achieved. Indeed, there is often a sizable minority of cases to which the nomothetic concept and general law do not seem to apply. For example, most people characterized as high in need for achievement will work harder than most people characterized as low. But some people called *high* will not work, whereas some people called *low* will resemble beavers. This is not surprising to Allport (1961, pp. 332–356), who believes that nomothetic concepts are merely convenient fictions that are useful only insofar as they resemble the true personality of some people. If a moderate degree of understanding and predictive accuracy is sufficient to satisfy the investigator, Allport is not seriously opposed to the nomothetic approach. But the paramount goal of the personologist requires a greater approximation to the truth.

In the attempt to achieve this goal, it will be necessary, according to Allport, to develop concepts and laws that are derived from and applicable to the data of each individual case. At first he called such theorizing *idiographic* (Allport, 1937, pp. 3–23) and seemed to take such an extreme view that virtually no generalization across persons would be possible (Allport, 1942, p. 57). Whatever organization of behaviors into classes that is attempted is considered properly done only within not across persons. Thus, if the need for achievement were used as an idiographic concept, it would refer to a class of behaviors in one person only and would not be used on anyone else. More recently Allport (1961, pp. 257–361; 1962) substituted the term *morphogenic* for *idiographic,* and seemed to be formulating a position that is less extreme, permitting the use of concepts that are not in principle restricted in their applicability across persons. He still overwhelmingly emphasized concepts and laws that reflect the individuality of the person studied, but he at least considered it possible that those concepts and laws would turn out to apply to some other people as well. Allport made a strong plea for freedom from the restricting nomothetic mold of other sciences, which he believed have not been confronted with uniqueness on a grand scale, and offered a number of suggestions for concrete morphogenic methods of study (Allport, 1962).

Allport poses an alternative to the traditional view of science that he believed would lead to the highest level of prediction and control. Although the morphogenic approach certainly should be tried in research, it raises a keen sense of futility when couched as a replacement for an approach that encourages generalization across persons. Must knowledge of individuals remain as unrelated, odd bits of information? How can significant systematization of knowledge be achieved? It should be established with certainty that nomothetic methods have been adequately tested before they are discarded on the grounds that they typically leave some individual cases unexplained.

Whether or not other sciences have been faced with overwhelming individuality, they certainly recognize the necessity for deduction, from the general law and the characteristics of the situation involved, of explanations and predictions that apply to the individual case. For this to be done well, the general law must provide exhaustive specification of the conditions under which it does and does not apply, and the investigator must have sufficient knowledge of the concrete prediction situation in order to determine whether or not the law should be used. For example, the law contending that need for achievement leads to hard work might be applicable only under conditions of permissiveness and opportunity rather than of authoritarianism or lack of resources. Furthermore, complex phenomena may well call for the application of more than one law, and hence the relationships among laws must be clearly specified. For example, in addition to the law relating need for achievement to hard work, there may be laws determining whether the person will approach or avoid permissive situations. You would have to be able to apply these latter laws to a person in order to understand whether or not his or her need for achievement level was readily expressed in work intensity. Only if all this information were available would it be possible to evaluate the explanatory adequacy of nomothetic methods, and even then particular general laws could turn out to be incorrectly formulated without this constituting a demonstration of the inadequacy of the methods they represent. The degree of theoretical and methodological care and precision involved in the valid application of nomothetic methods often is not recognized as important or attempted in psychology. Hence, the development of truly useful nomothetic concepts and laws may be stifled, and individuality may loom overly large as an explanatory problem.

It is by no means clear that any personologist who believes in individuality must reject the nomothetic approach in order to be true to this belief. To the contrary, the nomothetic approach is so natural to science that it seems straightforward to use it in the absence of evidence showing it to be inadequate. What the personologist believing in individuality should do is use the nomothetic approach in the manner most calculated to do justice to individuality.

Let me be more specific about what constitutes the nomothetic approach. Essentially it involves specifying not only the kinds of concepts at the peripheral level of personality but their content as well. I emphasize specification of content in peripheral-level theorizing because it is so much more to the point than is core-level specification of content. The latter is nice to have, but it speaks to what is common to all persons and therefore is not useful in understanding individuality. It is the specification of peripheral content that is crucial because it allows you to designate the classes of behavior in people that your theory will recognize. This means that even though you may recognize differences among particular people, you nonetheless expect to achieve understanding of them with a standard, unchanging set of concepts. You are assuming that while individuality may exist, true uniqueness does not. The differences that exist among people are relative, not absolute.

Even with this assumption, it is possible to use the nomothetic approach in a manner that will facilitate the understanding of individual differences. This involves postulating as many different kinds of peripheral characteristics and types as seems practical and intuitively accurate. Clearly the more peripheral characteristics you have and the more ways they can be combined to yield types, the more differences among people your theory will recognize. In other words, the nomothetic approach should be used complexly in order to permit an understanding of individuality. In what I have said you should recognize a strong argument for the kind of theorizing about peripheral characteristics found in McClelland, who offers the most categories of concept (motive, trait, schema) and a goodly number of content distinctions (e.g., needs for achievement, affiliation, power, and so forth) within each category. Fromm's theory is another example of complex use of the nomothetic approach. While he offers only the trait concept for the base unit, he lists some forty-seven traits. And while he organizes these traits into only five types, he does indicate that there are many combinations or mixtures of types, at least some of which he specifies. Maddi's activation approach exemplifies the complex use of the nomothetic approach at the level of the type concept. He suggests twenty-four types of peripheral personality. Spirited support for this position on the study of individuality is provided by Beck (1953).

But the matter is far from settled. As Marceil (1977) makes clear in his review, there have been arguments presented on both the morphogenic and nomothetic sides. He advocates that we distinguish between forms of this controversy that apply to theories of personality and those that relate to methods of doing research. As to the latter, a good argument can be made for including both research dealing with single cases (or a very few cases studied in depth) and that dealing with aggregates. One learns different things from each kind of research, but their results are not in principle incompatible.

THE CONTENT OF PERIPHERAL PERSONALITY

My emphasis up to this point has been on the various kinds of concepts one finds in theorizing about the periphery of personality. In this section, I will shift emphasis to the content of this theorizing, giving no regard to the kind of concept in which this content is found. In the content of peripheral personality, we can get a more vivid picture of what the theorist thinks characterizes life than would be possible in considerations of the fine points of the form of concepts. One can certainly quibble about whether the theorist has expressed his or her views in the most elegant and precise form, but in the final analysis differences and similarities among peripheral-level theories will be carried primarily in matters of content or substance. And peripheral-level content is more useful in understanding the concrete ways in which adults lead their lives than is core-level content, the latter being unconcerned with particular types of people.

Although the three models for personality theorizing that we have been considering do not appear to have been a determining influence on the kinds of peripheral concepts employed, they do have definite implications for the content emphasized. In pinpointing these content implications, I have found it useful to use the distinction between the ideal and nonideal peripheral personalities.

The Conflict Model

You will recall that at the core level the essence of the conflict model is expressed in the inevitable opposition of two great forces. In the psychosocial form of this model, one of the forces expresses the human as an individual and the other as a member of society. As society is more powerful than individuals, this version of the conflict model makes all behavior defensive. Persons will try to get what they want only if they can find a way of doing so that will be consistent with the corporate good, for fear of what would happen otherwise. One would expect such theories, at the peripheral level, to stress ideal functioning indicative of socialization (dependability, adaptation, adjustment to social pressures, attitudes and values consistent with and justificatory of the social order) and nonideal functioning indicative of social immaturity (irresponsibility, competitiveness, impulsivity, withdrawal, rebelliousness, conformity).

Sure enough, in the pure psychosocial conflict theory of Freud we see much that conforms to the expectations stated above. The ideal or genital type is someone who can truly love and work. But remember that loving and working occur on the basis of a defensive process—sublimation—and hence even this highest form of living does not transcend societal regulations. It is not too inaccurate to say of this theory that it explains adults as loving on the rebound (having had to give up the original love object—the opposite-sexed parent) and working as a way of channeling anti social instincts into acceptable behavior. Hence, the giving and receiving of love at biological, social, and psychological levels and the commitment to regular, productive enterprise will each involve stability, dependability, and adjustment to pressures. There will be generosity, responsibility, and predictability more than flamboyance and impulsivity. The picture is of solidity in whatever one does. In contrast, the nonideal or pregenital types are bogged down in self-preoccupation with how, when, why, and whether to take and receive, give and withhold, and heterosexualize living. The task-oriented process of straightforward, dependable, productive living is frequently interrupted by these signs of insecurity, self-preoccupation, selfishness, and rigidity. Pregenital persons are too concerned with themselves to be good citizens. Freud's content emphases at the periphery consistently derive from his emphases at the core.

Two variants on the psychosocial conflict model, Murray and Erikson, generally show the expected peripheral content emphases in considering non-ideal functioning. Murray endorses, with some elaboration, the pregenital types of Freud. So does Erikson, although he adds some nonideal emphases such as identity-diffusion, social isolation, stagnation, and despair. But as you can see, these additions are quite in character with the psychosocial conflict model. With regard to the characteristics of ideal functioning, Murray and Erikson are only partially expressive of this model. In addition to the solid virtues designated by Freudians, Murray and Erikson consider the possibility of at least some degree of imaginativeness, originality, and changeability. These additional emphases have not always seemed convincingly articulated with core assumptions. You will recall, for example, that White criticized Erikson's view of ideal peripheral characteristics as being too optimistic in their socially transcendent implications for a conflict model, with its inevitable subjugation of the individual to society. Further, I called to your attention in Chapter 7 the odd fact that Murray's peripheral theorizing, emphasizing needs and need-integrates, did not seem to fit, or be fitted by him, into the core characteristics of id, ego, and superego. Perhaps the most meaningful conclusion to reach is that the theories of Murray and Erikson are in transition away from the psychosocial conflict model.

Although the peripheral content emphases of Kohut and Berne are not particularly predictable from their classification under the psychosocial conflict model, neither is there any sense of incompatibility. The socially ineffective behaviors of persons with narcissistic disorders or unfortunate life scripts clearly indicate that the ideal for these theorists emphasizes social adjustment. In a way, it is surprising that their peripheral theorizing is so compatible with Freud's, as they so clearly appear to be breaking away from his views.

In the intrapsychic version of the conflict model, all of the inevitably opposed forces emanate from within the person. As there is no assumption of a powerful society bent on detecting and thwarting the individual, ideal functioning does not emphasize defensiveness. This is not to say that the relationship between individuals and their society is irrelevant. It is always relevant, because one of the opposing forces leads in the direction of individuation and isolation, whereas the other leads in the direction of dependence and gregariousness. The best that can be achieved is a compromise in which both forces are expressed. Thus, at the peripheral level, ideal functioning should show a commitment to being an individual in some fashion that can be respected by those around one, and to associating oneself with people and ideas without hampering one's own growth. These adjustments will be made with flexibility and awareness, as there is little defensiveness. Nonideal functioning should express the defensive negation of either the force toward individuality or the force toward union. The first alternative would stress rebelliousness and rejection of other people and the second anxious conformity. Both alternatives would involve inflexibility, because they are defensive in nature. As you can perceive, nonideal functioning in both intrapsychic and psychosocial conflict theories is similar. Ideal functioning is a bit less steady and more flamboyant in the intrapsychic version. Actually, the intrapsychic version comes quite close to the variant of the psychosocial version.

Of the intrapsychic conflict theories, only those of Rank and Jung make an extensive statement concerning peripheral personality. The content emphases of Rank conform very well to expectation. The two nonideal types are the average person (emphasis on conformity, passivity, and dependence) and the neurotic (emphasis on rebelliousness and insistent alienation from people). The ideal type, or artist, transcends conventional society, but in a fashion that can be respected by others and therefore permits retention of relationship to them. Artists essentially are heroes. What they do is extraordinary, but they do not do it simply for themselves.

At first blush, Jung's position does not seem to conform so well to expectation. The ideal for him is to achieve selfhood, which involves developing a kind of universal personality, not individualistic so much as expressive of what is in us all. Consciousness is only one aspect of selfhood and must make way for acceptance and expression of the collective unconscious if the ideal is to be achieved. But in a way, Jung is agreeing with the other intrapsychic conflict theorists. After all, the ego, or seat of consciousness, is an individualistic force with which persons navigate in the external world of events, affairs, and outcomes. They need to incorporate the collective unconscious into their day-to-day functioning in order for it to temper the individualistic ego with the accumulated, shared wisdom of humankind. Thus, in achieving selfhood, the person strikes a balance between individualistic and communal tendencies. The other personality types (e.g., introverted rational, extroverted irrational), in that they do not give an important role to the collective unconscious, can be interpreted as being too individualistic to be ideal. But it must be admitted that at the peripheral level Jung's position is less clearly expressive of the intrapsychic conflict model than is Rank's.

The Fulfillment Model

The fulfillment model postulates only one great force, thereby avoiding the assumption that conflict is inevitable. But the one force does express human individuality, and hence persons may come in conflict with society. This happens only when they have been failed by society, but the consequence for them is, nonetheless, nonideal functioning. As society is stronger than the individual, nonideal functioning is defensive.

At the core level, the actualization version of the fulfillment model stresses the humanistic belief that the content of the great force is the person's inherent potentialities and the inexorable attempt to realize them in tangible form. One need do nothing more to be ideal than give oneself over to one's genetic blueprint and follow it wherever it leads. The intentional, self-conscious actions one might wish to take will corrupt expression of the actualizing tendency. At the peripheral level, the actualization version of the fulfillment model should stress spontaneity, changeability, unself-conscious acceptance of self and others, simple confidence, sensitivity, imaginativeness, and impulsivity. In contrast, nonideal functioning should involve premeditation, an evaluative attitude, planfulness, anxious conformity, lack of confidence, and an overwhelming sense of obligation to a monolithic duty.

The peripheral statements of Rogers, the pure actualization theorist, conform almost exactly to these expectations. Fully functioning, or ideal, persons will show openness to experience, existential living, organismic trusting, creativity, and congruence between their view of themselves and what their potentialities really suit them to be. In contrast, nonideal, or maladjusted, persons will show strong preoccupation with how, when, why, and what they are or what they should do. These rigidifying concerns introduce a constraint in the direction of conformity and fixity that interferes with the more mature process of continually enlarging and experiencing one's capabilities. Maslow, the variant of the actualization version of the fulfillment model, shares these emphases with Rogers but adds to them certain ideological considerations. Ideal persons, according to Maslow, also possess democratic and humanitarian values that presumably also guide their behavior. Nonideal persons possess authoritarian and materialistic values. In this emphasis on values, both ideal and nonideal, Maslow seems to approach the perfection version of the fulfillment model.

In the perfection version, there is little concern with inherent potentialities as a basis for individuality. Instead, there is a conception of what perfect life, or essential human nature, is like. It is this goal toward which the human is impelled, often regardless of real or imagined inferiorities. At the peripheral level, perfection theorizing should emphasize evidence of transcendence over one's own limitations and those of society, guided always by ideals and principles that are superordinate to humans. In contrast, nonideal functioning should stress concern with mere biological survival and satisfaction, anxious conformity, and the avoidance of risk. As you can see, the content implications of the actualization and perfection versions of the fulfillment model are quite similar. The mild differences between the positions show the actualization version emphasizing intuitive functioning, sensitivity, spontaneity, and impulsivity and the perfection version rational functioning and consistent striving toward goals that have little to do with either inherent potentialities or societal pressures. These differences all stem from the actualization emphasis on a genetic blueprint and the perfection emphasis on the best in living regardless of endowment.

Happily, the perfection theorists include much in their peripheral theorizing that matches what I have just said. In Allport's emphasis on maturity as the presence of a consistent philosophy of life, a religious sentiment, and a generic conscience, we see how ideals are expected to infuse ideal functioning. Nonideal functioning, for Allport, is opportunistic, erratic, impulsive, pleasure seeking, defensive, and conforming. In more rudimentary form one sees similar implications in Adler, whose peripheral position unfortunately is not very elaborate. Taking the active-constructive and passive-constructive styles of life as indicative of the ideal, we emerge with a view that stresses ambition to reach certain goals and charmingness with regard to other people. Adlerians may intend in such emphases to imply transcendence of self and society in the service of ideals, but this will not be entirely certain until their peripheral theorizing is further clarified. White's emphasis on consistent, perfectionist striving and rationality can be seen in his adoption of the peripheral theorizing of Erikson, with its concern at the ideal level with ego integrity, generativity, intimacy, and identity, and at the nonideal level, with its emphasis on despair, stagnation, isolation, and identity diffusion. It is interesting that White has explicitly borrowed Erikson's theorizing. Not only is Erikson a variant of the conflict model, moving toward the fulfillment model; White may also be an incipient fulfillment variant, with something of the conflict theorist in him. I say the latter because, in an important paper on competence and the psychosexual stages of development, White (1960) does accept that there is some value to the psychosocial conflict model, even though it must be supplemented by his fulfillment emphasis.

The key to understanding Fromm is his suggestion that ideal functioning be defined as the most constructive aspects of the nonproductive (nonideal) orientations. Generally speaking, from the receptive orientation, one would derive tolerance, acceptance, trust, and the ability to be dependent; from the exploitative orientation, initiative, impulsivity, and effectiveness in grappling with external pressures; from the hoarding orientation, conservation of resources, loyalty, and a sense of the value of things; and from the marketing orientation, adaptability, curiosity, changeability, and open-mindedness. Fromm includes both the qualities of spontaneity and openness of the actualization position and the striving and sense of industry of the perfection position. As I pointed out in Chapter 4, this combining of emphases is also apparent in his core statements. The opposites of the qualities mentioned above define nonideal functioning, which strongly emphasizes conformity, pleasure seeking, and concern with biological survival.

In existential psychology, ideal functioning is called *individualism* or *authenticity* and stresses the development of sufficient consciousness to permit proper understanding of the true nature of life as a series of decisions. With this understanding comes the ability to make decisions well, evaluate ontological anxiety against ontological guilt, and take responsibility for what one does. The emphasis here is on rationality, self-reliance, independence, and honesty. Nonideal functioning, or conformism, is the opposite. In conformism, consciousness is not highly developed and the stereotypes and conventions of society are clung to in the vain attempt to avoid making decisions. Clearly existential psychology expresses in its peripheral statements what we would expect of the perfection fulfillment model.

The Consistency Model

As the consistency model makes minimal content assumptions at the core level, there is little that can be formulated by way of expected content at the peripheral level. Any or no specification of peripheral content would be understandable. If content is specified, however, it should at least reflect the procedures whereby people can ensure maximal consistency.

Turning to the actual theories, we find that the pure cognitive dissonance theorist, Kelly, specifies no peripheral content. The variant of this position, McClelland, does specify content, but it is an eclectic, omnibus specification and, as such, does not deviate from what we would expect. The activation theorist, Maddi, specifies content in a less omnibus fashion than McClelland. Virtually all the content in Maddi's peripheral theorizing refers to specialized procedures for anticipating activation requirements or correcting discrepancies between actual and customary levels of activation. This is true for tendencies to approach or avoid intensity, meaningfulness, and variety of stimulation and for the development of differentiation and integration of functioning. The content emphases of the activation version of the consistency model do not appear as important considerations in the other models. The major basis in Maddi's thinking for differentiating ideal from nonideal functioning is the activeness-passiveness trait. This trait is, at the same time, not strictly derivable from the core assumptions of the activation position and similar in emphasis and implications to the bases for distinguishing ideal from non ideal that appear in the perfection version of the fulfillment model.

CHAPTER 11
Empirical Analysis of Peripheral Considerations

In the end, any conceptualization is only as adequate as its empirical support. It would be of no use to have a theory that is beautiful from the standpoint of reason but does not account for the relevant facts or is contradicted by them. We should hasten, therefore, to consider the empirical studies that bear on peripheral theorizing. An analysis of empirical studies could yield evidence concerning which of the postulated peripheral characteristics really exist and how they actually organize themselves into larger units, or types. Empirical analysis can also indicate the amount of behavior (data) explained by each of the existing peripheral characteristics. Having all this information, it would be easy to decide on the relative fruitfulness of the various peripheral theories and the models they represent.

From what I have said, you can see that an empirical analysis could do great things. In the analysis we will conduct, however, it will be possible only to reach more modest conclusions, many of them tentative at that. Although it is possible to specify the kinds of studies that would permit the strong conclusions mentioned above, such ideal studies have not been done in the main. Nonetheless, I will outline studies that should be undertaken, organized in the form of a three-step strategy. If you comprehend this ideal strategy and the kinds of inferences it would permit, you will have no difficulty understanding why the actual studies we will subsequently consider are relevant. And who knows—when you see the discrepancies between the conclusions we can and might have reached, you may find yourself motivated to conduct studies that more closely approximate the ideal.

THE IDEAL STRATEGY

Step One: Measuring Concrete Peripheral Characteristics

In approaching an adequate empirical analysis of peripheral theorizing, the first step is to attempt to develop an empirical measure for each peripheral characteristic specified in the various theories under consideration. Arduous though this is, there is no way around it. An attempt must be made to measure all the traits mentioned by Freud, all the needs of Murray, and so forth down

402

the list of personologists. Here and there on the list you will encounter some theorists, such as Allport and Kelly, who offer literally nothing on which to base a measurement attempt. Others, such as White, are so unspecific in describing personality types that it takes much guesswork to decide which peripheral characteristics they consider important. Here is striking demonstration of the drawback of lack of theoretical elaboration at the peripheral level. How are you supposed to measure something if it is not clear what it is? Whoever attempts to carry out the first step of this ideal strategy will sigh with relief and gratitude on encountering a personologist who is explicit concerning the form and content of peripheral characteristics.

In any event, in attempting to measure the various peripheral characteristics that have been postulated, you must be guided not by what you think a characteristic really means but by what the personologist under consideration thinks about it. Only in this fashion can the success or failure of the measurement attempt be considered a reflection of the adequacy of the theorizing. We have little trouble being guided by the theorist's meaning when he or she has provided us with an operational definition of the postulated characteristic. An *operational definition* is a literal specification of what you must do in order to observe the entity under consideration. Unfortunately, only McClelland, Murray, and Maddi even try to provide operational definitions, with McClelland's being a little more useful because they are less ambiguous. And even McClelland offers complete operational definitions for only some motives.

To see the value of operational definitions, recall McClelland's discussion of motives. In Chapters 9 and 10, we saw that in a formal sense, a motive is a personal goal and the instrumental capability for pursuing it in a wide variety of situations. In discussing measurement operations, McClelland (1961) recognizes the formal attributes of motives that distinguish them from traits and schemata. A motive involves a personal goal, and therefore the measurement operation must elicit mentation rather than merely actions. But not just any mentation will do. The goal to be measured is personal, not social, and hence one must favor measurement operations that will not suggest to persons that their behavior will be judged as to its social desirability. As soon as you start asking persons questions about their goals or actions, you are too likely to get responses in terms of what is considered socially appropriate. Such questioning may be useful in the measurement of schemata, but it is misleading for measuring motives. Taking the requirement of personal mentation into account, McClelland concludes that the best measurement operations involve eliciting fantasy from the person in the form of stories composed about pictures of fictitious people and then analyzing the content of the stories for evidence of goals and predispositions to instrumental behavior relevant to them. The meaning of the pictures should be ambiguous enough and the task of making up stories sufficiently unstructured to render it unlikely the person will respond with socially desirable rather than personal goals. Further, since the human content of the pictures arouses mentation concerning what the fictitious people are doing and may want, one is likely to get information about motives rather than traits, as the latter are so habitual as to be virtually unrepresented in the composition of stories. Some of you may recognize the task described here as Murray's (1943) famous *Thematic Apperception Test*. Although this technique was available prior to McClelland's attempt to measure motives, it is extremely well suited to his operationalization. And anyway, Murray devised the test primarily for the measurement of his very similar need concept, though he never provided the compelling operational rationale available in McClelland's theorizing. It is to Murray's credit that McClelland had his ground-breaking work on which to build.

McClelland (1961) is almost as precise about the manner in which the form of schemata is to be measured. If you want to know about persons' social goals, defined by their values and sense of social roles, you might as well just ask them straightforwardly. It matters little whether they spruce up their answers because they think they will be evaluated by society, for it is just their sense of what society stands for that you want to measure. Questionnaires concerning the directionalities and goals in people's behavior tend to elicit schemata, as opposed to fantasies, or so-called projective tasks, which tend to elicit motives. Finally, from a formal standpoint, traits are to be measured by creating familiar circumstances in which action is called for and then observing the regularities in people's functioning.

My summary of McClelland's operational attempts is of necessity brief, but I want you to appreciate that no other personologists come close to him in precision. Indeed, going beyond the formal attributes, McClelland even offers very workable operational definitions for the content of the motives he has most strongly emphasized (achievement, affiliation, and power). For example, the operational definition for the achievement motive is *competition with a standard of excellence* (McClelland et al., 1953, pp. 110–112). Along with this overall definition, you are provided with a carefully devised scoring system with which to analyze fantasy for evidence of interest in competition with a standard of excellence (McClelland et al., 1953, pp. 107–138). With varying emphases and degrees of precision, Murray and Maddi provide measurement specifications in a fashion similar to McClelland.

Once you leave McClelland, Murray, and Maddi, you are on your own in measuring the peripheral characteristics offered by personologists. The best you can find are vivid descriptions of the application of a characteristic to life events. If such descriptions are extensive enough, you can form an impression of what the theorist means that is sufficiently precise to help you in deciding on measurement operations. Once you have selected the appropriate measurement operations for the entire set of peripheral characteristics, you can proceed with the tedious but unavoidable and important job of attempting to provide adequate measures. Assuming that the measure already has theoretical adequacy (or face validity) by virtue of the careful selection of measurement operations, it remains to be seen whether it can be demonstrated to have empirical existence.

In major part, a peripheral characteristic will be considered as having empirical existence if its measure has adequate *reliability*. There are two kinds of reliability: called internal consistency and stability.

In order to appreciate *internal consistency,* you must keep in mind that a measure almost always has a number of parts. For example, if you are measuring need for achievement with a scoring system to be used on fantasy productions, the different categories in the scoring system will be the parts of the measure. If your measure is a questionnaire, each question will be a part of the measure. Internal consistency refers to the degree to which the parts of the measure, presumably put there for theoretical reasons, appear to go together at an empirical level of analysis. On a questionnaire, this will involve determining the likelihood that a person answering one of the questions will answer the others in a similar fashion. On a scoring system applied to fantasy, internal consistency will be expressed as the tendency to apply the various scoring categories in the same way to a given person's productions. If you demonstrate sufficient internal consistency, you will have found empirical support for the contention that your measure gets at some genuine entity. The entity is genuine in the sense that its postulated parts really do seem to hang together.

But exactly how internally consistent a measure should be before you conclude that it reflects something real is a ticklish question. For some concepts, such as trait, you would expect a high degree of internal consistency because, theoretically, the range of behaviors that comprises it should be small and the behaviors very similar to one another. But a concept such as need or motive is inherently more heterogeneous, comprising not only goals but instrumental sequences of action, all of which wax and wane. In short, even though peripheral characteristics are supposed to be the basic unit of peripheral personality, we should recognize that the degree of internal consistency required of such characteristics partially depends on their postulated status. Nonetheless, unless a measure has at least moderate internal consistency, there is little empirical ground for considering it as reflecting a genuine entity.

When you assess the stability of a measure, you are determining the likelihood that you will get the same result with it when you apply it to the same people on two or more similar occasions separated in time. Generally speaking, the closer the results from the different testing sessions, the more justified you will feel in considering your measure as getting at some genuine entity. This is because peripheral characteristics are assumed to be reasonably stable in life. But exactly how stable we should require a measure to be is, once again, a partially theoretical question. In theory, some peripheral characteristics, such as Rogers's openness to experience and McClelland's need for achievement, should be less stable over time than some others, such as Freud's stinginess. If you are open to experience, you will literally be different from moment to moment, and your need for achievement should be high when it is frustrated but low when it is satisfied. So the degree of stability that we require as evidence of empirical existence is partially determined by how the theorist describes the nature of the characteristic assessed by the measure. But as with internal consistency, there must be at least moderate stability before you have empirical grounds for considering the measure as reflecting a genuine entity.

From an empirical point of view, a measure must be made up of parts that are homogeneous and that work the same way more than once. If these two things are not true, it may well be that the rational, or theoretical, adequacy of the peripheral characteristic being measured was more apparent than real. We want peripheral characteristics that are convincing not only rationally but empirically. If the attempt to measure a characteristic has been capably undertaken and internal consistency and/or stability is found to be lacking, you can be sure there is a heretofore unrecognized theoretical problem to blame. A common theoretical problem in such cases is the choice of peripheral characteristics that are less irreducible than they might have seemed (Fiske, 1963). If a peripheral characteristic can be subdivided further, when you attempt to measure it you will find a lack of internal consistency because the measure incorporates disparate parts. If you build your theory of personality on peripheral characteristics that turn out to be inconsistent at the empirical level, you are building on shifting sands.

The failure of attempts to develop reliable measures can well be the occasion for theorists' returning to the drawing board. They can revamp a peripheral characteristic in the hope of making it more homogeneous, or they can undertake a more sweeping reconsideration of all their peripheral-level theorizing. Clearly evidence on the reliability of measures of currently postulated peripheral characteristics can aid us in empirically evaluating the theories of personality they represent. We may find that one or another theory or model for theorizing seems to do a better job from the standpoint of this initial empirical criterion of reliability of measures. If so, we will be justified in reaching the tentative conclusion that this theory or model for theorizing is more empirically genuine. The conclusion would be tentative, because assessment of the reliability of measures is only the first step in the ideal strategy for empirical analysis of peripheral-level theorizing.

Step Two: Interrelationships among Measures

The completion of the first step in the empirical analysis of peripheral-level theorizing should leave you with measures of those peripheral characteristics that indeed lend themselves to reliable measurement. Some concrete peripheral characteristics postulated by certain theorists undoubtedly will have fallen by the wayside. In other words, they will not have met the empirical criterion of reliable measurement. Indeed, it is possible that most of some unfortunate personologist's peripheral theory will not have survived the first step in empirical analysis.

The second step begins with the surviving peripheral characteristics and concerns peripheral-level theorizing about types. You take all the reliable measures you have been able to develop and determine the relationships among them. You would do this by applying the measures to the same group of people and then analyzing the results with available statistical techniques for determining *relationship*. A useful technique for what I have in mind is *factor analysis*. This technique not only determines how strongly a number of measures are related to one another but organizes those that are most closely interrelated into clusters, called *factors*. Factor analysis is a very powerful and important technique in the empirical assessment of peripheral-level theorizing.

Take Fromm's peripheral-level theorizing as an example for explaining the value of factor analysis. Assume all of the traits that he presents under the five character orientations have been reliably measured and that all the measures have been applied to the same group of people. One thing a factor analysis will tell us is whether these traits cluster together in the manner predicted by his theory. There should be clusters of trait measures (factors) corresponding to the receptive, exploitative, hoarding, marketing, and productive orientations. If there is nothing like this, we can say that there is no empirical support in the clustering of traits for Fromm's peripheral-level theorizing about types of people. Whatever the organization of traits does show does not conform to the theory. Alternatively, we could find that Fromm's theorizing is quite strongly supported by empirical evidence or even that it is only moderately supported.

Another important thing about this second step is that all measures could be applied to all people studied. Hence, it becomes possible to determine the correlations and factor clusterings of the peripheral characteristics of not only one theory but of all theories under consideration. This is an ideal empirical procedure for determining the overlap among theories. We no longer have to rely on our rationality alone to determine whether, for example, what Fromm talks about as the hoarding orientation is essentially what Freud means by the anal character type.

Step Three: Construct Validity of Peripheral Theorizing

The third and final step in the ideal strategy for the empirical analysis of peripheral theorizing concerns the *validity* of peripheral characteristics. Obviously these characteristics are meant to be used in explaining something. It would be meaningless for them to explain nothing more than their own measures, for these measures are, after all, only the empirical form of the concept. It is important for you to grasp the idea that each peripheral characteristic has been theoretically developed so as to serve as the explanation for a particular set of human behaviors (other than the measure of the characteristic). For example, take McClelland's need for achievement and its measure involving fantasy behavior. In general, such a characteristic would be used to explain such entities—call them *variables*—as competitive social relationships, an interest in accumulating money, a strong commitment to work, an uneasiness with leisure time, and so forth. These variables can be said to be explained by the need for achievement. The higher a person is on this need, the more pronounced should such variables be in his or her everyday life.

The hypothesized relationships between the need for achievement and these other variables can be tested empirically due to the existence of a measure for the need that involves behavior that differs radically from that involved in the variables. If data obtained from a group of subjects showed that the fantasy measure participates in a network of relationships with the relevant variables, we would be in a position to conclude that the construct—need for achievement—had validity. To be extra careful, we would also want to demonstrate that the fantasy measure did not correlate with variables that bore no theoretical relationship to it.

What I have described comes very close to the assessment of construct validity as formulated by Cronbach and Meehl (1955). It is not the only kind of validity, but it seems the most relevant to the empirical analysis of peripheral theorizing. Other forms of validity investigation are more appropriate when the measure under consideration is intended to predict one variable to a very high degree (e.g., measure of high school grades as a predictor of college success). In contrast, each peripheral characteristic is usually conceptualized as influencing a reasonably wide selection of variables of human behavior. And the degree of influence is usually considered only moderate, as can be seen from the fact that personologists believe that in order to fully explain any one behavioral variable, a number of peripheral characteristics acting simultaneously must be invoked. Taking this seriously, it becomes clear that we can consider a peripheral characteristic as being valid if its measure shows moderate intercorrelation with a set of theoretically relevant variables (*convergent validation*) and an absence of intercorrelation with theoretically irrelevant variables (*discriminant validation*). For further discussion, see Campbell and Fiske (1959).

Thus far, we have discussed the validation of only single characteristics. A further goal within the third step of our strategy is to determine whether the entire list of peripheral characteristics offered by a theorist really does account for all the variables of human behavior. Although each peripheral characteristic, taken by itself, is not intended to account for all behavior, the entire list offered really should do this job. Virtually all personologists say, at one place or another in their writing, that they accept the goal of explaining all behavior. So two criteria—namely, that each peripheral characteristic actually explain only the variables it was postulated to explain and that the entire set of characteristics offered explain all variables—define the assessment of empirical validity.

In order to carry out this step, we need to know a good deal about what are to be considered the variables of human behavior. Here we encounter extraordinary difficulty. Of the personologists considered in this book, only Murray even touches the question of data categories. He offers the data designations of *proceedings* and *serials* (see Maddi, 1963; Maddi & Costa, 1972). A *proceeding* is a psychologically meaningful unit of behavior, having a specifiable beginning and end and some duration in time. A proceeding might be having a conversation, solving a problem in your head, or writing a paper. Proceedings can be social or solitary, passive or action oriented, as long as they are meaningful to the person engaging in them. A *serial* is a number of proceedings organized in a sequential fashion, as in a marriage or a college career. It is proceedings and serials, Murray argues, that are to be explained by peripheral characteristics. Unfortunately, Murray gives us no help in deciding how we are to identify proceedings and serials. There is only the hint—in the insistence that they be meaningful to the person—that they are to be introspectively defined. In other words, persons will virtually define them for themselves.

Generally speaking, the other personologists offer no more along the lines of a data language than the notion that a theory of personality ought to explain all behavior. This statement is so excessively general as to be arid, but it corresponds with what I have already said in Chapter 1: that personologists tend to define behavior as having regularity across situations and continuity over time. If the person is competitive, or generous, or idealistic over a range of situations and time, the personologist is interested. As you can see, this position is even more vague than Murray's. How in the world are we to proceed with the third step?

Probably, the most feasible thing to do is read the descriptions and examples of life made by personologists when discussing the peripheral level of personality. In this reading, you should remain alert for indications of the variables considered relevant to particular peripheral characteristics and, in a more general vein, the full range of variables discussed. Even from the descriptions quoted in Chapters 7 through 9 you can get an idea of what I am suggesting. Recall, for example, the vivid description of the anal personality type by Rado (1959, p. 326) and Fromm's (1947, pp. 68–72) descriptions of marketing and other orientations, so replete with behavioral references separate from what you would use as measures of the relevant peripheral characteristics. In addition, the behaviors relevant to the need for achievement mentioned earlier in this chapter are straight from McClelland's descriptions. All the variables in the life descriptions offered by the personologists we are considering would constitute the behavior we have to work with in our empirical analysis. Perhaps it would be helpful to adopt, as a heuristic device to facilitate alert reading, the distinctions in Chapter 10 between repetitive behaviors and directional behaviors, each of which may have personal or social goals. These distinctions are implied in many personologists' writings.

With this large group of variables in hand, we could in principle proceed with the empirical analysis of validity. It would be best to have available the same group of people on whom the second step of our analysis was performed. It would be necessary to agree on how to best identify the existence and intensity of the variables constituting data in each of the people being studied. Perhaps, for this purpose, they could be asked to give extensive descriptions of their own behavior, and we could then scrutinize these descriptions. Even better, though more cumbersome, would be to observe these people over some period of time in many different situations and to use these observations as estimates of the variables' intensity. Or the two possibilities could be combined. Murray (1938) tried such a combination in his path-finding attempt to understand personality.

We could then combine in the same factor analysis not only variables but measures of peripheral characteristics. What we would expect is that clusters composed of theoretically appropriate variables, plus measures, would emerge from the analysis. If, for example, the measure of need for achievement appeared in the same cluster with such variables as (1) competitive actions, (2) the sense of time as important, and (3) a commitment to hard work, we could conclude that there is convergent validational evidence for McClelland's theorizing. Further support would be the finding that the need-for-achievement measure did not appear in any other cluster, thus indicating discriminant validation. Although factor analysis usually is considered an exploratory technique, what I am suggesting amounts to using it deductively to test hypotheses concerning the relationship of certain peripheral characteristics to specific behaviors. Nor are we necessarily restricted to factor analysis, for that matter; there are now several forms of multi variate analysis that would serve. All that is important is that you grasp the logic of what is intended here.

Clearly, if a theorist's peripheral characteristics are to have empirical validity, they must show a relationship with the relevant variables. Overall, if peripheral-level theorizing is to be considered complete by empirical standards, there should also not be a large proportion of variables unrelated to one or another of the peripheral characteristics. This is so, incidentally, even if the unrelated behavior is not of the kind referred to in the theorizing, because the personologists included here have committed themselves to explaining virtually all behavior. If they say that personality explains all behavior, without being more specific, they must account for all viable behavioral variables, even those they do not specifically mention in their descriptions. What one says as a theorist is important; hence, one should say only what one means.

A Word of Practicality

The strategy just described seems to me close to ideal for determining which of the postulated peripheral characteristics are homogeneous and stable enough to be considered genuine, for discerning the nature of their organization into types, and for specifying the validity of peripheral theorizing. Although the strategy has a potentially great yield for personology, carrying out its procedures would be extraordinarily difficult and time consuming. Clearly scoring and analyzing the data on the huge scale advocated could be done only with the help of giant computers and the financing of large foundations supporting basic research in psychology. Also necessary would be the services of a large staff which could count on the cooperation of many personologists not directly involved in the work. As to the results, it must be expected with such large amounts of initial data that some of the factors obtained in the third, and perhaps even the second, step of the strategy will be virtually impossible to interpret in an intellectually satisfying manner. These uninterpretable factors would reflect such irrelevant things as common but theoretically unimportant procedures for measuring variables and even accidental similarities of data. To be sure, all large-scale research in the personality area is likely to uncover some results that are ambiguous or irrelevant to personality theorizing. If one avoids panicking, it will be possible to simply accept that some factors will be uninterpretable and still carry out the strategy reasonably effectively by requiring that those that are interpretable conform to what would be expected in one or another of the theories. Nonetheless, it must be noted that this ideal strategy would be difficult to carry out in a practical manner at this time because of its massiveness.

It will be valuable to keep this strategy in mind, however, so that it may serve as a goal toward which simpler, more feasible efforts can be pointed. For example, it may be more practical at this time to focus on single theories of peripheral personality rather than on all of them at once. But in focusing on a single theory, we could still employ the various steps in the strategy. Such a program of research would include only the variables and measures relevant to the particular theory in question, with the results clarifying which variables, peripheral characteristics, and types, if any, were not empirically viable. And if different groups of investigators were working on different theories, one could soon begin to gain an overall view of the most fruitful approaches to peripheral theorizing by comparing the results of these various research projects. Even such approximations to the ideal strategy would be a big improvement over current research practice. As Carlson (1971) pinpoints ably in her review, broad (to say nothing of comprehensive) efforts to measure personality are virtually absent from the contemporary research literature.

Having discussed a proposed ideal strategy and a practical version of it, I would like to move on to procedures that are actually practiced in personology. As you may have surmised, the empirical evidence available on the basis of current practice falls short in various ways of the evidence required in the ideal strategy. Nonetheless, we must turn to what is available in the hope of gaining some increased knowledge concerning the peripheral theories. Perhaps having considered an ideal strategy will alert you to the shortcomings of the work we will be considering. But lest I arouse too much cynicism in you, let me point out that some of the work reviewed in the following pages is striking, dramatic, and important. Without it, the personality field would be far less vital.

FACTOR ANALYTIC STUDIES

As you will recall, the third step in the ideal strategy calls for employing factor analysis in determining the intercorrelations among a large group of variables and measures of peripheral characteristics. The characteristics would be considered empirically validated when their measures correlated only with theoretically relevant variables. Although I advocated a particular use of factor analysis, you should recognize that it is a general procedure for determining the empirical clustering of any variables based on their intercorrelations. It is not at all necessary that measures of peripheral characteristics be included along with other variables. Indeed, such measures have almost never been included in the available factor analytic studies relevant to personality. Typically the investigator obtains data on a group of variables, performs a factor analysis on them, and then attempts to interpret the meaning of the clusters or factors obtained. It might be concluded that the factors expressed some particular peripheral characteristics described in the personological literature. Going further, it would be possible to perform another factor analysis on the factors already obtained. The result of this would be a set of so-called second-order factors, describing the way the original factors grouped themselves into larger units. It would then be possible to try to interpret these larger units as expressive of particular personality types described in the personological literature.

The above procedure can constitute an inductive strategy for empirical evaluation of peripheral theorizing. It is inductive mainly because no measures of peripheral characteristics are included; hence, you cannot really test hypotheses concerning the relationship of such characteristics to behavioral variables. The best you can do with the inductive use of factor analysis is arrive at clusterings of behavioral variables that suggest—but only suggest—the relevance of particular peripheral characteristics. This may sound acceptable, but believe me, once you include in the factor analysis a sufficient number of variables to do justice to even a small number of theories, you obtain factors so complex and ambiguous that the task of interpreting just which peripheral characteristics and types they express becomes extremely arduous. One of the most vulnerable points of inductive factor analytic studies has been the almost inevitably intuitive, crude nature of the interpretation of factors. The aura of empirical rigor and objectivity attending the inductive use of factor analysis is deceptive. In contrast, the deductive use of factor analysis advocated in the ideal strategy involves much more straightforward interpretation of factors. Only when a factor includes both the measure of a peripheral characteristic and the major variables deemed expressive of it theoretically can that characteristic be considered empirically valid.

Most currently available factor analytic studies have been of the inductive type. Indeed, virtually all of these studies have fallen short of the ideal procedure in yet another way: They have not started with all the variables that seem to crop up in the writings of all personologists. To be sure, it would be acceptable, in the interest of practicality, for a study to concern itself with all of the variables in one theory alone; at least it could then be said that the study comprehensively treated that theory. Fortunately, some available studies have approximated this goal. But sometimes the variables included in a study are not really specifiable in an intellectually satisfying way (such as comprehensively treating a theory). The investigator, perhaps out of an atheoretical bias or theoretical naïveté, will include some heterogeneous array of variables, and not be concerned with the implications of doing so. The outcome of such factor analytic studies is of dubious value, for to consider the resulting evidence comprehensive or even representative with regard to life in general or some particular theory is erroneous and often seriously misleading. You get out of a factor analysis only what you put into it, and therefore it is never acceptable to be ignorant of the implications of the variables you have decided to consider. The set of variables considered should be either comprehensive or at least specifiable in a theoretically meaningful way. Fortunately, the naïve use of factor analysis is decreasing in psychology.

Cattell, Guilford, Eysenck, and others

Among factor analysts, the work of three people—Cattell, Guilford, and Eysenck—is especially pertinent to empirical evaluation of peripheral theorizing. First I will describe something of their procedures, leaving communication of their results for later.

The factor analytic work of Raymond Cattell closely approximates the inductive procedure mentioned in the preceding section. Cattell has attempted to obtain comprehensive behavioral information so that his results will reflect on the question of what peripheral characteristics it is most fruitful to postulate. Actually, like many factor analysts, Cattell has been much concerned with building comprehensive, valid tests of personality. This task is not really very different from that of clarifying the peripheral characteristics that should be represented in personality theory. In an effort to obtain behavioral observations comprehensively, Cattell (1946, 1957) began by assembling all personality-variable names occurring in the dictionary (as compiled by Allport & Odbert, 1936) or in the psychological literature. This list was first reduced to 171 variable names by combining obvious synonyms. Then a sample of 100 adults from many walks of life was selected. Associates of these people, who knew them well, were asked to rate them on these 171 variables. Intercorrelations and factor analyses of these ratings were followed by further ratings of 208 people on a shortened list of variables. Factor analyses of the latter ratings led to the identification of what Cattell describes as "the primary source traits of personality." Cattell and his associates then set out to build a personality test that would give evidence of these source traits. The end result of considerable investigation was the *16 Personality Factor Questionnaire* (Cattell & Stice, 1957), which is made up of many items concerning life activities for which the respondent must indicate liking or disliking. Twelve of the sixteen factors, which have been obtained through factor analyzing the answers to these items given by many people, are similar to those obtained in the earlier work with ratings, while four appeared only on the test.

In considering the findings most relevant to the task of empirical evaluation of peripheral theorizing, we should focus on the sixteen factors of Cattell's test. Each factor can be considered as reflecting a peripheral characteristic. Cattell has also factor analyzed the sixteen primary factors, or *source traits,* as he calls them, deriving from this analysis seven second-order factors that link the first-order factors together. The second-order factors might be considered as reflecting the organization of peripheral characteristics into types.

Before turning to the actual substance of Cattell's findings, a brief summary of the procedures of Guilford and Eysenck is in order. In finding behavioral data on which to perform factor analyses, Guilford and his associates (Guilford, 1959; Guilford & Zimmerman, 1956) collected the items from a number of personality tests already in common use. These tests had, by and large, been constructed along rational, theoretical lines rather than by some empirical clustering procedure such as factor analysis. Guilford had a sample of people answer all the items from these tests, which required them mainly to indicate whether or not they liked the various kinds of activities presented. The answers to items were then intercorrelated and factor analyzed. Through a long process of refining, pruning, and interpreting the resulting factors, a number of personality tests were constructed. The last of these is the most authoritative. Called the *Guilford-Zimmerman Temperament Survey* (Guilford, Zimmerman, & Guilford, 1976), it includes a large number of items to be endorsed as being liked or disliked and yields ten factors. These factors, like those in Cattell's test, can be considered as reflecting peripheral characteristics. Three to four second-order factors are also identified.

Of the three factor analysts being considered, Eysenck samples the possible range of behavioral observations least widely. Although his work is therefore less valuable to us than the others', it is nonetheless capable of teaching us something. In his first study (Eysenck, 1947), the sample was 700 neurotic soldiers. The behavioral data of the study included some answers given by the soldiers to factual questions about themselves and also some ratings of the soldiers made by psychiatrists. The total number of information items on which the factor analysis was performed was only thirty-nine. Eysenck finds two factors, or peripheral characteristics, to be sufficient to describe the clustering of items. Subsequently, Eysenck (1947) added more subjects to this original sample in an attempt to determine whether these two factors were still sufficiently descriptive of people to be considered basic. The final sample totaled roughly 10,000 normal and neurotic subjects, and the available information on them varied from responses on test items to behavior in performance situations. Eysenck has reported that the same two factors found to describe the original 700 neurotic soldiers continued to be descriptive of the larger sample.

We are in a difficult position in evaluating the relevance of Eysenck's work to our present concerns. He has, in toto, included more kinds of behavioral observation in his studies than have the other two factor analysts, who have relied primarily on responses to test items. But, following the original study, Eysenck has used a procedure called *criterion analysis,* which is essentially deductive rather than inductive. In criterion analysis, you already have in mind a hypothesis as to what the important factors are and, hence, plan your study so as to test that hypothesis. You select behavioral observations that you think will be theoretically relevant to the factors you consider important. You design your study to include *criterion groups,* which should possess discriminably different degrees of the hypothesized factors. The end result of this procedure is that you get information largely relevant to your hypotheses only rather than more general data. Since the two factors that have preoccupied Eysenck were originally found descriptive of neurotic soldiers—a rather unusual group of people—all that the generalization of these results to other people may mean is that some evidence of these two factors can be found in people in general. It does not at all mean that these two factors are as basic in describing people in general as they might have been in describing neurotic soldiers. The conclusion that people in general can be adequately and comprehensively described by two factors alone may be quite spurious.

There has been an ongoing and lively debate among factor analysts as to whether the factors offered by the three psychologists under discussion are the definitive ones. The intricacies of these contentions cannot be chronicled here. Suffice it to say that although none of the factor analytic schemes has gone uncriticized (e.g., Howarth, 1976; Howarth & Browne, 1971), there have also been defenses of them (e.g., Cattell, 1972; Eysenck, 1970, 1977; Guilford, 1975, 1977). Some investigators (e.g., French, 1973; Sells, Demaree, & Will, 1971) have attempted to compare the three factor schemes in the same research. Of these attempts, the work of Coan (1974) is especially noteworthy, because he not only included measures relevant to the factors of Cattell, Eysenck, and Guilford but tried to include measures reflecting various theoretical views of ideal personality. These latter measures were of such concepts as emotional adjustment, psychological differentiation and integration, experiential openness, personal control, and social activity. In addition, his measures were not only of self-report but of fantasy and performance ratings. Another important factor analytic study (Costa & McCrae, 1980) included many of Coan's measures and others selected from the existing literature.

Actually, it is not surprising that there is such dispute concerning which are the real first- and second-order factors. Relevant studies use different samplings of persons and vary considerably in the content and form (e.g., self-report, fantasy, performance ratings) of measures included. Also, the number of measures encompass a broad range as do the particular mathematical procedures for factor analysis. Given all this variation, it will be some time before clarity and agreement concerning a definitive list of factors are reached. Nonetheless, let us push on in our attempt to determine the implications of this body of research for the adequacy of peripheral theorizing. Needless to say, our conclusions will have to be tentative.

Number of Factors

The most obvious question on the relevance of factor analytic studies for peripheral personality theorizing concerns the number of factors that emerge. The number of first-order factors should tell us how many peripheral characteristics it is fruitful to assume. The number of second-order factors should suggest the number of types that might be theorized about.

Much debate over how many first- and second-order factors exist has been generated. To some degree, this debate has been fueled by unfortunate differences from study to study in the number of measures included, the size of sample used, and the data analysis decisions made. It is therefore difficult to arrive at any definite answer to the question. After all, you get out of a factor analysis only some version of what you put in! But there is certainly a range of first- and second-order factors that can be observed with some regularity. This range appears to be roughly three to twenty-one for first-order factors. Eysenck, of course, agrees, but you will recall that his original work was done on a small number of psychopathological subjects. Although his three factors certainly can be uncovered in other larger and more representative samples, it is not clear that the behavior of the subjects in these samples is exhaustively described by so few factors. Further, some investigators have argued that what Eysenck calls *first-order factors* are really second-order factors (e.g., Costa & McCrae, 1980). Agreeing with Eysenck's low estimate are Peabody (1984), who derives 3 factors from influences concerning 120 traits, and Norman (1963), who estimates 5 factors from personality ratings made by peers. Despite the recent popularity of Norman's so-called "big five," other investigators continue to report more than this number of factors, even when working with such small databases as one personality test. For example, Costa, Zonderman, Williams, and McCrae (1985) find 9 factors (only one of which matches Norman's in content) on 1,576 subjects, and Johnson, Null, Butcher, and Johnson (1984) report fully 21 factors from their sample of 20,000 subjects! The clearest conclusion to be reached is that the number of first-order factors is probably more than five and maybe closer to twenty. If we interpret Eysenck's factors as being second order, putting his work alongside that of others already mentioned suggests that the number of higher-order factors is about three.

What are the implications of these conclusions for peripheral theorizing? Let us say tentatively that theories should include between five and twenty concrete peripheral characteristics and about eight personality types. The number of personality types may sound odd, but consider that persons may be high or low on each of the three second-order factors. For example, if the second-order factors are introversion versus extroversion, anxiety versus calmness, and openness versus defensiveness, possible types would be introversive-anxious-open, introversive-calm-open, introversive-anxious-defensive, introversive-calm-defensive, extroversive-anxious-open, extroversive-calm-open, extroversive-anxious-defensive, and extroversive-calm-defensive. Moreover, these estimates are bound to be on the low side, because even the best factor analytic studies do not sample types of behaviors or subjects comprehensively. As a case in point, Knapp (1976) utilized only a few measures and nonetheless extracted ten first-order factors. Consequently, we should be more willing to accept theorizing that exceeds the estimates rather than theorizing that falls short of them.

Among the theorists who are specific concerning the periphery, two—the conflict theorist, Erikson, and the fulfillment theorist, Adler—seem to suggest fewer than ten characteristics. In Erikson's case this is not actually true, for, as you will recall, his eight developmental conflicts are probably intended as summaries of clustered peripheral characteristics. Those eight developmental conflicts would seem to correspond to second-order rather than first-order factors. Although Erikson has not then specified peripheral characteristics, it cannot be said that he has theorized about too few. Although one suspects a similar state of affairs for Adlerians, who probably would not really want to defend the position that there is only one peripheral characteristic associated with each lifestyle, they are, unfortunately, as unclear on this matter as is Erikson.

Although the upper limit ventured for peripheral characteristics undoubtedly is an underestimation, one wonders whether a more accurate figure would be great enough to justify the theorizing of Murray, McClelland, and Fromm. They have postulated a great many peripheral characteristics, you will recall. A perusal of the content of their lists suggests that at least some of the items are too synonymous to be considered separately. Given the relatively heterogeneous nature of Murray's need construct and the great number of needs postulated, there is bound to be some overlap among them at the empirical level. This difficulty will also be found in McClelland's position, since it adopts Murray's list of needs. And to convince yourself that Fromm has included some synonyms in his clusters of traits, simply go back to Chapter 8 and reread them.

Turning to types, you will recall that several theories consider only two types (Rogers, Maslow, existential psychology). Some others are at between four and six (Freud, Kohut, Rank, Adler, Fromm). This appears to be too few given the findings of factor analytic studies. It should be noted that at least existential psychology (see Kobasa & Maddi, 1977) is developing more types, but it has quite a distance to go. Among the theories that are reasonably specific concerning types, only activation theory specifies more than can be easily justified from factor analytic studies. Undoubtedly, several of the types in this theory will fall by the wayside as more attempts to measure them are made.

Kinds of Factors

Factor analysts tend to label their factors *traits*, though on closer scrutiny it becomes clear that they do not mean this in the narrow sense of habitual behaviors alone. They use the term *trait* broadly enough for it to be synonymous with our usage of the term *peripheral characteristic*. When one looks at the content of their factors, it becomes apparent that distinctions could be made among habitual behaviors (or traits, in the narrow sense), cognitive behaviors (or such things as values), and motivational behaviors. Indeed, one factor analyst, Cattell (1950), even offers the distinction between dynamic and nondynamic traits, calling the former *ergs* and the latter *traits*. This is very close to McClelland's distinction between motive and trait. These distinctions will be discussed along with the factors' content.

Content of Factors

Summarizing not only the first-order factors originally presented by Guilford and Cattell but also the results of other, more recent, studies, we can arrive at a reasonably clear picture of the general content that should be taken into account in peripheral theorizing. Costa and McCrae (1980) offer a well-documented and extensive list of first-order factors that is representative of the work of many other investigators. They list *anxiety, hostility, depression, self-consciousness, impulsiveness, vulnerability, attachment, gregariousness, asser-consciousness, impulsiveness, vulnerability, attachment, gregariousness, asser-sense, emotional variability, rigidity, theoretical orientation,* and *traditional values.* Persons may score high or low on any of these factors. Thus, the name listed above for a factor needs to be thought of along with its opposite. For example, a person high on the first factor is anxious, but one low on the same factor is calm.

The first matter for consideration is whether the grouping of peripheral characteristics into traits, motives, and schemata made by some theorists is supported by factor analytic studies. In truth, it is very difficult to say. On the list of factors, there are some (e.g., traditional values, self-consciousness) that suggest schemata, with their emphasis on social-role playing and conscience. But it is unclear whether many of the others (e.g., gregariousness, assertiveness) are traits, in the sense of habitual and repetitive behaviors, or motives, in the sense of goal-directed behavioral change. It must be concluded that factor analytic studies do not at present shed much light on classification of peripheral characteristics.

How can we use results concerning first-order factors to evaluate the content emphases of peripheral theorizing? In approaching this question, there are two points to keep in mind. One is that the list of factors may, as mentioned earlier, be an underestimation. Hence, if a content theme on the factor list is not included in a theory, the theory may be criticized. But if the theory includes a content theme not on the factor list, we cannot conclude that a theoretical error has been made. The other point is that considerable interpretation goes into designating the meaning of a factor by a label and verbal description. All in all, it is very difficult to find fault with a peripheral theory of personality as long as its content themes come anywhere close to those on the factor list.

You will recall from Chapter 10 that confict and fulfillment positions do not differ in the content of their peripheral-level theorizing. The difference between them is in what content is considered ideal and nonideal. The ideal in conflict theories stresses adjustment, dependability, and stability, whereas the ideal in fulfillment theories emphasizes transcendence, voluntary commitment, and changeability. Each position characterizes the other as the opposite of its ideal.

The findings of factor analytic studies provide no empirical bases for favoring conflict over fulfillment positions. Factors have been found that refer to traditional values, gregariousness, and self-consciousness on the one hand and impulsivity, assertiveness, and excitement seeking on the other. Persons can be high or low on each of these. There is little in the factor studies that would lead us to interpret one or another factor as ideal or nonideal. Therefore, we must conclude that the adaptation-transcendence content of factor analytic studies shows the plausibility of both conflict and fulfillment models. The content themes on the factor list concerning social interaction (e.g., attachment, gregariousness) are also understandable from the standpoint of both models.

In peripheral theorizing, the consistency model leads either to eclecticism of content or to content expressing the maintenance of consistency. It is difficult, therefore, to prove or disprove such theorizing on the basis of the factor list. What emerges is that the three personality models are sufficiently comprehensive and the factor list sufficiently heterogeneous that it is really very difficult to determine the relative merits of the models in this particular empirical fashion. Factor analysis studies would have had to be done with the specific models of personality in mind in order for there to be much hope of concluding otherwise.

Perhaps more can be learned through scrutinizing the content of second- or higher-order factors and the types conceptualized in peripheral statements. It would appear that there is broad consensus on the two most important second-order factors. This is especially true if you accept the interpretation of Eysenck's factors as being of the second order and discount some of Cattell's highly disputed entries. The two higher-order factors are *introversion versus extroversion* (so called by Cattell, Costa and McCrae, and by Eysenck, and *social activity* by Guilford) and *emotional health versus neuroticism* (called *emotional health* by Guilford, *neuroticism* by Eysenck and by Costa and McCrae, and *anxiety* by Cattell). Other second-order factors that have been posited either have achieved much less acceptance (e.g., Eysenck's psychoticism) or involve content that can be subsumed under the two already mentioned (e.g., Costa and McCrae's openness to experience, which includes content some investigators subsume under introversion-extroversion; and Guilford's social activity, which can be subsumed under-extroversion). Thus, for purposes of considering content for peripheral theorizing, we shall lose little by focusing only on the two second-order factors that everyone seems to recognize.

In order to be high on emotional health, persons must be composed, secure, trustful, adaptable, mature, stable, and self-sufficient. To be high on neuroticism, the other pole of the factor, persons must be tense, anxious, insecure, suspicious, jealous, emotionally unstable, hostile, and vulnerable. To be high on extroversion involves warmth, sociability, enthusiasm, talkativeness, adventurousness, resourcefulness, friendliness, assertiveness, high activity level, and positive emotions. The introverted pattern involves aloofness, coldness, shyness, conventionality, practicality, emphasis on thoughts, and low activity level.

These two second-order factors suggest four personality types. The first, *neuroticism-introversion,* is tense, excitable, insecure, suspicious, jealous, emotional, unstable, lax, and unsure and also aloof, cold, glum, silent, timid, shy,

Bohemian, unconcerned, and resourceful. The second type, *emotional health–introversion,* is phlegmatic, composed, confident, unshakable, trustful, adaptable, mature, calm, and self-sufficient in addition to being aloof, cold, glum, silent, timid, shy, Bohemian, unconcerned, and resourceful. The third type, *neuroticism-extroversion,* is tense, excitable, insecure, suspicious, jealous, emotional, unstable, lax, and unsure and also, warm, sociable, enthusiastic, talkative, adventurous, thick-skinned, conventional, practical, imitative, and dependent. The final type, *emotional health–extroversion,* is phlegmatic, composed, confident, unshakable, trustful, adaptable, mature, calm, and self-sufficient and also warm, sociable, enthusiastic, talkative, adventurous, thick-skinned, conventional, practical, imitative, and dependent.

Do these personality types seem strikingly in line with any theory under consideration here? Some theories, such as those of Murray, Kelly, and McClelland, do not postulate personality types and thus need not be considered further. Others, such as those of Erikson, White, and Allport, are so nebulous concerning personality types that it is not really feasible to evaluate their positions with regard to the factorial information presented above. Among the remaining theories, those of Freud, Rogers, Maslow, and Fromm are not strikingly confirmed by the factorial evidence concerning personality types. Here and there, a bit of one of these theories seems to match one of the types presented above. So, for example, the *emotional health–extroversion* type seems somewhat similar to Freud's *genital character,* and there is some, albeit less, correspondence between the *emotional health–introversion* type and the fully functioning person of actualization theory. But neither Freud nor the actualization theorists have provided peripheral theorizing capable of rendering the other factorial types easily understandable.

The only peripheral theories that closely fit the types derived from factorial studies are those of Adler, Maddi, and, to some extent, Jung. It seems to me that the *emotional health–extroversion* and *emotional health–introversion* types bear much similarity to Adler's *active-constructive* and *passive-constructive* styles of life, respectively. Further, the *emotional health–extroversion* and *neuroticism-introversion* factorial combinations are reminiscent of Adler's *active-destructive* and *passive-destructive* styles of life, respectively. From the descriptions of the factors given above, it seems clear that high and low anxiety are much like high and low activation. Further, extroversion and introversion suggest the external and internal traits emphasized by Maddi. Although the emphasis on introversion-extroversion is quite accurate for Jung, it is not clear how low and high anxiety would fit his position. So once again we find the empirical support tending toward the fulfillment model and the activation version of the consistency model.

OTHER STUDIES OF PERIPHERAL PERSONALITY

The studies just reviewed did not involve selection of the behavioral variables coinciding with those considered important by any one personality theory. In general, they included a broad, eclectic sampling of variables so that the factors emerging from the data analysis would not be biased in favor of one kind of theory over another. The virtue of inductive factor analytic studies, when they sample broadly, is that they aid us in determining the relative fruitfulness of different approaches to peripheral theorizing.

Some studies restrict their concerns explicitly or implicitly to only one peripheral theory of personality. In order to be included here, such single-theory studies must focus primarily on the measurement of one or more peripheral characteristics or types and also be concerned with the assessment of construct validity for the entities measured. Less relevant here are those studies in which peripheral characteristics or types are used as explanatory concepts but not measured. In the main, I shall also exclude studies done on children, whose personalities may not be well formed. In addition, I shall emphasize only studies that are reasonably rigorous in their measurement attempts, systematic in their sampling of subjects, and appropriate in the data analyses undertaken. These restrictions are necessary in order for us to have any chance of obtaining a clear empirical analysis of peripheral considerations. There are many studies in the literature that are either so methodologically poor or so theoretically indirect and ambiguous as to be better left unchronicled here.

Even with the restrictions suggested, it must be said at the outset that the studies to be considered are of limited utility because they focus on one—and only one—peripheral theory of personality. Usually these single-theory studies have a partisan flavor; that is, they are performed by investigators who already believe the theory. Such partisanship often gives the theory the benefit of the doubt when findings can be interpreted in more than one way. All things considered, it would not be surprising to find some solid empirical evidence for each of the peripheral theories given the fact that all these theories have been devised by especially sensitive, serious, and intelligent personologists.

Of major value in the empirical evaluation of peripheral considerations are studies that pit the various theories against one another by comparing their explanatory capabilities. But lacking enough carefully devised studies of this kind to make a difference, we will have to make do with what we have. Do not be too ready to give the laurel wreath to a theory, even if it is the one you believe in, just because a few limited studies seem to lend it some empirical support. Look instead for a heavy accumulation of empirical support, for many studies pointing in the same direction, and for studies that truly impress you with their relevance to living.

We might tend to be especially skeptical of a peripheral theory that cannot boast empirical support even from partisan research. This would be a logical conclusion if we could be sure that personologists had attempted to conduct empirical studies stemming from that theory and had failed to turn up any support. But we cannot conclude that a peripheral theory is unfruitful if, though reasonably clear, it simply has never been the focus of research efforts. All in all, the best policy to adopt in reading the following pages is to be duly impressed when there is formidable empirical support for a peripheral theory while keeping an open mind concerning theories that lack such support unless it is clear that research attempts in their behalf have been mounted but have failed.

I will organize the following discussion in the simplest way—by individual theories. All the studies involve one or more of three basic ways of measuring peripheral characteristics and types. The first is *self-description,* which involves presenting subjects with a set of questions or adjectives and explicitly instructing them to depict themselves in their responses (the approach most common in the factorial studies covered earlier). Which characteristic of the subjects the investigator hopes to glean from the responses need not be apparent, but the subjects must know that they are describing themselves in some way. The second measurement technique is the *analysis of fantasy.* Obtaining the fantasy productions involves providing subjects with an ambiguous, unstructured stimulus that they are to render clear and structured through an act of imagination. The presumption is that subjects' fantasy will disclose the characteristics of their personalities. The final measurement technique is the *rating of performance or action.* This technique involves the investigator in classifying and quantifying the subjects' behavior on some explicit and structured task. The task requires action and choice but depends little on fantasy. You may wish to refer to Chapter 2 for more details of measurement.

Freud's Position

In order to be considered especially pertinent, research must involve measurement of some traits or defenses presumed to form the oral, anal, phallic, and genital character types. The subjects should be old enough to at least have attained puberty. By and large, the single traits comprised in the types are not so specific to Freudian theory alone that their study is definitive to someone interested in testing that theory. Understandably, we should prick up our ears only when a study includes clusters of traits that represent one or more types. Also of some interest are studies that, while focusing on only one trait, have singled out a trait that is fairly unique to the Freudian tradition (e.g., castration anxiety).

Having established these specifications, what comes immediately to mind are the studies concerning the Blacky Test (Blum, 1949). The stimuli in this test are twelve cartoons portraying the adventures of a male dog named Blacky, his mother, his father, and a sibling. The cartoons were carefully devised in order to pose familial situations reminiscent of the psychosexual themes and conflicts considered important in psychoanalytic theory. Subjects are asked to compose stories in response to the pictures, this constituting fantasy data. After doing so, they are asked to answer a series of multiple-choice and short-answer questions pertaining to the psychoanalytic theme or conflict presumably posed in the picture. Finally, subjects are asked whether they like or dislike each cartoon. The final two types of data resemble self-description. Blum (1949) has offered a scoring procedure for these three sources of data, the end result of which are scores reflecting the intensity of the subjects' disturbances on thirteen dimensions. The content of these dimensions is shown in Table 11–1. You should realize that these dimensions do not actually reflect either the traits or the defenses listed in Chapter 7 under the various character types. Instead, some of the dimensions seem indicative of the character types (or possibly subtypes) themselves (e.g., oral eroticism and anal retentiveness). Other dimensions seem to refer to general qualities that transcend any particular character type but probably indicate the overall degree of defensiveness and conflict (e.g., guilt feelings, sibling rivalry). In theoretical terms, it is certainly clear that the content of the dimensions is germane to Freud's position, though their precise status as peripheral characteristics, types, or conglomerates of these is unclear.

Consistent with this ambiguity is the necessity of global, intuitive scoring of the so-called dimensions. But even with intuitive scoring, Blum (1949) reports acceptable levels of agreement between himself and another psychologist

TABLE 11–1 Spontaneous Story Scoring Agreement

Dimension	Obtained Percent Scoring Agreement	Percent Expected by Chance
Oral eroticism	100	56
Oral sadism	96	61
Anal expulsiveness	84	43*
Anal retentiveness	96	44*
Oedipal intensity	96	53
Masturbation guilt	84	50
Castration anxiety (males)	100	56
Penis envy (females)	76	53
Positive identification	100	79
Sibling rivalry	92	56
Guilt feelings	80	51
Positive ego ideal	100	92
Narcissistic love object	92	54
Anaclitic love object	100	85

	Obtained	Expected by Chance
Mean	92.6½	59.5½
Median	96.0½	55.0½
Range	76½–100½	43½–92½

*These two dimensions were scored on a four-point scale instead of a two-point scale. Hence, the chance expectancy of agreement is somewhat lower.

SOURCE: "A Study of the Psychoanalytic Theory of Psychosexual Development" by G. S. Blum, 1949, *Genetic Psychology Monograph, 39.*

working independently on the same protocols. As can be seen from Table 11–1, the percentages of agreement on the various dimensions range from 76 to 100, with an average of 92.6. In major part, the scoring procedure involves deciding whether a story shows a strong or weak emphasis on the dimension being considered. For example, Blum (1949) lists the following story, in response to a card showing Blacky nursing, as strong on oral eroticism:

> Blacky has just discovered the delightful nectar that Mama can supply—it is an endless supply and she is enjoying it. She doesn't know where it comes from, but she doesn't care. Mama is pacific throughout it all—she doesn't particularly like this business of supplying milk, but she is resigned to it. It is a pretty day and they are both calm and happy.

In contrast, consider a story for the same card that is considered weak on oral eroticism (Blum, 1949):

> Blacky, a male pup of a few weeks, is having his midday lunch. Mama is bored with the proceedings but as a mother with her maternal interests is letting Blacky have his lunch to Blacky's satisfaction.

In this story, there is none of the elaboration so indicative of lingering oral conflict seen in the first story.

Having encountered at least some evidence that well-trained investigators can agree on scoring the stories, we should now turn our attention to the question of whether the dimensions of the test have sufficient internal consistency and stability to be considered empirically genuine. Charen (1956) reports stability correlations for the thirteen dimensions that range from a high of .52 through very low positive and even some negative values. The implication of low negative correlations is that people's responses changed almost completely from the first to the second testing. But we are justified in looking into the matter of reliability further, for Charen's study involved a period between testing of four months, which is long enough for one to expect certain real changes in personality not indicative of test inadequacy. The possibility of real personality change is heightened by the fact that in that four-month period the subjects were recovering from a serious illness, tuberculosis.

Granick and Scheflen (1958) have reported a study concerning stability, internal consistency, and interscorer agreement for the Blacky Test. Their results on interscorer agreement, which ranged on the thirteen cards from 58 percent to 95 percent, with an average of 77.5 percent, are poorer than those Blum obtained, but they are still somewhat acceptable. In considering stability and temporal consistency, these investigators adopted an unorthodox approach that is not really very relevant to the thirteen dimensions as used. Fortunately, Berger and Everstine (1962) have studied stability in a more direct fashion. With an interval between testings of four weeks, they obtained stability correlations on fifty college males for the thirteen dimensions that ranged from .20 to .54, with an average of .44. The stability of the dimensions seems quite modest, especially for a theory that considers significant development and change to be largely over by the time puberty is reached. The difficulty, of course, may lie in the test rather than the theory. After all, the so-called dimensions do have the heterogeneity and ambiguity mentioned before. An analysis of internal consistency could help determine whether this is the source of the difficulty. Unfortunately, there do not seem to be extensive studies on internal consistency. I suggest that we push on to consider studies of validity, keeping in mind that in the case of these dimensions we are hardly working with the stable characteristics envisioned by psychoanalytic theory.

First we should consider two factor analytic studies performed on the same set of data. The data were originally obtained by Blum (1949) by administering the Blacky Test to 119 male and 90 female college students. On the basis of scores obtained on these subjects, Blum computed the intercorrelations among the dimensions, separately for males and females, and felt that he had uncovered strong support for psychoanalytic theory. But instead of going over his results and conclusions, I will give attention to two factor analytic studies done by other investigators on Blum's data, because the statistical procedures they employed are more sophisticated than were his. The aim of both studies was to clarify the clustering of dimensions. If the dimensions really represent peripheral characteristics, such studies will yield evidence as to whether the psychoanalytic view on the subsuming of characteristics into types is accurate (think of the second step of the ideal strategy). But an air of ambiguity permeates the enterprise because of the difficulty in determining whether the dimensions are unitary enough to represent concrete peripheral characteristics. Nonetheless, let us push on.

The first factor analytic study was done by Neuman and Salvatore (1958) and the second by Robinson and Hendrix (1966). Neuman and Salvatore obtained six factors for males that corresponded reasonably well to the oral, anal, phallic, latency, and genital characters. But the six factors they extracted for females seemed contradictory to psychoanalytic theory. They could not stretch their conclusions to grant any more than partial confirmation to the theory of character types. Working with the same data, Robinson and Hendrix applied a factor analytic technique deemed more sophisticated and accurate than that employed in the earlier study. The factor matrices they obtained are reproduced for males in Table 11–2 and for females in Table 11–3. The thirteen dimensions appear down the side of the table and the factors obtained across the top. The terms in parentheses under the factor numbers represent the interpretation that the investigators deemed best suited to the results appearing in the body of the table. In order to follow these interpretations, you should know that the numbers in the body of the table are correlations and that the higher they are (whether positive or negative), the more the dimension involved is a defining attribute of the factor.

Considering the results Robinson and Hendrix obtained for males, it would seem that the first factor represents orality because of the high positive contribution to the factor made by *oral eroticism* and *oral sadism*. The negative contribution made by *anal retentiveness* adds support to this interpretation,

TABLE 11–2   Principal Component-Varimax Analysis of 13 Blacky Dimensions for 119 Males

	Factors						
Dimensions	*I* *(Oral)*	*II* *(Latent)*	*III* *(Anal)*	*IV* *(Genital)*	*V* *(Phallic)*	*VI* *(Guilt)*	h²
Oral eroticism	59†	10	50*	−22	−15	−10	71
Oral sadism	75†	01	05	−32	19	14	71
Anal expulsiveness	20	04	57*	−09	54*	−16	65
Anal retentiveness	−54*	−34	04	17	−32	00	54
Oedipal intensity	79†	−30	−12	24	−09	−06	74
Masturbation guilt	−10	08	−04	17	83†	−01	70
Castration anxiety	−15	−06	91†	08	04	14	88
Positive identification	09	30†	−03	14	−08	−04	68
Sibling rivalry	18	−22	11	−08	65†	09	54
Guilt feelings	04	−07	04	01	02	97†	95
Positive ego ideal	−17	−16	−30	87†	01	−08	91
Narcissistic love object	28	−83†	03	21	−01	06	80
Anaclitic love object	−02	08	21	86†	07	−09	79

*Significant at .05 level.
†Significant at .01 level.

SOURCE: "The Blacky Test and Psychoanalytic Theory: Another Factor-Analytic Approach to Validity" by S. A. Robinson and V. L. Hendrix, 1966, *Journal Project. Tech. Pers. Assessment, 30.*

though the positive loading of *Oedipal intensity* is, strictly speaking, a complication. The third factor is characterized by positive loadings for *oral eroticism, anal expulsiveness* and *castration anxiety*. This seems to represent a developmental situation that in psychoanalytic terms would span from the oral through the phallic stages and, hence, can only roughly be considered as expressive of the anal character. But Fenichel (1945) does point to the frequency with which castration anxiety is intermingled with anal-sadistic fears, and thus, there is some justification for the interpretation offered by Robinson and Hendrix. The fifth factor is characterized by positive loadings for *anal expulsiveness, masturbation guilt,* and *sibling rivalry.* Except for *anal expulsiveness,* contributing dimensions accurately accord with the psychoanalytic view of the phallic stage. But once again even more consistent with the results would be some conglomerate of anal and phallic character types. The second factor includes a positive loading for *positive identification* and negative loadings for *narcissistic love object* and *anal retentiveness.* Robinson and Hendrix suggest that this represents something like a latency character type, because the latency period

TABLE 11–3   Principal Component-Varimax Analysis of Thirteen Blacky
Dimensions for Ninety Females

	Factors					
	I	II	III	IV	V	
Dimensions	*(Anal)*	*(Phallic)*	*(Genital)*	*(Guilt)*	*(Oral)*	h²
Oral eroticism	42	05	00	31	57*	60
Oral sadism	− 09	− 21	− 21	40	54*	54*
Anal expulsiveness	83†	04	− 13	03	03	71
Anal retentiveness	− 73†	31	− 12	11	07	66
Oedipal intensity	71*	06	04	07	04	51
Masturbation guilt	16	01	− 17	90†	− 13	88
Penis envy	− 10	72†	13	14	08	57
Positive identification	− 04	− 09	− 08	22	− 83†	76
Sibling rivalry	46	12	32	13	− 59*	69
Guilt feelings	17	− 12	− 47	− 56*	− 10	59
Positive ego ideal	− 19	36	74†	− 17	− 09	74
Narcissistic love object	09	85†	− 08	− 11	− 12	76
Anaclitic love object	26	− 27	80†	− 01	− 10	79

*Significant at .05 level.
†Significant at .01 level.

SOURCE: "The Blacky Test and Psychoanalytic Theory: Another Factor-Analytic Approach to Validity" by S. A. Robinson and V. L. Hendrix, 1966, *Journal Project. Tech. Pers. Assessment, 30.*

is supposed to be one in which the child is trying out identifications with various adults and social roles and relinquishing the selfish loves of the phallic period. The fourth factor is characterized by positive loadings for *positive ideal* (or personal aspirations and values) and *anaclitic love object* (choice of a love object resembling the person on whom the individual depended for comfort in infancy). If you had to call this factor anything, you might conclude, in light of the other factors, that it represents the genital period. But in all seriousness, it should be recognized that the two strong positive loadings are somewhat contradictory. Finally, the sixth factor for males seems clearly expressive of *guilt feelings.*

The results for females are somewhat similar to those for males. The fifth factor is clearly oral, with its positive loadings for *oral eroticism* and *oral sadism* and negative loadings for *sibling rivalry* and *positive ego ideal.* The first factor is defined positively by *anal expulsiveness, sibling rivalry,* and *Oedipal intensity* but shows a negative loading for *anal retentiveness.* If anything, this factor seems a conglomerate of anal and phallic periods, but even in such an interpretation the negative contribution of anal retentiveness is difficult to understand. But the second factor, defined by positive loading for *penis envy* and *narcissistic love object,* does conform reasonably well to the phallic character type in women. Interestingly, no factor was obtained for women that seemed relevant to the latency period. This finding seems consistent with many psychoanalysts' belief that the latency period is a cultural artifact. Finally, the fourth factor seems to express *guilt feelings.*

In the results reported by Robinson and Hendrix, more so than in those of Neuman and Salvatore, there is reason to believe that the theory of character types has some empirical viability. But a note of caution is necessary, because the so-called dimensions are probably not the bedrock, irreducible, minimally interpretive, peripheral characteristics on which the theory of character types is built. Instead, the dimensions seem to be general, perhaps rather heterogeneous, conglomerates requiring considerable interpretation in their scoring. The results of factor analyses can be predetermined by such interpretation. If the scoring of dimensions presupposes the truth of the theory of character types, the ensuing factor analysis may be doing little more than celebrating the scorer's acumen in putting his or her belief in the theory of character types into action. Were the dimensions of the Blacky Test less general and interpretive, one could well be impressed by results showing them as grouping themselves into types in a manner consistent with psychoanalytic theory.

Let us now turn from the factor analytic studies to research investigating the construct validity of the thirteen dimensions of the Blacky Test. Blum and Hunt (1952) reviewed much of the early work of this nature. We will concentrate on studies that test psychoanalytic hypotheses concerning peripheral personality.

In one such study, Aronson (1950) focused on the Freudian theory of paranoia. He administered the Blacky Test to thirty paranoid schizophrenics, thirty nonparanoid schizophrenics, and thirty normal control subjects. The three groups were comparable in age, intelligence, occupation, religion, and status as veterans. The basis for distinguishing paranoid schizophrenics from nonparanoid schizophrenics was the presence or absence of delusions (common in paranoid people).

In the psychoanalytic theory, paranoia and schizophrenia are considered breakdown products of the anal and oral character types, respectively. Consequently, Aronson hypothesized that the paranoid schizophrenics would show greater intensity of *anal retentiveness, anal expulsiveness, oral sadism,* and *oral eroticism* than would the normal subjects. Further, the paranoid schizophrenics would be stronger than the nonparanoid schizophrenics on only *anal retentiveness* and *anal expulsiveness.* The results supported his hypotheses in all instances except *anal expulsiveness,* indicating considerable support for the Freudian position. But Aronson also found the paranoid group as showing greater evidence of *masturbation guilt,* conscious attempts at denial of strong underlying *castration anxiety,* a consistent tendency toward feminine identification; severe superego conflicts, and a preference for narcissistic types of love-object choice. Many of these differences could not have been precisely predicted from psychoanalytic peripheral theorizing.

A number of other studies (e.g., Blum & Kaufman, 1952) investigated scores on the Blacky Test of people with certain psychological disorders. In the main, these studies are less pertinent than Aronson's for illuminating the empirical validity of Freudian peripheral theorizing. Actually, the explicit intent of these studies is often to develop, rather than test, a psychoanalytic explanation of the disorder under consideration. Such studies assume the adequacy of the test and the validity of the theory, but actually clarify neither. In what is probably the most rigorous of these studies, Linder (see Blum & Hunt, 1952) administered the Blacky Test to sixty-seven male sexual offenders and sixty-seven male non–sexual offenders matched for age, race, IQ, education, socioeconomic and marital status, length of sentence, and previous convictions. Analysis of the data showed that the sexual offenders were significantly higher (more disturbed) on nine of the thirteen Blacky dimensions. Although this study may provide evidence that sexual offenders are very sick people, it does not really clarify psychoanalytic peripheral theorizing.

In a radically different study, Swanson (1951) attempted to use the Blacky Test to test certain psychoanalytic predictions about the interpersonal behavior of groups of people. Scores on the Blacky dimensions were obtained on the twenty members of each of two training groups at the National Training Laboratory for Group Development at Bethel, Maine. The aim of the members of such groups is to get to know one another and themselves more deeply through their meetings. Swanson predicted that high scores on *oral sadism, anal expulsiveness, Oedipal intensity, sibling rivalry,* or *guilt feelings* would raise the total amount of a person's actual participation in permissive groups such as those at the Training Laboratory. Swanson used the pattern of a person's scores on the Blacky dimensions just mentioned to reach an overall judgment concerning the likelihood of his or her participation in the group's interaction. These judgments were then correlated to several measures of actual participation. In general, the correlations obtained in both groups were sufficiently positive to indicate that Swanson's judgments had validity. It is quite difficult, however, to see how this study bears on the validity of psychoanalytic theory except in an indirect fashion.

Adelson and Redmond (1958) did a very pertinent study concerning the anal character type. They obtained the Blacky Test scores on *anal retentiveness* and *anal expulsiveness* for sixty-one college women. The hypothesis was that anal-retentive subjects should have greater ability to recall verbal material than anal-expulsive subjects. The basis for this hypothesis is clear in the Freudian belief that fixation occurs later in the anal period for retentive than for expulsive subtypes. The later the anal fixation occurs, the greater the emphasis on "holding on" rather than "letting go." Of the sixty-one subjects, thirty-two were classified as expulsives, eighteen as retentives, and eleven as neutral. Subjects read two prose passages, each containing several hundred words. One passage included sexual and aggressive themes, whereas the other was innocuous. Subjects were asked to reproduce the passages immediately after presentation and again one week later. As you can see from Table 11–4, the retentives showed greater recall under all conditions. In general, neutral subjects scored

TABLE 11–4   Differences between Expulsives and Retentives in Verbal Recall
(Expulsives, N = 32; Retentives, N = 18)

Tests	Group	M	SD	t	P
Innocuous passage—	Expulsive	19.9	12.84	2.25	.05
immediate recall	Retentive	28.3	12.08		
Innocuous passage—	Expulsive	9.9	6.00	2.60	.02
delayed recall	Retentive	15.1	8.66		
Disturbing passage—	Expulsive	21.6	9.59	2.68	.02
immediate recall*	Retentive	28.7	12.29		
Disturbing passage—	Expulsive	11.1	5.92	3.66	.001
delayed recall*	Retentive	19.3	8.94		

*The mean scores for the disturbing passages refer to thought units.

SOURCE: "Personality Differences in the Capacity for Verbal Recall" by J. Adelson and J. Redmond, 1958, *Journal of Abnormal and Social Psychology, 57.*

midway between the other two groups. Adelson and Redmond also presented evidence that these differences in verbal recall cannot be accounted for by differences in intellectual capacity. This very clear and rigorous study provides strong support for the construct validity of the psychoanalytic notion of anal-expulsive and anal-retentive subtypes of the anal character.

In another study, Kline (1968) attempted to determine the relationship between obsessional traits (which are considered expressive of extreme anality) and characteristics of toilet training (the conditions under which an anal fixation would have occurred). He used the Blacky Test and four obsession scales to measure anality, attempting to correlate them with information about toilet training. Although his results are ambiguous and indicate the importance of sex differences, there is some small support for the hypothesis. Tribich and Messer (1974) put 107 male students in a group situation in which the task was to judge the magnitude of apparent movement of a light. Confederates of the experimenter, with the status of authority figures, were members of the group and tried to influence the students' judgments. Students with oral characters, as measured by the Blacky Test were positively influenced by the "authorities," whereas those who were anal reacted against the attempted influence. This result appears to be solid support for Freudian peripheral theorizing.

This sampling of studies using the Blacky Test will have to suffice. Annotated bibliographies for the test are available (Schaeffer, 1968; Taulbee & Stenmark, 1968), and there is even a form for females (Robinson, 1968).

There are, of course, studies pertinent to Freudian peripheral theorizing that have not employed the Blacky Test. Although I cannot hope to be complete in reviewing them, I shall try to be representative. In presenting the studies, I shall cover the various character types in their presumed developmental order.

Sarnoff (1951) reported a study concerning the defense mechanism of *identification* (or *introjection*), which is a primitive technique for avoiding anxiety generally attributed to the oral stage of development. More specifically, he focused on identification with the aggressor, a notion found nowhere else but in Freudian theory. This defense involves becoming more like the person who is hurting you in order to avoid the anxiety associated with the threat of pain and of your own destructive anger. Sarnoff reasoned that anti-Semitism among Jews was prima facia evidence of identification with the aggressor and proceeded to construct a questionnaire to assess it. Jews receiving a high score on this questionnaire "were regarded as having taken, toward their own Jewish group, the same anti-Semitic attitudes that are expressed by majority group bigots in our society" (Sarnoff, 1951). On the basis of this questionnaire, 100 Jewish college students were divided into two groups of 45 high in anti-Semitism and 55 low in anti-Semitism. Several personality tests were also administered to these subjects in order to measure the personality differences between the two groups. The results, shown in Table 11–5, are offered by Sarnoff in support of hypotheses from Freudian theory. In the study, anti-Semitic Jews (highs) were likely to be insecure, chronically fearful people who had been severely rejected by their parents. They tended to dislike themselves through having experienced parental dislike. They also hated their parents. Being unable to accept themselves, these people seemed compelled to search for devious means of increasing their adequacy and, at the same time, fulfilling the urge to reject themselves. In Sarnoff's (1951) words, "In becoming anti-Semitic, these Jews may be vicariously appropriating the power position of the majority-group chauvinists and simultaneously achieving a vehicle for perpetuating the negative images of themselves and their parents." Although this study provides some evidence for the validity of the concept of identification with the aggressor, it does not tie down this personality characteristic to the oral stage of development.

Another defense mechanism associated with the oral stage is *projection,* which involves attributing to others characteristics that are really your own in order that you can remain unconscious of their presence in you and therefore be free of anxiety. Remaining alert to this precise meaning will aid us in what follows, for projection often is given the general meaning of simply expressing the characteristics of one's personality in external situations, especially if they are ambiguous. This general meaning, however, is not what Freud meant.

One relevant and intriguing study was done by Sears (1936). He obtained from nearly 100 college fraternity men character trait ratings of themselves and one another. The traits rated were stinginess, obstinacy, disorderliness, and bashfulness. The degree of a given trait attributed to others by a subject was compared with the amount attributed to him by the others. No clear relationships were found. But when a rough measure of insight was taken into account, it was found that those men who possessed more than the average degree of a trait tended to attribute more than average degrees to others provided insight was lacking. In essence, this means that projection of these

TABLE 11-5   Differences between the Number of Highs and Lows on Each of the
Personality Variables

Personality Variables	Number of Highs[*]	Number of Lows[*]	p[†]
Death of mother, father, and parents-as-a-group	25	13	.01
Disparaging remarks about mother	19	11	.04
Disparaging remarks about father	12	6	.05
Derogatory remarks about home and home life	8	5	.13
Fear of parental disapproval	6	2	.05
Favorable comments about mother	16	32	.09
Favorable comments about father	5	11	.15
Favorable comments about home and home life	8	19	.08
Self-negation	15	6	.01
Fear of the future	5	1	.04
Fear of rejection by others	12	5	.03
Admission of psychic stress	21	13	.05
Self-derogatory remarks	20	21	.34
Self-assertion	0	4	.05
Absence of fears	2	7	.09
Favorable remarks about the self	5	11	.15
Passivity in response to aggression	20	12	.05
Suppression of desires to retaliate against aggression	3	0	.05
Turning hostility against the self	9	4	.05
Active retaliation in response to aggression	14	31	.06

*For the variables based on the Thematic Apperception Test, these differences represent a
comparison between 43 Highs and 54 Lows. Three of the 100 TAT protocols were either lost or
had to be omitted from the analysis because subjects did not adhere to the instructions. All of
the other differences, those based on the Sentence Completion, involved 45 Highs and 55 Lows
as previously stated.
†Since all of our specific predictions were made on an a priori basis which took into account
the direction of the differences, only one half of the probability curve is used in determining
levels of significance. The level of significance of these predicted results was obtained by
reducing by one half the probabilities reported to the conventional "t" tables since these tables
use both halves of the probability curves.

SOURCE: "Identification with the Aggressor: Some Personality Correlates of Anti-Semitism among Jews"
by I. Sarnoff, 1951, *Journal of Personality, 20.*

character traits appeared to be a function of lack of insight. This finding is not
inconsistent with the concept of projection, which includes not only the attribution of one's own characteristics to others but the debarment from consciousness of those characteristics in oneself. The latter aspect of projection
may have been tapped by Sears's insight measure. Although the study provides
no information as to whether the four traits involved were indeed undesirable
to the subjects, it is fairly safe to assume that they were, as they are generally
undesirable. In addition, the traits are relevant to the psychoanalytic notions

concerning psychosexual stages of development (as you noted in Chapter 7, stinginess, obstinacy, and disorderliness are anal traits, while bashfulness is either oral or phallic). The chief difficulty with this study as evidence for projection is that Sears also found that subjects very low on a trait would attribute lowness to others if insight was lacking. But theoretically, being low on an undesirable trait should not lead to projection, because there is no personal basis for conflict with the superego and subsequent guilt and anxiety. This latter finding throws into serious question the interpretation of the prior finding as projection. Of course, one could say that for some people an absence of these traits is a potential source of guilt due to particularly peculiar early life experiences and that both findings were obtained because these kinds of people existed in the sample alongside the more usual ones. But the study provides no information with which to check this possibility, and it seems rather farfetched anyway.

Actually, the methodology Sears used has come under considerable criticism (see Holmes, 1968), because the manner in which he measured "insight" essentially forced the negative correlation that he then interpreted as evidence of projection. The subject was considered as lacking insight if his peers rated him high on a trait but he placed himself below the rating he assigned to the group. That for an equal trait score low-insight subjects attributed a greater amount of that trait to other people than did high-insight subjects becomes a statistical artifact of method! The negative correlation Sears reported would have been found regardless of whether or not the subject was insightful. This is because an insightful subject (who, by Sears's definition, would have given himself a higher rating than his peers) would have had to see others as low on the trait.

Rokeach (1945) attempted to replicate Sears's findings, only to discover that the correlation supporting the hypothesis of projection occurred only when the data were analyzed in the erroneous manner described above. When the data were analyzed in a fashion that did not force the predicted relationship, it did not occur. Since then, the absence of relationship has been found by several investigators, such as Lemann (1952) and Wells and Goldstein (1964). In other studies (e.g., Murstein 1956; Page & Markowitz, 1955), what appeared evidence for projection was thrown into considerable doubt by the existence of groups in whom the attribution of traits also occurred, but with the subjects' being conscious of it.

In an intriguing attempt to demonstrate projection, Wright (1940) took care to create conditions that would provoke guilt in his subjects. A pair of toys, one preferred and the other nonpreferred, were given to the subjects, who were eight-year-old children. Then the children were asked to give away one of the two toys to a friend. Immediately after this, they were asked which toy they thought the friend would have given away. Control-group children were asked this question without first having been asked themselves to give away one of the toys. The number of times that the friend was considered generous (giving away the preferred toy) was much lower after the conflict situation, in which the child was forced to give away a toy, than it was under the control condition. This indicates that stinginess is projected when one feels guilty about one's own stingy thoughts.

While this study certainly seems consistent with projection as a defense, it is a little weak in that it cannot be demonstrated that the attribution of stinginess occurred with no conscious relationship to the subjects' own stingy thoughts. If one's own stinginess were consciously appreciated, attributing stinginess to a friend would be generalization more than defensive projection. It appears that whenever a study in this area avoids being plagued by statistical artifacts, it only manages to demonstrate that projection may well take place with the subject's full awareness. This has led Holmes (1968) to contend that simple generalization is superior to projection as an explanation of the phenomenon. Here and there, studies of projection (Adler, 1967; Katz, Sarnoff, & McClintock, 1956; Sarnoff & Katz, 1954) have been designed in such a way that it is difficult to determine whether subjects were aware of their presumed defense. In light of what was said above, it is difficult to know what to make of these studies.

Let us now turn to research on traits rather than defenses associated with the oral character. A particular oral activity, smoking, is easily measured and has received considerable research attention. This research has sought mainly to determine the nature of general differences between smokers and non-smokers. Matarazzo and Saslow (1960) concluded from a careful review of forty-four such studies that despite much speculation about the relationship between early nursing experiences and smoking, no clear-cut pattern of personality peculiar to smokers has yet emerged from the literature. Although smokers seem to be more extroverted—which sounds plausible as an oral trait—they are also more anxious than nonsmokers. In a particularly extensive study, Schubert (1959a, 1959b) tested hypotheses derived from Freud and Fenichel concerning smoking as expressive of oral fixation, only to find that the smokers among his 1,500 college students showed as much evidence of being arousal or activation seekers as of being oral in character. It seems fair to conclude that if striking empirical support for the concept of oral character is to be found, it should not be sought in the literature on smoking.

More supportive of Freud's position is a study by Masling, Weiss, and Rothschild (1968), which tested the hypothesis that oral-dependent persons need support and approval from others. Subjects were introduced into a type of conformity experiment, invented by Asch, in which a pseudo-subject actually in the experimenter's employ insists on an apparently wrong judgment of some perceptual phenomenon, such as the length of a line. The true subject may or may not conform to the confederate's erroneous response. Masling et al. accumulated twenty-three undergraduate males who conformed and twenty-one who did not. On scrutinizing their performance on the Rorschach Test, a fantasy method of assessing personality (see Chapter 2), they discovered that the conforming subjects tended to show evidence of an oral character type. Also promising is the work of Cooperman and Child (1969), who utilized

115 undergraduate males to determine the relationship between aesthetic preference and food preference. Certain hypotheses they derived from psychoanalytic theory were confirmed when eight of the twelve oral personality variables they studied correlated significantly with the aesthetic preference score. Recently Masling, O'Neill, and Katkin (1982) reported that subjects judged oral on a projective test responded to interaction with a cold interviewer with increased physiological arousal (skin conductance), whereas there was no such arousal for oral subjects interacting with a warm interviewer or for nonoral subjects regardless of interviewer warmth or coldness.

Turning to the anal character type, we encounter another study by Sarnoff (1960). His aim was to investigate the empirical validity of the defense mechanism of reaction formation, which is a cornerstone of the Freudian position on the anal character. Sarnoff reasoned that warm, accepting, loving feelings toward others are anxiety provoking because they are socially unacceptable in our crass, market-oriented society. Therefore, when such warm feelings are aroused, people who tend to use the defense mechanism of reaction formation should show an increase in cynical, critical feelings toward others. In order to test this hypothesis, Sarnoff gave eighty-one male undergraduates one of two experimental manipulations. One of these manipulations, designed to arouse strong feelings of affection, involved listening to a live presentation of a portion of William Saroyan's play *Hello Out There*. The other manipulation involved listening to a taped version of the same thing and was supposed to arouse only mild feelings of affection. Before the presentations, all subjects filled out questionnaires yielding measures of cynicism and of reaction formation. Following the play, subjects again filled out the cynicism questionnaire. The results showed, contrary to expectations, that regardless of the strength of the tendency to use reaction formation and of the degree of affection arousal, all subjects decreased in cynicism. The subjects who tended toward reaction formation decreased in cynicism the least, but this is very meager support for the hypothesis. This study can be attacked on a number of grounds, not the least of which is the theoretically unconvincing assumption that feelings of affection are disapproved of socially. In addition, the measurement of defensive tendencies through self-description in the form of answers to questions is not really in the spirit of Freudian thinking. After all, one is not supposed to be aware of one's defenses.

Nalven (1967) compared thirty subjects who relied on repression with thirty who relied on intellectualization (a defense mechanism often associated with the anal character type) on a task of some complexity requiring perceptual decisions. The measurement of repressive and intellectualizing defenses was accomplished using a sentence completion test (which primarily taps fantasy). As one would expect from psychoanalytic theory, the intellectualizers could formulate more alternatives in the decision-making task than could the repressers. Although this study certainly supports Freud's position, it should be pointed out that an important basis for deciding that subjects were repressers was their sparsity of response on the sentence completion test. The same sparsity was looked for in the perceptual decision task. Thus, someone of a different theoretical persuasion could insist that no more has been demonstrated than a difference in productivity between the groups. To be convincing, studies of defense mechanisms must provide some basis in their design for believing that the mechanism under consideration has indeed been aroused. But putting the findings of this study together with those on sensitizing defenses reviewed in Chapter 6 makes the existence of such mechanisms a reasonable surmise. Of course, there is little, if anything, in any of this research that demonstrates sensitizing defenses to be strongly associated with the anal character.

Turning from defenses to the traits of the anal character, we encounter an interesting study by Pettit (1969) concerning attitudes toward time. He constructed a time scale of forty items with which to ascertain the ways in which time has special meaning and serves to organize a person's experience. This scale was administered to ninety-one undergraduates along with two questionnaire measures of anality and one of spontaneity. As one would expect from Freud's position, the preoccupation with time as an organizing principle correlated positively to the measures of anality and negatively to the measure of spontaneity. While it is likely that one feature of the anality measures is concern with time, the correlations obtained seem too high to be explained away in this fashion.

Centers (1969) tested the hypothesis that persons with an anal character type would express tough attitudes in regard to the mischievous behavior of teenagers and the dependence of social welfare recipients. A sample of 562 adults answered his attitude questionnaire and two questionnaires devised to reflect anality. Modest support is reported for the hypothesis. In a similar study, Koutrelakos (1968) tested 100 males on the Authoritarianism (F) Scale and a questionnaire concerning perceptions of their attitudes toward their fathers. As will be discussed later, the Authoritarianism Scale is an instrument in general use that Freudians would interpret as indicating the severe conscience and aggressiveness of anality. As predicted, highly authoritarian subjects perceived their fathers as more authoritarian and more similar to their ideal person than did subjects low in authoritarianism. Although both these studies provide support for the Freudian position, it must be said that the measures employed may well overlap on methodological (but not theoretical) grounds. Hence, some amount of relationship found may be spurious. In addition, the measures (e.g., Authoritarianism Scale) are sufficiently general in content to be claimed as relevant to personality theories other than Freud's.

In a review, Pollak (1979) reaches several conclusions concerning studies of the anal character. He finds little evidence for the Freudian etiological hypothesis. But there does appear to be evidence in both factor analytic and construct validity studies for the various traits of the anal character. Once again we see some, but not complete, support for the Freudian position.

There have been few studies of the clustering of traits constituting the phallic character. But one finds some studies that concentrate on one of the defenses or traits that has been considered relevant. These studies concern repression and were reviewed in Chapter 6. As a totality they are rather convincing, even though many of them can be strongly criticized. Of the studies concerning single traits, the most uniquely relevant to Freudian theory are those of *castration anxiety, castration wish,* and *penis envy,* all matters that are supposed to derive their importance in the adult personality from events during the phallic stage of development. Virtually all of these studies have employed fantasy measures of the various castration and envy themes. This kind of measurement clearly is appropriate, as such themes supposedly are unconscious. Blum (1949) found significantly more responses to the Blacky Test indicative of castration anxiety among males than among females, a finding that obviously supports Freudian thinking. Schwartz (1955, 1956) devised a method of scoring the Thematic Apperception Test for castration anxiety and found that male homosexuals displayed significantly more castration anxiety than normal males. In addition, males obtained higher castration anxiety scores than females. In a self-descriptive approach to measurement, Sarnoff and Corwin (1959) used a multiple-choice questionnaire on castration anxiety to show that males with high-castration scores have a significantly greater increase in fear of death than low-castration males after being exposed to sexually arousing stimuli. This finding supports Freudian thinking in that the sexually arousing stimuli should lead to guilt and fear of punishment most often in those males who experienced fixation during the phallic stage as a result of harsh punishment of their sexual desires for their mothers. Castration anxiety presumably is indicative of the harshness of such punishment. Intriguing though this finding is, it has required considerable interpretation and assumption making in order to be construed as support for Freud's position.

Finally, Hall and Van de Castle (1965) looked for evidence of castration anxiety, castration wish, and penis envy in reported dreams. Their study was particularly careful. The scoring system for *castration anxiety* involved such themes as difficulty with the penis, the changing of a man into a woman, and threatened or actual damage to or loss of part of the body. The criteria for *castration wish* were the same except that the events occured not for the dreamer but for another person in the dream. The scoring system for *penis envy* included the changing of a woman into a man, admiration of man's physical characteristics, and the acquisition of male objects. As scoring dreams for such characteristics involves some interpretation, it is important to demonstrate that the scoring systems result in adequate agreement among different investigators. Hall and Van de Castle reported interscorer agreement of over 95 percent on each of the three scoring systems. The subjects were male and female college students, who reported their recent dreams as part of a class assignment. The results of this study show that there is more evidence of castration anxiety among men than women and that women show more penis envy and castration wish than do men. The findings of this and the other studies mentioned above are quite in line with Freudian thinking concerning the phallic character type. But it must be said that there is nothing that could testify to the accuracy of the Freudian viewpoint on development.

I am at a loss for words concerning research relevant to the genital character type. Freudians do not themselves seem to do such research, probably because this type represents an ideal to them. There are virtually no fully genital people according to Freudians. In addition, the peripheral characteristics of the genital character are hardly peculiar to Freudian theory; hence, research concerning them would not provide vivid support of disconfirmation of the position. Personologists not of Freudian persuasion, particularly actualization theorists, have conducted research bearing on the kinds of emphases to be found in descriptions of the genital character. But these researches are more appropriately presented elsewhere in this review.

Before concluding this section, I should mention research themes involving the development of two paper-and-pencil tests of defensiveness. Both tests involve several defenses and, hence, imply several character types. One of the tests, the *Defense Mechanism Inventory,* was introduced by Gleser and Ihilevich (1969) in an attempt to measure the relative intensity of five major groups of defenses. The test is composed of twelve brief stories (two for each of the conflict areas of authority—independence, masculinity, femininity, competition, and situation), each followed by four questions regarding the person's actions, fantasies, thoughts, and feelings in the situations involved. Five responses exemplifying the five sets of defenses are provided for each question, and persons select the one most and the one least representative of their reactions. The five sets of defenses are *Turning Against Object* (displacement and identification with the aggressor), *Projection, Principalization* (intellectualization and isolation), *Turning Against Self* (masochism and autosadism), and *Reversal* (denial, reaction formation, and repression). Although Gleser and Ihilevich indulge in a confusing tendency to relabel well-known defenses with different names, their inventory appears at face value to have much bearing on Freudian theory.

Gleser and Ihilevich report internal consistency correlations that are comparable for males and females and range from $-.31$ to $.83$. Even if the two lowest (and quite unacceptable) correlations are omitted, the range is still large—from $.57$ to $.83$. These unimpressive findings suggest that at least some of the defensiveness scores are too heterogeneous as presently measured to be convincing as to empirical existence. The test fares better with regard to stability over a one-week interval, with correlations ranging from $.85$ to $.93$ and an average of $.89$.

As to validity, Gleser and Ihilevich report that psychologists were quite able to match stories with conflict areas and responses to questions with defense mechanisms. So the test appears to fit accepted beliefs of experts concerning defensiveness. It was also found that subjects who relied mainly on global defenses (Turning Against Self and Reversal) were more field dependent (unable to break up the visual field into component parts) than subjects who relied on differentiated defenses (Turning Against Object and Projection). Not only would there be disagreement among psychologists concerning the interpretation of this last finding; its relevance to Freudian thinking is far from clear.

Gleser and Sacks (1973) report a further validational attempt in which the Defense Mechanisms Inventory was administered to eighty-five college students after they had been exposed to a conflict situation in which they were led to believe their scholastic ability had proven deficient. Included were several measures of the effects of this conflict on mood and estimates of self-worth. In general, subjects with a tendency to defend by Turning Against Self reacted to the conflict with self-depreciation, anxiety, and depression. In contrast, subjects with a tendency to defend by Reversal but not by Turning Against Others showed no decrease in self-worth or increase in anxiety and depression. But there were some sex differences in this study, and the results are far from conclusive. Clearly the Defense Mechanisms Inventory will require more reliability and validational evidence before we can unequivocally adopt it as strong evidence for Freudian thinking.

The other test of defenses enjoying research attention is the *Repression-Sensitization Scale* introduced by Byrne (1961b) and later revised by Byrne, Barry, and Nelson (1963). Considerable research has been done with this scale, as indicated in several reviews (e.g., Byrne, 1964; Chabot, 1973). Originally devised to measure the same dimension on a paper-and-pencil test that is involved in perceptual defense and vigilance, the scale is best considered as incorporating several defenses at each of its two poles. The scale is constructed out of items from the Minnesota Multiphasic Personality Inventory, and it has proven acceptable with respect to internal consistency and stability.

Various studies (see Byrne, 1964; Chabot, 1973), have contributed construct-validational evidence that repressers differ from sensitizers in theoretically interesting ways in such areas of functioning as self-ideal discrepancy, physical illness, free associative sex responses to double-entendre words, effects of task familiarity on stress responses, and various cognitive skills. But some nagging problems also have emerged. For example, the high correlation between the Repression-Sensitization Scale and Welsh's anxiety factor on the Minnesota Multiphasic Personality Inventory (.97 for males, .96 for females) that has been reported by Gleser and Ihilevich (1969) raises serious questions as to whether it is defenses or merely anxiety that is being measured. In addition, Chabot (1973) has amassed evidence of a number of unresolved procedural and sampling problems surrounding the Repression-Sensitization Scale and alerts us to equivocal areas, such as sex differences, in which available findings are anything but clear. It would be difficult at this time to persuasively argue that this scale provides strong empirical validation for Freudian theorizing.

Silverman (1976) has summarized an interesting series of studies that have general significance for Freudian theory. These studies tend to employ the tachistoscopic (very brief) method of exposing stimuli to subjects. When the subjects respond to sexual and aggressive stimuli with physiological signs of recognition (e.g., increased sweating) but cannot yet identify the stimuli verbally (the exposure times being very short), it is assumed that the stimuli are having an unconscious effect (this kind of interpretation was discussed in terms of the first issue in Chapter 6). A number of studies conducted by Silverman and others influenced by him have shown that stimuli having this presumed unconscious effect increase signs of depression and other symptoms in subjects more than do stimuli to which there is no physiological reaction or that are accurately identified verbally. There is evidence here for the undermining effect of sexual and aggressive perceptions or thoughts that lie outside of awareness.

The studies we have covered tend to support Freudian theory in a general way, sometimes falling short of the comprehensiveness and incisiveness we should expect. Although the studies tend to reveal something suggestive, they also suffer from inconsistency of results or methodological shortcomings.

Murray's Position

Murray (1938) pioneered the modern emphasis on empirical measurement and validation of the peripheral characteristics present in a peripheral theory of personality. He and a capable staff of personologists collected huge amounts of data relating to his list of needs (e.g., for achievement, affiliation, power, nurturance, succorance, change) on a small group of college males. Over a period of six months or so, these investigators employed all methods of measurement—self-description, fantasy, and behavior ratings—toward the end of understanding the peripheral personalities of these young men.

To read the results of this extraordinary undertaking today is to invite a mixture of awe at the pioneering zeal of this group and a definite sense of the unsophisticated manner in which the business of measurement actually went forward. Instead of ensuring sufficient objectivity to permit use of measurement techniques that would result in high agreement by different investigators working independently, Murray instituted a diagnostic council. In this council, debate would ensue as to what was actually being observed in a subject and a conclusion reached by majority vote. Laudably democratic though this procedure is, it is not very objective in the scientific sense of different people being able to observe the same thing independently. It is very difficult for me to be critical, however, because I sincerely believe that Murray's approach was the most constructive thing that could be done at the time. The measurement of personality had not had sufficient time and use to achieve sophistication. Murray's procedures were brave beginnings, even if his findings cannot be taken as demonstrating the empirical existence and validity of his concepts. A gauge of his influence is that some of the techniques he and his colleagues invented, such as the *Thematic Apperception Test* (Murray, 1943), are still very much in use.

Another gauge of his influence is that his peripheral theory has had by far the greatest impact of any on the personologists whose major function is developing tests for assessing personality. Murray's list of needs has been a ready starting point for many investigators wanting to provide a comprehensive test of peripheral characteristics. Dramatic as this fact is, however, one must be careful not to conclude in the absence of additional information that Murray's theorizing is necessarily more accurate than other personologists'. The popularity of his needs is probably as much a function of their commonsense appeal and of Murray's care in trying to define them operationally as anything else. We must see how fruitful tests built on his needs are before concluding anything.

A popular test influenced by Murray's thinking is the *Activities Index* of Stern (1958). This test is composed of more than 300 items describing activities for which the person is supposed to indicate preference or dislike. Embedded in the test are thirty of Murray's needs, each measured by ten of the items. Stern gathered the original items for the test on the basis of Murray's own descriptions of the needs. He used a number of procedures, including factor analysis, to pare down the items to only those relating to needs that highly intercorrelated. The items relevant to one need also had to be relatively separate from those relevant to other needs. The resulting need measures have adequate internal consistency and stability. It can therefore be said that most of the needs postulated by Murray in his peripheral theory of personality have some claim to empirical existence.

But this conclusion needs to be qualified in certain ways. First is the disconcerting fact that a number of the need measures correlate fairly highly with one another. This could call into question whether the postulated needs are really so different from one another. The second qualification involves the fact that Stern's test uses only self-description in the form of answers to questions. Although Murray has advocated the use of self-description in measuring needs, he has also insisted that relevant fantasy and even performance be used in order to obtain the most accurate picture. Stern's decision to use only self-description reflects the test developer's bias that such information is more objective and quantifiable than is fantasy. If McClelland is right in presuming that self-description elicits schemata more than motives, we would expect Stern's test to fail in that it reflects culturally appropriate images of persons more than accurate descriptions of their true personal goals. Indeed, the current testing literature is replete with evidence that self-description used as a method of obtaining information about traits and motives suffers from the effects of what have been called *response styles* (e.g., Jackson & Messick, 1958). The most pervasive response style seems to be the tendency on the part of the test taker to respond to the items in a socially desirable fashion (e.g., Edwards, 1957). There is no guarantee whatsoever that people taking Stern's test will respond in terms of their actual personal goals rather than the goals they think are proper and socially constructive to have.

Were the Activities Index the only empirical evidence of the tangible measurability of Murray's needs, we could not conclude strongly for their empirical reality. But there are other tests based on his needs. Though these too employ the self-description format, they aim to obviate the hazard of socially desirable responding. One such test is the *Edwards Personal Preference Schedule* (Edwards, 1953). Edwards started with fifteen needs drawn from Murray's list and prepared sets of items whose content appeared to fit each need. At first he presented these items to a group of college students in the same form Stern used, namely, as descriptions of activities they were to indicate they liked or disliked. Being alert to the problem that people, when describing personal goals, tend to respond in a socially desirable fashion, Edwards also had other people judge each item for its social desirability. He found an extremely high correlation (.87) between the frequency with which the college students indicated preference for items and their judged social desirability! As a result of this disturbing finding, Edwards adopted what is called the *forced-choice format* for the presentation of items. In other words, he presented items not singly but in pairs, taking care to ensure that each item in a pair was similar in judged social desirability. Then respondents were asked to choose which item in each pair they preferred. Need strength was estimated through totaling the number of times each item relevant to a need was chosen. The result presumably was free of the influence of social desirability. The resulting need scores were correlated with a separate scale, developed at another time, for the purpose of measuring the strength of people's tendency to respond in a socially desirable fashion. The correlation between the need scores and socially desirable responses was quite low, indicating the success of Edwards's procedure.

Table 11–6 shows that the fifteen need measures on this test have reasonable internal consistency (split-half correlations of from .60 to .87) and stability (test-retest correlations of from .74 to .88). Table 11–7 shows that the intercorrelations of the need measures are satisfactorily low, the highest being .46 and the lowest close to zero. Later studies (e.g., Waters, 1967) have reported varying stability and internal consistency estimates, but this is to be expected when samples and testing conditions vary. In particular, evidence has accumulated that the scale scores may vary with shifts in the instructions given subjects. This, of course, is to be expected and is a problem only if too gross. But there is evidence in at least some studies (e.g., Weigel & Frazier, 1968) indicating some stability of scores despite instructional changes. It may be reasonably concluded, then, that there is empirical evidence in Edwards's test for the existence of many of Murray's peripheral characteristics. It would still be valuable, however, to attempt measurement of the needs utilizing the person's fantasy. I say this not simply out of insistence that if Murray thought fantasy an important means of measuring his needs, it should be tried. More important, it is apparently not clear that Edwards's procedure completely avoided socially desirable responding. Anastasi (1961) raises the possibility that the

TABLE 11–6   Coefficients of Internal Consistency and Stability for the
PPS Variables

Variable	Internal Consistency* $r_{1/}$	Stability†		
		$r_{1/}$	Mean	SD
1. Achievement	.74	.74	14.46	4.09
2. Deference	.60	.78	12.02	3.68
3. Order	.74	.87	11.31	4.45
4. Exhibition	.61	.74	14.43	3.67
5. Autonomy	.76	.83	13.62	4.48
6. Affiliation	.70	.77	15.40	4.09
7. Intraception	.79	.86	17.00	5.60
8. Succorance	.76	.78	12.09	4.59
9. Dominance	.81	.87	15.72	5.28
10. Abasement	.84	.88	14.10	4.96
11. Nurturance	.78	.79	14.04	4.78
12. Change	.79	.83	16.17	4.88
13. Endurance	.81	.86	12.52	5.11
14. Heterosexuality	.87	.85	15.08	5.66
15. Aggression	.84	.78	11.55	4.57
Consistency score				
N	1,509		89	

*Split-half, based on 14 items against 14 items, corrected.
†Test and retest with one week interval. Means and standard deviations are for first testing.

social desirability of items changes when they are paired and cites research indicating precisely this:

> Edwards, however, did not recheck the [social desirability] scale values of his statements when presented in pairs. Later research suggested that the [social desirability] values do change under these conditions. Not only are there significant differences in [social desirability] scale values of paired items, but a correlation of .88 was found between the predetermined scale values of paired items and their frequency of endorsement. It is also relevant to note that studies on faking indicate that scores on the [Edwards Personal Preference Schedule] *can* be deliberately altered to create more favorable impressions, especially for specific purposes. The latter possibility, of course, exists in any forced-choice test in which items were equated in terms of general social norms only. On the whole, it appears that the social desirability variable was not as fully controlled in the [Edwards Personal Preference Schedule] as had been anticipated. (p. 516)

Perhaps the best way to summarize the attempts of Stern and Edwards to develop tests of peripheral personality utilizing Murray's list of needs is to say

TABLE 11-7 Intercorrelations of the Variables Measured by the PPS ($N = 1,509$)

Variable	2 Def.	3 Ord.	4 Exh.	5 Aut.	6 Aff.	7 Int.	8 Suc.	9 Dom.	10 Aba.	11 Nur.	12 Chg.	13 End.	14 Het.	15 Agg.	Consistency Score
1. Achievement	-.17	-.05	.03	.14	-.33	-.09	-.14	.19	-.28	-.30	-.14	.07	.02	.09	.10
2. Deference		.26	-.22	-.30	.08	.10	-.09	-.22	.16	.05	-.09	.22	-.28	-.31	-.12
3. Order			-.21	-.15	-.16	-.06	-.08	-.16	.02	-.16	-.18	.33	-.16	-.16	-.06
4. Exhibition				.09	-.08	-.22	-.02	.11	-.18	-.17	.12	-.27	.12	.11	.00
5. Autonomy					-.33	-.10	-.21	.07	-.26	-.36	.15	-.13	.09	.29	.11
6. Affiliation						-.01	.09	-.12	.09	.46	.06	-.15	-.21	-.33	-.04
7. Intraception							-.16	-.12	-.01	.07	-.10	.03	-.19	-.20	.06
8. Succorance								-.22	.11	.16	-.18	-.31	.07	-.01	-.05
9. Dominance									-.34	-.20	-.11	-.16	.04	.21	.02
10. Abasement										.23	-.11	.07	-.29	-.25	-.05
11. Nurturance											-.12	-.12	-.21	-.33	.00
12. Change												-.14	-.07	-.08	.00
13. Endurance													-.27	-.22	-.06
14. Heterosexuality														.15	.01
15. Aggression															.05

SOURCE: *Edwards Personal Preference Schedule* by A. L. Edwards, 1953. New York: Psychological Corporation. Reproduced by permission from the manual for the Edwards Personal Preference Schedule. Copyright © 1953 by The Psychological Corporation. All rights reserved.

that especially with the corrections for socially desirable responding Edwards employed, there is empirical evidence that Murray's needs do indeed exist in people. This conclusion is supported by a similar test devised by Jackson (1974) to be less vulnerable to response biases than the others. Whether these measured entities have the status of needs is still unclear. It is ambiguous not simply on the rational grounds suggested by McClelland and partially agreed to by Murray—that motivational entities are best measured in fantasy productions—but on the empirical grounds of the pervasive influence on self-description of such response styles as socially desirable responding. From McClelland's point of view, it is understandable that tendencies toward socially desirable responding are aroused by the testing procedure that requires respondents to answer questions about what they are like. This procedure is, after all, best suited to the measurement of schemata. Therefore, no more precise conclusion is possible here than that there is empirical evidence for the existence of entities having the content specified by Murray, leaving open the matter of the kind of entities they may be.

Although the means of measuring these entities is not solidly in the spirit of Murray's theorizing, they still could be primarily motivational in nature. And in principle, one could garner additional information relevant to an empirical conclusion on this question of motivation through a vigorous attempt to determine the construct validity of the measures. Note that this is like the third step of the ideal strategy suggested earlier. But we do have little to go on in assessing construct validity. The manuals describing the tests of Edwards, Stern, and Jackson report such meager investigation of validity as to be insufficient. Since the publication of these tests, however, they have been used extensively in research. But rarely has the aim of the research been to investigate the validity of the various measures; rather, their validity has been more or less assumed, with the aim of the research banking on the adequate measurement of the range of needs specified in the test. For this reason, it is difficult to validate the status of the various measures. Nonetheless, indirect evidence suggests the probable validity of some of the needs measured on the two tests.

In a representative example of a study (Bernardin & Jessor, 1957) concerning the Edwards Personal Preference Schedule, people were put through three experimental task situations requiring the explicit demonstration of dependent or independent behavior. As shown in Table 11–8, Dependents (those scoring high on the need for deference and low on the need for autonomy) relied more on others for help and approval than did Independents (people low on the need for deference and high on the need for autonomy). No relationship was found, however, between these need measures and conformity to the opinions and demands of others. This study suggests that the measures of needs for deference and autonomy on Edwards's test are sufficiently free of the influence of schemata to be interpretable as motivational.

Other studies have attempted to compare the need scores obtained on the Edwards Personal Preference Schedule with other tests of the same needs. Poe

TABLE 11–8   Differences between Dependents and Independents in Both
Suggestion and Corroboration Scores

	Suggestion Score		Corroboration Score	
	Independents	Dependents	Independents	Dependents
Mean	.95	3.50	1.45	10.90
SD	1.24	2.31	1.63	7.53
H value	12.42		22.98	
p level	<.01		<.01	

SOURCE: "A Construct Validation of the Edwards Personal Preference Schedule with Respect to Dependency" by A. C. Bernardin, & R. A. Jessor, 1957, *Journal of Consulting Psychology, 21.*

(1969) administered to a sample of 132 male and female undergraduates an adjective checklist and both the standard form and a normative modification of the Edwards tests. Following the validational criteria formulated by Campbell and Fiske (1959), Poe attempted to determine whether scores for a particular need agreed more closely across tests than with scores on other needs within tests. This joint criterion of so-called convergent and discriminant validation was satisfied to a minimal extent.

In a similar study, Megargee and Parker (1968) employed first one sample of seventy adolescent delinquents and then another of eighty-six female Peace Corps trainees. It is of special interest that they compared Edwards's questionnaire test with ratings made of Thematic Apperception Test stories. In general, they found that the thematic apperception and questionnaire methods of measuring Murray's needs cannot be considered equivalent or parallel. They contend that "investigators who study these variables using one of these tests as their operational definition should be cautious in generalizing the results to the construct as operationally defined by the other instrument." At first encounter, findings such as this may well produce skepticism as to the very existence of the needs Murray has postulated. And insofar as he accepts that they should be measurable not only in fantasy but in self-description questionnaires, this skepticism is justified. But, as I will detail later, in a position such as McClelland's, which posits a strong theoretical rationale for fantasy as the only appropriate basis for assessing needs, the findings just mentioned represent little challenge. We shall have to consider once again in this chapter whether self-descriptive tests measure motivational entities.

Erikson's Position

Erikson's theorizing has comprised a fair amount of research in recent years. Most of it, however, is not really relevant here, for either of two reasons. In one instance, you find research concentrating on childhood and adolescence. While it is understandable that such research gets done, for much of Erikson's emphasis is on the early years of life, it is the period of adulthood that concerns us most here. The other kind of irrelevant study attempts to tie together a mass of findings by referring in some vague, post hoc fashion to Erikson's peripheral theorizing. This is a far cry from planning a study for the purpose of testing the empirical adequacy of his position. In order for a study to be valuable to us, it would at least have to try to measure the subject's status with respect to the psychosocial stages of development and then apply this information to an understanding of his or her adult functioning. Such studies are few compared to the many that refer to Erikson in one manner or another.

Certainly the studies relevant to the Freudian position on peripheral personality are also appropriate here. To be sure, Erikson's theorizing is less biologically oriented, even for the childhood years. But the Freudian conceptualization of oral, anal, and phallic character types bears resemblance to the types covered by Erikson in the first three stages of human development. Erikson's position, then, receives the same general but somewhat unincisive support that we found for Freud's position. But Erikson's unique contribution to peripheral theorizing concerns adolescence and adulthood. Therefore, only if there is empirical support for these aspects of his position can we seriously say that fruitfulness has been demonstrated.

Of the few studies available, we will review several that are particularly sound and relevant. The first, done by Peck and Havighurst (1960), has the advantage of comprehensiveness. It involved following the character development of youngsters in the period from ages ten to seventeen. The traits or groups of traits studied showed consistent development during this period such that the youngsters tended to keep their rank order in the group. This suggests that whatever determined the rank order in the first place must have occurred sometime before ten years of age. Fortunately, parental behavior that might have set the youngsters' traits had been examined three years before the beginning of the study. Meaningful relationships were obtained between themes of parental behavior and certain traits in the youngsters. Ego strength and moral stability in the youngsters were most closely related to mutual trust and consistency within the family. Superego strength was most highly related to parental consistency and friendliness to familial trust and democracy. A pattern of hostility and guilt in the youngsters was highly related to parental behaviors displaying severe discipline, lack of trust, and lack of democracy. Apparently, if children receive trust, warmth, and love from their parents, and if they are permitted to exercise their own processes of choice, they will appear more psychologically vigorous and affluent than if they experience the opposite parental attitudes. This study suggests the empirical validity of Erikson's conception of the first two stages of the human as involving trust versus mistrust and autonomy versus shame and doubt.

In contrast to this broad, somewhat vague study with many loose ends is one by Bronson (1959), which concerns itself with the period of adolescence designated by Erikson as relevant to the development of firm identity versus role diffusion. Bronson focused on the attempt to determine whether a group of peripheral characteristics, referring at one pole to a firm sense of identity and at the other to identity diffusion, had actual empirical existence. Starting with a sensitive reading of Erikson's (1956) descriptions of identity and diffusion, Bronson decided on four such characteristics for measurement: (1) to be certain or uncertain that there is a relationship between one's past and current notions of oneself; (2) to show a low or high degree of internal tension or anxiety; (3) to be certain or uncertain about which are one's dominant personal characteristics; and (4) to be stable or fluctuating in one's feelings about oneself. Bronson correctly hypothesized that significant positive intercorrelation among these bipolar characteristics would constitute support for Erikson's conceptualization of the fifth stage of development (identity versus role diffusion).

The subjects were forty-six college students, mainly female. Bronson measured the first two characteristics mentioned above through investigators' ratings of the subjects' behavior during a twenty-minute interview. The investigators were three trained clinical psychologists, and the average of their ratings was used as the data. A self-descriptive procedure was used to measure the final two characteristics, with the procedure being repeated after a four-week interval in order to estimate the stability or flux required in the fourth characteristic. As can be seen in Table 11–9, the correlations among the four measures ranged from .47 to .71, and all were highly significant from a statistical point of view. Apparently there are some adolescents who are anxious, do not perceive a relationship between who they are now and who they were before, are not sure what their dominant attributes are, and change their minds

TABLE 11–9   Correlations among Measures Relating to Aspects of Identity Diffusion

	1 *Continuity* *with* *Past*	*2* *Freedom* *from* *Anxiety*	*3* *Certainty* *of Self-* *Conception*
1. Continuity with the past (interview rating)	—		
2. Freedom from anxiety (interview rating)	.59†	—	
3. Certainty of self-conception (semantic differential measure)	.71†	.47*	—
4. Temporal stability of self-rating (semantic differential measure)	.53*	.47*	.54†

Note: $N = 18$ for the correlations involving the interview measures; $N = 46$ for the remaining value.
*$p < .05$, two-tailed test.
†$p < .01$, two-tailed test.

SOURCE: "Identity Diffusion in Late Adolescents" by G. W. Bronson, 1959, *Journal of Abnormal and Social Psychology, 59*.

about these matters as well. These people show identity diffusion. That some adolescents have a firm sense of identity is shown by the existence of a type with the opposite characteristics.

Recent studies provide further support for Erikson's thinking on ego identity. Tobacyk (1981) reported that subjects with a stable identity show less mood variability than do subjects with ego diffusion. In a similar vein, Rappaport, Enrich, and Wilson (1985) found that subjects showing strong ego identity think more in terms of the future than do ego-diffuse subjects. Both findings concern definite implications of Erikson's theorizing.

In another relevant study, Yufit (1969) attempted to determine whether the behavioral expressions of persons classifiable as intimate relaters differed from those classifiable as isolates. You will recall that intimacy versus isolation is the sixth of Erikson's eight stages. A large battery of paper-and-pencil tests plus interviews were collected on sixty-one undergraduates, who were classified as *intimates, isolates,* or *controls* (i.e., neither one nor the other). Complex and sometimes intuitive scoring procedures were employed on interviews and other tests. Then the data were factor analyzed. The emerging factors suggested the value of classifying people as intimates and isolates.

In an unusual study employing fairly rigorous methods, Waterman, Buebel, and Waterman (1970) addressed themselves to Erikson's hypothesis that a positive outcome in any stage of development is rendered more likely by positive outcomes in earlier stages. In the first part of their study, Waterman et al. employed a questionnaire, the *Internal-External Locus of Control Scale* (James, 1957), concerning whether one believes the events of one's life are determined personally or by force of external circumstance, as an index of whether autonomy or shame and doubt had been the outcome of the second stage of development. They also used questionnaire methods to assess whether trust or distrust had taken place in the first stages. Their dependent variable was outcome in the identity-versus-role-diffusion stage, which they also measured via questionnaire. As predicted, identity went along with internal locus of control (autonomy) and role diffusion with external locus of control (shame and doubt). But the hypothesized relationships linking identity with trust and role diffusion with distrust did not occur. In the second part of their study, these investigators employed a self-concept measure to test the predicted relationships mentioned above. This procedure produced more consistent support for Erikson's view. But it should be noted that in this part of the study, one source of data was employed to measure several characteristics, raising the possibility that the relationships were somewhat spurious reflections of overlap of method. In a similar vein, Tesch and Whitbourne (1982) reported that young adults who show adequate ego identity (versus diffusion) are also likely to show intimacy (versus isolation).

Constantinople (1969) developed a sixty-item self-rating scale called the *Inventory of Psychosocial Development*. This scale was based methodologically on a previous technique offered by Wessman and Ricks (1966) and theoretically on Erikson's stages. Constantinople reported a median stability correlation of

.70 on 150 subjects with a six-week interval between testings. Although reliability is by no means overwhelming, it is sufficient to entertain the notion that
this scale measures successful and unsuccessful development at the stages of
*trust versus mistrust, initiative versus guilty functioning, autonomy versus
shame and doubt, industry vs. inferiority, identity versus role diffusion,* and
intimacy versus isolation. Information concerning the validity of this scale is
slowly developing. In a particularly relevant study, Reimanis (1974) reasoned
that unsuccessful resolution of conflicts in psychosocial development should
give rise to feelings of anomie, or social disorganization. To test this prediction,
he administered both the Inventory of Psychosocial Development and a commonly used anomie scale to two samples (100 male veterans and 141 male and
female students). Table 11–10 shows the resulting correlations. As expected,
unsuccessful psychological development tends to be associated with anomie,
whereas successful psychosocial development tends not to be. These findings
are similar to those of Constantinople (1969), who found successful development to be associated with happiness.

Marcia (1966) has elaborated on Erikson's stage of ego identity versus role
diffusion, which is certainly the most heavily emphasized period. According to
Marcia, it is possible to distinguish no fewer than five orientations in Erikson's

TABLE 11–10   Correlations between Anomie and the Inventory of
Psychosocial Development

	Srole Scale Measurement of Anomie		
Inventory of Psychosocial Development Item	*Veterans Administration Members*	*College Males*	*College Females*
Basic trust	−.17	−.17	−.28*
Mistrust	.31*	.21	.25*
Initiative	−.08	−.05	−.36*
Guilt	.31*	.40*	.25*
Autonomy	−.14	.26	−.14
Shame and doubt	.28*	.40*	.13
Industry	−.17	.06	−.36*
Inferiority	.16	.44*	.29*
Identification	−.10	−.14	−.35*
Role diffusion	.24	.43*	.22*
Intimacy	−.06	−.24	−.28*
Isolation	.42	.29*	.16

Note: Veterans Administration members, $N = 74$; college males, $N = 55$; college females,
$N = 86$.
*$p < .05$.

SOURCE: Adapted from "Psychological Development, Anomie, and Mood" by G. Reimanis, 1974, *Journal
of Personality and Social Psychology, 29.*

thinking about this period: *identity achievement* (persons who have experienced the crisis and are committed to an occupation and an ideology); *moratorium* (persons currently in the crisis with only vague commitments to occupation and ideology); *foreclosure* (persons who, while committed to an occupation and ideology, seem to have experienced no crisis, their commitments being largely parentally determined); *identity diffusion* (persons who may or may not have experienced the crisis, but who exhibit no commitment); and *alienated achievement* (persons who have experienced the crisis and exhibit no commitment but have worked out an ideology condemning the social system). Determination of a subject's identity status is made by rating his or her responses to a standardized interview according to rules provided by Marcia (1966). Interscorer agreement on ratings has hovered between 80 and 90 percent in several studies (e.g., Toder & Marcia, 1973; Orlofsky, Marcia, & Lesser, 1973). Apparently no internal consistency or stability information is available, so we cannot be sure that the statuses have solid empirical support.

Orlofsky et al. (1973) studied the relationship of the various identity statuses described above to measures of intimacy, isolation, social desirability, affiliation, and heterosexuality in an attempt to determine whether difficulties in identity would jeopardize later development. As expected from Erikson's theorizing, *foreclosure* and *identity diffusion* subjects had the most superficial and stereotyped interpersonal relationships. *Moratorium* subjects were the most variable. And whereas *identity achievement* subjects were characterized by social intimacy rather than isolation, it was actually the *alienated achievement* subjects who were most marked in this regard. The last finding is a bit surprising, but the investigators reasoned that the capability of alienated achievement subjects indicates that they have forgone the identity crisis in favor of the intimacy crisis. This is an intriguing notion, but not one readily derivable from Erikson's present theorizing.

Toder and Marcia (1973) studied the role of identity status in the response-to-conformity pressure by placing sixty-four college females into a task situation in which confederates of the researchers would attempt to mislead the subjects in the judgments they were asked to make. Females with identity statuses that might be regarded as stable (*achievement* and *foreclosure*) conformed to the pressure less than did those with unstable statuses (*moratorium* and *diffusion*). While not unequivocally supportive of Eriksonian thinking, this and the previous study represent a beginning that bears further attention.

The studies we have reviewed suggest the fruitfulness of Erikson's peripheral theorizing. But more carefully planned work will have to be conducted before the position can be comprehensively evaluated from an empirical standpoint. I might mention that some investigators (e.g., Neugarten, 1964) especially concerned with the aging process believe Erikson's emphasis on such conflicts of maturity as ego integrity versus despair to be very helpful in ordering research findings dealing with the problems of old people. There are currently several studies charting the increase in depression as age advances (e.g., Grant, 1969; Lehr & Rudinger, 1969) and the possibility that a commitment to useful work may stem the tide (e.g., Rybak, Sadnavitch, & Mason, 1968). In general, however, these studies do not attempt to measure ego integrity versus despair so much as use it as an explanatory construct.

The Object-Relations Position

In its peripheral theorizing, the object-relations position tends to reinterpret and recombine the Freudian character types. As such, the preceding discussion of research is somewhat relevant here, too. The primary emphasis of object-relations approaches is on psychopathology, however, and as such is outside the scope of this discussion. There are some points made about ideal functioning, but these are too new and ambiguous to have generated relevant, systematic research as yet. Nonetheless, some of the discussions in later sections of this chapter may be partially relevant here.

Kohut's and Berne's Positions

There appears to be no systematic research on the peripheral theorizing in these positions. This is perhaps understandable at this early stage, in which the peripheral statements are barely developed and the major emphasis is still on clinical practice.

Rank's Position

Although Rank's peripheral personality types are clearly delineated, his theorizing has provoked scant research. Of all the professionals for whom personality theory is important, it is the psychologists who have the sophistication and inclination to conduct rigorous empirical research on a regular basis—and among psychologists, Rank's theorizing has never become popular. I am frankly unable to understand why this is so. Nonetheless, it is by no means true that Rank's position has been insufficiently pruned and developed to warrant the attempt at empirical analysis. Far from it.

There is one large-scale research program that indirectly suggests the empirical promise of Rank's peripheral theorizing. MacKinnon (1965) has conducted a complicated study of creativity in architects. Admittedly at a loss for a theory that would pull together his numerous findings in a coherent fashion, MacKinnon rediscovered Rank and found him very useful. MacKinnon felt that his creative architects displayed the acceptance of their own individuality coupled with the interest in and involvement with other people that Rank considered so characteristic of the type he called the *artist*. MacKinnon's ordinary architects seemed much like Rank's average persons, with their emphasis on conformity and mediocrity. Finally, MacKinnon even found an intermediate group of respected, productive, but not highly creative architects who resembled Rank's descriptions of the neurotic type, replete with a commitment to personal individuality without willingness to risk rejection.

Helson (1973a; 1973b) has reported parallel studies focusing on the personalities of male and female creative writers. Utilizing interviews with the writers and various ratings of their works, she abstracted through cluster analysis personality types reminiscent of Rank's artist, neurotic, and average person. The most creative of the writers tended to display the artist's temperament and life style.

There are also a few studies that attempted to evaluate Bakan's constructs of agency and communion. Agency is sufficiently similar to the Rankian fear of death, and communion to the fear of life, that these studies are of interest here. In one of them, Brown and Marks (1969) administered a questionnaire concerning these two tendencies to 150 maladjusted subjects and 150 normal subjects, with the intent of determining whether unmitigated agency was higher in the former group, as Bakan would expect. The results provided some support for this expectation.

Carlson (1971a) studied sex differences in agency and communion in two ways. The first involved obtaining from eighteen male and twenty-three female undergraduate subjects descriptions of seven remembered instances of intense emotion that they considered important. The instances were rated by judges as being agentic, communal, or mixed, and the interscorer agreement was a high 93 percent. As Bakan would expect, 60 percent of the male responses were coded agentic as compared with only 40 percent of female responses. Also, when each subject was classified as either agentic or communal on the basis of the predominance of his or her responses, ten of the fourteen males emerged as agentic as compared with only five of the twenty females (this finding achieved statistical significance). It was also possible to determine whether "unmitigated agency" represents something undesirable (as Bakan contends) by determining whether agentic responses tended to be unpleasant emotions (e.g., fear, anger) and communal responses pleasant emotions (e.g., joy, love). The results supported this contention.

Carlson's second procedure was a bibliographic study in which she employed data already collected by others for other purposes. She looked at 100 studies in which differences between males and females could have been found, with a view toward determining whether such differences conformed to Bakan's general views on agency and communion. Although her results overwhelmingly support those views, they must be taken with a grain of salt, because it may be that the investigators who originally collected the data were already biased in line with Bakan's views.

There is very little else by way of rigorous research that is sufficiently relevant to Rankian thought to be mentioned here. Further, what has been reviewed tends either to end by recognizing the utility of Rank's conception of types rather than beginning by testing it or to involve another, though admittedly related, theorist. It is premature, therefore, to evaluate Rank's peripheral theorizing empirically, though there are some interesting leads to be followed.

Perls's Position

At this time, there is essentially no peripheral statement in Perls's theorizing. Needless to say, no research has been conducted with individual emphases of this position in mind, nor is it possible to construe research from other traditions as relevant.

Jung's Position

Believers in Jung's theory do not themselves seem to do much research. But others have performed intriguing studies. Notable among them is Stephenson's (1950), which considers not only extroversion versus introversion and the thinking, feeling, sensing, and intuiting modes but consciousness versus unconsciousness of these characteristics. He considered the sixteen combinations of these aspects of personality that would be of interest to Jung (e.g., conscious-thinking introvert, unconscious-intuitive extrovert) and set about finding descriptions of them in that theorist's writings. He selected five descriptive sentences for each of the sixteen combinations. This led to a pool of twenty descriptive sentences for each mode, forty for each level of consciousness, and forty each for introversion and extroversion. This approach is of special interest because it employs a theorist's own words in measuring the peripheral considerations he or she is defining.

Armed with these descriptive sentences, how does one measure a subject's peripheral personality? Stephenson had each descriptive sentence written on a card and asked subjects to determine for each statement whether it applied to them (1) very definitely, (2) not at all, or (3) somewhere in between. The subject does this by sorting the cards into the three relevant piles. This technique came to be known as the *Q-sort*. When subjects are done, it is possible to determine, by counting the sorted cards, to what degree they are introverted, extroverted, conscious, thinking, and so forth. The Q-sort procedure is extremely flexible in that it is possible for subjects to describe not only themselves but others if so instructed.

Stephenson chose for study Jung's contention that differences in personality type cause misunderstandings among persons. For data, Stephenson described himself by a Q-sort and then had several judges supposedly familiar with him describe him by the same procedure. In addition, the judges described themselves. By Stephenson's own Q-sort, he was an extrovert. Five of the judges were introverts by their self-sort, and their Q-sort of him correlated with his own .46, .45, .61, .59, and .61, for an average of .54. Two of the judges were extroverts, and their Q-sorts of him correlated with his own .47 and .40, for an average of .44. Contrary to what Jung would have expected, the extroverts were certainly not superior in perceiving a fellow extrovert. This conclusion is strengthened by evidence that the extroverted judges were drawing on their own personality characteristics to a much greater degree than the introverts in attempting to describe Stephenson. Correlations between judges' self-sorts and their sorts of Stephenson were, on the average, .23 for the introverts and .50 for the extroverts. Unfortunately, this study does not seem to have been followed up, and it employed a very small sample. Nonetheless, it does raise questions as to whether it is differing personality types that misunderstand one another.

Actually, the introversion-extroversion dimension has led to considerable research, but with neither the procedure nor the hypothesis presented above. The work I shall now describe was inspired by the eminent English psychologist Hans Eysenck (1947), whose personality questionnaire, called the *Maudsley Personality Inventory,* was devised to measure not only introversion-extroversion but neuroticism. Many of the studies relevant to the Jungian types were actually done by followers of Eysenck. In addition, Raymond Cattell (Cattell & Stice, 1957), in his *16 Personality Factor Questionnaire* (mentioned earlier), found evidence for a first-order factor of introversion-extroversion and a second-order factor that he thought came even closer to what Jung had in mind. The studies I will review have, in the main, employed one or the other of these measures.

First, let us consider works directed toward the adequacy of these measures. Marshall (1967), though he reports no new data of his own, cites existing evidence for the validity of Cattell's first- and second-order factors of introversion-extroversion as measures of Jung's distinction of the same name. Once this correspondence is established, the construct validation work on Cattell's factors is relevant to Jung's theory as well. It has been found that on the average (Cattell, 1957) introversion is high among researchers, artists, and planning executives, as well as in creative workers in both art and science. In contrast, extroversion is high in mechanical occupations (e.g., engineers) and those requiring alertness (e.g., cooks, firefighters). Among teamsters, those high in introversion are accident prone. Introversion is also slightly correlated with certain psychopathological symptoms, particularly depressive reactions. Finally, women are higher than men in introversion, though there is no change in the average value of this characteristic over the age range of sixteen to sixty years. As you would expect, the second-order factor of introversion-extroversion operates similarly to the first-order factor.

It has also not escaped investigators that there might well be some relationship between the introversion-extroversion scales offered by Cattell and by Eysenck. Crookes and Pearson (1970) compared scores on the two procedures obtained from sixty maladjusted subjects. Correlations between the separate measures of introversion-extroversion "are all very similar and quite substantial."

Several normative studies suggest that more needs to be known about the meaning of the questions and testing situations used for both these tests. For example, McQuaid (1967) reports on the basis of a sample of 1,733 Scottish subjects compared with available U.S. norms for Cattell's measure that there is a definite trend toward greater extroversion among Americans. Salas (1967) and Skinner, Howarth, and Browne (1970) report that Eysenck's measure of introversion-extroversion can be shifted by instructional set. When subjects are asked to simulate a "nice personality," extroversion scores go up, and the opposite is true when they are asked to fake being "bad." It is at present difficult to determine how much of a problem is involved.

Eysenck's measure does seem to have some validity in terms of subjects' self-perceptions. Kramer (1969) administered the measure to 242 undergraduates who previously had rated themselves for (1) how extroverted they felt they really were, (2) how extroverted they felt they appeared to others, and (3) the ideal amount of extroversion one should have. The first two ratings correlated with Eysenck's measure of extroversion—.46 and .48, respectively. The 243 undergraduates used by Harrison and McLaughlin (1969) first took Eysenck's measure and then were read descriptions of the typical introvert and extrovert. Following this, they rated themselves on these two dimensions. Introversion-extroversion scores correlated .72 with the self-ratings of the same characteristics. It would seem that measures such as Eysenck's and, for that matter, Cattell's provide convenient ways of determining a person's level of introversion and extroversion.

The remaining studies to be discussed here concern the relationship between introversion-extroversion and various behaviors other than self-rating. As Carrigan (1960) has indicated, the body of research involved has produced ambiguous and even contradictory results over the last thirty years. Some of this may be a function of the extreme generality of the theorizing behind introversion-extroversion. This generality has permitted investigators to work with particular corners of the theorizing that may not coincide with what other investigators are doing. But it also may be that other variables moderate the effect of introversion-extroversion such that its relationship to behavior is clear only when they are controlled. Wallach and Gahm (1960) introduced the use of moderator variables to good advantage, and their approach has been adopted by some investigators working with introversion-extroversion.

Taft (1967) attempted to determine the effects of introversion-extroversion on the expressive behavior involved in writing. He used eighty-six undergraduates who took Eysenck's test and also gave a sample of handwriting. It was found that extroverts wrote either larger or smaller than introverts but that in order to understand which it would be, one had to take anxiety or neuroticism level into account. Extroverts low in neuroticism wrote the largest and extroverts high in neuroticism the smallest. Geen (1984) permitted subjects to determine level of background noise while performing a task. As expected, it was found that extroverts preferred more noise than introverts. When Graziano, Rahe, and Feldesman (1985) had their subjects play a competitive game, they found that introverts disliked the game but remembered their opponents' traits better than those of their teammates. This pattern was not found in extroverts. Such results are generally consistent with Jungian thinking.

Some studies bear on the affiliative behavior of introverts and extroverts. On the basis of Jung's theorizing, Bieler (1966) hypothesized that extroverted persons should prefer paintings in which humans are present and introverts paintings without humans. He too employed Eysenck's test and also discovered that in order to make sense out of his data, it was necessary to use anxiety or neuroticism level as a moderator variable. He found that extroverts low in neuroticism indeed preferred paintings including people and that introverts low in neuroticism preferred paintings devoid of people. But there was no difference between highly neurotic introverts and extroverts.

Shapiro and Alexander (1969) did a careful investigation following Bieler's lead. They chose another measure of introversion-extroversion, the *Myers-Briggs-Type Indicator* (Myers, 1962), a questionnaire specially devised to yield information on both Jung's introversion-extroversion dimension and the four modes of thought. The final sample was 130 undergraduates, all of whom not only took the Myers-Briggs-Type Indicator but also were led to believe that they were to receive electric shocks. Anxiety was strongly aroused in those subjects who expected the shocks to be painful and only minimally aroused in others who were told that the shocks would be mild. They were also told that there would be a brief waiting period before the shocks, during which they could elect to either talk with other subjects or remain alone. Choosing to be with others was considered evidence of affiliative behavior. Several checks on the effectiveness of the procedure for arousing anxiety carried out following the experiment yielded positive results.

The principal results concerning the effects of introversion and extroversion on affiliative behavior moderated by anxiety appear in Table 11-11. As you can see, highly anxious extroverts showed the strongest affiliation tendencies, whereas highly anxious introverts showed the weakest. This difference was statistically significant. But the difference between introverts and extroverts low in anxiety was not large enough to achieve significance. The last two studies taken together suggest that the potential differences between introverts and extroverts in affiliative behavior are actualized only in anxiety-producing circumstances or when neuroticism exists. Perhaps, then, neuroticism is a chronic state of anxiety.

Many other studies utilizing Eysenck's questionnaire measure have considered various aspects of affiliative behavior. For example, Brown and Hendrick (1971) found extroverts to be generally more popular because they were seen as more interesting, warm, and influential than introverts. This would seem to go along with findings that extroverts talk more and sooner in an interview situation than do introverts, but caution is necessary, since several studies have failed to replicate this finding (see Wilson, 1977). But the notion that extroverts are more socially oriented seems to persist. For example, Eysenck (1976) found extroverts reporting more sexual behavior and being more permissive in that regard than introverts. But results of many studies concerning whether extroverts are more suggestible than introverts have yielded conflicting results (see Wilson, 1977). What does appear clear, however, is that extroverts are more field dependent than introverts (Fine & Danforth,

TABLE 11–11   Relation of Induced Anxiety and Extroversion-Introversion to Intensity of Affiliation for Males*

	I		*E*	
	Mean	N	*Mean*	N
High anxiety	−4.80	(25)	4.42	(21)
Low anxiety	3.36	(13)	1.18	(11)

Note: The higher the score, the higher the affiliation tendency. Isolation scores subtracted from affiliation scores for intensity. Means collapsed across birth order.
*Interaction: (Anxiety $\times$ *EI*)F = 4.9, *df* = 1.62; *p* = .03.

SOURCE: "Extroversion-Introversion, Affiliation, and Anxiety" by K. J. Shapiro and I. E. Alexander, 1969, *Journal of Personality, 37.*

1975); that is, extroverts are less able to discard the cues coming from background characteristics of the visual field in attempting to discern something in an independent fashion.

In a particularly interesting study, Duckworth (1975) tested the notion that introverts, being more sensitive in general, should be better able than extroverts to judge the feelings of others. He employed thirty-six married couples, split into experimental and control groups. The experimental group was subjected to emotionally provocative disagreements. Then both groups were asked to judge the vocally expressed feeling of their spouses. The introverts indeed judged more accurately despite having been subjected to the disagreements as long as they were also low in anxiety. When subjects were high in anxiety, there was no difference between introverts and extroverts.

Turning from manifestly social behaviors, we find evidence (Shaw & Sichel, 1971) that when driving, extroverts take more risks and have more accidents than introverts. In intellectual performance (Wankowski, 1973), introverts are superior in long-term memory tasks and get better grades, even though there is no difference in general intelligence between them and extroverts. But extroverts benefit more from "discovery learning" programs, which are informal, spontaneous, individualistic, and social compared with more traditional programs (Leith, 1974).

Before turning to other matters, I should mention a group of studies exploring the origins of introversion-extroversion. These studies employ one or more of the measuring instruments for introversion-extroversion mentioned above and focus either on parent-child relations or on heredity. The most consistent conclusion is that accepting, loving, positive parents frequently have extroverted children, whereas rejecting, cold, negative parents have introverted children (see Siegelman, 1968). Studies attempting to determine the relationship between birth order and introversion-extroversion differences have yielded contradictory results (see Siegelman, 1968). Finally, there seems clear evidence of hereditary differences in introversion-extroversion from studies of identical and fraternal twins, and these differences have been shown to persist over time (see Wilson, 1977). As Jung's position concerning the origins of introversion-extroversion is not clear, it is difficult to determine what role these studies should have in evaluating his theory.

Carlson and Levy (1973) have reported an intriguing set of studies in which predictions concern the effect of Jungian personality types on memory, social perception, and social action. The Myers-Briggs Type Indicator was taken by all the female college students serving as subjects. As predicted, the results of the first study showed that introverted-thinking types performed best on a memory task involving impersonal stimuli (numbers), whereas extroverted-feeling types performed best when the stimuli were social and emotionally toned (faces with various expressions). The second study replicated the first, utilizing a task that was comparable in structure for both types of subjects. The task in the third study was to interpret (rather than merely remember) emotions from facial expressions. A series of pictures of the same person, each showing a different emotional expression, were shown to subjects (the emotional expressions had previously been labeled with a high level of agreement among 100 judges). Results showed that intuitive-feeling types were significantly more accurate in interpreting emotional expressions than were sensing-thinking types, a finding predicted by Jung. In the final study, the predicted tendency for social service volunteers to be extroverted intuitive types was confirmed by comparing the Myers-Briggs Type Indicator scores of such volunteers with a control group.

Also using the Myers-Briggs Type Indicator, Hanewitz (1978) collected personality profiles over four years on 1,282 veterans and police recruits, 96 undergraduate social work students, 88 public school teachers, and 946 dental students. For police recruits, the usual type was sensing-thinking, coupled most often with extroversion but also to some degree with introversion. The dental students showed the same picture. In contrast, teachers and social work students revealed much higher concentrations of intuition and feeling orientations. This study suggests that certain Jungian types are drawn differentially to professions. Helson (1982) reported similar findings with different methods. She analyzed the content of writings by literary critics and found evidence for all four of the Jungian modes of thinking.

In recent years, research on psychological androgyny has become popular. This combination of traditionally feminine and masculine characteristics can be found in persons regardless of whether they are biologically female or male. You will recall that an expression in behavior of both the male and female principles in each of us is considered by Jung as consistent with the ideal of selfhood. Consequently, evidence that androgynous subjects perform best would support Jung's position.

At present, androgyny research is fraught with controversy. Championed by Sondra Bem (1974), androgyny has raised both measurement and substantive issues. As expected, Tunnell (1981) found that psychologically feminine women used more feminine and less masculine constructs on the Role Repertory Test than did psychologically androgynous women. Further, Shaw (1982) reported that androgynous females found life events less stressful than did psychologically feminine females. In addition, both androgynous males and females rated themselves as happier than did nonandrogynous subjects. In a related finding (Major, Carnevale, & Deaux, 1981), androgynous males and females were rated by peers as more adjusted and better liked than nonandrogynous subjects of both genders. Such findings support the notion that being psychologically both masculine and feminine is developmentally advantageous.

But some studies have yielded more complex or ambiguous results. In a simulation study, for example, Senniker and Hendrick (1983) found that while androgynous females came to the aid of a supposedly "choking" confederate more quickly than did feminine females, so too did males whether they were psychologically androgynous, masculine, or feminine! Also, Heilbrun (1981) reported that androgynous males were higher in social cognition and lower in defensiveness than other males but that androgynous females showed the reverse pattern by comparison with other females. In another study, Heilbrun (1984) found that although androgynous females showed less ambiguity tolerance and greater social competence than other females, this pattern did not emerge with male subjects. To add further complexity, Harrington and Andersen (1981) found only slight support for androgyny as a predictor of creativity; male gender, regardless of psychological sexual orientation, was an equally good predictor. Taken together, these studies may be highlighting that androgyny is more of a developmental advantage for females than it is for males, a possibility not really consistent with Jungian thinking regarding selfhood.

Some studies even suggest that androgyny does not differ from masculinity or femininity per se (e.g., Lubinski, Tellegen, & Butcher, 1981, 1983). Consistent with this is the finding by Feather (1984) that no values distinguish androgynous males and females from others and the complex results concerning leadership in mixed-sex groups reported by Porter, Geis, Cooper, and Newman (1985). It is also possible that there is deficiency in the questionnaire measure of masculinity, femininity, and androgyny introduced by Bem and used by the researchers mentioned here. In this regard, Hall and Taylor (1985) offer several methodological suggestions that are important when the interaction of two dimensions (masculinity and femininity) are combined into a third, supposedly distinct dimension (androgyny). In any event, it presently is unclear how much support for the Jungian position on selfhood exists in the androgyny research.

The research discussed in this section provides some support for the Jungian emphasis on introversion-extroversion, which seems a seminal dimension for understanding human behavior. But the studies reported by Carlson and Levy and by Hanewitz are very important, because the aspect of Jung's peripheral theorizing most unique to him inheres in the combination of peripheral characteristics (such as introversion-extroversion) with others into types. There should be more of this kind of research. However, I must caution you about the existence of many studies yielding negative or conflicting results (see

Wilson, 1977). Although there are too many to be mentioned here, that by Domino (1976) is particularly telling. He obtained three dream reports from each of sixty-two male college students, which were rated on fifteen personality dimensions by five judges. Interested in the Jungian prediction that dreams have a compensatory or contrast function, he correlated the personality scores obtained from the dreams with scores on the same dimensions as measured by self-report questionnaires of personality. The close correspondence he found between the dream and questionnaire scores is inconsistent with a compensation hypothesis.

Rogers's Position

Although Rogers's position on the periphery of personality is hardly elaborate, it does have some fairly definite empirical implications. In order to see this, recall that the fully functioning person has five groupings of peripheral characteristics, referred to as *openness to experience* (including emotionality and reflectiveness), *existential living* (including flexibility, adaptability, spontaneity, and inductive thinking), *organismic trusting* (including congruence between what you believe yourself to be and what you believe to be worthy), *experiential freedom* (a sense of free will and personal control over life), and *creativity* (an interest in producing new things). The groupings of peripheral characteristics comprised in the maladjusted personality are the opposite of these, namely, *defensiveness, living according to a preconceived plan, conditions of worth, feelings of being manipulated,* and *conformity.* There are two ways in which empirical study could evaluate this theorizing. It could focus on whether or not the peripheral characteristics postulated for each personality type really show evidence of covarying. It could also focus on one or more of the postulated characteristics with the aim of determining whether they are associated with successful living if part of the fully functioning type or unsuccessful living is part of the maladjusted type.

Although there is much research that by its topic appears relevant to the second focus, little of it has been done with particular Rogerian emphases in mind. What I cover here is selected so as to be as close to his emphases as possible. Needless to say, however, some research mentioned elsewhere might also be construed as lending some general support to the Rogerian emphasis. This is true of many of the fulfillment positions.

In a study done to evaluate Rogerian theory directly, Pearson (1969, 1974) focused on the existence and interrelationship of openness to experience and organismic valuing as peripheral characteristics. Each characteristic was conceptualized as containing several parts. The parts or phases of openness to experience were considered to be (1) attention, or symbolizing the recognition of affective cues in a significant event; (2) reaction, or symbolizing the personal impact or significance of the event; and (3) exploration, or differentiating and symbolizing the personal impact or significance of the event. These phases were measured with paper-and-pencil performance tests (not questionnaires) and carefully developed for adequate reliability. The phases of organismic valuing were construed as (1) information collection, relevant to eventual decision; (2) information appraisal; (3) decision making, or choosing from among formulated alternatives; and (4) decision implementation. These phases were measured by three paper-and-pencil tests, two of them performance tests and one a questionnaire on decision making. Once again these measures were carefully devised and showed adequate reliability. The scores obtained from ninety male and female undergraduates showed that the various phases of each characteristic were reliable, indicating support for their existence. But contrary to what Rogerians would expect, openness to experience and organismic trusting scores did not intercorrelate. This rigorously done study suggests that the various peripheral characteristics postulated by Rogers do not organize themselves neatly into his two personality types. This may even provide a basis for considering the existence of subtypes, thereby rendering his formal theorizing more capable of dealing with individuality (see Chapter 8).

There have been other attempts to develop measures of openness to experience. Tittler (1974) has offered a thirty-eight-item questionnaire, with the item content drawn from encounter and sensitivity group protocols. Scores on these items from 105 undergraduates were subjected to factor analysis. The result was nine openness-to-experience factors, four of which seemed to have construct validity in the sense of negative correlations with measures of dogmatism and conventionality. In a similar approach, Coan (1972) administered theoretically relevant questionnaire items to 383 college students and factor analyzed the resulting scores. Sixteen factors resulted, many of which seemed reasonably valid on the basis of correlations between them and a battery of personality tests. In an attempt at cross-validation, Coan repeated this study on 219 college students, using a combination of original and fresh items. The end result was an openness-to-experience instrument containing eighty-three items that yielded seven factors corresponding very closely to the original sixteen. This instrument, called the *Experience Inventory,* contains scales concerning (1) aesthetic sensitivity, (2) openness to hypothetical ideas, (3) constructive utilization of fantasy, (4) openness to unconventional views of reality, (5) indulgence in fantasy, (6) unusual perceptions and associations, and (7) deliberate and systematic thought. Although it is too early in our empirical knowledge of these measures to be at all sure that they are reliable and valid indicators of the Rogerian concept of openness to experience, their emergence signifies growing interest in this concept.

In a more general vein, Rogers contended that for the fully functioning person, the self-concept undergoes continual change and has distinct dimensions or parts whereas the self-concept of the maladjusted person is just the opposite. There are a few studies indicating that the self-concept does not undergo major changes (e.g., Block, 1962; Havener & Izard, 1962) but disagreeing as to whether self-consistency is a positive or negative indicator of effective adjustment. Concerning the possible dimensionality of the self-concept, Akeret (1959) provides evidence that it includes at least four major divisions, defined by academic, interpersonal, sexual, and emotional content. He finds that these four dimensions are not highly intercorrelated. The trouble with this study is that it does not bear on Rogers's contention that the self-concept is unitary only in the maladjusted person. Although the studies mentioned in this paragraph have a ring of relevance to Rogers's theory, they actually are not very helpful in evaluating that position.

The aspect of full functioning that has received extensive research attention is that of organismic trusting. According to Rogers, fully functioning persons will have faith in their organisms, in the intuitive, even impulsive urges to action they experience, because they will not have developed the conditions of worth that could dictate which aspects of them are valuable and which are to be shunned. In contrast, maladjusted persons live lives controlled so as to pass muster with regard to their conditions of worth. The operational clue to understanding the research effort concerning these matters is that in organismic trusting there would be little difference between how persons described themselves and what they wanted to be, whereas the difference between these two frames of reference would be great for persons with conditions of worth. Virtually all the studies I will review below concern the magnitude of the difference between descriptions of the perceived self and those of the ideal self. Moreover, the typical means of measuring the so-called self-ideal discrepancy is to present subjects with a list of statements taken from actual verbalizations made by clients in Rogerian therapy and to ask them to sort these into a set number of categories ranging from very inaccurate to very accurate as descriptions of themselves. Then they sort the same group of statements into categories ranging from very inaccurate to very accurate as expressions of their ideals for themselves. As you may recognize, this is a variant on the Q-sort technique (Stephenson, 1953) described earlier, which yields information that can be factor analyzed to produce a quantitative index of the discrepancy between the perceived and ideal selves. This operationalization of organismic trusting and conditions of worth is very much in the spirit of Rogers's theory.

The first and most widely quoted study employing the self-ideal discrepancy measure is that of Butler and Haigh (1954). They measured self-ideal discrepancy in a group of patients both before and after therapy and also in a number of follow-ups. On the average, the size of the discrepancy decreased over time. Matched control groups started out with a smaller discrepancy but the discrepancy did not decrease as time went by. The decrease in discrepancy shown by the patient group was considerable and, for the most part, involved a movement of the self-description toward the ideal description. These results are presented in detail in Tables 11–12 and 11–13.

It is not clear whether the findings support Rogers's viewpoint. Certainly the closer the person is to fully functioning, the smaller should be the discrepancy between self and ideal. To be sure, psychotherapy should bring people nearer to full functioning. But statements of ideals are operational representations of conditions of worth; hence, one function of therapy should be to

TABLE 11–12 Self-Ideal Correlations in the Client Group

Client	*Pre-counseling* r	*Post-counseling* r	*Follow-up* r
Oak	.21	.69	.71
Babi	.05	.54	.45
Bacc	−.31	.04	−.19
Bame	.14	.61	.61
Bana	−.38	.36	.44
Barr	−.34	−.13	.02
Bayu	−.47	−.04	.42
Bebb	.06	.26	.21
Beda	.59	.80	.69
Beel	.28	.52	−.04
Beke	.27	.69	−.56
Bene	.38	.80	.78
Benz	−.30	−.40	.39
Beri	.33	.43	.64
Beso	.32	.41	.47
Bett	−.37	.39	.61
Bico	−.11	.51	.72
Bifu	−.12	−.17	−.26
Bime	−.33	.05	.00
Bina	−.30	.59	.71
Bink	−.08	.30	−.20
Bira	.26	−.08	−.16
Bixy	−.39	−.39	.05
Blen	.23	.33	−.36
Bajo	.16	.29	.47
Mean z	−.01	.36	.32
Corresponding r	−.01	.34	.31

SOURCE: "Changes in the Relation between Self-Concepts and Ideal-Concepts Consequent upon Client-Centered Counseling" by J. M. Butler and G. V. Haigh, in C. R. Rogers and R. F. Dymond (Eds.), *Psychotherapy and Personality Change*, 1954, Chicago: University of Chicago Press.

remove these aspects of maladjustment. Ideals would be considered beneficial from the standpoint of a perfection theory but not of an actualization theory. In this context, it is unfortunate for the Rogerian position that Butler and Haigh found the reduction in self-ideal discrepancy occurring as a function of therapy to be brought about primarily by a movement of self-description toward ideals. My interpretation of the results of this study as somewhat inconsistent with Rogerian theory is bolstered by the report that the ideal descriptions tended to be fairly uniform, indicating a shared cultural context. Ideal descriptions seem the stuff of conditions of worth, that is, socially imposed beliefs as to what is important.

TABLE 11–13 Self-Ideal Correlations in the Control Group

Client	Pre-counseling r	Follow-up r
Aban	.80	.50
Abor	.00	.30
Acro	.86	.89
Agaz	.75	.83
Akim	.84	.86
Akor	.48	− .03
Ajil	.49	.45
Afit	.73	.71
Abul	.58	.77
Adis	.42	.65
Abri	.35	.30
Abbe	.35	.36
Acme	.80	.65
Abco	.65	.76
Abet	− .01	.43
Adir	.30	.07
Mean z	.66	.68
Corresponding r	.58	.59

SOURCE: "Changes in the Relation between Self-Concepts and Ideal-Concepts Consequent upon Client-Centered Counseling" by J. M. Butler and G. V. Haigh, in C.R. Rogers and R. F. Dymond (Eds.), *Psychotherapy and Personality Change*, 1954, Chicago: University of Chicago Press.

The difficulty I have mentioned has led to a modified Rogerian view concerning self-ideal discrepancy. Some Rogerians (see Shlien, 1962) have considered large discrepancies as representing poor adjustment and moderate discrepancies as reflecting full functioning. And extremely small discrepancies are suspected to be defensive statements made by maladjusted people (Chodorkoff, 1954a, 1954b). The thinking behind such statements is that a very large self-ideal discrepancy can come about only if the self-description is viciously critical, and a very small self-ideal discrepancy requires that the persons twist their views of themselves to conform to what is socially desirable. Perhaps both large and small discrepancies signify strong conditions of worth. In that case, only moderate self-ideal discrepancies would signify the absence of maladjustment.

Of direct importance to the empirical evaluation of this modified Rogerian viewpoint are the studies determining the relationship between self-ideal discrepancy and general adjustment and happiness. Brophy (1959) collected from eighty-one female nurses self-reports of general satisfaction, vocational satisfaction, adjustment and values, and occupational and life roles. The results suggest that congruence between perceived and ideal selves is necessary for general happiness and for satisfaction in specific life areas. Turner and Vander-lippe (1958) obtained a broad range of information relating to effectiveness and satisfaction with life from 175 college students on whom they also had self-ideal descriptions. The range of information obtained included measures of general health, extracurricular participation, sociometric indices, scholastic adjustment, and a test of temperament. Subjects with low self-ideal discrepancy needed fewer days in the hospital and less frequent visits to the clinic. Further, the lower the self-ideal discrepancy, the greater was the tendency to be preferred as a companion. Finally, the results of the temperament test, which are shown in Table 11–14, indicated that people with low self-ideal discrepancy tend toward general activity, ascendance, sociability, emotional stability, and thoughtfulness. The authors concluded that

> The emergent composite picture of the college student high in self-ideal congruence (as contrasted with the student low in self-ideal congruence) is that of one who participates more in extracurricular activities, has a higher scholastic average, is given higher sociometric ratings by his fellow students, and receives higher adjustment ratings on . . . certain traits.

A similar picture is presented by Rosenberg (1962) in a study relating self-ideal discrepancy to the various scales of the California Personality Inventory. This personality test includes such variables as sociability, dominance, flexibility, and achievement. Rosenberg found that the greater the self-ideal discrep-

TABLE 11–14   Correlations between Self-Ideal Congruence Expressed as Z Values and Traits Measured by the Guilford-Zimmerman Temperament Survey

Trait	Correlation with Self-Ideal Congruence
1. General activity	.50*
2. Restraint	−.10
3. Ascendance	.58*
4. Sociability	.36*
5. Emotional Stability	.36*
6. Objectivity	−.03
7. Friendliness	−.16
8. Thoughtfulness	.41*
9. Personal relations	−.25
10. Masculinity	.10

*Significant at the .01 level.

SOURCE: "Self-Ideal Congruence as an Index of Adjustment" by R. H. Turner and R. H. Vanderlippe, 1958, *Journal of Abnormal and Social Psychology, 57.*

ancy, the lower the score on fifteen of the eighteen variables of this personality test. What this means is that people with large self-ideal discrepancies generally are inept in the kinds of interests and capabilities relevant to successful living. A contribution to the emerging picture has been made by studies concerning the tendency to agree with statements regardless of their content. This acquiescent response style is most marked in people having a large self-ideal discrepancy (Murstein, 1961). Another study (Schulberg, 1961) suggests that acquiescent responding occurs in people who seem to be smiling on the outside while jeering on the inside. Hence, we can take Murstein's (1961) findings as indicating yet another dimension of the ineptitude for living that accompanies a large self-ideal discrepancy. Similarly, Mahoney and Hartnett (1973) found that male and female subjects high on a self-actualization measure had much smaller self-ideal discrepancies than did subjects low in self-actualization. All in all, the modified Rogerian notion that both large and small self-ideal discrepancies would be indicative of maladjustment rather than full functioning seems to lack empirical support.

A final group of studies stems from another implication of the notion of organismic trusting. According to Rogers, if one has accepted oneself—that is, if the self-ideal discrepancy is small—one will also accept, respect, and value other people. As you will recall from Chapter 4, this expectation reflects the assumption made by actualization theorists that there is nothing in the basic nature of humans that is necessarily selfish and hostile. In this assumption, actualization theories are very different from psychosocial conflict theories. Suinn (1961) proceeded to test whether male high school seniors who accepted themselves would show a generalized acceptance of their fathers and male teachers. On a set of adjectives, his subjects described their perceived and ideal selves, perceived and ideal fathers, and perceived and ideal male teachers. Suinn found that the smaller the self-ideal discrepancy, the smaller the father-ideal and teacher-ideal discrepancies. This supports the contention that if you accept yourself, you also accept other people.

Medinnus and Curtis (1963) studied the relationship between self-acceptance and child acceptance in mothers. Their fifty-six mothers filled out a questionnaire and a semantic differential scale, each of which yielded a measure of the degree to which self and ideal differed. There was also a semantic differential measure of the general degree to which their children were accepted by them. Medinnus and Curtis found that the two measures of self-acceptance intercorrelated, as you would expect, and that both of them were positively related to the measure of child acceptance. So not only do male high school students who accept themselves accept their fathers and male teachers; mothers who accept themselves accept their children. The relevant literature includes other studies supporting the notion that self-acceptance occurs in the context of acceptance of others (e.g., Berger, 1953, 1955; Rosenman, 1955; Sheerer, 1949; Stock, 1949). Even though some of these studies are methodologically less relevant to the Rogerian frame of reference, they yielded results similar to the previously described studies. The substantial evidence that people who accept themselves also accept others supports not only Rogerian theory but the theories of Maslow, Fromm, and existential psychology. Of course, it is possible that the tendency to respond in socially desirable fashion may have contaminated the studies just considered, thereby weakening our conclusion.

Another Rogerian research theme involves the *Experiencing Scale,* developed by Gendlin and Tomlinson (1967). Experiencing is described as "the quality of an individual's experiencing of himself, the extent to which his ongoing, bodily, felt flow of experiencing is the basic datum of his awareness and communications about himself, and the extent to which this inner datum is integral to action and thought" (Klein, Mathieu, Gendlin, & Kiesler, 1969, p. 1). As you can see, the organismic trusting characteristic of full functioning is heavily involved here as it is in the above-mentioned self-ideal discrepancy. Though the name might imply it, the Experiencing Scale is not a questionnaire filled out by the subject; rather, the subject verbalizes in some manner—usually in psychotherapy—about anything of interest or importance to him or her. Then the verbalizations are rated by the psychologist as to the degree of "experiencing." There are seven stages of experiencing, running from the lowest, in which subjects seem distant or remote from their feelings, through the middle range, in which subjects get their feelings into clearer perspective as their own and may even be able to focus on them as their inner reality, to the highest, in which feelings have been scrutinized and explored such that they become a trusted and reliable source of self-awareness. Klein et al. (1969) provide a scoring manual for the Experiencing Scale and report adequate interscorer reliabilities after practice.

Most of the research involving this scale has concerned clients' progress through psychotherapy and, as such, is not of great relevance here. Suffice it to say that there is evidence to the effect that clients who are judged by their Rogerian therapists as having improved during treatment have moved up the stages of experiencing (see Klein et al., 1969). There is also some evidence that the Experiencing Scale may be an adequate measure of organismic trusting, construed as a peripheral characteristic (as a predisposition that persists over time and stimulus situations). For example, it has been found (see Klein et al., 1969) that successful therapy clients start, continue, and end therapy at a higher level of experiencing than do less successful clients. Once you conclude that those who profit most from psychotherapy are those who needed it least to begin with, you are dealing with the kind of behavioral regularity that signifies the presence of a peripheral characteristic. In other studies amplifying this theme, neurotics showed higher levels of experiencing than schizophrenics, who would, of course, be considered the sicker of the two groups (see Klein et al., 1969). Also of note, though not specifically directed at a test of some Rogerian hypothesis, is the study of Gorney and Tobin (1969), in which it was shown that as persons make the transition from adulthood to old age their level of experiencing drops. The Experiencing Scale would seem to be an intriguing tool with which to test Rogerian notions.

Another promising beginning at translating Rogerian theorizing into manageable empirical observations has been made by Wexler (1974), who reasons that the self-actualizing process can be discerned in mental content as progressively greater differentiation and integration and in verbal style as a vivid, focused quality not unlike the higher levels of experiencing mentioned above. In considering verbal style, Wexler was influenced by the prior work of Rice and Wagstaff (1967). Using a sample of undergraduate males and females, Wexler demonstrated that there was a positive correlation between degree of differentiation and integration and degree of focused voice style during the subjects' descriptions of emotional episodes. Further, both of these variables correlated positively with another purported test of full functioning. But as you will see later, there are additional studies that lend general empirical support to Rogers's position, though these studies are even more directly relevant to other theories.

Finally, recent work on the effects of intrinsic and extrinsic motivation are relevant here, as Rogers theorized that conditions of worth (extrinsic motivation) are a sign of maladjustment. Many studies have shown that extrinsic motivation actually decreases various indices of performance. Quite supportive of the Rogerian position is Amabile's (1985) recent demonstration that the imposition of extrinsic motivation to perform actually decreased the creativity of poems composed by subjects.

Maslow's Position

Maslow's position is sufficiently similar in empirical implications to that of Rogers that anything supporting the latter also tends to support the former. There is, however, a cognitive emphasis in Maslow that is less explicit in Rogers. This is the emphasis upon democratic values as part of the self-actualizing person as opposed to authoritarian and traditionalistic values in the non-actualizing person. While Rogers would probably agree, he does not stress such matters. But Allport, Fromm, and the existentialists clearly agree with Maslow. The body of personological research on the authoritarian personality (Adorno, Frenkel-Brunswik, Levinson, & Sanford, 1950), though planned independently, is especially relevant to Maslow's emphasis on this subject.

Adorno et al. developed a fascism, or F scale for purposes of assessing the degree to which people have authoritarian values. As is proper for studying values, the scale derives from self-descriptions obtained through giving the subjects a list of relevant questions to answer. Examples of the items appearing on the F scale are "Obedience and respect for authority are the most important virtues children should learn" and "Familiarity breeds contempt," with "yes" answers considered authoritarian. The first version of the F scale had internal consistency of .74, but removal of some poor items increased reliability to .90.

Adorno et al. set about determining the kinds of behavior and attitudes that occur in people high and low on the F scale. Their large group of subjects included a majority of white, native-born, middle-class Americans functioning as university students, public school teachers, public health nurses, prison inmates, psychiatric patients, and labor union and other club members. The results reveal a fairly coherent group of correlates for the F scale. Persons high in fascistic values are also ethnocentric in the sense that they not only are opposed to other cultures but attribute correspondingly high importance to their own. They are hostile not only toward minority groups but toward everyone whose ways or values differ from their own. Further, they are hostile toward and contemptuous of anything that is weak. This was shown not only in the dislike for weakness but indirectly in the admiration and valuing of power and strength, as exemplified by money, masculinity, and age-status authority. Also, persons high in fascistic values are essentially conformists, moralists with absolute values. They are intolerant of ambiguity in such social roles as those of parent-child, sex, and teacher-child. Finally, they see the world as a dangerous place, full of chaos and unpredictability, with uncontrollable catastrophes imminent.

Also included in the study by Adorno et al. are interviews and unstructured tests of fantasy. By and large, the results obtained with these procedures corroborate the other findings. But the interviews and fantasy tests are seriously flawed methodologically (see Hyman & Sheatsley, 1954). To be sure, the F-scale findings have also been criticized, mainly on the grounds that the sample may not have been fully representative of the general population and that the test items may have been contaminated by response sets. Although these criticisms have some justification, attempts to explain away the attributes of the authoritarian personality as presented above have not been very convincing.

Since the appearance of the work of Adorno et al., a huge number of studies tracing the correlates of the fascism scale have been done. Many of these studies have complemented and extended the findings reported above. For example, in a study unusual for having been conducted in a "real-life" context involving performance rather than self-description, Vroom (1959) showed that among supervisors in a large delivery company, authoritarians were affected less positively by the opportunity to participate in company decisions than were nonauthoritarians. Presumably people high in fascistic values feel most comfortable in authoritarian work situations, even when they are not in power.

There are, of course, some studies using the F scale that yield equivocal results. It has been suggested that this situation may be due to a lack of purity in the fascism scale in that it measures not only authoritarian values but many unintended things (see Peabody, 1966). One such unintended factor may be the tendency to agree or disagree in answering questions regardless of their content. Another may be our old friend, socially desirable responding. To date, a great deal of effort has been expended in the attempt to rid the fascism scale of such contaminations (Peabody, 1966; Byrne, 1974). Most recent studies use one or another of the newer scales, though the tendency toward conflicting results appears to persist. I am not especially surprised by this state of affairs, as it has never been clear to me that an authoritarian value orientation can be accurately measured if the tendencies to acquiesce and to respond in socially desirable fashion are excluded. After all, the authoritarian person deeply believes in the importance of acquiescence and conformity. Perhaps we will come closer to clarity by assuming that the authoritarian orientation can be expressed not only in fascistic values but in acquiescent and conforming traits. Once we adopt this point of view, we are not likely to hasten to exclude acquiescent and conforming tendencies from a measure of authoritarianism.

By now, the mass of authoritarianism research does permit some generalizations. Concerning the antecedents of authoritarianism, several studies have found that authoritarian parents tend to use autocratic child-rearing practices whereas equalitarian parents are more democratic (e.g., Levinson & Huffman, 1955). Byrne (1965) studied the tie between parents' and children's personalities directly and found that the F scores of both mother and father are positively related to their son's whereas only mother's F score shows this pattern with the daughter. He also reported that if either parent is equalitarian, that is sufficient for producing an equalitarian child. These findings generally support the actualization theory emphasis on unconditional positive regard as the important rearing practice for the encouragement of self-actualization.

Research has also accumulated on the behavioral expressions of authoritarianism. Persons high in authoritarianism tend to endorse conservative political candidates (e.g., Leventhal, Jacobs, & Kudirka, 1964), favored American intervention in Vietnam (Iyzett, 1971), and attend church more frequently (Byrne, 1977). Concerning thought processes, Kirscht and Dillehoy (1967) conclude on the bases of several studies that authoritarian persons show rigidity and are quick to attempt resolution of ambiguities. Elms and Milgram (1966) conducted an important experiment in which subjects were instructed to administer shocks to another subject of sufficient intensity to be painful and dangerous. In reality, the "victim" was a confederate of the investigators, and despite much screaming, no shocks actually took place. In the condition under which the victim was in another room and could not be seen, most subjects were willing to give what was presumed to be a shock! But when the condition called for being in the same room and even touching the victim, a number of subjects refused to participate. Elms and Milgram found that subjects who were willing to administer shocks when not confronted with the victim were more authoritarian than those who refused to participate when seated next to the victim. In general, it would appear that authoritarian subjects show some of the signs of maladjustment proposed by Maslow.

Lest we make a hasty conclusion, we should note the appearance of a theme in the research literature to the effect that not only highly authoritarian but highly equalitarian persons show tendencies inconsistent with self-actualization. In studying attitudes of punitiveness toward victims, Epstein (1965) manipulated high and low socioeconomic status by varying the victims' dress, incomes, employment goals, and so forth. He found that while authoritarian subjects were punitive toward low-status victims, equalitarian subjects were punitive toward high-status victims. In an ingenious study, Mitchell (1973) described for the subjects a scenario involving a rock concert that gets out of hand. In one version, a citizen, variously described in positive or negative terms, was killed. In another a police officer, also presented negatively or positively, was killed. When the scenario involved a citizen, authoritarian subjects were more abusive toward the person when described negatively than when described positively. The negativity or positivity of the description made no difference to equalitarian subjects. But when the scenario involved a police officer, the findings were reversed: Equalitarian subjects were more punitive toward someone negatively described, whereas the description made no difference to authoritarian subjects. It would seem that the highly liberal, flexible, democratic subject, here called *equalitarian,* is in certain situations just as punitive, insensitive, and hasty as is the authoritarian in other situations. These findings are not really in keeping with Maslow's theorizing about the self-actualized person, whom he describes as possessing democratic values. But, of course, democratic values are only one peripheral characteristic of self-actualization. Studies that measure the type more comprehensively are needed.

Rokeach (1960) has offered a *dogmatism scale* in the hope of avoiding this problem of being authoritarian that seems to characterize both high and low scores on the *F* scale. Much research has been done attempting to show that low dogmatism scores indicate flexibility, openness, and emotional maturity. As part of this effort, various investigators have studied the relationship of dogmatism to political beliefs, with conflicting results. The upshot of this theme seems to be that the dogmatism scale is primarily a measure of underlying cognitive orientation and only slightly tinged with ideological or political beliefs (e.g., Granberg & Corrigan, 1972).

Many studies tracing the effects of dogmatism on various behaviors have been performed. Ehrlich (1955, 1961a, 1961b) compared the performance of fifty-seven undergraduates enrolled in a sociology course on precourse and postcourse tests, separated by ten weeks, and on a follow-up several months later. The higher the dogmatism scores, the poorer was the performance on all three sociology tests, even when academic aptitude skills were controlled. Five years later, Ehrlich (1961b) obtained from many of the original subjects dogmatism scores, sociology test scores, and their reported final grade-point averages on graduation. Essentially the same results as before were obtained. But Costin (1965) attempted to replicate Ehrlich's findings and was unsuccessful. Baker (1964) performed a similar study of fifty-six student nurses, the measures of performance being the number of correct identifications of definitions for psychological concepts they were supposed to have learned. Oddly enough, he found that the higher the dogmatism scores, the better the performance! To make matters worse, Costin (1968), employing a design similar to that of his earlier work, obtained results indicating that dogmatism correlated positively with the students' retention of psychological misconceptions he had purposely given them but not with their acquisition of basic psychological principles that also had been taught. The contradictory nature of these findings suggests the action of important variables that were not measured (Ehrlich & Lee, 1969).

The studies reported above all occurred in classroom settings, where it was not possible to adequately control situations and experiences. Under more rigorous laboratory conditions, a consistent picture of the effects of dogmatism on learning begins to become apparent. Adams and Vidulich (1962) compared the eighteen highest and lowest dogmatism scorers in the number of errors made while learning two lists of fifteen belief-congruent word pairs (e.g., ball-round) and fifteen belief-incongruent word pairs (e.g., ball-square). As expected, the high-dogmatism subjects made more errors in retaining the belief-incongruent list. But they also, unexpectedly, made more errors retaining the belief-congruent list. That there may still be some tendency among high-dogmatism subjects to learn only belief-congruent or personally interesting materials well is indicated in studies by Kleck and Wheaton (1967) and Pyron and Kafer (1967). Consistent with this is the research of Restle, Andrews, and Rokeach (1964), which found that low-dogmatism subjects were able to solve a difficult problem more quickly than high-dogmatism subjects when the solution involved choosing an unusual alternative rather than a usual one. The implication that dogmatic persons do not learn well when operating in an unfamiliar situation or when the solution is novel is supported by further studies done by Rokeach, Swanson, and Denny (1960), Mikol (1960), Zagona and Zurcher (1965), and Jacoby (1967).

Not only are dogmatic persons unable to learn effectively in conditions of novelty; they are also swayed in their judgments by the contradictory judgments of high-status persons. Vidulich and Kaiman (1961) tested thirty high- and thirty low-dogmatism undergraduates in a situation requiring perceptual judgments (how far a spot of light had moved in a darkened room). All subjects were tested in the company of the experimenters' confederate, whose task was to try to sway judgments. Sometimes the confederate was introduced as a college professor and sometimes as a high school student. The results indicated a tendency for high-dogmatism subjects to acquiesce to high-status judgments. Support for this finding is found in research by Powell (1962) and Bettinhaus, Miller, and Steinfatt (1970), among others. The implications of conformity on the part of dogmatic persons were authenticated by Zagona and Zurcher (1964) in observational evidence, gleaned over four months of contact, to the effect that in small groups dogmatic persons are leader oriented, are unspontaneous, and prefer lectures to class discussion. Similarly, Gold, Ryckman, and Rodda

(1973) found that dogmatic subjects exposed to information contradicting their attitudes in a group discussion changed their attitude toward the group position. That the conforming effect of dogmatism is not merely a cognitive or attitudinal thing is suggested by Clark (1968), who investigated the relationship between dogmatism scores and the ability to discern a previously observed simple figure embedded in a more complex one (*field dependence-independence*). In his sample of 523 undergraduates, dogmatism was negatively correlated with this ability.

Of special relevance are studies charting the pattern of other personality characteristics that accompany dogmatism. Plant, Telford, and Thomas (1965) administered the *California Psychological Inventory,* a general test of personality, along with the dogmatism scale to their subjects and concluded that those high in dogmatism were also psychologically immature and characterized as impulsive, highly defensive, and stereotypic in their thinking. In contrast, subjects low in dogmatism were outgoing, enterprising, calm, mature, forceful, clear thinking, and responsible. Similarly, Hjelle and Lomastro (1971) found low-dogmatic subjects less accepting of traditional religious beliefs, more tolerant of ambiguities in their environment, and displaying fewer signs of emotional disturbance. Filling out the picture, Lee and Ehrlich (1971) found that dogmatic subjects held more negative and more contradictory beliefs about themselves and also had more negative attitudes toward others. Several studies (see Vacchiano, 1977) have attempted to demonstrate through performance tests that dogmatic subjects are more defensive than others, but the procedures are intricate and the interpretations elaborate. Nonetheless, there is evidence (e.g., Vacchiano, Strauss, & Schiffman, 1968; Richek, Mayo, & Pirgean 1970) that subjects high in dogmatism are more maladjusted than those who are low in the sense of emotional instability, poor self-concept, and occupational impairment.

There is much more support for Maslow's peripheral theorizing in the dogmatism research than there is in the authoritarianism research. Unfortunately for Maslow's emphasis on democratic values as a peripheral characteristic, it would appear that the ideological, political flavor of the authoritarianism scale is theoretically closer to him as a measure than is the dogmatism scale, with its emphasis on rigidity of thought processes regardless of content. In this there is a basis for theoretical revision. Actually, as it stands, the dogmatism research is more easily interpreted as support for Rogerian than Maslowian peripheral theorizing. Also, this research provides some general support for Allport, Fromm, and existential psychology.

In recent years, a general questionnaire aimed at measuring the various facets of self-actualization has been devised in strict adherence to Maslow's theorizing (Shostrom, 1965, 1966). Called the *Personal Orientation Inventory* (*POI*), this test consists of 150 paired, opposing statements. In each instance, the subjects must choose one of the two as more relevant to them. The test is scored as two major scales—*inner-directedness* and *time competence*—and ten complementary scales—*self-actualizing values, existentiality, feeling reactivity, spontaneity, self-regard, self-acceptance, nature of man, synergy, acceptance of aggression, and capacity for intimacy.* An adequate degree of reliability is reported for the scales (Ilardi & May, 1968; Klavetter & Mogar, 1967; Shostrom, 1966).

Thus far, the POI displays considerable construct validity (see Fox, Knapp, & Michael, 1968; Guinan & Foulds, 1970; Shostrom, 1966). One facet of this validity concerns behavioral ratings made by trained personologists. Various POI scales correlate positively with the degree to which subjects are rated as self-actualizing (McClain, 1970; Shostrom, 1965). POI scales also correlate negatively with alcoholism (Zaccaria & Weir, 1967), felony (Fisher, 1968), and hospitalization for psychopathological symptoms (Fox, Knapp, & Michael, 1968). The relationship of the POI to other personality tests also has been studied. All POI scales correlate negatively with Eysenck's neuroticism score (Knapp, 1965). Also, the inner-directed scale of the POI correlates positively with the autonomy scale and negatively with the abasement scale of the Edwards Personal Preference Inventory (Grossack, Armstrong, & Lussieu, 1966). Positive correlations have also been found between POI scales and various tests of creativity (Braun & Asta, 1968; Damm, 1969). Finally, there have been some studies involving actual performance. The main scale scores of the POI are positively related to academic achievement (LeMay & Damm, 1968; Stewart, 1968). In addition, high scores on the POI are associated with teacher and therapist effectiveness (Dandes, 1966; Graff & Bradshaw, 1970). Also relevant is the finding that subjects scoring high in self-actualization seek novelty more than those scoring low (Schwartz & Gaines, 1974).

Several studies have investigated whether responses to the POI are seriously affected by the tendency to present oneself in a socially desirable light. Fisher and Silverstein (1969) and Foulds and Warehime (1971) found that instructions to fake responses in a favorable direction actually produced lower self-actualization scores in subjects! This is in striking contrast to other tests, which appear so vulnerable to subjects' putting their best feet forward. Also, it has been shown that the POI scales are actually negatively related to measures of the tendency to respond in a socially desirable direction (Warehime & Foulds, 1973) and of conformity behavior (Crosson & Schwendiman, 1972). Perhaps subjects who dissimulate on questionnaires do so in terms of cultural stereotypes of ideal behavior. If self-actualization differs from such stereotypes, it is understandable that encouragement to present oneself in a good light would have no or even adverse effects on POI scores.

In an attempt to determine just how resistant to faking the POI is, Warehime, Routh, and Foulds (1974) presented subjects with instructions concerning the content of the self-actualization concept. They reasoned that given this clue, subjects high in the tendency to respond in a socially desirable direction would be able to increase their self-actualization scores. Although they used 276 subjects, they were unable to demonstrate this effect. Only when they combined instruction about the self-actualization concept with practice in answering some of the very items of the POI was there some tendency for subjects bent on appearing socially desirable to increase their self-actualization scores—and the tendency was very small at that. It seems likely that the POI is remarkably resistant to faking. This strengthens its claim to construct validity.

Lest we become too enthusiastic, I should point out that there have also been failures to establish the validity of this test (see Fox et al., 1968; Guinan & Foulds, 1970). A particularly interesting finding that is difficult to reconcile with Maslow's thinking was reported by de Grace (1974). Using 30 subjects, he demonstrated that there is no difference in level of anxiety between high and low self-actualization scores on the POI. Nonetheless, the POI seems a promising lead in investigating broad patterns of functioning clearly associated with the positions of Maslow and Rogers.

Several studies stimulated by Maslow have not employed the POI. Leith (1972) obtained scores on three verbal creativity tests from 106 subjects immediately after they had been subjected to two kinds and degrees of stress that should have constituted a threat to needs at the lower end of Maslow's hierarchy. Oddly enough, the effect of stress seems to have been to increase the number and originality of responses. According to Maslow, the opposite should have taken place, because unsatisfied or frustrated lower needs should render higher needs unsalient, and creativity is an expression of higher needs. Graham and Balloun (1973) attempted to show that in any pair of needs at different levels in Maslow's hierarchy satisfaction of the lower need should be greater than that of the higher need. Of the three scores derived from interviews testing this prediction, one produced the expected results, one did not, and the last yielded equivocal findings. Adding to this the scanty information that was provided concerning the interscorer agreement and the reliability of the ratings made from interviews, it is difficult to conclude that there was the support for Maslow's thinking that the researchers claimed. Finally, Ebersole (1973) interviewed students about their peak experiences, and found that in 55 percent of such instances, the subject regarded the experiences' effect on his or her life transitory. Although Ebersole regards this as supporting evidence for Maslow's position, it could easily be taken the opposite way. And besides, 55 percent is barely a majority.

Adler's Position

When we turn to the first perfection theorist, Adler, we are struck by the absence of research relevant to his peripheral theorizing in general. I believe the theorizing on life styles, fictional finalism, and traits is clear enough to have yielded meaningful research. Perhaps the Adlerian view simply has not been popular enough among psychologists for it to have captured their research attention. The one notable exception to what I have said is in regard to birth order, which, as you will recall, is an important determinant of lifestyle according to Adler. Since Toman's (1959) elaboration of the Adlerian position on family constellation as a character and marriage determinant and Schachter's (1959) intriguing research on birth order and affiliative tendencies in females, there has been a virtual flood of related studies. Here we see another instance, to go along with Eysenck's stimulation of Jungian research and Rokeach's of Maslowian, of how a primarily research-oriented personologist can capture the imagination of others like him in the service of broader theoretical concerns. And we shall see this again.

In that path-breaking study, Schachter (1959) observed that under stress, firstborn college girls tended to seek the company of others while later-born girls tended to withdraw into themselves. As part of the same study, he also offered evidence that the general preference for affiliation and withdrawal on the part of firstborn and later-born children, respectively, who are under stress permitted understanding of such diverse behaviors as combat-flying effectiveness and alcoholism. With such dramatic findings, it is not surprising that researchers were attracted to the area. A general search for correlates of birth order began.

One consistent finding concerns attendance at college. Schachter (1963) concluded, on the basis of reviewing earlier studies, that eldest children are more likely to become eminent than later-born children. Soon it became apparent that 50 to 65 percent of the student bodies in many colleges around the country, such as Columbia University (Schachter, 1963), Kansas State University (Danskin, 1964), Reed College (Altus, 1966), the University of Florida (Hall & Barger, 1964), were firstborn children. These percentages are larger than one would expect from the corresponding figures in the population at large (Schachter, 1963). This seems to be striking confirmation of Adler's contention that being born first precipitates ambition.

Although firstborn children more often go to college, there is inconsistent evidence that they do better there than later-born children. Campbell (1933) found no differences between these two groups in achievement. But Pierce (1959), Schachter (1963), and Falbo (1981) did find that firstborn children had higher grade-point averages. Although there is some evidence that these children have a higher need for achievement than later-born children (Sampson, 1965), it is known that this need is not a good predictor of grades (McClelland, 1961). In light of the general evidence that families place greater demands on firstborn children and expect them to reach greater heights (Bossard & Boll, 1955; Dittes, 1961; Rosen, 1961), it would seem that their going to college expresses the ambition mentioned above whether or not this eventuates in excellent grades.

But the ambition suggested in firstborn children does not have the connotation of independence. Indeed, Sears (1950) and Schachter (1964) found that firstborn children are actually more dependent on others and more easily influenced than those born later. That later-born children are more accepted by their peers (Sells & Roff, 1963) suggests a more relaxed attitude in them. In this regard, Dimond and Munz (1967) found later-borns more able to break through social barriers by self-disclosure. But it does seem that when expected to undergo painful electric shock, firstborn females have a stronger desire than later-born females to await the experience in the company of others (Gerard & Rabbie, 1961; Schachter, 1959). Zucker, Manosevitz, and Langon (1968) have found evidence of the same effect in a naturally occurring catastrophe. This again suggests that the apparent ambition of firstborn children is sufficiently tinged with dependency to constitute a wish for approval rather than success in personal terms. Consistent with this interpretation are the results of Radloff (1961), who designed a study in which he was able to make some of his female subjects believe that their opinions varied with those of a large majority of their peers. Among firstborn females, those in presumed conflict with their peers expressed a stronger desire for further discussion than did those in agreement with their peers. This effect did not appear for later-born females. Similarly, Koenig (1969) found that firstborns gave consensual or group-related answers when asked to describe themselves. Other studies are consistent with these findings (e.g., Wrightsman, 1960), though it is possible that the picture for males is more complicated (Connors, 1963; Dember, 1964; Sampson, 1962).

There is also some intriguing information concerning birth order and psychopathology. Although the contention that firstborn children are more resistant to alcoholism than later-born children (Schachter, 1959) has not held up in later study (Smart, 1963), later-borns do seem more prone to being "problem children" (Rosenow & Whyte, 1931) and are more apprehensive about dangerous situations (Longstreth, 1970). Actually, the highest proportion of delinquents seem to be middle children (Sletto, 1934). There is some rather inconclusive evidence that later-born children (at least females) are more prone to schizophrenia than those born earlier (Schooler, 1961). Last-born children also seem to have lower social competence in general (Schooler, 1964). Although some studies find laterborn children to be more creative (Staffieri, 1970), others report the opposite (Eisenman & Schussel, 1970). The picture simply is not clear as yet.

Several studies have concerned the interaction and marriage patterns related to family constellation. Here again the evidence for Adler's position is inconsistent. Some studies (e.g., Mendelsohn, Linden, Griven & Curran, 1974; Birtchnell & Mayhew, 1977) find support for the theory in the relationship among sibling configuration, friendship formation, and mate selection. But there are also contradictory findings. For example, Hall (1965) reported that males who are only children have high divorce rates and female only children have low divorce rates! Further, Ickes and Turner (1983) found that having had an older, opposite-sexed sibling makes it easier to interact with the opposite sex, a family constellation effect that contradicts that hypothesized by Toman (and Adler). It will take some careful sampling and measurement to sort out the confusing elements in what admittedly is an exciting and booming research area.

In one of the few studies planned to test a specific Adlerian hypothesis concerning family constellation, Croake and Hayden (1975) considered whether pairs of siblings show oppositeness of traits. Contrary to Adlerian expectation, no such oppositeness was found in the 16 Personality Factors Questionnaire responses of ninety college students and their siblings.

Worthen and O'Connell (1969) have done one of the rare studies directly concerned with Adler's concept of social interest. As they refer to this tendency's cooperative (rather than competitive) form, which can develop through learning, their study concerns Adler's peripheral statement and is relevant here. Constructive social interest was measured with a test of values formulated by the first author and humor appreciation with a test constructed by the second. A positive correlation was obtained between social interest and humor appreciation. It remains to be seen how close to Adlerian construals the measurement operations come.

Recently, Greever, Tseng, and Friedland (1973) developed a paper-and-pencil test called the *Social Interest Index* for determining the degree of positive social interest in four areas of life—work, friendship, love, and self-significance. On the basis of agreement among three prominent Adlerians, thirty-two items were selected, each of which was responded to by subjects on a five-point scale of personal relevance. It was demonstrated that these items did not correlate with a scale of socially desirable responding. Internal consistency was .81, and stability over a fourteen-day period was .79.

Having tested 228 male and female subjects, Greever et al. found that social interest scores are higher for females than males, increased with age and grade-point average, but were unrelated to socioeconomic level. With the possible exception of the finding concerning grade-point average, the results are consistent with Adlerian thought. The results of correlating the Social Interest Index with a standard, comprehensive test of personality, the California Personality Inventory, are shown in Table 11–15. A claim to construct validity is made because the Index shows correlates referring to communality, responsibility, socialization, sense of well-being, and achievement via conformance. This test seems worthy of additional empirical study.

White's Position

As White's peripheral theorizing is the same as Erikson's, everything I have said concerning the ego psychologists is relevant here. There is surprisingly little research to go on, which renders us unable to assess the position from an empirical standpoint. In one study, Wherry and Waters (1968) attempted an objective measure of motivation by administering to 235 undergraduates a 150-item questionnaire about usual feelings involving individual, social, and accomplishment states. Through a factor analysis, they obtained factors best described as competence motivation and general satisfaction. Accordingly, they believed White's position to be supported. Also, Smith (1966) reports the results of a factor-analytic study of Peace Corps volunteers as indicating that an important difference among people is whether or not they have a basic attitude of self-confidence and self-reliance. This finding provides

TABLE 11–15   Correlations between the Social Interest Index Score and Eighteen California Personality Inventory (CPI) Scores

CPI Attribute	r^a	r^b	r^c
Dominance	.27[‡]	.20[†]	.35[‡]
Capacity for status	.27[‡]	.25[‡]	.26[†]
Sociability	.27[‡]	.24[‡]	.27[‡]
Social presence	.07	.08	.08
Self-acceptance	.16[†]	.09	.20[*]
Sense of well-being	.36[‡]	.27[‡]	.36[‡]
Responsibility	.39[‡]	.29[‡]	.32[‡]
Socialization	.39[‡]	.31[‡]	.28[‡]
Self-control	.19[†]	.10	.26[†]
Tolerance	.26[‡]	.17[*]	.27[‡]
Good impression	.21[‡]	.14[*]	.35[‡]
Communality	.40[‡]	.37[‡]	.18[*]
Achievement via conformance	.35[‡]	.25[‡]	.35[‡]
Achievement via independence	.13[*]	.05	.14
Intellectual efficiency	.33[‡]	.24[†]	.30[‡]
Psychological mindedness	.09	− .02	.34[‡]
Flexibility	− .22[‡]	− .27[‡]	− .17[*]
Femininity	.29[‡]	.03	.08

[a]Total N = 344.
[b]Males n = 189.
[c]Females n = 155.
*$p < .05$.
†$p < .01$.
‡$p < .001$

SOURCE: "Development of the Social Interest Index" by K. B. Greever, M. S. Tseng, and B. U. Friedland, 1973, *Journal of Consulting and Clinical Psychology, 41.*

support for a number of fulfillment positions in addition to White's, just as certain results reviewed elsewhere can be construed as general support for them.

Goldfried and D'Zurilla (1969) have developed an inventory, the *Survey of Problematic Situations,* that attempts to determine the subject's level of competence. The Survey consists of a series of situations sampled from academic and social incidents provided by college freshmen, staff, and faculty and from clinical folders. Responses to these situations were obtained from a group of college freshman and high school seniors and then evaluated as inferior, average, or superior by teachers and counselors. These evaluations provided the scoring rules with which to assess competence. Although Goldfried and D'Zurilla have made an interesting beginning, there is simply too little information available about this inventory at this time to make any judgment about its empirical adequacy or its theoretical relevance to White's position.

Although it is also too early to tell in the case of Good and Good (1973), they developed a test called the *Fear of Appearing Incompetent Scale*. Comprised of 36 true-false items, the reliability of this scale was tested on 355 undergraduate subjects, with a resulting internal consistency correlation of .89. It is possible that this scale will prove relevant to White's emphasis on *sense* of competence (Good and Good may be measuring its opposite), whereas Goldfried and D'Zurilla's inventory assesses *actual* competence.

White's (1959) important paper on competence has stimulated research on what is being called *intrinsic motivation,* or the tendency to get involved in activities or work for which there is no tangible external reward. Most of this research has been done with either subhuman organisms or children. The work on animals is not really relevant here, though it is interesting to find that even they seem to get involved in an activity for its own sake. Although I said earlier in this chapter that research involving children would not be emphasized, this is one place where such work is relevant. For White, affectance and competence motivation certainly appear early in human life.

Lepper, Greene, and Nisbett (1973) and Deci (1975) have accumulated evidence indicating that children initially involved in some activity will actually do it less following the introduction of external reinforcement. In the former case, children who chose to draw with felt-tip pens (over other activities) were reinforced by receiving a "Good Player" certificate and subsequently chose the activity less frequently than similar children not given the reinforcement. Deci's series of studies shows that tangible reinforcements, such as money, reduced initially preferred activities. Negative reinforcements had the same effect. Further, Greene, Sternberg, and Lepper (1976) have shown that subjects rewarded for their most (rather than least) preferred activities decreased more in their subsequent willingness to choose the initially most preferred activity than did subjects who had been rewarded for their least preferred activity.

Lest you conclude that this research literature is without disagreement, you should recognize that various explanations of supposedly intrinsic motivation have been offered (see deCharms & Muir, 1978), and all seem to have some empirical support. Much more needs to be known about this research area before firm conclusions can be drawn. An interesting attempt in this direction is the work of Csikszentmihalyi (1975) which indicates that when persons are asked why they work on activities that do not promise external reward, they report getting satisfaction out of the functioning if the task difficulty just exceeds their current capabilities. This finding is especially in keeping with the connotations of White's concept that it is a core tendency to achieve competency. Perhaps in intrinsically motivated activities persons are trying to increase their competence.

Allport's Position

It would be quite possible to pass over Allport with no attention, as he is so nonspecific concerning the periphery of personality. Nonetheless, he does give us some inkling of a peripheral viewpoint in stating his criteria of maturity. Research could be done, even at this rudimentary stage in his peripheral theorizing, to determine whether these criteria of maturity occur in people whose lives are successful, proactive, and propriate rather than unsatisfactory, reactive, and opportunistic. Although research has not been explicitly directed to such matters, there are some findings in the literature that can be interpreted as relevant. For example, the research on dogmatism and authoritarianism cited for Maslow is relevant here as well. So is the work on the self-concept reviewed in connection with Rogers. The studies on internal versus external locus of control, which we will cover when we get to existential psychology, could also be considered as clarifying the existence and nature of proactive as opposed to reactive behavior, a distinction dear to Allport's heart.

But there are two considerations more nearly unique to him that should be mentioned here. One concerns the sense of humor, which Allport incorporated into his criteria of maturity. Actually, as he also believed it was mature to have a philosophy of life and stable bases for social intimacy, the study by Worthen and O'Connell (1969) that we reviewed for Adler could just as well have appeared here. In any event, O'Connell (1960) has reported results suggesting that a sense of humor is indeed associated with successful living. Working with 332 college student subjects for whom self-ideal discrepancies were available, he found that those with small discrepancies appreciated humor more than those with large discrepancies. In addition, those with small discrepancies tended to appreciate nonsense wit, whereas those with large discrepancies tended to appreciate hostile wit. Further, Martin and Lefcourt (1983) have reported that subjects with a sense of humor show less mood disturbance in response to negative events.

The other consideration involves Allport's emphatic peripheral statement that there exist not only dynamic (motivational) traits but expressive (stylistic) traits. This statement may have even stimulated McClelland's distinction between motives and traits. In any event, Allport and Vernon (1933) did a pioneering study of performance (rather than self-description or fantasy) aimed at determining whether there is sufficient consistency to expressive movements to justify the belief in the importance of expressive traits. In one part of this large research program, a group of twenty-five subjects was tested in three different sessions, each separated by about four weeks. During each session, the subjects responded to a large number of different tests providing measures of speed of reading and counting; speed of walking and strolling; length of stride; estimation of familiar sizes and distances; estimation of weights; strength of handshake; speed and pressure of finger, hand, and leg tapping; drawing squares, circles, and other figures; various handwriting measures; muscular tension; and so forth. In addition, observer ratings were obtained for various measures, such as voice intensity, speech fluency, amount of movement during natural speech, and neatness of appearance. First, Allport and Vernon assessed the stability of the various expressive measures over the three testing sessions. In general, these estimates of reliability were reasonably high and compared favorably with stability for self-descriptive measures of personality. It would seem that expressive characteristics have claim to empirical existence. Next, Allport and Vernon examined the relationship among scores for the same tasks performed by different muscle groups, such as left and right side of the body, arms, and legs. Strikingly enough, they found about the same level of consistency as had been reported for the same muscle groups over time. This important finding suggests a general or central integrating factor that produces a consistent style no matter what peripheral manifestation is observed.

The final analysis attempted in this study was the intercorrelation of the major variables from all the tasks. A total of thirty-eight measures were intercorrelated by a form of cluster analysis roughly comparable to factor analysis. Three factors seemed to emerge, as indicated in Table 11–16. The first, the *areal factor,* included such variables as area of total writing, area of blackboard figures, area of foot squares, and length of self-rating checks. Motor expansiveness is what seems to have been involved here. The second factor, called *centrifugal-centripetal,* seemed to involve introversion-extroversion, including such measures as overestimation of distance from body and underestimation of weights. The third factor, called the *factor of emphasis,* included such measures as voice intensity, movement during speech, writing pressure, tapping pressure, and pressure of resting hand. In this kind of research lies the basis for determining the content of expressive traits that should be included in peripheral theorizing. Subsequent studies of expressive characteristics (e.g., Allport & Cantril, 1934; Estes, 1938; Huntley, 1940) are not very useful in this regard, having focused on the degree to which people can predict other features of persons' personalities from their expressive movements. These studies seem to make the assumption that the expressive movements are not themselves aspects of personality.

From time to time, studies emerge championing the idiographic (or morphogenic) approach so close to Allport's heart. Pervin's (1983) work is in this tradition of studying individuals rather than groups. Also, Lamiell, Foss, Larsen and Hempel (1983) argue persuasively for the effectiveness of individual rather than aggregate data in understanding personality.

Fromm's Position

As I have already indicated, the studies cited under the discussion of Rogers on the relationship between self-acceptance and acceptance of others also provide support for the emphasis in Fromm on the inextricably intermingled destiny of individuals and groups. In an even more general sense, other studies discussed in relation to fulfillment theorists lend indirect support for

TABLE 11–16 Three Factors Based on Expressive Movements

Area group factor	
Area of total writing	.69
Total extent of figures	.67
Area of blackboard figures	.64
Slowness of drawing	.52
Area of foot squares	.48
Overestimation of angles	.45
Ratings on movement during idleness	.39
Length of self-rating checks	.38
Length of walking strides	.37
Centrifugal group factor	
Overestimation of distance from body with legs	.66
Overestimation of distance from body with hands	.55
Extent of cubes	.53
Underestimation (reverse of overestimation) of weights	.53
Verbal speed	.34
Underestimation of distances toward body with hands	.33
Ratings on speech fluency	.33
Group factor of emphasis	
Ratings on voice intensity	.71
Fewness of parallel lines	.65
Ratings on movement during speech	.53
Writing pressure	.52
Overestimation of weights	.46
Finger pressures on stylus	.45
Tapping pressure	.42
Underestimation of distances between hands	.42
Verbal slowness	.38
Ratings on forcefulness	.38
Overestimation of angles	.36
Pressure of resting hand	.32
Unoccupied space in drawing figures	.31

SOURCE: Adapted from *Studies in Expressive Movement* by G. W. Allport and P. E. Vernon, 1933, New York: Macmillan.

Fromm's position. But none of this bears on the receptive, exploitative, hoarding, marketing, and productive character types themselves. It is true that the first three types bear considerable similarity to the oral-incorporative, oral-aggressive, and anal types postulated by Freudians. Therefore, much of the research already discussed for Freud bears on Fromm's position as well. You will recall that there was some empirical support for the Freudian oral and anal types.

One large-scale field study (Fromm & Maccoby, 1970) bears directly on the hoarding, receptive, and exploitative character types. This is a naturalistic, anthropological study of a Mexican village, far from urban life. The coauthors came to know and help the villagers over a period of years, studying them all the while. The portion of this large and interesting project of most relevance here concerns a long, detailed questionnaire they administered to the villagers in the hope of obtaining information about character types that could aid in their understanding of day-to-day behavior and the social forces shaping it. Three questions are listed here as examples:

14. Describe your idea of a good mother.
   •
   •
   •

16. When you were a child, did you fear the anger of your father more, or that of your mother?
   •
   •
   •

47. Should women have the same rights as men? Why? (pp. 240–241)

Although these questions may appear easy to fake, let me remind you that Fromm and Maccoby knew their subjects well and had reason to believe they could be trusted.

The questionnaire was scored for 406 adult villagers, or 95 percent of the adult population. The scoring attempted to disclose which character types were present in a protocol and which was dominant. In attempting to accomplish this, the various traits Fromm (1947) has listed under the types were used. The areas of concern were mode of assimilating experience, mode of relatedness, sociopolitical relatedness, parental centeredness, and other behavioral traits. In addition to the supposedly nonideal character types, an attempt was made to score for productiveness directly. The scoring was inevitably somewhat global, and the scorers had to steep themselves in Fromm's position and the procedures involved. Nonetheless, reasonably adequate interscorer reliability was achieved for work of this kind (percentage of agreement ranged from 72 to 100). In addition, the Thematic Apperception and Rorschach tests were employed in a subsidiary way, yielding some interesting agreements and disagreements with the primary measure, the questionnaire (Fromm & Maccoby, 1970, pp. 271–191). Finally, the scored questionnaires were subjected to a factor analysis in order to determine whether the emerging factors conformed to character types. As you can see, this procedure conforms well to the first two steps of the ideal strategy discussed at the beginning of this chapter. Scores for traits relevant to Fromm's types were factor analyzed to see whether those types did in fact emerge. Of course, the scoring was rather interpretative, and the investigators can be presumed to have already believed in the value of the types. Nonetheless, emerging evidence for the position can be taken seriously.

The factors obtained include ones properly interpreted as receptive, exploitative, hoarding, and productive orientations. True to expectation, the last of these relates to the others such that one can speak of productive or non-productive versions of them. Although an age factor accounted for the biggest slice of the sample's behavior, productiveness-unproductiveness, exploitative-ness-nonexploitativeness, and hoarding-receptivity followed in that order. In addition, there was a masculinity-femininity factor and one for mother-father centeredness. It is interesting to note that Fromm's marketing orientation did not seem to emerge. The investigators contend that this orientation was simply not present in this rather traditional, rural village. This is consistent with Fromm's position, which makes the marketing orientation a product of modern industrialization and urbanization.

In interpreting the results, the investigators make some interesting and persuasive interpretations of how the existing orientations reflect long-standing cultural, social, and political realities of Mexican society. For example, the receptive orientation was found to be less often associated with productiveness than either the hoarding or exploitative orientations. Considering the authoritarian tradition of the wealthy landowner and the serfs that has existed in Mexico for centuries, it is not surprising that villagers would be pushed into developing receptive orientations of an unproductive variety (they succumbed to excessive dependency on their masters). But the hoarding orientation is more likely to occur in a productive mode because it was also possible, given the sociopolitical situation, for a few villagers to own their own tiny plot of land, which would provide them with a slim but possible means for independence. That they had to hold onto this valuable parcel of land for dear life, as it were, encouraged a hoarding form of productiveness. Finally, some with an exploitative orientation were able to achieve a productive mode due to the social changes taking place in Mexico, which are opening up the possibility for entrepreneurship among villagers who otherwise would be damned to poverty and dependence. My conclusion is that this comprehensive study, despite all its faults, provides general, if not the most precise, support for Fromm's position. Studies of its ilk should be mounted with regard to the other positions.

Understandably, no information has emerged concerning the marketing orientation. This is unfortunate, as it is the part of Fromm's peripheral theorizing that is most unique to him. There is some available research, however, that bears on the phenomenon of alienation, which is central to the definition of the marketing personality. Unfortunately, work on alienation is often more polemical than scientifically rigorous. Exemplary of the alienation research on adults is the work of Keniston (1966), in which twelve college males were studied intensively via repeated interviews, tests, and observations concerning their life situations and values. Unfortunately, Keniston does not see fit to include careful discussion of his procedures for selecting subjects, scoring their responses, and conducting statistical analyses of the data. These omissions are consistent with Keniston's preference for intuitive, impressionistic portraits of people, used as examples to elucidate his theoretical views. In any event, Keniston contends that there is an alienated personality type, which includes such peripheral characteristics as a futile quest for positive values, possession of a pessimistic orientation, a distrust of commitment, and a disaffection for adulthood. His students emerge as people who know what they are not but have little conviction as to what they are. Although the general emphasis in Keniston's work is consistent with the marketing orientation, it can hardly be said that his research is rigorous enough to have unequivocally demonstrated the empirical validity of Fromm's theorizing.

Indeed, Keniston (1966) thought he was providing a basis for understanding alienation in Freudian or at least ego psychology terms. He suggests that his alienated males had unresolved Oedipal conflicts, stemming from their being mother's darling in the context of either literal absence of father or his extreme detachment from and unimportance in the home. As such, Keniston's research would not really be so supportive of Fromm's position. But Keniston's Freudian explanation is very nebulous. It is not at all clear how or if the data bear him out in it. In this context, we can interpret the research conservatively to indicate the existence of a pattern of personality not unlike Fromm's marketing orientation. For that matter, these data are also generally relevant to existential psychology.

Maccoby (1976) has reported a study of male business executives studied in depth with interview techniques. Several types of personality were present among his subjects. One type, the "company man," is described in much the same terms as the marketing orientation. According to Maccoby, the company man is no longer making it big because businesses are becoming progressively bureaucratized and competition in the marketplace is diminishing. Thus, the company man is less able than before to get ahead by cleverly assessing what will sell about himself and expressing that above all. Although interesting, this study is so impressionistic as to data and so replete with assumptions regarding trends in our society that it really does not constitute empirical support for Fromm's theorizing regarding the marketing orientation.

There are a few studies (e.g., Benson, 1966; Klein & Gould, 1969; Reimanis, 1966) concerning children in school situations that indicate the existence of such characteristics as fatalism, meaninglessness, and powerlessness. While these studies are rigorous enough in their measurement procedures and sampling, it is not clear what relationship their results bear to the adult personality. After all, the childhood school years normally may be ones characterized by a sense of powerlessness without this auguring an adult personality of the marketing type.

Existential Psychology

Although Kobasa's and Maddi's (Maddi, 1967, 1970; Kobasa & Maddi, 1977) peripheral theorizing might not be acceptable to those existential psychologists who prefer such an extreme position on the individuality issue that no such theorizing is considered useful, we shall work with it nonetheless. The alternative would be to find very little research of any relevance to existential-ism. In specifying the two main personality types as individualism and con-formism, Kobasa and Maddi gear into a good deal of ongoing research in psychology. Some of this research might have been mentioned in other places, for it is certainly relevant to other theories. But it is perhaps most relevant here.

First is the burgeoning literature on whether people believe their lives to be controlled by them (internal locus of control) or by society and others (external locus of control). This research theme was pioneered by Julian Rotter (1954), who did not aim to provide any special support for existential psychol-ogy. Nonetheless, the findings are relevant here insofar as persons perceive themselves as having a mental life through which they can understand and influence their experiences and treat life as a series of decisions they must make responsibly (Kobasa & Maddi, 1977). This would clearly involve an in-ternal locus of control. In addition an external locus of control would bespeak the social reductionism of conformists, who perceive their lives as being ma-nipulated by social forces uninfluenceable by them.

After several refinements, an *Internal versus External Locus of Control (I-E) Scale* was made available for general use (Rotter, Seeman, & Liverant, 1962). This scale consists of twenty-three items from which the following have been chosen:

I more strongly believe that:

6. a. Without the right breaks one cannot be an effective leader. (*External*)
   b. Capable people who fail to become leaders have not taken advantage of their opportunities. (*Internal*)
   - •
   - •
   - •

9. a. I have often found that what is going to happen will happen. (*External*)
   b. Trusting to fate has not turned out as well for me as making a decision to take a definite course of action. (*Internal*)
   - •
   - •
   - •

17. a. As far as world affairs are concerned, most of us are the victims of forces we can neither understand, nor control. (*External*)
    b. By taking an active part in political and social affairs, the people can control world events. (*Internal*)

Reliability for this scale seems quite adequate (Rotter, 1966). By now several other, similar measures have been developed (e.g., Bialer, 1961; Crandall, Kat-kovsky, & Crandall, 1965).

The first group of construct validation studies concerns the ramifications of belief in internal as opposed to external control of events on characteristics of primarily personal versus socially relevant behavior. Crandall et al. (1965)

found that schoolboys high in internal control beliefs spent more time in intellectual free-play activities and scored higher on both reading and arithmetic achievement tests. The more effective study habits and school performances of internally oriented persons was further attested to in other studies (e.g., Procink & Breen, 1974, 1975; Findley & Cooper, 1983). Similarly, Seeman (1963) and Seeman and Evans (1962) found differential learning between internals and externals in two field settings. The latter investigators reported that among hospitalized tuberculosis patients, those believing in external control had obtained less knowledge about their own conditions than those believing in internal control. This finding was not attributable to socioeconomic or hospital experience factors. Controlling for intelligence and the novelty of stimulus materials presented for learning, Seeman (1963) demonstrated that prison inmates scoring low in externality were high in retention of information presented to them concerning procedures relating to successfully achieving parole. Generalizing these findings to people at large, Pines and Julian (1972), Wolk and Du Cette (1974), and several others have shown that internally oriented persons gather more information in a range of situations and show more incidental learning, than do externally oriented persons. Maddi, Hoover, and Kobasa (1979), using a measure of powerlessness similar to that of the I-E Scale, reported that subjects who believed they are powerless did not bother to explore an unfamiliar room in which they were asked to wait.

As might be expected from the above, it has also been shown that subjects high in externality tend to be conformists both when conformity is measured by questionnaire (Odell, 1959) and by performance (Crowne & Liverant, 1963). Typical of such studies is that of Ryckman, Rodda, and Sherman (1972), who exposed college students to influence from a high-prestige source who was depicted as having either relevant or irrelevant expertise. Externals changed opinion in the direction of the influence more often than internals, regardless of the relevance of expertise. This definite link between feeling externally controlled and conforming provides support for existential theorizing.

Consistent with the general picture of competence emerging from the studies above-mentioned are findings concerning risk taking. In a situation in which subjects were required to bet on the outcome of thirty trials of dice throwing, with the alternatives having objective probabilities, Liverant and Scodel (1960) showed that the more the subjects believed in an internal locus of control, the more they could choose bets of intermediate probability and avoid low-probability bets. Similar results reported by Lefcourt (1965) also indicated that internally oriented subjects tended to regulate their performances in terms of the realistic constraints contained in the probabilities. The only deviation from this conclusion concerns the observation made by Liverant and Scodel (1960) to the effect that internally oriented subjects never seemed to select an extremely high or low probability bet. In reflecting on the meaning of the risk-taking findings, it is perhaps valuable to consider Butterfield's (1964) study concerning anxiety, the results of which are presented in Table 11–17. Using questionnaire measures of anxiety, he found that the stronger the sense

TABLE 11–17 Intercorrelations of Measures

Measures	1	2	3	4	5	6	7	8	9	10	10	11	12	13
1. Locus of Control	—													
Frustration reactions														
2. Intropunitive	184	—												
3. Extropunitive	149	135	—											
4. Constructive	−366*	623*	−042	—										
Anxiety reactions														
5. Debilitating	233	−081	267	−050	—									
6. Facilitating	−677*	−206	−139	488*	−766*	—								
Academic aspirations														
7. Range	398*	287	252	133	098	132	—							
8. Lowest grade	368*	044	722*	458*	199	123	027	—						
9. Actual grade	−073	063	−159	130	220	−035	−090	684*	—					
10. Satisfaction	246	−073	−019	−223	299*	−172	−475*	−415*	−075	—				
Fear of failure														
10. Satisfaction	246	−073	−019	−223	299*	−172	−475*	−415*	−075	—	—			
11. Satisfaction difference	064	093	020	−341	675*	−339*	010	−496*	187	888*	888*	—		
12. UE-LS	248	−033	149	−336*	014	126	218	−492*	124	277	277	−022	—	
13. (UE-LS) range	207	112	008	−342*	096	114	−419*	−463*	024	250	250	−020	093	—
Intelligence														
14. WAIS vocabulary	−174	210	037	601*	−429*	466*	091	−453*	387*	469*	469*	−367*	−055	042

*$p < .05$.

SOURCE: Adapted from "Locus of Control, Test Anxiety, Reactions to Frustration, and Achievement Attitudes" by E. C. Butterfield, 1964, *Journal of Personality, 32.*

of external control, the greater the evidence that anxiety has a debilitating rather than facilitating effect on the person (see rows 5 and 6 of Table 11–17). Perhaps the seemingly unrealistic behavior of highly external persons in risk-taking situations reflects the debilitating effects on them of anxiety concerning evaluation. In addition, row 4 of Table 11–17 indicates that the more external persons are, the less constructive their reactions to frustration. Additional support for this position is provided by the studies of Platt and Eisenman (1968) and Feather (1967).

The general theme that internally and externally oriented persons are sharply different in perception and performance is amplified by several recent studies. Using 98 male and female subjects, Alegre and Murray (1974) demonstrated that externally oriented persons are more susceptible to verbal conditioning, which, of course, utilizes extrinsic reinforcements. That this may indeed reflect the generally greater experience of possibility or choice enjoyed by internally-oriented persons is suggested by the findings of Harvey and Barnes (1974), who presented their subjects with choice situations in which the two options differed as to attractiveness or were either both attractive or both negative. Characteristically, internally oriented subjects experienced a greater sense of personal choice when the options were similar in attractiveness. Cherulnik and Citrin (1974) induced their 100 male and female subjects to express preferences for objects promised to them at a later time and then failed to make good on the promise. They found that internally oriented subjects increased in preference for the preferred and undelivered object when the reasons for its not being delivered were made personally meaningful. In contrast, preference for the undelivered object increased for externally oriented subjects when the reason given was impersonal and arbitrary. It would seem that externally oriented persons feel more comfortable in arbitrary, uncontrollable conditions, whereas the opposite is true for internally oriented persons. Consistent with this are findings (e.g., Sosis, 1974; Lefcourt, Hogg, Struthers, & Holmes, 1975) indicating that internally-oriented subjects tend to attribute success and failure in task performances to themselves and consider the driver of a car in an accident to be at fault. In contrast, externals see good or bad luck as responsible for both their own performances and others'. Internally oriented persons appear to approximate the existential ideal in the sense that they regard life as a series of decisions that they can influence.

There are also interesting, if somewhat contradictory, findings concerning interpersonal behavior. Nowicki and Roundtree (1974) found internally oriented youngsters to be more popular with peers. That this is not for any lack of discernment on the part of internals is suggested by Sherman (1973), who reports that when teamwork was important for success at a task, internals tended to select partners of equal ability whereas externals chose inferior partners. Further, Holmes and Jackson (1975) found internals to be less angry toward a person who gave both rewarding and punishing feedback to the subjects' responses on an interactive task. Externals were more angry at the feedback, seeing the communicator as less friendly and attractive than did the internals. All in all, it appears that internally oriented persons are more task oriented and balanced in their social interactions and, perhaps for this reason, are more valued by others. Once again there is evidence to support existential theorizing concerning the authentic or individualistic type.

Let us now turn to some studies that compare various socially significant groupings of people as to the external or internal nature of their beliefs concerning control. In one of a series of studies on racial or ethnic groups, Battle and Rotter (1963) found that lower-class blacks were significantly more external (measured by the Children's Picture Test of Internal-External Control) than lower-class whites or middle-class blacks and whites. Using adult subjects, Lefcourt and Ladwig (1965, 1966) reported higher rates of belief in external control among black prison inmates than among their white counterparts. In a third ethnic group investigation, Graves (1961) adapted the I-E Scale for high school students and found whites to be more internal, followed by Spanish-Americans and then American Indians. Concerning males enrolled in a southern black college, Gore and Rotter (1963) found that subjects scoring most internal (I-E Scale) signed statements expressing the greatest amount of interest in social action concerning civil rights. That these statements did not represent empty commitments is shown by Strickland (1965), who found that black activists had a stronger belief in their own power than did blacks who did not take part in the civil rights movement. Pawlicki and Almquist (1973) found members of women's liberation groups to be more internal than college female nonmembers. Similar results were obtained by Colemen, Campbell, Hobson, McPartland, Mood, Weinfeld, and York (1966) in their study of 645,000 pupils in grades 3, 6, 9, and 12 in 4,000 American public schools. In summarizing this amazing study, they (Coleman et al., 1966) say:

> A pupil attitude factor, which appears to have a stronger relationship to achievement than do all the "school" factors together, is the extent to which an individual feels that he has some control over his own destiny. . . . The responses of pupils to questions in the survey show that minority pupils, except for Orientals, have far less conviction than whites that they can affect their own environments and futures. When they do, however, their achievement is higher than that of whites who lack that conviction. (p. 23)

In all of the ethnic studies, groups whose social positions were lowly by either class or race tended to score higher in the external control direction. And to judge from the already reported attitudinal and action correlates of the belief in external control, it is easy to see why disadvantage due to class or race tends to perpetuate itself. Supporting the dire implication of the ethnic studies are the findings of Cromwell, Rosenthal, Shakow, and Kahn (1961) to the effect that schizophrenics have a stronger belief in external control (using three measures) than do normals. If, as Maddi (1967, 1970) has contended, some proportion of people diagnosed as schizophrenic are actually suffering from existential sickness, this result lends some support to the contention that conformity is the premorbid state for this malaise.

A final group of studies concerns locus of control and health-related behaviors. Sampling from this already vast body of literature, we find that externals are more likely than internals to experience debilitating rather than
facilitating anxiety (e.g., Strassberg, 1973), to show more severe psychiatric
symptoms, particularly schizophrenia (Lefcourt, 1976), to be more likely to
contemplate suicide (e.g., Crepeau, 1978), and to suffer more from alcoholism
(Naditch, 1975). Kobasa (1979) found powerlessness or externality to be one
factor rendering business executives more likely to become physically or psychologically ill when confronted with highly stressful life circumstances. Needless to say, there are also some negative and equivocal findings in the literature
(see Lefcourt, 1976; Strickland, 1977). But there is general support for the
existential hypothesis that conformists are vulnerable to breakdown partially
because they feel themselves to be victims of outside forces.

The investigators whose work I have summarized obviously want to reach
the conclusion that internal control beliefs have a causal influence on actions.
To be sure, this seems a sensible position, especially with regard to some of
the studies, such as that of Coleman et al. (1966), in which beliefs concerning
locus of control seem intimately related to school achievement. But all of the
studies discussed are correlational in nature, making conclusions of causality
highly inferential. It could be, for example, that it is actual experiences of
competence and effectiveness that incline one to believe in the internal control
of rewards rather than the other way around. In defense of their interpretation
of belief as that which causes action, Rotter and his associates have marshaled
experimental rather than correlational evidence. For example, Phares (1957)
had two groups of subjects perform the same task of predicting a sequence of
events. One group was told that success in the task depended on skill in
deciphering the ordering of events; the other was told that success was due to
chance, there being no rational ordering. Despite the fact that both groups
received the same number and sequence of reinforcements, subjects with skill
instructions changed expectancies more frequently and more in the direction
of previous experience than did subjects with chance instructions. The differences in action between the two groups seemed understandable on the basis of
whether subjects did or did not believe that they could influence their own
destinies. Analogous findings have been obtained concerning perceptual
thresholds for nonsense syllables (Phares, 1962) and resistance to extinction
(Holden & Rotter, 1962; James & Rotter, 1958; Rotter, Liverant, & Crowne,
1961). The evidence from these studies indicating that people who believe they
can influence the occurrence of reward through their own skill act differently
from people not having this belief certainly strengthens the inference concerning the direction of causality in the correlational studies (see Phares, 1976).

But before leaving the I-E Scale, I should point out that several recent
studies have questioned its homogeneity. Collins (1974) administered the test
to 300 college students and factor analyzed the scores. He found a common
theme running through the items, but he was also able to abstract four fairly
distinct and unrelated factors. The factors seemed to distinguish the belief in

the world as (1) a difficult place, (2) an unjust place, (3) a place governed by luck, or (4) a politically unresponsive place. Abramowitz (1973) separated the I-E Scale items into those of a political nature and those of a more personal nature. Utilizing 166 male and female subjects, he found that the political items correlated positively with membership in sociopolitical action groups, whereas the personal items did not. Through studies of this sort we may learn more about what admittedly is an intriguing test.

Turning from the I-E Scale, we find a gradually developing body of studies quite relevant to, and for the most part inspired by, existential theorizing. For example, Houston and Holmes (1974) exposed their subjects to conditions of threat involving temporal uncertainty. Some of the subjects were induced to avoid thinking about the threat by immersing themselves in distracting activities, while the other subjects were left to their own devices. Physiological measurement showed that the subjects who engaged in avoidance thinking actually experienced a greater stress reaction to the threat than did the other subjects. Through interviews, it was determined that the subjects who did not engage in avoidance activities spent the time thinking about the threat and reappraising it as less serious than originally believed. Insofar as a temporal uncertainty differs only slightly from ontological anxiety, this study provides support for the existential belief that accepting such anxiety rather than avoiding it is consistent with personal growth. Liem (1973) permitted some students in an undergraduate course to choose the type of recitation section they preferred, granting them considerable choice in the ongoing conduct of the section, and denied such choice to other students in the course. Subjects who were permitted choice performed better than the others on a course examination and gave higher ratings of satisfaction with their sections than did subjects not permitted choice. This is another demonstration of the value of control over one's own life for personal comfort and growth.

Some interest is developing in devising ways to measure the sense of meaninglessness that results from an accumulation of ontological guilt. Crumbaugh and Maholick (1964) and Crumbaugh (1968) have offered a questionnaire, called the *Purpose in Life Test,* aimed at assessing Frankl's concept of existential vacuum. Although their study of the reliability of the questionnaire is quite incomplete, they do report an estimate of internal consistency of .85 with 120 subjects. The construct validation of the instrument is also scant, but there is a correlation of .44 with the Depression Scale of the Minnesota Multiphasic Personality Inventory and another of .48 for males and .32 for females with a measure of anomie. Sharpe and Viney (1973) administered the *Purpose in Life Test* to fifty-eight college students and interviewed them concerning their world views. Then three judges rated the interviews for indications of meaninglessness. Subjects showing existential vacuum on the *Purpose in Life Test* had world views that were negative, lacking in purpose, and devoid of transcendent goals. In one recent study, Soderstrom and Wright (1977) showed that among 427 college student subjects, those who appeared on other questionnaires to be intrinsically motivated, religiously committed, and true believers had lower existential-vacuum scores on the *Purpose in Life Test.* Further, Paloutzian (1981) reported that following religious conversion, subjects showed higher purpose-in-life scores. Although this test is probably of value, much more care must be given to its development than has been offered thus far.

Another related test, called the *Existential Study,* was developed by Thorne (1973), Pishkin and Thorne (1973), and Thorne and Pishkin (1973). The 200-item questionnaire has been produced factor analytically to yield seven scales on self-status, self-actualization, existential morale, existential vacuum, humanistic identification, existence and destiny, and suicidal tendency. In one study, the test was administered to 193 felons, 89 alcoholics, 153 adherents to Ayn Rand's rational philosophy, 336 unwed mothers, 159 students, and 338 schizophrenics. The Rand followers were highest in existential morale, followed by students and felons, alcoholics and unwed mothers demoralized, and schizophrenics disintegrated. However interesting this test may be, it should be recognized that (1) little information regarding internal consistency and stability is available, (2) little has been done to determine its construct validity, and (3) it has not been guided by a consistent and definite set of existential ideas (e.g., self-actualization is not really an existential concept).

Maddi, Kobasa, and Hoover (1979) have devised a sixty-item questionnaire, called the *Alienation Test,* for assessing the powerlessness, adventurousness, nihilism, and vegetativeness aspects of meaninglessness that appear in existential theorizing. Each of these dimensions can be measured across relationships to work, persons, social institutions, family members, and self. The internal consistency of the dimensions and relationships ranges from .62 to .96, with an average of .86. Stability figures range from .54 to .87, with an average of .80. Relevant to discriminant validation are the findings that the *Alienation Test* is uncorrelated to intelligence or sex, though it does show a small and understandable relationship to socioeconomic class and age. A beginning on convergent validation has been made in that the scales of the *Alienation Test* show negative correlation of varying degree with a measure of creative attitudes toward living. Also, persons scoring high on meaninglessness in interpersonal relationships and alienation from family spend more time watching TV and in solitary activities (Csikszentmihalyi, 1975). So apparently pervasive is the sense of powerlessness and vegetativeness that subjects high on these measures do not even bother to explore an unfamiliar room when left alone to wait for the experimenter (Maddi, Hoover, & Kobasa, 1982). Further, Kobasa (1979) has shown that business executives high on alienation from self, on vegetativeness, and on powerlessness are more likely to react to stressful life events with illness symptoms than are other executives. These findings indicate the general passivity and vulnerability involved in existential sickness as theorized by Maddi (1967, 1970). But an emerging difficulty with the *Alienation Test* is a rather high intercorrelation among the various dimensions, raising the possibility that there are in reality fewer usable scores than presumed.

There is also a large body of research on the regular tendency of some persons to conform by trying to be socially desirable. This literature is clearly important for the existential position, though it is also relevant for Rogers, Maslow, and Allport.

But at the outset, I should address a ready criticism. Much of the research in which conformity is measured on some performance task suggests that conforming tendencies are specific to situations (e.g., Hollander & Willis, 1967). This could be taken as evidence that no conformist personality type exists. But such a conclusion seems premature, however mystifying the performance results may be. There is, after all, a considerable body of research suggesting that the tendency to conform indeed may be quite general. I refer to the research employing questionnaire measures of socially desirable responding and internal versus external locus of control.

Crowne and Marlowe (1960) have reported an extensive attempt at construct validation for their carefully developed Social Desirability Scale (M-C SDS). On the face of it, the tendency to respond in a socially desirable direction should express conformity and an emphasis on social role playing. By and large, the empirical findings bear this out. In an extensive research program (Crowne & Marlowe, 1960), it was determined that persons scoring high in socially desirable responding show greater attitude change after being induced to deliver an appeal for an attitude they did not originally endorse (thereby resolving cognitive dissonance), express higher need for affiliation, and terminate psychotherapy sooner (perhaps out of unwillingness to face themselves) than is true of low scorers. In addition, the higher the M-C SDS score, the greater the tendency to give common word associations and fewer, more concrete responses on the Thematic Apperception, Rorschach, and Sentence Completion tests. In their fantasy productions, high M-C SDS scorers are especially rejecting of people but tend to underestimate the extent to which their friends really reject them. The highest threshold in a perceptual task requiring the recognition of obscene words belongs to these high social-desirability scorers.

There is also a group of findings concerning socially desirable responding and performance of simple laboratory tasks. Subjects high on the M-C SDS generally perform better on the pursuit rotor (Strickland & Jenkins, 1964) and perform more skillfully a motor steadiness task (Strickland, 1965) and other simple motor tasks (Willington & Strickland, 1965). Although the results may indicate superior motor ability in these subjects, it seems more likely that we are observing the heightened attentiveness created by a wish to appear socially desirable. Consistent with this interpretation is the finding (Crowne & Marlowe, 1960) that subjects high in M-C SDS are less likely to rate a monotonous spool-packing task as dull.

In general, the picture emerging is that of a personality type characterized by intense interest in appearing attentive, consistent, competent, and acceptable in the context of conformity, superficial interest in but lack of deep commitment to others and a general unwillingness to face these facts. The implications of defensiveness are supported by Conn and Crowne (1964), who found that high M-C SDS scorers selected euphoria as an alternative to the expression of anger in a manner suggestive of reaction formation. Similarly, Fishman (1965) found that subjects high in M-C SDS expressed less verbal aggression toward the experimenter when nonarbitrary frustration was imposed (whereas arbitrary frustration did not differentiate high from low M-C SDS scores). Apparently persons high in socially desirable responding can express anger only when they can find justification (or rationalization) for it.

Any information concerning the relationship of M-C SDS to psychopathology should be of interest, as Maddi (1967, 1970) has contended that conformism is the premorbid state for existential sickness. Even though the M-C SDS was specifically designed to be independent of frank psychopathology, there is some research indicating that this is not so. Katkin (1964) reports the correlations between the M-C SDS and the MMPI scales commonly used to assess psychopathological trends. Eight of the ten correlations reached significance but were negative, suggesting that conformity does not predispose one toward sickness. Further research is needed to determine whether Maddi's position requires reformulation. The additional research should involve measures of actual symptomatology rather than questionnaires such as the MMPI.

Although research on socially desirable responding continues to be done, the pace has slowed. Often these days this conforming tendency is studied not alone but along with other tendencies that may even be regarded as more important (see Strickland in Blass, 1977). Nonetheless, there is much support in this research theme for existential psychology, Rogers, Maslow, Allport, and Fromm.

Before closing this section, I should mention Tyler's (1978) book integrating a wide range of research studies toward the end of understanding individuality. This is an especially interesting approach given the emphasis on the nonideal, conforming states in the work discussed thus far. Reviewing hundreds of studies, Tyler found considerable evidence of what she calls *possibility-processing structures* in persons that underlie choice as a sign of individuality and creative living. This placing of the decision-making capabilities and the pursuit of possibility at the heart of the matter of individuality is, of course, quite consistent with existential theorizing. The emphasis Tyler identified has continued since her book appeared, as shown in a review by Singer and Kolligian (1987).

Though not available to Tyler, a previously mentioned study by Kobasa (1979) initiated a relevant program of research bearing directly on existential psychology. This study introduced the personality style of *hardiness,* which, as indicated in Chapter 8, is considered a concrete manifestation of existential courage (see Maddi, 1988; Kobasa & Maddi, 1977). Hardiness involves three interrelated beliefs about self and world, namely, that (1) you can always find something in what you are doing that will make it interesting and worthwhile (*commitment* rather than alienation); (2) you can influence the events going on around you if you try (*control* rather than powerlessness); and (3) life changes frequently in an ongoing growth process (*challenge* rather than threat). Kobasa

(1979) reasoned that persons showing hardiness (existential courage) should be able to resist the otherwise debilitating effects of stressful events because of their high level of awareness, their tendency toward future-oriented decisions, and the general individuality involved in this style. On the basis of questionnaire responses, Kobasa formed two groups of business executives, both high in stressful events, one also high in illness symptoms, and the other low in illness symptoms. As can be seen in Table 11–18, on various personality questionnaires, the group low in illness symptoms showed greater evidence of all three aspects of hardiness than did the group high in illness symptoms.

To bolster the direction of causal inference from hardiness to illness, Kobasa, Maddi, and Kahn (1982) used a time lag design (in which hardiness and stressful event scores were obtained a year before illness scores) plus a statistical control for prior illness scores in their study of business managers. As hypothesized, the results showed that hardiness buffers against illness most as stressful events mount. In explicating the mechanism whereby hardiness buffers, subsequent research shows that subjects high in this personality style respond to stressful events with less physiological arousal (measured by skin conductance and blood pressure) and with greater efforts to make the events less stressful (Hull & Schwartz, 1987; Holahan & Moos, 1985; Kobasa, 1982; Kobasa, Maddi, Donner, Merrick, & White, 1987). As to discriminant validity, it is also clear that personality hardiness is neither merely a mental reflection of a strong constitution (Kobasa, Maddi, & Courington, 1981) nor simply the glow that comes through physical exercise (Kobasa, Maddi, & Puccetti, 1982). In comparing the relative effectiveness of buffers in the stress-illness relationship, Kobasa, Maddi, Puccetti, and Zola (1986) found personality hardiness to be almost twice as powerful as either social support or physical exercise.

Although the hardiness research theme appears quite promising support for existential psychology, Ganellen and Blaney (1984) found a buffering effect in their subjects for the commitment but not the challenge and control components of hardiness. This discrepant finding may reflect the use of college students (rather than business managers) as subjects or use of measures of social support and stressful events by Ganellen and Blaney that appear to have correlated more highly with the hardiness measure than is true in the studies by Kobasa and associates. In any event, a study by Jensen (1987) that uses quite different methods appears to support the existential notion that high levels of awareness are consistent with mental and physical health. It was found that among women with breast cancer, those who were most defensive (repressive or relying on escapist fantasies) showed greater spread of their illness. The implications of this finding are quite consistent with hardiness research.

Ellis's Position

Rational-emotive therapy is so devoid of peripheral theorizing that it is not even possible to determine how to construe research done in other traditions as in any way relevant.

TABLE 11–18   Differences between High Stress/Low Illness[*] and High Stress/ High Illness[*] Executives

Variable	High Stress/ Low Illness (M)	(SD)	High Stress/ High Illness (M)	(SD)	t Value	Standardized Discriminant Function Coefficient
Control						
Nihilism	196.05	133.61	281.02	169.86	2.49[‡]	.73
External locus of control	5.92	4.10	7.90	4.61	2.03[†]	.22
Powerlessness	301.15	188.93	388.47	188.44	2.11[†]	—
Achievement	16.50	2.10	15.12	3.20	−1.20	—
Dominance	14.60	3.26	13.85	4.46	.86	—
Leadership	33.47	7.34	34.63	6.80	.73	.43
Commitment						
Alienation from self	102.35	117.24	219.15	185.77	3.36[†]	1.04
Alienation from work	181.67	122.04	223.73	175.09	1.22	.43
Alienation from friends	256.02	162.76	316.10	165.24	1.64	—
Alienation from family	158.47	139.02	198.72	144.33	1.27	—
Alienation from society	202.15	100.21	226.95	133.93	.94	—
Role consistency	29.22	6.42	29.50	6.44	.19	.30
Challenge						
Vegetativeness	155.50	140.24	216.27	160.94	1.98[†]	.99
Security	21.11	6.33	22.19	8.60	.34	.35
Cognitive structure	13.35	2.81	14.10	2.85	1.10	.21
Adventurousness	269.00	164.58	337.54	174.95	1.78[†]	—
Endurance	15.97	2.35	14.37	3.19	−.96	—
Interesting experiences	34.97	6.83	32.52	7.02	−.92	
Perception of personal stress	3.00	1.21	3.83	1.73	2.46[‡]	.43

Note: For all variables, the higher the number, the greater the degree of the variable observed. Superior hardiness is indicated by higher scores on achievement, role consistency, endurance, and interesting experiences, and lower scores on nihilism, external locus, powerlessness, dominance, leadership, alienation (from self, work, social institutions, interpersonal relationships, and family), vegetativeness, security, cognitive structure, and adventurousness. A subject's scores on all areas of alienation, measured by the Alienation Test, have a possible range of 0 to 1,200. Vegetativeness, nihilism, powerlessness, and adventurousness scores, also from the Alienation Test, may range from 0 to 1,500. External locus has a low of 0 and an upper limit of 23. The scales taken from the Jackson test—achievement, dominance, cognitive structure, and endurance—have a minimum value of 0 and a maximum of 20. The California Life Goals scale—leadership security, and interesting experiences—may range from 0 to 60. Role consistency has a low of 0 and a high of 40; perception of personal stress can range from 0 to 7.
[*]$n = 40$.
[†]$p < .05$.
[‡]$p < .01$.

SOURCE: "Stressful Life Events, Personality, and Health: An Inquiry into Hardiness" by S. C. Kobasa, 1979, *Journal of Personality and Social Psychology, 37.*

Kelly's Position

Kelly, the consistency theorist, says virtually nothing substantive concerning the periphery of personality. Consequently, there is virtually nothing we can do in our attempt to determine the empirical validity of his position. Using Kelly's Role Constructs Repertory Test (see Chapter 5), Bieri (1961) has shown that people differ in the number of bipolar constructs they have available to them. The notion of psychological complexity has been picked up by other investigators who do not necessarily use Kelly's test in measuring it. For example, Porter and Suedfeld (1981) reported that the more complexity shown in the writings of literary figures, the less they were interested in war, but the more they supported social unrest. Also, Tetlock (1984) found that the rank ordering of members of the British House of Commons on complex views regarding political issues was moderate socialists, moderate conservatives, and extremes of both. However interesting these differences in psychological complexity or differentiation are, they do not really bear on the peripheral point of view that is explicitly Kelly's. They are potentially important, however, to any theory that conceptualizes degrees of differentiation in peripheral personality (e.g., Allport, existential psychology). The same is true for studies showing that the constructs one holds influence the way one perceives and makes decisions. Studies such as those of Swann and Read (1981) and Leitner and Cado (1982) chronicle how perceptions of self and major values influence performance and stress levels. But such findings are as supportive of Allport, Rogers, and existential psychology as they are of Kelly.

There is an intriguing study by Sechrest (1968), admittedly inductive rather than hypothesis testing, in which two samples of fifty-seven and sixty-seven nursing students participated. They all filled out the Role Constructs Repertory Test and also took the Minnesota Multiphasic Personality Inventory (MMPI) and a sociometric instrument requiring them to specify how pleasant they thought each member of their group was. Sechrest determined that the personal constructs of intelligent-unintelligent, anxious-nonanxious, and friendly-unfriendly were among the most common in the group. His attempt, then, was to determine whether the personal constructs one employs are expressive in some sense of the realities of one's existence. This hypothesis is consistent with the general emphasis in Kelly's approach on a kind of rational trial and error in finding the best bases for navigating life. Sechrest also had available to him his subjects' linguistic ability scores on the American Council of Education (ACE) Test (a kind of intelligence measure). He tried to evaluate scores on this against reliance on intelligence-unintelligence as a construct. From the MMPI, he extracted an anxiety score (the Psychasthenia Scale) to evaluate against reliance on the anxious-nonanxious construct. For similar purposes with regard to the friendly-unfriendly construct, he utilized the number of the subjects' sociometric nominations of other people as friendly. His results appear in Table 11-19.

As you can see, moderately intelligent subjects are more likely to use intelligence as a personal construct than are highly intelligent ones. Those

TABLE 11–19   Relationships between Employment of Certain Personal Constructs and Corresponding Personal Characteristics

Personal Characteristic Measurement Instrument	Score	Personal Construct			
		Sample 1 (N = 57)[*]		Sample 2 (N = 67)	
		Nonuse	Use	Nonuse	Use
		Intelligent-Unintelligent			
ACE Aptitude test					
Linguistic ability score	70+	15	4	16	9
	60–69	6	11	8	14
	−59	12	9	10	10
	x^2	7.02; $p < .05$		3.57; $p < .20$	
		Anxious-Nonanxious			
MMPI					
Psychosthenia raw score	20+	2	13	2	12
	10–19	15	15	18	21
	−9	1	9	7	7
	x^2	8.66; $p < .02$		5.03; $p < .10$	
		Friendly-Unfriendly			
Nominating					
Number of nominations	10+	6	22	5	25
	−9	14	15	15	22
	x^2	4.52; $p < .05$		4.52; $p < .05$	

*For personal construct "anxious-nonanxious" $N = 55$ only.

SOURCE: "Pesonal Constructs and Personal Characteristics" by L. Sechrest, 1968, *Journal of Individual Psychology, 24.*

subjects who employ anxious-nonanxious as a construct are likely to be either extremely high or extremely low on the MMPI measure of anxiety. But the findings concerning the low end of the scale on Sample 1 are washed out on Sample 2. The safest conclusion is that highly anxious subjects use anxious-nonanxious as a construct. Similarly, subjects relying on friendly-unfriendly in their construct systems receive a large number of nominations as "most pleasant." This study provides evidence of correspondence between the way one construes the world and the way one behaves in it. It is not possible, however, to specify which comes first. Although the use of such presumably uninfluenceable variables as intelligence suggests that construals follow objective features of experience, this inference is not convincing with regard to anxiety and popularity.

The work of Adams-Webber (1970) on the discriminant validity of various forms of the Role Constructs Repertory Test does seem to have anticipated an increase in interest in this assessment technique. Fransella (in Bannister, 1970) has used this test to study construct change over the course of group psychotherapy, in which context it seems to be a useful tool for quantifying directions that are perennially difficult to chart. Also Bonarius (in Cole, 1976) has found Kelly's test a useful instrument for studying continuing interactions among persons. And Mancuso (in Cole, 1976) shows that children in kindergarten and sixth grade perceive situations of coercion and rational explanation differently as measured by this test. Although interesting in their own right, these studies really do not test anything about Kelly's theory; rather, they show that his general approach and assessment device can be useful where quantification is difficult.

There should be correspondence between Rosenberg's studies (in Cole, 1976) of the implicit "personality theories" persons carry around with them and Kelly's emphasis on personal construction of experience. Rosenberg indicates that the Role Constructs Repertory Test should be a useful instrument in getting at persons' implicit notions. Using his own assessment devices, Rosenberg has summarized typical content categories observable in people. It would be quite valuable for psychologists of Kelly's persuasion to take this work seriously and use it as a basis for some peripheral theorizing. If that happened, Kelly's position might become truly predictive rather than merely descriptive of behavior (Mischel, 1964). Unfortunately, a recent collection of Kellyian writings (Fransella, 1978) does not seem to be going in this direction.

McClelland's Position

Fantasy techniques for measuring personality produce an ambiguous or incomplete stimulus, requiring people to structure or complete it by exercising their own imaginations. In utilizing their own fantasies to structure or complete the stimulus, they presumably are displaying their personalities. Although fantasy techniques have been criticized for being so uncontrolled that it is truly difficult to determine the real meaning of the person's responses, they have the great advantage over self-descriptive techniques of being more likely to circumvent response styles. There are no right or wrong answers on a fantasy task, and the investigator encourages the subject to realize this. If it is not clear what the investigator is trying to find out, it is unlikely that the subject will find some basis for being acquiescent or for responding in socially desirable fashion. This is why McClelland has considered fantasy measures the most relevant to the motive construct, with its personal rather than societal goals. The technique of eliciting fantasy on which he has relied is the *Thematic Apperception Test* (Murray, 1943), with its ambiguous pictures about which the subject must compose a story with a beginning, middle, and end.

The first motive concentrated on was the need for achievement (McClelland, Atkinson, Clark, & Lowell, 1953). McClelland et al. first devised a scoring system for thematic apperception that suited the definition of the need as goal-directed fantasy expressing competition with a standard of excellence. After reading a story composed by the subject, the investigator applies the first, or general, component of the scoring system. This component calls for an overall judgment as to whether the study includes imagery *definitely relevant* (scored 1), *doubtfully relevant* (scored zero), or *definitively irrelevant* (scored − 1) to competition with a standard of excellence. If the story is scored as definitely relevant, the second (or specific) and third (or weighting) components of the scoring system are employed. The second component involves scoring for the presence (1) or absence (zero) of each of the specific categories of goal-directed functioning. These categories are *achievement wish, instrumental activity* toward an achievement goal, *block* or obstacle to reaching the goal, *goal anticipation,* and associated *goal affect.* The third component is for weighting purposes and involves giving an additional point to a story that is completely devoted to an achievement theme. All of the stories the person composes are scored in this fashion, with the intensity of need for achievement indicated by the algebraic sum of the scores.

As you know from the ideal research strategy previously discussed, the first thing to consider is the reliability of this measure of the need for achievement. Since fantasy measures require considerable judgment on the investigator's part, one kind of reliability that is important is that between two independent users of the scoring system. It has repeatedly been demonstrated (Atkinson, 1958; McClelland et al. 1953) that two experienced scorers working independently can obtain need-for-achievement scores from the same protocols that agree to the tune of correlations exceeding .90. This is excellent interscorer reliability. The situation concerning the internal consistency and stability of the need-for-achievement measure is not nearly as satisfactory. Correlations range from .22 to .54 for stability (Haber & Alpert, 1958; Lowell, 1950) and are approximately .65 for internal consistency (Atkinson, 1950). Recognizing that one might conclude that there was no compelling empirical evidence here that the peripheral characteristic, need for achievement, really exists, McClelland (1958) has pointed out that validity is much more important than reliability, especially in a fantasy measure. After all, fantasy tests by their nature involve considerable measurement error, as the investigator cannot be sure in any particular instance whether he or she has properly understood the respondent's real meaning. McClelland recommends that we consider the internal consistency and stability results as indicating that the measure's reliability is somewhere above zero and proceed with due haste to an assessment of validity. Supporting this approach is the conceptualization of a motive as something that waxes and wanes depending on its satisfaction. Because of this, we should expect no more than moderate reliability from a motive measure (McClelland, 1958).

A great many studies investigating the construct validity of the fantasy measure of the need for achievement have been done. One of these is experimental in nature, whereas the others are correlational. The experimental study and most of the correlational studies concern the effects of high and low levels of the need for achievement on the behavior of individual people; the remainder of the correlational studies concern the effects of the need on the social system phenomenon of economic growth. Let us first consider the studies concerning individuals.

An experiment by McClelland, Atkinson, and Clark (1949) launched the study of individuals. Its major aim was to demonstrate that an investigator can arouse the need for achievement by experimental manipulation of a theoretically relevant sort. Included were two groups of male college students, both of which were given a series of tasks to perform. In the experimental group, the tasks were introduced as tests of intelligence that are often used to select people of high administrative capacity for positions in Washington. There was further elaboration of the ability of the tasks to disclose a person's capacity to organize material, evaluate crucial situations quickly and accurately, and be a leader. In short, the instructions given to the experimental group were calculated to arouse a high level of need for achievement. In contrast, the control group was given the same task to perform but with neutral, relaxing instructions stressing that the investigator just wanted to try out some tests of uncertain utility. Following the brief but difficult tasks, the people in both groups were asked to compose stories about four ambiguous pictures showing human beings in work situations.

The important data of the study were these expressions of fantasy. There were striking and theoretically reasonable differences in the stories composed by the two groups. To make the differences vivid, I shall quote one story from the control group and one from the experimental group. Both stories were composed in response to a picture of a boy sitting at a desk with a book open in front of him. First, the control group story:

> A boy in a classroom who is daydreaming about something. He is recalling a previously experienced incident that struck his mind to be more appealing than being in the classroom. He is thinking about the experience and is now imagining himself in the situation. He hopes to be there. He will probably get called on by the instructor to recite and will be embarrassed.

Nothing in this story deals with achievement or with standards of excellence, but compare it with the experimental group story:

> The boy is taking an hour written. He and the others are high-school students. The test is about two-thirds over and he is doing his best to think it through. He was supposed to study for the test and did so. But because it is factual, there were items he saw but did not learn. He knows he has studied the answers he can't remember and is trying to summon up the images and related ideas to remind him of them. He may remember one or two, but he will miss most of the items he can't remember. He will try hard until five minutes is left, then give up, go back over his paper, and be disgusted for reading but not learning the answers.

Thinking in terms of the scoring system mentioned earlier, this story certainly qualifies as *definitely relevant* to competition with a standard of excellence under the first component. As to the second component of the scoring system, there is evidence for *obstacle* of a personal variety ("he saw but did not learn"), *instrumental activity* ("trying to summon up the images and related ideas to remind him of them"), *goal anticipation* ("he may remember one or two, but he will miss most of the items he can't remember"), and *goal affect* ("and be disgusted for reading but not learning the answers"). Clearly this story would also be weighted under the third component of the scoring system, because there is nothing but an achievement theme represented.

To be more precise about the results of this experiment, I should report two things. First, the average intensity of need for achievement, relying on total score attributed to each protocol through use of the entire scoring system, was significantly greater in the experimental group than in the control group. In addition, the scores for each specific category of goal-directed fantasy comprised in the second component of the scoring system were significantly greater in the experimental than in the control group. These results provide evidence of the validity of the fantasy measure of need for achievement.

But some of you may be wondering, since reading the high-need-for-achievement story above, whether obstacles that are not surmounted, instrumental activity that is unsuccessful, and negative affect concerning the goal have a proper place in a measure of the need for achievement. Should not such a measure include only fantasy positively oriented toward achievement? From the beginning, McClelland and his associates have contended that fantasy references to obstacles, instrumental activity, goal anticipation, and goal affect referring to competition with a standard of excellence are relevant regardless of the pessimism or optimism of their content. Pessimistic and optimistic content may well define the avoidance and approach versions of the need, respectively, but both are relevant. Some empirical support for this distinction between approach and avoidance versions of the need for achievement is to be found in the experiment we are considering. The experimental group was subdivided into two subgroups that experienced failure and success, respectively, on performing the tasks following the achievement-arousing instructions. In the failure subgroup, pessimistic content in achievement-relevant fantasy was more common than it was in the latter subgroup. Atkinson (1960) has interpreted many findings of the performance of people high in test anxiety as indicating fear of failure rather than as suggesting the more positive need for achievement.

Over the last twenty-five years, a great deal of correlational work has been done in an attempt to determine whether the fantasy measure of need for achievement predicts the sorts of actions and life patterns that one would expect. I cannot possibly review all the studies here, nor would that be necessary. It will suffice to summarize major findings so as to establish the significance of the need for achievement.

First, there is a group of findings suggesting the social and intellectual significance of high or low levels of the need for achievement. American males with high need for achievement come more often from the middle class than from the lower or upper class. They have better memory for incompleted tasks in situations arranged so that everyone must complete an equal number of tasks but fail to do so. They are more apt to volunteer as subjects for psychological experiments, participate more in college and community activities, choose experts over friends when asked whom they want as partners to work on difficult problems, and are more resistant to social pressure to conform (Atkinson, 1958; McClelland et al., 1953).

Of even more theoretical importance is a group of findings concerning how people high and low in need for achievement actually perform when confronted with a work situation. Lowell (see McClelland, 1961) presented people with a task requiring them to unscramble many scrambled words and recorded how many words a person unscrambled in each of five consecutive periods of four minutes each. As you can see in Figure 11–1, people high and low in need for achievement started at about the same level of performance. But as time went on, those with high levels of the need did progressively better than those with low levels. The people high in need for achievement appeared to be sufficiently concerned about doing the task well to learn to do it better as they went along. But you should not assume that these people would have done better at just any kind of task. Indeed, with a routine, ordinary task, which one cannot learn to do better as one proceeds—crossing out the S's in printed material, for example—there is no difference in the performance of people with high and low need for achievement. Similar results were obtained by French (1955) using a decoding task, presented under instructional conditions encouraging relaxation. Indeed, another group of people performed the decoding task under instructional conditions relevant to motives other than the need for achievement. The instructions indicated that those people who did the work the fastest would be allowed to leave the room, whereas the others would have to continue working. Under these instructional conditions, the people low in need for achievement actually did a little better than the others, indicating that the possibility of getting out of work is what appealed to them the most.

All these results taken together suggest that high need for achievement will lead persons to perform better when they perceive that they can display significant excellence through their attempts. If the task is routine or if finishing it sooner implies cooperating with someone or getting some nonachievement reward such as time off, subjects low in need for achievement (and presumably high in some other needs) will perform better.

That people high in need for achievement are challenged by situations in which they can display significant excellence is echoed in studies concerning risk taking. McClelland (1958) reports that people high in need for achievement will choose to take moderate risks in a ring-toss game permitting persons to stand as close to the ring as they want, whereas those low in need for achievement will take either large or small risks. You can convince yourself of this by observing, in Figure 11–2, that the biggest differences between the curves for high- and low-need-for-achievement groups occurred in conjunction with moderate probability of success. McClelland suggests, ingeniously, that taking both

FIGURE 11–1   Mean Output of Scrambled Words per Four-Minute Period for
Subject with High and Low *N* Achievement Scores

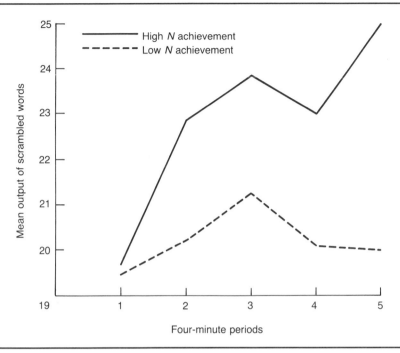

SOURCE: *The Achieving Society* by D. C. McClelland, 1961, Princeton, N.J.: Van Nostrand.

large and small risks has the function of removing the outcome from implication for your own skill and excellence. Success or failure is then either ensured or a matter of chance. But in taking a moderate risk, you are trying to be successful in a context that properly tests your skill. It is the high-need-for-achievement person who would be challenged by such a possibility.

Recent studies have used sophisticated methods of analysis in providing general support for McClelland's formulations regarding achievement motivation. For example, Cooper (1983) has reported a network of interrelated variables indicating that need for achievement finds expression in choice of task difficulty, persistence and performance at the task, importance of success and failure, and subjects' estimates of task difficulty. Using causal modeling, Reuman, Alwin, and Veroff (1984) demonstrated that need for achievement predicts work satisfaction in adult males. Lest we think achievement motivation is inevitably good, there is Johnson's (1981) findings that it predicts cheating on an examination among college students.

Summarizing thus far, it seems clear that it is possible to develop a fantasy measure of the peripheral characteristic of need for achievement that though

FIGURE 11–2   Percentage of Throws Made by Five-Year-Olds with High and Low "Doodle" *N* Achievement at Different Distances from the Peg and Smoothed Curve of Probability of Success at Those Distances.

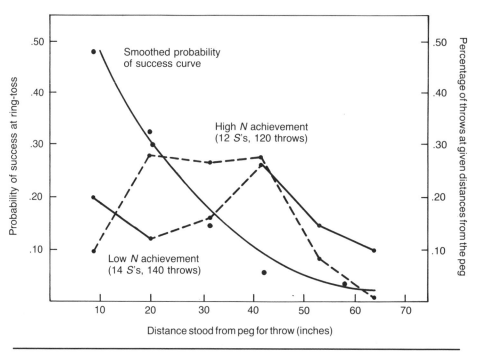

Note: 26 *S*s, 10 throws each. Plotted at midpoints of intervals of 11 inches beginning with closest distance stood (4″–14″, 5″–15″, etc.).

not distinguished from the viewpoint of internal consistency and stability, operates in a theoretically meaningful fashion in both experiment and correlational study.

Having found a measure that has brought us this far, we can ask the more precise question of whether it is clear that the measure has motivational status. There are three things one would expect of a measure if it had motivational status in McClelland's terms: It would refer to striving toward a goal; it would reflect at least momentary satiation when the goal is reached; and it would concern personal rather than societal goals. The first expectation is shown in the results already covered. Not only does the measure itself indicate striving toward a standard of excellence; so too do its work-relevant correlates. The evidence concerning momentary satiation, though not extensive, is very intriguing. In an attempt to better understand the measure's reliability, Atkinson (1958) correlated the need-for-achievement score obtained on each story with that of every other story. The results indicate a kind of saw-toothed effect, in which writing a story high in need for achievement seems to satiate one momentarily, leading to the immediately following story being low in the need; the story immediately following this will be high again, and so forth. This effect occurs in most persons, regardless of their overall score on need for achievement. The effect is just what we would expect in a motive measure, and it helps us take a more sophisticated view of the low reliability that results from actually measuring a motive—which is, after all, a waxing and waning thing. On the basis of such findings, measurement experts (e.g., Reuman, 1982; Jackson & Paunonen, 1980) are beginning to agree with McClelland that traditional reliability theory does not really apply to thematic apperception measures.

The final requirement of a motive measure is that it tap personal rather than societal goals. There is evidence that the fantasy measure does just this. It seems clear that the fantasy measure of need for achievement is either unrelated or only slightly related to structured self-descriptive measures purporting to assess the same need (de Charms, Morrison, Reitman, & McClelland, 1955; Lindzey & Heineman, 1955; McClelland, 1958; McClelland et al., 1953). Whereas the fantasy measure is based on those of the person's thoughts that are unencumbered by societal restrictions, the structured self-description measures are based on the degree to which the person subscribes to universalistic achievement sentiments posed by other people. As such, the latter measures should tap achievement values or schemata more than motives, with the opposite being true of the fantasy measure. The absence or meager correlation between the two types of measure is therefore understandable. This interpretation is strengthened by the nature of the correlates obtained for the two kinds of measure. De Charms et al. (1955) found that whereas the fantasy measure was correlated to behaviors involving memory and performance, a structured self-description measure involving achievement values was not related to such behaviors but did relate to the tendency to be influenced by the opinions of experts in an ambiguous situation.

The fantasy measure seems to tap an achievement motive in McClelland's sense, and the structured self-description measure may well tap an achievement schema. This conclusion requires discussion of the position put forward by Campbell and Fiske (1959) to the effect that one must be able to measure a peripheral characteristic by more than one method in order to be sure that it exists. If the characteristic shows up on only one measurement operation, there is too much risk that one is measuring no more than a peculiar attribute of that type of operation and nothing of substantive significance for personality. Although this seems like a sound position, results such as those mentioned above alert us to the need for greater precision. For example, to require that attempts to measure the need for achievement in fantasy and in structured self-description agree before concluding that the need really exists would directly contradict theoretical formulations of the nature of the need. The only form of Campbell and Fiske's position warranted here is that one might want to develop two fantasy measures of need for achievement in order to ensure that the current measure is not somehow an artifact of the thematic apperception task.

In general, attempts to measure peripheral characteristics with more than one method should be guided by theorizing concerning the nature of the characteristic. One should not require a characteristic to show generality across any arbitrary selected measurement operations. Thus, the negative findings in studies such as that of Gelbort and Winer (1985) are not really problematic for McClelland, as these investigators failed to use thematic apperception measures and therefore may not have been tapping motives at all.

Convincing as the thematic apperception studies are, there do exist some perplexing results as well (see Katz, 1967; Klinger, 1966). Notable among these is the role of achievement motivation in women. It had long been recognized that this motive measure was less than useful in understanding the actions of females, though this was poorly understood. Then Horner (in Atkinson & Raynor, 1975) proposed that the usual male-relevant achievement cues produce the avoidance motive of *fear of success* rather than the approach motive of *need for achievement*. This, she speculated, was because females do not really feel they can or should succeed in traditionally male activities. She provided evidence for this position from the imaginative productions of female college students asked to contemplate medical school application. Her findings have been criticized on methodological grounds (e.g., Zuckerman & Wheeler, 1975) and have received little support in recent studies (e.g., Peplau, 1976). It is possible that only some women holding traditional sex-role stereotypes respond as Horner contends (Peplau, 1976).

It should also be mentioned that some empirical support has emerged for the extension of McClelland's position formulated by Atkinson and Raynor (1975). From this extension, Raynor and Sorrentino (in Atkinson & Raynor, 1975) derived the surprising prediction that success-oriented persons will work harder and perform better when steps in a long, contingent path are perceived as easy than when they are perceived as hard. They reported two studies that tend to confirm this prediction. Also, several studies reported in Atkinson and Raynor (1975) chart how persistence and risk taking relate to achievement orientation differently in future-oriented contingent paths than in individual task situations. Additional studies are needed to determine the precise relationship between the original and this new formulation of achievement motivation.

I shall now turn to the correlational studies linking the need for achievement to the social system phenomenon of economic development. These studies constitute the most exciting demonstration of the effects of personality on the social system that exist in the social science literature, however much one may criticize fine points of method and interpretation. The theoretical impetus for considering the need for achievement as a determinant of economic development comes from the classical sociologist Max Weber (1930). In his view, it was the impact of Protestantism that spurred industrialization and capitalism. As a sociologist, Weber sought causes for social system phenomena in the social system itself. Protestantism is a social institution of a religious nature and, as such, is not an attribute of individuals. The explanation thus obtained, therefore, is bound not to cover every person—indeed, the explanation is too gross to hold even for all societies. Although the most important societies to become industrialized were predominantly Protestant, there were definite exceptions. Belgium, for example, had as vigorous an industrial revolution as any northern European country, even though its orthodox religion was Catholicism. And Renaissance Venice achieved a form of capitalism that was perhaps more pure and vigorous than any seen in modern times all the while it was officially Catholic. Such observations lead the personologist to speculate that Weber was right insofar as his social system "cause" mirrored an underlying psychological or individual cause. An even more accurate version of the supposed cause than Protestantism might be protestantism, or the existence of a set of values in people stressing the importance of hard work, excellence, and self-reliance. These values generally overlap with Protestantism as a religious form but need not always do so. McClelland theorized that values such as these lead parents to create the kinds of developmental experiences for their children that lead to high levels of need for achievement in much the same manner as described in Chapter 9. If enough parents in a society bring up their children this way, there eventually will be many citizens who choose a way of life involving the challenge of competition with a standard of excellence. Following Weber, McClelland contends that this challenge is most vivid and salient in entrepreneurial activity, which is basic to economic development.

Utilizing this general theoretical framework, three extraordinary studies have been performed. In the first of these, Berlew (1956) attempted to determine the relationship between the modal (or most frequent) level of need for achievement and economic growth in ancient Greece. Following accepted historical belief, Berlew considered three time periods for this society: the period of growth, from 900 B.C. to 475 B.C; the period of climax, from 475 B.C. to 362 B.C.; and the period of decline, from 362 B.C. to 100 B.C. For each time period, he tried to measure both need for achievement and economic development. For the first, Berlew decided to use as raw material surviving literature and to analyze this in much the same manner described previously for the analysis of thematic apperception stories. From each time period, he selected literature in the following categories: man and his gods, farm and estate management, public funeral celebrations, poetry, epigrams, and war speeches of encouragement. He selected these categories in an attempt to widely sample literature that was more imaginative than realistic or descriptive and, hence, thus expressive of the writers' personal motives. Because these writers were all famous and excellent men, Berlew felt sure that in measuring their need-for-achievement levels he was obtaining a representative picture of the modal level of this need in the society at large. If these men were so valued by their society, they must have mirrored it fairly accurately. Finally, the number of lines in each category of literature and in each time period was the same in order to ensure that there was no bias in the measurement of need for achievement. In this manner, Berlew was able to obtain average levels of the need associated with each of the three time periods.

The measurement of economic development was, if anything, more diffi-cult to obtain. After considering and rejecting various possible measures, Ber-lew decided on a measure that is intriguing though somewhat indirect: vases. To understand the significance of this, you must remember that the economic life of the Greek city-states was organized around agriculture and overseas trade. Above all, it was maritime commerce that brought prosperity, and Ath-ens and its seaport, Piraeus, were at the very center of Greek commerce. What Greece had to trade was largely surplus wine and olive oil. These were sent overseas to trade for grain from Sicily, rugs from Persia, perfumes from Arabia, foodstuffs, basic metals, and other materials. Olive oil and wine were carried in large, earthenware jars, which remained in the cities of delivery after their contents had been consumed. These jars, many of which were made by potters in or near Athens, have been found in regions all around the Mediterranean, and many of them date back at least to the century in which they were pro-duced and used. From the anthropological literature concerning the location of these vase remains, Berlew was able to calculate the area of Greek trade in millions of square miles. He contends that, especially for Greece, whose pros-perity depended so much on commerce, extent of trade area is a plausible measure of economic development.

What were the results of this ground-breaking study? In the periods of growth, climax, and decline, the average levels of need for achievement were 4.74, 2.71, and 1.35, respectively, a trend that is statistically significant. The levels of economic growth associated with these three time periods were 1.2, 3.4, and 1.9 million square miles, respectively. These dramatic results, depicted in Figure 11–3, led Berlew to the conclusion that the high level of need for achievement in the period of growth had the effect of spurring economic de-velopment, as shown by the sharp increase in trade area from this period to the period of climax. In addition, the decrease in level of need for achievement in the period of climax determined a decrease in economic growth, as shown by the sharp decrease in trade area from this period to the period of decline.

In truth, these results, however striking, can be criticized on many meth-odological grounds. One might commend the investigator on his courage in attempting to demonstrate the effect of personality factors on societal phenom-ena in a historical situation. But the results obtained and the conclusions formulated are upheld in equally striking fashion by two similar studies con-cerning different societies. One study (Cortes, 1960) involved Spain in the late Middle Ages. Cortes identified the following periods: economic growth, 1200 A.D. to 1492 A.D.; climax, 1492 A.D. to 1610 A.D.; and decline, 1610 A.D. to 1730 A.D. The measure of modal level of need for achievement was very similar to that of Berlew. Literary categories of fiction, verse, history, and legends were sampled with the same precautions used in the previous study. The measure of economic growth was shipping cleared from Spain for the New World in thousands of tons per year. The results of this study are strikingly similar to Berlew's. Cortes found a level of need for achievement that was highest in the period of growth and lowest in the period of decline. Economic

FIGURE 11–3   Average *N* Achievement Level Plotted at Midpoints of Periods of Growth Climax, and Decline of Athenian Civilization as Reflected in the Extent of its Trade Area.

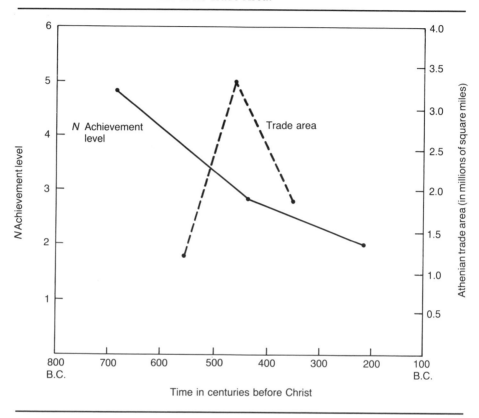

Time in centuries before Christ

SOURCE: "The Achievement Motive and the Growth of Greek Civilization" by D. E. Berlew, 1956, Unpublished bachelor's thesis, Wesleyn University, Middletown, Conn.

growth, in contrast, was highest in the period of climax and quite low in both of the other periods.

The final study indicating that modal level of need for achievement in a society will exert an influence on subsequent economic activity is that of Bradburn and Berlew (1961) concerning England from Tudor times to the Industrial Revolution. The investigators divided this span of time into fifty-year segments. For purposes of measuring need for achievement, they sampled the literary categories of drama, sea voyages, and street ballads, also with the same precautions employed by Berlew. Their measure of economic development was gains in coal imports at the port of London above and beyond what would have been expected on the basis of past figures. This method of using gain estimates is a more sophisticated measure, economically speaking, than relying on gross amounts of coal imported. The results of the study are shown in Figure 11–4. The average level of need for achievement continued to be fairly stable from 1500 A.D. through 1600 A.D., then declined sharply to a low point at 1650 A.D., which was maintained through 1700 A.D., and then increased sharply from that time on to a high point in 1800 A.D. Strikingly enough, the measure of economic activity follows a very similar course, but fifty years later in time. This study improves on the previous two because it shows for the first time that level of need for achievement can go up as well as down and that economic activity will follow these vicissitudes fairly precisely.

Important as these three studies are, they are dwarfed by the magnitude of a similar study done by McClelland (1961). Taking the world as his frame of reference, he endeavored to determine the influence of need for achievement on economic development. Needing raw material available on all nations in which to search for need for achievement, McClelland decided on stories appearing in the readers used in the education of children. These stories are fictional and imaginative, sometimes even articulating with the mythology of the society. As such, they are appropriate raw material for the measurement of level of need for achievement in their composers. But they are also representative of the level of the need in the society, argues McClelland, because the society has decided to use them as instructional material for its children. Thus, the level of need for achievement obtained in children's readers can be considered modal for the society. McClelland was able, albeit with considerable difficulty, to obtain twenty-one stories from the children's readers used in each of twenty-three countries in 1925 and twenty-one stories used in each of forty countries in 1950. The twenty-three countries in the 1925 sample also appeared in the 1950 sample. All the stories were translated into English and mixed together so that scorers would have no clues as to their origin. The original form of the need-for-achievement scoring system was employed (McClelland et al., 1953), with the usual high level of interscorer agreement and unusually high internal consistency. Estimates of internal consistency based on the split-half method corrected for length of test in the 1925 and 1950 samples was .75 and .80, respectively. This is very adequate reliability for a fantasy measure. In addition, McClelland found virtually no relationship between level of need for achievement and story length.

Obtaining a measure of economic development that could be applied to so many countries at the same time was even more difficult than measuring the need for achievement. After much consideration and investigation, McClelland decided on two economic measures. The first one, offered by an economist (Clark, 1957) involves international units of income. Obviously income is the best gauge of economic development, but the difficulty is that money has different value in different societies. In an attempt to overcome this difficulty, Clark advocated translation of each currency into international units of income, each unit representing the quantity of goods exchangeable in the United States for $1.00 over the average of the decade from 1925–34. In this way, all currencies could be translated into a common scale. Although there are certain difficulties with this measure of national income, McClelland adopted it as one

FIGURE 11–4   Averaged *N* Achievement Levels in English Literature
(1550 A.D.–1800 A.D.) Compared with Rates of Gain
in Coal Imports at London Fifty Years Later.

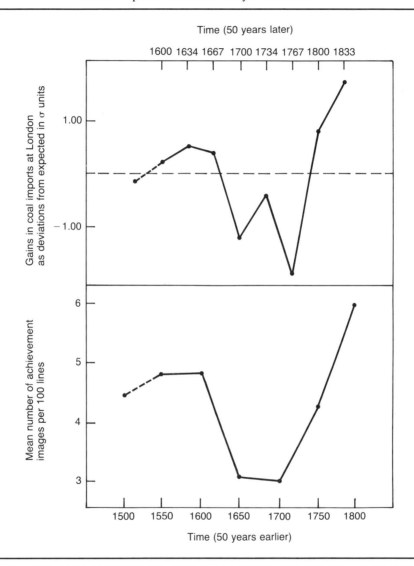

SOURCE: "Need for Achievement and English Industrial Growth" by N. M. Bradburn and D. E. Berlew, 1961, *Economic Development and Cultural Change, 10.*

of the few that permitted comparisons across many nations. Because of the difficulties, however, he decided to include another economic measure as well: the amount of electricity produced in a given country. Conveniently enough, there is a worldwide standard unit for measurement of electricity, the kilowatt-hour. In justifying the theoretical utility of the kilowatt-hour as a measure of economic growth, McClelland (1961) says:

> We have argued that economic growth, in its most unambiguous sense, is growth in the production, service, and use of the most modern technology ("hardware") known to society at a given moment in history. Certainly in our time the production and use of electricity in a country should be highly diagnostic of the level of its technology, since it is the form into which most of the energy is converted which runs our complex civilization. Though the sources of energy may be quite varied (water power, animal power, wind, coal, oil), electricity has become the *form* in which energy is most economically stored and transmitted. (pp. 85–96)

Armed with two reasonably adequate measures of economic growth, McClelland next faced the problem of determining whether or not a country made substantial gains in the period from 1925 to 1950. Some manner of determining the *rate* of growth seemed proper, for the absolute size of gains did not seem useful. The trouble with absolute size of gain is that it is highly correlated with the initial level of development. In other words, a society relatively high in kilowatt-hours per capita in 1925 would show more absolute gain from 1925 to 1950 than would a society relatively low in 1925. After considering many faulty methods of obtaining a measure of economic growth rate, McClelland settled on a procedure that involves predicting from the regression line that best fits the overall relationship between initial level and gain the amount of gain that can be considered normal. A gain exceeding or failing to meet this amount is considered extraordinary. It is unusually high or low economic gain that is to be related to the level of need for achievement.

Let us pass over much of the interesting and complex results of this huge study to the overall findings most directly relevant to our discussion of the economic effects of need for achievement. As indicated in Table 11–20, McClelland (1961, p. 92) found that the higher the need for achievement level in a country in 1925, the greater its rate of economic growth from 1925 to 1950 as measured by both international units of income ($r = .25$) and kilowatt-hours of electricity per capita ($r = .53$). Strikingly, there was virtually no relationship between need-for-achievement level in 1950 and the measures of economic growth from 1925 to 1950. These results, obtained from a truly grand-scale study, lead to the same conclusion as that suggested by the three studies described previously. The level of need for achievement in a society is a clear influence on the subsequent rate of economic development. It is equally apparent that the influence does not work the other way around.

More than any other psychological studies, those inspired by McClelland render in tangible form the contribution to the personologist's understanding

TABLE 11–20   Correlations of Reader N Achievement Scores with Deviations
from Expected Economic Gains

N Achievement Level by Year	I.U./Cap 1925–50 $N = 22$	Kw-hr./Cap 1929–50 $N = 22$	Both combined $N = 21$
1925	.25	.53, $p < .01pd$	.46, $p < .02pd$
1950	$-.10$	.03	$-.08$

pd = predicted direction.

SOURCE: *The Achieving Society* by D. C. McClelland, 1961, Princeton, NJ: Van Nostrand.

of social system phenomena. Neither economists nor other social scientists besides personologists would have seriously pursued in research the possibility that a motivational variable has a causal role in the explanation of economic growth. I assume that the far-reaching implications of McClelland's work for international economic and political policy are apparent. In terms of our more immediate concern in this chapter, it is clear that the need for achievement has motivational status and should be included in peripheral-level theorizing about personality.

McClelland's work with the need for achievement has stimulated similar studies of the needs for affiliation and power. These studies are not as extensive or convincing as those cited above. Fantasy in the form of stories composed about pictures also served as the raw material for measuring the needs for affiliation and power, the scoring systems for which were patterned after that described above for the need for achievement. The scoring or operational definition of the need for affiliation in thematic apperception involves evidence of concern in one or more of the characters over establishing, maintaining, or restoring a positive affective relationship with another person. This affective relationship is most adequately described by the word *friendship*. In contrast, the scoring definition for the need for power stresses concern with control of the means of influencing a person, expressed in such ways as pleasure in situations of dominance and reference to dominance and persuasion activities. Although the interscorer agreement associated with both scoring systems is high (generally correlations of .85 to .90), their internal consistency appears to be even lower than that for need for achievement. Reliability estimates are in the neighborhood of only .43 and .32, corrected to full test length for the needs for affiliation and power, respectively (McClelland, 1961, pp. 161, 168). But if we were willing to rely on the validity studies of the need for achievement measures as a gauge of the acceptability of its underlying concept, why not do so for these two measures as well?

Heyns, Veroff, and Atkinson (1958) conducted an experiment to determine whether the need for affiliation could be measured as higher using this scoring system in a group of people in whom the need was aroused when in a group in which no arousal took place. The thirty-one college fraternity brothers in the arousal (experimental) group performed a sociometric task before composing stories about pictures of people. The sociometric task consisted of (1) ranking a given set of traits according to the degree to which possession of the trait would make a person likable, (2) describing themselves and the other group members in terms of these traits, and (3) choosing at least three persons as the most desirable personal friends in the group. Heyns et al. felt that this task would arouse a high level of the need for affiliation. A control group of thirty-six college males was drawn from a psychology class without experiencing any arousal condition before composing stories about the same pictures used in the experimental group. The overall score for need for affiliation was considerably higher in the experimental group than in the control group, and the various subcategories of the scoring system also tended to distinguish the groups in this direction. So it can be concluded that the measure of need for affiliation operates as it should experimentally and therefore has a claim to construct validity.

There are also a few correlational studies indicating that the measure of need for affiliation has empirical validity. Atkinson and Walker (1958) indicate that people high in need for affiliation tend to be approval seeking and to be especially sensitive to faces presented along with other stimuli in a perceptual task. This task involved having subjects decide which of four simultaneous stimuli, presented tachistoscopically at speeds too short for complete perception, was a face. People high in the fantasy measure of need for affiliation picked out the face more accurately than people who were low. McClelland, Sturr, Knapp, and Wendt (1958) also report that people high in the need for affiliation generally are considered likely to succeed by their peers. That this reflects the strong interpersonal commitment these people have made is suggested by French's (1956) evidence that people high in the need for affiliation choose friends over experts to work with them on performance tasks, even though skill is important in completing the task that offers the greatest reward. In addition, Atkinson, Heyns, and Veroff (1954) found that persons scoring high in need for affiliation were considered unpopular by their peers on a sociometric rating. This result has been confirmed in similar circumstances by Groesbeck (1958) and Byrne (1961a). De Charms (1957) found that with cooperative task instructions those high in need for affiliation perform best whereas under competitive instructions they perform more poorly than those low in this need. Additional studies have been reviewed by Mehrabian and Ksionzky (1970).

There is now a variant on affiliation motivation called *need for intimacy*, introduced by McAdams and various associates. In one study (McAdams & Powers, 1981), it was shown that intimacy motivation measured in thematic apperception is expressed in the themes and activities of subjects in a psychodrama task. Specifically, those high in the need for intimacy develop drama scenarios involving mutual delight in interaction, rich reciprocal dialogue among characters, and the surrender of manipulative control. Also, subjects high in intimacy motivation are seen by others involved in the psychodrama task as being especially sincere, likable, and natural. McAdams and Constantian (1983) extended this kind of construct validation approach to demonstrate that subjects high in need for intimacy engage in more relevant social interactions than do other objects.

There is also considerable research available on the fantasy measure of need for power. In developing the scoring system, Veroff (1958) tried to perform a natural experiment that would show the scoring system to be sensitive to a situation of high power motivation. This arousal situation involved people who were candidates for election as student leaders at their college. The candidates had to petition for their candidacy and, following this declaration, were given one month for campaigning before the actual election. After two days of balloting, the candidates congregated at the polls to see what the balloting had decided. At least two hours elapsed after they had congregated before the results of the election were known. In this time period, the candidates were asked to compose stories about pictures of people in the manner of previous studies. Veroff reasoned that whatever other motives would be aroused in these candidates, the need for power certainly would be high. The control group consisted of thirty-four college males from the same school who were asked merely to compose the stories as part of a psychology course. The average need-for-power score, based on the entire scoring system, was higher in the experimental group than in the control group. In addition, most of the subcategories of the scoring system discriminated between the two groups in the same direction. There are also two other measures of need for power available (Uleman, 1965; Winter, 1971), both derived from arousal experiments; the latter claims to emphasize the positive wish for power rather than the negative fear of powerlessness.

Construct validational research on the need for power is now available. McClelland, Davis, Kalin, and Wanner (1971) report, primarily from Winter's (1971) findings, that men with a high drive for personal power tend to drink and gamble more, to own prestige items (such as power cars and credit cards), and to confess to more aggressive impulses (such as wanting to walk out on a date and to yell at someone in a traffic jam). These seem to be ways of feeling big and important. Failing them, a tendency toward alcoholism may develop, which is interpreted as being powerful in one's fantasy without the usual requirement of consistent, effective social action. If the inclination of power motivation is tempered by a sense of social responsibility, it tends to express itself more in political and social commitments and actions (McClelland, 1975). Further, Fodor and Smith (1982) found that groups having a leader low in need for power used more of the information available to them in trying to reach goals and developed more action proposals than did groups with high-power leaders. Regarding physiological reactions, Fodor (1984) reported that leaders high in need for power responded with more bodily arousal to group criticisms. Evidence tends to support the finding that the need for power leads persons to manipulate and gain control over others.

There is also a research theme concerning the joint effects of the needs for affiliation and power. McAdams, Healy, and Krause (1984) report that subjects high in affiliation motivation show much self-disclosure, listening, and social concern for friends, while those high in power motivation prefer large-group interactions and goal-oriented group activities. Further, McAdams (1982) showed that the experiences remembered by subjects high in the needs for intimacy or power were consistent with those motives. Accumulating evidence indicates that although both power- and affiliation-oriented persons are interested in social activities, the types of people, interactions, and experiences that they find rewarding are quite different.

McClelland (1961) included measures of need for affiliation and need for power in his previously mentioned large-scale study of social system phenomena. Although his primary focus concerned the relationship between need for achievement and economic growth, he felt it valuable to include these other measures for two reasons. The first was that it should be only the need for achievement and not other motives such as affiliation and power that relates to economic development. If it could be shown that affiliation and power motivations bear little on economic growth, the case for the relevance of need for achievement would be all the stronger. The second reason concerned to what, other than economic development, these other two needs would be relevant at the social system level. In the process of obtaining information concerning economic development, much other social system information was obtained as a matter of course and put to use in assessing the empirical value of the other motive measures.

The results concerning need for affiliation indicate that it bears a complex relationship to population growth, a matter that should not be too surprising. The need for affiliation is positively related to birthrate in 1950 ($r = +.41$) and negatively related to birthrate in 1925 ($r = -.41$). But why should high need for affiliation have led to having more children in 1950 and fewer children in 1925? McClelland's reasoning is complex and will only be summarized here.

Generally speaking, there seems to be evidence that prior to the introduction of large-scale public health measures, the birthrate was largely controlled by the death rate. But although the correlation between birthrate and death rate was high prior to 1950, by that time it had been significantly reduced by modern public health measures. Perhaps the meaning of the positive relationship between need for affiliation and birthrate in 1950 is that people determine how many children to have by how many they want, without fear that many will die. But the negative relationship between need for affiliation and birthrate in 1925 is more difficult to understand. It will help to know that even though there is a general positive relationship between birthrate and death rate in 1925, there turns out to be a negative relationship between need for affiliation and death rate at that time. This negative relationship does not appear for 1950. All these data taken together suggest that in the pre–public health era, how many children of those born would survive depended more on how much care and attention their parents gave them than is true in contemporary times. McClelland (1961) concludes that in 1925:

> The parents with higher need for affiliation care more for their children, fewer of them die, and there is therefore less need for "excess" children to take the

place of those who die off. In other words, those countries with a high [need for] affiliation have a lower infant mortality rate, and a lower birth rate. (p. 163)

Although it can hardly be claimed that this indirect but plausible and intriguing chain of reasoning really substantiates the validity of the need for affiliation measure, further research seems worthwhile.

The final matter of relevance from McClelland's study concerns both the need for affiliation and the need for power. It turns out (McClelland, 1961, p. 168) that a combination of high need for power and low need for affiliation is very closely associated with a nation's tendency to resort to totalitarian methods of governing its people. Strikingly enough, every one of the notorious police states (e.g., Germany, Japan, Spain, Russia, Argentina, Portugal, Republic of South Africa) in the sample showed this particular pattern of the two motives! I take this to mean that in countries whose residents are personally motivated to dominate others and avoid warm relationships with them, political forms will tend in the direction of denial of equality and individual freedom.

McClelland (1971) has prepared an especially useful discussion of the intertwining of needs for affiliation, achievement, and power in both personal and socially relevant behaviors. Notable among studies on such matters is that of LeVine (1966), in which the percentage of achievement dreams in the Yoruba and other tribes in northern Nigeria is used as a basis for understanding the tribes' social patterns and interrelationships. Also, Donley and Winter (1965) have coded the inaugural addresses of American presidents from Theodore Roosevelt to Richard Nixon for the needs for achievement and power. The scores seem surprisingly accurate in predicting administrative decisions of these men while in office. These results are schematically presented in Table 11–21.

What do these intriguing findings tell us concerning peripheral level theorizing? Despite their poor reliabilities, the measures of need for affiliation and need for power act empirically in a theoretically sound manner in relating to both individual and social system phenomena. It would appear that peripheral-level theorizing ought to include these two needs along with need for achievement.

This conclusion is further strengthened by an important book (Winter, 1973) on the need for power. In this book, Winter amassed an enormous amount of empirical information concerning how this need, as measured in fantasy, influences personal and social action. It is impossible to recount these vast findings here, so an example or two will have to suffice.

Following from the proposition that persons high in need for power want to control the existing social system whereas those high in need for achievement want to change it, Winter and his associates predicted that among student activists members of the Black Power Movement would he high in n power but members of the New Left Movement would be high in n achievement. This prediction was confirmed with various student samples. These results are seen as consistent with those concerning the average level of n power among per-

TABLE 11–21   Motive Characteristics of American Presidents and Associated Trends in Office

President	High n Achievement	High n Power	Associated Trends in Office
T. Roosevelt	6.2	8.3	Strong and active presidents,
F. Roosevelt	5.2	6.3	attempting to accomplish
Truman	4.1	7.3	much, quite willing to use po-
Kennedy	6.8	8.3	litical influence and expand
Johnson	7.5	6.8	government to gain ends.
	Low n *Achievement*	*High* n *Power*	
Wilson	3.0	5.4	Stubborn desire to impose his will, even at cost of accomplishments [George & George, 1956]
	High n *Achievement*	*Low* n *Power*	
Hoover	4.0	3.0	Stress on accomplishing more
Nixon	8.5	5.1	at less cost, smaller government involvement, willing to sacrifice political influence for goals of economy and efficiency
	Low n *Achievement*	*Low* n *Power*	
Taft	.9	2.0	Relatively inactive, not trying
Harding	2.3	3.4	to achieve major accomplish-
Coolidge	1.7	3.1	ments or use the power poten-
Eisenhower	2.8	4.1	tial office of the president

SOURCE: Adapted from "Measuring the Motives of Public Officials at a Distance: An Explanatory Study of American Presidents" by R. E. Donley and D. G. Winter, 1965, *Behavioral Science, 3.*

sons in various occupations. The highest average was in business management, followed by teaching, psychotherapy, and the religious vocation. Although these findings would not always be expected by the assumptions it is common to make, they are consistent with McClelland's peripheral theorizing. Most recently, McClelland (1978) has been involved in attempts to alter motivation levels in groups of persons in various underdeveloped countries. Important for such training efforts is an understanding of how motives develop during early life. McClelland and Pilon (1983) found that parents of children who went on to have high need for achievement used definite feeding schedules and severe toilet training approaches, whereas those whose children developed high need for power were permissive regarding sexual and aggressive activities.

Overall, there is no more striking evidence of the empirical fruitfulness of postulated peripheral characteristics than that offered by McClelland and his associates. But the great bulk of characteristics designated in the peripheral theorizing have not been touched. Further, the numerous characteristics are not organized into a few types that could be manageably studied empirically. The soundest conclusion is that while there is support for some of the theory, most of it has not been tested.

Maddi's Position

Most of the research directly relevant to Maddi's peripheral theorizing has concentrated on the need for variety and the traits of activeness-passiveness and internal-external orientation. In this research, Maddi and his associates followed McClelland in utilizing thematic apperception as the raw material for measurement. They did this because the need for variety is considered a motive, and they were swayed by McClelland's arguments concerning the proper measurement of such entities. In addition, they conceptualized different forms of the need for variety according to the trait characteristics that occur with it. Because of this, they consider it potentially valuable to have a rich, multifaceted source of information such as fantasy. They turned to the analysis of thematic apperception with the idea that the need for variety would take *active-internal, active-external, passive-internal,* and *passive-external* forms. As you will recall from Chapter 9, these forms of the need for variety actually constitute four of the personality types supposedly characterized by high activation requirements.

Attempts to devise measures of these four motivational types evolved over a number of studies. In the first of these, Maddi, Charlens, Maddi, and Smith (1962) selected the two types that would have the most obvious kind of expression in thematic apperception. Clearly a person could compose stories about pictures of people that imbued them with a sense of boredom and dissatisfaction with the status quo, coupled with interest in the possibility that something more unusual might happen. But it would be equally possible for persons to simply compose stories that are themselves novel and unusual, thereby producing their own variety. Scrutiny of some sample stories inclined Maddi et al. to the belief that the former orientation toward novelty is passive and external and the latter active and internal.

So Maddi et al. defined two scoring systems to be studied for construct validity. The scoring system for the passive-external form of the need for variety was patterned after those pioneered by McClelland. Called *desire for novelty,* it refers to the extent to which stories reflect dissatisfaction with the status quo because of its boring nature and an appreciation of externally caused, novel occurrences. The scoring system has the same three components as that for the need for achievement and can be used by different scorers with a high level of agreement—correlations range from about .80 to about .90 (Maddi & Andrews, 1966; Maddi & Berne, 1964; Maddi et al., 1962; Maddi, Propst, & Feldinger, 1965). Estimates of internal consistency range from .31 to .41 (Maddi & Andrews, 1966; Maddi et al., 1965), and an estimate of stability is .47 (Maddi & Andrews, 1966). If anything, these reliability results are better than those reported for the need-for-achievement measure.

Maddi et al. (1962) also developed a scoring system for the active-internal form of the need for variety. Called *novelty of productions,* the scoring system concerns how unusual or novel are the stories themselves, regardless of how much goal-directed striving toward novelty is attributed to characters. The scoring system includes three aspects each of character treatment and plot treatment. The categories of plot treatment are *unusual event, unusual interpretation* (scored when a story is strange, humorous, or ironic), and *unexpected ending* (scored when the end of a story violates a definite expectation built up by the preceding narrative). The categories of character treatment are *unusual role designation* for characters actually pictured in the stories (such designations as "spy" and "diplomat"), *unusual role designation* for characters the subject introduces into the story, and *uncommon naming.* That the agreement in the use of this scoring system is high is shown by estimates of interscorer reliability ranging from .84 to .92 (Maddi & Andrews, 1966; Maddi et al., 1962; Maddi et al, 1965). Also high for fantasy measures are estimates of internal consistency of the scoring system, which have ranged from .63 to .80 (Maddi & Andrews, 1966; Maddi et al., 1965). The sole estimate of stability is adequate—.65 (Maddi & Andrews, 1966). It seems as if the tendency to infuse fantasy with a desire for novelty and the tendency to fantasize in unusual ways are distinct and homogeneous entities in people.

Maddi et al. (1962) performed an experiment to see whether the scoring systems would be sensitive to conditions that should arouse the need for variety. People in the aroused (experimental) group were made to be bored by being required to listen to a tedious recording of the physical characteristics of a town delivered in monotonous tones and with much repetition. Following this experience, the people composed stories about four pictures of people in the standard manner. There were two control groups. In one, the period of time prior to composing stories was taken up by whatever the people chose to do that could be accomplished in a classroom setting. In the other, a novel, unusual, and somewhat humorous recording was played prior to the story composition task. Maddi et al. reasoned that in neither control group should there have been much arousal of the need for variety. The experimental treatment was expected to arouse not only the need for variety but the trait of passivity. The tendency to be passive should have been strong, because the subjects were asked to give their full attention to the recording. They could comply with these instructions only by relinquishing the many active procedures (e.g., tapping feet, daydreaming, walking out) whereby people avoid monotonous situations. Thus, people in the experimental group should have shown on the thematic apperception task an increase in passive expressions and a decrease in active expressions of the need for variety. The results of this experiment conformed to expectation: The aroused group showed a higher level of desire for novelty and a lower level of novelty of productions than did either control group. In addition, the control groups did not differ from each other in desire for novelty or novelty of productions. In the control groups, desire for novelty and novelty of productions were negatively correlated, and this relationship was even stronger in the aroused group. Maddi et al. concluded that their arousal condition had the joint effects of arousing the need for variety and stimulating the trait of passivity.

Although it certainly is reasonable to consider novelty of productions and desire for novelty as being active and passive measures, respectively, of the need for variety, there is at least one major alternative view that questions whether novelty of productions is motivational at all. Certainly this measure does not include the obviously goal-directed fantasy characteristic of other motive measures. Perhaps novelty of productions is a stylistic expression of a flexible, original, creative turn of mind. Further, perhaps desire for novelty is the only real measure of the need for variety. If it is also true that vigorous expression of flexibility and originality require freedom from strong motivational states, the negative relationship between desire for novelty and novelty of productions and the effects on each of the experimental manipulation would be very understandable: When the need for variety, or any motive, is strong, flexibility and creativity will be low.

The alternative explanation to that of Maddi et al. is reminiscent of White's contention that the expression of effectance motivation in exploration of the world occurs only when the major survival needs have been satisfied. It also recalls Harlow's (1953) demonstration that the hunger drive interferes with puzzle solution in the monkey. Maddi and Berne (1964) did a correlational study to determine which of the two interpretations of the desire for novelty and novelty of productions measures was more adequate. From the thematic apperception tests of a group of people, they obtained scores not on only these two measures but on the needs for achievement, affiliation, and power. They reasoned that if the alternative explanation considered above were accurate, there would be a negative correlation between novelty of productions and each of the motive measures, whereas if the interpretation of Maddi et al. were accurate, there would be only the negative correlation between novelty of productions and desire for novelty. The latter result was obtained, clearly supporting the position that novelty of productions and desire for novelty are alternative forms of the need for variety.

The next step for Maddi and his associates was a series of correlational studies (Maddi, 1968; Maddi & Andrews, 1966; Maddi et al., 1965) aimed at determining the construct validity of the two posited measures of need for variety. Indeed, at this point a third measure was devised. Also involving analysis of thematic apperception, this measure, called *curiosity*, reflects the degree to which stories are infused with the asking of questions and the posing of problems with concomitant interest in obtaining additional, new information with which to resolve the perplexities. On rational grounds, it was presumed that this measure is an active expression of the need for variety, as is novelty of productions, but differs from the latter in that is reflects an external rather than internal trait. In other words, in the active pursuit of variety, novelty of productions involves favoring internal sources of stimulation whereas curiosity involves favoring external sources. The curiosity measure, like the other two, can be used with adequate agreement by different scorers (.83 to .90) and has sufficient reliability to justify further consideration (internal consistency = .50 to .68; stability = .39).

The correlational studies support the claim of the novelty of productions and desire for novelty measures to construct validity but suggest an interpretation of the curiosity measure different from that postulated above. Some of the findings of these studies are presented in Table 11–22. Working down the first column, you can see that the higher persons are in novelty of productions,

TABLE 11–22   Selected Correlates of Novelty of Productions, Curiosity, and Desire for Novelty

	Fantasy Variables			
	Novelty of Productions	*Curiosity*	*Desire for Novelty*	*Number of Ss*
Performance variables				
Time spent exploring a room	$-.42^†$	$.38^†$	.11	62
Introspective productivity	$.27^*$	.06	$-.07$	62
Complexity of line-drawing completions	$.39^†$	$-.05$	$-.20$	62
Original uses for common objects	$.42^†$	$-.05$	$-.22$	42
Self-description variables				
n change	$.31^*$	$-.26$	$.44^*$	42
n order	$-.27$	$.42^†$	.27	42
Conjunctivity-disjunctivity	$-.32^*$	$.36^*$	.11	42
Impulsivity	.21	$-.10$	$-.34^*$	42
Rigidity factor	$-.38^*$	$.38^*$	.20	42
n understanding	$-.02$	.25	$-.41^†$	42
Reflectiveness	$.33^*$	$-.02$	$-.36^*$	42
Exteroception	$-.48^†$	.27	.18	42
n sentience	.13	$-.01$	$-.43^†$	42
Energy	.12	$-.03$	$-.50^†$	42

*Significant at .05 level.
†Significant at .01 level.

SOURCE: Adapted from "Three Expressions of the Need for Variety" by S. R. Maddi, B. Propst, and I. Feldinger, 1965, *Journal of Personality, 33*; "The Need for Variety in Fantasy and Self-Description" by S. R. Maddi and S. Andrews, *Journal of Personality, 34*; and "The Seeking and Avoiding of Variety" by S.R. Maddi, 1968, unpublished manuscript, Chicago.

the less they will explore the objects in a room with which they are unfamiliar but the more they will examine their internal environment through introspection. A high degree of novelty of productions also predisposes people to complete fragmentary line drawings in a complex way and to be original in thinking up uses for common objects. The active, internal search for novelty indicated in these performance characteristics is also shown in self-description. People high in novelty of productions describe themselves as being interested in change, disjunctive thinking, and contemplative activities. In complementary fashion, they are uninterested in order, in appearing rigid, or in the practical external world of affairs (exteroception). The performance correlates of the fantasy measure of novelty of productions suggest that it reflects behavior indicative of striving toward variety; its self-descriptive correlates clarify that variety is indeed a personal goal.

In contrast, the desire-for-novelty measure has shown no performance correlates to date, a fact that would cause alarm concerning its empirical validity were it not for the reasonable argument that something measuring passivity should not, after all, reflect such active tendencies as performance, which actually create novelty. People high in desire for novelty should appreciate novelty when they encounter it but not be active creators of it themselves. They are consumers rather than producers of novelty. Indeed, as shown in the third column of Table 11–22, people high in desire for novelty describe themselves as interested in change and offer insight into their passivity by also describing themselves as without initiative, interest in understanding, contemplativeness, sentience, energy, or anything else that might aid in pursuit of novelty. You may wonder what good is motivation that does not provide a format for action. But that is another question, the answer to which may lead to the study of psychopathology. For the moment, it can be safely concluded that there is empirical support for viewing desire for novelty as a passive form of the need for variety.

The original conceptualization of the fantasy measure of curiosity has not received empirical support. It is true that people high in curiosity actively explore the objects in an unfamiliar room. But that this finding should not be construed as indicating an active, external form of the need for variety is disclosed by the self-descriptions of people high in curiosity. As you can see in the second column of Table 11–22, these descriptions indicate an interest in order, conjunctivity of thought, and rigidity. Maddi and his associates seem to have inadvertently developed a measure of the active tendency to fear variety rather than revel in it! Once again we are alerted to the wisdom of McClelland's distinction between approach and avoidance versions of each of the needs. People with fantasy high in curiosity seem to be concerned with variety because it is a threat to them and wish to avoid the threat by ordering their experience so as to minimize or at least dampen novelty and change.

Especially because the novelty-of-productions and curiosity measures deviate from the usual format stressing obviously goal-directed fantasy, Maddi and his associates planned a further demonstration of the motivational nature of these measures. A definite implication of the motivation construct is that you can manipulate persons to learn something if it leads to satisfaction of motivation. The stronger the motive, the more you can manipulate them to learn. Thus, if novelty of productions and desire for novelty are really approach versions of the need for variety, people high in one or the other ought to learn something when rewarded by novelty more thoroughly than people low on these measures. Further, if curiosity really measures an avoidance version of the need for variety, people high in it ought to learn less well when rewarded by novelty than people low on that measure.

Feldinger and Maddi (1968) did an experiment to test these predictions. First they obtained thematic apperception stories from a large group of people and, by applying the scoring systems, were able to isolate groups high and low on each of the three measures. All groups were given the learning task, which consisted of viewing cards presented one at a time. Each card contained two pairs of lines, one pair parallel and the other unparallel but symmetrical. The subjects were asked to choose one pair of lines from each card. For half the people in each group, choosing parallel lines led to viewing a line drawing of a usual object. But when they chose the nonparallel lines, they viewed a line drawing showing an unusual version of the usual object. The only difference in procedure for the people in the other half of each group was that choice of the nonparallel lines led to seeing the usual object whereas choice of the parallel lines was associated with the unusual object. There were forty-five cards with parallel and nonparallel lines, and the measure of learning employed was the number of choices leading to viewing unusual or novel objects. For novelty of productions, the high group showed more choices that led to viewing novel objects than did the low group. There was a similar trend in the high- and low-desire-for-novelty groups. The people high in curiosity made fewer choices leading to novelty than did the group low in curiosity. These results, taken along with those of the correlational studies reviewed above, are thoroughly consistent with the consideration of novelty of productions and desire for novelty or measures of approach versions of the need for variety and of curiosity as an avoidance version.

The combination of high need for variety with active-internal or passive-external traits defines two of the high-activation types postulated by Maddi. Also, the combination of high fear of variety with active-external traits constitutes one of his low-activation types. Strictly speaking, in assessing the position's construct validity it would be important to determine whether the activation requirements of people high in novelty of productions, desire for novelty, or curiosity conform to the theoretical expectations.

A study by Thayer (1967) purports to have solved the problem of simple measurement of customary level of activation. He devised the Activation-Deactivation Adjective Check List, composed of a number of adjectives relevant to activation that subjects endorse in the manner most descriptive of them. The self-descriptions of 221 male and female college students were factor analyzed, with four of the resulting factors clearly indicating activation. Thayer listed the factors and the adjectives loading highest on each as follows: *general activation* (lively, active, full of pep, energetic, peppy, vigorous, activated); *high activation* (clutched up, jittery, stirred up, fearful, intense); *general deactivation* (at rest, still, leisurely, quiescent, quiet, calm, placid); *deactivation sleep* (sleepy, tired, drowsy). According to Thayer, these factors roughly constitute four points on a hypothetical activation continuum running from sleep to anxious tension. Although complete reliability information is unavailable, estimates of stability were obtained for some of the adjectives and ranged from .57 to .87, with a median of .75.

Thayer attempted two kinds of validation of these factors as points on an activation continuum. The first involves other self-descriptions and the second physiological recordings of autonomic nervous system activity. One of the validation attempts involving self-description was based on the conceptualization of the characteristic curve of activation as being low on awaking, rising to a peak near the middle of the day, and falling thereafter until sleep occurs (see Chapter 5). In one study (Thayer, 1967), subjects filled out the adjective checklist in the middle of the day and again in the evening. As expected, general-activation and high-activation scores went down, while general-deactivation and deactivation-sleep scores went up from one testing to the next. In a similar study (Thayer, 1967), subjects took the checklist four times, at roughly 9:00 A.M., 12:30 A.M., 5:00 P.M., and 11:00 P.M. As shown in Figure 11–5, general-activation and high-activation scores went from low to high to low again, while general-deactivation and deactivation-sleep scores did just the opposite. These findings provide striking evidence that the adjective checklist indeed measures characteristic level of activation and that the four factors do represent points on a continuum of characteristic activation. Further support for this conclusion is found in studies involving physiological correlates of the adjective checklist. Thayer (1967) obtained recordings of heart rate and degree of sweating (skin conductance, as you may recall from Chapter 6) for a small number of undergraduates who had also filled out the adjective checklist. The four activation factors were correlated with heart rate and sweating measures taken singly and also combined into a composite indicator of autonomic activity. In the three separate studies he reported, the composite indicator of autonomic activity correlated with the four activation factors in such fashion as to indicate that the factors represent points on a continuum of activation. The heart rate and sweating measures, taken singly, correlated less strongly and dependably with the activation factors but yielded no information contradictory to that already presented. All in all, Thayer's work seems to have demonstrated the reasonableness of theorizing about a customary level of activation and provides the opportunity to further evaluate the construct validity of Maddi's peripheral theorizing by determining whether the two approach and avoidance orientations to variety described earlier really do have the expected activation characteristics.

Costa (1970) attempted such a demonstration in the course of a large-scale investigation of the interrelationships among measures of activation, need for variety, originality, and other cognitive abilities. He administered many tests

FIGURE 11–5   Mean Scores of Four AD-ACL Factors at Four Diurnal Periods

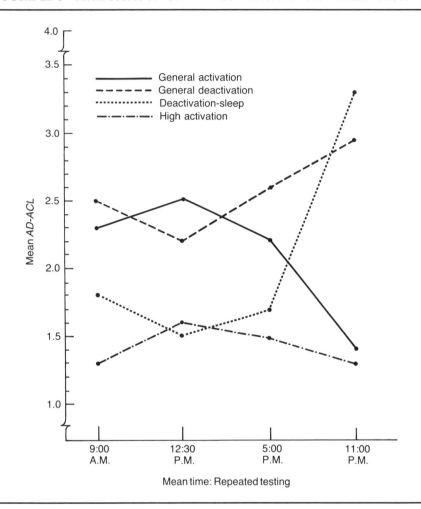

SOURCE: Thayer, R. E. Measurement of Activation through Self-Report. *Psychological Reports*, 1967, 20, 663-678 (Monogr. Suppl. 1-V26). Fig. 1.

to a group of sixty male and female undergraduates and subjected the data to an elaborate procedure of analysis (not unlike factor analysis) permitting the test of hypotheses concerning interrelationships. His results indicated little support for Maddi's position in that customary and actual levels of activation (measured by Thayer's adjective checklist) did not relate to thematic and questionnaire measures of personality types expressive of novelty orientation. But neither the novelty nor the cognitive measures intercorrelated among themselves in the same way as in previous studies, raising the question of whether the testing situation or subjects somehow contributed to the negative findings.

In another study, Maddi, Hoover, and Kobasa (1982) seem to have found some supporting evidence for the notion that not only the customary level of activation but whether the person is internally or externally oriented must be taken into account in understanding behavior. Customary level of activation was measured by means of Thayer's checklist and subjects were also given Eysenck's introversion-extroversion scale. In addition, subjects composed stories to ambiguous pictures, which were then scored for richness of imagination. Subjects also waited alone in an unfamiliar room sometime during their participation, and their activities were observed and scored for evidence of exploratory behavior. It was hypothesized that external exploration (of the room) would be engaged in most by persons with a combination of high customary activation and an external orientation (extroversion), whereas internal exploration (richness of imagination) would be done most by persons with a combination of high customary activation and an internal orientation (introversion). That the results supported this expectation suggests the value of further empirical efforts to test activation theorizing.

Perusing the general implications of this position, Wolters (1976) interpretively reviewed much research in quest of a motivational component for creativity. He concluded that it is an active-internal form of the need for variety that predisposes toward creative functioning.

Further evidence of the value of assuming that there is a characteristic level of activation with implications for under-and overactivation is suggested by Zuckerman, Persky, Miller, and Levin (1969). They measured anxiety and activation (adrenocortically) and manipulated stimulation. Their twenty-two male subjects were tested first on two control (normal) days and then on one understimulation day and one overstimulation day. Understimulation consisted of confinement in darkness and silence; overstimulation consisted of an eight-hour, multichannel, multimedia program. The overstimulation condition resulted in greater autonomic and adrenocortical activity than the understimulation condition. In contrast, the understimulation condition produced greater increases in anxiety, depression, and feelings of unreality. With both under- and overstimulation, subjects showed greater activation adrenocortically than they had on the control (normal) days. To some degree, under- and overstimulation seem to have comparable effects on the body. The study by Carrol, Zuckerman, and Vogel (1982) report similar findings. In an intriguing approach, Lesnik-Oberstein and Cohen (1984) report a similar pattern of sensation seeking in couples.

There are by now several other measures of variety seeking that involve questionnaire technique rather than fantasy (e.g., Garlington & Shimota, 1964; Zuckerman, Kolin, Price, & Zoob, 1964). These are less relevant to Maddi's position and, hence, will not be discussed at length here. In an attempt to provide normative data on three of these questionnaire measures, McCarroll,

Mitchell, Carpenter, and Anderson (1967) found them to overlap considerably.

Mehrabian and Russell (1973) regard the various questionnaires mentioned above as being sufficiently in agreement concerning underlying assumptions about activation level and sufficiently overlapping without being comprehensive to warrant an attempt to derive from them one overall measure. Through a careful process of excluding from this large pool items that were either unrelated to the others or tainted with the tendency to respond in socially desirable fashion, the investigators devised a final questionnaire of forty items. This measure of arousal-seeking tendency has internal consistency of .87 and stability of .88 with a seven-week interval between testings. Information concerning construct validity shows that the test correlates negatively with anxiety and neuroticism measures and positively with extroversion, affiliation, and preference for arousing situations. It is unclear at this time whether this test measures activation per se or a conglomerate of novelty and intensity preferences, though subsequent empirical work should provide further clarification.

CONCLUDING REMARKS

We have reached the end of our empirical analysis. The time has come to integrate the conclusions reached in this chapter with those in Chapter 6 on the empirical validity of core considerations. It must be admitted that the studies performed under the aegis of the various theories are of limited value in the empirical analysis of peripheral considerations. There is danger of deciding that a theory is empirically sound for no better reason than that it is championed by personologists who are especially energetic and capable concerning empirical inquiry. At most, we should use the results of the essentially partisan research just reviewed to supplement the other empirical conclusions reached in this chapter and in Chapter 6.

Recall that in Chapter 6 we found considerable empirical support for both versions of the fulfillment model and the activation version of the consistency model. There is nothing in this chapter to change that view. Both the factor analytic studies presented earlier and the more partisan studies that followed suggest empirical support for the peripheral theorizing associated with these models. It is true that there is little research associated with some of the fulfillment theories, but this should not be held against them, as it seems that little research effort has been mounted. Further, the research listed under each theory has been arbitrary to some extent. Little research has been done in the personality field that is so specific to a particular theory that it is relevant to that theory alone. More frequently than not, theories near to the one under consideration in the sense of belonging to the same class are also supported by the findings.

From the analysis of core considerations presented in Chapter 6, it emerged that the only little-supported models are the pure psychosocial version of the conflict model and the pure cognitive dissonance version of the consistency model. Although the review of factor analytic studies conducted earlier in this chapter seems to support conflict as well as fulfillment models, it should be kept in mind that this may be due in part to the studies' generality and ambiguity. In addition, the partisan studies show spotty but intriguing support for Freudian peripheral theorizing. While the evidence in this chapter is not persuasive enough to change the conclusions drawn in Chapter 6, there is certainly cause for wishing that more frankly comparative analytic research would be done.

One vexing problem (to which I hope you are now alert) in a field dominated by research that concerns only small, isolated corners of particular theories is that most theories seem to have reasonable empirical support even though they generate a disquieting suspicion that they have not been tested at all. There is great need for personology research that stems from a comparative analytic orientation. Such research, whether on a specific issue or more comprehensive, will yield evidence of the relative fruitfulness of the theories involved. The problem of lack of comparative orientation is further aggravated when the research does not even follow in any precise way from any particular personality theory. Because this is true of much of the research reviewed in the latter part of this chapter, it has been difficult to reach definite conclusions concerning whether the theories are really supported empirically. This is not to say that the research is uninteresting or even methodologically unrigorous. But even had the research considered here as relevant to single theories been more partisan, as long as it was precise in its relevance to its personality theory, definite conclusions might have been drawn. And think of what might have been accomplished with more comparative analytic studies!

CHAPTER 12

The Behavioristic Alternative

From the early days of this century to modern times, the movement known as *behaviorism* has exerted an enormous influence on psychology. But what behaviorism actually entails has been less apparent. Even a highly regarded behaviorist, Berlyne (1968), has been provoked to say,

> It is extremely difficult to say exactly what "behavior theory" is and to delineate its boundaries. Is it a branch of psychology, a school of psychology, a theoretical position, a methodological approach? It is certainly not quite any of these, and yet it is all of them to some extent. What is the relation of behavior theory to the rest of psychology? All sorts of answers to these questions have been put forward at one time or another. There are those who have felt that behavior theory is destined to assimilate more and more of psychology as time goes on, so that everything in psychology will eventually be marked with its stamp, and the sooner the better. Others, of course, have felt that behavior theory is a transitory aberration whose pernicious influence will soon be seen for what it is and annihilated. Some have maintained that all psychologists are behavior theorists, but that some realize it and some do not; the implication is that those who are aware of what they are doing will do it better.

When ranking behaviorists themselves make such statements, behaviorism could justifiably be excluded from consideration here on the grounds that its form and content are not yet sufficiently clear. But such an exclusion would be unfortunate, as behaviorism, for all the confusion over what it really is, has penetrated every fiber of psychology today.

Actually, for all the ambiguity about the boundaries of behaviorism, its main thrust has been clear all along and has not changed. This thrust is *learning*—the increase or decrease in frequency of overt, easily discernible movements (called *responses*), when followed by stimuli that act as positive or negative reinforcers. Berlyne (1968) is quite definite about this emphasis of behaviorism on learning:

> The term "behavior theory" has been used fairly interchangeably with the term "learning theory." "Learning theory" seems to have come into use rather earlier, and some writers, notably Mowrer, have favored it. Hull and Spence have preferred to speak of "behavior theory." There have been some not very happy attempts to distinguish between the theory of learning and "behavior theory"

534

as the theory of performance, but, although, according to most theories, there are differences between the principles that determine the acquisition of habit-strength and those that determine the probability and vigor of responding, it is certainly impracticable to separate the two completely, let alone to assign them to two distinct bodies of theory. The term "behavior theory" is perhaps to be preferred, on the grounds that "learning theory" has come to encompass much more than a statement of the principles that govern learning. (p. 629)

It is only to be expected that a theory of learning would have ramifications into many areas of psychology. What does need careful scrutiny is the nature and extent of the impact of behaviorism on these areas. In the personality area, we should identify what is of relevance and determine its similarities and differences to the other theories in this book. In this regard, we should consider whether behaviorism represents a frank alternative to personality theory as an explanation of behavior.

As I have said many times, a personality theory must include statements about a core, a periphery, and a developmental process linking the two. The core statement concerns assumptions about what is unchangeable in human nature; the peripheral statement concerns the lifestyles that people can acquire; and the developmental statement shows how each peripheral style derives from the interaction of the core with the environment. As the developmental statement heavily involves learning, behaviorism should be important in this aspect of personality theorizing. This is all the more so because many personality theorists merely assume some process of learning that is capable of linking the core with the periphery and focus all their attention on those. Actually, it is hardly inaccurate to say that behaviorism does just the opposite, namely, focus on the process of learning with little emphasis on core and peripheral considerations. Behaviorists are loath to make pronouncements about unchangeable human nature and are almost equally unwilling to elaborate on lifestyles. For the behaviorist, to consider inherent human nature is to stray too far from tangible observations, and to assume styles is to overemphasize predispositions to behave that are not a function of the stimulus characteristics of situations.

I find that behaviorism is less concerned with the personality domain than with other areas of psychology. Berlyne (1968, p. 638) seems to agree when he says, "It can hardly be overlooked that problems of personality have figured much less prominently in the writings of the behavior theorists than in psychological literature as a whole." He does lay some responsibility for this on ambiguity as to what personality is and is not, but he recognizes that the primary factor is the differing emphases of behaviorism and personology. Whatever else it considers, personology must be concerned with individual differences. It studies both when individuals act differently under the same stimulus conditions and act similarly under several different stimulus conditions. Behaviorism understandably has little to say about such individual differences, because it has sought general laws stating invariant relationships between stimuli and responses (Berlyne, 1968). If the responses of two individuals differ, the most likely explanation, according to behaviorists, is that the stimuli that elicited or reinforced the responses also differed. And if an individual responds the same way twice, the most likely reason is that the stimulus situation also was the same. But in order to get a more differentiated view of behaviorism as it relates to personality, it will be necessary to go into greater detail.

MODERATE BEHAVIORISM

In understanding the behaviorist movement, one should recognize that it has not been wholly uniform. The moderate, as opposed to the radical, form of the position has been fashioned by psychologists such as Clark Hull (1943) and Kenneth Spence (1948). As you will see, moderate behaviorism is more willing to consider organismic factors (e.g., biological needs, habits) than is radical behaviorism. Hull's work at Yale University stimulated such similarly inclined associates as Dollard and Miller (1950). At Iowa State University, Spence's colleagues included Farber (1948) and Taylor (1953). These psychologists, along with many others (e.g., Berlyne, 1960; Brown, 1961) have continued over the years to produce a corpus of research and theorizing that represents a reasonably distinct form of behaviorism. It derives, in essence, from the pioneering work of Ivan P. Pavlov (1927).

In explaining learning, moderate behaviorism has focused on stimulus-response, or S-R, bonds. An S-R *bond* is formed when a specific stimulus regularly elicits a particular response from the organism. With an occasional exception, moderate behaviorists have contended that the strength of an S-R bond is increased when the occurrence of the response in question is followed by a reward and decreased when followed by punishment. In other words, the stimulus comes to elicit the response dependably because the response obtains for the organism something of positive value. In order to pinpoint just what this positive value is, moderate behaviorists have theorized about the nature of organisms. They have assumed the existence of drives, such as hunger, thirst, and sex, which have the status of biological imperatives in that they support physical survival. So, if an organism is thirsty, it can be taught to emit a particular response in the presence of a stimulus if response is regularly followed with something to drink. The organism will learn that the stimulus is a reliable sign that it can reduce its drive if it performs in a particular fashion.

Although the main thrust of moderate behaviorism clearly is on learning, the various assumptions mentioned above can be considered as framing a position on the core and periphery of personality. The core tendency is the *attempt to reduce the tension of biological drives.* The drives having received most emphasis are *hunger, thirst, sex, activity, curiosity,* and *pain.* Since increments in each of these drives are experienced bodily as tension, it is possible to speak of *general drive,* or the total amount of tension across all the aroused drives at any given time. The core characteristics are the appropriate goals, or *rewards,* corresponding to the various drives. Food is the reward for the hunger drive and the removal of food the punishment. The reward for thirst is liquid; for sex, sexual experience; and for activity, exercise. In order to discern the presumed reward for the curiosity drive, remember that all drives are uncomfortable tension states that must be reduced. Thus, the tension of curiosity (or uncertainty) is reduced by *information* (Berlyne, 1960). The pain drive is ambiguous. In one sense, it is nothing more than another way of stating the core tendency of tension reduction. In another, it is associated with the reward of *safety.* In any event, as in the example concerning removal of food, the opposite of the reward in the case of each drive is the punishment. All of the above drives are inherent and unlearned. For this reason, moderate behaviorists call them *primary drives* and their corresponding goals *primary rewards.*

Moderate behaviorism also has something to say about the periphery of personality. After all, a strong S-R bond, or *habit* (Dollard & Miller, 1950), is in our terminology a concrete peripheral characteristic. The habit is learned on the basis of expression of the core tendency in the stimulus environment and is suited to the discussion of individual differences. Certainly two persons encountering the same stimulus conditions and response contingencies for reward or punishment will learn identical habits. But if the learning history of two persons is different, their habits will differ even though their core drives are the same. Once learned, habits persist for some time (this is called *resistance to extinction*) even if reward no longer follows the emission of the response. A male who had learned to be intimidating toward females because doing so frequently led to their having sexual intercourse with him would continue in his ways, at least for a while, even if gentility eventually became more valued. This is one way in which moderate behaviorism could recognize that a person's behavior sometimes imposes itself on the environment rather than being controlled by it. But if the reward for responding in a particular way continues to be absent, the habit eventually will be extinguished. The number of trials to extinction of a no longer rewarded habit is one measure of its strength.

From its inception, behaviorism was appealing largely because it promised a simple, clear understanding of learning. The stimuli serving as signals for responses and the rewards or punishments contingent on the responses were all observable, concrete aspects of the external environment. Indeed, the aspect of behavior chosen for study—the response—was a movement rather than a thought or feeling and, therefore, also clear and observable directly. It is true that influential behaviorists, such as Hull, recognized that such simple depictions of the learning process as the S-R bond should take into account certain complications concerning individual differences. Hull believed that though individual and species differences exist, they need not jeopardize the search for general laws governing learning in all organisms. If such general laws are possible, individual differences can be considered no more important than something to be taken into account in the application of the laws to everyday life. For example bridge designing is governed by general laws, even though the building of a particular bridge involves unique problems of application. So for Hull (1945), it was important to search for general laws by "assuming that the forms of the equations representing the behavioral laws of both individuals and species are identical, and that the differences between individuals and species will be found in the empirical constants which are essential components of such equations." In other words, researchers should cancel out, or neutralize, individual and species differences by adding to their equations those constants (which are, after all, arbitrary numbers) that will help make learning data seem identical across the individuals and species studied. But if there are important individual and species differences in the nature of learning, researchers will fail to recognize them because their methods of study are not suited to identification of these differences. The only way you can have any sort of test of the validity of the assumption that there are general laws governing learning is to observe how easy or difficult it actually is to find and manipulate the constants that must be employed to yield general laws.

In this regard, it must be admitted that the elegant emphasis on S-R bonds has been an oversimplification. Berlyne (1968) summarizes much research and theorizing as follows:

> Contemporary . . . behavior theorists make copious use of "intervening variables," as we have noted. These are essentially mathematical devices to make cumbersome relations between inputs (stimulus-variables) and outputs (response-variables) conceptually manageable. There must be some sort of correspondence, but not necessarily a one-to-one correspondence, between values of these variables and conditions within the organism that are not directly observable. Spence recognizes this and mentions two additional types of psychological laws, the one (O-R laws) identifying response variables as functions of "organic variables" (i.e., measurements of neuroanatomical or neurophysiological properties of the organism) and the other (S-O laws) identifying organic variables as functions of stimulus variables. Most psychological laws must surely be placed in a final category, containing what we may call "S-O-R laws," stating how response variables are determined jointly by stimulus and organic (i.e., intervening) variables. (p. 642)

Berlyne has said that it is necessary to include organismic variables, which are internal and therefore unobservable, in formulations of the stimulus control of behavior. He goes on to list four classes of organismic variables:

1. *Transient intervening variables,* whose values change within a matter of minutes or hours (e.g., emotional state, motivational condition).

2. *Age as a variable,* which focuses on how stimulus-response relationships change over long periods of time.

3. *Variables whose values can remain fixed* over long periods of time (e.g., habits).

4. *Constitutional* or *congenital predispositions* to particular kinds of behavior.

It seems to me that when one has devised a theory that fills out Berlyne's outline of what is needed, it will have considerable relevance to the understanding of individual differences, with personality as an important subject matter. The statement about learning as being inviolably constant will have so many exceptions and be shored up by so many intervening variables as to lose its position of centrality and elegant simplicity. Moderate behaviorism will then be closer to personality theory.

Actually, developments in this direction have been taking place, mainly in the attempt to apply behaviorism to human beings, who are obviously so much more complex than lower animals. The initial emphasis on responses as tangible, directly observable movements, and stimuli as manipulatable aspects of the external environment has been considerably modified. Now behaviorists consider thoughts and feelings as responses along with movements. Such internal, relatively unobservable states as thoughts and feelings may even be considered implicit or incipient movements in an attempt to save the old emphasis on that which is tangible. Perhaps more striking is the declaration that internal events (e.g., thoughts, feelings, metabolic states) can be considered stimuli with potential for influencing responses. Recently, it has become common to see, inserted between the old S and R of the S-R bond, s's and r's that stand for the internal, unmeasured stimuli and responses that have been assumed.

In addition, the moderate behaviorist's position on drives has undergone considerable elaboration. It became too cumbersome and unconvincing to try to explain the myriad forms of human behavior as attempts to reduce the tension of some few biological drives, such as hunger and thirst, and rewards, such as food and water. So the concepts of *secondary drive* and *secondary reward* were devised. In contrast to the primary drives and rewards, these are learned and changeable. According to Berlyne (1968, p. 664), "The principle of *secondary* reinforcement postulated that neutral stimuli accompanying primary rewards (i.e., conditions in which primary drives are reduced) would acquire a conditioned reward-value in their own right." Thus, if a person always ate food in a blue room, the color blue would come to have a pleasant, comforting effect on him or her even when encountered in a noneating context. Blue would have become a secondary reward.

A secondary drive is assumed to be evoked as "a consequence of conditioning by any stimulus (warning signal) that has habitually preceded or accompanied pain" (Berlyne, 1968, p. 664). So if the person were locked in a blue room with no food available, the pain of mounting hunger would become associated with the color blue. Subsequently, on encountering blue in a context unrelated to food deprivation, the person would experience discomfort, or anxiety. If some stimulus such as blue is associated with primary-drive increase, it becomes a secondary drive. In order to continue functioning as a secondary drive or reward, a stimulus such as blue must at least occasionally be paired once again with the primary drive or reinforcement from which it derived its power. Consistent with the notion of secondary (nonbiological) drives is Miller's (1959) assumption that any strong stimulus functions as a drive.

Because they are learned and changeable, secondary drives and rewards qualify as peripheral characteristics in the terminology of this book. Along with habits, they constitute the statement on peripheral personality that can be derived from moderate behaviorism. Secondary drives and rewards play a major role in the behaviorist's attempt to understand human behavior. Thus, such diverse goals as money, fame, and truth can be conceptualized as secondary rewards linked by past association with such primary rewards as food and water. Further, such uncomfortable states as anxiety and aggression can be considered secondary drives learned by association with primary drives. Since learning histories are likely to differ, secondary drives and rewards can show considerable variation from individual to individual. The same, of course, is true of habits.

Anxiety Research

Moderate behaviorism has produced an enormous amount of research. Most of it is experimental, focuses on learning, and employs subhuman organisms as subjects. Despite the emphasis on learning, much of this research supports the assumption that biological needs exist and that tension reduction is rewarding. Thus, an organism deprived of food or water will learn an S-R bond more rapidly the greater the deprivation, at least when the learning task is relatively simple, but when the learning task is relatively complex, there may actually be a level of drive too great to permit effective learning (e.g., Farber & Spence, 1953; Yerkes & Dodson, 1908). Although the bulk of the research has concerned the hunger and thirst drives, or the more general avoidance of pain, more recent work has also indicated that the postulated curiosity drive exists. Various organisms will perform work in order to obtain information (e.g., Berlyne, 1960) or to experience stimulus change (e.g., Dember in Fiske & Maddi, 1961). Although most of the research has employed subhuman subjects, enough of it has been done with humans to suggest that one can safely conclude the existence of various biological drives in them as well.

Of course, the existence of such drives is hardly surprising. Also, as they would be relevant to a behaviorist theory of personality as core characteristics, they would play an insignificant role in explaining those persisting individual differences that are at the heart of the personological enterprise. Further, the putative core tendency of moderate behaviorism, which makes tension reduction the aim of all functioning, is not so unassailably supported by research. The research both supporting and questioning the tension reduction assertion was reviewed in Chapter 6.

A representative theme in behavioristic research that is especially relevant here concerns manifest anxiety. This research has focused exclusively on human beings and concerns itself with individual differences. There is ambiguity, however, in the behavioristic conceptualization of anxiety. In the main, anxiety has been viewed as an expression of general drive or tension. But it is also possible to consider anxiety a secondary drive, learned through association with primary drives. The latter formulation, though less common in the literature, would actually be more consistent with the focus on individual or group differences in the research and the implication carried in many of the measurement operations employed that it is truly anxiety and not just tension that is being studied.

In the 1950s and 1960s, a great deal of behavioristic research on anxiety was done, but the emphasis appears to have dwindled. Most of the studies employed the *Manifest Anxiety Scale,* a questionnaire devised by Taylor (1953), which included such items as "I have very few headaches" and "I am very confident of myself." This test proved to have adequate reliability. Before long, several other anxiety scales became available (e.g., Sarason, 1958; Welch, 1956). Endler, Hunt, and Rosenstein's (1962) was unusual in that it assessed the degree of subjective anxiety in a number of different situational contexts.

Several hypotheses following from the assumption that anxiety functions like general drive were tested in what was for years a lively research area. This research has been ably reviewed by Spence and Spence (1966). One such hypothesis is that high anxiety should facilitate learning in simple tasks but disrupt it in complex ones. Although many studies support this contention, a goodly number do not. Another hypothesis is that anxiety should show a positive relationship to physiological indices of emotionality or tension. Although it must be said that this expectation has been neither fully nor sophisticatedly researched, the available findings are generally negative. But most available studies do confirm the hypothesis that highly anxious persons are more disrupted in their functioning by personal threat or stress than are low-anxiety persons. It would not be surprising to find highly anxious persons generally self-depreciatory and tending toward psychopathology—and indeed there is such evidence (e.g., Lauterback, 1958; Trapp & Kausler, 1958). In general, there are more confirming than contradicting findings for the interpretation of anxiety as general drive. There is, of course, extensive modern literature on anxiety that I will not summarize here because it is so far removed from the explicit attempt to test moderate behavioristic theorizing that it is not especially relevant to our purposes. Some of this research was considered in Chapter 11.

As you can tell from the preceding paragraphs, the Manifest Anxiety Scale and similar anxiety questionnaires have been employed in numerous studies that go beyond the specific predictions stemming from the concept of general drive alone. The correlation of anxiety scores with scores on other performances constitute the makings of R-R (response-response) rather than S-R laws in the terminology of moderate behaviorism (Spence, 1948). In searching for R-R laws, the investigator tries to determine invariances in the relationship among responses without tying the responses in any rigorous way to antecedent stimuli. It is my impression that when moderate behaviorists become interested in human behavior per se, they tend to abandon strict emphasis on the stimulus control of behavior and focus instead on how the various facets of behavior go together. This seems appropriate given the enormous complexity of human as opposed to subhuman behavior. Research themes such as that concerning manifest anxiety show an implicit distinction in moderate behaviorism between subhuman and human behavior, even though in explicit, formal theorizing no such distinction is assumed.

Moderate Behaviorism and Psychoanalytic Theory

Several other research themes traditionally have been considered part of the behavioristic movement. For example, there is the research stemming from the proposition that frustration breeds aggression. Although Berlyne (1968) classifies this research as being concerned with aggression construed as a secondary drive, it is not clear in behavioristic theory just how this interpretation can be made. As in the case of manifest anxiety, one could as easily consider aggression to be primary, or unlearned drive, because the tie between frustration and aggression is thought to be invariant. Other investigators loosely in the behavioristic tradition (e.g., Berkowitz, 1974) have considered aggression as a learned drive by detaching it from any necessary connection with frustration. In general, these investigations have focused on how experiences of success and failure in fighting lead to learned patterns of dominant and submissive behavior.

But aggression research is deviating even further from any pure behavioristic orientation. For example, Tedeschi, Smith, and Brown (1974) suggest the central importance of the concept of coercive power, with emphasis on the subject's attempt to influence. Investigators (e.g., Nickel, 1974) are reporting evidence that intent must be taken into account along with various other personality variables (e.g., Scarpetti, 1974). That some of these more personalistic recent emphases have been supported from within the behaviorist camp may be partially due to the long-standing affinity between behaviorism and psychoanalytic theory.

This affinity becomes even more apparent in research themes within the behaviorist movement that appear to bear an uncertain relationship to behavioristic thinking. An example is conflict, a subject that has provoked considerable study among moderate behaviorists (e.g., Berlyne, 1964; Brown & Farber, 1951; Miller, 1959). Although one might, by doing theoretical handstands, derive this interest in conflict from behavioristic thinking, it does not seem to follow from it naturally. I do not think behaviorists would have so emphasized conflict had it not been for the impact on them of psychoanalytic theorizing. I feel similarly about the study of defenses, which has been mounted with great energy by behaviorists (e.g., Farber, 1948; Miller & Dollard, 1941; Mowrer, 1940; Sears, 1943). In general, these studies have employed subhuman subjects and focused on observable responses without regard to underlying mentation.

Indeed, the behaviorists who have done the most to elaborate on the position so as to account for individual differences in human behavior (e.g., Dollard & Miller, 1950) explicitly consider themselves to be dealing with the same range of phenomena important to Freud. From their viewpoint, Dollard and Miller were focusing on those aspects of Freud most amenable to operationalization and empirical test and, by dispensing with the rest, improving on psychoanalytic formulations. In the main, they have dispensed with Freud's mentalistic aspects and his theoretical statements about the necessarily incompatible nature of individuals and society. What they have emphasized instead are the most biological aspects of his thinking and tangible movements rather than thoughts.

In my estimation, behaviorism seems to only resemble psychoanalytic theory while in reality being quite different from it. Although it is true, for example, that Freud would have endorsed the behaviorist's assumption of primary drives, such as hunger, thirst, and sex, he would not have agreed to defining them as devoid of mentality and therefore similar to what is present in lower animals. Freud saw the instincts as *wishes* and *attendant emotions*, present in the mind, and, although derived from metabolism, not merely biological phenomena. In addition, he considered the chief importance of instincts to be their incompatibility with the social requirements of maintaining the common good. From this assumption, as you know, comes Freud's emphasis on conflict and defense. But for him, conflict is not merely the presence of incompatible response tendencies. More important, conflict also involves a mental dilemma in which guilt and fear of punishment are inevitable participants. Defensiveness, for Freud, is a mental operation, denoting conscious and unconscious thoughts, only one small expression of which occurs in some actual movement or response.

On the basis of these differences in theoretical emphasis, Freud would have justifiably disagreed with the behaviorist's reliance on subhuman subjects for experimentation. Further, he would not have accepted such experimental designs as that of Mowrer (1940), mentioned in Chapter 6, in which the measure of defensive behavior is the substitution of a weaker habit for a stronger one in the face of stress. The defense mechanism of regression, which Mowrer thought he was demonstrating, makes no sense in Freud's thinking unless it derives from his conceptualization of psychosexual stages of development. It is clear neither that rats have psychosexual stages of development nor how, if they do, pushing a bar or rearing on their hind legs articulate with such stages in any important way.

Strictly speaking, research emphasis on conflict and defense proceeds mostly from Freudian-style theorizing, replete with the very assumptions that behaviorists have found objectionable. In addition, the frustration-leading-to-aggression hypothesis follows much more readily from Freud's thinking concerning the anal stage of psychosexual development than it does for moderate behaviorism. Even the study of manifest anxiety has, among behaviorists, involved more focusing on mental content (e.g., socially desirable responses, experiences of low self-confidence, obsessive thinking) than they can easily justify. It is not enough for behaviorists to insist that they are studying what Freud believed important when the changes in psychoanalytic thinking that have been made radically alter its emphases.

I am drawn to the conclusion that the rudimentary theory of personality contained in moderate behaviorism is either a pseudo-conflict theory, with its assumptions about the inevitability of hidden but implicit conflict, or a kind of fulfillment theory, in which the story of human behavior is to be understood as nothing more than the styles each person learns for reducing tension from drives. If the former, a fuller embracing of Freud's mentalistic and social assumptions would lead to research of greater relevance. If the latter, one probably would want to expend less research effort on such topics as conflict and defensiveness.

RADICAL BEHAVIORISM

Radical behaviorism derives from Watson (1924) more than from Pavlov and finds its contemporary expression in Skinner (1938, 1953, 1957) and those he has influenced (e.g., Krasner & Ullmann, 1965; Lundin, 1974; Verplanck, 1954). Like moderate behaviorism, it focuses on the way in which stimuli control actions and considers the laws of learning whereby this control takes place as being invariant across individuals and species. But what makes radical behaviorism radical is its unwillingness to make assumptions about the existence and importance of drives—primary or secondary—and its insistence that even the minimally mentalistic concept of habit is unnecessary for understanding. Apparently in radical behaviorism there are not even the rudiments of a position on the core and periphery of personality. Yet radical behaviorism claims to be able to predict, control, and understand all behavior. As such, it should represent a frank alternative to personality theorizing (and, for that matter, *any* kind of theorizing in psychology).

Radical behaviorists have championed many useful concepts and distinctions in understanding learning and in this have influenced all areas of psychology, including moderate behaviorism. Speaking for all radical behaviorists, Skinner asserts that the only appropriate criterion for scientific explanation is prediction and control. To accept an explanation merely because it seems to make sense or has coherence (i.e., appeals to intuitive and rational knowledge) is to be deluded. The extreme emphasis on prediction and control leads to a preoccupation with changing behavior. You must be able to change behavior in order to demonstrate the ability to control. Thus, the first break with personality theorizing is the radical behaviorist's lack of interest in behavior that remains the same over many different situations. ,

Radical behaviorists' distinctions concerning stimuli and responses are all aimed at providing a basis for understanding how responses change by increasing or decreasing in frequency. At the outset, it should be recognized that for an event to be classified as a stimulus it must be observable and manipulable and for an event to be classified as a response it must be observable and quantifiable. There are two classes of response. In Frankel's (1971) words:

> When a response is regularly elicited by a stimulus as the result of the inherited characteristics of the organism, it is called an *unconditioned respondent*. If we were to change the diaper of an infant and accidentally stick him with a pin, he would probably start crying. Since the response of crying when pin-pricked is not the result of previous experience but the consequence of the inherited structure and capacities of the infant, it is an unconditioned respondent. When

a previously neutral stimulus can elicit a response, it is called a *conditioned respondent*. The process whereby neutral stimuli function as conditioned eliciting stimuli is called *respondent conditioning*. Thus the sight of the pin may now cause the infant to cry. (p. 447)

Respondent conditioning was heavily emphasized by Pavlov (1927) and forms much of the basis of moderate behaviorism. Because it was recognized earlier, respondent conditioning is often called *classical*. Emotional behaviors often have respondent components; for example, a slap in the face may elicit crying from a child. The respondent components of our emotions (i.e., their unlearned tie to particular eliciting stimuli) may well underlie our feeling of helplessness about our moods (Frankel, 1971).

But much more important than respondent conditioning for radical behaviorism is *operant conditioning*. Although some of our behaviors are reflexive in nature, most of them usually pass as voluntary. These responses are called *operant* to emphasize that they "operate" on the environment and their shaping or control is achieved by operant conditioning. In Frankel's (1971) words:

Opening a refrigerator is an operant response insofar as it is a function of subsequent stimuli (food). If the refrigerator were always empty we would not open refrigerator doors. The presence of the food increases the strength of the operant response. When a stimulus following an operant response increases the strength of the operant, it is called a *reinforcing stimulus*. The difference between a reinforcing stimulus and an *eliciting stimulus* is that the former always follows an operant response whereas the latter always precedes a respondent.

A reinforcer is said to be positive when the effect of the operant response is experimentally observed to "produce" the reinforcing stimulus. Food is therefore a *positive reinforcer* for opening refrigerator doors. In contrast, whenever the effect of an operant response is experimentally observed to "eliminate" a stimulus, that stimulus is called a *negative reinforcer*. Let us suppose that the infant is now six months old, and he has not forgotten that we stuck him with pins. If we discover that whenever we enter the room the infant turns to the wall, we might hypothesize that we were an aversive stimulus that negatively reinforced facing the wall. By regularly facing the wall in our presence, the child eliminates us from his visual field. (pp. 447–448)

Thus, the organism performs an operant (or voluntary) response in order to bring about a positive reinforcing stimulus or eliminate a negatively reinforcing stimulus. If the investigator wishes to increase the frequency of an operant response, he or she must wait until it occurs and then follow it with either the presence of a positive reinforcer or the absence of a negative reinforcer. An increase in the frequency of an operant response indicates that learning (operant conditioning) has taken place.

Radical behaviorists also distinguish between *unconditioned* and *conditioned* reinforcers. When it is not the organism's past training that has produced the ability of a reinforcer to increase the rate of an operant response, the stimulus is considered an unconditioned reinforcing stimulus. Examples are food and water, which are presumed to be intrinsically reinforcing. But we also seek stimuli that are not immediately relevant to food and drink. For example, adults work for money and students work for grades, though they are not born with needs for money or grades. A neutral stimulus (money or grades) may subsequently function as a conditioned reinforcer when it has been present during the occurrence of an unconditioned reinforcer. Unconditioned and conditioned reinforcers are similar to the primary and secondary rewards (or punishments) of moderate behaviorism.

A final class of stimuli are those that supply information rather than elicit or reinforce responses. Information is provided by *discriminative stimuli,* which in large measure control our lives. In our society some people's functions are advertised by their uniforms. In this case, the uniforms are discriminative stimuli. Frankel (1971) clarifies how the classifications radical behaviorists offer are used in understanding complex human behavior:

> A stimulus may function as a discriminative stimulus at one point in time and as a conditioned reinforcer at another. In the presence of our mother (a discriminative stimulus) we may ask (an operant response) for money (a conditioned reinforcer). With the money in our hand (a discriminative stimulus) we may go (an operant response) to the grocer (a discriminative stimulus) for candy (an unconditioned positive reinforcer). (p. 449)

You will note from this example that the discriminative stimulus must precede or accompany the operant response whereas the conditioned reinforcer always follows the operant response. You should also keep in mind that radical behaviorists (and their more moderate counterparts) emphasize stimulus and response generalization. A response associated with a particular discriminative stimulus may occur, through *stimulus generalization,* in the presence of some similar discriminative stimulus that was not involved in the original learning. *Response generalization* refers to the tendency of very frequent (strongly learned) responses to occur in the context of stimulus conditions other than those in which they were learned. The concepts of stimulus and response generalization carry a distinct possibility for personalistic exploration; some responses occur in stimulus circumstances other than those that were learned.

Schedules of Reinforcement and the Extinction Process

Radical behaviorists have been especially adept at determining the effects of different contingencies (or relationships) of reinforcement on the strength of a learned response. An operant response that is reinforced every time it is emitted is called a *continuous schedule of reinforcement.* But reinforcements are more often intermittent, especially in the natural world outside the laboratory. *Intermittent reinforcement* can occur according to a *ratio schedule,* in which a relationship exists between the number of responses emitted and the number of reinforcements taking place (e.g., every third response is reinforced), or an *interval schedule,* in which reinforcement occurs after a certain period of time regardless of the number of responses that have occurred.

Many other reinforcement contingencies have been recognized. Suffice it to say that each reinforcement schedule has a different effect on the acquisition, maintenance, and weakening (extinction) of an operant response. Frankel (1971) gives evidence of this in an extended example that is close to everyday life:

> A child asks his father for money to buy bubble gum. Whenever he makes this request, he is given the money for the gum. Suppose that in the course of two months the child has received money two hundred times. When reinforcement follows an operant every time, the schedule is one of continuous reinforcement. Imagine now that another child makes the same request for the same time period and the same number of times, but his father does not always grant the request. This is an intermittent schedule of reinforcement. Suppose the dentist subsequently tells both parents that their children must stop chewing bubble gum. The parents agree, and from that day on they refuse to grant the request of their children. In operant terms, a previously rewarded operant response (asking for bubble gum) will undergo *extinction* as a result of non-reinforcement. Extinction refers to the procedure of continuous non-reinforcement which results in a lowering of response rate. Both children on discovering that their requests were going to be refused (non-reinforced) would suddenly begin asking more frequently. At first non-reinforced trials result in a rise in the frequency of the operant. This observation has been confirmed in hundreds of experiments. It is also not uncommon in our experience to find ourselves trying harder after frustration. However, as the non-reinforcement of the operant response continues over trials, the weakening of the response manifests itself in lower and lower rates of responding, until finally it returns to its initial level (prior to the first reinforcement), or disappears altogether. In our example, both children will gradually stop asking their parents for bubble gum. However, the child who has been reinforced on a continuous schedule will extinguish faster than the child who has been reinforced on an intermittent schedule. If we observe an individual seemingly struggling in vain, and we wonder how someone can work so hard when achieving so little reinforcement, we may speculate that a history of intermittent reinforcement for that individual effects the present drawn-out extinction process. Ironically, the very perseverance of an individual who has refused to give up and has inspired us with a sustained effort despite repeated failures may be at that moment undergoing extinction. (pp. 452–453)

Apparently intermittent reinforcement schedules can produce response patterns that are difficult to unlearn even when no further reward is forthcoming. Here too is something of personalistic relevance; some response patterns continue unchanged even if they do not lead to reinforcement.

There is little point in inquiring as to whether there is empirical support for the various tenets of radical behaviorism, which are largely the result of painstaking and rigorous research. It shows, of course, the same problem as moderate behaviorism, namely, that lower organisms such as pigeons and rats are subjects much more often than are humans. As long as one is willing to assume that the laws of learning are universal, this emphasis on subhuman species is no special limitation. But it arouses the skepticism of personologists, who are loath to make that assumption, even about learning. Some psychologists (e.g., Kohler, 1925; Tolman, 1948) believe that learning in humans takes place much more cognitively, through processes labeled *insight* and the like, than behaviorism would ever admit. Indeed, one criticism of behaviorism mounted on cognitive grounds appears in Chapter 13 of this book. Nonetheless, it must be said that, within its own set of assumptions, radical behaviorism has achieved considerable empirical support.

The Absence of Core and Periphery in Radical Behaviorism

As indicated earlier, the moderate behaviorist's emphasis on primary and secondary drives and on habits can be construed as a rudimentary position on the core and periphery of personality. There is not even this much of a position on personality in radical behaviorism. According to Skinner, the organism should be treated as a "black box," which, though perhaps not empty, need not be explored in order for understanding of behavior to be achieved. The responses constituting behavior are tangible and can be controlled by manipulating the external stimulus environment—and that is that. Of course, the emphasis of such a position would be on behavior modifications or learning. But radical behaviorists disapprove of their moderate counterparts for diagrams linking external stimuli to observable responses by way of a series of internal stimuli and responses.

Do radical behaviorists really deny the existence of common, unchangeable aspects of human nature? No, but they will not speculate about them and consider them unimportant in behavior modification. Any enduring, relatively unmodifiable behavior that might stem from, say, a particular genetic constitution would not be of interest. Skinner (1957) puts it this way:

> Even when it can be shown that some aspect of behavior is due to season of birth, gross body type, or genetic constitution, the fact is of limited use. It may help us in predicting behavior, but it is of little value in an experimental analysis or in practical control because such a condition cannot be manipulated after the individual has been conceived. The most that can be said is that the knowledge of the genetic factor may enable us to make better use of our causes. If we know that an individual has certain inherent limitations, we may use our techniques to control more intelligently, but we cannot alter the genetic factor. (p. 371)

It should be recognized that in his single-minded emphasis on behavior modification, Skinner is disagreeing to some extent with the personologist over what is to be explained. The personologist would include as important data behavior that does not change.

But what of the drives that moderate behaviorists and virtually everyone else in psychology recognize as important influences on behavior? Here surely are inherent or core characteristics that can have a variable influence on behavior (e.g., one may be more active when hungry than when satiated). In general, radical behaviorists abhor concepts that refer to unobservable, internal states construed as causes of behavior. What virtually every personologist does is thus regarded as unscientific. To radical behaviorists, to theorize about unconscious motivation, defenses, life fear, will to power, achievement motivation, or even hunger drive is to deny the external stimuli that supposedly control the various behaviors.

Although the primary drives of the moderate behaviorist are less abhorrent because they are more believably biological than these other concepts, the radical behaviorist still does not consider them useful explanatory devices. For the radical behaviorist, one gains nothing of scientific value in "explaining" that persons eat at one time and not at another by saying that they were hungry at first and not subsequently. One gains nothing because it is then necessary to determine the mechanism governing the waxing and waning of whatever it is that is called *hunger*. The tangible, observable, external stimulus situation that governs eating behavior turns out to be the number of hours since one has last eaten. To talk of a hunger drive is at best superfluous (if we know the external stimuli controlling the responses to be explained) and at worst misleading (by dulling our curiosity to find the external stimuli if we do not yet know them).

It is instructive to observe how radical behaviorists attempt to maintain this unwillingness to assume the existence of internal motivating states. All experimenters know that animals are more active when deprived of food or water and an active animal is easier to train. So radical behaviorists indeed deprive their subjects of food and water. But in describing their experimental procedure, they do not say that the animal was hungry or thirsty. At most they refer to the effects of deprivation on the body. A pigeon will be described as at "80 percent of its free-feeding weight." The more active the animal, the greater the likelihood that it will emit the desired operant response along with others. When the desired operant occurs, it can be reinforced with the same food or water that had been withheld before the beginning of the experimental task. Soon enough, the food or water reinforcement will increase the rate at which the operant is emitted, and learning will be said to have occurred. But once again the effectiveness of the food or water will not be discussed in terms of its drive-reducing properties as would be done in moderate behaviorism. For the radical behaviorist, a stimulus qualifies as a reinforcement if it increases the rate of an operant, and nothing else need or should be asked.

To me, the gymnastics that radical behaviorists must perform in order to avoid the mentalistic, personological implications of the learning process are, in the final analysis, unconvincing. One problem is the definition of reinforcement as the stimulus that increases or decreases the rate of emission of an operant response. But the reinforcement concept is also a major part of the explanation of learning. How do we know that learning has taken place? Because an operant response has changed in rate through the action of a reinforcement. How do we know that a stimulus has reinforcing properties? Because it can change the rate of an operant response. With all their rigor and concern for science, radical behaviorists have fallen into a serious circularity here. Moderate behaviorists have avoided this circularity by defining a reinforcing stimulus in terms of the drive or tension it reduces rather than of the change in response rate it may produce. With reinforcement defined in terms of tension-reducing capability, it becomes an empirical question whether a reward or punishment affects response rate. Hence, the use of reinforcement as an explanation of such rate changes is not circular in moderate behaviorism.

Of course, radical behaviorists do not think they deny the existence of physiological processes that might be called drives; rather, they prefer to refer only to observable and manipulable things—hence the emphasis on body weight rather than hunger. But then why not tie the definition of reinforcement to such body states as weight rather than to the very data (operant rate) that reinforcement is supposed to explain? This is not done because radical behaviorists insist that physiological processes such as drives affect not learning but only activity level. One reduces a subject's body weight only because the ensuing high activity level means that many operant responses are being emitted, so it is easier to focus on one of them for conditioning purposes. To define reinforcement in terms of bodily states would be to admit that they too affect learning.

But not only would it be more scientific to define reinforcements in terms other than what they are supposed to explain; it would also be thoroughly consistent with the commonsense, or intuitive, knowledge. Radical behaviorists are coming perilously close to functionally decorticating themselves (Murray, 1959) in their concern for scientific purity. Are we really supposed to believe that the procedure of decreasing subjects' body weight by depriving them of food was hit on by empirical exploration alone and not assumed all along to increase activity level because of its effect on hunger? Are we really supposed to believe that food qualifies as a positive reinforcer merely because it has been observed to affect the rate of operant responding, with no tie to already known nutritional requirements of organisms? Why was food tried as a possible reinforcer in the first place? Do we all not know that it was tried because we all accept the fact that food-deprived subjects want food and will do almost anything to get it? Did we need all the elegant experiments of the radical behaviorist to tell us that? And is not the substitution of rigorous-sounding terminology (e.g.,"80 percent of free-feeding body weight") for the commonsense terms that cover the same phenomena a sleight of hand intended to convey that some new, grand knowledge has been obtained?

However, I must admit that some empirical knowledge deriving from radical behaviorism is striking and useful. In particular, I would point to the research showing the differential effects of various schedules of reinforcement on acquisition, maintenance, and especially extinction of operant responses. It is of considerable value in attempting to explain human behavior to know that something learned according to an intermittent schedule of reinforcement extinguishes more slowly than if a continuous schedule has been involved. I suspect even here, however, that the plan for the radical behaviorist's research comes from his or her intuitive knowledge, which heavily includes the very speculations concerning what is inside the black box that supposedly are inadmissible in psychological science. If that is so, the radical behaviorist is really doing nothing that different from the moderate behaviorist, who is, as indicated before, rather unwilling to make assumptions constituting personality theory.

If it is true that intuition and common sense play a greater role in the radical behaviorist's enterprise than is admitted or should be expected from the noninferential terminology, one might expect to find little slips of the tongue, as it were, that belie the rigor. Frankel (1971) believes he has found evidence of one such slip in Skinner's explanation of superstitious behavior. As you know, it is common for personologists such as Freud (1960) to refer to such mentalistic considerations as repressed hostile feelings projected onto others in explaining superstitious (excessively fearful) behavior. Thus, one thinks of the world as dangerous because of one's own projected anger. Skinner, of course, will have none of this, preferring to search for the external manipulable stimulus conditions producing superstitious behavior.

In offering a laboratory demonstration of superstitious behavior, Skinner (1961) started with a pigeon maintained at 75 percent of its free-feeding body weight and placed it in an experimental chamber arranged so that food was presented every five seconds no matter what the pigeon was doing (fixed-interval reinforcement). In such a situation, if the "clock is arranged to present the food . . . at regular intervals *with no reference whatsoever to the bird's behavior,* operant conditioning usually takes place" (Skinner, 1961). Skinner (1961) goes on to describe the results of such conditioning:

> One bird was conditioned to turn counterclockwise about the cage, making two or three turns between reinforcements. Another repeatedly thrust its head into one of the upper corners of the cage. A third developed a "tossing response," as if placing its head beneath an invisible bar and lifting it repeatedly.

These responses involved orientation to some aspect of the environment rather than mere execution of movements. Skinner interprets these findings as the development of superstitious behavior. Apparently, such superstitious behavior is very resistant to extinction. With learning taking place according to a time interval of fifteen seconds between presentations of food, one conditions an operant response that will then be emitted 10,000 times despite the absence of food (Skinner, 1961)! In accounting for this superstitious behavior, Skinner does not have recourse to covert stimuli and responses such as impulses, emotions, repressions, or projection, relying instead on an analysis of the stimulus conditions under which an organism will behave as if its actions were effective in determining the reinforcing consequences.

What makes it possible to call this *superstitious behavior* is that *Skinner and we know that the pigeon's responses are not really effective* in bringing about the reinforcement, which occurs only after some time interval regardless of the responses being made. Frankel (1971) asks:

> How did Skinner know that the bird was superstitious? Presumably because Skinner was outside the pigeon's universe, and thus was able to know that the

ritualistic behavior . . . was not instrumental in getting the pellet of food. But is it really possible to call one behavior superstitious and another behavior unsuperstitious within the framework of the operant model? (p. 455)

In elaborating on the challenge in the last sentence, Frankel (1971) presents a lengthy but pithy parable:

Let me make the point clearer through the use of a pigeon parable. Imagine that one of the pigeons, Max, begins to wonder whether it is necessary for him to walk in circles in order for the food to arrive. Max decides to perform an experiment and walks to another section of the cage, only to discover that the food is delivered. Shall he conclude that the reinforcement is unrelated to his behavior? He might also conclude that there are two behaviors related to the delivery of food. Max may try another experimental excursion to another part of the cage and once again discover that a pellet of food is delivered. He then might conclude either that his behavior is unrelated to the delivery of food or that three behaviors are related to the food. Suppose Max now decides to see whether doing nothing leads to the same result. He discovers that again food is delivered and again he is faced with the dilemma of deciding whether the *behavior of doing nothing* is related to food delivery or whether food delivery is unrelated to behavior. Suppose Max had access to a philosopher pigeon, whom he asks for advice. He may say to the philosopher, "Food is a life and death matter and it comes at intervals so long as I am doing something. When I purposely do nothing it also comes. Must I worry about it or think about it at all?" The philosopher may reply, "The ways of the world are strange. Life is given and life is taken (reinforcement) both in the experimental chamber and back in the cage (present reinforcement and historical contingencies), and it is difficult for us to comprehend the ways of our Lord, B. F. Skinner. Sometimes he is benevolent in the experimental chamber and sometimes he is not. It is a question of deciding ultimates. If what we do is irrelevant to life and death, then it becomes a problem to decide what is relevant to behavior and if anything can be "relevant" in the context of a universe that remains ultimately beyond reach. The teachings of Skinner are clear about this—Man must assume control and behave as if his behavior is relevant to important goals. One of our prophets has developed a system whereby it would have been possible to kill many German men and women—because German men and women killed many Polish men and women. Thus the prophet, an American, developed a missile system carrying one of our own species to eventual destruction. The judgement of Skinner (1961, p. 426), as related in the book, is simply: "The ethical question of our right to convert a lower creature into an unwitting hero is a peacetime luxury." It is clear that Skinner is concerned with our species and more concerned with us than he appears to be with German men and women. So, in practical matters, one must assume there is a meaning, a reinforcement, to which our operants are directed.

Max may reply: "Philosopher, I take it you are not an atheist, but that you do believe that there is a God, called Skinner, though his ways are inscrutable." The philosopher answers, "Yes, I do believe." "Are you not merely superstitious?" asks Max. The philospher replies: "You come to me with a problem and I provide you with a solution which implies that inscrutability need not eliminate meaningfulness—go about your daily affairs as if things mattered, as Skinner suggests." Max walks away from the philosopher and ponders the solution.

He doesn't want to be superstitious. He doesn't want to live as if anything he does matters, if it does not, in fact, matter. Max then hits upon a clever idea. "If my behavior is irrelevant (no God—no Skinner) then I may as well commit suicide or do nothing. However, if my behavior is relevant, then I must commit myself accordingly. It is also true that life would be better if behavior mattered. Since I will never understand even if he 'is,' I will never know the solution to my problem. However, it makes sense to choose the alternative that would be better if true, and that alternative is to act *as if* my behavior were relevant to the consequences." Max then returns to his experimental chamber and continues his walking in circles.

Are we not all like Max insofar as we are inhabitants of a Skinner box? As inhabitants of a Skinner box, can any of us discover whether a given behavior is superstitious or non-superstitious? Skinner, the scientist, informs us that through the operation of contingencies of reinforcement our behavior is controlled. Skinner also informs us that the only relationship necessary to establish the effectiveness of a reinforcer is the "order and proximity of response and reinforcement." Such a formula does not allow for distinctions such as right and wrong, superstitious or non-superstitious, unless these refer to receiving reinforcement after a response. Clearly, the pigeons accomplish this. They do get reinforced; therefore, they are as correct as they can be within the confines of an operant conditioning paradigm. Since reinforcement will always take place when the organism is doing one thing or another, there is no way for it to decide the relevance of its behavior to reinforcement.

The best the organism can hope to accomplish is to discover that the reinforcement is delivered on a certain time schedule, but this would require that the organism leave his universe and consult with the controlling network outside of his universe. By definition, this is not possible. At best, one may infer, deduce, or extrapolate that there must be a universal clock (interval schedule of reinforcement), and indeed, such deductions, inferences, and extrapolations on the parts of priests, medicine men, and philosophers take place. This is what Skinner calls superstitious behavior. He seems to think that science is freed from such superstitions. If so it is also uninvolved in the nature of that "universal clock" that regulates the reinforcement schedule. In fact, scientists are as superstitious as anyone else. It is the scientist who has developed the extraordinary ritual of the scientific method in an effort to understand the nature of the universe, or, as in the case of our pigeons, the nature of Skinner.

The scientist is searching for meaning in the form of laws. But what proof is offered that a law has been discovered? For the behaviorist, the ultimate criterion as to whether we know anything is contingent on reinforcements. A law must be proven to have reinforcing consequences. To say we will discover other laws is to do nothing more than express the faith that we shall find behaviors that lead to reinforcing consequences. Of course, the Pope will also undoubtedly tell us that belief in Christ has reinforcing consequences, and further religiosity will lead to behaviors that lead to other reinforcements. We have already seen that "persevering" may become an interpretation of another person's behavior when he does not extinguish a response. If he is on an extinction schedule of non-reinforcement, then we would know whether such a response is right or wrong, but we can never know that unless we could get outside our universe. Thus, like our pigeons we require *faith* to believe that behavior is relevant to the universal clock.

When Skinner writes an essay concerning the ways in which the world operates and the ways in which it should operate, he is presuming to have an insight
into the nature of that clock as a result of his scientific background. Skinner's
statement (1961, p. 4) "Let us agree to start with, that health is better than
sickness, wisdom better than ignorance, love better than hate, and productive
energy better than neurotic sloth" ignores the implication of his own writings.
It was Skinner who argued that one reinforcement is not better or worse than
another. Reinforcements simply reinforce behavior. To say love is better than
hate is to say nonsense, unless he adds that it is better to love X reinforcement
than to hate Y reinforcement. This is absurd because loving or hating a reinforcement is contingent upon a history of other reinforcements or present contingencies. Thus, to hate or love a reinforcement is to love or hate the law of
gravity. Yet Skinner writes as though knowledge of reinforcement effects the
law of reinforcement. (pp. 455–458)

Of course, Skinner is careful to put the term *superstitious* in quotes, on
the grounds that he will not interpret behavior or make value judgments about
it. Because of his own assumptions, he knows he cannot know anything more
than what he observes. Actually, here and there (e.g., Skinner, 1961), he also
uses drive names such as *hunger,* again in quotes. But as Frankel (1971, p. 458)
aptly charges, words such as "hunger" or "superstitious" are interpretations of
behavior, not mere descriptions. And interpretations are miniature theories
insofar as they purport to describe the "meaning" of what is seen. Although
Skinner considers theory to be explanatory fiction at worst and irrelevant at
best, he is in fact theorizing when he interprets movements as if he knew their
meaning. That the interpretations make good common sense should not dull
our recognition that he is theorizing nonetheless.

What Frankel has pinpointed is hardly unimportant. Consider another
ramification of radical behaviorists' theorizing intuitively without admitting
that doing so affects their actions and conclusions. Skinner has provided a
powerful technology with which to change and control behavior; hence, it is
not surprising to find his approach utilized in psychotherapy (e.g., Ayllon &
Azrin, 1968; Goldiamond & Dyrud, 1967). But especially in something
as crucial as psychotherapy, it becomes necessary to consider what behavior
shall be changed and in what direction change shall be implemented. Skinner
asserts again and again that his is merely a technology for behavior modification that is all the more scientific for carrying no value judgments within it.
And when behavioristic psychotherapists discuss cases, they refer to the cur-
ing of stuttering, or autism, or some such gross abnormality the correction
of which is such an unquestionable good that no value judgment seems to be
involved.

When pressed further on just what changes should and should not be
made, behavioristic psychotherapists are likely to say that they bring about
specifically those changes that the patient wants. The therapist is not so much
a manipulator as a helper. But suppose that a patient came to the radical
behaviorist's office asking for aid in becoming courageous enough to assassi-

nate the President. What would the therapist say or do? He or she might turn the patient away, indicating lack of interest in or even opposition to such an aim. If therapists did this, they would be admitting that their behavior modification technology is in the service of their theory as to what is good and bad, constructive and unconstructive. Alternatively, they might engage the patient in conversation, on the expressed or private presumption that the stated aim was not the real one. Perhaps the patient just wants to feel more effective or substantially change his or her life. In choosing this alternative, the radical behaviorists would be showing the subjugation of technology to a theory no less than they would by turning the patient away. It is only by helping the patient gain courage to murder that the therapists would be true to their non-evaluative position. And yet, we all know they would not do that. Once again we see the operation of theory—rife with value judgments similar to those forming the corpus of personology—in the decisions, plans, and conclusions of the radical behaviorists.

The upshot of all this is that radical behaviorism as an alternative to personality theorizing is not as pure as it purports to be. There is the distinct possibility that insofar as it is relevant to the understanding of complex human behavior, it is so by virtue of implicit, intuitive theorizing similar to what takes place more explicitly in moderate behaviorism. To refer to "hunger" and to maintain subjects at some fraction of body weight at the same time that one chooses food as a reinforcer is to assume the existence of hunger as a primary drive and the effectiveness of the reinforcer as a tension reducer. To try to explain the resistance to extinction of "superstitious" behavior is to admit that there are learned traits or habits that affect behavior relatively directly even though the stimulus justification of such behavior in the environment may not be particularly apparent. And, for that matter, to turn patients away or to become convinced that they do not know their own minds is to have a theory of psychopathology and mental health. If radical behaviorism indeed contains the intuitive seeds of a personality theory, the theory should be brought to flowering so that its strengths and weaknesses can be clearly judged in the marketplace of ideas.

If it still be insisted that radical behaviorism includes no theorizing with implications for core and peripheral statements on personality, the sorts of slips and therapeutic decisions discussed above should be ruthlessly weeded out. Radical behaviorists ought to behave as if they really believed the presently stated tenets of their position. They are describers and manipulators of physical movements and nothing more. If the radical behaviorist adhered strictly to this, Frankel's (1971) words would be well worth noting:

> One can wonder what Skinner's appeal would be if he described only movements and did not add theoretical projections. Would the reader have the patience to project his own interpretations upon the movements or would he read someone like Freud who at least makes systematic projections? Skinner and Freud are similar in that both have an ingenious ability to take a unit of behavior

and establish its meaning. Freud interprets dreams. Skinner interprets movements. The *undemonstrable conjectures* of Freud are perhaps no worse than the *meaningless movements* of Skinner. (p. 459)

To say that all behavior is the result of learning and then say nothing about developmentally common themes as to what is learned is to make very little headway in understanding human life. To say that learning is dependent on reinforcers and give no basis for discovering or identifying reinforcers except as learning actually occurs is to damn us to a minute analysis of every event of human life that amounts to searching for a needle in a haystack. To insist that we need not speculate about the contents of that black box we call *the organism* is to force us to act as if those wonderfully simplifying and organizing inferences about the true nature of complex phenomena we wish to understand, which have produced rapid advances in every other science, are irrelevant in ours.

Toward a Rapprochement

Until recently, the debate between radical behaviorists and personologists was quite intense. But a spirit of reconciliation is developing now in which the personality theories becoming most influential are those that give weight to situations as one determinant of behavior, and behaviorism is acknowledging its implicit theorizing about human core and peripheral characteristics. For behaviorists, this shift is most apparent when attempts at psychotherapy are made. According to those "card-carrying" behaviorists, Hunt and Dyrud (1968),

> innate proclivities of man have an important bearing on behavioral modification. They can lie waiting as traps or can be employed as powerful allies . . . . There is no reason why we cannot devise methods to play into man's ethology, to turn the apparent rigidities of innate tendencies to our advantage . . . . In a sense, the important part of the modification would consist of putting the individual into a position in which "nature would take its course," in a new and better direction. (pp. 149–150)

In another statement, Hunt (1975) admits implicit theorizing among behaviorists far beyond core characteristics alone:

> Identification of the effective reinforcers for a particular person and his particular behavior can be quite difficult, requiring shrewd guesses based on personal experience and empathy, clinical knowledge and dynamic theory, plus a good green thumb for behavior-in-context.

It is understandable that in the act of finding reinforcers that will work for the client, the behavior therapist's implicit personality theory will be shown.

Hand-in-hand with the growing willingness to make implicit personality assumptions explicit is increasing self-criticism among behaviorists. Where earlier there was an optimistic, almost incautious attitude of invincibility, there is now a more sober appraisal of the whole approach. Hunt (1975) provides a good example of this evaluative attitude. He identifies three related weaknesses in behaviorism as a scientific approach and a psychotherapy that are beginning to gain wide discussion.

First is the problem of unexpected side effects. It is now apparent that schedules of reinforcement may have unintended but important and systematic effects on behavior other than the behavior that is the target of the treatment or shaping. Examples are (1) aggression as a side effect of aversive conditioning (e.g., Ulrich, Dulaney, Kucera, & Colasacco, 1972); (2) behavioral "contrast," in which changes in the reinforcement schedule in one segment of a session changes behavior in another segment though the schedule there remains unchanged (e.g., Reynolds in Hunt, 1975); and (3) "auto-shaping," in which even pigeons seem to acquire an operant-pecking response without there having been direct reinforcement of it (e.g., Jenkins, 1973).

The second or ethological weakness of radical behaviorism is its inadequate ability to deal with species-specific behaviors, especially the differences among lower organisms, higher primates, and human beings. Specifically, it is the human's symbolization and active use of it to control his or her own and others' behavior that create havoc with attempts at behavior shaping (Hunt, 1975). Not only therapists and experimenters can shape behavior; so can clients and subjects! Related is the accumulating evidence (e.g., Medin, 1972) that even in monkeys "reward can function to decrease as well as increase the probability of choosing an object," thus casting doubt on positions based on an automatic strengthening function of reinforcement. There are also humorous examples of animal research in which strange "misbehavior" results from the shaping of responses that are not a natural part of the relevant organism's repertoire (e.g., Hinde & Stevenson-Hinde, 1973). At the human level, recent research on empathy and prosocial behavior has led many investigators (e.g., Feshbach, 1982; Hoffman, 1981; Staub, 1978) to conclude that children are not the "blank screens" at birth that radical behaviorism would have us believe; rather, children appear ready early in life to behave altruistically.

The third weakness of radical behaviorism that is gaining increasing attention from behaviorists is the difficulty in rigorously accounting for self-regulation of behavior. Just what this mysterious self is that can control its actions is a vexing problem in a position that has been as situational as radical behaviorism (Hunt, 1975). According to Hunt and Dyrud (1968), an entirely new set of assumptions may be necessary in order to understand human symbolization instead of the earlier attempt to generalize from lower organisms with rudimentary mentation. The experimental evidence is consistent with this clinical conclusion in showing that human adults do not seem to learn without awareness of doing so. Dulany (1962, 1968), Spielberger (1962), and Bandura (1969) have convincingly demonstrated that in order for learning to occur in humans, it is necessary for the person to be able to verbalize not only the relationship between the target response class and the reinforcement but his or her intention to cooperate with the learning task! In situations in which this cooperative attitude is presumed not to exist, it has been shown (e.g., Calder & Staw, 1975a, 1975b) that extrinsic reinforcement (the usual kind recognized by behaviorists) does not add to, but rather interacts with, intrinsic reinforcement (the inherent value in the task), decreasing overall performance.

Early in his presidential address before the American Psychological Association, Bandura (1974) said:

> After individuals discern the instrumental relation between action and outcome, contingent rewards may produce accommodating or oppositional behavior depending on how they value the incentives, the influencers and the behavior itself, and how others respond. Thus reinforcement, as it has become better understood, has changed from a mechanical strengthener of conduct to an informative and motivating influence . . . . Theories that explain human behavior as the product of external rewards and punishments present a truncated image of man because people partly regulate their actions by self-produced consequences. (p. 860)

For Bandura, recent research developments of the sort we have been discussing have shifted the emphasis of behaviorism from the study of response learning to analyses of memory and cognition. The rest of his address theorizes about these mental functions. In this new emphasis, Bandura is joined by other behaviorists (e.g., Boneau, 1974; Dember, 1974; Mischel, 1973). Self-regulation research currently is gathering force, documenting a cognitive influence on action that is way beyond anything accountable by radical behaviorism (e.g., Bandura, 1978; Kuhl & Beckman, 1985).

Reluctantly, Holland (1978) suggests that behavior modification therapy has deviated from its parent discipline, radical behaviorism. He observes that whereas behaviorism assumes behavior to be the result of contingencies and that lasting behavior change involves altering these contingencies, most behavior modification programs do no more than arrange special contingencies in a specific environment. Behavior modification therapy is itself the result of certain contingencies imposed on it by current social structure (e.g., once-a-week therapy on an outpatient basis). Lazarus (1977) notes that behavior modification therapy is no longer the rallying cry for rigorous intervention that it once was. He blames this change on accumulating evidence that cognitive mediation of human functioning is paramount and radical behaviorism's inability to account for this. It is best, he counsels, to adopt a more comprehensive framework than radical behaviorism.

Volpe (1978), a leader of the behavior modification movement, is far from ready to give up. He argues that this form of therapy has always considered actions, feelings, *and* thoughts, treating all of them as learned phenomena subject to the laws of radical behaviorism. In attempting to account for the current emphasis on thought processes as determinants of action, he argues that this conception is mistaken in failing to recognize recent work on internal, neuronal sources of reinforcement (e.g., Olds, 1975). Although the reinforcement contingencies for thoughts may be internal, they operate by the same laws as external reinforcers. But in this very argument itself, one sees how far we have come from radical behaviorism, which insisted on regarding the organism as a "black box." In his attempt to save the child, behavior modification therapy, Volpe may have sacrificed the parent, radical behaviorism. It certainly is clear that Skinner (1975) would adopt a much more restrictive view of the nature of behaviorism.

The dissenting voices from within behaviorism are by no means restricted to behavior modification therapists. Recently Hernstein (1977) concluded that "new data undermine traditional assumptions." He believes that self-control and other phenomena require a conceptualization involving motivation. Once again this will require looking into the black box. All of the elements of a rapprochement are present. On their part, behaviorists can start developing more comprehensive approaches to human behavior, cognition, and choice. And personologists can freely avail themselves of the methodological and cognitive rigor of behaviorists.

CONCLUDING REMARKS

In considering the relative merits of personality theorizing and the behavioristic approach, it is important to recognize that to some extent they have been oriented toward different empirical phenomena. In data terms, the emphasis of behaviorism on the learning process means that it is oriented toward behavior that changes. In contrast, personology emphasizes behavior that remains the same or at least changes only slowly. The main concepts in behaviorism concerning stable behavior are stimulus and response generalization and resistance to extinction. These concepts are not at the heart of behaviorism. In addition, personology emphasizes individual and species differences, whereas behaviorism attempts to hold them constant in order to attempt specification of that which is universal in the learning process. In a sense, it is the constants in learning formulae that most directly refer to the personologist's concerns, and these constants could hardly be construed as central in behaviorism.

But although their emphasis lies elsewhere, behaviorists do accept that some aspects of behavior are at least relatively stable. Insofar as this is true, it becomes worthwhile to consider how much their theorizing about behavioral stability resembles what the personologist does. We have seen that moderate behaviorism makes assumptions that can be construed as statements about the core and periphery of personality. Radical behaviorism, in contrast, attempts to explain behavior without recourse to such organismic variables as primary and secondary drives, tied definitionally to primary and secondary rewards. Nor does radical behaviorism use terms, such as *habit,* that refer to lifestyles. But it does seem extraordinarily difficult to maintain this extreme purity from interpretations based on the contents of what is within the skin, or black box. If such purity were strictly adhered to, behaviorism might even be too cumbersome, too dependent on empirical study of each and every minute external stimulus and manipulatable movement to be of much practical use. While the risk of being wrong is certainly present once one theorizes about what is important, that risk is minimized if theorizing is done carefully enough to lead to hypothesis testing. Fortunately, even radical behaviorists now seem more willing to theorize explicitly.

What remains an unanswerable question at this time is just what kind of personality theorizing will go on in behaviorism. The persistent reference of behaviorists to Freud and their choice of such research topics as conflict and defense suggest that they are utilizing the conflict model. But they exclude the dynamic aspects of Freudian theory so that defenses become habits learned as the result of certain reinforcement schedules rather than ego operations that render certain thoughts unconscious. The very things that make psychoanalytic formulations expressive of the conflict model are disputed. And recent emphases in behaviorism have been on human choice, memory, and perception, topics that at least imply human intention. In the final analysis, it may be that behavioristic personality theorizing follows the fulfillment model, with life being understood as the general attempt to satisfy primary, biological drives through cognitive effort and intention. Understood in this way, behaviorism ceases to be a frank alternative to personology. Instead, it becomes an approach to understanding learning—which, in some of its statements, is not so different from the enterprise of personality theories covered in this book.

CHAPTER 13
The Rise of Social Learning Theory

Recently an emphasis called *social learning theory* has been gaining considerable popularity in psychology. It has implications for the study of personality and therefore should be considered here. Initially an offshoot of moderate behaviorism, the social learning position seems to have emerged in response to the difficulty human behavior has posed to learning emphases developed in laboratory experiments on rats and other lower organisms. Human beings are so complex that their behavior often seems different both in kind and in degree from that of other animals. Faced with this problem, some behaviorists have clung steadfastly to their simple S-R, associationist emphases, shoring up their theories with an additional assumption here and there and attempting wherever possible to translate apparent human complexity into the simple response repertoires of their rats and pigeons. But other behaviorists have chosen instead to develop more complex theoretical approaches that, though retaining something of the flavor of behaviorism, provide understanding of human complexity without seeming to explain it away. It is from the work of this latter group of behaviorists that social learning theory arose. As the name of this approach suggests, there is still emphasis on learning rather than inherent characteristics and on the social surroundings rather than internal dispositions as the determinant of behavior.

The main architects of social learning theory are Albert Bandura (1969), Richard Walters (Bandura & Walters, 1963), Julian B. Rotter (1964), Walter Mischel (1968, 1971), and, to some extent, Hans J. Eysenck (1957) and Joseph Wolpe (1958, 1969). Although there certainly are differences among their views, the substantial similarities have begun to define a consistent approach to understanding and influencing human behavior.

THE BREAK WITH PSYCHOANALYTIC THOUGHT

You will recall from Chapter 12 that moderate behaviorism has had a fascination with psychoanalytic theory. This has taken the form of trying to purge psychoanalytic theory of its most metaphysical features, such as the unconscious and defenses, by translating everything possible into the behavioristic concepts of habit and drive. Although it can fairly be questioned whether

561

what emerged from this translation was still psychoanalytic theory, behaviorists nonetheless were cheered that they could appear to retain the clinical insights of Freud without doing violence to their view of scientific rigor.

It is significant that the social learning theorists have explicitly detached themselves from psychoanalytic theory even though they are, if anything, more interested in abnormal or neurotic behavior than are the general run of moderate behaviorists. This is happening mainly because social learning theory emphasizes cognition, or information processing, which implies thought that is rational and logical. Although Freud certainly emphasized mental functioning, it was unconscious wishes, impulses, and conflicts that emerged as the major determinants of behavior. One cannot engage in vigorous rational trial and error if unconscious mental processes are paramount. One is left with rationalization or that which appears to be rational but really is not.

It is the intent on the part of social learning theorists to emphasize a rational process of learning from experience that prompts Eysenck and Rachman (1965) to say:

> How does our theory compare with the psychoanalytic one? In the formation of neurotic symptoms, Freud emphasized the traumatic nature of the events leading up to the neurosis, as well as their roots in early childhood . . . . The Freudians' stress seems to be rather misplaced in allocating the origins of all neuroses to this period. It is possible that many neurotic symptoms find their origin in this period, but there is no reason at all to assume that neurotic symptoms cannot equally easily be generated at a later period, provided conditions are arranged so as to favor their emergence.
>
> The point, however, on which the theory here advocated breaks decisively with psychoanalytic thought . . . is in this. Freudian theory regards neurotic symptoms as adaptive mechanisms which are evidence of repression; they are "the visible upshot of unconscious causes." Learning theory does not postulate any such "unconscious" causes, but regards neurotic symptoms as simply learned habits; there is no neurosis underlying the symptoms, but merely the symptom itself. *Get rid of the symptom (skeletal and autonomic) and you have eliminated the neurosis.* (pp. 9–10)*

In attributing psychopathology to certain learned habits alone, social learning theorists are also rejecting Freud's emphasis on the inherent conflict between instincts and society or superego. Where Dollard and Miller (see Chapter 12) retained an intuitive reliance on this conflict formulation, all the while trying to divest Freud of seemingly untestable metaphysics, the social learning theorists want to make their break complete.

But it must be recognized that some social learning theorists, especially Eysenck and Wolpe, are very close to their moderate behaviorist ancestors. These social learning theorists recognize the existence and importance of the

---

*Reproduced with permission from *The Causes and Cures of Neuroses*, Eysenck, H.J. & Rachman, S. Copyright 1965, R. R. Knapp/EdITS, San Diego, CA.

primary drives (see Chapter 12). Their main emphasis is on the drive for avoidance of pain, and the anxiety they see as the heart of neurotic symptomatology is considered a secondary drive deriving from this primary one. Anxiety is a conditioned reaction, brought about by the conjunction on one or more occasions of an initially neutral stimulus with a painful event. This emphasis on habits and secondary drives rather than on conflicts and defenses stems in part from research evidence. Psychoanalysts commonly refer to Masserman's (1943) classical studies of "neurosis" in cats as justification for a conflict explanation of psychopathology. Masserman trained cats to receive food at a given location and later shocked them at that location. They developed what looked like intense anxiety reactions, which were explained in terms of conflict over whether to approach or avoid the location. Wolpe (1958) repeated Masserman's experiment but added another group of animals. This additional group was shocked in the experimental apparatus but had not had the prior approach training with food that was given to the conflict group. The "anxiety responses" observed were similar in both groups, suggesting that pain but not necessarily conflict is the essential ingredient in anxiety reactions.

If anxiety is simply a learned reaction, it should be removable, however persistent it has become, by some process of new learning that cancels out the old S-R bond. This statement underlies the psychotherapeutic efforts of the branch of social learning theory closest to moderate behaviorism. Wolpe (1958), for example, employs what he calls *systematic desensitization therapy,* in which persons are encouraged to think of anxiety-provoking thoughts while relaxing. As soon as anxiety occurs, they are to think of something else. They try this over and over until they can contemplate the previously anxiety-arousing thoughts without this emotion. As you can see, this is very far from the psychoanalyst's encouragement to patients to freely associate and thereby rediscover suppressed experiences.

When systematic desensitization therapy and other behavioristic techniques of psychotherapy became available, there was an initial flood of enthusiasm for them. They promised a simple and quick antidote for nagging symptoms that clients seemed capable of talking about forever without any behavioral change. By now, however, sobriety is replacing overenthusiasm. One has only to read relevant case histories to recognize that even direct attempts to remove symptoms with no concern for underlying problems are long, arduous, and not invariably successful.

For example, Wolpe (Krasner & Ullman, 1965) reports the use of systematic desensitization therapy with a woman who suffered with an intense fear that she would be involved in a collision whenever she was driving a car. Wolpe regards this phobia as having developed when a collision occurred while her husband was driving. It took more than sixty sessions of concentrated, arduous attention to nothing more than getting this symptom to go away. At that, Wolpe considers his patient fortunate, indicating that sometimes fears simply cannot be treated effectively by this approach. An additional vexing problem with this case (and many others like it) is that despite Wolpe's insistence that it is systematic desensitization therapy that finally produced symptom remission, many psychoanalytically inclined readers will find many descriptions suggesting otherwise. Wolpe mentions near the end of his discussion that as the woman was questioned further, it became clear that her fear was more generalized than it had originally appeared. In addition, the only two men besides her husband whom she had loved were her first fiancé, who died in an airplane crash just before they were to marry, and her father, who had died some time after that in the same year that she married her present love. It may be that behind what seemed a simple phobia deriving from an accident was the deeper fear of abandonment by beloved males. If one were so inclined, it would be easy to implicate the Oedipal triangle as an abandonment that she never fully resolved. Further, Wolpe's claim that systematic desensitization therapy must have produced symptom remission because no transference was permitted to develop is also less than convincing. The therapist even went riding in a car with the client at one point in his attempt to help her overcome her fear. Events of this sort would be regarded by psychoanalysts as definitely courting transference.

It is probably too early in our experience with behavioristic psychotherapies to evaluate them fully and well. Suffice it to say that they are not the dramatic end to all our searching for methods to alleviate human suffering—if any psychotherapy ever could be. Further, the claim that they do not implicitly employ techniques deriving from more dynamic, mentalistic theories of personality has not been definitely proven. What we can be sure of is that psychotherapy research seeking to study outcome could profit from an explicit comparative analytic stance. I do not mean anything as simple as comparing proportions of cures across various psychotherapies, though this is certainly a useful step in accumulating information with which to evaluate. At some point in the near future, it will be necessary to determine whether therapists employing a particular technique use it and no other and, if they do, whether it leads to more or less symptom remission than other single techniques. We cannot rely for this determination on what the therapist says he or she did and did not do. There seems no alternative to detailed and painstaking observational studies of ongoing psychotherapy sessions.

To summarize, Wolpe's approach, whose assumptions are very similar to those of Eysenck's position, conceptualizes learning as S-R bonds cemented by reinforcement, with primary and secondary drives providing the motive force for activity. In this regard, the positions are similar to the older moderate behaviorism mentioned in Chapter 12. The core tendency is still tension reduction, and the core characteristics are still the primary drives and rewards. The peripheral characteristics are habits and secondary drives and rewards.

COGNITION AS PARAMOUNT

It is common to regard Bandura, Rotter, and Mischel as moderate behaviorists. But with them the notion of social learning has reached a peak that virtually removes them from the behaviorist camp. To me this seems true for two reasons: (1) the assumption that learning can take place without the person emitting a response and receiving positive or negative reinforcement for it and (2) the paramount importance of learning that is attributed to cognition (which is, after all, internal and not directly observable). Turning first to Bandura (Bandura & Walters, 1963; Krasner & Ullmann, 1966), we find that he emphasizes what might be called *S-S* (stimulus-stimulus) laws, in contrast to the S-R laws of behaviorism. He believes that one need not actually emit a response in the presence of a stimulus cue, with a reinforcement following the response, in order for learning to take place. For him, it is possible for persons to observe someone else behaving in a particular way in response to a given situation and learn just by seeing what happens to them. Then, when the observers themselves are in such a situation, they are likely to behave in similar fashion. The person observed has served as a *model* for imitative learning on the part of the observers.

In this view, modeling behavior is the most common and important form of learning in humans. In making this point, Bandura (Krasner & Ullmann, 1966) argues that

> one does not employ trial-and-error or operant conditioning methods in training children to swim, adolescents to drive an automobile, or in getting adults to acquire vocational skills. Indeed, if training proceeded in this manner, very few persons would ever survive the process of socialization. It is evident from informal observation that the behavior of models is utilized extensively to accelerate the acquisition process, and to prevent one-trial extinction of the organism in situations where an error may produce fatal consequences.

Going further, Bandura (Krasner & Ullmann, 1966) contends that operant conditioning is not only a less common but also a less effective procedure for learning at the human level. He quips that if a child had no occasion to hear the phrase "successive approximations" or any other combination of unusual words, it is doubtful whether such a verbal response could ever be shaped by differential reinforcement of the child's random utterances. This frontal assault on radical behaviorism would probably produce the rejoinder that verbal behavior is not sufficiently universal across animal species to warrant granting it such importance for purposes of theorizing about the learning process. Anticipating this, Bandura (Krasner & Ullmann, 1966) concludes that such a position "simply highlights the inadvisability of relying too heavily on infrahuman organisms for establishing principles of human behavior." He is incredulous that we would actually be asked to believe that verbal communication in humans is unimportant merely because no researcher has ever succeeded in teaching a rat to talk in a recognizable language. Instead, we might be well advised to conclude that modeling procedures are superior to operant conditioning procedures in promoting learning. He suggests that we relegate the role of operant conditioning in humans to that of regulating performance of behavioral sequences once they already have been learned through modeling.

To get a vivid sense of what is being said, consider one of the many research studies (see Bandura & Walters, 1963; Mischel, 1968) supporting learning by imitation. Bandura (1965) had his child subjects watch a film about an adult who displayed novel aggressive responses, such as hitting and kicking a Bobo doll. The subjects were split into three groups based on the consequences of the adult's behavior. In one group the adult's aggression was punished, in another it was ignored, and in the third it was rewarded. When tested after the film, children who had observed aggression punished expressed less aggression in their behavior than did children who had observed it either ignored or rewarded. But in subsequent testing, when the children were offered attractive incentives to reproduce the adult's behavior, the differences among the groups vanished! Presumably all of the subjects had learned the observed aggressive behavior. The effect of punishing the observed behavior seems to have been merely to inhibit its exhibition in the children. On this basis, it is argued that reward and punishment increase or decrease not what is learned but the likelihood that it will be expressed in performance.

Cognition, or information processing, or thought must be very active and important, even in children, in order to learn by observing others and then decide whether to express what has been learned on the basis of presumed outcomes. Cognition is definitely not given such a major role in moderate behaviorism, even when it makes some concession to mentalistic matters in considering the human being.

In what sense, then, is the position of Bandura and his colleagues a behaviorism at all? It does not consider rewards and punishments important to learning and emphasizes cognition as much as, if not more than, action. According to Mischel (1968), whose own position is quite similar, Bandura is a behaviorist in that while he emphasizes cognition he does not assume elaborate motivations, impulses, conflicts, and the like to be underlying the behavior being observed. Mischel and the others attempt to explain expectations and imitative (heavily cognitive) learning in terms of a relatively uninterpretive analysis of the observable stimulus conditions that are occurring. This new body of theory is, according to him, truly a "social learning" position in that it attempts to explain thoughts and actions in terms of concrete social, functional realities. Mischel (1971) sees social learning theory as an alternative to other personological approaches, which seem to emphasize either traits (broad, cross-situational consistencies in behavior) or motivational states (which underlie many, apparently dissimilar behaviors).

In discriminating the social learning approach from positions emphasizing traits, Mischel (1971, p. 75) considers the case of a woman who seems hostile and fiercely independent some of the time but passive, dependent, and feminine on other occasions. His position is that the woman is all of these seemingly contradictory things, but with each behavior being tied to the particular stimulus conditions that elicit it. This seems a very reasonable position. But Mischel contends that trait theorists would have difficulty understanding the woman, because traits are general dispositions presumably finding expressions across a great many unspecified stimulus situations. But surely it is a vague use of the trait concept that Mischel criticizes rather than any use one would want to defend. I grant that some personality theorists name traits and then leave them hanging there, as if there were no limits to their influence on behavior. But if this were not mere sloppiness why would theorists ever postulate more than one trait? They postulate many because they at least implicitly recognize that the sphere of influence of each is limited. Traits are, after all, used primarily in explaining individual differences. In personology, one certainly can point to a use of the trait concept rigorous enough to make it hard to distinguish from what Mischel advocates. Allport (see Chapter 8), for example, considers personal dispositions as rendering a definite delimited range of stimuli and responses functionally equivalent. Also, McClelland (see Chapter 9) defines a motive as a predisposition that becomes active only in the presence of certain situational cues. Murray (see Chapter 7) shares this view, taking pains to implicate, both subjectively and objectively, perceived situational cues (alpha and beta presses) arousing the motive. It is my impression that when used carefully, the trait or motive concept is very similar to Mischel's emphasis.

This becomes even more apparent when Mischel (1971, p. 77) stresses that social learning theory is interested in "the functional relations between what [one] does and the psychological condition of [one's] life." Clearly he does not want to be restricted to a mindless listing of the links between particular cognition and particular stimulus situations. He wishes to consider how these links go together into larger functional units relevant to the main enterprises of life.

How does this differ from Allport's intent, or, for that matter, from the intent of theorists who emphasize underlying motivations for observed behaviors? I certainly grant that many personality theorists have used the motivation concept loosely. But once again we must distinguish loose from rigorous usage, for it is only the latter that is a proper target for Mischel if he were to demonstrate the *inherent* superiority of his position. In carving out the relevant domain of social learning theory, Mischel (1971, pp. 78–79) emphasizes "covert representation" (for learning that is unexpressed externally), the whole matter of "the individual's interpretation of events and experiences," and the occurrence of "mediation." In discussing mediation, Mischel (1971, p. 81) emphasizes the importance of the human as an active organism that "evaluates, judges, and regulates his own performance" and "in addition to being rewarded and punished by the external environment . . . [learns] to monitor and evaluate [his] own behavior and to reward and punish [himself], thus modifying [his] own behavior and influencing [his] environment." Is there any personality theorist who would find this emphasis different from his or her own? Hardly, unless it were those who so stress unconscious motivation that they would find the self-deterministic ring of Mischel's words objectionable. But then, at the very least, Mischel might do well, at this early stage in the development of social learning theory, to oppose it to theories of unconscious motivation alone rather than to all motivational emphases.

Indeed, from the examples and cases he raises, Mischel does seem to have psychoanalytic theory as his main objection. A notable case in point concerns Pearson Brack, an American pilot during World War II, whose famous problem is discussed by two psychoanalysts, Grinker and Spiegel (1945, pp. 197–207). During a bombing mission, Brack's plane was severely damaged by flak and he was rendered unconscious. The plane began to dive, and Brack barely regained consciousness in time to right it before it crashed. Seriously injured, Brack was hospitalized for a month. After this time, he seemed fully recovered and was returned to duty. But on his next two missions, he fainted when the plane reached about 10,000 feet, the elevation at which the original flak damage had occurred.

After intensive interviewing, the psychoanalytically oriented psychiatrist at the hospital concluded that Brack's fainting was connected to deep, unconscious anxieties rooted in his childhood experiences. The diagnosis involved basic immaturity, long-standing insecurity, and faulty identification with father. The incident of nearly being shot out of the sky was perceived as rather trivial except as it precipitated anxiety in an already insecure and immature person. In contrast, Mischel (1968) offers a social learning analysis of the case that emphasizes the severe emotional reaction that had been conditioned to altitude cues specific to 10,000 feet. According to Mischel, it explains sufficiently the fainting for one to recognize that the occurrence of any cues specific to the near fatal incident would be enough to re-elicit the emotional debilitation associated with that trauma.

It is my impression that virtually all fulfillment and consistency theorists would tend to agree with Mischel in his interpretation of the Brack case. This further underscores the fact that Mischel's main dispute regarding motivation is with the Freudians, who persist in postulating basically unconscious conflicts and purposes underlying behavior. But if what I am saying is so, it would be wise for Mischel to acknowledge that there indeed are personalistic approaches to the motivation construct that are much more compatible with his own.

The final social learning theorist we will consider is Rotter (1954), who takes as his task an understanding of the probability that a particular act will occur. He calls this probability the *behavior potential*. You will recall that in moderate behaviorism the probability of a response is determined by the strength of the habit or S-R bond. The more times in the past the response has followed a particular stimulus cue and been stamped in by a reinforcement, the greater the likelihood that the cue will elicit the response in the future. Radical behaviorism offers a similar formulation, except that it does not use the terminology of habit and explicitly recognizes that intermittent reinforcement may produce a higher response probability than invariant reinforcement. The differences between these formulations and Rotter's pinpoints what is new about social learning theory. For Rotter (1954), *behavior potential is a function of both the expectancy that reinforcement will follow the behavior and the perceived value of the expected reinforcement*. First, the emphasis on expectancy and perceived value shows the strong cognitive commitment that Rotter has made. Expectancies and perceived values are internal, mental events and are given the role of jointly determining whether or not action will take place.

Second, Rotter is dealing with a subjective rather than objective basis for predicting behavior. One person's expectancy that reinforcement will follow a response may differ from another person's expectancy. Similarly, there may well be individual differences in the perceived value of any particular reinforcement. Consequently, what is being said is that if you wish to understand why humans behave or fail to, you must refer to their own individualized views of the world. Indeed, Rotter has a name for this: the *psychological situation*. This is clearly intended to be the person's general construction of the value and likelihood of the stimuli making up his or her environment.

True to his social learning assumptions, Rotter does not regard individual differences in reinforcement expectancy and value to stem merely from instincts or underlying motives; rather, he believes that such differences strongly reflect differences in previous experience. Having assumed this, Rotter could take a reasonably conservative stance that would come as close as possible to an objective position. He could say that the value one places on a reinforcement reflects what its actual utility has been in one's past. Thus, sports cars would have more reinforcement value for a male who has won the company of attractive females by owning them than for someone whose female associates regard fancy cars as ostentatious. Further, he could say that the expectancy of a reinforcement mirrors its actual frequency of occurrence in a person's past. Such an approach certainly would generate an ability to understand individual differences, for it could be safely assumed that the chances are great for the occurrence of objective differences among people in their past experiences.

Certainly Rotter recognizes these actuarial bases for differences in reinforcement value and expectancy in the present. But he goes even further than this. In a leap into subjectivism from which there is no return, he (Rotter, Chance, & Phares, 1972) asserts that "people's probability statements, and other behaviors relating to the probability of occurrence of an event, often differ systematically from their actuarial experience with the event in the past." A variety of factors are regarded as influencing one's probability estimates away from objective occurrence. Among these factors are the way in which a situation is categorized, various patterning and sequential considerations, the uniqueness of events, the degree of generalization that occurs, and how the person perceives causality. These factors are not meant to be derived from the person's reinforcement history in any precise way; rather, they are best understood as cognitive commitments or decisions that interact with the objective frequency and utility of reinforcements to produce each person's particular reinforcement expectancies and values, or psychological situation. It is this psychological situation that determines the relative likelihood of the person taking various actions in the future.

In his reference to factors that influence cognition and perception away from actuarial experience, Rotter shows the influence of his longtime colleague, George A. Kelly (see Chapter 5 especially). Interestingly, Mischel studied for his Ph.D. with Rotter and Kelly. It should be clear by now why I think that the cognitive emphasis of these social learning theorists and Bandura is so extreme as to place them outside behaviorism. To try to somehow subsume not only the notion of observational learning but that of subjective perceptions as determinants of reinforcement value and expectancy under behaviorism would literally destroy its original intent. When social learning theorists assert that they remain behaviorists nonetheless, it seems to me that what they really mean is that they still wish to be regarded as serious scientists. They are still concerned with the prediction and control of behavior, and they fervently believe that the cognitive concepts they employ are measurable and manipulable experimentally. In this, most personologists would agree with them. But that does not make any of them behaviorists.

If you are wondering whether the conclusion that social learning theory is beyond the limits of behaviorism really applies to Bandura, set your mind at rest. In his presidential address before the American Psychological Association, Bandura (1974) went as far as Rotter.

Bandura first reasserted the preeminence of cognition by indicating that in his judgment research has shown that there is no operant conditioning at all without both awareness on the subject's part of the contingencies existing between responses and reinforcements and his or her consent to being manipulated by the experimenter in this fashion!

Second, he regarded self-regulation of one's own behavior through manipulation of the environment as the hallmark of human functioning. According to him, humans progress toward maturity by gaining greater and greater control over their behavior through a combination of internal or self-reward and actual shaping of the external environment to make it more self-rewarding. Moreover, the procedure whereby certain events become more or less rewarding than others is for Bandura an essentially internal one. Not only is it internal; it is also subjective in the sense that there may not be complete correspondence between reinforcement value and reinforcement histories.

His third point that is important here was an amplification of the previously mentioned assumption that persons learn largely through observing the reinforcement consequences of action without having to perform any act or experience any reinforcement themselves. Bandura did not intend that this imitative learning imply a slavish following of the literal behaviors that have been observed. If this were so, nothing new would ever happen. In attempting to explain how new behaviors could occur through imitative learning, Bandura considered how it is possible to learn by merely observing. The key is the human capacity to represent observed behaviors symbolically, not just literally. In other words, persons can generalize from what they see to categories of behavior. Said Bandura (1974):

> From observing others, one forms an idea of how certain behavior is performed, and on later occasions the coded information serves as a guide for action . . . . Some of the limitations commonly ascribed to behavior theory are based on the mistaken belief that modeling can produce at best mimicry of specific acts. This view is disputed by growing evidence that abstract modeling is a highly effective means of inducing rule-governed cognitive behavior.

Going further, he gave clear recognition to the fact that in the process of abstracting from specific acts observed the person utilizes internal "judgmental orientations, conceptual schemes, linguistic styles, information-processing strategies, as well as other forms of cognitive functioning." It goes without saying at this point that when Bandura calls himself a behaviorist, what he really means is that he is still a rigorous scientist.

THE IMPACT OF SOCIAL LEARNING RESEARCH

To some psychologists the cognitive, internal, subjective emphasis of social learning theory will indeed brand it as no longer fully scientific. But Bandura, Mischel, Rotter, and others who share their beliefs consider themselves quite interested in and capable of articulating, measuring, manipulating, and predicting the cognitive variables and learning process they have assumed. Although in a purist sense a behaviorist might argue that there is no way to measure a thought or an idea because it is internal and intangible (remember that to a philosopher it would be spiritual, not material), a social learning theorist would insist that adequate measurement is possible through oral and written verbal report. This is the same assumption all personologists make. Were it not for the subject's verbalizations, be they spontaneous or in response to interview questions or paper-and-pencil tests, little by way of empirical study of personality would be possible. Thus, it would be hard for personologists to fault social learning theorists in their claim to being serious scientists.

Moreover, if impact is any gauge of research soundness, the work of social learning theorists certainly has been important. It is not irrelevant that Bandura was President of the American Psychological Association in 1974. He and his colleagues have provided a body of research, an example of which was mentioned before, showing that observational learning takes place in humans, is more rapid than standard conditioning, and can lead to generalization beyond what is literally observed. The studies' content has often been aggressive behavior (e.g., Bandura & Walters, 1963). By choosing in this fashion, Bandura and his associates have brought their work close to present concerns in our society. Their conclusion is clear: By merely observing on TV or in the movies aggressive behavior that is rewarded or at least not punished, a person can learn that it pays to be aggressive! And this will happen even if the program or film contains only cartoon characters. Such findings raise an insistent question for a society beset by a steadily increasing rate of violence: When and under what circumstances is censorship of public communications appropriate? You may be appalled by the merest posing of the question of censorship. But recall that Plato, in *The Republic,* puts into Socrates' mouth the defense of censorship in order to preserve the ideal state and foster sound character in its members. And, after all, the work of Bandura and his associates does not lead to the conclusion that all portrayals of violence breed violence in the observer. When what is observed is aggression leading to punishment, aggressive behavior is learned but its performance is not likely.

Another important research theme that Bandura shares with Mischel concerns self-control, a matter that is one of the major differences between social learning theory and ordinary behaviorism. A general procedure has been devised for studying the person's criteria for self-reward. The usual subjects are schoolchildren, who are asked to work on a performance task that seems to require skill. In reality, their scores on the task are predetermined by the experimenter so that they will experience varying degrees of success or failure. They also have available to them a large supply of rewards (e.g., candy, cake, toys), and they are usually left alone, though secretly observed, during testing. But before testing, the children observe adults performing the same or a similar task and rewarding themselves according to a high or low criterion of success. Often the adult models also verbalize rationales that are consistent with self-reward decisions.

Using such a procedure, Bandura and Kupers (1964) demonstrated that patterns of self-reward are acquired through imitating models. Children who observed adult models rewarding and praising themselves after low scores on the performance test tended to do the same when they were subsequently tested. Children who observed self-reward and praise only after high scores followed that example. These findings are shown in Figure 13–1.

It is important to note that the children were alone when tested and, hence, should not have experienced any direct social pressure influencing self-reward. That they did not deviate from the self-reward pattern they had previously observed is quite consistent with social learning theory. There are several additional studies consistent with this one. As a whole, these studies have entailed a range of performance tasks, performance criteria, and model characteristics. The consistency of the findings that self-reward patterns are strongly influenced by observed behavior in models therefore can be considered to have some generality.

A particularly interesting direction in self-control research involves the decision for immediate or delayed gratification. It can certainly be argued that adequate adjustment to our society requires the ability to delay rewards. If, as social learning theorists contend, persons are at least partially able to manipulate reinforcement contingencies in the environment rather than passively succumb, they must be able to delay reinforcement to some later time even though it is within their power to have it immediately. In research on this matter, subjects usually must choose among actual rewards that differ in time of occurrence and in value. Typically the choice of immediate reinforcement brings a smaller reward, whereas delaying reinforcement qualifies one for a larger reward. Again children are the common subjects, and again subjects observe an adult model making choices similar to those they will subsequently be asked to make.

In such a study, Bandura and Mischel (1965) preselected children such that their sample included both subjects who characteristically sought immediate though small rewards and others who sought delayed and larger rewards. There were some of these children in each treatment group of the experiment. In one

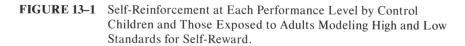

FIGURE 13–1   Self-Reinforcement at Each Performance Level by Control Children and Those Exposed to Adults Modeling High and Low Standards for Self-Reward.

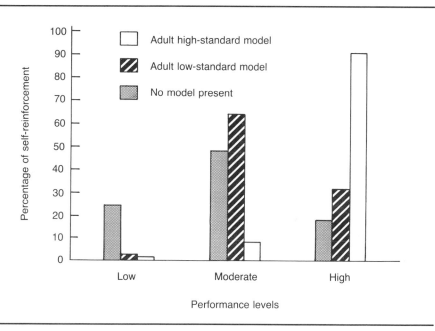

SOURCE: Adapted from "Transmission of Patterns of Self-Reinforcement through Modeling" by A. Bandura and C. J. Kupers, 1964 *Journal of Abnormal and Social Psychology, 69.*

treatment group, children observed an adult model who exhibited delay-of-reward choices that were counter to their own self-reward patterns. For example, if the child was initially high in delay of gratification, the adult model chose immediate rewards, and children who preferred immediate gratification during the pretest period observed a model who chose the delayed, larger rewards. Also, models always gave verbal rationales for their choices. In another treatment group, subjects were again exposed to information about a model performing counter to their pretest patterns, but rather than viewing an actual model, they received the model's choices in written form. Children in a control group had no exposure to or information about models.

The children's own choices to have immediate or delayed gratification were tested immediately after they had observed the model. Figure 13–2 shows clearly that the subjects' choices were strongly influenced in the direction of the model's choices. The effects of the treatment persisted in a different social setting one month later. Further, they occurred even with the written responses rather than the "live" model. These findings are impressive, especially when you keep in mind that observing the model actually reversed a predilection that the child had brought to the experimental situation!

FIGURE 13–2 Mean Percentage of Immediate-Reward Responses by High-Delay Children on Each of Three Test Periods for Each of Three Experimental Conditions.

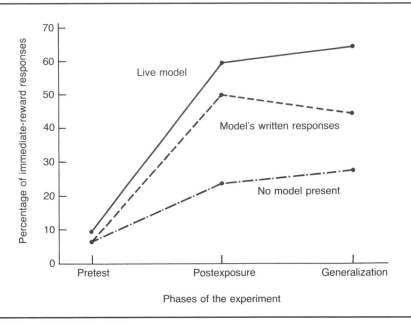

SOURCE: Adapted from "Modification of Self-Imposed Delay of Reward through Exposure to Live and Symbolic Models" by A. Bandura and W. Mischel, 1965, *Journal of Personality and Social Psychology, 2.*

A fair amount of work attempting to pinpoint the mental state of subjects who are able to delay gratification had been done. The subjects must have the expectation or "trust" that the delayed reward will indeed be granted (e.g., Mischel, 1966). Also, in order to choose the delayed reward, the subjects must be able to spend the time period preceding the reward either not thinking about anything in particular (Mischel & Ebbesen, 1970) or distracting themselves with other pleasant thoughts (Mischel, Ebbesen, & Raskoff, 1971).

Despite the many intriguing findings in this and other research themes involving imitative learning, an important question remains unanswered. To what extent is the learning and performance of adults influenced by observing models? After all, research to this point has almost invariably utilized children as subjects and adults as models. But adult subjects might be less impressionable in observing other adults or children as models.

The concern with the mental state of subjects who delay gratification forms a natural transition to research that more squarely involves personality. This research treats the preference for *delayed versus immediate gratification* as a peripheral characteristic. Mischel (1958) measured this in a simple fashion. After subjects had filled out a questionnaire, he displayed a large and a small piece of candy and indicated that he wished to give a piece to each of them but that he did not have enough of the larger ones just then to go around. The subjects were given their choice of getting the smaller piece immediately or the larger one a week later, when another shipment would arrive. Since this early study, the simple measure of immediacy or delay of gratification has been extended to include more choice situations. The resulting test seems to have adequate internal consistency and stability (e.g., Mischel, 1961).

Considerable research correlating the measure of delayed versus immediate gratification with other behaviors has been done. Persons who prefer delayed rewards are high in achievement orientation, social responsibility, and resistance to temptation; they are older, are future oriented, live in a home with no father present, and plan carefully for distant goals (see Mischel, 1966; Klineberg, 1968). Socioculturally, preference for delayed gratification tends to be found most often in the middle and upper classes and in industrialized societies (e.g., Mischel, 1958). There clearly is empirical overlap between delay versus immediate gratification and McClelland's need for achievement (see Chapters 9 and 11). The extent of this overlap remains to be determined. For the present, however, we can accept delay versus immediacy of gratification as a peripheral characteristic with sufficient empirical support to be taken seriously.

Turning to Rotter's research, its most influential theme, *internal versus external locus of control,* was discussed in Chapter 11 under existential psychology. In this, Rotter is concerned with people's generalized and pervasive expectancy that they have control over and responsibility for what happens to them as opposed to feeling manipulated and controlled by external factors. Strictly speaking, this peripheral characteristic derives from the least explicit part of Rotter's theorizing. Generalized expectancies, such as that concerning locus of control, are not as concrete as the expectancies and values attributed to reinforcements; rather, generalized expectancies are what form the psychological situation, according to Rotter.

By now, considerable research correlating various questionnaire measures of locus of control with other variables has been done. But there is no point in repeating what we covered in Chapter 11. Suffice it to say that persons with an internal locus of control at a personal level are more individualistic, assertive, interested in gaining knowledge, and willing to rely on their skill in risky situations than are persons who believe they are externally controlled. At the societal level, persons with internal locus of control are more concerned with social problems and more activistic in attempting to solve them than are persons who feel extremely controlled. It should also be kept in mind that Rotter and his associates have done experimental studies in this area that bolster the claim that internal versus external locus of control has a causal influence on behavior. Recent evidence (e.g., Lao, 1970) has begun to suggest that the internal-versus-external-locus-of-control construct is not as unitary as initially thought. Persons who regard themselves as able to influence their own and their friends' lives do not necessarily believe they can influence events in the broader society, and vice versa. Paralleling this empirical complication is the theoretical likelihood of overlap between locus of control and McClelland's need for achievement. And, as you know from Chapter 11, the overlap between locus of control and the emphasis in existential psychology on the individualist's self-definition and world view is so great that Rotter's research is as relevant to that body of theory as it is to his own. Despite all these complications, the personologists' reaction to locus of control research has been enthusiastic. It seems to be an intuitively and rationally compelling peripheral characteristic.

The emphasis on cognitive control seen in social learning theory has fueled a general reconsideration of the self-concept (cf. Markus & Wurf, 1987). In this, some studies have focused on the sources of information people use when they formulate self-representations. People appear to make conclusions about themselves from (1) direct attempts to evaluate their own actions (e.g., Trope, 1986), (2) communications from and comparisons with others (e.g., McGuire, 1984), and (3) inferences concerning their own physiological reactions (e.g., Bandura, 1977). Further, the generalizations people make from these sources appear to be influenced by their ability to cognitively process information (e.g., Harter, 1983).

A growing body of research concerns the processes whereby the self-concept is formed, changes, and influences behavior (e.g., Cantor & Kihlstrom, 1986; Carver & Scheier, 1981). As to regulation of action by the self-concept, Bandura (1977, 1985, 1986) and Kirsch (1985) have demonstrated an impressive range of effects. In emphasizing self-efficacy, Bandura (1977, 1985, 1986) refers to both a generalized perception of controllability over action and a specific perception of ability to execute a particular task. It appears that the self-efficacy concept is similar to the internal locus of control discussed earlier.

Bandura (1986) identifies the four principal sources of perceived self-efficacy as *mastery experiences* (successes incline you to believe you will be successful), *modeling* (we judge our abilities partially through comparison with others), *social persuasion* (we sometimes believe what others tell us about ourselves), and *physiological state inferences* (we try to make sense out of our bodily events). These serve as the cornerstone for teaching self-efficacy to persons in the hope that this will have a beneficial effect on their actions. Bandura (1986) reports that postcoronary recovery patients who perceived themselves (through training) as having greater physical efficacy complied more fully with prescribed exercise programs. Further, a wife's support of her postcoronary husband is more likely to lead to his curtailing efforts to become physically active if she regards his heart function as impaired than if she judges it to be robust (Taylor, Bandura, Ewart, Miller, & DeBusk, 1985). There is also some evidence (e.g., O'Leary, 1985) that enhancing a patient's self-efficacy increases the likelihood that needed changes in health habits, once made, will be maintained. Although such results are not surprising, they are consistent enough with social learning theory to recommend that position to us.

Perhaps more remarkable are the findings suggesting a link between perceived self-efficacy and physiological reactivity. For example, Bandura, Taylor, Williams, Mufford, and Barchas (1985) showed that in order to understand elevated catecholamine secretions in the blood (usually interpreted as a stress reaction) one must compare task demands with level of perceived self-efficacy. Only with discrepancies between demands and self-efficacy is there an elevated catecholamine secretion. Though dramatic, this result would appear to be as supportive of consistency theories (Chapters 5 and 9) as social learning theory. Nonetheless, the lively research effort surrounding the self-efficacy concept seems well worth following in the coming years.

There is further evidence that recent research on social learning theory is going in an applied direction. Topics to which this theoretical approach has been considered relevant are drug use (Sadave & Forsyth, 1977), Japanese socialization (Sukemune, Haruki, & Kashiwagi, 1977), witchcraft (Spanos, 1978), and moral development (Brody, 1978). But there is a problem with the last of these. According to Loevinger and Knoll (1983), research on empathy and prosocial behavior (e.g., Feshbach, 1982; Hoffman, 1981; Staub, 1978) shows that there may be an inborn basis for altruistic behavior in children. This seems inconsistent with the heavy emphasis on morality as learned that we find in social learning theory. In a set of interrelated papers, some writers found social learning theory useful in understanding how children learn, but Berlin (1978) felt that it cannot adequately explain rule invariance in the face of capricious and informationally impoverished situations and the process whereby abstract rules are acquired. Although there is always controversy surrounding social learning theory, it continues to have a lively reception.

PERSONAL VERSUS SITUATIONAL DETERMINATION OF BEHAVIOR

For all Mischel's emphasis on self-control and a cognitively based ability to delay gratification, he has somewhat reluctantly played a major role in the recent controversy over whether it is personal dispositions or situational forces that determine behavior. The controversy seems to have begun with Mischel's (1968) attempt to demonstrate that there is scant empirical support for the view that traits and underlying motivational states control behavior. In this argument, he was criticizing the view that traits and underlying motives have a pervasive, even ubiquitous influence on behavior to the exclusion of situational forces. In the context of such a view, the modest reliability and validity correlations associated with nearly all measures of peripheral characteristics seem a damaging empirical fact. If a person's score on the measure of a trait or motive varies over time, and if its relationship to behavior is small, how can traits and motives be conceived as important in determining action? Moreover, Mischel amassed evidence that situational factors seem to have a much larger role in controlling action.

As I have indicated earlier, this seemingly damning criticism must be examined more closely. For one thing, it takes as its starting point a version of trait theory that many personologists would recognize as sloppy. There is ample precedent among personality theorists (e.g., Allport, McClelland, Murray, Fiske & Maddi) for a conceptualization of peripheral characteristics as potentialities that await situational cues for arousal. Only when these potentialities are aroused should one expect them to influence action. This more rigorous usage than Mischel considered is not only rationally more satisfying; it would also lead to the empirical prediction of only moderate rather than large relationship between measures of peripheral characteristics and the behavioral variables they are supposed to explain. Something very similar is true of the best examples of theorizing about underlying motivational states. As Mischel clearly would have to shoot down the best usage in order to demonstrate the inherent superiority of the view that it is the situation alone that controls behavior, what appeared at first to be a damning criticism ends up being considerably blunted (see Maddi, 1979). As I indicated earlier, his criticism seems most cogent in the case of such views as psychoanalysis, which emphasize the constant effect on action of underlying unconscious motivations. Such views indeed explain even opposite behaviors as expressive of the same motivation. But Mischel has much less quarrel with fulfillment and consistency positions.

Mischel's critique ignited heated controversy that raged for several years and now shows signs of having abated. Defending the personological view, Alker (1972) argued that Mischel, in his zealous situationalism, had overlooked several available studies crucial for the issue of whether the person or the situation determines action. These studies are important because they permit evaluation of the contribution to behavior of not only traits and situations but the interaction between them. In perhaps the best known of these studies, Endler, Hunt, and Rosenstein (1962) constructed an *S-R Inventory* of anxiousness consisting of eleven anxiety-provoking situations and fourteen modes of response indicating anxiety. Subjects indicated the intensity of each of their modes of response in each situation. Through their analysis of the data, Endler et al. initially concluded that the situation was more predictive of behavior than the mode of response. But in reanalysis of the data, Endler and Hunt (1966) revised their conclusion to the position that the interaction between mode of response and situation is by far the best predictor of behavior. This finding was confirmed for the *S-R Inventory* in several subsequent studies (e.g., Endler & Hunt, 1969; Endler, 1973).

But the *S-R Inventory* is, after all, a questionnaire, which means that subjects were merely describing how they would respond in various situations without actually being in them. Moos (1968, 1969, 1970) improved on this by putting subjects in a range of situations and observing their reactions in addition to obtaining their self-descriptions. His results also showed that the interaction between the person and the situation is a far better predictor of behavior than either the person or the situation alone.

Although Alker's citation of such studies seemed persuasive, the situationalist argument was raised again by Bem (1972). He identified certain weak spots in Alker's position and insisted that the situationists be given a chance since, he asserted, personology had failed. Although Mischel expressed discomfort with this extreme, the argument raged on for a time. It has now subsided in the face of strong agreement on an interactionist position. Many now believe that the controversy was a pseudo-issue in the first place (e.g., Carlson, 1971; Hogan, DeSoto, & Solano, 1977; Bowers, 1973; Maddi, 1984; McClelland, 1981) in the sense that personality theories uniformly aim to predict behavioral regularity across situations and time rather than literal behavioral repetitions.

In what seems to be a definite settlement of the disagreements, Bowers (1973) amassed no fewer than eleven studies of the sort mentioned above demonstrating that behavior is largely a function of the interaction between personality and situation. Bowers also demonstrated the rational implausibility of asserting that either personality or situation is the whole explanation of behavior. A broader perspective on the controversy and its end has been provided by Ekehammar (1974), who reminds us of the various personologists and other psychologists who, years ago and now, have called for an interactionist approach. Recently Mischel himself (1973) endorsed interactionism. And no less a figure than Cronbach (1975) has reminded us that he called for the same thing years ago.

Just what is the nature of the interactionist solution? It rejects the idea of traits as determinant of literal response repetition across situations regardless of their characteristics and demands. It also rejects the idea that the person is without structure and shifts behavior passively from one situation to the next. Instead, it focuses on the way persons construe the situation and the effects of this construed or subjective environment on their behavior. It is assumed that there will be individual differences in response to what has been construed. There is sufficient enthusiasm for this new accord that the difficulties it creates for empirical study do not seem to be a deterrent at this time.

The interactionist position is, of course, very similar to the emphases of several personologists, including Lewin, Angyal, Sullivan, Murray, Allport, McClelland, and the existentialists (see Maddi, 1979). True, some personologists put more emphasis on personality and less on situation than is consistent with the interactionist stance (e.g., Freud, Jung), essentially regarding reality as an internal mental state. But they are in the minority, however influential they may have been in the past.

I do not mean to suggest that there has been no value in the person-situation controversy. It has alerted psychologists to the need for an articulate theory of situations. A start on this has been made (see Ekehammar, 1974) that distinguishes (1) an a priori definition of physical and social stimuli, (2) need concepts, (3) single reactions elicited by situations, and (4) perceptions of situations. Bem and Funder (1978) have even begun to speak of situations as having "personalities," by which they refer to the shared interpretations observers make. The controversy has also pinpointed the need for personality theory to have a cognitive emphasis in order that we be able to explain how the person construes the environment. This emphasis expresses itself not only in *prototype theory* (Cantor & Kihlstrom, 1986), which is an outgrowth of the social learning approach, but in other cognitive approaches, such as *script theory* (Tompkins, 1979; Carlson & Carlson, 1984) and *schema* (Helson, 1984; McAdams, 1985). Although these cognitive emphases clearly are consistent with the social learning approach and many personality theories, they are oddly out of place as moderate behaviorism, with its emphasis on mindless habits and automated responses.

Also, psychologists have begun to theorize specifically about the nature of the interaction between person and situation (e.g., Endler & Magnusson, 1976). Although these attempts have aroused reactions of hurt concerning the similar insights of earlier theorists presently overlooked (e.g., Krauskopf, 1978), the ferment seems constructive. Recently Bandura (1978) has reminded us of the rudimentary stage of our thinking about interactions by postulating *reciprocal determinism,* a process in which person and situation not only influence each other but cease to be independent entities because each ends by changing the other. In this theorizing he relies on a concept of self not unlike that found in Rogerian and existential positions.

Further, there seems to be renewed interest in theorizing more precisely about the nature of peripheral characteristics. In their return to the concept of *acts,* Buss and Craik (1983) are rethinking for personology such matters as the conceptual distinctions (such as behavioral versus dispositional consistency in actions) needed in order to understand the person's contributions to stable individual differences in behavior. Though similar in some respects to the early work of Allport (Chapter 8) and Murray (Chapter 7), there is freshness in what Buss and Craik are attempting. Similarly, Cantor and Kihlstrom (1986) suggest that the concept of *prototypes* carries the implications needed for a viable peripheral characteristic. Roughly, a prototype is more in the nature of a hypothetical construct held in the person's mind than of some precisely and operationally defined category. Thus, the person may not be able to enumerate in advance of experience everything encompassed by this vague notion existing in his or her mind. But this idea may well serve as a basis for interpreting experience once it has happened. Through interpreted experiences, prototypes may also change. Cantor and Kihlstrom believe that the peripheral characteristics personologists postulate have been vulnerable to situationist critiques because they have not been of the prototype sort. But what, if not prototypes, are the traits of Fromm, the needs of Murray, and the personal dispositions of Allport? Although Cantor and Kihlstrom seem to exaggerate the novelty of their approach, it is nonetheless heartening to see a rekindling of interest in peripheral theorizing.

Lingering Controversies

Although the controversy is largely over and the accord is fairly general, there still lingers a splinter position of situationalism. Fiske (1974, 1978) is troubled not only by the low reliability of most personality trait measures but by the many and diverse disagreements in personologists' theorizing. Adopting the behaviorists' pessimism about theorizing, Fiske asserts that personologists can never reach agreement or measure reliably as long as they are focusing on personality constructs because they probably do not really exist empirically. Disregarding the recently offered methodological and theoretical criticism of extreme situationism (and extreme personalism) cogently presented by Bowers (1973) and Ekehammar (1974), Fiske advocates that personologists abandon theorizing and devote themselves instead to the observational study of small, and therefore objective, actions and their controlling stimuli. He cites his work with Duncan (Duncan & Fiske, 1977) as a model for personological research. In their studies, they have observed persons interacting together and have abstracted from those data the nonverbal cues or rules signaling that someone is starting or ending speech. The study does not consider individual differences at length.

But if the interactionist accord mentioned earlier is correct, there really is no virtue in assuming an objective environment that affects all persons similarly. Duncan's and Fiske's work is as interpretive as anyone's. Though they have tried to de-emphasize individual differences, it undoubtedly would be possible to scrutinize the relationship between their data and findings, noting which cues for initiating and ending speech they choose to observe, and thereby discover their own subjective construction of the environment. It would also be possible to discern individual differences among subjects in perception and action. Similarly, Fiske's (1974, 1978) proposed direction for personology expresses a behavioristic preference on his part rather than a necessary conclusion for anyone else. Indeed, one might as easily be moved to excitement by the disagreements among personality theorists, because they provide the occasion for comparative analytic research. Once the disagreements are taken seriously enough to be organized into precise issues, empirical and rational effort can well be expended in resolving them.

The sting is even being taken out of the argument that virtually all personality measures are too unreliable to signify empirical existence for the underlying construct. Rejoinders to the effect that the level of reliability desirable in a measure is a function of the theoretical nature of the underlying construct (e.g., McClelland, 1981; Maddi, 1984) have been supplemented by supportive extensions of classical reliability theory (cf. Jackson & Panounen, 1980). Very systematic psychometric proofs now show that high reliability is not necessary in order for a measure to show validity. Even if this were not so, Epstein (1984) has accumulated considerable evidence that the more observations you make on a subject, the more reliable his or her behavior appears to be.

Another splinter position of lingering controversy is identified with D'Andrade (1974) and Shweder (1975), who argue that behavior is indeed less reliable than personality theory construes it. They believe that people (from lay persons to personality theorists) engage in a *systematic distortion* whereby they imagine more regularity in behavior than there really is. The distortion, they claim, is based on similarity in word meanings rather than accurate observations of actions. But Block, Weiss, and Thorne (1979) have effectively counterargued that the meaning structure in personality ratings must accurately reflect behavioral regularity and pointed to several serious weaknesses in empirical data supporting the systematic-distortion hypothesis. Shweder (1982) counterattacked. And so the controversy lingers. Perhaps the most sensible position to take is that as the existing data support both positions equally well, there is no empirical basis for concluding counterintuitively that personality does not exist (Brown, 1986; Rohrer & Widiger, 1983).

PERSONALITY IMPLICATIONS OF SOCIAL LEARNING THEORY

Social learning theorists clearly intend to have an impact on personality theory in addition to their emphasis on learning. In their statements, they recognize full well that the aim of personality theory is to specify those characteristics and tendencies of persons that partially determine behavior. They also recognize that individual differences in perception, cognition, emotionality, and action form the main subject matter of personology. And they have indeed offered some theoretical statements that lead in the direction of a viewpoint on personality. These statements are not sufficiently extensive or developed to constitute a full personality theory, but they do make a recognizable start.

Core Considerations

It is at the level of core assumptions that the personality implications of social learning theory are least clear. Certainly the statements they make about learned dispositions, which qualify as peripheral considerations, suggest underlying assumptions about core considerations. But discerning these core conditions is not particularly easy. Mischel (1973b) is clearest in the recognition that core assumptions are necessary in personology. He suggests that *all persons have an inherent tendency to construe the events of their experience and thereby give them meaning.* As a core tendency, this bears resemblance to that of Kelly (see Chapter 5), though with less emphasis on prediction and control of events. Indeed, much of what Mischel has to say about personality shows the unmistakable stamp of Kelly. But a word of caution is necessary. Mischel's main interest is in emphasizing individual differences in the ability to construe one's world. As these differences are conceived of as inherent rather than learned, it is possible to regard them as aspects of a core statement. But it is quite rare for core statements to refer to individual differences. In any event, Mischel nominates the kinds of cognitive capabilities and skills that appear on intelligence tests (e.g., memory, perception of similarities, discernment of differences, ability to abstract) as what he means. He suggests that much of what others have referred to as *ego strength, maturity,* and *competence* is really a reflection of inherent differences in the cognitive abilities whereby meaning is attributed to events.

There is little else in social learning theory concerning core considerations. Little or no direction is provided whereby one can understand why persons construe in one direction or another. Rotter (1964, p. 58) makes passing reference to "unlearned or biologically based satisfactions of the organism" but says no more than that. The rest of the personality emphasis in social learning theory is at the peripheral level. That is, I suppose, understandable in a position that derived from behaviorism and its preoccupation with the learning process.

Development

Whatever notion of personality development in social learning theory exists is simple enough. Endowed with a particular level of cognitive capabilities, you encounter the social world, which is comprised of models to observe and persons who will apply positive and negative reinforcements. The greater your cognitive capabilities, the more actively you will construe the events and people of your world, accept or resist the reinforcements applied to you, and engage in the self-control that mitigates the effects of those reinforcements.

The major form of learning is assumed to be observational. Although models are important in this, that does not neccessarily mean a slavish repetition of just what is observed. Presumably the more cognitive capabilities you have, the more you will generalize and transform what you observe into something more unique to you. Although there are no notions of developmental periods or stages in social learning theory, Bandura (1974) has indicated that the process of maturing involves progressively greater freedom from reinforcements imposed by others all the while there is progressively greater self-control of reinforcements.

Peripheral Considerations

Most of what social learning theory has to say about personality involves learned orientations. There is general agreement that peripheral characteristics develop out of the interaction between persons and their environment. But

Rotter and Mischel disagree on how to conceptualize these learned characteristics.

According to Rotter (1964, pp. 58–60), development results in *motives* or *needs,* which vary from very specific to very general. He considers a need as having three essential components. The first is the set of behaviors, all directed toward the same goal, that together define the expression of the need. The second is expectancies that certain behaviors will lead to satisfactions or goals that are valued. The third component is the need's value, or the degree to which a person prefers the goal state associated with a need to some other goal state. You will recognize the three components as the behavior potential, reinforcement expectancy, and reinforcement value we considered earlier in this chapter.

To get a more complete sense of Rotter's approach, let us consider six very broad needs he offers as examples. They are listed in Table 13–1. According to Rotter, the needs for *recognition-status, dominance, independence, protection-dependency, love and affection,* and *physical comfort* are very common among people, though they are learned. He believes that each of the six broad needs would have to be broken down into subneeds in order to approach the level of specificity necessary for predicting behavior. For example, the need for recognition-status could be regarded as including needs for certain social, occupational, and intellectual activities.

Mischel's (1973b) approach is really quite different from Rotter's. He considers any conceptualization that resembles the traditional approach concern-

---

TABLE 13–1   List of Needs for Rotter

1. *Recognition-status:* The need to excel, to be considered competent, good or better than others in school, occupation, profession, athletics, social position, physical appeal, or play; that is, the need to obtain high position in a socially valued competitive scale.
2. *Dominance:* The need to control the actions of other people, including family and friends; to be in a position of power, to have others follow one's own ideas and desires.
3. *Independence:* The need to make one's own decisions, to rely on oneself, to develop the skill necessary to obtain satisfaction and reach goals without the help of others.
4. *Protection-dependency:* The need to have another person or persons prevent frustration, provide protection and security, and help obtain other desired goals.
5. *Love and affection:* The need for acceptance and liking by other people, to have their warm regard, interest, concern, and devotion.
6. *Physical comfort:* The need for physical satisfactions that have become associated with security and a state of well-being, the avoidance of pain, and the desire for bodily pleasures.

SOURCE: J. B. Rotter, *Clinical Psychology,* 2/e, © 1971, p. 60. Reprinted by permission of Prentice-Hall, Inc., Englewood Cliffs, New Jersey.

ing traits and needs unwise. He is unwilling to consider content definitions of person variables. Instead, he offers cognitive and response styles and strategies as peripheral characteristics. One set of these is *encoding strategies,* which are very similar in emphasis to Kelly's personal constructs. According to Mischel, people do not passively absorb external stimulation; rather, they reflect on and transform stimulation, thereby rendering it more personally meaningful. These processes of transformation constitute how the information is coded, which in turn determines how it can be used then and in the future. Another set of peripheral characteristics offered by Mischel are expectancies concerning behavior-outcome and stimulus-outcome. *Behavior-outcome expectancies* concern the perceived consequences of action, whereas *stimulus-outcome expectancies* concern perceptions as to how components of the stimulus surround relate to one another (the S-S laws mentioned previously). Behavior-outcome and stimulus-outcome expectancies give the person a sense that the environment is familiar and predictable. Also at the peripheral level are what Mischel calls *subjective stimulus values.* This concept is very similar to Rotter's reinforcement value and is intended to refer to the varying degrees to which events are satisfying or dissatisfying for persons. The final set of peripheral characteristics are *self-regulatory systems and plans,* which essentially are contingency rules that guide the person's behavior in the absence of, or even despite, immediate external situational pressures and rewards. Such rules indicate to persons their own sense of the kinds of behavior appropriate under particular conditions, the performance levels they will require of themselves, and the consequences of reaching or falling short of these standards.

As you can see from the discussion of self-regulatory systems, the five sets of peripheral characteristics are conceived of as interacting complexly in the determination of behavior. In order to know what persons will do, you must know how they have coded information (what their personal constructs are), what relationships among stimuli and consequences of their actions they expect, what value they place on various outcomes of their actions, and their plans for regulating their own behavior. As if this were not complicated enough, Mischel insists that it is foolhardy to try to specify the typical content of these characteristics. He feels that they will reflect in each person some combination of actual reinforcement history, observational learning, and the fruits of internal cognitive competencies and transformations.

Echoing Allport's morphogenic approach (see Chapter 8), Mischel contends that each person is indeed unique in the sense that the specific content of one's personality cannot be determined in advance of studying it, and that one's present peripheral characteristics cannot accurately be discerned from a simple analysis of one's past. Part of Mischel's objection to traditional trait and motive terms is, as Allport also contended, that they are too general to permit precise understanding or prediction of individual behavior. But in championing the morphogenic view, Allport gives us very little conceptual apparatus with which to know even how to scrutinize individuals in order to determine their peripheral personalities. Fortunately, Mischel gives us much more guidance by offering as concrete peripheral characteristics the five sets of cognitive styles and strategies.

As you might imagine, Mischel does not provide anything remotely approaching a typology. He does not regard such general categories as having any empirical value. Perhaps Rotter (1964) is less extreme, offering the notion of *generalized expectancies*. These are more or less conglomerates of need potentials, reinforcement expectancies, and reinforcement values and together define the psychological situation as the person construes it. Internal versus external locus of control, as mentioned before, is an example of a generalized expectancy. But it is difficult to pursue this lead further, as Rotter has not been sufficiently explicit concerning the relationship of generalized expectancies to other peripheral aspects of personality.

The work of Cantor and Kihlstrom (1986) on *prototypes* is properly understood as an extension of Mischel's thinking in the area of peripheral characteristics. They believe that prototypes are constructs persons hold in their minds that are not precisely defined. These prototypes are models used in the effort to understand and influence experience. Cantor and Kihlstrom believe that the trait concepts in more common use among personality theorists imply a greater precision than is possible for persons as they go through their lives. As indicated earlier, although the prototype concept is consistent with social learning theory and has been the focus of some spirited research, it is not so dissimilar from the peripheral characteristics of other personologists such as Allport, Murray, Fromm and McClelland.

CONCLUDING REMARKS

Although the social learning approach was born in the attempt to understand human learning and has been critical of certain aspects of personology, it does have the beginnings of a theory of personality. It is too early in this development for extensive criticism to be a constructive enterprise. But in order to fulfill an important mission of this book, we should briefly consider toward which model of personality theorizing the social learning position seems to be developing.

It seems apparent that there is little in the approach that suggests the conflict model. Indeed, social learning theorists are ardent critics of the psychoanalytic approach to theorizing and psychotherapy. It is possible, however, that the consistency model best illuminates the social learning approach. After all, Mischel's approximation to a core tendency nominates cognitive capabilities not at all unlike Kelly's approach. The expectations and plans the person forms do not follow any content lines that are necessary in the sense of reflecting some inner nature. And the feedback obtained through interaction with the environment is regarded as important in changing one's expectations. Rotter's emphasis on needs is not inconsistent with this classification, because they are conceptualized as learned, not inherent.

But one point provokes me to at least mention the fulfillment model as possibly being relevant. Social learning theorists emphasize a very active use of cognitive processes. Persons do not just sit back passively and receive information and meaning from outside; rather, they actively develop encoding strategies, expectancies, reinforcement values, and plans. In this way, they exercise considerable self-control. This suggests the existence of an implicit assumption, perhaps of the sort made by existential psychology, to the effect that the core tendency is to search for meaning. Actually, Mischel (1973a) mentions existential psychology as a compatible approach to his own. Bandura's (1974, 1978) discussion of freedom is similarly suggestive. He considers it important to conceptualize the human being's struggle to escape externally imposed reinforcement and emerge into autonomous self-control. When there is conflict between what the person wants and what others want, the person is in difficulty, according to Bandura. But this conflict is not inherent and can be surmounted through the person's gaining control of the reinforcement contingencies at play in his or her life.

It is probably best to regard the current personality theorizing in the social learning approach as expressive of the consistency model. But I suspect that the theorizing is moving steadily toward the fulfillment model. The direction is away from Kelly and toward existential psychology.

CHAPTER 14

Psychotherapy and Assessment

By now you know a good deal about personality theories. You have experienced how they are put together out of various parts, each of which has a logic and a function. You have also seen how these theories influence research and are in turn influenced by it. In Chapter 1, I called all these things the *intellective functions* of personality theory to highlight that what is involved is more the pursuit of new knowledge than the application of what is already known.

As you read, however, you also encountered many applications of personality theory. These were contained mainly in examples I used in the hope of making these theories more tangible and vivid for you. It is now time to pull these examples (and others) into a more systematic expression of typical applications. It will not surprise you, after reading Chapter 1, that the major applications involve psychotherapy and assessment.

In this chapter, my aim is to alert you to the main features of psychotherapy and assessment according to the conflict, fulfillment, and consistency models on which we have focused. I will also include the behavioristic and social learning approaches. Although the comparison and contrast of approaches will certainly mark a comparative analytic inquiry, do not expect any marshaling of research evidence to resolve issues. The psychotherapy and assessment research literature is just too vast and complex to permit evaluation and review here. These research areas are rightly the subject matter of their own courses in the psychology curriculum. It will be enough in this course for you to appreciate the stark differences in psychotherapy and assessment practices that the three models for personality theorizing produce.

LOGICAL REQUIREMENTS OF PSYCHOTHERAPY AND ASSESSMENT

Before we examine the three models' emphases in psychotherapy and assessment, let us clarify the logical requirements of these two practical activities. This will guide us in identifying the particular parts of a personality theory that are most relevant.

The general aim of assessment is to characterize a person in terms of how he or she differs from others. This is true whether the assessment concerns only one aspect of behavior or the totality of characteristic thoughts, feelings, and actions. Theoretically, the peripheral statement of a personality theory is the most relevant here. If you were a Freudian, it would not help you much in the assessment task to conclude that both Mary and John have a sex instinct, especially as you would believe all humans to be so endowed. But it would help to conclude that John expresses his sex instinct in the form of an oral character type and Mary as an anal character type.

Further, the assessment task commonly involves an evaluation of the person assessed against some norm, usually a standard of maturity. Thus, you might conclude that although Mary is developmentally more advanced than John (for Freud, the anal stage is later than the oral stage), neither has reached maturity (for Freud, the ideal is the genital character type). Even when the assessment concerns one peripheral characteristic (rather than the pattern forming types), there is an at least implicit notion of the desirability of being well supplied with or devoid of that characteristic. As you have come to know, personality theories conceptualize maturity by evaluating the peripheral types as to how fully they permit expression of the core tendency (or purpose of human life).

Turn your attention to psychotherapy and you will find the same thing. In order to be helpful, the therapist must have a sense of what the person is like as to personality and whether or not it is fully mature. If it is not, the therapist may decide that there is a good reason for psychotherapy and also will discern the developmental direction that the treatment should take. So you can see that psychotherapy too relies on the peripheral statement of a personality theory and its relationship with the core statement.

In its additional reliance on the developmental statement of a personality theory, psychotherapy somewhat differs in emphasis from assessment. This is because the therapeutic task is to stimulate development from the initial immature personality type seen toward the ideal type as conceptualized in the theory. Indeed, you might look at the psychotherapy itself as a constructed microcosm of the developmental interactions thought to lead to the ideal type. Thus, the therapist may act toward clients the way their parents should have, whether that involves giving freedom, advice, or support.

The other thing you must recognize is that the various theories of personality carry implications as to the specific content of observations (data) about persons that are most relevant in assessment and psychotherapy. Also, these theories often suggest the kinds of approaches that should work in obtaining the assessment data and doing the psychotherapy.

THE CONFLICT MODEL

In both the psychosocial and intrapsychic versions of the conflict model, there is agreement that the most revealing data about personality are dreams, followed by waking-state fantasies (or daydreams). The least revealing observations are the person's more controlled, instrumental attempts to do things (reach goals, solve problems, shoulder responsibilities) in the social world.

This data orientation is thoroughly consistent with the emphasis on defensiveness that is inherent in the conflict model. In the psychosocial version, there is, of course, no alternative to defensiveness in dealing with the inevitable antagonism between antisocial instincts and society as the protector of the common good. In the intrapsychic version, the conflict is no less real or inevitable because it arises from two aspects of the mind rather than from the individual and the society. In dreaming, people are as close to being undefended as is tolerable for them. This is why, according to conflict theorists, dreams are sometimes so frightening. Daydreams can also be frightening, but they are usually less so because they are believed to involve a greater level of defensiveness, being the products of the waking state. It is certainly true that the psychosocial and intrapsychic versions of the conflict model differ in that the latter emphasizes defensiveness less, but this difference appears not to matter in the construal by both approaches of dreams and fantasies as the most revealing data.

The Assessment Task

It is not surprising that assessment devices common in conflict approaches are designed to stimulate the person's fantasies. Because the person is given wide latitude in concocting responses to the items of such assessment devices, it is assumed that private fantasies will be revealed. It is even expected that some of these fantasies will reveal unconscious thoughts and feelings. In this, the approach of the conflict model to assessment seems quite consistent with its theorizing.

A technique example is Jung's *Word Association Test,* in which the tester presents various words, one at a time. The respondent is instructed to react to each word with the first word that comes to mind, regardless of its sense or propriety. In this rather unstructured approach, the tester is free to choose whatever stimulus words might elicit areas of fantasy of particular interest. The assumption is that the response "nasty" to the stimulus word "mother" reveals something quite different from the response "father." You can see how in such an approach respondents might reveal things they intended to keep private or may even have been unaware of themselves.

Murray's (1943) *Thematic Apperception Test,* discussed in Chapter 2, and the *Rorschach Test* (Rorschach, 1942) are also imagination-stimulating techniques. The former is a set of ambiguous pictures about each of which the client is supposed to compose a story; and the latter is a set of ten inkblots for the client to identify. Composing a story about persons stealing nuclear secrets is a lot different from imagining a father and son having a friendly chat. Similarly, seeing an inkblot as a menacing gorilla is not at all like imagining a fuzzy teddy bear. Such assessment devices for stimulating fantasy tend to stem from conflict theorizing, with its emphasis on the compromise that involves persons in lying to others (not revealing private thoughts and feelings in order to avoid punishment) and to themselves (not being aware of the full truth about themselves).

The major assessment devices that express conflict theorizing provide test responses that the tester must interpret in order to arrive at conclusions about personality. This is to be expected from a line of thinking that emphasizes unconscious processes as the basis of personality. For Freud, persons cannot reveal underlying truths about themselves because their defenses are designed to drop these antisocial concerns from awareness lest they be too anxiety provoking or clamor too strongly for raw expression. For Jung, even if this (as he would have termed it) personal unconscious is eliminated, there is still the collective unconscious, which cannot ever be squarely in awareness. Thus, in conflict approaches the tester needs as raw material for interpretations expressions of the respondent's imagination, for it is these that are likely to reveal the underlying nature of personality.

Certainly there are questionnaires that have been used as assessment devices in the conflict approach, but this usage is understandably uncommon. After all, questionnaires restrict the elaborateness of responses (often to "true" or "false" reactions to items) and tend to emphasize events in everyday life (rather than stimulating fantasy). In assessing personality, it is much more difficult to obtain revealing information in questionnaires than in relatively unstructured tests that provoke imagination.

The Psychotherapeutic Task

In the relevant psychotherapies (usually called *psychoanalysis* whether done by Freudians, ego psychologists, Rankians, or Jungians), clients are encouraged to recount their dreams. Also, they are instructed to relate anything and everything that comes into their minds without regard for coherency, orderliness, or propriety. For Freudians, this is the cardinal principle of *free association,* and other conflict approaches agree with it. Clients are even encouraged to free associate to their dreams once they have recounted them.

Psychoanalytic therapies are so weighted toward dreams and fantasies that they have engendered various other techniques for supporting free association. The hope of stimulating imagination was one reason, for example, why Freud felt that the client should be lying down on a couch in a quiet, simple, darkened room while the therapist sat out of the client's view. These arrangements are not very common anymore, even in Freudian psychoanalysis. Jung and his followers have, from time to time, encouraged sensitivity to the collective unconscious by playing music and burning incense during therapy sessions, by reading poetry to clients or having them read or compose it themselves, and even with carefully controlled use of drugs that heighten the senses and induce fantasies.

Needless to say, psychoanalysis is more than only an opportunity for the client to exercise imagination. In all forms of this therapy that so well expresses the conflict model, therapists feel free to interpret the meanings of their clients' fantasies and dreams once those meanings have clearly emerged. Typically the therapist discerns the meaning before the client does. Again this should not surprise you, as the therapist assumes that the true significance of what clients say will be unavailable to them (since it is unconscious). It is considered good practice for the therapist to withhold an interpretation until there is enough evidence for it in the client's accumulated utterances for it to be reasonably convincing. Psychoanalysts like to insist that the client's reaction to the interpretation is an important source of new information with which to evaluate the accuracy of understanding. Certainly interpretations sometimes are refined, changed, or even abandoned by therapists, but you should not expect that this is any straightforward result of counterpersuasion on the client's part.

It is the therapist who decides whether the interpretation is accurate, and in this the client's response to it is, once again, more raw material for interpretation. If the client vigorously protests the inaccuracy of the interpretation, the therapist may well take that as a sign of its accuracy (considering the protest an expression of the very defenses that have protected the client against true self-knowledge). If the client readily accepts the interpretation, the therapist may conclude the same thing on the same grounds or decide that he or she has missed the real mark. The latter is likely because in order to be accurate, an interpretation must be threatening (a defensive unconsciousness must be assailed). And if the client responds to an interpretation with indifference, that too can be interpreted by the therapist as a sign of accuracy or inaccuracy. The conflict assumptions that psychoanalysts make lead them to expect *resistance* to any accurate interpretations. So clients who think they can enter into a logical dialogue with their psychoanalysts have another think coming.

What I have said thus far applies reasonably well to all forms of therapy in the conflict tradition. Freudians, ego psychologists, Rankians, and Jungians certainly emphasize and adopt the various techniques differently. But they share the assumption that in order for development to be stimulated, it is the client's job to focus on dreams and fantasies and the therapist's job to convincingly express interpretations.

Among conflict therapies, however, Freudian psychoanalysis has a cardinal feature that distinguishes it from the rest, namely, that the therapist is regarded as having the job of interpreting not only dreams and fantasies but the transference as well. *Transference* is the thoughts, feelings, and actions that the client experiences about the therapist. The therapist assumes that these thoughts, feelings, and actions are not accurate responses to the therapist's role in the therapy. For Freudians, that role is to be a shadowy stranger who stands prepared to help but is not to be known by the client. This is the other reason why Freud advocated that the therapist always sit out of the client's view. Although most Freudians no longer go to these lengths, they try very hard not to disclose themselves. Certainly they do not answer questions about themselves that clients may raise, nor do they engage in ordinary conversation, even about simple things like the weather. This insistence on remaining anonymous may sometimes lead in strange directions. If, for example, a therapist is thirty minutes late in seeing a client, no explanation may be given. In any explanation, there is too much risk that the client will learn something personal about the therapist or have reason to expect some normal, social relationship.

So the assumption the Freudian makes goes like this: If the client has no basis in knowledge of the therapist for strong thoughts, feelings, or actions toward him or her, these reactions must be defensively transferred from past relationships—hence, the term *transference*. Interpreting the transference is yet another way whereby the Freudian assesses client's personalities and attempts to persuade them about themselves, all in the hope of stimulating needed development.

You are now ready to appreciate a final characteristic of therapies expressing the confict model: They concern themselves primarily (sometimes even exclusively) with the contents of the mind. In technique terms, they have been called *talk therapies*. The talk may or may not get around to problems of action or inaction in the social world, such as whether one gets along with one's boss or is making a lot of money. If such practical problems are resolved as a result of psychoanalysis, that will be because interpreting dreams and fantasies will have increased the maturity of personality. Psychoanalysts generally consider it an unnecessary waste of time to focus heavily on practical, everyday problems. What is important to them is the client's pervasive personality type, the limitations on overall outlook (or immaturity) it represents, how it all developed, and whether the outlook can be improved. If outlook is improved, it is assumed that at least the most important practical problems will solve themselves.

The therapist must be initially concerned with determining what is wrong with the client. In content terms, the assessment task is to identify the client's personality type. As long as the type (or mixed type) identified falls short of the ideal or mature type, there is reason for psychotherapy. There may also be some *psychopathological state,* which also is grounds for psychotherapy. In general, psychopathological states are conceptualized as breakdowns in functioning produced by excessive stress operating on the weaknesses inherent in immaturity. In identifying psychopathology, most therapists endorse the classification of psychopathological states offered by the *Diagnostic and Statistical Manual of Mental Disorders,* third edition (1980). It includes such states as major depression and obsessive-compulsive disorder.

For Freud (see Chapter 7), the immature personality types are designated as oral, anal, and phallic, all of which deviate from the ideal, or genital, type. As the client free associates, recounts, and works on dreams and responds to interpretations, the therapist forms conclusions about the person's personality type. In doing this, the therapist looks for whether traits and defenses expressive of *receiving* and *taking* (oral type), *giving* and *withholding* (anal type), or excessive and insufficient *sexualization* (phallic type) predominate in the client (see Chapter 7). If one or another predominates, the therapist looks for evidence of relevant *fixations* through the client's recounting of early life. The therapist knows that therapy is complete when predominance of oral, anal, or phallic modes gives way to a balancing and combination of them such that the client is fully able to *love* and *work*.

For Freud, this process of increasing maturity does not connote that the client now knows the full, stark truth about his or her antisocial impulses. As genitality is still a defensive state (relying on sublimation), maturity is more a matter of adjustment to and acceptance of social norms than of radical self-knowledge (see Chapter 3). Ego psychologists are, of course, less pessimistic than Freud was about how possible and worthwhile radical self-knowledge may be.

Although the intrapsychic conflict theorists also emphasize dreams and free associations in therapy, what they are looking for in content terms differs from that sought in the psychosocial conflict approach. For example, Rankian therapists would be listening for evidence of neuroticism which suppresses the fear of life (such a client would be alienated from others, institutions, and belief systems) or awareness which suppresses the fear of death (such a client would avoid changes, challenges, and critical thought). Having identified either immature style, the therapist would look for corroborating evidence in the client's report of early punitive reactions of parents toward negativistic behaviors signifying the emergence of self. Finally, through supportive and instructive interventions, the therapist would hope to stimulate the client to become more aware of both fears and to achieve a pattern of behavior that would balance them.

Content Emphases

Also concerned with dreams and waking fantasy life, Jungians try to determine whether the client is introverted or extroverted and rational or irrational in thinking mode (see Chapter 7). Having identified the client's *psychological type,* the therapist would use the treatment techniques to stimulate development of selfhood—the balance of ego and collective unconscious that transcends the psychological types in the direction of universality (maturity). For most Western clients, achieving this balance means becoming more sensitive to and receiving guidance from the collective unconscious (as shown in accepting intuitions, mysteries, and one's limited control over self and world). Here you can see a clear example of how conflict positions really do not adopt radical self-knowledge as the definition of maturity and the goal of therapy.

Though a conflict position, Jung's intrapsychic emphasis is very different from Freud's psychosocial emphasis. Nowhere is this more starkly shown than in dream interpretation as it occurs in therapy. As you may know, Freudians assume that dreams are almost always wish fulfillments. Even when your dream is so frightening that you wake up in a cold sweat, there is assumed to be some unconscious fantasy being fulfilled. If a client dreams of being attacked by persons of the same sex, the unconscious wish may be for homosexual experience. So you can see that even dreams usually are defensive expressions for Freudians—the client is aware of being afraid but not of the unacceptable desire. The work of dream interpretation is to unravel the defensive expressions the better to glimpse the underlying truths. In this process, the therapist uses such interpretive assumptions as that some dream content may stand for itself, its opposite, a condensation of many related thoughts, or a symbolic expression of one concrete element. Thus, the therapist has many ways of tracing the dream back to its essential meaning, which invariably is something sexual or aggressive of an antisocial nature (see Chapter 3).

Freudian interpretation is incorporated as one element of Jung's approach to the meaning of dreams. But Jungian interpretation of what he called the *personal unconscious* (see Chapter 3) is not limited to underlying sexual or aggressive meanings. Jungians assume a larger range of antisocial unconscious thought. The main difference between the two approaches, however, is in Jung's emphasis on dreams as expressive of the collective unconscious. Themes from the collective unconscious are universalistic (see Chapter 3). This is shown either by their directly mythic or archetypal quality (e.g., hero figures, wise old men, or earth mothers), by their recurrence in a sequence of the client's dreams, or even sometimes by the strangely elevating effect of having dreamt.

Jungians assume that archetypal material appears in dreams because greater expression of the collective unconscious is needed than the client permits in waking life. It is not surprising, therefore, that Jungians use the principle of *symmetry* in discerning dream meanings. This indicates the lines along which functioning must proceed in order for the balancing of ego by collective unconscious called *selfhood* (maturity) to be achieved. To illustrate, Jung (1933a) recounted a male client's frightening dream of killing his father. The fear was no defensive expression of father hatred, according to Jung; rather, the client loved and admired his father too much to be able to engage in the developmentally valuable struggle for independence. Jung assured the client that his dream was nothing more than a symbolic expression that it was time to grow up by drawing away from (not literally killing or having homosexual relations with) his father. The dream was necessary for symmetry because the client, in the waking, or ego, state, was so affectionately tied to his father that it was jeopardizing his development.

Jungians also believe in the *prophetic* quality of dreams. It certainly is not new in the history of thought to believe that dreams foretell the future. But it is odd to include such an idea in a personality theory! Recall that we have encountered Jung's mysticism before (see Chapter 3). Actually, the emphasis on prophecy is not that strange given the focus on symmetry already covered. If the male client in Jung's example understood the meaning of his dream, he might well have taken steps to detach himself from his father by tempering his affection. This developmental process often lies at the root of the criticality and anger that adolescents generate toward their parents. Symbolically it constitutes a kind of "killing" of the parent and, in that sense, the dream is prophetic. But you should recognize that Jung very likely also means something more mystical related to the individual features of the collective unconscious (see Chapter 3). In any event, you now have some sense of the differences in dream interpretation between psychosocial and intrapsychic versions of the conflict model.

THE FULFILLMENT MODEL

In fulfillment approaches, there is much less emphasis on dreams and fantasies. These phenomena are not regarded as any more revealing of clients or important in helping them than are any other thought processes and experiences. Indeed, fulfillment positions are more likely to focus on problems of everyday working life, such as attempts at intimate relationships or difficulties at work or school, than on dreams and fantasies. It is in these problems that personality style is most clearly revealed, according to fulfillment theorists. Dreams, while also potentially revealing, are considered more indirect and difficult to understand.

This data orientation is quite consistent with the general de-emphasis on defensiveness seen in fulfillment positions. While it is true that defensiveness can happen, maturity is a state of true openness in this approach (see Chapter 4). This leads to taking what persons are aware of in themselves literally as a guide to understanding them and not as an occasion for interpretation. Approaches that are literal in this sense have been called *phenomenological*.

The Psychotherapeutic Task

In fulfillment therapies, clients are encouraged to talk about their problems. They are not instructed to free associate. On the contrary, they are supposed to recount ongoing interactions with others and social institutions, clarifying as much as possible their perceptions, feelings, frustrations, and anxieties. There is no emphasis on recounting dreams, unless these constitute special problems. The whole thrust of these therapies is on what is going on here and now. Although past experiences are of some interest, there is no insistence that present problems can be understood only as reflections of past ones. Superimposed on the general fulfillment approach are several telling differences in technique that distinguish its two versions. In the actualization fulfillment approach, the emphasis is on accepting and supporting clients in whatever they experience and recount. In contrast, the perfection fulfillment approach is much more confrontational (though the confrontation is done in a caring manner).

In the actualization approach, the person-centered psychotherapy of Rogers is rather simple in technique. The client presents and discusses current problems, and the therapist gives *unconditional positive regard* (you will remember this from Chapters 4 and 8 as the way in which parents must react to their offspring in order to ensure ideal development). To do this, the therapist must reflect back to the client the emotional essence of what the person is saying. This is not done by merely repeating. The client's remark "Nothing ever happens, and I could scream" is not well reflected by the therapist who responds, "You feel that nothing ever happens, and you could scream." A helpful reflection that summarizes or identifies emotional essences in the client's statement might be "You're terribly bored and restless." Or, if a female client said, "We sit there all evening watching TV, barely talking to each other. It's not like it used to be, and I don't know why. He's a fine person, but nothing ever happens," a sensitive reflection might be "The romance seems gone— maybe you're not sure you love him anymore."

I gave the second example so that you can see how the reflective response can appear to interpret the client's statements. And yet, person-centered therapists insist that they, unlike the Freudians, do not interpret. What they mean is that they strive to identify essences without adding any frame of reference to the client's statement that is not already there. In contrast, an interpretation would shift attention away from the statement itself by trying to understand it in terms of the frame of reference of unresolved past conflicts. Such an interpretation in response to the above female client's statement might be "Your relationships with men all seem to end up this way—notice how differently you feel when you have those wonderful visits with your father on weekends." In contrast to such interpretations, reflections intensify rather than shift attention from what is being experienced right here and now.

Perceptive reflections give clients the sense that they have really been heard and encourage them to go further in expressing themselves. Sometimes clients will respond to sensitive reflections in a fashion such as "That's exactly what I meant—I couldn't have put it so well." They feel stimulated and freed in a way that leads to additional emotional experiences in the area under discussion. This is why Rogerians feel that unconditional positive regard is the major technique of therapy—it leads clients to feel so understood and appreciated that they can drop their defenses and experience more completely. Through being acceptable to another, they learn to temper their own conditions of worth and be more open to their organismic experience. In that way, they develop more fully (see Chapters 4 and 8).

An implication of giving unconditional positive regard is so basic to this approach that it deserves mention here: The person-centered therapist characteristically avoids giving advice. Clients often ask the therapist's opinion, especially as they come to feel understood and appreciated. "What should I do?", "I'm right, aren't I?", and "Will you help me?" are frequent client questions. These too are reflected by the therapist, who may say, "It's hard to be making these decisions alone" or "You wish there were some definite way to know." If the client's requests for help are insistent and show much suffering, the therapist may explain the reticence to offer advice, as in "I wish I could help you, so that the uncertainty wouldn't hurt so much, but I know that the best answers for you are the ones that you find for yourself." This is very consistent with the Rogerian assumption that persons (including clients) know themselves better than anyone else (including therapists) ever can.

In the early days of Rogerian therapy, therapists did nothing more than has been discussed. Now, however, they are willing to share their own feelings with clients, especially if these feelings might interfere with listening carefully. So the therapist might say, "Today I feel as if I'm not helping you enough, and it's making it hard for me to listen to you fully" or "I'm really preoccupied with something in my life, and it made me miss what you were saying." You can see in such remarks, and in the general emphasis on reflection, that there is simply no basis in person-centered therapy for identifying transference in the client, much less interpreting it (Shlien, 1987). I hope you are seeing just how different psychotherapies can be!

This sense of difference can only be heightened as we turn to therapies that represent the perfection version of the fulfillment model. The major relevant approach is existential, and that means a confrontational approach to here-and-now problems. Once again clients are encouraged to focus on their current everyday problems rather than on dreams or waking fantasies. In listening and reacting, the existential therapist is guided by several content emphases that will be mentioned shortly. First, a word on existential techniques is in order.

Until recently, existential therapy borrowed techniques from other approaches, and its distinctiveness lay mainly in content. But techniques have started emerging from this approach that are consistent with its perfection fulfillment stance. Perhaps the earliest was *paradoxical intention* (Frankl, 1985), which recognizes that we call something a *psychological symptom* specifically when we cannot control it. For example, a persistent fear or obsession may so fill one's mind that there is little chance of doing whatever else one feels is important. Extreme symptoms often require dramatic treatment. With paradoxical intention, the therapist encourages the client to intensify the symptoms even further rather than fight against them. This can have the effect of outmaneuvering the symptom so that it will recede and no longer appear troublesome.

Another existential technique is *focusing* (Gendlin, 1973). By going through a series of steps, clients temporarily push aside everyday conventional meanings and attend instead to the messages coming from their bodies in the hope of reaching some more personal, individualized meaning. The starting point for focusing may be quite general (e.g., contemplating what stands in the way of feeling well) or more specific (e.g., what it is about a particular problem that disrupts well-being). Whatever the starting point, clients are led to progressively greater awareness of bodily states (e.g., rumbling stomach, neck muscles tightened, lumps in the throat) for their potential clues to personal reactions.

Recently introduced, the techniques of *situational reconstruction* and *compensatory self-improvement* are meant to be used along with focusing to provide a comprehensive basis for coping with stressful circumstances (Maddi, 1984b). In situational reconstruction, clients are stimulated by the steps of the exercise to stretch their imagination in construing stressful circumstances. Through considering how the circumstances could be better and worse than they are, and pinpointing just what constitutes the problem, clients develop a perspective that facilitates effectively coping. In this sense, they feel more in control.

But not all stressful circumstances (such as serious physical illness) can be controlled. When attempts at control fail, the technique of compensatory self-improvement aids clients in accepting unchangeable "givens" without giving up on themselves. In this technique, the client identifies another problem that though related to the given, appears changeable and works on changing that instead. Perhaps a male client's wife is diagnosed as having a severe breast cancer. Beyond obtaining medical care, there is little that can be done with this given. But compensatory effort can be expanded on the psychosocial features of the relationship and working along these lines will have a therapeutic effect.

In the existential techniques outlined here, you can see how different this approach is from person-centered counseling. The existential techniques are more directive and confrontational. They deal with the here and now. Their general aim is to increase clients' sense of control and individualized meaning. Notice, however, that they do not involve interpretation in the sense that the therapist imposes his or her sense of meaning on the client. All in all, the techniques are quite consistent with existential theorizing and the perfection version of the fulfillment model.

The Assessment Task

It must be said at the outset that Rogerians do spend little time and energy assessing whether and how clients are maladjusted (as indicated in Chapter 8, maladjustment is their view of the nonideal personality). Generally, client's requests for therapy are sufficient justification for giving it. And Rogerians assume that if they can give unconditional positive regard, clients will develop in the direction of greater maturity no matter what their problems. So there does not seem much point in assessing whether there exist conditions of worth, defensiveness, or the other characteristics of maladjustment.

Sometimes—usually for research purposes—Rogerians collect empirical data on client's personality characteristics. When they do, the measurement devices they utilize tend to be of the self-report variety—either interviews or questionnaires (see Chapter 2). The *Personal Orientation Inventory* (Shostrom, 1965, 1966) is a commonly used example. Self-report measures are thoroughly consistent with the fulfillment roots of the position, which insists that persons know themselves better than others can ever hope to.

The same is true of existential psychology. Its practitioners do not emphasize assessment as a precursor to therapy. And when they do assess—also usually for research purposes—they use interviews and questionnaires out of a conviction of the validity of self-report. But existential psychologists are more willing than their Rogerian counterparts to evaluate clients' self-reports in order to reach conclusions regarding personality. In this, existential psychologists pay special attention to self-reports that reflect on clients' decision-making processes (future versus past oriented) and conventionality versus individuality (see Chapter 8). A recent example of the approach is the *Hardiness Test* (Kobasa, Maddi, & Kahn, 1983).

Content Emphases

Little remains to be said regarding actualization fulfillment positions. Insofar as they consider content, person-centered psychologists are interested in whether clients express such characteristics of maladjustment as conditions of worth and defensiveness or of maturity such as organismic trusting and openness to experience (see Chapter 8). As the former decrease and the latter increase, the therapist assumes the client is improving.

Existential psychologists, being more inclined to influence the direction of therapeutic interactions, concern themselves more than Rogerians with evaluating content. Summarizing many relevant themes, Yalom (1980) indicates that existential psychotherapy deals especially with responsibility, isolation, and death. These topics may be raised by either the client or the therapist, but they must be considered, as they underlie a sense of meaning in life.

In order to experience a sense of freedom and vitality, persons must assume responsibility for their own lives. This is exceedingly difficult to do, because we have indeed been shaped by our pasts. It is necessary to accept the effects of the past on our present functioning as a given but still recognize that because we know and understand that given, we can transcend it with future-oriented decision making.

Isolation is omnipresent because no matter how well we know another person, there will always be some things unknown. The key to overcoming a sense of isolation is accepting the limits on knowing others. This is analogous to achieving freedom by accepting that we are shaped by the past and making future-oriented decisions anyway. We need to try for intimacy with others even though we cannot fully succeed.

As the ultimate given, death has a special place in existential therapy. We cannot live fully without accepting that death is beyond our control—it is both inevitable and unpredictable (Yalom, 1980). Once death has been truly accepted, life is enhanced by appearing more vivid and precious by comparison. This requires trying to make the most of one's life despite its fragility and poignancy.

Persons who have hardiness or courage (Maddi, 1984) are considered as dealing with responsibility, isolation, and death more effectively. Therefore, a content emphasis in existential therapy is the building of hardiness through the various techniques mentioned above.

THE CONSISTENCY MODEL

As mentioned before (see Chapters 5 and 9), consistency theories de-emphasize content in their core and peripheral personality statements. It is understandable, therefore, that they are quite eclectic concerning what is most revealing in thoughts, feelings, and actions. Fantasies, dreams, practical problems, and decision points all reveal personality equally, according to consistency theorists.

The Assessment Task

The cognitive dissonance version of the consistency model leads one to look for signs of the various constructs clients use and how these constructs are organized into construction systems (see Chapter 5). A particularly useful way of doing this involves the Role Repertory Test (Kelly, 1955). The first step in taking this test is for clients to provide the names of persons fulfilling certain roles (e.g., mother, father, siblings, lovers, major teachers, close friends) in their lives. Then every possible combination of three of these names is presented in turn to the clients with the same instruction, namely, to say how two of the persons are similar to and different from the third. As you can tell, this is a performance test (see Chapter 2) that involves sorting persons (or roles) into categories. The names given to these categories define the client's categories. Thus, if a client said that "mother" and "father" were similar to each other and different from "major teacher" in being "family," "family-nonfamily" would have been identified as a relevant bipolar construct.

The more frequently a client uses a construct in going through all the combinations of three names (roles), the higher it is in his or her hierarchically organized construct system (see Chapter 5). Various other relationships of constructs to each other can also be determined through the Role Repertory Test.

As you can see, this test is very appropriate for the cognitive dissonance version of the consistency model. Clients reveal their constructs by performing a classificatory task. Clients will be very aware of some of the constructs thus revealed. Other constructs will have been difficult to articulate except for the requirements imposed by the task. When the Role Repertory Test cannot be given to clients, interviews can be (and have been) used to glean information about constructs. In general descriptions that clients make of the persons, activities, and things in their lives, the assessor tries to discern the content and frequency of constructs.

McClelland's variant on the cognitive dissonance approach and Maddi's activation approach use a plurality of assessment strategies. Peripheral characteristics that are motivational (motives for McClelland and Maddi) typically are measured through such fantasy tasks as the Thematic Apperception Test, because motives are regarded as being private goals (see Chapter 10). Peripheral characteristics that involve habits (traits for McClelland and Maddi) have been measured through performance tasks designed to reveal repetitive responses or through questionnaires. Finally, McClelland's schemata concept, being expressive of societal norms, has been measured through self-report of values. As you can see, consistency theories consider a wide range of content and assessment approaches.

The Psychotherapy Task

Of all the personality models, the consistency approach is the least developed regarding psychotherapy. Among consistency theorists, only Kelly has a relevant procedure; it is called *fixed role therapy* (Kelly, 1955). It begins with the therapist listening to the new client's problems. When the therapist believes he or she has understood how the client's constructs have led to the problems, a role is constructed for the client to play that is calculated to end the difficulty.

For example, a male client may complain of being lonely because he is too shy to date girls. Perhaps behind this is the superordinate construct "unworthy-worthy" and, parallel to it, the subordinate construct "male-female." Being a male, the client considers himself unworthy and females worthy. This makes it hard for him to approach females for dates and to interact with them as equals. With such a set of beliefs, it is not surprising that he is without female company and lonely. A possibly corrective role that the therapist might construct for this client to play is that of an extroverted, assertive, worthy person. How such a person would act toward women would be carefully reviewed with the client. Then the client's assignment would be to enact this fixed role, even if it did not feel right and was painful. Each time the client returned for a session, he would report his experiences in enacting the role, and modifications to it might be made as needed. The general aim of this fixed role therapy would be to ease his loneliness at the same time as the relationship of the construct "worthy-unworthy" and "male-female" was shifted ninety degrees. This would mean that males and females would not invariably be considered unworthy and worthy, respectively. Once this was accomplished, a male (including himself) might be considered by the client either worthy or unworthy, presumably on other grounds. In the process of the interaction with females forced by the fixed role, the client might well have obtained signs of his worthiness. The problem that brought him into therapy would have been solved!

Despite the simplicity of this example, it helps one grasp the essential features of fixed role therapy. Therapist and client interact in conversational style concerning the latter's experiences and constructs. The emphasis is on the present and the lines along which new experience can influence construction systems.

Although McClelland's variant on the cognitive dissonance approach does not have a psychotherapy in the sense of something with which to remediate behavior problems, it does have a training program for persons who want to increase such motives as the need for achievement, which is characterized by fantasies involving competition with a standard of excellence (see Chapter 9). McClelland's (1971b) notion of increasing the need for achievement involves simply teaching persons to fantasize along these lines. A characteristic mechanism for doing this is for the person to read stories composed about pictures that are high in the need for achievement and take these stories as a model for his or her own fantasy efforts. These fantasy efforts are then evaluated by the trainer, who gives feedback and supervises the person in correcting stories to make them even more achievement oriented, if necessary. McClelland's assumption here is that learning to fantasize about achievement will lead one to act accordingly in the real world. A similar approach would be taken regarding other motives.

In both Kelly's and McClelland's approaches to intervention, we see a cardinal feature of the consistency position, namely, feedback as a basis for corrective effort. The therapist or trainer devises a task for the client to perform that is calculated to produce shifts in behavior in the desired direction. The feedback from all this is then used to fine-tune behavior even more. All in all, the assumption is that desired change takes place by a process of trial and error. In the intervention effort, there is little concern for the past, for dreams, for the unconscious, or for the client's discovering directions on his or her own. The approaches of Kelly and McClelland closely fulfill the thrust of the consistency model.

Content Emphases

At first, the content aims of consistency approaches to assessment and therapy (intervention) are clear. The content goal is defined by the client (e.g., to become less lonely or to increase in need for achievement) and accepted by the therapist (trainer). Assessment focuses on determining how the client's thought processes (e.g., constructs, fantasies) obstruct reaching his or her content goals. The intervention is planned in terms of where the client is and wants to be. In considering approaches, there are no content criteria of maturity and immaturity. This general eclecticism with regard to content accurately expresses the consistency model.

But Kelly's position requires a bit more scrutiny before we move on. Let us return to the example of the young man who felt lonely. In Kelly's approach, he could not have felt lonely unless he had a relevant construct—say, "lonely-socially fulfilled"—and placed himself on the "lonely" pole of it. But if this were so, why, in Kelly's system, would the young man have had any problem at all? If his expectations about being lonely were confirmed by his experience, he would not have cognitive dissonance and, hence, no problem that would lead him to seek therapy. You and I may feel that loneliness is painful, even if expected, but Kelly has no theoretical basis for regarding a confirmed construct as problematical. Kelly (1955) does consider it possible for a person to have two partial construction systems that are inconsistent with each other, and this may be a theoretical way out of the dilemma just identified. Perhaps in one construction system the young man expects to be lonely and has this confirmed, but in the other construction system he expects to be loved and has this confirmed. In this case, the complaint he brought to psychotherapy about being lonely would have to be regarded as imprecise, to say the least. Perhaps the complaint should have been something like "Sometimes I'm lonely and sometimes I'm loved, and the difference is confusing." Although this may clarify our dilemma somewhat, Kelly's position certainly does seem difficult to pinpoint.

BEHAVIORISTIC AND SOCIAL LEARNING APPROACHES

There is much in behavioristic and social learning approaches that touched on what we have already encountered in the positions of Kelly, McClelland, and the existential psychologists. All these positions emphasize that change in thoughts, feelings, and actions takes place through guided trial and error.

Consistent with its de-emphasis on personality, behaviorism has not developed an assessment approach. When measurement of such factors as general drive has been necessary in research, behaviorists have used experimental manipulations, such as shocks, or questionnaires concerning self-report of tension (see Chapter 12). In their therapeutic efforts, behaviorists have emphasized operant conditioning techniques (see Chapter 12). In this, the therapist accepts the client's definition of the problem but recasts that problem in terms of a response that needs to be either increased or decreased in rate of occurrence (an example of the former might be studying for exams and of the latter smoking). This so-called *behavior modification* therapy involves altering the rate at which the target response is emitted in the relevant stimulus circumstance by carefully planned applications of reinforcements. Thus, if eating candy is determined as being reinforcing for the client, he or she will be permitted to do that following desired studying or nonsmoking responses. Over time, the rate of studying or smoking will be changed. When the aim of the therapy is to decrease the client's fear responses, and the imagination of pleasant scenes is used as the reinforcement, the approach is called *systematic desensitization* (Volpe, 1969).

These approaches are quite consistent with behavioristic principles in their avoidance of elaborate theorizing (notice that the client determines what the problem is and, hence, what the desired direction of therapy will be), focus on actions or responses, and reliance on reinforcement as the mechanisms of change. This approach is distinct from more personological positions on therapy.

The distinction is dwindling lately, however, due to the increased role given by behavioristic therapists to their clients' cognitive processes. A good example of the shift in what is now called *cognitive behaviorism* is the new emphasis on self-control.

Behavioristic therapists have also begun to use a technique called *flooding* (Goldstein, 1973), which at first consideration seems similar to existential psychology's paradoxical intention. Typically flooding involves the client in sitting with closed eyes, imagining and feeling, as the therapist paints word pictures of situations known to be anxiety provoking to the client. The client is "flooded" with negative emotions, hour after hour, until "reactive inhibition" takes place, and these emotions subside. Sometimes, subject to feasibility, flooding is conducted *in vivo,* that is, by immersing the client in anxiety-provoking situations (Wilson & O'Leary, 1980). Certainly a client engaging in paradoxical intention will also experience negative emotions. But in paradoxical intention, the client is the one who tries to increase the symptom through willing and doing. By comparison, the flooding technique renders the client passive, and the reduction of anxiety is more likely to be an exhaustion phenomenon than a renewed sense of personal control. Once again the similarity between cognitive behaviorism and existential approaches is more apparent than real.

Like behaviorism, the social learning approach has de-emphasized personality and, hence, has spent little effort on an approach to assessment. When social learning psychologists need to measure subjects in research, they too tend to rely on either experimental manipulations or questionnaires (see Chapter 13). The social learning approach has only recently concerned itself with therapy, with the resulting emphasis on *self-efficacy* (Bandura 1977, 1986). Here the therapeutic approach builds on theorizing concerning the four principal sources of perceived self-efficacy, namely, *mastery experiences* (successes incline you to the belief that you will be successful), *modeling* (you judge your abilities partly through emulating others), *social persuasion* (you believe what others tell you about yourself), and *physiological state inferences* (you try to make sense out of what is going on in your body). Various combinations of these sources are employed by the social learning therapist in an effort to convince clients that they can be efficacious. Typically particular tasks or goals are taken as the problems to be worked on.

At this stage in its development, social learning therapy is rather eclectic in technique. This is consistent with its greater concern with how learning takes place rather than what learning content is important. It is not surprising, given its eclecticism, that self-efficacy therapy appears somewhat similar in part to a range of behavioristic and personological approaches.

CONCLUDING REMARKS

I have not considered every theory in this chapter because my aim was to give you a sense of how the various models conduct assessment and therapy. The theories covered well exemplify the general approaches. Some of the theories not considered are fairly mixed or eclectic at the practical level of therapy and assessment, even though they are more consistent at the level of theorizing about personality. This applies to the therapeutic approaches of Berne (1964), Kohut (1971, 1977), Perls (1969a), and Ellis (1962). At the level of technique, the therapies of Berne and Kohut resemble not only conflict but fulfillment approaches. In the case of Perls and Ellis, the resemblance is to existential, Kellian, and cognitive-behavioristic approaches. Perhaps the eclectic nature of the therapies associated with Berne, Kohut, Perls, and Ellis is a function of their recent inception.

Throughout the chapter, I have presented assessment and psychotherapy as practical applications of personality theories, as indeed they are. This is not to say, however, that the direction is only one way (from theory to application). As in any application, the practice of psychotherapy and assessment often provides vivid observations, unexpected successes, or abysmal failures that provoke the practitioner to theory revision or elaboration. In a real sense, the processes whereby knowledge is developed and applied are intertwined.

This intertwining is one reason that I have not tried to evaluate here the relative effectiveness of psychotherapy and assessment as done through conflict, fulfillment, and consistency models. No sooner does some practical application reveal a theoretical shortcoming than that shortcoming is corrected. No sooner does some practical application achieve remarkable success than it is adopted by practitioners of other theoretical persuasions. In trying to help suffering persons through assessment and psychotherapy, the stakes are just too high for practitioners to worry about logical niceties such as whether their pet theories really lead to the particular practice they observe as being successful. What works is adopted! I believe this is an important factor in the currently eclectic nature of the assessment and psychotherapeutic approaches of Berne, Kohut, Perls, and Ellis. Ultimately, positions that have become eclectic through the headlong attempt to do an important, practical job well will be subject to a pruning period. External and internal scrutiny will, over time, render such positions more internally consistent in their assumptions. To my mind, this will involve becoming less eclectic in the sense that all their explicit and implicit assumptions will move in the same core and peripheral directions. Any of these pruned positions may, of course, transcend the conflict, fulfillment, and consistency modeis of current relevance and express some new, clear, internally consistent model that you and I may not have imagined.

The other reason that I have not attempted a comparative analysis of psychotherapies and assessment approaches here is that of complexity. Although much psychotherapy outcome and process research has been done in recent years, it is extremely difficult to reach convincing conclusions due to a host of methodological and theoretical problems.

Regarding psychotherapy, some approaches (e.g., psychoanalysis) require more time—years—than is practically possible in a research design, whereas others (e.g., person-centered counseling) can sometimes be completed in months. Also, when the researcher arbitrarily decides on a term of therapy for the study, that time line may be too short for some techniques to be effective. You can see how this could prejudice results. Further, in comparing psychotherapeutic approaches it is difficult to separate the effectiveness of the particular therapist from that of his or her technique. This is because it is difficult to get the therapist to consent to applying not only his or her favored technique but some other one as well. Even in the unlikely event that therapists would be swayed to cooperation by the requirements of research, they might not be effective with their non preferred, less practiced techniques. This would have a homogenizing effect on results even with a counter balanced design in which all therapists participating would utilize all therapeutic techniques being evaluated comparatively. Also, it is difficult (if not unethical) in a practical setting in which clients need help to institute the kind of control conditions really necessary for the evaluation of therapy effectiveness. To have some clients merely wait longer than others to get therapy is sometimes ethically justifiable (if there are not enough therapists to handle demand anyway) but does not provide a sufficiently precise control (the best that one could conclude is that some therapy was more effective than the mere passage of time—and that is not saying much). Furthermore, there is the unresolved question of what are the best criteria of therapy outcome, or process along which to compare approaches. The difficulty here is that there are sharp disagreements stemming from the approaches themselves (e.g., psychoanalysis aims at changing underlying belief systems about self and world, whereas behaviorism attempts to change unwanted actions).

If these matters are not complicated enough, add to them the difficulty in determining what measurement operations are the best in evaluating therapy outcome and process. Shall we ask the client, the therapist, or some third party whether a session or an entire therapy was effective or when it is time to terminate? Even if using all three were practically feasible (and it would be very hard), the resulting complexities would be overwhelming, as each source of data would involve different assumptions as to which criteria are important in judging effectiveness.

It is not surprising, given the problems mentioned (and others as well), that the empirical evidence regarding the relative effectiveness of therapeutic approaches is unclear. Earlier, Eysenck (1952) reviewed much research and reached the pessimistic conclusion that psychotherapy is no more effective than the mere passage of time. Although this view has receded with the advent of more sophisticated research, it is still echoed from time to time (e.g., Rachman, 1973). And conclusions that used to be offered concerning empirical evidence favoring one psychotherapy or another seem to be receding in favor of the identification of effective factors that seem to be present across many psychotherapies (e.g., Bergin & Lambert, 1978). However interesting and useful this trend is, it does not further comparative analysis very much. The comparative analysis of assessment approaches is only slightly less complex than that concerning therapies. Battles have raged concerning whether projective or questionnaire or structured or unstructured techniques are more supported by research findings (e.g., Ciminero, Calhoun, & Adams, 1977; Waskow & Parloff, 1975). Behind these battles stand the differing theoretical views on personality contained in the conflict, fulfillment, and consistency models, to say nothing of behaviorism and social learning theory. There appear to be no easy resolution to these disputes despite their lower intensity nowadays than before.

Perhaps this has given you enough of a flavor for the complexity of doing psychotherapy and assessment research to allow you to appreciate why I will not enter into a full-fledged comparative analysis of these matters here. The detail necessary for doing a creditable job would easily fill another book and comprise the subject matter of another course.

CHAPTER 15

Formal and Substantive Characteristics of the Good Theory of Personality

In the preceding chapters, I compared and contrasted theories, posed issues, and conducted rational and empirical analyses. My overall aim has been to identify the most promising bases for conceptualizing personality. In pursuit of this goal, I have made statements concerning the value of certain models for personality theorizing. Hopefully these statements will serve as a guide to the development of theories of personality that are more sophisticated and effective than those considered in this book. What remains to be done in this concluding chapter is to set forth in one place the implications of preceding discussions for future personality theorizing. This amounts to considering the formal and substantive characteristics that the good theory of personality will have. What I say here will not always agree with current orthodoxy. If I do not convince you entirely, perhaps you will at least be provoked to rethink the nature of the task of personality theorizing.

FORMAL CHARACTERISTICS

In this section, we will consider the form that a good theory of personality should take, delaying discussion of content until later. There will be two aspects for discussion. One refers to the parts that properly compose a personality theory; the other refers to the overall criteria of formal adequacy that it should fulfill.

The Parts of a Personality Theory

It will come as no surprise to you that I believe the good theory of personality will include both core and peripheral levels. The first level will include one or more core tendencies. Everything pertaining to the core of personality will be common to all persons. Emphasized here will be inherent attributes of persons, whether viewed individually or as part of a social aggregate. The attributes will tend to be inherent in the sense that they are not learned so

much as comprising part of the nature of the organism. Although core characteristics may be physiological in nature, it is not at all necessary that they be
so, except when the theorist assumes that the only commonalities in people
are biological. It would be just as possible, however, to consider ideals as being
inherent attributes of the person, as do perfection theorists. From the formal
point of view, it is necessary only that core-level statements refer to the inherent characteristics common to all persons. What content is desirable in such
statements is a matter to be evaluated later.

At the peripheral level of theorizing, emphasis is on the easily discernible
regularities in functioning that distinguish one person from another. Theorizing
at this level should include a minimum of two kinds of concept. One I have
called the *peripheral characteristic*. It refers to those entities in people that
cannot sensibly be subdivided further and differ across people in intensity and
content. From the formal point of view, the peripheral characteristic is the
smallest, most homogeneous unit of personality. It should be quantitative in
nature so a person can be said to have more or less of it than another. It is also
necessary that more than one peripheral characteristic be assumed if the peripheral theorizing is to have any success in celebrating the differences among
people. The other kind of concept necessary for good peripheral-level theorizing is what I have called the *type*. It has the function of indicating how the
peripheral characteristics get organized into broader units, more nearly approximating the styles of living that people show. Here too theorists must
include a minimum of two types if their peripheral theorizing is to permit
understanding of differences among people. We have every reason to expect of
the theorist a typology, or exhaustive listing, of the types of peripheral personality considered important, each type with its array of peripheral characteristics. With such a typology in hand, we can be sure of what the theorist
considers an adequate description of the different ways it is possible for people
to be.

Also necessary are developmental statements that express the nature of
the relationship between the core tendencies and characteristics on the one
hand and the peripheral characteristics on the other. Generally, it will be
assumed that the core tendencies and characteristics are at such a high level
of generality as to permit expression in a wide range of concrete forms. The
actual forms of expression that become fixed are shaped by interaction with
the external environment in the form of parents, culture, social and economic
conditions, and so forth. Thus, the personality theorist will disclose his or her
position on the relationship between core and peripheral considerations
through assumptions concerning development.

Finally, the good theory of personality will include a data language, or set
of conventions for observation, having the function of indicating what it is
important to explain. Application of a data language yields a group of behavioral variables arrived at through minimal interpretation of observations—
certainly less interpretation than is involved in peripheral characteristics.
Because it involves minimal interpretation, a behavioral variable usually is
considered descriptive rather than explanatory.

Thus far, I have been somewhat abstract about the parts of a personality theory, asserting their necessity rather than attempting to convince you of it. In the following paragraphs, I shall try to be more concrete about why each of these parts is valuable and exactly what explanatory capability would be lost without each one.

Let us start with what is to be explained. The whole point of theory is to foster understanding of something hitherto not understood. Once the function of theory is stated this way, it becomes very clear that there must be some well-developed sense of what is to be explained. The data or phenomena that are perplexing must be clear enough in the theorists' minds that they can direct their theoretical efforts in a problem-oriented way. This means that the good theory of personality must include a clear statement of the data it is attempting to explain. In other areas of theorizing, this point is so obvious that it need not be articulated. But in the personality area, one tends to find an emphasis on developing a theory with the data it is to explain left open for future discovery. This is perhaps understandable in that the personality field is so broad that one is hard-pressed to be very specific about the data to be considered. Everything rushes to mind whenever one attempts to determine just which behavioral observations need understanding in personality terms.

But the difficulty of specifying data does nothing to diminish the necessity of doing it—indeed, perhaps the opposite is true. In any event, theorizing about the nature of personality without keeping in mind just what you want to understand about human behavior is like building a boat without knowing what water is like. The organization of the things people do, feel, and think into specifiable, communicable, tangible behavioral variables requires a data language. Personologists have sadly failed in developing or adopting a data language, however basic to theorizing such a step is. Rather than criticize further, however, let me simply conclude that a good theory of personality will specify a language for describing human functioning in terms that indicate what the theory needs to explain. Whether the language has been invented by the theorist or adopted from more widespread usage is unimportant as long as it is clear what needs to be explained.

There is some guidance to be found in formulating the behavioral variables from numerous discussions in this book. An appropriate data language for the personologist will be heavily psychological rather than biological or sociological. It will describe complete human thoughts, feelings, and actions, especially recurrent ones. Although personology does not yet have a consistently developed data language, current rudimentary descriptions of data lead in the above direction. So in saying that a good theory of personality ought to specify a data language that is psychological in nature, I am at least not doing violence to the apparent intent of personologists.

The first level of explanation of the behavioral variables is the peripheral characteristic. This characteristic is a postulated entity in the person that renders a number of behavioral variables understandable by indicating their similarity or functional equivalence. For example, the behavioral variables of competitiveness with work associates, moderate risk taking in situations whose outcomes can be influenced by skill, and greater involvement in complex rather than simple tasks might all be explained as expressions of a particular peripheral characteristic—the *need for achievement*. Invoking the need for achievement would not amount to merely describing the behavioral variables; rather, it would entail interpreting or explaining them. Some personologists who strongly emphasize core level theorizing would dispute the explanatory value of what I am calling *peripheral characteristics,* considering them no more than descriptive generalizations of behavioral variables. In order to convince yourself that peripheral characteristics are more than data descriptions, consider in the above example how easy it would be to devise some characteristic other than the need for achievement to explain the observations. Ready alternatives would be *insecurity* and *dominance*. Considering the observations expressive of need for achievement rather than of these alternatives indicates that what has been done is an interpretation or explanation, not a description.

The criticism that peripheral characteristics are descriptive rather than explanatory may imply a more valid criticism: that the peripheral characteristic has no logical existence apart from the behaviors it is supposed to explain, and hence its adequacy as an explanation cannot be determined. Suppose, as in the previous example, that the presence or absence of the need for achievement could be decided on only by inference from the presence or absence of the behaviors concerning risk taking and so forth. If this were so, the need-for-achievement characteristic would have no existence apart from the data it is used to explain. Another personologist could easily invoke an alternative characteristic, such as dominance, with equal persuasiveness. It would not be possible to determine which explanation was the better. The criticism being made here is not that the need for achievement would have no explanatory value but that the explanation offered would be inconclusive.

Fortunately, there is a simple way around this criticism. It involves offering an *operational definition* of each peripheral characteristic. An operational definition tells you how to measure the characteristic in terms that differ from the data it is meant to explain. In our example, once an operational definition of need for achievement is offered, it becomes possible to conduct an empirical test of the adequacy of explaining those particular behaviors with that particular characteristic. One would measure the strength of need for achievement in, say, fantasy and then determine the relationships between achievement fantasy and the relevant behavioral variables. It is in order to render the explanatory power of peripheral characteristics more compelling that I conclude that the good theory of personality will include operational definitions of its peripheral characteristics.

The concept of personality types is at a more general level of behavior than peripheral characteristics, but it is similar in other respects. The behavior explained by a type is a composite of the behaviors explained by each of the peripheral characteristics it subsumes. The typology explains differences among people that are more gross and, in common sense terms, more obvious than those explained by single peripheral characteristics. Perhaps I should mention that types need not include operational definitions, for they do no more than subsume a specified set of peripheral characteristics, each of which already is operationally defined. The general style and directionality of individual lives are best understood in terms of the type concept and the associated typology. This is true even though it is possible to pinpoint a more restricted, less sweeping directionality at the level of peripheral characteristics, as do Murray and McClelland with their motive concepts.

We have reached a natural transition to the discussion of the explanatory value of core-level theorizing. Core-level theorizing explains the attributes and directions found in all persons by virtue of their common human nature. It is a necessary kind of theorizing insofar as one thinks in terms of humankind as a whole and of contrasting it with other forms of life. In addition, the core tendency has the vital function of explicating the overall directionality of life. The concrete directions identified at the peripheral level must be derived from the overall directionality and are not themselves understandable without it. The core tendency and characteristics are a level of theorizing further removed from the behavioral observations that prompt peripheral-level theorizing. As such, the core of personality only indirectly explains behavior through its relationship to the periphery. There is no point, therefore, in attempting operational definition of core tendencies and characteristics. Empirical validity of core-level theorizing is not to be assessed directly; rather, in the process of testing empirically peripheral theorizing, one can determine the adequacy of core theorizing equally well by weight of evidence. In theory that is only indirectly related to data, weight of evidence is the most sensible empirical standard.

But the weight of evidence cannot be brought to bear on core-level theorizing unless it is carefully articulated with peripheral-level theorizing. This means that developmental statements relating core and periphery through the mediation of experience in the world are essential to a good theory of personality.

As core theorizing refers to data only indirectly, its explanatory value may be questioned. Indeed, some personologists who prefer to stay very close to data in their attempts to understand would consider core-level theorizing not only dispensable but a waste of time and effort. But anyone who feels it is valuable to consider persons as sharing some inherent nature and direction will find it hard to agree. And anyone who considers it important in an explanation of human behavior to understand how there is an initial impetus to behave before any learning takes place could never agree. Core-level theorizing explicates the prime mover of behavior and clarifies the restrictions imposed on what is subsequently learned by the common characteristics of human nature. Any theory of personality that makes a claim to comprehensiveness must explain these matters and, therefore, requires a core statement.

In summary, each part of a theory of personality has a definite and important function. Without articulating with a data language, a theory cannot specify what it intends to explain. A theory in such a position is less an explanatory device than a world view, religion, or myth. Peripheral characteristics are necessary if one seriously believes that there are many obvious, though concrete and small, differences among people. Without a typology, a theory is mute concerning larger patterns of difference among people. If a theory does not include a statement of core tendencies and associated core characteristics, it is not possible to consider persons as sharing some attributes by virtue of their common species, nor is it possible to consider how any functioning occurs in the absence of considerable learning. And the explication, through statements about development, of the process whereby core considerations come to be expressed in particular peripheral styles of life, is essential if the core statements are ever to be even indirectly accessible to an empirical test of adequacy.

Obviously complete personality theories do not spring full-blown from the theorist's mind. One part or another may well be developed before the rest. Theorists may want to—and should—express their views even before they can make as comprehensive a statement as would be ideal. Nonetheless, the ideal defines what the theorist should be trying to accomplish. Failure to include any part of a personality theory leads to a particular, recognizable kind of drawback. Comprehensive understanding of personality requires all the parts.

Overall Criteria of Formal Adequacy

Even assuming that the good theory of personality will have all the parts discussed above, there are still some overall principles of theorizing that are generally considered important. These frequently mentioned principles are that a theory should be *important, operational, parsimonious, precise, empirically valid* and *stimulating*. It is generally believed that a theory is adequate only if it can fulfill these formal criteria. I agree with some of the criteria more than others and will therefore discuss each separately. Much of what I am about to say has been implicit or even directly mentioned before. But it is high time now to be explicit.

A Theory Should Be Important.   Although it is not unusual for psychologists to evaluate theories on the basis of their triviality versus importance, this is a very difficult kind of evaluation to justify. Mandler and Kessen (1959) make this point forcefully:

> Were there at hand a rigorous criterion for triviality, the psychological community could agree with confidence on the study of genuinely important issues, the ones that "really matter." Unfortunately no such criterion of exclusion can be stated. The polemic use of terms such as "inconsequential," "limited," "far from reality," and so on, when applied to theories of behavior, misses the fact that science has no dead-end markers. We can look back into the past and see with relatively high acuity the junctures at which a line of theory went awry, but no satisfactory method can be proposed for making a similar judgment about contemporary systems of explanation. A responsible scientist may choose to work on whatever problems interest him but he is fooling himself if he claims to

know that he is on a more direct route to some future truth than his colleagues. Franklin and Faraday were both asked "What good is it?" by curious and puzzled friends who were watching the demonstration of a new device. Franklin's famous reply "What good is a new-born child?" was a pointed recognition of our ignorance of future utilities, but Faraday expressed more accurately the disdain of the pure scientist for questions of applicability when he responded to Gladstone, "Why, sir, there is every probability that you will soon be able to tax it." . . . . Much the same answers can be made to attacks against psychological theories on grounds of triviality; their ultimate contribution to knowledge is determined by so many unknown considerations that it seems wisest to recognize that attacks of this order cannot be justified by reference to an unambiguous criterion. (pp. 253–254)

As a spirited argument for theoretical freedom, this statement is very effective. Yet we must consider just how far we would endorse it. Consider, in this regard, an equally spirited indictment of a theory made by Bruner on the grounds of triviality. The theory criticized is Spence's version of general behavior theory, which holds that the hallmark of human and animal learning is the associative bonding of stimuli and responses that have been experienced as contiguous in time. This theory has been formulated mainly on the basis of experiments performed on rats that involved learning a particular route through a maze. Railing out against this concretistic theory of learning, Bruner (1957a) says:

> Let me illustrate one source of my discouragement in attempting to evaluate this truly distinguished book. It is estimated that there are 10^{75} possible sentences in the English language 50 words in length, and that in the course of a year we hear perhaps 10^6 sentences altogether. If one learned the sentences we uttered by a process that is Markovian [associationistic] in nature, eliminating alternatives according to the gradual build-up of excitatory strength, our lives would be far too short to master even the simple prattle of a child. And there is little doubt, moreover, that we would be able to indicate which sentences among the 10^{75} constructed by an algorithm were proper sentences and which were not, even though we have never encountered them. It is obvious that "verbal responses" are not what is "learned" but, rather, rules and principles of structuring that make it possible for us to *generate* sentences. The answer to such a point as this is by now familiar: You cannot criticize a thing for what it does not attempt to account for. But the ultimate end of such a defense is that the critic is then forced to celebrate behavior theory of this type as the applied psychology of CS-US linkages, T mazes, and straight runways. (p. 156)

Elsewhere in his review, Bruner (1957a) says in the same vein:

> Donald Hebb recently remarked that if one made a set of microphotographs of Cambridge, inch by inch, very likely one would fail to discover the Charles River. (p. 156)

In pointing out that Spence's theory will either have to answer his criticism or be celebrated as the applied psychology of mazes, Bruner is raising the question of triviality. He does not really dispute the fact that humans can learn in an associationistic fashion. What he disputes is that such learning is to be considered characteristic of how the human operates. He feels that it obviously cannot be, from his example concerning language learning. One does not need to do empirical research to recognize that Spence has trivialized human beings by failing to attribute to them the principle learning they obviously show. It will not help Spence to say, with Mandler and Kessen, that one could hardly have known in advance of theorizing that people are predominantly principle rather than association learners. This is because Bruner, in his very example—which is rational rather than empirical—is saying that he and lots of other psychologists would have known in advance. This is why he is so disappointed in the book.

What brought about the trivialization of learning theory constituted by Spence's approach? Surely it was not a necessary concomitant of adopting a laboratory paradigm for the investigation of learning. Indeed, the value of laboratory paradigms can be great if they truly represent simpler, more controllable forms of the naturalistic phenomenon under consideration. Through systematically varying one variable at a time while holding the others constant, a phenomenon such as learning can be analyzed more effectively in the laboratory than in a natural setting. But in order for the promise of the laboratory to be realized, the paradigm chosen must be representative of, or at least homologous with, the phenomenon as it occurs in a naturalistic setting. If humans learn primarily principles rather than associations, the T maze is not a suitable paradigm because it is too simple to lend itself to principle learning. Further, if rats are primarily association rather than principle learners, no matter how carefully they are studied application of the conclusions to human beings is likely to be an oversimplification. Whenever theorizing about some phenomenon is not directed toward understanding it as it naturally occurs—being directed instead at some laboratory paradigm supposedly similar but in reality not representative of it—it runs a great risk of being trivial. The difficulty with Spence's approach is not that it relied on a laboratory paradigm but that there was insufficient grappling with the question of the suitability of the paradigm as a basis for generalizing to human learning as it occurs outside the laboratory.

In theorizing, one can minimize the risk of being trivial by deciding what should constitute the major phenomena to be explained on the basis of primary reliance on naturalistic observation. If truly representative laboratory paradigms are available, observations from them can be relied on as well. But theorists need not be especially alarmed at finding their position unable to account for laboratory observations whose relationship to natural occurrences is unclear (e.g., hypnotic behavior, because hypnosis does not occur naturally). Reliance on naturalistic observation in theorizing is especially important for personologists, whose aim of understanding the whole human being can be so easily trivialized by oversimplification. After formulating the rudiments of their theory through reliance on naturalistic observation, they can, of course, design laboratory experiments to their hearts' delight in order to determine whether their theorizing is really sound. If they start with naturalistic observation, they are unlikely to be working on a trivial problem or designing laboratory experiments that are so oversimplified that they no longer represent the phenomenon under consideration.

Actually, most personality theorists would agree with much of what I have said. They certainly rely on naturalistic observation, as can be seen from the case histories and even appeals to common experience that are often made the bases for theorizing. The more formal and systematic ratings of subjects' behavior in various tasks, so effectively employed by such personologists as Murray (1938) and Cattell (1946), are still close enough to everyday functioning to be considered naturalistic. Also close to naturalistic observation are those personality tests that are least structured (e.g., Thematic Apperception Test), permitting persons to disclose themselves in their own way. Rarely do personologists heavily rely on laboratory forms of phenomena as a guide in theorizing.

But the danger with some personologists is that they use the psychotherapeutic interaction with much of the same alacrity that Spence exhibits with the T maze. After all, the psychotherapeutic situation is a highly specialized one, created to facilitate treatment. It is a contrived rather than natural situation. To my mind, it is only partially representative of naturally occurring interactions. When personologists devise a personality theory on the basis of psychotherapy observations alone, they run a large risk of being trivial in the depth and breadth of their understanding of life. Perhaps you will recall that in Chapter 8 I suggested that the reason Rogers offers only two personality types—thereby simplifying life—is that his theory was developed almost exclusively on the basis of observation of client's behavior. A theory of psychotherapy is one thing; a theory of personality is another.

A Theory Should Be Operational.   Simply put, the doctrine of *operationism* indicates that the meaning of a concept is determined by the measurement operations associated with it. This has been a very useful notion to scientists, because it forces them to be really precise about what they mean lest someone else measure it in a manner at variance with their intended meaning. Further, it alerts them to the implications of various measurement operations for influencing what they mean. But some overzealous psychologists have interpreted the doctrine of operationism in ways that to me do not seem at all advantageous.

One disadvantageous version of operationism is that concepts mean whatever we want them to mean—nothing more and nothing less. This seems a misuse of operationism, which was never meant to be a substitute for theorizing. When we use our measurement operations to define a concept rather than first defining the concept and then choosing the measurement operations most relevant for it, we assume that the concept is nothing more than an arbitrary symbol. This assumption is virtually always violated in psychology, which uses as concepts not mathematical symbols so much as words. Words acquire fairly consistent meanings as conventions of usage for them develop. And these conventions are not merely semantic; distinctions among words generally co-incide with perceived differences among events in experience. Denying this "real" meaning of a concept (see Mandler & Kessen, 1959, pp. 93–101) and defining it merely in terms of a set of measurement operations (e.g., intelligence is the score on the Stanford-Binet Test) would lead us into even more blind alleys than it already does were it not for the fact that in reality we rarely give up the real meaning completely. It usually hovers on the fringe of conscious-ness all the while it is disavowed and exercises an intuitive influence on our investigations. This intuitive influence is what probably keeps us from making too many mistakes all the while we are foolishly saying that we know nothing of the meanings of our concepts except the steps we took in measuring them. We do not land in blind alleys unequivocally enough to force a reconsideration of the madness of capitulating, as theorists, to arbitrarily chosen measurement operations. After all, there are an infinite number of measurement operations, and if we have no theory to guide us in choosing among them, the choice will be arbitrarily made. Our undetected intuition leads to just enough reward to perpetuate our misguided belief in the value of remaking concepts in the image of our measurement operations!

Clearly, then, I believe that concept definition is a matter of theory and that only when definition has already been achieved does it make sense to select measurement operations. These may well provoke a reconsideration of the concept's meaning. But the contribution of measurement operations to the meaning of a concept is secondary to that made by the theorist using all the intuition and reason available to him or her. In the good theory of personality, therefore, the cart will not lead the horse; the measurement operations for concepts will follow from their theoretical definitions rather than themselves constituting the definitions.

The other disadvantageous version of the doctrine of operationism is sim-ply that all concepts, regardless of their logical function, must be operational-ized in order for their inclusion in a theory to be justifiable. You already know that I disagree with this from my indicating that only peripheral characteristics need have operational definitions. I see little reason why a concept should have an operational definition if its primary function is not to explain data directly but to indicate the relationship and organization among concepts. To require that only operationalized concepts be included in theories might have the unfortunate effect of decreasing emphasis on core statements. In the good theory of personality, only peripheral characteristics will be equipped with operational definitions.

Most personality theorists are lax in providing operationalizations of their peripheral characteristics. It is not likely, therefore, that they will fall prey to the two versions of operationism I have called disadvantageous. These versions are common in other fields of psychology, however, and perhaps what I have said can aid personality theorists in defending themselves against critics. Hopefully, I have also been convincing concerning the need for operational definitions of peripheral characteristics. In providing such definitions, the theorist has much to gain and nothing to lose.

A Theory Should Be Parsimonious.   For a long time in psychology, it has been orthodox to believe that parsimony is a standard of adequacy in theorizing. What *parsimony* means is that given a set group of phenomena to be explained the best explanation among those available is the one that makes the fewest assumptions. Assumptions, for present purposes, are roughly equivalent to concepts and the interrelationships among them. The aim of parsimony is simplicity in theorizing. Sensible and sound though it may seem, the principle of parsimony may be virtually impossible to apply in psychology. In order to do so, one would have to specify the domain of behavioral variables to be explained and the assumptions of all theories that claim to explain them. Specification of theoretical assumptions is difficult, because psychological theory generally is incomplete and based on implicit assumptions (Mandler & Kessen, 1959). Personality theories in particular are formulated more implicitly than is consistent with an application of the principle of parsimony. Specification of the domain of behavioral variables cannot be done meaningfully because even similar personality theories show little agreement in the data they attempt to explain. As you know, some theories do not even specify the data to which they pertain. And even if there were both more specification of relevant data and more agreement or overlap among the specifications, at current rates of information increase in psychology the data personality theorists would want to explain would not remain constant long enough to permit any meaningful assessment of parsimony. These conditions render the principle of parsimony virtually useless as a basis for evaluating alternative theories. After all, can anyone remember a personality theory being definitely found unparsimonious not only by its opponents but by its adherents and disinterested persons? What this means is that the principle of parsimony has not been useful as a guide to theoretical fruitfulness in the personality area.

Indeed, even if parsimony were capable of assessment in the personality area, I am not sure I would want to put much stock in it. Let us say that you could, at some point in time, specify some domain of data that theorists agreed was what they wanted to explain. Let us also say that you could make all the assumptions of the various theories explicit. Further, let us suppose that one theory emerged as the one that explained the facts with the fewest assumptions. Would you be willing, on the basis of this possibly transitory victory, to discard the unparsimonious theories? I would not, because the victory would tell us little about the ability of the parsimonious theory to continue providing good explanations of whatever additional data were uncovered in the future. Indeed, it is distinctly possible that a theory that looks parsimonious in explaining today's facts may actually be such an oversimplification in terms of explaining all human functioning as to be wholly inadequate to cope with tomorrow's facts without major overhaul. Recognizing this, it does not seem important in theorizing to strive for simplicity for its own sake. Better to use all your intuition, reason, and empirical knowledge in striving for a theory that is as comprehensive concerning human functioning as you can make it. Happily, personality theorists seem to have done this, being rather indifferent to the parsimony of their formulations.

A Theory Should Be Precise.   A criterion so obviously important that it requires little elaboration here is that a theory be as clear and precise as possible. In defining concepts and relating them to one another and to data, the theorist should avoid being implicit and using figurative, metaphorical, or analogical language. The trouble with implicit formulations is that they are not recognized and therefore exert an ambiguous, frequently inconsistent influence on the use of a theory. Figurative, metaphorical, and analogical formulations also create ambiguity and inconsistency. To make statements such as "The superego does battle with the id" or "The ego is the *executive organ attempting to strike a compromise* between the id and superego" is inconsistent with clarity and precision. As I pointed out in Chapter 6, such statements cannot be true literally, for doing battle and striking compromises are attributed to whole organisms whereas id, ego, and superego are intended to be only parts of organisms. To theorize in this loose fashion is to court misunderstanding.

At the earliest, most intuitive phase of theory formulation, metaphorical usage and some general implicitness is probably inevitable and perhaps even a stimulant to imaginativeness. But the theorist nonetheless should strive toward the goal of precision and clarity in his or her formulations. All too often personality theories remain characterized by implicitness and metaphorical usage long after their inception. Actually, were theories of personality more precise, my task of analysis in this book would be much simpler and my conclusions less equivocal.

There is a fairly simple way to determine whether a theory is sufficiently precise. Try to use it for what it was intended. Try to apply it to observations of people so as to understand them better. Or try to generate predictions concerning the behavior of particular kinds of people whom you have not yet observed. Try to decide how, in the theory's terms, these predictions should be tested. When you encounter difficulty in using the theory, it will be for one of two reasons: The theory is incomplete (recall the parts of a personality theory previously listed as necessary), or it is imprecise. If all the necessary parts are present in some form, imprecision is the flaw. Often a careful scrutiny of the theory will even disclose where the imprecision lies. Remember that a precise theory can be used readily even by someone who has no special faith in it. Indeed, theories that can be applied only by people who believe in their truth usually lack some degree of precision, which can sometimes be overcome by zealous utilization of intuition. But it would be better to use the zeal to decrease the implicitness and metaphorical qualities of the theory so that it can communicate to all would-be users.

A Theory Should Be Empirically Valid.   In discussing the previous principles of theorizing, I have been considering rational rather than empirical standards of adequacy. Demonstrating the rational adequacy of a theory is the first step, following which assessment of empirical validity becomes relevant. The crucial evidence on *empirical validity* involves systematic empirical tests of the predictions made by the theory. Explanations generated for data known before the explanation was formulated are interesting and useful, but they do not directly clarify the matter of empirical validity. Such explanations are called *post hoc,* to indicate that they do not involve putting yourself out on the limb of *predicting* the kind of data you will find before you have looked. In determining empirical validity, the empirical test of such predictions is much more important than the fineness of post hoc explanation. Given that theories of personality are very complex and inevitably somewhat elastic in construction, it is just too possible that post hoc explanations sound as good as they do because of some degree of unintentional twisting and stretching of the theory in order to square it with what you already know the data to be. No such theoretical body English can operate in predictions, whose relevant data are not yet available. To test a prediction, one must determine whether the relevant data, obtained under strict scientific standards, are indeed as expected. If a theory's predictions are disconfirmed often enough, it will be thrown into serious doubt, regardless of its rational adequacy and the apparent adequacy of its post hoc explanations.

The assessment of empirical validity, though a basic method of evaluation, is premature until the theory is sufficiently developed that the kinds of data that are actually relevant and the precise manner in which the theory addresses itself to them, can be unequivocally discerned. The rational standards already discussed are concerns prior to that of empirical validity in that they are marks of sufficient development. Before rational adequacy has been attained, empirical observations probably are more effectively used for theory construction and refinement rather than testing.

A Theory Should Be Stimulating.   It is often said that a theory justifies its existence if it provokes others to thought and investigation. Personologists might find a theory congenial and be motivated to enhance and support it; they might simply associate freely to it and be caught up in the novel ideas thus generated; they might react against it and be driven to demonstrate its inadequacies. It makes little difference which course is taken as long as it generates careful thought and research that otherwise might not occur. Clearly a theory need not meet any other criterion of adequacy, rational or empirical, in order to be considered worthwhile by the stimulation standard. And I certainly would agree that a theory that stimulates is a good thing.

But legitimate and important as stimulation value is, a theory will not make a lasting, specific contribution to understanding in a scientific discipline such as personology unless it achieves rational adequacy and empirical validity. It is fruitless, however, to be condemnatory because personology has made little progress in producing such theories. The standards discussed here simply define a goal to be worked toward. But personologists should not permit themselves to avoid the tedious and difficult work of rendering their theories more rationally and empirically adequate by satisfying themselves with the thought that their theories have been stimulating.

SUBSTANTIVE CHARACTERISTICS

It is the content, or substantive characteristics, of a theory that determines the predictions it will make. If the predictions are supported by empirical research, it will be because the theory's substantive characteristics were wisely chosen. Therefore, in attempting to develop better theories of personality, it would be sensible to take into account the substantive conclusions we have reached in analyzing the various positions included in this book. For vividness, I have organized substantive considerations into broad, somewhat interpretative units and italicized the most important statements.

One of the most salient substantive conclusions coming out of Chapter 6 is that *defensiveness is a common, though not ubiquitous, occurrence in living.* There are likely to be differences among people in their degree of defensiveness and in the areas of living in which defensiveness occurs. The evidence suggests two general techniques of defense; *to repress,* by failing to remember or perceive, and *to be hypersensitive,* by remembering or perceiving only some especially problematic things. The stimuli shown to elicit defensiveness have been of an anxiety-provoking or socially taboo nature. All of these findings suggest that *defensiveness occurs in the attempt to avoid anxiety that arises out of some conflict pitting the person and society against each other.* But such conflict is not an inevitable outcome of interaction between individuals and groups, for defensiveness is not ubiquitous.

Consistent with the view that the conflict involves person and society are the conclusions from Chapter 11 to the effect that two common characteristics on which people show differences in intensity are *conscience* (a set of values bearing on the regulation of personal action) and *commitment to or endorsement of existing social institutions and role structures.* Apparently some people are more accepting of the importance of society and its restrictions than are others. The complementary findings from Chapter 11 are that people differ in the degree to which they are *stable, predictable,* and *dependable,* which characteristics probably refer to the conformance of behavior to social responsibilities. At a more abstract level, Chapter 11 also testifies to the existence in people of *personal goals* (motives) as well as *social goals* (schemata). It is important to recognize that personal goals can have a wide range of content.

Let us conclude that there can, but need not, be anxiety-inducing conflict between personal and social goals. Let us also conclude that this anxiety is often reduced by defensiveness aimed at convincing oneself and others of the social purity of one's intent. We are left with the insistent question of whether defensiveness is a good thing. The evidence summarized in the next two paragraphs suggests that whatever the possible short-term gains, defensiveness is disadvantageous to the individual and, in a general sense, even to the vigorous development of his or her society. Clearly defensiveness implies conformity to what people around you do and believe. That people differ in the strength of such conforming tendencies when interacting with others is suggested by evidence in Chapter 11. Common bipolar characteristics emerging from factor analytic research are *gregariousness-aloofness, cooperativeness-competitiveness,* and *dominance-dependence.* The existence of *needs for power, achievement, and affiliation* is also well documented.

Knowing that it is possible to be conforming or individualistic, we can then ask what are the implications of these ways of being. From Chapter 6, we learned that *people who transcend the roles and institutions of society and are individualistic rather than conforming in their interpersonal behavior are more likely to be creative in their work.* Chapter 11 contributes evidence that *people who conform by answering questions about themselves in a socially desirable fashion show less initiative and self-confidence and can be more easily influenced by others.* In contrast, *people who accept themselves and their individuality are involved in a broader range of activities, have a more positive impact on other people, and are especially able to accept them.* A number of studies suggest that *people who do not see themselves as masters of their own fates are less likely to show initiative and proaction in the service of not only their own goals but of social problems.* These kinds of findings suggest that transcendent persons are not only more capable of fulfilling their own personal goals but are more socially useful than are conforming persons. Supporting this conclusion is the evidence that *a personal goal, the need for achievement, is an important factor in the socially crucial matter of economic development.*

There is another group of findings that prompt the substantive conclusion that activation and its adjustment are important attributes of the person. From the factor analytic studies reviewed in Chapter 11, we find that an important characteristic in which people show differences is *general energy or activation.* Chapter 6 made it clear that *people decrease tension in some of their functioning and actually increase tension in the rest.* You will recall that *tension* and *activation* are virtually interchangeable terms. Another aspect of the picture is the evidence in Chapter 6 that *people seek moderate degrees of variety while avoiding large degrees of it.* Additional evidence is provided in Chapter 11 to indicate that *there are individual differences in the strength of the motivation to seek or avoid variety.* It is not hard to believe that the seeking and avoiding of variety is in the service of increasing or decreasing activation, respectively. Other behaviors of possible relevance for increasing or decreasing activation that Chapter 11 shows to be differentially represented in people are *stability-impulsivity* and *rigidity-flexibility.*

Also apparent from Chapter 6 is the fact that people differ in the degree to which their personalities show *differentiation,* or *complexity.* Moreover, *differentiation increases from birth at least until some time in early adulthood.* Further, *integrative processes may well increase as the years pass.* Differentiation and integration are the two aspects of psychological growth, and hence these findings are important for that concept. Chapter 6 provides general evidence for the *occurrence of significant change in personality over the life span.*

The Aims of Comparative Analytic Research

The substantive considerations mentioned above are provocative as a basis for improving personality theorizing. But there remains some uncertainty about what is crucial substantively, because true comparative analytic research is still rare in personology. One way in which research qualifies as comparative analysis is its intent to resolve an issue or issues separating two or more theories or models (Chapter 6 gives examples of such issues). Another kind of comparative analytic research aims to determine the relative ability of one or more theories or models to account for the dimensions of individual differences that are observed (Chapter 11 is relevant). The methods employed may vary widely—from experimental to correlational analysis, from naturalistic observation to structured tests, from longitudinal to cross-sectional approaches. As long as the methods are appropriate to the problem, the main thing that qualifies a study as comparative analysis is an explicit emphasis on assessing the relative merits of differing theories. A concerted effort at such research on the part of many researchers would at the same time lead to a giant step forward in knowledge and give personology the boost in vitality it currently needs.

Ideally comparative analysis deals with models or families of theories because in that manner one gets the greatest return for the effort. But such a grand approach is not always feasible or practical. Comparative analysis can also deal fruitfully with mini-issues concerning two individual theories rather than broader models. It seems likely that most comparative analytic research that gets done in the near future will be of this sort.

Perhaps an example or two of what might be done will be helpful. One might address the issue concerning whether defensiveness facilitates or inhibits sound functioning (for example, Rogers would regard it as inhibiting and Freud as facilitating). Adopting an experimental approach, one might use the same threatening treatment on several experimental groups to arouse defensiveness and then have each group perform some relevant task. The threatening treatment would have to be theoretically appropriate to the arousal of defensiveness in both theories (e.g., constituting what Rogers would call *conditional positive regard* and Freud *psychosexual trauma*). The tasks performed by each group together would have to constitute a broad and reasonably representative cross-section of life's activities (e.g., problem-solving performance, creative endeavor, interpersonal functioning). It would also be useful to have a built-in manner (e.g., post test interviews) of determining whether (and in which subjects) defensiveness actually occurred. Control groups for each experimental group would perform the same tasks without prior defensiveness arousal. The aim of the study would be to chart the actual effect of defensiveness on the various tasks. The results would show either a general inhibition (favoring Rogers) or facilitation (favoring Freud) of performance or some more complex pattern of inhibition on some tasks and facilitation on others. The latter result would also be quite valuable in that it would constitute a basis for modification of both theories or for new theorizing.

Another example would be to use correlational methodology in comparing the existential and Freudian views of guilt. As the actual experience of guilt is similar (e.g., self-criticism, feelings of unworthiness, pessimism, depression, lack of energy, self-destructiveness) in the conceptualizations of both theories, a common measure of this state (probably questionnaire or interview) could be applied to a group of subjects. The subjects could also complete tests (probably other questionnaires or interviews) indexing the explanations of guilt that prevail in the two theories (for existential psychology, the chronic tendency to choose the past or status quo rather than the future or change; for Freud, an unresolved love for the opposite-sexed parent and hatred for the same-sexed parent and their representation in contemporary life). Then, by correlating the measure of guilt with the measures of ontological choice and psychosexual conflict, one could determine whether guilt is best explained by Freudian or existential psychology. Once again even complex patterns of results (e.g., some subjects appear more "Freudian" and others more "existential") would be useful in theory modification or new theorizing.

The Psychology of Possibility

One of the most constant and unique features of personality theory is the identification of ideal lifestyles and developmental directions. As you will recall from Chapter 1, this willingness to make value judgments about the good life is basic to statements and techniques in the area of psychotherapy, with its aim of changing destructive behavior to something better. Personologists are often criticized by their colleagues for making such value judgments, which frequently are seen as unscientific and appropriate, if at all, only in the nonempirical disciplines of philosophy and theology.

But it seems to me that personologists have a definite contribution to make to science through their concern with ideal functioning. Whereas most empirical psychologists are preoccupied with what is actual, with preponderance or majority, generalizing from this to the way things inevitably must be, personologists have the ability, because of their theoretical concerns, to explicate bases for human improvement. They carry the seeds of a psychology of possibility (Maddi, 1984).

All they need do is study persons approximating their theoretical ideal in a rigorous empirical fashion. By definition, few persons achieve ideal functioning. But some approximate it and, by searching them out, a sample large enough for rigorous study can be accumulated. Then these supposedly ideal persons can be compared on many theoretically relevant dimensions of living with a group of supposedly less ideal persons. Empirical information on how the ideal persons live and how they got to be that way can then be translated into prescriptions for personal development, parental actions, and psycho-therapy so that those who wish to follow suit will have some guidance. Indeed, one might even have a comparative analysis of conceptualizations of the ideal life! There is nothing at all unscientific about this—quite the contrary. And there is much for the human species to learn and become.

CONCLUDING REMARKS

I believe that the substantive considerations just summarized indicate the fruitfulness for personality theorizing using some combination of the ful-fillment model and the activation version of the consistency model. But it certainly is possible for someone to order the important substantive consider-ations in an even more powerful fashion by developing some other kind of personality theory. I will be satisfied if reading this book has rendered the task of personality theorizing more understandable, tangible, important, and engag-ing for you. As I mentioned in the preface, this book carries within it the seeds of its own demise. The demise will happen when a comparative analytic orien-tation takes such root as to lead to theories of personality more precise and powerful than any mentioned here. But the demise could also take the form of the promulgation of a more trenchant comparative analysis than I have been able to manage. If this book spurs others to better comparative analyses, then it will have fulfilled its purpose.

Appendix of Theoretical Summaries

FREUD'S THEORY

Core of Personality

Core Tendency. *To maximize instinctual gratification while minimizing punishment and guilt* (called the *reality principle*). This is a compromise necessitated by the inevitable conflict between the individual (whose instincts are selfish) and society (which aims at the common good). The reality principle involves *secondary process* thinking, which is characterized by formulating and testing strategies for maximizing instinctual gratification while minimizing punishment and guilt.

Core Characteristics.

Id: Consists of the *instincts,* which are the original contents of mind. All instincts have their *source* in the biological (metabolic) requirements of the organism and derive their *energy* from this source. The *aim* of all instincts is tension reduction (or satisfaction), which is achieved by obtaining objects appropriate to the source and aim. Instincts function according to the *pleasure principle,* or tendency to maximize instinctual gratification without regard for external reality. The pleasure principle involves *primary process* thinking, in which imagined objects give hallucinatory (and therefore only partial) satisfaction and tension reduction. All persons possess life, death, and sexual instincts, the last being by far the most important.

Ego: With experience, a portion of the person's mind becomes differentiated for the purpose of facilitating reality principle functioning through secondary process thinking. The major function of the ego is defensive in that it permits only the forms and portions of instincts unlikely to engender punishment and guilt to remain in consciousness. The reality principle is largely engineered by the defensive process, which is itself unconscious.

Superego: A portion of the mind, differentiated from the ego, which contains the traditional *values* and *taboos* of society as interpreted for the child by its parents. It is the superego that makes *guilt* possible, which

627

is the internal version of *punishment*. The values and taboos set restrictions on the forms of instinctual gratification that can be sought. When some instinctual impulse threatens to produce punishment or guilt, *anxiety* occurs as a warning. Some form of *defensiveness* occurs in order to avoid the anxiety by removing the instinctual impulse from consciousness. Because conflict between id and either society or superego is inevitable, all behavior is defensive.

Development

Psychosexual Stages

Oral (first year of life), in which the erogenous zone is the mouth and the primary activities are *receiving* (oral incorporative) and *taking* (oral aggressive). Feeding is the important area of conflict.

Anal (second year of life), in which the erogenous zone is the anus and the primary activities are *giving* (anal expulsive) and *withholding* (anal retentive). Bowel training is the important area of conflict.

Phallic (third through fifth year of life), in which the erogenous zone is the genitals and the primary activities involve *heterosexualizing interaction*. This is the time of the Oedipus conflict, when the child vies with the same-sexed parent for the affection of the opposite-sexed parent. Especially important for the boy is *castration anxiety* and for the girl *penis envy*.

Latency (sixth year through puberty), in which the sexual instinct is dormant and the child is learning skills not directly related to sexuality.

Genital (puberty to death), characterized by mature sexuality that combines all that is learned in the pregenital stages and relies primarily on *intercourse* and *orgasm*. The person reaching genitality is fully able to *love* and *work*.

Fixation.   When the inevitable conflict encountered at each psychosexual stage is minimal in intensity, the stage is successfully traversed. But when the parents intensify the conflict by *depriving* or *indulging* the child unduly or inconsistently, growth is arrested through the occurrence of massive defensiveness aimed at avoiding anxiety through avoiding conflict. This arresting of growth is called *fixation,* and it signifies that the activities of the psychosexual stage involved will remain especially important to the person, even after he or she has achieved puberty.

Periphery of Personality

Character Types Composed of Traits.   In adulthood, the types are expressive of the activities and conflicts of the various psychosexual stages of development and of the *defenses* common to those stages.

Oral character: Major defenses are *projection* (attributing to others an objectionable trait that one really possesses), *denial* (failing to perceive some threatening object or event in the external world), and *introjection* (incorporating other persons in order to avoid threat posed by them or one's own instincts). Some typical traits are *optimism-pessimism, gullibility-suspiciousness, manipulativeness-passivity,* and *admiration-envy.*

Anal character: Major defenses are *intellectualization* (substituting a fictitious, socially acceptable reason for the genuine, instinctual reason behind one's behavior), *reaction formation* (substituting for one's own true wishes the directly opposite wishes), *isolation* (severing the connecting links normally present between the cognitive and emotional components of wishes so that something of their true nature can remain conscious without a concomitant sense of threat), and *undoing* (certain thoughts and actions are engaged in so as to cancel out, or atone for, previous threatening thoughts or actions). Some typical traits are *stinginess-overgenerosity, stubbornness-acquiescence, orderliness-messiness,* and *precision-vagueness.*

Phallic character: Major defense is *repression* (the active debarring from consciousness of instinctual wishes and actions of a threatening nature). Some typical traits are *vanity–self-hatred, pride-humility, blind courage–timidity, stylishness-plainness,* and *chastity-promiscuity.*

Genital character: Major defense is *sublimation* (changing the object of the sexual instinct to make it more socially acceptable than the original but in no other way blocking the instinct). Traits indicate full socialization, adjustment, and potency.

MURRAY'S THEORY

Core of Personality

Core Tendency.   Similar to Freud. Raises the possibility that not all functioning is determined by the attempt to avoid conflict between individual and society.

Core Characteristics.

Id: Similar to Freud, but with the addition that not all of the instincts are selfish and socially deleterious in nature.

Ego: Similar to Freud, but with considerable elaboration of nondefensive processes whereby the socially acceptable instincts can be vigorously expressed. These nondefensive ego processes include such cognitive and actional procedures as *rational thought* and *accurate perception.*

Superego: Similar to Freud, but with proviso that the values and taboos it contains are not fixed in childhood. Following childhood, one's peers, events, and reading matter can influence the superego.

Development

Psychosexual Stages.   Similar to Freud, but with the addition of the following stages:

Claustral (intrauterine period of life), in which there is no clearly definable erogenous zone but there is passive dependency on mother.

Eurethral (between oral and anal stages), in which the urinary apparatus is the erogenous zone and the primary activities involve urinary display.

Fixation.   Similar to Freud.

Periphery of Personality

Complexes.   Similar to Freud's character types, with the addition of two types corresponding to the two additional psychosexual stages:

Claustral complex: Major defense is *denial;* traits are expressive of *passivity* and *withdrawal.*

Eurethral complex: Major defenses resemble the anal character type; traits stress *competitiveness* or *acquiescence.*

Needs.   A major contribution of uncertain relation to the rest of the theory is the concept of *need,* which is defined as an entity that organizes perception, apperception, intellection, conation, and action in such a way as to transform in a certain direction an existing, unsatisfying situation. A list of forty needs (e.g., achievement, power, affiliation, nurturance) is offered, along with several overlapping classifications of their functions and attributes. Needs are triggered by *press,* or environmental forces, real or perceived, that have arousing properties. Associated with the need concept is the *need-integrate,* or set of stable values and action patterns that are learned as a function of need expression.

ERIKSON'S THEORY

Core of Personality

Core Tendency.   Similar to Freud, but with a definite emphasis on some proportion of functioning that is not determined by the attempt to avoid conflict between individual and society.

Core Characteristics.

Id: Similar to Freud.

Ego: Similar to Freud, but with considerable elaboration of ego processes (such as rational thought and realistic perception) that are unrelated to the conflict between id and society. Ego is believed to be partially innate and to have a facsimile of its own instincts.

Superego: Similar to Freud.

Development

Psychosexual Stages.   Similar to Freud, but with biological sexuality de-emphasized in favor of the psychosocial features of conflict between child and parents. Development is seen as a process extending throughout life, which is divided into either periods or stages. In all stages, the amount of conflict determines whether the positive or negative pole is learned. The greater the conflict, the more likely the negative pole.

Trust versus mistrust (similar to Freud's oral stage), in which the issue is whether the child can feel dependent on and comfortable with others.

Autonomy versus shame and doubt (similar to Freud's anal stage), in which the issue is whether the child can feel independent of others.

Initiative and responsibility versus guilty functioning (similar to Freud's phallic stage), in which the issue is whether the youngster can feel competent and be active.

Industry versus inferiority (similar to Freud's latency stage), in which the issue is whether the youngster can feel satisfied in working hard.

Identity versus role diffusion (puberty to the end of adolescence), in which conflict is produced by the socially imposed task of becoming an independent and effective adult and the difficulty for the adolescent of performing this task.

Intimacy versus isolation (young adulthood), in which conflict is produced by the socially imposed task of developing close and comprehensive relationships and the difficulty of doing so.

Generativity versus stagnation (middle adulthood), in which conflict is produced by the socially imposed task of forgoing one's own immediate concerns in favor of fostering children and others and the difficulty in doing this.

Ego integrity versus despair (middle adulthood through death), in which conflict is produced by the decrease in important social and biological roles as old age approaches and the difficulty in accepting this.

Fixation.   Similar to Freud in that conflict is intensified through excessive deprivation or indulgence.

Periphery of Personality

Erikson is not explicit but presumably assumes *character types* comprised of combinations of the sets of *traits* related to the eight stages of development. As development continues throughout life, one must know not only a person's history of fixation but his or her approximate age in order to access the individual's personality. For example, a person in late adulthood who had not experienced fixations would show ego integrity, generativity, intimacy, identity, industry, initiative, autonomy, and trust, whereas a person also without fixations but only in young adulthood probably would not yet show generativity and ego integrity. Whenever a fixation occurs, it is likely to jeopardize sound development in subsequent stages as well. Thus, a young adult who shows isolation rather than intimacy is likely to also exhibit at least one negative quality relevant to earlier stages.

OBJECT-RELATIONS THEORY

Core of Personality

Core Tendency. *To develop a self.* This tendency, according to most object-relations theorists, is parallel to but independent of (and perhaps even more basic than) the Freudian core tendency.

Core Characteristics. These are the components of the self, namely:

Self-image, or what one thinks of and expects from oneself.

Object-images, or what one thinks of and expects from other persons.

Affect-dispositions, or tendencies toward emotional states that reflect how one felt during formative interpersonal relations.

Development

Stages of Self-Differentiation and Integration.

Autism (first several months of life), in which there is little differentiation of self and objects (others). Characterized by the defense mechanism of *splitting,* or vacillation between the ways of being of self and others as a response to feeling overwhelmed.

Symbiosis (about two to seven months of age), in which there is some differentiation of self and other but frequent confusion of the two. Characterized by the gradual diminution of splitting, if development is ideal, in favor of the defense of *introjection* (literal incorporation of objects into the mind). Self and object, though differentiated, remain an inseparable unit in the child's mind.

Differentiation (from one to two years of age), in which self and objects are clearly separate, are no longer confused, and have separate destinies. Characterized by the process of *identification,* usually regarded as a defense, in which objects have influence on the child through imitation.

Integration (beyond two years of age), in which the self and object representations independently perceived are fit into relationship with each other. Although identification processes are still important, the self is sufficiently formed to constitute an *identity*, with definiteness and uniqueness. It is unclear whether this stage is defensive or nondefensive under ideal developmental conditions.

Developmental Implications of Interactions.   Also unclear is the precise nature of interactions between child and others that is ideal and nonideal. Presumably something like the Freudian notion that there should not be too much frustration or indulgence operates for object-relations theorists.

Periphery of Personality

Mature Self-Identity.   Deep and stable relations with others, tolerance of ambivalence toward loved objects, capacity for tolerating guilt and separation, having an integrated self-concept, and correspondence between behavior patterns and self-concept.

Pathological States.   Three levels of self-pathology are mentioned. Important are how disintegrated the self is, how punitive the superego is, and how much social relations and work are impaired. Many of the traditional neuroses and psychoses are subsumed under self-pathology.

KOHUT'S SELF-PSYCHOLOGY

Core of Personality

Core Tendency.   *To enhance and order functioning through the experience of self.* When the self has developed well, it is a consciously appreciated sense of who and what one is that lends meaning and direction to behavior.

Core Characteristics.

Need to be mirrored, expressed in the child's wish to have its expressions and products recognized, approved of, and admired. The most important mirroring person in the child's life is the mother. Early mirroring experiences underlie *ambitions*.

Need to idealize, expressed in the child's admiration of and identification with others more powerful and developed than itself. The most important object of idealization in the child's life is the father. Early idealization experiences underlie *goals*.

Development

The *nuclear self* emerges during the second year of life if development is ideal. This nuclear self is defined as bipolar, including archaic nuclear ambitions on the one hand and archaic nuclear goals on the other. The "tension arc" between these two poles stimulates the expression (and hence development) of the child's rudimentary skills and talents.

Conditions for Ideal Development.   The mother must mirror her child, and the father must permit himself to be idealized. When parents are too preoccupied, ungenerous, or unable to accept their own selves, the child's development will be jeopardized.

Periphery of Personality

Autonomous Self.   This ideal type is characterized by *self-esteem* and *self-confidence*. One is not dependent on others and has both *ambition,* in a general sense, and specific *goals. Talents* and *skills* are developed in the service of ambitions and goals.

Narcissistic Personality Disorders.   Involve thought processes more than action.

The *understimulated self* (resulting from lack of parental response) will do anything (e.g., promiscuity, perversion, gambling, drug and alcohol abuse, hypersociability) to create excitement and ward off feelings of deadness.

The *fragmented self* (resulting from lack of parental response) is extremely vulnerable to setbacks, responding with sharp decrease in self-esteem and disorganization.

The *overstimulated self* (resulting from excessive parental response) shies away from creative and leadership activities for fear of being flooded by unrealistic fantasies of greatness.

The *overburdened self* (resulting primarily from frustrated idealizing need) perceives others as hostile, reacting with irritability and suspicion to hardly noticeable events as frustrations or attacks.

Narcissistic Behavior Disorders.   Expressed primarily in action rather than in thought.

The *mirror-hungry personality* (resulting from failure to mirror parental response) is famished for admiration, leading to incessant displays in an insatiable attempt to get attention.

The *ideal-hungry personality* (resulting from lack of parental response) can experience self as real only when related to others who conform slavishly to the person, though full satiation of the hunger is never really achieved.

Other types mentioned are considered frankly pathological.

BERNE'S TRANSACTIONAL ANALYSIS

Core of Personality

Core Tendency. *To strive for a socially satisfying and meaningful life.* Something like the Freudian instincts and their gratifications are still there, but increasingly they form the background, with social and psychological matters gaining greater emphasis. There is little to suggest the assumption of necessary, inevitable conflict.

Core Characteristics. In addition to the usual biological survival drives (which are relatively unimportant), there are the following psychological needs:

Stroke hunger, for physical contact of a soothing sort.

Structure hunger, which refers specifically to how persons invest their lives with meaning by deciding how to fill up their time.

Excitement hunger, which recognizes that persons wish not to be bored.

Recognition hunger, for social approval and respect.

Leadership hunger, which shows persons' need for influence and control.

Ego States. All persons have within them the *Child* (dependent, biologically oriented, undisciplined views of life), the *Parent* (morally oriented, disciplined, authoritative views of life), and the *Adult* (unevaluative, realistic perceptions of life). The content of these three ego states is influenced by learning.

Periphery of Personality

At the moment there is no definitive statement on types, but there are some leads.

Life Script. A plan (typically not conscious) that organizes energies and direction. It develops through parental interaction and other cultural forces (e.g., fairy tales). All scripts include a *life position,* or learned assumptions about acceptability of self and others. The four basic life positions are: "I'm OK and you're OK," "I'm OK but you're not OK," "I'm not OK but you're OK," and "Neither you nor I are OK."

Games. A series of social transactions with a well-defined climax or *gimmick.* The particular life position and script influences the games that are played. Examples of games are *alcoholic, debtor, kick me, frigid woman,* and *look how hard I've tried.*

Ego States. Games and life scripts involve various configurations of the three ego states: Child, Parent, and Adult.

RANK'S THEORY

Core of Personality

Core Tendency.   *To minimize the fear of life while minimizing the fear of death.* As these two fears are inherent and opposed, conflict is inevitable and compromise must be sought.

Core Characteristics.

Fear of life, where *life* refers to the inevitable process of separation and individualization, starting with being born and continuing through being weaned, locomoting independently, leaving the home for school, and so forth.

Fear of death, where *death* refers to the inherent tendency toward union, fusion, and dependency.

The *will,* or organized sense of who and what one is that in its most vigorous form is not defensive and functions to establish a basis for minimizing both the life and death fears.

Development

Counterwill and Will.   Soon after birth, the child begins to differentiate between itself and others and develops a rudimentary form of the will. This is the *counterwill* and involves the child's learning that it can say no to the pressures of adults and to its own impulses. If this negativistic counterwill shatters the union between child and parents, the result will be *guilt* (a specialized expression of fear of life). But if union between child and parent is not shattered, counterwill will mature into will. No precise developmental stages are specified.

Periphery of Personality

Personality Types Composed of Traits.

Artist: Expresses ideal development, in which the fears of life and death are effectively minimized and will is strong. Characterized by high degree of *differentiation* and *integration* of thoughts, feelings, and actions; *intimacy* without slavish loyalties or concern for propriety; creation of products that are *unusual* but also *useful.*

Neurotic person: Expresses the tendency toward separation (fear of death) but has denied the tendency toward union (fear of life) and shows counterwill more than will. Such persons have committed themselves to the pain of separation from the herd but have not, like the artist, also won through to constructive interactions with the world. They are *hostile, negativistic, arrogant, isolationistic, critical of others, guilty,* and so on. When developing counterwill, they were made to feel wrong and unworthy.

Average person: Expresses the tendency toward union (fear of life) but has denied the tendency toward separation (fear of death). Out of fear of life, such persons never entertain the possibility of their own individuality. They are *conforming, dependable, superficial, suggestible,* and *self-satisfied.* The developmental handicap is an overwhelming negative response of parents to first expressions of counterwill.

ANGYAL'S THEORY

Core of Personality

Core Tendency.   *To maximize both the expression of autonomy and the expression of surrender.* Autonomy and surrender are inherent and opposing tendencies; thus, conflict is inevitable and compromise must be sought.

Core Characteristics.   *Autonomy* refers to separation from others and the physical environment, with emphasis on independence and aloofness. *Surrender* refers to functioning leading to merger or union with other people, ideals, or the inanimate environment, with emphasis on dependency. Expressing both characteristics leads to simultaneous differentiation and integration. Relevant to Angyal's theorizing about the interaction between the person and the environment is the concept of *biosphere,* which encompasses individuals and their worlds. The personality is one component of the biosphere. The *symbolic self* is the sum total of the person's self-conceptions, but little specification of its content is available.

Development

No specific position is taken.

Periphery of Personality

Although the distinction is made between periphery and core, little specification of periphery is offered. Of possible relevance is the notion of *dimensions* (which may be somewhat like traits).

Vertical dimension: Refers at one pole to concrete, overt behavior and at the other to deep, underlying forces.

Progressive dimension: Comprises a series of surface actions, which are organized in such fashion as to bring the person nearer to a goal.

Transverse dimension: Involves the coordination of discrete actions into a larger, better integrated, and more effective behavior unit (e.g., the type).

BAKAN'S THEORY

Core of Personality

Core Tendency.   *To maximize the expression of both agency and communion.* Agency and communion are inherent, opposed tendencies; thus, conflict is inevitable and compromise must be sought.

Core Characteristics.

Agency: Separation from others and the physical environment, with emphasis on manipulativeness.

Communion: Merging with or joining other people, ideas, or the inanimate environment, with emphasis on unity.

Development

No specific position taken.

Periphery of Personality

No formal position taken, although implicit emphasis is put on the importance of living according to the compromise involving expression of both agency and communion. The result is simultaneous differentiation and integration. When agency is expressed with communion denied, the end result is psychological or physical illness.

PERLS'S GESTALT THERAPY

Core of Personality

Core Tendency.   *To strive to comprehend life by identifying bits of experience and construing them in relationships of simultaneous attraction and repulsion.* Intrapsychic conflict is a characteristic of mental life in this theory.

Core Characteristics.

Bits: Things, events, times, places, persons, parts of a person, and so on. The person breaks up experience into bits in an attempt to comprehend what is going on.

Process: Two bits and a happening. A *happening* is the simultaneous attraction and repulsion that characterizes all relationships between bits. The whole involved in the process is sometimes called a *gestalt*.

Personality: Comprised of *being* (the biological organism construed by the mind), *self* (awareness of one's dimensions and purposes as distinct from others and nature), and *self-image* (what one ought to want to be).

Development

Three Phases or Modes of Thinking.

Social phase, developmentally earliest, is so named because the child requires interaction with others for survival. The child begins to develop an awareness of others as they aid and frustrate it.

Psychosocial phase, which encompasses most of life, involves awareness of self and resultant sharpening of social awareness. Most construing of bits and relationships takes place at this time, as does the emergence of personality.

Spiritual phase, or an intuitive apprehension of meanings beyond being, self, and self-image. This phase is not reached by everyone.

Acknowledgment and Approbation.   Progression from one phase to another is hastened by these reactions from others. *Acknowledgment* refers to recognition of the person and his or her actions by others. It implies acceptance with little criticality. *Approbation* is critical (positive or negative) response from others.

Periphery of Personality

No firm position is taken. In ideal development, the relationships between bits run their course and end, whereupon the bits enter into other relationships with other bits. Thus, new occasions of conflict are always being born, and the personality has fluidity. In the nonideal state, some particular relationship between some bits will become frozen, presumably through failures of acknowledgment or negative approbation. These frozen relationships are called *blisters,* which are as close to personality types as this position comes. The aim of psychotherapy is to remove blisters.

JUNG'S THEORY

Core of Personality

Core Tendency.   *To attain selfhood.* Selfhood represents a balance between the opposing forces of personality and includes both conscious and unconscious material. Energy concepts instrumental in achieving selfhood are the *principle of equivalence* (if the value of any aspect of personality increases or decreases, this shift will be compensated for by an opposite shift in another aspect) and the *principle of entropy* (the distribution of energy in the personality seeks an equilibrium, or balance). Of uncertain relationship to the rest is the *transcendent function,* whose aim is to integrate personality elements into an overall whole.

Core Characteristics.

The *ego* (or conscious, individualistic mind), which is in conflict with the *personal unconscious* (formed of socially unacceptable mental content that was once conscious but has been forced out of awareness by defenses).

The *collective unconscious* (a communal, species memory, never achieving consciousness, representing the accumulated experiences of humankind and possibly even subhuman life). Comprised of archetypes, or essences (universal forms) that predispose toward characteristically human thoughts and feelings. Although these thoughts and feelings can become conscious, the underlying archetypes cannot. Major archetypes are the *shadow* (the animalistic possibilities of persons), the *anima* (the feminine possibility in persons), the *animus* (the masculine possibility in persons), and the *persona* (the conventional mask adopted by persons in the face of social pressures).

Development

There is little emphasis on stages, though a distinction is made between early life and later adulthood. In early life, sexuality and the individualistic concerns of the ego are dominant. In later adulthood, there is a shift to spirituality and the universal emphases of the collective unconscious. Concepts employed in understanding development are:

Causality (influence on behavior of the past) versus *teleology* (influence on behavior of the anticipated future).

Progression (forward thrust) versus *regression* (shrinking to a safe past).

Sublimation (energy transformed from primitive to cultural spiritual concerns) versus *repression* (defensive blocking of consciousness and energy).

Periphery of Personality

Personality Types Composed of Orientations and Modes.

Introversive-rational: Oriented toward the inner world of experience (introversion). Emphasizes either the thinking or feeling modes (both are considered rational in that they involve evaluation of experience). Subtypes are introversive-thinking and introversive-feeling.

Extroversive-rational: Oriented toward the outer world of experience (extroversion). Emphasizes either thinking or feeling modes, leading to subtypes corresponding to the above.

Introversive-irrational: Oriented toward the inner world of experience (introversion). Emphasizes either the sensing or intuiting modes (both are considered irrational in that they passively record but do not evaluate experience). Subtypes are introversive-sensing and introversive-intuiting.

Extroversive-irrational: Oriented toward the outer world of experience (extroversion). Emphasizes either sensing or intuiting modes, leading to subtypes corresponding to the above.

Selfhood: The ideal peripheral personality. Involves a form of transcendence of the other personality types such that the introversion-extroversion and rational-irrational modes are balanced. Selfhood can be approached, but never completely attained.

ROGERS'S THEORY

Core of Personality

Core Tendency.   *To actualize one's inherent potentialities.* This tendency serves to maintain and enhance living not only for the individual but for the species. As there is nothing in inherent potentialities that is unacceptable to society, conflict is not inevitable. The actualizing tendency, as stated above, is common to all living things. In humans, the tendency takes the additional form of the *attempt to actualize the self* (discussed below).

Core Characteristics.   Important in the *self-actualization tendency* are the need for positive regard, the need for positive self-regard, and the self. Both needs are offshoots of the self-actualizing tendency. The *need for positive regard* (from other people) renders one influenceable by social approval and disapproval. The *need for positive self-regard* refers to the satisfaction involved in finding one's experience of oneself consistent with one's self-concept. The *self* refers to one's conscious sense of who and what one is.

Development

No developmental stages are specified. In general, the important consideration is whether the person receives *unconditional positive regard* (basic, complete acceptance and respect) or *conditional positive regard* (acceptance of some and rejection of other behaviors) from significant others. If unconditional positive regard is received, the self-concept will reflect all that there is in the inherent potentialities, that is, the self will be *congruent* with the potentialities. But if the person encounters conditional positive regard, he or she will develop *conditions of worth* (evaluative notions concerning which behaviors are worthy and which unworthy). The self-concept will have been socially determined and therefore will be *incongruent* with the inherent potentialities. In order that this incongruence not become conscious and, hence, the source of *anxiety* concerning unworthiness, *defenses* are instituted. Defensive functioning involves either *repression* or *distortion*.

Periphery of Personality

Personality Types Composed of Traits.

Fully functioning person (or ideal person): Has received unconditional positive regard. Hence, there are no conditions of worth, no defensiveness, and congruence between self and potentialities. Such persons are characterized by *openness to experience* (emotional depth and reflectiveness), *existential living* (flexibility, adaptability, spontaneity, and inductive thinking), *organismic trusting* (intuitive living, self-reliance, confidence), *experiential freedom* (subjective sense of free will), and *creativity* (penchant for producing new and effective ideas and things).

Maladjusted person: Has received conditional positive regard. Therefore, there are *conditions of worth, incongruence* between self and potentialities, and *defensiveness*. Also, such persons *live according to a preconceived plan* rather than existentially, *disregarding their organism* rather than trusting it, feeling *manipulated* rather than free, and *common and conforming* rather than creative.

For all his emphasis on individuality, Rogers specifies only these two personality types. Subclassifications within each broad category might be possible if the contents of inherent potentialities were stated.

MASLOW'S THEORY

Core of Personality

Core Tendencies. *The push toward actualization of inherent potentialities* and *the push to satisfy needs ensuring physical and psychological survival.* The actualizing tendency leads to the enhancement of life (called *growth motivation*), whereas the survival tendency merely ensures the maintenance of life (called *deprivation motivation*). Although these tendencies are hierarchically organized such that the survival tendency must be satisfied before the actualization tendency can be strongly expressed, they are not really in conflict with each other.

Core Characteristics. Associated with the survival tendency are *physiological needs* (food, water, etc.), *safety needs* (avoidance of pain), *needs for belongingness and love* (intimacy, gregariousness, identification), and *esteem needs* (approval of self and others). Each of these needs becomes important only when those preceding it are satisfied. When all the needs associated with survival are satisfied, those associated with actualization become salient. They are the *need for self-actualization* (emphasis on the person's special capabilities) and the *need for cognitive understanding* (emphasis on information and stimulation hunger).

Development

Not much specification, though what there is agrees with Rogers. If the survival tendency is not blocked by other people, the actualization tendency will be vigorously expressed. Blockage leads to defense.

Periphery of Personality

Personality Type Composed of Traits and Values.   The *self-actualized person* (has had satisfaction of the survival tendency) is characterized by *realistic orientation; acceptance* of self, others, and natural works; *spontaneity; task orientation* (rather than self-preoccupation); *sense of privacy; independence;* vivid *appreciativeness; spirituality* that is not necessarily religious in a formal sense; sense of *identity with mankind;* feelings of *intimacy* with a few loved ones; *democratic values;* recognition of the *difference between means and ends; humor* that is philosophical rather than hostile, *creativeness;* and *nonconformism.*

ADLER'S THEORY

Core of Personality

Core Tendency.   *To strive toward superiority or perfection.* This tendency applies to functioning not only as an individual but as a member of society. Hence, there is no necessary conflict between the person and society. An earlier form of the core tendency, the *will to power,* had more competitive implications.

Core Characteristics.   The bases of the perfection tendency are *organ inferiorities* (actual physical weaknesses and incapacities), *feelings of inferiority* (psychic states of inferiority regardless of physical condition), and *compensation* (the attempt to overcome real or imagined inferiorities). The direction of the compensations can be seen by the nature of the inferiorities but also by the ideals of perfect living (which are called *fictional finalisms)*. There is also the somewhat mysterious notion of *creative self,* which essentially expresses persons' capability of exercising free will to transcend the forces acting on them.

Development

No stages are postulated. Instead, there is emphasis on family constellation and family atmosphere. *Family constellation* refers to the sociological facts of the family as they affect each member. Included are such matters as ordinal position of the child and presence or absence of the father. *Family atmosphere* refers more to the quality of emotional relationship among family members. Family constellation affects development by giving the child a particular set of problems (e.g., only child or oldest child) with which to cope. Family atmosphere influences whether the child is active or passive and constructive or destructive in striving toward perfection. Cooperative atmospheres of mutual trust and respect encourage constructiveness, whereas the opposite atmosphere encourages destructiveness. Family emphasis on personal initiative encourages activeness, while the opposite atmosphere encourages passiveness.

Periphery of Personality

Styles of Life Composed of Fictional Finalisms and Traits.

Active-constructive style: Includes the fictional finalism of *service* and the set of traits that can be summarized as *ambitiousness* or orientation toward success. This style may be the Adlerian ideal.

Passive-constructive style: Includes the fictional finalism of *attention getting* and the set of traits summarized as *charm,* or receiving special attention for what one is rather than for what one does. This style is also considered desirable.

Active-destructive style: Includes the fictional finalisms of abrogation of *power,* achievement of *revenge,* and the bid to be *left alone.* The traits include *being a nuisance, rebelliousness, viciousness,* and *degeneration.*

Passive-destructive style: Includes the fictional finalisms mentioned for the active-destructive style but the additional traits of *laziness, stubbornness, passive aggression,* and *despair.*

WHITE'S THEORY

Core of Personality

Core Tendency. *To produce effects through one's actions (effectance motivation)* and *to achieve competence in one's functioning (competence motivation).* Probably effectance motivation occurs first and with maturation becomes competence motivation.

Core Characteristics. Associated with effectance motivation is the requirement of the nervous system for *information,* or stimulation. Associated with competence motivation is *actual competence* and *sense of competence,* though it is not yet clear what role in personality these characteristics play.

Development

Not specified, though White adopts some of the most psychosocial (least biological) features of Erikson's views on the eight developmental stages.

Periphery of Personality

Not specified extensively, but partially endorses Erikson's emphases on trust versus mistrust and so on.

ALLPORT'S THEORY

Core of Personality

Core Tendencies.   *To function in a manner expressive of the self or proprium (propriate functioning)* and *to satisfy biological survival needs (opportunistic functioning)*. The self is phenomenologically defined, and functioning in terms of it is considered more important, human, and extraordinary than functioning in terms of survival needs. There is little real conflict between the two tendencies. The survival tendency must be satisfied first, but once it is, the attempt to express the self becomes paramount.

Core Characteristics.   Opportunistic functioning involves biological characteristics such as the *needs for food, water,* and *air*. Propriate functioning includes *sense of body, self-identity, self-esteem, self-extension, rational coping, self-image,* and *propriate striving*. Propriate functioning is *proactive* (influences the world), whereas opportunistic functioning is *reactive* (is influenced by the world).

Development

No specific stages are postulated. It is assumed that the organism is opportunistic at birth and that it requires nurturance and affection. If the biological needs are satisfied easily, propriate functioning will develop vigorously. The first signs of a sense of body begin to develop by the end of the first year. The second and third years see the beginnings of self-identity and then self-image. From six to twelve, the rational coping qualities of the proprium become apparent. In adolescence, propriate striving is in increasing evidence. Although the various propriate functions begin their development at different times, they all act interdependently by the time adulthood is reached. All this presupposes nurturance and support of the child early in life. If this does not occur, propriate development will not be vigorous and opportunistic functioning will continue to predominate in adulthood. The process of shifting from opportunistic to propriate functioning involves the principle of *functional autonomy,* which indicates that a behavior pattern originally instrumental to satisfaction of a biological need can persist as a fully independent aspect of living even after the biological need is no longer an important force.

Periphery of Personality

No typology is offered. The major peripheral characteristic is the *personal disposition,* which is a generalized neuropsychic structure (peculiar to the individual), with the capacity to render many stimuli functionally equivalent and to initiate and guide consistent (equivalent) forms of adaptive and stylistic behavior. Personal dispositions can be primarily *dynamic* (motivational) or *expressive* (stylistic). Personal dispositions are virtually unique to particular individuals, being expressive of individuality. In studying personal dispositions, Allport advocates the *morphogenic* (idiographic) approach, in which laws applying to individuals rather than groups are sought. Of secondary importance is the concept of *common trait,* an abstraction that describes the average rather than individual case. To study common traits, one adopts a *nomothetic* approach, which seeks to arrive at laws by generalizing across people.

With Allport's strong emphasis on individuality, it is not surprising that little specification of content for personal dispositions is offered. The closest Allport comes to content specification is in his criteria of maturity: enduring *extensions of the self;* techniques for *warm relating to others* (such as tolerance); stable *emotional security* or self-acceptance; habits of *realistic perception, skills,* and *problem centeredness;* established *self-objectification* in the form of *insight* and *humor;* and a *unifying philosophy of life,* including particular *value orientations,* differentiated *religious sentiment,* and a generic, *personalized conscience.* In stable aspects of behavior these criteria of maturity seem to be the results of expressing the propriate functions.

FROMM'S THEORY

Core of Personality

Core Tendency. *To express one's human nature.* A person's human nature differs radically from his or her animal nature. Yet the two are not really in conflict (1) because one's animal nature is the least important thing about one and (2) because one's animal nature is usually satisfied continuously.

Core Characteristics.

Need for relatedness (to be in contact with people and physical nature).

Need for transcendence (to be separate from other people and things).

Need for rootedness (to have a sense of belongingness).

Need for identity (to know who and what one is).

Need for a frame of reference (to have a stable way of perceiving and comprehending the world).

Development

There are three types of relationship between parents and child: *symbiotic relatedness,* in which the people are related but never attain independence; *withdrawal-destructiveness,* in which there is a negative relatedness or distance and indifference; and *love,* in which there is mutual respect, support, and appreciation. Development is more a function of the type of relationship between child and parents than one of stages.

Periphery of Personality

Orientations (or Types) Composed of Traits.

Receptive orientation: Stems from the masochistic patterns of behavior learned by the child who is the passive party in a symbiotic relationship with its parents. In this orientation, persons feel the source of all good to be outside themselves and expect to receive things passively. Typical traits show *passivity, lack of character, submissiveness,* and *cowardliness.*

Exploitative orientation: Stems from the sadistic behavior patterns learned by the child who is the dominant party in a symbiotic relationship with the parents. In this orientation, persons believe the source of all good to be outside themselves but do not expect to receive it so much as take it forcibly. Typical traits show *aggression, egocentrism, conceit, arrogance,* and *seductiveness.*

Hoarding orientation: Stems from the behavior pattern of destructiveness learned by the child who is reacting to parental withdrawal in the withdrawal-destructiveness type of relationship. In this orientation, there is little faith in anything new to be obtained from the outside world; security is based on hoarding and saving what one already has. Typical traits are *stinginess, unimaginativeness, suspiciousness, stubbornness,* and *possessiveness.*

Marketing orientation: Stems from the behavior pattern of withdrawal learned by the child who is reacting to parental destructiveness in the withdrawal-destructiveness type of relationship. In this orientation, the person experiences self as a commodity obeying the laws of supply and demand and has the values of the marketplace. Typical traits are *opportunism, inconsistency, aimlessness, lack of principle, relativism,* and *wastefulness.*

Productive orientation: Stems from the behavior patterns learned through a love relationship with the parents. In this orientation, the person values self and others for what they are and experiences security and inner peace. Typical traits reflect the potentially useful aspects of the other orientations (e.g., *modesty, adaptability, trust, activeness, pride, confidence, practicality, patience, loyalty, flexibility, open-mindedness,* and *experimenting spirit.* Clearly the productive orientation is Fromm's ideal.

EXISTENTIAL PSYCHOLOGY

Core of Personality

Core Tendency. *To achieve authentic being. Being* signifies the special quality of human mentality (aptly called *intentionality*), that makes life a series of decisions, each involving an alternative that precipitates persons into an unknown future and an alternative that pushes them back into a routine, predictable past. Choosing the unknown future brings *ontological anxiety* (fear of the unknown), whereas choosing the safe status quo brings *ontological guilt* (sense of missed opportunity). Authenticity involves accepting this painful state of affairs and finding the *courage* or *hardiness* to persist in the face of ontological anxiety and choose the future, thereby minimizing ontological guilt.

Core Characteristics. *Being-in-the-world* emphasizes the unity of person and environment, since, in this heavily phenomenological position, both are personally or subjectively defined. Being-in-the-world has three components: *Umwelt* (the construed biological and physical world), *Mitwelt* (the construed social world), and *Eigenwelt* (the internal dialogue of relationship to oneself). It is assumed that behind these three components lie the person's inherent biological, social, and psychological (symbolization, imagination, and judgment) needs.

Development

Early Development.   The period during which the child is dependent and requires parental guidance in order to develop *courage*. Ideally, parents (1) expose the child to a richness of experience, (2) freely impose limits expressing their own views, (3) love and respect the child as a budding individual, and (4) teach the value of vigorous symbolization, imagination, and judgment directly and by example. Experiencing these things, the child develops courage, or the willingness to consider what is *facticity* and what *possibility,* and the tendency to chose the *future* rather than the *past,* tolerating *ontological anxiety* (fear of unknown) rather than building up *ontological guilt* (sense of missed opportunity).

Later Development.   Begins when courage has been developed (presumably sometime in adolescence, if conditions have been ideal). This period, which continues throughout life, involves self-initiated learning from failure experiences. There are two transitional stages to go through before authenticity or individuality can be reached. The first is the *aesthetic phase,* which takes place as soon as the person leaves the family. It is characterized by living in the moment (without regard for past or future) and failing to form deep relationships. The loneliness and aimlessness of this orientation teaches the person its shortcomings. Thus, the *idealistic phase* begins, characterized by undying commitments and uncompromising principles. Sooner or later the person recognizes, through failures, that commitments cannot be made forever and that the relationship between principles and any particular persons or events is problematical. With this learning, the phase of authenticity or individuality begins.

Nonideal Development.   If the conditions for learning courage are not present during early development, later development never really takes place. In other words, the person is unable to discern what is facticity and what possibility, does not choose the future, and shrinks from failure too often to learn anything from it.

Periphery of Personality

Personality Types Emphasizing Self-Definition and World View.

Authenticity or *individuality* (ideal type) involves the self-definition as someone with a mental life permitting comprehension and influence over one's social and biological experiences. The world view is characterized by considering society the creation of persons and properly in their service. The individualist's functioning has unity and shows originality and change. Biological and social experiencing show subtlety, taste, intimacy, and love. Doubt (or ontological anxiety) is experienced as a natural concomitant of creating one's own meaning and does not undermine the decision-making process. There is a minimum of ontological guilt, or sense of missed opportunity.

Conformism (nonideal type) is the expression in adulthood of not having learned courage in early development and, hence, being unable to learn from failures. The self-definition is nothing more than a player of social roles and an embodiment of biological needs. Expression of symbolization, imagination, and judgment is inhibited, leading to stereotyped, fragmentary functioning. Biological experiencing is isolated and gross, and social experiencing is contractual rather than intimate. The conformist feels worthless and insecure because of the buildup of ontological guilt through frequently choosing the past rather than the future. The relevant world view stresses materialism and pragmatism. This type represents a vulnerability to existential sickness, which tendency becomes an actuality when environmental stresses occur that are sufficient to disconfirm the conformist's self-definition and world view.

ELLIS'S RATIONAL-EMOTIVE THERAPY

Core of Personality

Core Tendencies.   *To think irrationally and harm oneself* and *to gain understanding of one's folly, training oneself to change self-destructive ways.* This is not a conflict position, because the second tendency corrects the first. No compromise is advocated.

Core Characteristics.   Various characteristics are implied, such as *self-pity* and *irrationality,* which express the personally destructive core tendency, and *patience* and *levelheadedness,* which express the constructive core tendency. However, very little systematic theorizing is available.

Development

Little systematic theorizing has been done. It is assumed that parents generally intensify the person's destructive, irrational tendencies.

Periphery of Personality

Little emphasis is given, the concern being mainly with psychotherapeutic considerations.

KELLY'S THEORY

Core of Personality

Core Tendency   *To predict and control the events one experiences.* The model adopted for understanding persons is that of the scientist, construing events and subjecting the resulting constructs to testing, retaining those that are confirmed and rejecting or changing those that are disconfirmed.

Core Characteristics.   *Constructs* are abstractions or generalizations from concrete experience. All constructs take the form of a dichotomy, with the two poles having opposite meanings (e.g., good-bad). Constructs are organized into *construction systems* on the basis of two hierarchical principles:

1. A construct may be superordinate to another because each pole of the subordinate construct forms a part of the context for the two poles of the superordinate.
2. An entire construct may fit in one pole of another construct without relevance to the remaining pole.

In anticipating events, one selects the constructs that seem relevant and then chooses which poles of the relevant constructs to apply. Choosing the pole of the construct is called the *elaborative choice,* and it reflects deciding on the alternative through which one anticipates the greater possibility for extension and definition of one's construction system.

Although constructs that are disconfirmed by actual events are changed or discarded, Kelly is not explicit about the procedure for testing constructs. But he does indicate something of the emotional conditions surrounding construct disconfirmation and change:

> *Anxiety:* The awareness that the events with which one is confronted lie outside the predictive capabilities of one's construction system.

> *Hostility:* The continued effort to extort validational evidence in favor of a social prediction that already has been recognized as a failure.

> *Guilt:* The awareness of dislodgement of the self from one's core role structure.

Development

There is no consideration of development aside from the statements concerning the construing of events and the changing of disconfirmed constructs. The nature of significant relationships in childhood and adulthood is not considered important.

Periphery of Personality

There is no specification of typical constructs or organization of constructs into personal styles. Some differentiations concerning constructs are offered, however, that could be of use in understanding individual differences. Constructs differ in their degree of *permeability* (hitherto unencountered events can be subsumed within a construct if it is permeable) and *preemptiveness* (a preemptive construct renders the events it subsumes unavailable for subsumption within other constructs). In addition, constructs can be *preverbal* (having no consistent word symbols to represent them), *comprehensive* (subsuming a wide variety of events), *incidental* (subsuming a narrow variety of events), *superordinate* (including other constructs as one of their elements), *subordinate* (being included as an element of other constructs), and *loose* (leading to varying predictions while maintaining their identity).

McCLELLAND'S THEORY

Core of Personality

Core Tendency.   *To minimize large discrepancies between expectation and occurrence while maximizing small discrepancies between them.* People are perceived as craving small degrees of unpredictability in order to offset boredom and avoiding large degrees of unpredictability in order to avoid threat.

Core Characteristics.   *Expectancies* are cognitive units, referring to what one believes will be the content and timing of events in the future. *Positive* (pleasurable) and *negative* (displeasurable) *affect* (emotion) are inherent reactions to small and large discrepancies between expectation and occurrence, respectively. Also on an inherent basis, positive affect leads to *approach* whereas negative affect leads to *avoidance*.

Development

There is little emphasis on stages. More simply, the developmental position is that if the parents arrange to make most of the child's experiences in a particular area of endeavor small rather than large discrepancies, the child will learn stable patterns of approach behavior for that area. If large discrepancies predominate, the child will learn stable patterns of avoidance behavior. If there is little discrepancy, the child will be indifferent to the area.

Periphery of Personality

No personality types are postulated. For peripheral characteristics, motives, traits, and schemata are offered.

A *motive* is a strong affective association characterized by an anticipatory goal reaction and based on past association of certain cues with positive or negative affect. There are *approach motives,* in which persons try to act such that their anticipations will indeed become a reality, and *avoidance motives,* in which persons work to keep their anticipation from becoming a reality. Approach motives are the stable behavior patterns learned on the basis of a predominance of small discrepancies between expectation and occurrence. Avoidance motives are the result of large discrepancies between expectation and occurrence. McClelland adopts Murray's needs (e.g., achievement, affiliation, power), postulating an approach and an avoidance version of each one.

A *trait* is a learned tendency in persons to react as they have reacted more or less successfully in the past in similar situations when similarly motivated. The trait is much like the habit and is not considered motivational because it leads to repetitive rather than goal-directed behavior. It is not clear how the trait is developed, and it almost certainly does not express the core tendency mentioned above. No list of traits is offered.

A *schema* is a unit of cognition or mentation that symbolizes past experience. Three major classes of schemata are *ideas, values,* and *social roles.* For content, McClelland suggests that ideas and values primarily concern *economic, aesthetic, social, political, religious,* and purely *theoret-*

ical realms. Social roles can be understood as involving *age, sex, family position, occupation,* and *association group membership*. The manner in which schemata are developed is not clearly specified, although they are considered as cultural knowledge communicated socially. They also do not seem expressive of the core tendency mentioned above.

FISKE AND MADDI'S THEORY

Core of Personality

Core Tendency.   *To maintain the level of activation to which one is accustomed (that is characteristic of one).* At any given moment, activation may be higher or lower than what is customary, leading to an avoidance of or search for additional activation.

Core Characteristics.   *Activation* refers on the psychological side to excitement or tension and on the physiological side to the state of excitation in a postulated brain center. *Customary* or *characteristic activation* refers to the typical levels of activation a person experiences over the course of many days. The level of activation at any time is determined by the *impact of stimulation,* meaning the degree of *intensity, meaningfulness,* and *variety* of stimulation emanating from *internal* and *external sources*.

When the actual level of activation has fallen below what is customary, *impact-increasing behavior* occurs. When the actual level of activation is above what is customary, *impact-decreasing behavior* occurs.

Development

No specific developmental statements are made. However, it is assumed that early experience contributes to the development of a customary level of activation. People differ in the amount of activation they require depending on their customary activation level. High-activation requirements lead to development of *needs* for stimulus *intensity, meaningfulness,* or *variety*. Low-activation requirements will lead to *fears* of stimulus *intensity, meaningfulness,* or *variety*. Further, it is assumed that some people learn to *anticipate* activation requirements well (through an *activeness trait*), whereas others are frequently in the position of having to *correct* (through a *passiveness trait*) for discrepancies between actual and customary activation levels. The former show simultaneously increasing differentiation and integration of thoughts, feelings, and actions (future impact is increased by differentiation and decreased by integration). Also, it is assumed that some people learn to rely on external sources of stimulation and others on internal sources.

Periphery of Personality

Personality Types Composed of Motives and Traits.

High-activation persons with *active* and *external* traits will be "go-getters," seeking out challenges to meet in the physical and social environments. Such persons will be energetic and voracious in their appetites. If they also have a high *need for meaningfulness*, they will pursue causes and problems. But if they have a high *need for intensity*, they may pursue action and tumult per se. If they have a high *need for variety*, they will show curiosity, adventurousness, and impulsiveness.

High-activation persons with *active* and *internal* traits will pursue impact through thinking, daydreaming, and responding to challenges posed by limitations of mind and body, with little regard for the tangible affairs of the external world. Such persons will be subtle and complex. With a high *need for meaningfulness*, they will lead the life of the mind. With a high *need for intensity*, they will pursue sensations and emotions. With a high *need for variety*, they will strive for originality in some creative endeavor.

Low-activation persons with *active* and *external* traits will be external conservationists, bent on heading off social and physical disorganization and conflict through negotiation and control. Such persons will tend to be conformists and show simplicity in their tastes. If they also have a high *fear of meaningfulness*, they will try to oversimplify problems and avoid ambiguity. With a high *fear of intensity*, they will exert a dampening effect on vigorous, disorganized external events. If they have a high *fear of variety*, they will seek to force routine on the environment, preferring the familiar to the new.

Low-activation persons with *active* and *internal* traits will be conservative with their own organisms by advocating the golden mean, taking care to avoid excesses and indulgences of any kind. Such persons will be uncomplex and devoid of inconsistencies. With a high *fear of meaningfulness*, they will show absence of detailed or diverse thoughts and daydreams. With a high *fear of intensity*, they will have an especially ascetic aura. With a high *fear of variety*, they will force themselves to function consistently and stably, in a manner devoid of flamboyance.

For all of the above personality types, there are counterparts in which the passive rather than active trait occurs. All these passive personality types will seem similar to those with the active trait in stated aims, values, and interests. But on finer analysis, those with the passive trait will emerge as somewhat unable to practice what they preach. If they have high-activation requirements, they will be consumers rather than producers of impact. They will frequently be in the uncomfortable position of having to correct for activation levels that have become too low.

If they are low in activation requirements, they will not actively and effectively manipulate the world or themselves to keep impact low. Instead, they will just try to renounce stimulation, ending frequently in the uncomfortable position of having to correct for activation levels that have become too high.

MODERATE BEHAVIORISM

Core of Personality

Core Tendency.   *To reduce tension or general drive. Tension* is defined as the somatic effect of drives.

Core Characteristics.   The *primary drives* (e.g., hunger, thirst, sex, pain, avoidance, curiosity) are biological in nature, and their satisfaction is consistent with physical survival. *General drive* is the tension from all drives at any given time. Also relevant are the *primary reinforcements,* which are the rewards and punishments corresponding to the primary drives (e.g., food, water, sexual experience, cessation of pain, information). Cognitive behaviorism now emphasize memory and choice as human capabilities.

Development

No stages are specified. Development amounts to *learning,* which is defined as an increase in the probability of a response in the presence of a particular stimulus. This increase in probability occurs when the response is followed by a reinforcement. In effect, tension reduction can be brought about by performing the response. *Resistance to extinction,* a major measure of the strength of what is learned, refers to the number of times a learned response will occur when it has ceased to lead to reinforcement.

Periphery of Personality

For peripheral characteristics, there are habits, secondary drives, and secondary reinforcements.

A *habit* is a stable stimulus-response bond established through the regular occurrence of reinforcement. Through *stimulus generalization,* a learned response can occur in the presence of stimuli similar (but not identical) to the original stimulus. Through *response generalization,* responses similar (but not identical) to the original learned response can occur in the presence of the original stimulus.

A *secondary drive* (e.g., anxiety) occurs when the stimulus conditions that have been regularly associated with primary drive arousal take on arousing properties themselves.

A *secondary reinforcement* occurs when the stimulus conditions that have been regularly associated with primary reinforcement take on reinforcing properties.

Although secondary drives and reinforcements are learned, both can mediate further learning.

RADICAL BEHAVIORISM

Core of Personality

Core Tendency.   None specified.

Core Characteristics.   None specified.

Development

Operant conditioning refers to the process of bringing a voluntary (spontaneously occurring) response under stimulus control. Learning has taken place when a particular stimulus serves as a cue (*discriminative stimulus*) for the operant response. This learning is brought about by following the operant response with a *positive* or *negative reinforcement*. A *reinforcement* is defined as anything that can increase or decrease the rate of occurrence of an operant response.

Respondent conditioning refers to the occurrence of responses in the presence of stimuli where the responses are "natural" sequels to the stimuli (e.g., an eyeblink response to the stimulus of a puff of air in the eye).

Schedules of reinforcement of various kinds have different effects on the rate of acquisition and extinction of a learned response. *Partial reinforcement* (where reinforcements occur intermittently) produce learned responses with greater resistance to extinction than does *continuous reinforcement*.

Periphery of Personality

No position taken. However, statements about a response's *resistance to extinction* and *stimulus* and *response generalization* have some relevance (see Moderate Behaviorism).

SOCIAL LEARNING THEORY

Core of Personality

Core Tendency.   *Expressions of inherent individual differences in cognitive capabilities (e.g., memory, differentiation, generalization). This approach* is rare in that it considers certain cognitive differences among persons to be unlearned and important for personality. These inherent differences underlie differences in amount and content of meaning.

Development

Observational learning is emphasized. Learning does not require the occurrence of either responses or reinforcements on the learner's part. It is enough to observe a model responding. In such observation, the person associates stimuli with one another (S-S laws). Whether the observed model receives positive or negative reinforcement for responses will determine if and when the learner will perform what he or she has learned.

Operant conditioning is also believed to occur but is given little importance at the human level. Persons mature by gaining greater and greater autonomy from reinforcements applied by others and increasing their ability to apply reinforcements to themselves through a process of self-control that changes their environment.

Periphery of Personality

For peripheral characteristics there are *needs,* comprised of reinforcement values, reinforcement expectancies, and behavior potentials. *Reinforcement value* refers to how satisfying the goal of the need is to the person. *Reinforcement expectancy* refers to how likely he or she thinks the attainment of the goal is. *Behavior potential* summarizes the implications of the other two components for actual performance and specifies the set of actions that such performance would entail. Examples of broad sets of needs common in people are *recognition-status, dominance, independence, protection-dependency, love and affection,* and *physical comfort.*

Other peripheral characteristics offered are more strategies and styles and fewer content considerations. These include encoding strategies, behavior and stimulus outcome expectancies, stimulus values, and self-regulatory systems and plans. *Encoding strategies* emphasize the manner in which persons transform and lend meaning to information and the resulting personal constructs. *Behavior and stimulus outcome expectancies* and *stimulus values* are similar to the reinforcement expectancies and reinforcement values mentioned above. *Self-regulatory systems and plans* involve settled procedures for controlling oneself and regulating one's environment and, as such, constitute combinations of the other strategies and styles. The emerging conception of peripheral characteristics in this tradition is the *prototype,* which structures the person's perceptions and actions around several exemplary expressions of content but leaves other possible expressions to be discovered through experience. As such, prototypes are similar to Kelly's *permeable constructs.*

Strictly speaking, no types are specified. But one theme in social learning theory does refer to broader peripheral characteristics such as *generalized expectancies*. An example is people's view as to whether they are controlled externally or control themselves. Related to this is the notion of *self-efficacy,* which includes both generalized and task-specific views as to whether one can perform effectively.

Glossary of Terms

Activation-Deactivation Adjective Check List   A checklist devised by Thayer to measure customary level of activation according to Fiske and Maddi. (See Chapter 11.)

Activities Index   A questionnaire of 300 items, devised by William Stern, that yields scores on some of Murray's needs. (See Chapter 11.)

adaptation   Usually refers to adjusting to social and physical pressures rather than avoiding or changing them. (See Chapter 6 and *transcendence*.)

Adler's position   See Appendix.

Alienation Test   A sixty-item questionnaire, devised by Maddi, Kobasa, and Hoover, that measures powerlessness, adventurousness, nihilism, and vegetativeness in the person's relationship to work, persons, social institutions, family, and self. (See Chapter 11.)

Allport's position   See Appendix.

Analysis of Variance (and Covariance)   A statistical test to determine the significance of effects in such research studies as experiments, whether continued or natural (see *experiment*). In analysis of covariance there is a statistical control for relevant factors that have not been controlled through the design of the study. This statistical control is frequently necessary in natural experiments because they are usually less rigorous as to design than are continued experiments (see Chapter 2).

Angyal's position   See Appendix.

assessment   One of the practical applications of personology that involves determining through some sort of measurement (interview, questionnaire, performance test) the lifestyle of personality type of the person and evaluating his or her development with regard to its level of maturity. Often done as a precursor to the other practical application of personology, psychotherapy. (See Chapters 1 and 14.)

Bakan's position   See Appendix.

behavior modification therapy   Originally the radical behavioristic means of therapy, which did not consider thought processes as being any different from actions. All behavior is regarded as controlled by stimulus cues and the principles of reinforcement. Therapy involves manipulating schedules of reinforcement so as to alter unwanted behaviors. By now, this approach is becoming more eclectic, and thought processes are emerging as the source of self-control, with implications that set it apart from other behaviors in some practitioners' minds. (See Chapter 12.)

benevolent eclecticism   An attitude toward inquiry in which all points of view are accepted as plausible and there is little effort to pinpoint and evaluate differences among them. (See Chapter 1, *partisan zealotry,* and *comparative analysis.*)

Berne's position   See Appendix.

Blacky Test   A set of pictures, devised by Gerald S. Blum, that depict a young dog in various situations, mainly with its parents, having special significance in psychoanalytic theory. The subject composes stories about the pictures, thereby projecting his or her personality for the tester to observe. (See Chapters 6 and 11.)

Briggs-Myers Type Indicator   A questionnaire, devised by Myers, to measure introversion-extroversion and the thinking, feeling, sensing, and intuiting modes of Jung. (See Chapter 11.)

California Personality Inventory (CPI)   A questionnaire yielding scores on many peripheral characteristics covering mentally healthy functioning. (See Chapter 6.)

chi-square   A statistical test of significance for the data of frequency of occurrence of various categories of two or more characteristics (see contingency table).

client-centered or person-centered therapy   A Rogerian approach that involves the therapist in reflecting the client's verbalizations clearly enough that the client realizes the therapist understands, cares, and approves. Through this empathic and unconditional positive regard, it is believed that the client will drop defenses and grow in confidence to be able to actualize inherent potentialities. (See Chapter 14 and Appendix.)

comparative analysis   An attitude toward inquiry in which similarities and differences are sought among the various viewpoints on a subject matter, with the aim of posing issues for resolution by thought and research. (See Chapter 1, *benevolent eclecticism,* and *partisan zealotry.*)

comprehensive understanding   Occurs when empirical, rational, and intuitive knowledge match. (See Chapter 1, empirical knowledge, intuitive knowledge, and rational knowledge.)

conflict model   A form of personality theorizing that postulates that the person is continuously in the grips of the clash between two great, opposing forces. Life is necessarily a compromise, which at best involves a balance of the two forces and at worst a foredoomed attempt to deny the existence of one of them. In the *psychosocial version,* the source of one great force is in the individual and of the other in society. In the *intrapsychic version,* both great forces arise from within the person. (See Chapters 3–11, *fulfillment model, consistency model,* and *personality theory.*)

consistency model   A form of personality theorizing in which there is little emphasis on great forces whether single or dual and in conflict or not. Instead, emphasis is on the formative influence of feedback from the external world. Life is to be understood as the extended attempt to maintain consistency. But consistencies and inconsistencies can have any content, themselves having been determined by prior experience. In the *cognitive dissonance version,* the relevant aspects of the person in which there may or may not be consistency are cognitive in nature. In the *activation version,* it is the degree to which bodily tension is consistent or inconsistent with what is customary that is important. (See Chapters 3–11, *conflict model, fulfillment model,* and *personality theory.*)

content analysis Application of a set of interpretive rules to performance whereby the content of that performance can reveal personality characteristics. Content analysis is an integral part of the use of performance tasks such as projective tests (see performance tasks and projective test). As content analysis is interpretive, it is important to demonstrate that two or more raters can agree in the application of the interpretive rules. (See Chapter 2.)

contingency table When two (or more) characteristics are measured by determining the number of persons falling into such categories as presence-absence, or low-medium-high, the resulting data can be recorded into a table the cells of which are defined jointly by the categories of the characteristics. This is called a contingency table, and the statistical significance of the emerging pattern is often evaluated by the chi-square test.

core characteristic An unlearned, inherent structural entity of personality shared by all human beings. (See Chapters 1, 2–6, 13, 14, and *core of personality.*)

core of personality The unlearned, inherent aspects of human nature that all persons share. Included are one or two core tendencies, which give the overall directionality or purpose of human life, and core characteristics, or structural entities, that the tendencies imply. (See Chapters 1, 2–6, 13, 14, and *personality theory.*)

core tendency The unlearned, inherent, overall direction or purpose of life shared by all human beings. (See Chapters 1, 6, 13, 14, and *core of personality.*)

correlation A statistical measure of covariation (see covariation). The product-moment correlation is computed when both characteristics are measured on a continuous numerical scale having more than two values (e.g., 0 to 3, or 1 to 10). When both characteristics are measured in a dichotomous fashion (e.g., 0 and 1 for absence-presence or low-high, respectively), then the contingency coefficient is computed to assess covariation. When one characteristic is measured continuously and the other dichotomously, the point bi-serial correlation is computed. In the case where persons are rank ordered with regard to the degree to which each of two characteristics are expressed in them relative to other persons, then rank-order correlation is computed.

correlational research Relatively naturalistic research in which information on the intensity of two or (usually) more aspects of behavior are obtained from all subjects with the intent to determine how the aspects are related. If many aspects are included, factor analysis can be used on the data to determine how the aspects cluster. Correlational research is especially relevant to identifying peripheral characteristics and types. (See Chapters 2, 6, 11, 13, and *peripheral characteristic, type,* and *experimental research.*)

covariation The degree to which two characteristics (in the case of personality, they may be core or peripheral characteristics) vary interdependently. When increases in one characteristic involve increases in the other as well, that shows positive covariation. Negative covariation involves decreases in one characteristic for increases in the other. A typical statistical measure of covariation is the correlation.

creativity   In a person, the predisposition to produce ideas and things that are new and useful. In an idea or thing, the quality of novelty and utility. (See Chapter 6.)

criterion analysis   A special case of factor analytic method that is deductive (hypothesis testing) rather than inductive (exploratory). (See Chapter 11 and *factor analysis*.)

data language   The designation of the form and content of thoughts, feelings, and actions (dependent variables) that are to be explained in personology. No such language has yet been generally adopted. (See Chapters 2 and 11.)

Defense Mechanism Inventory   Devised by Gleser and Ihilevich, a test that requires subjects to respond to stories and yields scores on five sets of defenses (turning against object, projection, principalization, turning against self, and reversal). (See Chapter 11.)

defensiveness   The tendency to distort reality in order to make what one is conscious of conform to what is socially acceptable. Theorists differ in their reliance on this concept, in what they think is defended against, and in the elaborateness and precision with which they conceptualize the techniques of defense. But all agree that the technique of defense must itself operate unconsciously. (See Chapters 3–11 and 14.)

development   The interaction between expressions of the personality core and social and physical influences in the external world that culminates in the particular lifestyle or personality type that is learned. (See Chapters 1–14, *core of personality, periphery of personality*, and *personality theory*.)

Dogmatism Scale   A questionnaire, devised by Rokeach, for measuring inflexibility in thinking. (See Chapter 11.)

drive   Often used synonymously with *need, motive,* or *motivation,* but connotes something more biological and mechanical, less self-conscious and intellective than the term *motive.* (See Chapter 10, *motive, motivation,* and *need.*)

Edwards Personal Preference Schedule   A preference test, devised by Edwards, that uses the forced-choice format to obtain scores on several of Murray's needs. (See Chapter 11.)

ego psychology   See Appendix.

Ellis's position   See Appendix.

empirical knowledge   Hypotheses, derived carefully from theories, that have been confirmed in rigorous, systematic, and relevant research studies. This knowledge is public, precise, and systematic. (See Chapters 1, 2, *rational knowledge,* and *intuitive knowledge.*)

Erikson's position   See Appendix.

experiment   A contrived procedure in which a characteristic or environmental factor is artificially increased or decreased in order to determine the effect of so doing on subsequent behavior. The magnitude and direction of the produced effect is evaluated by comparing the experimental (manipulated) group (of subjects) with one or more control groups. For rigor of method, the control group(s) must be similar in all respects to the experimental group except in the characteristic or factor manipulated. Sometimes experiments are impractical or unethical. In such cases, the natural experiment is useful if less rigorous. The natural experiment involves capitalizing on the natural (rather than continued) increase or decrease in the target characteristic or environmental factor, and compares the group to which this has happened to one or more control groups not having this experience. (See Chapter 2 for example.)

Existential Psychology   See Appendix.

Existential Study   A questionnaire, devised by Thorne, for measuring several dimensions of general relevance to the existential position, including self-status, self-actualization, existential morale, existential vacuum, humanistic identification, and existence and destiny. (See Chapter 11.)

existential therapy   Although hardly a homogeneous movement, the core of this approach involves the therapist in stimulating, confronting, supporting, and urging the client to recognize decisions made in life and begin to choose the future, however fearful, rather than the past, however safe. The client is encouraged to symbolize, imagine, and judge vigorously in order to take responsibility for his or her life. A technique employed in severely uncontrollable symptoms is *paradoxical intention,* or the willful attempt to exaggerate a symptom in order to outmaneuver it. Other techniques include situational reconstruction, focusing, and compensatory self-improvement. (See Chapter 14 and Appendix.)

Experience Inventory   A factor analytically developed questionnaire, devised by Coan, for measuring various aspects of openness to experience, such as aesthetic sensitivity, openness to hypothetical ideas, constructive utilization of fantasy, unconventional ideas of reality, and unusual perceptions and associations. (See Chapter 11.)

experimental research   Research in which subjects in an experimental group are treated in a particular manner in order to determine what the effect of the treatment will be. Subjects not receiving the treatment are used as a control group to ensure that the effect observed in the experimental group really did not result from the treatment. Experiments are best employed in the testing of hypotheses. (See Chapters 2, 6, 11, 13, and *correlational research.*)

exploratory behavior   Behavior that brings the subject into contact with previously unfamiliar aspects of the environment. A special case of this is *spontaneous alternation,* in which an organism that chose one portion of the environment (usually a maze) on the first trial chooses the other on the next trial. (See Chapter 6.)

Eysenck (formerly Maudsley) Personality Inventory   A questionnaire, devised by Eysenck, for measuring neuroticism and introversion-extroversion. (See Chapter 10.)

factor analysis   A statistical procedure for determining the covariation (see covariation) among some number of characteristics (see characteristics) larger than two. Employing a correlational approach (see correlation), factor analysis results in the smallest number of clusters of characteristics (called factors) that define the data. The researcher can force the factors to be unrelated to each other (orthogonal factors) or permit them to covary with each other (oblique factors). First-order factors are those that emerge from the covariation in the characteristics. Second-order factors are those that emerge from the covariation in the first-order factors.

fantasy test   Frequently called a *projective test,* an unstructured technique for obtaining scores on some variable or variables often used in personality research. The subject is presented with ambiguous stimuli (usually pictures) and given the task of rendering them less ambiguous (by identifying them or using them in a story). The test should be shown to have adequate interscorer agreement, reliability, and validity. Such a procedure can be regarded as an indirect test of performance. (See Chapters 2, 6, 11 14, *unstructured test, personality research, questionnaire, performance test, reliability,* and *validity.*)

Fascism (F) Scale   A questionnaire, devised by Adorno and colleagues, for measuring fascistic attitudes and values. (See Chapter 11.)

Fear of Appearing Incompetent Scale   A thirty-six-item questionnaire, devised by Good and Good, for measuring White's emphasis on sense of incompetence. (See Chapter 11.)

field dependence-independence   Individual differences, studied by Witkin and associates, in the degree to which a person is able to utilize gravitational rather than visual cues to orient the body or other objects in space. The term *psychological differentiation* tends to be substituted when emphasizing the related phenomenon of discerning a simple figure embedded in a complex one. Typical tests are the *Body Adjustment Test* and the *Embedded-Figures Test.* (See Chapter 6.)

Fiske and Maddi's position   See Appendix.

fixed role therapy   Introduced by Kelly (see Appendix), an approach that involves the therapist in planning a role for the client to play that will provide corrective or broadening experiences. The ensuing experiences are discussed in therapy as a basis for producing change in the client's constructs and construction system. (See Chapters 9 and 14.)

forced-choice format   A variant of the questionnaire in which each item is presented as a pair with each other item and the subject's task is to choose which of each pair he or she prefers or considers correct. The items can be ranked on the basis of number of choices. This test is regarded as less vulnerable to response sets than the ordinary questionnaire, but it should be shown to have reliability and validity. (See Chapters 2, 6, 11, *questionnaire, personality research, reliability,* and *validity.*)

formal criteria of theoretical adequacy   Criteria for evaluating theories that include the theories' importance, operationalization, parsimony, precision, stimulating nature, and empirical validity. (See Chapter 15, *operational definition, parsimony, precision of a theory,* and *importance of a theory.*)

Freud's position   See Appendix.

Fromm's position   See Appendix.

fulfillment model   A form of personality theorizing that postulates that the person embodies one great force. Life involves a progressively greater expression of this force at best and inhibition of it at worst. Conflict between individual and society is possible (indeed, causes inhibition) but not necessary as it is in the conflict model. In the *actualization version,* the great force is in the form of a genetic blueprint of the person's special capabilities. In the *perfection version,* the great force constitutes ideals of what is fine, excellent, and meaningful. (See Chapters 3–11, *conflict model, consistency model,* and *personality theory.*)

gating   A phenomenon, promulgated by Bruner, in which some central nervous system process "tunes" peripheral sense organs as to what stimulation they shall receive and reject. Could be a physiological substratum of defensiveness. (See Chapter 6 and *defensiveness.*)

Gestalt psychotherapy   Introduced by Perls, an approach that involves reestablishing the flow of experience that has been interrupted by some reversal or punishment. Often practiced in groups, it encourages the client to take all points of view in a situation in order to gain a comprehensive *gestalt,* or understanding. Contrasts among viewpoints are regarded as being rich in insight. (See Chapter 3 and Appendix.)

Guilford-Zimmerman Temperament Survey   A questionnaire, devised by Guilford and Zimmerman, that yields ten personality factors from a large pool of items. (See Chapter 11.)

habit   See *trait.*

Hardiness Test   A questionnaire, introduced by Kobasa and Maddi, for measuring a concrete expression of existential courage. This test has gone through three revisions and now appears to have adequate reliability and construct validity. (See Chapter 11.)

idiographic (or morphogenic) law   A law that concerns the functioning of particular individuals rather than the average case. The term is emphasized by Allport. (See Chapter 10 and *individuality.*)

importance of a theory   A formal criterion for evaluating a theory. There is disagreement as to whether the importance of a theory can be determined except after the fact. One viewpoint is that in order to ensure its importance, a theory should take as its subject matter (data to be explained) that which can be observed naturalistically rather than behavior produced in the laboratory by experimental manipulation and hence contrived. (See Chapter 15.)

individual commonalities   Similarities on one or more dimensions or variables among persons in any group. Of special interest to personology are those commonalities that seem to reflect the inherent nature of humans rather than the regularizing effect (or demand characteristics) of stimulus or social pressures. (See Chapters 1, 2, and *individual differences.*)

individual differences   Differences on one or more dimensions or variables among persons in any group. Of special relevance for personology are differences that occur under what appear to be the same stimulus situations and differences that persist over time and across situations. (See Chapters 1, 2, and *individual commonalities*.)

individuality   The uniqueness of a person, usually considered as residing in the total pattern of the personality rather than in one aspect of it. This is an extreme case of individual differences, especially emphasized by theorists such as Allport, Kelly, Rogers, Maslow, ego psychologists, and existential psychologists. (See Chapter 1, Appendix, and *individual differences*.)

Internal-External Locus of Control (I-E) Scale   A questionnaire, introduced by Rotter and refined by James, that measures whether subjects believe they are in control of their own fate or externally controlled. (See Chapter 11.)

inter-scorer reliability   The degree to which two scorers analyzing the same ambiguous data agree as to what is there. (See Chapters 2 and 11.)

interview   A procedure, which can be relatively structured or unstructured, whereby information about the subject is obtained through a face-to-face question-and-answer session. This technique is more flexible than the questionnaire and therefore is useful when the investigator is exploring. Also, the option of patterning one's questions on the subject's responses to prior questions sometimes makes this technique more desirable than even performance and fantasy tests, which are more restrictive. (See Chapters 2, 6, 11, *structured test, unstructured test, questionnaire, performance test,* and *fantasy test*.)

intrinsic versus extrinsic motivation   Behavior engaged in for its own sake and interfered with by external (or extrinsic) reinforcement is considered intrinsically motivated. Curiosity, play and exploratory behavior are examples of intrinsic motivation. (See Chapter 11.)

intuitive knowledge   The relatively inarticulate, private, and emotional, though vivid, immediate, and compelling, sense of the meaning of things. (See Chapter 1, *empirical knowledge,* and *rational knowledge*.)

Inventory of Psychosocial Development   A questionnaire, developed by Constantinople, for measuring the salience of Erikson's stages of development. (See Chapter 11.)

Jung's position   See Appendix.

Kelly's position   See Appendix.

Kohut's position   See Appendix.

latent learning   The phenomenon whereby a subject seems to learn a maze (or other task) even when he or she receives no reinforcement for doing so. (See Chapter 6.)

lifestyle   See *type*.

Manifest Anxiety Scale (MAS)   A questionnaire, devised by Taylor and Spence, for measuring general drive in the framework of moderate behaviorism. (See Chapter 12.)

Marlowe-Crowne Social Desirability Scale (M-C SDS)   A questionnaire, devised by Marlowe and Crowne, for measuring the tendency to respond in a socially desirable fashion. (See Chapter 11.)

Maslow's position   See Appendix.

maze   Usually in the form of a T, a ubiquitous apparatus for studying learning in rats. In more complex, paper-and-pencil, or stylus form, mazes have also been used on human subjects. (See Chapter 6.)

McClelland's position   See Appendix.

Minnesota Multiphasic Personality Inventory (MMPI)   A questionnaire comprising many items to be answered "true" or "false" that provides several scores concerning psychopathological trends in personality. The scales from which the scores derive have adequate reliability and have been validated by determining that they predict the psychopathological entities assumed. (See Chapters 6 and 11.)

modeling behavior   Imitative or observational learning, in which it is assumed that what is learned is linkage among stimuli rather than between stimuli and responses. Learning takes place without need for responses and reinforcements. (See Chapter 13.)

moderate behaviorism   See Appendix.

motivation   The pressure or energy to produce activity and the goal or direction that guides it. Some core tendencies are considered motivational even though they are probably too abstract to achieve mental representation as goals. Some theorists reserve the concept of motivation for peripheral characteristics. (See Chapters 1 through 13.)

motive   Usually refers to a kind of peripheral characteristic having motivational properties in that it produces directional behavior aimed at reaching a goal. (See Chapters 2, 7–11, *motivation*, and *peripheral characteristic*.)

Murray's position   See Appendix.

narcissistic behavior disorders   In Kohut's position, personality types characterized by acting out lack of confidence and insufficient sense of self. (See Chapter 7 and Appendix.)

narcissistic personality disorders   In Kohut's position, personality types characterized by persistent thoughts of personal unworthiness and vulnerability to slights. (See Chapter 7 and Appendix.)

need   Often used synonymously with *drive, motive,* or *motivation.* Usage varies widely by theorist. (See Chapter 10, *motive, motivation,* and *drive*.)

nomothetic law   A law that concerns the functioning of the average case rather than of any particular individual. The term is emphasized by Allport. (See Chapter 10.)

Object-Relations Positions   See Appendix.

operational definition   A precise, literal statement of which operations to perform in order to measure concepts and variables. In personology, such definitions are especially important for identifying peripheral characteristics. (See Chapters 2, 11, 13, and *peripheral characteristic.*)

parsimony   The criterion that, other things being equal, the best of several explanations of a phenomenon is the one that makes the fewest assumptions. This criterion is difficult to apply to personality theory and may stifle imagination. (See Chapter 15.)

partisan zealotry   An attitude toward inquiry in which the viewpoint one already holds is regarded as true and championed energetically regardless of plausible contrary arguments and disagreements. (See Chapter 1, *benevolent eclecticism,* and *comparative analysis.*)

perceptual defense   The phenomenon whereby subjects require longer tachistoscopic exposures of threatening rather than nonthreatening stimuli in order to recognize them. (See Chapter 6, *tachistoscope,* and *perceptual vigilance.*)

perceptual vigilance   The phenomenon whereby subjects require shorter tachistoscopic exposure times in order to recognize threatening as opposed to nonthreatening stimuli. (See Chapter 6, *tachistoscope,* and *perceptual defense.*)

performance task   A source of personality data in which the person performs some task and the performance is judged as to the personality characteristics it reveals by the investigator or some specific group. In contrast to the interview and the questionnaire, performance tasks need not rely on the person's self-report. Hence, performance tasks may reveal to the investigator things that persons do not understand or recognize in themselves. The psychotherapy session and projective tests are examples of performance tasks that have been useful in personality. (See Chapter 2.)

performance test   A standardized technique, usually structured, for obtaining scores on some variable or variables that is sometimes used in personality research. The subjects reveal themselves by their effectiveness at and manner of performing the task rather than in describing themselves directly. The test should be shown to have reliability and validity. (See Chapters 2, 6, 11, 14, *structured test, personality research, questionnaire, reliability,* and *validity.*)

peripheral characteristic   The smallest, most homogeneous learned aspect of personality that a theorist believes can properly be conceptualized. Exerts an influence on thoughts, feelings, and/or actions such that they show continuity over time and across stimulus situations. (See Chapters 1, 7–11, 13, and *periphery of personality.*)

periphery of personality   The learned, relatively concrete aspects of personality that develop out of the interaction of the personality core and the external, mainly social world. Included in peripheral statements are the types of personality (or lifestyles) it is possible to develop and the peripheral characteristics (motives, traits, schemata) that comprise the types. (See Chapters 1, 2, 7–11, 13, 14, and *personality theory.*)

Perls's position   See Appendix.

personality   A stable set of characteristics and tendencies that determine those commonalities and differences in the psychological behavior (thoughts, feelings, and actions) of people that have continuity over time and that may or may not be easily understood in terms of the social and biological pressures of the immediate situation alone. (See Chapter 1.)

personality change   Theorists differ in their views as to the degree of personality change that occurs as a function of aging. For some, little real change takes place after childhood, whereas others see change as continual throughout life. Most believe that even radical change can take place through psychotherapy. (See Chapter 6.)

personality data   Thoughts, feelings, and actions that show continuity over time and across various stimulus situations. (See Chapter 1, *personology,* and *data language.*)

personality research   May be designed primarily to test hypotheses (deductive method) or to explore in order to generate hypotheses (inductive method). Naturalistic observation and correlational data analyses seem well suited to exploratory research, whereas experimental designs seem more appropriate for hypothesis testing. Research is particularly relevant to personality when, whether exploratory or hypothesis testing, it concerns thoughts, feelings, and actions having continuity over time and across situations. Usually this involves stable individual differences. Often personality research also concerns large amounts of each person's behavior rather than only one or two elements. (See Chapters 1, 2, 6, 11, 13, and *personality theory, personality data, correlational research,* and *experimental research.*)

personality theory   A set of interconnected and logically consistent assumptions having the aim of explaining personality data (thoughts, feelings, and actions having continuity over time and across situations). Consists of a *core statement* (concerning the inherent nature that is unlearned and common to all), a *peripheral statement* (concerning the lifestyles that are learned and that differentiate persons), and a *developmental statement* (explicating how expressions of the core lead, through interaction with the external, mainly social environment, to the periphery). (See Chapters 1, 6, 10, 13, and *personality data, core of personality, periphery of personality,* and *development.*)

Personal Orientation Inventory (POI)   A questionnaire, devised by Shostrom, for measuring various characteristics of actualization fulfillment theory, for example, Rogers and Maslow. (See Chapter 11).

personologist   Someone who practices personology. (See Chapter 1 and *personology.*)

personology   A field of psychology concerned with the holistic study of entire persons. The data for the field are thoughts, feelings, and actions that characterize a person over time and across situations, and the explanations employed concern personality (a set of concepts that are within the skin rather than in the surround and may or may not have biological substrata). In addition to this theorizing function, personology includes the conducting of research (to test the theorizing), the practical application of knowledge in the form of assessment (the systematic identification of a person's personality), and psychotherapy (the systematic attempt to change personality to more greatly approximate some theoretical ideal). (See Chapters 1, 14, *personality, personality theory, personality research, personality data, personality assessment,* and *psychotherapy.*)

point-biserial correlation   A statistical measure of covariation (see *correlation,* and *covariation*).

precision of a theory   A formal criterion for evaluating a theory. Effort should be made to avoid inconsistencies, loose ends, and metaphorical language. (See Chapter 14.)

product-movement correlation   A statistical measure of covariation (see correlation, and covariation).

projective test   A source of personality data of the performance-task sort (see performance task) in which the person is presented with ambiguous stimuli which must be identified or incorporated into a composed story. Because they require the use of imagination, projective tests are thought to reveal aspects of personality that persons are unwilling to reveal or of which they are unaware. (See Chapter 2.)

prototype   A peripheral characteristic proposed by Mischel and Cantor that is defined by the person in terms of one or two definite expressions and other, more ambiguous examples. The prototype is gradually defined as the person's experience accumulates. Mischel and Cantor believe that prototypes differ from traits. (See Chapter 13.)

psychoanalysis   A general body of theory in which fantasy, especially dreams, is believed to reveal persons most clearly. Persons are construed as distorting reality through defensiveness, but fantasy comes closest to revealing the truth. As a therapy, psychoanalysis includes various techniques (e.g., free association) for stimulating waking fantasy and interprets these and nighttime dreams in terms of the transference of the client's pent-up emotions from past conflicts onto the therapist. The therapist analyzes the patient's free verbalizations, attempting thereby to get behind the defenses. Originally Freudian, psychoanalysis has been developed in various directions by ego psychologists, object-relations psychologists, and self analysts. (See these and Rank, Jung, Adler, and Fromm; see also Appendix.)

psychobiography   A personologist's interpretation of the personality characteristics and their organization into an holistic pattern as revealed in a person's life history. Relevant to this task are written documents (e.g., diaries, speeches, scholarly works, and interviews) with the person and significant others. The emphasis of a psychobiography is usually on the overall pattern of the person's life, the underlying causal factors, and the individuality that emerges. Usually, psychobiographies are done on historically important persons.

psychological growth   Progressively greater differentiation and integration of experience, especially emphasized by Allport, Adler, Maslow, Fiske, Maddi, and existential psychology. (See Chapters 2–8.)

psychotherapy session   As considered in this book, the psychotherapy session is a source of personality data falling in the category of performance tasks. (See *performance task.*) In relating his or her problems to the therapist, the person reveals much about personality. (See Chapter 2.)

questionnaire   A source of personality data involving printed items to which the person responds. These items are usually questions, which, because they are printed, tend to be specific and delimited. Because of this, the questionnaire is usually considered a structured technique most useful when the data that is needed is known, and richness of responses is not necessary. The questions used may be of the true-false (dichotomous) or rating scale (continuous) sort. Sometimes, questions are paired, and the person is asked which member of each pair is most true or relevant (this is called the forced-choice format). Checklists are also used, in which the person checks which of a number of descriptive words are most true or relevant. Although questionnaires can be administered to large groups of person, this advantage is mitigated by the prevalence of response biases (tendencies to answer in particular ways because of the form rather than content of the questions, and to maintain a socially-acceptable image). When questionnaires are used in assessing personality characteristics, it is important to minimize response biases and to demonstrate the reliability (internal consistency and stability) of the measurement. (See Chapter 2.)

radical behaviorism   See Appendix.

rank-order correlation   A statistical measure of covariation (see correlation, and covariation).

Rank's position   See Appendix.

rational-emotive therapy   Introduced by Ellis, an approach that involves strenuous confrontations in which the therapist cajoles, exposes, and encourages the client to recognize destructive self-pity and wasteful repetition of ineffective functioning. (See Chapter 4 and Appendix.)

rational knowledge   Conclusions that are deduced from a set of assumptions by the careful, reflective use of logic rather than arrived at by systematic observation. (See Chapter 1, *empirical knowledge,* and *intuitive knowledge.*)

reliability   In measuring personality characteristics, it is useful to show that the various presumed expressions of the characteristic covary (internal consistency) and that they show consistency over time (stability). Especially when using questionnaires (see *questionnaire*), the internal consistency and stability of the measurement should be demonstrated. (See Chapter 2.)

Repression-Sensitization Scale   A questionnaire, devised by Byrne, for measuring the defensiveness dimension concerning too little and too much sensitivity to stimuli. (See Chapter 11.)

response set   It has been discovered that subjects, particularly when taking questionnaires, respond in set ways that bear little relationship to the questions' content. Major response sets are to be socially desirable and to be acquiescent. (See Chapters 2 and 11.)

Rogers's position   See Appendix.

Role Constructs Repertory (REP) Test   A categorizing performance test, devised by Kelly, that measures the subject's personal constructs and their organization into a construct system. (See Chapter 11.)

Rorschach Test   A series of inkblots, devised by Rorschach, that the subject is asked to identify. In indicating what the blots resemble, the subject's personality is disclosed. (See Chapters 2, 6 and 14.)

schema   Usually refers to a kind of peripheral characteristic that is mainly cognitive in nature and expressive of cultural or social influences. Examples are values and social roles. (See Chapters 7–11, 13, and *peripheral characteristic*.)

self-analysis   Practiced by Kohut and object-relations theorists, an approach that involves reflecting the client's statements and serving as a model for him or her to admire. Little confrontation or interpretation takes place. It is believed that in this fashion the patient's narcissistic needs will be filled and development can progress. (See Chapter 3 and Appendix.)

self-control   An emphasis in social learning theory (see Chapter 13) and a bit in behaviorism (see Chapter 12) on the person's gaining control over the reinforcements influencing his or her behavior. This is considered a sign of maturity.

Self-Ideal Q Sort   A test, devised by Stevenson, employing a procedure for sorting statements into groups that has been used to measure the discrepancy between self-concept and self-ideal in a Rogerian framework. Butler and Haigh devised this particular Q sort. (See Chapter 11.)

sensory deprivation   An experimental procedure whereby the amount of stimulation from external (and sometimes internal) sources is markedly decreased. Sleep and disordered thought frequently ensue. (See Chapter 6.)

sentence completion test   A semi unstructured test in which the subject is provided with a series of sentence beginnings that he or she is to finish in some way. The test should be shown to have adequate interscorer agreement, reliability, and validity. (See Chapters 2, 6, 11, *personality research, unstructured test, interscorer agreement, reliability,* and *validity.*)

Sixteen Personality Factor Questionnaire   A questionnaire, devised by Cattell, yielding scores on sixteen first-order and eight second-order factors. The factors result from numerous factor analyses of the items, and the test offers a comprehensive description of personality. (See Chapters 6 and 11.)

skin conductance (or galvanic skin response)   A procedure for measuring increases in sweating (considered emotional arousal) by the ease with which a mild electric current passes over the skin. Sweating increases skin conductivity. (See Chapters 5, 10, and 11.)

Social Interest Index   Devised by Greever, Tseng, and Friedland, a questionnaire that measures Adler's emphasis on constructive interest in other persons and society. (See Chapter 11.)

social learning theory   An offshoot of moderate behaviorism that stresses the importance of imitative or observational learning. Children especially are frequent learners by observing a model, with subsequent performance of what they learned dependent on anticipated reinforcement contingencies. In its emphasis on cognition and de-emphasis of reinforcement as necessary for learning to take place, this position, as developed by Bandura, Walters, and Mischel, deviates significantly from moderate behaviorism. (See Chapter 13.)

S-R Inventory   Devised by Endler, Hunt, and Rosenstein, a questionnaire that measures various types of anxiety response over a range of situations. (See Chapter 11.)

stages of development   Stages demarcated by some theorists during which particular core functions mature and certain types of social experiences can have special impact on personality. (See Chapters 3–11 and *development.*)

Strong Vocational Interest Blank   A questionnaire, devised by Strong, often used to assess vocational interests. (See Chapter 6.)

structured test   Often called *objective,* a type of test that presents the subject with a structured, organized, specific situation to which to respond. Structured tests usually are questionnaires, but they can also be performance tasks. Some techniques, such as the interview, can be either somewhat structured or unstructured. Structured tests have greater reliability than unstructured tests and are regarded by some theorists as being especially valuable in assessing socially directed personality characteristics. (See Chapters 2, 6, 11, 14, *unstructured test, performance test, questionnaire, interview, reliability,* and *validity.*)

subception   A phenomenon in which a subject responds physiologically (e.g., by sweating) even when stimuli are presented tachistoscopically at exposure times too brief for conscious recognition. (See Chapter 6, *perceptual defense,* and *tachistoscope.*)

Survey of Problematic Situations   A questionnaire, developed by Goldfriend and D'Zurilla, for measuring White's emphasis on actual competence. (See Chapter 11.)

systematic desensitization   Wolpe's psychotherapy, in which the person is encouraged to relax while thinking of threatening material in the the hope that it will become less threatening. (See Chapter 12.)

tachistoscope   A device for presenting visual stimuli for controllable and very brief lengths of time. Has been used extensively in personality research to study how and whether there are differences among subjects and among types of stimuli in recognition time. (See Chapter 6, *perceptual defense,* and *perceptual vigilance.*)

tension reduction or increase   Tension (sometimes called *arousal* or *activation*) is usually regarded as a state of bodily discomfort or pent-up energy. Many theorists believe tension reduction to be pleasurable and the major aim of life. Other theorists define aims otherwise and believe that tension increases will be tolerated (even enjoyed) in order to achieve the aims. (See Chapter 6.)

Thematic Apperception Test   A set of pictures, devised by Murray, showing persons alone or in various relationships with one another. In composing stories for the pictures, the subject projects his or her personality for the tester to observe. (See Chapters 2, 6, 11,14).

Glossary

trait   Usually refers to kinds of peripheral characteristics producing habitual, routinized, unreflective behaviors having little or no apparent motivational significance. (See Chapters 6–11, 13, and *peripheral characteristic*.)

Transactional Analysis   Introduced by Berne, an approach typically practiced in groups. Through scrutiny of group behavior, the therapist clarifies the destructive features of the client's life script and life position and the associated games that are played. (See Chapter 3 and Appendix.)

transcendence   Usually refers to transforming or surmounting social and physical pressures rather than adjusting or acquiescing to them. (See Chapter 6 and *adaptation*.)

type   A learned lifestyle composed of peripheral characteristics (motives, traits, schema) that exert an influence on thoughts, feelings, and actions. (See Chapters 1, 7–11, 13, 14, and *periphery of personality*.)

typology   A classification of types that is part of a statement of the periphery of personality. (See *type* and *periphery of personality*.)

unstructured test   Often called *projective,* a type of test that presents the subject with an unstructured, ambiguous situation to which to respond. Unstructured tests usually engage the subject's fantasy, but they can also involve other aspects of performance. Some techniques, such as the interview, can be either somewhat structured or unstructured. Although unstructured tests have lower reliability than structured tests, many theorists regard them as more appropriate for assessing underlying defenses, conflicts, and unconscious material that may not be readily apparent in overt behavior. (See Chapters 2, 6, 11, 14, *structured test, personality research, performance test, interview, fantasy test, reliability,* and *validity*.)

validity   The degree to which a test or scale predicts the naturally occurring behavior it was intended to forecast. In personality research, construct validity is most relevant. Here there is no one naturally occurring behavior crucial in the validation of a scale; rather there are several, each linked to the scale (perhaps indirectly) by theory. The process for validating the scale is the same as that for validating its underlying constructs. (See Chapters 2, 11, 13.)

White's position   See Appendix.

Word Association Test   A procedure for studying personality, devised by Jung, in which a series of words are presented to subjects one at a time and they associate a word to each of them as quickly as they can. (See Chapter 11.)

References

Abelson, R., Aronson, E., McGuire, W., Newcomb, T., Rosenberg, M., & Tannenbaum, P. (Eds.). (1969). *Theories of cognitive consistency: A sourcebook*. Chicago: Rand McNally.

Aborn, M. (1953). The influence of experimentally induced failure on the retention of material acquired through set and incidental learning. *Journal of Experimental Psychology, 45,* 225–231.

Abraham, K. (1927a). The first pregenital stage of the libido. In K. Abraham (Ed.), *Selected papers*. London: Institute for Psychoanalysis and Hogarth Press.

Abraham, K. (1927b). The influence of oral erotism on character formation. In K. Abraham (Ed.), *Selected papers*. London: Institute for Psychoanalysis and Hogarth Press.

Abraham, K. (1927c). Contributions to the theory of the anal character. In K. Abraham (Ed.), *Selected papers*. London: Institute for Psychoanalysis and Hogarth Press.

Abraham, K. (1927d). Character formation on the genital level of libido development. In K. Abraham (Ed.), *Selected papers*. London: Institute for Psychoanalysis and Hogarth Press.

Abramowitz, S. (1973). Internal-external control and sociopolitical activism: A test of the dimensionality of Rotter's internal-external scale. *Journal of Consulting and Clinical Psychology, 40,* 196–201.

Adams, H. E., & Vidulich, R. N. (1962). Dogmatism and belief congruence in paired-associate learning. *Psychological Reports, 10,* 90–94.

Adams, J. S. (1961). Reduction of cognitive dissonance by seeking consonant information. *Journal of Abnormal and Social Psychology, 62,* 74–78.

Adams-Webber, J. R. (1970). An analysis of the discriminant validity of several repertory grid indices. *British Journal of Psychology, 60,* 1, 83–90.

Adelson, J., & Redmond, J. (1958). Personality differences in the capacity for verbal recall. *Journal of Abnormal and Social Psychology, 57,* 244–248.

Adler, A. (1917). *Study of organ inferiority and its physical compensation*. New York: Nervous and Mental Diseases Publishing Company.

Adler, A. (1927). *The practice and theory of individual psychology*. New York: Harcourt, Brace & World.

Adler, A. (1930). Individual psychology. In C. Murchinson (Ed.), *Psychologies of 1930*. Worchester, MA: Clark University Press.

Adler, A. (1931). *What life should mean to you*. Boston: Little, Brown.

Adler, A. (1939). *Social interest*. New York: Putnam.

Adler, A. (1956). *The individual psychology of Alfred Adler*. New York: Basic Books.

Adler, A. (1964). *Problems of neurosis*. New York: Harper Torchbooks.

Adorno, T. W., Frenkel-Brunswik, E., Levinson, D. J., & Sanford, R. N. (1950). *The authoritarian personality*. New York: Harper.

Adrian, E. D. (1954). The physiological basis of perception. In E. D. Adrian et al. (Eds.), *Brain mechanisms and consciousness*. Oxford, England: Blackwell.

Adler, H. A. (1967). Cognitive controls and the Hoan-Kroeker model of ego functioning. *Journal of Abnormal and Social Psychology, 72*, 434–440.

Akeret, R. U. (1959). Interrelationships among various dimensions of the self-concept. *Journal of Counseling Psychology, 6*, 199–201.

Alegre, C., & Murray, E. (1974). Locus of control, behavioral intention, and verbal conditioning. *Journal of Personality, 42*, 668–681.

Alker, H. A. (1972). Is personality situationally specific or intrapsychically consistent? *Journal of Personality, 40*, 4–16.

Allport, F. H. (1955). *Theories of perception and the concept of structure*. New York: Wiley.

Allport, G. W. (1937). *A psychological interpretation*. New York: Holt.

Allport, G. W. (1942). *The use of personal documents in psychological research*. New York: Social Science Research Council.

Allport, G. W. (1955). *Becoming: Basic considerations for a psychology of personality*. New Haven, CT: Yale University Press.

Allport, G. W. (1961). *Pattern and growth in personality*. New York: Holt, Rinehart & Winston.

Allport, G. W. (1962). The general and the unique in psychological science. *Journal of Personality, 30*, 405–422.

Allport, G. W., & Cantril, H. (1934). Judging personality from voice. *Journal of Social Psychology, 5*, 37–55.

Allport, G. W., & Odbert, H. S. (1936). Trait names: A psychological study. *Psychological Monographs, 47*, (1–171, No. 211).

Allport, G. W., & Vernon, P. E. (1933). *Studies in expressive movement*. New York: Macmillan.

Allport, G. W., Vernon, P. E., & Lindzey, G. A. (1951). *A study of values* (2nd ed.). Boston: Houghton Mifflin.

Altus, W. D. (1966). Birth order and its sequelae. *Science, 151*, 44–49.

Amabile, T. (1985). Motivation and creativity: Effects of motivational orientation on creative writers. *Journal of Personality and Social Psychology, 48*, 393–399.

Anastasi, A. (1961). *Psychological testing* (2nd ed.). New York: Macmillan.

Anderson, J. D. E. (1960). Prediction of adjustment over time. In I. Iscoe & H. A. Stevenson (Eds.), *Personality development in children*. Austin, TX: University of Texas Press.

Angyal, A. (1941). *Foundations for a science of personality*. New York: Commonwealth Fund.

Angyal, A. (1951). A theoretical model for personality studies. *Journal of Personality, 20*, 131–142.

Angyal, A. (1965). *Neurosis and treatment: A holistic theory*. New York: Wiley.

Ansbacher, H. L. (1967). Life style: A historical and systematic review. *Journal of Individual Psychology, 23*, 191–231.

Ansbacher, H. L., & Ansbacher, R. (1956). *The individual psychology of Alfred Adler*. New York: Basic Books.

Aronson, E. (1961). The effect of effort on the attractiveness of rewarded and unrewarded stimuli. *Journal of Abnormal and Social Psychology, 63,* 375–380.

Aronson, E., & Mills, J. (1959). The effect of severity of initiation on liking for a group. *Journal of Abnormal and Social Psychology, 59,* 177–181.

Aronson, M. L. (1953). A study of the Freudian theory of paranoia by means of the Blacky Pictures. *Journal of Projective Techniques, 17,* 3–19.

Atkinson, J. W. (1950). *Studies in projective measurement of achievement motivation.* Unpublished manuscript, University of Michigan, Ann Arbor, MI.

Atkinson, J. W. (1957) Motivational determinants of risk-taking behavior. *Psychological Review, 64,* 359–372.

Atkinson, J. W. (Ed.). (1958). *Motives in fantasy, action, and society,* Princeton, NJ: Van Nostrand.

Atkinson, J. W. (1960). Personality dynamics. In P. R. Farnsworth & Q. McNemar (Eds.), *Annual Review of Psychology.* Palo Alto, CA: Banta.

Atkinson, J. W., & Birch, D. (1970). *The dynamics of action.* New York: Wiley.

Atkinson, J. W., Heyns, R. W., & Veroff, J. (1954). The effect of experimental arousal of the affiliation motive on thematic apperception. *Journal of Abnormal and Social Psychology, 49,* 405–410.

Atkinson, J. W., & Raynor, J. Q. (1975). *Motivation and achievement.* Washington, DC: Winston.

Atkinson, J. W., & Walker, E. L. (1958). The affiliation motive and perceptual sensitivity to facts. In J. W. Atkinson (Ed.), *Motives in fantasy, action, and society.* Princeton, NJ: Van Nostrand.

Ayllon, T., & Azrin, N. (1968). *The token economy.* New York: Appleton-Century-Crofts.

Bachman, J. R., O'Malley, P. M. & Johnston, G. (1978). *Adolescence to adulthood: Change and stability in the lives of young men.* Ann Arbor, MI: Institute for Social Research.

Bakan, D. (1966). *The duality of human existence.* Chicago: Rand McNally.

Bakan, D. (1968). *Disease, pain, and sacrifice.* Chicago: University of Chicago Press.

Bakan, D. (1971). *Slaughter of the innocents.* San Francisco: Jossey-Bass.

Baker, S. R. (1964). A study of the relationship of dogmatism to the retention of psychological concepts: A research note. *Journal of Human Relations, 12,* 311–313.

Bandura, A. (1965). Vicarious processes: A case of no-trial learning. In L. Berkowitz (Ed.), *Advances in experimental social psychology* (Vol. II). New York: Academic Press.

Bandura, A. (1966). Behavioral modifications through modeling procedures. In L. Krasner & I. P. Ullman (Eds.), *Research in behavior modification.* New York: Holt, Rinehart & Winston.

Bandura, A. (1969). *Principles of behavior modification.* New York: Holt, Rinehart & Winston.

Bandura, A. (1974). Behavior theory and the models of man. *American Psychologist, 29,* 859–869.

Bandura, A. (1977). Self-efficacy: Toward a unifying theory of behavioral change. *Psychological Review, 84,* 191–215.

Bandura, A. (1978). The self system in reciprocal determinism. *American Psychologist, 33,* 344–358.

Bandura, A. (1986). Self-efficacy mechanism in physiological activation and health-promoting behavior. In J. Madden IV, S. Matthysse, & J. Barchas (Eds.), *Adaptation, learning and affect.* New York: Raven Press.

Bandura, A., & Kupers, C. J. (1964). Transmission of patterns of self-reinforcement through modeling. *Journal of Abnormal Social Psychology, 69,* 1–9.

Bandura, A., & Mischel, W. (1965). Modification of self-imposed delay of reward through exposure to live and symbolic models. *Journal of Personality and Social Psychology, 2,* 698–705.

Bandura, A., Taylor, C. B., Williams, S. L., Mufford, I. N., & Barchas, J. D. (1985). Catecholamine secretion as a function of perceived self-efficacy. *Journal of Consulting and Clinical Psychology, 53,* 406–414.

Bandura, A., & Walters, R. H. (1963). *Social learning and personality development.* New York: Holt, Rinehart & Winston.

Bannister, D. (Ed.). (1970). *Perspectives in personal construct theory.* New York: Academic Press.

Bannister, D., & Fransella, K. (1971). *Inquiring man.* Baltimore: Penguin.

Bannister, D., & Mair, J. M. M. (1988). *The evaluation of personal constructs.* London: Academic Press.

Barker, R., Dembo, T., & Lewin, L. (1941). Frustration and regression: An experiment with young children. *University of Iowa Studies of Child Welfare, 18,* no. 1, 1–314.

Barron, F. (1963). *Creativity and psychological health.* Princeton, NJ: Van Nostrand.

Battle, E., & Rotter, J. B. (1963). Children's feelings of personal control as related to social class and ethnic group. *Journal of Personality, 31,* 482–490.

Beck, S. (1953). The science of personality: Nomothetic or idiographic? *Psychological Review, 60,* 353–359.

Bem, D. J. (1972). Constructing cross-situational consistencies in behavior: Some thoughts on Alker's critique of Mischel. *Journal of Personality, 40,* 17–26.

Bem, D. J., & Funder, D. C. (1978). Predicting more of the people more of the time: Assessing the personality of situations. *Psychological Review, 85;* 485–501.

Bem, S. L. (1974). The measurement of psychological androgyny. *Journal of Consulting and Clinical Psychology, 42,* 155–162.

Benson, J. K. (1966). *Alienation and academic achievement: An empirical study of the reactions of college students to academic success and failure.* Unpublished doctoral dissertation, University of Texas, Austin, TX.

Berger, E. M. (1953). The relation between expressed acceptance of self and expressed acceptance of others. *Journal of Abnormal and Social Psychology, 47,* 778–782.

Berger, E. M. (1955). Relationships among acceptance of self, acceptance of others and MMPI scores. *Journal of Counseling Psychology, 2,* 279–284.

Berger, L., & Everstine, L. (1962). Test-retest reliability of the Blacky Pictures Test. *Journal of Projective Techniques, 26,* 225–226.

Bergin, A. E., & Lambert, M. J. (1978). The evaluation of therapeutic outcomes. In S. L. Garfield & A. E. Bergin (Eds.), *Handbook of psychotherapy and behavior change: An empirical analysis* (2nd ed.). New York: Wiley.

Berkowitz, L. (1974). Some determinants of impulsive aggression: Role of mediated associations with reinforcements for aggression. *Psychological Review, 81,* 165–176.

Berlew, D. E. (1956). *The achievement motive and the growth of Greek civilization.* Unpublished bachelor's thesis, Wesleyan University, Middletown, CT.

Berlin, H. (1978). An alternative to social learning theory. *Contemporary Educational Psychology, 3,* 27–31.

Berlyne, D. E. (1955). The arousal and satiation of perceptual curiosity in the rat. *Journal of Comparative and Physiological Psychology, 48,* 238–246.

Berlyne, D. E. (1957). Uncertainty and conflict: A point of contact between information-theory and behavior-theory concepts. *Psychological Review, 64,* 329–339.

Berlyne, D. E. (1960). *Conflict, arousal, and curiosity.* New York: McGraw-Hill.

Berlyne, D. E. (1964). Emotional aspects of learning. *Annual Review of Psychology, 15,* 115–142.

Berlyne, D. E. (1967). Arousal and reinforcement. *Nebraska Symposium on Motivation,* 1–110.

Berlyne, D. E. (1968). Behavior theory as personality theory. In E. F. Borgatto & W. W. Lambert (Eds.), *Handbook of personality theory and research.* Chicago: Rand McNally.

Bernardin, A. C., & Jessor, R. A. (1957). A construct validation of the Edwards Personal Preference Schedule with respect to dependency. *Journal of Consulting Psychology, 21,* 63–67.

Berne, E. (1964). *Games people play.* New York: Grove Press.

Bettinhaus, E., Miller, G., & Steinfatt, T. (1970). Source evaluation, syllogistic content, and judgments of logical validity by high and low dogmatic persons. *Journal of Personality and Social Psychology, 16,* 238–244.

Bialer, I. (1961). Conceptualization of success and failure in mentally retarded and normal children. *Journal of Personality, 29,* 303–320.

Bieler, S. H. (1966). Some correlates of the Jungian typology: *Personal style variables.* Master's thesis, Duke University, Durham, NC.

Bieri, J. (1961). Complexity-simplicity as a personality variable in cognitive and preferential behavior. In D. W. Fiske & S. R. Maddi (Eds.), *Functions of varied experience.* Homewood, IL: Dorsey Press.

Binswanger, L. (1958). The existential analysis school of thought. In R. May, E. Angel, & H. F. Ellenberger (Eds.), *Existence: A new dimension in psychiatry and psychology.* New York: Basic Books.

Binswanger, L. (1963). *Being-in-the-world: Selected papers of Ludwig Binswanger.* New York: Basic Books.

Birtchnell, J. & Meyhew, J. (1977). Toman's theory: Tested for mate selection and friendship formation. *Journal of Individual Psychology, 33,* 18–36.

Blass, T. (Ed.). (1977). *Personality variables in social behavior.* Hillsdale, NJ: Erlbaum.

Block, J. (1962). Some differences between the concepts of social desirability and adjustments. *Journal of Consulting Psychology, 26,* 527–530.

Block, J. (1971). *Lives through time.* Berkeley, CA: Bancroft.

Block, J., Weiss, D. S., & Thorne, A. (1979). How relevant is a semantic similarity interpretation of personality rating. *Journal of Personality and Social Psychology,* 37, 1055–1074.

Blum, G. S. (1949). A study of the psychoanalytic theory of psychosexual development. *Genetic Psychology Monograph, 39,* 3–99.

Blum, G. S. (1955). Perceptual defense revisited. *Journal of Abnormal and Social Psychology, 51,* 24–29.

Blum, G. S., & Hunt, H. F. (1952). The validity of the Blacky Pictures. *Psychological Bulletin, 49,* 238–250.

Blum, G. S., & Kaufman, J. B. (1952). Two patterns of personality dynamics in male ulcer patients, as suggested by responses to the Blacky Pictures. *Journal of Clinical Psychology, 8,* 273–278.

Boneau, C. A. (1974). Paradigm regained? Cognitive behaviorism restated. *American Psychologist, 29,* 297–309.

Bootzin, R. R., & Natsoulas, T. (1965). Evidence for perceptual defense uncontaminated by response bias. *Journal of Personality and Social Psychology, 1,* 461–468.

Boss, M. (1963). *Psychoanalysis and Daseinanalysis.* New York: Basic Books.

Bossard, J. H. S., & Boll, E. S. (1955). Personality roles in the large family. *Child Development, 26,* 71–78.

Bowers, K. S. (1973). Situationism in psychology: An analysis and a critique. *Psychological Review, 80,* 307–336.

Bowers, K. S. (1977). There's more to Iago than meets the eye: A clinical account of personal consistency. In D. Magnussen & N. S. Endler (Eds.), *Personality at the crossroads.* Hillsdale, NJ: Erlbaum.

Bowlby, J. (1969). *Attachment: Vol. 1: Attachment and loss.* New York: Basic Books.

Bradburn, N. M., & Berlew, D. E. (1961). Need for achievement and English industrial growth. *Economic Development and Cultural Change, 10,* 8–20.

Bradley, R. W. (1968). Birth order and school-related behavior: A heuristic review. *Psychological Bulletin, 70,* 45–51.

Braun, J., & Asta, P. (1968). Intercorrelations between the Personal Orientation Inventory and the Gordon Personal Inventory scores. *Psychological Reports, 23,* 1197–1198.

Brehm, J. W. (1965). Comments on "Counter-norm attitudes induced by consonant versus dissonant conditions of role-playing." *Journal of Experimental Research in Personality, 1,* 61–64.

Brehm, J. W., & Cohen, A. R. (1959). Re-evaluation of choice alternatives as function of their number and qualitative similarity. *Journal of Abnormal and Social Psychology, 58,* 373–378.

Brehm, J. W., & Cohen, A. R. (1962). Explorations in cognitive dissonance. New York: Wiley.

Breuer, J., & Freud, S. (1936). Studies in hysteria. *Nervous and Mental Diseases Monograph* (No. 61).

Brody, G. H. (1978). A social learning explanation of moral development. *Contemporary Educational Psychology, 3,* 20–26.

Bronson, G. W. (1959). Identity diffusion in late adolescents. *Journal of Abnormal and Social Psychology, 59,* 414–417.

Brophy, A. L. (1959). Self, role, and satisfaction. *Genet. Psychol. Monogr., 59,* 236–308.

Brown, D., & Marks, P. A. (1969). Bakan's bi-polar constructs: Agency and communion. *The Psychological Records, 19,* 465–478.

Brown, J. S., & Farber, I. E. (1951). Emotions conceptualized as intervening variables with suggestions toward a theory of frustration. *Psychological Bulletin, 38,* 465–495.

Brown, N. O. (1959). *Life against death.* Middletown, CT: Wesleyan University Press.

Brown, N. O. (1961). *Apocalypse.* Phi Beta Kappa address. *Harper's, 222,* 46–49.

Brown, R. (1986). *Social psychology: The second edition.* New York: Free Press.

Brown, S. R., & Hendrick, C. (1971). Introversion, extroversion and social perception. *British Journal of Social and Clinical Psychology, 10,* 313–319.

Bruner, J. S. (1956). You are your constructs. *Contemporary Psychology, 1,* 355–358.

Bruner, J. S. (1957a). Mechanism riding high. *Contemporary Psychology, 2,* 155–157.

Bruner, J. S. (1957b). Neural mechanisms in perception. *Psychological Review, 64,* 340–358.

Bruner, J. S. (1962a). *On knowing: Essays for the left hand.* Cambridge, MA: Harvard University Press.

Bruner, J. S. (1962b). The creative surprise. In H. E. Gruber, G. Terrell, & M. Wertheimer (Eds.), *Contemporary approaches to creative thinking.* New York: Atherton.

Bruner, J. S., & Postman, L. (1947a). Emotional selectivity in perception and reaction. *Journal of Personality, 16,* 69–77.

Bruner, J. S., & Postman, L. (1947b). Tension and tension-release as organizing factors in perception. *Journal of Personality, 15,* 300–308.

Bugental, J. F. T. (1965). *The search for authenticity.* New York: Holt, Rinehart & Winston.

Bugental, J. F. T. (1976). *The search for existential identity.* San Francisco, Jossey-Bass.

Buss, D. M., Craik, K. H. (1983). The act frequency approach to personality. *Psychological Review, 90,* 105–26.

Butler, J. M., & Haigh, G. V. (1954). Changes in the relation between self-concepts and ideal-concepts consequent upon client-centered counseling. In C. R. Rogers & R. F. Dymond (Eds.), *Psychotherapy and personality change.* Chicago: University of Chicago Press.

Butler, J. M., & Rice, L. (1963). Adience, self-actualization, and drive theory. In J. M. Wepman & R. W. Heine (Eds.), *Concepts of personality*. Chicago: Aldine.

Butler, R. A., & Alexander, H. M. (1955), Daily patterns of visual exploratory behavior in the monkey. *Journal of Comparative and Physiological Psychology, 48,* 247–249.

Butterfield, E. C. (1964). Locus of control, test anxiety, reactions to frustration, and achievement attitudes. *Journal of Personality, 32,* 298–311.

Byrne, D. (1961a). Anxiety and the experimental arousal of affiliation need. *Journal of Abnormal and Social Psychology, 63,* 660–662.

Byrne, D. (1961b). The Repression-Sensitization Scale: Rationale, reliability, and validity. *Journal of Personality, 29,* 344–349.

Byrne, D. (1964). Repression-sensitization as a dimension of personality. In B. A. Maher (Ed.), *Progress in experimental personality research*. New York: Academic Press.

Byrne, D. (1965). Parental antecedents of authoritarianism. *Journal of Personality and Social Psychology, 1,* 369–373.

Byrne, D. (1977). Authoritarianism. In T. Blass (Ed.), *Personality variables in social behavior*. Hillsdale, NJ: Erlbaum.

Byrne, D., Barry, J., & Nelson, D. (1963). Relation of the revised Repression-Sensitization Scale to measures of self-description. *Psychological Reports, 13,* 323–334.

Calder, B. J., & Staw, B. M. (1975a). Interaction of intrinsic and extrinsic motivation: Some methodological notes. *Journal of Personality and Social Psychology, 31,* 76–80.

Calder, B. J., & Staw, B. M. (1975b). Self-perception of intrinsic and extrinsic motivation. *Journal of Personality and Social Psychology, 31,* 599–605.

Campbell, A. A. (1933). A study of the personality adjustments of only and intermediate children. *Journal of Genetic Psychology, 43,* 197–206.

Campell, A., Converse, P. E., Miller, W. E., & Stokes, D. E. (1960). *The American voter*. New York: Wiley.

Campbell, D. T., & Fiske, D. W. (1959). Convergent and discriminant validation by the multitrait-multimethod matrix. *Psychological Bulletin, 56,* 81–105.

Camus, A. (1955). *The myth of Sisyphus and other essays* (J. O'Brien, Trans.). New York: Knopf.

Cannon, W. B. (1929). *Bodily changes in pain, hunger, fear, and rage*. New York: Appleton.

Cantor, N., & Kihlstrom, J. (1986). *Personality and social intelligence*. Englewood Cliffs, NJ: Prentice-Hall.

Cantor, N., Smith, E. E., French, R. D., & Mezzich, J. (1980). Psychiatric diagnosis as prototype categorization. *Journal of Abnormal Psychology, 89,* 181–193.

Carlson, L., & Carlson, R. (1984). Affect and psychological magnification: Derivations from Tomkins' script theory. *Journal of Personality, 52,* 36–45.

Carlson, R. (1971a). Sex differences in ego functioning: Exploratory studies of agency and communion. *Journal of Consulting and Clinical Psychology, 37,* 267–277.

Carlson, R. (1971b). Where is the person in personality research? *Psychological Bulletin, 75*, 203–219.

Carlson, R., & Levy, N. (1973). Studies of Jungian typology: 1. Memory, social perception and social action. *Journal of Personality, 41*, 559–576.

Carrigan, P. (1960). Extraversion-introversion as a dimension of personality: A reappraisal. *Psychological Bulletin, 57*, 329–360.

Carrol, E. N., Zuckerman, M., & Vogel, W. H. (1982). A test of the optimal level of arousal theory of sensation seeking. *Journal of Personality and Social Psychology, 42*, 572–575.

Carver, C. S., & Scheier, M. F. (1981). *Attention and self-regulation: A control theory approach to human behavior*. New York: Springer-Verlag.

Cattell, R. B. (1946). *Description and measurement of personality*. New York: World Book.

Cattell, R. B. (1950). *Personality: A systematic, theoretical, and factual study*. New York: McGraw-Hill.

Cattell, R. B. (1957). *Personality and motivation structure and measurement*. New York: World Book.

Cattell, R. B. (1972). The 16 PF and basic personality structure: A reply to Eysenck. *Journal of Behavioral Science, 1*, 169–187.

Cattell, R. B., & Delhees, K. (1973). Seven missing normal personality factors in the questionnaire primaries. *Multivariate Behavior Research, 8*, 173–194.

Cattell, R. B., & Stice, G. F. (1957). *Sixteen Personality Factor Questionnaire* (rev. ed.) Champaign, IL: *Institute for Personality & Abilities Testing*.

Centers, R. (1969). The anal character and social severity in attitudes. *Journal of Projective Techniques & Personality Assess., 33*, 501–506.

Chabot, J. A. (1973). Repression-sensitization: A critique of some neglected variables in the literature. *Psychological Bulletin, 80*, 122–129.

Chapanis, N. P., & Chapanis, A. (1964). Cognitive dissonance: Five years later. *Psychological Bulletin, 61*, 1–22.

Charen, S. (1956). Reliability of the Blacky Test. *Journal of Consulting Psychology, 20*, 16.

Cherulnik, P. D., & Citrin, M. M. (1974). Individual difference in psychological reactance: The interaction between locus of control and mode of elimination of freedom. *Journal of Personality and Social Psychology, 29*, 398–404.

Chodorkoff, B. (1954a). Adjustment and the discrepancy between perceived and ideal self. *Journal of Clinical Psychology, 10*, 266–268.

Chodorkoff, B. (1954b). Self-perception, perceptual defense, and adjustment. *Journal of Abnormal and Social Psychology, 49*, 508–512.

Ciminero, A. R., Calhoun, K. S., & Adams, H. E. (1977). *Handbook of behavioral assessment*. New York: Wiley.

Clark, C. (1957). *The conditions of economic progress* (3rd ed.) London: Macmillan.

Clark, S. L. (1968). Authoritarian attitudes and field dependence. *Psychological Reports, 22*, 309–310.

Clark, W. C., & Hunt, H. F. (1971). Pain. In J. A. Powney & R. C. Darling (Eds.), *Physiological basis of rehabilitation medicine*. Philadelphia: Saunders.

Coan, R. W. (1972). Measurable components of openness to experience. *Journal of Consulting and Clinical Psychology, 39,* 346.

Coan, R. W. (1974). *The optimal personality*. New York: Columbia University Press.

Cohen, A. R., Brehm, J. W., & Fleming, W. H. (1958). Attitude change and justification for compliance. *Journal of Abnormal and Social Psychology, 56,* 276–278.

Cole, J. K. (Ed.). (1976). *Nebraska symposium on motivation*. Lincoln, NE: University of Nebraska Press.

Coleman, J. S., Campbell, E. Q., Hobson, C. J., McPartland, J., Mood, A. M., Weinfeld, F. D., & York, R. L. (1966). *Equality of educational opportunity*. (Superintendent of Documents, Catalog No. FS 5.238.38001), Washington, DC: U. S. Office of Education.

Collins, B. E. (1974). Four components of the Rotter Internal-External Scale: Belief in a difficult world, a just world, a predictable world, and a politically responsive world. *Journal of Personality and Social Psychology, 29,* 381–391.

Conant, J. B. (1947). *On understanding science*. New Haven, CT: Yale University Press.

Conley, J. J. (1984). Longitudinal consistency of adult personality: Self-reported psychological characteristics across 45 years. *Journal of Personality and Social Psychology,* 1325–1333.

Conn, L. K., & Crowne, D. P. (1963). Instigation to aggression, emotional arousal and defensive emulation. *Journal of Personality, 32,* 163–179.

Conners, C. K. (1963). Birth order and needs for affiliation. *Journal of Personality, 31,* 408–416.

Constantinople, A. (1969). An Eriksonian measure of personality development in college students. *Developmental Psychology, 1,* 357–372.

Cook, J. R. (1985). Repression-sensitization and approach-avoidance as predictors of response to a laboratory stressor. *Journal of Personality and Social Psychology, 49,* 759–773.

Cook, P. (1958). Authoritarian or acquiescent: Some behavioral differences. *American Psychologist, 13,* 338.

Cooper, J., & Goethals, G. R. (1974). Unforeseen events and the elimination of cognitive dissonance. *Journal of Personality and Social Psychology, 29,* 441–445.

Cooper, J., & Scalise, C. J. (1974). Dissonance produced by deviations from life styles: The interaction of Jungian typology and conformity. *Journal of Personality and Social Psychology, 29,* 556–571.

Cooper, W. H. (1983). An achievement motivation nomological network. *Journal of Personality and Social Psychology, 44,* 841–861.

Cooperman, M., & Child, I. L. (1969). Esthetic preference and active style. *Proceedings of the 77th Annual Convention of the American Psychological Association, 4,* 471–472.

Cortes, J. B. (1960). The achievement motive in the Spanish economy between the 13th and 18th centuries. *Economic Development and Cultural Change, 9,* 144–163.

Costa, P. T., Jr. (1970). *Multivariate analysis of the Maddi model of forms for variety.* Unpublished doctoral dissertation, University of Chicago, Chicago.

Costa, P. T. & McCrae, R. R. (1976). Age differences in personality structure: A cluster analytic approach. *Journal of Gerontology, 31,* (5), 564–570.

Costa, P. T. & McCrae, R. R. (1977). Psychiatric symptom dimensions in the Cornell Medical Index among normal and adult males. *Journal of Clinical Psychology, 33,* (4), 941–946.

Costa, P. T., & McCrae, R. R. (1977–78). Age differences in personality structure revisited: Studies in validity, stability, and change. *International Journal of Aging and Human Development, 8,* (4), 261–275.

Costa, P. T., Jr., & McCrae, R. R. (1980). Still stable after all these years: Personality as a key to some issues in aging. In D. Baltes & O. G. Brim (Eds.), *Lifespan development and behavior (Vol. III).* 1981.

Costa, P. T., Jr., McCrae, R. R., & Arenberg, D. (1970). Enduring dispositions in adult males. *Journal of Personality and Social Psychology,* 1981.

Costa, P. T., Jr., McCrae, R. R., & Arenberg, D. (1980). Enduring dispositions in adult males. *Journal of Personality and Social Psychology, 38,* 793–800.

Costa, P. T., Jr., Zonderman, A. B., Williams, R. B., Jr., & McCrae, R. R. (1985). Content and comprehensiveness in the MMPI: An item factor analysis in a normal adult sample. *Journal of Personality and Social Psychology, 48,* 925–933.

Costin, F. (1965). Dogmatism and learning: A follow-up of contradictory findings. *Journal of Educational Research, 59,* 186–188.

Costin, F. (1968). Dogmatism and the retention of psychological misconceptions. *Educational & Psychological Measurement, 28,* 529–534.

Cowen, E. L., & Beier, E. G. (1954). Threat expectancy, work frequencies, and perceptual prerecognition hypotheses. *Journal of Abnormal and Social Psychology, 14,* 469–477.

Crandall, V. C., Katkovsky, W., & Crandall, V. J. (1965). Children's beliefs in their own control of reinforcement in intellectual-academic achievement situations. *Child Development, 36,* 91–109.

Crepeau, J. J. (1978). The effects of stressful life events and locus of control on suicidal ideation. Unpublished research, University of Massachusetts.

Croake, J. W., & Hayden, D. J. (1975). Trait oppositeness in siblings: Test of Adlerian tenet. *Journal of Individual Psychology, 31,* 175–178.

Cromwell, R., Rosenthal, D., Shakow, D., & Kahn, T. (1961). Reaction time, locus of control, choice behavior and descriptions of parental behavior in schizophrenic and normal subjects. *Journal of Personality, 29,* 363–380.

Cronbach, L. J. (1975a). The two disciplines of scientific psychology. *American Psychologist, 12,* 671–684.

Cronbach, L. J. (1975b). Beyond the two disciplines of scientific psychology. *American Psychologist, 30,* 116–127.

Cronbach, L. J., & Meehl, P. E. (1955). Construct validity in psychological tests. *Psychological Bulletin, 52,* 281–302.

Crookes, T. G., & Pearson, P. R. (1970). The relationship between EPI scores and 16 PF second order factors in a clinical group. *British Journal of Social and Clinical Psychology, 9,* 189–190.

Cross, P. G., Cattell, R. B., & Butcher, H. J. (1967). The personality pattern of creative artists. *British Journal of Education Psychology, 37,* 292–299.

Crosson, S., & Schwendiman, G. (1972). Self-actualization as a predictor of conformity behavior. Unpublished manuscript, Marshall University, Huntington, WV.

Crowne, D. P., & Liverant, S. (1963). Conformity under varying conditions of personal commitment. *Journal of Abnormal and Social Psychology, 66,* 547–555.

Crowne, D. P., & Marlowe, D. (1960). A new scale of social desirability independent of psychopathology. *Journal of Consulting Psychology, 24,* 349–354.

Crumbaugh, J. C. (1968). Cross-validation of the Purpose in Life Test based on Frankl's concepts. *Journal of Individual Psychology, 24,* 74–81.

Crumbaugh, J. C., & Maholick, L. T. (1964). An experimental study in existentialism: The psychometric approach to Frankl's concept of noogenic neurosis. *Journal of Clinical Psychology, 20,* 200–207.

Csikszentmihalyi, M. (1975). *Beyond boredom and anxiety.* San Francisco: Jossey-Bass.

Damm, V. J. (1969). Overall measures of self actualization derived from the Personal Orientation Inventory. *Educational & Psychological Measurement, 29,* 977–981.

Dandes, H. M. (1966). Psychological health and teaching effectiveness. *Journal of Teaching Education, 17,* 301–306.

D'Andrade, R. G. (1974). Memory and the assessment of behavior. In T. Blalock (Ed.), *Social measurement.* Chicago: Aldine-Atherton.

Danskin, D. G. (1964, September). *An introduction to KSU students.* Unpublished report, Kansas State University, Student Counseling Center. Cited in J. B. Warren (1966). Birth order and social behavior. *Psychological Bulletin, 65,* 38–49.

Davis, A., & Dollard, J. (1940). *Children of bondage.* Washington, DC: American Council on Education.

Davis, P. J., & Schwartz, G. (1986). Repression and the inaccessibility of affective memories. *Journal of Personality and Social Psychology, 49,* In press.

de Charms, R. C. (1957). Affiliation motivation and productivity in small groups. *Journal of Abnormal Social Psychology, 55,* 222–226.

de Charms, R. C., Morrison, H. W., Reitman, W., & McClelland, D. C. (1955). Behavioral correlates of directly and indirectly measured achievement motivation. In D. C. McClelland (Ed.), *Studies in motivation.* New York: Appleton-Century-Crofts.

deCharms, R., & Muir, M. S. (1978). Motivation: Social approaches. In M. R. Rosenzineig & L. W. Porter (Eds.), *Annual Review of Psychology* (Vol. 29). Palo Alto, CA: Annual Reviews.

Deci, E. L. (1975). *Intrinsic motivation.* New York: Plenum.

de Grace, G. R. (1974). The compatibility of anxiety and actualization. *Journal of Clinical Psychology, 130,* 566–568.

Dember, W. N. (1956). Response by the rat to environmental change. *Journal of Comparative and Physiological Psychology, 49,* 93–95.

Dember, W. N. (1961). Alternation behavior. In D. W. Fiske & S. R. Maddi (Eds.), *Functions of varied experience.* Homewood, IL: Dorsey Press.

Dember, W. N. (1964). Birth order and need affiliation. *Journal of Abnormal and Social Psychology, 68,* 555–557.

Dember, W. N. (1974). Motivation and the cognitive revolution. *American Psychologist, 29,* 161–168.

Dennis, W. (1939). Spontaneous alternation in rats as an indicator of persistence of stimulus effects. *Journal of Comparative Psychology, 28,* 305–312.

Diamond, R. E., & Munz, D. C. (1967). Ordinal position of birth and self-disclosure in high school students. *Psychological Reports, 21,* 829–833.

DiCaprio, N. S. (1974). *Personality theories: Guides to living.* Philadelphia: Saunders.

Dittes, J. E. (1961). Birth order and vulnerability to differences in acceptance. *American Psychologist, 16,* 358.

Dollard, J., & Miller, N. E. (1950). *Personality and psychotherapy: An analysis in terms of learning, thinking, and culture.* New York: McGraw-Hill.

Domino, G. (1976). Compensatory aspects of dreams: An empirical test of Jung's theory. *Journal of Personality and Social Psychology, 34,* 658–662.

Donley, R. E., & Winter, D. G. (1965). Measuring the motives of public officials at a distance: An exploratory study of American presidents. *Behavioral Science, 3,* 227–236.

Dorfman, D. D. (1965). Esthetic preference as a function of pattern information. *Psychonomic Science, 3,* 85–86.

Douglas, W., & Gibbins, K. (1983). Inadequacy of voice recognition as a demonstration of self-deception. *Journal of Personality and Social Psychology, 44,* 589–592.

Dreikurs, R. (1963). Individual psychology: The Adlerian point of view. In J. M. Wepman & R. W. Heine (Eds.), *Concepts of personality.* Chicago: Aldine.

Duckworth, D. H. (1975). Personality, emotional state and perception of nonverbal communications. *Perceptual and Motor Skills, 40,* 325–326.

Duffy, E. (1963). *Activation and behavior.* New York: Wiley.

Dulany, D. E., Jr. (1962). The place of hypotheses and intentions: An analysis of verbal control in verbal conditioning. In C. W. Eriksen (Ed.), *Behavior and awareness.* Durham, NC: Duke University Press.

Dulany, D. E., Jr. (1968). Awareness, rules, and propositional control: A confrontation with S-R behavior theory. In T. R. Dixon & D. L. Horton (Eds.), *Verbal behavior and general behavior theory.* Englewood Cliffs, NJ: Prentice-Hall.

Duncan, S. D., Jr. (1972). Some signals and rules for taking speaking turns in conversations. *Journal of Personality and Social Psychology, 23,* 283–292.

Duncan, S. D., Jr., & Fiske, D. (1977). *Face to face interactions: Research methods and theory.* Hillsdale, NJ: Erlbaum.

D'Zurilla, T. (1965). Recall efficiency and mediating cognitive events in "experimental repression." *Journal of Personality and Social Psychology, 3,* 253–256.

Ebersole, P. (1973). Effects and classifications of peak experiences. *Psychological Reports, 40*, 22–28.

Edwards, A. L. (1957). *The social desirability variable in personality assessment and research*. New York: Dryden Press

Edwards, A. L. (1963). *Edwards Personal Preference Schedule*. New York: Psychological Corporation.

Ehrlich, D., Guttman, I., Schonbach, P., & Mills, J. (1957). Postdecision exposure to relevant information. *Journal of Abnormal and Social Psychology, 54*, 98–102.

Ehrlich, H. J. (1955). Dogmatism and intellectual change. Unpublished master's thesis, Ohio State University, Columbus, OH.

Ehrlich, H. J. (1961a). Dogmatism and learning. *Journal of Abnormal and Social Psychology, 62*, 148–149.

Ehrlich, H. J. (1961b). Dogmatism and learning: A five-year follow-up. *Psychological Reports, 9*, 283–286.

Ehrlich, H. J., & Lee, D. (1969). Dogmatism, learning and resistance to change: A review and a new paradigm. *Psychological Bulletin, 71*, 249–260.

Eisenberger, R. (1972). Explanation of rewards that do not reduce tissue needs. *Psychological Bulletin, 77*, 319–339.

Eisenberger, R., Myers, A. K., Sanders, R., & Shanab, M. (1970). Stimulus control of spontaneous alternation in the rat. *Journal of Comparative and Physiological Psychology, 70*, 136–140.

Eisenman, R., & Schussel, N. R. (1970). Creativity, birth order and preference for symmetry. *Journal of Consulting and Clinical Psychology, 34*, 275–280.

Ekehammar, B. (1974). Interactionism in personality from a historical perspective. *Psychological Bulletin, 81*, 1026–1048.

Elder, G. H., Jr. (1965). Family structure: The effects of size of family, sex composition and ordinal position on academic motivation and achievement. In B. A. Maher (Ed.), *Progress in experimental personality research*. New York: Academic Press.

Elliot, L. L. (1961). Effects of item construction and respondent aptitude on response acquiescence. *Educational & Psychological Measurement, 21*, 405–415.

Ellis, A. *Reason and Emotion in Psychotherapy*. (1962). New York: Lyle Stuart.

Elms, A. C. (1967). Role playing, incentive, and dissonance. *Psychological Bulletin, 68*, 132–148.

Elms, A. C., & Janis, I. L. (1965). Counter-norm attitudes induced by consonant versus dissonant conditions of role-playing. *Journal of Experimental Research in Personality, 1*, 50–60.

Elms, A. C., & Milgram, S. (1966). Personality characteristics associated with obedience and defiance toward authoritative command. *Journal of Experimental Research in Personality, 1*, 282–289.

Emerson, R. W. (1940). In B. Atkinson (Ed.), *The selected writings of Ralph Waldo Emerson*. New York: Modern Library.

Endler, N. S. (1973). The person versus the situation—a pseudo issue? A response to Alker, *Journal of Personality, 41*, 287–303.

Endler, N. S., & Hunt, J. McV. (1966). Sources of behavioral variance as measured by the S-R Inventory of Anxiousness. *Psychological Bulletin, 65,* 338–346.

Endler, N. S., & Hunt, J. McV. (1969). Generalizability of contributions from sources of variance in the S-R inventories of anxiousness. *Journal of Personality, 37,* 1–24.

Endler, N. S., Hunt, J. McV, & Rosenstein, A. J. (1962). An S-R Inventory of anxiousness. *Psychological Monograph, 76,* (Whole No. 536).

Endler, N. S., & Magnusson, D. (1976). Toward an interactional psychology of personality. *Psychological Bulletin, 83,* 956–974.

Epstein, R. (1965). Authoritarianism, displaced aggression, and social status of the target. *Journal of Personality and Social Psychology, 2,* 585–589.

Epstein, S. (1984). The stability of behavior across time and situations. In R. A. Zucker, J. Aronoff, & R. I. Rabin (Eds.), *Personality and the prediction of behavior.* New York: Academic Press.

Erdelyi, M. H. (1974). A new look at the new look: Perceptual defense and vigilance. *Psychological Review, 81,* 1–25.

Eriksen, C. W. (1951a). Perceptual defense as a function of unacceptable needs. *Journal of Abnormal and Social Psychology, 46,* 557–564.

Eriksen, C. W. (1951b). Some implications for TAT interpretation arising from need and perception experiments. *Journal of Personality, 19,* 283–288.

Eriksen, C. W. (1952). Defense against ego-threat in memory and perception. *Journal of Abnormal and Social Psychology, 47,* 430–435.

Eriksen, C. W. (1954). Psychological defenses and ego strength in the recall of completed and incompleted tasks. *Journal of Abnormal and Social Psychology, 49,* 45–50.

Eriksen, C. W. (1963). Perception and personality. In J. M. Wepman & R. W. Heine (Eds.), *Concepts of personality.* Chicago: Aldine.

Eriksen, C. W., & Brown, C. T. (1956). An experimental and theoretical analysis of perceptual defense. *Journal of Abnormal and Social Psychology, 52,* 224–230.

Eriksen, C. W., & Davids, A. (1955). The meaning and clinical validity of Taylor Anxiety Scale and the Hysteria-Psychasthenia Scales from the MMPI. *Journal of Abnormal Social Psychology, 50,* 135–137.

Erikson, E. H. (1950). *Childhood and society.* New York: Norton.

Erikson, E. H. (1956). The problem of ego identity. *Journal of the American Psychoanalytic Association, 4,* 56–121.

Erikson, E. H. (1959). Identity and the life cycle. *Psychological Issues.* Monograph 1, 1 (1). New York: International Universities Press.

Estes, S. G. (1938). Judging personality from expressive behavior. *Journal of Abnormal and Social Psychology, 33,* 217–236.

Eysenck, H. J. (1947). *Dimensions of personality.* London: Routledge & Kegan Paul.

Eysenck, H. J. (1952). The effects of psychotherapy: An evaluation. *Journal of Consulting Psychology, 16,* 319–324.

Eysenck, H. J. (1957). *The dynamics of anxiety and hysteria: An experimental application of modern learning theory to psychiatry.* London: Routledge & Kegan Paul.

Eysenck, H. J. (1970). *The structure of human personality* (3rd ed.). London: Methuen.

Eysenck, H. J. (1976). *Sex and personality*. London: Open Books.

Eysenck, H. J. (1977). Personality and factor analysis: A reply to Guilford. *Psychological Bulletin, 84*, 405–411.

Eysenck, H. J., & Rachman, S. (1965). *The causes and cures of neuroses*. San Diego: Knapp.

Fairbairn, W. R. D. (1954). *An object-relations theory of personality*. 1954. New York: Basic Books.

Falbo, T. (1981). Relationships between birth category, achievement, and interpersonal orientation. *Journal of Personality and Social Psychology, 41*, 121–131.

Farber, I. E. (1948). Response fixation under anxiety and non-anxiety conditions. *Journal of Experimental Psychology, 38*, 111–131.

Farber, I. E., & Spence, K. W. (1953). Complex learning and conditioning as a function of anxiety. *Journal of Experimental Psychology, 45*, 120–125.

Feather, N. T. (1967). Some personality correlates of external control. *Australian Journal of Psychology, 19*, 253–260.

Feather, N. T. (1984). Masculinity, femininity, psychological androgyny, and the structure of values. *Journal of Personality and Social Psychology, 47*, 604–620.

Feldinger, I., & Maddi, S. R. (1968). The motivational status of measures of the need for variety. Unpublished manuscript, University of Chicago.

Fenichel, O. (1945). *The psychoanalytic theory of neurosis*. New York: Norton.

Feshbach, N. D. (1982). Sex differences in empathy and social behavior in children. In N. Eisenberg-Berg (Ed.), *The development of pro-social behavior*, pp. 315–38. New York: Academic Press.

Festinger, L. (1958). *A theory of cognitive dissonance*. Stanford, CA: Stanford University Press.

Festinger, L. (1958). The motivating effect of cognitive dissonance. In G. Lindzey (Ed.), *Assessment of human motives*. New York: Holt, Rinehart & Winston.

Festinger, L., & Carlsmith, J. M. (1959). Cognitive consequences of forced compliance. *Journal of Abnormal and Social Psychology, 58*, 203–210.

Findley, M. J., & Cooper, H. M. (1983). Locus of control and academic achievement: A literature review. *Journal of Personality and Social Psychology, 44*, 419–427.

Fine, B. J., & Danforth, A. V. (1975). Field-dependence, extroversion and perception of the vertical: Empirical and theoretical perspectives of the Rod and Frame Test. *Perceptual and Motor Skills, 40*, 683–693.

Fink, D. R., Jr. (1958). Negative evidence concerning the generality of rigidity. *Journal of Abnormal and Social Psychology, 57*, 252–254.

Fisher, G. (1968). Performance of psychopathic felons on a measure of self-actualization. *Educational & Psychological Measurement, 28*, 561–563.

Fisher, G., & Silverstein, A. G. (1969). Simulation of poor adjustment on a measure of self-actualization. *Journal of Clinical Psychology, 25*, 198–199.

Fishman, C. G. (1965). Need for approval and the expression of aggression under varying conditions of frustration. *Journal of Personality and Social Psychology, 2*, 809–816.

Fiske, D. W. (1961). Effects of monotonous and restricted stimulation. In D. W. Fiske & S. R. Maddi (Eds.), *Functions of varied experience*. Homewood, IL: Dorsey Press.

Fiske, D. W. (1963). Problems in measuring personality. In J. M. Wepman & R. W. Heine (Eds.), *Concepts of personality*. Chicago: Aldine.

Fiske, D. W. (1974). The limits for the conventional science of personality. *Journal of Personality, 42,* 1–11.

Fiske, D. W. (1978). *Strategies for research in personality: Observations vs. interpretation of behavior*. San Francisco: Jossey-Bass.

Fiske, D. W., & Maddi, S. R. (Eds.). (1961). *Functions of varied experience*. Homewood, IL: Dorsey Press.

Flavell, J. (1955). Repression and the "return of the repressed." *Journal of Consulting Psychology, 19,* 441–443.

Fodor, E. M. (1984). The power motive and reactivity to power stresses. *Journal of Personality and Social Psychology, 47,* 853–959.

Fodor, E. M., & Smith, T. (1982). The power motive as an influence on group decision making. *Journal of Personality and Social Psychology, 42,* 178–185.

Foulds, M. L. (1969). Self-actualization and the communication of facilitative conditions during counseling. *Journal of Counseling Psychology, 16,* 132–136.

Foulds, M. L., & Warehime, R. G. (1971). Effects of a "fake good" response set on a measure of self-actualization. *Journal of Counseling Psychology, 18,* 279–280.

Fox, J., Knapp, R., & Michael, W. (1968). Assessment of self-actualization of psychiatric patients: Validity of the Personal Orientation Inventory. *Educational & Psychological Measurement, 28,* 565–569.

Frankel, M. (1971). Personality as a response: Behaviorism. In S. R. Maddi (Ed.), *Perspectives on personality*. Boston: Little, Brown.

Frankl, V. (1960). *The doctor and the soul*. New York: Knopf.

Fransella, F. (Ed.). (1978). *Personal constructs 1977*. New York: Academic Press.

Freedman, M. B., & Bereiter, C. (1963). A longitudinal study of personality development in college alumnae. *Merrill-Palmer Quarterly, 9,* 295–302.

Freeman, G. L. (1933). The facilitative and inhibitive effects of muscular tension upon performance. *American Journal of Psychology, 45,* 17–52.

Freeman, G. L. (1938). The optimal muscular tension for various performances. *American Journal of Psychology, 51,* 146–150.

Freeman, G. L. (1940). The relationship between performance level and bodily activity level. *Journal of Experimental Psychology, 26,* 602–608.

French, E. G. (1955). Some characteristics of achievement motivation. *Journal of Experimental Psychology, 50,* 232–236.

French, E. G. (1956). Motivation as a variable in work partner selection. *Journal of Abnormal and Social Psychology, 53,* 96–99.

French, J. W. (1973). *Toward the establishment of non-cognitive factors through literature search and interpretation*. Princeton, NJ: Educational Testing Service.

Freud, A. *(1946). The ego and the mechanisms of defense*. New York: International Universities Press.

Freud, S. (1893). Quelques considerations pour une étude comparative des paralysies motrices organiques et hystèriques. *Archives de Neurologie, 26,* 29–43.

Freud, S. (1900). *The interpretation of dreams.* In J. Strachey (Ed.), *The standard edition of the complete psychological works of Sigmund Freud.* (Vols. IV & V). London: Hogarth Press.

Freud, S. (1922a). *Beyond the pleasure principle.* London: International Psychoanalytic Press.

Freud, S. (1922b). *Reflections* (A. A. Brill & A. B. Kuttner, Trans.). New York: Moffat Yard.

Freud, S. (1925a). Character and anal erotism. In S. Freud, *Collected papers* (Vol. 2). London: Institute for Psychoanalysis and Hogarth Press.

Freud, S. (1925b). Instincts and their vicissitudes. In S. Freud, *Collected papers* (Vol. 4). London: Institute for Psychoanalysis and Hogarth Press.

Freud, S. (1925c). On the transformation of instincts with especial reference to anal erotism. In S. Freud, *Collected papers* (Vol. 2). London: Institute for Psychoanalysis and Hogarth Press.

Freud, S. (1925d). Some character types met with in psychoanalysis work. In S. Freud, *Collected papers* (Vol. 4). London: Institute for Psychoanalysis and Hogarth Press.

Freud, S. (1925e). The infantile genital organization of the libido. In S. Freud, *Collected papers* (Vol. 2). London: Institute for Psychoanalysis and Hogarth Press.

Freud, S. (1927). *The ego and the id.* London: Institute for Psychoanalysis and Hogarth Press.

Freud, S. (1930). *Civilization and its discontents.* New York: Norton.

Freud, S. (1933). *New introductory lectures in psychoanalysis* (W. J. H. Sprott, Trans.). New York: Norton.

Freud, S. (1936). *The problem of anxiety.* New York: Norton.

Freud, S. (1938). Three contributions to the theory of sex. In *The basic writings of Sigmund Freud.* New York: Modern Library.

Freud, S. (1952). *Totem and taboo.* New York: Norton.

Freud, S. (1957). The history of the psychoanalytic movement. In J. Strachey (Ed.), *The standard edition of the complete psychological works* (Vol. 14). London: Hogarth Press.

Freud, S. (1960). *The psychopathology of everyday life* (Vol. 6, standard ed.). London: Hogarth Press.

Frick, J. W., Guilford, J. P., Christensen, P. R., & Merrifield, P. R. (1959). A factor-analytic study of flexibility of thinking. *Educational Psychological Measurement, 19,* 469–496.

Fromm, E. (1941). *Escape from freedom.* New York: Rinehart.

Fromm, E. (1947). *Man for himself.* New York: Holt, Rinehart, & Winston.

Fromm, E. (1955). *The sane society.* New York: Rinehart.

Fromm, E. (1956). *The art of loving.* New York: Harper.

Fromm, E., & Maccoby, M. (1970). *Social character in a Mexican village.* Englewood Cliffs, NJ: Prentice-Hall.

Fuerst, K., & Zubek, J. P. (1968). Effects of sensory and perceptual deprivation on a battery of open-ended cognitive tasks. *Canadian Journal of Psychology, 22,* 122–130.

Galambos, R. (1956). Suppression of auditory nerve activity by stimulation of efferent fibers to cochlea. *Journal of Neurophysiology, 19,* 424–431.

Galambos, R., Sheatz, G., & Vernier, V. G. (1956). Electro-physiological correlates of a conditioned response in cats. *Science, 123,* 376–377.

Ganellen, R. J., & Blaney, P. H. (1984). Hardiness and social support as moderators of the effects of life stress. *Journal of Personality and Social Psychology, 47,* 156–163.

Garlington, W. K., & Shimota, H. (1964). The change seeker index: A measure of the need for variable stimulus input. *Psychological Reports, 14,* 191–924.

Geen, R. G. (1984). Preferred stimulation levels in introverts and extraverts: Effects on arousal and performance. *Journal of Personality and Social Psychology, 46,* 1303–1312.

Gelbort, K. R., & Winer, J. L. (1985). Fear of success and fear of failure: A multitrait-multimethod validation study. *Journal of Personality and Social Psychology, 48,* 1009–1014.

Gelfand, D. M. (1962). The influence of self-esteem on rate of verbal conditioning and social matching behavior. *Journal of Existentialism, 65,* 259–265.

Gendlin, E. T. (1965–1966). Experiential explication and truth. *Journal of Existentialism, 6,* 131–146.

Gendlin, E. T. (1973). Experiential psychotherapy. In R. Corsini (Ed.), *Current psychotherapies.* Itasca, IL: Peacock.

Gendlin, E. T., & Tomlinson, T. M. (1967). The process conception and its measurement. In C. R. Rogers, E. T. Gendlin, D. J. Kiesler, & C. B. Truax (Eds.), *The therapeutic relationship and its impact: A study of psychotherapy with schizophrenics.* Madison, WI: University of Wisconsin Press.

Gerard, H. B., & Rabbie, J. M. (1961). Fear and social comparison. *Journal of Abnormal and Social Psychology, 62,* 586–592.

Getzels, J. W., & Csikszentmihalyi, M. (1976). *The creative vision: A longitudinal study of problem finding in art.* New York: Wiley.

Gibbins, K. & Douglas, W. (1985). Voice recognition and self-deception: A reply to Sackheim & Gur. *Journal of Personality and Social Psychology, 48,* 1369–1372.

Gleser, G. C., & Ihilevich, D. (1969). An objective instrument for measuring defense mechanisms. *Journal of Consulting Clinical Psychology, 33,* 51–60.

Gleser, G. C., & Sacks, M. (1973). Ego defenses and reaction to stress: A validation study of the Defense Mechanisms Inventory. *Journal of Consulting Clinical Psychology, 40,* 181–187.

Glover, E. (1925). Notes on oral character formation. *International Journal of Psychoanalysis, 6,* 131–154.

Glover, E. (1926). Einige probleme der psychoanalytischen Characterologie. *Internationale Zeitschrift für Psychoanalyse, 12,* 326–333.

Glover, E. (1928). The etiology of alcoholism. *Proceedings of the Royal Society of Medicine, 21,* 1351–1356.

Gold, J. A., Ryckman, R. M., & Rodda, W. C. (1973). Differential responsiveness of dissonance manipulations by open and closed-minded subjects in a forced compliance situation. *Journal of Social Psychology, 90,* 73–83.

Goldfriend, M. R., & D'Zurilla, T. J. (1969). A behavioral-analytic model for assessing competence. In C. D. Spielberger (Ed.), *Current topics in clinical and community psychology* (pp. 151–196). New York: Academic Press.

Goldiamond, I. (1968). Moral behavior: A functional analysis. *Psychology Today,* pp. 31, 31–34, 70.

Goldiamond, I., & Dyrud, J. (1967). Some applications and implications and behavioral analysis for psychotherapy. In *Research in psychotherapy* (Vol. 3). Washington, DC: American Psychological Association.

Goldstein, A. (1973). Behavior therapy. In R. Corsini (Ed.), *Current psychotherapies.* Itasca, IL: Peacock.

Goldstein, K. (1963). *The organism.* Boston: Beacon Press.

Good, L. R., & Good, K. (1973). An objective measure of the motive to avoid appearing incompetent. *Psychological Reports, 32,* 1075–1078.

Gore, P. M., & Rotter, J. B. (1963). A personality correlate of social action. *Journal of Personality, 31,* 58–64.

Gorney, J. E., & Tobin, S. S. (1969). Experiencing the age: Patterns of reminiscence among the elderly. Reported at the Eighth International Congress of Gerontology, Washington, DC.

Graff, R., & Bradshaw, H. (1970). Relationship of a measure of self-actualization to dormitory assistant effectiveness. *Journal of Counseling Psychology, 17,* 502–505.

Graham, W. K., & Balloun, J. (1973). An empirical test of Maslow's need hierarchy theory. *Journal of Human Psychology, 13,* 97–108.

Granberg, D., & Corrigan, G. (1972). Authoritarianism, dogmatism and orientations toward the Vietnam War. *Sociometry, 35,* (3), 468–476.

Granick, S., & Scheflen, N. A. (1958). Approaches to reliability to projective tests with special reference to the Blacky Pictures Test. *Journal of Consulting Psychology, 22,* 137–141.

Granit, R. (1955). *Receptors and sensory perception.* New Haven, CT: Yale University Press.

Grant, C. H. (1969). Age differences in self-concept from early adulthood through old age. *Proceedings of the 77th Annual Convention of the American Psychological Association, 4,* 717–718.

Graves, T. D. (1961). *Time perspective and the deferred gratification pattern in a tri-ethnic community* (Research Report No. 5, Tri-Ethnic Research Project). Boulder, CO: University of Colorado, Institute of Behavioral Science.

Gray, J. J. (1969). Effect of productivity on primary process thinking and creativity. *Proceedings of the 77th Annual Convention of the American Psychological Association, 4,* 157–158.

Graziano, W. G., Rahe, D. F., & Feldesman, A. B. (1985). Extraversion, social cognition, and the salience of aversiveness in social encounters. *Journal of Personality and Social Psychology, 49,* 971–980.

Greene, D., Sternberg, B., & Lepper, M. R. (1976). Overjustification in a token economy. *Journal of Personality and Social Psychology, 34,* 1219–1234.

Greever, K. B., Tseng, M. S., & Friedland, B. U. (1973). Development of the Social Interest Index. *Journal of Consulting and Clinical Psychology, 41,* 454–458.

Griffin, G. A., & Harlow, H. F. (1966). Effects of three months of total social deprivation on social adjustment and learning in the rhesus monkey. *Child Development, 37,* 533–547.

Grinker, R. R., & Spiegel, J. P. (1945). *Men under stress.* Philadelphia: Blakiston.

Groesbeck, B. L. (1958). Toward description of personality in terms of configurations of motives. In J. W. Atkinson (Ed.), *Motives in fantasy, action, and society.* Princeton, NJ: Van Norstrand.

Grossack, M., Armstrong, T., & Lussieu, G. (1966). Correlates of self-actualization. *Journal of Human Psychology, 37.*

Guilford, J. P. (1959). *Personality.* New York: McGraw-Hill.

Guilford, J. P. (1967). *The nature of human intelligence.* New York: McGraw-Hill.

Guilford, J. P. (1975). Factors and factors of personality. *Psychological Bulletin, 82,* 802–814.

Guilford, J. P. (1977). Will the real factor of extroversion-introversion please stand up? A reply to Eysenck. *Psychological Bulletin, 84,* 412–416.

Guilford, J. P., & Zimmerman, W. S. (1956). Fourteen dimensions of temperament. *Psychological Monograph, 70,* (10).

Guilford, J. P., Zimmerman, W. S., & Guilford, J. P. (1976). *The Guilford-Zimmerman temperament survey handbook: Twenty-five years of research and application.* San Diego, CA: Robert R. Knapp.

Guinan, J., & Foulds, M. (1970). Marathon group: Facilitator of personal growth? *Journal of Counseling Psychology, 17,* 145–149.

Gur, R. C., & Sackheim, H. A. (1979). Self-deception: A concept in search of a phenomenon. *Journal of Personality and Social Psychology, 37,* 147–169.

Gurin, P., Lao, R. C., & Beattie, M. (1969). Internal-external control in the motivational dynamics of Negro youth. *Journal of Social Issues,* 29–53.

Haan, N., & Dey, D. (1974). A longitudinal study of change and sameness in personality development: Adolescence to later adulthood. *International Journal on Aging Human Development, 5,* 11–39.

Haber, R. N., & Albert, R. (1958). The role of situation and picture cues in projective measurement of the achievement motive. In J. W. Atkinson (Ed.), *Motives in fantasy, action, and society.* Princeton, NJ: Van Nostrand.

Hall, C. S., & Lindzey, G. (1970). *Theories of personality.* New York: Wiley.

Hall, C. S. & Lindzey, G. (1985). *Introduction to theories of personality.* New York: Wiley.

Hall, C. S., & Van de Castle, R. L. (1965). An empirical investigation of the castration complex in dreams. *Journal of Personality, 33,* 20–29.

Hall, E. (1965). Ordinal position and success in engagement and marriage. *Journal of Individual Psychology, 21,* 154–158.

Hall, E., & Barger, B. (1964). Background data and expected activities of entering lower division students. *Mental Health Project Bulletin, 7,* May. Gainesville, FL: University of Florida.

Hall, J. A. & Taylor, M. C. (1985). Psychological androgyny and the masculinity × femininity interaction. *Journal of Personality and Social Psychology, 49,* 429–435.

Hall, W. B., & MacKinnon, D. W. (1969). Personality inventory correlates of creativity among architects. *Journal of Applied Psychology, 53,* 322–326.

Hanewitz, W. B. (1978). Police personality: A Jungian perspective. *Crime and Delinquency, 24,* 152–172.

Harlow, H. F. (1953). Mice, monkeys, men, and motives. *Psychological Review, 60,* 23–32.

Harlow, H. F. (1959). Learning and satiation of response in intrinsically motivated complex puzzle performance by monkeys. *Journal of Comparative and Physiological Psychology, 43,* 289–294.

Harlow, H. F., Harlow, M. K., Dodsworth, R. O., & Arling, G. L. (1966). Maternal behavior of rhesus monkeys deprived of mothering and peer associations in infancy. *Proceedings of the American Philosophical Society, 110,* 58–66.

Harlow, H. F., Harlow, M. K., & Meyer, D. R. (1950). Learning motivated by a manipulation drive. *Journal of Experimental Psychology, 40,* 228–234.

Harrington, D. M., & Andersen, S. M. (1981). Creativity, masculinity, femininity, and three models of psychological androgyny. *Journal of Personality and Social Psychology, 41,* 744–757.

Harrison, A. A. (1967). *Response competition and attitude change as a function of repeated stimulus exposure.* Unpublished doctoral dissertation, University of Michigan, Ann Arbor, MI.

Harrison, N. W., & McLaughlin, R. J. (1969). Self-rating validation of the Eysenck Personality Inventory. *British Journal of Social and Clinical Psychology, 8,* 55–58.

Harter, S. (1983). Developmental perspectives on the self-system. In P. H. Mussen (Ed.). *Carmichael's manual of child psychology* (Vol. 4). New York: Wiley.

Hartmann, H., Kris, E., & Loewenstein, R. M. (1947). Comments on the formation of psychic structure. In A. Freud et al. (Eds.), *The psychoanalytic study of the child.* New York: International Universities Press.

Harvey, J. H., & Barnes, R. (1974). Perceived choice as a function of internal-external locus of control. *Journal of Personality, 42,* 437–452.

Havener, P. H., & Izard, C. E. (1962). Unrealistic self-enhancement in paranoid schizophrenics. *Journal of Consulting Psychology, 26,* 65–68.

Hebb, D. O. (1955). Drives and the C.N.S. (conceptual nervous system). *Psychological Review, 62,* 243–254.

Heilbrun, A. B., Jr. (1984). Sex-based models of androgyny: A further cognitive elaboration of competence differences. *Journal of Personality and Social Psychology, 46,* 216–229.

Heilbrun, A. B. (1981). Gender differences in the functional linkage between androgyny, social cognition, and competence. *Journal of Personality and Social Psychology, 41,* 1106–1118.

Helson, R. (1973a). The heroic, the comic, and the tender: Patterns of literary fantasy and their authors. *Journal of Personality, 41,* 163–184.

Helson, R. (1973b). Heroic and tender modes in women authors of fantasy. *Journal of Personality, 41,* 493–512.

Helson, R. (1977). The creative spectrum of authors of fantasy. *Journal of Personality, 45,* 310–326.

Helson, R. (1982). Critics and their texts: An approach to Jung's theory of cognition and personality. *Journal of Personality and Social Psychology, 42,* 409–418.

Helson, R., & Crutchfield, R. S. (1970). Creative types in mathematics. *Journal of Personality, 38,* 177–197.

Helson, R., Mitchell, V., & Moane, G. (1984). Personality and patterns of adherence and nonadherence to the social clock. *Journal of Personalilty and Social Psychology, 46,* 1079–96.

Hendrick, I. (1943). The discussion of the "instinct to master." *Psychoanalysis Quarterly, 12,* 561–565.

Hernandez-Peon, R., Scherrer, H., & Jouvet, M. (1956). Modification of electric activity in the cochlear nucleus during "attention" in unanesthetized cats. *Science, 123,* 331–332.

Hernstein, R. J. (1977). The evolution of behaviorism. *American Psychologist, 32,* 593–603.

Hess, E. H. (1958). Attitude and pupil size. *Scientific American, 212,* 46–54.

Heyns, R. W., Veroff, J., & Atkinson, J. W. (1958). In J. W. Atkinson (Ed.), *Motives in fantasy, action, and society.* Princeton, NJ: Van Nostrand.

Hielbun, A. B. (1981). Gender differences in the functional linkage between androgyny, social cognition, and competence. *Journal of Personality and Social Psychology, 41,* 1106–1118.

Hilgard, E. R. (1956). *Theories of learning* (2nd ed.) New York: Appleton-Century-Crofts.

Hill, W. F. (1978). Effects of mere exposure on preference in nonhuman mammals. *Psychological Bulletin, 85,* 1177–1198.

Hinde, R. A., & Stevenson-Hinde, J. (Eds.). (1973). *Constraints on learning.* New York: Academic Press.

Hjelle, L. A., & Lomastro, J. (1971). Personality differences between high and low dogmatic groups of Catholic seminarians and religious sisters. *Journal for the Scientific Study of Religion, 10,* 49–50.

Hoffman, M. L. (1981). Perspectives on the difference between understanding people and understanding things: The role of affect. In J. H. Flavell & L. Ross (Eds.), *Social cognitive development,* pp. 67–81. Cambridge, MA: Cambridge University Press.

Hoffman, M. L. (1981). Is altruism part of human nature? *Journal of Personality and Social Psychology, 40,* 121–137.

Hogan, R., DeSoto, C. B., & Solano, C. (1977). Traits, tests and personality research. *American Psychologist, 32,* 255–264.

Holahan, C. J., & Moos, K. H. (1985). Life stress and health: Personality, coping and family support in stress resistance. *Journal of Personality and Social Psychology, 49*, 738–747.

Holden, K. B., & Rotter, J. B. (1962). A nonverbal measure of extinction in skill and chance situations. *Journal of Experimental Psychology, 63*, 519–520.

Holland, J. G. (1978). Behaviorism: Part of the problem or part of the solution? *Journal of Applied Behavior Analysis, 11*, 163–174.

Holland, J. M. (1968). Creativity in relation to socioeconomic status, academic achievement, and school, personal and school adjustment in elementary school children. *Dissertation Abstracts, 29*, (I-A), 147.

Hollander, E. P., & Willis, R. H. (1967). Some current issues in the psychology of conformity and nonconformity. *Psychological Bulletin, 68*, 62–76.

Holmes, D. S. (1968). Dimensions of projection. *Psychological Bulletin, 69*, 248–268.

Holmes, D. S. (1974). Investigations of repression: Differential recall of material experimentally or naturally associated with ego threat. *Psychological Bulletin, 81*, 632–653.

Holmes, D. S. (1979). Projection as a defense mechanism. *Psychological Bulletin, 86*, 225–241.

Holmes, D. S., & Jackson, T. H. (1975). Influence of locus of control on interpersonal attraction and affective reactions in situations involving reward and punishment. *Journal of Personality and Social Psychology, 31*, (1), 132–136.

Holmes, D. S., & Shallow, J. R. (1969). Reduced recall after ego threat: Repression or response competition? *Journal of Personality and Social Psychology, 13*, 145–152.

Houston, B. K, & Holmes, D. S. (1974). Effect of avoidant thinking and reappraisal for coping with threat involving temporal uncertainty. *Journal of Personality and Social Psychology, 30*, 382–388.

Howarth, E. (1976). A psychometric investigation of Eysenck's personality inventory. *Journal of Personality Assessment, 40*, 173–185.

Howarth, E., & Browne, J. A. (1971). Investigation of personality factors in a Canadian context: I. Marker structure in personality questionnaire items. *Canadian Journal of Behavioral Science, 3*, 161–173.

Howes, D., & Solomon, R. L. (1950). A note on McGinnies' emotionality and perceptual defense. *Psychological Review, 57*, 229–234.

Howes, D., & Solomon, R. L. (1951). Visual duration threshold as a function of word probability. *Journal of Experimental Psychology, 41*, 401–410.

Hull, C. L. (1943). *Principles of behavior*. New York: Appleton-Century-Crofts.

Hull, C. L. (1945). The place of innate individual and species differences in a natural science theory of behavior. *Psychological Review, 52*, 55–60.

Hull, J. G., & Schwartz, R. M. (1987). *Physiological and attributional responses of hardy individuals to situational stress*. Unpublished manuscript, Dartmouth College, Hanover, N.H.

Hunt, H. F. (1975). Problems in the interpretation of "experimental neurosis." *Psychological Report, 15*, 27–35.

Hunt, H. F. (1975). Behavior therapy for adults. In S. Arieti (Ed.), *American handbook of psychiatry*. New York: Basic Books.

Hunt, H. F., & Dyrud, J. E. (1968). Commentary: Perspective in behavior therapy. *Research in Psychotherapy, 3*, 140–152.

Huntley, C. W. (1940). Judgments of self based upon records of expressive behavior. *Journal of Abnormal and Social Psychology, 35*, 398–427.

Hutt, L. D., & Anderson, J. P. (1967). The relationship between pupil size and recognition threshold. *Psychonomic Science, 9*, 477–478.

Hyman, H. H., & Sheatsley, P. B. (1954). "The authoritarian personality"—a methodological critique. In R. Christie & M. Jahoda (Eds.), *Studies in the scope and method of "the authoritarian personality."* New York: Free Press.

Ickes, W. & Turner, M. (1983). On the social advantages of having an older, opposite-sex sibling: Birth order influences in mixed-sexed dyads. *Journal of Personality and Social Psychology, 45*, 210–222.

Ilardi, R., & May, W. (1968). A reliability study of Shostrom's Personal Orientation Inventory. *Journal of Human Psychology, 8*, 68–72.

Isaacson, G. S., & Landfield, A. W. (1965). Meaningfulness of personal vs. common constructs. *Journal of Individual Psychology, 21*, 160–166.

Iyzett, R. R. (1971). Authoritarianism and attitudes toward the Vietnam war as reflected in behavioral and self report measures. *Journal of Personality and Social Psychology, 17*, 145–148.

Jackson, D. N. (1974). *Personality research from manual*. Goshen, NY: Research Psychologists Press.

Jackson, D. N., & Messick, S. (1958). Content and style in personality assessment. *Psychological Bulletin, 55*, 243–252.

Jackson, D. N. & Panounen, S. V. (1980). Personality structure and assessment. In M. R. Rosenzweig & L. W. Porter (Eds.), *Annual Review of Psychology*. Palo Alto, CA: Annual Reviews.

Jackson, P. W., & Messick, S. (1965). The person, the product, and the response: Conceptual problems in the assessment of creativity. *Journal of Personality, 33*, 309–329.

Jacoby, J. (1967). Open-mindedness and creativity. *Psychological Report, 20*, 822–823.

James, W. (1957). *Internal versus external control of reinforcements as a basic variable in learning theory*. Unpublished doctoral dissertation, Ohio State University, Columbus, OH.

James, W., & Rotter, J. B. (1958). Partial and 100% reinforcement under chance and skill conditions. *Journal of Experimental Psychology, 55*, 397–403.

Janis, I. L., & Gilmore, J. B. (1965). The influence of incentive conditions on the success of role playing in modifying attitudes. *Journal of Personality and Social Psychology, 1*, 17–27.

Jasper, H. H. (1958). Reticular-cortical systems and theories of the integrative action of the brain. In H. F. Harlow & C. N. Woolsey (Eds.), *Biological and biochemical bases of behavior*. Madison, WI: University of Wisconsin Press.

Jenkins, H. M. (1973). Effects of the stimulus-reinforcer relation on selected and unselected responses. In R. A. Hinde & J. Stevenson-Hinde (Eds.), *Constraints on learning*. New York: Academic Press.

Jensen, M. (1987). *Psychobiological factors in the prognosis and treatment of neoplastic disorders*. Unpublished doctoral dissertation, Yale University, New Haven, CT.

Johnson, J. H., Null, C., Butcher, J. N., & Johnson, K. N. Replicated item level factor analysis of the full MMPI. *Journal of Personality and Social Psychology, 49,* 105–114.

Johnson, P. B. (1981). Achievement motivation and success: Does the end justify the means? *Journal of Personality and Social Psychology, 40,* 374–375.

Jones, E. (1955). *The life and work of Sigmund Freud*. New York: Basic Books.

Jones, H. E. (1960). Consistency and change in early maturity. *Vita Humana, 3,* 17–31.

Jung, C. G. (1933a). *Modern man in search of a soul*. New York: Harcourt, Brace, & World.

Jung, C. G. (1933b). *Psychological types*. New York: Harcourt, Brace, & World.

Jung, C. G. (1953a). The psychology of the unconscious. In H. Read, M. Fordham, & G. Adler (Eds.), *Collected works* (Vol. 7). Princeton, NJ: Princeton University Press.

Jung, C. G. (1953b). The relations between the ego and the unconscious. In H. Read, M. Fordham, & G. Adler (Eds.), *Collected works*. Princeton, NJ: Princeton University Press.

Jung, C. G. (1959a). Concerning the archetypes, with special reference to the anima concept. In H. Read, M. Fordham, & G. Adler (Eds.), *Collected works*. Princeton, NJ: Princeton University Press.

Jung, C. G. (1959b). The archetypes and the collective unconscious. In H. Read, M. Fordham, & G. Adler (Eds.), *Collected works* (Vol. 9). Princeton, NJ: Princeton University Press.

Jung, C. G. (1959c). The shadow. In Arion, *Collected works* (Vol. 9, Part II). Princeton, NJ: Princeton University Press.

Jung, C. G. (1960a). On psychic energy. In H. Read, M. Fordham, & G. Adler (Eds.), *Collected works* (Vol. 8). Princeton, NJ: Princeton University Press.

Jung, C. G. (1960b). Synchronicity: An acausal connecting principle. In H. Read, M. Fordham, & G. Adler (Eds.), *Collected works* (Vol. 8). Princeton, NJ: Princeton University Press.

Jung, C. G. (1960c). The stages of life. In H. Read, M. Fordham, & G. Adler (Eds.), *Collected works* (Vol. 8). Princeton, NJ: Princeton University Press.

Jung, C. G. (1961). The theory of psychoanalysis. In H. Read, M. Fordham, & G. Adler (Eds.), *Collected works* (Vol. 4). Princeton, NJ: Princeton University Press.

Kagan, J. (1972). Motives and development. *Journal of Personality and Social Psychology, 22,* 51–66.

Kagan, J., & Moss, H. A. (1962). *Birth to maturity: A study in psychological development*. New York: Wiley.

Katkin, E. S. (1964). The Marlowe-Crowne Social Desirability Scale: Independent of psychopathology? *Psychological Report, 15,* 703–706.

Katz, D., Sarnoff, I., & McClintock, C. (1956). Ego defense and attitude change. *Human Relations, 9,* 27–45.

Katz, I. (1967). The socialization of academic motivation in minority group children. In D. Levine (Ed.), *Nebraska symposium on motivation.* Lincoln, NE: University of Nebraska Press.

Keen, E. (1970). *Three faces of being: Toward an existential clinical psychology.* New York: Appleton-Century-Crofts.

Kelly, E. L. (1955). Consistency of the adult personality. *American Psychologist, 10,* 659–681.

Kelly, G. A. (1955). *The psychology of personal constructs* (Vol. 1). New York: Norton.

Kelly, G. A. (1962). Europe's matrix of decision. In M. R. Jones (Ed.), *Nebraska symposium on motivation.* Lincoln, NE: University of Nebraska Press.

Keniston, K. (1966). *The uncommitted: Alienated youth in American society.* New York: Harcourt, Brace, & World.

Kernberg, O. F. (1976). *Object relations theory and clinical psychoanalysis.* New York: Jason Aronson, Inc.

Kierkegaard, S. (1954). *The sickness unto death.* New York: Doubleday.

Kiesler, C. A., & Pallak, M. S. (1976). Arousal properties of dissonance manipulations. *Psychological Bulletin. 83,* 1014–1025.

Kirsch, I. (1985). Self-efficacy and expectancy: Old wine with new labels. *Journal of Personality and Social Psychology, 49,* 824–830.

Kirscht, J. P., & Dillehay, R. C. (1967). *Dimensions of authoritarianism: A review of research and theory.* Lexington, KY: University of Kentucky Press.

Klavetter, R., & Mogar, R. (1967). Stability and internal consistency of a measure of self actualization. *Psychological Report, 21,* 422–424.

Kleck, R. E., & Wheaton, J. (1967). Dogmatism and responses to opinion-consistent and opinion-inconsistent information. *Journal of Personality and Social Psychology, 5,* 249–252.

Klein, E. B., & Gould, J. (1969). Alienation and identification in college women. *Journal of Personality, 37,* 468–480.

Klein, M. (1948). *Contributions to psychoanalysis.* London: Hogarth Press.

Klein, M. H., Mathieu, P. L., Gendlin, E. T., & Kiesler, D. J. (1969). *The Experiencing Scale: A research and training manual* (Vol. 1). Madison, WI: Wisconsin Psychiatric Institute.

Kleitman, N. (1939). *Sleep and wakefulness.* Chicago: University of Chicago Press.

Kleitman, N., & Ramsaroop, A. (1948). Periodicity in body temperature and heart rate. *Endocrinology, 43,* 1–20.

Kline, P. (1968). Obsessional traits, obsessional symptoms and anal erotism. *British Journal of Medical Psychology, 41,* 299–305.

Klineberg, S. L. (1968). Future time perspective and the preference for delayed reward. *Journal of Personality and Social Psychology, 8,* 253–257.

Klinger, E. (1966). Fantasy need achievement as a motivational construct. *Psychological Bulletin, 66,* 291–308.

Knapp, R. J. (1965). Relationship of a measure of self actualization to neuroticism and extraversion. *Journal of Consulting Psychology, 29,* 168–172.

Knapp, R. J. (1976). Authoritarianism, alienation, and related variables: A correlational and factor-analytic study. *Psychological Bulletin, 83,* 194–212.

Kobasa, S. C. (1979). Stressful life events, personality, and health: An inquiry into hardiness. *Journal of Personality and Social Psychology, 37,* 1–11.

Kobasa, S. C. (1982). Commitment and coping in stress resistance among lawyers. *Journal of Personality and Social Psychology, 42,* 707–717.

Kobasa, S. C., & Maddi, S. R. (1977). Existential personality theory. In R. Corsini (Ed.), *Current personality theories.* Itasca, IL: Peacock.

Kobasa, S. C., Maddi, S. R., & Courington, S. (1981). Personality and constitution as mediators of the stress-illness relationship. *Journal of Personality and Social Psychology, 42,* 168–177.

Kobasa, S. C., Maddi, S. R., Donner, E., Merrick, W., & White, H. (1987). *The personality construct of hardiness.* Unpublished manuscript, University of Chicago, Chicago, IL.

Kobasa, S. C., Maddi, S. R., & Kahn, S. (1982). Hardiness and health: A prospective study. *Journal of Personality and Social Psychology, 42,* 168–177.

Kobasa, S. C., Maddi, S. R., & Kahn, S. (1982). Hardiness and health: A prospective study. *Journal of Personality and Social Psychology, 42,* 168–177.

Kobasa, S. C., Maddi, S. R. and Puccetti, M. Personality and exercise as buffers in the stress-illness relationship. *Journal of Behavioral Medicine, 4,* 391–404.

Kobasa, S. C., Maddi, S. R., Puccetti, M. & Zola, M. (1986). Relative effectiveness of hardiness, exercise and social support as resources against illness. *Journal of Psychosomatic Research, 29,* 525–533.

Kobasa, S. C., & Puccetti, M. C. (1983). Personality and social resources in stress resistance. *Journal of Personality and Social Psychology, 45,* 839–850.

Koenig, F. (1969). Definitions of self and ordinal position of birth. *Journal of Social Psychology, 78,* 287–288.

Koestler, A. (1960). *The lotus and the robot.* London: Hutchinson.

Kohler, W. (1925). *The mentality of apes* (E. Winter, Trans.). New York: Harcourt, Brace.

Kohut, H. (1971). *The analysis of the self.* New York: International Universities Press.

Kohut, H. (1977). *The restoration of the self.* New York: International Universities Press.

Konrad, K. W., & Bagshaw, M. (1970). Effect of novel stimuli on cats reared in a restricted environment. *Journal of Comparative and Physiological Psychology, 70,* 157–164.

Koutrelakos, J. (1968). Authoritarian person's perception of his relationship with his father. *Perceptual Motor Skills, 26,* 967–973.

Kramer, E. (1969). The Eysenck Personality Inventory and self-ratings of extraversion. *Journal of Projective Techniques and Personality Assessment, 33,* 59–62.

Krasner, L., & Ullmann, L. P. (Eds.). (1965). *Research in behavior modification.* New York: Holt, Rinehart & Winston.

Krauskopf, C. J. (1978). Comments on Endler and Magnusson's attempt to redefine personality. *Psychological Bulletin, 85,* 280–283.

Kris, E. (1952). *Psychoanalytic explorations in art.* New York: International Universities Press.

Kuhl, J., & Beckman, J. (eds.). (1985). *Action control: From cognition to behavior.* New York: Springer-Verlag.

Kuhlen, R. G. (1945). Age differences in personality during adult years. *Psychological Bulletin, 42,* 333–358.

Lamiell, T. T., Foss, N. A., Larsen, R. J., & Hempel, A. M. (1983). Studies in intuitive psychology from an idiothetic point of view: Implications for personality theory. *Journal of Personality, 51,* 438–467.

Landfield, A. W. (1977). The Complaint: A confrontation of personal urgency and professional construction. In D. Bannister (Ed.), *Issues and approaches in psychological therapies.* New York: Wiley.

Lao, R. C. (1970). Internal-external control and competent and innovative behavior among Negro college students. *Journal of Personality and Social Psychology, 14,* 263–370.

Lauterbach, C. G. (1958). The Taylor A scale and clinical measures of anxiety. *Journal of Consulting Psychology, 22,* 314.

Lazarus, A. A. (1977). Has behavior therapy outlived its usefulness? *American Psychologist, 32,* 550–554.

Lazarus, R. S., Eriksen, C. W., & Fonda, C. P. (1951). Personality dynamics in auditory perceptual recognition, *Journal of Personality, 19,* 471–582.

Lee, D., & Ehrlich, H. J. (1971). Beliefs about self and others: A test of the dogmatism theory. *Psychological Review, 28,* 919–922.

Lefcourt, H. J. (1965). Risk-taking in Negro and white adults. *Journal of Personality and Social Psychology, 2,* 765–770.

Lefcourt, H. J. (1976). *Locus of control: Current trends in theory and research.* Hillsdale, NJ: Erlbaum.

Lefcourt, H. J., Hogg, E., Struthers, S., & Holmes, C. (1975). Causal attributions as a function of locus of control, initial confidence, and performance outcomes. *Journal of Personality and Social Psychology, 32,* 391–397.

Lefcourt, H. J., & Ladwig, G. W. (1965). The effect of reference group upon Negroes' task persistence in a biracial competitive game. *Journal of Personality and Social Psychology, 1,* 668–671.

Lefcourt, H. J., & Ladwig, G. W. (1966). Alienation in Negro and white reformatory inmates. *Journal of Social Psychology, 68,* 153–157.

Lehr, U., & Rudinger, G. (1969). Consistency and change of social participation in old age. *Human Development, 12,* 255–267.

Leith, G. O. M. (1972). The relationships between intelligence, personality, and creativity under two conditions of stress. *British Journal of Educational Psychologists, 42,* 240–247.

Leith, G. O. M. (1974). Individual differences in learning: Interactions of personality and teaching methods. *Association of Educational Psychologists 1974 Conference Proceedings,* London.

Leitner, L. M., & Cado, S. (1982). Personal constructs and homosexual stress. *Journal of Personality and Social Psychology, 43,* 869–872.

Lemann, G. F. J. (1952). Group characteristics as revealed in sociometric patterns and personality ratings. *Sociometry, 15,* 7–90.

LeMay, M., & Damm, V. (1968). The Personal Orientation Inventory as a measure of self actualization of underachievers. *Measurement and Evaluation in Guidance,* 110–114.

Lepper, M. R., Greene, D., & Nisbett, R. E. (1973). Undermining children's intrinsic interest with extrinsic rewards: A test of the "overjustification" hypothesis. *Journal of Personality and Social Psychology, 28,* 129–137.

Lesnik-Oberstein, M., & Cohen, L. (1984). Cognitive style, sensation-seeking, and assortative mating. *Journal of Personality and Social Psychology, 46,* 112–117.

Lessac, M. S. & Solomon, R. L. (1969). Effects of early isolation on later adaptive behavior of beagles: A methodological demonstration. *Developmental Psychology, 1,* 14–25.

Leventhal, H., Jacobs, R. L., & Kudirka, J. (1964). Authoritarianism, ideology, and political candidate choice. *Journal of Abnormal and Social Psychology, 69,* 539–549.

LeVine, R. (1966). *Dreams and deeds: Achievement motivation in Nigeria.* Chicago: University of Chicago Press.

Levinson, D. (1977). *Psychiatry, 40,* 99–112.

Levinson, D. J., & Huffman, P. E. (1955). Traditional family ideology and its relation to personality. *Journal of Personality, 23,* 251–273.

Liebert, R. M., & Spiegler, M. D. (1982). *Personality: Strategies and issues* (4th ed.). Chicago: Dorsey Press.

Liem, G. R. (1973). Performance and satisfaction as affected by personal control over salient decisions. *Journal of Personality and Social Psychology, 31,* 232–240.

Lindzey, G., & Heineman, P. S. (1955). Thematic Apperception Test: A note on reliability and situational validity. *Journal of Projective Techniques, 19,* 36–42.

Linton, R. (1945). *The cultural background of personality.* New York: Appleton-Century-Crofts.

Liverant, S., & Scodel, A. (1960). Internal and external control as determinants of decision-making under conditions of risk. *Psychological Report, 7,* 59–67.

Loevinger, J., & Knoll, E. (1983). Personality: Stages, traits and the self. In M. R. Rozensweig & L. W. Porter (Eds.), *Annual Review of Psychology.* Palo Alto, CA: Annual Reviews.

Longstreth, L. E. (1970). Birth order and avoidance of dangerous activities. *Developmental Psychology 2,* 154.

Lowell, E. L. (1950). *A methodological study of projectively measured achievement motivation*. Unpublished master's thesis, Wesleyan University, Middleton, CT.

Lubinski, D., Tellegen, A., & Butcher, J. N. (1981). The relationship between androgyny and subjective indicators of emotional well-being. *Journal of Personality and Social Psychology, 40,* 722–730.

Lubinski, D., Tellegen, A., & Butcher, J. N. (1983). Masculinity, femininity, and androgyny viewed and assessed as distinct concepts. *Journal of Personality and Social Psychology, 44,* 428–439.

Lundin, R. W. (1974). *Personality: A behavioral analysis* (2nd ed.). New York: Macmillan.

Maas, H. S., & Kuypers, J. A. (1974). *From 30 to 70: A forty-year longitudinal study of adult life styles and personality.* San Francisco: Jossey-Bass.

Maccoby, M. (1976). *The gamesman.* New York: Simon & Schuster.

MacKinnon, D. W. (1965). Personality and the realization of creative potential. *American Psychologist, 20,* 273–281.

MacKinnon, D. W., & Dukes, W. (1962). Repression. In L. Postman (Ed.), *Psychology in the making.* New York: Knopf.

Maddi, S. R. (1961a). Exploratory behavior and variation-seeking in man. In D. W. Fiske & S. R. Maddi (Eds.), *Functions of varied experience.* Homewood, IL: Dorsey Press.

Maddi, S. R. (1961b). Unexpectedness, affective tone, and behavior. In D. W. Fiske & S. R. Maddi (Eds.), *Functions of varied experience.* Homewood, IL: Dorsey Press.

Maddi, S. R. (1961c). Affective tone during environmental regularity and change. *Journal of Abnormal and Social Psychology, 62,* 338–345.

Maddi, S. R. (1963). Humanistic psychology: Allport and Murray. In J. M. Wepman & R. W. Heine (Eds.), *Concepts of personality.* Chicago: Aldine.

Maddi, S. R. (1965). Motivational aspects of creativity. *Journal of Personality, 33,* 303–347.

Maddi, S. R. (1967). The existential neurosis. *Journal of Abnormal Psychology, 72,* 311–325.

Maddi, S. R. (1968a). *The seeking and avoiding of variety.* Unpublished manuscript, University of Chicago.

Maddi, S. R. (1968b). Meaning, novelty, and affect: Comments on Zajonc's paper. *Journal of Personality and Social Psychology* (Monogr. Suppl.), *9* (2), 28–30.

Maddi, S. R. (1970). The search for meaning. In M. Page (Ed.), *Nebraska symposium on motivation.* Lincoln, NE: University of Nebraska Press.

Maddi, S. R. (1971). Novelty, meaning, and intrinsic motivation. In H. I. Day, D. E. Berlyne, & D. E. Hunt (Eds.), *Intrinsic motivation: A new direction in motivation.* Toronto: Holt, Rinehart & Winston.

Maddi, S. R. (1979). The uses of theorizing in personology. In E. Staub (Ed.), *Personality: Basic issues and current research.* Englewood Cliffs, NJ: Prentice-Hall.

Maddi, S. R. (1984). Personology for the 1980s. In R. A. Zucker, J. Aronoff, & A. I. Rabin (Eds.), *Personality and the prediction of behavior.* New York: Academic Press.

Maddi. S. R. (1986). Existential psychotherapy. In J. Garske & S. Lynn (Eds.), *Contemporary psychotherapy,* Columbus, OH: Merrill.

Maddi, S. R. (1988). On the problem of accepting facticity and pursuing possibility. In S. B. Messer, L. A. Sass, & R. L. Woolfolk (Eds.). *Hermeneutics and psychological theory: Interpretive perspectives on personality, psychotherapy and psychopathology.* New Brunswick, NJ: Rutgers University Press.

Maddi, S. R., & Andrews, S. (1966). The need for variety in fantasy and self-description. *Journal of Personality, 34,* 610–625.

Maddi, S. R., & Berne, N. (1964). Novelty of productions and desire for novelty as active and passive forms of the need for variety. *Journal of Personality, 32,* 270–277.

Maddi, S. R., Charlens, A. M., Maddi, D., & Smith, A. (1962). Effects of monotony and novelty on imaginative productions. *Journal of Personality, 30,* 513–527.

Maddi, S. R., & Costa, P. T., Jr. (1972). *Humanism in personology: Allport, Maslow, Murray.* Chicago: Aldine-Atherton.

Maddi, S. R., Hoover, M., & Kobasa, S. C. (1979). *Alienation and exploratory behavior.* Unpublished manuscript, University of Chicago.

Maddi, S. R., Hoover, M., & Kobasa, S. C. (1982). Alienation and exploratory behavior. *Journal of Personality and Social Psychology, 42,* 884–890.

Maddi, S. R., Kobasa, S. C., & Hoover, M. (1979). An alienation test. *Journal of Humanistic Psychology, 19,* 73–76.

Maddi, S. R., & Kobasa, S. C. (1984). *The hardy executive: Health under stress.* Homewood, IL: Dow Jones-Irwin.

Maddi, S. R., & Propst, B. (1971). Activation theory and personality. In S. R. Maddi (Ed.), *Perspectives on personality: A comparative approach.* Boston: Little, Brown.

Maddi, S. R., Propst, B., & Feldinger, I. (1965). Three expressions of the need for variety. *Journal of Personality, 33,* 82–98.

Mahoney, J., & Hartnett, J. (1973). Self-actualization and self-ideal discrepancy. *Journal of Psychology, 85,* 37–42.

Major, B., Carnevale, P. J. D., & Deaux, K. (1981). A different perspective on androgyny: Evaluations of masculine and feminine characteristics. *Journal of Personality and Social Psychology, 41,* 988–1001.

Mancuso, J. C. (1977). *Current motivational models in the elaboration of personal construct theory.* In A. W. Landfield (Ed.), *Nebraska symposium on motivation.* Lincoln, NE: University of Nebraska Press.

Mandler, G., & Kessen, W. (1959). *The language of psychology.* New York: Wiley.

Marceil, J. C. (1977). Implicit dimensions of idiography and nomothesis. *American Psychologist, 32,* 1046–1055.

Marcia, J. E. (1966). Development and validation of ego-identity status. *Journal of Personality and Social Psychology, 3,* 551–558.

Markus, H., & Wurf, E. (1987). The dynamic self-concept: A social psychological perspective. In M. R. Rosenzweig & L. W. Porter (Eds.), *Annual Review of Psychology,* Palo Alto, CA: Annual Reviews.

Marshall, I. N. (1967). Extraversion and libido in Jung and Cattell. *Journal of Analytical Psychology, 12,* 115–136.

Martin, R. A., & Lefcourt, H. M. (1983). Sense of humor as a moderator of the relation between stressors and moods. *Journal of Personality and Social Psychology, 45,* 1313–1324.

Maslach, C., Stapp, J., & Santee, R. T. (1985). Individualization: Conceptual analysis and assessment. *Journal of Personality and Social Psychology, 49,* 729–738.

Masling, J., O'Neill, R., & Katkin, E. S. (1982). Autonomic arousal, interpersonal climate and orality. *Journal of Personality and Social Psychology, 42,* 529–534.

Masling, J., Weiss, L., & Rothschild, B. (1968). Relationships of oral imagery to yielding behavior and birth order. *Journal of Consulting and Clinical Psychology, 32,* 89–91.

Maslow, A. H. (1955). Deficiency motivation and growth motivation. In M. R. Jones (Ed.), *Nebraska symposium on motivation.* Lincoln, NE: University of Nebraska Press.

Maslow, A. H. (1962). Some basic propositions of a growth and self-actualization psychology. In *Perceiving, behaving, becoming: A new focus for education.* Washington, DC: Yearbook of the Association for Supervision and Curriculum Development.

Maslow, A. H. (1967). A theory of metamotivation: The biological rooting of the value-life. *Journal of Human Psychology, 7,* 93–127.

Maslow, A. H. (1968). *Toward a psychology of being* (2nd Ed.). Princeton, NJ: Van Nostrand.

Masserman, J. H. (1943). *Behavior and neurosis: An experimental psychoanalytic approach to psychobiological principles.* Chicago: University of Chicago Press.

Matarazzo, J. D., & Saslow, G. (1960). Psychological and related characteristics of smokers and nonsmokers. *Psychological Bulletin, 57,* 493–513.

May, R. (1958). Contributions of existential psychotherapy. In R. May, E. Angel, & H. F. Ellenberger (Eds.), *Existence: A new dimension in psychiatry and psychology.* New York: Basic Books.

McAdams, D. P. (1982). Experiences of intimacy and power: Relationship between social motives and autobiographical memory. *Journal of Personality and Social Psychology, 42,* 292–302.

McAdams, D. P. (1985). *Power, intimacy, and the life story: Personological inquiries into identity.* Homewood, IL: Dorsey Press.

McAdams, D. P., & Constantian, C. A. (1983). Intimacy and affiliation motives in daily living: An experience sampling analysis. *Journal of Personality and Social Psychology, 45,* 851–861.

McAdams, D. P., Healy, S., & Krause, S. (1984). Social motives and patterns of friendship. *Journal of Personality and Social Psychology, 47,* 828–838.

McAdams, D. P., & Powers, J. (1981). Themes of intimacy in behavior and thought. *Journal of Personality and Social Psychology, 40,* 573–587.

McCarroll, J. E., Mitchell, K. M., Carpenter, R. J., & Anderson, J. P. (1967). Analysis of three stimulation-seeking scales. *Psychological Report, 21,* 853–856.

McClain, E. (1970). Further validation of the Personal Orientation Inventory: Assessment of the self-actualization of school counselors. *Journal of Consulting and Clinical Psychology, 35,* 21–22.

McCleary, R. A., & Lazarus, R. S. (1949). Autonomic discrimination without awareness. *Journal of Personality, 18,* 171–179.

McClelland, D. C. (1951). *Personality.* New York: Dryden Press.

McClelland, D. C. (1958). Risk taking in children with high and low need for achievement. In J. W. Atkinson (Ed.), *Motives in fantasy, action, and society.* Princeton, NJ: Van Nostrand.

McClelland, D. C. (1961). *The achieving society.* Princeton, NJ: Van Nostrand.

McClelland, D. C. (1971a). *Assessing human motivation.* New York: General Learning Press (No. 4021V00).

McClelland, D. C. (1971b). *Motivational trends in society.* New York: General Learning Press (No. 4020V00).

McClelland, D. C. (1975). *Power: the inner experience.* New York: Irvington.

McClelland, D. C. (1978). Managing motivation to expand human freedom. *American Psychologist, 33,* 201–210.

McClelland, D. C. (1981). Is personality consistent? In A. I. Rabin, J. Aronoff, A. M. Barclay, & R. A. Zucker (Eds.), *Further explorations in personality* (pp. 87–113). New York: Wiley.

McClelland, D. C., Atkinson, M. W., & Clark, R. A. (1949). The projective expression of needs: III. The effect of ego-involvement success and failure on perception. *Journal of Psychology, 27,* 311–330.

McClelland, D. C., Atkinson, J. W., Clark, R. A., & Lowell, E. L. (1953). *The achievement motive.* New York: Appleton-Century-Crofts.

McClelland, D. C., Davis, W. N., Kalin, R., & Wanner, H. E. (1971). *Alcohol and human motivation.* New York: Free Press.

McClelland, D. C., & Pilon, D. A. (1983). Sources of adult motives in patterns of parent behavior in early childhood. *Journal of Personality and Social Psychology, 44,* 564–574.

McClelland, D. C., Sturr, J. F., Knapp, R. H., & Wendt, H. W. (1958). Obligations to self and to society in the United States and Germany. *Journal of Abnormal and Social Psychology, 56,* 245–255.

McGinnies, E. (1949). Emotionality and perceptual defense. *Psychological Review, 56,* 244–251.

McGuire, W. J. (1984). Search for the self: Going beyond self-esteem and the reactive self. In R. A. Zucker, J. Aronoff, & R. I. Rabin (Eds.), *Personality and the prediction of behavior.* New York: Academic Press.

McGuire, W. J., McGuire, C. V., & Cheever, J. (1986). The self in society: Effects on social contexts on the sense of self. *British Journal of Social Psychology.*

McQuaid, J. (1967). A note on trends in answer to Cattell personality questionnaire by Scottish subjects. *British Journal of Psychology, 58,* 455–458.

Medin, D. L. (1972). Role of reinforcement in discrimination learning set in monkeys. *Psychological Bulletin, 77,* 305–318.

Medinnus, G. R., & Curtis, F. J. (1963). The relation between maternal self-acceptance and child acceptance. *Journal of Counseling Psychology, 27,* 542–544.

Megargee, E. I., & Parker, G. V. (1968). An exploration of the equivalence of Murrayan needs as assessed by the Adjective Check List, the TAT and Edwards Personal Preference Schedule. *Journal of Clinical Psychology, 24,* 47–51.

Mehlman, J. (1972). The "floating signifier": From Levi-Strauss to Lacan. *Yale French Studies, 48,* 10–37.

Mehrabian, A., & Ksionzky, S. (1970). Models for affiliative and conformity behavior. *Psychological Bulletin, 74,* 110–126.

Mehrabian, A., & Russell, J. A. (1973). A measure of arousal seeking tendency. *Environmental Behavior, 5,* 315–333.

Meichenbaum, D. (1976). Cognitive behavior and modification. In J. T. Spence, R. C. Carson, & J. W. Thibaut (Eds.), *Behavioral approaches to therapy.* Morristown, NJ: General Learning Press.

Melendy, M. R. (1901). *Maiden, wife, and mother: How to attain health, beauty, happiness.* Chicago: American Literary and Musical Association.

Melzack, R., & Wall, P. D. (1968). Gate control theory of pain. In A. Soulairac, J. Cahn, & J. Charpentier (Eds.), *Pain.* New York: Academic Press.

Mendelsohn, M. B., Linden, J., Gruen, G., & Curran, J. (1974). Heterosexual pairing and sibling configuration. *Journal of Individual Psychology, 30,* 202–210.

Mikol, B. (1960). The enjoyment of new musical systems. In M. Rokeach, *The open and closed mind.* New York: Basic Books.

Miller, N. E. (1959). Liberalization of basic S-R concepts: Extension to conflict behavior, motivation, and social learning. In S. Koch (Ed.), *Psychology: A study of science* (Vol. 2). New York: McGraw-Hill.

Miller, N. E., & Dollard, J. C. (1941). *Social learning and imitation.* New Haven, CT: Yale University Press.

Mischel, T. (1964). Personal constructs, rules and the logic of clinical activity. *Psychological Review, 71,* 180–192.

Mischel, W. (1958). Preference for delayed reinforcement: An experimental study of a cultural observation. *Journal of Abnormal and Social Psychology, 56,* 57–61.

Mischel, W. (1961). Delay of gratification, need for achievement, and acquiescence in another culture. *Journal of Abnormal and Social Psychology, 62,* 543–552.

Mischel, W. (1966). Theory and research on the antecedents of self-imposed delay of reward. In B. A. Maher (Ed.), *Progress in experimental personality research* (Vol. 3) New York: Academic Press.

Mischel, W. (1968). *Personality and assessment.* New York: Wiley.

Mischel, W. (1971). *Introduction to personality.* New York: Holt, Rinehart & Winston.

Mischel, W. (1973a). On the empirical dilemmas of psychodynamic approaches. *Journal of Abnormal Psychology, 82,* 335–344.

Mischel, W. (1973b). Toward a cognitive social learning reconceptualization of personality. *Psychological Review, 80,* 252–283.

Mischel, W. (1981). *Introduction to personality* (2nd ed.). New York: Holt, Rinehart & Winston.

Mischel, W. (1981). *Introduction to personality.* (3rd ed.). New York: Holt, Rinehart & Winston.

Mischel, W., & Ebbesen, E. (1970). Attention in delay of gratification. *Journal of Personality and Social Psychology, 16,* 329–337.

Mischel, W., Ebbesen, E. B., & Roskoff, Z. (1972). Cognitive and attentional mechanisms in delay of gratification. *Journal of Personality and Social Psychology, 21,* 204–218.

Mitchell, H. E. (1973, May). *Authoritarian punitiveness in simulated juror decision-making: The good guys didn't always wear white hats.* Paper presented at the Midwestern Psychological Association Convention.

Modell, A. H. (1975). A narcissistic defense against affects and the illusion of self-sufficiency. *International Journal of Psychoanalysis, 56,* (3), 275–282.

Modell, A. H. (1976). The holding environment and the therapeutic action of psychoanalysis. *Journal of the American Psychological Association, 24,* (2), 285–307.

Moos, R. H. (1968). Situational analysis of a therapeutic community milieu. *Journal of Abnormal Psychology, 73,* 49–61.

Moos, R. H. (1969). Sources of variance in responses to questionnaires and in behavior. *Journal of Abnormal Psychology, 74,* 405–412.

Moos, R. H. (1970). Differential effects of psychiatric ward settings on patient change. *Journal of Nervous and Mental Disease, 5,* 316–321.

Morgan, C. D., & Murray, H. A. (1935). A method of investigating fantasies: The Thematic Apperception Test. *Archives of Neurological Psychiatry, 34,* 289–306.

Mosak, H. H. (1971). Life style. In *Techniques for behavior change: Applications of Adlerian theory.* Springfield, IL: Charles C Thomas.

Mowrer, O. H. (1940). An experimental analogue of "regression" with incidental observations on "reaction formation." *Journal of Abnormal and Social Psychology, 35,* 56–87.

Mowrer, O. H. (1950). *Learning theory and personality dynamics.* New York: Ronald Press.

Munroe, R. (1955). *Schools of psychoanalytic thought.* New York: Holt.

Munsinger, H., & Kessen, W. (1964). Uncertainty, structure and preference. *Psychological Monograph, 78,* (9).

Murray, H. A. (1938). *Explorations in personality: A clinical and experimental study of fifty men of college age.* New York: Oxford.

Murray, H. A. (1943). *Thematic Apperception Test.* Cambridge, MA: Harvard University Press.

Murray, H. A. (1954). Toward a classification of interaction. In T. Parsons & E. A. Shils (Eds.), *Toward a general theory of action.* Cambridge, MA: Harvard University Press.

Murray, H. A. (1959). Preparations for the scaffold of a comprehensive system. In S. Koch (Ed.), *Psychology: A study of a science* (Vol. 3). New York: McGraw-Hill.

Murray, H. A., & Kluckhohn, C. (1956). Outline of a conception of personality. In C. Kluckhohn, H. A. Murray, & D. M. Schneider (Eds.), *Personality in nature, society, and culture* (2nd ed.). New York: Knopf.

Murstein, B. I. (1956). The projection of hostility on the Rorschach and as a result of ego-threat. *Journal of Projective Techniques, 20*, 418–428.

Murstein, B. I. (1961). The relation of the Famous Sayings Test to the self- and ideal-self-adjustment. *Journal of Consulting Psychology, 25*, 368.

Myers, I. B. (1962). *Manual (1962), the Myers-Briggs type indicator*. Princeton, NJ: Educational Testing Service.

Naditch, M. P. (1975). Locus of control and drinking behavior in a sample of men in army basic training. *Journal of Consulting and Clinical Psychology, 43*, 96.

Nalven, F. B. (1967). Some perceptional decision-making correlates of repressive and intellectualizing defenses. *Journal of Clinical Psychology, 23*, 446–448.

Natsoulas, T. (1965). Converging operations for perceptual defense. *Psychological Bulletin, 64*, 393–401.

Neugarten, B. L. (1964). A developmental view of adult personality. In J. E. Birren (Ed.), *Relations of development and aging*. Springfield, IL: Charles C Thomas.

Neugarten, B. L. (1979). Time, age and the life cycle. *American Journal of Psychiatry, 136*, 887–894.

Neugarten, B. L. (1980). Acting one's age: New rules for old. *Psychology Today, 13*, 66–80.

Neuman, G. G., & Salvatore, J. C. (1958). The Blacky Test and psychoanalytic theory: A factor-analytic approach to validity. *Journal of Projective Techniques, 22*, 427–431.

Nickel, T. W. (1974). The attribution of intention as a critical factor in the relationship between frustration and aggression. *Journal of Personality, 42*, 482–492.

Norman, W. T. (1963). Toward an adequate taxonomy of personality attributes: Replicated factor structure in peer nomination personality ratings. *Journal of Abnormal and Social Psychology, 66*, 574–583.

Nowicki, S., & Roundtree, J. (1974). Correlates of locus of control in secondary age students. *Developmental Psychology, 10*, 33–37.

Nunnally, J. (1971). Visual attention to novel pictures. In H. I. Day, D. E. Berlyne, & D. S. Hunt (Eds.), *Intrinsic motivation: A new direction in education*. Toronto: Holt, Rinehart, & Winston.

O'Connell, W. E. (1960). The adaptive function of wit and humor. *Journal of Abnormal and Social Psychology, 61*, 263–270.

Odell, M. (1959). *Personality correlates of independence and conformity*. Unpublished master's thesis. Ohio State University, Columbus, OH.

Olds, J. (1975). Mapping the mind onto the brain. In F. G. Worden, J. P. Swazey, & G. Adelman (Eds.), *The neurosciences: Paths of discovery*. Cambridge, MA: Colonial Press.

O'Leary, A. (1985). Self-efficacy and health. *Behavior Research and Therapy, 23*, 437–451.

O'Leary, J. T., & Coben, L. A. (1958). The reticular core—1957. *Physiology Review, 38*, 243–276.

Oliveus, D. (1978). *Aggression in the schools*. New York: Halsted.

Orlofsky, J. L., Marcia, J. E., & Lesser, I. M. (1973). Ego identity status and the intimacy versus isolation crisis in young adulthood. *Journal of Pesonality and Social Psychology, 27*, 211–219.

Osgood, C. (1962). Studies on the generality of affect meaning systems. *American Psychologist, 17*, 10–28.

Page, H. A., & Markowitz, G. (1955). The relationship of defensiveness to rating scale bias. *Journal of Psychology, 40*, 431–435.

Paloutzian, R. F. (1981). Purpose in life and value changes following conversion. *Journal of Personality and Social Psychology, 41*, 1153–1160.

Pavlov, I. P. (1927). *Conditioned reflexes*. Oxford, England: Oxford University Press.

Pawlicki, R. E., & Almquist, C. (1973). Authoritarianism, locus of control, and tolerance of ambiguity as reflected in membership and nonmembership in a women's liberation group. *Psychological Reports, 32*, 1331–1337.

Peabody, D. (1966). Authoritarianism scales and response bias. *Psychological Bulletin, 65*, 11–23.

Peabody, D. (1984). Personality dimensions through trait inferences. *Journal of Personality and Social Psychology, 46*, 384–403.

Pearson, P. H. (1969). Openness to experience as related to organismic valuing. *Journal of Personality, 37*, 481–496.

Pearson, P. H. (1974). Conceptualizing and measuring openness to experience in the context of psychotherapy. In D. A. Wexler & L. N. Rice (Eds.), *Innovations in client-centered therapy*. New York: Wiley.

Peck, R. F., & Havighurst, R. J. (1960). *The psychology of character development*. New York: Wiley.

Penn, N. (1964). Experience improvements on an analogue of repression paradigm. *Psychological Record, 14*, 185–196.

Peplau, L. A. (1976). Impact of fear of success and sex-role attitudes on women's competitive achievement. *Journal of Personality and Social Psychology, 34*, 561–568.

Perls, F. (1969a) *Gestalt therapy verbation*. Lafayette, CA: Real People Press.

Perls, F. (1969b). *In and out of the garbage pail*. Lafayette, CA: Real People Press.

Perls, F. (1969c). *Ego, humor and aggression*. New York: Random House.

Pervin, L. A. (1983). The stasis and flow of behavior: Toward a theory of goals. In M. M. Page (Ed.), *Personality: Current theory and research*. Lincoln, NE: University of Nebraska Press.

Pervin, L. V. (1970). *Personality: Theory, assessment, and research*. New York: Wiley.

Peters, R. S. (1958). *The concept of motivation*. New York: Humanities Press.

Petersen, R. C., & Hergenhahn, B. R. (1968). Test of cognitive dissonance theory in an elementary school setting. *Psychological Report, 22*, 199–202.

Pettit, T. F. (1969). Anality and time. *Journal of Consulting and Clinical Psychology, 33*, 170–174.

Phares, E. J. (1957). Expectancy changes in skill and chance situations. *Journal of Abnormal and Social Psychology, 54*, 339–342.

Phares, E. J. (1962). Perceptual threshold decrements as a function of skill and chance expectancies. *Journal of Psychology, 53,* 399–407.

Phares, E. J. (1976). *Locus of control in personality.* Morristown, NJ: General Learning Press.

Phillips, W. S., & Greene, J. E. (1939). A preliminary study of the relationship of age, hobbies, and civil status to neuroticism among women teachers. *Journal of Educational Psychology, 30,* 440–444.

Pierce, J. W. (1959). *The educational motivation of superior students who do not achieve in high school.* Washington, DC: U.S. Department of Health, Education, and Welfare, Office of Education.

Pines, H. A., & Julian, J. W. (1972). Effects of task and social demands on locus of control differences in information processing. *Journal of Personality, 40,* 407–416.

Pishkin, V., & Thorne, F. C. (1973). A factorial study of existential state reactions. *Journal of Clinical Psychology, 29,* 392–402.

Plant, W. T., Telford, C. W., & Thomas, J. W. (1965). Some personality differences between dogmatic and non-dogmatic groups. *Journal of Social Psychology, 67,* 67–75.

Platt, J. J., & Eisenman, R. (1968). Internal-external control of reinforcement, time perspective, adjustment, and anxiety. *Journal of Genetic Psychology, 79,* 121–128.

Poe, C. A. (1969). Convergent and discriminant validation of measures of personal needs. *Journal Educational Measurement, 6,* 103–107.

Pollak, J. M. (1979). Obsessive-compulsive personality: A review. *Psychological Bulletin, 86,* 225–241.

Porter, C. A., & Suedfeld, P. (1981). Integrative complexity in the correspondence of literary figures: Effects of personal and societal stress. *Journal of Personality and Social Psychology, 40,* 321–330.

Porter, N., Geis, F. L., Cooper, E., & Newman, E. (1985). Androgyny and leadership in mixed-sex groups. *Journal of Personality and Social Psychology, 49,* 808–823.

Postman, L., Bruner, J. S., & McGinnies, E. (1948). Personal value as selective factors in perception. *Journal of Abnormal and Social Psychology, 43,* 142–154.

Powell, F. A. (1962). Open- and closed-mindedness and the ability to differentiate source and message. *Journal of Abnormal and Social Psychology, 65,* 61–64.

Procink, T. J., & Breem, L. J. (1974). Locus of control, study habits and attitudes, and college academic performance. *Journal of Personality and Social Psychology, 88,* 91–95.

Procink, T. J., & Breem, L. J. (1975). Defensive externality and its relation to academic performance. *Journal of Personality and Social Psychology, 31,* 549–556.

Pryon, B., & Kafer, J. (1967). Recall of nonsense and attitudinal rigidity. *Journal of Personality and Social Psychology, 5,* 463–466.

Qualls, P. J. (1983). The physiological measurement of imagery: An overview. *Imagination, Cognition and Personality, 2,* 89–101.

Rachman, S. (1973). The effects of psychological treatment. In H. Eysenck (Ed.), *Handbook of abnormal psychology.* New York: Basic Books.

Radloff, R. (1961). Opinion evaluation and affiliation. *Journal of Abnormal and Social Psychology, 62,* 578–585.

Rado, S. (1959). Obsessive behavior. In S. Arieti (Ed.), *American handbook of psychiatry* (Vol. 1). New York: Basic Books.

Rank, O. (1929). *The trauma of birth.* New York: Harcourt, Brace.

Rank, O. (1945). *Will therapy and truth and reality.* New York: Knopf.

Rapaport, D. (1958). The theory of ego autonomy: A generalization. *Bulletin of Menninger Clinic, 22,* 13–25.

Rappaport, H., Enrich, K., & Wilson, A. (1985). Relation between ego identity and temporal perspective. *Journal of Personality and Social Psychology, 48,* 1609–1620.

Raven, B. H., & Fishbein, M. (1961). Acceptance of punishment and change in belief. *Journal of Abnormal and Social Psychology, 63,* 411–416.

Razik, T. A. (1965). *Bibliography of creativity studies and related areas.* Buffalo, NY: State University of New York at Buffalo.

Reich, W. (1931). Character formation and the phobias of childhood. *International Journal of Psychoanalysis, 12,* 219–230.

Reich, W. (1933). *Charakteranalyse.* Berlin: Selbstverlag des Verfassers.

Reimanis, G. (1966). Childhood experience memories and anomie in adults and college students. *Journal of Individual Psychology, 22,* 56–64.

Reimanis, G. (1974). Psychosocial development, anomie, and mood. *Journal of Personality and Social Psychology, 29,* 355–357.

Restle, F., Andrews, M., & Rokeach, M. (1964). Differences between open- and closed-minded subjects on learning-set and oddity problems. *Journal of Abnormal and Social Psychology, 68,* 648–654.

Reuman, D. A. (1982). Ipsative behavioral variability and the quality of thematic apperceptive measurement of the achievement motive. *Journal of Personality and Social Psychology, 42,* 1098–1110.

Reuman, D. A., Alwin, D. F., & Veroff, J. (1984). Assessing the validity of the achievement motive in the presence of random measurement error. *Journal of Personality and Social Psychology, 47,* 1347–1362.

Rhine, R. J. (1967). Some problems in dissonance theory research on information selectivity. *Psychological Bulletin, 68,* 21–28.

Rice, L. N., & Wagstaff, A. K. (1967). Client voice quality and expressive style as indexes of productive psychotherapy. *Journal of Consulting Psychology, 31,* 557–563.

Richek, J. G., Mayo, C. D., & Pirgean, H. B. (1970). Dogmatism, religiosity, and mental health in college students. *Mental Health, 54,* 572–574.

Riesen, A. H. (1961). Stimulation as a requirement for growth and function in behavioral development. In D. W. Fiske & S. R. Maddi (Eds.), *Functions of varied experience.* Homewood, IL: Dorsey Press.

Robinson, S. A. (1968). The development of a female form of the Blacky Pictures. *Journal Projective Techniques and Personality Assessment, 32,* 74–80.

Robinson, S. A., & Hendrix, V. L. (1966). The Blacky Test and psychoanalytic theory: Another factor-analytic approach to validity. *Journal of Projective Techniques and Personality Assessment, 30,* 597–603.

Rogers, C. R. (1959). A theory of therapy, personality, and interpersonal relationships, as developed in the client-centered framework. In S. Koch (Ed.), *Psychology: A study of a science* (Vol. 3). New York: McGraw-Hill.

Rogers, C. R. (1961). *On becoming a person.* Boston: Houghton Mifflin.

Rogers, C. R. (1963). Actualizing tendency in relation to "motives" and to consciousness. In M. R. Jones (Ed.), *Nebraska symposium on motivation.* Lincoln, NE: University of Nebraska Press.

Rogers, C. R. (1977). *Carl Rogers on personal power: Inner strength and its revolutionary impact.* New York: Delacorte Press.

Rohrer, J. H., & Edmonson, M. S. (Eds.). (1960). *The eighth generation.* New York: Harper.

Rohrer, L. G. & Widiger, T. A. (1983). Personality structure and assessment. In M. R. Rosenzweig & L. W. Porter (Eds.), *Annual Review of Psychology.* Palo Alto, CA: Annual Reviews.

Rohrer, L. G., & Widiger, T. A. (1983). Personality structure and assessment. *Annual Review of Psychology, 34,* 431–463.

Rokeach, M. (1945). Studies in beauty: II. Some determiners of the perception of beauty in women. *Journal of Social Psychology, 22,* 155–169.

Rokeach, M. (1960). *The open and closed mind.* New York: Basic Books.

Rokeach, M., Swanson, T. S., & Denny, M. R. (1960). The role of past experience: A comparison between chess players and non-chess players. In M. Rokeach, *The open and closed mind.* New York: Basic Books.

Rorschach, T. (1921). *Psychodiagnostik.* Bern, Switzerland: Huber.

Rosen, B. C. (1961). Family structure and achievement motivation. *American Sociological Review, 26,* 574–585.

Rosenbaum, M. E., Horne, W. C., & Chalmers, D. K. (1962). Level of self-esteem and the learning of imitation and non-imitation. *Journal of Personality, 30,* 147–156.

Rosenberg, L. A. (1962). Idealization of self and social adjustment. *Journal of Consulting Psychology, 26,* 487.

Rosenberg, M. J. (1965). When dissonance fails: On eliminating evaluation apprehension from attitude measurement. *Journal of Personality and Social Psychology, 1,* 28–42.

Rosenman, S. (1955). Changes in the representations of self, others and interrelationship in therapy. *Journal of Counseling Psychology, 2,* 271–277.

Rosenow, C., & Whyte, A. H. (1931). The ordinal position of problem children. *American Journal of Orthopsychiatry, 1,* 430–444.

Rosenzweig, S. (1933). The recall of finished and unfinished tasks as affected by the purpose with which they were performed. *Psychological Bulletin, 30,* 698.

Rosenzweig, S. (1943). An experimental study of "repression" with special reference to need-persistive and ego-defensive reactions to frustrations. *Journal of Experimental Psychology, 32,* 64–74.

Rosenzweig, S., & Mason, G. (1934). An experimental study of memory in relation to the theory of repression. *British Journal of Psychology, 24,* 247–265.

Rotter, J. B. (1954). *Social learning and clinical psychology.* Englewood Cliffs, NJ: Prentice-Hall.

Rotter, J. B. (1964). *Clinical psychology* (2nd ed.). Englewood Cliffs, NJ: Prentice-Hall.

Rotter, J. B. (1966). Generalized expectancies for internal versus external control of reinforcement. *Psychological Monograph, 80,* (1, Whole No. 609).

Rotter, J. B., Chance, J. E., & Phares, E. J. (Eds.). (1972). *Applications of a social learning theory of personality.* New York: Holt, Rinehart & Winston.

Rotter, J. B., Liverant, S., & Crowne, D. P. (1961). The growth and extinction of expectancies in chance controlled and skill tasks. *Journal of Personality, 52,* 161–177.

Rotter, J. B., Seeman, M., & Liverant, S. (1962). Internal versus external control of reinforcements: A major variable in behavior theory. In N. F. Washburne (Ed.), *Decisions, values, and groups* (Vol. 2, pp. 473–516). London: Pergamon Press.

Runyan, W. M. (1982). In defense of the case study method. *American Journal of Orthopsychiatry, 52,* 440–446.

Rutter, M. (1984). Continuities and discontinuities in socioemotional development. In R. N. Emde & R. J. Harmon (Eds.), *Continuities and discontinuities in development* (pp. 41-68). New York: Plenum.

Rybak, W. S., Sadnavitch, J. M., & Mason, B. J. (1968). Psycho-social changes in personality during foster grandparents program. *Journal of American Geriatrics Society, 16,* 956–959.

Ryckman, R. M., Rodda, W. C., & Sherman, M. F. (1972). Locus of control and expertise relevant as determinants of changes in opinion about student activism. *Journal of Social Psychology, 88,* 107–114.

Sackheim, H. A., & Gur, R. C. (1978). Self-deception, self-confrontation, and consciousness. In G. E. Schwartz & D. Shapiro (Eds.), *Consciousness and self-regulation: Advances in research* (Vol. 2). New York: Plenum.

Sackheim, H. A., & Gur, R. C. (1979). Self-deception, other-deception, and self-reported psychopathology. *Journal of Consulting and Clinical Psychology, 47,* 213–215.

Sackheim, H. A., & Gur, R. C. (1985). Voice recognition and the ontological status of self-deception. *Journal of Personality and Social Psychology, 48,* 1365–1368.

Sadave, S. W., & Forsyth, R. (1977). Person-environment interaction and college student drug use: A multivariate longitudinal study. *Genetic Psychology Monographs, 96,* 211–245.

Salas, R. G. (1967). Some characteristics of the Eysenck Personality inventory (EPI) found under Australian conditions. *Australian Military Forces Research Report, 6.*

Sampson, E. E. (1962). Birth order, need achievement, and conformity. *Journal of Abnormal and Social Psychology, 64,* 155–159.

Sampson, E. E. (1965). The study of ordinal position: Antecedents and outcomes. In B. A. Maher (Ed.), *Progress in experimental personality research*. New York: Academic Press.

Samuels, I. (1959). Reticular mechanisms and behavior. *Psychological Bulletin, 56,* 1–25.

Sanford, N. (Ed.). (1962). *The American College*. New York: Wiley.

Sarason, I. G., (1957a). The effect of anxiety and two kinds of failure on serial learning. *Journal of Personality, 25,* 383–392.

Sarason, I. G., (1957b). Effect of anxiety and two kinds of motivating instructions on verbal learning. *Journal of Abnormal and Social Psychology, 54,* 166–171.

Sarason, I.G. (1958). Interrelationships among individual differences variables, behavior in psychotherapy, and verbal conditioning. *Journal of Abnormal and Social Psychology, 56,* 339–344.

Sarnoff, I. (1951). Identification with the aggressor: Some personality correlates of anti-Semitism among Jews. *Journal of Personality, 20,* 199–218.

Sarnoff, I. (1960). Reaction formation and cynicism. *Journal of Personality, 28,* 129–143.

Sarnoff, I. (1962). *Personality: Dynamics and development*. New York: Wiley.

Sarnoff, I., & Corwin, S. M. (1959). Castration anxiety and the fear of death. *Journal of Personality, 27,* 374–385.

Sarnoff, I., & Katz, D. (1954). The motivational bases of attitude change. *Journal of Abnormal and Social Psychology, 49,* 115–124.

Sartre, J. P. (1956). *Being and nothingness*. New York: Philosophical Library.

Scarpetti, W. L. (1974). Autonomic concomitants of aggressive behavior in repressors and sensitizers: A social learning approach. *Journal of Personality and Social Psychology, 30,* 772–781.

Schachter, S. (1959). *The psychology of affiliation: Experimental studies of the sources of gregariousness*. Stanford, CA: Stanford University Press.

Schachter, S. (1963). Birth order, eminence, and higher education. *American Sociological Review, 28,* 757–767.

Schachter, S. (1964). Birth order and sociometric choice. *Journal of Abnormal and Social Psychology, 68,* 452–456.

Schaefer, C. E. (1969). The self-concept of creative adolescents. *Journal of Psychology, 72,* 233–242.

Schaeffer, D. L. (1968). Addenda to an annotated bibliography of the Blacky Test (1949–1967). *Journal of Projective Techniques and Personality Assessment, 32,* 55–555.

Schooler, C. (1961). Birth order and schizophrenia. *Archives of Genetic Psychiatry, 4,* 91–97.

Schooler, C. (1964). Birth order and hospitalization for schizophrenia. *Journal of Abnormal and Social Psychology, 69,* 574–579.

Schubert, D. S. P. (1959a). Impulsivity and other personality characteristics of cigarette smokers. *American Psychologist, 14,* 354–355.

Schubert, D. S. P. (1959b). Personality implications of cigarette smoking among college students. *Journal of Consulting Psychology, 23*, 376.

Schulberg, H. (1961). Authoritarianism, tendency to agree, and interpersonal perception. *Journal of Abnormal and Social Psychology, 63*, 101–108.

Schultz, D. P. (1964). Spontaneous alternation behavior in humans: Implications for psychological research. *Psychological Bulletin, 62*, 394–400.

Schwartz, B. J. (1955). The measurement of castration anxiety over loss of love. *Journal of Personality, 24*, 204–219.

Schwartz, B. J. (1956). An empirical test of two Freudian hypotheses concerning castration anxiety. *Journal of Personality, 24*, 318–327.

Schwartz, D. W., & Carp, S. A. (1967). Field dependence in a geriatric population. *Perceptual and Motor Skills, 24*, 495–504.

Schwartz, M., & Gaines, L. (1974). Self-actualization and the human tendency for varied experience. *Journal of Personality Assessment, 38*, 423–427.

Sears, R. R. (1936). Experimental studies of projection: I. Attribution of traits. *Journal of Social Psychology, 7*, 151–163.

Sears, R. R. (1943). *Survey of objective studies of psychoanalytic concepts.* New York: Social Science Research Council.

Sears, R. R. (1944). Experimental analysis of psychoanalytic phenomena. In J. McV. Hunt (Ed.), *Personality and the behavior disorders* (Vol. 1). New York: Ronald Press.

Sears, R. R. (1950). Personality. In C. P. Stone & D. W. Taylor (Eds.), *Annual review of psychology.* Stanford, CA: Annual Reviews, Inc.

Sechrest, L. (1963). The psychology of personal constructs: George Kelly. In J. M. Wepman & R. W. Heine (Eds.), *Concepts of personality.* Chicago: Aldine.

Sechrest, L. (1968). Personal constructs and personal characteristics. *Journal of Individual Psychology, 24*, 162–166.

Sechrest, L. (1977). Personal constructs theory. In R. Corsini (Ed.), *Current personality theories.* Itasca, IL: Peacock.

Seeman, M. (1963). Alienation and social learning in a reformatory. *American Journal of Sociology, 69*, 270–284.

Seeman, M., & Evans, J. (1962). Alienation and learning in a hospital setting. *American Sociological Review, 27*, 772–782.

Sells, S. B., Demaree, R. G., & Will, D. P. (1971). Dimensions of personality: II. Separate factor structures in Guilford and Cattell trait markers. *Multivariate Behavior Research, 6*, 136–165.

Sells, S. B., & Roff, M. (1963). Peer acceptance-rejection and birth order. *American Psychologist, 18*, 335.

Senniker, P., & Hendrick, C. (1983). Androgyny and helping behavior. *Journal of Personality and Social Psychology, 45*, 916–925.

Shapiro, K. J., & Alexander, I. E. (1969). Extraversion-introversion, affiliation, and anxiety. *Journal of Personality, 37*, 387–406.

Sharpe, D., & Viney, L. (1973). Weltanschaung and the Purpose of Life Test. *Journal of Clinical Psychology, 29*, 489–491.

Shaw, J. S. (1982). Psychological androgyny and stressful life events. *Journal of Personality and Social Psychology, 42,* 145–153.

Shaw, L., & Sichel, H. (1971). *Accident proneness.* New York: Pergamon Press.

Sheerer, E. (1949). Analysis of the relationship between acceptance of and respect for self and acceptance of and respect for others. *Journal of Consulting Psychology, 13,* 169–175.

Sheffield, F. D., & Roby, T. B. (1950). Reward value of a non-nutrient sweet taste. *Journal of Comparative and Physiological Psychology, 43,* 471–481.

Sherman, S. J. (1973). Internal-exernal control and its relationship to attitude change under different social influence techniques. *Journal of Personality and Social Psychology, 23,* 23–29.

Shlien, J. M. (1962). The self-concept in relation to behavior: Theoretical and empirical research. *Religious Education* (Research Suppl.).

Shlien, J. M. (1963). Phenomenology and personality. In J. M. Wepman & R. W. Heine (Eds.), *Concepts of personality.* Chicago: Aldine.

Shlien, J. M. (1987). A countertheory of transference. *Person Centered Review, 2,* 15–49.

Shostrom, E. (1965). An inventory for the measurement of self actualization. *Educational and Psychological Measurement, 24,* 207–218.

Shostrom, E. (1966). *Manual for the Personal Orientation Inventory (POI): An inventory for the measurement of self actualization.* San Diego: Educational and Industrial Testing Service.

Shostrom, E., & Knapp, R. (1966). The relationship of a measure of self actualization (POI) to a measure of pathology (MMPI) and to therapeutic growth. *American Journal of Psychotherapy, 20,* 193–202.

Shweder, R. A. (1975). How relevant is an individual differences theory of personality? *Journal of Personality, 43,* 455–483.

Shweder, R. A. (1982). Fact & artifact in trait perception: The systematic distortion hypothesis. In B. A. Maher (Ed.), *Progress in experimental personality research* (Vol. II). New York: Academic Press.

Sidis, B. (1908). An experimental study of sleep. *Journal of Abnormal and Social Psychology, 3,* 1–32, 63–96, 170–207.

Siegelman, M. (1968). "Origins" of extraversion-introversion. *Journal of Psychology, 69,* 85–91.

Silverman, I. (1964). Defense of dissonance theory: Reply to Chapanis & Chapanis *Psychological Bulletin, 62,* 205–209.

Silverman, L. H. (1976). Psychoanalytic theory: "The reports of my death are greatly exaggerated." *American Psychologist, 31,* 621–637.

Singer, J. L., & Kolligian, J., Jr. (1987). Personality: Developments in the study of private experience. In M. R. Rosenzweig & L. W. Porter (Eds.), *Annual Review of Psychology, 38,* 533–574.

Skinner, B. F. (1938). *The behavior of organisms: An experimental analysis.* New York: Appleton-Century-Crofts.

Skinner, B. F. (1950). Are theories of learning necessary? *Psychological Review, 57,* 193–216.

Skinner, B. F. (1953). *Science and human behavior.* New York: Macmillan.

Skinner, B. F. (1957). *Verbal behavior.* New York: Appleton-Century-Crofts.

Skinner, B. F. (1961). *Cumulative record.* New York: Appleton-Century-Crofts.

Skinner, B. F. (1971). *Beyond freedom and dignity.* New York: Knopf.

Skinner, B. F. (1974). *About behaviorism.* New York: Alfred A. Knopf.

Skinner, B. F., Howarth, E., & Browne, J. A. (1970). Note on the role of neuroticism and extroversion in the "nice personality" stereotype. *Psychological Report, 26,* 445–446.

Slettoo, R. F. (1934). Sibling position and juvenile delinquency. *American Journal of Sociology, 39,* 657–669.

Smart, R. G. (1963). Alcoholism, birth order, and family size. *Journal of Abnormal and Social Psychology, 66,* 17–23.

Smith, M. B. (1966). Explorations in competence: A study of Peace Corps teachers in Ghana. *American Psychologist, 21,* 555–566.

Smith, M. B. (1968). Competence and socialization. In J. A. Clausen (Ed.), *Socialization and society.* Boston: Little, Brown.

Soderstrom, D., & Wright, E. W. (1977). Religious orientation and meaning in life. *Journal of Clinical Psychology, 33,* (1), 65–68.

Solomon, R. L., & Howes, D. (1951). Word frequency, personal values, and visual duration thresholds. *Psychological Review, 58,* 256–270.

Sosis, R. H. (1974). Internal-external control and the perception of responsibility of another for an accident. *Journal of Personality and Social Psychology, 30,* 1031–1034.

Spanos, N. P. (1948). Witchcraft in histories of psychiatry: A critical analysis and an alternative conceptualization. *Psychological Bulletin, 85,* 417–439.

Spence, K. W. (1948). The postulates and methods of "behaviorism." *Psychological Review, 55,* 67–78.

Spence, K. W., & Spence, J. T. (1966). Sex and anxiety differences in eyelid conditioning. *Psychological Bulletin, 65,* 137–142.

Spielberger, C. D. (1962). Role of awareness in verbal conditioning. In C. W. Eriksen (Ed.), *Behavior and awareness.* Durham, NC: Duke University Press.

Spranger, E. (1928). Types of men (W. Pigors, Trans.). Halle, Germany: Niemeyer.

Staffieri, J. R. (1970). Birth order and creativity. *Journal of Clinical Psychology, 26,* 65–66.

Staub, E. (1978). *Positive social behavior and morality: Vol. 1. Social and personal influences.* New York: Academic Press.

Stein, M. I. (1968). Creativity. In E. F. Borgatta & W. W. Lambert (Eds.), *Handbook of personality theory and research.* Chicago: Rand McNally.

Stephenson, W. (1950). The significance of Q-technique for the study of personality. In M. L. Reymert (Ed.), *Feeling and emotions: The Mooseheart symposium.* New York: McGraw-Hill.

Stephenson, W. (1953). *The Study of behavior: Q-technique and its methodology.* Chicago: University of Chicago Press.

Stern, G. G. (1958). *Preliminary record: Activities index—College Characteristics Index.* Syracuse, NY: Syracuse University Psychological Research Center.

Stevenson, I. (1957). Is the human personality more plastic in infancy and childhood? *American Journal of Psychiatry, 14,* 152–161.

Stewart, R. A. C. (1968). Academic performance and components of self actualization. *Perceptual and Motor Skills, 26,* 918.

Stock, D. (1949). An investigation into the interrelations between self-concept and feelings directed toward persons and groups. *Journal of Consulting Psychology, 13,* 176–180.

Stotland, E., & Cottrell, N. B. (1961). Self-esteem, group interaction, and group influence on performance. *Journal of Personality, 29,* 273–284.

Strassberg, D. S. (1973). Relationships among locus of control, anxiety, and valued goal expectations. *Journal of Consulting and Clinical Psychology, 2,* 319.

Strickland, B. R. (1965). The prediction of social action from a dimension of internal-external control. *Journal of Social Psychology, 66,* 353–358.

Strickland, B. R. (1978). Internal-external expectancies and health-related behaviors. *Journal of Consulting and Clinical Psychology, 46,* (6) 1192–1211.

Strickland, B. R., & Jenkins, O. (1964). Simple motor performance under positive and negative approval motivations. *Perceptual and Motor Skills, 19,* 599–605.

Stong, E. K., Jr. (1943). Vocational interests of men and women. Stanford, CA: Stanford University Press.

Suinn, R. M. (1961). The relationship between self-acceptance and acceptance of others: A learning theory analysis. *Journal of Abnormal and Social Psychology, 63,* 37–42.

Sukemune, S., Haruki, Y., & Kashiwagi, K. (1977). Studies on social learning in Japan. *American Psychologist, 32,* 924–933.

Swann, W. B., Jr., & Read, S. J. (1981). Acquiring self-knowledge: The search for feedback that fits. *Journal of Personality and Social Psychology, 41,* 1119–1128.

Swanson, G. E. (1951). Some effects of member object-relationships on small groups. *Human Relations, 4,* 355–380.

Symonds, P. M. (1961). *From adolescent to adult.* New York: Columbia University Press.

Taft, R. (1967). Extraversion, neuroticism and expressive behavior: An application of Wallach's moderator effect to handwriting analysis. *Journal of Personality, 35,* 570–584.

Taulbee, E. S., & Stenmark, D. E. (1968). The Blacky Pictures Test: A comprehensive annotated and indexed bibliography (1949–1967). *Journal of Projective Techniques and Personality Assessment, 32,* 102–137.

Taylor, C. B., Bandura, A. Ewart, C. K., Miller, N. H., & DeBusk, R. F. (1985). Exercise testing to enhance wives' confidence in their husbands' cardiac capabilities soon after clinically uncomplicated acute myocardial infarction. *American Journal of Cardiology, 55,* 635–638.

Taylor, C. W. (1963). *Creativity: Progress and potential.* New York: McGraw-Hill.

Taylor, I. A., & Getzels, J. W. (1975). *Perspectives in creativity.* Chicago: Aldine.

Taylor, J. A. (1953). A personality scale of manifest anxiety. *Journal of Abnormal and Social Psychology, 48*, 285–290.

Tedeschi, J. T., Smith, R. B., III, & Brown, R. C., Jr. (1974). A reinterpretation of research on aggression. *Psychological Bulletin, 81*, 540–562.

Terman, L. M., & Miles, G. C. (1936). *Sex and personality.* New York: McGraw-Hill.

Terman, L. M., & Oden, M. H. (1959). *The gifted group at mid-life.* Palo Alto, CA: Stanford University Press.

Tesch, S. A., & Whitbourne, S. K. (1982). Intimacy and identity status in young adults. *Journal of Personality and Social Psychology, 43*, 1041–1051.

Tetlock, P. E. (1984). Cognitive style and political belief systems in the British House of Commons. *Journal of Personality and Social Psychology, 46*, 365–375.

Thayer, R. E. (1967). Measurement of activation through self-report. *Psychological Reports, 20*, 663–678.

Thompson, W. R., & Schaefer, T. (1961). Early environmental stimulation. In D. W. Fiske & S. R. Maddi (Eds.), *Functions of varied experience.* Homewood, IL: Dorsey Press.

Thorndike, E. L., & Lorge, I. (1944). *The teacher's word book of 30,000 words.* New York: Teachers College, Columbia University.

Thorne, F. C. (1973). The Existential Study: A measure of existential status. *Journal of Clinical Psychology, 29*, 387–392.

Thorne, F. C., & Pishkin, V. (1973). The Existential Study. *Journal of Clinical Psychology, 29*, 389–410.

Tillich, P. (1952). *The courage to be.* New Haven, CT: Yale University Press.

Tittler, B. (1974). A behavioral approach to the measurement of openness to experience. *Journal of Personality Assessment, 38*, 335–340.

Tobacyk, J. (1981). Personality differentiation, effectiveness of personality integration, and mood in female college students. *Journal of Personality and Social Psychology, 41*, 348–356.

Toder, N. L., & Marcia, J. E. (1973). Ego identity status and response to conformity pressure in college women. *Journal of Personality and Social Psychology, 26*, 287–294.

Tolman, E. C. (1948). Cognitive maps in rats and men. *Psychological Review, 55*, 189–208.

Toman, W. (1959). Family constellation as a character and marriage determinant. *International Journal of Psychoanalysis, 40*, 316–319.

Tompkins, S. S. (1979). Script theory: Differential magnifications of affects. In *Nebraska symposium on motivation.* Lincoln, NE: University of Nebraska Press.

Trapp, E. P., & Kausler, P. H. (1958). Test anxiety level and goal-setting behavior. *Journal of Consulting Psychology, 22*, 31–34.

Tribich, D., & Messer, S. (1974). Psychoanalytic character type and status of authority as determiners of suggestibility. *Journal of Consulting and Clinical Psychology, 42*, 842–848.

Trope, Y. (1986). Self-enhancement and self-assessment in achievement behavior. In R. M. Sorrentino & E. T. Higgins (Eds.), *Handbook of motivation and cognition: Foundations of social behavior*. New York: Guilford.

Truax, C. B. (1957). The repression response to implied failure as a function of the hysteria-psychasthenia index. *Journal of Abnormal and Social Psychology, 55*, 188–193.

Tuddenham, R. D. (1959). Constancy of personality ratings over two decades. *Genetic Psychology Monograph, 60*, 3–29.

Tudor, T., & Holmes, D. (1973). Differential recall of successes and failures: Its relationship to defensiveness, achievement motivation, and anxiety. *Journal of Experimental Research in Personality, 7*, 208–224.

Tunnell, G. (1981). Sex role and cognitive schemata: Person perception in feminine and androgynous women. *Journal of Personality and Social Psychology, 40*, 1126–1136.

Turner, R. H., & Vanderlippe, R. H. (1958). Self-ideal congruence as an index of adjustment. *Journal of Abnormal and Social Psychology, 57*, 202–206.

Tyler, L. E. (1978). *Individuality: Human possibilities and personal choice in the psychosocial development of men and women*. San Francisco: Jossey-Bass.

Uleman, J. S. (1965). *A new TAT measure of the need for power*. Unpublished doctoral dissertation, Harvard University Press, Cambridge, MA.

Ulrich, R. E., & Azrin, N. H. (1962). Reflective fighting in response to aversive stimulation. *Journal of Experimental Analysis of Behavior, 5*, 511–520.

Ulrich, R. E., Dulaney, S., Kucera, T., & Colasacco, A. (1972). Side effects of aversive control. In R. M. Gilbert & J. D. Keehn (Eds.), *Schedule effects*. Toronto: University of Toronto Press.

Vacchiano, R. B. (1977). Dogmatism. In T. Blass (Ed.), *Personality variables in social behavior*. Hillsdale, NJ: Erlbaum.

Vacchiano, R. B., Strauss, P. S., & Schiffman, D. C. (1968). Personality correlates of dogmatism. *Journal of Consulting Psychology, 32*, 83–85.

Veroff, J. S. (1958). A scoring manual for the power motive. In J. W. Atkinson (Ed.), *Motives in fantasy, action, and society*. Princeton, NJ: Van Nostrand.

Verplanck, W. S., & Skinner, B. F. (1954). In W. K. Estes, S. Koch, K. MacCorquodale, P. E. Meehl, C. G. Mueller, W. N. Schoenfeld, & W. S. Verplanck (Eds.), *Modern learning theory*. New York: Appleton-Century-Crofts.

Vidulich, R. N., & Kaiman, I. P. (1961). The effects of the information source status and dogmatism upon conformity behavior. *Journal of Abnormal and Social Psychology, 63*, 639–642.

Vitz, P. C. (1966). Affect as a function of stimulus variation. *Journal of Experimental Psychology, 68*, 176–183.

Volpe, J. (1969). *The practice of behavior therapy*. Elmsford, NJ: Pergamon Press.

Vroom, V. H. (1959). Projection, negation, and self-concept. *Human Relations, 12*, 235–244.

Wallach, M. A., & Gahm, R. C. (1960). Personality functions of graphic construction and expansiveness. *Journal of Personality, 28*, 73–88.

Wankowski, J. A. (1973). *Temperament, motivation and academic achievement.* Birmingham, AL: University of Birmingham Educational Survey and Counseling Unit.

Warehime, R. G., & Foulds, M. L. (1973). Social desirability response sets and a measure of self-actualization. *Journal of Human Psychology, 13*, 89–95.

Warehime, R. G., Routh, D. K., & Foulds, M. L. (1974). Knowledge about self-actualization and the presentation of self as self-actualized. *Journal of Personality and Social Psychology, 30*, 155–162.

Warren, J. R. (1966). Birth order and social behavior. *Psychological Bulletin, 65*, 38–49.

Waterman, C. K., Buebel, M. E., & Waterman, A. S. (1970). Relationship between resolution of the identity crisis and outcomes of previous psychosocial crises. *Proceedings of the 78th Annual Convention of the American Psychological Association, 5*, 467–468.

Waters, L. K. (1967). Stability of Edwards PPS need scale scores and profiles over a seven-week period. *USNAMI Report, 1019*, 6 pp.

Watson, J. B. (1924). *Behaviorism.* New York: Norton.

Watson, J. B. (1929). *Psychology from the standpoint of a behaviorist* (3rd ed.). Philadelphia: Lippincott.

Watts, A. W. (1957). *The way of Zen.* New York: Pantheon.

Weber, M. (1930). *The Protestant ethic and the spirit of capitalism* (T. Parsons, Trans.). New York: Scribner.

Weigel, R. G., & Frazier, J. E. (1968). The effects of "feeling" and "behavior" instructions on responses to the Edwards Personal Preference Schedule. *Journal of Educational Measurement, 5*, 337–338.

Weinberger, D. A., Schwartz, G., & Davidson, R. (1979). Low-anxious, high-anxious and repressive coping styles: Psychometric patterns and behavioral and physiological responses to stress. *Journal of Abnormal Psychology, 88*, 369–380.

Welker, W. I . (1959). Escape, exploratory, and food seeking responses of rats in a novel situation. *Journal of Comparative and Physiological Psychology, 52*, 96–111.

Wells, W., & Goldstein, R. (1964). Sears' study of projection: Replications and critique. *Journal of Social Psychology, 64*, 169–179.

Welsh, G. S. (1956). Factor dimensions A and R. In G. S. Welsh & W. G. Dahlstrom (Eds.), *Basic readings on the MMPI in psychology and medicine.* Minneapolis, MN: University of Minnesota Press.

Wessman, A. E., & Ricks, D. F. (1966). *Mood and personality.* New York: Holt, Rinehart & Winston.

Wexler, D. (1974). Self actualization and cognitive processes. *Journal of Consulting and Clinical Psychology, 42*, 47–53.

Wherry, R. J., & Waters, L. K. (1968). Motivational constructs: A factor analysis of feelings. *Educational and Psychological Measurement, 28,* 1035–1046.

White, R. W. (1959). Motivation reconsidered: The concept of competence. *Psychological Review, 66,* 297–333.

White, R. W. (1960). Competence and the psychosexual stages of development. In M. R. Jones (Ed.), *Nebraska symposium on motivation.* Lincoln, NE: University of Nebraska Press.

White, R. W. (1961). Competence and the psychosexual stages of development. In D. W. Fiske & S. R. Maddi (Eds.), *Functions of varied experience.* Homewood, IL: Dorsey Press.

White, R. W. (1963). Ego and reality in psychoanalytic theory. *Psychological Issues, 3,* 1–210.

Willington, A. M., & Strickland, B. R. (1965). Need for approval and simple motor performance. *Perceptual and Motor Skills, 21,* 879–884.

Wilson, G. (1977). Introversion-extroversion. In T. Blass (Ed.), *Personality variables in social behavior.* Hillsdale, NJ: Erlbaum.

Wilson, G. & O'Leary, V. (1980). *Principles of behavior therapy.* Englewood Cliffs, NJ: Prentice-Hall.

Winter, D. G. (1971). The need for power in college men. In D. C. McClelland, W. N. Davis, R. Kalin, & H. E. Wanner (Eds.), *Alcohol and human motivation.* New York: Free Press.

Winter, D. G. (1973). *The Power motive.* New York: Free Press.

Witkin, H. A., Dyk, R. B., Faterson, H. F., Goodenough, D. R., & Karp, S. A. (1962). *Psychological differentiation.* New York: Wiley.

Witkin, H. A., Lewis, H. G., Hertzman, M., Machover, K., Meissner, P. B., & Wapner, S. (1954). *Personality through perception.* New York: Harper.

Wolff, P. H. (1959). Observations on newborn infants. *Psychosomatic Medicine, 21,* 100–118.

Wolk, S., & DuCette, J. (1974). Intentional performance and incidental learning as a function of personality and task dimensions. *Journal of Personality and Social Psychology, 29,* 91–101.

Wolpe, J. (1958). *Psychotherapy by reciprocal inhibition.* Stanford, CA: Stanford University Press.

Wolpe, J. (1969). *The practice of behavior therapy.* New York: Pergamon Press.

Wolpe, J. (1978). Cognition and causation in human behavior and its therapy. *American Psychologist, 33,* 437–446.

Wolpe, J. (1978). Self-efficacy theory and psychotherapeutic change: A square peg in a round hole. In S. Rochman (Ed.), *Advances in behavior research and therapy* (Vol. 1). Oxford: Pergamon Press.

Wolters, B. J. (1976). The "Need for Variety" by Maddi et al. in connection with creativity. *Gedrag: Tijdschrift voor Psychologic, 4* (5–6), 307–324.

Worthen, R., & O'Connell, W. E. (1969). Social interest and humor. *International Journal of Social Psychiatry, 15,* 179–188.

Wright, B. P. (1940). *Selfishness, guilt feelings, and social distance.* Unpublished doctoral dissertation, State University of Iowa, Iowa City, IA.

Wrightsman, L. S., Jr. (1960). Effects of waiting with others on changes in level of felt anxiety. *Journal of Abnormal and Social Psychology, 61,* 216–222.

Yalom, I. D. (1980). *Existential psychotherapy.* New York: Basic Books.

Yarrow, L. J. (1961). Maternal deprivation: Toward an empirical and conceptual reevaluation. *Psychological Bulletin, 58,* 459–490.

Yerkes, R. M., & Dodson, J. D. (1908). The relation of strength of stimulus to rapidity of habit formation. *Journal of Comparative and Neurological Psychology, 18,* 459–482.

Yufit, R. I. (1969). Variations of intimacy and isolation. *Journal of Projective Techniques and Personality Assessment, 33,* 49–58.

Zaccaria, J. S., & Weir, W. R. (1967). A comparison of alcoholics and selected samples of non-alcoholics in terms of a positive concept of mental health. *Journal of Social Psychology, 71,* 151–157.

Zagona, S. V., & Zurcher, L. (1964). Participation, interaction, and role behavior in groups selected from the extremes of the open-closed cognitive continuum. *Journal of Psychology, 58,* 225–264.

Zagona, S. V., & Zurcher, L. A. (1965). The relationship of verbal ability and other cognitive variables to the open-closed cognitive dimension. *Journal of Psychology, 60,* 213–219.

Zajonc, R. B. (1968). Attitudinal effects of mere exposure. *Journal of Personality and Social Psychology, 9,* Monograph Suppl. 2).

Zeigarnik, B. (1927). über das Behalten von erledigten und unreledigten Handlungen. *Psychologische Forschrift, 9,* 1–85.

Zeller, A. (1950). An experimental analogue of repression: II. The effect of individual failure and success on memory measured by relearning. *Journal of Experimental Psychology, 40,* 411–422.

Zeller, A. (1951). An experimental analogue of repression: III. The effect of induced failure and success on memory measured by relearning. *Journal of Experimental Psychology, 42,* 32–38.

Zucker, R. A., Manosevitz, M., & Langon, R. I. (1968). Birth order, anxiety, and affiliation during a crisis. *Journal of Personality and Social Psychology, 8,* 354–359.

Zuckerman, M., Kolin, E. A., Price, L., & Zoob, I. (1964). Development of a sensation-seeking scale. *Journal of Consulting Psychology, 28,* 477–482.

Zuckerman, M., Persky, H., Miller, L., & Levin, B. (1969). Contrasting effects of understimulation (sensory deprivation) and overstimulation (high stimulus variety). *Proceedings of the 77th Annual Convention of the American Psychological Association, 4,* 319–320.

Zuckerman, M., & Wheeler, L. (1975). To dispel fantasies about the fantasy-based measure of fear of success. *Psychological Bulletin, 82,* 932–946.

Index

ABOUT THE AUTHOR

Salvatore R. Maddi is currently Professor of Psychology in Social Ecology at the University of California in Irvine. Prior to this position, Dr. Maddi was for many years Professor in the Department of Behavioral Sciences at the University of Chicago. He received a B.A. degree from Brooklyn College in 1954 and a Ph.D. in Clinical Psychology from Harvard University in 1960. The author of numerous books and articles, Dr. Maddi has been President of Divisions Ten (Psychology and the Arts) and One (General Psychology) of the American Psychological Associations. He has also been a visiting professor at Harvard University, the Educational Testing Service, and the University of Rome, as well as a Fulbright Scholar in Brazil. He founded the Hardiness Institute, Inc., a consulting company of which he is President, that offers various services concerning personal and organizational development and stress management.

Más Joven que Nunca

Más Joven que Nunca

Recursos rejuvenecedores para la mujer

Las medidas
que usted
puede tomar
ahora para
lucir y sentirse
como nueva

Por los Editores de **PREVENTION** Magazine Health Books en Español

Doug Dollemore, Mark Giuliucci, Sid Kirchheimer,
Ellen Michaud, Elisabeth Torg, Laura Wallace-Smith, Mark D. Wisniewski

Editado por Patricia Fisher y Abel Delgado

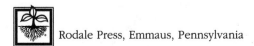

Rodale Press, Emmaus, Pennsylvania

NOTA

La intención de este libro es que se use como referencia solamente, y no como un manual médico. La información contenida aquí está diseñada para ayudarle a usted a tomar decisiones inteligentes sobre su salud. No tiene la intención de ser una sustitución para cualquier tratamiento que le hubiera sido recetado por su médico. Si usted sospecha que tiene algún problema médico, le exhortamos a buscar asistencia médica competente.

Library of Congress Cataloging-in-Publication Data

Más joven que nunca: recursos rejuvenecedores para la mujer / las medidas que usted puede tomar ahora para lucir y sentirse como nueva / por los editores de Prevention Magazine Health Books en español.

    p. cm.
Incluye índice.
ISBN 0–87596–444–3 tapa dura

1. Middle aged women—Health and hygiene. 2. Aged women—Health and hygiene.
3. Middle aged women—Mental health. 4. Aged women—Mental health. 5. Longevity.
I. Prevention Magazine Health Books. II. Title.
RA778.A3318 1997
613'.04244—dc20   97–6592
                                     CIP

2 4 6 8 10 9 7 5 3   tapa dura

> *Nuestro objetivo es demostrar que toda persona puede usar*
> *el poder de su cuerpo y de su mente para mejorar su vida.*
> *El mensaje en cada página de nuestros libros y revistas es:*
> *¡Usted sí puede mejorar su vida!*

MÁS JOVEN QUE NUNCA: PERSONAL EDITORIAL Y DE DISEÑO

EDITOR DE PREVENTION® MAGAZINE HEALTH BOOKS EN ESPAÑOL: ABEL DELGADO

TRADUCCIÓN AL ESPAÑOL Y MAQUETACIÓN: GRANDA INTERNATIONAL INTERPRETERS, BELLFLOWER, CALIFORNIA

ÍNDICE EN ESPAÑOL: FRANCINE CRONSHAW

EDITORA EJECUTIVA SÉNIOR: PATRICIA FISHER

EDITOR SÉNIOR: RUSSELL WILD

ESCRITORES: DOUG DOLLEMORE, MARK GIULIUCCI, SID KIRCHHEIMER, ELLEN MICHAUD, ELISABETH TORG, LAURA WALLACE-SMITH, MARK D. WISNIEWSKI

ESCRITORES COLABORADORES: STEFAN BECHTEL, JEFF CSATARI, LISA DELANEY, TIM FRIEND, MARK GOLIN, MARCIA HOLMAN, CLAIRE KOWALCHIK, RICHARD LALIBERTE, JEFF MEADE, MELISSA MEYERS, RICHARD TRUBO, JOSEPH M. WARGO, STEPHEN WILLIAMS

DIRECTOR ARTÍSTICO: STAN GREEN
DISEÑADORA DE LA TAPA: DEBORA SFETSIOS
DISEÑADOR DE INTERIORES: ACEY LEE
ILUSTRADORA: SUSAN ROSENBERGER

ASESORA EDITORIAL: TANIA RODRÍGUEZ

ASISTENTE EDITORIAL: LINDA MOONEY

INVESTIGADORA DE DATOS REFERENTES A LOS LATINOS: KATHRYN PIFF CASTAÑO
INVESTIGADORES Y VERIFICADORES DE DATOS: SUSAN E. BURDICK, HILTON CASTON, CHRISTINE DREISBACH, VALERIE EDWARDS-PAULIK, JAN EICKMEIER, THERESA FOGARTY, CAROL J. GILMORE, DEBORAH PEDRON, SALLY A. REITH, SANDRA SALERA-LLOYD, ANITA SMALL, CAROL SVEC, MICHELLE M. SZULBORSKI, JOHN WALDRON

PREVENTION MAGAZINE HEALTH BOOKS EN ESPAÑOL

VICEPRESIDENTA Y DIRECTORA EDITORIAL: DEBORA T. YOST
DIRECTOR DEL DISEÑO Y PRODUCCIÓN: MICHAEL WARD
DIRECTORA ARTÍSTICA: FAITH HAGUE
GERENTE DE INVESTIGACIÓN: ANN GOSSY YERMISH
GERENTE DEL TEXTO: LISA D. ANDRUSCAVAGE

LOS ASESORES MÉDICOS DE PREVENTION® MAGAZINE HEALTH BOOKS EN ESPAÑOL

HÉCTOR BALCAZAR, PH.D., es profesor asociado de nutrición comunitaria y salud pública en el Departamento de Recursos Familiares y Desarrollo Humano así como catedrático asociado en el Centro Hispano de Investigación en la Universidad Estatal de Arizona en Tempe, Arizona.

HANNIA CAMPOS, PH.D., es profesora asistente de nutrición en la Escuela de Salud Pública de la Universidad de Harvard en Boston, Massachusetts, y miembro del comité que está actualizando la Pirámide Dietética Latinoamericana. Ella también es profesora asociada visitante del Instituto de Investigación de la Salud en la Universidad de Costa Rica.

VÍCTOR CONTRERAS, DOCTOR EN MEDICINA, es el director médico de la Clínica de Medicina Ocupacional en Santa Paula, California.

ELENA RÍOS, DOCTORA EN MEDICINA, es la presidenta de la Asociación Nacional de Médicos Hispanos en Washington, D.C.

HELEN RODRÍGUEZ-TRIAS, DOCTORA EN MEDICINA, fue presidenta de la Asociación de Salud Pública de los Estados Unidos y actualmente es la codirectora del Instituto Pacífico de la Salud de la Mujer en Los Ángeles, California.

ÍNDICE

Tercera Parte: Recupere su juventud

Introducción

Es más temprano de lo que usted se imagina

Es posible que los impuestos y la muerte sean inevitables, pero para la mayoría de nosotras, estos no representan un miedo tan grande como el de envejecer. Envejecer, ¡ay, ay, ay! Las puras palabras son suficientes para congelar el corazón de cualquier mujer. Y nos encogemos ante las desgastadas imágenes que acompañan estas palabras: canas, arrugas pronunciadas, brazos fláccidos, muslos colgantes, y el fin de la atracción, del romance y de las posibilidades.

Le quedaba bien a Gloria Steinem decir orgullosamente, durante unas de sus décadas importantes: "Así es cómo una se ve a los 40 años." Y lo dijo otra vez cuando cumplió 50 años, añadiendo alegremente otros diez años a su edad.

Pero la mayoría de nosotras no somos tan displicentes y seguras de nosotras mismas. Y, ciertamente, no nos reímos en público mientras que los cumpleaños pasan uno tras otro. Dejamos de admitir nuestra edad después de los 29 y cambiamos el tema cuando alguien más joven que nosotras pregunta: "Así que, ¿cuándo fue que se graduó de la universidad?"

Por eso es que escribimos *Más joven que nunca: Recursos rejuvenecedores para la mujer.*

Después de un año de hablar con expertos y efectuar un estudio extenso sobre cómo ponerle freno al paso del tiempo, nuestro equipo de escritores encontró que, de hecho, sí es posible para cualquier mujer "atrasar al reloj" —o por lo menos detenerlo donde está. Como mínimo, este libro le ayudará a redefinir la imagen que usted tiene del envejecimiento, para que pueda moverse hacia el mañana con energía y expectación.

Nos embarcamos en este proyecto después de que ustedes nos dijeron en nuestras encuestas que el envejecer era una de sus preocupaciones más grandes. Es una preocupación que nosotros compartimos, ¿por qué no? En los Estados Unidos, la juventud es reina, especialmente para las mujeres.

Cuando un hombre empieza a tener canas alrededor de las sienes, se ve distinguido. Cuando empieza a mostrar una barriga, se ve simpático. Cuando empieza a jugar golf en lugar de fútbol con muchachos de 18 años de edad, está madurando.

Cuando eso le sucede a una mujer, se está haciendo vieja.

Pero no tiene que ser así. Las múltiples medidas simples contenidas en este libro le ayudarán a sentirse y verse más joven, sin importar su edad.

Por lo tanto, tome este libro, por favor, y diviértase con él. El futuro es mejor de lo que usted se imagina.

Patricia Fisher
Editora Ejecutiva Sénior
Rodale Books

Primera Parte

Cómo envejece una mujer

Detenga el tiempo

Y haga que los años la traten bien

Pepper Herman juega al golf fabulosamente, conduce un carro deportivo y vuela para arriba y para abajo entre su casa en Charlottesville, Virginia, y sus trabajos como locutora para agencias de publicidad en Wilmington, Delaware y Filadelfia.

Su cabello es largo y oscuro. Su cutis es suave. La gente le dice que se parece bastante a Cher.

Ah, y otra cosa: Pepper Herman tiene 60 años de edad.

Allá cuando ella se encontraba entre los 30 y los 40 años de edad, Pepper empezó a crear la mujer vibrante y llena de energía que es hoy. Usted también puede lograr esto.

Lo que realmente la envejece

Hoy en día, el envejecer no es lo que era para nuestras madres.

Muchas de nosotras teníamos madres que engordaron 10 libras cuando tenían 30 años de edad. Empezaron a tener arrugas a los 35, piel reseca a los 40, articulaciones tiesas a los 45, alto colesterol a los 50, problemas de corazón a los 55, pérdida de memoria a los 57, y osteoporosis a los 60 años de edad.

Nosotras, no.

Nosotras no, porque hoy sabemos que una dieta con bajo contenido de grasa evita el subir de peso y el aumento en el colesterol asociado con la edad.

Sabemos que manteniéndonos fuera del sol y usando lociones antisolares evitamos la proliferación de arrugas.

Sabemos que los ácidos alfahidróxidos —ácidos que se encuentran en frutas y leche— previenen la piel reseca y dispareja que viene acompañada de manchas de edad y piel abolsada.

Sabemos que el ejercicio —especialmente nadar y aeróbicos en el agua— retrasa la aparición de la artritis.

Sabemos que el ejercicio aeróbico, una dieta de bajo contenido de grasa, aspirina y ejercicios de relajamiento previenen la evolución de arterias obstruidas en enfermedades del corazón.

Sabemos que hacer crucigramas y leer la sección de opinión y editorial del periódico puede contrarrestar la pérdida de memoria que resulta de un cerebro envejeciendo.

También sabemos que hacer ejercicios de cargar con su propio peso y tener suficiente calcio pueden evitar el adelgazamiento de los huesos que conduce a la osteoporosis en una mujer.

En otras palabras, sabemos que aunque el sobrepeso, las arrugas, la piel reseca, la artritis, el colesterol alto, las enfermedades del corazón, la pérdida de memoria, la osteoporosis y una multitud de otras cosas pueden robarnos nuestra juventud, lo que realmente nos hace envejecer no es físico; es la actitud mental que permite que vegetemos enfrente de la televisión, comamos alimentos con alto contenido de grasa, fumemos, no comamos verduras, nos tostemos bajo el sol y nos olvidemos cómo jugar y desafiarnos a nosotras mismas.

El envejecimiento, en su mayor parte, nos lo causamos nosotras mismas.

El proceso biológico del envejecimiento

"El cuerpo humano está preparado para durar 110 años", dice Ben Douglas, Ph.D., profesor de anatomía en el Centro Médico de la Universidad de Misisipí, en Jackson y autor de *"AgeLess: Living Younger Longer"* (Sin edad: viviendo joven por más tiempo). "Exactamente igual que otros miembros del reino animal, nuestros cuerpos están diseñados para durar aproximadamente cinco veces la edad que teníamos cuando alcanzamos nuestra madurez sexual. Por lo tanto, con un cuidado apropiado, así debería ser."

Entonces, ¿qué es lo que tiene el envejecer que nos detiene? Echemos una mirada, parte por parte, teniendo en mente que lo que llamamos envejecer puede superarse.

Piel. Cuando usted se encuentra entre los 20 y los 30 años de edad, el daño acumulado debido al sol puede causar que su piel se arrugue a través de su frente. Y luego entre los 30 y los 40 años de edad puede arrugarse entre los ojos. Al llegar a los 40 años, aparecen las patas de gallo, y al llegar a los 50 años, las arrugas empezaron a formarse en las comisuras de su boca. Con el tiempo, su piel se volverá más delgada, más seca y menos elástica —debido mayormente a una reducción en el abastecimiento de tejido conectivo y estrógeno que comienza al cumplir 40 años de edad.

Sistema cardiovascular. Después de los 25 años de edad, se produce un descenso pequeño pero constante en la capacidad de su sistema cardiovascular para suministrar sangre oxigenada a través de todo su cuerpo al hacer ejercicio. Típicamente, la capacidad aeróbica de una mujer disminuye de 5 a 10 por ciento por década entre los 25 y los 75 años de edad, lo cual en términos prácticos, significa que usted se queda sin aliento más fácilmente al envejecer. El corazón mismo se achica y palpita a un ritmo más lento. Los vasos capilares se estrechan y se vuelven menos flexibles. La presión sistólica de la sangre —el número más alto al tomarse la presión— aumenta aproximadamente 20 a 30 por ciento entre los 30 y los 70 años de edad.

Músculos. Después de los 45 años de edad, más o menos, sus músculos empiezan a encogerse a medida que los depósitos de grasa se expanden. La fuerza en los músculos decrece aproximadamente 30 por ciento entre las décadas de los 20 y los 70 años de edad, mientras que la masa muscular se reduce hasta en un 40 por ciento.

Huesos. Los minerales —particularmente calcio— se agregan y retiran de sus huesos constantemente a lo largo de toda la vida. Los depósitos exceden los retiros hasta alrededor de los 35 años de edad. Después de esa edad, hay una reducción constante en fuerza ósea y densidad. En parte porque los esqueletos de las mujeres son más pequeños que los de los hombres, y en parte debido a que los cambios hormonales después de la menopausia aceleran la pérdida ósea, la osteoporosis tiende a ser más un problema para las mujeres que para los hombres. El peligro de una fractura de la cadera empieza a aumentar entre los 40 y los 50 años de edad, y después se duplica cada seis años a partir de esa edad. De hecho, los investigadores estiman que es probable que una mujer haya perdido 30 por ciento de su masa ósea pico para cuando llega a los 70 años de edad, volviéndose más propensa a fracturas.

Articulaciones. Una ligera rigidez en las rodillas, caderas y cuello empieza entre los 40 y los 50 años de edad. Gradualmente empeora hasta que su médico lo diagnostica como artritis cuando está entre los 60 y los 70 años de edad. Los discos entre sus vértebras empiezan a degenerarse y su espina se endurece más o menos entre los 70 y los 80 años de edad.

Metabolismo. Comenzando alrededor de los 20 años de edad, el número de calorías que su cuerpo requiere se reduce gradualmente. Para cuando usted cumple 70 años de edad, necesitará 500 calorías menos por día.

Cerebro. Nosotras empezamos la vida con un número determinado de neuronas diseñado para prestar un servicio de por vida. Aunque perdemos algunas células nerviosas durante nuestra vida, si no sufrimos alguna enfermedad, las células nerviosas funcionan, se reparan, regeneran y hacen nuevas conexiones durante nuestra vida entera. Entonces, ¿qué causa la senilidad? La mayor parte de lo que pensamos que es un comportamiento senil en las personas mayores es causado por enfermedad, no por la pérdida de neuronas.

Sistema inmune. Después de los 60 años de edad, la baja gradual de su sistema inmune la hace a usted más propensa a infecciones. Si hay un microbio alrededor, hay más probabilidad de que usted lo contraiga.

Colesterol. La cantidad de colesterol en su sangre —el cual es producido por el hígado de las grasas saturadas y el colesterol en su dieta— tiende a aumentar con su edad. Generalmente, alcanza un pico entre los 60 y los 70 años de edad, aproximadamente una década después del pico de los hombres.

Cabello. Las canas pueden empezar en cualquier momento. Para los 50 años de edad, la mitad de nosotras tendrá canas. A los 80 años de edad, el 40 por ciento de nosotras tendrá más vello en la cara del que quisiéramos.

(continúa en la página 8)

Ante el espejo

La mayoría de nosotras seguimos el proceso de envejecimiento con nuestros espejos. Esto es lo que una mujer puede y no puede ver mientras observa su cara y su cuerpo a lo largo de los años adultos.

Entre los 20 y los 30 años de edad. Se ve bien y se siente fantástica. Pero al principio de la decada de los veinte años, las primeras señales ligeras de envejecimiento empiezan a aparecer. Sus músculos empiezan a perder lo lleno y lo firme debido a la pérdida de fibras musculosas. El ritmo al cual su cuerpo quema calorías empieza a hacerse más lento, decreciendo en un dos por ciento por década a partir de ahora. Su oído para tonos agudos empieza a desaparecer.

Entre los 30 y los 40 años de edad. Líneas de risa y arrugas pequeñas aparecen alrededor de sus ojos y boca, y si es muy aficionada a un bronceado à la California, puede tener otras arrugas también, así como manchas de la edad. Eso es porque su cutis está disminuyendo lentamente la producción de melanocitos productores de pigmento, pequeñas células que ayudan a proteger contra los rayos ultravioleta. Más o menos al cumplir los 30 años de edad, las patas de gallo se le pueden aparecer. También tiene que mantenerse activa para hacer más lenta la disminución de la salud cardiovascular, que empieza ahora y puede bajar 30 a 40 por ciento para los 65 años de edad. La pérdida gradual en la fuerza de los huesos empieza a los 35.

Entre los 40 y los 50 años de edad. A medida que las glándulas sebáceas en su piel reducen la producción y las fibras de apoyo se vuelven menos elásticas, primordialmente como resultado del daño solar, ella nota que su cutis se vuelve reseco, más delgado y con más tendencia a arrugarse. Puede notar bolsas bajo los ojos. Para su

20 a 30   **30 a 40**   **40 a 50**

sorpresa, encontrará que necesita anteojos para leer —las lentes en su ojos empiezan a endurecerse alrededor de los 40 años de edad y ahora tiene dificultad para enfocar objetos cercanos. Puede ser que también empiece a notar un pequeño aumento en su peso.

Entre los 50 y los 60 años de edad. En la mayoría de las mujeres, los ovarios dejan de producir estrógeno y progesterona a aproximadamente los 50 años de edad. El cambio acelera la pérdida ósea, reduce la lubricación vaginal y aumenta los niveles de colesterol —aumentando el riesgo de osteoporosis, ataques al corazón y derrame cerebral. Su piel se aflojará y colgará a la mitad de sus mejillas, parte inferior de los carrillos y cuello. El tono de la piel se vuelve más irregular.

Entre los 60 y los 70 años de edad. Ella empieza a pedirle a la gente que le repita lo que dijeron porque su oído ha comenzado a debilitarse. También puede descubrir que de hecho, está empezando a perder peso —principalmente porque ha perdido masa muscular y aumentado grasa. Dado que la grasa pesa menos que los músculos, ella tiene aproximadamente una talla menos. Asimismo, ella empieza a hacerse ligeramente más corta de estatura, perdiendo media pulgada durante los próximos veinte años. Su cutis es más áspero y ha perdido su color uniforme, resultando en más manchas. Es posible que note que está siendo más fácil pescar cualquier microbio que ande circulando, debido a una disminución en su sistema inmune que la hace más propensa a infecciones.

Entre los 70 y los 80 años de edad. Ella toma ahora la vida con más calma. Su fuerza muscular ha disminuido desde su ápice entre los 30 y los 40 años de edad, y una reducción en el tono muscular significa que ahora puede tener dificultad en controlar su orina o hacer que los alimentos pasen a través de sus conductos digestivos. Ahora necesita el doble de luz para ver tan claramente como antes, pero lo más probable es que mentalmente esté tan despierta como siempre lo fue.

50 a 60   60 a 70   70 a 80

Nuestra ventaja de longevidad

Es posible que las mujeres sean más resistentes que los hombres desde el momento de la concepción.

La razón sigue siendo un misterio, según dicen los científicos. Pero notan que aunque se desarrollan 170 embriones masculinos por cada 100 embriones femeninos, solamente nacen 106 niños por cada 100 niñas.

También más bebés del sexo masculino mueren durante la infancia y niñez, de tal manera que cuando las hormonas reproductoras empiezan a fluir durante la adolescencia, la relación de muchachos a muchachas es aproximadamente de uno a uno.

Después de eso, los hombres parecen estar resueltos a dejar el planeta. Tienen el doble de posibilidades de morir de una lesión no intencional que las mujeres, y cerca de tres veces la posibilidad de morir por suicidio o crimen.

Parte de la razón del deceso prematuro de tantos hombres —según dicen los expertos— es la expectativa social que anima a los hombres a desarrollar trabajos peligrosos. Por eso es que los hombres tienen 29 veces más probabilidades que las mujeres de caerse de una escalera a su muerte; 23 veces más probabilidades de que los mate una máquina, o cerca de 20 veces más probabilidades de ser electrocutados.

Por supuesto, a medida que las oportunidades aumentan para las mujeres en el lugar de trabajo, probablemente van a tener oportunidades iguales de

Vejiga. Cuando empieza a disminuir el estrógeno al final de la década de los 40 años de edad, usted puede perder orina al estar haciendo ejercicio. Después de la menopausia, usted puede ser más susceptible a infecciones de la vejiga.

Reproducción. Los ovarios pueden producir menos estrógeno y progesterona después de los 35 años de edad. La fertilidad cesa gradualmente y la menopausia comienza.

Ojos. Cuando usted empieza a sostener el periódico con los brazos extendidos —entre los 40 y los 45 años de edad— la lente de su ojo está perdiendo su elasticidad haciendo más difícil enfocarse en objetos cercanos o ajustarse de cerca a lejos. Para los 65 años de edad, es posible que empiece a desarrollar cataratas, y para los 80 años de edad usted puede necesitar tres veces más luz para ver tan claramente como ve ahora.

Oídos. Su capacidad para oír empieza a declinar gradualmente en la década de los 60 años de edad. Declina también en los hombres, pero a un paso más rápido.

ser aplastadas, destrozadas y electrocutadas. Por ello, hay una fuerte posibilidad según los expertos, de que la diferencia en los índices de muertes entre hombres y mujeres relacionados con su ocupación desaparezca.

Entretanto, las estadísticas indican que hay tres factores que aparentemente aumentan la longevidad en las mujeres: educación, trabajo y un ingreso arriba del promedio.

Una mujer de 25 años de edad que vive en los Estados Unidos que tiene estudios de postgrado puede anticipar que va a vivir 59 años más, mientras que una mujer de la misma edad que sólo terminó el cuarto grado probablemente vivirá solamente otros 54 años, reporta la Oficina de Censos de los Estados Unidos.

Una mujer de 25 años de edad que trabaja fuera de su casa puede anticipar que va a vivir otros 61 años, mientras que una mujer de la misma edad que trabaja en su casa probablemente viva otros 56 años. Y una mujer de ascendencia europea con ingresos familiares de más de $50.000 anuales puede anticipar que vivirá otros 58 años más, mientras que una mujer de la misma edad cuyo ingreso familiar es de aproximadamente $5.000 probablemente vivirá sólo 54 años más.

Pero, como quiera que sea que las mujeres logran años adicionales, el hecho es que para cuando hombres y mujeres alcanzan los 65 años, habrán ocho mujeres por cada siete hombres.

Nariz. Su capacidad para oler decrece gradualmente después de cumplir los 45 años de edad.

Boca. Su capacidad para notar diferencias sutiles entre sabores se reduce al disminuir el número de papilas gustativas de la lengua.

Las medidas rejuvenecedoras

A pesar de lo que usted acaba de leer, muy poco de lo que llamamos envejecer tiene que suceder. Alrededor de los 40 años de edad, por ejemplo, Pepper Herman se dio cuenta de que si quería mantener su cuerpo joven y su personalidad llena de energía al llegar a las decadas de los 60 y 70 años de edad era mejor que desarrollara un plan para rechazar la irrupción de la edad.

Pepper enfocó esto en su forma característica: habló con sus amigas, vio médicos y leyó todo lo que pudo encontrar acerca de la preservación de un cuerpo saludable. Entonces comenzó a experimentar para encontrar lo que era más conveniente para ella.

Empezó con un régimen de alimentación que incluía frijoles (habichuelas), arroz integral, brócoli, sopa miso y pastelillos de arroz junto con tomates, pimientos verdes y pollo.

La dieta tuvo tal éxito que la hizo verse y sentirse alrededor de diez años más joven. "Mi colesterol bajó de 300 a 167 y perdí peso", dice. "Pero no hice ejercicio, así que no tenía una buena figura."

Finalmente, una amiga la arrastró a una clase de aeróbicos que trataba de formar todo al mismo tiempo: "trasero de acero", "vientre potente" y "pectorales espectaculares". "Fue horrible", declara Pepper. "Todas se veían como estrellas de cine y yo no podía mantener el paso. Sólo podía hacer una cuarta parte de lo que ellas hacían."

Exhausta, Pepper decidió que podía ser que necesitara ejercicio, pero no a ese nivel de intensidad. "Encontré localmente una clase de ejercicio en la cual me sentí más cómoda, y fui a ella dos veces por semana", dice. "También empecé a caminar con mi cuñada y a jugar golf."

"Comencé a perder más peso, y a ponerme más a tono y a endurecerme", añade. "Mi cuerpo se volvió mejor de lo que había sido cuando tenía entre los 20 y los 30 años de edad."

Eventualmente, dice Pepper, agregó una técnica de relajamiento, tragó algunas vitaminas —especialmente vitaminas C y E más betacaroteno— , empezó a mascar un chicle enriquecido con calcio, completó y se graduó con una maestría, empezó a andar con gente creativa que estimulaba su mente, se involucró en grupos de acción política y sedujo a su esposo durante viajes vigorizantes a Santa Fe, Anguilla, Vermont y a cualquier parte que se le antojaba.

¿El resultado? La Pepper que tenemos ahora: el prototipo de una mujer excitante, para la que aparentemente no pasan los años —una mujer que hace pedazos el concepto de "vejez" que tenían todas las generaciones anteriores.

No todas pueden volverse una Pepper, por supuesto. Pero todas pueden detener el envejecimiento al cambiar la forma en que ven el envejecer.

Para mantenerse joven, dice Mary M. Gergin, Ph.D., profesora asociada de psicología del Campus Delaware de la Universidad Estatal de Pennsylvania, "Necesitamos liberarnos de las nociones anticuadas sobre envejecer. Necesitamos no tener miedo, ser desafiantes y tener la voluntad de tomar riesgos. Y necesitamos estar dispuestas a romper el molde del envejecimiento."

Una vez que lo hacemos, dice la doctora Gergin, necesitamos usar las medidas rejuvenecedoras que más se conforman a nuestras necesidades individuales tal y como Pepper Herman lo hizo. ¿Cuáles? Aquí hay una muestra de medidas que usted puede tomar en cuenta.

Salga a sudar la gota gorda

Si hay algo cercano a una droga genuina de la juventud, es el sudor.

"No hay nada que la ciencia pueda hacer por usted que pueda ser de más beneficio que el ejercicio", dice William Evans, Ph.D., director de Laboratorio

Noell para la Investigación del Desempeño Humano, en la Universidad Estatal de Pennsylvania en University Park, y coautor de *Biomarkers: The Ten Determinants of Aging You Can Control* (Bioindicadores: Los 10 determinantes de edad que usted puede controlar).

Un solo experimento clásico ilustra gráficamente su punto. Al final de los años 1960, un fisiólogo sueco de nombre Bengt Saltin pidió a cinco hombres jóvenes, dos de ellos atletas, que se acostaran en cama por tres semanas mientras él medía la reacción fisiológica de sus cuerpos a un desuso prolongado.

¿El resultado? En un espacio de 21 días, no hacer nada redujo la capacidad aeróbica tan dramáticamente que el Señor Saltin concluyó que era equivalente a casi 20 años de envejecimiento.

Afortunadamente, investigación subsecuente encontró que el ejercicio no sólo podía invertir los resultados del Señor Saltin, sino que de hecho podía invertir los resultados de la edad. En un estudio, por ejemplo, 11 hombres y mujeres saludables entre los 62 y los 68 años de edad fueron puestos por seis meses en un programa moderadamente extenuante de caminar; éste logró aumentar su capacidad aeróbica en un promedio de 12 por ciento. Al continuar con este programa por otros seis meses, al doble de intensidad, su capacidad aeróbica aumentó un 18 por ciento adicional.

Muchos otros cambios fisiológicos que antes normalmente se asociaban con el envejecimiento también se pueden evitar o retrasar por medio de un ejercicio moderado. ¿Qué quiere decir "moderado"? Cerca de 20 minutos de actividad aeróbica, tres veces por semana, deben lograrlo.

Investigadores en la Universidad Tufts pusieron un grupo de voluntarios mayores de edad en un programa de ocho semanas de entrenamiento de fuerza, y encontraron que mujeres de hasta 96 años de edad tenían la capacidad de incrementar el tamaño y fuerza de sus músculos en más de 200 por ciento.

Otros investigadores han descubierto que los ejercicios de cargar con su propio peso como son caminar, trotar y bailar pueden mantener los huesos fuertes y evitar la osteoporosis.

Y aún otros investigadores han encontrado que el ejercicio puede evitar los aumentos de peso, triglicéridos, colesterol y presión arterial diastólica —el número pequeño en una lectura de la presión arterial.

En un estudio en la Escuela de Medicina de la Universidad de Pittsburgh, los investigadores registraron peso, triglicéridos, colesterol y presión arterial a 500 mujeres entre los 42 y los 50 años de edad tanto al empezar el estudio, como después otra vez tres años más tarde. En los años entre una medición y la otra, la presión diastólica de la sangre, el peso, los triglicéridos y el total de los niveles de colesterol se fueron para arriba en todas. Pero, las mujeres que hacían más ejercicio aumentaron menos de peso y disfrutaban de niveles más saludables de colesterol en la sangre.

¿Cuánto ejercicio es necesario para mantener su cuerpo joven en las décadas de los 60 y los 70 años de edad?

(continúa en la página 15)

¿Cuánto vivirá usted?

Las decisiones que usted hace cada día sobre lo que come, si es que hará ejercicio, y qué tan estresada se permitirá estar se combinan con los problemas genéticos para determinar su longevidad.

Haga la siguiente prueba para ver si tiene una buena posibilidad de longevidad. Vaya sumando o restando la puntuación a medida de que responda a las siguientes preguntas:

Historia familiar
(Escoja todo lo que corresponda)

1. −1   Uno o ambos padres vivieron más allá de los 75 años y no tuvieron cáncer o enfermedades del corazón.
2. +2   Cáncer en uno de los padres o hermanos.
3.   Enfermedad coronaria del corazón antes de los 40 años en:
   +2   Uno de los padres
   +4   Ambos padres
4.   Alta presión arterial antes de los 50 años en:
   +2   Uno de los padres
   +4   Ambos padres
5.   Diabetes *mellitus* antes de los 60 años en:
   +2   Uno de los padres
   +4   Ambos padres
6.   Derrame cerebral antes de los 60 años en:
   +2   Uno de los padres
   +4   Ambos padres

Tipo de vida y salud
(Escoja todo lo que corresponda)

7. +2   Vive y/o trabaja en una zona con alta contaminación en el aire
8.   Fumar:
   −1   Nunca fumó o dejó de fumar hace más de cinco años
    0   Dejó de fumar hace uno a cinco años
   +1   Dejó de fumar durante el año pasado
   +5   Ha fumado más de 20 años
9.   Usted fuma cigarrillos:
   +2   Menos de una cajetilla por día
   +3   Una cajetilla por día
   +5   Más de dos cajetillas por día

10.   Su consumo de alcohol:
- −1   Nunca o rara vez
- 0   Bebe no más de 1,5 onzas (44 ml) de licor fuerte, 5 onzas (148 ml) de vino o 12 onzas (360 ml) de cerveza por día
- +2   Tres o más bebidas diarias

11.   Su presión arterial:
- −2   Abajo de 121/71
- 0   121/71 a 140/85
- +2   141/86 a 170/100
- +4   171/101 a 190/110
- +6   Arriba de 190/110

12.   Su nivel de colesterol en la sangre:
- 0   190 o menos
- +1   191 a 230
- +2   231 a 289
- +4   290 a 320
- +6   Más de 320

13.   Su nivel HDL de colesterol:
- −1   Arriba de 60
- 0   60 a 45
- +2   44 a 36
- +4   35 a 28
- +6   27 a 22

14.   Su peso:
- 0   Normal o dentro del 10 por ciento de lo normal
- +1   Sobrepeso de 20 a 29 por ciento
- +2   Sobrepeso de 30 a 39 por ciento

15.   Usted hace ejercicio:
- −2   Vigoroso, más de 45 minutos, cuatro a cinco veces por semana
- −1   Vigoroso, por lo menos 30 minutos, tres veces por semana
- 0   Moderado, por lo menos 30 minutos, tres veces por semana
- +2   Moderado, dos veces por semana
- +3   Rara vez o nunca

Personalidad y evaluación de estrés
(Escoja todo lo que corresponda)

16. +2   Intensamente competitiva
17. +2   Enojada y hostil

(continúa)

¿Cuánto vivirá usted? —continuado

18. **+2** No expresa su enojo
19. **+2** Trabaja duro sin sentir satisfacción
20. **+2** Rara vez se ríe; a menudo deprimida
21. **+2** Rara vez discute problemas o sentimientos con otros
22. **+2** Trata constantemente de complacer a otros en lugar de a sí mismo
23. **−2** Nada de lo anterior

Dieta
(Escoja todo lo que corresponda)

24. **−2** Usted come repollo, brócoli, coliflor, zanahorias o frijoles (habichuelas) tres o más veces por semana
25. **−2** Usted come granos con alto contenido de fibra (tales como pan de trigo integral, arroz integral, cereal de salvado) casi diariamente
26. **−2** Usted come tres o más porciones de frutas y verduras al día
27. **+1** Usted hace una o dos dietas de moda para perder peso por año
28. **+2** Usted come mantequilla, crema y queso frecuentemente
29. **+2** Usted come carne, tocino o carnes procesadas frecuentemente
30. **+2** Usted le echa sal a la comida antes de probarla
31. **+2** Usted come más de seis huevos por semana
32. **+2** Usted come helado de crema, pastel o postres ricos casi diariamente

Otros factores

33. **+3** Usted usa píldoras anticonceptivas y fuma
34. **+1** Usted ha pasado la menopausia y no toma estrógeno

Cómo interpretar su puntuación

-16 a 0. Riesgo bajo. Usted debería disfrutar de una vida larga y saludable sin cáncer, enfermedades del corazón, ataques de apoplejía o diabetes. Continúe su estilo de vida.

1 a 34. Riesgo moderado. Usted tiene algún riesgo de desarrollar mala salud y puede esperar vivir un término promedio de vida. Estudie la prueba para ver dónde puede usted bajar su riesgo.

35 a 60. Riesgo alto. Usted está corriendo un riesgo considerable de contraer una enfermedad con peligro de muerte temprano en su vida y de morir antes de lo que debería. Use la prueba para ver dónde puede usted reducir su riesgo. Vea al médico para que la aconseje.

Más de 60. Riesgo muy alto. Su salud está corriendo un riesgo extremo, y usted puede morirse prematuramente. Use esta prueba para identificar sus hábitos poco saludables y consulte a su médico para que le dé mayores consejos.

"Por años, los fanáticos del ejercicio han estado diciendo que usted debe de hacer ejercicio por 30 ó 40 minutos, tres veces por semana, a fin de obtener un beneficio", dice el doctor Evans. "Pero ahora, hay evidencia clara que un nivel de ejercicio relativamente bajo también es beneficioso."

Nivel bajo significa subir por las escaleras cuando se puede tomar el elevador, añade. Significa estacionar el coche lejos de la entrada a los centros comerciales (*malls*), supermercados, lugares de trabajo —en resumen, donde quiera que usted vaya. También significa caminar diez minutos en la mañana o a la hora del almuerzo, y otros diez minutos cerca de la hora de la cena o antes de irse a la cama.

"Todo funciona", dice el doctor Evans. Y el resultado final es que usted eliminará muchos de los problemas que la están envejeciendo antes de tiempo.

Coma verduras para su longevidad

Unas cabezuelas de brócoli, un montón de zanahorias cocidas al vapor o unas cuantas hojas de col rizada parece no ser tan importantes en el gran esquema de la vida. Pero estas verduras sencillas son de hecho "alimentos para longevidad"—se compara a los combustibles que arden limpiamente, con alto octanaje, que pueden evitar muchas causas de envejecimiento prematuro.

Brócoli, col de brusela (*brussels sprouts*), zanahorias y la mayoría de las verduras verdes hojosas están llenas de betacaroteno, la substancia productora de vitamina A que ha mostrado poder impedir al cáncer y prevenir ataques al corazón.

La col rizada y otras verduras están llenas de calcio, el mineral que su cuerpo necesita para mantener fuerza juvenil en sus huesos.

Y todos los vegetales casi no tienen grasa o colesterol, lo cual le ayudará a mantener controlados los aumentos de peso relacionados con la edad, las lecturas altas de presión arterial y las arterias taponadas.

Dese un festín de fruta

Los nutrientes llamados antioxidantes —vitaminas C y E y betacaroteno— resultan ser ingredientes clave en lo que se podría describir como una "dieta antienvejecimiento". Contenidos en frutas, nueces y algunos vegetales, los antioxidantes son la defensa del cuerpo contra lo que los científicos llaman radicales libres —moléculas altamente reactivas moviéndose alrededor del cuerpo, causando toda clase de daños celulares. Estas moléculas están involucradas en la iniciación del cáncer, enfermedades del corazón y aun el envejecimiento mismo, tanto así que algunos científicos creen que el proceso de envejecer se produce en su mayor parte por toda una vida de pequeñas hendiduras, abolladuras, y golpes celulares causados por los radicales libres al oxidar diferentes células.

Los antioxidantes, como su nombre lo indica, proporcionan al cuerpo una defensa natural contra estos radicales libres. Por eso es que los especialistas en nutrición recomiendan frecuentemente que usted ingiera alimentos ricos en vitaminas C y E y betacaroteno.

Las fuentes de la vitamina C incluyen frutos cítricos, pimientos (ajís) rojos y repollo. Otras fuentes buenas son las fresas y los tomates.

Las mejores fuentes de betacaroteno son las zanahorias, la espinaca, el brócoli y la lechuga.

La vitamina E se encuentra principalmente en los aceites de nueces como son las avellanas, girasoles y almendras —todos ellos contienen más de 100 calorías por cucharada. Usted podría comer las nueces solas, por supuesto, pero tendría que comer tantas para obtener suficiente vitamina E que estaría masticando todo el tiempo —sin mencionar toda esa grasa que también estaría ingiriendo. Por consecuencia, muchas mujeres prefieren obtener su vitamina E de un suplemento.

Comprométase con la vida

"La literatura científica es absolutamente clara en un punto", dice el doctor Evans. "Las personas que llevan vidas significativas y algo que les da un propósito —una carrera satisfactoria, participación en la comunidad o en trabajo de la iglesia— viven más tiempo y más saludablemente que aquellas que no cuentan con esto."

Camine a la luz de la luna

Usted puede llamar a los efectos del sol en su piel broncearse, pero los dermatólogos lo llaman fotoenvejecimiento. Eso es porque la exposición a los rayos ultravioletas en la luz solar causan literalmente las arrugas, las motitas, pigmentación irregular y manchas de la edad que nosotras normalmente atribuimos a una piel envejeciendo. Con suficiente exposición al sol, la piel se hace más gruesa, cuelga y desarrolla una textura áspera y como de cuero. Y mientras más blanca sea su piel, mayor será el daño.

También, usted se verá más vieja de lo que realmente es. Los dermatólogos estudiaron a 41 mujeres, oscilando en edad entre los 25 y los 51 años, que habían vivido en Tucson, Arizona por un mínimo de diez años. Algunas eran adoradoras inveteradas del sol; otras se mantenían la mayor parte del tiempo dentro.

Se fotografiaron las caras de las mujeres, sin maquillaje en inmutables acercamientos de primer plano. Las fotos se mostraron entonces a un panel de jueces femeninas a quienes se les preguntó: "¿De qué edad se ven estas mujeres?"

En aquellas mujeres que se encontraban entre los 20 años y a principios de la década de los 30 años de edad, no se notó diferencia en la edad aparente entre aquellas que se habían expuesto al sol para broncearse, y las que habían rechazado el sol. Pero entre las mujeres mayores (con un promedio de 47 años de edad), la situación no era tan agradable. De hecho, a las mujeres con las caras tostadas por el sol se les calculó que tenían por lo menos cinco años más que aquellas que se habían mantenido lejos del sol.

Aún más, ya que los estudios han demostrado que la exposición al sol por largo plazo aumenta su riesgo de cataratas, demasiado sol también puede envejecer sus ojos.

Por eso es que los expertos dicen que usted debería guardarse del sol tanto como sea posible y aprender a gustar de los sombreros grandes que dan mucha sombra. Los anteojos (gafas) para sol curvados alrededor de sus ojos y una loción antisolar con un factor de protección (o *SPF*, por sus siglas en inglés) de 15 también le ayudarán a proteger del sol a sus ojos y cutis.

Evite el humo

Fumar cigarrillos es una forma estupenda de gastar mucho dinero para envejecerse más rápidamente, sentirse mal y enfermarse más pronto.

A pesar de que el fumar acostumbraba a verse como un problema de salud de los hombres, hoy también es un problema de la mujer. Y ahora, si usted fuma, tiene las mismas probabilidades de morirse de cáncer de pulmón que los hombres.

Usted también puede sumarse a los hombres para obtener una bonificación adicional: aquellas de ustedes que realmente inhalan, van a lograr tener una "cara de fumadora", la cual incluye arrugas alrededor de la boca, nariz y ojos que se deben exclusivamente a las contorsiones faciales necesarias para aspirar el humo de un cigarrillo.

"Trabaje" esas neuronas

La mejor manera de mantener su mente alerta, su intelecto agudo y su memoria despierta es mantener activo su cerebro. Eso se debe a que las células del cerebro tienen pequeñas ramas que crecen y se esparcen cuando se usan —tal y como las raíces de una planta cuando se las riega— o se marchitan y mueren cuando no se las usa.

Los investigadores han encontrado que las células del cerebro de ratas habitando un entorno intelectualmente estimulante —eso quiere decir juguetes para ratas y otras ratas— están más densamente llenas de estas ramas de células en el cerebro que los animales que se mantienen en aislamiento sombrío y sin juguetes.

Lo mismo puede ser verdad en los humanos. Los estudios indican que cuando una u otra área del cerebro se usa intensivamente, esa área casi explota con crecimiento. El área del cerebro destinada a la comprensión de palabras, por ejemplo, está mucho más desarrollada en los graduados de universidad que en los de escuela secundaria. Y la razón probablemente se debe al hecho de que los estudiantes de universidades se pasan más tiempo trabajando con palabras.

En resumen, el mantener su mente trabajando —tratando de obtener un grado más avanzado, leyendo sobre una amplia variedad de tópicos, aprendiendo un nuevo idioma o proporcionando al cerebro de cualquier manera un estímulo mental— mantiene sus filamentos neurales funcionando hasta una edad bien avanzada.

Segunda Parte

Detenga los ladrones de la juventud

ALERGIAS

Ayuda para la que estornuda

Este día parece ser una obra maestra de la naturaleza, con sus cielos azules, flores perfumadas y la brisa que acaricia suavemente. Tan sólo al estar afuera, usted se siente más joven. Sale al parque para disfrutar el buen tiempo, pero de repente la atacan. No es un ladrón que le está robando la cartera, sino un ataque por un ejército microscópico —¡el polen! Entre los estornudos y la congestión, en vez de sentirse como un capullo que florece, se siente como una flor vieja y marchitada. Logra escaparse al entrar a su casa, pero su día ya está arruinado, y el único consuelo que le queda es la cajita de antihistamínicos en la gaveta.

Las alergias de estación como esta afectan a unos estimados 45 a 50 millones de habitantes de los Estados Unidos, o uno en cada cinco, según los Institutos Nacionales de Salubridad. Pero el polen no es su único enemigo en las alergias. Docenas y docenas de cosas pueden provocar reacciones, desde ácaros de polvo, moho y caspa de las mascotas a camarones y cacahuates (maníes). Incluso un par de guantes de látex puede dar problemas.

Y las alergias no son siempre algo que se puede tomar a la ligera, tampoco. En casos de asma y reacciones alérgicas severas, pueden ser fatales.

"Afortunadamente, hay bastante que se puede hacer para mejorar la situación", dice el doctor Harold S. Nelson, médico sénior en el Centro Nacional Judío para Medicina de Inmunología y Respiración en Denver, y un miembro del Panel Nacional de Expertos para Educación sobre Asma del Instituto Nacional de Corazón, Pulmón y Sangre. "Aunque parezcan terribles cuando usted las tiene, las alergias no necesitan dominar su vida."

Un caso de identificación equivocada

Cuando se trata de combatir enfermedades, su sistema inmune es normalmente bastante inteligente. Puede identificar rápidamente substancias extrañas dañinas tales como gérmenes y virus, y destruirlos con eficiencia letal.

Pero algunas veces su cuerpo se confunde un poco. Por razones que nadie entiende completamente, su sistema inmune puede identificar erróneamente y atacar a substancias inofensivas como son el moho, polen y productos derivados de alimentos. Las células cebadas, parte de su sistema inmune, se pegan a estas substancias conocidas como alergenos. Las células cebadas entonces desprenden unos químicos potentes llamados mediadores alérgicos, incluyendo histamina, para combatir los alergenos.

El resultado, dice el doctor Nelson, es un caso clásico de síntomas de alergia: una nariz congestionada, estornudos y ojos acuosos. En algunos casos, usted también puede terminar con sarpullido, urticaria, retortijones en el estómago, náusea o vómito. Y 5 a 12 horas después, cuando otras partes del sistema inmune se unen a la batalla, una segunda ola de síntomas similares puede atacar.

La herencia desempeña un papel importante en muchas alergias. Usted puede heredar la capacidad de producir un anticuerpo llamado inmunoglobulina E, o IgE, dice el doctor alergólogo David Tinkelman, profesor de pediatría en el Departamento de Alergias e Inmunología en el Colegio Médico de Georgia, en Augusta. Si una persona no hereda IgE, dice él, es menos propensa a desarrollar alguna alergia.

Las alergias a alimentos son más raras de lo que usted se imagina. Sólo 0,1 a 5 por ciento de la población sufre de ellas, dice el doctor Nelson —y la mayor parte de la gente las pierden a la edad de tres años. Sin embargo, algunos adultos son altamente alérgicos a las nueces, los mariscos y pescados, la leche, los huevos y otros alimentos. Y en algunas ocasiones, las reacciones se empeoran con el tiempo.

Las mujeres rara vez contraen alergias nuevas después de los 30 años de edad, dice el doctor Nelson, a menos que usted esté expuesta a algún alergeno nuevo como es una mascota o polen. La buena noticia es que las alergias tienden a disminuir aproximada a los 55 años de edad, dice el doctor Edward O'Connell, profesor de pediatría, alergias e inmunología en la Escuela de Medicina Mayo, en Rochester, Minnesota. Eso es porque su sistema inmune empieza a declinar, haciendo menos factible que ataque a una espora invasora de moho u otro alergeno.

Pueden ser una cosa seria

Las alergias son usualmente nada más que una molestia. Los medicamentos que se pueden obtener con o sin receta pueden aliviar los síntomas cuando se toman correctamente, dice el doctor Nelson. Pero, algunas alergias pueden ser mucho más serias.

En el caso de picaduras de abejas y otros encuentros desafortunados con insectos, aproximadamente 1 por ciento de la población puede desarrollar una reacción alérgica peligrosa llamada anafilaxia, según la doctora Susan Rudd Wynn, una alergista de Médicos Asociados para Alergia y Asma de Fort Worth, en Texas.

Poco después de que una abeja la ha picado usted puede notar síntomas tales como picazón en las palmas de las manos, una tensión en el pecho, ronquera o incluso un sentimiento de que algo muy desagradable va a pasar. "Si se siente así, váyase rápido a una sala de emergencia", dice la doctora Wynn. "La anafilaxia no es algo que se puede tomar a la ligera." De hecho, dice, hasta 50 personas mueren anualmente de la reacción —muchas de ellas porque se sofocaron cuando sus gargantas se inflaman y cierran. En casos raros, las alergias a alimentos también pueden causar anafilaxia, dice la doctora Wynn.

No existe una prueba que permita predecir la anafilaxia, pero los doctores pueden proporcionar juegos de jeringas a las personas que ellos saben que sufren de reacciones alérgicas severas, para inyectarse adrenalina ellas mismas. "Eso le da a usted un poco de tiempo valioso, para que pueda llegar a un hospital para recibir tratamiento adicional", dice la doctora Wynn.

También hay evidencia de que las mujeres con alergias pueden tener un mayor riesgo de desarrollar ciertos tipos de cáncer, incluyendo cáncer de mama. Un estudio de seis años a más de 34.000 Adventistas del Séptimo Día en California mostró que las mujeres con tres o más alergias pueden ser 1,25 veces más propensas a desarrollar cáncer de mama. La buena noticia es que el estudio encontró un pequeño descenso en el riesgo de cáncer en los ovarios en mujeres con alergias.

Los investigadores no entienden la posible conexión entre alergias y cáncer. De hecho, dice el doctor Nelson, otros estudios han demostrado que las probabilidades de desarrollar ciertos tipos de cáncer realmente parecen disminuir en personas con alergias. "Toda esta área se presta a todo tipo de especulaciones", dice.

Medidas de auxilio

¿Cuál es el mejor consejo para vencer las alergias? Evite cualquier cosa que la haga estornudar o que le provoque un sarpullido. Un alergista puede hacerle unas simples pruebas de sangre o piel para determinar sus alergias. "Una vez que usted sabe qué causa sus problemas, puede tratar de evitarlo", dice la doctora Wynn. Aquí hay algunos consejos para mantener sus alergias bajo control.

Conozca sus medicinas. Dos tipos de medicamentos, disponibles sin receta, atacan síntomas de alergia. Los antihistamínicos alivian los estornudos, y la nariz con picazón que gotea. Los descongestionantes ayudan a aliviar una nariz tapada. Algunas medicinas combinan ambos; lea la etiqueta para saber qué es lo que usted necesita.

"La mayor desventaja de los antihistamínicos es que la pueden hacer sentir somnolienta", dice el doctor Edward Philpot, profesor asistente de medicina en el Departamento de Reumatología, Alergia e Inmunología, en la Escuela de Medicina de la Universidad de California, en Davis. "Si todo lo que usted tiene es una nariz congestionada, tome solamente un descongestionante." O, si usted necesita un antihistamínico, trate una de las nuevas recetas de antihistamínicos como terfenadina (*Seldane*) que no la hacen sentir somnolienta. Si está descontenta con la efectividad de un antihistamínico, trate otras marcas hasta que encuentre la que funciona.

Dé el primer golpe. Si usted sabe que el conteo de polen es alto, o si va a visitar a la tía Juanita y su gato peludo, tome su medicina antes de que los síntomas se hagan notar. "Es mucho más efectivo de esa manera", dice el doctor Philpot. "Le da una ventaja de anticipo al antihistamínico con su alergia." Asegúrese de tomar la medicina por lo menos 30 minutos a una hora antes de exponerse a los alergenos.

Evite el alcohol. El alcohol puede empeorar síntomas tales como la congestión, dice la doctora Wynn, y mezclar alcohol con antihistamínicos puede causar problemas serios de salud. Lea la etiqueta en la medicina para alergias antes de beber cualquier cosa.

Mire bien a su mascota. La caspa de perros y gatos es un alergeno doméstico importante. Si usted es alérgica a la caspa, la forma más sencilla de aliviar el problema es deshacerse de sus mascotas. Pero, emocionalmente, eso es muy difícil de hacer —y puede ser innecesario. El doctor Nelson dice que siguiendo estos pasos puede corregir el problema y de paso dejar que se quede con sus queridos animales:

• Mantenga a sus mascotas fuera de la recámara.
• Limítelas a partes de la casa donde no hay alfombra.
• Bañe semanalmente a sus mascotas para eliminar la caspa.

Barra con el polvo. El mayor enemigo en su casa también es el más pequeño. El ácaro de polvo es un organismo microscópico —pero bajo aumento, se ve como el Chupacabras. Si respira esos pequeños bichos puede causarle toda clase de síntomas de alergia. Para ayudarla a reducir el problema, los expertos sugieren tomar estas medidas:

• Cubra sus fundas de almohadas y colchones con cubiertas de plástico. Lave las sábanas, los protectores de colchones y las mantas semanalmente en agua a una temperatura mínima de 130°F (54° C).
• Limpie regularmente la casa. Limpie con la aspiradora por lo menos una vez por semana, y trate de no tener cosas amontonadas ya que eso almacena polvo.
• Siempre que sea posible, escoja pisos de madera o vinilo en lugar de alfombra. Un estudio en la Universidad de Virginia en Charlottesville encontró que la alfombra atrae y guarda alergenos 100 veces más que los pisos de madera barnizada. Use tapetes lavables en lugar de alfombrillas, especialmente en el baño.

¿Puede usted ser alérgica al frío?

Usted sale a la calle en una fría mañana de invierno para recoger el periódico. Dos minutos más tarde, está llena de urticaria. ¿Por qué?

Es raro pero es posible ser alérgica a descensos súbitos de temperatura, dice el doctor Martin Valentine, un experto en alergias y profesor en el Centro Johns Hopkins de Asma y Alergias en Baltimore. Un descenso de 30 grados (17° C) —tal y como usted experimenta cuando sale de su casa caliente para recoger el periódico— puede causar la urticaria e inflamación que puede durar hasta dos horas. Los cambios drásticos, como echarse a una piscina (alberca) helada, pueden causar un shock a algunas personas.

Si usted cree que es alérgica al frío, haga una prueba colocando una bolsa para sándwich llena de hielo sobre su brazo y dejándola ahí de 30 segundos a dos minutos. Si usted es alérgica, se le formará allí un verdugón con picazón. Su médico le puede recetar el antihistamínico apropiado para ayudarla con su problema, dice el doctor Valentine.

Ayune a su alergia. La única manera en que usted va a evitar las alergias a alimentos es con evitar a los alimentos que la están causando. Si usted no está totalmente segura de cuales alimentos le causan problemas, el doctor Nelson dice que un médico puede efectuar pruebas para estudiar su sensibilidad. Usted también puede llevar un diario de alimentos, en el que anote qué comió cada día para descubrir así qué es lo que le provoca una reacción alérgica.

Deshágase del látex. Un estudio de más de 1.000 dentistas del Ejército de los Estados Unidos descubrió que entre 9 y 14 por ciento de la gente es alérgica al látex que se encuentra en guantes. Otros estudios encontraron alergias similares a productos de caucho desde botas hasta condones.

¿En conclusión? Si una marca le provoca un sarpullido, trate otra. Ya que los fabricantes usan diferentes aditivos en sus productos, el doctor Nelson dice que tratar varias marcas puede ayudarla a encontrar la que no le causa problemas.

Quédese en la cama. Los conteos de polen usualmente llegan a su máximo en las primeras horas de la mañana, entre las cinco y las ocho de la mañana. Si usted se puede quedar en su casa hasta media mañana, el doctor Philpot asegura que será mejor. Y no importa qué tan agradable se siente allá afuera, no duerma con las ventanas abiertas en días de mucho polen. "Usted se garantizará una llamada de despertador miserable", dice.

Detenga la humedad. Mantenga su casa o apartamento seco para reducir los alergenos. Eso significa usar el aire acondicionado que seca el aire al mismo tiempo que lo enfría, o usar un deshumectador. Un humectador o vaporizador es una mala idea. "Los ácaros del polvo adoran la humedad adicional causada por un humectador", dice la doctora Wynn. "Y lo mismo pasa con el moho. Si usted tiene alergias, simplemente olvídese del humectador completamente."

Arranque su problema de la raíz. La Asociación del Pulmón de los Estados Unidos dice que las siguientes plantas pueden causar fuertes alergias: robles y nogales, enebros, cipreses, arbustos de alheña y todo tipo de pasto *Bermuda*. Si usted está buscando reemplazos antiestornudos para su jardín, trate con estos: morera, abeto, peral y árboles de seda; hibisco, arbustos de yuca y *pyracantha*, y *dichondra*, musgo irlandés y céspedes *bunchgrass*.

Deje que la piquen. Si sus alergias resisten todas las medidas, usted probablemente necesita inyecciones contra la alergia, dice el doctor Philpot. Los doctores la pueden inyectar con pequeñas cantidades de lo que le causa a usted las alergias para ayudar a su cuerpo a que produzca inmunidad contra los alergenos. Usualmente, esta es una medida de última instancia ya que usted necesitará de seis meses a un año de inyecciones semanales más otra inyección cada mes, por cerca de cinco años.

"Realmente se requiere una gran dedicación", dice el doctor Philpot. "Pero es lo único que puede ayudar a las personas que sufren de alergias." El doctor Philpot recomienda evitar las inyecciones de corticosteróides, las cuales, dice él, pueden suprimir su sistema inmune y permanecer en su cuerpo. "Es como usar una bazuca para eliminar las termitas en su casa", dice. "Se va usted a deshacer de las termitas, pero también va a dañar su casa considerablemente."

ARRITMIAS

Cuando su corazón
se salta un latido

¿Cuándo fue la última vez que usted sintió dentro del pecho el golpeteo de latidos rápidos o caprichosos de su corazón? Posiblemente fue momentos antes de presentar un informe en el trabajo. O quizás fue durante una sesión fuerte de ejercicio en el gimnasio.

Bienvenida al mundo de las arritmias, las cuales son perturbaciones en el ritmo normal de los latidos de su corazón.

Puede ser que su corazón sea la máxima abeja obrera, palpitando cerca de 100.000 veces al día, año tras año, década tras década. Si usted tuviera un programa así de intenso también daría pitiditos, se sacudiría y saltaría. Afortunadamente, su corazón es suficientemente listo y protesta sólo brevemente. La mayor parte del tiempo, casi más rápidamente de lo que usted puede sentirlo, su corazón vuelve por sí mismo a su curso normal, y la vida continúa como si nada hubiera pasado.

Pero a medida que nos envejecemos, esas idiosincrasias del corazón pueden a veces ser algo más que una molestia inofensiva. Algunas formas de arritmia pueden minar su energía, dejándola débil y desgastada. En ocasiones, las perturbaciones grandes en el ritmo del corazón amenazan al corazón mismo. "Por lo general, cuando las arritmias empiezan tarde en la vida, se deberían investigar mucho más cuidadosamente y tratarse más seriamente", dice la doctora Marianne J. Legato, profesora asociada de medicina clínica en el Colegio de Médicos y Cirujanos de la Universidad Columbia, en la ciudad de Nueva York y autora de *The Female Heart* (El corazón femenino).

La conexión con la placa

Pongamos las cosas en perspectiva: no importa cuál es su edad, la mayor parte de las vibraciones del corazón no son una señal de una catástrofe por ocurrir. "En algún momento de nuestras vidas, todos tenemos latidos extras", dice el doctor Gerald Pohost, director de la División de Enfermedad Cardiovascular en la Escuela de Medicina de la Universidad de Alabama, en Birmingham. "Y ciertamente, la gran parte de esos latidos extras son inofensivos."

Pero si usted desarrolla una enfermedad de las arterias coronarias —en especial, la acumulación de placa (ateroma), que consiste en depósitos grasos y otros depósitos que pueden contribuir a un ataque al corazón— entonces esas arritmias podrían necesitar algo más de atención. Si la placa priva a su corazón de la sangre y el oxígeno que necesita, su corazón puede temblar y estremecerse con arritmias que son potencialmente más serias y pueden poner su vida en peligro.

Por suerte, las mujeres en edad previa a la menopausia tienen algo de protección adicional contra problemas del corazón porque nuestros cuerpos producen la hormona sexual estrógeno, que protege al corazón contra enfermedades. Como resultado, las mujeres van diez años atrás de los hombres

Un problema en el corazón de una mujer

No es precisamente una condición inquietante, pero en algunas mujeres puede causar un dolor ligero en el pecho, desmayo, mareo —y ritmo irregular en el corazón. Se le llama prolapso de la válvula mitral (o *MVP*, por sus siglas en inglés), una condición congénita que afecta al 5 por ciento de la población, y tanto como las dos terceras partes de ésta son mujeres.

¿Qué es exactamente MVP? Es una irregularidad en una válvula del corazón en la cual los folíolos (o faldones) de una de las válvulas del corazón, sobresale o prolapsa cuando el corazón se contrae. "En las mujeres, es una de las causas más comunes de palpitaciones y disturbios en el ritmo del corazón", dice el doctor Richard H. Helfant, vicepresidente de medicina y director del Programa de Entrenamiento de Cardiología del Centro Médico de la Universidad de California, en Irvine, y autor de *Women, Take Heart* (Mujeres, anímense).

Si usted sufre de MVP y está preocupada acerca de esos pitiditos irregulares en su pecho, consulte con su médico.

en desarrollar un endurecimiento de las arterias. Pero todo lo bueno tiene su fin. Después de la menopausia, las mujeres se emparejan rápidamente con los hombres al reducirse su estrógeno a un hilito. Así es que al envejecer, tenemos mayores probabilidades de una enfermedad del corazón, ataque al corazón y desórdenes de ritmo potencialmente serios.

Si usted ha tenido un ataque al corazón, es posible que su médico le haya advertido que el músculo lesionado de su corazón tiene más probabilidades de causar anarquía en los impulsos eléctricos rutinarios del corazón, produciendo posiblemente latidos peligrosamente anormales llamados arritmias ventriculares. Cuando esto sucede, el corazón puede acelerar de un trote a una carrera supersónica, palpitando a un paso frenético y caótico de quizás 150 a 300 veces por minuto en lugar de 60 a 100 que es lo normal. En su peor momento, esta condición puede deteriorarse en tales temblores y estremecimientos que el corazón dejará de bombear sangre adecuadamente, y el resultado puede ser la muerte súbita.

Esta situación puede hacer que usted se preocupe. Pero no entre en pánico. Recuerde, la mayoría de los latidos irregulares del corazón son bastante habituales —y si usted toma el control de su salud, puede reducir las posibilidades de experimentar tanto los inofensivos como los más serios desasosiegos y fluctuaciones en los latidos de su corazón.

Cómo recobrar su ritmo

Ya que muchas de las irregularidades más preocupantes en los latidos del corazón están relacionadas con enfermedades coronarias, probablemente su mejor defensa contra esos indeseables estremecimientos y temblores del corazón sea prevenir en primer lugar problemas tales como un ataque al corazón. Aunque usted haya experimentado palpitaciones, usted puede mantenerlas a un mínimo a través de cambios en su estilo de vida. Aquí hay algunas formas de hacerlo, ya sea por medio de prevenirlas completamente o reduciendo su frecuencia.

Apague el cigarrillo. Demasiadas mujeres —cerca de la cuarta parte de la población femenina— fuma. Y como grupo, empezamos a fumar más jóvenes. Esos cigarrillos están aumentando nuestro riesgo de enfermedades del corazón y ciertos tipos de latidos irregulares del corazón. Pero si usted elimina la nicotina de su vida, le será más fácil a su corazón mantener un latido regular, dice el doctor Richard H. Helfant, vicepresidente de medicina y director del Programa de Entrenamiento de Cardiología del Centro Médico de la Universidad de California, en Irvine, y autor de *Women, Take Heart* (Mujeres, anímense).

Venza el estrés. Ahora que las mujeres están ascendiendo la escalera corporativa más que nunca, hay un mayor número experimentando estrés relacionado con su trabajo. Añada a eso la tensión producida por los otros papeles de las mujeres —esposa, madre y ama de casa— y no es de extrañar que algunas mujeres sienten que la presión las está aplastando.

Muchos expertos creen que el estrés tiene algo que ver en el desarrollo de las enfermedades de arterias coronarias así como que contribuye a las arritmias. Para disminuir el efecto del estrés, trate de hacer mucho ejercicio, dese unos baños calientes y masajes y mantengase ocupada con pasatiempos creativos, dice el doctor Fredric J. Pashkow, director médico del Programa de Mejoría y Rehabilitación de la Salud Cardíaca en la Fundación Clínica Cleveland, en Cleveland y autor de *The Woman's Heart Book* (El libro del corazón de la mujer).

Tenga cuidado con su cafecito. Un estudio británico a 7.300 personas encontró que nueve o más tazas de café pueden hacer que un corazón se salte palpitaciones. Algunos estudios más pequeños sugieren que las cantidades menores de café pueden tener efectos similares, particularmente en aquellas personas que no están acostumbradas a tomar mucha cafeína. Vaya a lo seguro: si usted es propensa a arritmias, vaya despacio con la cafeína.

Beba con mesura. Aún cuando usted no consuma alcohol regularmente, no piense que está fuera de peligro. Las rachas de beber sin control —seis o más bebidas en un día, según un estudio de los Estados Unidos— pueden aumentar el riesgo de un palpitar rápido del corazón asociado con una irregularidad llamada taquiarritmia supraventricular. Algunos doctores le llaman a este síndrome "corazón de fiestas" ya que ocurre a menudo en personas que consumen durante días festivos más alcohol del que están acostumbradas.

Amparo profesional

Las arritmias pueden ser en lo que usted menos piensa cuando va a la doctora para un examen físico. Pero con un electrocardiograma —una prueba que mide la regularidad de los latidos de su corazón— ella le puede confirmar un desorden en el ritmo. La doctora también puede diagnosticar arritmias si usted llega a su oficina quejándose de palpitaciones y mareo. Usted tiene varias opciones cuando se requiere algo más que un cambio en el estilo de vida para controlar un latido seriamente irregular del corazón.

Los medicamentos son una opción. "Los medicamentos pueden controlar muchas arritmias y sus síntomas. Algunas de las drogas nuevas son bastante efectivas", dice el doctor Pohost. Estos medicamentos usualmente pueden calmar su temor de una muerte súbita estabilizando la actividad eléctrica de su corazón, pero su médico debe escogerlos cuidadosamente ya que pueden provocar efectos secundarios, incluyendo arritmias más graves, trastornos gastrointestinales y baja presión arterial. En muchos casos, la gente termina tomando estas drogas por el resto de sus vidas.

Su médico también puede recomendar el implante de un desfibrilador cardíaco. Su médico puede insertar este dispositivo a pilas en su pecho o abdomen desde donde controlará el latido de su corazón. Si el latido se vuelve peligrosamente rápido o caótico, mandará un choque eléctrico al corazón que puede sentirse como una palmada o golpe en el pecho. Esto tiene por objeto sobresaltar al corazón para que regrese a su actividad normal.

¿Qué tan efectivos son estos dispositivos? Un estudio encontró que entre 650 pacientes (edad promedio de 60 años), los desfibriladores implantados mantuvieron al 60 por ciento de ellos vivos por diez años como mínimo. Los investigadores estimaron que prácticamente todos ellos se hubieran muerto sin este dispositivo de alta técnica.

Cuando el latido de su corazón simplemente no quiere agarrar la onda, los médicos tienen otra opción de alta técnica a su disposición, llamada catéter de ablación. Este tratamiento está reservado para tipos particulares de desorden de ritmo que pueden ser resistentes a otras terapias. Es particularmente útil para condiciones en las cuales los latidos anormales del corazón se originan en las cámaras superiores del corazón. Consiste en hacer pasar un tubo delgado a través de una de sus venas e insertarlo en el corazón.

Una vez que el catéter está colocado correctamente, se activa una frecuencia débil de radio para matar las áreas minúsculas del tejido del corazón que están causando las arritmias. Al destruir las células en una sección no mayor a la quinta parte de una pulgada en diámetro, este procedimiento elimina los impulsos locos que causan ciertos tipos de arritmias de alto riesgo.

ARRUGAS

Cómo liquidar
las líneas prematuras

Concentrada y con el ceño fruncido, usted se pone muy seria cuando se maquilla. Entrecierra los ojos para aplicarse un toque de sombra de ojos. Levanta las cejas ligeramente al ponerse rímel y darse una pasada de rubor. Luego frunce la boca para el lápiz de labios. Muy bien. Usted se recompensa con una sonrisa en el espejo.

Y entonces se da cuenta. El ceño fruncido todavía está allí, junto con los ojos entrecerrados y las líneas de la sonrisa.

¿Arrugas, ya? Tener carácter está bien, y usted siempre ha admirado a las mujeres que envejecen con dignidad, pero estas líneas se sienten prematuras —como un mensaje del futuro entregado demasiado temprano. Usted simplemente no está lista para las arrugas todavía.

De repente, usted se siente vieja. Y probablemente menos atractiva. Por eso, le preocupa que una sonrisa amplia vaya a dejar translucir sus arrugas grandes. Y mantiene sus ojos bien abiertos para borrar esas patas de gallo.

Las raíces de los surcos

Los médicos dicen que las inevitables arrugas de origen genético y de la gravedad realmente no deberían llegar hasta que usted se acerca a su década de los 60 años de edad. Pero estas llegan mucho más temprano —a finales de su década de los 20 años de edad y durante su década de los 30 años de edad— para muchas de nosotras. Aquí está la razón por qué.

Primero, muchos conocen el viejo refrán que dice "No se puede tapar el sol, y muchos menos con un dedo". Pues un refrán nuevo para evitar las arrugas debería de ser: "Si al salir al sol te tapas, de las arrugas te escapas". La razón es sencilla, el sol es el causante número uno de las arrugas prematuras y el cáncer de la piel. A pesar de esto, las personas siguen tostándose como nueces para un *look* aparentemente "saludable". Y no se crea que este daño se limita sólo a las personas muy blancas de tez, aunque sí es cierto que éstas se queman más fácilmente que las personas trigueñas. Aun en una piel naturalmente oscura, el daño del sol causa entre un 80 a un 90 por ciento de las señales visibles del envejecimiento, incluyendo las arrugas, dicen los doctores.

La causa número dos de las arrugas es fumar, porque acelera el envejecimiento de su piel en hasta diez años. El fumar reduce el flujo de la sangre a la piel, lo cual disminuye su capacidad de reparar el daño. También libera enzimas que atacan los tejidos de su piel de la misma forma en que los ablandadores para la carne debilitan las fibras de esta. Y debido a que la piel "memoriza" cuando se la dobla en el mismo lugar una y otra vez, la mecánica de fumar también causa arrugas. El continuo fruncir la cara para aspirar el cigarrillo forma arrugas en los labios, y entrecerrar los ojos para evitar el humo abre el camino para las patas de gallo.

Algunas líneas se van a formar simplemente porque expresamos emociones, con una sonrisa pronta o un entrecejo preocupado. La forma en que usted duerme puede también dejar grabada una arruga en la memoria de su piel, especialmente si usted duerme boca abajo.

Pero, ¿qué puede hacer usted si lleva años practicando hábitos que fomentan las arrugas? ¿Puede deshacerse del daño? Sí, se puede. Usted puede evitar que se formen la mayoría de las arrugas nuevas y quitar las peores de las antiguas con la ayuda de su doctor.

Más vale prevenir...

Si usted está decidida a combatir las arrugas, aun cuando signifique abandonar el bronceado por una belleza más pálida y más saludable, aquí está dónde empezar.

Use un parasol químico. La loción antisolar es su arma número uno contra el daño adicional del sol, dice el doctor Albert M. Kligman, profesor de dermatología en la Escuela de Medicina de la Universidad de Pensilvania, en Filadelfia. Use una loción antisolar de espectro completo que bloquee los dos tipos de radiación ultravioleta (*UVA* y *UVB*, por sus siglas en inglés), y úsela diariamente, durante todo el año, dice el doctor Kligman. Después de que usted se lava la cara en la mañana, déjela ligeramente húmeda y aplique gotitas del tamaño de un chícharo (guisante) de loción antisolar en sus mejillas y frente, frótela por la piel en toda la cara. No se olvide de los dorsos de sus manos, el cuello y el escote.

Usted necesita usar una loción con un *SPF* de 15 o más alto. *SPF* (por sus siglas en inglés), significa el factor protector del sol, y SPF 15 —el que la mayoría de los médicos recomiendan— significa que usted puede estar en el sol 15 veces más tiempo sin quemarse que lo podría estar si no usara la loción.

Recuerde también, que aunque el uso diario de una loción antisolar SPF 15 la protegerá adecuadamente mientras usted sale y entra de los edificios, para pasarse muchas horas afuera necesitará usar productos con un SPF más alto y volverse a aplicar frecuentemente.

Sin embargo, los doctores no concuerdan en qué tan alto ir con los números SPF. Algunos dicen que los números superiores a 25 pueden darle una falsa sensación de seguridad. Aunque los números más altos sí la protegen de los rayos UVB que queman, pueden dejar pasar más radiación UVA. Los rayos UVA penetran más profundamente en la piel y causan la mayoría de los daños relacionados con la edad, como las arrugas, dice el doctor Melvin L. Elson, director médico del Centro Dermatológico, en Nashville.

El doctor Joseph Bark, un dermatólogo en Lexington, Kentucky, y autor de *Retin-A and Other Youth Miracles* (La *Retin-A* y otros milagros de la juventud) no está de acuerdo. Él dice que la investigación muestra que la piel se va a quemar algo aun con las lociones SPF 15, y él recomienda usar el SPF más alto que pueda encontrar, incluso para el uso diario.

Y lea el contenido de las lociones antisolares. "Las mejores lociones de espectro amplio contienen dióxido de titanio (*titanium dioxide*) —partículas finas que permanecen en su piel y son resistentes al lavado y frotado", dice el doctor Kligman. Un ejemplo es *Sundown*.

Confíe en los cosméticos sólo para maquillarse. Su mostrador favorito de cosméticos puede ofrecer bases o humectantes que contienen loción antisolar con SPF bajos, pero estos son muy débiles para una protección real, dice el doctor Kligman.

Proteja el área de sus ojos. Mientras que está haciendo ejercicio, usted no quiere una loción antisolar que irrite sus ojos al sudar. Pruebe este consejo del doctor Elson para cuando hace ejercicio. "Tome una loción antisolar con base de cera hecha para los labios y aplíquela alrededor de los ojos. No se correrá", dice él. Usted también se debería proteger los ojos con un buen par de anteojos (gafas), preferentemente del tipo que se curva alrededor. Asegúrese de que la protegen de los rayos UV.

Vístase para el sol. Los fabricantes de ropa innovadores han salido con una colección básica de blusas, trajes de baño y ropa informal de una tela que está especialmente tejida para evitar que la radiación del sol llegue a su piel.

Bote ese hábito desagradable. Sí, sí, ya le han dicho antes que fumar ya no está de moda. Ahora usted tiene otra razón más para dejarlo.

Alimente su rostro. Para la salud de la piel en general, coma una dieta balanceada de frutas, granos integrales y verduras. Puede ser que también quiera probar suplementos que han probado reducir el daño del sol en su piel, dice la doctora Karen Burke, Ph.D., una dermatóloga en práctica privada en la Ciudad de Nueva York. Ella recomienda suplementos diarios de 100 microgramos de selenio (tomado mejor como *l-selenomethionine*), más 400 unidades de vitamina E. Use las formas de la vitamina E *d-alpha tocopheryl acetate*, *d-alpha tocopheryl acid succinate* o *d-alpha tocopherol* —no la forma "*dl tocopherols*", la cual es mucho menos activa. Usted no debería sufrir ningún efecto secundario de estas dosis seguras, dice la doctora Burke. Aunque la investigación no se ha diseñado específicamente para vincular estos nutrientes con la reparación de las arrugas, estos pueden ayudar, agrega ella.

Obsérvese en el espejo. Coloque un pequeño espejo de mano junto a su teléfono por unos cuantos días y obsérvese cuando habla. Puede ser que tenga algunos hábitos de arrugar la cara de los cuales no está usted consciente, tales como fruncir el entrecejo o entrecerrar los ojos mientras está reflexionando. El espejo le ayudará a aprender a relajar los músculos de la cara que usted está haciendo trabajar horas de más y a reducir las líneas de expresión.

Mueva el cuerpo, no la cara. Aunque los ejercicios faciales han sido promocionados en muchos libros sobre la belleza, la mayoría de esos realmente aumentan las arrugas, dice la doctora Burke. Cuando usted hace muecas o contorsiona su rostro a través de los ejercicios, termina por trabajar los mismos músculos que causan las arrugas en primer lugar, dice ella.

Duérmase boca arriba. "Es la mejor posición para un rostro de aspecto joven y sin líneas", dice el doctor Gary Monheit, profesor asistente de dermatología en la Escuela de Medicina de la Universidad de Alabama, en Birmingham. Si usted ha enterrado su cara de frente en la almohada por años, acostarse sobre la espalda todas las noches con una almohada debajo de sus rodillas puede ayudarle a cambiar el hábito.

Los puntos básicos para reparar las arrugas

Ahora que usted se ha comprometido a evitar arrugas nuevas, ¿tiene usted que seguir sufriendo por las que ha tenido por años? De ninguna manera. Hay muchas tendencias nuevas en la dermatología y la cirugía plástica que pueden quitarle sus arrugas. Abarcan desde lociones y cremas con receta para *peeling* (descamación de la piel en capas) a reparaciones de superficie y cirugía.

Pero recuerde esto: "No es posible ir y que le hagan una cantidad ilimitada de cirugía plástica. Hágase lo menos posible para obtener la cantidad máxima posible de mejoras", dice el cirujano plástico doctor Geoffrey Tobias, de la Escuela de Medicina Monte Sinaí de la Universidad de la Ciudad de Nueva York. "Usted nunca volverá a tener 21 años de edad otra vez o a borrar 20 años de su cara. Pero si dos o tres arrugas la molestan, hágase cargo de ellas. Se verá y se sentirá mejor."

Considere esto.

Alíselas con *Retin-A*. El *tretinoin* (*Retin-A*), derivado de la vitamina A, se ha ganado su reputación como una crema excelente para alisar las arrugas, particularmente para las líneas finas causadas por años de gozar bajo el sol. Pero esté prevenida: la crema *Retin-A* sólo está disponible con receta. La multitud de ingredientes con nombres similares en muchos de los cosméticos y las lociones son sólo eso: similares en nombre. Vea a su dermatólogo. (Para consejos en el uso de *Retin-A*, vea la página 461)

Detenga el tiempo con *Retin-A*

La *Retin-A* no es solamente para el acné.

"Yo no sé cómo tratar a una paciente con arrugas sin recetarle *Retin-A*", dice el doctor Melvin L. Elson, director médico del Centro Dermatológico, en Nashville. "La crema *Retin-A* funciona al cambiar la piel para hacerla normal y más lisa." Aumenta el flujo sanguíneo en la piel para darle otra vez un tono rosado juvenil y también atrae las células fabricantes de colágeno más cerca de la superficie de la piel, lo cual tiende a rellenar las arrugas.

Los efectos de la *tretinoin* (*Retin-A*) sobre las arrugas fueron descubiertos por el doctor Albert M. Kligman, profesor de dermatología en la Escuela de Medicina de la Universidad de Pensilvania, en Filadelfia. Muchos de sus pacientes que estaban usando *Retin-A* para el acné grave observaron su piel notablemente más tersa y firme. Desde entonces, los efectos contra el envejecimiento de la *Retin-A* se han comprobado en numerosos estudios, el doctor Kligman recomienda usarla temprano en la vida para tener una ventaja en la prevención de las arrugas.

"Si usted tiene muchas arrugas y está joven, aun en su década de los veinte años de edad, no espere hasta llegar a los 40 ó 50 años de edad y tener arrugas profundas y muchas manchas en la piel", dice él. "Si usted es una persona de tez clara quien tuvo una niñez normal en los Estados Unidos, usted debería empezar con la *Retin-A* temprano y ponerse en un programa que le dure por el resto de su vida."

La *Retin-A* para arrugas se vende en forma de jalea y crema en varias concentraciones, y usted y su dermatólogo probablemente necesiten experimentar para descubrir cuál es la adecuada para usted. Al principio, su piel puede irritarse y escamarse, pero dentro de un mes o dos, debería adaptarse. Si usted tiene una piel muy sensible, pruebe aplicándola una vez cada tercer día y después cada segundo día hasta que su piel se adapte, o bien empiece con la concentración más baja (crema de 0,25 por ciento), y aumente gradualmente a concentraciones más altas, sugiere el doctor Kligman. Una forma menos irritante de *Retin-A*, llamada *Renova* está esperando la aprobación de la Administración de Alimentos y Drogas.

Si usted está determinada a combatir las arrugas con *Retin-A*, necesita saber que esta es una relación de por vida. Si usted deja de usar la droga, sus arrugas finas volverán. Y debido a que la *Retin-A* aumenta la sensibilidad de su piel al sol, es vital un tratamiento de loción antisolar diario con un factor de protección solar (o *SPF*, por sus siglas en inglés) alto.

Pruebe las lociones *AHA*. Su dermatólogo tiene un nuevo método gradual para la reducción de las arrugas, dice el doctor Elson. Las lociones altamente concentradas hechas de ácidos alfahidróxidos (o *AHA*, por sus siglas en inglés), derivadas del vino, la leche, las manzanas, los limones o la caña de azúcar, gradualmente desprenderán las capas superiores de piel muerta. "Con el transcurso del tiempo, harán menos visibles las patas de gallo y las arrugas finas", dice el doctor Elson. Algunas de las lociones más populares contienen ácido glicólico de la caña de azúcar, el cual tiene pequeñas moléculas que son fáciles de absorber por la piel. Los AHAs de baja concentración también están disponibles en su botica o mostrador de cosméticos en algunos limpiadores y humectantes tales como *Avon's Anew Alpha Hydrox Skin Treatment System* y *Eucerin Plus Alphahy-droxy Moisturing Lotion*, pero estos son menos efectivos que los productos de mayor fuerza que su dermatólogo le puede proporcionar.

Hasta la fecha, los AHAs son la única competencia real para la capacidad de combatir arrugas de la *Retin-A*. Las lociones AHA proporcionan resultados menos dramáticos que *Retin-A*, pero también tienen menos probabilidades de irritar su piel.

Quítese las líneas con el *peeling*. Aunque esto puede sonar drástico, el *peeling* (descamación de la piel en capas) químico puede ser un procedimiento relativamente sutil, dice la doctora Sorrel S. Resnik, profesora clínica de dermatología y cirugía cutánea en la Escuela de Medicina de la Universidad de Miami. El dermatólogo limpia su rostro con acetona, un solvente fuerte para limpieza, y entonces aplica ácido en su cutis con un algodón. El cutis se vuelve blanco y arde brevemente mientras que la acetona penetra; entonces, un día o dos después, varias capas de cutis (y arrugas finas) se desprenden. Muchos doctores ofrecen una serie de tres a seis *peelings* de ácido leves con intervalos de varias semanas, para obtener resultados que son un poco menos efectivos que un *peeling* medio o profundo. Con las series, usted tendrá menos molestia y una cura más rápida, usualmente en unos cuantos días. El ácido tricloroacético tiene un buen récord de seguridad y efectividad, y el ácido glicólico, que es menos penetrante, también es popular.

Los *peelings* muy profundos pueden ser peligrosos, dice la doctora Resnik, y por lo general se ofrecen sólo a las personas con la piel extremadamente curtida y áspera. El químico usado más a menudo para los *peelings* profundos es el fenol, el cual puede causar problemas cardíacos o en el riñón. El fenol se debe aplicar en la sala de operaciones ya que requiere una supervisión cercana del corazón.

Pregunte acerca de los rellenos. Rellenar la piel debajo de una arruga es una alternativa al *peeling* de las arrugas desde la superficie, dice el doctor Monheit. Los dermatólogos usan varias substancias para rellenar las arrugas, pero la más conocida es el colágeno, derivada del ganado. El colágeno es un tejido fibroso que forma una red de apoyo justo debajo de la superficie de la piel. El doctor inyecta el colágeno en su arruga, y aparece un bulto debajo de la superficie de la piel. Cuando el bulto desaparece (en tan poco como seis horas), la arruga se habrá desaparecido.

¿Los problemas con el colágeno? Que es temporal —los resultados duran de 4 a 15 meses, dice el doctor Monheit. Y algunas personas pueden ser alérgicas a esta forma de colágeno, así que los doctores deben primero hacer una prueba alérgica.

Si usted resulta ser alérgica al colágeno del ganado, pregunte acerca de un nuevo método llamado implante autógeno de tejido, dice el doctor Elson. Un parche de piel obtenido de otra parte de su cuerpo se manda a una empresa que procesa su propio colágeno de la piel. Esta empresa entonces regresa a su doctor una jeringa llena con el colágeno para una inyección.

Un relleno de arrugas llamado *Fibrel* puede durar hasta cinco años, dice el doctor Monheit. El *Fibrel* es un material de base gelatinosa que se mezcla con su propio suero de la sangre y se inyecta debajo de la arruga. Su cuerpo reacciona fabricando su propio colágeno el cual, a su vez, llena la arruga. ¿Desventajas? Las inyecciones de *Fibrel* duelen más que las inyecciones de colágeno, y el proceso toma más tiempo, dice el doctor Monheit.

"El mejor relleno sería algo natural de su propio cuerpo", dice el doctor Michael Sachs, un cirujano plástico en práctica privada en la Ciudad de Nueva York. Una técnica para llenar arrugas que todavía se encuentra en la etapa experimental se llama transferencia de grasa o *microlipoinjection* (inyección pequeña de grasa). El doctor extrae una cantidad minúscula de grasa de otra parte de su cuerpo, como por ejemplo de su barriga o asentadera, y la inyecta debajo de la arruga. No hay peligro de una reacción alérgica ya que esto es realmente inyectarse a usted misma dentro de usted misma. Sin embargo, los resultados duran poco. Los investigadores no están seguros por qué, pero las células grasosas no parecen durar mucho en su nueva ubicación.

El hilo quirúrgico también puede hacer rellenar una arruga, dice el doctor Sachs. "El cirujano coloca un hilo de base proteica directamente debajo de la línea de la arruga, donde estimula las células locales para que produzcan su propio colágeno. En unos seis meses o algo así, el hilo se disuelve, y el colágeno que queda rellena la arruga por dos a cinco años." El doctor Sachs desarrolló este procedimiento. Verifique con su doctor acerca de su disponibilidad.

Quítelas raspando. Un procedimiento llamado dermabrasión, el cual a menudo se usa para quitar cicatrices de acné, también puede ser muy efectivo sobre las arrugas alrededor de la boca pero no en áreas donde la piel es muy delgada, como alrededor de los ojos, dice el doctor Sachs. Un instrumento especial llamado *dermabrader* literalmente lija y quita la capa superior de la piel dejando una costra que sanará en unos diez días, dice él. Una desventaja es que a menudo la dermabrasión quita el pigmento de la piel, agrega la doctora Resnick. Así que si usted escoge este método de quitar las arrugas, siempre necesitará ponerse maquillaje en las áreas tratadas.

Y si piensa en la cirugía . . .

Hay una amplia gama de opciones quirúrgicas para quitar las arrugas, dice el doctor Tobias. Algunas cirugías levantarán y tensarán la piel facial, alisando las arrugas en el proceso. Otros procedimientos quitan las bolsas arrugadas o rellenan los pliegues de arrugas en la piel. Aquí hay dos opciones.

Alise el área de los ojos. A lo largo de los años, los párpados pueden arrugarse en forma de pliegues pesados que hacen a sus ojos verse cansados todo el tiempo. Con una blefaropastia tradicional, o estiramiento de los ojos, un cirujano corta y quita la piel excesiva para hacer el aspecto del área de los ojos más firme y de aspecto juvenil. O usted puede tener bolsas arrugadas arriba o abajo de los ojos que están compuestas primordialmente de grasa. Un nuevo procedimiento inventado por el doctor Sachs, llamado blefaroplastia para derretir la grasa, puede ayudar. Un cirujano inserta una sonda caliente a través de una incisión diminuta en la esquina del ojo y vaporiza el contenido de agua de la grasa, que literalmente derrite las bolsas. El tiempo de recuperación puede variar entre unos cuantos días a una semana o más, depende del procedimiento usado, dice el doctor Sachs.

Deshágase del aspecto demacrado. Uno de los procesos naturales del envejecimiento es la pérdida gradual de hueso a lo largo de la mandíbula y del tejido suave debajo de las mejillas. Los implantes de silicón sólido pueden rellenar los resultantes huecos y pliegues de arrugas avejentados, dice el doctor Tobias. Los implantes sólidos de silicón no se han asociado con las dificultades que se han visto en los implantes de silicón líquido, agrega. Operando a través de incisiones dentro de la boca, un cirujano puede insertar estas fórmulas debajo de las mejillas y a lo largo de la línea de los carrillos.

ARTRITIS

Cómo puede usted vencer el dolor

Según un estudio publicado en la revista *Arthritis Care and Research* (Tratamiento e Investigaciones Sobre la Artritis), casi el 7 por ciento de los latinos que viven en los Estados Unidos, más de dos millones de personas, padecen de la artritis. Pero a menudo no es quien usted espera.

Seguramente, usted entendería si fuera su madre o abuela. Después de todo, aproximadamente la mitad de las personas mayores de 60 años de edad sufren de alguna forma de esta enfermedad, haciéndola la condición crónica más común entre los estadounidenses mayores.

¿Pero, artritis en personas de su edad?

Puede suceder.

A pesar de su reputación de ser tan parte de envejecer como es el tener canas, la artritis no discrimina —despliega dolor con igualdad. "Mucha gente no se sorprende de oír que la artritis es la causa principal de incapacidad en personas arriba de los 45 años de edad", dice el doctor Paul Caldron, D.O., un reumatólogo clínico e investigador en el Centro de Artritis, en Phoenix. "Pero sí se sorprenden de saber que es la causa principal de incapacidad en todas las edades." Las estadísticas apoyan lo que dice el doctor Caldron. Casi un millón de mujeres latinas de la edad de 15 años y mayores padecen de la artritis. Quiere decir que no sólo afecta a las personas mayores, sino también a mujeres muy jóvenes.

El vínculo con las hormonas

Aunque hay más de 100 tipos diferentes de artritis, los más comunes son la osteoartritis y la artritis reumática. Las mujeres tienen tres veces más probabilidades que los hombres de adquirir la artritis reumática, la forma más debilitante de la enfermedad.

A diferencia de la osteoartritis, la artritis reumática afecta todo el cuerpo. Es especialmente dolorosa y normalmente ataca a las mujeres entre los 20 y los 40 años de edad.

"Lo que realmente es triste es que muchas personas sufren de fuertes dolores y pérdida de funciones, y no hay nada que usted pueda hacer para prevenirla, ya que no sabemos qué es la causa", dice el doctor Arthur Grayzel, vicepresidente de asuntos médicos en la Fundación de la Artritis. "Sabemos que la artritis reumática es una enfermedad inmunológica, y como otras enfermedades inmunológicas como el asma, lupus y problemas de la tiroides, afecta a las mujeres en índices más altos debido a que ellas tienden a tener sistemas inmunes sobreactivos. Pero también hay información sólida apoyando que la artritis reumática está relacionada con las hormonas."

Los investigadores especulan que durante nuestros años de fertilidad, a algunas de nuestras hormonas se les asigna la protección del feto contra ataques inmunológicos, dice el doctor Grayzel. En el proceso, otras partes de nuestros cuerpos se dejaron más vulnerables, y algunos investigadores creen que por esa razón algunas de nosotras nos volvemos víctimas de la artritis reumática. Aun cuando una mujer nunca tiene niños, estos cambios hormonales ocurren de todas maneras, y es por eso que muchas de las mujeres sin niños se encuentran entre los casi dos millones de mujeres con artritis reumática que viven en los Estados Unidos.

La forma más común de artritis, la osteoartritis, afecta a 16 millones de estadounidenses y se produce cuando el cartílago en las articulaciones se deteriora por estrés, sobrepeso o lesión a menudo relacionada con algún deporte. "Eso no quiere decir que si usted practica algún deporte, sufrirá de artritis. Pero aquellos que han sufrido una lesión repetida en una articulación, sin importar qué tan pequeña, tienen una probabilidad mayor de sufrir de osteoartritis", dice el doctor Caldron. Ataca a unos 12 millones de mujeres, quienes usualmente la adquieren después de cumplir los 55 años de edad. Los lugares problemáticos típicos incluyen los dedos, pies, la espalda, las rodillas y caderas.

Una pesadez para el cuerpo y la mente

Cualquiera de las formas de artritis pueden afectar una vida activa. La artritis puede hacer que sus movimientos sean más lentos y causar algo de dolor en sus músculos, articulaciones o tendones. En su peor momento, puede causar suficiente agonía como para requerir hospitalización o cuidado día y noche, dice el doctor Jeffrey R. Lisse, director de la División de Reumatología, y profesor asociado de medicina en la División Médica de la Universidad de Texas, en Galveston. La artritis también puede resultar en problemas para dormir, actividad sexual disminuida debido al dolor y un sistema cardiovascular más débil, ya que los que la sufren dejan de hacer ejercicio cuando tienen dolor y articulaciones inflamadas.

Pero la artritis no envejece sólo al cuerpo. "La depresión es casi universal entre los pacientes de artritis", dice el doctor Lisse. "Pero mucha gente con artritis también adquiere lo que se conoce como incapacidad aprendida. Eso ocurre cuando alguien empieza saludable y capaz de hacer cosas por sí misma, pero al paso del tiempo, a medida que el dolor empeora, ella es menos capaz de cuidarse a sí misma. Alguien más debe asumir esas funciones, así que la persona con artritis se vuelve más y más inútil. De hecho, algunos de los pacientes más jóvenes en asilos de ancianos son personas que sufren de artritis grave, que están allí por su incapacidad de cuidarse a sí mismos."

El doctor Grayzel agrega: "Yo creo que la sociedad casi espera que la gente tenga artritis cuando se hace vieja, de tal manera que cuando una mujer mayor cojea o usa un bastón, realmente no sorprende a nadie. Pero cuando usted es joven y la imagen de su cuerpo es muy diferente, los efectos pueden ser devastadores. El hecho es que muchas personas que tienen artritis —atletas, estrellas de cine y otras bajo la vista del público— no lo admitirán porque parece tener una imagen negativa. Tener artritis la hace verse vieja antes de tiempo."

Una estrategia inteligente

Pero no tiene que ser así. Puede ser que usted no pueda evitar la artritis reumática, pero sí puede reducir los efectos de envejecimiento sobre usted. Y puede ser que pueda prevenir o reducir el dolor de la osteoartritis. Aquí le decimos cómo.

Pierda peso. "Tener sobrepeso es un factor de mayor riesgo, especialmente para artritis de las rodillas y caderas", dice el doctor Grayzel. "Aun cuando se encuentre entre los 20 y los 40 años de edad, usted debe tratar de reducir el peso a cerca del promedio normal para su estatura. Si usted tiene 20 por ciento de sobrepeso —cerca de 160 libras (72 kilos) o más para la mujer normal— usted es una candidata ideal para la osteoartritis. Pero cualquier pérdida de peso ayuda. Si pierde solamente 10 libras (4,5 kilos) y se mantiene así por diez años, no importa cuál es su peso actual, usted puede reducir el riesgo de osteoartritis en sus rodillas en un 50 por ciento."

Cuide lo que come. Varios estudios muestran que los alimentos desempeñan un papel crucial en la gravedad de la artritis. Investigadores noruegos descubrieron que pacientes con artritis reumática vieron una mejoría dramática en sus condiciones dentro del mes de comenzar dietas vegetarianas. Otros científicos han encontrado que los ácidos grasos omega-3, abundantes en peces de aguas frías como el salmón, arenque y sardinas, también alivian los dolores de la artritis reumática.

"Una dieta que es baja en grasas saturadas y grasas animales también parece ayudar", dice el doctor Caldron. Comer bastantes frutas frescas y verduras y fuentes de grasa de carne no roja como pescado y pollo pueden hacer que el cuerpo produzca menos substancias pro-inflamatorias. Eso no quiere decir que una dieta va a curar la artritis, pero puede modificar sus efectos.

"Algunas personas reaccionan a ciertos alimentos, casi como una alergia", agrega el doctor Caldron. "Esto puede resultar del trigo o frutos cítricos, lentejas o aun alcohol. El problema es que no hay una forma de hacer pruebas para esto. Pero si usted nota una reacción significativa y consistentemente más dolor dentro de un período de 48 horas después de comer ciertos alimentos, elimínelos de su dieta."

Póngase en movimiento. El ejercicio regular para fortalecer sus músculos y adquirir flexibilidad puede mantener a raya a la osteoartritis o reducir sus efectos. El ejercicio también se recomienda para la artritis reumática, aunque el ejercicio debe estar bajo la supervisión de un médico y enfatizar ejercicios de alcance-de-movimiento, (en inglés, se llaman *range-of-motion exercises*).

"El ejercicio mejora la fuerza y la flexibilidad, por lo tanto se ejerce menos tensión sobre las articulaciones y éstas se pueden mover más fácil y eficientemente", dice el doctor John H. Klippel, director clínico del Instituto Nacional de Artritis y Enfermedades Musculoesqueléticas y de la Piel en Bethesda, Maryland. "La inactividad, por otro lado, de hecho incita al dolor, rigidez y otros síntomas."

Levantar pesas es especialmente útil ya que fortalece el tono muscular, que es especialmente importante en los que sufren de artritis. Enfatice el fortalecimiento de los músculos abdominales para reducir el dolor en la espalda, y los músculos de los muslos para el dolor en las rodillas, aconseja el doctor Grayzel. Entretanto, el ejercicio aeróbico como correr, andar en bicicleta y nadar también es útil para mejorar la flexibilidad.

Vaya más despacio cuando sea necesario. Cuando una articulación está hinchada e inflamada, no ayuda que se la continúe usando. "No ejercite cuando tenga dolor", dice el doctor Grayzel. "De lo contrario, se va a lastimar más." Así que aun cuando usted esté en un programa de ejercicio regular, deje de hacerlo un día (o dos) cuando sus articulaciones o músculos empiezan a doler.

Equípese bien. "Una causa frecuente de la osteoartritis son las lesiones, por lo que usted debe aprovechar de los diferentes equipos de protección para atletas", dice el doctor Caldron. "Al usar equipo protector, usted va a disminuir la posibilidad de lesiones o de volver a lastimar sus articulaciones, tendones y músculos, lo cual reduce el riesgo de la osteoartritis." Eso quiere decir que usted debería usar almohadillas en las rodillas, codos y otros lugares de posibles problemas para reducir las lesiones. Estas almohadillas están disponibles en cualquier tienda de artículos deportivos.

Caliéntese. Para alivio inmediato, mucha gente encuentra que colocar calor húmedo directamente sobre las áreas inflamadas ayuda a reducir el dolor, dice el doctor Lisse. Las botellas de agua caliente, mantas eléctricas y baños calientes ayudan. Pero use el calor juiciosamente —no más de 10 ó 15 minutos a la vez. Y asegúrese de hacer una pausa de por lo menos una hora antes de volver a aplicarlo. Los bálsamos analgésicos de venta libre como por ejemplo *Ben-Gay*, también pueden ayudar a calmar el dolor cuando las articulaciones están calientes, sensibles e inflamadas. Pero no las use con calor, advierte el doctor Caldron. Las dos cosas juntas pueden provocar reacciones desagradables tales como quemaduras y ampolladuras.

O congélese. El hielo, entretanto, se recomienda algunas veces para prevenir dolor cuando las articulaciones están sobretrabajadas o abusadas. El doctor Lisse sugiere que usted envuelva algo de hielo en una toalla y lo aplique suavemente a sus articulaciones varias veces al día, 15 minutos sí y 15 minutos no.

También practique la otra forma de enfriarse —al encontrar maneras de enfrentarse al estrés en su vida. Cuando usted está tensa, tendrá más dolor. Pero cualquier cosa que usted haga para aprender a relajarse —sea escuchar música, meditar o practicar un pasatiempo— puede ayudar, especialmente cuando el dolor es fuerte.

ATAQUE AL CORAZÓN

No descarte la posibilidad

De vez en cuando usted se entera de una mujer en la flor de su edad cuya vida fue arrebatada por un ataque al corazón. Y entonces usted piensa "¿me podría suceder esto a mí?"

No entre en pánico. Hasta que no llegan a la menopausia, la mayoría de las mujeres tienen una protección natural contra los ataques al corazón. De hecho, los expertos dicen que apenas arriba de la mitad de un 1 por ciento de los ataques al corazón ocurren a las mujeres de 44 años de edad para abajo.

Pero mientras que los ataques al corazón son poco comunes entre las mujeres premenopáusicas, eso no quiere decir que usted no debería hacer todo lo que pueda ahora para estar segura de que no va a sufrir uno.

Pocas cosas en la vida pueden envejecerla tan rápidamente como un ataque al corazón.

Puede caer como un rayo, aunque el escenario se puede haber estado preparando por años con depósitos de grasa formándose en sus arterias coronarias.

Cuando se termina la suerte

Por definición, un ataque al corazón es una reducción o bloqueo del flujo de sangre en una arteria coronaria lo cual causa un daño al corazón que potencialmente pone su vida en peligro. Y aunque nuestra sociedad tiende a pensar que los ataques al corazón son un problema de los hombres, más de 500.000 mujeres sufren ataques al corazón cada año, a menudo acompañados por un dolor agobiante en el pecho, mucho sudor y falta de aliento que son señales de un coágulo súbito en una arteria coronaria y de sus efectos en el corazón. Un tercio de estos ataques al corazón son fatales. Cuatro en cinco muertes por ataques al corazón ocurren en aquellas mujeres de 65 años de edad o mayores.

Cuando se trata de nuestros corazones, las mujeres somos más afortunadas que los hombres. En nuestros años premenopáusicos, la hormona femenina estrógeno proporciona una protección natural contra las fuerzas siniestras que son los ataques al corazón, los cuales empiezan a afectar a gran cantidad de hombres antes de llegar a una edad madura. Pero una vez que nosotras atravesamos la menopausia, esas defensas naturales prácticamente desaparecen. Al envejecer, nuestros corazones y los vasos sanguíneos que los alimentan empiezan a mostrar y sentir su edad, aun sin la intrusión dramática de un ataque al corazón. El corazón comienza gradualmente a bombear un poco menos eficientemente, y las paredes de las arterias se vuelven un poco más duras y menos flexibles.

Cuando le da un ataque al corazón, en sólo minutos u horas, éste puede afectar en forma devastadora su cuerpo, tal y como si usted agregara 20 a 30 años a su edad de la noche a la mañana. Cuando el abastecimiento de sangre a su corazón se daña, las células del corazón pueden perjudicarse gravemente. Mientras más tiempo se obstaculiza este flujo de sangre, mayor es la posibilidad de un daño irreversible, que produzca la muerte de células y de parte del músculo del corazón.

Pero también hay buenas noticias. La mayoría de los ataques al corazón son evitables, sin importar cuál sea edad, si usted adopta hábitos en su estilo de vida que pueden hacer más lenta la acumulación de depósitos grasosos en sus arterias coronarias. Sí, hay excepciones a esta regla. En algunas raras ocasiones, el estrés puede provocar un ataque al corazón, aun en una mujer joven que no tiene los vasos sanguíneos fuertemente obstruidos. "Las arterias coronarias pueden entrar en espasmo en situaciones estresantes, y esto puede reducir el flujo sanguíneo al corazón", dice el doctor James Martin, un médico familiar en el Instituto para la Salud de la Familia Urbana del Centro Médico Beth Israel, en la ciudad de Nueva York. "Si el espasmo dura lo suficiente —cerca de siete a diez minutos— usted puede tener un ataque al corazón."

Pero ese tipo de escenario es extremadamente raro. Lo más probable es que usted tenga bastante control sobre la salud y la longevidad de su corazón.

Cómo atacar el problema

Entonces, ¿dónde debe de empezar para evitarlo? Aquí hay algunas estrategias cruciales para tener en mente.

Conózcase a sí misma. "Es importante saber cuál es su situación", aconseja el doctor Richard H. Helfant, vicepresidente de medicina y director del Programa de Entrenamiento de Cardiología en el Centro Médico de la Universidad de California, Irvine y autor de *Women, Take Heart* (Mujeres, anímense). Eso quiere decir estar consciente de los factores de riesgo que pueden aumentar las posibilidades de que usted tenga problemas con el corazón. Como mujer, usted cuenta con el estrógeno como uno de sus más grandes aliados para combatir un ataque al corazón —pero, la producción de estrógeno de su cuerpo se reduce después de la menopausia. También, si parientes cercanos han tenido ataques al corazón a edades tempranas —menos de 55 años de edad— usted necesita ser aun más precavida. Y si tiene una condición que aumenta su riesgo pero que usted puede cambiar —alta presión arterial, un nivel alto de colesterol en la sangre, diabetes o el hábito del cigarrillo— necesita atacarla y controlarla antes de que ésta ataque a su corazón. Hable con su doctor sobre cómo hacer eso.

Sea disciplinada. Nadie le está pidiendo que sea una fanática. Usted no tiene que dejar la carne roja o hacer ejercicio en el gimnasio hasta querer caerse al suelo. Pero si usted lleva un estilo de vida razonablemente cuidadoso y vigoroso, usted puede mantener a su corazón palpitando con el vigor de una mujer mucho más joven, sin tener que preocuparse acerca de un ataque al corazón.

Vuélvase activa. Si usted es una de esas mujeres que se siente más cómoda con un control remoto del televisor en la mano que con una raqueta de tenis, es hora de cambiar. El ejercicio regular, como es caminar vigorosamente por 30 a 45 minutos tres veces a la semana o nadar varias veces el largo de la piscina (alberca), puede hacer de esa bomba dentro de su pecho una máquina impresionante.

"El ejercicio es beneficioso para su corazón en muchas formas", dice el doctor Stephen Havas, profesor asociado de epidemiología y medicina preventiva en la Escuela de Medicina de la Universidad de Maryland, en Baltimore. "Puede impulsar su colesterol *HDL* (lipoproteína de alta densidad), el cual es el componente protector del nivel de colesterol en su sangre. También puede reducir modestamente su presión arterial y ayudarle a controlar su peso." Y puede ayudar a mantener su corazón en forma y en condición, tal y como lo hace con los otros músculos en su cuerpo.

Coma correctamente. No es una varita mágica, pero una dieta apropiada puede ser el cuerpo y alma de cualquier programa de cuidado cardíaco personalizado. Según el doctor Fredric J. Pashkow, director médico del Programa de Rehabilitación y Mejora de la Salud Cardíaca en la Fundación Clínica de Cleveland, en Cleveland y autor de *The Woman's Heart Book* (El libro del corazón de la mujer), la investigación muestra que la mejor manera de mantener a su corazón fuera de peligro es recortando la grasa y el colesterol en su dieta. Eso significa que cuando se trata de planificar el menú, escoja pescado más a menudo que bistec (biftec), leche descremada más frecuentemente que leche entera, claras de huevo en lugar de los huevos enteros y yogur congelado bajo en grasa en lugar de helado de crema. Conserve su consumo diario de grasa dietética en un 25 por ciento o menos del total de las calorías.

Considere las hormonas. La terapia de reposición de estrógeno puede reducir su riesgo de un ataque al corazón a la mitad o a una tercera parte, según el doctor Helfant.

Pero usted debe hablar con su doctor sobre sus opciones. "Hay un inconveniente potencial con la terapia hormonal", dice el doctor Helfant, "y éste es un riesgo en el aumento de cáncer endometrial y quizás también, cáncer de mama". Si tiene una historia familiar de cáncer endometrial o de mama u otros factores de riesgo, puede ser que usted y su doctor decidan que la terapia hormonal no es para usted.

Después de sufrir un ataque

La prevención puede sonar bien, pero ¿qué si usted ya sufrió la terrible experiencia de un ataque al corazón? Bueno, agradezca haberlo sobrevivido y entonces comprométase a observar algunos hábitos saludables que podrían evitar que lo sufra por segunda vez, y esto podría ponerla en el camino más rápido a una vida vigorosa y saludable. Si usted cree que un ataque al corazón afectará permanentemente su movilidad, nivel de actividad, funcionamiento en el trabajo o vida sexual, es hora de que haga desaparecer esos mitos. A pesar de su ataque al corazón, todavía puede tener sus mejores años por delante.

Con los cambios de estilo de vida, usted debería ser capaz de reducir el riesgo de sufrir otro ataque al corazón, dice el doctor Helfant. "Estos cambios también le permitirán tomar el control de su salud y vivir una vida con sentido y significativa mientras que usted se protege al máximo grado posible."

Entonces, ¿cuál es el curso de acción que debe tomar? Las recomendaciones pueden sonar familiares, pero aquí está el impacto específico que pueden tener cuando un ataque al corazón es parte de su historia clínica.

Coma saludablemente. Después de algo tan trascendental como un ataque al corazón, usted podría pensar que el daño que su corazón ha sufrido hace que las medidas simples tal como una alimentación más saludable sea tan útil como poner un *Band-Aid* (curita) sobre su pecho. Pero cuando los investigadores del Instituto Nacional de Corazón, Pulmón y Sangre llevaron a cabo un análisis de estudios a sobrevivientes de ataques al corazón, encontraron que las personas podrían reducir significativamente sus posibilidades de sufrir otro ataque al corazón al disminuir sus niveles altos de colesterol en la sangre. Varios estudios han mostrado que una reducción del 10 por ciento en los niveles de colesterol en la sangre disminuye entre el 12 y 19 por ciento el riesgo de sufrir un segundo ataque al corazón. Una clave para bajar el colesterol en la sangre es bajar el consumo de grasa saturada (el tipo que se encuentra en productos animales y aceites tropicales) y colesterol dietético (encontrado en la mayoría de los productos animales).

Muévalo. En muchos programas para la recuperación de un ataque al corazón, la actividad física es el centro de atención, a menudo comenzando con niveles muy mesurados incluso mientras las mujeres están todavía hospitalizadas. La mayoría de los programas de rehabilitación recomiendan hacer ejercicio por 15 a 30 minutos al menos tres veces por semana.

"Las personas que no han hecho ejercicio en el pasado ciertamente estarían mejor haciendo por lo menos un poco ahora", dice Peter Wood, Ph.D., profesor emérito de medicina y director asociado del Centro de Investigación en Prevención de Enfermedades de la Universidad de Stanford, en Palo Alto, California. Al aumentar gradualmente la cantidad de actividad física que usted haga —bajo la guía de su doctor— su corazón cosechará aún más beneficios, dice el doctor Wood.

Tome aspirina. En esta era de medicamentos de gran poder y alto precio, ¿podría la humilde aspirina convertirla a usted en la viva imagen de la salud? Un equipo de investigadores de la Asociación del Corazón de los Estados Unidos analizó seis estudios en los cuales se les dio aspirina a los pacientes después de sufrir ataques al corazón. Esta píldora blanca y barata redujo el índice de fallecimiento por enfermedades del corazón entre el 5 y el 42 por ciento, y disminuyó el índice de subsecuentes ataques al corazón no fatales entre el 12 y el 57 por ciento.

Otra buena noticia: usted no necesita excederse en las dosis de aspirina. "Una aspirina para bebés al día es todo lo que necesita", dice el doctor Helfant. No obstante y a pesar de sus beneficios potenciales, algunas personas probablemente deberían evitar la aspirina por completo. "Si usted tiene un trastorno de sangramiento o una úlcera, por ejemplo, tomar aspirina no es una buena idea", dice Julie Buring, Sc.D., investigadora principal del Estudio de la Salud de las Mujeres y profesora asociada de cuidado ambulante y prevención en la escuela de Medicina de Harvard, en Boston. Ella sugiere hablar con su doctor antes de tomar aspirina.

BURSITIS Y TENDONITIS

Cómo aliviar esas articulaciones agotadas

Usted ha estado en la máquina escaladora por una hora. Ha estado paleando nieve toda la tarde. Puso tapiz de empapelar en la cocina durante el fin de semana.

¿Qué tienen todas estas cosas en común? Todas ellas son formas magníficas de terminar con un caso tremendo de bursitis o tendonitis. Estas condiciones dolorosas se superponen tan a menudo que los médicos frecuentemente las diagnostican como bursitis/tendonitis, ya que puede ser difícil decir dónde una termina y la otra empieza.

Y pueden suceder más a menudo en personas entre los 40 y los 50 años de edad, particularmente en aquellas que no han hecho nada para mantener su flexibilidad. Sin un estiramiento regular, los músculos y los tendones se tensan y se frotan más entre sí, aumentando el riesgo de inflamación.

Una vez que usted tiene bursitis y tendonitis, usted se mueve con la precaución de una persona mucho más mayor. Y usted se puede olvidar del placer de su deporte favorito, porque un movimiento súbito puede sentirse como si alguien la hubiera golpeado con un atizador caliente al rojo vivo.

Estas son las razones por la que duele.

El síndrome del desuso

Sus bolsas (*bursae*) son pequeños sacos llenos de fluido que acojinan los espacios donde los músculos pasan sobre el hueso y donde dos músculos se frotan entre sí. En sus rótulas y codos, forman un acojinamiento entre la piel y el hueso. Pueden inflamarse cuando usted se lesiona o abusa de una articulación o cuando usted acelera su ejercicio más allá de lo que está acostumbrada, dice el doctor Pekka Mooar, director del Centro de Medicina Deportiva Delaware Valley, en Filadelfia.

Si usted tiene tendonitis, lo que duele no es realmente su tendón sino un anillo de tejido alrededor del tendón donde éste se sujeta al hueso o músculo. El dolor está causado por un abuso del tendón lo cual produce inflamación.

"Todos tenemos más achaques con la edad; no hay controversia acerca de eso", dice el doctor Phillip E. Higgs, un cirujano reconstructivo en la Escuela de Medicina de la Universidad Washington, en St. Louis. Pero si usted se mantiene flexible a través de los años, un estallido de esfuerzo tiene menos probabilidades de causar bursitis y tendonitis, dice él.

Es el poco ejercicio, no el envejecimiento mismo, lo que aumenta su riesgo de sufrir estos dolorosos padecimientos. Esa es la conclusión a la que el doctor Higgs y sus colegas llegaron después de contar casos de bursitis y tendonitis en un estudio de 157 trabajadores avícolas y 118 procesadores de datos. Aunque los trabajadores oscilaban en edad entre los 20 y los 71 años de edad, los trabajadores más jóvenes que hacían poco ejercicio sufrían de aproximadamente el mismo número de inflamaciones que los trabajadores mayores que tampoco hacían mucho ejercicio.

La bursitis y la tendonitis varían mucho de persona a persona, dice el doctor Higgs. Por ejemplo, un día de hacer deportes al máximo puede causar síntomas en una persona, mientras que otra puede no tener dificultad hasta después de pasar muchos años de trabajar en una línea de ensamblaje.

Donde duele

Los hombros, codos, las caderas, rodillas y los tobillos son especialmente vulnerables a la bursitis y tendonitis. Las mujeres tienden a sufrir inflamaciones en las caderas más que los hombres porque nuestras caderas están colocadas en un ángulo más amplio desde la pelvis, colocando una mayor tensión en las articulaciones de las caderas. Para los hombres, el área problemática es por lo regular los hombros, porque ellos tienden a lanzar más o a tener empleos que requieren levantar a menudo por encima de la cabeza.

Años atrás, cuando nosotras éramos las únicas fregando pisos, a una bolsa inflamada en la rodilla se le llamaba rodilla de criada. Y una forma de tendonitis raramente vista en alguien hoy en día solía ocurrir casi exclusivamente en las muñecas de las mujeres. ¿La causa? Exprimir pañales de tela y trapos para limpiar. Actualmente, muchas de nosotras todavía sufrimos de otras formas de tendonitis por actividades como mecanografiar, dicen los médicos. Cualquier trabajo o pasatiempo que requiere un movimiento repetitivo, desde trabajar en una línea de ensamblaje hasta coser, aumenta el riesgo.

La bursitis y tendonitis también son causadas por practicar su deporte favorito en demasía. El tenis puede causarlas en los codos y muñecas y nadar puede irritar las bolsas de los hombros; correr puede agravar los tobillos y el tendón de Aquiles, particularmente si usted corre sobre superficies duras en zapatos inadecuados. Y los ejercicios aeróbicos, particularmente los aeróbicos de *step*, pueden causar que sus caderas y rodillas estallen de dolor.

Muchas veces no se detecta la bursitis como una causa del dolor en la parte inferior de la espalda, dicen los expertos. Y muchas veces acompaña al trastorno llamado fibromialgia, el cual causa dolor muscular y rigidez en todo el cuerpo.

Afortunadamente, la bursitis y tendonitis pueden tratarse. Y usted puede hacer bastante para prevenirlas.

Cómo proteger sus articulaciones

Lo más importante es ponerse en condición gradualmente y empezar con cuidado a hacer ejercicio vigoroso, dice el doctor Stephen Campbell, un reumatólogo de la Universidad de Ciencias de la Salud de Oregon, en Portland. Aquí hay algunas sugerencias.

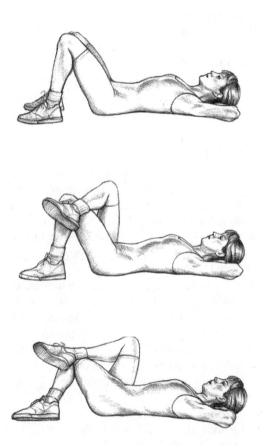

Acuéstese derecha en el piso boca arriba con las rodillas flexionadas y los pies planos en el piso (arriba). Enlace las manos atrás de la cabeza. Cruce la pierna derecha sobre la pierna izquierda, colocando el pie derecho en la parte exterior de la pierna izquierda apenas abajo de la rodilla izquierda (centro). Incline ligeramente su pelvis (esto es, presione suavemente la curvatura de su espalda hacia el piso). Conservando los hombros y la parte superior de la espalda estacionarios, use su pie derecho para jalar la rodilla izquierda a un ritmo constante hacia el piso a su lado derecho (fondo). Usted debe sentir un estiramiento en la parte izquierda de la región inferior de la espalda o parte exterior del muslo al tratar de hacer que su rodilla izquierda toque el piso. Mantenga este estiramiento por seis segundos. Regrese a la posición del principio. Descanse. Repita el ejercicio usando el pie izquierdo en la parte exterior de la pierna derecha (ligeramente abajo de la rodilla derecha) para jalar la rodilla derecha hacia el piso a su lado izquierdo. Repita tres a cinco veces, dos veces diarias.

Estírese antes de hacer ejercicio. "En preparación para una actividad vigorosa, usted necesita estirar más los músculos que va a usar", dice el doctor Mooar. "Mantenga un estiramiento lento y sostenido por diez segundos, y no salte. Repita el estiramiento tres a cinco veces antes de hacer ejercicio." Y no se estire a alta velocidad, o corre el riesgo de rasgar las fibras de músculos o los ligamentos, dice. Si no está segura de qué tipo de estiramiento es el mejor para usted, pregúntele a un entrenador.

Empiece nuevas actividades lentamente. Si usted empieza con un nuevo deporte, empiece gradualmente aumentando la fuerza y flexibilidad de los músculos que va a usar, dice el doctor Mooar. Si usted escoge tenis, por ejemplo, juegue un *set* a la vez al principio. "No tome la raqueta y juegue varios *sets* enseguida, porque su hombro va a sentir como que se está desprendiendo", dice.

Prepárese para trabajar o jugar. Si su trabajo o pasatiempo requiere movimiento repetitivo, pida a un entrenador que le recomiende ejercicios de fortalecimiento y resistencia especiales para ese movimiento, dice el doctor Mooar. "Si hace eso", dice, "usted puede detener la bursitis y tendonitis antes de que sucedan una y otra vez". Muchas personas desarrollan una inflamación crónica al volverse a lesionar sus articulaciones, dice.

Apóyese usted misma. Escribir a máquina (o computadora) y archivar puede causar problemas en sus muñecas y espalda. Para escribir, use un apoyo de muñecas para el teclado, dice el doctor Campbell. Y verifique que su silla esté ajustada correctamente para que su espalda tenga apoyo y sus brazos y muñecas estén nivelados entre sí.

Tenga piedad de sus rodillas. Fuera de una pequeña bolsa entre su rótula y la piel que la cubre, dice el doctor Mooar, hay muy poco. Así que si está haciendo el trabajo de la casa o jardinería sobre las rodillas, arrodíllese sobre un pedazo de espuma de caucho o use almohadillas en las rodillas para acojinarlas. Muchos centros de productos para el jardín, tiendas de productos deportivos y ferreterías tienen espuma de caucho o almohadillas para las rodillas.

Consejos para una pronta recuperación

¡Ay! Usted ya tiene bursitis o tendonitis y quiere alivio, pronto. La primera pregunta que usted debe hacerse es ¿qué es lo que ha hecho diferente? "Usted está haciendo demasiado, sea lo que sea", dice el doctor Campbell. "Primero, deje de hacerlo." Luego:

Dese un masaje con hielo. "Aplique una taza de papel llena de hielo a la zona dolorida", dice el doctor Robert L. Swezey, director médico del Centro de Artritis y Dolor de Espalda en Santa Mónica, California. Frote el fondo helado de la taza en el lugar dolorido de dos a cinco minutos, tres o cuatro veces al día, para controlar la inflamación, dice el.

Altérnelo con calor. Para calmar el dolor, después del hielo aplique una compresa de esas que se calientan en el horno de microondas, o una compresa

Ejercicios sin dolor

No hay necesidad de dejar que la bursitis o la tendonitis le eche a perder su participación en su deporte favorito. El acondicionamiento gradual es la clave a la prevención —o para preparar un retorno cuidadoso si la bursitis o la tendonitis ya la atacó. Aquí hay algunos consejos para varias actividades.

Ejercicios aeróbicos. Aprenda la rutina a su propio paso; no se esfuerce. Siempre haga ejercicios de calentamiento y estiramientos antes de hacer ejercicio y enfríese después, dice el doctor Robert L. Swezey, director médico del Centro de Artritis y Dolor de Espalda en Santa Mónica, California.

Tenis. Para evitar sufrir de dolor en las muñecas o del codo de tenis, escoja una raqueta de mango largo, disminuya la tensión en las cuerdas y use una banda elástica alrededor de su antebrazo para soportar los músculos, dice el doctor Stephen Campbell, un reumatólogo en la Universidad de Ciencias de la Salud de Oregon, en Portland. Si su problema es el hombro, modifique su servicio para evitar hacer girar su brazo enérgicamente por encima de su cabeza.

Correr. Acondiciónese muy gradualmente antes de correr distancias grandes, dice el doctor Campbell. No corra demasiado vigorosamente si apenas está comenzando, evite superficies duras, y use zapatos con suelas suaves y plantillas y soportes de calidad para el arco del pie.

Nadar. Aunque el nadar es muy moderado para la mayoría de las articulaciones, el hombro puede hacer demasiado ejercicio, dice el doctor Campbell. Para prevenir o curar la bursitis o tendonitis del hombro, evite el estilo libre, el crol y la brazada de mariposa, dice. En lugar de eso, use la brazada de pecho o de lado o una tabla de patear.

Regresar al entrenamiento. Después de un encuentro con la bursitis o tendonitis, es crucial esperar hasta que el dolor se ha ido para volver a empezar el ejercicio enérgico, dice el doctor Campbell. Cuando usted tiene la aprobación de su médico para empezar de nuevo, ejercítese a una frecuencia e intensidad más baja y reacondicione su articulación lesionada a través de semanas o meses, dice él.

eléctrica, dice el doctor Campbell. Las compresas para el horno de microondas se encuentran disponibles en la mayoría de las farmacias, dice el.

Arrópese para meterse a la cama. Use una camisa de franela o un suéter de lana en la noche para darle calor adicional a su hombro dolorido. Si usted duerme sin mangas en un cuarto frío, la rigidez y el dolor de las mañanas van a ser mayores.

Use el analgésico apropiado. Escoja un analgésico con aspirina o ibuprofen para calmar el dolor, dice el doctor Campbell. La aspirina y el ibuprofen bloquean la producción de los químicos llamados prostaglandinas, que contribuyen a la hinchazón y el dolor de los tejidos inflamados. El acetaminófeno no controlará la inflamación porque no bloquea las prostaglandinas.

Balancéelo. Algunas veces la bursitis en el hombro progresa hasta una condición dolorosa llamada capsulitis adhesiva u hombro congelado. Cuando esto sucede, los límites de movimiento del hombro se restringen completamente y la articulación queda prácticamente inmóvil. Para evitar el hombro congelado, usted necesita empezar a mover su hombro tan pronto como el dolor agudo haya pasado, dice el doctor Campbell. Acuéstese boca abajo sobre una superficie acojinada como una cama, y deje que el brazo afectado cuelgue por un lado. Con cuidado haga oscilar su brazo como un péndulo, aumentando gradualmente la amplitud hasta que lo puede balancear en un círculo completo. Haga esto por 15 a 30 minutos, tres a cinco veces a la semana, para restablecer su amplitud de movimiento, dice él.

Considere cuidado quiropráctico. Si su dolor no cesa, una técnica llamada masaje de fricción puede eliminar el problema, dice Warren Hammer, D.C., un quiropráctico con práctica privada en Norwalk, Connecticut. Cuando la inflamación es crónica, las adherencias fibrosas no permiten que las bolsas se deslicen suavemente. El masaje de fricción puede romper esas adherencias, dice el doctor Hammer, aliviando la causa del dolor de la bursitis. "También, un tendón inflamado se hace más grueso y corto lo cual crea más inflamación en la bolsa sobre la que está frotando", dice el doctor Hammer. "La presión profunda del masaje a través de la bolsa y el tendón puede estirar las fibras del tendón otra vez." Use hielo para calmar la inflamación antes del tratamiento quiropráctico, dice el.

Cómo prevenir el congelamiento

Si la bursitis o tendonitis persisten por demasiado tiempo, es posible que necesite ver a su doctora para que la ayude a combatir el dolor. Aquí hay algunos remedios que usted le puede pedir a ella.

Considere alivio recetado. Si usted no tiene una historia de problemas estomacales, pregunte a su doctora acerca de las drogas antiinflamatorias (o *NSAIDs* por sus siglas en inglés) para el dolor, de fuerza sujeta a receta, que no son esteroidales y son desinflamantes, dice el doctor Campbell. Como la aspirina y el ibuprofen, las NSAIDs trabajan bloqueando la producción de prostaglandinas. Pero también pueden irritar el estómago como lo hace la aspirina y por ello usualmente no se recetan por períodos prolongados.

Tome las inyecciones con precaución. Prácticamente el último recurso para el dolor, los esteroides son "atajos, no curaciones", dice el doctor Mooar. La mayoría de los doctores recomiendan inyectar una articulación, tendón o bolsa dolorido no más de dos veces al año. Las inyecciones frecuentes pueden debilitar o desgarrar un tendón.

"La mayoría de las personas están sobreinyectadas con drogas similares a la cortisona", dice el doctor Swezey. "La mayoría de los doctores usan de 10 a 20 miligramos para inyecciones bursales, pero yo he encontrado que 2,5 miligramos funcionan bastante bien."

Haga que la cirugía sea su último recurso. Para bursitis extremadamente severa, su doctor puede usar una aguja para extraer líquido de una articulación dolorida o recomendar que un cirujano ortopédico remueva una bolsa inflamada completamente, dice el doctor Mooar. Pero antes de consentir a la cirugía, usted debería pedir una segunda opinión.

CAFEÍNA

Ojo con la temblorina colombiana

Para muchas de nosotras las latinas, levantarnos por la mañana y pasar el día entero sin tomar por lo menos una tacita de café sería como salir a la calle en piyamas. Y no sólo para nosotras —el café es parte de la rutina diaria de millones de personas por todo el mundo. Además del hecho de que sabe bien, el café contiene cafeína, una sustancia química que estimula el cuerpo, "aclara" la mente, y nos llena de energía.

Como nosotras, más de la mitad de la gente que vive en los Estados Unidos usa cafeína para "arrancar" el día. Una taza de café o té, o aun una lata de cola, puede en algunas ocasiones aclarar su cabeza, reanimar su cuerpo y regresarla rápidamente al mundo de los vivos.

Pero tenga cuidado de no abusar. Demasiada cafeína puede hacerla sentirse fatigada, nerviosa, irritable o las tres cosas a la vez. También puede ponerla en riesgo de tener problemas relacionados con la salud y con la edad, desde dolores de cabeza e insomnio hasta enfermedades del corazón.

"Consuma la cafeína con moderación", dice Mary Sullivan, R.D., especialista de apoyo en nutrición en los Hospitales de la Universidad de Chicago. "Puede realmente ayudarle a hacer que su mente y cuerpo estén más despiertos cuando se toma en pequeñas cantidades. Pero también puede causar daño si usted la toma en exceso dentro de su dieta."

Motivo de preocupación

La cafeína estimula el sistema nervioso central, provocando la secreción de adrenalina en el torrente sanguíneo y aumentando los niveles de azúcar en la sangre. Eso la vuelve más alerta y enfocada y reduce la fatiga a corto plazo.

Pero demasiada cafeína puede llevar a una condición llamada cafeinismo, más comúnmente conocida como nervios de café. Este problema se distingue por mareo, inquietud, estómago revuelto, diarrea, orinar continuo, insomnio y dolor de cabeza. Para eliminar todo esto, usted tiene que reducir el consumo de cafeína.

Los estudios también advierten acerca de vínculos posibles entre la cafeína y los niveles elevados de colesterol, problemas en aumento de alta presión arterial y síntomas graves de síndrome premenstrual y enfermedad de seno fibrocístico. Pero los resultados de pruebas han sido inconsistentes y a menudo contradictorios. Manfred Kroger, Ph.D., profesor de ciencia de los alimentos en la Universidad Estatal de Pennsylvania, en University Park dice que eso se debe a que muchos estudios usan café para proporcionarle cafeína a los sujetos de las pruebas, y el café puede contener otros ingredientes que causan problemas por sí solo.

¿Cuánta cafeína es demasiada? Eso depende. "No hay dos personas iguales", dice el doctor Richard Podell, profesor clínico de medicina familiar en la Escuela de Medicina Robert Wood Johnson de la Universidad de Medicina y Odontología de New Jersey, en Piscataway, New Jersey. "Una taza de café puede causar problemas en algunas mujeres, otras parecen tener una mayor tolerancia."

La Administración Federal de Alimentos y Drogas incluye la cafeína en su lista titulada "Generalmente reconocidos como seguros", pero advierte que la gente debería ingerirla con moderación. Los estadounidenses consumen en promedio 200 miligramos de cafeína por día, el equivalente a cerca de 2 tazas de 5 onzas (148 ml) de café o 4 latas de cola. Sullivan dice que esa cantidad de cafeína no va a perjudicar a la mayoría de las personas.

"Use su cabeza nada más", dice ella. "Si usted tiene problemas para dormir o se siente nerviosa, probablemente es una buena idea tomar menos café."

El doctor Kroger advierte que nadie debería tomar más de dos o tres tazas al día, sin importar como el individuo reacciona a la cafeína. "Nosotros simplemente no sabemos lo suficiente acerca de lo que puede hacerle a usted", dice él. "Equivóquese mejor para el lado de la moderación."

Cómo cuidarse con la cafeína

Si usted está pensando limitar la cafeína en su dieta pero no quiere eliminarla por completo, los expertos ofrecen estos consejos.

Rehuse tomarla antes de acostarse. La cafeína permanece en su sistema por más tiempo que la mayoría de los otros estimulantes. La mitad de la cafeína que usted tomó en una taza de café puede todavía estar recorriendo por sus venas cinco horas más tarde. Así que si usted tiene problemas para dormir, Sullivan dice que usted debería evitar la cafeína desde las últimas horas de la tarde.

Use algo de descafeinado. ¿No puede soportar la idea de una vida sin café? Los cafés descafeinados pueden ser una respuesta, pero el doctor Kroger advierte que aun el café descafeinado puede contener los elementos dañinos del café regular que no se han investigado completamente. "Cambiar a 'descafeinado' no debe verse como una invitación a continuar tomando diez tazas diarias", dice el doctor Kroger.

Usted también puede tratar los nuevos cafés medio-descafeinados en el mercado, que son cafés semiregulares. O bien cambie a café hecho de granos de *arabica*. Estos granos pueden contener aproximadamente un tercio menos de cafeína que los granos más baratos de *robusta*, que a menudo se usan en cafés instantáneos.

Fíjese en las otras fuentes de cafeína. El café y el té no son los únicos "escondites" de la cafeína. Los refrescos contienen de un tercio a la mitad de la

LA CUENTA DE CAFEÍNA

¿Cuántos miligramos de cafeína hay en esa bebida o barra de confitura? Aquí están los números.

Alimento/Bebida	Cafeína (mg.)
Café (por taza de 5 onzas/148ml)	
Filtrado en cafetera eléctrica	115
Filtrado en cafetera regular	80
Instantáneo	68–98
Descafeinado	4
Té (por taza de 5 onzas)	
Tetley	64
Lipton	52
Tender Leaf	33
Constant Comment	29
Refrescos (por lata de 12 onzas/355 ml)	
Tab	57
Mountain Dew	54
Coca-Cola	46
Diet Coke	46
Pepsi	38
Diet Pepsi	36
Chocolate (por 1 onza/28 g)	
Ghirardelli dark chocolate (Chocolate oscuro de Ghirardelli)	24
Hershey's milk chocolate (Chocolate de leche de Hershey's)	4

UN GOLPE FURTIVO

Algunas drogas sin receta contienen una sorprendente cantidad de cafeína. La siguiente tabla muestra el contenido de cafeína en una tableta de cada uno de estos medicamentos que no están sujetos a receta.

Droga	Cafeína (mg.)
Maximum Strength No Doz (No Doz de fuerza máxima)	200
Vivarin	200
No Doz	100
Aspirin Free Excedrin (Excedrin sin aspirina)	65
Excedrin Extra Strength (Excedrin de fuerza extra)	65
Anacin (regular strength) (Anacin de fuerza normal)	32
Maximum Strength Anacin (Anacin de fuerza máxima)	32

cafeína en el café. El tomar una marca sin cafeína puede reducir su ingestión de ésta por hasta 60 miligramos, dice Sullivan.

También tenga cuidado con el chocolate oscuro. Usted necesitaría comerse más de una libra de chocolate de leche *Hershey's* para ingerir la misma cantidad de cafeína contenida en una taza de café hervido —pero sólo 3 onzas (85 g) de chocolate oscuro *Ghirardelli* casi equivalen a la cafeína en una taza de café.

Las drogas sin necesidad de receta también pueden contener una cantidad sorpresiva de cafeína. Algunos analgésicos contienen el equivalente de un refresco o más. Y las pastillas para dietas y píldoras estimulantes como *Maximun Strength No Doz* y *Vivarin* contienen tanto como 200 miligramos de cafeína.

Rompa su rutina. Probablemente usted no es tan adicta a la cafeína como es adicta a la rutina. "Si usted se encuentra agarrando una taza de café cada vez que se sienta para hacer algo, probablemente sólo tiene una mala costumbre", explica Sullivan. "Pregúntese si usted realmente quiere esa taza o si puede pasársela sin ella."

Usted podría poner alguna otra cosa en su taza (quizás agua, ya que la mayoría de nosotras no toma suficiente).

Lea la etiqueta. Cualquiera que ha trabajado en alguna ocasión toda la noche sabe que las píldoras estimulantes como *No Doz* y *Vivarin* están completamente atestadas de cafeína. Ese es el objeto. Pero usted se sorprendería encontrar que algunos analgésicos (tales como *Anacin* y *Excedrin*) contienen tanta cafeína como una lata de cola. Si usted es sensible a la cafeína, vea qué dicen las letras pequeñas en su caja de aspirina.

Retroceda lentamente. Si usted decide reducir su ingestión de cafeína, Sullivan sugiere que lo haga gradualmente, durante el transcurso de unos cuantos días. Si suspende de pronto el consumo de cafeína puede ocasionarle síntomas desagradables de abstinencia, incluyendo dolores de cabeza, ansiedad y sentimiento de depresión. Los estudios muestran que estos síntomas ocurren aun en personas que son bebedores moderados de café.

CAMBIOS EN EL METABOLISMO

La crisis de energía fisiológica

¿**R**ecuerda cuando se podía poner a dieta por unos cuantos días y fácilmente perder unas diez libras? Bueno, ahora eso ya no es tan fácil. Y sí, seguro, usted está comiendo menos que comía cuando estaba en la década de los 20 años de edad, además de que se ha acostumbrado a omitir el postre y la barra de confitura a media tarde. Pero, por alguna razón, usted usa vestidos unas cuantas tallas más grandes. Y sin importar el sistema de medir, las libras (o los kilos) siguen acumulándose.

Aquí está lo que sucede: su metabolismo —la forma en que su cuerpo convierte alimentos en energía y después quema esa energía en forma de calorías— está haciéndose más lento. Este es un proceso natural que comienza aproximadamente a los 30 años de edad. De allí en adelante, cada diez años su cuerpo quema energía de un 2 a un 4 por ciento más despacio. Así que se están quemando menos calorías y se están almacenando más como grasa. Usted puede ver que si no hace nada para contrarrestar esta tendencia, engordará cada vez más y tendrá menos energía. Y se pondrá en un mayor riesgo de tener problemas serios de salud tales como la presión arterial alta y las enfermedades del corazón. No exactamente una receta para una vida juvenil.

Algo de lo que está sucediendo está fuera de su control. Usted naturalmente quema las calorías más despacio que un hombre. Y su cuerpo tiene también un contenido más alto de grasa que el de un hombre, con su porcentaje de grasa corporal inevitablemente aumentando con el pasar del tiempo. "Los cambios en el metabolismo son una respuesta directa a los cambios en la composición de su cuerpo", dice el doctor Robert Kushner, director de la Clínica de Nutrición y Control del Peso de la Universidad de Chicago. "Al envejecer, tendemos a perder el músculo y a aumentar la grasa. Dado que el músculo quema mucha

Descriminación metabólica

¿Se ha preguntado alguna vez por qué los hombres que usted conoce comen el doble de lo que usted come y difícilmente aumentan una libra? Llámele sexismo biológico: el hombre común quema calorías más eficientemente que la mujer común —y durante la misma cantidad de tiempo y con la misma cantidad de actividad física, él perderá más peso que usted.

Los hombres queman calorías más rápidamente por dos razones. Una, por lo general ellos son más pesados y están quemando más calorías todo el tiempo. Dos, tienen una mayor proporción de músculo para quemar calorías. Como resultado, el índice de metabolismo basal promedio en las mujeres es 5 a 10 por ciento más bajo que en los hombres.

Los hombres, también, tienen más probabilidades de poner la grasa alrededor de la barriga, que casualmente es el lugar más fácil para perder grasa. Pero gracias al estrógeno, las mujeres tienden a llevar la grasa en los muslos, las caderas y asentaderas —esos lugares difíciles de adelgazar. Esto hace aún más lento nuestro metabolismo.

El estrógeno, que manda la grasa a las áreas donde no la queremos, desempeña otro papel en nuestro metabolismo, debido a que también influye en nuestros apetitos. Los investigadores han observado que el consumo de alimento se reduce durante el tiempo de la ovulación, cuando los niveles de estrógeno están en su punto más alto, y después aumenta en la segunda mitad del ciclo menstrual.

energía, nuestras necesidades de energía disminuyen a medida que perdemos músculo y nuestro metabolismo se hace más lento."

Pero mucha de esta disminución metabólica la provocamos nosotras mismas. Sí, perdemos algo de músculo al envejecer, pero "la causa principal de esta pérdida de músculo es la inactividad", dice Eric T. Poehlman, Ph.D., profesor asociado de medicina en el Departamento de Medicina de Baltimore en la Universidad de Maryland. "Mientras más inactivas nos volvemos con la edad, menos músculo delgado tendremos. Mientras menos músculo delgado tengamos, más inactivas nos volveremos. Al pasar los años, los dos se alimentan el uno del otro y nuestro metabolismo se viene a pique."

¿Cómo se sale de esta trampa? A menos que usted sufra de una enfermedad de la glándula tiroides, la cual puede causar gran confusión en la manera en que

¿Cuál es su cuota de calorías?

Si usted supiera exactamente cuántas calorías su cuerpo quema en el transcurso de un día, usted sabría cuántas calorías necesita comer para mantener o perder peso. Aquí hay una fórmula práctica para balancear su ecuación de energía.

Primero multiplique su peso por diez. Ese es su índice de metabolismo basal, el número mínimo de calorías que usted necesita para mantener a su sistema funcionando.

Luego, determine su nivel de actividad de la tabla a continuación y multiplique su índice de metabolismo basal por el porcentaje apropiado. Esto le da las calorías adicionales que usted requiere para el día.

La actividad sedentaria se refiere al tiempo que usted gasta sentada en algún lugar de la casa viendo televisión, leyendo su revista favorita o hablando por teléfono. Actividades ligeras incluyen cosas como quehaceres del hogar, cocinar y dar un paseo alrededor de la manzana después de la cena. La actividad moderada incluye nadar o caminar a paso vigoroso mientras es capaz de hablar sin jadear. La actividad extenuante incluye ejercicios que hacen latir fuertemente a su corazón como correr o aeróbicos.

su cuerpo quema la energía, usted puede volver a poner en marcha su metabolismo al hacer algunos cambios en su estilo de vida. Pero primero, aquí está lo que sucede por dentro.

Mucho combustible, poca actividad

Sume toda la energía que necesita para ejercer las actividades de un cuerpo en descanso —todo, desde respirar y digerir, hasta la actividad de la células nerviosas durante la función de pensar— y entonces tiene su índice del metabolismo basal, el mínimo de energía que usted requiere para conservarse con vida. Para la mayoría de las mujeres, está entre 1.000 y 1.200 calorías diarias.

Después agregue las calorías que necesita para ejercer sus actividades adicionales —todo, desde jugar a las canicas con su pequeña hasta saltar en la clase aeróbica— y entonces tiene el número total de calorías que necesita cada día.

Esto significa, por supuesto, que dos mujeres pueden tener el mismo índice de metabolismo basal pero quemar muy diferentes cantidades de calorías diariamente. Por ejemplo, una mujer de 125 libras (56 kilos) muy activa puede

Nivel de actividad   Porcentaje

Sedentario   30 a 50
Ligero   55 a 65
Moderado   65 a 70
Extenuante   75 a 100

Sume estos dos números y entonces usted tiene sus necesidades totales diarias de calorías. Si usted es una mujer que pesa 120 libras cuyo nivel de actividades diarias está en el extremo inferior de la escala extenuante, necesitaría 2.100 calorías.

$$120 \times 10 = 1.200$$
$$1.200 \times 0,75 = 900$$
$$1.200 + 900 = 2.100$$

Esta cantidad es sin embargo sólo una estimación. Su metabolismo puede ser medido más exactamente por un fisiólogo de ejercicio o un médico especializado en pérdida de peso y metabolismo.

fácilmente quemar 2.200 calorías diarias, mientras que una mujer también de 125 libras pero poco activa apenas quemará 1.750.

Esto nos lleva a lo más importante de esta breve lección en calorías —la formula metabólica para no aumentar de peso. Las calorías que entran deben igualar a las calorías que salen. Las calorías que no se "salen" son almacenadas en su cuerpo como grasa. Pero si usted quema más calorías de las que ingiere, la grasa almacenada se quema, y usted pierde peso.

Por consiguiente, la manera de no aumentar de peso al envejecer es simple: disminuya las calorías. Pues, siga la rutina alimenticia que le ha dado resultado en el pasado. Comida insípida, privaciones y pequeñas porciones —todo esto la hará rebajar de peso, ¿no? Sí, pero hay un pequeño problema. Su cuerpo no sabe que usted está a dieta; él piensa que usted está muriéndose de hambre. Así que en lugar de quemar grasa, su metabolismo se pone en la modalidad de hambruna, y trata de conservar sus reservas de grasa.

"Una dieta muy baja en calorías puede reducir su índice de metabolismo basal entre el 15 y el 30 por ciento, haciendo la pérdida de peso más difícil", dice el doctor Kushner. Una dieta muy baja en calorías es aquella que consiste de menos de 600 calorías diarias. Debido a que su cuerpo está tratando de salvarla manteniendo su nivel de grasa intacto, escoge entonces otra fuente de combustible: músculo. Usted ha oído la frase "las dietas no funcionan". Ahora sabe por qué.

Su índice metabólico no regresa al nivel normal después de que usted termina de hacer dieta, porque su cuerpo piensa que otra hambruna puede estar en camino. En realidad, ponerse a dieta evita una pérdida de peso permanente a largo plazo.

Y por si eso fuera poco, las que se ponen a dieta cortan calorías sin poner mucha atención a qué tipo de calorías están cortando. Un gramo de grasa contiene el doble de calorías que un gramo de carbohidratos —y los carbohidratos tienen el beneficio adicional de quemarse más rápidamente que las grasas. Así que en lugar de cortar las calorías en general, sería mejor que no cortara las calorías y mantuviera una dieta baja en grasas, alta en carbohidratos que ponga énfasis en las frutas, verduras, pastas y los granos. "La grasa que usted consume tiene una mayor probabilidad de convertirse en la grasa que usted lleva", dice el doctor Kushner.

Ejercicio: el mejor amigo de su metabolismo

Muy bien, ponerse a dieta no es la solución. Por lo tanto, ¿qué puede hacer usted cuando su edad hace que el metabolismo en su cuerpo cambie a una velocidad más baja y lenta?

Ejercicio.

El ejercicio aeróbico —caminar, andar en una bicicleta estacionaria, baile aeróbico, cualquier actividad que aumente el ritmo de su corazón por 20 minutos o más— es la mejor forma de quemar calorías. Y los beneficios del ejercicio realmente no tienen límite. El ejercicio pone a su metabolismo en un ritmo más alto, así que las calorías se incineran por horas después de que usted deja de hacerlo.

La mejor manera de estimular su metabolismo es participar en una actividad aeróbica y un período regular de entrenamiento de fuerza, como levantar pesas. "La razón más importante por la cual una persona quema 1 caloría por minuto y otra quema 1,5 es que la segunda persona tiene una masa muscular mayor, y el músculo es un tejido extremadamente hambriento de energía", dice el doctor Poehlman. "Los ejercicios de formación de fuerza como es levantar pesas agregarán masa muscular a cualquier edad. Y mientras más haga estos ejercicios, mejor será para su metabolismo."

Para comprobar este punto, el doctor Poehlman y sus asociados midieron el índice metabólico basal de 96 personas: 36 efectuaron una actividad aeróbica, 18 levantaron pesas y 42 no hicieron nada. El grupo aeróbico tuvo un índice metabólico 13 por ciento más alto que el grupo sedentario; el grupo de fuerza tuvo un índice metabólico 18 por ciento más alto que el grupo sedentario.

Este estudio, dice el doctor Poehlman, muestra que tanto el ejercicio aeróbico como el entrenamiento de fuerza puede estimular a su metabolismo.

Eleve al máximo su metabolismo

¿Está usted convencida de que el ejercicio es la mejor manera de vencer la gordura de la edad madura? Aquí está lo que usted puede hacer para acelerar su motor.

Apresure el paso. Una forma sencilla de quemar más calorías en la misma cantidad de tiempo es poner un poco más de velocidad en su sesión actual de ejercicio aeróbico. Supóngase que usted es una persona que cuando camina cubre 1 milla en unos 15 minutos (cerca de 4 millas / 6,4 km por hora), quemando aproximadamente 365 calorías por hora (o cerca de 90 calorías por milla / 1,6 km). Si usted aumenta la velocidad y camina 1 milla en 12 minutos (5 millas / 8 km por hora), su cantidad de calorías quemadas aumenta a 585 por la misma hora. Eso es una ganancia de 27 calorías por milla / 1,6 km. Esas calorías extras que usted quema por día pueden traducirse en una pérdida de peso de aproximadamente 15 libras (6,8 kg) en menos de un año.

Dure más tiempo. Si usted ya está haciendo ejercicio a su velocidad máxima, no vaya más rápido, pero trate de durar más. "Al igual que un carro, su cuerpo quemará más combustible —en este caso, grasa— mientras más tiempo se mantiene activo", dice el doctor Kushner.

Haga trabajar a sus brazos y piernas. Los ejercicios que usan vigorosamente tanto los brazos como las piernas son mejores quemadores de grasa que los que incluyen sólo a sus piernas. "Según las pruebas de laboratorio el esquiar a campo traviesa se considera como el mejor para quemar la mayor cantidad de calorías por minuto, debido a que se usa las piernas, la parte superior del cuerpo y aun el torso", dice Wayne Westcott, Ph.D., consultor de entrenamiento de fuerza para la Asociación Internacional de Profesionales en Buen Estado Físico. Las máquinas estacionarias para remar y las bicicletas estacionarias con palancas de mano móviles también se consideran buenas.

Empiece su día con un desayuno. Los expertos dicen que su cuerpo quema calorías a un ritmo más lento cuando usted duerme. El desayuno actúa como un despertador para su metabolismo, poniéndolo en una modalidad de quemar calorías. Si usted no come algo en la mañana, en última instancia va a quemar menos calorías durante el día. Y es más probable que cuando sí coma, devorará el primer bocadillo (merienda o *snack*) alto en grasa que usted vea.

Distribuya sus comidas. Ingerir comidas pequeñas a lo largo del día en lugar de tres comidas completas puede ser mejor para quemar grasa. Después que usted come, su cuerpo secreta la hormona insulina, la cual causa que su cuerpo almacene grasa. Mientras más grande la comida, su cuerpo secretará más insulina. Pero las comidas más pequeñas y frecuentes mantienen los niveles de insulina bajos y más estables. Mientras menos insulina tenga usted en su sangre, más grasa quemará usted y menos almacenará.

No se olvide de comer. Saltar comidas y después comer una comida grande en la noche puede ser un arma de doble filo, dice el doctor Kushner. Primero, la pone a usted en una modalidad de quemar lentamente durante el día. Segundo, la comida grande proporciona una sobrecarga de energía: el cuerpo puede metabolizar sólo una cierta cantidad de alimento a la vez, así que el exceso probablemente se convertirá en grasa. Tercero, la mayor parte de la metabolización se llevará a cabo mientras usted duerme —cuando su índice metabólico está en su nivel más bajo.

Haga ejercicio después de comer. El hacer ejercicio moderado inmediatamente después de una comida le da a usted un beneficio adicional para quemar grasa. Una caminata vigorosa de tres millas con el estómago vacío quema aproximadamente 300 calorías. Pero caminar con el estómago lleno quemará cerca de 345 calorías. Eso es porque el comer estimula a su metabolismo; agregue ejercicio, y su metabolismo recibe un doble estímulo y quema aún más calorías.

Póngale sazón. Vigilar su metabolismo no significa que usted tiene que dejar de comer alimentos sabrosos. De hecho, los alimentos muy condimentados, picantes, como son la mostaza y el chile pueden incluso cambiar la velocidad de su metabolismo a una más alta por un corto período de tiempo. En un estudio hecho por investigadores británicos, se mostró que la comida condimentada aumentaba el índice de metabolismo basal en un promedio del 25 por ciento.

Aléjese de los estimulantes. La cafeína, el alcohol y otros estimulantes pueden aumentar su índice metabólico, pero una vez que salen de su cuerpo, su metabolismo baja en forma violenta al índice normal o aún más abajo. Lo inteligente, dice el doctor Poehlman, es evitar todas las formas artificiales de aumentar su metabolismo a menos que le haya sido recetado por un médico.

Haga que le revisen su glándula tiroides. Una glándula tiroides poco activa causa que el cuerpo queme energía a un ritmo más despacio que el normal, y una glándula tiroides muy activa tiene el efecto opuesto. Más mujeres que hombres tienen una enfermedad de la glándula tiroides. Así que si usted sospecha que la suya no está funcionando bien, hágasela revisar por un médico. Si una deficiencia hormonal existe en la glándula tiroides, a menudo puede regularizarse con las drogas recetadas.

CAMBIOS EN LA VISTA

Échele un vistazo a la prevención

Es el fin de otro semestre, y usted tiene que firmar las boletas de calificaciones (*report cards*) de sus hijos. A su hijo mayor por poco lo reprobaron en matemáticas el semestre pasado, y ahora vamos a ver si sus notas han mejorado. Pero espérese —¿sacó una "D" o una "B"? Usted entrecierra los ojos para ver mejor, y al final puede ver que el muchacho logró una "B". Todo parece estar bien para él, pero no para usted. Tenga calma, a pesar de este incidente, aún no le pueden llamar "abuelita". Lo que sucede es que con el tiempo su visión se va a empeorar un poco. Nueve de cada diez mujeres entre los 40 y los 64 años de edad usan anteojos (gafas) o lentes de contacto para facilitar la lectura y otros trabajos de cerca.

Pero no pierda las esperanzas. Usted puede hacer más lento el proceso con exámenes regulares de sus ojos, una dieta saludable y quizás algunos ejercicios de la vista que usted misma puede hacer. Aún más importante, usted puede tomar medidas ahora para enfrentarse con los problemas serios de la vista como el glaucoma, las cataratas y la degeneración macular que podría conducir a una vista muy reducida o aun ceguera.

De cerca y borroso

¿Recuerda todas las mariquitas en el viejo jardín de flores de mamá? Usted las cogía cuidadosamente y dejaba que caminaran por sus dedos, llevándolas hasta cerca de la nariz para poder contar los pequeños puntos negros en sus dorsos.

Pruebe hacer eso ahora. Lo más probable es que usted no podría ver la diferencia entre una mariquita y una pastilla de menta hasta que estuvieran a 7 u 8 pulgadas (18 ó 20 cm) de su rostro. Eso es porque las lentes en sus ojos se empiezan a endurecer con la edad. Y mientras menos flexibles son, más difícil es enfocar en algo cercano.

La condición es una forma de hipermetropía llamada presbicia, y es tan inevitable como la lluvia en un día de picnic. "Realmente no hay forma de evitarlo", dice el doctor Richard Bensinger, un oftalmólogo en el área de Seattle y portavoz para la Academia de Oftalmología de los Estados Unidos. "Es fácil de corregir, pero eso quiere decir que usted probablemente tiene que usar anteojos o lentes de contacto."

Si usted termina por necesitar anteojos correctivos, la elección entre los anteojos y los lentes de contacto está realmente en usted. "En la mayoría de los casos, es una cuestión de preferencia", dice el doctor Bensinger. "A algunas personas les gustan los anteojos porque se los pueden quitar cuando no los necesitan. Y otras prefieren los lentes de contacto, ya que les permiten ver bien sin demostrar que necesitan anteojos."

Aun cuando usted eventualmente necesite bifocales, los cuales ayudan a corregir su visión tanto de cerca como de lejos, no necesita anunciárselo al mundo. Los médicos han desarrollado los lentes que eliminan la línea reveladora cruzando el centro de cada lente. Usted también puede probar los lentes bifocales de contacto, que le permiten cambiar de foco al mover sus ojos hacia arriba o hacia abajo. Sin embargo, el doctor Bensinger dice que estos pueden ser mucho más caros que los lentes de contacto normales, y advierte que no cualquiera se puede adaptar a estos.

Su oculista también puede recetarle los que se conocen como lentes de contacto de monovisión. Usted coloca un lente de contacto para vista de lejos en su ojo dominante (usualmente el derecho) y el lente para leer en su otro ojo. "No es tan difícil como suena acomodarse a esto", dice el doctor Bensinger. "Usted no tiene que ajustarse a esto conscientemente cada vez que cambia de

Mitos comunes sobre los ojos

Leer con luz débil puede perjudicar a sus ojos. Mito. La luz débil puede causar fatiga en los ojos pero no dañarlos.

Ver la televisión lastima sus ojos. Mito. No hay pruebas que sentarse demasiado cerca del televisor o ver la televisión por períodos prolongados cause algún problema.

Demasiado leer desgasta sus ojos. Mito. De nuevo, leer puede cansar sus ojos, pero no hay pruebas que a la larga pueda perjudicarlos.

Comer muchas zanahorias mejora su vista. Casi un mito. Usted necesita vitamina A para ver, pero sólo una pequeña cantidad —menos de una zanahoria al día. Una dieta saludable, con o sin zanahorias, le dará toda la vitamina A que usted necesita.

foco." Los lentes de monovisión están hechos como los lentes normales de contacto y son menos caros que los lentes bifocales, dice él.

Además de la presbicia, las manchas y los depósitos flotantes pueden aparecer con más frecuencia a medida que usted envejece. Estos son pequeñas manchas o puntos que aparecen ocasionalmente en su campo visual, desapareciendo después de una hora, un día o a veces más. El doctor Bensinger dice que estos son causados cuando partes del líquido vítreo transparente que llena su ojo se vuelve un poco filamentoso o grumoso.

"Por lo general, no es nada serio", dice el doctor Bensinger. "Las manchas simplemente se desvanecen, y eso es todo. Pero si usted súbitamente ve muchas manchas o destellos de luz en sus ojos, esto puede ser una señal de que algo serio está pasando, y debería ver a un médico inmediatamente."

Y si usted vive en un área especialmente polvorosa o ventosa, puede correr el riesgo de desarrollar ptérigions, los cuales son crecimientos carnosos, benignos, alrededor de los ojos. Estos pueden empezar a crecer alrededor de los 25 años de edad, por lo general en los lados de sus ojos, más cerca de la nariz. El doctor Bensinger dice que estos son solamente un problema cosmético a menos que crezcan lo suficiente como para bloquear su visión. Los ptérigions se pueden extirpar fácilmente con cirugía menor.

Adopte una perspectiva amplia

Descontando una lesión accidental, sus ojos probablemente le servirán hasta bien entrada en los 65 años de edad. Puede ser que usted necesite en unos cuantos años un juego de anteojos nuevos para leer, pero probablemente no notará ningún deterioro serio en su vista.

De todas maneras, los expertos advierten que usted nunca debería dejar de apreciar el valor de sus ojos. Las enfermedades más serias de los ojos son indoloras y no muestran ningún síntoma por años. Si usted no se hace revisar los ojos regularmente, puede no darse cuenta de lo mal que se han puesto las cosas hasta que es demasiado tarde para ayudar. Aquí hay algunas enfermedades que vigilar.

Glaucoma. Esta enfermedad progresiva causa el 12 por ciento de todas las cegueras en los Estados Unidos. Se caracteriza por una presión creciente del líquido en el ojo, la cual, al pasar los años, puede causar un daño irreversible a los nervios que mandan impulsos visuales a su cerebro.

Los médicos no saben qué causa la mayor cantidad de los glaucomas, y no saben cómo curarlos. La vista que se pierde debido al glaucoma no puede reponerse, pero cuando el glaucoma se descubre lo suficientemente temprano, se puede controlar. A veces las gotas para los ojos o las pastillas orales pueden ayudar a disminuir la presión en el ojo. Si eso falla, la cirugía con láser puede ayudar a destapar los drenajes naturales del ojo, permitiendo que el líquido escape y reduciendo la presión. Y si eso tampoco funciona, los cirujanos oftalmólogos pueden crear un drenaje artificial para extraer el líquido.

Aproximadamente unos tres millones de estadounidenses tienen glaucoma, y la mitad de ellos ni siquiera lo saben. Otros cinco a diez millones de personas tienen la acumulación de la presión en el ojo que antecede a la enfermedad, y

¿Está usted en riesgo de glaucoma?

Sí. Cualquiera está en riesgo, pero algunos más que otros. Para descubrir dónde está usted, conteste las siguientes preguntas de *Prevent Blindness America* (Prevenga la ceguera Estados Unidos).

1. ¿Alguno de los miembros de su familia inmediata tiene glaucoma?
2. ¿Tiene usted más de 40 años de edad?
3. ¿Toma usted algún medicamento con esteroides?
4. ¿Ha sufrido alguna lesión o cirugía en los ojos?
5. ¿Tiene diabetes?

Si usted contesta sí a alguna de las preguntas, programe un examen de ojos para hablar sobre glaucoma con su médico. Si usted contestó sí a dos o más, está en un riesgo alto y probablemente necesite ver a un especialista de ojos anualmente.

mucho menos de la mitad lo saben. ¿Cuál es el mejor consejo para saber qué hacer con el glaucoma? Investigue para saber si usted lo tiene, ahora. "Mientras más temprano se descubre esta enfermedad, más capaces seremos de controlarla", dice el doctor Carl Kupfer, director del Instituto Nacional de los Ojos, en Bethesda, Maryland. Eso significa exámenes regulares de los ojos, especialmente si usted tiene un riesgo de glaucoma.

Cataratas. Aunque estas no se vuelven un problema hasta que usted está cerca de la edad de jubilarse, las cataratas empiezan a formarse mucho antes en la vida, especialmente si usted ha sufrido alguna lesión en el ojo o se ha sometido a procedimientos tales como tratamientos de radiación, quimioterapia o el trasplante de un órgano.

A través de los años, el cristalino en cada ojo que una vez fueron transparentes pueden volverse amarillas debido a la acumulación de proteína. Después de un tiempo, el cristalino puede hacerse blanco como la leche y traslúcido, opacando la vista hasta el punto en que usted necesita el implante de un cristalino artificial. Este cristalino plástico de reemplazo no se flexionan para enfocar la luz, como lo hacía el cristalino original. Pero con los anteojos correctores, su vista puede restablecerse bastante bien. "Aunque no podemos todavía curar las cataratas, ciertamente podemos proporcionar a los pacientes una buena visión", dice el doctor Bensinger.

Las cataratas, como el glaucoma, pueden tener un vínculo hereditario. Así que si alguien en su familia ha tenido cataratas, usted puede estar en un riesgo más alto y debería examinarse los ojos más seguido que la norma de cada tres años.

Degeneración macular. Esta insidiosa enfermedad de los ojos la despoja a usted de sus habilidades visuales excelentes. "En los casos más avanzados, usted podría notar que alguien está parado enfrente suyo, pero no podría saber quién", dice el doctor Bensinger. "Usted podría ver que un autobús viene por la calle, pero no podría saber cuál, porque no podría leer los letreros."

La causa permanece desconocida, pero la condición de alguna manera causa el deterioro de la mácula, la parte central de la retina responsable del enfoque agudo. Desafortunadamente, hay poca esperanza por lo pronto de restablecer la vista perdida por el deterioro macular, aunque la cirugía de láser puede ayudar a estabilizar la vista por un tiempo. Hay algunas noticias alentadoras, no obstante: debido a que el deterioro macular ataca casi exclusivamente a las personas mayores de 60 años de edad, usted puede empezar ahora —quizás con la ayuda de una dieta mejorada— a protegerse antes de que comience.

Retinopatía diabética. Ataca primordialmente a las personas con diabetes y es la causa principal de la ceguera en las personas entre los 20 y los 50 años de edad. La pérdida de visión empieza a ocurrir cuando los vasos sanguíneos en la parte de atrás del ojo gotean, empañando la vista y a veces denegando nutrientes al ojo.

"Si usted tiene diabetes", dice el doctor Bensinger, "le recomiendo enfáticamente que se haga revisar los ojos regularmente. Esto puede literalmente salvar su vista".

Los tratamientos con láser pueden ayudar a hacer más lento el daño de los vasos que gotean. Pero nuevamente, la ayuda está disponible solamente si usted se hace examinar sus ojos regularmente. "La detección precoz de la retinopatía diabética es aún más una historia de éxito que hacer pruebas para el glaucoma" dice el doctor Kupfer. Si se descubre temprano, hay un 95 por ciento de probabilidades que usted pueda conservar su vista por lo menos cinco años, dice el doctor Kupfer.

El enfoque debe estar en la prevención

Usted no puede cambiar sus genes, así que no hay mucho que pueda hacer acerca del mayor de todos los riesgos de la vista: la herencia. Sin embargo, aquí hay algunos consejos para darle a usted la mejor posibilidad de mantenerse 20/20 en el siglo 21.

Hágase examinar sus ojos. Los médicos no pueden repetirlo suficientes veces.

"Los exámenes regulares de los ojos son por lejos lo más importante que usted puede hacer para ayudarse a conservar su vista", dice el doctor Bensinger.

Si usted está entre los 30 y los 50 años de edad y no tiene ningún problema previo de los ojos, la Academia de Oftalmología de los Estados Unidos sugiere ver a un oftalmólogo cada tres años. Si usted tiene una historia familiar de glaucoma o diabetes o ya está usando anteojos o lentes de contacto, su médico puede sugerir visitas más frecuentes.

Ojo-rcicios: ejercicios para sus ojos

Usted hace ejercicios todas las semanas para aplanar su estómago, moldear sus muslos y afirmar sus brazos. Así que ¿por qué no tomar unos cuantos minutos para ejercitar sus ojos?

No todos los expertos piensan que los ejercicios ayudan a sus ojos. Pero un número creciente de terapeutas para la vista creen que unos cuantos ejercicios diarios pueden ayudarla a mantener sus ojos jóvenes.

"La lógica detrás de la terapia para la vista", dice Steven Ritter, O.D., del Colegio de Optometría de la Universidad Estatal de Nueva York, en la Ciudad de Nueva York, "es que si usted puede perjudicar su sistema visual haciendo tareas muy de cerca, debería ser posible rehabilitarlo".

Los terapeutas de la vista pueden recetar tantos como 280 ejercicios diferentes. Ninguna de las series de ejercicios puede curar los problemas de la vista de todos. Sin embargo, estos deben ayudarle un poco.

Mire por sus intereses. Si usted trabaja en la terminal de una computadora por horas a la vez, pruebe esto: fije una página de un periódico a la pared a aproximadamente ocho pies (dos metros y medio) de donde usted normalmente se sienta. Interrumpa su trabajo cada diez minutos o algo así y mire hacia el periódico. Enfoque sus ojos en las letras. Entonces vuelva a mirar la pantalla de la computadora. Haga esto repetidamente por 30 segundos, unas seis veces por hora. Esto puede ayudarle a eliminar la vista borrosa que muchas personas experimentan al final del día de trabajo.

Golpee contra la pared. Si usted juega frontón (*handball*), frontenis (*racquetball*), *squash* o tenis, este ejercicio para dos personas puede ser muy conveniente. Párese de tres a cinco pies (un metro a un metro y medio) de una pared vacía. Pídale a su compañero que se pare detrás suyo y que lance una pelota de tenis contra la pared. Cuando la pelota rebote en la pared, trate de agarrarla. Este ejercicio puede ayudarle a mejorar su coordinación de manos y ojos.

Enfóquese en su pulgar. Con el brazo extendido sostenga su pulgar. Muévalo en círculos, en équises y cruces, de cerca y de lejos. Sígalo con los ojos. Al hacer esto, mantenga dentro de su campo visual lo que más

La academia sugiere una visita inmediata al médico si ocurre algo de lo siguiente:

- Cambios visuales súbitos en uno o en los dos ojos
- Enrojecimiento inexplicable
- Dolor que no cesa en el ojo

pueda del cuarto. Continúe el ejercicio cerrando un ojo. Repita con el otro ojo. Esto puede mejorar su visión periférica.

Siga a la linterna eléctrica. Este ejercicio divertido puede mejorar su capacidad para seguir un objeto visualmente. Requiere de otra persona y de dos linternas eléctricas. Párese en un cuarto oscuro mirando hacia una pared. Haga que la otra persona dirija la luz de su linterna eléctrica sobre la pared y que mueva el disco de luz en movimientos amplios. Trate de eclipsar el círculo de luz con la luz de su linterna eléctrica mientras que balancea un libro sobre su cabeza. Esto la obligará a seguir la luz sólo con los ojos en lugar de mover la cabeza también.

Conviértalo en un juego. Escriba letras o números en una pelota de *softball* o de espuma de poliestireno, entonces atornille un gancho sobre la parte de arriba de la pelota y cuélguela del techo con un hilo. Mientras más pequeños los caracteres, más difícil será el ejercicio. Empuje la pelota en cualquier dirección. Trate de leer en voz alta los números o las letras que usted ve. Este ejercicio le ayuda a mantener enfocado un objeto en movimiento.

Haga la cuenta. Este ejercicio adiestra a ambos ojos a converger en un objeto. También adiestra a su cerebro a dejar de ver con un ojo. Pase un hilo de unos 6 pies (1,8 m) a través del agujero de tres cuentas de colores. Fije un extremo del hilo a la pared a la altura de su vista y sostenga el otro extremo del hilo a su nariz. Deslice una de las cuentas hasta cerca de la pared, coloque la otra cuenta a 4 pies (1,2 m) de la nariz y coloque la tercera cuenta a 16 pulgadas (40 cm) de su nariz.

Mire hacia la última cuenta. Usted verá dos hilos formando una V convergiendo en la cuenta. Mueva ambos ojos hacia la cuenta del medio. Note la X donde los dos hilos parece que convergen sobre esta. Mueva ambos ojos a la cuenta más cercana, y observe una X similar. Mueva la vista rápidamente de una cuenta a la otra, siempre observando la V o la X. Si ambos ojos están funcionando como un equipo, usted siempre debería ver dos hilos cruzando cuando usted se enfoca sobre una cuenta. Si sus ojos no están trabajando al unísono, usted verá diferentes patrones o solamente un hilo.

• Contacto accidental con químicos, especialmente la lejía

• Ver una cantidad de manchas o depósitos flotantes o lluvias de chispas en las orillas de sus ojos

(continúa en la página 78)

Examine su vista en casa

Más de diez millones de personas mayores de 25 años de edad que viven en los Estados Unidos sufren de algún tipo de pérdida de la vista. Muchos ni siquiera lo saben. Estas pruebas sencillas podrían ayudarlo a descubrir si su vista requiere algún tipo de atención.

Recuerde: las pruebas no son un substituto para un examen profesional de los ojos. Solamente pueden servir como una advertencia para ir a ver a un oculista.

Prueba de la vista Nº 1: Vista de distancia *(página opuesta). Si es posible, haga que alguien la ayude con esta prueba. No la tome si está cansada. Y, si usa anteojos (gafas) o lentes de contacto, asegúrese de que los tiene puestos. (1) Coloque la gráfica a 10 pies (3 m) suyo, contra una pared o puerta vacía. Asegúrese de que el cuarto está bien iluminado y evite el reflejo de las ventanas. (2) Cúbrase el ojo izquierdo ligeramente con un pedazo de papel. Con ambos ojos abiertos, dígale a su asistente (o escríbalo) dónde están las aberturas de cada C en la gráfica. Empiece con la C más grande y recorra la página hacia abajo. Repita con el ojo derecho cubierto. (3) Si usted no acierta todas las Cs en la penúltima línea, repita la prueba otro día.*

Casi la mitad de todas las cegueras pueden evitarse.
Todos deberían tener exámenes periódicos de los ojos.

Prueba de la vista Nº 2: Vista de cerca. *Use sus lentes de contacto o anteojos sólo si usted los usa para leer. (1) Siéntese en un cuarto bien iluminado lejos de los reflejos de las ventanas. (2) Con ambos ojos abiertos, sostenga la prueba de vista de cerca a unas 14 pulgadas (36 cm) de sus ojos. (3) Lea la frase de la prueba o escriba lo que a usted le parece que dice. (4) Escriba dónde están las aberturas para cada una de las Cs. Si no acertó con todas, haga la prueba otro día.*

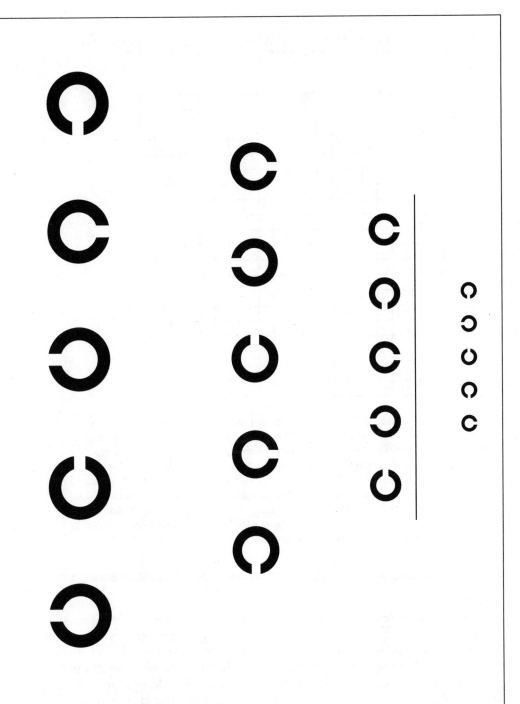

Examine su vista en casa —continuado

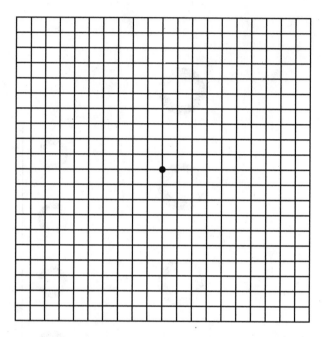

Prueba de la vista N.º 3: Degeneración macular. *Para esta prueba, use sus anteojos o lentes de contacto solamente si los usa para leer. (1) Haga que alguien sostenga la cuadrícula contra una pared o una puerta vacía en un cuarto bien iluminado sin los reflejos de las ventanas. Asegúrese de que el punto en la cuadrícula está a la altura de la vista. (2) Párese a 14 pulgadas (36 cm) de la cuadrícula. Mire el punto dentro de la cuadrícula y cúbrase el ojo izquierdo con un pedazo de papel. Usted debería ver todas las cuatro esquinas de la cuadrícula. Si la cuadrícula se ve distorsionada o usted ve partes en blanco o líneas onduladas, haga una nota mental de esto. Repita cubriendo su ojo derecho.*

Escóndase detrás de los anteojos oscuros. Los anteojos para el sol que bloquean tanto los rayos *UVA* como *UVB* (por sus siglas en inglés) y la luz azul visible pueden ayudar a disminuir el riesgo de cataratas, dice el doctor Bensinger. Los anteojos curvos que cubren los lados de sus ojos son una buena idea, ya que le protegen los ojos completamente. Y trate de usar un sombrero con un visor para bloquear la luz solar directa a sus ojos. "La exposición a la luz solar disminuye la edad en la cual usted puede empezar a desarrollar cataratas", dice el doctor Bensinger. "Así que si usted va a estar afuera, tiene sentido reducir la luz solar tanto como sea posible."

Suspenda el fumar permanentemente. El cáncer. Las arrugas. La ropa apestosa. Los dientes amarillos. El enfisema. Si usted realmente necesita otra razón para dejar de fumar, aquí está: el fumar cigarrillos puede causar cataratas. Un estudio de la Escuela de Medicina de Harvard a 120.000 enfermeras mostró que las mujeres que fuman 35 o más cigarrillos al día tienen un 63 por ciento más de riesgo de desarrollar cataratas.

La razón no se conoce, pero los investigadores especulan que fumar puede reducir el nivel de antioxidantes en su sangre, promoviendo el crecimiento de las cataratas.

Alimente a la vista. Los vínculos entre la dieta y la vista todavía son débiles. Pero existe evidencia creciente que una substancia llamada glutatión puede ayudar a controlar la propagación del deterioro macular. Esta se encuentra en los vegetales frescos, verdes, rojos y amarillos. Los vegetales enlatados o congelados pierden todo su glutación en el procesamiento.

El cinc también puede ayudar. Aunque no hay pruebas concluyentes todavía, el doctor Bensinger dice que tomar suplementos multivitamínicos que contienen cinc "probablemente no es una mala idea, siempre y cuando no esté gastando demasiado dinero en marcas lujosas".

Los antioxidantes —vitaminas A, C y E más betacaroteno— mostraron ser prometedoras como combatientes de las cataratas en el Estudio de Harvard de la Salud de Enfermeras. Un reporte en la *American Journal of Clinical Nutrition* (Revista norteamericana de nutrición clínica) alega que las personas que comen 3,5 porciones de frutas y verduras diariamente también tienen un riesgo menor de cataratas.

"Comer una dieta saludable puede retardar el envejecimiento usual del cristalino de los ojos y retardar también las cataratas", dice Paul F. Jacques, Sc.D., un epidemiólogo con el Centro de Investigación de la Nutrición Humana sobre el Envejecimiento, del Departamento de Agricultura de los Estados Unidos, ubicado en la Universidad de Tufts en Boston.

CAMBIOS POR LA MENOPAUSIA

Inevitables pero soportables

Su amiga la llamó el otro día y usted todavía no puede borrar la conversación de su mente.

"Últimamente he notado algunos cambios en mi cuerpo", dijo ella. "Y no puedo dejar de pensar si estoy empezando."

"¿Empezando qué?", le preguntó usted, media distraída por estar pensando en sus próximas vacaciones.

"La menopausia."

¡La menopausia! Eso sí la hizo prestar atención. Aquí estaba su mejor amiga —la que sólo tiene unos cuantos años más que usted— hablando acerca de un tema de salud sobre el que usted no se imaginaba que debía preocuparse todavía. Usted sabía que eventualmente le iba a suceder a las dos. Pero no ahora. No tan pronto. Ninguna de ustedes había llegado todavía ni a los 50 años de edad. La menopausia es para su madre, su tía abuela. Es algo... para las mujeres más viejas.

Para la mayoría de las mujeres, la menopausia es un hito del envejecimiento, dice Ellen Klutznick, Psy.D., una sicóloga en práctica privada en San Francisco quien se especializa en temas de salud de la mujer. La manera en que una mujer reacciona a esto varía enormemente.

Mientras que las mujeres que ya han pasado por la menopausia a menudo la ven como un nuevo comienzo, las mujeres jóvenes que no han llegado allí todavía tienden a sentirse especialmente ansiosas acerca de la transición, dice la doctora Klutznick. "Se preocupan acerca de cómo se van a sentir cuando lleguen a los 50 años de edad y acerca de sentirse viejas. Lo ven como envejecer", dice ella.

Primero, la menopausia marca el fin de los años reproductivos de una mujer. "El reloj biológico interno está marcando el paso del tiempo para muchas de estas mujeres jóvenes y es aterrador", dice la doctora Klutznick. Para ellas la menopausia se trata de la pérdida de su fertilidad y en una sociedad que pone tanto énfasis en la juventud, belleza y reproducción, esto puede ser difícil, dice ella. La pérdida de la capacidad de tener niños puede ser dura aun para las mujeres que ya terminaron de tener niños o para aquellas que nunca lo planearon, asiente el doctor Brian Walsh, director de la Clínica de Menopausia, en Brigham, y del Hospital para Mujeres, en Boston. "Ellas han perdido la posibilidad de escoger. Una puerta se les ha cerrado", dice él.

Las mujeres también están preocupadas acerca de cómo la menopausia va a afectar su apariencia física. Les preocupa que sus cuerpos y cutis no van a ser los mismos —que sus senos van a colgar, sus rostros se van a arrugar y sus cinturas van a engordar, dice la doctora Klutznick. Y todo eso está relacionado con su sexualidad, dice ella. Les preocupa que cuando entren en los bares (cantinas) o restaurantes, los hombres ya no las van a mirar —mirarán a las mujeres más jóvenes en el establecimiento o el juego de fútbol americano en la televisión, dice ella. El envejecimiento en una sociedad que idolatra a la juventud hace que algunas mujeres se sientan invisibles y devaluadas, dice la doctora Klutznick. No es que las mujeres se sientan viejas físicamente sino que la sociedad las ve viejas. Las mujeres de esta edad preguntan a la doctora Klutznick "¿Qué es lo que puedo esperar excepto hacerme vieja? ¿Quién me va a querer?"

¿Qué es la menopausia?

Literalmente hablando, la menopausia se refiere al último período de una mujer. Técnicamente, una mujer no debe haber menstruado por todo un año para ser menopáusica. La edad promedio para la menopausia en los Estados Unidos es 51, aunque las mujeres pueden tenerla antes. Aproximadamente un 1 por ciento de las mujeres experimentan la menopausia antes de llegar a los 40 años de edad.

Las mujeres a quienes se les han extirpado los ovarios durante una histerectomía se vuelven menopáusicas virtualmente de la noche a la mañana, dice Joan Borton, una consejera con licencia en salud mental, en Rockport Massachusetts, y autora de *Drawing from the Women's Well: Reflections on the Life Passage of Menopause* (Extrayendo de la fuente femenina: reflexiones sobre el paso de la menopausia por la vida). A menudo se sienten como si hubieran sido lanzadas a la menopausia sin ninguna preparación. Las mujeres que han recibido quimioterapia también pueden experimentar una menopausia prematura.

En la menopausia natural, el último período de una mujer está rodeado por una cantidad de años durante los cuales ocurren otros cambios físicos. Eso es lo que se conoce como el climatérico o perimenopausia. Por lo general comienza varios años antes de que la menstruación se suspenda, dice el doctor Walsh. Durante este tiempo, las mujeres pueden experimentar una gama completa de cambios físicos, incluyendo sofocos, sudores nocturnos, dificultad para dormir, sequedad vaginal, cambios en la piel, pérdida de cabello, cambios de estado de ánimo, depresión y aumento de peso. Los sofocos, que a menudo son los síntomas de mayor preocupación para las mujeres que se están acercando a la menopausia, afectan a aproximadamente el 75 al 85 por ciento de las mujeres postmenopáusicas.

Todos estos cambios y la pérdida de los períodos mismos, están provocados por los niveles en disminución del estrógeno, una de las varias hormonas producidas por los ovarios. Cuando una mujer envejece, lo mismo le sucede a sus ovarios; se encogen de tamaño, dejan de expulsar óvulos y producen menos estrógeno.

Sus riesgos para el futuro

El estrógeno también aumenta la calidad y fuerza de sus huesos, por lo que su declinación en la menopausia puede colocar a las mujeres en un mayor riesgo de osteoporosis, una enfermedad en la cual los huesos se vuelven más quebradizos y frágiles. La osteoporosis resulta en aproximadamente 1,5 millones de fracturas por año. Un tercio de todas las mujeres mayores de 65 años de edad experimentan fracturas espinales, y una de cada tres mujeres en su década de los 90 años de edad se fractura las caderas (comparado con uno en seis hombres). En total, entre el 25 y el 44 por ciento de las mujeres experimentan fracturas después de la menopausia debido a la enfermedad.

La reducción en estrógeno que acompaña a la menopausia aumenta el riesgo de las enfermedades del corazón, el asesino número uno de las mujeres estadounidenses. Eso es porque el estrógeno es un protector natural contra las enfermedades del corazón. Sin él, las mujeres y los hombres están parejos en sus esfuerzos para evitar las enfermedades del corazón. Eso significa que el riesgo de una mujer de sufrir un ataque al corazón y derrame cerebral aumenta después de la menopausia. Antes de los 65 años de edad, una en cada nueve mujeres experimentará un ataque al corazón según la Asociación del Corazón de los Estados Unidos. Después de los 65 años de edad, esa proporción aumenta tremendamente a una en cada tres.

Cómo planificar de antemano

Usted no puede evitar la menopausia. Pero hay algunas cosas que puede hacer ahora, antes de llegar a ese punto, que pueden hacer la experiencia total un poco más fácil para usted. La menopausia no tiene que ser una etapa difícil, y no tiene que hacer que se sienta y se vea vieja. Aquí está lo que usted puede hacer.

Manténgase en movimiento. El ejercicio es una de las mejores cosas que las mujeres pueden hacer con anticipación para que les vaya mejor durante sus años menopáusicos, dice el doctor Walsh. El ejercicio pone tensión sobre el hueso, aumentando su densidad y fuerza. Los huesos de las mujeres pierden densidad después de la menopausia —en una proporción de 4 a 6 por ciento en los primeros cuatro o cinco años. Así que mientras más fuertes estén al principio, mejor. Los ejercicios de cargar su propio peso como son el caminar y el correr son los mejores, dicen los expertos. El ejercicio también ayuda a mantener sus niveles de colesterol bajos, ofreciendo protección contra las enfermedades del corazón.

Coma mejor. Póngase en una dieta nutritiva baja en grasas saturadas, dice el doctor Walsh. Esto ayudará a reducir el colesterol y el riesgo de una enfermedad del corazón, dice él, ambos de los cuales aumentan después de la menopausia. Los expertos recomiendan que usted mantenga su consumo de grasa en un 25 por ciento o menos del total de calorías que consume.

Vigile el síndrome premenstrual. Si usted tiene síndrome premenstrual o *PMS* (por sus siglas en inglés), lleve un diario de sus síntomas y esté atenta a cualquier cambio. Algunas veces los síntomas del síndrome premenstrual se pueden hacer mucho más intensos cuando las mujeres entran en la menopausia, dice la doctora Klutznick, y pueden ser una señal para usted que está volviéndose menopáusica. Algunos de los cambios posibles que usted puede notar son síntomas del síndrome premenstrual que duran más de lo acostumbrado y una sensación de confusión en su mente, dice ella. Si usted nota cambios, dígale a su doctora. Ella le puede hacer un examen simple de sangre llamado la prueba *FSH* (por sus siglas en inglés), la cual mide la cantidad de FSH o *follicle-stimulating hormone* (hormona estimulante de folículos). Antes de la menopausia, su cuerpo produce suficiente FSH para ayudar a que los folículos se desarrollen y a provoquen la ovulación. En la menopausia, sin embargo, usted tiene menos folículos y se necesita más FSH para hacer que uno madure y ovule. Por ello su cuerpo bombea más de la hormona de lo que solía bombear antes. Si su prueba muestra un nivel alto de FSH —digamos, arriba de 40— eso quiere decir que usted está oficialmente en la menopausia.

Bote los cigarrillos. Si usted deja de fumar cuando es más joven, le puede ayudar a experimentar una menopausia más ligera, dice el doctor Walsh. Las fumadoras tienen más probabilidades que las no fumadoras de sufrir síntomas de menopausia, dice él. Las fumadoras tienen también una tendencia a una masa ósea más baja, poniéndolas en mayor riesgo de osteoporosis. El fumar puede causar que usted experimente la menopausia antes, dicen los expertos. Ellos creen que eso se debe a que la nicotina puede de alguna manera contribuir a una disminución en el estrógeno. Así que dejando de fumar ahora puede demorar un poco a la menopausia.

Tome ahora su calcio. Aunque la disminución en la masa ósea se acelera durante la menopausia, ésta empieza alrededor de los 35 años de edad. Después de los 35 años de edad, las mujeres pierden un 1 por ciento de su masa ósea por año. Por esa razón, asegúrese de tomar suficiente calcio. La Asignación Dietética Recomendada actual para adultos es de 800 miligramos de calcio, pero algunos expertos sugieren 1.000 miligramos diarios para las mujeres premenopáusicas y 1.500 miligramos para las mujeres postmenopáusicas.

Desafortunadamente, la mayoría de las mujeres consumen solamente cerca de 500 miligramos diarios a través de su dieta. Usted puede acercarse a las cantidades protectoras añadiendo productos lácteos bajos en grasa y pescado enlatado con espinas (como el salmón) a su dieta diaria. Por ejemplo, una porción de leche descremada le da a usted 300 miligramos de calcio, y una porción de yogur bajo en grasa contiene 415 miligramos.

Usted también puede aumentar su consumo de calcio a través de los alimentos que no son lácteos: 3 onzas de salmón de Alaska enlatado contienen 203 miligramos de calcio, y media taza de tofu crudo contiene 258 miligramos.

Otra forma de aumentar su consumo de calcio es a través de los suplementos. La cantidad que usted debería tomar y el tipo de tableta que debería usar —carbonato de calcio, lactato de calcio o citrato de calcio— dependerá de sus necesidades individuales de salud, así que consulte con su médico.

Sepa cuales son sus niveles de colesterol. Haga que le controlen sus niveles de colesterol, dice el doctor Walsh. La menopausia puede causar que los niveles de la lipoproteína de alta densidad (o *HDL*, por sus siglas en inglés) de colesterol, el tipo "bueno", bajen y los niveles de la lipoproteína de baja densidad (o *LDL*, por sus siglas en inglés) de colesterol, el tipo "malo", aumenten. Así que cuanto mejor sea su perfil de colesterol antes de la menopausia, mayores serán sus posibilidades de mantenerlo bajo una vez que usted llega a ésta. Los expertos dicen que las mejores medidas para usar son la relación entre el total de colesterol y el colesterol HDL. Una relación de menos de 3,5 se considera baja, entre 3,5 y 6,9 moderada, y arriba de 7, alta.

Hable con su mamá. A menudo las mujeres siguen los mismos patrones que sus madres, dice el doctor Walsh, particularmente si tienen las mismas experiencias de salud. Así que pregúntele a su mamá cuándo ella empezó con la menopausia y cuál fue su experiencia con esta.

Al llegar el momento

Si usted cree que está entrando en la menopausia, o si ya está usted allí, aquí hay algunas cosas que puede hacer.

Busque apoyo. "Lo más valioso es juntarse con otras mujeres", dice Borton. Al hablar con otras mujeres, ya sea individualmente o en grupos de apoyo, usted puede aprender acerca de los varios síntomas y obtener información acerca de los doctores y otros profesionales en el cuidado de la salud que otras mujeres ven, les gustan y recomiendan, dice ella. "El hablar con otras mujeres y compartir experiencias ayuda a las mujeres a sentirse apoyadas y no aisladas", asiente la doctora Klutznick. Una opción es unirse a un grupo de apoyo. Llame a su hospital local para informarse acerca de los grupos en su área. O hable con otras mujeres.

Encuentre un médico que la comprenda. La menopausia traerá consigo muchos cambios físicos y muchas preguntas, en especial acerca de la terapia de reposición de hormonas (o *HRT*, por sus sigla en inglés). El HRT se recomienda para ayudar a reemplazar el estrógeno faltante y para mantener a sus huesos fuertes. Pero también es problemático, principalmente porque puede aumentar su riesgo de ciertos cánceres. "La clave es tener un doctor que esté de acuerdo en trabajar con usted —uno que respete su decisión", dice Borton. Pregunte a sus amigas acerca de sus doctores. Y no tenga temor de buscar hasta que encuentre un doctor que le agrade.

Elija una consejera. Encuentre a una mujer de 10 a 15 años mayor que usted que haya pasado por la menopausia y a quien usted admira y respeta, dice Borton. "Pase tiempo con mujeres mayores, explorando con ellas qué es lo que le da significado y propósito a sus vidas", dice ella. "Muchas de nosotras sentimos que el hacer esto nos ha ayudado a cruzar el umbral para podernos ver como mujeres mayores y aceptarlo de una manera que se siente realmente maravilloso." Además de identificar o encontrar mujeres que puedan servir como consejeras en su vida cotidiana, observe a las mujeres muy conocidas a quienes usted puede emular y de las cuales puede aprender, dice ella.

Manténgase lubricada. La reducción del estrógeno que las mujeres experimentan con la menopausia puede causar sequedad vaginal. La elasticidad y el tamaño de la vagina cambian, y las paredes se hacen más delgadas y pierden su capacidad de humedecerse. Esto puede hacer que las relaciones sexuales provoquen dolor e incluso se hagan indeseables, dice la doctora Klutznick. Las encuestas indican que esto sucede en el 8 al 25 por ciento de las mujeres postmenopáusicas. Mientras que las mujeres premenopáusicas generalmente pueden lubricarse en 6 a 20 segundos cuando están excitadas, puede tardar uno a tres minutos para las mujeres postmenopáusicas.

Las mujeres pueden permanecer lubricadas usando lubricantes vaginales solubles en agua como las jaleas *K-Y, Replens* y *Astroglide,* los cuales están disponibles sin necesidad de receta, dice la doctora Klutznick. Evite los lubricantes de base aceitosa como la jalea de petróleo; los estudios indican que estos no se disuelven tan fácilmente en la vagina y por lo tanto pueden provocar infecciones vaginales. El HRT también puede ayudar a aliviar el problema, dice la doctora Klutznick.

Manténgase activa sexualmente. Los estudios indican que las mujeres que se mantienen sexualmente activas experimentan menos cambios vaginales que aquellas que no lo están. La actividad sexual promueve la circulación en el área vaginal, lo cual ayuda a mantenerla húmeda. Para las mujeres que no tienen compañeros, la masturbación ayuda a promover la circulación y humedad en la vagina, dice ella.

Refrésquese. Los sofocos que las mujeres experimentan durante la menopausia pueden ir desde una sensación templada a una muy caliente en que la mujer se pone roja y suda. Puede ayudar si se viste en capas y mantiene el medio ambiente fresco, dicen los expertos. Algunas mujeres chupan cubos de hielo y beben líquidos fríos o se imaginan que están caminando en la nieve o nadando en un lago transparente. Los líquidos calientes y los alimentos muy condimentados pueden provocar los sofocos, así que mantenga estos al mínimo. Los expertos no entienden completamente qué causa los sofocos, pero creen que la disminución de estrógeno de alguna manera altera el termómetro interno del cuerpo.

CANAS

Conquístelas con color a su favor

Usted se baja de la cama, despacio se dirige al baño y prende la luz. Se inclina hacia el espejo para mirarse más de cerca.

¿Cuántas canas más habrán hoy?

Además de las arrugas y la piel colgante, pocas cosas dejan translucir el "envejecimiento" en una mujer de una manera tan notable como las canas. Mientras que a algunas de nosotras nos encanta como nos vemos y las llevamos bien, a una gran cantidad de nosotras no nos gustan. Y hay una industria de muchos millones de dólares ahí lista para satisfacer nuestras necesidades y mantener nuestros colores verdaderos en secreto.

"Si se está volviendo canosa, yo le garantizo que usted no está muy feliz al respecto", dice Philip Kingsley, un especialista en el cuidado del cabello con base en la ciudad de Nueva York. "Yo he visto decenas de miles de personas a través de los años, y ninguna quiere las canas. Esto realmente puede hacer que las personas se sientan viejas antes de tiempo."

Las raíces de su árbol genealógico

La mayoría de nosotras tenemos cerca de 100.000 cabellos en nuestras cabezas. Antes de hacernos canosas, cada uno de esos cabellos contiene el pigmento melanina, que da color a su cabello. Pero por razones que los doctores no entienden, las células pigmentarias cerca de la raíz de cada cabello comienzan a cerrarse al hacernos viejas. De esa manera, cuando un cabello rubio, castaño o rojo se cae, a menudo es reemplazado por uno gris.

Uno blanco, en realidad —no obstante le llamamos gris porque así es como se ve en contraste con el cabello que todavía tiene color.

Falsedades sobre los folículos: los mitos de las canas

Hay un millón de leyendas por ahí acerca de las canas —y muy pocos, hechos sólidos. A pesar de que los doctores pueden no saber todavía qué causa las canas, sí saben de algunas cosas que no las causan.

Mito de las canas Nº 1: Usted puede volverse canosa instantáneamente debido a un suceso espantoso. Es físicamente imposible —el cabello existente no se vuelve canoso. La doctora Diana Bihova, profesora clínica asistente del Centro Médico de la Universidad de Nueva York, en la ciudad de Nueva York, explica que a usted le salen las canas solamente cuando el cabello normal se cae y es reemplazado por una cana en el mismo folículo.

Mito de las canas Nº 2: Su cabello puede volver al color normal después de haber sido canoso. Lo sentimos mucho, pero no. Cuando un folículo del cabello empieza a producir canas no se invierte el proceso.

Hay algunas excepciones, dice la doctora Bihova. Su cabello puede volverse canoso temporalmente si usted tiene un desorden de la glándula endocrina, está desnutrida, sufre una herida o una enfermedad del sistema nervioso o tiene un desorden autoinmune. Y aun así, puede ser que el cabello no vuelva en su color original, dice ella.

Mito de las canas Nº 3: Si usted se arranca una cana, le saldrán dos. No. Usted se vuelve canosa folículo por folículo. Si usted se arranca una cana, será reemplazada por otra cana en el mismo folículo. "Usted no puede detener el proceso", dice la doctora Bihova. "Pero el arrancarse las canas tampoco lo acelerará."

Si usted está buscando a alguien a quien culpar, empiece con papá, mamá, la tía Julieta, o el bisabuelo Pedro. "Hay una relación hereditaria muy estrecha con el cabello canoso", dice la doctora Diana Bihova, profesora clínica asistente de dermatología en el Centro Médico de la Universidad de Nueva York, en la ciudad de Nueva York. "Si su familia se vuelve canosa prematuramente, es muy probable que a usted también le ocurra."

Sea lo que sea, no lo atribuya al estrés. Haciendo el papel de mamá, jefa, cocinera, chofer, jardinera y compañera amorosa, todo al mismo tiempo, no hará que su cabello se vuelva canoso, dice la doctora Bihova —a menos que el estrés sea tan fuerte que usted reduce su reserva de algunas vitaminas B. La evidencia no está clara en esto.

La sobreexposición al sol también podría causar que el cabello se volviera canoso, dice la doctora Bihova. La teoría es que los rayos ultravioleta provocan que las células pigmentarias en su cuero cabelludo trabajen de más, tal y como sucede con sus brazos y piernas cuando usted se broncea. Si trabajan demasiado y se consumen prematuramente, dice la doctora Bihova, el resultado pueden ser las canas. No hay evidencia concreta para esto. Pero la doctora Bihova aún sugiere usar un sombrero o usar productos para el cuidado del cabello que contengan un producto antisolar. "Digamos simplemente que no puede hacer daño", dice.

A la típica mujer de ascendencia europea le empiezan a salir las canas a la edad de 34 años, mientras que la típica mujer de ascendencia africana goza de un aplazamiento de 10 años. Hasta ahora, no hay estadísticas sobre cuándo les empiezan a salir canas a las mujeres latinas. La doctora Bihova dice que las mujeres empiezan a encanecer a los lados, después en la coronilla y finalmente en la parte de atrás del cuello. El proceso puede darse por rachas, saliéndole más canas en algunos años y menos en otros.

Para la edad de 50 años sin embargo, el 50 por ciento de las mujeres estarán canosas en un 50 por ciento, dice la doctora Bihova.

Por lo general, el cabello en su cabeza empieza a cambiar primero, seguido un poco tiempo después por los vellos en sus piernas, en las axilas y en sus cejas y, finalmente, en la zona púbica. Pero de nuevo, cada persona es diferente.

La buena noticia de todo esto es que usualmente no hay nada físicamente malo con tener canas —no significa que usted está envejeciendo más rápidamente que las amigas que no tienen ni una sola cana. Los estudios muestran que las personas que se vuelven canosas a una edad temprana por lo general no están sufriendo de nada más que de un caso de características genéticas familiares indeseables.

La mala noticia es que volverse canosa es irreversible.

Para muchas de nosotras, es teñir o morir

Las canas vienen en camino, le guste o no. Eso la deja con dos opciones. Lo puede aceptar como una parte ineludible, aun deseable de la madurez. O las puede detener por un tiempo, usando algún tipo de tinte para el cabello.

"Algunas personas llegan a sentirse muy cómodas con las canas", dice Kingsley. "El punto más importante para recordar acerca de las canas, o el cabello en general, es que usted debe sentirse cómoda con éste. Si la hace sentirse inteligente o digna, entonces está bien."

Aquí hay algunos consejos de expertos sobre cómo manejar esas canas.

Córtelo. Si usted decide quedarse canosa, Kingsley sugiere conservar su cabello corto. "Es realmente simple", dice Kingsley. "Si usted no quiere canas o no está segura al respecto, entonces los estilos cortos mostrarán menos las canas."

Acondiciónelo. Al pasar el tiempo, su cabello y su cuero cabelludo pueden resecarse. Para que su cabello canoso se vea saludable, Kingsley sugiere usar un acondicionador cada vez que usted se lava el cabello con champú. Y sugiere también, dejar que el aire seque su cabello de vez en cuando, en lugar de usar una secadora eléctrica para el cabello.

Así que pruebe el aspecto canoso por un tiempo corto. Si no le gusta, puede usted optar por algo de color. Aquí hay algunas opciones que usted puede probar en el salón o en su casa.

Pruebe los rayitos. El aplicar rayitos (claritos, *highlights*), lo cual consiste de usar tinte en algunos cabellos diseminados por la cabeza, puede ocultar sutilmente algunas canas. Escoja un color que sea un par de tonos más claros que su color natural.

Los tintes más claros también ayudan a evitar las raíces canosas desagradables. Cuando su cabello crezca lo canoso no se verá tanto.

Tíñalo todo. Los expertos llaman a este proceso colorear, y significa que todo su cabello será teñido de un solo color. Si usted opta por esto, evite los tonos más oscuros que tienden a hacer que su cabello se vea apagado y poco natural. "Los colores negros realmente no funcionan muy bien", dice Kingsley. "Todo el cabello se tiñe exactamente del mismo color, y se puede ver enseguida que está teñido."

Existe también la duda de que si los tintes oscuros para cabello pueden causar cáncer. Algunos estudios han vinculado el uso de tales tintes con un riesgo en el aumento de cáncer de los huesos y linfoma.

¿Y la conclusión final? "No hay ninguna, todavía", dice Sheila Hoar Zahm, Ph.D., una epidemióloga en el Instituto Nacional del Cáncer, en Rockville, Maryland. "El riesgo de contraer cáncer de un tinte para el cabello no es tan alto como contraer cáncer por fumar. Pero definitivamente necesitamos estudiar más la relación."

Kingsley dice que usted debería tener cuidado con los tintes progresivos que prometen ir ocultando lentamente sus canas. Él piensa que estos productos pueden dar a su cabello un tinte poco natural y de un color verde amarillento. También pueden resecar su cabello, haciéndolo quebradizo y difícil de manejar.

Y una vez que usted empieza a usarlos, es difícil cambiar a los tintes normales. "Estos pueden darle a su cabello toda clase de colores que usted nunca quisiera que su cabello tuviera", dice Kingsley.

Los tintes semipermanentes que se desaparecen al cabo de varias semanas al lavarlos ofrecen un color un poco mejor pero no son tan buenos como los tintes permanentes. Si usted quiere probar un camino lento a un cabello más oscuro, Kingsley sugiere que trate de usar tintes gradualmente más oscuros cada vez que se tiñe el cabello.

CÁNCER

Cómo puede ayudarse a sí misma

Cuando se le dice a una mujer que tiene cáncer, muchas preguntas pasan por su mente: "¿Me voy a morir?" "¿Me va a desfigurar la cirugía?" "¿Va a pensar mi esposo que soy menos mujer?" "¿Qué les voy a decir a mis amistades y familia?" "¿Cómo vamos a pagar las cuentas?" "¿Quiere esto decir que ya no voy a poder tener más niños?"

El cáncer es un envejecedor particularmente poderoso. Es una enfermedad desalmada que puede causar un dolor debilitante y exprimir la juventud y el vigor de cualquiera de nosotras.

La enfermedad puede realmente acelerar el proceso del envejecimiento al causar cambios químicos en el cuerpo que conducen a articulaciones doloridas, apetito apagado, pérdida de peso, debilidad, fatiga y pérdida de resistencia, dice el doctor Ernest Rosenbaum, un oncólogo en la Universidad de California, San Francisco/Mount Zion.

"El cáncer la agota. Si usted tiene cáncer, puede sentir que envejece muy rápidamente", dice el doctor Charles B. Simone, un oncólogo en Princeton, New Jersey y autor de *Cancer and Nutrition* (El cáncer y la nutrición).

La verdad acerca del cáncer

El cáncer pone su vida en peligro porque sus células anormales crecen en forma incontrolada, puede extenderse a través de su cuerpo y puede dañar las células normales a su alrededor, dice el doctor John Laszlo, vicepresidente nacional para investigación de la Sociedad de Cáncer de los Estados Unidos. En realidad no se trata de una enfermedad sino de una serie de más de 100 tipos de enfermedades malignas que atacan diferentes órganos del cuerpo en una variedad de formas. Por ejemplo el cáncer del pulmón puede extenderse a otros tejidos en forma ligeramente diferente al cáncer de mama.

"Existe la percepción de que el cáncer es una entidad única y que nosotros vamos a encontrar una píldora mágica que evitará la enfermedad totalmente o que será la cura final de todas las formas de cáncer. Desafortunadamente, el cáncer es más complicado que eso", dice el doctor Ronald Ross, director de investigación de causa y prevención del cáncer en el Centro Comprensivo de Cáncer Kenneth Norris, Jr., de la Universidad de California del Sur, en Los Ángeles.

Los investigadores sospechan que del 5 al 10 por ciento de los cánceres pueden ser heredados, lo que significa que la enfermedad pasa de una generación a la otra a través de un gene anormal. Pero en la gran mayoría de los casos, el cáncer se desarrolla a través de una serie compleja de pasos que a menudo incluye una exposición prolongada a carcinógenos, los cuales son substancias que causan cáncer como el tabaco y el asbesto, dice el doctor Laszlo. Estos carcinógenos afectan usualmente células en órganos específicos. El asbesto, por ejemplo, aumenta el riesgo de la persona al cáncer del pulmón, mientras que una exposición excesiva al sol se vincula con un mayor riesgo de cáncer de la piel.

Algunos investigadores creen que los carcinógenos causan la formación de radicales libres, moléculas inestables de oxígeno que pueden dañar las cadenas de moléculas ADN que indican a las células cómo reproducirse. Cuando el ADN se daña en lugares críticos, se puede formar una célula de cáncer.

"Los radicales libres que causan envejecimiento son las mismas cosas que causan cáncer", explica el doctor Simone. "¿Cómo prevenimos eso? Necesitamos

Siete señales que usted no debería ignorar

Aquí hay siete señales comunes de advertencia del cáncer. Si usted desarrolla alguna de ellas, póngase en contacto con su médico inmediatamente.

1. Una masa o engrosamiento en el seno
2. Cambio en una verruga o lunar
3. Una llaga que no se cura
4. Cambio en los hábitos de evacuar u orinar
5. Una tos persistente o ronquera
6. Indigestión constante o dificultad al tragar
7. Sangrado o evacuación de pus o fluido extraño

reducir nuestra exposición a las cosas que causan radicales libres, incluyendo alimentos grasosos, tabaco y alcohol."

Cada año se diagnostican aproximadamente 576.000 nuevos casos de cáncer entre mujeres que viven en los Estados Unidos, de acuerdo con la Sociedad de Cáncer de los Estados Unidos. Los tipos más comunes de cáncer entre las mujeres se encuentran en los senos, el colon y el recto, los pulmones, el útero, el tejido linfático y los ovarios. En las mujeres menores de 35 años de edad, el cáncer de mama y la piel, y los linfomas como es la enfermedad de Hodgkins son los tres más frecuentes.

El cáncer mata anualmente a cerca de 255.000 mujeres y es la segunda causa principal de muerte en estadounidenses de todas las edades. Para el año 2000, se espera que el cáncer afecte a dos de cada cinco personas viviendo en los Estados Unidos y va a superar a las enfermedades del corazón como el asesino principal de la nación, dice el doctor Simone.

Pero tener cáncer no es una sentencia de muerte automática. De hecho, más de la mitad de todos los estadounidenses diagnosticados con cáncer lo sobreviven, según la Sociedad de Cáncer de los Estados Unidos. Si se descubren temprano, algunos tipos de cáncer como los de la piel y de mama, tienen índices de sobrevivencia de cinco años que van más allá del 90 por ciento. Si una paciente aparece libre de síntomas de cáncer por cinco años, los médicos pueden considerarla "curada", aunque con algunos tipos de cáncer se puede sufrir una recaída después de diez o más años.

"En los últimos 50 años hemos progresado lenta pero constantemente en la lucha contra el cáncer. Paso por paso, estamos ganando esta guerra", dice el doctor Harmon Eyre, el vicepresidente ejecutivo adjunto para investigación y asuntos médicos de la Sociedad de Cáncer de los Estados Unidos.

La mayoría de los cánceres ocurren en las mujeres mayores de 50 años de edad, y el 66 por ciento de las muertes debido a cáncer ocurren después de los 65 años. De hecho, de los 182.000 casos de cáncer de mama —el tipo de cáncer más común entre las mujeres— diagnosticados anualmente, menos de 11.000 son entre mujeres menores de 40 años.

"En su mayor parte, las jóvenes no tienen que tenerle miedo al cáncer. Es algo que acecha en el futuro distante, en algunas ocasiones a 30 ó 40 años de distancia", dice el doctor Carl Mansfield, profesor y presidente del Departamento de Radiación, Oncología y Medicina Nuclear en el Hospital de la Universidad Thomas Jefferson, en Filadelfia.

Lo que usted puede hacer

Algunos cánceres, sin embargo, pueden tomar más de 30 años para desarrollarse. Así que lo que usted haga ahora puede tener un tremendo impacto en su capacidad para gozar de una vida larga y saludable libre de cáncer, dice el doctor Laszlo. De hecho, los oncólogos estiman que quizás un 50 por ciento de los cánceres se podrían evitar si las mujeres simplemente hicieran unos cuantas ajustes sencillos en sus estilos de vida. Aquí está dónde empezar.

Vuélvase una ex-fumadora. El cáncer del pulmón era una enfermedad rara antes que el fumar cigarrillos se hizo popular. Ahora mata a cerca de 59.000 mujeres anualmente y ha sobrepasado al cáncer de mama como la causa número uno de muertes relacionadas con cáncer entre las mujeres, dice el doctor Dennis Ahnen, director asociado para prevención y control del cáncer en el Centro del Cáncer de la Universidad de Colorado, en Denver. (El cáncer de mama, sin embargo, es todavía el tipo más común de cáncer que afecta a las mujeres). Las fumadoras tienen diez veces más probabilidades de desarrollar cáncer en el pulmón, y hasta un 30 por ciento de todas las muertes por cáncer se deben a fumar, dice el doctor Rosenbaum, autor de *You can prevent cancer* (Usted puede prevenir el cáncer). Los estudios también sugieren que las mujeres que fuman tienen el doble de probabilidades de tener cáncer cérvico. Así que si usted no fuma, no empiece, y si fuma, deje de hacerlo.

Cuídese del humo pasivo. Hasta 8.000 muertes al año por cáncer al pulmón entre no fumadores se pueden atribuir al humo de segunda mano, dice el doctor Simone. Investigadores en la Universidad de California en Berkeley y del Programa de Residencia de Medicina Preventiva de la Universidad de California en San Francisco encontraron que los trabajadores en restaurantes están expuestos al doble de humo pasivo que las personas que viven en hogares donde por lo menos una persona fuma. Los barmans (cantineros), por ejemplo, están expuestos a 4,5 veces más humo pasivo. Comparados con la población en general, se encontró que estos trabajadores de servicio de alimentos tienen 50 por ciento más probabilidades de desarrollar cáncer del pulmón, una diferencia que se atribuye —por lo menos en parte— al fumar pasivo en el lugar de trabajo. Evite bares (cantinas) con mucho humo y siempre pida que la sienten en la sección de no fumadores en los restaurantes, sugiere el doctor Simone. Si alguna persona fuma en su hogar, pídale que lo deje o determine una zona donde ellos puedan fumar sin ponerla a usted en peligro.

Tenga cuidado con los tragos. Un consumo fuerte de alcohol aumenta el riesgo de cáncer en el hígado, la boca, el esófago y la laringe. Los estudios que tratan de vincular el alcohol con el cáncer de mama han tenido resultados contradictorios, pero es mejor tener cuidado, dice Louise Brinton, Ph.D., jefe de la Sección de Estudios Ambientales del Instituto Nacional del Cáncer en Rockville, Maryland. La doctora Rosenbaum recomienda que usted se limite diariamente a no más de una cerveza de 12 onzas (360 ml), un vaso de vino de 4 onzas (120 ml) o 1 onza (30 ml) de licor en un cóctel o puro.

Llénese de fibra. Las mujeres que comen muchas frutas fibrosas, verduras y granos integrales tales como el brócoli, col de bruselas (*brussels sprouts*), repollo, manzanas, plátanos (guineos) amarillos, mangos, y cereales y panes integrales, pueden tener menos cánceres en los senos, colon y recto que aquellas que no ingieren estos alimentos, dice el doctor Simone. La fibra reduce la cantidad de estrógeno en la sangre. El estrógeno posiblemente altera la estructura de las células y promueve el cáncer de mama, dice el doctor Mansfield. Además, la fibra ayuda a que la materia fecal pase más rápidamente por su cuerpo, y reduce la exposición de su tracto digestivo a carcinógenos.

La fibra también puede ayudar a prevenir otros tipos de cáncer. En un estudio de 399 mujeres con cáncer endometrial y 296 mujeres libres de enfermedades, la doctora Brinton encontró que las mujeres que comían más de dos porciones diarias de panes y cereales con alto contenido de fibra tenían 40 por ciento menos riesgo de desarrollar cáncer endometrial.

El Instituto Nacional del Cáncer recomienda que las mujeres coman por lo menos 20 a 30 gramos de fibra al día. Si usted empieza su día con un cereal que tiene por lo menos siete gramos de fibra por porción, añada otros tres gramos de fibra agregando a su cereal un medio plátano rebanado y dos cucharadas de pasas. De esa forma usted ya va a la mitad de la recomendación mínima diaria de 20 gramos, dice Gladys Block, Ph.D., profesora de nutrición de salud pública en la Universidad de California, Berkeley. Entonces, todo lo que usted tiene que hacer es asegurarse de consumir tres porciones más de frutas, verduras y/o granos durante el resto del día. Los frijoles (habichuelas), por ejemplo, tienen un contenido particularmente alto de fibra.

Échele ganas a las verduras. Coma por lo menos cinco porciones de frutas y verduras al día, dice el doctor Rosenbaum. Estos alimentos contienen vitaminas y minerales antioxidantes como es el betacaroteno, selenio y vitaminas A y E que combaten la formación de radicales libres.

Tome un suplemento. Los suplementos que contienen vitaminas C y E y otras vitaminas y minerales antioxidantes pueden ayudar a neutralizar ciertos carcinógenos como son las nitritas encontradas en el tocino, las salchichas, los perros calientes y las carnes curadas, según Kedar N. Prasad, Ph.D., director del Centro para Vitaminas e Investigación del Cáncer, en el Centro de Ciencias de la Salud de la Universidad de Colorado, en Denver y autor de *Vitamins in Cancer Prevention and Treatment* (Las vitaminas en la prevención y tratamiento del cáncer). Los suplementos también pueden fortalecer el sistema inmune de su cuerpo para que pueda destruir células de cáncer recién formadas antes de que se multipliquen, dice el doctor Prasad. Él sugiere tomar 15 miligramos de betacaroteno una vez al día, 2.500 UI de vitaminas A dos veces al día, 500 miligramos de vitamina C dos veces al día, 200 miligramos (o 134 UI) de vitamina E dos veces al día y 50 microgramos de selenio dos veces al día.

Recorte la grasa. Una dieta con alto contenido de grasa —como la que comen muchas mujeres en los Estados Unidos— se cree que provoca cáncer. Investigadores en la Universidad de Hawai en Manoa compararon el consumo de grasa de 272 mujeres que habían pasado la menopausia y que habían sufrido de cáncer de mama, con el de 296 mujeres que estaban libres de cáncer. Los investigadores encontraron una asociación significativa entre el cáncer de mama y comer salchichas, fiambres procesados, res y carne de cordero. Los doctores no están seguros de por qué la grasa provoca tumores, pero varios factores pueden desempeñar un papel, dice el doctor Mansfield. Algunos sospechan que los alimentos grasosos provocan la producción de ácidos biliares que interactúan con bacterias en el colon para formar carcinógenos. También puede ser que las células grasosas sean más susceptibles a carcinógenos que otras células. Cualquiera que sea la causa, muchos expertos sugieren reducir su consumo de grasa dietética a no más del 25 por ciento de las calorías. Para lograr eso, coma más frutas, verduras y alimentos de grano integral, recorte toda la grasa visible en las carnes y no coma más de una porción de 3 onzas (85 g) de carne roja, pescado o aves al día.

Deshágase de la freidora. Freír simplemente agrega más grasa a la comida, y la grasa promueve el cáncer. En lugar de eso, ase a la parrilla, cocine al vapor o al horno, o hierva sus alimentos, dice el doctor Mansfield. Dore o saltee en sartenes antiadherentes, o use aceite vegetal en atomizador o caldo de pollo.

Tenga cuidado con la barbacoa. El humo y el calor al asar al carbón producen varias substancias causantes de cáncer, incluyendo nitrosamina, uno de los carcinógenos más potentes conocidos, dice el doctor Mansfield. Si a usted le gusta asar a la barbacoa, hágalo con cuidado y moderación, sugiere el doctor Prasad. Coloque la parrilla tan separada como sea posible del carbón, y envuelva papel de aluminio alrededor de la parrilla para evitar que la grasa gotee sobre la llama causando humo y carbonización excesiva.

Pierda peso. Si usted tiene peso de más, puede estar produciendo más estrógeno del que necesita. Se cree que las cantidades excesivas de estrógeno, una hormona reproductora, alteran la estructura de las células y están vinculadas con un mayor riesgo de cáncer de mama, dice el doctor Mansfield. Mantenga su peso dentro de los límites sugeridos por su ginecólogo o médico familiar.

En un estudio, los investigadores de la Escuela de Salud Pública de Harvard llegaron a la conclusión de que las mujeres que permanecen físicamente activas a lo largo de su vida son 2,5 menos susceptibles a sufrir cáncer cérvico y otros del sistema reproductor. Trate de hacer ejercicio aeróbico regular como nadar, caminar o correr por 20 minutos al día, por lo menos tres veces por semana, dice el doctor Simone.

Quédese en la sombra. El cáncer de la piel, uno de los cánceres más comunes (afecta a más de 700.000 personas viviendo en los Estados Unidos), es causado primordialmente por quemarse al sol. Para prevenir el cáncer de la piel, evite exposiciones prolongadas al sol, use sombreros y blusas de manga larga, y no ande con las piernas descubiertas sin usar una loción antisolar que tenga un factor de protección al sol (SPF) de por lo menos 15. Usted debería ponerse loción antisolar en la piel descubierta cuando se encuentra afuera, dice el doctor Rosenbaum.

No se dé duchas vaginales muy a menudo. Los investigadores de la Universidad de Servicios Uniformes de las Ciencias de la Salud, en Bethesda, Maryland encontraron que el riesgo de cáncer cérvico era cuatro a cinco veces mayor en mujeres que se daban duchas vaginales más de cuatro veces al mes. Las mujeres que se daban menos duchas vaginales no tenían mayor riesgo. El tipo de líquido de las duchas vaginales no mostró diferencia en el grado de riesgo. Los investigadores especularon que una limpieza muy frecuente puede alterar el balance químico normal, diluyendo secreciones o destruyendo bacterias amigas que pueden proteger contra invasores virales.

Tenga relaciones sexuales seguras. El papilomavirus humano (o *HPV*, por sus siglas en inglés), una enfermedad transmitida sexualmente, se ha vinculado con cambios precancerosos en la cérvix llamados displasia. Los compañeros sexuales múltiples y la falta de protección al tener relaciones sexuales son los dos factores principales de riesgo para contraer HPV. Use condones y mantenga una relación mutuamente monógama, sugiere el doctor Rosenbaum.

Estudie su árbol genealógico. Aunque menos del 10 por ciento de los cánceres tienen raíces genéticas, descubrir que existe cáncer en la familia puede ayudar a su doctor a evaluar su riesgo y a recomendar formas de prevenir la enfermedad o de descubrirla temprano, dice el doctor Rosenbaum. Incluya a tantos parientes como pueda de ambos lados de su familia. Si alguien ha tenido cáncer, anote la edad en que se le diagnosticó y el órgano en que se originó.

Someterse a revisiones médicas protege su salud

Aunque usted coma bien, no fume y no tenga una historia de cáncer en la familia, de todas maneras puede adquirir la enfermedad. De hecho, el 75 por ciento de las mujeres que desarrollan cáncer de mama no tienen un factor de riesgo conocido, dice el doctor Charles Taylor, director de oncología médica en el Programa de Cáncer de mama en el Centro de Cáncer de Arizona, en Tucson. Pero mientras más temprano se detecte el cáncer mayores serán las probabilidades de que se la pueda curar.

Por eso es importante para las mujeres autoexaminarse mensualmente los senos, tener sus primeras mamografías entre los 35 y los 40 años de edad y hacer sus pruebas de Papanicolau (*Pap smear*) por lo menos un año sí y otro no.

Aquí las ponemos al tanto de las mamografías y pruebas de Papanicolau. (Para mayor información sobre el autoexamen de senos, vea Cuidado de los senos en la página 463.)

Mamografías: cómo descubrir los problemas a tiempo

Una mamografía, una radiografía del seno, detecta las masas que tanto el médico como la paciente no pueden sentir, dice el doctor Taylor. Aquí hay un par de consejos que pueden hacer su mamografía más agradable.

Hágala acompañada. Arregle con una amiga para que mutuamente se recuerden programar y no faltar a sus citas para mamografía. O mejor aún, vayan juntas, sugiere la doctora Phyllis Kornguth, Ph.D., jefa de imaginología de senos en el Centro Médico de la Universidad Duke, en Durham, Carolina del Norte. Después, almuercen en un restaurante o váyanse de compras —hagan de esto una ocasión especial para disfrutar mutuamente de su compañía.

Hágase cargo. Las mamografías pueden no ser placenteras porque para encontrar cánceres pequeños, se deben comprimir los senos. Pero si usted tiene control sobre cuánta presión se aplica, puede hacer el examen más confortable, dice la doctora Kornguth. "De hecho, los estudios muestran que las mujeres que comprimen sus propios senos van a obtener igual de buenas imágenes pero con menos dolor", añade ella. Durante su mamografía, pregunte: "¿Tiene usted inconveniente en que yo opere el aparato de compresión?" También, usted puede convenir en una señal verbal. Dígale a la técnica "yo le voy a decir 'es suficiente' cuando yo quiera que usted disminuya la presión". La mayoría de las técnicas están dispuestas a complacerla.

Pruebas de Papanicolau: cómo verificar la salud de sus células

Una prueba de Papanicolau (*Pap smear*) es una prueba para detectar células anormales en y alrededor de la cérvix, la abertura estrecha del útero en forma de *donut*. Su médico recoge una muestra de las células de la cérvix y parte alta de la vagina con una raspadora de madera, con un algodón o con un cepillo para la cérvix y coloca la muestra en una platina de vidrio. Esta platina se manda a un laboratorio médico para evaluación.

Aproximadamente del 15 al 40 por ciento de las pruebas de Papanicolau se reportan como normales cuando, de hecho, están presentes anormalidades en las células. Aquí hay algunas maneras de mejorar la exactitud de sus resultados.

Evite el contacto sexual. Absténgase de tener relaciones sexuales por lo menos 12 horas antes de una prueba ya que el semen puede interferir con los resultados de la prueba.

Enfoque el punto medio. Programe su prueba de Papanicolau para la mitad de su ciclo menstrual. Calcular exactamente el tiempo no es crítico, pero deben evitarse los días de su período menstrual ya que la sangre puede oscurecer las células en la platina.

Absténgase de la prueba si tiene infección por hongos. Posponga su prueba de Papanicolau si tiene una infección activa de hongos. La inflamación producida por la infección puede ocultar las células anormales en la cérvix.

Manténgalas vivas. No se dé duchas vaginales o use un tampón por lo menos 72 horas antes de la prueba. Si lo hace, puede reducir el número de células disponibles para el examen.

Usted lo tiene, ¿y ahora qué?

Nadie quiere oír a su médico decirle que tiene cáncer, pero si a usted se le diagnostica, no entre en pánico, dicen los oncólogos.

"Para muchos cánceres, la cura es claramente posible", dice el doctor Eyre. "La mayoría de los individuos que viven en este país y que tienen cáncer pueden esperar vivir una duración normal de vida."

Los tratamientos incluyen cirugía, radiación, quimioterapia e inmunoterapia, la cual consiste de inyecciones de proteínas y anticuerpos que asisten o estimulan el sistema inmune para combatir el cáncer. Las nuevas combinaciones de tratamientos también son prometedoras. En muchos casos, la extirpación de masas en el seno, en la cual se remueve una parte pequeña del seno, combinada con la radiación está siendo tan efectiva en el tratamiento del cáncer de mama como una mastectomía, la extirpación del seno, dice el doctor Taylor. También es posible tener la mastectomía y cirugía reconstructiva del seno durante la misma operación.

Cuáles tratamientos son los apropiados para usted dependerá del tipo de cáncer, su tamaño, qué tan rápidamente está creciendo y si se ha extendido más allá del sitio original.

Pero cualquiera que sea el tipo de cáncer que usted tenga, la tensión sicológica puede ser enorme.

"La mujer con cáncer siente que es algo completamente injusto", dice Karen Syrjala, Ph.D., una sicóloga en el Centro de Investigación del Cáncer Fred Hutchinson, en Seattle. "Ellas piensan 'A los 30 ó 40 años de edad, ¿cómo me puede estar pasando esto a mí?' Esto no es realmente lo que usted había planeado estar haciendo con su vida en este momento, así que se siente como una intrusión. Se siente como una equivocación. Toda la familia se puede sentir así."

Aun las más cercanas de las amistades pueden empezar a distanciarse de una mujer que tiene cáncer debido a su propio terror al cáncer o por el temor de que se va a morir, dice el doctor Mansfield. Como resultado, la mujer con cáncer termina aislada socialmente.

Aquí hay algunas estrategias para hacer frente al cáncer.

Vuélvase una sabelotodo. Descubra todo lo que pueda acerca del cáncer y su tratamiento. Hágales pregunta tras pregunta a sus doctores y enfermeras. "La primera cosa es reunir información, para que usted entienda lo que le está ocurriendo y cuáles son sus opciones", dice la doctora Syrjala. "En el momento en que usted sepa que tiene opciones, se va a sentir más en control de la situación."

Evita culparse. "Eso es algo que las mujeres hacen a veces", dice la doctora Syrjala. "Usted no se causó el cáncer. Sí, hay cosas que usted puede hacer para reducir las posibilidades de tener cáncer, pero nada lo va a prevenir absolutamente."

Mantenga el sentido del humor. El sentido del humor es extremadamente importante porque puede ayudarla a sobrellevar los peores aspectos del cáncer y su tratamiento, dice la doctora Syrjala. Hágase tiempo para ver películas cómicas o para echarse una buena carcajada con una amiga.

Evite ser una paciente pasiva. El tratamiento no debe ser algo que su doctor le da a usted; debe ser algo en el cual usted lleva un papel activo. Piense acerca de lo que puede hacer usted misma para ayudar a su recuperación, dice la doctora Syrjala, y discútalo con su doctor.

Sea honesta con su doctor. Su oncólogo no sabrá que el tratamiento la está molestando a menos que usted le diga algo. Si usted no tiene una buena relación con su médico, piense en ver a algún otro, dice la doctora Syrjala.

Hable al respecto. "Ayuda hablar acerca de su miedo y tristeza, porque si usted habla de esto puede descubrir que hay algo que puede hacer respecto a esos sentimientos", dice la doctora Syrjala. "Si no habla acerca de sus temores, usted tiende a no hacer nada acerca de ellos. Algunas veces hablar le quita fuerza a sus temores." Posiblemente, la terapia emocional podría ayudarla.

Sepa que no está sola. Encuentre un grupo de apoyo para personas con su tipo de cáncer. "Las personas en grupos de apoyo viven más tiempo", dice la doctora Syrjala. "No sabemos por qué, pero obviamente, hay algo acerca de participar sus experiencias con personas que se encuentran en circunstancias similares, que la puede ayudar a vivir una vida más larga y complacente." Su doctor o la afiliada local de la Sociedad de Cáncer de los Estados Unidos debería estar en condiciones de ayudarle a encontrar tal grupo.

Siga comiendo. Hasta el 40 por ciento de las mujeres que tienen cáncer en realidad mueren de desnutrición, dice el doctor Simone. Eso es porque las células del cáncer sueltan una hormona llamada caquectina que inhibe el apetito. Esa pérdida de apetito se ve aumentada por algunos tipos de tratamiento de cáncer que causan náusea y vómito como es la quimioterapia. "El fundamento de la cura es una buena nutrición. Yo les digo a mis pacientes que aun cuando una comida no se vea apetitosa, que traten de comer algo de ella. Solamente mastiquen y traguen; porque usted necesita ese alimento", dice el doctor Mansfield. Él sugiere comer pequeñas comidas tales como un medio sándwich y un vaso de jugo de naranja varias veces al día, y mordisquear bocadillos (meriendas o *snacks*) saludables como zanahorias, manzanas y otras frutas y verduras.

CÁNCER DE LA PIEL

El lado oscuro del sol

Durante la década de los 20, la diseñadora francesa Coco Chanel era una de las primeras personas quien popularizó la costumbre de broncearse. Desde ese entonces, según la leyenda popular, la piel bronceada se convirtió en moda, mas se hizo un símbolo de salud. Y aún persiste: cada verano, las playas se llenan de personas recostadas "tostándose" para un *look chic*. Si usted es una de esas personas, antes de salir a la playa con una toalla en una mano y el bronceador en la otra, pregúntese lo siguiente: para usted, ¿las arrugas forman parte integral de su *look* personal? ¿Piensa que el cáncer de la piel es un accesorio imprescindible? Si responde que no (¿y quién diría que sí?), debería reconsiderar broncearse.

La verdad es que con sólo una mala quemadura de sol durante la niñez, se multiplica por dos su riesgo de tener cáncer de la piel en la edad adulta. Agregue algunas décadas más de exposición al sol —aun cuando usted siempre se haya bronceado sin quemarse— y su riesgo aumenta aún más, así como también aumenta la edad cosmética de su piel, la cual se verá vieja por el daño del sol. Los ancestros de piel blanca y ojos claros también incrementarán su riesgo. Además, si a alguno de sus padres o abuelos le han extirpado un cáncer de la piel, usted puede ser la siguiente en la línea.

Como muchas mujeres, usted probablemente le presta mucha atención a la apariencia de su piel. Si se ve bien, usted asume que es saludable. Esa es la razón por la cual el cáncer de la piel puede ser un choque tan fuerte —parece como un ataque sorpresa. (Pueden pasar 20 años entre el daño inicial y el cáncer.) Y muchas de nosotras estamos siendo emboscadas al fin de nuestra década de los 40 años de edad o al principio de la década de los 50 años de edad en lugar de a los 70 años de edad o más adelante, las edades que solían proporcionar la mayoría de las víctimas. Los investigadores especulan que el daño a la capa de ozono del planeta, que nos protege de lo peor de la radiación del sol, es una razón probable.

Cuidado con los salones de bronceado

No se crea el bombo publicitario de que el bronceado bajo una lámpara solar o en una cama para broncear es de alguna manera más seguro que la radiación que usted recibe del sol. O que un "bronceado básico" que le dan en un salón de bronceado de alguna manera la va a proteger de un daño mayor del sol.

Ambas afirmaciones son peligrosamente falsas, dice el doctor Vincent DeLeo, profesor asociado de dermatología en el Centro Médico Presbiteriano Columbia, en la Ciudad de Nueva York.

"Los salones de bronceado y las lámparas solares son cosas sin ningún valor por las que usted paga dinero, y muy dañinas para la piel," dice él. Un informe de los Institutos Nacionales de Salud dice que algunas lámparas para broncearse generan cinco veces más radiación ultravioleta (o *UVA*, por sus siglas en inglés) de que la que usted recibiría si se sentara por la misma cantidad de tiempo en una playa en el ecuador.

Si usted está desesperada por el *look* dorado, use una loción de autobronceado, sugiere el doctor DeLeo. Pero no se le olvide usar también una loción antisolar.

Afortunadamente, los cánceres de la piel que ocurren más a menudo —las formas conocidas como célula basal y célula escamosa— muy raramente se propagan, aunque si son obstinadas pueden reaparecer, dice el doctor Thomas Griffin, un dermatólogo con el Hospital de Graduados y profesor clínico asistente de dermatología en la Escuela de Medicina de la Universidad de Pensilvania, ambas en Filadelfia. Estos aparecen como abultamientos pequeños en la piel, usualmente en las áreas expuestas al sol incluyendo su espalda, la cual recibe la radiación a través de las telas livianas. Pueden ser del mismo tono de la piel o entre café y gris y algunos tienen úlceras diminutas en el centro del crecimiento que sangran fácilmente. Los cánceres de células escamosas también pueden tener un punto duro dentro del crecimiento.

El tiburón de los cánceres de la piel es el melanoma. Ocurre mucho menos frecuentemente que otros cánceres de la piel, pero puede ser mortal. Una vez que el melanoma crece más profundamente que un milímetro dentro de la piel, presenta un mayor riesgo de propagarse a otros órganos. Puede empezar como un lunar, aunque también puede empezar como una peca grande, plana y de color café o como un punto sangrante.

Un broncceado seguro en una botella

Afortunadamente, las lociones de autobronceado de hoy no le darán a usted el horrible color anaranjado en franjas que las tinturas para la piel solían dar hace años. La nueva generación de bronceado en una botella es fácil de aplicar, se ve natural y no perjudicará a su piel.

Un autobronceador, en realidad, interactúa con su piel para volverla de un color dorado natural, dice Yveline Duchesne, directora internacional de entrenamiento para Clarins Cosmetics con base en la Ciudad de Nueva York. El bronceado se desvanece gradualmente cuando usted pierde las células muertas de la piel, usualmente en unos cuantos días.

El ingrediente activo principal en las lociones de autobronceado es un químico llamado dihidroxiacetona (o *DHA*, por sus siglas en inglés). Para producir el color, la DHA se combina con ciertos aminoácidos y queratina en las capas de las células superficiales de la piel.

Con los productos nuevos, usted puede estar atractivamente bronceada sin dañar a su piel siempre y cuando continúe usando la loción antisolar. La mayoría de los autobronceadores tienen una loción antisolar aunque con un factor bajo de protección (SPF), así que es mejor que usted use su propia loción antisolar con un SPF de 15 o más alto. ¿El mejor momento? Ya que los autobronceadores toman unas cuantas horas para aparecer, aplíquelos la noche anterior, sugiere Duchesne. Entonces aplique su loción antisolar a la mañana siguiente, por lo menos una hora antes de salir.

Otros consejos para sacar el mayor provecho de su autobronceador:

Aunque los hombres tienen un índice mayor de melanoma que las mujeres, está aumentando más rápidamente en las mujeres jóvenes que en ningún otro grupo de edades, dice el doctor David J. Leffell, jefe de cirugía dermatológica en la Escuela de Medicina de la Universidad de Yale, en New Haven, Connecticut. "No estamos seguros por qué, pero puede ser que las mujeres que hoy se encuentran en su década de los 30 años de edad tuvieron una gran cantidad de exposición al sol durante los años 60 cuando eran niñas", dice él.

Sin embargo, los doctores dicen que el cáncer de la piel es motivo de precaución, no de alarma. En la mayoría de los casos es casi 100 por ciento curable, siempre y cuando se descubra a tiempo. Y lo mejor de todo, es evitable.

Siempre pruébelo contra las alergias. Antes de que usted pruebe un autobronceador por todo el cuerpo, aplique la loción sobre una pequeña porción de la piel y déjela toda la noche para ver si su piel es alérgica a la DHA. (Si reacciona, una jalea de bronceado o loción antisolar con tintura son sus mejores opciones para color).

Exfóliese antes de aplicarlo. La DHA puede no tomar uniformemente en las áreas donde hay una acumulación de células muertas. Asegúrese de incluir las manos, los codos y las rodillas.

Empiece desde arriba. Aplíquese la loción a partir de su frente, cubriendo todas las áreas expuestas, pero omita las cejas donde el color puede concentrarse. Aplique uniformemente incluyendo sus orejas y abajo de su mandíbula.

Humedezca los lugares ásperos. Los codos y las rodillas se verán más naturales si usted los humedece primero y aplica el autobronceador ligeramente.

Espere los resultados. Qué tan a menudo vuelve usted a aplicarla, no cuánto, determina el tono de su bronceado. El color toma de tres a cinco horas para aparecer, así que no se vuelva a aplicar hasta que no vea los resultados finales.

Déjela secar. Espere una media hora antes de vestirse o meterse a la cama, ya que algunos autobronceadores pueden manchar las telas.

Lávese. Lávese las manos después de aplicarse el autobronceador, o usted va a terminar con las palmas bronceadas.

Reduzca sus probabilidades

Aun cuando haya pasado un gran número de veranos en el sol, usted puede reducir dramáticamente sus probabilidades de desarrollar cáncer de la piel si controla su exposición al sol de ahora en adelante. Usted también necesita saber cómo detectar el cáncer en la piel que está expuesta al sol o en un lunar anormal antes de que crezca a un punto peligroso. Aquí hay algunas tácticas importantes para "salvarle el pellejo".

Resguárdese. Use una loción antisolar de espectro completo que bloquee ambos tipos de radiación ultravioleta (*UVA* y *UVB*, por sus siglas en inglés), y úsela diariamente, verano e invierno, dice el doctor Perry Robins, profesor asociado de dermatología de la Universidad de Nueva York, en la Ciudad de Nueva York, presidente de la Fundación del Cáncer de la Piel y autor de *Sun Sense* (El sol con sentido). Verifique que su loción tenga un factor de protección solar (o *SPF*, por sus siglas en inglés) de por lo menos 15.

Quédese adentro a la hora del mediodía. Trate de limitar sus actividades afuera durante las horas cuando los rayos del sol son más intensos, de las 10 de la mañana a las 2 de la tarde, dice el doctor Griffin.

Busque cambios. Examine su piel detenidamente dos veces al año con un espejo de mano o con la ayuda de un amigo (a) o su esposo. Busque cualquier tipo de mancha que cambia, dice el doctor Robins. El cambio puede ser en color, textura o tamaño (la mancha se hace más grande), o la mancha empieza a sangrar, dice él. Si usted tiene una historia familiar de cáncer en la piel o ha tenido quemaduras serias de sol, pida a su dermatólogo que haga un "mapa" de su cuerpo para localizar los lugares potencialmente problemáticos y para que pueda tener control de cualquier cambio durante las visitas posteriores.

Memorice los ABCDs. Esto le ayudará a observar los lunares para ver si encuentra señales de melanoma, dice el doctor Vincent DeLeo, profesor asociado de dermatología en el Centro Médico Presbiteriano Columbia, en la Ciudad de Nueva York:

- A es por asimetría (una forma no simétrica).
- B es por borde (un borde irregular).
- C es por cambio de color (una mancha oscura se eleva dentro de un lunar, o un lunar muestra áreas que se aclaran).
- D es por diámetro (el lunar se agranda o es más grande que el borrador de un lápiz).

Si usted tiene alguno de los ABCDs, vaya inmediatamente al doctor, dice el doctor DeLeo.

Detección temprana, curación temprana

¿Qué pasa cuando sus esfuerzos de detección temprana tienen éxito? Usted le llamó la atención de un crecimiento a su dermatóloga, y ella confirma que debe extirparse.

Para la mayoría de los cánceres, todo lo que usted necesita es anestesia local y la extirpación no dejará una cicatriz notable. Dependiendo de la profundidad y naturaleza del crecimiento, su doctora usará un procedimiento o una combinación de los mismos. Estos incluyen quemar, raspar, congelar y cortar el crecimiento. Algunos cánceres poco profundos pueden ser tratados con una crema de quimioterapia para uso local.

Para los cánceres difíciles o recurrentes, un cirujano puede extirpar las células malignas en capas muy delgadas, sin tocar la piel saludable. Aun el melanoma tiene un nuevo enemigo poderoso —una vacuna de células de melanoma que significativamente aumenta los índices de sobrevivencia.

CELULITIS

Es grasa, y nada más

En la playa, usted envuelve la toalla de playa más grande que encuentra alrededor de sus caderas y muslos.

En el gimnasio, usa mallas oscuras de *Lycra* ajustadas al cuerpo debajo de sus *shorts* de gimnasia.

Y para un baile, usted se pone un vestido ceñido con una abertura al lado —la cual sólo llega a su rodilla.

¿Qué está tratando de esconder? Sus muslos, por supuesto. Y mas específicamente, la celulitis que apareció por primera vez en ellos más o menos cuando usted cumplió 30 años de edad. Además de que se ve como si usted tuviera requesón borboteando bajo la piel (lo que algunos le llaman "piel de naranja"), la celulitis la hace sentirse vieja, fea y gorda —especialmente cuando está parada en la playa junto a una muchacha de 19 años de edad en un bikini.

Pero no se preocupe. Usted no está sola.

"El 99 por ciento de las mujeres desarrollan por lo menos algo de gordura con hoyuelos después de los 30 años de edad", explica el doctor Donald Robertson, director médico del Centro de Nutrición Bariátrica, en Scottsdale, Arizona.

Parte del problema es la genética. Pero mucho de ello es simplemente debido al envejecimiento. En algún momento, cuando una mujer se encuentra entre los 30 y los 40 años de edad, una disminución natural en los niveles de estrógeno junto con el daño del sol acumulado a través de los años, causa que la piel pierda su elasticidad, dice el doctor Ted Lockwood, profesor clínico asistente de cirugía plástica en la Escuela de Medicina de la Universidad de Missouri-Kansas City. La piel cuelga un poco aquí, se abolsa un poco allá y generalmente ya no tiene la elasticidad firme de la juventud.

Al mismo tiempo, la red de apoyo de fibras que anclan la piel a los músculos subyacentes está también empezando a estirarse. Eso, combinado con las libras adicionales que todas nosotras aumentamos al aproximarnos a la madurez —y

¿Le conviene la liposucción?

Usted ha mantenido una dieta sensata de baja grasa y una campaña fuerte de aeróbicos por varios años. Pero ninguna cantidad de motivación parece ayudar a su estómago redondo o muslos de alforja. Y estos nada más la hacen sentirse más vieja y fuera de forma. ¿Hay algo que un cirujano pueda hacer?

La forma más solicitada de cirugía cosmética es la liposucción —una técnica de aspiración que literalmente absorbe células de grasa subcutáneas. Y el cambio es permanente. Como adulta, usted ya no puede hacer crecer nuevas células de grasa para remplazar las que se removieron.

"La liposucción puede hacer milagros", dice el doctor Alan Matarasso, un cirujano plástico en el Hospital de Ojos, Oídos y Garganta, en la ciudad de Nueva York. "Pero no existe un procedimiento quirúrgico que pueda sustituir una dieta saludable, ejercicio y pérdida de peso."

Y la liposucción está lejos de ser un plan de pérdida instantánea de peso. Debido a que remover cantidades grandes de grasa puede ser peligroso, funciona mejor en personas que están en su peso ideal o cerca de él y que tienen bolsas de gordura pertinaz que permanecen a pesar de dieta y ejercicio. Además, después de la operación, usted tiene que mantener esos hábitos saludables. Si usted empieza a comer demasiado, esas calorías en exceso serán almacenadas en las células de grasa restantes en otra parte de su cuerpo, dice el doctor Matarasso.

Esta es la forma en la que se realiza la operación. Mientras usted está bajo anestesia general o adormecida con una anestesia local y sedación, un cirujano hace una pequeña incisión en su vientre o ingle. A continuación, él inserta un tubo de metal con un extremo romo llamado cánula. Con movimientos enérgicos, él guía la cánula de un lado a otro debajo de la piel. La cánula está conectada a una máquina similar a una aspiradora que chupa hasta cuatro libras (dos kilos) de células de grasa, junto con sangre.

Después de la cirugía, a usted la visten con una ropa estirable, tipo faja, que debe usar de una a cuatro semanas para mantener el hinchazón a un mínimo y su piel suave. En la mayoría de los pacientes, los moretones desaparecen en unas dos semanas y el hinchazón decrece completamente en unos seis meses. Los resultados continúan mejorando con el tiempo. A menudo usted puede regresar al trabajo después de un fin de semana de descanso y a una actividad normal en 7 a 14 días.

¿Es usted una buena candidata para la liposucción? Es importante estar en buena salud, sin un sobrepeso significativo (aunque algunos cirujanos le darán más latitud que otros) y entre los 40 y los 50 años de edad, cuando su piel todavía es flexible y elástica.

las cuales por orden de las hormonas irán directamente a las caderas, muslos y asentaderas de las mujeres— lleva a la *celulitis*, una palabra elegante para describir lo que en realidad es gordura y piel que ha perdido su elasticidad.

Esto no estaría tan mal si los hombres en nuestras vidas estuvieran colgándose y abolsándose junto con nosotras.

Pero no lo están.

Una razón es que los hombres tienden a poner peso alrededor de sus estómagos más que en sus caderas, muslos y traseros. Otra es que la piel de los hombres es más gruesa y más elástica, así que conserva la grasa abajo de ella más firmemente que la nuestra. Y todavía otra razón es que las fibras que anclan la piel a los músculos está estructurada de manera diferente en los hombres que en las mujeres: mientras que las fibras que sostienen la piel de la mujer corren en una sola dirección, los hombres tienen fibras apretadas y entrecruzadas que forman una red para mantener la grasa firmemente en su lugar.

¿Qué le vamos a hacer? La vida no es siempre justa.

No se haga de la vista gorda

Mientras que usted no puede evitar tener celulitis, usted no tiene que conservarla. Porque la celulitis es grasa. Y al igual que otras formas de grasa, usted se puede deshacer de ella. Aquí está cómo hacerlo.

Trabaje para eliminarla. Las mujeres que tratan de deshacerse de la celulitis haciendo ejercicios solamente para los muslos o asentaderas fallan miserablemente. "La reducción localizada no funciona", dice Susan Olson Ph.D., directora de servicios sicológicos en el Centro de Nutrición Bariátrica del Sudoeste, en Tempe, Arizona.

La mejor manera de reducir la celulitis —así como la grasa en cualquier otra parte de su cuerpo— es con actividad aeróbica que quema calorías a través de todo el cuerpo. La mejor actividad es la que aumenta el ritmo de su corazón y se mantiene allí por 20 minutos continuos por lo menos tres veces por semana.

Correr, caminar, andar en bicicleta, patinar, bailar y nadar —todos los cuales atizan el metabolismo para que queme la grasa más eficientemente— son perfectos.

Solamente recuerde: si usted ha llevado una vida sedentaria, verifique con su médico antes de embarcarse en cualquier programa de ejercicios.

Levante pesas. Un buen ejercicio aeróbico le ayudará a dar tono a sus músculos. Pero hacer que se desarrollen por medio de entrenamiento con pesas también puede ayudar a esconder la piel con hoyuelos. "Hacer que sus músculos ganen en volumen puede significar una ligera mejoría", dice el doctor Lockwood. "Pero no espere milagros." Pregúntele a un entrenador en su gimnasio si hay un programa que la pueda ayudar a usted.

Bote la grasa de su dieta. Además de ejercicio, comer una dieta baja en grasas es la mejor manera de mantener la llamada celulitis a un mínimo. "Mucha de la celulitis viene por comer alimentos con alto contenido de grasa", dice Maria Simonson, Sc.D., Ph.D., profesora emérita y directora de la Clínica de Salud, Peso y Estrés en las Instituciones Médicas Johns Hopkins, en

---

"Maravillas" mentirosas

Cada año, las mujeres que viven en los Estados Unidos gastan mas de $20 millones tratando de deshacerse de la celulitis usando jaleas, cremas, corrientes eléctricas y otros productos incredulentes. Desafortunadamente, lo único que estos productos logran adelgazar es su cartera.

La Administración de Alimentos y Drogas está ahora controlando las quejas hechas a los fabricantes de estos productos, muchos de los cuales son importados de Francia donde la protección al consumidor es menos estricta. Pero esos pregonados productos para la celulitis están prometiendo demasiado desde hace mucho tiempo, ya que la *celulitis* es un término de mercadotecnia, no un diagnóstico médico.

Un equipo de investigación de la Clínica de Salud, Peso y Estrés de las Instituciones Médicas Johns Hopkins, en Baltimore, probaron 32 productos para quitar la celulitis, dice Maria Simonson, Sc.D., Ph.D., profesora emérita y directora de la clínica.

Ninguno funcionó.

Baltimore. "Así que mientras menos grasa haya en su dieta, menor será el problema que usted va a tener."

Trate de limitar su ingestión total de grasa a alrededor del 25 por ciento de sus calorías, añade la doctora Simonson. Usted puede llevar un control de su consumo de grasa leyendo las etiquetas de los productos y alejándose de los alimentos con mucha grasa tales como pasteles, quesos, comidas fritas y fiambres procesados como el jamón o la bologna.

Frótese con los nudillos. "Un masaje intenso usando los nudillos puede ayudar a deshacer los hoyuelos", dice el doctor Robertson. Cuando se combina con pérdida de peso y comidas inteligentes, un masaje dos veces por semana ayuda a desgastar las bolsas de grasa más resistentes.

Llénela de crema. Frotando cualquier crema para el cutis que contenga ácidos alfahidróxidos —esencialmente, ácidos hechos de frutas o leche— en su piel le dará a su cuerpo una apariencia más suave. Pero recuerde: ninguna crema o loción eliminará la celulitis.

Camúflajela. Use una crema de broncearse para camuflar la celulitis. El color oscuro emparejará el tono de su piel y hará las sombras causadas por las masas de grasa bajo la piel menos aparentes.

Úntese loción antisolar. Usted no puede enmendar los años de exposición al sol que eliminó la elasticidad de su piel y le ayudó a la celulitis "colarse" en su cuerpo. "Pero, limitando su exposición al sol o usando una buena loción antisolar cuando se encuentra afuera, puede evitar que su piel se degenere aún más", dice el doctor Lockwood. Los rayos de sol más dañinos para la piel son entre las diez de la mañana y las dos de la tarde, por lo que es esencial mantener muslos y otras áreas vulnerables cubiertas durante esas horas. Y siempre que usted esté expuesta al sol, asegúrese de usar una loción antisolar con un factor de protección solar (o SPF, por sus siglas en inglés) de por lo menos 15.

Considere un ajuste. Si todo lo demás falla y usted siente que sus muslos con piel de naranja están arruinando su vida, hay un procedimiento quirúrgico que puede reducir su celulitis, dice el doctor Lockwood. Al efectuarse un ajuste por cirugía —que cuesta miles de dólares y generalmente no está cubierto por el seguro médico— un cirujano plástico puede estirar la piel en las zonas problemáticas para esconder los depósitos de grasa que se encuentran debajo. Como es el caso con cualquier otra cirugía, considere la experiencia y reputación del profesional. Puede ser que usted quiera una segunda opinión antes de proceder.

COLESTEROL

Mientras menos, mejor

Algunas veces parece que todo el mundo está hablando del colesterol: cómo reducirlo; cómo mantenerlo; cuál fue su último recuento de colesterol.

Y no para allí. Los paquetes de alimentos proclaman a gritos "sin colesterol". Los platos en los menúes de restaurantes están a veces marcados con corazones rojos, recordándole a usted que si sabe lo que le conviene, limitará su selección a platillos bajos en colesterol.

Nos hemos encontrado con el enemigo, y éste está disfrazado de una substancia blanca, tipo cera, grasosa, llamada colesterol. Pregunte a los expertos, y ellos le dirán que el colesterol alto es uno de los mayores contribuyentes a uno de los más temidos problemas relacionados con la edad en los Estados Unidos: la enfermedad del corazón. Y si usted piensa que puede dar un suspiro de alivio porque las enfermedades del corazón afectan sólo a los hombres, piense otra vez. Es una enfermedad de las mujeres, también.

Razón para preocuparse

Sí, sus hormonas femeninas le proporcionan a usted cierta protección natural contra los niveles altos de colesterol durante sus años anteriores a la menopausia. El estrógeno puede bajar la parte mala (lipoproteína de baja densidad, o *LDL*, por sus siglas en inglés) de colesterol en la sangre y subir la parte buena (lipoproteína de alta densidad, o *HDL*, por sus siglas en ingles). Pero ese tipo de protección —debido al proceso de envejecimiento— no va a durar siempre. Al disminuir su cuerpo la producción de estrógeno durante la menopausia, también declina su refugio tipo Teflón contra el colesterol. Bienvenida al mundo real de las mujeres y el colesterol alto.

Estos son los hechos brutales: un buen nivel de colesterol se encuentra abajo de los 200 miligramos de colesterol por decilitro de sangre. Antes de los 45 años de edad, las mujeres tienen un promedio total de colesterol en la sangre de 190; entre los 45 y los 64 años de edad, esas cantidades de colesterol aumentan a entre 217 y 237. En total, cerca de 55 millones de mujeres adultas tienen niveles de colesterol de 200 o más. Y al aumentar las cantidades de colesterol, también aumenta la avalancha de problemas de corazón en las mujeres.

Por ejemplo, un estudio importante —la investigación de las Clínicas de Investigación de los Lípidos, realizada en centros médicos a través del país— mostró que las mujeres con niveles totales de colesterol arriba de 235 tienen un riesgo de muerte 70 por ciento mayor que las mujeres con recuentos más bajos de colesterol.

Una en cada siete mujeres entre los 45 y los 64 años de edad tiene algún tipo de enfermedad del corazón o ha tenido un derrame cerebral. Para aquellas de 65 años o más, estas cantidades aumentan a una en cada tres. No es de asombrarse entonces que la Asociación Del Corazón de los Estados Unidos llame a las enfermedades del corazón una epidemia silenciosa entre las mujeres.

Pero aun en medio de estas arenas movedizas de malas noticias, hay cierta razón para el optimismo. Aún vivimos más que los hombres por cerca de siete años, y debido al estrógeno tenemos una protección extra contra enfermedades del corazón en nuestros años antes de la menopausia. De todas maneras, mientras más baja puede usted tener su recuento de colesterol, mejor. Si usted toma la iniciativa, puede burlar al colesterol, no importa cuál sea su edad, y hacer de esos años adicionales años saludables.

La ironía de la vida

Hay cierta ironía en las malas noticias acerca del colesterol. Después de todo, algo del colesterol flotando en su torrente sanguíneo está de hecho producido por su propio hígado. Sin colesterol, sus células no funcionarían correctamente, y la vida misma se vería amenazada.

Así que mientras tener algo de colesterol no es problema, tener demasiado sí lo es. Debido a que el colesterol se consume en su dieta (exclusivamente de alimentos de origen animal), puede terminar circulando en la sangre en exceso, uniendo fuerzas con el colesterol producido por su hígado así como con la grasa saturada que usted come. Y al navegar estas substancias por su torrente sanguíneo, algunas de ellas atacan y se adhieren a las paredes de sus arterias, formando placas que al pasar el tiempo angostan sus arterias e impiden el flujo de la sangre al corazón. Este proceso que no presagia nada bueno, llamado ateroesclerosis, puede envejecerla antes de tiempo y conducirla a la angustiosa angina de pecho (dolor en el pecho) y ataque al corazón.

Para burlarse del colesterol, el primer paso es controlar su colesterol. Su médico debería medir no sólo el nivel total del colesterol en su torrente sanguíneo sino también su nivel de colesterol HDL. Si estas pruebas muestran señales de problemas potenciales, su médico también debería medir su nivel LDL, ya que el evaluar todos estos números puede ser importante para determinar su riesgo.

El número mágico

Una vez que usted llega a la edad adulta de 20 años, los expertos dicen que ese es el momento de tener su primera prueba de colesterol. Después de allí, usted debería tener una por lo menos cada cinco años.

Una de las lecturas que esta prueba va a producir es su nivel total de colesterol. Echemos aquí una mirada a lo que ese número significa (todos los números se refieren a miligramos por decilitro de sangre):

Menos de 200 —deseable

200 a 239 —bordeando en alto

240 o más —alto

Aun cuando usted se encuentre colocada cómodamente en el índice "deseable", de todas maneras necesita medir su colesterol regularmente, junto con una revisión de su HDL (lipoproteína de alta densidad), el tipo bueno. Algunas veces un nivel HDL alto ayudará a compensar por un número total de colesterol en el índice "bordeando en alto" (aunque se le aconseja mantener su colesterol total tan bajo como sea posible). Sin embargo, si su lectura HDL es de menos de 35, cae dentro de la categoría "baja", y usted debe hacer algo para elevarla. Sus mejores opciones son perder peso, hacer más ejercicio, dejar de fumar y reducir la cantidad de azúcar que usted ingiere.

¿Y qué acerca del colesterol LDL (lipoproteína de baja densidad), el tipo malo? Si sus otras pruebas muestran un problema potencial, su doctor también debería medirle su nivel LDL. Menos de 130 se considera generalmente deseable.

Finalmente, para ayudarle a interpretar lo que todos estos números significan, su médico puede determinar su proporción de colesterol, la cual es la proporción entre su colesterol total y su número HDL. Si la proporción es de 3,5 a 1 o más baja, usted está bien.

Veamos un poco más de cerca estas facetas del colesterol. El colesterol se mueve por su torrente sanguíneo haciéndose llevar por serviciales moléculas llamadas lipoproteínas. Mientras que el colesterol conducido en los transportadores LDL es el instigador de problemas en sus arterias, los transportadores HDL son los buenos, acorralando al colesterol y echándolo fuera de su cuerpo. En otras palabras, mientras que el colesterol LDL es el bravucón en su torrente sanguíneo, el colesterol HDL es el buen samaritano.

Desafortunadamente, muchos de los torrentes sanguíneos en los Estados Unidos tienen demasiados LDLs y muy pocos HDLs, una combinación que resulta en números totales de colesterol insaludables. En los Estados Unidos, el total promedio de colesterol es de 206, el cual es más alto que el nivel deseable de menos de 200.

Darle la vuelta a la tortilla

Los expertos dicen que haciendo algunos pequeños ajustes en el estilo de vida, usted puede reducir dramáticamente su colesterol. Los estudios muestran que por cada 1 por ciento que reduzca en su nivel de colesterol, usted puede disminuir las posibilidades de sufrir un ataque al corazón en un 2 por ciento. Con cambios en la dieta solamente, usted puede reducir en un promedio de 10 por ciento su lectura de colesterol —y probablemente más. La doctora Margo Denke, profesora asistente de medicina en el Centro Médico del Sudoeste de la Universidad de Texas, en el centro para Nutrición Humana de Dallas, y miembro del Comité de Nutrición de la Asociación del Corazón de los Estados Unidos, dice que mientras más alta esté el recuento de su colesterol, mayor será el impacto que una dieta saludable tendrá en el corazón. Por ejemplo, una mujer con una lectura de colesterol de 280 puede ser capaz de recortarle 25 por ciento a este número comiendo correctamente. Si la longevidad y no envejecer son sus metas, éste es un balance final que usted no puede ignorar.

Para evitar el colesterol alto y los estragos que éste puede causar, trate estos cazadores de colesterol.

Cambie el tipo de grasa. "Disminuir la grasa saturada es la estrategia más efectiva contra el colesterol que usted puede usar", dice Karen Miller-Kovach, R.D., especialista principal en nutrición para *Weight Watchers International,* en Jericho, Nueva York. Eso significa comer menos carne roja, mantequilla, queso, leche entera y helados de crema, todo lo cual eleva los LDL y el total de los niveles de colesterol. Por otro lado, grasa monoinsaturada, conocida como grasa buena, puede de hecho reducir el colesterol.

"Cuando usted cambia de una dieta alta en grasas saturadas a una alta en grasas monoinsaturadas, y su peso permanece más o menos igual, su colesterol LDL caerá mientras que el colesterol HDL permanecerá estable", dice el doctor Robert Rosenson, director del Centro de Cardiología Preventiva en el Centro Médico Rush-Presbyterian-St. Luke, en Chicago. "Por eso el aceite de oliva es tan popular, ya que es alto en moninsaturados." Mejor aún, aumente su consumo de pescado grasoso, como son el salmón y el atún. La grasa en estos pescados es monoinsaturada.

Ingiera menos colesterol. Tan importante como puede ser reducir la grasa saturada, es que no se le olvide el colesterol dietético. El colesterol en su sangre que no está producido por su propio organismo proviene de su dieta. Aquí está cómo mantenerlo bajo control.

Trate de eliminar carnes de órganos (como hígado) de su dieta. Limite la cantidad de carne magra, aves y pescado a tres onzas al día. Y cuando se trata de huevos, limite su consumo de yemas a no más de dos por semana. Haga sus propias galletitas, pasteles y pasteles de frutas, y use claras de huevo y sustituto de huevos cuando horneé o cocine.

Finalmente, cuando usted está pasando por la línea del buffet, sírvase con gusto verduras, frutas y granos, los cuales no contienen en lo absoluto colesterol dietético. Pero muestre fuerza de voluntad en resistirse a los aliños (aderezos) para ensaladas con alta grasa, las salsas y la mantequilla.

Aliméntese de fibra. La fibra es justamente lo que el doctor recomendó para ayudarle a llenar el vacío que dejaron las grasas saturadas al ser eliminadas en su planificación de comidas. Concéntrese en las fibras solubles, el tipo que está atiborrado en frijoles (habichuelas) secos, lentejas, frutas cítricas, chícharos (guisantes) y manzanas. Agregar fibra soluble a su dieta puede ayudarle a bajar su colesterol en la sangre del 5 al 10 por ciento.

Cómase su avena. El salvado de avena ha sido popular desde hace años. ¿Pero cuánto es bombo publicitario y cuánto es verdad? Investigadores en la Universidad de Minnesota en Minneapolis revisaron todos los estudios examinando el poder de la avena y llegaron a una conclusión "limpia-arterias": agregue una y un tercio de tazas de cereal de salvado de avena (o tres paquetes de harina de avena instantánea) a su dieta diaria, y vea cómo su colesterol desciende de 2 a 3 por ciento. Si su nivel de colesterol ya es alto, usted cosechará aún más beneficios, al recortarle el salvado de avena de 6 a 7 por ciento del total.

Póngase en forma. Esto no va a sorprenderla: el ejercicio le hace bien al cuerpo. De hecho, para hacer que su nivel HDL se eleve, métase en una clase de ejercicio y sude la gota gorda. Y no se preocupe de tener que ir al extremo. "Hemos aprendido que aun ejercicios aeróbicos moderados (caminar vigorosamente, trotar, nadar) eleva los HDLs, aunque esto toma a menudo de seis meses a un año para ocurrir", dice el doctor Rosenson.

Adelgace su pancita. Demasiadas mujeres llevan vidas de dietas desesperadas, sin tener mucho que mostrar por sus esfuerzos aunque sí bastante frustración. Pero un programa sensato y moderado de pérdida de peso puede darle un golpe bajo a su colesterol. La doctora Denke ha encontrado que cuando las mujeres jóvenes están llevando a cuestas peso excesivo en sus cuerpos, sus niveles de colesterol total y LDL tienden a ser más altos, y sus niveles HDL más bajos. Al perder peso ocurre lo contrario.

Fuera la fumadera. Hay muchas buenas razones para dejar de fumar y aquí hay una más: fumar puede hacer que su lectura de HDL baje, algo que ninguna persona consciente de su salud puede darse el lujo de permitir.

Pero aun cuando usted sea una persona que fuma un cigarrillo tras otro, hay algunas noticias alentadoras —si está dispuesta a tirar sus cigarrillos para siempre. Al dejar de fumar, usted puede invertir la declinación en su nivel HDL en unos 60 días. No se requieren años para eliminar el daño que se hace al fumar.

Ofrezca un brindis. Quizás usted escuchó informes que una bebida o dos de alguna bebida alcohólica diariamente puede elevar el componente HDL de su colesterol. Pues bien, escuchó correctamente. Sin embargo, acérquese cuidadosamente a esta estrategia para combatir el colesterol. Las bebidas alcohólicas están llenas hasta el borde con calorías, así que pueden derrotar sus esfuerzos para perder peso. Aun beber moderadamente puede aumentar sus probabilidades de desarrollar cáncer de mama. Finalmente, si usted está embarazada o tratando de embarazarse, aléjese del alcohol completamente por la salud de su bebé.

¿Otra opción? Beba jugo de uva —del tipo morado. La cáscara de las uvas contiene un ingrediente reductor de colesterol, según Leroy Creasy, Ph.D., profesor de pomología en el Colegio de Agricultura y Ciencias de la Vida de la Universidad Cornell, en Ithaca, Nueva York.

Considere el estrógeno. Ya que el estrógeno natural la protege contra problemas de colesterol durante sus años premenopáusicos, ¿no es lógico pensar que una terapia de reposición de estrógeno después de la menopausia pudiera hacer lo mismo? De hecho, eso es exactamente lo que muestra la investigación: una terapia de reposición de estrógeno puede cortar su colesterol LDL y subir su colesterol HDL en aproximadamente 15 por ciento cada uno, según un informe sobre enfermedades cardiovasculares en las mujeres de la Asociación del Corazón de los Estados Unidos.

Al mismo tiempo, sin embargo, la terapia de reposición de estrógeno tiene algunas señales de alerta propias, particularmente un vínculo con cánceres del endometrio y quizás de mama. Usted y su médico necesitan tener en mente estos factores cuando pesen los pros y los contras de usar una terapia de reposición de estrógeno en la lucha contra el colesterol. Afortunadamente, los médicos creen que combinando estrógeno con progestina (otra hormona femenina) usted puede tener la posibilidad de reducir su riesgo de cáncer.

¿Qué tan mágica es la medicina?

Hasta los esfuerzos más heroicos para bajar un colesterol alto pueden encallar. Una posible fuente de ayuda pueden ser los medicamentos anticolesterol, los cuales pueden reducir las lecturas de colesterol en un promedio de 20 por ciento. Antes de que usted tome estos medicamentos, sin embargo, muchos doctores aconsejan tratar un enfoque más conservador (dieta, ejercicio, pérdida de peso) por cerca de seis meses. Si eso no funciona, las drogas pueden ser la respuesta, particularmente si su colesterol LDL todavía está alto, o usted tiene otros factores de riesgo de sufrir enfermedades del corazón (como puede ser una historia familiar con alta presión arterial), o usted ya está enferma del corazón.

El ácido nicotínico y aglutinadores de ácido biliar pueden ser las primeras selecciones de su médico.

El ácido nicotínico (tal como el *Niacor*) es una forma de niacina, la vitamina que se puede comprar sin necesidad de receta. Pero ya que usted necesita tomar ácido nicotínico en dosis altas para que se note una diferencia en sus lecturas de colesterol, los médicos lo consideran una droga. Y usted también debería. Las altas dosis pueden causar serios problemas secundarios. Asegúrese de tomar sólo la forma recetada de esta droga e informe a su médico de cualquier problema.

"Acaloramiento y estómago revuelto pueden ocurrir con la niacina", advierte el doctor Richard H. Helfant, vicepresidente de medicina y director del Programa de Entrenamiento de Cardiología del Centro Médico de la Universidad de California, Irvine y autor de *Women, Take Heart* (Mujeres, anímense). Él sugiere evitar la niacina completamente si usted tiene diabetes, úlceras, enfermedad del hígado o algún problema importante con el ritmo de su corazón.

Otros medicamentos también tienen efectos secundarios potenciales, por lo que su médico debería controlarla de cerca cuando usted los está tomando. Algunas de estas drogas recetadas, incluyendo aglutinadores de ácido biliar *cholestyramine* (tal como *Questran*) y hidrocloruro de colestipol (*Colestid*), están disponibles en forma de polvo. La mayoría de los otros incluyendo lovastatin (*Mevacor*) y *gemfibrozil* (*Lopid*), viene en forma de píldoras. Algunas de estas drogas —ácido nicotínico y aglutinadores de ácido biliar— han existido desde hace bastante tiempo para que existan estudios que muestren no sólo que pueden reducir bastante su nivel LDL de colesterol, sino que también pueden disminuir las probabilidades de desarrollar una enfermedad al corazón.

De hecho, aun cuando su doctor le recete medicamentos, no piense que está usted a salvo, advierte la doctora Denke. "Las drogas no son un substituto de comer saludablemente, perder peso, hacer ejercicio y otras estrategias de estilo de vida que necesitan ser parte de mantener su colesterol bajo control."

DEPRESIÓN

Cómo triunfarle a la tristeza

La mayor parte del tiempo, Bonnie Brand se siente realmente bien. Pero ocasionalmente, cuando la presión de balancear una carrera y las necesidades de su familia la abruman, una sombra oscura de depresión desciende, y entonces siente que está envejeciendo sin darse cuenta.

"Como la mayoría de las mujeres, yo me preocupo acerca de mi peso, me preocupo acerca de mi apariencia, y sí, me preocupa envejecer", dice la supervisora de procesamiento de textos, de 33 años de edad, en un bufete de abogados en Newport Beach, California. "Cuando me siento bien, me siento atractiva. Pero cuando estoy deprimida, definitivamente me siento más vieja. Cuando me siento así cada achaque y cada dolor en mi cuerpo parece magnificarse."

Esto no sorprendería a muchos médicos que aseguran que la depresión afecta tanto al cuerpo como a la mente.

"Naturalmente, la depresión hace que vaya más lentamente y que se vea y se sienta más vieja", dice la doctora Janice Peterson, una siquiatra clínica en el Centro de Ciencias de la Salud de la Universidad de Colorado, en Denver. "Si observa algunos de los síntomas mayores de depresión —falta de energía, libido reducida, pérdida de apetito, dificultad para concentrarse, cambios en los hábitos de dormir, y achaques y dolores generalizados— usted vería algunas cosas que podría considerar como parte normal de envejecer. Por lo tanto, si ve una persona con esos problemas, usted podría pensar 'bueno, ella se está haciendo vieja' cuando en realidad lo que tiene es una fuerte depresión."

Los efectos de la depresión en el cuerpo son tan potentes que a menudo pueden hacer que se vea más de una década mayor de lo que realmente es. "Algunas personas que están deprimidas crónicamente pueden verse muy viejas —tienen los hombros encorvados, líneas de surcos alrededor de los ojos y todas esas otras cosas que hacen que una persona se vea avejentada. Yo he visto algunas personas deprimidas que parece que andan en sus sesenta y tantos cuando en realidad tienen 35 ó 40 años de edad", dice el doctor Harry Prosen, presidente del Departamento de Siquiatría y Ciencias de Salud Mental del Colegio Médico de Wisconsin, en Milwaukee.

Lo triste del caso

Todas nosotras nos sentimos tristes en un momento u otro. La muerte de una persona querida, un divorcio, la pérdida de un empleo o alguna otra penuria nos puede hacer sentir tan por el suelo que dudamos si podremos levantarnos otra vez. Mientras que la mayoría de nosotras logramos salir de eso, muchas otras no lo logran. En el transcurso de su vida, una mujer tiene un 8 a 12 por ciento de probabilidades de sufrir de una depresión fuerte, lo cual significa que tiene cinco o más síntomas de depresión durante al menos dos semanas, incluyendo sentimientos de falta de valor o pensamientos de muerte o suicidio.

Durante una vida, la mujer tiene el doble de posibilidades que el hombre de que se le diagnostique con una depresión fuerte. Esta diferencia desconcierta a los investigadores, dice el doctor Dan Blazer, Ph.D., profesor de siquiatría en el

¿Queda todo entre familia?

Usted no es la única que se deprime. La abuela, mamá, papá y su hermano todos caen regularmente en una depresión de la cual parece que no se pueden desprender. ¿Coincidencia, o eso significa algo?

"Es claro que las personas con historia de depresión en la familia tienen más probabilidades de sufrir de ella que las personas que no tienen esta historia en la familia", dice el doctor Allan Mellow, Ph.D., profesor asistente de siquiatría en la Escuela de Medicina de la Universidad de Michigan, en Ann Arbor. "Existe evidencia bien documentada que al igual que el cáncer, la diabetes y la alta presión arterial, la depresión grave tiene un componente genético."

Muy bien, usted no puede escoger a sus padres. Pero sabiendo que su familia tiene una historia de depresión debería ayudarla a entender por qué usted puede sentirse particularmente con el ánimo bajo más frecuentemente que otras personas, dice el doctor Mellow. Si se siente extraordinariamente triste, en especial si usted tiene una historia de depresión grave en la familia, debería considerar buscar la orientación de un profesional e investigar acerca de terapia con drogas antidepresivas.

Centro Médico de la Universidad Duke, en Durham, Carolina del Norte. Pero la herencia, las diferencias biológicas y una disparidad en las expectativas de nuestra sociedad sobre cómo deberían comportarse los hombres y las mujeres pueden contribuir a esta diferencia.

"Hay una teoría sobre la depresión que gira alrededor de la ira", dice la doctora Kimberly Yonkers, profesora asistente de siquiatría y ginecología en el Centro Médico del Sudoeste de la Universidad de Texas, en Dallas. "Según esta teoría, las mujeres tienden a reprimir su ira, volviéndola hacia el interior y, como resultado, se deprimen. Los hombres, por otro lado, expresan su ira y cólera hacia el exterior volviéndose agresivos." Sin embargo, también podría ser que las mujeres, más probablemente que los hombres, hablen acerca de sus emociones y busquen tratamiento para la depresión, dice la doctora Yonkers.

El costo físico

Aun una leve tristeza que dure sólo uno o dos días puede hacerla más susceptible a muchas de las enfermedades y cambios de apariencia que se consideran parte de envejecer. "Definitivamente, la depresión se hace sentir físicamente en las personas. No sabemos todos los mecanismos que están involucrados, pero sí sabemos que el bienestar general del cuerpo se desorganiza totalmente cuando una persona está deprimida", dice el doctor Blazer.

La reducción del tono muscular es uno de los cambios físicos inmediatos que ocurren cuando usted empieza a deprimirse. "Eso causa que los músculos cuelguen y contribuye a la expresión facial triste y mala postura que usted ve en las personas deprimidas", dice el doctor Elmer Gardner, un siquiatra en práctica privada en Washington, D.C.

Pero los cambios causados por la depresión pueden ser más que superficiales. Los investigadores creen que la depresión puede debilitar el sistema inmune, acelerar el endurecimiento de las arterias y provocar algunas formas de artritis.

Si usted está deprimida, su actividad celular inmune puede caer a los niveles de una persona que es 25 a 30 años mayor, dice el doctor Michael Irwin, profesor asociado de siquiatría en la Escuela de Medicina de la Universidad de California, San Diego. El doctor Irwin no ha estudiado la depresión en las mujeres, pero en un estudio de hombres deprimidos entre los 40 y los 45 años de edad, encontró que tenían actividad de células asesinas naturales que se veía asombrosamente similar a la de los hombres en sus setenta y tantos que no estaban deprimidos. Las células asesinas naturales son parte del sistema inmune que la protege de los virus tales como el herpe simple, el virus de herpe labial, y estas células asesinas se vuelven normalmente menos activas a medida de que envejecemos.

La depresión provoca una reacción de inmunidad baja, pero nosotros todavía no sabemos hasta qué punto eso conduce a enfermedades", dice el doctor Irwin. "Sí sabemos, sin embargo, que los virus contra los cuales las

¿Está usted realmente deprimida?

Aquí hay una lista de síntomas, según la Asociación Siquiátrica de los Estados Unidos, que puede ayudarla a determinar la intensidad de su depresión. Si usted tiene cinco o más de estos síntomas en un lapso de dos semanas, o si se siente deprimida por más de dos semanas, debería pedir la ayuda de su médico o de un terapeuta calificado.

- Se siente triste la mayor parte del día o ha perdido interés en actividades agradables incluyendo las relaciones sexuales.
- Se siente cansada o sin energía para hacer las tareas cotidianas.
- Se siente inquieta y no puede permanecer sentada.
- Tiene insomnio o duerme más de la cuenta.
- Tiene dificultad en concentrarse o tomar decisiones.
- Tiene fluctuaciones en su apetito o peso.
- Se siente sin esperanza, sin valor y culpable.
- Piensa en la muerte y el suicidio.

células asesinas nos ayudan a protegernos son más comunes en personas que están deprimidas."

La depresión también puede estimular la ateroesclerosis, una formación de depósitos grasos en las paredes de las arterias que contribuye a la enfermedad coronaria del corazón, dice George Kaplan, Ph.D., un epidemiólogo y jefe del Laboratorio de Población Humana del Departamento de Servicios de Salud de California, en Berkeley.

La artritis reumática es una enfermedad mas que la depresión puede agravar o aun provocar, dice el doctor Stanford Roth, un reumatólogo y director médico del Centro de Artritis en Phoenix. "No es fuera de lo corriente para una persona que sufre la pérdida devastadora de uno de sus padres o cónyuge desarrollar una enfermedad como artritis reumática", dice el doctor Roth. "Debido a que la artritis reumática puede asociarse con una raíz genética, estas personas tenían todo el tiempo el potencial de desarrollar esta enfermedad. Sólo tomó un episodio depresivo para causarla."

Siempre sale el sol después de la tormenta

Así que ahora que usted sabe que la depresión puede causar un fuerte impacto en cómo envejece, ¿qué puede hacer para prevenirla o tratarla? Bastante, dicen los médicos.

Tenga en mente que una depresión grave —aquella que persiste por más de dos semanas— puede requerir la atención de un médico y tratamiento con drogas antidepresivas. Pero si su depresión dura unos cuantos días y no interfiere con sus actividades, aquí hay algunas sugerencias que pueden levantarle el ánimo.

Tenga una meta en mente. "Las personas que tienen sueños y visiones de logros tienen menos probabilidades de deprimirse que aquellos que no tienen metas a corto y largo plazos", dice el doctor Dennis Gersten, un siquiatra en práctica privada en San Diego. Haga una lista de las metas. Divida la lista en secciones que incluyan cosas que usted quiere hacer esta semana, este mes, dentro de un año y dentro de cinco años. Coloque la lista en un lugar que esté a la vista, como por ejemplo sobre su refrigerador, y marque como completas las metas cuando las ha alcanzado. Trate de poner su lista al día por lo menos una vez al mes.

Ocúpese en algo. "Si usted se mantiene ocupada le ayudará, porque al mantenerse activa puede evitar que usted piense demasiado en lo que sea que la está haciendo sentir infeliz", dice Linda George, Ph.D., profesora de sociología médica en el Centro Médico de la Universidad Duke.

Siga riéndose. El humor es su mejor aliado, dice el doctor Prosen. Recorte caricaturas y artículos divertidos del periódico o revistas y póngalos en una carpeta que usted pueda hojear cuando se siente deprimida.

Apóyese en familiares y amistades. Ellos le han ayudado a sobrevivir malas relaciones y otros desastres; ahora ellos la pueden ayudar superar de este período sombrío. "Eso no quiere decir que les está pidiendo que resuelvan sus problemas por usted", dice la doctora George. "Sólo quiere decir que les está pidiendo que la escuchen, que le permitan desahogarse y que la apoyen."

Exprese sus pensamientos negativos por escrito. Escribiendo sus sentimientos cuando usted está deprimida puede ayudarle a reconocer formas de pensar erróneas y a reemplazar esos pensamientos con otros que levantan más el ánimo, dice la doctora Peterson. Por cada pensamiento negativo que usted escriba, como por ejemplo "yo soy la peor persona del mundo", escriba también uno positivo, como "yo no soy perfecta, pero tengo bastantes cualidades buenas". Después de un rato, los pensamientos positivos pueden reemplazar a los negativos.

Aléjese de los tragos. Aunque sea tentador ahogar sus penas en unas cuantas copas de vino, no lo haga, advierte la doctora Yonkers. El alcohol es un depresivo que puede arrastrarla aún más a sentirse con el ánimo por el suelo. "Beber en exceso trastornará también su sueño y puede hacer que sus amistades y familiares se distancien de usted precisamente cuando usted necesita más de su apoyo", dice.

Actívese y anímese. "El ejercicio es una forma fabulosa de aliviar la depresión", dice el doctor Gersten. "El ejercicio aeróbico como caminar, correr, nadar o andar en bicicleta estimula su actividad cerebral y puede invertir los efectos de incluso una depresión fuerte." Él sugiere hacer ejercicio por lo menos 20 minutos diarios, tres veces por semana.

Deje sus tarjetas de crédito en la cartera. "Algunas personas que se deprimen tratan de curar eso con una receta de tarjetas de crédito", dice la doctora Yonkers. "Ellas piensan que si se van de compras y compran algo, les va a levantar el ánimo. Pero a menudo terminan por sentirse culpables porque hicieron compras de valor que en realidad no podían darse el lujo de hacer y eso las deprime aún mas." Si usted está deprimida y se va de compras, póngase un límite para gastar antes de salir, y pague en efectivo.

Sea una buena actriz. Una manera fantástica de rechazar la depresión es actuar en forma feliz por una hora, dice la doctora Yonkers. Luego trate por una hora más y así sucesivamente. Para el final del día, se sorprenderá de encontrar que ya no está fingiendo.

DERRAME CEREBRAL

No es demasiado temprano para la prevención

De todos los ladrones de la juventud, el derrame cerebral es el más veloz y el más trágico. En un instante, una mujer vital y vibrante puede perder su capacidad para hablar, para moverse libremente —incluso para pensar tan claramente como lo hacía unos segundos atrás.

Y a pesar de su reputación por ser un problema de las personas mayores —en realidad un problema de los hombres mayores— el derrame cerebral no discrimina.

Más de 8.000 mujeres estadounidenses entre los 30 y los 44 años de edad sufren derrames cerebrales cada año. Casi uno en cada tres derrames cerebrales es mortal. Y los efectos del envejecimiento en aquellos que sobreviven pueden ser brutales. Los sobrevivientes pueden sufrir daños al cerebro que afectan el habla, la memoria, los patrones de pensamiento y la conducta. Algunas veces hay parálisis temporal, o permanente.

La buena noticia es que usted puede reducir significativamente su riesgo de un derrame cerebral.

"Estamos empezando a darnos cuenta de que el derrame cerebral no es un proceso inevitable", dice el doctor Michael Walker, director de la División de Derrame Cerebral y Trauma en el Instituto Nacional de Trastornos Neurológicos y Derrame Cerebral, en Bethesda, Maryland. "Es evitable, y es tratable."

Tomar medidas preventivas puede consistir en cambios difíciles de hacer al principio, como hacer más ejercicio y fijarse más en su presión arterial. Pero cuando usted considera que puede evitar un cruel derrame cerebral que la puede dejar incapacitada, bien vale la pena hacer estos cambios.

El riesgo para las mujeres

El derrame cerebral es una enfermedad súbita y grave que ataca el cerebro. Hay dos tipos básicos. Los derrames cerebrales isquémicos, que representan el 80 por ciento de todos los derrames cerebrales, ocurren cuando se interrumpe el flujo sanguíneo a una parte del cerebro, causando que las células cerebrales mueran por falta de oxígeno. Esto ocurre frecuentemente debido a un endurecimiento y obstrucción en sus arterias carótidas, las cuales alimentan de sangre del cuello a su cabeza. Los derrames cerebrales isquémicos también pueden ser causados por fibrilación atrial, un latido irregular del corazón que conduce a coágulos que puedan viajar a través de su cuerpo y alojarse en las arterias del cerebro.

Los derrames cerebrales hemorrágicos representan el 20 por ciento restante. Estos derrames cerebrales son causados debido a rupturas ya sea de un vaso sanguíneo en la superficie de su cerebro o de una arteria en el cerebro mismo. Estos derrames cerebrales pueden ser aún más fatales que los derrames cerebrales isquémicos, con un índice de mortalidad de cerca del 50 por ciento.

Las mujeres entre los 30 y los 44 años de edad tienen la mitad de probabilidades de tener un derrame cerebral que los hombres en el mismo grupo de edades, según los números de la Asociación del Corazón de los Estados Unidos. Las mujeres de ascendencia africana tienen un riesgo mayor que las mujeres de ascendencia europea de morirse de un derrame cerebral. Una historia familiar de derrames cerebrales también puede desempeñar un papel, aunque en qué proporción todavía no está claro. Y el riesgo de un derrame cerebral aumenta a medida que la mujer envejece. Las estadísticas de la Asociación del Corazón de los Estados Unidos muestran que la incidencia de los derrames cerebrales aumenta a más del doble cada década para una mujer después de que ella llega a los 55 años de edad.

Las mujeres más jóvenes tienen algo de protección contra los derrames cerebrales debido a que sus cuerpos producen grandes cantidades de estrógeno. Eso ayuda a mantener los niveles de colesterol bajos y contiene la aparición de la arteriosclerosis o el endurecimiento de las arterias. Después de la menopausia, no obstante, el índice de derrames cerebrales aumenta rápidamente. Al llegar a los 65 años de edad, los hombres y las mujeres tienen aproximadamente la misma incidencia de derrames cerebrales.

El embarazo puede causar un ligero aumento en el riesgo de un derrame cerebral, aunque las probabilidades son todavía bastante bajas. Existen unas cuantas razones para este aumento de riesgo, dice el doctor Harold Adams, Jr., profesor de neurología en el Hospital y Clínica de la Universidad de Iowa, en la Ciudad de Iowa. La sangre de una mujer coagula en forma diferente durante el embarazo. Y su presión arterial tiende a ser un poco más alta. Los estudios además muestran que ciertos tipos de píldoras anticonceptivas también pueden aumentar el riesgo de un derrame cerebral, especialmente para las fumadoras mayores de los 35 años de edad o para las mujeres con presión arterial alta.

Por supuesto, usted no puede hacer nada con respecto a la edad o el sexo. Pero según el doctor Adams hay muchos riesgos que usted definitivamente puede controlar.

Las señales de advertencia de un derrame cerebral

La acción rápida puede ser la diferencia entre la tragedia y la recuperación cuando se trata de un derrame cerebral. Preste atención a estas señales de advertencia, dice la Asociación del Corazón de los Estados Unidos:

- Debilidad súbita o adormecimiento en la cara, el brazo o la pierna de un lado del cuerpo
- Pérdida del habla, o dificultad para hablar o entender cuando alguien habla
- Oscurecimiento súbito o pérdida de la visión, especialmente en un solo ojo
- Fuerte dolor de cabeza de repente sin una causa aparente
- Mareo sin explicación, inestabilidad o caída inesperada, especialmente en combinación con alguno de los síntomas anteriores

Si usted nota alguno de estos síntomas, pida ayuda inmediatamente llamando al 911 o al número telefónico de emergencia en su área. Un estudio de los tiempos de tardanza mostró que las personas con señales de derrame cerebral que llamaron a este número de emergencia llegaron al hospital de dos a tres veces más rápido que aquellas que llamaron a sus médicos y trataron de transportarse ellas mismas al hospital. Y con un derrame cerebral, los minutos cuentan.

Lo que parece ser un derrame cerebral en realidad puede ser un ataque isquémico momentáneo (o *TIA*, por sus siglas en inglés). A estos se les llama a veces derrames cerebrales temporales, ya que los síntomas desaparecen rápidamente. Pero usted no debe ignorar un TIA, ya que es la advertencia más importante de un derrame cerebral inminente, según lo indica el doctor Harold Adams, Jr., profesor de neurología en el Hospital y Clínica de la Universidad de Iowa, en la Ciudad de Iowa.

La presión arterial alta, por ejemplo, también conocida como hipertensión, es el factor de riego más importante para el derrame cerebral. "Casi la mitad de todos los derrames cerebrales están causados por presión arterial alta", dice el doctor Edward S. Cooper, ex presidente de la Asociación del Corazón de los Estados Unidos.

La presión arterial alta causa el derrame cerebral al acelerar la arterioscle-rosis y dañar los pequeños vasos sanguíneos. Y, en las palabras del doctor Cooper, puede causar que los diminutos vasos sanguíneos en su cerebro "se revienten como una llanta sobreinflada".

El fumar la pone a usted en un riesgo creciente de tener un derrame cere-bral al acelerar la obstrucción de las arterias carótidas, dice el doctor Jack P. Whisnant, investigador principal para un estudio de las enfermedades de la arteria carótida en la Clínica Mayo, en Rochester, Minnesota. Las mujeres que fuman tienen más de 2,5 veces de probabilidad de sufrir un derrame cerebral que las no fumadoras, según un Estudio de la Salud de Enfermeras de Harvard que examinó a 117.000 enfermeras diplomadas entre los 30 y los 55 años de edad, cuando se comenzó a hacer el estudio. Mientras más fumaban las mujeres en el estudio, mayor era su riesgo. Comparadas con las no fumadoras, las muje-res que fumaban de 1 a 14 cigarrillos por día tenían el doble de riesgo de un derrame cerebral, mientras que las mujeres que fumaban de 35 a 44 cigarrillos al día —cerca de dos cajetillas— aumentaban a cuatro veces el riesgo. Aquellas que fumaban más de 45 cigarrillos diarios tenían 5,4 veces más probabilidades de sufrir un derrame cerebral.

Las mujeres con diabetes también tienen un mayor riesgo de derrame cerebral. Y las mujeres obesas y aquellas con niveles altos de colesterol pueden tener un riesgo mayor de desarrollar arteriosclerosis y por lo tanto de sufrir un derrame cerebral.

Una estrategia de intervención

Los derrames cerebrales todavía están envueltos en misterio. Parece que atacan sin previo aviso. Incluso a veces es difícil decir cuando usted se encuen-tra en peligro.

Pero la prevención temprana puede ser la clave para mejorar sus probabili-dades de sufrir un derrame cerebral. "El proceso que lleva al derrame cerebral empieza cuando usted está entre los 40 y los 50 años de edad, aún antes, así que el momento de intervenir es ahora", dice el doctor David G. Sherman, jefe de neurología en el Centro de Ciencias de la Salud de la Universidad de Texas, en San Antonio.

Para ayudarle a reducir su riesgo, pruebe estos consejos.

Alivie la presión. Muchas personas ni siquiera saben que tienen presión arterial alta, debido a que esta muestra pocos indicios externos. Por eso es que la Asociación del Corazón de los Estados Unidos recomienda que usted se haga revisar la presión arterial por un médico u otro profesional en el cuidado de la salud por lo menos una vez al año, si su presión es de 130/85 o más alta. Si su presión arterial es más baja, haga que se la revisen cada dos años. Muchos casos de presión arterial alta empiezan a desarrollarse entre los 35 y los 45 años de edad.

La investigación muestra que al controlar la presión arterial alta se puede reducir el riesgo de derrame cerebral en hasta un 40 por ciento. Cualquier lectura superior a 140/90 se considera alta.

Su médico le podrá recetar tratamientos para la presión arterial alta incluyendo cambios dietéticos, hacer más ejercicio y terapia de drogas. Siga las indicaciones como si su vida dependiera de ello. Así podría ser.

"Controlar la hipertensión es absolutamente vital en la prevención de los derrames cerebrales", dice el doctor Adams.

Quítese ese vicio. El estudio sobre la Salud de las Enfermeras mostró que las mujeres que dejaron de fumar redujeron su riesgo notablemente. De hecho, el riesgo de un derrame cerebral cayó en los niveles normales para las mujeres dos a cuatro años después de que dejaron de fumar.

"No solamente reduzca el número de cigarrillos", dice el doctor Adams. "No existe tal cosa como fumar moderadamente. Usted debe abstenerse completamente, totalmente, ahora."

Cuidado con la píldora anticonceptiva. Por años, los médicos han advertido a las mujeres acerca de las píldoras anticonceptivas y el riesgo creciente de derrame cerebral. Pero con las píldoras anticonceptivas que contienen una dosis baja de estrógeno que se usan ahora, el doctor Adams dice que el riesgo de derrame cerebral es menor.

"Estamos viendo más y más pruebas de que los anticonceptivos orales con dosis bajas de estrógeno son más seguros", dice él. "El estrógeno en dosis bajas es probablemente seguro."

Existen sin embargo dos advertencias. El fumar y la píldora anticonceptiva forman una mezcla peligrosa, especialmente para las mujeres mayores de los 35 años de edad. Y la presión arterial alta, combinada con la píldora anticonceptiva, también puede aumentar el riesgo de derrame cerebral. "Si usted tiene esos factores de riesgo, las píldoras anticonceptivas no son aconsejables", dice el doctor Adams.

Chequee su cuello. Pida a su médico que escuche a ver si oye un ruido murmoroso, un sonido como un silbido en las arterias carótidas de su cuello. Este es causado por un bloque parcial y turbulencia en los vasos sanguíneos cruciales que alimentan de oxígeno al cerebro.

"Esto es especialmente importante si usted tiene arteriosclerosis que está bloqueando los vasos sanguíneos en otra parte de su cuerpo", dice Patricia Grady, Ph.D., directora interina del Instituto Nacional de Trastornos Neurológicos y Derrame Cerebral.

Asegúrese también de que el médico le revise el corazón. Si se trata la fibrilación atrial puede reducir su riesgo de un derrame cerebral en hasta un 80 por ciento.

Manténgase activa. La inactividad física puede ser un riesgo para el derrame cerebral, pero hacer ejercicio por un total de 20 minutos al día, tres veces por semana, puede reducir su riesgo de un derrame cerebral. Caminar, jugar al tenis, andar en bicicleta, subir escaleras, aeróbicos y aun la jardinería y el ping-pong pueden ser destructores potenciales de los derrames cerebrales.

Un estudio británico mostró que mientras más pronto empieza usted a hacer ejercicio, mejor. Las mujeres que empezaron a hacer ejercicio entre los 15 y los 25 años de edad tenían un 63 por ciento de reducción en su riesgo de un derrame cerebral. Aun cuando usted empiece un poco tarde, todavía puede beneficiarse del ejercicio: el estudio mostró que las personas que empezaron a hacer ejercicio entre los 25 y los 40 años redujeron su riesgo en un 57 por ciento y aquellas que comenzaron entre los 40 y los 55 años lo redujeron en un 37 por ciento.

"El ejercicio tiene tantos beneficios", dice el doctor Adams. "Si usted no está haciendo ejercicio podría estar robándole años a su vida más adelante."

Derrote los derrames con zanahorias. El mismo Estudio de la Salud de Enfermeras que observó el fumar también descubrió un vínculo entre el nutritivo betacaroteno y el derrame cerebral.

"Encontramos una reducción del 22 por ciento en el riesgo de ataques al corazón y una reducción del 40 por ciento en el riesgo de derrames cerebrales para aquellas mujeres con un consumo alto de frutas y verduras ricas en betacaroteno comparado con aquellas con un consumo bajo", dice la doctora JoAnn E. Manson, una de las investigadoras principales del componente cardiovascular en el Estudio de la Salud de Enfermeras, quien es codirectora de salud femenina en el Hospital de Brigham y Mujeres y profesora asociada de medicina en la Escuela de Medicina de Harvard, ambos en Boston.

Sólo una zanahoria grande, que tiene 15 miligramos de betacaroteno, proporciona la cantidad de alimento nutritivo que se asoció con el riesgo más bajo en el estudio. Otros alimentos que dieron resultado fueron *sweet potatoes* (camotes, boniatos), los mangos, los albaricoques y la espinaca. El betacaroteno se puede encontrar en la mayoría de las frutas y verduras verde oscuro y anaranjadas.

Páseme el potasio. Los investigadores en la Universidad de California, San Diego han encontrado que al agregar a su dieta una porción individual diaria de un alimento rico en potasio podría reducir su riesgo de un derrame cerebral mortal en hasta un 40 por ciento. La razón de este beneficio no está completamente clara. Aunque se sabe que el potasio ayuda a bajar la presión arterial, la cantidad de potasio que los sujetos de la prueba ingirieron tuvo poco efecto directo en sus lecturas de la presión arterial. Los estudios en el Centro Médico de la Universidad de Misisipí, en Jackson mostraron que el potasio puede ayudar a prevenir la formación de coágulos en la sangre, uno de los factores primordiales en los ataques al corazón y derrames cerebrales.

Si usted está buscando un refuerzo con alto contenido de potasio, coma una papa asada diariamente. Las papas son una de las fuentes más ricas en potasio. Otros alimentos ricos en potasio incluyen los albaricoques secos, las habas blancas (*lima beans*), las acelgas suizas, los plátanos (guineos) amarillos, la leche descremada, las castañas tostadas, el quimbombó (calalú) y las naranjas.

Infórmese sobre la aspirina. La aspirina puede protegerla contra el derrame cerebral isquémico al adelgazar los coágulos potenciales en la sangre, dice el doctor Adams. Pero a menos que usted ya tenga un factor de riesgo, como por ejemplo arteriosclerosis o un derrame cerebral anterior, puede ser que no le haga mucho beneficio. De hecho, la investigación muestra que la aspirina puede estar vinculada con una incidencia ligeramente más alta de derrame cerebral hemorrágico.

Exactamente cuánta aspirina usted debería tomar también es algo discutible. Algunos estudios han encontrado beneficios con una dosis diaria de 81 miligramos (una aspirina para niños). Otros promueven una dosis diaria de 325 miligramos (una aspirina de fuerza normal para adultos). Y ahora algunos investigadores dicen que puede ser necesario tomar tres tabletas de aspirina diariamente. En resumen, vea a su médico antes de empezar en un régimen de aspirinas para prevenir el derrame cerebral.

Manténgala balanceada. Lo que es bueno para su corazón también es bueno para su cerebro. Si conserva su colesterol bajo control puede retrasar la arteriosclerosis y detener los derrames cerebrales isquémicos. Así que coma una dieta baja en grasas. La recomendación actual de la mayoría de los médicos e investigadores es limitar la grasa a no más del 25 por ciento de su total de calorías.

"Junto con hacer ejercicio y dejar de fumar, lo que usted come es un factor clave para prevenir un derrame cerebral", dice el doctor Adams. "Nos estamos refiriendo a una dieta buena que le ayudará a disminuir el riesgo de que sus arterias se endurezcan." Esta dieta no necesita ser extrema, dice él. Pero sí necesita ser una dieta bien balanceada y baja en grasas.

Recuerde: nada en exceso, todo con medida. Beber en exceso significa un riesgo creciente de derrame cerebral. Numerosos estudios muestran que tomar más de cuatro tragos al día aumenta mucho sus probabilidades de un derrame cerebral hemorrágico.

Pero algunos estudios muestran un vínculo entre el consumo moderado de alcohol y una reducción leve en el riesgo de sufrir un derrame cerebral isquémico, por lo menos entre las personas de ascendencia europea.

"Puede haber algo acerca del alcohol que en niveles reducidos ayuda. Puede prevenir tanto los ataques al corazón como los derrames cerebrales. Yo no les estoy diciendo a mis pacientes que beban por su salud", dice el doctor Adams. "Si usted no bebe ahora, no le recomiendo que empiece. Si usted toma más de dos tragos diarios, las complicaciones potenciales del alcohol probablemente la van a dañar a la larga. La clave con el uso del alcohol es la moderación."

DIABETES

Cómo desarmar a un asesino potencial

No sería una mentira decir que el azúcar es popular en nuestra sociedad. Sin ella, el café estaría amargo, los dulces agrios, y la "Reina de la Salsa" Celia Cruz no tendría su palabra favorita que "endulza" sus canciones.

Desafortunadamente, el azúcar no es tan popular, e incluso es algo amargo para la gente que tiene una demasiada cantidad en su sangre, la cual es una forma de diabetes. Esta enfermedad es la cuarta causa de muerte en los Estados Unidos y afecta a muchas personas, tanto a los latinos como a los otros grupos étnicos. Según el Instituto Nacional de la Salud, 1,3 millones de latinos mayores de 21 años de edad padecen de la diabetes.

No hay salidas fáciles

Pero aun el tratar de manejar esta enfermedad puede envejecerla antes de tiempo. Las mujeres con diabetes deben observar una dieta estricta con respecto a qué comen y cuándo comen. "Posiblemente puedan comer un pedazo de pastel de vez en cuando, en el cumpleaños de un niño o en un aniversario, pero eso es todo", dice Audrey Lally, R.D., una educadora certificada de diabetes y especialista de nutrición de la Clínica Mayo, en Scottsdale, Arizona. "Pero en su mayor parte, yo trato de convencer a mis pacientes con diabetes que no consuman alimentos que contengan grandes cantidades de azúcar puro."

Este régimen va más allá de la cocina. Las mujeres con diabetes no pueden pasearse descalzas en un día de verano como si nada. Debido a los daños en los nervios que resultan de una pérdida de sensación en sus piernas y pies, pueden no darse cuenta cuando se causan heridas en sus pies. Según la Asociación de la

Diabetes de los Estados Unidos, más de 54.000 personas que padecen de diabetes pierden sus pies o piernas por amputación cada año debido a la enfermedad.

"Cada vez que usted cambia la química en su sangre, está cambiando virtualmente cada sistema afectado por la sangre", dice Steve Manley, Ph.D., un sicólogo en práctica privada en Denton, Texas. "Y eso serían todos ellos."

Incluyendo sus órganos sexuales. Debido a que la diabetes puede debilitar tanto el sistema neurológico como el sistema vascular —y usted necesita buenos nervios y flujo de sangre para funcionar sexualmente— muchas mujeres pierden el placer que antes encontraban en las relaciones sexuales. "Los hombres a menudo se vuelven impotentes por la diabetes, y en cierta forma, ésta afecta a las mujeres de la misma manera", dice el doctor Manley. "La fase de lubricación en las mujeres es similar a la fase de erección en los hombres."

Sus efectos mentales

La diabetes puede afectar su mente en más de una forma. "Cuando el azúcar en su sangre está fuera de control, tiene un efecto en su función cognoscitiva", dice Patricia Stenger, R.N., una consejera en diabetes y vicepresidenta sénior para la Asociación de la Diabetes de los Estados Unidos. "Puede ser que usted reaccione más lentamente y se sienta aletargada y fatigada."

El doctor Manley agrega: "En efecto, la diabetes la sume a usted en una reacción de pena profunda, porque usted ha perdido algo. Algunas personas se sienten sin recursos y sin esperanzas debido a que sienten que sus cuerpos, de alguna manera, se rebelaron contra ellas. Algunas sienten que ya no tienen control sobre sus propios destinos. Pueden perder la creencia, por lo menos temporalmente, que en algún momento en su futuro van a estar bien. La enfermedad comienza a interactuar con sus personalidades básicas".

Un dulce agrio

La diabetes ocurre cuando el cuerpo no produce suficiente insulina o no la usa correctamente. Esta es una hormona secretada en el páncreas que se necesita para convertir el alimento en energía. Mucho de lo que comemos para energía se descompone en un azúcar llamado glucosa, el combustible que alimenta cada una de nuestras células para mantenernos vivas. La enfermedad no es causada por comer dulces, aunque la gente con diabetes debe limitar su consumo de azúcar porque los dulces pueden hacer que el azúcar en la sangre se eleve drásticamente.

En las personas saludables, las células absorben automáticamente la glucosa. El cuerpo usa justamente lo que necesita y lo demás lo almacena. Pero sin insulina para abrir los receptores de la célula a fin de que la glucosa pueda entrar, la cantidad en exceso de este azúcar se acumula en el torrente sanguíneo donde puede causar una gran cantidad de dificultades. Las personas con diabetes tienen cinco veces el riesgo de un derrame cerebral y de dos a cuatro veces el riesgo de enfermedades del corazón en comparación con las personas que no sufren de esta enfermedad. Una de cada diez personas que padecen de diabetes desarrolla enfermedades de los riñones y entre 15.000 y 39.000 al año pierden la vista debido a la enfermedad.

Cambios sutiles pero significantes

Hay dos tipos de diabetes. Con la diabetes Tipo I (o juvenil), la cual representa sólo el 10 por ciento de los casos, el cuerpo deja de producir insulina completamente, por lo que se necesitan inyecciones diarias de esta hormona. El Tipo I se diagnostica a veces durante la pubertad y los síntomas, que pueden imitar a los de la gripe, son súbitos y muy notables: hambre y sed en extremo, pérdida de peso sorpresiva y fatiga e irritabilidad extremas.

En la más común, la diabetes Tipo II (o que aparece en la edad adulta), que usualmente ataca a las mujeres después de los 45 años de edad, el páncreas produce insulina, pero no suficiente. Puede haber algunos síntomas —corta-duras o moretones que tardan en sanar, infecciones recurrentes en la piel, encía o vejiga, o un cosquilleo o adormecimiento en las manos o los pies— pero muchas mujeres no notan estos cambios sutiles o simplemente hacen caso omiso de ellos. Y eso es exactamente por qué más de la mitad de las mujeres con diabetes no están conscientes de su condición. La diabetes es una enfermedad imperceptible que llega a la gente furtivamente —y con resultados devastadores, dice el doctor Xavier Pi-Sunyer, profesor de medicina en la Universidad Columbia en la ciudad de Nueva York y ex-presidente de la Asociación Americana de la Diabetes.

Por eso es importante que usted se haga examinar la sangre para determinar si hay niveles elevados de la glucosa, especialmente, si usted tiene una historia de la enfermedad en su familia, tiene peso de más, tiene más de 40 años de edad o tuvo un bebé que pesó más de nueve libras (cuatro kilos) al nacer. "La gente muchas veces no está consciente de que tiene la enfermedad porque se siente bien", dice Stenger.

Tomar la sartén por el mango

"La mejor forma de evitar la diabetes es cuidando su peso", dice Lally. "Eso significa comer una dieta saludable que se concentre en frutas y verduras. Tener sobrepeso es el factor de mayor riesgo para la diabetes que aparece en la edad adulta. Esto es importante para cualquiera pero es esencial si usted tiene una historia familiar con diabetes o tuvo diabetes durante su embarazo."

Aun cuando usted esté entre las 650.000 personas diagnosticadas este año —eso es una cada 60 segundos— un estilo saludable de vida puede ser todo lo que se necesite para dominar la situación con la diabetes. Aunque algunas personas con diabetes Tipo II requieren drogas orales o inyecciones para estabilizar su azúcar en la sangre, la mayoría pueden controlar la enfermedad simplemente adoptando estilos de vida más saludables. Al comprometerse a ciertos cambios en su estilo de vida, usted puede ser capaz de reducir su necesidad de medicamentos —y posiblemente librarse de y mantenerse sin las drogas para la diabetes por el resto de su vida, dice James Barnard, Ph.D., profesor de ciencia fisiológica en la Universidad de California, Los Ángeles. Aquí está cómo.

Comparta sus sentimientos. Enterarse de que usted tiene diabetes puede ser un golpe duro, y muchas mujeres encuentran consuelo en compartir sus experiencias con otras personas que están pasando por lo mismo.

El reunirse regularmente con un grupo de apoyo puede ayudarla a sobrellevar la enfermedad, mental y físicamente; es también una buena forma de vencer a la depresión. Llame a las oficinas locales de la Asociación de la Diabetes de los Estados Unidos para que le den una lista de los grupos de apoyo en su área.

Controle el estrés. Aun cuando usted no esté preocupada acerca de la depresión, los estudios de los investigadores de la Universidad Duke en Durham, Carolina del Norte, muestran que cuando usted está bajo estrés, ciertas hormonas se activan y bombean glucosa almacenada a su torrente sanguíneo. A la inversa, el manejo del estrés y tomar tiempo para relajarse mejora el control de la glucosa, un factor significativo para aquellos con diabetes. Además de la terapia de grupo que es una forma de relajarse, existen otras como meditación y yoga.

Coma correctamente. Eso significa baja grasa y mucha fibra, por lo menos cinco porciones de frutas y verduras al día, dice Lally. Por cada 40 gramos de grasa que se coma al día —la cantidad que se encuentra en una hamburguesa y una orden grande de papas fritas— su riesgo de desarrollar diabetes se eleva tres veces, y si usted ya tiene diabetes, tiene una mayor posibilidad de complicaciones, según encuentra un estudio en la *American Journal of Epidemiology* (Revista Norteamericana de Epidemiología). El problema: la grasa dietética se convierte inmediatamente en grasa en el cuerpo, y la grasa en el cuerpo induce a las células a resistir la insulina, dice el doctor Frank Q. Nuttall, Ph.D., jefe de la Sección Endocrina, Metabólica y de Nutrición del Centro Médico de la Administración de Veteranos de Minneapolis.

Entretanto, trate de consumir por lo menos 25 gramos de fibra de alimentos con carbohidratos complejos diariamente, los cuales ayudan a frenar la glucosa que entra en su torrente sanguíneo y también mantiene el colesterol bajo — importante para las personas con diabetes, quienes se enfrentan con un riesgo más alto de enfermedades del corazón. Eso es entre dos y tres veces lo que la mayoría de los estadounidenses comen. Las mejores fuentes de carbohidratos complejos son las papas, panes de grano integral, las pastas, las legumbres, las avenas y la cebada.

Prográmelas exactamente. "Si usted tiene diabetes, necesita comer cada cuatro o cinco horas", dice Lally. Lo mejor es comer menos varias veces ya que las comidas grandes le hacen más difícil a su cuerpo satisfacer la demanda creciente de insulina. La clave es distribuir uniformemente su alimento a lo largo del día, para que ninguna comida por sí sola abrume al páncreas.

Evite el azúcar y la sal. Es obvio que usted debería evitar el azúcar; aun en pequeñas cantidades, puede hacer subir mucho su azúcar en la sangre. Por supuesto, el consumir poco azúcar y poca sal es una buena regla dietética para que la siga cualquier persona, pero aquellas con diabetes deben ser especialmente cuidadosas. En su lugar, satisfaga su antojo de dulces con endulzantes artificiales como *aspartame* (*NutraSweet*). Vea también si puede encontrar productos con bajo sodio o sodio reducido. Los alimentos salados pueden aumentar la presión arterial, un peligro para personas con diabetes.

Haga palpitar a su corazón. El ejercicio aeróbico regular no solamente ayuda a controlar su peso sino que también hace que sus células sean más receptivas a la insulina. "Usted necesita poner a su corazón en marcha y mantenerlo marchando por lo menos 20 minutos", dice Stenger. "No necesita hacer nada especial; una caminata rápida es suficiente."

Mientras tanto, investigadores en la Universidad de Harvard, en Cambridge, Massachusetts encontraron que el ejercicio es una forma excelente de ayudar a prevenir la diabetes Tipo II. En su Estudio de Salud de Médicos a 22.000 doctores, los investigadores notaron que aquellos que hacían ejercicio por lo menos cinco veces a la semana disminuyeron su riesgo de desarrollar diabetes en más de un 40 por ciento.

Pero las personas con diabetes necesitan hacer ejercicio cuidadosamente. "La principal preocupación para el ejercicio y la diabetes es el riesgo de hipoglicemia, o baja azúcar en la sangre", dice Greg Dwyer, Ph.D., profesor de educación física en la Universidad Estatal Ball, en Muncie, Indiana. Para evitar esto, él sugiere adherirse a una rutina que requiere la misma cantidad de ejercicio a la misma hora diariamente.

Pruebe las pesas, también. Levantar pesas también desempeña un papel en mejorar la tolerancia a la glucosa, la capacidad del cuerpo para metabolizar el azúcar correctamente, según un estudio realizado por investigadores de la Universidad de Maryland College Park y la Universidad Johns Hopkins en Baltimore. Verifique con su médico antes de comenzar un programa de levantamiento de pesas. El entrenamiento de resistencia puede causar aumentos en la presión arterial.

Tome vitaminas E y C. Estos dos antioxidantes tienden a escasear entre las personas con diabetes —investigadores italianos han encontrado que la vitamina E ayuda a mejorar la acción de la insulina. Buenas fuentes alimenticias incluyen germen de trigo, aceite de maíz y nueces, pero usted debería tomar diariamente un suplemento que contenga 400 UI.

Entretanto, debido a que aquellas personas con diabetes son propensas a enfermedades vasculares, pueden necesitar aumentar su consumo de vitamina C, sugiere el doctor Ishwarial Jialal, profesor asistente de medicina interna y nutrición clínica en el Centro Médico del Sudoeste de la Universidad de Texas, en Dallas. La Asignación Dietética Recomendada es de 60 miligramos diarios, pero el doctor Jialal sugiere un mínimo de 120 miligramos de vitamina C diariamente, la cantidad que usted encontraría en una guayaba o un vaso de jugo de naranja.

Deje actuar a la aspirina. La aspirina puede reducir hasta en un 20 por ciento el riesgo de ataques al corazón y derrames cerebrales entre los que padecen de diabetes, según una investigación realizada por los Institutos Nacionales de Salud a 3.711 personas con ambos tipos de la enfermedad. "Las personas con diabetes tienen muchas más probabilidades de tener una enfermedad cardiovascular, así que la recomendación de aspirina es mucho más pertinente para ellos", dice el doctor Frederick Ferris, jefe de la Agencia de Ensayos Clínicos en los Institutos Nacionales de Salud, en Bethesda, Maryland.

La mayoría de los investigadores recomiendan una dosis diaria de media aspirina para adultos o una aspirina infantil, pero verifique antes con su médico: la terapia de la aspirina no se recomienda para personas que están tomando adelgazadores de la sangre o que sufren de úlceras.

DIETAS

Las privaciones no funcionan

Usted se acuerda cómo se hace: Mamá siempre estaba empezando una dieta, especialmente al envejecer. Así que, tal como solía hacer Mamá, usted se dirige a la cocina, tarareando por todo el camino. . . .

Un pedazo grande y jugoso de lechuga con repollo. Remátelo con una cucharada pequeña de requesón. ¿Qué tal un medio melocotón (durazno) enlatado? Hmm, veamos. ¿Qué más? ¡Ah, por supuesto!, tostadas *Melba*. Ponga tres; son pequeñas. Oye, esto no está tan mal —¿verdad? Ahora agregue un poco de endulzante artificial al café y ya está lista. Buen provecho.

De repente, usted ya no se siente con ganas de tararear —ni de comer.

Las dietas no funcionan. Seguro, usted puede perder algo de peso al principio. Pero eventualmente, cuando esté tan hambrienta que se podría comer hasta sus pantuflas, usted dejará la dieta con rencor. Y usted va a recuperar más peso que el que perdió, dice John Foreyt, Ph.D, director de la Clínica de Investigación sobre Nutrición del Colegio Baylor de Medicina, en Houston.

¿Quién no ha pensado: "Si yo pudiera perder estas últimas 10 libras (5 kilos), me vería más joven"? Pero la triste realidad es que la ganancia neta de grasa en su cuerpo resultante de este ciclo de perder y ganar impone un tremendo esfuerzo a su cuerpo. Usted lo ve en su piel que se arruga y cuelga, dice el doctor George Blackburn, Ph.D., profesor asociado de cirugía en la Escuela Medica de Harvard y jefe del Laboratorio de Nutrición/Metabolismo del Hospital Deaconess de Nueva Inglaterra, ambos en Boston.

Pero lo que usted no ve es el envejecimiento interno —órganos y sistemas que se envejecen antes de su tiempo.

Sube y baja como un yoyo

Toda una vida de hacer dieta puede afectar su corazón. En una investigación realizada por Kelly Brownell, Ph.D., una sicóloga e investigadora de la

¿Qué tan buenas son las píldoras de dieta?

¿Funcionan realmente las píldoras de dieta, o sólo ofrecen una falsa esperanza?

"Algunos antidepresivos pueden ayudar a la gente que tiene problemas serios con su peso que incluyen comer sin control y que son causados por desórdenes de comportamiento o siquiátricos", dice David Schlundt, Ph.D., un sicólogo clínico y profesor asistente de sicología en la Universidad Vanderbilt, en Nashville. "Pero asegúrese de combinarlos con alguna forma de sicoterapia."

¿Y qué con respecto a las píldoras para dietas sin receta? La mayoría de los expertos no las recomiendan. Su ingrediente activo, hidrocloruro de fenilpropanolamina (*PPA*), es un estimulante tipo adrenalina. "Para las personas que en primer lugar no están tan saludables —que padecen de alta presión arterial, enfermedades del corazón, asma o diabetes— el PPA puede causar problemas reales", dice el doctor Schlundt. Aun pequeñas dosis pueden elevar la presión arterial y aumentar el ritmo del corazón. Y dosis grandes pueden causar ansiedad, pérdida de sueño, hasta convulsiones. El PPA también tiene el potencial de que se le abuse, hace notar el doctor Schlundt. Causa una excitación similar a la que provocan las anfetaminas que pueden volverse adictivas.

Para personas con un serio sobrepeso, hay un prometedor "bloqueador de grasa" en el horizonte, dice John Foreyt, Ph.D., director de la Clínica de Investigación sobre la Nutrición del Colegio Baylor de Medicina, en Houston. Se le llama *orlistat* (*Xenical*), y esta siendo probado en los Estados Unidos y Europa. "El *orlistat* no es para alguien que necesite perder 5 ó 10 libras (2 ó 5 kilos) sino para la obesidad moderada a grave", dice. La droga opera bloqueando la absorción de grasa.

"Pero ninguna píldora es una bala mágica", dice el doctor Foreyt. "Aun con *orlistat* usted todavía tiene que seguir una dieta baja en grasa y un programa sensato de ejercicio."

obesidad en la Universidad de Yale, en New Haven, Connecticut, encontró que hacer dieta repetidamente puede predisponerla a una enfermedad del corazón. Los estudios de la doctora Brownell mostraron que las personas con grandes fluctuaciones de peso tienen un riesgo 75 por ciento mayor de morir de una enfermedad del corazón, que las personas cuyo peso se mantiene relativamente estable. "Se requiere bastante fluctuación de peso para colocarla a usted en esta categoría, no cinco libras (dos kilos) de vez en cuando", dice el doctor Brownell.

Las dietas de yoyo también pueden causar alta presión arterial y redistribuir la grasa a partes de su cuerpo donde hace más daño, como por ejemplo pasando de sus asentaderas a su barriga. Las personas con mucha grasa abdominal, por ejemplo, son más propensas a desarrollar enfermedades del corazón, dicen los expertos.

Ponerse a dieta también hace imposible para usted cosechar los beneficios completos de la actividad física. Un estudio de la Universidad Estatal de Arizona, en Tempe, encontró que las mujeres que habían hecho por lo menos cuatro dietas diferentes el año anterior usaron menos calorías al hacer ejercicio que las que no hacían dieta. También, pesaban más y tenían más grasa en el cuerpo que las mujeres que no estaban a dieta.

Evite engaños y estafas

Los anuncios exclaman "¡Pierda una libra por día!", ¡"Yo perdí 100 libras en tres meses!", "¡Píldora milagrosa para perder peso!", "¡Alimento misterioso derrite las libras de más!", "¡Dieta de bajos carbohidratos!", "¡Dieta de alta proteína!"

¿Le suena conocido? Las dietas de pérdida de peso rápida simplemente no funcionan. Usted puede perder peso rápidamente al principio, pero la mayor parte es agua. En el momento que usted deje de matarse de hambre, repondrá todo —más grasa adicional.

Aquí está cómo distinguir un programa de control de peso legítimo de otro plan tonto de dieta.

Tenga mucha paciencia. No caiga presa de los planes hábiles de pérdida de peso que prometen rapidez, dice el doctor Blackburn. La gran virtud de una pérdida de peso con éxito es paciencia, porque la única forma de perder peso es despacio. Lo mejor es de media a una libra por semana, dice.

Nunca diga "nunca". Las privaciones no funcionan, pero los cambios de estilo de vida sí pueden funcionar, dice Janet Polivy, Ph.D., profesora de sicología de la Facultad de Medicina en la Universidad de Toronto. Un buen plan de comidas —uno que esté enfocado en la salud y no en la pérdida de peso— no le prohíbe darse un gusto de vez en cuando comiendo cosas favoritas con alto contenido de grasa, dice. "Si a usted le dicen que nunca coma alimentos fritos, se va a sentir terrible cuando coma alguno —lo cual es inevitable— y usted dejará de comer bien porque se siente como un fracaso."

Olvídese de las dietas con comidas de moda. "Este concepto no tiene ningún valor", dice el doctor Blackburn. "No hay alimentos mágicos que anulen las calorías consumidas, tal y como la toronja."

Ignore las recomendaciones. "Las recomendaciones son una parte importante en los planes falaces de pérdida de peso", dice el doctor Terrence Kuske, un nutriólogo y profesor de medicina en el Colegio Médico de Georgia, en Augusta. Una recomendación típica podría ser más o menos como esto: "¡Yo perdí 30 libras (17 kilos) en un mes con la Dieta Dinamita!, J. Smith, ciudad de Nueva York". Lo más probable es que J. Smith no exista —o si existe, ella es pariente del dueño de la compañía que está vendiendo este plan de dieta. Los programas de control de peso que funcionan están respaldados por estudios científicos, no por recomendaciones.

DOLOR DE ESPALDA

Cómo sobrellevar un dolor común

Hace unos años atrás, usted era una campeona en la pista de baile. No importaba que la música fuera cumbia, salsa, merengue o *rock and roll*, usted movía su cuerpo con una destreza que hubiera llenado a la misma Charytín de envidia. Pero el otro día en el concierto de Tito Puente, al dar una vuelta, sintió un dolor que era como si alguien le hubiera clavado un cuchillo en la espalda. Se tuvo que sentar para descansar, y se sintió como una anciana, mientras Puente, con sus setenta y tantos años, siguió tocando como si nada.

Usted se recuperó en unos cuantos días, pero ese episodio era un recordatorio muy doloroso de que su espina no está hecha de caucho y que la edad se está metiendo de puntillas en su vida por la puerta de atrás.

"Una mujer de 30 años de edad que sufre de dolor en la espalda y de movilidad limitada puede sentirse como si tuviera 90 años de edad", dice Joseph Sasso, D.C., presidente de la Federación de Quiroprácticos y Organizaciones de Quiroprácticos Tradicionales.

Por lo menos el 70 por ciento de las mujeres sufrirán de dolor en la espalda en algún momento de sus vidas. De ellas, el 14 por ciento tendrá dolores severos que duran por lo menos dos semanas, y un 7 por ciento sufrirá dolores crónicos que pueden durar más de seis meses, según el doctor Gunnar B. J. Andersson, Ph.D., profesor y presidente asociado del Departamento de Cirugía Ortopédica del Centro Médico Rush-Presbyterian–St. Luke, en Chicago. Aproximadamente 400.000 lesiones en la espalda ocurren en el trabajo cada año, y eso resulta en más productividad perdida que ninguna otra condición médica. El dolor en la espalda es la causa más frecuente de actividad restringida entre la gente de 45 años de edad para abajo y la segunda razón más común (después de resfriados/catarros y gripe) para visitar al doctor, según la Academia Norteamericana de Cirujanos

Ortopédicos. También es la quinta causa en importancia de hospitalización y la tercera razón más común para cirugía, dice el doctor Andersson.

"Dormir, sexo, sentarse —no puedo imaginarme una actividad que no esté afectada por la espalda. Está envuelta en casi todo lo que hacemos. Usted no puede entrar o salir de un carro, correr, saltar o caminar. Hasta que no sufre de dolor de espalda, usted no se da cuenta de todo lo que la espalda hace por usted", dice el doctor Alan Bensman, un siquiatra en Servicios de Salud Rehabilitativa, en Minneapolis.

¿Cuándo comienza la dolencia?

Muchas mujeres experimentan sus primeros encuentros con el dolor de espalda durante el embarazo, cuando el útero se expande para acomodar al bebé creciente, dice el doctor Bensman. El dolor de espalda puede ocurrir después de la menopausia, cuando la producción de estrógeno disminuye y una mujer se vuelve más propensa a la osteoporosis, una pérdida de masa ósea que debilita a la espalda y causa dolor. Pero el dolor de espalda es particularmente común en las mujeres entre los 30 y los 45 años de edad, dice Dan Futch, D.C., jefe del equipo de quiropráctica en la Cooperativa *HMO* de Salud de Grupo en Madison, Wisconsin.

"Esas edades son 'la ventana de oportunidad' para el dolor de espalda", dice él. "Aproximadamente al mismo tiempo que usted empieza con canas, usted probablemente empezará a notar punzadas de dolor en su espalda."

Entre los 30 y los 50 años de edad es cuando la artritis y otros tipos de degeneración natural en las articulaciones pequeñas de la espalda empiezan a alcanzarnos, dice el doctor Robert Waldrip, un cirujano ortopédico de la espina con práctica privada en Phoenix. La estenosis de la columna vertebral, por ejemplo, un estrechamiento del canal en las vértebras que rodean la médula espinal, ejerce presión sobre los nervios en la parte inferior de la espalda y causa dolor. En otros casos el problema es un disco herniado. Los discos son pequeñas almohadillas hechas de un recubrimiento exterior resistente y elástico (llamado el anillo) y un núcleo suave. Los discos actúan como amortiguadores de golpes entre las vértebras. Al pasar el tiempo, un disco puede herniarse, lo que significa que el anillo se ha rasgado y el núcleo central se ha extendido hacia afuera y presiona contra una raíz nerviosa, causando un dolor horrible. Una mala postura también aumenta la tensión en la espalda y puede agravar la artritis y conducir a problemas con los discos.

Pero por mucho, la causa más común de dolor de espalda es músculo y tensión. A medida que envejecemos, muchas de nosotras hacemos menos ejercicio. Como resultado, los músculos en el abdomen y la espalda que soportan la columna vertebral se debilitan y deforman, dice el doctor Bensman. Así que cosas que usted hacía antes con facilidad, como levantar y sacar una bolsa con comestibles del carro, cargar a un bebé fuera de su cuna o rastrillar las hojas, de repente la hacen sentir como si tuviera una docena de cuchillos clavados en su espalda.

Introducción a cómo levantar: empecemos por el principio

Todas nosotras pensamos que sabemos cómo se hace. Después de todo, usted ha alzado, arrastrado y levantado cosas por años. Pero aún cuando levantar parece ser una parte muy ordinaria de la vida, si se hace equivocadamente puede mandar una ola de shock doloroso y ondulante a través de la columna vertebral más resistente. Para evitar eso, la Academia Norteamericana de Cirujanos Ortopédicos sugiere que usted observe esta guías cuando levanta algo.

Acérquese tanto como sea posible al objeto que va a levantar. Separe sus pies al ancho de sus hombros para darse una base sólida de apoyo. Flexione las rodillas, tensione los músculos de su estómago y levante con sus piernas a medida que se para. No flexione la cintura y no trate de levantar un objeto que es demasiado pesado o de forma muy rara sin ayuda de otros.

Cuando usted esté sosteniendo un objeto conserve sus rodillas ligeramente flexiona- das para mantener su balance. Apunte los dedos de sus pies en la dirección en que quiere moverse. Evite girar su torso. En lugar de eso, gire sobre sus pies. Man- tenga el objeto cerca suyo cuando se está moviendo.

Para levantar un objeto muy liviano como un lápiz del suelo, inclínese, flexione una rodilla ligeramente, y extienda la otra pierna atrás de usted. Sosténgase de una silla o mesa cercana para apoyarse al agacharse para levantar el lápiz.

Levantar algo cuando su espalda no está en condiciones es como si alguien la arrancara del público mientras que está viendo la Maratón de Boston y la forzara a correr las 26 millas (42 kilómetros) de la carrera. Probablemente se va a lastimar, porque está esforzando a su espalda de una manera para la cual usted no está preparada.

Por supuesto, aun atletas bien entrenados pueden sufrir de dolor de espalda, pero en general si se encuentra en buena forma física, será menos probable que su espalda le cause problemas.

Vea a su médico si el dolor es tan intenso que no se puede mover, si se extiende a sus piernas o asentaderas, si sus piernas o pies se sienten adormecidos o cosquillean, si pierde control sobre su vejiga o si también tiene fiebre o dolor abdominal.

Cómo conservar su columna

A menudo el dolor de espalda se alivia fácilmente sin cirugía o drogas, dice el doctor Waldrip. En realidad, el 60 por ciento de la gente con dolor agudo de espalda regresa a trabajar en una semana, y el 90 por ciento está de regreso en el trabajo en unas seis semanas. Aquí hay algunos consejos para prevenir y tratar el dolor de espalda.

Estírese temprano en la mañana. "Yo les digo a mis pacientes que siempre empiecen su día estirándose mientras están todavía en la cama", dice el doctor Bensman. "Recuerde que usted ha estado tendida por ocho horas, y si usted salta enseguida, puede encontrarse con una espalda dolorida." Por lo tanto, antes de levantarse, estire lentamente los brazos sobre su cabeza y entonces pausadamente jale sus rodillas sobre el pecho, una a la vez. Cuando está lista para sentarse, dese la vuelta hacia el lado de la cama y use su brazo para ayudar a levantarse. Ponga las manos sobre las asentaderas e inclínese lentamente hacia atrás para extender su columna vertebral.

Camínelo. El caminar y otros ejercicios aeróbicos tales como nadar, andar en bicicleta y correr conservan sana a su espalda al condicionar todo su cuerpo. Hacen más fuertes los músculos para la postura de las asentaderas, piernas, la espalda y el abdomen. El ejercicio aeróbico puede ayudar a su cuerpo a secretar endorfinas, hormonas que atenúan el dolor. Trate de hacer un ejercicio aeróbico por 20 minutos diarios, tres veces por semana, dice el doctor Futch.

Mejórese con movimiento. Estar sentada causa más tensión en su espalda que estar parada. Si usted necesita estar sentada frente a su escritorio por largos períodos de tiempo o usted viaja por avión, tren o carro, cambie de posición a menudo y dele un descanso a su espalda levantándose y caminando más o menos cada hora, dice el doctor Augustus A. White III, profesor de cirugía ortopédica en la Escuela de Medicina de Harvard, en Boston y autor de *Your Aching Back* (Su espalda doliente).

Deje su equipaje ahí. En lugar de saltar del carro o avión y arrebatar sus maletas, tómese un par de minutos para estirarse, sugiere el doctor Bensman. Lentamente traiga sus rodillas hacia su pecho y gire suavemente los brazos alrededor para que los músculos tiesos se aflojen. Evite levantar con los brazos estirados y trate de mantener sus maletas cerca del cuerpo. Piense en adquirir un portaequipaje plegable con ruedas.

Arrodíllese, no se agache. Evite inclinarse desde la cintura para levantar algo. Eso crea tensión en la espalda y aumenta su riesgo de una lesión, dice el doctor Futch. En lugar de eso, use herramientas de mango largo y arrodíllese sobre un cojín o almohadilla para las rodillas cuando trabaje en el jardín, limpie con la aspiradora o efectúe otras actividades a "nivel bajo".

Deje que sus piernas hagan el esfuerzo. Si está levantando algo —no importa si pesa 5 libras ó 50 (2 ó 23 kilos)— flexione las rodillas, mantenga su espalda recta y levante con las piernas. "Las piernas son mucho más fuertes que la espalda y pueden cargar bastante más peso sin esforzarse", dice el doctor Futch.

Pruebe la carga. "¿Cuántas de nosotras hemos esforzado los músculos de la espalda cuando tratamos de levantar cajas que pensábamos que estaban vacías y en realidad estaban llenas de enciclopedias?", pregunta el doctor Sasso. Siempre toque la caja ligeramente con su pie o levántela apenitas con cuidado antes de realmente tratar de alzarla. Si está demasiado pesada para usted, pida ayuda.

Dele la espalda a las cosas pesadas. Si no puede encontrar a alguien que la ayude a mover un objeto pesado, trate esta maniobra como última instancia: si el objeto se encuentra a la altura de una mesa, dele la espalda para arrastrarlo o levantarlo. Usted también puede usar esta técnica para alzar ventanas. Esta posición reduce la presión que usted ejercería sobre su columna vertebral forzándola a usar las piernas para hacer palanca.

Enderécese. Mantener una buena postura es una de las mejores maneras de prevenir el dolor de espalda, dice el doctor Futch. Para mejorar su postura, trate esto. Párese contra una pared o siéntese en una silla del comedor, asegurándose de que sus hombros y asentaderas toquen la pared o silla. Deslice su brazo en el espacio entre la parte baja de su espalda y la pared o silla. Si hay algún punto donde su mano no está tocando ni su espalda ni la pared o silla, incline sus caderas para eliminar ese espacio extra. Mantenga esa posición mientras cuenta hasta 20 y se mira en el espejo para ver cómo se ve su postura. Trate de recordar cómo se siente, para que pueda mantener esa postura por el resto del día. Haga ese ejercicio una vez al día por tres semanas para asegurar que la buena postura se vuelve un hábito.

No taconee. Los tacones altos cambian su modo de andar, ponen un esfuerzo adicional sobre la parte baja de su espalda y afectan negativamente su postura, dice el doctor Bensman. "Los tacones altos no deberían ser parte de la vida diaria de una mujer. Deberían usarse sólo en ocasiones especiales. Durante la vida diaria normal, los tacones nunca deberían exceder una pulgada y media (3,8cm)", dice él. Si usted ocasionalmente usa tacones más altos que eso, úselos por no más de dos horas a la vez. Siempre tenga a la mano un par de zapatos de piso o tenis.

Revise su colchón. Su colchón debe proporcionar un soporte adecuado, conservarse plano y no hundirse en el medio. Por lo que si usted siente que está durmiendo en medio de un pan de *pita*, probablemente es hora de comprar un colchón nuevo, dice el doctor Sasso.

Enróllelo. Un rollo lumbar, una almohada redonda de espuma de caucho que se puede comprar en la mayoría de las tiendas de abastecimientos médicos, puede mantener la curvatura natural en el segmento dorsal de su columna vertebral y prevenir el dolor en la parte baja de su espalda, dice el doctor Hamilton Hall, director del Instituto Canadiense de la Espalda, en Toronto. Siempre que usted se siente, meta el rollo entre la parte baja de su espalda y la silla.

Vístase para la ocasión. Meterse dentro de un par de pantalones vaqueros (*jeans*) ajustados al cuerpo puede ser la gran cosa para su ego, pero también puede impedirle usar las biomecánicas apropiadas tales como flexionar sus rodillas, especialmente al levantar algo, dice el doctor White. Trate de usar ropa más suelta por un mes para ver si hay alguna diferencia.

No respalde a los cigarrillos. El fumar disminuye el flujo de la sangre a su espalda y puede debilitar los discos, dice el doctor Bensman. Así que si usted fuma, déjelo.

Tome su leche. Las mujeres entre los 30 y los 50 años de edad que hacen ejercicio regularmente y tienen dietas ricas en calcio tienen menos probabilidades más tarde en su vida de sufrir de dolor de espalda causado por osteoporosis, dice el doctor Bensman. La Asignación Dietética Recomendada de calcio para mujeres mayores de 25 años de edad es de 800 miligramos diarios. Eso es cerca del equivalente a un vaso de 8 onzas (237 ml) de leche descremada, una taza de yogur sin grasa y media taza de brócoli cocido por día. Otras buenas fuentes de calcio incluyen: salmón, sardinas, queso, suero de manteca, col rizada, brócoli, frijoles (habichuelas) pintos y almendras. Si usted no come bastantes alimentos ricos en calcio —y muchas mujeres no lo hacen— hable con su doctor acerca de suplementos.

Congélela. Ponga hielo en su espalda dolorida tan pronto como sea posible para reducir el dolor y la inflamación, dice el doctor Bensman. Envuelva una bolsa de hielo en la funda de una almohada o toalla (nunca ponga el hielo directamente sobre su piel) y colóquelo sobre el lugar que duele durante diez minutos por cada hora hasta que el dolor amaina.

Luego caliéntela. Una vez que el hielo alivia la inflamación —usualmente dentro de un período de 48 horas— usted puede empezar a usar calor. El calor aumenta el flujo de sangre a la herida, relaja tejidos y puede mejorar su movilidad, dice el doctor Bensman. Aplique un trapo templado —debe estar a aproximadamente la temperatura de la piel— a su espalda por 5 ó 10 minutos por cada hora, o dese una ducha tibia de 15 minutos o métase en una piscina (alberca) de hidromasaje.

Haga uso de los alivios que se compran sin receta. Si se toma una o dos tabletas de aspirina o *ibuprofen* cada cuatro a seis horas puede aliviar el dolor y reducir la inflamación, dice el doctor Bensman. Asegúrese de no exceder la dosis recomendada por el fabricante.

(continúa en la página 149)

Ocho ejercicios para minimizar el dolor de espalda

Si usted quiere un rendimiento grande para una inversión pequeña, trate estos ejercicios recomendados por la Academia Norteamericana de Cirujanos Ortopédicos. Fortalecer y estirar los músculos de su espalda, estómago, caderas y muslos, le ayudarán a mantener su espalda sintiéndose fuerte y flexible.

Confirme con su doctor antes de empezar cualquier programa de ejercicios.

Párese con su espalda contra una pared y sus pies separados al ancho de sus hombros. Deslícese hacia abajo hasta ponerse en cuclillas, con sus rodillas flexionadas a cerca de 90 grados. Mantenga esta posición mientras cuenta hasta cinco y deslícese hacia arriba sobre la pared. Repita cinco veces.

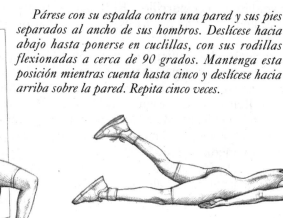

Acostada boca abajo, tensione los músculos de una pierna y levántela del piso. Mantenga esta posición contando hasta diez y regrese la pierna al piso. Repita con la otra pierna. Repita esto cinco veces con cada pierna.

Recuéstese boca arriba con los brazos a los lados. Levante una pierna del piso y manténgala así contando hasta diez. Regrésela al piso y levante la otra pierna. Repita esto cinco veces con cada pierna. Si esto es muy difícil, mantenga una rodilla flexionada al levantar la otra pierna.

Acuéstese boca arriba con la rodillas flexionadas y sus pies planos sobre el piso. Lentamente levante la cabeza y los hombros del piso y extienda ambas manos al frente hacia sus rodillas. Mantenga esa posición contando hasta diez. Acuéstese nuevamente y repita esto cinco veces.

Sosteniéndose del respaldo de una silla, levante una pierna hacia atrás. Mantenga sus rodillas derechas. Baje la pierna lentamente y repita con la otra pierna. Repita cinco veces con cada pierna.

Sobre el piso o sobre la cama, acuéstese boca arriba con sus rodillas flexionadas y sus pies planos. Levante ambas rodillas hacia su pecho. Ponga las dos manos abajo de sus rodillas y tire de sus rodillas ligeramente tan cerca de su pecho como sea posible. No levante la cabeza. Baje las piernas sin enderezarlas. Empiece con cinco repeticiones varias veces al día.

(continúa)

Ocho ejercicios para minimizar el dolor de espalda —continuado

Acuéstese boca abajo con las manos bajo sus hombros y sus codos flexionados. Empuje hacia arriba con sus brazos. Levante la mitad superior de su cuerpo tan alto como sea posible, dejando que sus caderas y piernas permanezcan planas sobre el piso o cama. Mantenga esta posición por uno o dos segundos. Repita diez veces varias veces al día.

Párese con sus pies ligeramente separados. Coloque sus manos en la región baja de la espalda. Manteniendo sus rodillas derechas, dóblese hacia atrás sobre la cintura tanto como sea posible y mantenga esa posición por uno o dos segundos.

Ponga sus pies en alto. Cuando un dolor pequeño en la espalda la ataca, acuéstese sobre el piso y ponga sus pies sobre una silla para que sus muslos estén a un ángulo de 90 grados con respecto a sus caderas, y sus pantorrillas descansen a un ángulo de 90 grados con respecto a sus muslos. Esta posición relaja músculos claves de la espalda y es una de las menos estresantes para su columna vertebral, dice el doctor White.

Manténgase en movimiento. Aunque antes se recomendaban descansos prolongados en cama para el dolor de espalda, los doctores creen ahora que cuanto más activa sea usted, más pronto se restablecerá. De hecho, dos semanas en cama debilita los músculos y la columna vertebral, y eso puede en realidad hacer más lento su restablecimiento y más probable que usted sufra una recaída, dice el doctor Hall. Así que no se quede en cama por más de dos días, y asegúrese de levantarse por lo menos una vez por hora para caminar o estirarse.

Busque alguien quien la manipule. Los quiroprácticos están ganando respeto en la comunidad médica, dice el doctor Bensman. Un análisis de 25 estudios de manipulación de la columna vertebral —el cuerpo y alma del tratamiento quiropráctico— encontró que esta manipulación sí proporciona por lo menos un alivio a corto plazo para dolores de espalda agudos sin complicaciones.

"Seguro, los quiroprácticos funcionan", dice el doctor Bensman. "Se están volviendo muy conocedores y están ofreciendo algunos beneficios reales." En un caso típico, un quiropráctico puede dar una serie de empujones con la base de sus manos a través del área problemática de su columna vertebral. Pida a su doctor que le recomiende un quiropráctico en su área.

Apriete el cinturón. Si usted sufre de dolor de espalda durante el embarazo, puede ser causado por una presión en la articulación sacroilíaca, que une la pelvis con la columna vertebral, dice el doctor Hall. Para aliviar ese dolor, que tiende a ocurrir más abajo en las asentaderas y se agrava al estar parada o caminar, use un cinturón alrededor de sus caderas, abajo de su embarazo, para estabilizar la pelvis. "Cuando mi mujer estaba embarazada, ella tenía ese tipo de dolor", dice el doctor Hall. "Le di un cinturón grande y ancho de uno de mis pantalones vaqueros (*jeans*). Ella sólo se ajustó eso, y fue bastante asombroso como alivió su dolor."

Obtenga una segunda opinión. Más de 400.000 cirugías, tales como fusión espinal y extirpación o destrucción de discos se realizan cada año para aliviar el dolor de espalda, según la Academia Americana de Cirujanos Ortopédicos. Sin embargo, un estudio de *Blue Cross y Blue Shield* encontró que casi el 13 por ciento de las operaciones de la columna vertebral se llevan a cabo por razones poco apropiadas. Obtenga por lo menos otra opinión cuando su doctor sugiere cirugía, dice el doctor White.

DROGODEPENDENCIA

Cómo aclarar la mente
y limpiar el cuerpo

Lo más probable es que usted no conozca a nadie que realmente trató de volverse adicta a las drogas. Pero la dependencia aparece sigilosamente, insidiosamente, una píldora o un cigarrillo de marihuana a la vez, hasta que una mujer debe enfrentar el problema con el cual ella nunca se imaginó que tendría que tratar.

Y a pesar de su reputación como un problema de las zonas urbanas deprimidas, el abuso de las drogas puede atacar en sus propios alrededores: la antigua compañera de cuarto en la universidad, que depende de los analgésicos desde que tuvo un accidente automovilístico hace tres años; el jefe exigente, que usa cocaína para ayudarle a soportar su horario de trabajo de 14 horas diarias.

Posiblemente, si no tenemos cuidado, hasta nosotras mismas.

"No cualquiera está en peligro de volverse drogodependiente", dice Joan Mathews Larson, Ph.D., directora del Centro de Recuperación de Salud, en Minneapolis, y autora de *Seven Weeks to Sobriety* (Siete semanas a la sobriedad). "Pero esto atraviesa todas las barreras. Usted ciertamente no tiene que ser una joven urbana pobre para volverse adicta a las drogas."

El uso de las drogas nos impone un costo brutal. Puede costarnos nuestro capital, nuestros trabajos, nuestras amistades, nuestros esposos, nuestra dignidad. Puede asolar y envejecer nuestros cuerpos. Puede hacernos dejar de comer u obligarnos a comer sin control. Puede hacernos abandonar el ejercicio o descuidar nuestra higiene. Podemos perder nuestra capacidad mental. La drogodependencia hasta puede ser fatal.

"No tiene que ser así", dice la doctora Larson. "Pero a menos que una persona decida hacer algo, lo más probable es que continúe deteriorándose. Las personas drogodependientes pueden caer desde muy alto."

Cómo llenar el vacío

Los estudios muestran lo extendido que se ha vuelto el problema de las drogas en el país. Un estudio de gran escala de residentes en cinco ciudades de los Estados Unidos mostró que al menos 1 entre 20 mujeres estadounidenses abusan o son dependientes de las drogas.

Y la drogodependencia es terriblemente cara. Los números de la Universidad de California en San Francisco, muestran que el uso de las drogas ilegales en los Estados Unidos cuesta casi $7.000 millones al año en tratamientos, pérdida de productividad y otros costos.

¿Por qué las personas se vuelven drogodependientes a pesar de los riesgos? Porque las drogas las hacen sentir bien —al menos al principio. "Las drogas llenan una necesidad en la vida de una persona", dice la doctora Larson. "La heroína, por ejemplo, puede ayudar a una persona a enfrentarse a su ansiedad natural. El alcohol actúa como un depresivo en la mayoría de las personas. Pero en otras, realmente las estimula. Compensa una deficiencia natural en algunos químicos del cerebro."

El alivio, sin embargo, siempre es pasajero. Al pasar el tiempo, el uso de las drogas interfiere con la producción de endorfinas, los químicos naturales del cuerpo para "sentirse bien". "Esto quiere decir que usted necesita usar más drogas para compensar la diferencia", dice el doctor Adam Lewenberg, un médico en la ciudad de Nueva York cuya práctica privada incluye el tratamiento de la adicción. "Se convierte en un ciclo donde usted ansía la droga más y más y eventualmente se vuelve dependiente de su uso."

Y no es sólo la cocaína, marihuana, heroína u otras drogas ilegales las que están causando el problema. Los doctores e investigadores han identificado muchísimas drogas de venta sin receta y con receta que causan dependencia, incluyendo los jarabes para la tos, las drogas para la ansiedad de la familia de la benzodiazepina, como por ejemplo el diazepam (*Valium*), y posiblemente aun el estrógeno tomado durante la terapia de reposición de hormonas.

Las mujeres, de hecho, tienen un riesgo más alto que los hombres de abusar de las drogas con receta tales como los tranquilizantes, sedantes y estimulantes simplemente porque se les dan a ellas más a seguido. También existen menos probabilidades de que ellas den a conocer su abuso, lo cual resulta en una drogodependencia más avanzada, dice la doctora Larson. "Más y más mujeres están admitiendo que tienen problemas. Eso se debe principalmente a que están teniendo dificultades en el trabajo", dice ella. "Pero las mujeres que no trabajan tienden a ser más reservadas acerca de sus problemas, y la drogodependencia puede progresar hasta volverse una condición más fuera de control."

Mientras que cualquiera puede volverse dependiente de las drogas, la herencia puede tener un papel importante. En su libro *The Good News about Drugs and Alcohol* (La buena noticia acerca de las drogas y el alcohol), el doctor Mark S. Gold estima que una en cada diez personas está predispuesta genéticamente a volverse drogodependiente. "No hay duda que la drogodependencia, como el alcoholismo, puede provenir de familia", dice la doctora Larson. Desafortunadamente, no podemos hacer pruebas para ello. Pero si usted sabe de alcohólicos o personas drogodependientes en su familia, debe ser extra cuidadosa."

El abuso de alcohol también aumenta sus probabilidades de volverse drogodependiente. Todos hemos oído acerca de cómo el alcohol es una "droga de acceso" que abre la puerta a mayor abuso de las drogas. Bueno, aquí está la prueba: el Instituto Nacional de Salud Mental entrevistó a más de 20.000 hombres y mujeres que viven en los Estados Unidos, mayores de 18 años de edad, de cinco localidades a través del país. Los investigadores encontraron que las mujeres que abusan del alcohol corren un riesgo seis veces mayor de también abusar de las drogas.

El mismo estudio encontró que si se tiene una historia de trastornos mentales también aumenta su riesgo. Las personas con trastornos tales como depresión pueden tener hasta 4,7 veces más probabilidades de abusar o volverse drogodependiente. Y aquellas con problemas de ansiedad como es el trastorno del pánico o el comportamiento obsesivo-compulsivo tienen 2,5 veces más probabilidades de volverse dependientes o abusar de las drogas.

Lo más importante para recordar acerca de la drogodependencia, dice la doctora Larson, es que le puede suceder a cualquiera. "No es algo de lo cual uno debe avergonzarse. No significa que usted tiene un defecto moral o de carácter", dice ella. "Nadie empieza con la intención de volverse drogadicto. Pero por una variedad de razones, muchas de ellas fuera del control de una persona, simplemente sucede. Y entonces usted tiene que enfrentar esto."

Ni siquiera hay que empezar

Definitivamente, la mejor manera de vencer la dependencia de las drogas es evitarla en primer lugar. Para ayudarle a no meterse en líos, considere estos consejos.

Conozca las señales de advertencia. "Cuando los pensamientos de una droga llenan su mente, usted tiene un problema", dice la doctora Larson. Si siente que no puede relajarse, ser feliz, irse a dormir o hacer nada en absoluto sin usar primero una droga, probablemente es tiempo de pedir ayuda.

Otras señales de problema incluyen mentir a los médicos para que le renueven las recetas, faltar al trabajo por usar las drogas sin control o por las resacas, atacar la cuenta de ahorros para pagar por las drogas y consistentemente renunciar a los alimentos, las amistades o los familiares para obtener y usar drogas.

Sacuda su árbol genealógico. Busque indicios de abuso de las drogas en su familia, ya que esto puede indicar que usted es más propensa a la dependencia. Incluya el alcoholismo en su búsqueda. Y no ignore cosas como los analgésicos del abuelo o el *Valium* de la Tía Sofía.

"Si usted encuentra señales de esto en su familia, sea extremadamente cuidadosa", dice la doctora Larson. "No experimente jamás con drogas, porque en su caso puede necesitar sólo una vez para enviciarse."

Resuelva los conflictos. Las personas usan las drogas para evitar tener que enfrentarse a los problemas como la ansiedad, el aburrimiento, la depresión, la frustración, las malas relaciones, la presión en el trabajo y el desempleo. "Encare estos problemas de frente", sugiere la doctora Larson. "Beber o tomar drogas para evitarlos no va a resolver nada. Solamente va a agregar otra capa más —la drogodependencia— a la mezcla."

Si usted está aburrida, encuentre un pasatiempo o haga algún trabajo voluntario. Si está teniendo dificultades en el trabajo o con su esposo, busque orientación. Cualquier cosa que usted haga, no acuda a las drogas para un alivio temporario, no importa qué tan atractivas suenen.

Siga lo que dice la etiqueta. Si su doctor le receta drogas, particularmente analgésicos y tranquilizantes, úselos exactamente en la manera en que le dijeron que lo hiciera. Y nunca trate de que le renueven la receta a menos que su doctor lo indique. "Las drogas con receta no actúan en su cuerpo en distinta manera a las drogas ilegales", dice el doctor Lewenberg. "En cierta manera, son más peligrosas porque están disponibles y son legales. Las personas que no pensarían en comprar cocaína no verían el mismo problema en usar mal una droga recetada. Pero deberían."

Cuando usted termine de tomar una droga, tire la botella. Si quedó algo, no la meta en el botiquín de las medicinas, porque si lo hace usted o alguien más puede estar tentado a usarla después, sin la aprobación de un médico.

Simplemente diga que no. Esta es una frase trillada, pero todavía suena a verdad. Evite las drogas ilegales. Porque para algunas personas, el uso de drogas "recreativas" puede conducir rápidamente a la dependencia. "Usted no puede volverse adicta a las drogas ilegales a menos que las use", dice el doctor Lewenberg.

Cuando usted necesita ayuda

Si usted cree que ya puede haber desarrollado una dependencia a las drogas, los expertos ofrecen estos consejos.

Busque ayuda. "Lo diré otra vez: no se avergüence", dice la doctora Larson. "Dígale a una amiga en quien confíe. Dígale a su esposo. Mientras más rápido se hace público, más rápidamente empezará usted a tratarlo de manera constructiva." No necesita usted anunciar su problema al mundo. Pero si hay aunque sea una sola persona que sepa y le importe, usted tendrá el apoyo que necesita para volver a andar por el buen camino.

Encuentre la fuerza en la unión. Los grupos de 12 pasos son de gran ayuda para algunas mujeres. Usted puede encontrar personas con problemas y esperanzas similares quienes pueden ayudarla a que logre atravesar por los caminos escollosos de la recuperación.

Empiece por localizar la organización local de Alcohólicos Anónimos, Cocaína anónima o Narcóticos anónimos. Llame o escriba a estos grupos para que le den mayor información:

• Narcotics Anonymous, World Services Office, P.O. Box 9999, Van Nuys, CA 91409

• National Clearinghouse for Alcohol and Drug Information, P.O. Box 2345, Rockville, MD 20847-2345

Haga ejercicio con moderación. Si usted ha estado abusando de las drogas, también ha estado abusando de su cuerpo. Puede ser que no haya hecho ejercicio durante meses, un factor que sólo puede aumentar la depresión o la ansiedad.

Así que empiece a hacer ejercicio. Comience con ejercicio moderado; lo mejor es caminar por unos 20 minutos diarios, por lo menos tres veces por semana. No es buena idea hacer ejercicio muy enérgico al principio, según el doctor Lewenberg. Usted probablemente ahora no se encuentra en su mejor forma y fácilmente podría lesionarse o desanimarse. Y también es posible volverse adicta al ejercicio, ya que estimula la producción de endorfinas. "No es un mal trueque realmente —drogas por ejercicio", dice el doctor Lewenberg. "Pero la idea es regresar su cuerpo a la normalidad lentamente."

Coma correctamente. Las drogas hacen cosas extrañas con su apetito. Las personas dependientes de la marihuana, por ejemplo, son propensas a la obesidad y a comer demasiado. Y el abuso de la cocaína puede llevar a la desnutrición y aun a los desórdenes de comer como la anorexia nerviosa. "Cuando usted depende de las drogas, el comer bien es rara vez una prioridad", dice la doctora Larson.

Trate de comer una dieta balanceada, sea que se sienta con ganas de comer o no. Reemplace los dulces por las frutas y verduras. "El alimentar su cuerpo y su cerebro con lo que precisa es un primer paso necesario para la recuperación", dice la doctora Larson.

Considere un tratamiento. Los centros de recuperación para pacientes hospitalizados y pacientes ambulantes ofrecen a la gente la oportunidad de destoxificar sus cuerpos al mismo tiempo que tratan las causas subyacentes de sus drogodependencias. "Cuando hay adicción, hay depresión", dice el doctor Lewenberg. "No es suficiente cortar en seco y no tratar los otros problemas." El programa del doctor Lewenberg ha incluido terapia de drogas no adictivas para manejar la depresión y aun electroacupuntura, la cual según él dice ayuda a estimular la producción de endorfinas y a hacer los medicamentos más efectivos.

Muchos empleadores y compañías de seguros cubrirán el costo de centros de recuperación.

ENDOMETRIOSIS

No se dé por vencida

La endometriosis siempre ha hecho que Allison McCormick con sus 35 años de edad se sienta mayor de lo que realmente es.

Cuando era una adolescente, la enfermedad le causó un dolor intenso y crónico que hizo que muchas de las actividades que ella anhelaba hacer, como viajar y correr distancias largas, fueran una prohibición. "No le permite a usted hacer las cosas que la gente de su edad haría", dice ella.

Cuando tenía veinte y tantos años de edad, McCormick, una asociada de investigación clínica en Aliso Viejo, California, trató de quedar embarazada, pero debido a la endometriosis ella era estéril. Entonces, a los 25 años de edad, le hicieron una histerectomía para parar el dolor y el avance de la enfermedad. El no tener un niño ha sido el punto más doloroso con el cual tratar, dice ella. Asimismo, la histerectomía la lanzó a una menopausia prematura. "Ya ni se diga de envejecer", dice.

Sufrir de endometriosis la hizo "sentirse muy diferente. Uno tiene que preocuparse de su salud todo el tiempo. Otras personas de mi edad no tenían que hacer eso", dice McCormick. "Yo me perdí una gran cantidad de años, una gran cantidad de cosas."

El dolor que agota a las mujeres

La endometriosis es una enfermedad crónica y debilitante que afecta a cinco millones de mujeres estadounidenses en la edad reproductiva. Es causada cuando un tejido similar al del revestimiento del útero, llamado tejido endometrial, crece fuera de la cavidad uterina. Esto puede ser doloroso para las mujeres, porque el tejido rebelde se comporta como un tejido uterino normal —puede causar calambres, sangrado y molestias antes y durante el período de una mujer.

Si crece en el intestino delgado o grueso, puede causar presión y dolor cuando una mujer va al baño. Y si se localiza en el área pélvica, puede causar molestias durante las relaciones sexuales. Para algunas mujeres, el dolor es leve o inexistente. Pero para otras, es insoportable —lo que algunas describen como una cuchillada o quemadura.

El dolor de la endometriosis muchas veces agota a las mujeres, dice Nancy Petersen, R.N., directora del Centro de Tratamiento de la Endometriosis del Centro Médico St. Charles, en Bend, Oregon, dejándolas con muy poca energía o capacidad para realizar las actividades que quieren y necesitan hacer.

"Yo creo que ellas se debilitan mucho por el intenso dolor crónico al que tienen que enfrentarse. La mayoría de ellas sufren de una fatiga considerable", dice Petersen. Muchas mujeres con endometriosis están "luchando, realmente, para vivir sus vidas. Tienen que realmente esforzarse", dice ella. Y cuando no pueden participar completamente, muchas veces quedan con una sensación de soledad y aislamiento.

El tema de los niños

Para las mujeres que quieren niños, el tener endometriosis puede representar un golpe particularmente fuerte, porque las puede hacer estériles. (De hecho, los problemas de fertilidad pueden ser los primeros indicios de que una mujer tiene la enfermedad). A menudo los tejidos endometriales mal colocados se adhieren a los ovarios y a las trompas de falopio uniéndose unos con otros y con las paredes de la pelvis haciendo que la fertilización sea imposible, dice la doctora Paula Bernstein, Ph.D., médica de cabecera en el Centro Médico Cedros del Sinaí, en Los Ángeles. "Debido a que todo está pegado a todo lo demás, los tubos no tienen la movilidad para recoger el óvulo" y hacerlo que se mueva correctamente para abajo hacia el útero, dice ella.

Si usted tiene endometriosis, es posible que no sepa si su fertilidad ha sido afectada hasta que no trate de quedar embarazada. Y mientras más tiempo usted espera, más tiempo tiene la enfermedad para progresar. A menudo muchas mujeres que tienen endometriosis se encuentran tratando de concebir antes de lo que hubieran preferido. "Hay mucha ansiedad al respecto", dice la doctora Deborah A. Metzger, Ph.D., directora del Centro de Endometriosis y Dolor Pélvico en el Centro de Salud de la Universidad de Connecticut, en Farmington. "Enfrentarse a la ansiedad puede ser difícil. A menudo las mujeres sienten que sus opciones están limitadas."

Lo que su doctor puede hacer

Los médicos diagnostican la endometriosis a través de un procedimiento quirúrgico llamado laparoscopía. Es la única manera de saber con certeza si usted tiene la enfermedad.

El procedimiento consiste en insertar un laparoscopio, un tubo de metal iluminado que tiene algo de aumento, a través de su ombligo y dentro de la cavidad pélvica, donde los médicos buscan las señales reveladoras de la enfermedad. Los médicos también pueden usar el mismo procedimiento para extirpar el tejido endometrial que se encuentra fuera de lugar.

La cirugía no es la única opción para tratar la endometriosis, aunque es muy efectiva para muchas mujeres. Otras opciones incluyen tratamiento con medicamentos tales como danazol (*Danocrine*) o agonistas GnRH, un tipo de drogas sintéticas casi idénticas a la hormona natural del cerebro que estimula la secreción de la hormona gonadotropina, o GnRH. Tanto el danazol como los agonistas GnRH evitan la ovulación y menstruación. Reducen el dolor de la endometriosis al detener el flujo menstrual.

Pero tienen sus inconvenientes.

El danazol tiene una gran cantidad de efectos secundarios. "Aquellos que las mujeres encuentran más difíciles de aceptar son el aumento de peso, algunos cambios en el estado de ánimo y a menudo calambres en los músculos, así como algunos sofocos y un poco de acné o cutis grasoso. Esas son las quejas más comunes", dice el doctor G. David Adamson, profesor clínico asociado en la Escuela de Medicina de la Universidad de Stanford, California, y director del Instituto de Fertilidad y Salud Reproductora de California del Norte, en Palo Alto.

Lo que las mujeres encuentran más inquietante, dice el doctor Adamson, es el aumento de peso. Las mujeres normalmente aumentan entre 8 y 12 libras (3,6 y 5,5 kg) mientras están tomando el danazol, dice. La mayor parte de este peso se pierde cuando una mujer deja de tomar esta droga, pero puede ser que ella conserve dos a tres libras (0,9 a 1,4 kg) adicionales aun después de dejar de tomarla.

El danazol también puede cambiar el perfil del colesterol de una mujer en manera que pueden no ser beneficiosas para el corazón, dice el doctor Adamson. El colesterol tipo lipoproteína de baja densidad (o *LDL* por sus siglas en inglés), el tipo malo, tiende a subir. "Intuitivamente, eso no parece ser favorable, y potencialmente puede ser dañino", dice el doctor Adamson. Pero no hay datos que digan que tomar danazol aumentará las probabilidades de una enfermedad del corazón. "Esa conexión no se ha hecho", dice él.

Los agonistas GnRH también tienen efectos envejecedores. "Los agonistas GnRH crean un estado de menopausia", dice el doctor Adamson. La menopausia es temporal y reversible, durando únicamente mientras la mujer está tomando los agonistas, pero no obstante puede ser difícil. El mayor efecto secundario son los sofocos, dice el doctor Adamson, y tienen la tendencia a ser más severos con los agonistas GnRH que con el danazol. En un estudio, el 90 por ciento de las mujeres que tomaban el agonista GnRH llamado *nafarelin* (*Synarel*) tuvo sofocos, comparado con el 68 por ciento de las mujeres que tomaban danazol. Para contrarrestar los sofocos, a menudo se les da a las mujeres otra droga, una forma de progestina llamada *norethindrone* (como es el *Nor-Q.D.*), dice el doctor Adamson.

Las mujeres que están tomando los agonistas GnRH a menudo son más irritables y tienen más dolores de cabeza que normalmente. Para las propensas a los dolores de cabeza esto puede ser un golpe bajo: usted probablemente va a tener más cuando tome los agonistas GnRH, dice el doctor Adamson.

Y como si eso no fuera suficiente, los agonistas GnRH también pueden causar pérdida ósea, razón por la cual los doctores no los recetan a las mujeres con riesgo de osteoporosis. Las mujeres tienden a perder de 6 a 8 por ciento de su masa ósea mientras están tomando estas drogas, y por ello es que los agonistas GnRH son sólo una solución a corto plazo para la endometriosis. No deberían tomarse por más de seis meses, dice el doctor Adamson. Una vez que las drogas se suspenden, la mayoría de las mujeres recuperan su hueso en 12 a 18 meses. Si usted tiene una densidad ósea normal cuando empieza a tomar estas drogas, no deberían ponerla en ningún riesgo de tener problemas con los huesos más adelante, dice el doctor Adamson. Pero si usted ya empezó a perder hueso como resultado de la osteoporosis, tiene muy poco calcio o algún otro problema con los huesos, los agonistas GnRH pueden no ser una opción para usted.

Histerectomía: "la cura" polémica

Por mucho, la histerectomía es el tratamiento más discutible para la endometriosis. Detiene a la enfermedad porque el útero, donde la enfermedad empieza y se desarrolla, se extirpa. Algunas veces también se extirpan los ovarios, poniendo a la mujer en un estado de menopausia prematura.

La endometriosis es la segunda razón más común por la cual las histerectomías se llevan a cabo en las mujeres que se encuentran entre los 25 y los 44 años de edad. (Para las mujeres entre los 25 y los 34 años de edad, el sangrado intenso y las complicaciones obstétricas ocupan en conjunto el primer lugar, y para las mujeres entre los 35 y los 44 años de edad, los fibromas son la razón número uno). En 1992, se realizaron 335.000 histerectomías a mujeres menores de los 45 años de edad.

Cuando se trata del envejecimiento, nada puede provocarlo más abruptamente que una histerectomía en la cual se remueven los ovarios. En el caso de las mujeres más jóvenes, hacer que les extirpen el útero y los ovarios pone fin a su capacidad de tener niños. Ellas también experimentan los síntomas comunes que las mujeres padecen en la menopausia: sofocos, cambios de estado de ánimo, aumento de peso. Y aunque la terapia de reposición de hormonas puede aliviar algunos de estos problemas, las mujeres todavía tienen que preocuparse del impacto físico y emocional del cambio de vida años o aun décadas antes de tiempo.

El factor de envejecimiento es sólo parte de la razón por la cual la histerectomía es tan discutible como tratamiento para la endometriosis. En algunos casos, el dolor que la cirugía supuestamente iba a aliviar puede no desaparecer, o puede regresar. Aproximadamente el 8 por ciento de las mujeres todavía experimenta dolor después de la operación, dice el doctor Adamson. Para las mujeres que optan por conservar sus ovarios, el estrógeno puede continuar estimulando la enfermedad, causando dolor. A veces el tejido endometrial se encuentra en otros órganos, tales como el intestino, dejando algo de la enfermedad en el cuerpo cuando se extirpa el útero. También, los niveles bajos de estrógeno aún en el cuerpo después de una histerectomía total, pueden ser suficientes para estimular a que el tejido endometrial que quedó ocasione una acción dolorosa, esto quiere decir que la histerectomía no es una cura segura.

Para muchas mujeres con síntomas serios, informa el doctor Adamson, la cirugía trae consigo un bienvenido alivio. Otras lamentan la decisión. Así que esto no es nada que pueda tomarse a la ligera. "Cada mujer necesita estudiar bien las consecuencias antes de pensar en la cirugía", dice él.

Lo que usted puede hacer

No hay manera de prevenir la endometriosis. Pero si usted la tiene, hay pasos que usted puede tomar para evitar que el dolor y la fatiga la agoten.

Aprenda a aceptar. "Aceptarla y hablar acerca de ella como una enfermedad crónica es realmente importante", dice la doctora Metzger. Muchas veces, las mujeres van de doctor en doctor con la esperanza de encontrar la cura mágica, dice ella. Entonces, cuando el dolor regresa, se desilusionan.

"Yo les digo 'miren, esta es una enfermedad crónica' ", dice la doctora Metzger. " 'Yo no voy a ser capaz de curarla. Voy a ayudarle, no obstante, a abordarla, y también podemos reducir significativamente su dolor.' " Cuando las mujeres escuchan esto, a menudo se dan cuenta de que están escuchando la verdad acerca de su enfermedad, y comprenden que ellas pueden y necesitan empezar a controlarla, dice.

Es importante reconocer que usted tiene endometriosis y darse cuenta de que se trata de una enfermedad crónica, asiente McCormick. "Por bastante tiempo, yo no aceptaba el hecho de que tenía un padecimiento crónico. Sólo cuando usted lo acepta, puede tratarlo." Una vez que usted lo hace, experimente con algunas técnicas para salir adelante, las cuales le proporcionarán una sensación de control sobre la endometriosis, aconseja ella. "Ponga algo de poder otra vez en sus manos." Algunas cosas que funcionan para ella, dice, son el ejercicio y los baños calientes.

Suba el calor. Aplicar una compresa de calor o una botella de agua caliente, o tomar un baño caliente, puede ayudar aliviar el dolor de la endometriosis, dice McCormick. El dolor acalambrante que las mujeres sienten es causado por las contracciones del tejido endometrial, y el calor puede ayudarla a interrumpir el ciclo de espasmos dolorosos.

Haga algo de ejercicio. Muchas mujeres encuentran que hacer ejercicio ayuda a controlar y a aliviar el dolor. Esto funciona, dicen los expertos, porque el ejercicio secreta endorfinas, los analgésicos naturales del cuerpo. La señora McCormick dice que mientras que correr le causa mucho dolor, levantar pesas y andar en bicicleta le proporcionan alivio. Caminar por lo menos 20 minutos al día también le puede ayudar, dicen los expertos. No hay receta, dicen los médicos, así que descubra qué es lo que funciona para usted.

Pruebe medicamentos. Los medicamentos sin receta que contienen ibuprofen pueden proporcionar alivio a las mujeres con las formas leves de la enfermedad, dice la doctora Bernstein. El ibuprofen opera contra las substancias en su cuerpo, llamadas prostaglandinas, que contribuyen a los calambres menstruales. Si un medicamento sin receta no es suficiente, puede pedirle a su médico una droga con receta como es el naproxen (*Anaprox*), el ibuprofen (*Motrin*), el piroxicam (*Feldene*) o el ácido mefenámico (*Ponstel*). Todos estos contienen agentes antiinflamatorios no esteroides que proporcionan alivio al dolor inhibiendo la síntesis de las prostaglandinas.

Pruebe la píldora anticonceptiva. Muchas mujeres logran alivio para el dolor tomando dosis bajas de anticonceptivos orales, dice la doctora Bernstein. La píldora anticonceptiva alivia algo de las molestias del acalambrado menstrual al disminuir el flujo menstrual. Pregunte a su doctor acerca de esto.

Estírese y reduzca el estrés. El yoga es una alternativa para las mujeres cuya endometriosis es tan grave que el ejercicio aeróbico es imposible, dice Petersen. La ayuda a mejorar su tono muscular y flexibilidad así como reducir el estrés, dice. Localice libros y clases que la puedan ayudar a empezar con éste.

Cuide su dieta. Reducir la cantidad de azúcar refinado y cafeína en su dieta evitará que el azúcar en su sangre fluctúe sin control, y la mantendrá calmada para que le sea más fácil sobrellevar su dolor, dice la doctora Metzger.

Enfóquese en la intimidad. Si su enfermedad hace las relaciones sexuales dolorosas en ciertos momentos, recuerde que hay otras formas de tener intimidad, dicen los expertos. Concéntrese en tocar, abrazar, besar y el sexo oral, sugiere una mujer con la enfermedad. Y recuerde que aunque una posición puede ser dolorosa en las relaciones sexuales, otra puede no serlo, así que trate de experimentar y explorar las distintas posibilidades con su compañero.

Pruebe la acupuntura. Algunas mujeres encuentran que la acupuntura les ayuda a sobrellevar la endometriosis, dice la doctora Metzger. Esta antigua técnica consiste en insertar agujas en puntos de la piel que están asociados con el alivio del dolor.

Trata de buscar apoyo. Las mujeres con endometriosis seguido encuentran que ayuda el hablar con otras mujeres que sufren de la enfermedad. Para más información acerca de la enfermedad y los grupos de apoyo, póngase en contacto con la Endometriosis Association (Asociación de la Endometriosis), escribiendo a 8585 North 76th Place, Milwaukee, WI 53223. Si no hay grupos de apoyo cerca suyo, McCormick sugiere que usted empiece uno por su cuenta.

ENFERMEDAD DEL CORAZÓN

Mientras más pronto actúe, mejor

Hay un mito que dice que la enfermedad del corazón es un problema de los hombres. Muchas mujeres así lo creen —y también muchos de sus doctores. Pero el mito no podría estar más equivocado.

Es cierto, los ataques al corazón les suceden por lo general a las mujeres más tarde en su vida, un promedio de siete a diez años después que a los hombres. Pero cuando pegan, pegan con fuerza. La enfermedad del corazón mata más mujeres que ninguna otra —casi seis veces más que el cáncer de mama y nueve veces más que el cáncer del pulmón.

La conexión con la menopausia

Cuando se trata de las mujeres y las enfermedades del corazón, la edad es un factor clave. Las posibilidades de desarrollar enfermedades del corazón aumentan constantemente después de la menopausia.

La razón supuesta: el estrógeno. A lo largo de la mayor parte de la vida de una mujer, esta hormona protege al corazón y a las arterias coronarias, defendiéndolas contra los depósitos grasosos que pueden incrustarse en las paredes arteriales y bloquear el torrente sanguíneo haciéndola más vulnerable a un ataque al corazón.

"Ahora estamos comenzando a pensar que el efecto protector del estrógeno está relacionado con su influencia en el nivel de la lipoproteína de alta densidad (o *HDL*, por sus siglas en inglés) del colesterol", dice el doctor Richard H.

Si sucede lo peor

Algunas veces aun los esfuerzos más cuidadosos para la prevención simplemente no son suficientes. Si usted empieza a sentir las señales de advertencia de un ataque al corazón —tal como presión o una sensación de opresión en el pecho, dolor moviéndose hacia los hombros, los brazos o el cuello, o la falta de aliento y náusea— necesita reaccionar rápidamente.

Debido a que las mujeres tienden a pensar que los ataques al corazón son algo que sólo sus esposos, padres o hermanos sufren, puede ser que no reaccionemos tan rápidamente a nuestros propios síntomas. Pero como la Asociación del Corazón de los Estados Unidos advierte: "¡La demora puede ser fatal!"

Las drogas para disolver coágulos llamadas trombolíticas son administradas en la sala de urgencia y pueden restablecer el flujo sanguíneo, minimizando de esa forma un daño al músculo del corazón.

Pero el tiempo es crucial. "Mientras más tarde usted llega a la sala de urgencia, es menos probable que una droga trombolítica sea efectiva", dice el doctor Gerald Pohost, director de la División de Enfermedad Cardiovascular en la Escuela de Medicina de la Universidad de Alabama, en Birmingham. "Las primeras dos horas son el mejor momento, pero al pasar el tiempo, la posibilidad de éxito de estas drogas disminuye."

Helfant, vicepresidente de medicina y director del Programa de Entrenamiento de Cardiología del Centro Médico de la Universidad de California, Irvine y autor de *Women, Take Heart* (Mujeres, anímense). "Existe evidencia creciente que el estrógeno aumenta la cantidad de este colesterol bueno, el cual ahora sabemos que protege las arterias de la infiltración de depósitos grasosos." Al mismo tiempo, el estrógeno puede hacer que su lipoproteína de baja densidad (o *LDL*, por sus siglas en inglés) caiga vertiginosamente que es justamente lo que usted quiere que ocurra.

Después de la menopausia, por supuesto, esta protección se agota rápidamente. Al reducirse el estrógeno natural producido en su cuerpo, usted se queda con un arma menos en su arsenal para combatir el ataque de la enfermedad del corazón. Alrededor de los 45 años de edad, su nivel de colesterol LDL por lo general empezará a subir, junto con su cuenta total de colesterol. Al suceder esto, también se elevará su riesgo de una enfermedad del corazón.

Esto puede sonar desalentador. Pero no tiene por qué resignarse a una vida de ansiedad. Cierto, usted no puede cambiar su edad o mantener su estrógeno natural fluyendo, aunque la investigación indica que la terapia de reposición de hormonas (una combinación de estrógeno y progestina) que se da a las mujeres en la menopausia puede tener un efecto protector. Tampoco puede usted cambiar una tendencia heredada a enfermedades del corazón. Pero eso no quiere decir que no hay otros factores de riesgo que usted sí puede cambiar.

Renovarse es vivir

La enfermedad del corazón no sucede de la noche a la mañana. La mayoría de las enfermedades del corazón son el resultado de un estrechamiento de las arterias coronarias durante décadas, conocido como arteriosclerosis. ¿Qué hace que las arterias se estrechen? En su mayor parte, es la forma en que nosotras vivimos nuestras vidas. En algunos otros países, donde los estilos de vida son más sencillos, las arterias están saludables y completamente abiertas, aun en las personas mayores de edad.

La noticia alentadora es muy directa: el progreso de una enfermedad del corazón puede hacerse más lento, y en algunos casos aun invertirse, sin drogas o cirugía. Pero no piense que usted tiene que ir a los extremos o tener una voluntad de acero para lograrlo. "Aun los cambios moderados pueden lograr bastante", aconseja el doctor Helfant. "Usted no tiene que ser una fanática o ser perfecta para influir en su salud."

Veamos algunas de las estrategias que pueden conservar a su corazón bombeando como si hubiera heredado una o dos décadas adicionales de vida.

Deje los cigarrillos, ya. Muy bien, posiblemente usted ha estado fumando por años e incluso ha tratado de dejarlo aunque sin suerte. Pero muchas ex-fumadoras no tuvieron éxito en dejar de fumar hasta después de su segundo, tercero o aun sexto intento. Así que no se dé por vencida.

¿Por qué no? Cuando usted fuma, sus vasos sanguíneos se contraen. Eso pone un esfuerzo adicional en su corazón. Pero eso no es todo. El humo del cigarrillo obliga a su corazón a latir más rápidamente y esto eleva su presión arterial.

El resultado es tan cruel como suena: según la Asociación del Corazón de los Estados Unidos, los cigarrillos causan directamente casi una quinta parte de todas las muertes por enfermedades del corazón.

Si usted fuma y toma anticonceptivos orales, está buscándose problemas. Juntos, la hacen a usted hasta 39 veces más propensa a sufrir un ataque al corazón que una mujer que no usa ni uno ni el otro.

Corte su colesterol. Cualquiera necesita al menos algo de esta substancia en su cuerpo para que éste realice algunas funciones esenciales. Pero el caso es que su propio hígado produce todo el colesterol que su cuerpo necesita.

Si su dieta tiende demasiado a los alimentos con alto contenido de grasa y colesterol, su lectura total de colesterol en la sangre puede llegar hasta los 240 miligramos por decilitro de sangre (mg/dl) o más, un nivel peligroso que doblará sus posibilidades de una enfermedad del corazón. Al escoger alimentos con menos grasa puede retomar el control y ponerse en camino a un corazón más saludable —quizás aun invirtiendo el sentido de la arteriosclerosis. Su meta debe ser un total de colesterol menor de 200 mg/dl.

Cuando el doctor Dean Ornish, presidente y director del Instituto de Investigación de Medicina Preventiva, en Sausalito, California, puso a varias personas en un programa extensivo de estilo de vida que incluía una dieta muy baja en grasas, ejercicio moderado, cesación de fumar y entrenamiento para el manejo del estrés, el 82 por ciento de ellas después de un año experimentaron una regresión significante de los depósitos grasosos que habían obstruido sus arterias coronarias.

Pero no piense que para prevenir una enfermedad del corazón usted necesita adoptar una dieta de privación que sólo esté un paso más arriba de una huelga de hambre. "Nadie tuvo un ataque al corazón provocado por un bistec o un pedazo de pastel (de fruta)", dice el doctor Helfant. "Estamos hablando acerca de un cambio total del estilo de vida y no preocupándonos por un desliz ocasional." La gracia está en ajustarse a las recomendaciones de limitar el consumo de grasa a no más del 25 por ciento de las calorías por un largo plazo.

¿Es usted una manzana o una pera?

En la canasta de frutas, las peras tienden a envejecer algo más rápido que las manzanas. Pero cuando se trata de su corazón —y si "peras" y "manzanas" se usan para describir las diferentes formas de cuerpo— las peras definitivamente envejecen más lentamente.

Afortunadamente, la mayoría de las mujeres obesas tienden a estar formadas como peras (con su peso adicional alrededor de las caderas) más que como manzanas (con su grasa metida en la zona central). Pero ese no es siempre el caso, especialmente en las mujeres después de la menopausia. Los estudios claramente muestran que una forma de manzana crea un riesgo mayor de ataque al corazón (así como de diabetes, derrame cerebral y presión arterial alta).

¿Por qué es tan peligrosa la pancita? Una teoría es que la grasa abdominal se convierte más fácilmente en colesterol.

No importa cuál es finalmente la causa, haga un esfuerzo para recortar el tamaño de su propia "manzana" perdiendo algunas de esas libras adicionales. Aquí hay una guía para que usted tenga en mente: para reducir su riesgo, la medida de su cintura no debería ser más del 80 por ciento de la medida de sus caderas.

Controle sus triglicéridos. Como si el colesterol no fuera suficiente para preocuparse, usted y su doctor también deben vigilar sus triglicéridos. Estos son un tipo de grasa en el torrente sanguíneo, y aunque parece que desempeñan un papel en la enfermedad del corazón, su papel exacto en ese proceso todavía no está tan claro como el vínculo entre el colesterol y los problemas del corazón.

Muchos expertos dicen que un nivel de triglicéridos arriba de los 200 mg/dl debería verse como una señal de advertencia. ¿Cuál es la mejor manera de atenuar sus triglicéridos? Ejercicio regular, dice Peter Wood, Ph.D., profesor emérito de medicina y director asociado del Centro para Investigación en la Prevención de Enfermedades de la Universidad de Stanford, en Palo Alto, California.

Conserve su peso ideal. Aunque estamos en un país que parece estar obsesionado con la delgadez, a muchas de nosotras no se nos podrían tomar por desnutridas. Cerca de 19 millones de mujeres estadounidenses están un poco más que rellenitas (pasadas de su peso deseado por aproximadamente un 20 por ciento o más). Es un poco como jugar a la ruleta rusa con sus corazones. En el Estudio de la Salud de Enfermeras en la Escuela de Medicina de Harvard, el 40 por ciento de los casos de enfermedad del corazón fueron atribuidos al exceso de peso acumulado.

Por lo tanto, ya sea que usted considere o no que la gordura es poco atractiva, es definitivamente peligrosa para su salud. "Si usted es obesa, el corazón tiene que trabajar más para mover nutrientes a las células adicionales en su cuerpo", dice el doctor James Martin, médico familiar con el Instituto para la Salud de la Familia Urbana, en el Centro Médico Beth Israel, en la ciudad de Nueva York. Ese esfuerzo adicional para el corazón puede ser particularmente preocupante si usted ya tiene otros factores de riesgo que pueden contribuir a una enfermedad del corazón, como son el colesterol alto o la presión arterial alta. Fíjese algunas metas para deshacerse de las libras de más al depender más de los alimentos con bajo contenido de grasa y haciendo más ejercicio.

Sude un poco. Seguro que es tentador tirar los zapatos de ejercicio, cancelar su membresía en el gimnasio y pasar cada fin de semana atrincherada como Gibraltar enfrente del televisor o acampada en la playa con su novela bestséller. Si esa es su idea del paraíso, no es usted la única —pero está pagando un precio. De hecho, casi el 60 por ciento de las mujeres estadounidenses no hace ningún ejercicio, una elección de estilo de vida que aumenta enormemente su riesgo de un ataque al corazón.

El ejercicio puede hacer más por usted que simplemente hacerla tomar un poco de aire fresco y sentirse mas vigorizada. "Fortalece el músculo del corazón", dice el doctor Wood. "Con ejercicio regular, el corazón se vuelve una bomba más eficiente. Como resultado, el ritmo del corazón se hace más lento para una cantidad determinada de esfuerzo." Cada latido es más eficiente, dice él, y de esa manera el corazón no tiene que trabajar tanto como sería si usted no estuviera en forma.

El ejercicio es particularmente importante si está tratando de perder peso. "Cuando las mujeres pierden peso, sus niveles de colesterol HDL tienden a disminuir", advierte el doctor Robert Rosenson, director del Centro Preventivo de Cardiología en el Centro Médico Rush-Presbyterian-St. Luke, en Chicago. "Para mantener sus HDLs al mismo nivel o incluso producir un ligero aumento, usted necesita hacer ejercicio mientras que está perdiendo peso a través de una dieta."

Rebaje su presión arterial. La presión arterial alta es llamada la asesina silenciosa, ya que calladita hace un trabajo siniestro que pone tanto esfuerzo adicional en el corazón y las arterias que al final puede provocar un ataque al corazón (ya no se diga un derrame cerebral o un fallo renal).

Pero al rebajar su presión arterial alta —lo cual usted puede lograr reduciendo el sodio en su dieta, perdiendo peso, haciendo ejercicio y (si es necesario) tomando uno de los tantos medicamentos disponibles— usted le puede dar un descanso a su corazón. Aquí hay algunas estadísticas alentadoras: por cada punto que logre bajar en su presión diastólica de la sangre (el número bajo), usted puede reducir su riesgo de un ataque al corazón en un 2 a 3 por ciento. Y con la terapia adecuada, no es raro para las personas con alta presión arterial bajar sus lecturas diastólicas en 20 puntos o más.

Considere la aspirina. Puede que no sea la "fuente de la juventud", pero la droga que puede mantener a su corazón vital puede estar tan cerca como el botiquín de las medicinas en su baño. La aspirina, esa pequeña píldora blanca de la cual ha dependido una cantidad enorme de veces para quitar los dolores de cabeza y otros dolores leves, parece que es también una salvadora de corazones.

Nuevamente, el Estudio de la Salud de las Enfermeras nos ha dado información crucial. Por un período de seis años, las mujeres que tomaron de una a seis tabletas de aspirina por semana tuvieron cerca de 32 por ciento menos probabilidades de tener un primer ataque al corazón comparado con las mujeres que no tomaron aspirina. Las mujeres mayores de 50 años de edad parece que obtienen la mayor protección. Pero, particularmente si usted tiene tendencia a los problemas de sangramiento, consulte con su doctor antes de autorecetarse la aspirina, ya que es un medicamento que inhibe la coagulación de sangre en su cuerpo.

Tome sus vitaminas. Por décadas, los doctores tradicionales solían considerar a los suplementos vitamínicos como algo relacionado con el curanderismo. Pero ya no más. Un estudio publicado por la *New England Journal of Medicine* (La Revista de Medicina de Nueva Inglaterra) involucrando a más de 87.000 mujeres concluyó que las mujeres que tomaron suplementos de vitamina E por más de dos años tuvieron un 40 por ciento menos riesgo de una enfermedad seria del corazón que aquellas que no tomaron los suplementos.

¿Cuál es el secreto de la vitamina E? Esta vitamina es un antioxidante, lo que quiere decir que protege a las células de moléculas maliciosas llamadas radicales libres las cuales ocasionan un proceso llamado oxidación, que puede contribuir a la obstrucción de las arterias.

"Yo les estoy dando vitamina E a mis pacientes en dosis normales que no representan riesgos", dice la doctora Marianne J. Legato, autora de *The Female Heart* (El corazón femenino) y profesora asociada de medicina clínica en el Colegio de Médicos y Cirujanos de la Universidad de Columbia, en la ciudad de Nueva York. La doctora Legato aconseja suplementos de 400 UI de vitamina E, junto con 1.500 miligramos de vitamina C y 6 miligramos de betacaroteno, estos dos últimos también son antioxidantes. Ella también aconseja 1.500 miligramos de calcio suplementario, el cual según han mostrado los estudios puede ayudar a prevenir la enfermedad del corazón.

Busque ayuda hormonal. Su doctor tiene la opción de recetarle estrógeno suplementario en sus años postmenopáusicos, el cual puede darle a usted la capacidad de defenderse de una enfermedad del corazón antes de que esta la ataque a usted. Un estudio de la Universidad de Harvard en Cambridge, Massachusetts, a más de 48.000 mujeres encontró que la terapia de reposición de estrógeno puede reducir el riesgo de una enfermedad coronaria grave y una enfermedad cardiovascular fatal a más de la mitad.

Pero hay una advertencia importante para tener en mente: ha habido cierta preocupación que el estrógeno puede aumentar su riesgo de cáncer del endometrio (el revestimiento del útero) y quizá de cáncer de mama. Pero al recetar dosis más bajas de estrógeno y combinando estrógeno con progestina (la forma sintética de otra hormona llamada progesterona), su doctor quizás pueda contrarrestar estas amenazas. Usted y su doctor necesitan pesar los pros y los contras antes de decidir si el estrógeno solo o en combinación con progestina es lo apropiado para usted.

Una multitud de tratamientos

Lo bueno acerca de la enfermedad del corazón —seguramente la única cosa buena— es que muy a menudo le da a usted señales de advertencia antes de azotar con fuerza. La señal de advertencia más común es la angina, un dolor en el pecho causado por un flujo sanguíneo insuficiente al corazón. Si usted experimenta una angina, su doctora podría recetarle nitroglicerina para relajar los vasos sanguíneos y permitir que el corazón tenga más sangre. O bien, para la angina crónica, ella podría sugerir otros medicamentos, tales como los bloqueadores beta, bloqueadores de canal de calcio o inhibidores *ACE* (por sus siglas en inglés), las enzimas que convierten la angiotensina.

"La selección de las drogas dependerá de su situación en particular", dice el doctor Martin. "Si usted tiene presión arterial alta así como enfermedad del corazón, puede haber una sola droga que pueda ayudar en estas dos condiciones. Si usted tiene una falla del corazón además de la enfermedad misma del corazón —es decir, si su corazón no está bombeando tan eficientemente como le es posible— un inhibidor ACE sería una buena elección. Algunos pacientes necesitan más de un medicamento. Por lo tanto, es una decisión individual."

Si la obstrucción de sus arterias coronarias se ha vuelto grave, entonces su doctor podría recomendar una operación a corazón abierto (cirugía de derivación coronaria o bypass) o bien una angioplastia. Aproximadamente el 30 por ciento de estas operaciones del corazón se efectúan en mujeres. Las angioplastias y la cirugía de derivación son igualmente comunes.

En la angioplastia, se guía un catéter con punta de globo por dentro de las arterias coronarias, donde el globo se infla para aplanar los depósitos grasosos que están causando la obstrucción.

Aunque la angioplastia tiene éxito en abrir las arterias en un 90 por ciento de los pacientes, estas arterias pueden volverse a obstruir, algunas veces meses después del procedimiento. En tal momento, la angioplastia debe repetirse o, en su lugar, el doctor puede sugerir cirugía de bypass.

En una operación de bypass, unos vasos sanguíneos sanos (a menudo transplantados de la pierna o del pecho) se injertan en el corazón para circunvalar las porciones obstruidas de las arterias coronarias. Aunque se trata de un procedimiento más serio, sus beneficios tienden a durar más. La doctora Legato dice que la cirugía se escoge por lo regular para la así llamada enfermedad de tres vasos, en la cual tres o más de las arterias coronarias más importantes están obstruidas, interfiriendo seriamente con el flujo sanguíneo al corazón.

Si usted termina optando entre las medicinas y la cirugía, todavía es importante —quizás doblemente importante— el mantener un estilo de vida saludable, activo y con un consumo bajo de grasa.

ENFERMEDADES RESPIRATORIAS

Consejos para que no se quede sin aliento

Después de un invierno casi eterno, ha llegado por fin la primavera. Usted se levanta temprano, y al ver las flores y oír los pajaritos cantando, abre la ventana. Inhala el aire fresco de la mañana, disfrutando su aroma.

Pero si tuviera la gripa, un resfriado (catarro) o enfisema, usted no podría hacer nada de esto. Usted tendría que tomar aire después de cada palabra que dice como si tuviera 100 años de edad. Usted tosería cada vez que respirara profundamente. Y usted resollaría.

Pero si usted mantiene sus pulmones saludables, no tiene que pasar por esto, dice el doctor Robert Bethel, un médico miembro del personal del Centro Nacional Judío para Medicina Inmunológica y Respiratoria, en Denver.

Nuestros pulmones están hechos para aguantar cualquier actividad que los pongamos a hacer, hasta bien avanzados en nuestra década de los 70 años de edad. Fumar, por supuesto, puede cambiar ese escenario, al obstruir los pulmones y hacernos jadear por aire. Los resfriados, la gripa, neumonía y otras enfermedades infecciosas pueden provocar lo mismo, pero sólo temporalmente. Otras enfermedades también pueden afectar los pulmones, pero estas son menos comunes.

Cómo fortalecer sus defensas naturales

Cada día, su sistema respiratorio aspira aproximadamente 9.500 cuartos de galón de aire y los mezcla con hasta 10.600 cuartos de galón de sangre

La TB: está de regreso

La tuberculosis (TB), una infección bacterial de los pulmones que los científicos pensaban que habían virtualmente eliminado en los Estados Unidos, no sólo está vivita y coleando sino prosperando.

Mientras que la enfermedad ha ido declinando desde la última parte de la década de los años 40, el número de casos de TB ha aumentado casi el 16 por ciento en un período de 6 años entre la última parte de la década de los años 80 y el principio de la década de los años 90.

Las ciudades han sido atacadas peor que ninguna otra zona. Para el principio de los años 90, la TB había aumentado en Atlanta a aproximadamente siete veces el promedio nacional, seis veces en Newark, New Jersey, y cinco veces en la ciudad de Nueva York, de acuerdo con los Centros para el Control y la Prevención de Enfermedades, en Atlanta.

¿La causa? La propagación incontrolable de la bacteria que causa la TB entre aquellos que tienen SIDA, los desamparados y aquellos que acaban de emigrar a los Estados Unidos —más el desarrollo de las variedades de la bacteria que son resistentes a las drogas.

La TB se propaga por gotitas transportadas por el aire al estornudar, toser y simplemente respirar. Las bacterias son inhaladas por los pulmones. En aquellos con sistemas inmunes resistentes, las bacterias son rodeadas por una legión de combatientes bacteriales que las vuelven

---

bombeada por el corazón a los pulmones. Sus pulmones mandan oxígeno a través de las carreteras arteriales para sostener al resto del cuerpo y para proporcionar un sistema de escape para la basura metabólica gaseosa como es el bióxido de carbono.

Dado que sus pulmones son órganos internos que atraen los microorganismos del mundo exterior cada vez que respira, la resistencia de su sistema natural de defensa es particularmente importante para mantener el flujo del oxígeno hacia y desde el resto del cuerpo. Afortunadamente para la mayoría de nosotras, los jugadores de defensa del cuerpo, incluyendo la mucosidad y los filamentos como pelos llamados cilios, pueden arrasar con los pólenes, el polvo, los virus y las bacterias fuera de la vía respiratoria.

La mayor parte del tiempo funcionan maravillosamente. Pero algunas veces se debilitan por irritantes tales como el humo de cigarrillos o se abruman por los microbios invasores.

inofensivas. En otros, las bacterias se acomodan en los pulmones y se multiplican. Con el tiempo, pueden destruir áreas extensas de los pulmones y dejar cavidades. Eventualmente, los pulmones parecen un queso suizo.

Hoy, 10 millones de estadounidenses portan la enfermedad, muchos sin los síntomas típicos de tos, fatiga y pérdida de peso.

"Yo pienso que la población en general está en peligro", dice el doctor Robert Bethel, un médico miembro del personal del Centro Nacional Judío para Medicina Inmunológica y Respiratoria, en Denver. "En gran parte, usted no puede controlar si está o no expuesta a la TB."

"No es que yo quiera alarmar a la gente", el doctor Bethel se apresura a agregar. "Pero si usted va en un autobús, tren subterráneo o avión con alguien que tiene TB activa y que está tosiendo, entonces las personas alrededor de esa persona están expuestas y son vulnerables."

Afortunadamente, un régimen complicado a largo plazo por lo general puede combatir la TB y relegarla a un estado latente. Pero el tratamiento temprano es importante. Si usted cree que ha estado expuesta a la TB, verifique con su doctor. Una simple prueba de la piel o una radiografía del pecho puede normalmente determinar si usted tiene o no la enfermedad.

Más de 14 millones de hombres y mujeres sufren de una obstrucción crónica pulmonar, la cual incluye tanto bronquitis crónica como enfisema. Y en sólo un año, 7 a 8 millones de hombres y mujeres tuvieron asma, 129 millones tuvieron gripa, 4 millones tuvieron neumonía, y prácticamente cada una de nosotras tuvo algún tipo de virus del resfriado (catarro).

¿Cómo puede usted proteger a sus pulmones de las enfermedades e irritantes que pueden hacerla aminorar la marcha? Aquí es lo que dicen algunos expertos.

Mantenga sobrios a sus cilios. El beber interfiere con los mecanismos de limpieza que mantienen a sus pulmones libres de gérmenes causantes de las enfermedades, dice el doctor Steven R. Mostow, presidente del Comité para la Prevención de la Neumonía y la Influenza de la Sociedad Torácica de los Estados Unidos y profesor de medicina en la Universidad de Colorado, en Denver. "Los cilios del sistema respiratorio se emborrachan al mismo tiempo que el resto de usted", explica él. Si usted está acostumbrada a beber uno o dos tragos diariamente, sus cilios estarán bien. Pero si usted de repente decide beber más de lo que acostumbra, sus cilios no van a ser capaces de hacer su trabajo.

Use ultrasonido. Para mantener a su sistema respiratorio en buena forma para luchar, humedezca su medio ambiente en el invierno con un humectador ultrasónico, dice el doctor Mostow. La humedad adicional ayudará a que sus cilios arrasen con el polvo, los virus, las bacterias y los pólenes.

Haga trabajar a sus pulmones. No sólo haga trabajar a sus bíceps. Métase en un programa de ejercicios aeróbicos que haga trabajar a su corazón y pulmones, dice el doctor Mostow. Esto ayudará a que sus pulmones se mantengan funcionando a una eficiencia óptima. Caminar, correr y nadar por 20 minutos por lo menos tres veces por semana seguramente será suficiente, pero verifique con su doctora antes de empezar, a fin de que ella acomode su receta de ejercicios específicamente a sus necesidades.

Asfixie los cigarrillos. Fumar un cigarrillo o incluso estar en un cuarto donde otros están fumando puede dañar a sus pulmones, dice el doctor Bethel. El humo puede causar que el sistema de defensa natural de su cuerpo secrete una enzima que al tratar de atacar los químicos del humo, literalmente daña el pulmón. Esto no sólo crea el marco para las enfermedades futuras, sino que también afecta a la respiración inmediatamente.

Cómo reprimir los síntomas del resfriado

Los resfriados (catarros), las infecciones del tracto respiratorio superior y la bronquitis pueden ser causados por cualquiera de los numerosos microorganismos que la pueden hacer sentir a usted como si hubiera perdido su capacidad para respirar.

Usted contrae estas enfermedades al inhalar los gérmenes de alguna otra persona o al tocar a alguien que tiene el virus y después se toca la nariz o boca, así haciendo posible que entren los gérmenes a su cuerpo.

Una vez que el virus la ha invadido, se instala en su garganta y empieza a producir virus bebés en cientos. Estos virus se esparcen por todo su cuerpo y provocan esos síntomas del resfriado: nariz tapada y goteando, garganta irritada, achaques y dolores y tos.

Hasta la fecha no hay una cura para el resfriado, pero aquí está como usted puede sobrellevar sus síntomas.

Pruébelo un poco picante. Los chiles muy picantes y las especias como el *curry* y el polvo de chile causan secreciones de la membrana mucosa. Este líquido adicional puede adelgazar la flema gruesa en sus pasajes nasales y lubricar una garganta irritada y con picazón.

Vaporícelo. Beba una sopa a sorbos o quédese por un buen rato debajo de una ducha que produzca vapor, sugiere Thomas A. Gossel, Ph.D., decano del Colegio de Farmacia y profesor de farmacología y toxicología en la Universidad de Ohio del Norte, en Ada. Los líquidos que usted tome o inhale diluyen la mucosidad en su nariz y parte superior de la garganta para que usted pueda respirar más fácilmente. Use descongestionantes en atomizador a la hora de irse a la cama por no más de cinco días para evitar la inflamación de los tejidos.

Dele duro con la D. La D en muchos de los supresores de tos sin receta (como el *Robitussin DM*) significa dextrometorfan. Los doctores tienen confianza total en éste. Solamente asegúrese de seguir las instrucciones en el paquete.

Chupe cinc. Desde hace años se ha sospechado que el cinc tiene la capacidad para eliminar un resfriado. Y por lo menos un estudio, del Colegio Dartmouth, en Hanover, New Hampshire, indica que las tabletas de cinc pueden reducir la duración de un resfriado en un 42 por ciento. Pero no cualquier tableta de cinc funcionará. Usted necesita esas que dicen *"zinc gluconate with glycine"* (gluconato de cinc con glicina). Estas son relativamente nuevas en el mercado así que probablemente va a necesitar la ayuda del farmacéutico para localizarlas. Si su farmacéutico no puede ayudarla, escriba a *Quigley Corporation* (Corporación Quigley), 10 South Clinton Street, Doylestown, PA 18901.

Entuma su garganta. Chupe una de esas pastillas sin receta para la garganta que se disuelven en la boca, para entumir y calmar el dolor de la garganta, sugiere el doctor Gossel. O dirija un atomizador con medicamento a la parte de atrás de su garganta, sostenga la respiración y rocíe. Siga las instrucciones en el paquete tanto para las pastillas como para el atomizador.

Purgue el dolor. Pruebe con la aspirina, el acetaminófeno o el ibuprofen para calmar los achaques y dolores de un resfriado, dice el doctor Gossel.

Combata el malestar. La sensación de que está muy cansada para moverse, que por lo general acompaña a un resfriado a menudo es causada por la deshidratación, según el doctor Gossel. Trate de beber por lo menos seis vasos de agua para evitarlo.

Cálmese. Un estudio de la Universidad Carnegie Mellon, en Pittsburgh indica que mientras más estrés tenga usted es más probable que reciba la visita de algún virus de resfriado que ande por los alrededores.

Los investigadores preguntaron a 394 hombres y mujeres entre los 18 y los 54 años de edad acerca del estrés en sus vidas —algún pesar reciente, ponerse a dieta, cambiar de trabajo, perder dinero, tener poco sueño y discutir con sus familiares— y entonces los dividieron en cinco grupos. Cada grupo recibió gotas nasales preparadas especialmente que contenían uno de los cinco virus conocidos como causantes de los resfriados.

¿El resultado? Aquellos que tenían el mayor estrés en sus vidas tenían una probabilidad cinco veces mayor de contraer un resfriado que aquellos que tenían el menor estrés.

Cómo sobrellevar el enfisema y la bronquitis

Una enfermedad con probabilidades de hacer que su sistema respiratorio se jubile antes de tiempo es una obstrucción crónica pulmonar. Este padecimiento incluye la bronquitis crónica, una condición en la cual los sacos de aire en los pulmones se destruyen, y el enfisema, una condición en la cual se pierde la elasticidad de los pulmones y el aire no puede fluir libremente hacia adentro o hacia fuera por la vía respiratoria. No incluye la bronquitis común que usted puede adquirir con un resfriado (catarro) —esa es simplemente una irritación de los tubos bronquiales que causa unos pocos días de toser y después desaparece.

Tanto la bronquitis crónica —definida en forma general como una tos productiva diaria que dura por tres meses o más— como el enfisema generalmente están causados por fumar. Los primeros síntomas de ambas enfermedades son la respiración dificultosa, la capacidad limitada para hacer esfuerzos, el expectorar mucosidad y la tos, y ambas condiciones van en aumento. El número de personas que sufre de estas enfermedades ha aumentado el 41 por ciento en los últimos diez años, y la bronquitis crónica y el enfisema representan el mayor número de las enfermedades respiratorias (aparte de resfriados) en personas entre los 30 y los 45 años de edad. Debido a que más hombres que mujeres fuman, los hombres tienen casi el doble de probabilidades de contraer enfisema aunque las mujeres los están alcanzando rápidamente. Cuando se trata de la bronquitis crónica, las mujeres tienen más probabilidades de contraerla. El enfisema y la bronquitis crónica juntos matan a aproximadamente 75.000 personas al año.

No hay una cura para la bronquitis crónica o para el enfisema, pero las estrategias siguientes pueden reducir la la respiración dificultosa que eventualmente ocurre cuando se obstruye una vía respiratoria, y pueden hacer un poco más fácil la vida con estas enfermedades.

Evite a la gente que estornuda. Cualquier tipo de infección respiratoria puede hacer que se empeoren el enfisema y la bronquitis crónica, dice el doctor Bethel. Evite áreas abarrotadas de gente o personas que tienen infecciones tanto como sea posible. Vea a su doctor si una enfermedad como el resfriado o la gripa está agravando sus problemas respiratorios.

Vacúnese. Evite las complicaciones de la influenza y neumonía bacterial haciéndose inmunizar contra ambos, gripa y neumonía, dice el doctor Bethel.

Aprenda a mantener la respiración. Si usted tiene enfisema, pida a su médico que le recomiende a un terapeuta ocupacional y a un terapeuta físico en su área.

"Un terapeuta ocupacional puede trabajar con las personas con respiración dificultosa quienes están limitadas en sus actividades cotidianas", dice el doctor Bethel. "El terapeuta puede enseñar a las personas formas más eficientes para ahorrar energía al realizar estas actividades."

Un terapeuta físico puede desarrollar un programa de ejercicios que entrenará a su cuerpo a usar el oxígeno que tiene a su disposición más eficientemente. El resultado será que el poco oxígeno que usted tiene durará más.

Dilate su vía respiratoria. Su doctor puede recetarle medicamentos para dilatar al máximo su vía respiratoria, dice el doctor Bethel. Úselos según las instrucciones.

Asma: una enfermedad cada vez más mortal

El asma es diferente a la bronquitis crónica y al enfisema ya que su obstrucción de la vía respiratoria es tanto intermitente como reversible.

Durante un ataque de asma, la vía respiratoria se contrae, las paredes se engruesan por la inflamación, y la mucosidad se acumula dentro de ésta. El resultado es una vía respiratoria que la hace sentir como si se estuviera asfixiando. Pero por lo regular, después del ataque la vía respiratoria regresa a la normalidad. Desafortunadamente, varios años de estos ataques pueden llevar a un daño permanente en la vía respiratoria.

Si usted nunca ha tenido asma, dé un respiro de alivio. Una vez que usted pasa los 30 años de edad, no es probable que usted la contraiga, dice el doctor Harold S. Nelson, médico sénior del personal en el Centro Nacional Judío para Medicina Inmunológica y Respiratoria y un miembro del Panel Nacional de Expertos en la Educación del Asma, del Instituto Nacional del Corazón, Pulmón y Sangre.

"El asma tiende a venir de familia", dice el doctor Bethel. "Puede haber una predisposición en algunas personas, pero nosotros pensamos que el asma es causada por una inflamación de la vía respiratoria."

"No todos los mecanismos están claros", agrega. "Algunas veces la inflamación es causada por alergenos que las personas inhalan. Algunas veces es la exposición en el lugar de trabajo. La exposición a un número grande de agentes —la soldadura usada en la industria electrónica o los vapores emanados en la fabricación de plásticos— pueden sensibilizar la vía respiratoria y hacer a una persona asmática. Y muchas veces las personas desarrollan asma, y no está claro qué la causó."

Lo que sí es claro, los doctores concuerdan, es que el asma, que afecta a cerca de 12 millones de estadounidenses está volviéndose más frecuente y más mortal cada año. Cerca de 5.000 personas mueren de esta enfermedad cada año —y con los años el índice de muerte asciende.

Lo que ocasiona el aumento en el número y la muerte de asmáticos es todavía un misterio, informa la Asociación del Pulmón de los Estados Unidos. Un número de factores puede provocar un ataque de asma, incluyendo alergias, humo de cigarrillos y otros irritantes, una infección viral en su sistema respiratorio y acidez, lo cual puede resultar en tos y espasmos en sus pulmones. Aun emociones y ejercicio fuertes —especialmente en tiempo frío— pueden causar problemas, dice el doctor Nelson.

Los casos nuevos o recurrentes de asma pueden empezar como si fueran infecciones normales del tracto respiratorio, dice el doctor Nelson. Si usted empieza a desarrollar un resuello, presión en el pecho o falta de aliento, vea inmediatamente a un doctor.

Si a usted se le diagnostica con asma, los médicos pueden recetar medicinas para aliviar los síntomas. Los inhaladores que contienen corticoesteroides son la forma más efectiva de reducir la inflamación y ayudarle a respirar más libremente. Las drogas sin receta rara vez tienen mucho efecto, dice el doctor Nelson.

"Esto no es algo que usted puede tratar por sí sola", dice él. "El asma es demasiada seria para eso." Aquí está lo que algunos expertos sugieren para tratar esta enfermedad.

Combata la contaminación. "Hay evidencia de que si se vive en ambientes contaminados aumenta la incidencia de enfermedades pulmonares como el asma", dice el doctor Bethel. Por eso es que usted debería tratar de evitar áreas sumamente contaminadas como son las zonas industriales y las carreteras urbanas.

Frecuentemente la calidad del aire se observa por varias agencias para ver si cumple con las normas federales y estatales. Para averiguar qué tan contaminada está el área donde usted vive o trabaja, llame a su agencia ambiental estatal. Las personas que trabajan allí tienen la información a mano o pueden recomendar a alguien que la tenga.

Respire a través de una bufanda. Si usted respira aire frío y seco puede estrechar la vía respiratoria y provocar resuello, tos y falta de aliento. ¿La solución? Use una bufanda con la que usted pueda cubrir su boca y nariz para respirar a través de ella durante períodos fríos. Y trate de respirar principalmente a través de la nariz. El respirar a través de la nariz calienta y humedece el aire antes de que llegue a sus pulmones.

Váyase a la cocina. Una revisión de lo que 9.000 adultos comen todos los días reveló que los consumos más altos de vitamina C y ácido nicotínico se asociaron con menos casos de resuello. Las buenas fuentes de vitamina C incluyen la grosella negra, guayaba, el jugo de naranja y los pimientos rojos. Las buenas fuentes de ácido nicotínico incluyen la pechuga de pollo, el atún envasado en agua y pez espada (*swordfish*).

Use un sistema que lo alerte con anticipación. El medidor de flujo óptimo (*peak-flow meter*) para el hogar, un dispositivo que mide su capacidad de respiración, puede ayudarle a identificar cuál es un flujo normal y cuál no lo es, dice el doctor Nelson. Ya que el flujo de aire a veces disminuye un par de horas o días antes de un ataque, el medidor le puede dar una advertencia por adelantado que le permita prevenirse contra el ataque con medicinas recetadas por su doctor.

Pida a su doctor que le diga dónde usted puede conseguir un medidor de flujo óptimo y cómo usarlo.

Tome los medicamentos correctos. Las medicinas con receta que tratan el asma incluyen drogas antiinflamatorias que contienen la inflamación de la vía respiratoria, como los esteroides, así como los broncodilatadores que dilatan la vía respiratoria misma.

Pero al notar que algunas personas solamente usan los broncodilatadores, el doctor Nelson añade: "Cualquier persona con algo más que el asma leve ocasional necesita estar en un tratamiento antiinflamatorio en lugar de usar solamente los broncodilatadores. Juntos, disminuirán los síntomas, probablemente reducirán el número de episodios serios que de otra manera necesitarían tratamiento en un hospital, reducirán también la necesidad de broncodilatadores y —los doctores esperan— prevendrán el desarrollo a largo plazo de las obstrucciones irreversibles".

Cómo sobrevivir la gripa y la neumonía

Ni la gripa ni las formas más comunes de neumonía presentan la probabilidad de dañar a sus pulmones, pero pueden hacer que usted esté tan corta de respiración que siente que no va a poder ni siquiera subir un tramo de las escaleras.

La gripa, que generalmente provoca fiebre, dolor de cabeza, garganta irritada, congestión nasal, dolores musculares y una sensación de agotamiento, típicamente ataca entre diciembre y marzo. Es causada por dos variedades de virus, A o B, que por lo general logran infectar todos los años entre el 33 y el 52 por ciento de los habitantes en los Estados Unidos. Debido a que la gripa afecta tan severamente a las personas más mayores, está considerada la sexta causa principal de muerte en los Estados Unidos.

La neumonía, que generalmente está caracterizada por tos, flema, fiebre, escalofríos y dolor en el pecho, puede ser causada por una variedad de agentes infecciosos, incluyendo los virus, los parásitos y las bacterias microplasmas. Ocurre en el 80 por ciento de aquellos que tienen SIDA. Llamada neumonía neumocística carinii, la provoca un parásito y rara vez se observa en personas sin SIDA.

Afortunadamente, ambas, la gripa y los tipos más mortales y comunes de neumonía frecuentemente se pueden prevenir o tratarse con éxito sin que dañen permanentemente sus pulmones. Aquí está cómo.

Prepárese para las señales de peligro. Algunos tipos de neumonía, como son *staph* o klebsiela, pueden seriamente dañar a los pulmones, dice el doctor Mostow, y "sus pulmones ya nunca serán los mismos de ahí en adelante". Así que vea a su doctor rápidamente si tiene fiebre, dificultad para respirar o una tos molesta que no se quita.

Defiéndase contra la neumonía. La vacuna contra la neumonía no evita la neumonía, dice el doctor Mostow, pero puede evitar que usted se muera cuando la ataca la neumonía. La vacuna es efectiva contra 23 variedades diferentes de gérmenes bacteriales, las variedades que son responsables por el 90 por ciento de las muertes por neumonía. Usted necesita vacunarse solamente una vez en su vida.

Protéjase contra la gripa. La vacuna contra la gripa es altamente eficiente, dice el doctor Mostow.

Cualquier persona con una enfermedad crónica de los pulmones o del corazón, diabetes, inmunidad dañada, enfermedad del riñón, anemia u otro problema con la sangre debería vacunarse todos los años en el otoño; también debería hacerlo cualquier persona mayor de los 65 años de edad, y cualquier persona que esté involucrada en el cuidado de pacientes.

¿Quién no debería hacerse vacunar? Ya que la vacuna se incuba en huevos, aquellas que son alérgicas a los huevos deberían evitarla. En general, si usted puede comer huevos, puede recibir con seguridad una vacuna contra la gripa.

Visite a su médico particular. Si a usted se le olvida su vacuna contra la gripa, hay dos drogas antivirales con receta que pueden parar la gripa, dice el doctor Mostow. Una es amantadina (*Symmetrel*), y la otra es rimantadina (*Flumadine*). Estos dos compuestos son activos contra la influenza A, el único virus de la gripa que mata. Una advertencia solamente: debe obtenerlas de su doctor dentro de las 48 horas siguientes a haber contraído la gripa.

Si a usted se le olvidó hacerse vacunar contra la neumonía —o si tiene la mala suerte de haber contraído una de las neumonías para la cual la vacuna no es efectiva— su doctor le recetará un antibiótico que está destinado especialmente a matar el virus o la bacteria que la haya atacado, dice el doctor Mostow. Si usted tiene la forma de neumonía que afecta a aquellos con SIDA, P. carinii, entonces su doctor le recetará sulfato de trimetropim (*Polytrim*), una droga que no la curará pero mantendrá la enfermedad bajo control.

ESTRÉS

La cura está en el control

Usted no logra descansar lo suficiente, y tampoco logra hacer lo suficiente. Y su estómago está siempre hecho un nudo.

"El estrés siempre le hará eso a usted", dice la doctora Leah J. Dickstein, profesora en el Departamento de Siquiatría y Ciencias de la Conducta en la Escuela de Medicina de la Universidad de Louisville, en Kentucky y ex presidenta de la Asociación Médica de Mujeres de los Estados Unidos. "Realmente la puede desgastar. Y el problema real es que usted está preparando el terreno para otros problemas más adelante."

El Instituto para el Estrés de los Estados Unidos, en Yonkers, Nueva York, estima que el 90 por ciento de todas las visitas al doctor son por trastornos relacionados con el estrés. En las mujeres, el estrés se ha vinculado con la fatiga, la pérdida del cabello, el mal semblante, el insomnio, la perturbación del ciclo menstrual, la libido reducido y la falta de orgasmo, entre otros. Incluso hay evidencia de que puede aumentar su riesgo de problemas más serios como son la presión arterial alta y la enfermedad del corazón.

"El estrés acelera todo su sistema y produce condiciones en las personas jóvenes que están generalmente asociadas con el envejecer", dice Allen J. Elkin, Ph.D., director del Centro de Manejo y Orientación del Estrés, en la Ciudad de Nueva York. "Virtualmente no hay una parte de su cuerpo que pueda escaparse de los estragos del estrés."

Hay muchas maneras en que nosotras podemos reducir el estrés en nuestras vidas. Pero antes de que podamos vencerlo, los expertos dicen que tenemos que entender lo que es el estrés, y cómo funciona.

Confusiones peligrosas

A pesar de su mala reputación, el estrés es uno de los mejores sistemas de defensa de nuestros cuerpos. Cuando presentimos el peligro —como un carro que se nos viene encima— nuestros cuerpos producen adrenalina y otros

¿Se está acumulando el estrés?

Recuerde: el estrés viene de adentro. Sus actitudes acerca de la vida tienen mucho que ver con cuánto estrés siente usted. Este examen del libro *Is It Worth Dying For?* (¿Vale la pena morirse por eso?), por el doctor Robert S. Eliot y Denis L. Breo, prueba su punto de vista y nivel total de estrés. Lea cada declaración y entonces anótese un punto si usted casi nunca se siente de esa manera, dos puntos si usted ocasionalmente se siente de esa manera, tres puntos si usted frecuentemente se siente de esa manera y cuatro puntos si usted siempre se siente de esa manera.

1. Las cosas tienen que ser perfectas.
2. Debo hacerlo yo misma.
3. Me siento más aislada de mi familia y amistades cercanas.
4. Siento que la gente debería escuchar mejor.
5. Mi vida me está controlando.
6. No debo fracasar.
7. No puedo decir que no a nuevas exigencias sin sentirme culpable.
8. Necesito generar excitación constantemente para evitar el aburrimiento.
9. Siento una falta de intimidad con las personas a mi alrededor.
10. No soy capaz de relajarme.
11. Soy incapaz de reírme de una broma sobre mi persona.

químicos que nos hacen más alertas, elevan nuestra presión arterial y aumentan nuestra fuerza, velocidad y tiempo de reacción.

Eso está muy bien si estamos respondiendo a una amenaza que requiere acción física. Desafortunadamente, dice la doctora Dickstein, nuestros cuerpos no reconocen la diferencia entre las amenazas físicas y mentales. Cuando nos ponemos nerviosas acerca de cumplir con un plazo, por ejemplo, podemos producir los mismos químicos de estrés que cuando vemos a ese carro que se nos viene encima. Y si no quemamos esos químicos a través del esfuerzo físico, pueden permanecer en nuestro torrente sanguíneo y empezar a causar problemas.

Los estudios muestran que el estrés puede reducir la fuerza de nuestro sistema inmune. Un estudio en Gran Bretaña expuso a 266 personas, la mayoría de ellas en su década de los 30 años de edad, a un virus del resfriado (catarro) común y después observaron quiénes se enfermaban. El estudio mostró que el

12. Evito decir lo que pienso.
13. Me siento bajo presión de triunfar todo el tiempo.
14. Automáticamente expreso actitudes negativas.
15. Me parece estar más atrasada al final del día que cuando comencé.
16. Se me olvidan los plazos, las citas y las pertenencias personales.
17. Soy irritable y estoy desilusionada de las personas a mi alrededor.
18. El sexo parece ser más problema que lo que vale.
19. Me considero explotada.
20. Me despierto temprano y no puedo dormir.
21. Me siento intranquila.
22. Me siento insatisfecha con mi vida personal.
23. Me siento insatisfecha con mi vida laboral.
24. No estoy donde quiero estar en la vida.
25. Evito estar sola.
26. Tengo dificultad para dormirme.
27. Tengo dificultad para despertarme.
28. No me siento con ganas de salir de la cama.

Sume sus puntos. Si su puntuación es de 29 o menos, usted muestra poco estrés. Los totales de 30 a 58 muestran estrés ligero. Si su puntuación es entre 59 y 87, usted muestra estrés moderado. Si está arriba de 87, usted puede estar bajo un fuerte estrés.

28,6 por ciento de aquellas personas con pocas señales de estrés contrajeron el resfriado. Pero la cantidad pegó un salto al 42,4 por ciento para aquellas que estaban bajo un estrés intenso.

¿La razón? El estrés puede inhibir las células que combaten las enfermedades en nuestro torrente sanguíneo. "Todo el mundo se enferma de vez en cuando", dice la doctora Dickstein. "Pero si usted se encuentra bajo mucho estrés, un virus que usted hubiera podido rechazar bajo otras circunstancias puede causar que usted se enferme."

Otros estudios muestran que las mujeres que tienen problema para sobrellevar el estrés pueden estar en riesgo de acumular grasa abdominal peligrosa. Un estudio de la Universidad de Yale, en New Haven, Connecticut, a 42 mujeres obesas encontró que aquellas con grasa abdominal —las llamadas "mujeres en forma de manzana"— secretaron más hormonas de estrés que aquellas con cuerpos "en forma de pera", quienes llevan el peso extra sobre sus caderas. Y

¿La está desgastando el trabajo?

Todos sentimos presión en el trabajo. Pero muchas veces esta se nos escapa de las manos, dejándola a usted enojada, cansada e improductiva.

Para verificar su nivel de estrés en el trabajo, haga esta pequeña prueba desarrollada por el doctor Paul J. Rosch, presidente del Instituto del Estrés de los Estados Unidos, en Yonkers, Nueva York. Anótese un punto por cada pregunta con la que usted no está de acuerdo, dos puntos por cada pregunta con la que está algo de acuerdo y tres puntos por cada pregunta con la que está totalmente de acuerdo.

1. Yo no puedo decir lo que realmente pienso en el trabajo.
2. Tengo bastante responsabilidad pero no mucha autoridad.
3. Yo podría hacer mejor el trabajo si tuviera más tiempo.
4. Rara vez recibo reconocimiento o aprecio.
5. Yo no estoy orgullosa ni satisfecha con mi trabajo.
6. Se meten conmigo o me discriminan en el trabajo.
7. Mi lugar de trabajo no es particularmente agradable o seguro.
8. Mi trabajo interfiere con las obligaciones de mi familia y necesidades personales.
9. Yo tiendo a discutir más a menudo con mis superiores, compañeros de trabajo o clientes.
10. Siento que tengo poco control sobre mi vida en el trabajo.

Aquí está cómo determinar los resultados de la prueba: 10 a 16 puntos significa que usted maneja bien el estrés; 17 a 23 puntos significa que usted lo está haciendo moderadamente bien y 24 a 30 puntos significa que usted necesita resolver los problemas que están causándole estrés excesivo.

---

los médicos saben que las personas en forma de manzana tienen mayor riesgo de una enfermedad del corazón.

Hasta la menopausia, las mujeres tienen una protección extra contra los problemas del corazón. Eso es debido al estrógeno, que evita la formación de placa (ateroma) en nuestras arterias. Pero una vez que dejamos de producir estrógeno, nuestro riesgo de ataques al corazón aumenta y se iguala al de los hombres. Y allí es cuando el estrés realmente puede causar problemas. "El estrés aumenta el ritmo del corazón y la presión arterial, cambiando así el recubrimiento interno de nuestros vasos sanguíneos y haciendo a nuestra sangre más susceptible a la coagulación", dice el doctor Robert DiBianco, director de investigación cardiológica en el Hospital Adventista de Washington, en Takoma

Park, Maryland. "El estrés puede cambiar la forma en que los vasos sanguíneos manejan el colesterol y, al hacer eso, puede aumentar la formación de placa."

A pesar de que generalmente nosotras tenemos un aplazamiento a enfermedades del corazón de dos o tres décadas, las mujeres jóvenes ya se están enfrentando a otras dificultades con el estrés. Un estudio a 5.872 mujeres embarazadas en Dinamarca mostró que las mujeres que se encuentran bajo un nivel de estrés entre moderado a alto en su último trimestre tienen 1,2 a 1,75 más probabilidades de dar a luz prematuramente. El ruido también nos provoca más estrés que a los hombres. Los estudios muestran que a las mujeres nos irritan los sonidos a la mitad del volumen que molesta a los hombres, y podemos oír mejor los sonidos de alta frecuencia, según Caroline Dow, Ph.D., profesora asistente de comunicación en la Universidad de Evansville, en Evansville, Indiana.

La doctora Dow ayudó a conducir un estudio que muestra lo que el ruido puede causar. A cien estudiantes femeninas de la universidad se les dio una prueba uniforme en una computadora. La mitad tenía terminales que emitían sonidos de tono alto, mientras que las otras no emitían ningún sonido. Las mujeres con las computadoras ruidosas alcanzaron una puntuación de 8,5 por ciento más bajo en la prueba. Estas estudiantes trabajaron más rápido y estaban más propensas a errores —una indicación, dice la doctora Dow, que estaban actuando bajo estrés.

Aun la sociedad misma puede causarnos estrés. Ahora que las mujeres estamos haciendo carrera como los hombres, estamos enfrentándonos al estrés del mundo del trabajo como nunca antes. De hecho, nuestros trabajos causan la mayor parte de nuestro estrés, dice la doctora Dickstein. Pero no para allí. Las mujeres con carreras aún deben cocinar, limpiar, cuidar de los niños y ser esposas cariñosas. Y ese tipo de estrés de doble cara puede ser pesado para nuestros sistemas. Un estudio sueco a hombres y mujeres que tenían entre 30 y 50 años de edad, todos gerentes en plantas automovilísticas, mostró que la presión arterial y los niveles de hormonas de estrés aumentaron para todos durante el día de trabajo. Pero cuando los hombres se iban a sus casas, sus lecturas de presión arterial y estrés bajaron drásticamente, mientras que las lecturas de las mujeres, porque ellas tenían aún más cosas por hacer en el día, se mantuvieron altas.

"Ese estudio lo dice todo", dice la investigadora de la salud de las mujeres Margaret A. Chesney, Ph.D., profesora en la Escuela de Medicina de la Universidad de California, San Francisco. "Es una prueba sicológica de que las mujeres se van a su casa para un segundo empleo. Los hombres saben que hay una distinción; que en sus hogares están libres de trabajo. Las mujeres no están libres de trabajo. Están bajo más coacción."

Pautas para pararlo en seco

¿Cuál es la clave para vencer al estrés? Crear una sensación de control. Tenemos que entender que algo de estrés es inevitable. De hecho, un poco de estrés nos ayuda a terminar los deberes y a alcanzar las metas, dice la doctora

Dickstein. Pero demasiado de las fuentes equivocadas —como discusiones con el esposo, o expectativas poco realistas en el trabajo o en el hogar— puede hacernos sentir indefensas e incapaces de sobrellevar las situaciones. Y allí es donde el estrés hace la mayor parte de su trabajo dañino.

Aquí hay algunos consejos para ayudarle a controlar el estrés.

Súdelo. Nada alivia más el estrés que el ejercicio, según David S. Holmes, Ph.D., profesor de sicología en la Universidad de Kansas, en Lawrence. "Las sesiones regulares de ejercicios aeróbicos reducen el estrés más efectivamente que la meditación, intervención siquiátrica, *biofeedback* y el manejo convencional del estrés", dice él.

El ejercicio ayuda a quemar todos los químicos relacionados con el estrés en su sistema. Durante una sesión de ejercicio, su cuerpo también secretará endorfinas relajantes para la mente, dice el doctor Holmes. Y el ejercicio también hace más fuerte a su corazón, protegiéndola aún más contra los estragos del estrés.

La investigación realizada por Robert Thayer, Ph.D., profesor de sicología en la Universidad Estatal de California, en Long Beach, mostró que 30 minutos de ejercicio aeróbico intenso reducen la tensión del cuerpo, y lo logra en forma aún más efectiva que el ejercicio moderado como es caminar.

No se pase de lista. Tantos proyectos y tan poco tiempo. Para vencer al estrés, usted tiene que aprender a dar prioridad, según Lee Reinert, Ph.D., director y conferencista para el Centro Bioconductista Brandywine, un centro de orientación en Downingtown, Pensilvania. Al empezar cada día, escoja la tarea más importante que se debe completar, y entonces termínela. Si usted es una persona que hace listas de cosas para hacer, nunca escriba una con más de cinco puntos. De esa manera, usted tendrá mayor probabilidad de terminar todas las cosas, y sentirá una sensación de logro y control, dice el doctor Reinert. Luego usted puede preparar una segunda lista con cinco puntos más. Ya que se encuentra usted en eso, haga una lista de las cosas que puede delegar a los compañeros de trabajo y miembros de la familia. "Recuerde: no tiene que hacer todo usted misma", dice el doctor Reinert. "Usted puede encontrar ayuda y apoyo en las personas que están a su alrededor."

Simplemente diga que no. Algunas veces usted tiene que aprender a poner un límite. "A menudo las personas estresadas no saben imponerse", dice Joan Lerner, Ph.D., una sicóloga de orientación en el Servicio de Orientación de la Universidad de Pensilvania, en Filadelfia. "Y por lo tanto se tragan las cosas. En lugar de decir 'no quiero hacer eso' o 'necesito que me ayuden', lo hacen todo ellas mismas. Entonces, tienen aún más trabajo que hacer."

Dele a escoger a su jefe. "Diga 'me gustaría hacer eso, pero no puede hacerlo a menos que deje de hacer alguna otra cosa', '¿cuál de las dos cosas quisiera usted que yo hiciera?' ", dice Merrill Douglass, D.B.A., presidente del Time Management Center, en Marietta, Georgia, una compañía que entrena a los individuos y a las corporaciones en el uso del tiempo y la energía, y coautor de *Manage Your Time, Manage Your Work, Manage Yourself* (Administre su tiempo, administre su trabajo y adminístrese a sí mismo). La mayoría de los jefes

Una solución a la mano

Cuando usted está demasiado estresada, a menudo el primer lugar donde lo siente es en su cuello. Pruebe estas cuatro formas de ejercicio para relajar el cuello recomendadas por el ex atleta de categoría mundial en atletismo Greg Herzog en su libro *The 15 Minute Executive Stress Relief Program* (El programa de 15 minutos para aliviar el estrés del ejecutivo). Repita cada uno de los siguientes ejercicios tres veces:

1. Pase la mano derecha por encima de la cabeza y por detrás de su oreja izquierda, agarrándose el cuello con los dedos. Jale con cuidado su cabeza hacia el hombro derecho.

2. Haga el mismo ejercicio, pero esta vez use la mano izquierda para inclinar la cabeza hacia su hombro izquierdo.

3. Enlace las manos detrás de la cabeza, con sus codos extendidos y la cabeza inclinada hacia su pecho. Descanse en esta posición por 30 segundos. Entonces mientras jala hacia abajo con sus manos, empuje lentamente la cabeza hacia atrás hasta que esté mirando al techo.

4. Coloque la palma de su mano izquierda sobre la frente, con la parte inferior de la palma sobre el caballete de la nariz. Mantenga el brazo derecho a través de su cuerpo para que pueda descansar el codo izquierdo sobre la muñeca derecha. Ahora empuje con la frente contra su palma izquierda mientras conserva su brazo derecho trabado. Cambie de manos y repita.

---

pueden entender la insinuación, dice el doctor Douglass. La misma estrategia funciona en la casa, con su esposo, los niños, parientes y amistades. Si usted tiene problema para decir que no, empiece con algo pequeño. Dígale a su marido que se haga su propio sándwich. O dígale a su hija que encuentre a otra persona que la traiga a la casa después de la práctica de vóleibol.

Dese tiempo de respirar. "Dese cuenta de que casi todo va a llevar más tiempo de lo que usted anticipaba", dice el doctor Richard Swenson, autor de *Margin: How to Create the Emotional, Physical, Financial and Time Reserves You Need* (Margen: cómo crear las reservas emocionales, físicas, económicas y de tiempo que usted necesita). Al asignarse suficiente tiempo para completar una tarea, usted reduce su ansiedad. En general, si cumplir con los plazos es un problema, siempre dese un 20 por ciento más de tiempo del que usted piensa que necesita para terminar la tarea.

Cambie su Jaguar por un Hyundai. El llevar un estilo de vida que va mas allá de sus ingresos realmente puede enfermarla. Un investigador de la

Universidad de Alabama, en Tuscaloosa estudió los datos del censo británico sobre 8.000 hogares y encontró que las familias que trataban de mantener estilos de vida que en realidad no podían mantener estaban más propensas a tener problemas de salud.

Siéntese derecha. Una buena postura vertical mejora la respiración y aumenta el flujo de sangre al cerebro. A veces nos encorvamos cuando estamos estresadas, lo cual restringe la respiración y el flujo de sangre y puede aumentar la sensación de impotencia.

Apriete las clavijas. Tenga un ejercitador para las manos o una pelota de tenis en su escritorio en el trabajo y dele unos cuantos apretones durante los momentos de tensión. "Cuando el estrés inyecta adrenalina en el torrente sanguíneo, eso pide acción muscular", dice el doctor Roger Cady, director médico del Instituto Shealy para el Cuidado Completo de la Salud, en Springfield, Misuri. "Apretar algo proporciona una liberación que satisface la reacción de nuestros cuerpos de luchar o salir corriendo."

Reviente una burbuja. Un estudio encontró que los estudiantes podían reducir sus sentimientos de tensión reventando dos de esas hojas con burbujas de plástico usadas para empacar. "Ahora sabemos por qué las personas juntan esas cosas", dice Kathleen Dillon, Ph.D., sicóloga y profesora del Colegio de Nueva Inglaterra del Oeste, en Springfield, Massachusetts y autora del estudio.

Remójese en su tina. ¿Quiere realmente relajar sus músculos? Remójese en una tina caliente. Para obtener la mayor relajación de un baño caliente, remójese por 15 minutos en agua que está unos cuantos grados más caliente que la temperatura de su cuerpo, o entre 100°F y 101°F (37,7°C a 38,3°C). Pero tenga cuidado, los remojos prolongados en agua caliente pueden en realidad hacer bajar demasiado su presión arterial.

Serénese y cómase una papa. Si usted quiere relajarse al final del día, coma una comida alta en carbohidratos, dice Judith Wurtman, Ph.D., una científica investigadora en el Instituto de Tecnología de Massachusetts, en Cambridge y autora de *Managing Your Mind and Mood with Food* (Administrando su mente y estado de ánimo con alimentos). Los carbohidratos provocan la secreción del neurotransmisor del cerebro serotonina, el cual la relaja. Las buenas fuentes de carbohidratos incluyen el arroz, las pastas, las papas, los panes, las palomitas de maíz hechas a presión y las galletitas de bajas calorías. La doctora Wurtman dice que sólo 1,5 onzas (43g) de carbohidratos, la cantidad en una papa asada o una taza de espagueti o arroz blanco, es suficiente para aliviar la ansiedad de un día estresante.

Pruebe algo de fibra. "A menudo el estrés se va directamente a la barriga", dice el doctor George Blackburn, Ph.D., profesor asociado de cirugía en la Escuela de Medicina de Harvard y jefe del Laboratorio de Nutrición y Metabolismo en el Hospital Deaconess de Nueva Inglaterra, ambos en Boston. Eso quiere decir calambres y estreñimiento. Para evitar estos problemas, el doctor Blackburn sugiere comer más fibra para mantener a su sistema digestivo en movimiento. Usted debería ir aumentando gradualmente hasta llegar por lo menos a los 25 gramos de fibra por día. Eso significa comer más frutas, verduras y granos. Pruebe comer las frutas enteras en lugar de sólo el jugo a la hora del desayuno, y pruebe cereales de grano integral y *muffins* fortificados con fibra.

Ríase. El humor es un reductor comprobado del estrés. Los expertos dicen que una buena risa relaja los músculos tensos, acelera más el oxígeno dentro de su sistema y reduce la presión arterial. Así que ponga en el televisor su programa cómico favorito. Lea un libro divertido. Llame a una amiga y ríase por unos cuantos minutos. Incluso ayuda forzar una risa de vez en cuando. Usted sentirá cómo su estrés desaparece casi instantáneamente.

Aguante la respiración. Esta técnica debería ayudarla a relajarse en 30 segundos. Respire profundamente y sostenga el aire adentro. Juntando sus manos palma con palma, presione los dedos juntos. Espere cinco segundos y entonces exhale despacio a través de sus labios mientras deja descansar sus manos. Haga esto cinco o seis veces hasta que se sienta relajada.

Imagínese unas vacaciones de 10 minutos. La meditación es un gran alivio para el estrés, pero algunas veces es difícil encontrar el tiempo o el lugar para esta. El doctor Reinert sugiere que en lugar de eso se tome una minivacación en su propio escritorio o mesa de la cocina. Nada más cierre los ojos, respire profundamente (desde su estómago) e imagínese a usted recostada en una playa en México. Sienta el calor del sol. Oiga las olas. Huela el aire salado. "Simplemente ponga una pequeña distancia entre usted y su estrés", dice el doctor Reinert. "Unos cuantos minutos al día pueden ser de gran ayuda."

Baje el volumen. Si usted trabaja, vive o hace deportes en un área muy ruidosa, considere usar tapones para los oídos. Asegúrese de que los que usted compre reduzcan el sonido por lo menos en 20 decibeles, dice Ernest Peterson, Ph.D., profesor asociado de otolaringología en la Escuela de Medicina de la Universidad de Miami.

Usted también puede usar los sonidos en su favor. Trate de escuchar música suave, con flautas u otros instrumentos de sonido suave, dice el doctor Emmett Miller, un experto en estrés conocido nacionalmente y director médico del Centro de Apoyo y Educación del Cáncer, en Menlo Park, California. Él también sugiere hacer caminatas en lugares tranquilos y oír el murmurar de las hojas o el susurrar de un arroyo. Las grabaciones de las olas del mar o los aguaceros leves también ayudan, dice él.

FATIGA

Cómo recobrar su energía

Usted se levanta en cuanto amanece. Hace el desayuno. Alista a los niños para irse a la escuela. Sale corriendo para el trabajo donde va de acá para allá como una loca durante nueve o diez horas. Vuela a la casa para improvisar una comida para los muertos de hambre. Lava los platos. Ayuda a los chicos con sus tareas. Echa una tanda de ropa en la lavadora. Y por ahí alrededor de la medianoche, cuando ya no puede moverse más, se va cojeando por el pasillo y se derrumba en la cama hasta que la alarma del reloj suena y la diversión comienza de nuevo.

¿Es de extrañarse que esa energía necesaria para saltar de la cama y echarse a andar se quedó entre las sábanas?

La fatiga es una de las diez quejas que los doctores escuchan más de las mujeres. ¿Y, por qué no? Nosotras llenamos nuestros días hasta el tope. Y eso deja nuestras baterías totalmente descargadas.

Por lo general es algo que podemos controlar, y no tenemos problema en recuperarnos rápido. Pero en otras ocasiones, una sensación abrumadora de fatiga se nos puede acercar sigilosamente y tomarnos por sorpresa. Nos sentimos débiles. Nuestros cuerpos duelen. Nuestras caras se ponen mustias. Nuestros espíritus decaen. Y antes de que nos demos cuenta, nos hemos transformado de activas y vigorosas amantes de la vida en zombies acabados y rendidos que se sienten como de 100 años.

"El mayor impacto de la fatiga es en la función y actividad humana", dice el doctor y teniente-coronel Kurt Kroenke, profesor asociado de medicina en la Universidad de Servicios Uniformes de las Ciencias de la Salud, en Bethesda, Maryland, y un experto en fatiga. "Cuando usted ya no tiene la fuerza o energía para moverse, aun las tareas simples se vuelven difíciles. Usted se vuelve sedentaria, su productividad decae, su motivación sufre. Para algunas, este cansancio persistente puede ser tan debilitante que ni siquiera pueden levantarse de la cama."

La fatiga puede afectar también su mente, asienten los expertos. Pensar se vuelve difícil y confuso. Las decisiones tardan en alcanzarse. Incluso su actitud ante la vida se vuelve sombría.

El resultado es que la fatiga puede conducir a un desempeño pobre en el trabajo, menos interacción con las amistades y familiares y menos participación en los deportes y las actividades que a usted le gustan.

Esta es una mala noticia si usted está acostumbrada a ser una mujer activa. Pero la buena noticia es que con un poco de trabajo detectivesco, usted puede casi siempre llegar a la raíz del problema y recuperar su energía y vitalidad.

¿Qué la tiene exhausta?

Es fácil no darle importancia a un caso de letargia pensando que es sólo otra señal de que se está haciendo vieja o que está por caer enferma de algo.

Pero para la mayoría de nosotras, no es ninguna de las dos cosas. "La mayor parte de la fatiga no se debe a envejecer o a un problema médico serio", dice el doctor Kroenke. "Muy a menudo es una señal de que el cuerpo está teniendo demasiado o muy poco de algo, y eso la hace sentirse agotada."

La mayor parte de la fatiga se debe a demasiado trabajo, demasiado estrés, demasiado peso, demasiada comida basura y muy poco ejercicio, dicen los doctores.

"La mayoría de nosotros vivimos y trabajamos en ambientes apresurados y llenos de presión", explica Ralph LaForge, un fisiólogo de ejercicio e instructor de promoción de la salud y ciencia del ejercicio en la Universidad de California, en San Diego. "Mucha de la fatiga que la gente experimenta realmente se debe a la incapacidad de ir a su propio paso, de distribuir en forma eficiente su volumen de trabajo o de poner orden en el caos a su alrededor."

Solamente luchar con las presiones de la vida cotidiana requiere bastante energía, dice Thomas Miller, Ph.D., profesor de siquiatría en el Colegio de Medicina de la Universidad de Kentucky, en Lexington. "Una de las primeras cosas que nosotros miramos cuando un paciente se queja de fatiga es el estrés. Siempre que alguien tiene una situación a la cual debe enfrentarse —problemas familiares, relaciones, presión en el trabajo— usualmente existe un tremendo factor de agotamiento tanto físico como emocional."

La fatiga también es a menudo una señal de que usted no está comiendo correctamente, dice Peter Miller, Ph.D., director ejecutivo del Instituto de Salud de Hilton Head, una clínica en Hilton Head, Carolina del Sur que desarrolla programas personales de salud. "Los hábitos de comer que nosotros establecimos cuando éramos jóvenes no son adecuados a medida de que vayamos madurando."

"Piense en su cuerpo como si fuera un carro y los alimentos fueran combustible", dice el doctor Peter Miller. "Cuando usted está joven, puede poner casi cualquier clase de gasolina en su tanque. Pero al envejecer, el cuerpo tiene dificultades para funcionar con esa gasolina de bajo octanaje. Por lo tanto, usted necesita llenar su tanque con un combustible de alta calidad y en las cantidades apropiadas."

Si usted come de más, por ejemplo, va a almacenar más combustible del que necesita en forma de grasa. Y el tener que cargar con ese peso del cuerpo en exceso por todos lados puede hacer que cualquier persona se sienta desganada. En el otro extremo, comer de menos también puede causar fatiga al privarla de suficientes calorías para impulsar su cuerpo a lo largo del día. Es por eso que muchas mujeres que hacen dietas muy estrictas o con muy bajas calorías seguido encuentran que sus niveles de energía caen por el suelo. Son como carros con el tanque vacío.

Su nivel de actividad también tiene un efecto directo sobre si usted se siente fatigada o no, dice LaForge. La falta de ejercicio puede fácilmente crear un patrón de inactividad que es difícil romper. "Un cuerpo en descanso tiende a permanecer en descanso", dice LaForge. "Generalmente, mientras más activa y en forma está usted, más resistencia y energía tendrá cotidianamente. Los carteros, por ejemplo, están siempre de pie. Sin embargo, se quejan de fatiga mucho menos que los empleados de oficina."

Por otro lado, demasiado ejercicio puede producir un efecto negativo. "Hacer un esfuerzo excesivo puede mandar su nivel de energía para abajo", dice LaForge. Eso es porque cuando hacemos ejercicio, el cuerpo produce ácido láctico, una substancia que se acumula en nuestros músculos, produciendo debilidad y dolores en el cuerpo. Esta acumulación normalmente no representa un problema, cuando nosotros evitamos trabajar hasta caer exhaustas y seguimos nuestras sesiones de ejercicio con períodos de descanso, porque entonces nuestros cuerpos son capaces de deshacerse del ácido láctico.

Pero cuando empujamos nuestros cuerpos durante las sesiones de ejercicio y no les damos tiempo a nuestros músculos para recuperarse, el ácido láctico se acumula más rápidamente de lo que nos podemos deshacer de él. Y esto nos puede hacer sentir fatigadas todo el tiempo.

¿Otros factores que pueden hacernos sentir cansadas todo el tiempo? Fumar, las así llamadas drogas recreativas, el alcohol y los patrones de comer y dormir irregularmente ponen un enorme esfuerzo sobre nuestra mente y cuerpo. Algunas veces, los expertos están de acuerdo, la fatiga es simplemente su cuerpo gritándole que su estilo de vida no es uno que le pueda servir de apoyo a un cuerpo saludable.

Pero la fatiga forma parte de la vida de una mujer. Tanto el embarazo como el período posterior al parto pueden ser los momentos más agotadores en la vida de cualquier mujer. La tensión física y emocional del embarazo y del parto — más el aumento de peso, enfermedad de las mañanas y alimentación de pecho asociados con esto— consumen una cantidad enorme de energía. Lo mismo ocurre con los cambios de estado de ánimo, los dolores de cabeza, la diarrea y los sofocos que algunas mujeres experimentan durante los cambios hormonales de menstruación, síndrome premenstrual o menopausia.

Recupere sus ganas de vivir

La fatiga puede ser un síntoma de cualquier cosa, desde el resfriado (catarro) común hasta el cáncer. Es un síntoma de hepatitis, diabetes, enfermedad del corazón, tuberculosis, problemas de la tiroides, enfermedad de Hodgkin's, esclerosis múltiple, anemia, SIDA, ansiedad y depresión. Y también es un efecto secundario de algunos de los medicamentos usados para tratar estas condiciones.

Pero la fatiga rara vez es algo de lo que haya que preocuparse a menos que venga acompañada por otros síntomas tales como dolor, inflamación o fiebre, o si dura más de una semana. Si su fatiga ha durado tanto así o tiene otros síntomas, vea a su doctor.

De lo contrario, aquí hay algunos consejos para revitalizar su vida.

Tómese su tiempo. "La fatiga es el precio que pagamos por empujarnos a nosotros mismos más allá del punto donde nuestras mentes y cuerpos dicen no", dice el doctor Kroenke. Así que piense dónde podría ser que usted está empujándose más allá de lo que son sus límites naturales. Reduzca algunas de sus actividades. No trabaje o haga ejercicio tan dura, rápida o prolongadamente como lo ha estado haciendo. Tome descansos frecuentemente. Y asegúrese de dormir la noche entera todas las noches —lo cual significa que duerme bien y suficiente para levantarse sintiéndose como nueva en la mañana.

Enfoque su energía. Romperse la cabeza por situaciones que están fuera de su control sólo logra consumir la energía personal, dice el doctor Thomas Miller. Aprenda a dejar a un lado las cosas que usted no puede cambiar y enfoque sus energías en aquellas que sí puede.

Ordene el desorden. ¿Se siente usted rendida con una lista de tareas antes de siquiera haber empezado? Ponga orden en el desorden de su vida poco a poco, dice LaForge. Empiece su día con una lista de cuatro o cinco tareas que usted seguramente puede completar, y trabaje sólo en ellas. Al día siguiente, pruebe cuatro o cinco más. Lo que al principio parecía como una montaña que usted no hubiera podido escalar se convierte en una serie de pequeñas colinas sobre las cuales camina usted con facilidad.

Diviértase. Mucho trabajo y nada de diversión pone más estrés en la mente y el cuerpo del que estos pueden manejar, dice el doctor Thomas Miller. Mezclar su programa diario con una combinación de experiencias sociales y actividades agradables proporciona el descanso necesario en la acción y alivia ese estrés antes de que éste agote su sistema de energía.

Póngase en marcha. Según un estudio de Robert Thayer, Ph.D., profesor de sicología en la Universidad Estatal de California, en Long Beach, una caminata de diez minutos a paso ligero provoca un cambio en el estado de ánimo que aumenta rápidamente los niveles de energía y los mantiene en alto por hasta dos horas.

Y un paseo después de comer puede contrarrestar el descenso de energía que usted experimenta después de una comida fuerte, agrega el doctor Peter

¿Tiene usted el síndrome de fatiga crónica?

El síndrome de fatiga crónica (o *CFS*, por sus siglas en inglés) es un padecimiento raro y extenuante que deja a quienes lo padecen débiles, exhaustas y apenas capaces de funcionar por meses o aun décadas.

La causa es todavía un misterio. "Debido a que CFS por lo general aparece después de una gripe u otra enfermedad, en alguna ocasión se pensó que era causado por el virus de Epstein-Barr", dice el doctor Nelson Gantz, un miembro del Grupo de Trabajo sobre el Síndrome de Fatiga Crónica de los Centros para el Control y la Prevención de Enfermedades (o *CDC*, por sus siglas en inglés), quien es profesor clínico de medicina en el Colegio de Medicina de la Universidad Estatal de Pensilvania, en Hershey y jefe de medicina y de la División de Enfermedades Infecciosas en el Centro Médico Policlínico en Harrisburg, Pensilvania. "Hoy estamos menos seguros de sus orígenes. Probablemente no tiene una sola causa sino que es una combinación de infecciones virales, alergias y factores sicológicos actuando sobre el sistema inmune."

No hay cura para el síndrome, dice el doctor Gantz. Hasta que se encuentre una, las personas con la enfermedad pueden encontrar alivio a través de un programa de buena nutrición, ejercicio cuidadoso y descanso que desarrollen con sus médicos personales. En casos graves, se están usando drogas antiinflamatorias no esteroides, y antidepresivos para aliviar parcialmente los síntomas, según el doctor Gantz.

¿Cómo sabe usted si tiene CFS? El equipo de trabajo CDC ha desarrollado un grupo de parámetros. Para que se le diagnostique con CFS, usted debe haber sufrido de fatiga persistente por al menos seis meses. La fatiga no debe haber existido previamente, debe persistir a

---

Miller. Digerir comidas fuertes aumenta el flujo de sangre y oxígeno al estómago e intestinos, y esto le quita energía a los músculos y al cerebro. Pero una caminata mantendrá sangre y oxígeno circulando uniformemente en todo el cuerpo.

Equilibre su dieta. Una dieta de comida basura alta en azúcar, grasa y alimentos procesados le proporciona a su cuerpo poco o nada de las vitaminas, los minerales y los nutrientes básicos que necesita para funcionar a niveles normales. Y algunas veces tan sólo la más pequeña deficiencia de cualquiera de estos nutrientes es suficiente para mandar los niveles de energía en picada.

pesar de un descanso en cama y debe reducir su nivel diario de actividades a la mitad por un mínimo de seis meses.

La existencia de alguna otra enfermedad, infección, malignidad o condición que pueda provocar síntomas similares así como el uso de algunas drogas, medicamentos o químicos, deben ser descartados por un médico.

Usted debe haber sufrido 8 de los siguientes 11 síntomas por al menos seis meses:

1. Fiebre ligera o escalofríos
2. Garganta irritada
3. Dolor en los ganglios linfáticos (glándulas en ambos lados del cuello)
4. Debilidad general inexplicable en los músculos
5. Molestia o dolor en los músculos
6. Fatiga por 24 horas o más después de niveles de ejercicio que antes se toleraban fácilmente
7. Dolores de cabeza fuera de lo normal
8. Achaques y dolores (sin hinchazón o enrojecimiento) que pasan de una articulación a otra
9. Alguna de estas quejas: pérdida de memoria, irritabilidad excesiva, confusión, dificultad para pensar, incapacidad para concentrarse, depresión
10. Dificultad para dormir
11. Desarrollo extremadamente rápido de estos síntomas, que van de unas cuantas horas a unos cuantos días

La respuesta, dice el doctor Peter Miller, es encontrar un equilibrio tanto en la cantidad como en el tipo de alimentos que usted come. "Es importante comer de todos los grupos principales de alimentos —frutas, verduras, granos y cereales, lácteos, nueces y carnes— diariamente para garantizar que usted está dándole a su cuerpo la combinación correcta de combustible y nutrientes básicos para seguir funcionando a niveles óptimos", dice el doctor Miller.

Idealmente, todos los días usted debería obtener un 60 por ciento (o más) de sus calorías de alimentos ricos en carbohidratos tales como la pasta, el pan, las papas y los frijoles (habichuelas); un 25 por ciento (o menos) de sus calorías de la grasa que se encuentra en alimentos tales como el aceite de *canola*, el aceite de oliva y la mantequilla de cacahuate (maní), y un 15 por ciento de sus calorías de alimentos ricos en proteínas tales como pollo y pescado.

Concéntrese en los carbohidratos. De los tres nutrientes proveedores de energía —carbohidratos, grasa y proteína— los carbohidratos son los más potentes para combatir la fatiga. "Los carbohidratos proporcionan una fuente de energía eficiente y de acción prolongada", dice el doctor Peter Miller. Para producir una reserva abundante de energía de carbohidratos, añada algunos de estos alimentos a su plato siempre que se siente a comer.

Coma más frecuentemente. El omitir comidas puede dejar sus reservas de combustible peligrosamente bajas, y digerir comidas fuertes puede ser un desgaste enorme de energía. Desafortunadamente, las tres comidas al día tradicionales pueden contribuir al problema.

"Su cuerpo necesita combustible en dosis moderadas a lo largo del día para continuar funcionando a niveles óptimos", dice el doctor Peter Miller. Él recomienda consumir cuatro o cinco comidas pequeñas todos los días. "El reducir la cantidad de comida que usted come en cada ocasión y el repartir su consumo de calorías más uniformemente durante el transcurso del día pone más energía a disposición de su cuerpo a lo largo del día", dice él.

Busque bocadillos buenos. Cuando su estómago está rugiendo y su energía declinando, los mejores bocadillos (meriendas o *snacks*) son los del tipo natural, dice el doctor Peter Miller. Las frutas, las verduras crudas, las nueces y las palomitas de maíz sin mantequilla —los cuales son bajos en grasa consumidora de energía— son unos vigorizantes excelentes.

Evite la solución momentánea. Los alimentos cargados de azúcar como son los dulces y los refrescos pueden cargar su nivel de energía por un rato, pero también causan que los niveles de azúcar en la sangre aumenten y bruscamente desciendan. Desafortunadamente, el resultado es que su nivel de energía bajará aún más de lo que estaba antes, dice el doctor Peter Miller.

Tome café. Unos estudios del Instituto Tecnológico de Massachussets han descubierto que la cafeína en una sola taza de café puede impulsar su nivel de energía por hasta seis horas, según informan los investigadores. Pero no abuse.

Ahóguese en seis vasos de agua. Sentirse debilitada es a menudo la primera señal de deshidratación, dice el doctor Peter Miller. Si toma por lo menos seis vasos de agua por día —más si usted es activa o está tratando de perder peso— evitará este tipo de fatiga.

Evite los tragos y las píldoras. El uso continuo de alcohol, píldoras para dormir y tranquilizantes hará que cualquiera actúe como un zombie, dice el doctor Kroenke. Y créalo usted o no, los estimulantes y las píldoras para levantar el ánimo la pueden hacer sentir allá bien arriba por las nubes y dejarla por el suelo cuando los efectos inmediatos hayan pasado.

Revise su botiquín de las medicinas. Los antihistamínicos y el alcohol, los cuales se encuentran en una gran variedad de medicamentos para el resfriado (catarro) de venta sin y con receta, pueden hacerla sentir mareada, dice el doctor Kroenke. Pregunte a su doctora o farmacéutica si ella le puede recomendar una alternativa que no la fatigue.

Piense en otras posibilidades. Muchas personas combaten la fatiga yendo más allá de los límites tradicionales de la ciencia occidental, dice LaForge. La meditación, el yoga y el masaje son solamente algunas de las opciones poco tradicionales que quienes las practican dicen que vigorizan, refrescan y reviven tanto al cuerpo como a la mente.

Los estudios de la Escuela de Medicina de Harvard muestran que si respira profundo, exhala, y después se sienta y se queda quieta por 20 minutos mientras se concentra en una palabra que refleje su fe personal —*Dios, Alá, Krishna* o *shalom,* por ejemplo— relajará y revigorizará tanto su mente como su cuerpo.

Busque en las páginas amarillas de su directorio telefónico local organizaciones que enseñen estas técnicas. En muchos casos, también las puede encontrar en su Asociación Cristiana de Jóvenes (o *YMCA* por sus siglas en inglés) local.

Pregunte a su doctor acerca de los suplementos. Además de una dieta balanceada, un suplemento de multivitaminas y minerales debería asegurar que usted va a tener todas las vitaminas y minerales que necesita, dice el doctor Kroenke. Hable con su doctor para ver cuál es el apropiado para usted.

FIBROMAS

No siempre es necesario hacer algo

Usted se siente hinchada, le duele la espalda, y tiene un período que parece que no va a terminar nunca. Se arrastra a ver a su doctora, quien encuentra que su corazón está bien, sus pulmones están perfectos y su presión arterial magnífica.

Entonces, ella le examina la pelvis.

"¡Ajá!", usted la oye decir desde el otro lado de los estribos. Ella oprime su útero, desde la vagina, y entonces rinde su veredicto. "Sí, es un fibroma. No muy grande. Ha agrandado su útero al tamaño de un embarazo de nueve semanas."

La doctora se quita los guantes. "Siéntese, y vamos a hablar acerca de lo que vamos a hacer."

Es una escena común. En algún momento de sus vidas, el 60 por ciento de las mujeres que viven en los Estados Unidos tendrá fibromas, los cuales son tumores benignos. Los fibromas empiezan como pequeñas aglutinaciones de células musculares que crecen desde adentro, afuera o dentro de la pared uterina.

El problema es que los fibromas pueden hacernos viejas antes de tiempo. Pueden romper el recubrimiento del útero y pueden crecer lo suficiente para aplicar una presión sobre los intestinos, la vejiga y los tubos que van de los riñones a la vejiga —todo lo cual puede conducir a la esterilidad, incontinencia, daños a los riñones, estreñimiento, dolor crónico y hemorroides.

No los pierda de vista

Qué causa los fibromas es todavía un misterio, dicen los doctores.

Los fibromas ocurren durante los años fértiles de una mujer, después de su primer período y antes de la menopausia, porque a estos les sienta de maravilla su abastecimiento de estrógeno. Son más comunes en mujeres embarazadas y con sobrepeso, y en aquellas que toman esos tipos de píldoras para el control de la natalidad o para reposición de hormonas que exponen a las mujeres a niveles más altos de estrógeno.

Pero además de la observación de que parece que viene de familia, nadie tiene idea de su causa.

"Siempre son benignos", dice el doctor Alvin F. Goldfarb, director de educación para obstetricia y ginecología en el Colegio Médico Thomas Jefferson de la Universidad Thomas Jefferson, en Filadelfia. "Pueden sufrir cambios malignos, pero el desarrollo de un tumor maligno es raro. Por ello, en la mayoría de los casos, si los fibromas no provocan síntomas, no se necesita hacer nada."

¿Qué clases de síntomas requieren hacer algo? "Dolores de espalda, estreñimiento, presión en la vejiga que cause urgencia y frecuencia de orinar o un útero más grande que un embarazo de 10 a 12 semanas", responde el doctor Goldfarb. Todos pueden indicar el principio de problemas con la vejiga, el intestino y los riñones estimulados por los fibromas.

Los fibromas también requieren que usted haga algo si empieza a sangrar excesivamente durante su período, si sangra entre períodos, si su ginecólogo detecta un crecimiento repentino que surge en los fibromas entre un examen rutinario y otro o si estos afectan la reproducción, ya sea evitando la implantación de un óvulo fertilizado o causando repetidos abortos, dice el doctor Goldfarb.

Sus opciones

Afortunadamente, sólo la mitad de las mujeres que tienen fibromas experimenta algún síntoma lo bastante severo como para necesitar tratamiento. Esto es lo que los doctores recomiendan cuando sí lo experimentan.

Mátelos de hambre. Su doctor puede recetar la hormona secretante de gonadotropina (o _GnRH_, por sus siglas en inglés), la cual puede reducir el tamaño de los fibromas en un 50 por ciento. Esta hormona suspende la producción de estrógeno por parte de los ovarios y de esa manera priva a los fibromas de lo que para ellos era un abastecimiento constante de alimento nutritivo.

Sin embargo, las mujeres que toman GnRH deben entender que cuando la terapia hormonal termina, los fibromas van a crecer otra vez, advierte la doctora Mary Lake Polan, Ph.D., profesora y presidenta del Departamento de Ginecología y Obstetricia en la Escuela de Medicina de la Universidad de Stanford, en California. Y nadie debería tomar la hormona por sí sola por más de seis meses, porque puede causar osteoporosis. Hay otras terapias que combinan los iniciadores GnRH con estrógeno y/o progestina, una forma sintética de la hormona progesterona. Esto permite a las mujeres usar la terapia GnRH por años, dice la doctora Polan.

Un momento apropiado para usar GnRH es cuando la mujer está cerca de la menopausia, dice la doctora Polan. Éste puede achicar los fibromas y conservarlos pequeños hasta que desaparecen naturalmente en la menopausia.

Considere la extirpación. Si usted quiere proteger su fertilidad, puede necesitar que le extirpen los tumores. La operación se llama miomectomía y se lleva a cabo de dos maneras, dice el doctor Goldfarb.

En un procedimiento laparoscópico, se hacen un par de pequeñas incisiones en el abdomen. En una de las incisiones se inserta un laparoscopio, un pequeño instrumento usado para ver el cuerpo por dentro; en la otra incisión se inserta un láser. El doctor localiza los fibromas y los elimina con el láser. Los restos se extraen con otro instrumento quirúrgico.

Este es el procedimiento que los doctores jóvenes se inclinan a usar, porque es más moderno, agrega el doctor Goldfarb. Es menos invasivo que otras opciones y realiza un trabajo excelente siempre que los fibromas no sean grandes.

El doctor Goldfarb sugiere que las mujeres que están pensando en este procedimiento se aseguren de que sus doctores estén bien versados en éste. Él sugiere que usted pregunte a su doctora cuántas laparoscopías realiza ella anualmente. Escoja un médico que realice por lo menos 50 por año, dice el doctor Goldfarb.

El segundo procedimiento es una operación en la cual el abdomen se abre por completo y los fibromas se extraen quirúrgicamente. La cirugía es mas invasiva y requiere un tiempo más largo de recuperación.

El doctor Goldfarb aconseja que, ya sea que los fibromas se extraen por cirugía de láser o mediante una operación abierta, usted siempre debería hablar con su médico sobre las posibles complicaciones de cada procedimiento.

Discuta la posibilidad de una histerectomía. Si sus tumores son muy grandes, usted puede necesitar una histerectomía. Y a menudo el médico no sabrá si usted la necesita o no hasta el momento en que esté practicando la miomectomía, dice el doctor Goldfarb.

"Yo he llevado a cabo muchas miomectomías donde he extirpado de 4 a 7 libras (1,8 a 3 kilos) de tumor y he salvado el útero, y las mujeres han podido llegar a tener niños", dice el doctor Goldfarb. "Pero nunca se puede garantizar nada hasta que se encuentra allí. Si usted es mi paciente, yo le diré para empezar: si tiene un tumor enorme y yo no lo puedo extirpar, quiero su permiso para efectuar una histerectomía."

Antes de una miomectomía, pregunte a su doctora acerca de la posibilidad de una histerectomía y las repercusiones de esta cirugía. Indíquele a ella si usted quiere este procedimiento o no.

FUMAR

Purifique el aire
y ponga al tiempo de su lado

Si usted se encuentra entre los millones de mujeres que empezaron a fumar durante su adolescencia porque se querían ver y sentir mayores, sus deseos se le cumplieron. A lo mejor en mayor proporción de lo que usted esperaba. Nada envejece más su apariencia, espíritu y salud que el vicio más practicado y más peligroso de los Estados Unidos.

Sólo pregúntele a la doctora Elizabeth Sherertz, una dermatóloga e investigadora en la Escuela de Medicina Bowman Gray de la Universidad de Wake Forest, en Winston-Salem, Carolina del Norte. "Hemos encontrado que en promedio, las fumadoras tienden a verse entre cinco y diez años mayores que sus edades reales debido a las arrugas causadas por fumar", dice ella. "Las personas que fuman tienen más probabilidades de desarrollar arrugas, porque el fumar daña el tejido elástico que mantiene a la piel tirante, además de que probablemente también aumenta los efectos dañinos del sol en la piel."

O pregúntele a Richard Jenks, Ph.D., un sociólogo en la Universidad del Sudeste de Indiana, en New Albany quien estudia los efectos que el fumar tiene en nuestro estado emocional, quien encontró una vez más, las fumadoras sufren. "Las fumadoras saben que su hábito es un camino seguro a los problemas de salud, y ellas con más probabilidad que las no fumadoras o las ex fumadoras lo describirán como algo sucio", dice él. "Pero lo que mi estudio encontró fue que las fumadoras tienden a sentir que tienen menos control sobre sus vidas, además que se sienten menos satisfechas con sus vidas que las no fumadoras."

O pregúntele a cualquier otro investigador o médico que haya estudiado alguna vez los efectos que el fumar tiene en nuestro bienestar físico y emocional. Estudio tras estudio —y ha habido cientos de ellos— respaldan lo que los expertos ya saben: si no la mata —y todos los años una de cada cinco

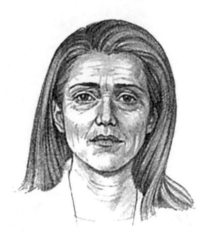

Fumadora, contemple su rostro futuro. Note las arrugas que salen de los labios y las comisuras de los ojos. Note, también, las mejillas con líneas profundas y las grietas que recorren desde arriba hacia abajo de la mandíbula inferior.

personas en todo el mundo se muere por las enfermedades relacionadas con fumar— sí seguramente le quitará años a su vida. Margaret A. Chesney, Ph.D., una investigadora de la salud femenina y de fumar dice: "Si usted quiere hacer radicalmente más lento el proceso del envejecimiento y vivir más, deje de fumar".

Una batalla dura para las mujeres

Pero siempre es más fácil decirlo que hacerlo, especialmente para muchas de nosotras. "Cuando en la década de los años 60 se publicó el primer informe del cirujano general sobre fumar y la salud, el número de hombres que fumaba duplicaba al de las mujeres," dice Douglas E. Jorenby, Ph.D., coordinador de actividades clínicas para el Centro de Investigación e Intervención del Tabaco en la Escuela de Medicina de la Universidad de Wisconsin, en Madison. "Hoy, la relación entre las mujeres y los hombres que fuman es casi igual, y en los próximos años va a invertirse por primera vez, y habrá más mujeres fumando que hombres."

En números reales, eso se traduce a más del 24 por ciento de las mujeres estadounidenses mayores de 18 años de edad que fuman; en disminución con respecto al 34 por ciento que fumaba cuando el informe del cirujano general se publicó en 1964. Hoy en día, cerca del 28 por ciento de los hombres estadounidenses fuma, una reducción drástica del 52 por ciento que fumaba en 1964. Según los Centros para el Control y la Prevención de Enfermedades, actualmente el 20 por ciento de los latinos y casi el 25 por ciento de las latinas son fumadores. La conclusión final alarmante es que debido al hecho de que más niños están empezando a fumar, los índices de fumar ya no van a seguir bajando. Y el cáncer del pulmón mata ahora a más mujeres todos los años que el cáncer de mama.

Una vez que las mujeres empezamos a fumar, las estadísticas muestran que nos cuesta más tanto física como emocionalmente dejarlo. "Hay evidencia de que un número igual de mujeres como de hombres tratan de dejarlo, pero los hombres tienen casi el doble de éxito", dice el doctor Jorenby. "Una razón es que las mujeres indican sufrir de más depresión cuando dejan de fumar, y sabemos por varios estudios que la depresión hace más posible que usted vuelva a fumar."

Pero él agrega, parece que las mujeres tienen menos deseos de dejar de fumar. "Muchas mujeres se sienten tan abrumadas por sus familias y trabajos que muchas de ellas manifiestan que los cigarrillos son su único refugio. Y por ello vacilan en dejarlo, aunque ellas saben que si lo dejan será de gran beneficio para su salud."

Las mujeres, particularmente aquellas menores de 25 años de edad, se han vuelto un objetivo comercial importante para las compañías de cigarrillos. "Uno de los mensajes importantes detrás de la publicidad dirigida a las mujeres es que el fumar les ayudará a controlar su peso", dice el doctor Jorenby. "En un anuncio para cigarrillos que yo vi, estaba la foto de una modelo que ya estaba bastante flaca. Pero la foto estaba distorsionada para que se viera aún más delgada —más delgada que cualquier ser humano podría realmente estar. El mensaje, dirigido a las mujeres en su adolescencia y a principio de su década de los 20 años de edad, es obvio: el fumar le ayuda a estar delgada y glamorosa."

El mensaje parece ser efectivo. Aunque los Centros para el Control y la Prevención de Enfermedades, en Atlanta, no mantienen estadísticas desglosando por sexo a los fumadores jóvenes, Suzie Gates, portavoz de su Oficina sobre Fumar y Salud dice que la mayoría de las 3.000 personas que empiezan

Deje de fumar sin aumentar de peso

Para muchas mujeres que quieren dejar de fumar, el mayor temor es aumentar de peso.

Bueno, ya no se inquiete más porque es oficial: según los Centros para el Control y la Prevención de Enfermedades, en Atlanta cuando usted deja de fumar, el promedio de peso que va a aumentar es de 5 libras (2,25 kilos). Y el aumento de peso puede ser evitado por medio de una dieta cuidadosa y manejo del estrés. De hecho, algunas personas pierden peso después de dejar de fumar.

Para muchas mujeres, dejar de fumar es parte de un programa completo para volverse saludable que incluye ejercicio regular y mejoras en la dieta, dice Douglas E. Jorenby, Ph.D., coordinador de actividades clínicas para el Centro de Investigación e Intervención del Tabaco en la Escuela de Medicina de la Universidad de Wisconsin, en Madison.

Entretanto, tome sus vitaminas

Mientras que no hay substitución para dejar de fumar, las vitaminas antioxidantes han mostrado ofrecer por lo menos algo de protección contra los efectos dañinos de fumar.

Jeffrey Blumberg, Ph.D., director asociado en el Centro de Investigación de la Nutrición Humana en la Vejez del Departamento de Agricultura de los Estados Unidos en la Universidad de Tufts, en Boston, recomienda estas vitaminas para conservar fuerte a su sistema inmune y para compensar algo del daño causado por el tabaco.

Vitamina C. 250 a 1.000 miligramos diarios. La Asignación Dietética Recomendada (o *RDA*, por sus siglas en inglés) es de 60 miligramos. Algunas buenas fuentes alimenticias incluyen las frutas cítricas, el brócoli, el cantaloup, los pimientos rojos, el kiwi y las fresas.

Vitamina E. 100 a 400 unidades diarias. La RDA es de 12 UI u 8 miligramos equivalentes de alfatocoferol. Las buenas fuentes alimenticias incluyen aceites para cocinar, germen de trigo y mangos.

Betacaroteno. 15 a 30 miligramos diarios. No hay una RDA establecida. Las mejores fuentes son las frutas y verduras amarillo-anaranjadas y verde oscuro tales como las zanahorias, *sweet potato* (camote, boniato) y *squash*, así como la espinaca y otros vegetales verdes frondosos.

con el hábito todos los días son mujeres menores de 25 años de edad y algunas tan jóvenes como de 12 años de edad.

Fumar no la pone flaca

A pesar de lo que las agencias de publicidad quieren que usted crea, las fumadoras no son más delgadas. Cierto, la nicotina suprime ligeramente el apetito, lo cual significa que las fumadoras consumen menos comidas. Pero cuando comen, las fumadoras más que las no fumadoras tienden a gravitar hacia los alimentos que son altos en calorías y grasa, dice Doris Abood, Ed.D., profesora asociada de educación sobre la salud en la Universidad Estatal de la Florida, en Tallahassee. En su estudio, el cual examinó los hábitos de fumar, comer, beber y hacer ejercicio de 1.820 personas, ella también encontró que los fumadores hacían menos ejercicio y consumían más alcohol, el cual es notablemente alto en calorías. La doctora Abood y otros investigadores encontraron que mientras más fuman las personas, más malos hábitos practican, y en gran volumen.

Sin embargo, sin importar estos otros hábitos, es el fumar mismo el que provoca el mayor daño, causando casi 419.000 muertes al año. También desempeña un papel principal en una cantidad de enfermedades, entre ellos cáncer, resfriados (catarros), enfermedades del corazón y hasta fracturas de la cadera. "Los efectos de fumar están tan distribuidos por todo el cuerpo que tienen un impacto en virtualmente cualquier enfermedad en la que usted pudiera pensar", dice el doctor Jorenby.

Por qué el fumar mata

El humo del cigarrillo contiene cerca de 4.000 químicos, incluyendo cantidades diminutas de venenos tales como arsénico, formaldehído y *DDT*. Con cada soplo, estos venenos se inhalan a través de los pulmones —los cuales retienen hasta un 90 por ciento de los compuestos— y después se pasan a través del torrente sanguíneo. Algunos de estos venenos, como el monóxido de carbono, son los llamados radicales libres que roban de oxígeno a las células de la sangre. Los radicales libres se han vinculado con una gran cantidad de problemas que van desde las arrugas al cáncer.

Entretanto, la nicotina en el humo del tabaco causa que las glándulas adrenales secreten hormonas que aumentan la presión arterial y el ritmo del corazón, lo cual hace que su corazón trabaje más intensamente —la razón primordial por la cual las mujeres que fuman tienen el doble de probabilidades de tener derrames cerebrales y casi tres veces más el riesgo de enfermedades del corazón. El riesgo aumenta aún más si ellas toman anticonceptivos orales.

Fumar la hace a usted más susceptible a las enfermedades infecciosas tales como resfriados (catarros) y gripa, ya que daña los cilios, pequeños cuerpos como pelos que atrapan y arrastran las substancias extrañas de los pulmones. Sin los cilios para cumplir con su trabajo, el alquitrán de los cigarrillos obstruye las vías respiratorias, conduciendo al enfisema y cáncer del pulmón. También perjudica su capacidad de estar en forma, privando a su cuerpo y mente de oxígeno vigorizante. En promedio, las mujeres fumadoras alcanzan la menopausia por lo menos un año antes que las no fumadoras, y la menopausia está asociada con un riesgo más alto de un ataque al corazón prematuro.

Pero aun los síntomas asociados con fumar causan su propio daño. Por ejemplo, las mujeres que fuman tienen un índice mayor de incontinencia urinaria debido a la tos causada por su hábito. "Aun cuando el fumar no sea un factor causante de una enfermedad determinada, sí ciertamente puede agravarla", dice el doctor Jorenby. "Por ejemplo, nosotros sabemos que el fumar no causa la diabetes, pero las personas con diabetes que fuman tienen un pronóstico mucho peor que aquellas que no fuman."

Otro ejemplo que hace al caso: un estudio de investigadores británicos encontró que los fumadores con el virus de inmunodeficiencia humano desarrollan el SIDA abiertamente declarado dos veces más rápido que los no fumadores, aunque los investigadores no saben por qué.

Cómo dejarlo —para siempre

La buena noticia es que algo de este daño se puede revertir. Sólo un año después de que usted deja de fumar, su riesgo de una enfermedad del corazón se reduce a la mitad, y después de tres años, su riesgo se vuelve comparable al de una persona que nunca ha tocado un cigarrillo. Su riesgo de otras enfermedades, tales como el enfisema, la bronquitis y el cáncer también disminuye. Además, usted se verá más joven, con más energía y resistencia, y menos arrugas.

Seguro, dejarlo es difícil. Menos del 10 por ciento de los 20 millones de fumadores que tratan de dejarlo todos los años realmente lo logran, dice Rami Bachiman, director de educación comunitaria de la Asociación del Pulmón de Nueva York, en la Ciudad de Nueva York. Hay varias estrategias para ayudarla —mantener ocupadas las manos, morder zanahorias, respirar aire fresco profundamente, tomar mucha agua o incluso recompensarse a usted misma con un regalo. Pero aquí está cómo usted puede aumentar sus posibilidades de tener éxito para dejarlo y no recaer durante esas cruciales primeras semanas.

Lleve un diario de su progreso. La primera cosa que usted debe hacer es ponerse un plazo de hasta tres semanas por adelantado para cuando va a dar su última fumada. Pero entretanto, anote cada cigarrillo que usted fuma —dónde lo fumó y bajo qué circunstancias, aconseja Don R. Powell, Ph.D., presidente del Instituto para Medicina Preventiva de los Estados Unidos, en Farmington Hills, Michigan, y un ex fumador. Eso le ayudará a identificar las situaciones que la incitan a fumar. Entonces busque otras cosas distintas para hacer que no sean fumar cigarrillos.

Retrase el deseo. Si usted está dejándolo gradualmente, cada vez que usted tenga ganas de fumar, aguántelas por unos cinco minutos, sugiere el doctor Powell. Después de unos cuantos días, aumente y aguante las ganas 10 minutos. Después de otros cuantos días, aumente la espera a 15 minutos y así sucesivamente. "Usted se dará cuenta de que las ganas reales de fumar en un momento determinado se desvanecen relativamente rápido", dice él.

Mejor bien acompañada que sola. Ya sea que usted decida parar en seco o hacerlo en forma gradual al disminuir lentamente el número de cigarrillos que fuma, a usted probablemente le irá mejor si le dan mucho ánimo. "Ya que tienen más dificultades para dejar de fumar, las mujeres van a necesitar todo el apoyo que puedan conseguir", dice el doctor Jorenby. "Si tiene algún tipo de apoyo de grupo puede representar una gran diferencia en cómo le va a ir a usted, ya sea que venga de amistades o familiares o de algún tipo de terapia de grupo." Hay probablemente grupos en su área ofreciendo orientación gratuita y terapia de grupo para las mujeres que están tratando de dejarlo. Póngase en contacto con la división local de la Asociación del Corazón de los Estados Unidos para que le den más información.

Hágale el juego al jugo. La parte más difícil de parar en seco de fumar —que es el método más popular— es soportar los síntomas de abstinencia de la nicotina, los cuales duran de una a dos semanas. Pero usted podrá superar más rápidamente la irritabilidad, ansiedad, confusión y dificultad para concentrarse y

¿Funcionan los atajos?

Los parches y chicles de nicotina y la hipnosis pueden quitar parte de lo doloroso de los síntomas de abstinencia que vienen con el dejar de fumar, pero no espere que estos medios auxiliares vayan a remplazar las agallas y la determinación.

Las fumadoras que lo dejan ayudadas por estas herramientas tienen dos a tres veces más probabilidades de tener éxito que aquellas que deciden suspenderlo en seco. Aunque el dejar de fumar en seco es el método más popular, es también el menos exitoso, teniendo un índice de éxito de sólo el 5 por ciento. La fumadora que usa parches o chicle de nicotina y además se inscribe en un programa comprensivo de conducta para cesar de fumar, aumenta sus probabilidades de dejar el hábito y en un año puede anticipar un índice de éxito del 23 al 40 por ciento. Entretanto, hay un índice de éxito del 15 por ciento cuando se usa la hipnosis.

No obstante, los parches y chicles de nicotina tienen algunos efectos secundarios.

El parche, un cuadrado adhesivo que secreta nicotina a través de la piel y en el torrente sanguíneo para ayudar a aliviar el dolor de los síntomas de abstinencia, puede causar picazón y ardor leve. Y si la que lo usa fuma aunque sea un cigarrillo mientras está usando el parche, puede tener un ataque al corazón.

La efectividad del chicle, entretanto, desaparece si usted come o bebe algo —especialmente diuréticos como café y cola— dentro de los 15 minutos de haber empezado a masticarlo. Y aunque el chicle no se supone que debe usarse después de cuatro meses de su último cigarrillo, 1 en cada 12 fumadoras continúa usándolo por más de un año después de haber dejado de fumar.

En resumen, si usted ha tratado de dejar de fumar y ha fracasado en el pasado, consulte a su médico acerca de estos productos. Pero, dice el sicólogo Mitchell Nides, Ph.D., de la Universidad de California, Los Ángeles, usted tiene que "aprender" a ser una persona no fumadora, y eso es algo que ningún producto farmacéutico puede hacer por sí solo.

para dormir que acompañan a la abstinencia de la nicotina, si bebe grandes cantidades de jugo de naranja todo el tiempo.

Eso es porque el jugo de naranja hace que su orina se vuelva más ácida, lo cual permite limpiar a su cuerpo de la nicotina más rápidamente, dice Thomas

Cooper, D.D.S., un investigador en dependencia de la nicotina y profesor de ciencias orales de la salud en la Universidad de Kentucky, en Lexington. "Además", agrega el doctor Jorenby, "el sabor cítrico en su boca hace muy desagradable el pensar en fumarse un cigarrillo".

Si usted está dejando de fumar con la ayuda de chicle o parches de nicotina recetados por un médico, evite el jugo de naranja y otras bebidas ácidas, ya que el propósito de estos productos es conservar la nicotina en su sistema.

Imagínese que es la gripa. "Antes de que tuviéramos el chicle y los parches de nicotina, yo solía decirle a las personas tratando de dejar de fumar que se imaginaran sufriendo de la gripa", dice el doctor Jorenby. "Muchos de los síntomas de abstinencia son similares a los de la gripa: usted pierde los estribos fácilmente, tiene dificultad para concentrarse, su resistencia disminuye. Y, como es el caso con la gripa, es poco lo que usted puede hacer excepto dejarla que siga su curso. Pero usted se repondrá. Si no recae y se fuma un cigarrillo, los síntomas de abstinencia desaparecerán y terminarán en el lapso de una semana o dos."

Aléjese de los bares. La mayor posibilidad de una recaída se encuentra en los bares (cantinas), dice el doctor Jorenby. "Para muchas personas, tener un trago en una mano significa tener un cigarrillo en la otra. Yo aconsejo que cualquiera que esté tratando de dejar de fumar se mantenga fuera de los bares por lo menos las dos primeras semanas después de haber dejado de fumar." En lugar de eso, él aconseja, vaya a las bibliotecas, los museos y otros lugares públicos donde se prohibe fumar. "Las personas que dejan de fumar no necesitan jurar que no volverán a ir a los bares, pero nosotros sabemos por varios estudios que a no ser que se alejen de ellos por las dos primeras semanas tienen un riesgo mucho mayor de volver a fumar."

Escriba una carta a un ser querido. Cuando le da un ataque de nicotina, tome una pluma en lugar de un cigarrillo y escriba una carta a un ser querido explicándole por qué el fumar es más importante que su vida misma, sugiere Robert Van de Castle, Ph.D., profesor emérito de medicina de la conducta en el Centro Médico de la Universidad de Virginia, en Charlottesville. En la carta, trate de explicar por qué usted continúa con un hábito que sabe que la va a matar en lugar de dejarlo y vivir para ver a un hijo graduarse de la universidad o casarse o ser testigo de otros eventos importantes. Cuando los pacientes del doctor Van de Castle hacen la prueba con esta carta, dice él, se sienten tan egoístas que a menudo les da el valor de enfrentarse a los síntomas de abstinencia y seguir sin fumar.

HISTERECTOMÍA

Infórmese bien sobre los hechos

La mayoría de nosotras a sabiendas no escogeríamos una operación que provoca una menopausia prematura. A sabiendas no escogeríamos una operación que acelera el proceso del envejecimiento y nos hace vulnerables —con una década de anticipación— a enfermedades del corazón, osteoporosis e incontinencia urinaria. Y sin embargo, eso es exactamente lo que más de medio millón de mujeres que viven en los Estados Unidos hacen cada año cuando deciden hacerse una histerectomía.

Lo triste del caso es que la cirugía posiblemente no es necesaria.

"Yo diría que el 80 por ciento de las histerectomías que no se efectúan debido a cáncer pueden ser evitadas", dice el doctor Herbert A. Goldfarb, instructor clínico de obstetricia y ginecología en la Escuela de Medicina de la Universidad de Nueva York, en la ciudad de Nueva York y autor de *The No Hysterectomy Option* (La opción de no hacerse la histerectomía). Éstas se hacen para resolver problemas para los cuales otras soluciones existen.

El 30 por ciento de las 567.000 operaciones realizadas anualmente se hacen para eliminar fibromas, crecimientos benignos dependientes de estrógeno que aparecen en la mitad de todas las mujeres en edad reproductiva y que experimentan una regresión por sí solas al llegar a la menopausia, según la investigación del Centro Nacional para Estadísticas sobre la Salud.

Solamente un poco más del 19 por ciento se llevan a cabo para eliminar la endometriosis, una condición en la cual grupos celulares del revestimiento uterino emigran fuera del útero y se localizan en la cavidad abdominal.

El 19 por ciento se hacen por razones que incluyen sangramiento entre períodos, dolor pélvico y complicaciones obstétricas.

Cerca del 16 por ciento se hacen para corregir un prolapso o un útero caído, una consecuencia común después de haber tenido varios embarazos.

Sólo el 15 por ciento de todas las histerectomías se hacen para tratar cáncer o condiciones precancerosas. Sin embargo, con excepción del cáncer, dice el doctor Goldfarb, "existen tratamientos efectivos para la mayoría de estos problemas sin tener que extirpar los órganos femeninos".

Menopausia instantánea

¿Por qué se realizan tantas histerectomías en situaciones donde la vida no está en peligro?

"A muchos doctores se les enseñó en la escuela de medicina que el útero no tiene un propósito fuera de ser un receptáculo para un feto", dice el doctor Goldfarb. Así que cuando los problemas ginecológicos surgen en una mujer entre los 30 y los 50 años de edad cuando la maternidad se ha completado, remover el útero parece ser una "solución prolija y ordenada —la panacea para todos los problemas de la pelvis", dice el doctor Goldfarb.

El problema es que no lo es —no cuando empuja a la mujer a la vejez antes de tiempo.

Hay cuatro tipos de histerectomía. Una histerectomía parcial extirpa la mayor parte del útero, dejando el cuello uterino intacto. Una histerectomía total extirpa el útero completamente, incluyendo el cuello uterino. Una histerectomía total con una salpingo-ooferoctomía bilateral también extirpa las trompas de Falopio y los ovarios. Y una histerectomía radical quita todo lo anterior más la parte superior de la vagina y algunos ganglios linfáticos.

El tipo de operación que tiene una mujer dependerá del problema que el doctor está tratando de resolver y cómo fue éste entrenado.

Todas las formas de histerectomía son cirugía seria, dice el doctor Goldfarb. Pero aquella en que se extirpan los ovarios —las cuales representan más o menos la mitad de todas las histerectomías— es probablemente la más difícil porque priva instantáneamente al cuerpo de su fuente más importante de las hormonas de estrógeno y andrógeno.

El andrógeno es lo que nos da nuestro deseo sexual. Así que sin los ovarios, las mujeres experimentan una pérdida significante de libido, dice el doctor Goldfarb. Y el estrógeno es ese elíxir mágico que mantiene a la piel suave, la vagina lubricada, las arterias flexibles, las aberturas de la vejiga tirantes y los huesos fuertes. Hasta puede contribuir a una noche de sueño tranquila.

Normalmente los ovarios empiezan a hacer más lenta su producción de estrógeno alrededor de los 35 años de edad. Mes a mes, año a año, la cantidad de estrógeno disminuye hasta ser un hilito, suspendiéndose completamente por lo general de tres a cinco años después de la menopausia.

Pero cuando se quitan los ovarios y se priva al cuerpo entero de estrógeno en forma repentina, el cuerpo reacciona en forma exagerada. "Los sofocos son más intensos, más prolongados y más frecuentes" de lo que serían durante una reducción gradual del estrógeno que ocurre naturalmente, dice el doctor Goldfarb.

Aun más, la ausencia súbita del estrógeno acelera instantáneamente varios problemas que una mujer no tendría que encarar por lo menos una década. El proceso de adelgazamiento de los huesos que conduje a la osteoporosis ocurre con el doble de rapidez, y un estudio de la Escuela de Medicina de Harvard que incluyó a 121.700 mujeres indica que aquellas a quienes se les extirparon los ovarios doblaron de riesgo de una enfermedad del corazón —a menos que tomaron suplementos de estrógeno.

Hable primero

Las mujeres nunca deberían consentir a una histerectomía hasta no haber sido informadas completamente sobre las alternativas y las consecuencias de la cirugía, agrega Nora W. Coffey, presidenta de Recursos y Servicios Educacionales sobre la Histerectomía (o *HERS*, por sus siglas en inglés), un grupo de consumidores sin fines de lucro con base en Bala Cynwyd, Pensilvania que ofrece información a las mujeres por todo el mundo sobre las alternativas a la histerectomía.

Un estudio del Colegio de Medicina de la Universidad de Cornell, en la ciudad de Nueva York indica que más de la mitad de todas las segundas opiniones sobre histerectomía encuentran que el procedimiento es inapropiado. Y éste no es un procedimiento inocuo. Cerca de una en cada siete mujeres que se sometieron a la operación necesita una nueva cirugía debido a las complicaciones de dicha operación.

Así que antes de programar una operación que podría envejecer su cuerpo y aumentar su riesgo de enfermedades, considere estas opciones.

Busque apoyo. A pesar de que hay millones de mujeres que han tenido histerectomías, muchas la enfrentaron solas, innecesariamente. Si usted está considerando este procedimiento, puede obtener ayuda de HERS. "Nosotros ofrecemos orientación gratuita acerca de las alternativas a la histerectomía que muchas mujeres no conocen, así como orientación a las mujeres que ya tuvieron una histerectomía", dice Coffey.

Consulte con otro especialista. Probablemente el problema no es realmente su útero. En un estudio a 200 mujeres con úteros de tamaño normal recomendadas a una clínica en San Diego, los investigadores encontraron que el 80 por ciento de las mujeres a quienes se les había dicho que deberían tener una histerectomía para aliviar sus dolores crónicos en la pelvis, en realidad tenían problemas gastrointestinales u otros no ginecológicos. "A usted se le puede extirpar su útero y todavía seguir con dolor", dice el doctor Francis Hutchins, profesor clínico asociado de obstetricia y ginecología en el Hospital de la Universidad Thomas Jefferson y vicecatedrático en el Hospital de Graduados, ambos en Filadelfia. Por ello, si usted tiene dolores pélvicos haga que la sometan a una evaluación minuciosa de varias causas antes de asumir que la causa es ginecológica, dice el doctor Hutchins.

Ejercite sus músculos pélvicos. En lugar de que le extirpen un útero por prolapso del mismo, trate ejercitarlo, dice el doctor Hutchins. Los ligamentos que sostienen el útero frecuentemente se debilitan después de un parto, pero los ejercicios *Kegel* pueden ayudar a aumentar el tono de los ligamentos de soporte, particularmente cuando se combinan con una crema de estrógeno aplicada vaginalmente.

Para hacer el útero y los ligamentos mas fuertes, simplemente endurezca sus músculos por varios segundos como si estuviera reteniendo orina y luego relájelos. Haga el ejercicio hasta 20 veces al día, dice el doctor Hutchins.

Pregunte acerca de un raspado. Si su problema es un sangramiento anormalmente fuerte —el cual puede ser resultado de fibromas, problemas hormonales u otras causas— pregunte a su médico acerca de eliminar por medio del raspado una porción de su revestimiento uterino para controlarlo. Este procedimiento, que elimina el sangramiento fuerte por medio de "limpiar" la parte del útero que tiene un abastecimiento rico en sangre, se realiza de dos maneras:

- Dilatación y curetaje (D & C) es un procedimiento en el cual se dilata el cuello uterino y se raspa y extirpa el revestimiento uterino con un instrumento en forma de cuchara.

- Ablación endometrial es un procedimiento más nuevo que usa un instrumento caliente en espiral llamado resectoscopio para destruir el revestimiento del útero. Hay menos dolor y la recuperación es más rápida que con una histerectomía, pero éste puede conducir a la infertilidad, y los estudios muestran que tiene un éxito completo sólo la mitad de las veces.

Planificar para después

Los expertos dicen que usted no debería precipitarse a una histerectomía sin una información completa sobre los efectos secundarios, tiempo de recuperación, y los cambios físicos y emocionales que usted puede esperar.

Si la histerectomía es lo que usted necesita, aquí está cómo sacar el mejor provecho de ésta.

Pregunte acerca de una histerectomía vaginal. En muchas histerectomías, el útero puede ser extirpado a través de la vagina mejor que a través de una incisión de 4 a 6 pulgadas (10 a 15 centímetros) de largo en el abdomen. Cuando se usa un laparoscopio para ayudar en este procedimiento, se le llama una histerectomía vaginal asistida laparascópicamente (*laparascopic assisted vaginal hysterectomy* o *LAVH*, por sus siglas en inglés). La LAVH no deja una cicatriz visible y puede llevarse a cabo como paciente ambulante, dice Joseph Gambone, D.O., profesor asociado de obstetricia y ginecología en la Escuela de Medicina UCLA de la Universidad de California, en Los Ángeles.

La LAVH requiere un cirujano bien entrenado, así que cuando su médico primario le haga recomendaciones, pida que le recomiende cirujanos certificados por el consejo (*board-certified*) en ginecología y obstetricia y que tengan experiencia en este procedimiento, aconseja el doctor Hutchins. Y no sea tímida acerca de entrevistar a más de un cirujano. Siga hablando hasta que encuentre uno con quien usted se sienta a gusto.

Luche por su cuerpo. Algunos médicos que llevan a cabo las histerectomías aconsejan quitar los ovarios como una medida preventiva contra el cáncer de los ovarios. Pero a menos que usted tenga cáncer o una historia familiar de la enfermedad, no deje que la convenzan al respecto. En toda la vida de una mujer, las probabilidades de que muera de cáncer en los ovarios son de sólo 2 en 100, dice el doctor Gambone. Entretanto, extirpar sus ovarios sin una terapia adecuada de reposición de hormonas puede duplicar su riesgo de desarrollar osteoporosis y enfermedad del corazón —el asesino número uno de las mujeres.

Pregunte acerca del estrógeno en dosis bajas. Si a usted le tienen que extirpar los ovarios, la terapia de reposición de estrógeno (*estrogen replacement therapy* o *ERT*, por sus siglas en inglés) es la mejor manera de protegerse contra las enfermedades del corazón y los síntomas de osteoporosis, dice el doctor Hutchins. Pero pregunte a su médico acerca de la dosis más baja posible, ya que el ERT puede aumentar su riesgo de cáncer de mama y otras condiciones, dice el doctor Goldfarb. Afortunadamente, los médicos creen que combinando el estrógeno con la progestina (otra hormona femenina), usted puede llegar a reducir su riesgo de cáncer.

Empiece a caminar regularmente. Si el tener una historia familiar de cáncer la hace a usted una mala candidata para ERT, es esencial que haga ejercicio regularmente y tome bastante calcio para hacer más lenta la pérdida ósea que puede conducir a la osteoporosis. Investigadores australianos encontraron que una caminata rápida y enérgica de 30 minutos por lo menos tres veces por semana ayudó a hacer más lento el ritmo de la pérdida ósea en las mujeres postmenopáusicas cuando se combinó con 1.000 miligramos de calcio suplementario diariamente.

Eso es porque los ejercicios de cargar su propio peso como es caminar, ayudan a formar la masa ósea. El ejercicio también es una forma excelente de mantener a su corazón saludable, ya que la falta de estrógeno puede cambiar la manera en que su cuerpo procesa el colesterol y puede ocasionar un endurecimiento de las arterias.

Incluya a su compañero. Si está contemplando la posibilidad de una histerectomía, hable con su compañero al respecto y piense en incluirlo en las discusiones con su ginecólogo acerca de sus efectos. Las mujeres notarán cambios en sus orgasmos al faltarles el útero. Las contracciones tipo terremotos que afectan el útero en el momento del orgasmo van a desaparecer, aunque otros tejidos van a ser igual de volátiles. El incluir a su compañero en la discusión de cómo sus sensaciones físicas pueden cambiar podría prevenir los problemas futuros en la recámara, dice el doctor Hutchins.

IRA

Encuentre la calma antes de la tormenta

A diferencia de nuestras madres, se nos ha alentado a expresar nuestros sentimientos, todos. Hasta la ira.

"La generación más vieja de mujeres —aquellas con 55 años o más— creció en la creencia de que las damas finas no se enojan. Pero las mujeres jóvenes recibieron otro mensaje: que no se necesita ser una 'dama fina' todo el tiempo", dice la investigadora de la ira Sandra Thomas, R.N., Ph.D., autora de *Women and Anger* (Las mujeres y la ira) y directora del Centro para Investigación de Enfermería de la Universidad de Tennessee, en Knoxville.

Eso es bueno, porque suprimir la ira es una forma segura de envejecer antes de tiempo. No saber cómo tratar la ira ha sido asociado con numerosos malestares físicos y mentales así como la muerte prematura, según Mara Julius, Sc.D., epidemióloga sicosocial de la Escuela de Salubridad Pública en la Universidad de Michigan, en Ann Arbor. Por más de 20 años, la doctora Julius ha estudiado cómo sobrellevar la ira afecta la salud de mujeres y hombres. En su primer estudio, encontró que las mujeres que reprimen la ira durante pleitos con sus esposos, tienen mayores probabilidades de morir prematuramente de una enfermedad cardiovascular, cáncer y otras causas que aquellas que la expresaron.

El destructor que no discrimina

Ahora que estamos expresando nuestra ira tan libremente como los hombres, estamos sufriendo como ellos. Los hombres han tenido la reputación desde hace tiempo, de poder desahogarse fácilmente —probablemente, muy fácilmente ya que su ira estaba a menudo mal dirigida. "Un hombre que esté enojado por una razón u otra llegará a la casa y pateará al perro", dice Sidney B.

Simon, Ed.D., un consejero y profesor emérito de educación sicológica en la Universidad de Massachusetts, en Amherst y autor que se especializa en la ira y el perdón.

Y parece que estamos siguiendo el ejemplo, según un estudio nuevo muy completo sobre las mujeres y la ira. "Encontramos que las mujeres tienden a expresar su ira más frecuentemente a los miembros de sus familias —especialmente a sus esposos— aun cuando sus familias no son la razón de su ira", dice la doctora Thomas, quien llevó a cabo un estudio sobre los hábitos de enojo de 535 mujeres. "Por un lado, esto se puede ver de una forma positiva: más mujeres se sienten suficientemente seguras en sus relaciones para expresar sus sentimientos reales sin temor a terminar con esas relaciones. Pero deben existir ciertas restricciones. Gritar y maldecir no resuelven nada pero sí pueden causar distanciamientos, especialmente cuando los niños están involucrados. Los niños pequeños no entienden por qúe Mami está tan enojada con Papi o con la gente en su trabajo, sin embargo les está gritando a ellos. Cuando esto ocurre, y ocurre frecuentemente, puede causar toda una nueva seria de problemas, incluyendo culpa."

No hay que tomarlo a pecho

"Cuando usted se enoja, varios cambios fisiológicos ocurren en su cuerpo, porque el enojo provoca una reacción de pelear o salir corriendo", dice Christopher Peterson, Ph.D., autor de *Health and Optimism* (Salud y optimismo) y profesor de

---

Comer para dominar su carácter

Una dieta mala puede hacer que usted se sienta malhumorada además de verse deforme, según los investigadores de la Universidad Estatal de Nueva York en Stony Brook, y la Universidad de Ciencias de la Salud de Oregon, en Portland.

Después de estudiar a 156 mujeres y 149 hombres por cinco años, ellos notaron que las personas que consumieron la dieta típica estadounidense con alto contenido de grasa se enojaban más fácilmente que aquellas que cambiaron a dietas más saludables. Aquellas que cambiaron a una alimentación con bajo contenido de grasa mostraron menos ira y estaban menos predispuestas a la depresión.

Los investigadores creen que reducir la cantidad de grasa en la dieta y en el torrente sanguíneo desempeña un papel: mientras menos grasa hay, mejor será el estado de ánimo en general.

sicología de la Universidad de Michigan. "La adrenalina aumenta, el corazón late más rápidamente, la respiración se vuelve más rápida y superficial, y la digestión se detiene."

Cuando esto ocurre a menudo, estos cambios se hacen sentir en su salud. Se ha determinado que enojarse frecuentemente es un factor que contribuye a índices más altos de enfermedades del corazón, alta presión arterial y otras enfermedades con peligro de muerte, especialmente si usted tiene una personalidad tipo A y se enoja fácilmente. "Todo lo malo que la ira produce en los hombres también lo produce en las mujeres", dice el doctor Redford B. Williams, director del Centro de Investigación Médica del Comportamiento y profesor de siquiatría en el Centro Médico Duke en Durham, Carolina del Norte, y autor de *Anger Kills* (La ira mata). Las mujeres empiezan con un menor riesgo de enfermedades del corazón que los hombres, dice él, pero la hostilidad aumenta ese riesgo, tal y como lo hace con los hombres.

La ira también afecta nuestra capacidad mental. "Todas las emociones tienen cierta influencia sobre la forma en que pensamos, pero las emociones fuertes pueden de hecho hacer más lenta nuestra capacidad para razonar, resolver problemas y tomar decisiones", manifiesta la doctora Julius. "Cuando siente ira, furia u hostilidad, éstas la abruman a usted. En algunas personas, el proceso de pensar se hace más lento; en otras, el proceso de pensar se detiene completamente."

Añade el doctor Peterson : "La ira sólo hace que perdamos el sentido del humor y nos distanciemos de la gente. Se manifiesta en nuestra energía, creatividad y en todas esas otras cosas que podrían hacernos sentir más jóvenes."

Entre en razón

Entonces, ¿qué podemos hacer? Después de todo, nos vamos a enojar; todo el mundo se enoja. Y, seguramente nadie nos va a aconsejar que escondamos la cólera, frustración y otros sentimientos que nos pueden comer por dentro, porque eso hace más daño que expresarlos.

¿La solución al problema? Enójese cuando la provocan, dice la doctora Julius, pero no se quede así. Cálmese e identifique la razón de su enojo. Elimine la razón al identificar el problema subyacente.

Si la ira se maneja correctamente, dice la doctora Julius, todos esos problemas de salud relacionados con ésta —alta presión arterial, obesidad, depresión y hasta problemas futuros del corazón o cáncer— se pueden evitar. "Durante una prolongación crónica del enojo usted se enfermará", dice la doctora Julius. "En otras palabras, no es tanto enojarse lo que daña. El daño se produce cuando permanece enojada. Si se enoja y enfrenta el problema rápida y efectivamente, el daño si acaso hay alguno es mínimo."

Por lo tanto, aquí está cómo poner el grito en el cielo sin gritar.

Muévase. Mientras que los hombres explotan más rápidamente, las mujeres tienden a permanecer agitadas como por una hora antes de que su ira desaparezca, dice la doctora Thomas. Es durante ese tiempo que mucho del

De la represión a la expresión

¿Así que usted es una de esas mujeres que simplemente no pueden expresar su ira? Pues bien, usted no es la única. A pesar de los hallazgos que las mujeres se sienten mejor expresando su ira, "muchas mujeres, aun mujeres jóvenes, todavía se sienten incómodas expresando sus sentimientos", dice la investigadora de la ira Sandra Thomas, R.N., Ph.D., autora de *Women and Anger* (Las mujeres y la ira) y directora del Centro para Estudio de Enfermería de la Universidad de Tennessee, en Knoxville.

Si usted parece ser así, aquí hay algunas formas de aprender a expresarse.

Aprenda a ser una persona segura de sí misma. Sí, es correcto, para muchas de nosotras este es un comportamiento que se aprende. Hay muchos cursos de entrenamiento sobre seguridad de sí misma (*assertiveness training courses*) que enseñan a las mujeres a manejar la ira. Llame a la organización local de una agencia de salud mental para que le den una lista de los cursos que se ofrecen en su área. "Ser más segura de sí misma muchas veces perturba el balance en una relación, a pesar de que al final pruebe ser útil", dice Emily Rosten, Ph.D., una sicóloga con práctica privada en Salt Lake City.

Asegúrese de hacerle saber a todos acerca de su nueva manera de ser. "Sin un aviso de su nueva actitud, usted puede desconcertar a la otra persona. Más importante aún, a menos que le haga saber a la persona que usted quiere cambiar, esa persona hará toda clase de cosas para hacer que usted se comporte como lo hacía antes", dice la doctora Rosten.

Responda por escrito. ¿Todavía no se siente usted cómoda con un encuentro cara a cara? Póngalo entonces por escrito. Nadie dice que usted debe hablar para expresarse. "Responda por escrito", dice Jerry L. Deffenbacher, Ph.D., profesor de sicología de la Universidad Estatal de Colorado, en Fort Collins. "Eso le da a usted la oportunidad de serenarse y organizarse para responder más racionalmente. Y usted se sentirá en control al haber eliminado la confrontación inmediata."

Llore a gusto. "Llorar es un escape emocional muy saludable que le ayudará a deshacerse de la ira en su sistema", dice la doctora Thomas.

daño físico ocurre. "Una cosa que es realmente efectiva, es hacer algo físico durante ese tiempo", aconseja. "Salga a caminar. Vaya a nadar. Limpie con la aspiradora o limpie sus clósets ... cualquier cosa física que usted haga ayudará."

Ya que la ira desencadena la reacción de pelear o salir corriendo, su cuerpo querrá luchar o moverse (correr), explica la doctora Thomas. El ejercicio quema esta adrenalina más positivamente que el permanecer agitada sin hacer nada, permitiéndole pensar más claramente acerca de cómo manejar su ira.

Encuentre la paz. El lugar de trabajo es una de nuestras fuentes más frecuentes de ira, pero la oficina no es siempre el mejor lugar para serenarse e ir a darse una vuelta. "En esas situaciones, cuando usted no puede hacer algún ejercicio, busque un lugar tranquilo y medite, respire profundamente o practique alguna otra técnica de relajamiento", dice la doctora Thomas.

Conozca sus límites. Mucha de nuestra ira es tocante cosas sobre las cuales no podemos hacer nada. "Fíjese en el tráfico, por ejemplo", dice la doctora Julius. "Todos se enojan con el tráfico, así que no voy a decir: 'No se enoje cuando esté atascada en tráfico.' Pero usted no tiene que ser consumida por esa ira si hace lo que puede pero se da cuenta que es todo lo que puede hacer."

En otras palabras, trate de evitar el tráfico reprogramando la hora en que va a conducir a su trabajo o tome el autobús o el tren. "Pero dese cuenta de que usted sola no puede parar el tráfico, así que enojarse a causa de él es un desperdicio de su energía. En lugar de eso, cuando esté en su carro, canalice sus sentimientos usando más efectivamente este tiempo desperdiciado —escuchando música o libros grabados, planificando su programa o cualquier otra actividad", sugiere la doctora Julius.

Y dé gracias por lo que tiene. "También es importante darse cuenta de las compensaciones —dar gracias por lo que se tiene, por un decir", añade la doctora Julius. "Cuando usted está atascada en el tráfico, piense en todas las cosas positivas: el hecho de que usted sea dueña de un carro, y que junto con el tráfico en la ciudad existen algunas ventajas —museos, buenos restaurantes, parques." Hacer esto toma algo de tiempo, pero ayuda a poner las cosas en perspectiva. Cuando usted está enojada con sus niños o su esposo, pensar qué tan afortunada es en tenerlos calmará su ira.

Escoja sus objetivos. "Es importante que usted exprese su ira, aunque en bastantes situaciones existen restricciones con respecto a esa expresión", dice la doctora Thomas. "Por ejemplo, usualmente es desventajoso si usted expresa sus sentimientos en el lugar de trabajo ya sea hacia su supervisor o aun hacia sus compañeros de trabajo. Aunque usted esté haciendo todo correctamente y hablando de una manera totalmente racional y mesurada, es posible que la otra persona se torne defensiva y más tarde se comporte vengativamente."

Usted debe tener cuidado con quién comparte sus sentimientos, o de lo contrario bien puede usted pagar caro el error. La doctora Thomas aconseja: "Escoja a una amiga íntima, confidente o alguien más en quien usted pueda confiar —y no necesariamente el objeto de su ira— y hágale saber cómo se siente".

Cuide cómo se expresa. Siempre es mejor expresar sus sentimientos que decirles a otros cómo se deberían haber comportado, dice Roland D. Maiuro, Ph.D., director del Programa de Manejo de la Ira y Violencia Doméstica en

Seattle. Una manera es concentrándose en dar mensajes tipo "Yo". Por ejemplo, es mejor decir "Yo me enojé porque tú no me dejaste el carro" en lugar de "Tú me dijiste que ibas a dejarme el carro, y no lo hiciste". Los mensajes tipo "Tú" suenan acusatorios y ponen a la gente a la defensiva, fomentando pleitos en lugar de resolverlos.

Rodéese de gente feliz. "Si usted no quiere enojarse, trate de asociarse con gente que no se enoja", aconseja el doctor Peterson. "Esas formas de sentirse y actuar son contagiosas. Por supuesto, el secreto está en no rodearse de esas personas irritantemente super-optimistas sino de gente racional que ve soluciones a los problemas."

Únase. La soledad motiva algo de ira, por lo tanto añadir a su calendario social puede ayudar. "Algunas veces, usted tiene que forzarse a involucrarse en algo. Puede ser que no todos le caigan bien, y que usted no le caiga bien a todos, pero ser activa termina con la depresión, y la depresión deja a mucha gente enojada", dice el doctor Peterson. "Además, el unirse a asociaciones y otros grupos le ayuda a usted a ver los logros en su vida, lo cual puede calmar sus sentimientos de ira, soledad y depresión."

LESIONES
Y ACCIDENTES

Son fáciles de evitar

La bolsa de hielo está funcionando bien. El dolor ha disminuido, el hinchazón está bajando, y su rodilla —con la excepción de una configuración interesante de cortaduras y colores— se ve como debería verse.

Pero van a pasar todavía unos días antes de que usted se restablezca. Y en este momento, restringida a una silla, sintiéndose rígida y dolorida, usted sabe que la próxima vez que esté jugando con su hijita tratando de agarrarla tendrá cuidado de no pisar uno de sus patines.

Nada la puede hacer sentirse como si su cuerpo tuviera 110 años de edad como una lesión que la manda a la cama o la restringe a una silla. Pero sea que la lesión haya sido causada en un accidente automovilístico, una caída o un movimiento raro en un juego de vóleibol, prácticamente todos tenemos el riesgo de lesionarnos tarde o temprano.

Según el Consejo Nacional de Seguridad, las lesiones matan a aproximadamente 83.000 estadounidenses cada año, primordialmente debido a accidentes de tráfico o caídas. A pesar de lo que usted podría pensar, el riesgo no está limitado sólo a los ancianos. De hecho, más de la mitad de todas las muertes accidentales ocurren en las mujeres y los hombres que se encuentran entre los 25 y los 44 años de edad.

Pero la mayoría de nosotras no vamos a morir de lesiones o accidentes; sólo vamos a estar fuera de acción temporalmente. Y para las personas entre los 25 y los 44 años de edad, usualmente la causa es un músculo torcido o desgarrado debido a una lesión deportiva.

La conexión deportiva

Las lesiones deportivas resultan en 6.000 muertes al año. Las lesiones no fatales en actividades recreativas como el béisbol, softbol, basquetbol, fútbol americano y ciclismo ponen a más de dos millones de personas en las salas de urgencia cada año. Agregue a esto los números gigantes de torceduras y esguinces que se tratan en los vestidores deportivos, más las lesiones sufridas en docenas de otros deportes, y usted podrá entender por qué el Consejo Nacional de Seguridad estima que el número total de las lesiones en los deportes excede los tres millones cada año.

Las personas entre los 25 y los 64 años de edad representan más del 74 por ciento de todas las visitas a las salas de urgencia por lesiones en buceo, 68 por ciento por lesiones en squash, frontenis y frontón a pala, 51 por ciento por lesiones al andar a caballo, 45 por ciento de lesiones pescando, 44 por ciento de lesiones en tenis, 42 por ciento por lesiones en vóleibol y 40 por ciento por lesiones al levantar pesas.

¿Por qué se lesionan tantas personas en este grupo de edad? "Para cuando cumplen los 25 años de edad, las personas se han vuelto 'atletas de fin de semana' ", explica el doctor Stephen J. Nicholas, médico asociado de equipo para los *Jets* de Nueva York y director asociado del Instituto Nicholas de Medicina Deportiva y Lesiones Atléticas en el Hospital Lenox Hill en la ciudad de Nueva York. "Están más involucrados en el trabajo, y las exigencias sociales empiezan a tomar prioridad sobre el bienestar físico."

"Es como si uno tiene el cuerpo enyesado y se quita el yeso solamente los fines de semana", dice el doctor Nicholas. "Los músculos se acortan, se debilitan y se entiesan. Y ya no son capaces de funcionar a sus niveles óptimos."

Los estudios muestran que las mujeres tienen mayores probabilidades de sufrir lesiones en los tobillos, dice Christine Wells, Ph.D., miembro del Comité de Salvaguardas Competitivas y Aspectos Médicos de Deportes de la Asociación Nacional Atlética Colegial, y profesora de ciencia del ejercicio y educación física en la Universidad Estatal de Arizona, en Tempe. Las mujeres también se lesionan los hombros y las rodillas —los hombros primordialmente por los remates y lanzamientos en vóleibol, y las rodillas por una variedad de estiramientos y giros.

Ya que tanto las mujeres como los hombres probablemente van a disminuir sus actividades deportivas después de los 25 años, ambos tienen la misma posibilidad de que su cuerpo no vaya a estar en condiciones de hacer actividades atléticas intensas los fines de semana.

Desafortunadamente, ellos aún podrían creer que están en condiciones óptimas, dice el doctor Nicholas. Así que cuando hacen deporte como por ejemplo tenis los fines de semana, empujan a sus cuerpos como lo hacían antes cuando jugaban varias veces por semana.

¿El resultado? Los músculos se fatigan, se acalambran, se esfuerzan, y se estiran hasta el punto en que de hecho pueden desgarrarse, dice el doctor Nicholas.

Cómo reducir su riesgo

Es difícil frenarse cuando se está tratando de lograr esa última milla o punto, agrega el doctor Nicholas. Pero aquí está cómo puede ayudar a su cuerpo mantenerse a nivel y a reducir su riesgo de lesiones.

Tome un examen de escuela secundaria. Si usted es mayor de 25 años de edad y participa en deportes los fines de semana, programe un examen físico con el médico familiar que efectúa los exámenes físicos a los equipos de la escuela secundaria local, sugiere la doctora Rosemary Agostini, una doctora dentro del personal directivo en la Clínica Deportiva Virginia Mason y profesora asociada clínica de la Universidad de Washington, ambas en Seattle.

Pídale que le haga el mismo tipo de examen físico que ella les hace a los equipos locales de fútbol americano o basquetbol, incluyendo una revisión de sus lesiones deportivas anteriores. Las lesiones antiguas combinadas con un enfoque de "atleta apasionado de fin de semana", encuentran una manera de regresar y perseguirlo, a veces en una forma crónica, dice la doctora Agostini. Una doctora puede evaluar la posibilidad de que eso suceda y hacer sugerencias específicas para evitar que vuelva a lesionarse.

Balancee su dieta. "Algunas mujeres atletas se involucran tanto en el ejercicio que no se alimentan correctamente", dice la doctora Agostini. "No terminan con trastornos para comer, pero sí tienen hábitos desordenados de comer", en los cuales en una semana sólo comen pastas y verduras o solamente frutas en otra.

Pero usted no puede formar musculatura o mejorar su rendimiento sin comer una dieta balanceada, explica la doctora Agostini. La falta de calcio para formar huesos fuertes, la falta de hierro para crear glóbulos rojos de sangre o la falta de proteína para formar y mantener la musculatura puede no sólo sabotear su rendimiento pero también predisponerla a las lesiones.

Pida a la doctora que le hace su examen físico que le recomiende una especialista en nutrición de deportes cerca suyo. Y entonces desarrolle con ella un programa de alimentación que satisfaga sus necesidades particulares.

Vigile sus períodos. Algunas mujeres dejarán de menstruar cuando alcancen ciertos niveles de ejercicio, dice la doctora Agostini. Este nivel es diferente para cada una, pero indica un desequilibrio hormonal que debería ser evaluado y corregido. De lo contrario, dice la doctora Agostini, usted tiene un mayor riesgo de fracturas por estrés u osteoporosis prematura. Por ello, vea a su doctora si sus períodos se suspenden por más de tres ciclos.

Cambie los zapatos cada 500 millas. Los zapatos necesitan proporcionar un buen soporte y absorción de impacto para prevenir las lesiones, dice la doctora Agostini. Reemplácelos cada seis meses o 500 millas, lo que ocurra primero. Y recuerde que el tamaño de su pie probablemente será mayor después del embarazo. Así que obséquiese un par de zapatos nuevos cuando nazca el bebé.

Siga en movimiento. "Usted será capaz de reducir al mínimo las lesiones si se pone en un programa de ejercicio regular —uno que incluye 30 a 40 minutos diariamente o por lo menos tres a cuatro veces por semana", dice el doctor Nicholas. El objeto es que no le permita a su cuerpo cinco o seis días seguidos en que se entumezca.

Estírese. Empiece su programa de ejercicios con por lo menos 25 minutos de estiramientos cada vez que va a hacer ejercicio, dice el doctor Nicholas. Los músculos en las partes de atrás y enfrente de sus muslos —los tendones de la corva y los cuadríceps— más aquellos en la parte baja de la espalda son los más importantes que usted debe aflojar.

"Estos músculos, por lo general, no reciben ningún estiramiento durante el día a menos que usted específicamente decida hacerlo", dice el doctor Nicholas. "Y sin embargo, una de las causas más comunes de dolor en la parte baja de la espalda es la tensión de los tendones de la corva que causan una inclinación de la pelvis.

"Si usted puede mantener sus tendones de la corva relajados," agrega él, "usted podría reducir al mínimo no solamente los tirones a esos tendones o lesiones a las extremidades inferiores sino también el grado de dolor en la parte baja de la espalda que usted pudiera desarrollar en el futuro".

Haga trabajar a su cuerpo. Después de estirarse, haga cualquier ejercicio aeróbico —caminar, correr, saltar— que acelere el ritmo de su corazón y la haga respirar agitadamente —agitada, no jadeando— por 20 minutos, dice el doctor Nicholas.

La única excepción es durante el último trimestre del embarazo, agrega él, cuando "el cuerpo secreta una hormona llamada relaxina, la cual relaja las estructuras de los tejidos suaves del cuerpo al prepararlos para el parto". Desafortunadamente, ésta también afloja todos los ligamentos que mantienen unidas a sus articulaciones.

Está bien que usted continúe con sus ejercicios aeróbicos regulares siempre y cuando su médico lo haya autorizado, dice el doctor Nicholas. Pero, durante este período, usted no debe tratar de alcanzar sus mejores niveles personales, porque el esfuerzo adicional en sus articulaciones relajadas debido a la relaxina la hacen vulnerable a las lesiones.

Levante. Refuerce sus músculos al levantar por lo menos una cantidad mínima de peso, dice el doctor Nicholas. Consígase un entrenador atlético para que revise el examen y las recomendaciones de su doctora y para que le recomiende y determine los pesos específicos y el número de repeticiones que usted debería hacer. Y no se olvide de estirarse antes de hacer ejercicio.

Las mujeres en el último trimestre de embarazo deberían evitar las pesas por completo. La relaxina más el esfuerzo en las articulaciones por las pesas pueden predisponerla a una lesión.

Active sus relaciones. "Yo estaba platicando con un amigo mío el otro día, y ambos admitimos que al envejecer, siempre hay algo que se interpone para que hagamos ejercicio", dice el doctor Nicholas. "Uno tiene que encontrarse con alguien para un trago, o está tratando de ver algo sobre una hipoteca, un paciente o los niños."

Pero si usted arregla encontrarse con las amistades para un juego de tenis en lugar de tomar un trago o lleva a los niños a la pista de hielo en lugar de al cine, dice él, tiene muchas más probabilidades de hacer el ejercicio adicional que necesita para mantenerse relajada y libre de lesiones.

Cuando usted comete un error

No importa cuán cuidadosamente mantiene usted a su cuerpo en forma, de vez en cuando usted va a estirar o forzar algo cuando gira para el lado equivocado, hace más intenso su programa de ejercicio o simplemente se tropieza con sus propios pies.

Por ello aquí está lo que el doctor Nicholas le recomienda hacer acerca de un ligamento, tendón o músculo estirado o forzado.

Pruebe un poco de "*RICE*". Aunque "RICE" significa "arroz" en inglés, no le estamos diciendo que debe literalmente comer arroz, porque RICE también es una sigla para "*Rest*", "*Ice*", "*Compression*", y "*Elevation*", que son cuatro tratamientos fundamentales para cualquier lesión nueva que sufra, según el doctor Nicholas. "*Rest*" significa reposo; "*Ice*" es hielo; "*Compression*" es compresión; finalmente, "*Elevation*" es elevación. La idea es reducir al mínimo la inflamación que se produzca. Es la inflamación la que produce el hinchazón que provoca el dolor, el cual puede limitar su movimiento.

"Aplique hielo sobre la lesión por tres o cuatro días", dice el doctor Nicholas. "Aplíquelo 20 minutos por cada hora en que está despierta." Después envuelva una banda elástica alrededor del área lesionada, y entonces eleve el músculo lesionado.

Tome ibuprofen. "Yo también les digo a las personas que tomen *Advil* si no tienen problemas estomacales", dice el doctor Nicholas. Eso también reduce la inflamación. Simplemente siga las instrucciones en el paquete.

Use calor húmedo. Una vez que usted se ha aplicado el método "RICE" por tres o cuatro días, es tiempo de hacer algo para recuperar sus funciones normales y evitar que el área lesionada se vuelva un problema crónico, dice el doctor Nicholas.

La dificultad es que después de tres o cuatro días, la sangre seca de las fibras de un músculo desgarrado o traumatizado se ha fijado en el sitio lesionado.

"Necesitamos sacarla fuera del área", dice el doctor Nicholas. "Entonces empezamos con lo que llamamos el programa de calor húmedo. Envolvemos una toalla templada, húmeda alrededor del área lesionada, ponemos plástico —el tipo de bolsa plástica que le dan en la tintorería— alrededor de la toalla para proporcionar aislamiento, y entonces ponemos encima una almohadilla de calor.

"La dejamos así por aproximadamente una hora y media, tres veces al día, teniendo cuidado de no quemar la piel", agrega él. "Esto va a derretir la sangre seca en el área lesionada, traerá la sangre a la superficie y ayudará al cuerpo a absorberla."

"Esto también ayuda con el proceso de curación al aflojar los músculos."

Vuelva a estirar los músculos lesionados. Una vez que un músculo se ha lesionado, tanto éste como los músculos a su alrededor se contraen y se hacen más cortos, dice el doctor Nicholas. Así que antes de que usted reanude sus ejercicios normales, tiene que volver a estirar los músculos hasta que recuperen su longitud normal cuando están en descanso. Pida a una entrenadora atlética que le diga qué estiramientos sugiere ella para su lesión en particular.

"Si usted no recupera esa longitud en descanso, usted estará más propensa a tirones crónicos que pueden volver una y otra vez", dice el doctor Nicholas.

Caídas en el trabajo

Las lesiones deportivas pueden ser costosas en términos de tiempo, dolor y fastidio, pero las caídas tienen más probabilidades de ocasionar la muerte. Y no solamente a las personas mayores. En un año casi 1.100 hombres y mujeres entre los 25 y los 44 años de edad murieron por caídas.

Mientras que las caídas que ocurren en el hogar probablemente le ocurrirán a las personas mayores con vista defectuosa o usando calzado muy flojo, las caídas de hombres y mujeres entre los 25 y los 44 años de edad van a ocurrir probablemente en el trabajo, dice el investigador John Britt, R.N., coordinador estatal para prevenir lesiones, en el Hospital Harborview, en Seattle.

Las personas se caen cuando se están moviendo de una altura a otra cuando están usando todo tipo de cosas desde escaleras y tablados hasta escaleras de mano y vigas, según los expertos en seguridad en la Administración de Seguridad Ocupacional y Salubridad (o *OSHA*, por sus siglas en inglés), en Washington, D.C. Los pasamanos se pueden interrumpir inesperadamente antes del último escalón, los escenarios movibles pueden no estar sujetos con abrazaderas en algunas partes de los tablados, las cuerdas de seguridad pueden estar desgarradas o desgastadas en las escaleras de mano, las herramientas se pueden haber quedado en las vigas sin darse cuenta.

¿Quiere usted asegurarse de que no será la próxima en caerse cabeza para abajo en el trabajo? Aquí está cómo Britt dice que usted puede reducir ese riesgo.

Localice al responsable de las caídas. Cada empresa tiene a alguien cuya responsabilidad es hacer informes detallados sobre accidentes a las compañías de seguros, comités de seguridad y la agencia de compensación al trabajador, dice Britt. Encuentre a esa persona. Y entonces pregúntele cuándo y dónde ocurrió cada lesión durante los últimos 12 meses. Asegúrese entonces de no caer en las mismas trampas en que los otros cayeron.

Haga visible a lo invisible. La gente tiende a prestar atención a los detalles pequeños ignorando los grandes, dice OSHA. Ven la pequeña navaja *X-acto* que puede rebanar sus dedos en el cuarto de producción artística pero no ven el charco de tinta que puede causar que se resbalen.

Entre en cualquier cuarto en su lugar de trabajo, párese en una esquina y busque cualquier cosa con que pueda tropezarse o que de alguna forma pueda lesionarla. Informe entonces del riesgo a la gerencia o corríjalo usted misma.

Deje los tacones en casa. Si su compañía sugiere que use zapatos bajos, suelas antideslizantes, botas u otro calzado diseñado para evitar que usted se caiga en el trabajo, hágalo.

Allane el camino

Muchos de los hombres y las mujeres que sobreviven los 10 millones o algo así de accidentes de tráfico en los Estados Unidos cada año no pueden ya esperar la compasión automática por parte de sus amistades y compañeros de trabajo.

En lugar de eso, dice Britt, la narración de sus accidentes será probablemente recibida con las preguntas "¿Tenías puesto tu cinturón de seguridad?" o "¿Hiciste una parada en el bar (cantina) antes de conducir a tu casa?"

"Ha habido un cambio sutil en la opinión pública acerca de los accidentes de tráfico en los últimos dos años", explica Britt. La gente solía sentir lástima por las víctimas de accidentes. Pero hoy —en parte debido a los programas nacionales de seguridad y los grupos de ciudadanos tales como Madres en Contra de Choferes Ebrios— existe más un sentimiento de que los accidentes son previsibles.

¿Qué puede usted hacer? Aquí hay tres estrategias que Britt considera que le ayudarán a prevenir —o sobrevivir— accidentes de vehículos motorizados.

Evite el alcohol. Los estudios de seguridad indican que entre el 40 y el 50 por ciento de todos los accidentes fatales incluyen conductores borrachos, dice Britt. Lo más probable es que el alcohol esté involucrado en los accidentes fatales con conductores adultos del sexo masculino entre los 20 y los 55 años de edad. Y mientras más violento haya sido el accidente, más probable es que un borracho iba detrás del volante. Así que no beba antes de conducir.

Esté alerta los viernes y sábados. Un tercio de todos los accidentes fatales ocurren entre las seis de la tarde y las seis de la mañana de los viernes y sábados, informan los investigadores. Así que esté particularmente alerta durante ese tiempo.

Use cinturones de seguridad para cintura y hombros. Muchas personas no usan cinturones de seguridad en la creencia errónea de que tienen un menor riesgo de lesionarse si están "libres" para salir del coche rápidamente. Desafortunadamente, estas son las personas que tienen las menores probabilidades de salir de sus coches en lo absoluto. Un estudio de la Administración Nacional de Seguridad en el Tráfico de las Carreteras indica que cuando se llevan correctamente, los cinturones para cintura y hombros reducen por un 45 por ciento las probabilidades de muerte de los ocupantes en un accidente.

MANCHAS DE LA EDAD

Qué hacer cuando el daño ya está hecho

Ella era una mujer muy atractiva de cierta edad. Estaba en forma y era esbelta, y era obvio que se cuidaba el cutis. Usted admiraba su estilo, su porte, su maquillaje. Envejecer no sería tan malo si una pudiera verse así de bien, usted pensó. Entonces, de pronto, usted notó sus manos. Estaban cubiertas de manchas cafés. ¡Uy, qué feas!

Uno de estos días, puede ser que se sorprenda mirando sus propias manos con cierta preocupación. Hasta ahora son sólo unas cuantas, pero allí están. Manchas de la edad. Manchas del hígado. Léntigos de sol. Pero, no importa cómo les llame: le están añadiendo años innecesarios a su apariencia, y son una razón por la cual sus manos pueden revelar su edad. Pero hoy en día, usted puede hacer mucho más acerca de las manchas de la edad que simplemente contarlas cuando aparecen.

Distinga entre sus manchas

Primero, usted necesita determinar qué es una mancha de la edad y qué no lo es. Hay varios tipos de estas manchas desagradables, pero hay una causa que es común a todas ellas, según los médicos, y esta es el daño causado por el sol. Posiblemente usted expuso su piel sin protegerla de los rayos ultravioleta, ya sea en un establecimiento para broncearse, una lámpara solar o años de asolearse sin ponerse loción antisolar. En respuesta, su piel ha tratado de protegerse por sí misma produciendo una superabundancia de melanina —las células pigmentadas en su piel— en manchas disparejas.

¿Cuál es la diferencia entre manchas de la edad y pecas? Las pecas aparecen cuando usted es joven, son más numerosas en el verano y tienden a desaparecer con la edad, dice el doctor Nicholas Lowe, profesor de dermatología en la Escuela de Medicina UCLA, de la Universidad de California, en Los Ángeles. Las manchas de la edad empeoran, y no desaparecen.

Si usted estuvo bajo el sol mientras se encontraba embarazada, se le puede haber desarrollado la "máscara del embarazo", una mancha que va de pálida a oscura en la piel. Esta no es una mancha de la edad. Propiamente llamada melasma, estas manchas aparecen a menudo en la cara y podrían desaparecer por sí solas.

Causas químicas

Ciertas substancias que entran en contacto con su piel pueden causar manchas de la edad, dice la doctora Karen Burke, una dermatóloga con práctica privada en la ciudad de Nueva York. Los químicos llamados *psoralens* están presentes en alimentos como el perejil, limas y chirivías. Cuando usted maneja estos alimentos y después sale al sol, su piel puede estar más sensible y quemarse más fácilmente donde los *psoralens* la tocaron. Cuando las pequeñas ampollas causadas por las quemaduras se han curado, puede ser que en su lugar aparezcan manchas de la edad.

Algunos antibióticos como la tetraciclina (*Achromycin*), algunos diuréticos (píldoras de agua) y las medicinas antisicóticas como la cloropromazina (*Thorazine*) también causarán que su piel produzca manchas de la edad cuando no está protegida contra el sol, dice la doctora Burke.

Y si su fragancia o loción favorita contiene almizcle o aceite de bergamota, los cuales son ingredientes comunes de perfumes, pueden darle a usted algo más que un aroma encantador. Cuando los perfumes o lociones que contienen estos ingredientes se aplican a las áreas expuestas al sol, pueden producir manchas de edad, dice la doctora Burke.

Más vale prevenir que curar

Lo más importante que usted puede hacer para detener la formación de nuevas manchas de la edad es usar loción antisolar —todo el tiempo. Y una onza (28 g) es todo lo que se necesita, dicen los dermatólogos.

Úsela diariamente. "Empiece a usar una loción antisolar con factor SPF 15 o más alto, diariamente", dice el doctor John E. Wolf, Jr., profesor y presidente del departamento de dermatología de la Universidad Baylor de Medicina en Houston. ¿Qué es SPF? Son las siglas de *sun protection factor* (factor de protección solar). SPF 15, por ejemplo, quiere decir que usted puede estar en el sol 15 veces más tiempo antes de empezar a quemarse que si no se hubiera puesto la loción.

"Aplíquela al dorso de sus manos y a su cara como primera cosa en la mañana, antes de ponerse cualquier humectante o maquillaje", dice el doctor Wolf. "Después de lavarse las manos, no se olvide de volverse a poner la loción. Si usted nota el principio de manchas de la edad o melasma, cambie a una loción antisolar con un factor más alto que el que está usando actualmente."

Y recuerde que si usted no está preparada para usar loción antisolar diariamente, todo el año, realmente no tiene sentido que se trate sus manchas de la edad, dice el doctor Lowe. Sin una loción antisolar diaria, "en unos meses su piel volverá a estar como estaba antes", dice.

Lávese. Lávese las manos minuciosamente después de manejar alimentos que contienen *psoralens* y vuélvase a poner loción antisolar antes de salir otra vez, dice la doctora Burke.

Perfúmese en un lugar "oscuro". Póngase su perfume o loción en áreas de su piel que no estén expuestas al sol, sugiere la doctora Burke.

Quitamanchas

Lo más importante que usted puede hacer acerca de las manchas de la edad es asegurarse primero que no son lesiones precancerosas, dice el doctor Wolf. "Si una mancha café aparece de la nada, o una de las antiguas manchas súbitamente cambia de forma, se levanta o sangra, haga que un dermatólogo la examine para tener la certeza de que no se trata de un melanoma prematuro", dice. El número de casos de melanomas, una forma potencialmente fatal de cáncer de la piel, está aumentando más rápidamente que cualquier otro tipo de cáncer. (Para más información sobre melanomas, vea Cáncer de la piel, en la página 100).

Si usted tiene sólo unas cuantas manchas que no son demasiado oscuras, puede probar con un remedio que se puede comprar sin receta. Pero para un montón de persistentes manchas de la edad, su dermatólogo tiene varios tratamientos muy efectivos.

Deshágase de ellas blanqueándolas. Diríjase al pasillo en su botica favorita donde están los productos para el cuidado del cabello para encontrar ayuda sin necesidad de receta. Toma tiempo, pero un producto para decolorar el cabello que es por lo menos 30 por ciento agua oxigenada puede ayudar a hacer que se desvanezcan las manchas de la edad pequeñas. Los productos con el más alto porcentaje de agua oxigenada son para los tonos rubios, como son *Nice'n Easy 97* y *98* y *Ultress 24, 25* y *26*. La doctora Burke sugiere usar un algodón humedecido en el agua oxigenada. Puede ser que necesite usarlo diariamente por varias semanas.

Trate con una crema desvanecedora. No estamos bromeando. Posiblemente usted se acuerda de los anuncios para *"Porcelana, the Fade Cream"* (Porcelana, la crema desvanecedora). Todavía se puede encontrar —y puede ser justamente lo que funcione. Porcelana y otras cremas, incluyendo las cremas desvanecedoras *Esotérica* y *Palmer's Skin Success*, contienen hidroquinona, que interfiere con la producción de melanina de su piel. La doctora Burke indica sin embargo, que estos productos funcionan lentamente. Las preparaciones de hidroquinona más fuertes, sujetas a receta, pueden lograr resultados más rápidamente.

Busque una solución más fuerte. *Melanex* y *Eldoquin*, cremas que contienen hidroquinona con una fuerza sujeta a receta, pueden alcanzar buenos resultados para hacer desaparecer sus manchas de la edad más grandes y más tenaces. *Tretinoin* (*Retin-A*), que viene en crema o jalea, es otro removedor potencial de manchas de la edad, aunque normalmente se usa contra el acné y las arrugas. La *Retin-A* regresa gradualmente la piel a su condición normal, haciendo que las manchas de la edad desaparezcan. A discreción de su médico, se puede usar en combinación con hidroquinona, dice la doctora Burke.

Considere una descamación o congelamiento. Su dermatólogo puede probar con ácido tricloroacético, que es usado a menudo para descamaciónes (*peelings*) químicas y es bastante efectivo sobre manchas de la edad. Podría ser una buena elección para sólo algunas cuantas manchas que no sean demasiado oscuras, dice el doctor Wolf. Otra alternativa es congelar las manchas con nitrógeno líquido. Con estos tratamientos, que deben efectuarse en el consultorio de un médico, hay cierto riesgo de que los químicos funcionen demasiado bien, dejando manchas blancas sin pigmentación donde antes estaban las manchas de la edad, dice.

Aprenda acerca de láser. Usado por un médico muy hábil, el rayo láser es la solución de alta técnica para las manchas de la edad, dice el doctor Lowe. Es, también, la más cara. "La gran ventaja acerca del tratamiento por láser de este problema es que en las manos de un experto, usted no corre el riesgo de tener manchas blancas donde antes estaban las manchas oscuras", dice. Pregunte a su dermatólogo si es que el tratamiento láser está disponible. ¿Le dolerá? Sólo por un instante. Y, según el doctor Lowe, el dolor es similar a cuando le pegan a una en la piel con una liga elástica.

Recuerde que con todos estos tratamientos, es esencial seguir usando loción antisolar. De lo contrario, seguramente se formarán nuevas manchas de la edad.

MEMORIA

Olvídese de este mito
del envejecimiento

Usted siempre ha manejado su casa con la eficiencia de un general con sus tropas. Puede ir a la tienda, y, casi sin mirar la lista, comprar todo lo necesario para la casa, desde el champú que está en venta especial hasta el cereal favorito de su hijo más pequeño. Pero recientemente, se ha olvidado de algunas cosas. El vestido que tenía que coser para su hija, la cuenta del teléfono, el regalo que había que comprar para su amiga —todo esto se le fue de la mente esta semana. ¿Serán estas faltas de memoria, como dice su hija en broma, una señal que usted se está "poniendo vieja"?

"No hay duda: cuando se le olvidan las cosas, usted se siente como si su mente se le estuviera escapando", dice Douglas Herrmann, Ph.D., un investigador de la memoria en el Centro Nacional para Estadísticas de la Salud, en Washington, D.C., y autor de *Super Memory* (Super memoria).

Pero el doctor Herrmann dice que hay bastante motivo para ser optimista. Posiblemente usted necesite poner un poco más de atención en su memoria, pero probablemente todavía es completamente funcional. "Lo más factible es que usted no esté perdiendo la memoria", dice él. "Con un poco más de enfoque y un poco de trabajo, su memoria será tan buena como lo fue en su adolescencia o en la década de los veinte años —posiblemente aún mejor."

Todavía un área oscura

Los expertos aún no saben realmente cómo es que almacenamos y recordamos información. Una teoría mantiene que las personas pueden guardar recuerdos en forma holográfica y tridimensional, usando redes de neuronas y reacciones químicas para tener acceso al sistema. Lo que sí saben los investigadores es que

Sea una rutinera

¿Está siempre perdiendo sus llaves? Designe un lugar para ellas en su casa u oficina. Si usted pone sus llaves —o anteojos (gafas) u otras cosas— en el mismo lugar todos los días, siempre va a saber dónde están, dice Douglas Herrmann, Ph.D., un investigador de la memoria en el Centro Nacional para Estadísticas de la Salud, en Washington, D.C., y autor de *Super Memory* (Super memoria).

uno puede llegar al mismo recuerdo a través de una cantidad de senderos diferentes. Los olores pueden activar un recuerdo, tal y como lo hace una visión, palabra o frase familiar.

La mayoría de los científicos descomponen la memoria en tres partes. La primera es la memoria de trabajo, llamada también la memoria de bloc para apuntes. El doctor Herrmann dice que las personas usan ésta para recordar números de teléfono u otra información que necesitan por un período muy corto de tiempo —por lo general cerca de un minuto. Y entonces generalmente se la olvidan.

La memoria de alcance medio o intermedia, guarda toda la información que usted absorbe consciente o inconscientemente durante las últimas horas o días. Eventualmente, usted olvida esas cosas porque no eran importantes (¿qué desayunó hace tres días?) o las transfiere a la memoria de largo alcance. Allí, usted almacena recuerdos permanentes, como son las direcciones y los nombres importantes, la receta de mamá para hacer flan y los recuerdos de las mañanas de Navidad durante su niñez.

Por años, los estudios siempre mostraron que las memorias de bloc de apuntes y de alcance medio empiezan a declinar relativamente temprano en la vida —aun en la década de sus 40 años de edad. Pero esa investigación tenía fallas, dice el doctor Herrmann. La nueva evidencia muestra que usted probablemente no va a sufrir de una pérdida seria de memoria hasta bien entrada en las décadas de sus sesenta o setenta años, dice él.

Entonces, ¿por qué se le están olvidando más cosas ahora que antes? El estrés puede ser el culpable. "Su capacidad para concentrarse y tomar decisiones, junto con su memoria de corto plazo, puede ser una de las primeras áreas del funcionamiento mental que el estrés ataca", dice el doctor Paul J. Rosch, presidente del Instituto Norteamericano del Estrés, en Yonkers, Nueva York. Y trate de no preocuparse acerca de olvidarse de las cosas; el doctor Herrmann indica que la ansiedad acerca de la memoria hace aún más difícil recordar.

Y también existe la simple sobrecarga sensorial. Cuando la vida la jala en cinco direcciones diferentes a la vez, dice el doctor Herrmann, usted tiene menos posibilidad de concentrarse en detalles. "Y mientras menos preste usted atención, menos será lo que usted va a recordar", dice él.

Para la mayoría de las mujeres, la pérdida de la memoria nunca ha sido un problema serio. Pero algunas enfermedades, más notablemente la de Alzheimer, conducen a un problema directo de la memoria. Si a usted se le olvidan citas importantes en el trabajo, no puede recordar los nombres de miembros de su familia o de buenos amigos, o se vuelve seriamente desorientada o confundida, vea a un doctor, dice el doctor Francis Pirozzolo, un neurosicólogo en el Colegio de Medicina de Baylor, en Houston.

Mantenga esa idea

Su cerebro no es una computadora. Usted no puede ir corriendo a la tienda y comprar más memoria; usted tiene que aprender a usar la que tiene.

Afortunadamente, usted tiene bastante lugar para almacenamiento. Aquí está cómo sacar el mayor provecho de éste.

Ejercite su mente. El ejercicio regular puede darle un impulso a su memoria. En un estudio, las personas que tomaron una clase aeróbica acuática de nueve semanas tuvieron una mejor puntuación en las pruebas generales de la memoria que un grupo similar que no había hecho ejercicio. "El ejercicio aeróbico puede haber aumentado la eficiencia del oxígeno al cerebro", dice el coautor del estudio, Richard Gordin, Ph.D., profesor en el Departamento de Salud, Educación Física y Recreación de la Universidad Estatal de Utah, en Logan.

El doctor Gordin hace hincapié en que los resultados son preliminares. Pero están llegando otros estudios con hallazgos similares. Y además, tenemos los

Hágala pedazos

Las computadoras recuerdan información en pequeñas partes, o *bytes*. Esa también es la mejor manera en que usted puede hacerlo, según el doctor Francis Pirozzolo, un neurosicólogo en el Colegio de Medicina de Baylor, en Houston.

El proceso se llama despedazar. Ya que su mente recuerda cosas en grupos de cinco a nueve, desglose las listas en segmentos de ese tamaño. Es mucho más fácil recordar cinco grupos con cinco artículos que recordar una lista de 25 artículos, dice el doctor Pirozzolo. Y si usted puede agrupar juntas cosas similares —frutas en una lista, productos de papel en otra— le irá aún mejor.

beneficios adicionales de un menor riesgo de enfermedades del corazón y derrames cerebrales y todos los otros provechosos efectos secundarios del ejercicio.

Preste atención. Esta es la ayuda más básica —y más olvidada— para la memoria. No espere memorizar la línea de productos de un cliente mientras que está hablando con otro en una llamada de larga distancia. No espere recordar el nombre de una persona si está pensando qué es lo que va a comer para el almuerzo cuando está haciendo sus presentaciones.

"Es sencillo", dice el doctor Herrmann, "Enfóquese, enfóquese, enfóquese. Si no se registra inicialmente en su cerebro, no hay posibilidad de recordarla después." Así que cuando tenga que recordar información clave, deje todo lo que está haciendo y pase un par de minutos concentrándose. Luego siga con la próxima tarea.

Consúltelo con la almohada. Una buena noche de descanso hará mucho por su memoria. La investigación muestra que las personas a quienes se les despierta cuando están soñando dejan de procesar memorias del día anterior y por lo tanto se olvidan más. El doctor Herrmann también dice que el sueño regular le permite recargarse a todo su cuerpo, haciéndola a usted más alerta y atenta al detalle. "Y evite las píldoras para dormir", dice él. "Usted no va a tener la misma calidad de sueño, y tiene menos probabilidades de recordar cosas al día siguiente."

Un consejo más: si usted estudia o trabaja por la noche, váyase a dormir tan pronto como termine. Si después va a salir a tomar un trago o un café, o se queda por un rato para ver las noticias, le será más difícil recordar la información al día siguiente.

Sea selectiva. Hemos inventado directorios telefónicos, libros de direcciones, archivos en la computadora, lápices, plumas y esos pequeños blocs

Hágalo poco a poco

Usted recordará información por más tiempo si la absorbe gradualmente en lugar de toda de una sola vez, según Harry P. Bahrick, Ph.D., profesor de sicología en la Universidad de Ohio Wesleyan, en Delaware, Ohio. En un estudio que duró ocho años, él encontró que la gente que practicaba su vocabulario de español una vez al mes recordaba cuatro veces más palabras que la gente que lo practicaba diariamente. El doctor Bahrick dice que el principio funciona de la misma manera para las habilidades físicas. "Si yo estuviera aprendiendo a jugar golf, practicaría una hora a la semana por siete semanas en lugar de una hora al día por siete días", dice él.

FÁCIL de recordar

Usted tiene que fregar los platos, arrancar unas malas hierbas de su jardín, comprar cebollas, ir a pagar una cuenta y lavar ropa. Para acordarse de esta lista, trate de formar una palabra usando la primera letra de cada cosa. En este caso, la palabra que se forma es "FÁCIL". Esto se llama mnemotecnia, según el doctor Francis Pirozzolo, un neurosicólogo en el Colegio de Medicina de Baylor, en Houston. Si usted convierte la información en una forma familiar, como es una palabra simple, tiene más probabilidades de recordarla, dice él.

adhesivos amarillos —todo para ayudarnos a recordar las cosas. Úselos entonces. "¿Para qué tratar de memorizar listas gigantescas de compras si simplemente las puede escribir?", pregunta el doctor Pirozzolo. "Si usted es una persona ocupada con muchas cosas que recordar, hacer listas le deja la memoria libre para recordar cosas más importantes."

Rompa el estereotipo. Los estudios muestran que muchas mujeres creen que los miembros de su mismo sexo son buenas para recordar "cosas femeninas" como por ejemplo, las listas de compras, y malas para recordar "cosas masculinas" como las direcciones. No es cierto. La investigación del doctor Herrmann muestra que las mujeres y los hombres tienen una capacidad de memoria parecida pero algunas veces la aplican en forma diferente debido a los persistentes estereotipos sociales. Si usted quiere mejorar cualquier área de su memoria —con las listas de compras, direcciones o cualquiera otra cosa— el doctor Herrmann sugiere que practique. "Esa es la única forma de volverse mejor en eso", dice él.

No se le olviden sus minerales. No hay nada mejor para su memoria que una dieta balanceada y saludable con bastantes frutas y verduras, dice el doctor Herrmann. También hay pruebas que manteniendo su consumo de cinc y boro puede revivir su memoria, según James G. Penland, Ph.D., sicólogo investigador con el Centro Grand Forks de Investigación de la Nutrición Humana en el Departamento de Agricultura de los Estados Unidos, en Dakota del Norte. Un estudio mostró que las mujeres en dietas bajas en cinc tuvieron una puntuación más baja en memoria a corto plazo que cuando tomaban la Asignación Dietética Recomendada de 12 miligramos. Una media docena de ostras al vapor le dan a usted la cantidad enorme de 76,4 miligramos de cinc. Otras buenas fuentes incluyen el germen de trigo, las carnes magras, y las semillas de calabaza y de *squash*.

Enfóquese en dos a la vez

¿Está obligada a veces a recordar información en medio del caos en la casa o el trabajo? La práctica puede ayudar. Ponga el volumen del televisor alto y trate de concentrarse en otra cosa por unos minutos, por ejemplo leer un libro o memorizar un número telefónico. Esto le ayudará a superar el ruido de fondo y poner atención, dice Douglas Herrmann, Ph.D., un investigador de la memoria en el Centro Nacional para Estadísticas de la Salud, en Washington, D.C., y autor de *Super Memory* (Super memoria). Usted también puede tratar de ver dos televisores al mismo tiempo. Eso la obliga a poner atención solamente en la información importante y le ayuda a afinar su concentración.

Lo mismo sucede con el boro, el cual su cuerpo necesita en cantidades pequeñas. Las mujeres que tomaron dietas altas en boro de cerca de tres miligramos por día tuvieron puntuaciones más altas en las pruebas de atención y memoria. Esa es la misma cantidad que usted encontrará en tres manzanas. Otras buenas fuentes de boro incluyen las ciruelas, los dátiles, las pasas y los cacahuates (maníes).

El doctor Penland hace notar que estos estudios muestran que usted estará en mejores condiciones tomando los niveles recomendados de boro y cinc que si usted toma niveles más bajos. Pero eso no significa que tomando altas dosis de los dos hará que su memoria mejore aún más; el comprobar eso requerirá más estudio.

Suspenda el café. La cafeína es un asesino probado de la memoria, dice el doctor Herrmann. Más de una taza durante el día de trabajo probablemente la estimulará demasiado y le hará más difícil concentrarse. "Es completamente un mito que el café le ayuda a recordar. Puede mantenerla despierta, pero destruyendo su sueño usted recordará aún menos", dice el doctor Herrmann.

Fumar provoca el mismo problema de estímulo en exceso, dice el doctor Herrmann. Y el alcohol, aun un trago, reduce la capacidad de las células individuales del cerebro para procesar y almacenar información. Beber por tiempo prolongado también mata a las células del cerebro, dice el doctor Herrmann.

Ignore las curas milagrosas. Una gran cantidad de píldoras y polvos se anuncian como "estimulantes milagrosos de la memoria". Estos no funcionan, según Thomas H. Crook, Ph.D., un sicólogo clínico y presidente de las Clínicas de Evaluación de Memoria, con base en Bethesda, Maryland. Ha habido una investigación prometedora sobre las drogas para mejorar la memoria, pero el doctor Crook dice que nada en el mercado hoy en día ayudará. "Estos realmente son nada más que suplementos nutritivos disfrazados de curaciones", dice él.

MIGRAÑAS

Cómo evitar estos dolores de cabeza

Entre los niños, su esposo y el trabajo, esta semana que acaba de pasar parece que duró un año. Pero es viernes, los niños están durmiendo y su esposo está trabajando el turno de noche. Finalmente, usted tiene un poco de paz. Prende el televisor para mirar su novela favorita. A estas alturas, usted está harta de la cocina, por lo tanto está comiéndose una comida china que ordenó. Y para celebrar que sobrevivió esta semana de ajetreo, prueba un poco de vino tinto que quedó de la fiesta del año nuevo. Bueno, después de enterarse si Pedro vuelve con María aunque ella está embarazada con el hijo de Francisco y quedarse asombrada porque el nuevo novio de Filomena es en realidad el hijo que nunca conoció, usted se duerme, cansada pero contenta.

Se levanta al día siguiente y ¡son las doce del mediodía! Ha dormido toda la mañana, pero en vez de sentirse refrescada y llena de energía, se siente mareada, está sudada y tiene náusea. Está sufriendo los dolores de una migraña, y en vez de ser un alivio, el fin de semana se ha convertido en una pesadilla.

Dieciocho millones de mujeres estadounidenses regularmente sufren de migrañas, y la mayoría son mujeres entre los 30 y los 45 años de edad. El estrés, ciertos alimentos y bebidas y una alteración en los patrones de sueño causan migrañas, pero el 60 por ciento de todas las migrañas que sufren las mujeres están relacionadas con el ciclo menstrual. Estos dolores de cabeza están causados por cambios hormonales antes y durante la menstruación, dice el doctor Seymour Diamond, director de la Clínica Diamond para dolores de Cabeza, en Chicago, y director ejecutivo de la Fundación Nacional de Dolores de Cabeza. Más de la mitad de todas las mujeres que sufren migrañas dejarán de tener los dolores de cabeza después de la menopausia, agrega él.

Pero no importa cuál es la causa, millones de nosotras estamos desperdiciando los años más productivos de nuestras vidas viviendo con el temor del

La receta para relajarse

Ese martilleo entre sus oídos puede estar diciéndole algo: relájese.

La Fundación Nacional para el Dolor de Cabeza informa que el 50 por ciento de las migrañas ocurren inmediatamente después de un período de estrés fuera de lo normal. Para combatir el estrés, los doctores pueden recetar hipnosis, *biofeedback* (donde se le conecta con cables a un monitor y se le enseña a relajar partes de su cuerpo) y otras técnicas de relajación, según el director ejecutivo de la fundación, el doctor Seymour Diamond, quien también es director de la Clínica Diamond para Dolores de Cabeza, en Chicago.

Si usted está buscando una forma de vencer al estrés, el doctor Diamond sugiere este ejercicio de relajación para hacer en casa, el cual no debería tomar más de cuatro a cinco minutos para completarlo.

Siéntese cómodamente en una silla. Deje que todos sus músculos se aflojen y se vuelvan pesados.

1. Frunza el ceño. Arrugue la frente y después alísela. Imagine que tanto su frente como su cuero cabelludo se vuelven más suaves al aumentar la relajación.

---

ataque de una migraña. Cuando el temido dolor azota, nos encontramos nosotras mismas hechas un ovillo en un cuarto oscuro por horas o aun días, deseando que regresaran esos días de nuestra juventud en que podíamos comer y beber lo que se nos viniera en gana, quedarnos despiertas para ver la salida del sol y no pagar por lo que hicimos.

"Una migraña es dolorosa, indeseable y a veces debilitante", dice el doctor Diamond. "Las personas no son capaces de hacer mucho hasta que desaparece."

¡Ay... cómo duele!

Las migrañas empiezan cuando los vasos sanguíneos en su cabeza se contraen por un período de 15 minutos a una hora y luego se expanden rápidamente, dice el doctor Diamond. Se cree que el culpable en este proceso es la serotonina, una substancia parecida a una hormona producida por las plaquetas de la sangre.

Cuando usted provoca una secreción de serotonina —al comer ciertos alimentos, tomar ciertas bebidas, estresándose o algunas veces sólo por dormir demasiado— los vasos sanguíneos en su cabeza se estrechan. Cuando los riñones procesan la serotonina el nivel de esta substancia parecida a la hormona se

Ahora frunza el ceño, arrugue las cejas, y sienta la tensión. Relaje la tensión otra vez. Alise la frente una vez más.

2. Cierre y apriete. Ahora cierre los ojos más y más apretados. Sienta la tensión, entonces descanse los ojos. Mantenga sus ojos cerrados ligeramente, cómodamente, y note la relajación.

Ahora apriete los dientes. Sienta la tensión a través de la mandíbula y entonces relájese.

3. Empuje y gire. Empuje su cabeza hacia atrás lo más que pueda, y sienta la tensión en su cuello. Gire la cabeza hacia la derecha y sienta como la tensión cambia; ahora haga girar su cabeza hacia la izquierda.

Enderece la cabeza, muévala hacia adelante y presione la barbilla contra el pecho. Deje que la cabeza regrese a una posición cómoda y sienta la relajación.

Encójase de hombros y mantenga la tensión. Deje caer los hombros y sienta la relajación. Mueva los hombros hacia arriba, hacia adelante y hacia atrás. Sienta la tensión en los hombros y en la parte superior de la espalda. Deje caer los hombros una vez más y relájese.

reduce, los vasos se dilatan en forma rápida, presionando los nervios circundantes y causando dolor e inflamación. El doctor Diamond dice que el dolor puede durar horas o días porque la inflamación persiste aun después de que los vasos sanguíneos han regresado a la normalidad.

Cerca de una en cada cinco personas que sufre migrañas experimenta un "aura" minutos antes de la aparición del dolor de cabeza. Las mujeres reportan ver destellos de luz y dibujos en zigzag, y algunas veces experimentan dificultad para hablar, confusión y adormecimiento en sus rostros y extremidades, según el doctor Diamond.

Cómo evitar el dolor

Los tratamientos para las migrañas han adelantado mucho durante los últimos 8.500 años. (Sí, las migrañas siempre han estado entre nosotros). En el antiguo Egipto, las personas con migrañas acostumbraban a mordisquear partes de los árboles —el ajenjo y el enebro eran los favoritos— para tratar de aliviar el dolor. Con el progreso de la ciencia médica, los doctores empezaron a recetar tratamientos tales como colocar hierros calientes en los lugares doloridos, cortar las sienes de un paciente y frotar ajo en la herida y hasta enrollar una anguila eléctrica alrededor de la cabeza del paciente.

Afortunadamente, esas "soluciones" ya no están de moda. Si usted está buscando la forma de parar las migrañas antes de que empiecen, los expertos ofrecen estos consejos.

Cuide lo que come. Muchos alimentos pueden causar que el cuerpo estimule los niveles de serotonina. El doctor Diamond dice que estos incluyen el vino tinto, el queso añejo, las carnes procesadas como son los perros calientes y las salchichas, las frutas cítricas, las lentejas, las vainitas de arvejas y los alimentos preparados usando el glutamato de monosodio o *MSG* (por sus siglas en inglés), para realzar el sabor. Para ver qué tiene MSG, lea las etiquetas en los alimentos que usted compra. A menudo la comida china tiene MSG, así que pida en el restaurante que no lo pongan en su orden si usted es sensible a éste.

Los alimentos afectan a las personas de manera diferente, así que es una buena idea mantener un diario que enumere lo que usted comió en las horas anteriores a la migraña. El doctor Diamond dice que es posible que usted pueda ver la formación de pautas e identificar los alimentos que provocan la migraña en su caso.

Tome una aspirina. Un estudio a 22.000 doctores estadounidenses del sexo masculino encontró que si se toma una tableta de aspirina de 325 miligramos un día sí y un día no puede ayudar a protegerse contra los dolores de cabeza. Los doctores del estudio que tomaron aspirina reportaron 20 por ciento menos migrañas que aquellos que tomaron placebos.

Los investigadores están tratando de descubrir si las mujeres tendrán los mismos resultados. Por ahora, los expertos dicen que usted debería ver a su doctor antes de tomar aspirina regularmente porque la aspirina puede causar trastornos estomacales, sangramientos internos y otras complicaciones que puedan ponerla a usted en riesgo de otros problemas de la salud.

Piense en la píldora anticonceptiva. Las píldoras anticonceptivas pueden causar migrañas en algunas mujeres, dice el doctor Diamond. Consulte con su médico si usted debería discontinuar el uso de la píldora anticonceptiva o cambiar a una dosis diferente.

Métase magnesio. Un estudio del Hospital Henry Ford, en Detroit, encontró una escasez de magnesio en los cerebros de la mayoría de los pacientes de migrañas. Así que comiendo alimentos ricos en magnesio, incluyendo los vegetales de color verde oscuro, frutas y nueces, podría obtenerse algo de alivio.

El doctor Kenneth Welch, presidente del Departamento de Neurología del Hospital Henry Ford, hace hincapié en que la información es muy preliminar. Se necesita más trabajo antes de que los investigadores establezcan una relación clara entre las migrañas y el magnesio. Sin embargo, si come unas cuantas porciones extras de frutas y verduras, no le van a hacer daño.

Duerma de acuerdo con un programa. Las pautas irregulares para dormir también contribuyen a las migrañas, aunque el doctor Diamond acepta que la razón exacta no está clara. "Vemos muchas migrañas de fin de semana, cuando las personas duermen hasta tarde", dice él. "Usted debería tratar de obtener la misma cantidad de sueño todas las noches, aun los fines de semana."

Controle su cafeína. Demasiada cafeína —cualquier cantidad de más de tres tazas de café dentro del transcurso de una hora o algo así— puede contraer sus vasos sanguíneos y provocar un dolor de cabeza, según el doctor Diamond. Pero él dice que si toma una taza de café o té justo en el momento en que un dolor de cabeza empieza, puede evitar que sus vasos se expandan demasiado y podría protegerla contra una migraña.

Serénese, después vea a su doctor. Una vez que un dolor de cabeza estalla, dice el doctor Diamond, nada puede quitarlo con excepción de las drogas recetadas. Él sugiere sobrellevar el dolor reclinándose en un cuarto tranquilo y oscuro. Nunca trate de hacer ejercicio durante un episodio de migraña, ya que el pulso en aumento sólo empeorará el dolor.

Puede ser que usted también quiera poner su cabeza en hielo, dice el doctor Lawrence Robbins, profesor asistente de neurología en la Universidad de Illinois, en Chicago y en el Colegio Médico de Rush en la Universidad de Rush, también en Chicago. Así tendrá un 50 por ciento de posibilidad de obtener algún alivio para el dolor dentro de dos a tres minutos después de aplicarse un paquete blando de hielo y presión moderada en su cabeza. Los paquetes blandos para hielo se venden en las farmacias y tiendas de abastecimientos médicos.

Algunas veces, dice el doctor Robbins, una migraña puede ser tan dolorosa que ponerse algo sobre la cabeza puede hacerla sentir aun peor. En esos casos olvídese de los paquetes de hielo.

Si usted no puede controlar las migrañas por sí sola, vea a su doctor. Una combinación de *biofeedback*, ejercicios relajantes y medicamentos pueden resolver sus problemas.

Una droga para disipar la agonía

Una nueva droga, *sumatriptan* (*Imitrex*), parece ser muy prometedora para combatir las migrañas. Un estudio mostró que el 70 por ciento de los pacientes que tomaron *sumatriptan* durante un episodio de migraña reportaron un alivio o incluso nada de dolor después de una hora. Esta droga con receta está libre de efectos secundarios tales como la sedación, náusea o el vómito comunes en medicamentos para las migrañas.

"Este es uno de los más grandes descubrimientos en la investigación de las migrañas", dice el doctor Diamond. "Realmente ofrece una gran esperanza a las personas que sufren de migrañas frecuentes." Desafortunadamente, no es para aquellas que tienen presión arterial alta o problemas del corazón. Pregunte a su doctor si usted podría ser una buena candidata.

OSTEOPOROSIS

Sea la guardia de sus huesos

Sus huesos parecen vigas de acero —fuertes, permanentes, una estructura de la cual usted puede depender.

Pero en una de cada cuatro mujeres, esta estructura esquelética se está erosionando, las vigas se están debilitando y desgastando.

La causa es la osteoporosis.

La osteoporosis es una enfermedad del desgaste de los huesos, caderas fracturadas y columnas vertebrales encorvadas, una enfermedad del envejecimiento que usted puede prevenir —si empieza hoy.

Ahora bien, usted no puede evitar que sus huesos se desgasten. Cada mujer pierde algo de hueso a través del tiempo, por lo general al paso de un 1 por ciento por año. Pero en las mujeres con osteoporosis, la pérdida es mucho más rápida que lo normal, y los huesos pueden volverse tan quebradizos y frágiles que se quiebran cuando se baja del bordillo (borde) de la acera o se pega con su cadera contra el filo de una mesa. De hecho, los huesos en su columna vertebral, las vértebras, aun se pueden quebrar por su propio peso.

Además de que la hace verse mayor, la osteoporosis puede hacer que usted se sienta así. "De repente, las mujeres tienen miedo de salir, dar paseos, lavar las ventanas, limpiar la tina. Tienen miedo de que si se tropiezan o se caen, van a quebrar un hueso", dice el doctor Clifford Rosen, director del Centro de Maine para Investigación y Educación sobre la Osteoporosis, en Bangor.

El doctor Rosen dice "mujeres" porque la osteoporosis ataca a cuatro mujeres por cada hombre. Las mujeres, para empezar, tienen menos hueso y durante la menopausia hay una reducción en la producción de la hormona femenina estrógeno, que contiene el calcio en sus huesos como una represa.

Pero sus huesos pueden empezar a desgastarse demasiado rápido aun antes de que llegue la menopausia, un agotamiento lento y sin síntomas de la fuerza interior de su cuerpo que comienza en las décadas de sus 30 y 40 años de edad.

Si usted no hace nada para pararla —cosas tales como tomar calcio, hacer ejercicio, probar con la terapia de reposición de hormonas o tomando otras acciones preventivas discutidas más adelante— se convierte en osteoporosis. Y eso, es serio.

Algunas mujeres con osteoporosis se encorvan y se hacen más bajas de estatura al quebrarse los huesos en su espina dorsal. Estas fracturas pueden ser indoloras o mal interpretadas como problemas de la espalda (por lo menos al principio). "Una mujer puede tener dolor en la espalda que duele por un tiempo y después desaparece. Ella puede atribuirlo a un espasmo muscular cuando en realidad tiene una fractura de compresión", dice el doctor Rosen.

Algunas mujeres se fracturan las muñecas, otro punto vulnerable.

Y algunas mujeres se fracturan las caderas. De estas mujeres, el 10 al 20 por ciento morirán durante el próximo año.

¿Es usted una candidata?

Si su madre tiene osteoporosis, usted también puede ser propensa a estas fracturas aterradoras, dice el doctor Rosen. "Hasta el 70 por ciento de su masa ósea máxima, la cual usted alcanza en la década de sus 20 años, está determinada por herencia", dice él. Las mujeres muy pequeñas o delgadas son también más susceptibles a la osteoporosis, añade él, ya que tienen una masa ósea menor que otras mujeres.

Una de las causas principales de la osteoporosis es muy poco calcio en su dieta. Aunque las estimaciones de cuántas mujeres tienen una deficiencia de este nutriente básico para la formación de los huesos varían del 10 al 25 por ciento, los expertos concuerdan en que la deficiencia de calcio es extremadamente común. Otro nutriente vital para la salud de los huesos es la vitamina D, porque ayuda en la absorción del calcio. Si usted no está tomando suficiente vitamina D, su cuerpo no tendrá la capacidad de aprovechar aun las cantidades más abundantes de calcio.

Y si su ejercicio no es del tipo que estimula el crecimiento de los huesos, sus huesos se volverán más porosos —y se fracturarán más fácilmente.

Los expertos dicen que otros factores que también contribuyen a la osteoporosis son el fumar y el beber mucho. Ciertas medicinas recetadas también pueden erosionar la fuerza de los huesos, especialmente si se toman durante muchos años en dosis extremadamente altas.

Pero usted no tiene que cruzarse de brazos y rendirse a la osteoporosis. Usted puede reducir al mínimo sus riesgos y tomar pasos decisivos para formar huesos más fuertes. Lo más importante es que usted empiece ahora.

Cuenta de huesos

Imagine que sus huesos son como un tipo de cuenta bancaria. A lo largo de su vida, su cuerpo está constantemente depositando hueso y retirando hueso de

¿Cuál es su riesgo?

No es difícil evaluar su riesgo de desarrollar osteoporosis, dice la doctora Susan Allen, Ph.D., profesora asistente de medicina interna en la Escuela de Medicina de la Universidad de Missouri-Columbia. Empiece con las siguientes preguntas:

1 ¿Tiene usted un cuerpo pequeño, delgado, o es usted caucásica o asiática?

2. ¿Tiene usted familiares con osteoporosis?

3. ¿Ya llegó usted a la menopausia?

4. ¿Ha sufrido usted una menopausia prematura o inducida quirúrgicamente?

5. ¿Toma usted dosis altas de un medicamento para la glándula tiroides o drogas similares a la cortisona para asma, artritis o cáncer?

6. ¿Evita usted tomar muchos productos lácteos u otras fuentes de calcio?

7. ¿No está usted haciendo regularmente ejercicios de cargar con su propio peso tales como caminar vigorosamente?

8. ¿Fuma usted cigarrillos o bebe alcohol en exceso?

Si usted contestó sí a dos o más de estas preguntas, su riesgo de desarrollar osteoporosis es alto, dice la doctora Allen. Es hora de hablar con su médico acerca del desarrollo de un plan preventivo de por vida.

su esqueleto. Cuando usted es joven, usted deposita más hueso del que retira, dice el doctor Rosen. Pero cuando usted llega a los 35 años de edad, esta tónica se invierte —usted retira más de lo que deposita. Para evitar una bancarrota de sus huesos, usted necesita depositar tanto hueso como sea posible antes de la menopausia.

Pero ¿y qué pasa si usted está sólo a unos cuantos años de la menopausia o ya está allí y realmente no sabe cuánto hueso hay en su cuenta? Aunque no todos los doctores están de acuerdo en que todas las mujeres deberían ser examinadas para osteoporosis, el doctor Rosen recomienda que usted vaya a lo seguro y haga que le tomen una medida de la densidad ósea en su cadera y en su columna vertebral cuando usted está entre los 45 y los 55 años de edad, que es cuando el desgaste del hueso es por primera vez perceptible. La mejor prueba se llama *dual energy x-ray absorptiometry* (absorciometría radiológica de doble energía o *DEXA*, (por sus siglas en inglés) y cuesta entre $100 y $250. La mayoría de los hospitales comunitarios y todos los hospitales en las ciudades grandes deben tener escáners para DEXA, dice el doctor Rosen. Pero si en su comunidad no hay una máquina DEXA disponible, en su lugar, su doctor puede, evaluar la salud de sus huesos con una tomografía axial computarizada o escáner TAC.

Los doctores están de acuerdo en que las mujeres con un mayor riesgo de la enfermedad —mujeres con historias familiares de osteoporosis o historias personales de fumar o beber en exceso— deberían ser examinadas antes de cumplir los 45 años de edad.

Si su prueba muestra un nivel de pérdida ósea más alto que el normal, no pierda las esperanzas —probablemente no es demasiado tarde para empezar a formar hueso.

Estrategias para su esqueleto

Aquí están las mejores maneras de reforzar su esqueleto.

Aumente su consumo de calcio. El calcio es para sus huesos lo que el aire es para sus pulmones —el elemento que necesitan para estar saludables. El 99 por ciento del calcio en su dieta se va directamente a sus huesos. Si usted no toma suficiente calcio, usted no puede formar suficiente hueso, es así de simple.

Aunque la Asignación Dietética Recomendada (*Recommended Dietary Allowance* o *RDA*, por sus siglas en inglés) para mujeres es de 800 miligramos por día, usted necesita más calcio en la adolescencia y después de la menopausia, dice el doctor Rosen. Las mujeres deben tomar por lo menos 1.000 miligramos antes de la menopausia y 1.500 miligramos después. Aunque los alimentos son la mejor forma de obtener calcio, lo que importa es que usted tome la cantidad recomendada, dice el doctor Rosen. Si eso es a través de los alimentos, magnífico; si es a través de una combinación de alimentos y suplementos de calcio, también está bien. Sólo asegúrese de que los números coincidan.

Onza por onza, la leche y los productos lácteos son las mejores fuentes de calcio dietético. Una porción de 8 onzas (227 g) de yogur sin grasa proporciona cerca de 450 miligramos de calcio. Una taza de leche descremada ofrece más de 300 miligramos. Muchos otros alimentos contienen calcio, pero el nutriente no se absorbe tan fácilmente de estos alimentos como de los productos lácteos.

No se olvide de la D. Los huesos no absorben calcio a menos que tengan bastante vitamina D, dice Michael F. Holick, Ph.D., director del Laboratorio de Investigación de Vitamina D, Piel y Hueso en el Centro Médico de la Universidad de Boston. Sin la vitamina D, su cuerpo absorbe cerca del 10 por ciento del calcio que ingiere; con vitamina D puede absorber del 80 al 90 por ciento. "La vitamina D le dice al intestino delgado 'aquí viene el calcio; abre y déjalo entrar' ", explica el doctor Holick. La RDA para la vitamina D es de 5 microgramos o 200 unidades —lo cual se encuentra fácilmente en los alimentos fortificados como son la leche, los panes y cereales.

Además de obtener algo de su vitamina D a través de los alimentos, su cuerpo puede fabricarla de la luz solar, lo cual provoca un proceso de manufactura de vitamina D en su piel. Entre 5 a 15 minutos de luz brillante de sol diariamente, antes de que se ponga la loción antisolar, puede abastecer sus necesidades, dice el doctor Rosen. Sin embargo, si usted vive al norte de la ciudad de Nueva York no

Ejercicios para fortalecer la columna vertebral

El hacer ejercicios que estiren su columna vertebral tan derecha como sea posible fortalecerá las vértebras más vulnerables a la osteoporosis. Pruebe estos ejercicios para extender la espalda sugeridos por la doctora Susan Allen, Ph.D., profesora asistente de medicina interna en la Escuela de Medicina de la Universidad de Missouri-Columbia.

"Haga tantos de estos ejercicios como pueda, una vez en la mañana y otra vez en la noche", dice la doctora Allen.

Acuéstese boca arriba con sus rodillas flexionadas. Traiga ambas rodillas tan cerca al pecho como le sea posible y manténgase así (sosteniendo las rodillas con las manos) por cinco segundos, luego baje los pies lentamente hacia el piso. Levante entonces una rodilla y llévela hacia su pecho tan lejos como pueda; manténgala por cinco segundos y bájela lentamente hacia el piso. Alterne las piernas derecha e izquierda repitiendo diez veces con cada una.

puede depender del sol. En ese caso, usted necesitará asegurarse de obtener suficiente vitamina D de las fuentes dietéticas. (Si usted ya está tomando bastante en su dieta, no necesitará nada de tiempo en el sol).

Revise su medicamento. Ciertos medicamentos —medicamentos para la glándula tiroides, esteroides antiinflamatorios tales como la hidrocortisona (*Locoid*), la cortisona (*Cortone Acetate*) y la prednisona (*Key-Pred 50*),

Acuéstese boca arriba con sus rodillas flexionadas. Oprima la región baja de la espalda contra el piso y mantenga por cinco segundos. Repita diez veces.

Acuéstese boca arriba con sus rodillas flexionadas. Coloque los brazos a través de su parte media, tomando el codo opuesto con cada mano, ahuecándola. Levante la cabeza y los hombros lo más que pueda sin llegar a sentarse. Mantenga por tres segundos. Repita diez veces.

Acuéstese boca arriba con sus piernas derechas y los brazos a sus lados. Levante la cabeza y los hombros lo más que pueda sin llegar a sentarse. Mantenga por tres segundos. Repita diez veces.

anticonvulsivos como es el phenytoin (*Dilantin*), depresivos tales como fenobarbital (*Barbita*) y el furosemida diurético (*Lasix*)— pueden causar la osteoporosis, particularmente cuando se toman regularmente en dosis altas o por varios años. Sin embargo, los medicamentos para la glándula tiroides en dosis normales no deben presentar problema alguno, dice el doctor Rosen, y el riesgo con los diuréticos se puede contrarrestar si se toma calcio adicional. El riesgo más serio de la osteoporosis es de los esteroides, dice el doctor Rosen. Si usted necesita medicación con esteroides a largo plazo, su doctor puede recomendar medicamentos adicionales contra la osteoporosis tales como la calcitonina (*Cibacalcin*) o una terapia de reposición de hormonas además de los suplementos de calcio y vitamina D, dice él.

Manténgalos secos. "El alcohol de hecho envenena las células que forman los huesos", dice la doctora Susan Allen, Ph.D., profesora asistente de medicina interna en la Escuela de Medicina de la Universidad de Missouri-Columbia. Una cerveza o una copa de vino de vez en cuando probablemente no le va a causar mucho daño. Pero evite beber en exceso, dice ella, más de dos o tres tragos diarios.

No eche humo. Fumar reduce sus niveles de estrógeno, dice Barbara S. Levine, Ph.D., profesora clínica asociada de nutrición en medicina y directora del Centro de Información Sobre el Calcio en el Colegio Médico de la Universidad de Cornell, en la ciudad de Nueva York. Y un estrógeno más bajo, dice ella, significa menos protección contra la pérdida ósea.

Considere la terapia de reposición de hormonas. Para algunas mujeres que han pasado la menopausia, la terapia de reposición de hormonas puede hacer que sus huesos se hagan más gruesos. Pregunte a su doctor si usted es una candidata para eso.

Fisiculturismo interior

Un programa de ejercicios forma músculo y hueso, dice Gail Dalsky, Ph.D., directora del Laboratorio de Investigación del Ejercicio en el Centro de Salud de la Universidad de Connecticut, en Farmington. "La densidad de hueso de las mujeres que hacen bastante ejercicio es 5 a 10 por ciento mayor que en otras mujeres", dice ella.

Y el ejercicio no sólo aumenta la densidad de los huesos sino que también mejora su destreza y reflejos, y por ello será menos probable que se caiga y se rompa un hueso, dice la doctora Allen.

Cargue con su cuerpo. Para reforzar los huesos, usted necesita actividades en las cuales usted está cargando peso sobre sus huesos, dice la doctora Allen. Los ejercicios de cargar peso incluyen caminar vigorosamente, trotar y bailar, lo cual de hecho estimula a las células de los huesos a formar más hueso, particularmente en su espalda y caderas, donde usted más lo necesita, dice la doctora Allen.

Usted está haciendo un ejercicio de cargar con su propio peso si sus pies están golpeando sobre el piso con al menos el impacto que produce el caminar vigorosamente, dice el doctor Rosen. "Básicamente, usted puede depender de cualquier ejercicio que hace uso intenso de la ley de gravedad", dice él. "Nadar, por ejemplo, no lo hace pero la mayoría de las clases aeróbicas y el tenis sí lo hacen."

Levantar pesas es también una forma ideal de aumentar la fuerza en los huesos, ya que aumenta el peso de la gravedad en sus huesos. Tiene sentido levantar pesas durante una parte de sus ejercicios de cargar con su propio peso. Cualquier levantamiento hecho mientras que está parada es particularmente útil para la columna vertebral y las caderas. Si usted nunca ha usado pesas, asegúrese de obtener el permiso de su médico y el consejo de un entrenador sobre la rutina más segura.

Hágalo regularmente. Una vez que usted ha encontrado los ejercicios de cargar con su propio peso que le gustan, practíquelos por lo menos de 30 minutos a una hora tres a cuatro veces por semana, dice la doctora Allen.

Enfóquese en la espalda y concéntrese en las caderas. Si usted está haciendo ejercicio para perder peso y tener tono muscular, usted probablemente está haciendo algo para la parte superior de su cuerpo, y eso está bien. Pero recuerde, dice la doctora Allen, los huesos más vulnerables a la osteoporosis son las caderas y las vértebras en la parte de la columna vertebral a la altura media y baja de la espalda. Caminar, trotar y el baile aeróbico son especialmente provechosos para su espalda y caderas, dice ella.

PAPADA

Qué hacer cuando la edad nos llega al cuello

La Madre Naturaleza no nos hizo ningún favor cuando inventó la gravedad. Desde el día en que nos quitamos nuestro vestido de quinceañera, nos ha estado jalando, jalando, y jalando, estirando partes de nuestro cuerpo a lugares que nunca nos hubiéramos imaginado cuando estábamos en nuestra adolescencia.

Y de todas nuestras partes del cuerpo, ninguna es tan sensible a la gravedad como el cuello. Agregue unas cuantas libras inocentes, unos cuantos años inofensivos y, —¡ay, ay, ay!— ahí viene la papada.

"Debo admitirlo, una papada realmente parece molestar a algunas mujeres. Las hace sentir como que están envejeciendo de prisa", dice el doctor Robert Kotler, un cirujano cosmético facial e instructor clínico de cirugía en la Universidad de California, en Los Ángeles. "Cada vez que se miran en el espejo, la ven. Están conscientes de ella en las fiestas y en el trabajo. Y les está diciendo que probablemente no son tan jóvenes como solían serlo."

A mandíbula suelta

Tres factores contribuyen a la papada (doble mentón, doble barbilla); grasa en el cuerpo, la anatomía y el tiempo. Las mujeres almacenan grasa en sus cuellos tan fácilmente como en sus caderas o muslos, dice el doctor Kotler. Así que si aumentamos unas cuantas libras, hay una buena posibilidad de que algunas de ellas encontrarán refugio bajo nuestras barbillas.

Pero las mujeres con sobrepeso no son las únicas en peligro. También las personas delgadas tienen papadas, usualmente debido a la forma de su mandíbula y garganta. "Mientras menos agudo sea el ángulo entre las líneas de la mandíbula y el cuello, mayor es el riesgo de un cuello carnoso", dice el doctor

Kotler. Pero mientras más abajo esté la manzana de Adán en su cuello, más posible es que a usted le cuelgue la barbilla.

La edad también aumenta las probabilidades. La piel de las mujeres empieza a perder su elasticidad después de los 35 a los 40 años de edad. Aun cuando usted se encuentre firme y en buena forma, puede tener una pequeña papada simplemente debido a la piel más suelta, dice el doctor Kotler.

Desde una perspectiva de salud, nada de esto es realmente importante. No hay nada peligroso en una papada a menos que usted tenga un serio sobrepeso, dice el doctor Kotler. Y aun así, es un síntoma de obesidad, no un problema por sí mismo. "Las papadas son simplemente una parte desafortunada del proceso de envejecer", dice el doctor Kotler. "Pero en el orden general de la vida, hay cosas más importantes de qué preocuparse."

Consejos para su cuello

Inofensiva o no, la mayoría de las mujeres encuentran a las papadas poco atractivas, de todas maneras. Para ayudarla a deshacerse de esos pliegues extras —o por lo menos esconderlos un poco— los expertos ofrecen estos consejos.

Pierda 10. O a lo mejor, 15 —libras, queremos decir. "La mejor forma de deshacerse de una papada es perdiendo peso", dice el doctor Kotler. "Muchas personas vienen a mi consultorio porque quieren una cirugía cosmética. Pero si tan sólo perdieran algo del peso excesivo, el problema disminuiría a tal grado que ya no necesitarían ayuda."

Las reglas normales son válidas. Haga ejercicio aeróbico regularmente. Coma menos grasa. Evite dietas estrictas que generalmente causan más daños que beneficios. Y no se confíe en los ejercicios milagrosos de "reducción por área" para su cuello. Estos no quitarán la grasa —y en algunos casos han causado mandíbulas dislocadas y músculos del cuello seriamente distendidos.

Acórtelo. El cabello largo atrae miradas a su cuello —precisamente lo que usted trata de evitar. Los cortes al estilo paje que se curvan abajo de la barbilla son los peores. "La regla es mantenerlo corto, en o arriba de la línea de la mandíbula", dice Kathleen Walas, directora de modas y belleza para la empresa Avon Products con base en la ciudad de Nueva York, y autora de *Real Beauty... Real Women* (Belleza real... mujeres reales).

Destaque otro detalle. Para hacer menos notable una papada, haga relucir otros aspectos físicos. La señora Walas sugiere usar colorete en la parte de arriba de sus pómulos. O pruebe con una sombra de ojos más brillante, con un tono de buen gusto. Si usa base de maquillaje, aplique una de tono ligeramente más oscuro abajo de la barbilla, y combínela con cuidado con la base de maquillaje en su cara. "Eso hará el resto de su rostro brillante y atractivo y su papada mucho menos notable", dice Walas.

Baje el escote. Los escotes abiertos y amplios son los más favorecedores para las mujeres con papadas, dice Walas. Los cuellos de tortuga deben descartarse definitivamente. Y en cuanto a joyas, evite gargantillas y pruebe con collares largos. Los aretes que cuelgan —cualquier cosa abajo de la línea de su mandíbula— pueden atraer atención hacia su cuello, según Walas.

Sepa lo que le espera con la cirugía. La cirugía cosmética es un último recurso, dice el doctor Kotler. Pero si usted ha probado todo y no puede perder esa papada —y tiene aproximadamente $4.500 a la mano— puede tener su cuello "esculpido". El cirujano hará un pequeño corte horizontal debajo de su barbilla, entonces succionará la grasa que se ha acumulado bajo la piel. Finalmente, hará una incisión vertical entre las capas del cuello y el músculo de la mandíbula y a continuación juntará y coserá los bordes, ajustando la capa de músculo como un corsé.

Es un procedimiento relativamente indoloro que requiere dos curitas para esconderla, dice el doctor Kotler. Los moretones son mínimos, y dentro de unos diez días usted no verá nada excepto que su barbilla sin papada de antes. "Es un procedimiento común", dice. "La técnica se ha vuelto muy refinada, y los resultados son bastante buenos." La operación se puede realizar bajo anestesia general o local con sedación.

Por $500 adicionales o algo así, el cirujano puede añadir un implante en la barbilla. Se trata de una pieza de silicona sólida que se desliza entre el hueso de su mandíbula y la funda de los tejidos que cubre el hueso. El implante le proporciona una mandíbula más prominente y acentúa aún más el ángulo entre la línea de su mandíbula y el cuello, dice el doctor Kotler. Esto no agrega nada al tiempo total de recuperación. Los cirujanos usan implantes en aproximadamente una cuarta parte de todos los procedimientos de papada, dice el doctor Kotler.

PÉRDIDA
DE CABELLO

Dele cabeza a la raleza

Su peinadora lo ha podido ocultar hasta ahora. Esos peinados cortos y crespos hacen que los mechones se vean abundantes, y nadie puede ver la diferencia.

Áun así, se hace difícil negar que al igual que los otros 20 millones de mujeres estadounidenses, usted está empezando a perder el cabello. Usted está muy preocupada ahora, y se mira en el espejo constantemente, sintiéndose más vieja cada minuto que pasa.

"El cabello es una parte importante de la imagen del cuerpo de una mujer", dice el doctor Dominic A. Brandy, director médico de Dominic A. Brandy, M.D., and Associates, un consultorio de restauración permanente del cabello, en Pittsburgh. "El perderlo puede causar bastante estrés y, en algunos casos, puede hacer que las mujeres pierdan también una cierta cantidad de respeto por ellas mismas."

No ayuda el hecho de que la pérdida de cabello normalmente empieza entre los 25 y los 40 años de edad, aun antes de llegar a una edad madura. "Eso no parece ser muy justo", dice el doctor Brandy. "Se supone que usted debería estar en su momento óptimo, y ya está pasando por algo que la hace sentirse vieja. Esto puede hacer que algunas mujeres se preocupen de que la juventud se les está yendo de las manos."

No sólo para los hombres

La herencia desempeña un papel de hasta un 85 por ciento en la pérdida de cabello en las mujeres. Si su mamá, abuela o tía tuvo cabello ralo, es posible que usted también lo tenga, dice Marty Sawaya, Ph.D., profesora asistente de dermatología en el Centro de Ciencias de la Salud de la Universidad de Florida, en Gainesville.

A diferencia de los hombres, quienes primero pierden el cabello en la coronilla y en el nacimiento del cabello, las mujeres tienen más probabilidades de perder el cabello uniformemente en todo el cuero cabelludo. Donde una mujer antes tenía cinco cabellos, puede ser que ahora tenga dos. También puede desarrollar una entrada en forma de V, con la línea de nacimiento del cabello en retroceso ligero y una pérdida de cabello más notable alrededor de las sienes.

Nadie está muy seguro qué causa que el cabello deje de crecer. La investigación muestra que las mujeres con niveles altos de hormonas masculinas —y aquellas con cueros cabelludos sensibles aun a niveles normales de hormonas— tienen más probabilidad de perder el cabello. Cualquiera que sea la causa, los cabellos individuales se adelgazan gradualmente y los folículos eventualmente dejan de producirlos completamente.

La triste realidad es que fuera de las drogas con receta o transplantes de cabello, realmente no hay mucho que usted pueda hacer para detener la pérdida de cabello. El doctor Ken Hashimoto, profesor de dermatología en la Escuela de Medicina de la Universidad Estatal Wayne, en Detroit, hace notar que los tratamientos milagrosos para el cabello —masajes, cremas locales, megavitaminas y todo el resto— no hacen absolutamente nada.

Pero no se dé por vencida todavía. Tiene algunas opciones.

Causantes de la caída

Usted puede abordar un número de factores no hereditarios que causan que las mujeres pierdan el cabello, dice la doctora Sawaya. Ella enumera:

• Las dietas de moda y muy estrictas. Las dietas deficientes en proteínas (como los planes de comer sólo toronjas, o aquellos que ignoran frijoles (habichuelas), carnes magras y otras fuentes de proteína) pueden privar al cuerpo de un componente básico vital para el cabello.
• Anemia.
• Parto.
• Las drogas incluyendo píldoras anticonceptivas, esteroides anabólicos, drogas para la presión arterial bloqueadores de beta y las drogas derivadas de la vitamina A.
• Condiciones tales como la artritis, el lupus (una enfermedad de la piel caracterizada por las lesiones), y el síndrome poliquístico de los ovarios, el cual causa que los ovarios se llenen de pequeños quistes.
• Los sucesos de estrés fuerte, tales como un divorcio o la muerte de un ser querido. Una dieta deficiente también puede estresar a su cuerpo.

La doctora Sawaya indica que algunas de estas causas no hereditarias pueden resultar en una pérdida temporal del cabello. Un examen médico minucioso, una

¿ Lo está perdiendo realmente?

No entre en pánico si encuentra un par de cabellos en el lavabo o en su cepillo todos los días. Las mujeres típicamente pierden de 50 a 100 cabellos por día, según la doctora Marty Sawaya, Ph.D., profesora asistente de dermatología en el Centro de Ciencias de la Salud de la Universidad de Florida, en Gainesville. Eso no es mucho —los adultos tienen más de 100.000 cabellos en la cabeza.

Si usted tiene temor de estar perdiendo el cabello, haga esta pequeña prueba. Tome un puñado de cabellos en una mano y jálelos firme pero cuidadosamente. Si se arrancó más de media docena de cabellos, puede ser que esté en las primeras etapas de la pérdida de cabello.

No se preocupe acerca del cabello que se cae cuando usted se lava el cuero cabelludo. Eso le pasa a todas.

mejor dieta, el manejo del estrés y un tratamiento médico podrían en algunos casos estimular un nuevo crecimiento, dice ella.

Búsquele la vuelta

No hay ninguna razón por la cual usted tiene que soportar el cabello que es demasiado delgado o lacio, no importa la causa. Usted puede darle cuerpo a su cabello ralo otra vez. Aquí está cómo.

Ocúltelo con ondas. La forma más rápida de ocultar el cabello ralo es con un permanente rizado, según David Cannell, Ph.D., vicepresidente corporativo de tecnología con Redken Product Laboratory, en Canoga Park, California.

"Con un estilo ondulado, los cabellos individuales se empujan uno contra el otro", dice el doctor Cannell. "El efecto total es de que empujan hacia arriba y hacia afuera, haciendo que su cabellera se vea más llena."

El doctor Cannell aconseja a las mujeres que eviten estilos de peinado que requieren rulos pequeños o estirar apretadamente el cabello. Mientras más presión ponga usted sobre su cabello, más probable es que lo arranque.

Acondiciónese. Evite los componentes aceitosos para el cabello y otros productos que anuncian resultados "cremosos y ricos". El doctor Cannell dice que estos tienden a aplastar el cabello por su peso, lo cual puede hacer que se vea más delgado.

Él recomienda probar con un acondicionador más ligero, de los que se dejan en el cabello, el cual puede añadir una cantidad microscópica de grosor a cada cabello individual.

Hacerlo crecer
nuevamente —algunas veces

Si usted acaba de notar que su cabello se vuelve ralo, recuerde esto: *Minoxidil* —la cura para la pérdida de cabello que viene en una fórmula con receta para uso local— no es sólo para los hombres.

"Las mujeres pueden lograr resultados significantes con el uso de *minoxidil*", dice el doctor Dominic A. Brandy, director médico de Dominic A. Brandy, M.D., and Associates, un consultorio para la restauración permanente de cabello, en Pittsburgh. "De hecho, en algunas de mis pacientes, los resultados parecen ser mejores que en los hombres."

El *minoxidil* es el ingrediente químico activo en el medicamento para uso local que se vende bajo la marca *Rogaine*. Las pruebas clínicas han mostrado que *Rogaine* puede ayudar a las mujeres a recuperar algo de la abundancia en su cabellera. Pero hay límites en la efectividad de *Rogaine* en las mujeres, al igual que los hay en los hombres.

Nadie está muy seguro cómo funciona *Rogaine*. Los investigadores especulan que al aumentar el flujo de sangre al cuero cabelludo, éste estimula el crecimiento del cabello.

El doctor Brandy dice que *Rogaine* no hará crecer el cabello en la línea frontal de nacimiento del cabello o en áreas que están completamente calvas. En el mejor de los casos, dice él, engrosará ligeramente el cabello existente y hará regresar un aspecto de más cuerpo a sus mechones.

"Pero en la mayoría de los casos, simplemente retarda el progreso de la calvicie", dice el doctor Brandy. "Eso es lo que le digo a la mayor parte de las personas que pueden esperar. Cualquier otra cosa viene de arriba."

Una cosa más en qué pensar: *Rogaine* es caro. Los tratamientos típicamente cuestan de $500 a $700 al año, y usted tiene que usar *Rogaine* para siempre. Si lo suspende, va a perder en seis meses todo lo que había ganado hasta la fecha.

La *Upjohn Company*, fabricante de *Rogaine*, continúa perfeccionándolo. Al mismo tiempo, otros investigadores están viendo tratamientos

Dese una palmadita en la cabeza. Después de la ducha, séquese el cabello con cuidado. Dele palmaditas ligeras con una toalla en lugar de frotarlo.

Péinese con cuidado. El doctor Cannell sugiere que se tenga cuidado con los cepillos y peines. Nunca se cepille el cabello cuando está mojado (nunca se debe jalar el cabello enredado). En lugar de eso, trate de usar un peine con los dientes bastante separados.

nuevos para el cabello ralo. Pero el problema más grande al que se enfrentan los investigadores de la pérdida de cabello es el hecho de que ninguno está seguro por qué las mujeres empiezan a perder el cabello en primer lugar.

"No estamos haciendo estos tratamientos a ciegas. Estos están basados en teoría", dice el doctor Ken Hashimoto, profesor de dermatología en la Escuela de Medicina de la Universidad Estatal Wayne, en Detroit. "Pero realmente no sabemos cuál es el mecanismo exacto que causa la calvicie."

Los investigadores están evaluando estos tratamientos alternativos. Puede ser que algunos no estén disponibles todavía.

Aromatasa. Las personas con el cabello ralo parecen que no tienen suficiente de esta enzima la cual, cuando está presente en niveles normales, causa que los folículos hagan crecer el cabello. La doctora Marty Sawaya, Ph.D., profesora asistente de dermatología en el Centro de Ciencias de la Salud de la Universidad de Florida, en Gainesville y otros investigadores están trabajando para mejorar un método de reponer los niveles naturales de aromatasa.

La doctora Sawaya predice que los tratamientos efectivos de hormonas pueden estar disponibles al público para el año 2000.

Solución de tricomin. Karen Hedine, vicepresidenta de desarrollo de negocios para el fabricante de drogas *ProCyte*, en Kirkland, Washington, dice que esta droga parece que funciona al estimular el crecimiento de nuevos folículos en el cuero cabelludo y al prevenir que los folículos existentes se vuelvan inactivos.

Dizóxido. Al igual que *Rogaine*, esta droga parece que funciona dilatando los vasos sanguíneos en el cuero cabelludo.

Estimulación eléctrica. Las pruebas que involucran dosis de electricidad a corrientes bajas sobre los cueros cabelludos de los hombres han mostrado ser prometedoras en pruebas canadienses. Los investigadores predicen que los tratamientos pueden estar disponibles en los Estados Unidos en unos pocos años.

Y olvídese de las letanías que su tía abuela solía predicar acerca de cepillarse 100 veces. El doctor Cannell dice que usted debe cepillar su cabello sólo por el tiempo que sea necesario para darle el estilo que quiere.

Aclárelo. Escoja un color nuevo, más claro, para su cabello. Los tonos que se asemejen al tono de su cutis son los mejores, dice el doctor Cannell, porque de esa manera armonizan con su cuero cabelludo.

"Lo peor que usted puede hacer es teñir su cabello de negro azabache", dice el doctor Cannell. "Eso realmente deja ver su cuero cabelludo, que es lo último que usted quiere hacer."

Controle sus manos. Deshágase de los hábitos nerviosos como estar jalándose el cabello o rizándoselo con los dedos. Puede estar jalando el cabello más de lo que usted cree, ya que está consciente de cómo se ve.

"Aun cuando el cabello esté listo para caerse, se mantendrá en su sitio por bastante tiempo —si lo deja en paz", dice el doctor Cannell. "Mientras más lo toque, más rápidamente se caerá."

Sepa que usted no está sola. Más que ninguna otra cosa, dice el doctor Brandy, usted debe recordar que otras mujeres están enfrentándose al mismo problema que usted.

"Millones de mujeres tienen el cabello ralo", dice él. "Usted no debería sentirse como que es la única, y tampoco debería sentirse como que ya no tiene opciones para tratar el problema."

El camino de la cirugía

Si su problema es hereditario, y no hay posibilidad de que su cabello vuelva a su aspecto juvenil por sí mismo, puede ser que quiera considerar la cirugía de reemplazo de cabello. Años atrás, los trasplantes de cabello se podían notar fácilmente y a menudo el costo no valía la pena. Pero la tecnología y la técnica han mejorado dramáticamente, dice el doctor Brandy. Y, sí, las mujeres se los están haciendo, aunque la mayoría de los pacientes todavía son hombres.

"Cuando se hace correctamente ahora, usted ya no ve la 'fila artificial de maíz' o 'el cabello de muñeca' ", dice el doctor Brandy. "El proceso puede ser caro para algunos, pero los resultados son bastante buenos."

Los doctores están realizando tres tipos principales de cirugía cosmética en las mujeres, dice el doctor Brandy.

Trasplantes de cabello. Existen desde hace unos 35 años. La práctica antigua incluía mover grupos grandes de folículos de cabello (8 a 20 a la vez) de la parte de atrás de la cabeza de un paciente, para después insertarlos en una región sin cabello. Esto resultaba a menudo en líneas de nacimiento del cabello irregulares y poco naturales.

El doctor Brandy dice que las nuevas técnicas quirúrgicas de microinjerto permiten a los doctores transplantar hasta un solo cabello por vez. El doctor Brandy dice que este procedimiento es especialmente bueno para las mujeres, quienes usualmente no tienen grandes áreas calvas que se necesiten cubrir.

Los costos totales pueden fluctuar entre $3.500 y $10.000.

Estiramiento de cabello. Esto no se usa comúnmente para las mujeres, ya que están diseñados para cubrir áreas extendidas de calvicie. El procedimiento incluye cortar y retirar cuero cabelludo sin cabello y entonces estirar el cuero cabelludo con cabello, de los lados y parte de atrás de la cabeza hacia la coronilla de una mujer. El procedimiento puede costar entre $3.500 y $5.000, dice el doctor Brandy.

Reducción del cuero cabelludo. Esta es una versión reducida del estiramiento de cabello. Consiste en deshacerse de pequeñas áreas sin cabello cubriéndolas al estirar cuero cabelludo con cabello sobre esas áreas con calvicie. El costo es de cerca de $2.500 a $3.000.

Entretejido de cabello. Estos son tratamientos cosméticos, no procedimientos quirúrgicos, en los cuales los técnicos empalman extensiones naturales o sintéticas al cabello existente para hacer que se vea con más cuerpo. Mientras que a corto plazo pueden ser más baratos que la cirugía, el doctor Brandy dice que deben ser reajustados cada cuatro a seis semanas a medida que el cabello crece.

PÉRDIDA DE LA AUDICIÓN

Rechace a los sonidos del silencio

A Kathy Peck le encantaba el tipo de música que retumba en la cabeza. Tocando el bajo eléctrico y como cantante principal en un conjunto femenino de *punk* rock, siempre creyó que mientras más fuerte sonara la música mejor era.

Durante cerca de cinco años, su grupo, las Contracciones, ensayaba cuatro veces por semana en un cuarto pequeño lleno de bocinas (parlantes) gigantescas, y se presentaba en la región de San Francisco por lo menos tres noches por semana sin usar tapones para los oídos.

"En los clubes *punk* de esos días, si uno se hubiera atrevido a usar tapones para los oídos alguien te habría dado una paliza", dice ella.

Pero después de que el conjunto tuvo su gran oportunidad de ser el que hiciera la apertura del concierto de Duran Duran en el Coliseo de Oakland, Peck notó que su oído se estaba desvaneciendo rápidamente. "Después de ese espectáculo, tenía un silbido en los oídos, y cuando trataba de hablar con mis amistades, podía ver cómo sus labios se movían pero no podía escuchar ningún sonido. Yo estuve prácticamente sorda por varios días."

Poco después, las pruebas revelaron que ella había sufrido una pérdida del 40 por ciento en su audición. Peck estaba deprimida y preocupada por su carrera y se preguntaba si el "tiempo implacable" ya la estaba alcanzando, a pesar de que ella solo tenía poco más de 30 años de edad.

"Perdí la confianza en mí misma, y sentía que yo ya no era buena en lo que estaba haciendo. Sentía como que estaba envejeciendo. Como muchas otras personas, yo pensaba que la pérdida de la audición le pasaba a las personas viejas", dice Peck, cofundadora y directora ejecutiva de Educación y (sobre el Oído para Roqueros (o *HEAR*, por sus siglas en inglés), una org sin fines de lucro con base en San Francisco, que alienta a los músicos ⅃ ₋ℶℶℶℸℴ₋ nados de música de altos decibeles a bajar el volumen y usar tapones para los oídos.

Pero como Peck y muchas otras mujeres están descubriendo, la pérdida de la audición entre los 30 y los 50 años de edad es muy común. "La pérdida de la audición está ocurriendo a edades cada vez más jóvenes y es más frecuente de lo que generalmente se pensaba", dice la doctora J. Gail Neely, profesora y directora de otología, neurotología y cirugía de la base del cerebro en la Escuela de Medicina de la Universidad Washington, en St. Louis.

En total, cerca de 10 millones de mujeres residentes en los Estados Unidos sufren de un deterioro significativo en la audición, y más de 2,5 millones de esas mujeres son menores de 45 años de edad, según la Asociación de Habla, Lenguaje y Oído de los Estados Unidos. En una encuesta a 2.731 personas con deterioro de la audición, casi el 57 por ciento dijeron que habían notado por primera vez el problema antes de cumplir los 40 años de edad, dice Laurel E. Glass, Ph.D., profesora emérita y directora anterior del Centro sobre Sordera en la Escuela de Medicina de la Universidad de San Francisco.

La pérdida de la audición tiene un costo enorme, dicen los doctores. Puede llevar al aislamiento social, limitar sus perspectivas de trabajo, complicar su vida sexual, privarla de su autoestima y hacerla sentir como si la vida la está pasando por alto.

¡Oigan bien!

Antes de ver por qué Kathy Peck y otras mujeres tienen problemas auditivos, es importante entender cómo funcionan sus oídos. Cuando su mejor amiga le dice la gracia de su último chiste, el sonido de su voz entra a su canal auditivo y golpea sobre el tímpano, una membrana elástica en forma de cono que se extiende hasta el extremo del canal. Cuando el tímpano vibra, causa que los huesos pequeños en el oído medio se muevan de un lado al otro. Estos movimientos provocan ondas pequeñas de fluido en el oído interior que ondulan a través de un órgano en forma de caracol llamado coclea. Dentro de la coclea, 30.000 células como pelo transmiten los impulsos al nervio auditivo, el cual transporta el sonido al cerebro. Allí son interpretados como el chiste más gracioso que usted jamás había escuchado, y entonces usted se ríe.

Algo de la pérdida de la audición es una parte natural del envejecimiento, dice Debra Busacco, Ph.D., audióloga y coordinadora del Instituto de Aprendizaje por Toda la Vida de la Universidad Gallaudet, en Washington, D.C., la única universidad de humanidades en el mundo para los sordos. El tímpano se hace rígido con la edad, reduciendo de esa manera su capacidad para vibrar. Los cambios que se producen en los huesos en el oído medio relacionados con la edad, tales como la degeneración de las articulaciones y los depósitos de calcio en esas articulaciones, causan que el sistema en el oído medio se endurezca resultando en una

La prueba de audición de cinco minutos

De repente, todos alrededor suyo hablan entre dientes, mascullan y susurran. ¿Podría ser que usted tiene un problema de audición? Para descubrirlo, tome esta prueba preparada por la Academia Norteamericana de Otolaringología y Cirugía de la Cabeza y el Cuello. Sus opciones son casi siempre (C), la mitad del tiempo (M), ocasionalmente (O) y nunca (N).

1. Tengo un problema para oír por teléfono.
2. Tengo dificultad para seguir una conversación cuando dos o más personas están hablando al mismo tiempo.
3. La gente se queja de que pongo el volumen del televisor muy fuerte.
4. Tengo que hacer un esfuerzo para entender las conversaciones.
5. Se me escapa oír algunos sonidos comunes, como el teléfono o el timbre de la puerta.
6. Tengo dificultad para oír conversaciones con un fondo ruidoso, tales como en una fiesta.
7. Me confundo acerca de dónde vienen los sonidos.
8. Yo entiendo mal algunas palabras en una frase y necesito pedirle a la gente que me repitan lo que dijeron.
9. Especialmente tengo dificultad para entender cuando las mujeres o los niños hablan.

transmisión menos eficiente del sonido. Al pasar el tiempo, las irremplazables células capilares en el oído interior se dañan por una combinación de envejecimiento, exposición a ruidos, medicamentos, abastecimiento reducido de sangre al oído e infección. Y una vez que estas se dañan, el nervio auditivo se vuelve menos eficiente. Pero la mayoría de estos cambios no ocurren hasta que la mujer tiene por lo menos 60 años de edad.

Si los síntomas de pérdida de la audición aparecen a una edad más joven, la causa puede ser tan simple como cerilla excesiva o el efecto secundario muy raro de un medicamento. También puede ser causada por un tímpano reventado, una lesión a la cabeza, alta presión arterial, una infección a los oídos, meningitis o un tumor. Algunos tipos de pérdida de la audición vienen de familia, como es la otosclerosis, una enfermedad que causa depósitos excesivos de hueso en el oído medio y evitan que éste conduzca los sonidos al oído interior, dice el doctor John House, profesor clínico asociado de otolaringología en la Universidad de California del Sur, en Los Ángeles.

Pero la causa más común de pérdida de la audición en los adultos menores de 50 años de edad es estar expuestos a sonidos excesivos, dice Susan Rezen,

10. He trabajado en ambientes ruidosos (en cadenas de montaje, con martillos neumáticos, cerca de motores a reacción y otras cosas así por el estilo).
11. Yo oigo bien —si la gente sólo hablara claramente.
12. La gente se molesta porque entiendo mal lo que dicen.
13. Entiendo mal lo que otros están diciendo y doy respuestas poco apropiadas.
14. Yo evito actividades sociales porque no puedo oír bien y temo que voy a dar respuestas poco apropiadas.
Para ser contestada por un miembro de la familia o amistad:
15. ¿Piensa usted que esta persona ha perdido la audición?

Puntuación

Anótese tres puntos por cada ocasión en que usted contestó "casi siempre"; dos puntos por cada "la mitad del tiempo"; un punto por cada "ocasionalmente", y ningún punto por cada "nunca."

0 a 5. Su oído está bien.

6 a 9. La academia sugiere que usted vea a un especialista en oído, nariz y garganta.

10 y más. La academia recomienda enérgicamente que usted vea a un especialista en oído, nariz y garganta.

Ph.D., profesora de audiología en el Colegio Estatal de Worcester, en Massachusetts y autora de *Coping with Hearing Loss* (Cómo sobrellevar la pérdida de la audición). Por lo regular, esto es todavía un problema de los hombres debido a que ellos están más expuestos a ruido en los deportes y en el trabajo. Pero al cambiar las vidas de las mujeres, la frecuencia de la pérdida de la audición inducida por ruido se espera que aumente. "Los efectos de la exposición a ruido son a largo plazo", dice la doctora Rezen. "No aparecen enseguida. Pero cuando las personas están expuestas continuamente, sus oídos se desgastan más rápidamente, y los efectos del envejecimiento se muestran más pronto."

"No hay sonidos fuertes continuos en la naturaleza como los de conciertos de rock o martillos neumáticos. Nuestros oídos están diseñados para ser sensibles, para que nuestros antepasados pudieran oír una rama quebrándose, lo que podía significar que el alimento o el peligro estaban cerca. De esa forma cuando usted entra en un ambiente ruidoso, se está poniendo a sí misma en un ambiente para el cual sus oídos no fueron diseñados", dice el doctor Flash Gordon, un médico de atención primaria en San Rafael, California y cofundador de HEAR.

Los sonidos súbitos fuertes cerca del oído, como los petardos o disparos, pueden causar una pérdida inmediata de la audición. Pero usualmente, la pérdida de la audición provocada por el ruido sucede gradualmente, a través de los años. En general, mientras más tiempo usted está expuesta a sonidos más fuertes que 85 decibeles, sea un concierto de rock o un soplador de hojas, lo más probable es que destruya los filamentos en el oído interior y dañe su oído, dice la doctora Rezen.

¿Qué tan fuerte es fuerte?

Los decibeles es lo que usan los expertos para medir la intensidad del sonido (presión de sonido), empezando con el sonido más suave que una persona puede oír en un entorno de laboratorio, el cual es de 0 decibeles. Usando este sistema, 20 decibeles es 10 veces más intenso que 0, 40 decibeles es 100 veces más intenso, 60 decibeles es 1.000 veces más intenso y así sucesivamente.

Entonces, ¿qué tan fuertes son 85 decibeles? Es más o menos la misma cantidad de ruido hecho por una aspiradora de polvo, una licuadora o una cortadora eléctrica de césped. En comparación, una conversación normal alcanza cerca de 65 decibeles. Los niveles de ruido en algunos conciertos de rock andan cerca de exceder los 140 decibeles, un nivel que puede causar daño rápido e irreparable en algunos oídos sensibles. Aun las orquestas sinfónicas pueden generar sonidos más fuertes que 110 decibeles, lo cual puede causar molestia y dolor en algunas personas.

En realidad, solamente un concierto de rock de dos horas puede potencialmente envejecer el oído de una mujer cerca de dos años y medio si ella no usa protección en los oídos, según los cálculos de Daniel Johnson, Ph.D., un ingeniero que prueba protectores de oídos para los militares en la Base Kirkland de la Fuerza Aérea, en Albuquerque, Nuevo México. Basándose en eso, él estima que después de 50 conciertos, la misma mujer puede tener una disminución en su audición similar a la de una mujer 16 años más vieja que no ha sido expuesta a niveles altos de ruido. Además, si una mujer de 30 años de edad que no usa tapones para los oídos empieza a trabajar ocho horas diarias cerca de maquinaria que produzca ruido promediando los 95 decibeles, para cuando tenga 40 años de edad puede haber sufrido una pérdida de la audición de altas frecuencias similar a la de una mujer de 70 años de edad.

Más fuerte no es mejor

Pero por supuesto, la mayoría de nosotras hemos ido a conciertos ruidosos, hemos estado paradas cerca de trenes que pasan, o trabajando cerca de equipo ruidoso como una motosierra. Entonces, ¿exactamente en qué forma están afectando esos ruidos a su oído?

Pruebe esto la próxima vez que vaya a un concierto de rock u otro evento ruidoso, sugiere el doctor Gordon. Antes de salir de su carro, ponga la radio en una estación de esas de puro hablar y baje el volumen a un punto en que usted apenas entiende todas las palabras. Entonces, prenda la radio después del concierto pero antes de arrancar el motor. Lo más posible es que las voces que antes se entendían ahora ya no se entiendan.

Eso es lo que los doctores llaman cambio temporal del umbral auditivo. Básicamente quiere decir que el ruido ha sobreestimulado las células capilares en su oído interior. Como resultado estas células capilares no están funcionando tan eficientemente como normalmente lo hacen, así que los sonidos tienen que ser más fuertes para que usted los oiga, dice la doctora Neely. Investigadores en la Universidad de Manitoba, en Manitoba, Winnipeg, por ejemplo, probaron el oído de diez mujeres antes y después de un concierto de rock de dos horas y media. Para la mayoría de las mujeres, el umbral de su capacidad para oír era diez o más decibeles más alto después del concierto que antes.

Eso puede no sonar a mucho, pero por varias horas usted probablemente tendría dificultad en oír el susurrar de las hojas o una conversación susurrante. Afortunadamente, su oído va a regresar a la normalidad dentro de 24 horas.

Pero un cambio de umbral auditivo es una señal de advertencia de que su oído corre un riesgo si usted continúa exponiéndose a los sonidos fuertes. Algunas personas nunca experimentan cambios de umbral auditivo y asumen erróneamente que son inmunes a los peligros de ruidos fuertes, dice la doctora Neely. En verdad, la exposición repetida a ruidos fuertes puede matar gradualmente las células capilares y dañar permanentemente su capacidad de oír, especialmente sonidos de frecuencia alta tales como las consonantes *sh, ch, t, f, h* y *s* que se usan frecuentemente durante una conversación.

Si usted deja de oír esos sonidos de frecuencia alta, la parte restante de la palabra no tendrá sentido para usted", dice la doctora Neely. "Usted literalmente no sabrá si la gente a su alrededor está hablando acerca de pescados o de latas. Eso puede ser muy confuso y frustrante."

Cómo proteger sus oídos

Aunque la mayoría de nosotras vamos a sufrir algo de pérdida de la audición debido al envejecimiento, si usted protege a sus oídos del ruido ahora puede mantener la agudeza de su oído hasta bien entrada en sus años de oro. "Imagínese que su oído es un barril grande de arena", dice el doctor Gordon. "Una de dos, usted lo puede vaciar gradualmente con una cuchara, para que la arena dure un tiempo largo, o bien puede usar una pala y acabar con ésta mucho más pronto". Aquí hay algunas maneras de prevenir la pérdida de la audición.

Baje el volumen. Usted probablemente no puede hacer mucho acerca del ruido del tráfico, los martillos neumáticos y muchas otras fuentes de sonido excesivo. Pero sí puede bajar el volumen de su estéreo, dice Stephen Painton, Ph.D., un audiólogo en el Centro de Ciencias de la Salud de la Universidad de Oklahoma, en la ciudad de Oklahoma. Algunos sistemas de sonido pueden producir un sonido igual al de los conciertos de rock más ruidosos. Aquí hay una forma de saber si su estéreo está demasiado fuerte. Préndalo, entonces salga fuera de la casa y cierre la puerta. Si puede oír la música, está muy fuerte. La

Cuando el silbido no para

A los 31 años de edad, Elizabeth Meyer se estaba encaminando. Tomaba lecciones de marimba y clases de teatro y tenía muchas ganas de empezar su carrera como música. Y de repente, la mañana siguiente a un concierto de música africana en Portland, Oregon, notó un silbido en sus oídos; durante las próximas semanas, también desarrolló una intensa sensibilidad al sonido. Pronto, sólo podía hablar por teléfono si colocaba una almohada entre su oído y el teléfono. Antes de dejar de ir a ver películas, estaba usando dos pares de tapones para los oídos y orejeras industriales como las que usan los cargadores de equipaje en los aeropuertos. No podía viajar por más de 15 minutos en un autobús porque el ruido y el silbido en los oídos la abrumaban.

"De la noche a la mañana, yo me sentí como si hubiera envejecido 30 años", dice Meyer, ahora de 36 años de edad. "Literalmente me sentí como si tuviera 60 años. Las cosas se han compuesto un poco, pero el primer año lo pasé solamente tratando de detenerme a mí misma para no empezar a saltar y golpear la cabeza contra una pared cada 30 segundos. Al principio, pasé por un período suicida. Finalmente, me di cuenta de que aunque mi condición podría no mejorar, mi capacidad para sobrellevarla sí ciertamente lo lograría."

Meyer es una de las 3,5 millones de mujeres estadounidenses que sufren de tinnitus crónico, un silbido, zumbido o susurro molesto en los oídos que puede ser un síntoma de cualquier cosa, desde cerilla en exceso a alta presión arterial hasta una enfermedad del corazón. Una en cada tres mujeres que tiene tinnitus, como Meyer, puede también desarrollar hiperacusia, la cual es una sensibilidad extrema a los sonidos. Tanto el tinnitus como la hiperacusia pueden también ser señal de una pérdida de la audición debida al ruido causada por el daño a los cilios, células capilares en el oído interior que ayudan a conducir el sonido al nervio auditivo en el cerebro, dice el doctor Christopher Linstrom, director de otología y neurotología en la Enfermería de Ojos y Oídos de Nueva York, en la ciudad de Nueva York.

misma regla se aplica para la radio de su carro. Y si usted usa auriculares o un estéreo personal, la persona que está parada junto a usted no debería ser capaz de oír el sonido.

Si tiene que gritar, váyase. Si usted tiene que elevar la voz para hacerse oír por alguien que se encuentra a un pie o dos de usted, es una clara advertencia de

La hiperacusia, por ejemplo, causa que las células capilares indivi-duales, cada una de las cuales es estimulada normalmente sólo por ciertas frecuencias, reaccionen a la misma gama de sonidos. Como resultado, más y más células capilares vibran al unísono, y eso puede hacer que los ruidos más leves parezcan fuertes y discordantes. Cuando este daño ocurre, los sonidos que son tolerables para muchas personas pueden ser dolorosos para usted, dice el teniente-coronel Richard Danielson, Ph.D., supervisor de audiología en el Centro de Audiología y Habla del Ejército de Centro Médico Walter Reed del Ejército, en Washington, D.C.

En algunos casos, el tinnitus puede ser tratado con drogas o cirugía, especialmente si es causado por un exceso de líquido en el oído medio, alta presión arterial, una arteria en el cuello parcialmente bloqueada, o alergias. Pero en la mayoría de los casos, no hay cura para el tinnitus o la hiperacusia, dice el doctor Linstrom.

Una vez que se le diagnostica el tinnitus o la hiperacusia, usted debería evitar ruidos fuertes y usar tapones en los oídos para evitar un daño mayor a su oído que puede empeorar estas condiciones. Algunos dispositivos que producen sonidos agradables como las gotas de lluvia o las olas del mar pueden ayudar a las personas con tinnitus a ahogar el silbido, dice el doctor Linstrom. La cafeína y la nicotina agravan ambos padecimientos, así que deje de fumar y evite el café, té y chocolate, dice él. Algunos medicamentos como la aspirina, los antibióticos y las drogas contra el cáncer también pueden causar tinnitus y sensibilidad auditiva. Un audífono podría ayudar, porque mientras mejor oiga usted, menos notable puede ser el silbido, dice el doctor John House, profesor clínico asociado de otolaringología en la Universidad del California del Sur, en Los Ángeles.

Si usted tiene preguntas acerca de estos problemas de la audición, vea a su médico o escriba a la *American Tinnitus Association* (Asociación de Tinnitus de los Estados Unidos), P.O. Box 5, Portland, OR 97207.

que el nivel de ruido puede ser peligroso, y debería irse de ahí tan pronto como sea posible o use protección para los oídos, dice el doctor House.

Tenga los tapones a mano. Meterse algodón o pedazos de una servilleta de papel desmenuzada en sus orejas no hará virtualmente nada para reducir el daño a su oído. En lugar de eso, hágase el hábito de llevar tapones para los oídos consigo, dice la doctora Busacco. La mayoría de los tapones para los oídos son pequeños y pueden ser llevados fácilmente en su cartera o bolsillo. De esa manera, dice ella, usted estará preparada para un ruido imprevisto, como puede ser una película especialmente fuerte. Los de espuma de caucho son buenos porque son baratos y están disponibles sin receta en la mayoría de las boticas, y fácilmente se pueden enrollar y poner dentro de sus orejas. Busque el índice de reducción de ruido en un lado de la caja, dice el doctor Painton. Esto le dirá cuántos decibeles de sonido estos tapones pueden amortiguar. Compre tapones que tengan un índice de por lo menos 15. Estos tapones reducirán el sonido por 15 decibeles y reducirán drásticamente las posibilidades de daño a su oído. Si usted quiere mejor protección, un audiólogo puede diseñar un par de tapones hechos a medida que reduzcan el ruido en unos 35 decibeles por alrededor de $80, dice la doctora Busacco.

Tómese un descanso. Mientras más tiempo usted está expuesta a los sonidos fuertes sin interrupción, más probable es que se cause un daño permanente a su oído, aun si está usando tapones para las orejas. Por ello, dele a sus oídos un descanso del ruido de 5 ó 10 minutos cada 30 minutos, dice el doctor Gordon. "Es como poner su cabeza bajo el agua por 20 minutos. Usted lo puede hacer si aguanta contener la respiración durante un minuto por vez, y entonces toma un descanso de 10 segundos. Pero si tratara de hacer esto en dos segmentos de 10 minutos cada uno, usted se moriría. Si le da a sus oídos un descanso ocasional, pueden descansar y recuperarse del trabajo excesivo que los sonidos fuertes los obligan a hacer."

Dilate el ruido. El colocar varios aparatos ruidosos o herramientas eléctricas muy cercanas entre sí va a agravar su problema de ruido. Así que si su televisor está en el mismo cuarto que su lavadora de vajillas, por ejemplo, usted podría estar tentada a subir excesivamente el volumen de su televisor cuando está lavando una tanda de platos. En lugar de hacer eso, mueva el televisor a un cuarto más callado, dice el teniente-coronel Richard Danielson, Ph.D., supervisor de audiología en el Centro de Audiología y Habla del Ejército en el Centro Médico Walter Reed del Ejército, en Washington, D.C.

Limpie la casa, no sus oídos. Tratar de extraer la cerilla de sus orejas usando un limpiador de algodón, fósforo de madera o cualquiera otra cosa va a hacer más daño que bien, dice el doctor House. La cerilla, de hecho, es buena para usted ya que repele el agua y ayuda a mantener el polvo lejos de su tímpano sensible. Si usted inserta pequeños objetos en su oreja empuja la cerilla más adentro y puede causar infección. "Lo mejor que puede hacer con la cerilla dentro del canal auditivo es dejarla en paz", dice el doctor House. Si le molesta, vea a su médico o compre sin receta un juego para remover cerilla que contiene gotas que la ablandarán y le permitirán fluir naturalmente fuera de sus orejas.

Controle sus medicamentos. Tomar seis a ocho aspirinas al día puede provocar un silbido en sus oídos y una pérdida temporal de la audición, dice el doctor Gordon. Los antibióticos tales como la gentamicina (*G-Mycin*), estreptomicina y tobramicina (*Nebcin*) pueden también dañar a su oído, dice el doctor

Barry E. Hirsch, un neurotólogo en la Escuela de Medicina de la Universidad de Pittsburgh. Si usted está tomando cualquier droga y desarrolla un problema con el oído, pregunte a su doctor si el medicamento puede estar causándolo.

Cancele los cigarrillos. Fumar reduce el flujo de sangre a los oídos y puede interferir con la curación natural de los pequeños vasos sanguíneos que ocurre después de estar expuestos a los ruidos fuertes, dice el doctor House. En un estudio de 2.348 trabajadores expuestos al ruido en una fábrica aeroespacial, investigadores de la Escuela de Medicina en la Universidad de California del Sur encontraron que los fumadores habían sufrido una pérdida mayor de la audición que los no fumadores. Así que si usted fuma, déjelo.

Corte la cafeína. Al igual que la nicotina, la cafeína corta el flujo de sangre a los oídos, aumentando sus posibilidades de una pérdida de la audición, dice el doctor House. No tome más de dos tazas de 8 onzas (237 ml) de café o té por día. Si es posible, tome bebidas descafeinadas.

Balancee su dieta. Los mismos alimentos grasosos y cargados de colesterol que son malos para su corazón también ponen en peligro a sus oídos, según el doctor House. La alta presión arterial y arteriosclerosis, una acumulación de placa en las paredes de sus arterias, no solamente causan enfermedades del corazón pero también pueden reducir el flujo de la sangre a los oídos y gradualmente estrangulan su oído, dice el doctor House. Por lo mismo, corte la grasa con una dieta diaria balanceada que incluya por lo menos cinco porciones de frutas y verduras, seis porciones de panes y granos y no más de una porción de 3 onzas (85 g) de carne roja magra, aves o pescados.

Haga ejercicio. Camine, corra, nade o haga cualquier otro ejercicio aeróbico por 20 minutos al día, tres veces por semana, recomienda el doctor House. Esto estimulará la circulación de la sangre, bajará su presión arterial y ayudará a mantener a sus oídos en una condición óptima.

Cómo sacar el mejor partido posible de la situación

La persona común espera de cinco a siete años después de notar por primera vez un problema con sus oídos para pedir ayuda. Esto puede significar años de aislamiento social y frustración innecesarios, dice la doctora Busacco, porque mientras más pronto usted solicite ayuda, más rápidamente se podrá diagnosticar y tratar su problema de la audición.

"Las personas están más acomplejadas acerca de su oído que lo están acerca de su vista", dice el doctor Hirsch. "Frecuentemente se trata de un aspecto de vanidad. Usar un audífono de alguna forma implica envejecer, mientras que usar anteojos (gafas) no."

Si usted sospecha que tiene un problema con la audición, particularmente si tiene un silbido en sus oídos o desarrolla una súbita sensibilidad a los ruidos fuertes que no la molestaban en el pasado, vea a su doctor o a un médico que se especialice en enfermedades del oído, nariz y garganta. Algunos problemas con los oídos como por ejemplo la enfermedad de Ménière, un desorden que causa un silbido en los oídos y desvanecimiento, puede ser tratada con medicamentos recetados o cirugía. Otras condiciones, tales como un tímpano reventado y otosclerosis, se pueden corregir con cirugía.

Aun cuando la pérdida no pueda corregirse completamente, hay disponibles audífonos potentes que no llaman la atención —algunos tan pequeños que pueden caber dentro de su canal auditivo— para ayudarle a permanecer en contacto con el mundo. Los precios varían de alrededor de $550 por un audífono básico a más de $2.500 por uno de los modelos computarizados más sofisticados. Un audiólogo, un profesional entrenado para instalar audífonos, puede ayudarle a escoger uno que satisfaga sus necesidades.

Aquí está cómo determinar si usted está perdiendo la audición y cómo sobrellevar esta situación.

Fíjese en las señales de aviso. Seguro, es molesto cuando usted conduce por la calle y se da cuenta que su señalador ha estado puesto por millas, pero también puede ser una señal de que usted tiene un problema de audición. Si usted prende su señalador y no puede oír el correspondiente sonido de clic en su carro, es hora de hacer que un audiólogo o un doctor le revisen su oído, dice el doctor Painton.

Dígaselos sin pena. Si usted tiene dificultad para oír o entender a la gente, dígaselos, dice el doctor Philip Zazove, profesor asistente de medicina familiar en la Escuela de Medicina de la Universidad de Michigan, en Ann Arbor quien ha tenido una profunda pérdida de la audición desde su nacimiento. Simplemente diciendo "Ya no oigo tan bien como acostumbraba", "¿Podría repetir eso?" y "Hable un poco más lento", puede evitar muchos malentendidos, frustración y enojo, dice él. Si es necesario, pida a la persona que le repita lo que dijo, o si tiene dificultad con una palabra clave, haga que la escriba en un pedazo de papel.

Ilumine su vida sexual. La pérdida de la audición puede causar estragos en la cama. Esas palabras tiernas susurradas que a usted tanto le gustaban cuando estaba teniendo relaciones sexuales a menudo son las primeras bajas. Déjese el audífono si hay alguna posibilidad de tener relaciones, o pida a su compañero que deje la luz prendida para que usted pueda ver lo suficiente como para leer sus labios, sugiere la doctora Rezen. Hable sobre lo que usted quiere sexualmente antes de hacer el amor. Si es necesario, desarrolle su propio código secreto, tal y como "dos toques en la espalda significan bésame". "Si usted no planifica, puede echar a perder por completo la ocasión", dice ella.

Encuentre un lugar tranquilo. Si usted realmente quiere platicar con un hombre interesante en una fiesta, llévelo de la mitad del cuarto a un rincón apartado. No solamente es eso más íntimo sino que podrá concentrarse en lo que él está diciendo y no tendrá que competir con las risas, la música y otro ruido de fondo que simplemente hace mucho más difícil oír, dice el doctor Zazove. En la casa, considere apagar el televisor, radio u otros aparatos ruidosos antes de tratar de oír a alguien.

Tómelo a risa. Un buen sentido del humor es vital si usted tiene un problema de audición, dice el doctor Painton. Total, ¿qué si usted malentiende una palabra o dos, o dice algo poco apropiado? Disfrute el momento y únase a la risa.

Haga su tarea. Si usted está participando en una reunión importante de negocios o conferencia, llegue temprano y trate de conseguir un asiento en la primera fila, de frente a la persona que usted cree que va a hablar más, dice el doctor Zazove. Si es posible, dígale a la oradora acerca de su pérdida de la audición y pídale que evite voltear la cara lejos de usted. Mantenga contacto visual con la oradora. Trate de obtener un resumen escrito del tópico o agenda, así usted estará preparada para las palabras o frases que podrían estar incluidas. De esa manera, si a usted se le escapan unas cuantas palabras, tendrá una mayor posibilidad de reponerlas con exactitud.

PÍLDORA ANTICONCEPTIVA

Igual a usted, ha cambiado con el tiempo

Qué no hubiera dado usted por haber hablado con su madre acerca del sexo cuando era una jovencita llena de preguntas, pero entre nosotras las latinas, ese tema jamás se tocaba. Sin embargo, los tiempos cambian, y ahora usted se encuentra con su hija hablándole de sexo y en particular de la píldora anticonceptiva. Por supuesto que ella tiene las preguntas básicas acerca del uso de ésta, pero en la época del SIDA y con las cuestiones acerca de los riesgos asociados con el uso de la píldora anticonceptiva a largo plazo, la conversación se pone un poco más complicada de lo que hubiera sido si su mamá y usted hubieran hablado de esto años atrás.

Siguiendo con el tema del tiempo, lo interesante es que tanto como nosotras, la misma píldora anticonceptiva ha cambiado con el tiempo, y parece que no hay tantas malas noticias acerca de ella como solían existir. De hecho, puede que hayan más beneficios que riesgos. Muchos expertos creen que para las mujeres entre los 30 y los 50 años de edad, los pros pesan más que los contras — siempre que estén saludables y no fumen.

Cosas del corazón

Cuando se trata del envejecimiento y la píldora anticonceptiva, las fumadoras enfrentan los riesgos mayores. En general, las fumadoras tienen un riesgo mayor de ataques al corazón y si toman la píldora anticonceptiva, ese riesgo aumenta dramáticamente. Las estadísticas muestran que las mujeres mayores

270

de los 30 años de edad que fuman entre 1 y 24 cigarrillos por día aumentan tres veces su riesgo de sufrir un ataque al corazón, y las mujeres que fuman 25 o más cigarrillos al día aumentan diez veces su riesgo de un ataque al corazón al tomar la píldora anticonceptiva.

La píldora anticonceptiva y los cigarrillos también son una mala combinación cuando se trata del riesgo de un derrame cerebral. Los números son similares a aquellos de un ataque al corazón: las mujeres mayores de 30 años de edad que toman la píldora anticonceptiva y fuman entre 1 y 24 cigarrillos al día aumentan su riesgo de un derrame cerebral tres veces, y las mujeres que fuman 25 o más cigarrillos al día aumentan su riesgo en casi diez veces.

Pero si usted no fuma y por lo demás está saludable, puede considerar a la píldora anticonceptiva relativamente segura. Los estudios muestran que la píldora de la década de los años 90 presenta poca amenaza a su salud en general.

Este mensaje es dramáticamente diferente al que las mujeres recibieron en los primeros días de la píldora anticonceptiva, la cual debutó en la década de los años 60. Eso es porque el estrógeno sintético, el ingrediente que da a la píldora anticonceptiva su acción protectora, es más bajo en contenido que nunca. Los investigadores han descubierto que sólo se necesita un pequeño porcentaje de los niveles hormonales usados en sus primeros días para hacer que la píldora anticonceptiva sea efectiva. Y se ha encontrado que esta pequeña dosis tiene efectos positivos.

En estos niveles reducidos, el estrógeno parece que reduce los niveles de colesterol de la lipoproteína de baja densidad (o *LDL*, por sus siglas en inglés), el colesterol malo que contribuye al taponamiento de las arterias. El estrógeno también parece que aumenta los niveles de colesterol de la lipoproteína de alta densidad (o *HDL*, por sus siglas en inglés), el colesterol bueno que ayuda a prevenir la obstrucción de las arterias al transportar al colesterol malo lejos de las paredes de los vasos. Y aun cuando el colesterol malo está presente, los estudios muestran que el estrógeno puede actuar sobre la pared del vaso de una forma beneficiosa que puede ayudar a prevenir la formación de placa.

La era de las *STD*

Es un alivio saber que la píldora anticonceptiva ya no representa la amenaza de antes. Y también es reconfortante saber que cuando se usa correctamente, la píldora anticonceptiva ofrece cierta protección contra lo que originalmente fue la razón para su creación: el embarazo. Pero allá en la década de los años 60, el SIDA y las enfermedades transmitidas sexualmente (*sexually transmitted diseases* o *STD*, por sus siglas en inglés) no eran una gran inquietud para las mujeres como lo son hoy.

Cuando se usa por sí sola, sin un condón u otro método de barrera, la píldora anticonceptiva no ofrece protección contra el virus de inmunodeficiencia humana que causa el SIDA, o contra las enfermedades transmitidas por las relaciones sexuales como son la clamidia, la gonorrea o el papilomavirus humano (o *HPV*, por sus siglas en inglés), o las verrugas vaginales. Según los Centros para el Control de Enfermedades, el SIDA es la segunda causa principal de muerte en los latinos entre los 25 a los 44 años de edad. A pesar de que los latinos representan sólo un 10 por ciento de la población total de los Estados Unidos, este grupo ocupa el 19 por ciento de todos los casos de SIDA, y las latinas solas constituyen el 20 por ciento de todos los casos femeninos de SIDA en los Estados Unidos.

Cada año, se piensa que las enfermedades transmitidas sexualmente son la causa de aproximadamente 150.000 casos de esterilidad en las mujeres y de 45.000 embarazos ectópicos con peligro de muerte, en los cuales el óvulo se fertiliza en la trompas de Falopio en lugar de en el útero. Algunas cepas de HPV o verrugas vaginales se han asociado con el cáncer cervical, el cual mata a más de 4.500 mujeres al año. Por lo que si una mujer usa la píldora anticonceptiva sin ninguna otra protección, está poniendo en peligro su vida y su salud.

Sin embargo, la píldora anticonceptiva ofrece algo de protección contra una enfermedad transmitida sexualmente. La investigación indica que la píldora anticonceptiva puede de hecho reducir el riesgo de la enfermedad de inflamación de la pelvis (*pelvic inflammatory disease* o *PID*, por sus siglas en inglés), una enfermedad en la cual ciertos organismos transmitidos por las relaciones sexuales infectan las trompas de Falopio y el útero de una mujer y pueden causar esterilidad. Por algunos medios que los investigadores aún no entienden completamente, la píldora anticonceptiva puede ayudar a prevenir que las infecciones en el tracto genital inferior, como la clamidia y la gonorrea, asciendan al tracto genital superior y causen PID.

Preguntas acerca del cáncer

Usted puede estar haciendo más preguntas de las que acostumbraba acerca de la píldora anticonceptiva y el cáncer. Ha oído que el cáncer de mama es el más frecuente en las mujeres y usted quiere saber qué papel, de haberlo, desempeña la píldora anticonceptiva en su desarrollo.

Desafortunadamente, algunas preguntas con respecto al cáncer de mama y la píldora anticonceptiva todavía no tienen una contestación. Varios estudios, incluyendo el estudio sobre el cáncer y la hormona esteroide, o *CASH* (por sus siglas en inglés), que llevaron a cabo los Centros para el Control y la Prevención de Enfermedades, en Atlanta, proporcionan algunas pistas.

El estudio CASH observó los efectos del uso de la píldora anticonceptiva en el cáncer de 10.000 mujeres estadounidenses. Los resultados indicaron que las mujeres de 35 años de edad o menores tenían 1,4 veces más probabilidades de desarrollar cáncer de mama si tomaban la píldora anticonceptiva que las mujeres de la misma edad que nunca usaron anticonceptivos orales. Las mujeres entre los 35 y los 44 años de edad que tomaron la píldora anticonceptiva tenían 1,1 veces más probabilidades de desarrollar cáncer de mama que las mujeres que no la tomaron. Y las mujeres mayores de 45 años de edad tenían en realidad un riesgo apenas menor; ellas tenían 0,9 veces más probabilidades de desarrollar cáncer de mama que las mujeres en su edad que nunca habían usado la píldora anticonceptiva. En otras palabras, tomar la píldora anticonceptiva puede aumentar ligeramente el riesgo de cáncer de mama.

Aunque no se ha establecido una conexión segura entre el cáncer de mama y la píldora anticonceptiva, sí hay información sobre la culpabilidad de la píldora anticonceptiva en otros cánceres femeninos, específicamente el de los ovarios y el uterino. El veredicto: no culpable.

De hecho, se ha encontrado que la píldora anticonceptiva en realidad ayuda a proteger contra estos cánceres. Los estudios muestran que después que una mujer ha estado tomando la píldora anticonceptiva durante un año, su riesgo de contraer alguna de estas formas de cáncer se reduce a cerca del 50 por ciento, dice el doctor Herbert Peterson, jefe de la División de Salud de la Mujer de los Centros para el Control y la Prevención de Enfermedades. Y el efecto protector se extiende hasta bastante después de que la mujer deja de tomar la píldora anticonceptiva, dice él.

¿Se afecta la fertilidad?

Otra preocupación para las mujeres entre los 30 y los 50 años de edad es que el tomar la píldora anticonceptiva va a afectar su fertilidad. "La fertilidad disminuye naturalmente a medida que la mujer envejece, sea que esté o no tomando la píldora anticonceptiva", dice el doctor Linn. Pero los anticonceptivos orales no han mostrado que aumentan la infertilidad, dice él.

Varios estudios indican que el uso de anticonceptivos orales puede retrasar ligeramente la capacidad de una mujer para concebir, pero el retraso es generalmente cosa de un par de meses.

En un estudio en Oxford, Inglaterra, las mujeres que usaron anticonceptivos orales experimentaron retrasos en la concepción de cerca de dos meses. Mientras más mayores eran las mujeres cuando dejaron de tomar la píldora anticonceptiva o algún otro método —digamos 35 años de edad comparado con 30 años de edad— más tardaron en embarazarse, aunque a menudo sólo tomó un mes o dos, dice la doctora Carolyn Westhoff, profesora asociada de la Universidad de Columbia, en la ciudad de Nueva York y una de las investigadoras en el estudio británico. Pero, dijo ella, el retraso puede ser más una cuestión de edad que de tomar la píldora anticonceptiva.

Otro estudio, realizado en la Universidad de Yale, en New Haven, Connecticut, también reportó retrasos en la concepción de las mujeres que tomaban la píldora anticonceptiva. De nuevo, el retraso era solamente de un par de meses. A las mujeres que usaron otros métodos anticonceptivos les tomó casi cuatro meses para concebir, mientras que a aquellas que tomaron la píldora anticonceptiva generalmente les tomó cerca de seis meses.

Su mejor protección

Si usted está tomando la píldora anticonceptiva o planea empezar, aquí está lo que necesita saber.

Vea a su doctora anualmente. Su decisión de empezar, seguir o dejar la píldora anticonceptiva debería estar basada en su propia historia clínica. Por ello es que usted debería ver a su doctora cada año. No vacile en hacer preguntas y obtener su opinión. No tenga temor de pedir una segunda opinión. Recuerde que muchas doctoras sienten que los beneficios generalmente pesan más que los riesgos para las mujeres saludables que no fuman.

Conozca su historia familiar. Si alguien en su familia ha tenido enfermedades del corazón, cáncer de mama, presión arterial alta, cáncer en los ovarios o uterino, discútalo con su doctor. Estos factores deberían tomarse en consideración, pero no van a prohibirle inmediatamente que usted tome la píldora anticonceptiva, dice el doctor Linn.

Protéjase. La píldora anticonceptiva puede protegerla de un embarazo, pero no la protegerá de las enfermedades transmitidas sexualmente o del SIDA. Una solución son los condones. Los condones de látex que contienen el espermicida *nonoxynol-9* son los más efectivos contra las enfermedades transmitidas sexualmente, dicen los expertos.

Practique la prevención. Hacerse un autoexamen mensual de los senos siempre es importante, pero si usted está tomando la píldora anticonceptiva, asegúrese de hacerlo rutinariamente. Los doctores también recomiendan que usted se haga su primer mamograma entre los 35 y los 40 años de edad, y después uno cada dos años durante la década de los 40 años de edad y a partir de allí uno cada año.

PREOCUPACIÓN

Tómela con calma

Usted ve a su hijo pequeño abordar el autobús de la escuela cada mañana. ¿Estarán bien los frenos? ¿Estará bien abrigado? ¿Se come su almuerzo?

Y después, se va al trabajo. La economía está tan mal, ¿la irán a descansar? ¿Qué va a hacer sin trabajo?

Regresa a la casa justo a tiempo para ver las noticias de la noche. La capa del ozono está desapareciendo. La guerra, el hambre y la violencia están por todas partes.

La vida proporciona suficientes razones para preocuparse. Y a veces es demasiado para soportar. Es posible que usted sufra de dolores de cabeza por la tensión continua o se sienta cansada todo el tiempo. A lo mejor la preocupación le deja su estómago hecho un nudo. Sólo unos cuantos años atrás, usted se sentía llena de esperanza juvenil y optimismo, lista para resolver los problemas del planeta. Pero ahora, puede ser que se empiece a sentir impotente, desgastada e incapaz de enfrentarse a los dilemas aún más pequeños.

"Las preocupaciones son como una camisa de fuerza", dice Mary McClure Goulding, coautora de *Not to Worry! How to Free Yourself from Unnecessary Anxiety and Channel Your Worries into Positive Action* (¡No se preocupe! Cómo librarse de ansiedad innecesaria y canalizar sus preocupaciones en acción positiva). "Usted siente como que no puede hacer nada, y entonces no hace nada. Es una forma totalmente improductiva de gastar los mejores años de su vida. Y es algo que usted debe cambiar —y que puede cambiar— empezando inmediatamente."

Los hechos aterradores

Todos nos preocupamos. La persona común (los hombres también se preocupan) gasta aproximadamente un 5 por ciento del tiempo que pasa despierta todos los días —cerca de 48 minutos— preocupándose sobre una cosa u otra. Las encuestas muestran que los orígenes más comunes de la preocupación para los que viven en los Estados Unidos son la familia y las relaciones, los trabajos y la escuela, la salud y las finanzas.

Para aproximadamente el 6 por ciento de las mujeres, preocuparse se vuelve crónico. Incluso puede evolucionar en una condición clínica llamada trastorno de ansiedad generalizado. Las personas con este trastorno se preocupan acerca de problemas múltiples al mismo tiempo incluyendo cosas sobre las que tienen poco o ningún control, como son el clima o la guerra nuclear. Y se preocupan excesivamente. Las personas que se preocupan en forma crónica reportan gastar un promedio del 50 por ciento de cada día en preocuparse, y algunos reportan que hasta el 100 por ciento, dice la sicóloga Jennifer L. Abel, Ph.D., directora asociada de la Clínica de Trastornos de Estrés y Ansiedad de la Universidad Estatal de Pensilvania, en University Park. Típicamente la preocupación crónica comienza en las décadas de los 20 y los 30 años de edad de una mujer.

No hay pruebas que preocuparse cause directamente una enfermedad, dice Timothy Brown, Psy.D., director asociado de la Clínica de Trastornos de Fobia y Ansiedad de la Universidad Estatal de Nueva York, en Albany. La preocupación puede conducir en muchos casos al mal dormir, lo cual resulta en fatiga, inquietud e irritabilidad. Pero la parte sicológica es la más devastadora. "Las personas que se preocupan no se pueden concentrar, sufren de dolores de cabeza y posiblemente son incapaces de enfrentar y resolver sus problemas efectivamente", dice él.

Las personas que se preocupan casi siempre vienen de familias que también se preocupan, dice Goulding. Usted puede haber aprendido a preocuparse al observar a su madre, padre, abuelo o una tía. Las personas que se preocupan pueden tener poca autoestima, dice Goulding, y a menudo se les ha enseñado a reprimir sus sentimientos, especialmente los de felicidad.

Todo esto lleva a un problema central: una sensación de impotencia. "Usted no se siente en control de su vida", dice Susan Jeffers, Ph.D., una sicóloga y autora de *Feel the Fear and Do It Anyway* (Sienta el temor y hágalo de todos modos). "Usted siente que todo va a salir mal. Eso hace difícil superar aun los problemas sencillos sin un gran esfuerzo y ansiedad."

Un estudio a 24 estudiantes universitarios en los Estados Unidos confirma esto. Cuando se les preguntó qué pasaría si no sacaban buenas calificaciones, un grupo de los que por lo general no se preocupaban hablaron acerca de terminar con trabajos malos y ganar menos dinero. Los que se preocupaban crónicamente hablaron acerca de las mismas inquietudes. Pero estos llevaron sus preocupaciones mucho más allá. Algunos se preocupaban acerca de volverse drogadictos. Otros se preocupaban de que estarían con un dolor físico constante. Y algunos otros decían que se morirían —o incluso que terminarían en el infierno.

"En ese momento, usted tiene que preguntarse si es que preocuparse vale el esfuerzo", dice la doctora Jeffers. "Usted tiene que decidir si se va a pasar el resto de su vida preocupándose acerca de las cosas o si es que va a hacer algo al respecto. Es una decisión difícil, pero ojalá, usted escoja esto último."

Calme a la preocupada que lleva adentro

Llámele Petra la Preocupada. Ella es la infeliz portadora de malas nuevas dentro de su cabeza quien no cesa de hablar acerca de cosas que pueden y van a salir mal.

Es tiempo de hacerla callar para siempre.

"Usted tiene que silenciar esa voz de autoacosamiento", dice Mary McClure Goulding, coautora de *Not to Worry! How to Free Yourself from Unnecessary Anxiety and Channel Your Worries into Positive Action* (¡No se preocupe! Cómo librarse de ansiedad innecesaria y canalizar sus preocupaciones en acción positiva). "Si usted la escucha, usted siempre estará preocupándose."

Tome consciencia de la voz. Siéntese en un lugar tranquilo y escuche sus pensamientos. Cuando usted empieza a oír pensamientos negativos, reemplácelos conscientemente con otros positivos. Las afirmaciones —declaraciones sencillas positivas que usted repite frecuentemente— podrían funcionar. Pruebe con frases tales como: "No hay nada que temer", "yo tengo control sobre mi vida", "yo lo voy a arreglar", "todo está funcionando perfectamente".

La repetición es la clave. Al principio usted ni siquiera necesita creer lo que se está diciendo a sí misma", dice Susan Jeffers, Ph.D., una sicóloga y autora de *Feel the Fear and Do It Anyway* (Sienta el temor y hágalo de todos modos). "El simple hecho de hablar positivamente cambia nuestra energía y nos ayuda a movernos hacia adelante."

Goulding sugiere ser más directa con su crítica interna. Párese, ponga las manos sobre sus caderas y grítele a Petra: "¡Cállate, yo ya no te voy a escuchar nunca más!" Maldiga, diga palabrotas, haga lo que la haga sentirse bien. "Deshágase de esa voz", dice ella. "Y entonces, en su lugar usted podrá llenar su mente con pensamientos felices."

Derrote a la preocupación

Lleva años construir un mundo de preocupaciones. Va a necesitar un tiempo para demolerlo todo. Pero el tiempo está de su lado. Un estudio tanto a personas jóvenes como viejas que se preocupaban mostró que tendemos a preocuparnos menos a medida que envejecemos. Las personas mayores entre las 163 que fueron estudiadas por los profesores de la Universidad de Massachusetts, en Amherst, estaban menos ansiosas acerca de los problemas sociales y financieros y no se preocupaban más acerca de las cuestiones de salud.

Pero ¿por qué esperar a que las cosas se mejoren? Si usted está lista para empezar enseguida a prohibirse la preocupación, aquí hay consejos de los expertos.

Considérelo detenidamente. Está bien, preocúpese un poco. Es mejor que tratar de suprimir toda la ansiedad. "Deje de tratar de evitar esos pensamientos infelices", dice Daniel Wegner, Ph.D., profesor de sicología en la Universidad de Virginia, en Charlottesville. "Mi investigación muestra que mientras usted más trata de suprimir los pensamientos indeseados, más probable es que se obsesione con estos. Eso es particularmente cierto cuando está bajo mucha presión, estrés o sobrecarga mental. Así que justo cuando esté tratando de evitar pensamientos infelices, en realidad usted se volverá más triste que si se enfrentara cara a cara con esos pensamientos infelices."

La doctora Jeffers hace notar que el 99 por ciento de las cosas sobre las que nos preocupamos nunca llegan a ocurrir. "Sienta el temor. Eso es parte de ser humano", dice ella. "Pero salga y haga cosas de todos modos, sabiendo que la mayoría de sus temores son infundados."

Tome su tiempo. Una cosa es pensar acerca de sus problemas. Otra es dejar que estos dominen sus pensamientos. El doctor Wegner dice que la investigación de las personas que se preocupan crónicamente muestra que si pasan tiempo durante la noche para preocuparse activamente acerca de sus problemas, el grado de preocupación de sus vidas desciende en general.

Michael Vasey, Ph.D., profesor asistente de sicología de la Universidad Estatal de Ohio, en Columbus, sugiere separar 30 minutos al día, siempre en el mismo lugar y a la misma hora, para preocuparse. "Enfóquese en sus preocupaciones durante todo ese período, y trate de pensar en las soluciones a los problemas", dice él. Si a usted le preocupa que la van a despedir, imagínese la escena —el despido y las consecuencias— y no deje que la imagen se desaparezca.

Usted probablemente estará más ansiosa al principio. Pero las cosas mejorarán. "Si practica enfocarse en las preocupaciones y en pensar en las soluciones por 30 minutos todos los días por varias semanas, su ansiedad empezará a disminuir", dice el doctor Vasey. "Usted mejorará su capacidad de generar soluciones o se dará cuenta que no vale la pena preocuparse."

Escriba un nuevo final. Las personas que se preocupan pueden ser asombrosamente creativas, dice Goulding. Estas convierten cualquier escena inofensiva en un desastre al imaginarse lo peor. Trate de hacer uso de esa creatividad para convertir sus temores en fantasías. Si usted se preocupa de un accidente al autobús escolar, trate de imaginarse a su hijo pequeño tomando el volante y salvando a todos. Después imagínese el desfile que la ciudad tendrá en su honor. A lo mejor hasta le dan la llave de la ciudad.

De esta manera usted está desarmando sus preocupaciones, dice Goulding. Al poner un final feliz, o tonto, a una preocupación, se está dando la oportunidad de ser positiva, dice ella. Y ese es un paso importante hacia el vencimiento de las preocupaciones.

Enumere sus dificultades. Haga una lista de todas sus preocupaciones. ¿Tiene temor de que va a llover en la reunión familiar este fin de semana?

Usted no tiene control sobre eso, por lo que Goulding sugiere que lo archive bajo el título "Más allá de mi capacidad". ¿La preocupa que otras personas la encuentren poco atractiva, aun cuando usted sabe que en realidad no lo es? Eso va en la lista "Ficción creativa."

¿Qué sentido tiene preocuparse de cosas en esas categorías? "No tiene ninguno," dice Goulding. "¿Para qué preocuparse acerca del clima? ¿Por qué preocuparse acerca de cosas que no son ciertas?" Una vez que usted expone estos pensamientos como preocupaciones sin valor, dice ella, es más fácil descartarlos.

Actúe. Algunas preocupaciones son más legítimas. ¿Está usted preocupada acerca de su salud? Bueno, haga una lista de todas las cosas que usted puede hacer para mejorarla. A lo mejor usted podría empezar a caminar todos los días. O a comer mejor. Entonces decida cuáles son las cosas que va a hacer. El secreto es hacer, hacer, hacer. "Cuando está trabajando activamente en una solución, es menos probable que la preocupación sea un problema", dice la doctora Jeffers. "Usted empezará a sentir que es la creadora de su vida, no una víctima de ésta."

Encuentre una amiga. Hable con alguien especial acerca de sus temores. "Cuando usted habla acerca de sus preocupaciones, las está desinflando. No pueden ser suprimidas. Ya salió el peine. Y, afortunadamente se trata de un peine y no de un piojo", dice el doctor Wegner.

Sólo tenga cuidado que su amiga no empeore las cosas sin querer. Por amabilidad, a lo mejor ella le dice que está bien preocuparse o le dice: "Sí, yo puedo entender por qué estás tan preocupada." Goulding dice que eso puede reforzar su necesidad de preocuparse. Si decide compartir sus pensamientos, asegúrese de que la otra persona acepte ser franca con usted y a ayudarla a encontrar las formas positivas y constructivas para enfrentarse a sus preocupaciones.

PRESIÓN ARTERIAL ALTA

El destructor silencioso de nuestra juventud

Las arrugas las podemos ver. Los músculos doloridos los podemos sentir.

Pero por ahí hay escondido un problema de envejecimiento, uno que es mucho más peligroso que las venas varicosas, la hiperopia o las canas. La presión arterial alta, también llamada hipertensión, está relacionada directamente con la muerte anual de más de 18.000 mujeres estadounidenses. Según la Asociación del Corazón de los Estados Unidos, el 14 por ciento de las mujeres latinas tiene alta presión arterial. Puede hacernos 12 veces más propensas a sufrir derrames cerebrales, 6 veces más propensas a sufrir ataques al corazón y 5 veces más propensas a morir de insuficiencia cardíaca congestiva. Es también un factor importante de riesgo de un fallo renal.

Y es más común entre las mujeres jóvenes de lo que muchas de nosotras nos podemos imaginar. Una de cada diez de las mujeres estadounidenses que se encuentra entre los 35 y los 44 años de edad tiene presión arterial alta. Una en cada cuatro de nosotras desarrolla presión arterial alta antes de cumplir los 55 años de edad. Y después de allí, nuestro riesgo es en realidad más alto que el de los hombres. Los expertos piensan que los cambios hormonales desempeñan un papel en el desarrollo tardío de la presión arterial alta en las mujeres.

Y sin embargo, casi la mitad de la gente en este país con presión arterial alta ni siquiera sabe que la tiene. "Realmente no hay ninguna señal externa notable. Pero si usted tiene presión arterial alta, está haciendo daño", dice el doctor Patrick Mulrow, presidente del Departamento de Medicina en el Colegio

Trate de recordar

Si necesitamos seguir recordándole a usted que controle su presión arterial, entonces quizás ya está muy alta. Eso es porque la presión arterial alta puede debilitar su memoria.

Un estudio a 100 adultos encontró que las personas con presión arterial alta tuvieron una puntuación más baja en un proceso llamado recuperación de la memoria a corto plazo. Eso significa que les tomó más tiempo a ellas recordar si un número que se les había mostrado había sido parte de una combinación original de números que habían visto anteriormente.

Nadie está seguro de por qué la presión arterial alta confunde su memoria. Es posible que esté relacionado con la forma en que la sangre circula por el cerebro o con una disminución en la cantidad de oxígeno que llega al cerebro. "Cualquiera que sea el mecanismo, esta es otra razón más para mantener su presión arterial bajo un control saludable", dice David J. Madden, Ph.D., profesor en el Departamento de Siquiatría del Centro Médico de la Universidad Duke, en Durham, Carolina del Norte.

Médico de Ohio y Toledo, y presidente del Consejo para la Investigación de la Presión Arterial Alta de la Asociación del Corazón de los Estados Unidos.

"Nosotros podríamos salvar vidas si la gente se diera cuenta de que tiene presión arterial alta y entonces tomara medidas para controlarla", dice el doctor Mulrow. En muchos casos es sólo una cuestión de ir al doctor y hacer que le revisen la presión arterial una o dos veces por año, de reducir el consumo de sal y de grasa, y de sudar unas cuantas veces por semana. Eso realmente es pagar un precio muy bajo, dice el doctor Mulrow, considerando que esto podría agregar años a su vida.

Productores de la presión

Los doctores toman dos medidas cuando revisen su presión arterial. La primera es llamada la lectura sistólica. Ésta indica qué tan vigorosamente está bombeando su corazón para impulsar sangre a lo largo de sus arterias. La segunda medida, llamada la lectura diastólica, muestra cuánta resistencia están poniendo sus arterias al flujo sanguíneo. La presión arterial se mide en milímetros de mercurio, o mm Hg, y una lectura sistólica de aproximadamente 120 mm Hg, y una diastólica de 80 mm Hg se consideran saludables. Eso lo leemos simplemente como 120/80.

La presión arterial de cada persona varía ampliamente a lo largo del día. Generalmente, se eleva cuando estamos haciendo ejercicio y baja cuando estamos dormidos. Pero cuando la lectura base o de descanso avanza lentamente a 140/90, usted está en los límites de la presión arterial alta. Eso significa que su corazón está trabajando demasiado para bombear sangre, sea porque sus arterias se han estrechado o endurecido con placa o porque tiene demasiada sangre en su sistema debido a que está reteniendo agua, o por otros problemas. El resultado de este estrés extra puede ser una enfermedad del corazón o coágulos peligrosos en la sangre que pueden ocasionar un derrame cerebral o un ataque al corazón.

La presión arterial tiende a elevarse con la edad. Esto lo causa una combinación de factores, incluyendo la actividad física reducida, el peso adicional en el cuerpo y los cambios hormonales, según el doctor Robert DiBianco, director de investigación cardiológica en el Hospital Adventista de Washington, en Takoma Park, Maryland.

En el 90 al 95 por ciento de los casos, dice el doctor Mulrow, se desconoce la causa exacta de la presión arterial alta. Pero los investigadores han identificado un número de factores de riesgo que pueden aumentar sus probabilidades de desarrollar presión arterial alta. La historia familiar es una. Si varios miembros de su familia inmediata tienen presión arterial alta, usted tiene más probabilidades de desarrollarla. Las mujeres afro-americanas y los miembros de otros grupos minoritarios tienen un riesgo más alto que las mujeres de ascendencia europea. La obesidad es otro factor importante. Los estudios muestran que el 60 por ciento de la gente con presión arterial alta tiene sobrepeso.

El vínculo entre el sodio y el estrés

La cantidad de sodio en los alimentos que comemos es uno de los factores que más contribuye a la presión arterial alta, dicen los expertos. El sodio nos hace retener agua, dice el doctor Mulrow, lo cual aumenta el volumen de sangre en nuestros cuerpos y hace que nuestros corazones trabajen más para bombearla. También, hay pruebas que el sodio en alguna forma daña los revestimientos de los vasos sanguíneos, haciendo más posible la cicatrización y obstrucción de las arterias.

La gran mayoría del sodio que consumimos viene de la sal en nuestros alimentos (cerca del 40 por ciento de la sal de mesa es sodio). Después de analizar docenas de estudios sobre el sodio y la presión arterial alta, un equipo británico de investigadores encontró que al reducir la sal a 3.000 miligramos por día —eso es un poco menos que el equivalente de una cucharadita— podría prevenir el 26 por ciento de todos los derrames cerebrales y el 15 por ciento de los ataques al corazón causados por los coágulos de sangre.

Algunas personas son más sensibles que otras a los efectos de la sal, o más específicamente, del sodio, dice el doctor DiBianco. "Es posible que usted

¿Qué tan bajo todavía es seguro?

Tratándose de la presión arterial, mientras más baja mejor.

"Realmente no importa qué tan baja es su lectura, aun cuando sea algo muy, muy bajo como 85 sistólica. Mientras usted no sienta efectos negativos debido a eso, todo está bien. De hecho, usted debería sentirse bien sabiendo que se encuentra en un grupo de bajo riesgo", dice el doctor Robert DiBianco, director de investigación cardiológica en el Hospital Adventista de Washington, en Takoma Park, Maryland.

El histórico Estudio Framingham del Corazón, que tomó toda una década para observar la salud en más de 5.200 residentes de Framingham, Massachusetts, encontró que las personas con lecturas de la presión sistólica de la sangre de menos de 120 mm Hg (milímetro de mercurio) tenían las menores probabilidades de sufrir ataques al corazón. El riesgo aumentó en forma constante al incrementar la presión. Las personas con las lecturas más altas, de 170 mm Hg o más, tenían más de tres veces la probabilidad de morirse de un ataque al corazón que aquellos en los 120 mm Hg o menos.

De todas maneras, hay un par de problemas de los que hay que cuidarse si se tiene presión arterial baja. Al envejecer las personas, hay una mayor posibilidad de que sufran de una forma temporal de presión arterial baja llamada hipotensión ortostática —la sensación que usted tiene cuando salta fuera de la cama y se siente débil de repente, como si el cuarto estuviera girando o las luces se hubieran atenuado. "Si usted alguna vez se ha desmayado por eso o si le sucede más que muy, muy raramente, usted debería ver a un doctor", dice el doctor DiBianco. El problema podría ser causado por una deshidratación ligera, la reacción a un medicamento, fiebre, enfermedad o agotamiento por el calor, dice él.

Para algunas personas, especialmente los ancianos y las personas con diabetes o enfermedad del corazón y posiblemente aquellos que están siendo tratados por presión arterial alta, las lecturas demasiado bajas pueden ser un riesgo particular. Si usted está en uno de estos grupos, consulte a su doctor, dice el doctor DiBianco.

pueda comer mucha sal, procesarla y deshacerse de ella rápidamente sin tener que preocuparse al respecto", dice él. Pero también puede ser que no. No hay una forma confiable de probar la sensibilidad a la sal. Si usted tiene sobrepeso, no hace mucho ejercicio o tiene una historia familiar de presión arterial alta o diabetes, el doctor DiBianco dice que usted probablemente tiene un mayor riesgo y necesita limitar su consumo de sal.

Los factores sicológicos también desempeñan un papel en la presión arterial alta. Un estudio de 129 estudiantes universitarios en la Universidad de British Columbia, en Vancouver mostró que las mujeres sintiendo que recibían poco apoyo social de parte de las amistades, miembros de la familia y colegas mostraban lecturas sistólicas ligeramente más altas. Los investigadores no están seguros por qué es esto. El estrés en el trabajo también puede conducir a la presión arterial alta. Otro estudio de 129 trabajadores adultos encontró que las mujeres en empleos de alto nivel y mucha presión mostraron aumentos considerablemente mayores en la presión arterial durante el día de trabajo que aquellas con empleos menos exigentes.

Los científicos han encontrado que la combinación de mucho sodio y mucho estrés pueden crear un problema de presión serio. Un estudio de 32 estudiantes en la Escuela de Medicina de la Universidad Johns Hopkins, en Baltimore, mostró que las personas que comían dietas con mucho sodio y se enfrentaban a condiciones de estrés intenso, notaron en un período de dos semanas cómo sus lecturas de presión arterial sistólica subieron más de 6 puntos. En comparación, las personas que ingirieron mucho sodio pero tenían menos estrés, notaron aumentos de sólo 0,6 puntos, y las personas con poco sodio y estrés intenso mostraron aumentos de sólo 0,1 puntos.

Hay también una relación entre las píldoras anticonceptivas y la presión arterial alta en algunas mujeres, dice el doctor Mulrow. Los nuevos anticonceptivos orales en dosis bajas han reducido notablemente el problema de la presión arterial elevada, aunque si fuma y toma píldoras anticonceptivas aumentará sus probabilidades de presión arterial alta, según el doctor Mulrow.

Y además, tenemos el alcohol. Los científicos desde hace tiempo saben que beber en exceso puede contribuir a la presión arterial alta. Pero un estudio del Instituto Investigador de Alcoholismo, en Buffalo, Nueva York, muestra que la frecuencia con que usted bebe puede ser tan importante como cuánto bebe. Los investigadores observaron a 1.635 residentes del Condado de Erie, en Nueva York, y encontraron que las personas que bebían diariamente tenían lecturas sistólicas 6,6 puntos más altas y lecturas diastólicas 4,7 puntos más altas que las personas que bebían sólo una vez a la semana. Pero el estudio no encontró una relación significativa entre la presión arterial y la cantidad total de alcohol consumida.

Cómo bajarla

Muchas de las drogas recetadas ayudan a reducir la presión arterial alta. Los diuréticos hacen salir los líquidos en exceso de su cuerpo. Los bloqueadores beta disminuyen el ritmo del corazón y la producción total de sangre del corazón. Los vasodilatadores ensanchan las arterias y facilitan el flujo de la sangre. Los inhibidores del nervio simpático también evitan que los vasos sanguíneos se contraigan.

Pero las drogas deberían ser el último recurso. Entre otros problemas éstas pueden causar fatiga e inhibir su vida sexual. La gracia está en evitar la presión arterial alta en primer lugar, y los consejos a continuación le ayudarán a empezar. Aunque usted ya tenga una leve presión arterial alta, los consejos podrían reducir su drogodependencia y a lo mejor hasta ayudarla a controlar las cosas en forma natural.

Revísela. Hay sólo una forma de saber con seguridad si usted tiene presión arterial alta: haga que su médico se la revise. Una vez al año debería ser suficiente, a menos que su doctor ordene más exámenes. Es un procedimiento rápido e indoloro. El doctor le pone un manguito inflable alrededor de su brazo y revise su pulso con un estetoscopio. Si usted muestra una lectura alta en el límite, el doctor puede recomendar que se vuelva a hacer varios de los exámenes durante un período de un par de semanas o meses.

Usted incluso puede encontrar monitores para tomarse la presión arterial usted misma en las farmacias, las tiendas de comestibles y los centros comerciales. Estos le pueden dar una estimación aproximada de su presión arterial, pero el doctor Mulrow advierte que estas máquinas no son un substituto de la visita anual al doctor. Algunas máquinas no están bien calibradas y proporcionan resultados bastante inexactos. Hay muchos factores externos —si usted ha estado caminando, o si tiene una manga muy gruesa— que pueden interferir.

Líbrese de esas libras de más. Si usted tiene sobrepeso, aun una pérdida moderada de peso puede ayudarle a bajar su presión arterial, dice el doctor Marvin Moser, profesor clínico de medicina en la Escuela de Medicina de la Universidad de Yale, en New Haven, Connecticut, y consejero sénior del Programa Nacional de Educación sobre la Presión Arterial Alta. En algunos casos, dice él, una pérdida de peso de 10 a 15 libras (4,5 a 6,8 kilos) puede ser suficiente para reducir ligeramente una presión arterial elevada a lo normal y ayudarle a evitar los medicamentos.

Un estudio por todo el país de 162 mujeres con sobrepeso entre los 30 y los 54 años de edad, mostró lo bien que puede funcionar una pérdida de peso. Durante un período de 12 meses estas mujeres, en un programa de pérdida de peso, perdieron un promedio de 6 libras (2,7 kilos). Sus lecturas sistólicas bajaron un promedio de 3,7 puntos, y las lecturas diastólicas bajaron 4,1 puntos.

Sacúdase. El ejercicio, combinado con una dieta baja en grasa, es la mejor manera de perder peso y mantener sus arterias libres de obstrucciones. La investigación muestra que las personas que no hacen ejercicio tienen 35 a 50 por ciento más probabilidades de desarrollar presión arterial alta. Y el Colegio Norteamericano de Medicina Deportiva dice que el entrenamiento regular aeróbico puede reducir la presión arterial sistólica y diastólica por hasta 10 puntos.

Usted tampoco tiene que ser una corredora de maratones para cosechar los beneficios. De hecho, algunos estudios han encontrado que los ejercicios de baja intensidad como el caminar son tan buenos o mejores para bajar la presión arterial que el correr u otras actividades aeróbicas fuertes. Muchos expertos recomiendan hacer ejercicio al menos tres veces por semana por 20 minutos cada vez.

Sea menos salada. Recuerde que no todas las personas son sensibles a los efectos del sodio. Pero hasta que los médicos pueden decir confiadamente quién lo es y quién no, es una buena idea limitar su consumo. "Ciertamente cortar la sal no va a dañar a nadie y probablemente tendrá mucho valor si usted tiene éxito", dice el doctor DiBianco.

Reduzca la sal en su dieta siempre que sea posible. Muchas de nosotras estamos comiendo dos veces y media más de lo que deberíamos. Dejar el salero tendrá algún efecto. Pero la investigación muestra que tres cuartas partes de toda la sal que consumimos proviene de los alimentos procesados como son el queso, la sopa, el pan, los alimentos asados y los bocadillos (meriendas o *snacks*).

"Usted necesita leer las etiquetas", dice el doctor Mulrow. Revise el contenido de sodio, y fíjese una meta total diaria de aproximadamente 2.400 miligramos. Cuando vaya de compras, busque las etiquetas que dicen *"low sodium"* (bajo en sodio). Eso quiere decir que no contiene más de 140 miligramos de sodio por porción. Y pase un poco de tiempo en el pasillo agrícola. Prácticamente cada fruta o verdura es naturalmente baja en sodio.

Tenga cuidado también cuando coma afuera. Se sorprendería de lo rápido que se acumula el sodio. Por ejemplo una hamburguesa de su restaurante favorito de comida rápida, puede darle a usted casi la mitad de su total para el día.

Acumule el potasio. Los estudios han mostrado que si toma 3.500 miligramos de potasio puede ayudar a contrarrestar el sodio y a mantener su volumen de sangre —y presión arterial— bajo. Y es fácil obtener lo suficiente. Una papa asada contiene 838 miligramos de potasio por sí sola, y una taza de espinacas tiene 800 miligramos. Otros alimentos con mucho potasio incluyen los plátanos (guineos amarillos), el jugo de naranja, maíz, repollo y brócoli. Consulte también a su doctor antes de tomar suplementos de potasio. Demasiado, puede agravar los problemas con los riñones.

Satisfaga sus necesidades de magnesio. Parece que los investigadores han encontrado una relación entre el consumo bajo de magnesio y la presión arterial alta. Pero exactamente cuánto magnesio necesita usted para combatir la presión arterial alta aún no está claro. Por ahora, dice el doctor DiBianco, lo mejor que puede hacer es tomar la Asignación Dietética Recomendada (*Recommended Dietary Allowance* o *RDA*, por sus siglas en inglés) de aproximadamente 280 miligramos.

Desafortunadamente, el consumo de magnesio en los Estados Unidos ha ido decreciendo durante un siglo, desde que empezamos a procesar los alimentos y a robarles sus microelementos. Las buenas fuentes de magnesio incluyen las nueces, la espinaca, las habas blancas (*lima beans*), los chícharos (guisantes), los pescados y mariscos. Pero no abuse tomando suplementos; el doctor Mulrow dice que demasiado puede provocarle una fuerte diarrea.

Mantenga su calcio. La relación entre el consumo de calcio y la presión arterial es discutible. Algunos estudios muestran que el calcio adicional puede bajar la presión arterial, en tanto que otros muestran que no tiene ningún efecto.

Pero los expertos todavía no están convencidos de que las dosis grandes de calcio vayan a ayudar. El doctor Mulrow dice que el tomar los 800 miligramos del RDA —tres vasos de leche descremada de 8 onzas (237 ml) cada uno proporcionarán más que suficiente— y el mantener los otros factores de riesgo bajo control es el mejor consejo a seguir por ahora. Otras fuentes de calcio son los quesos bajos en grasa, el salmón enlatado y otros pescados enlatados con espinas. Si usted quiere tomar suplementos de calcio, vea a su doctor ya que demasiado calcio puede causar otros problemas, como por ejemplo cálculos renales.

Llénese de fibra. Un estudio sueco a 32 personas con una ligera presión arterial alta encontró que tomar una tableta de siete gramos de fibra diariamente ayuda a bajar la presión arterial diastólica en cinco puntos. Nadie está seguro por qué; quizás es por la pérdida de peso debido a que la gente se llena más y come menos, o porque consumen menos sodio. Cualquiera sea la razón, siete gramos extras de fibra son fáciles de encontrar. Casi hay esa cantidad en un bol de cereal alto en fibra.

Beba con moderación. "Un poco de alcohol no es perjudicial", dice el doctor Mulrow. "Pero beber diariamente, y beber en exceso, puede traer problemas." Para las mujeres que están luchando con la presión arterial alta, tres onzas (89 mg) de alcohol a la semana parece ser el límite aproximado. Un estudio de 12 años a 1.643 mujeres en una edad promedio de 47 años, mostró que tanto la lectura de la presión sistólica como de la diastólica empezaron a aumentar en forma constante después de esa cantidad. Eso significa seis cervezas de 12 onzas (355 ml) cada una, seis copas de vino de 4 onzas (118 ml) cada una o seis cócteles que contengan cada uno 1 onza (29 ml) de licor fuerte a la semana.

Deje de fumar. El fumar notablemente aumenta su riesgo de sufrir un derrame cerebral o un daño en sus vasos sanguíneos debido a la presión arterial alta, dice el doctor Mulrow. Cuando usted fuma, alienta a su cuerpo a depositar el colesterol dentro de sus arterias coronarias. Esto disminuye el tamaño de sus vasos y fuerza a su corazón a trabajar más. "Cualquier persona con presión arterial alta debería dejar de fumar inmediatamente", aconseja el doctor Mulrow.

PROBLEMAS
DEL ALCOHOL

Cómo vencer a la botella

Ella piensa que es su pequeño secreto. Pero todos saben que guarda un frasco en su maletín. Ella trata de disfrazar el alcohol en su aliento con grandes cantidades de enjuague bucal. Su "almuerzo" consiste de tres copas de vino tinto. Después del trabajo, ella vuela a su bar (cantina) favorito y allí se queda hasta la hora de cerrar.

Esa es la imagen clásica de una mujer con un problema de alcohol. Pero el abuso de alcohol tiene muchas caras sutiles. Puede ser su socia de negocios, quien bebe solamente los fines de semana. Puede ser su vecina, quien continúa bebiendo a pesar de las imploraciones de sus hijos. Y sí, puede ser usted.

"Un problema de alcohol puede atacar a cualquiera, en cualquier momento, de cualquier profesión o condición social. Nadie está inmune a éste," dice el doctor Donald Damstra, un especialista en medicina para adicciones y consultor en abuso de substancias, en Phoenix.

Y no importa cómo le llama usted —alcoholismo, beber demasiado o "ese pequeño problema"— el abuso del alcohol es un envejecedor poderoso y muchas veces mortal. Puede destruir su hígado, diezmar su corazón, elevar peligrosamente su presión arterial, minar su energía, arruinar su estómago, destrozar su vida sexual, reducir su fertilidad, causar un corto en su cerebro, agravar la diabetes, disminuir su inmunidad, incrementar su riesgo de cáncer y provocar la depresión, el estrés y los problemas sociales, incluyendo las dificultades matrimoniales y laborales.

"Cuando usted observa a las personas que han estado bebiendo mucho por varios años, notará que tienden a verse mal. Algunas mujeres en sus cuarenta y tantos años pueden verse como si tuvieran sesenta y tantos. Su cutis simplemente se ve viejo, su modo de andar es desgarbado, tienen sobrepeso y a menudo han perdido masa ósea, por lo que se ven como pequeñas viejecitas mucho antes de lo que deberían", dice Frederick C. Blow, Ph.D., director de investigación del Centro de Investigación sobre el Alcohol de la Universidad de Michigan, en Ann Arbor.

¿Quién tiene un problema?

Casi todas las mujeres que beben han experimentado una resaca (cruda) y las otras torturas que ocurren cuando se toma de más. Pero después de que nos recobramos de uno de esos desastres autocausados, muchas de nosotras aprendemos a moderar nuestra manera de beber.

"Beber generalmente disminuye al envejecer", dice el doctor Blow. "Esto puede estar relacionado con las enfermedades crónicas como la diabetes y la alta presión arterial o por un exagerado uso de medicamentos, o puede ser que la gente simplemente ya no se siente con ganas de beber demasiado."

Las mujeres también suelen beber menos cuando se hacen mayores porque encuentran que el alcohol parece afectarlas más. Eso es porque al envejecer, su cuerpo es menos capaz de soportar el alcohol, dice el doctor Damstra.

De hecho, el consumo de alcohol en los Estados Unidos está en su nivel más bajo desde 1967, según el Instituto Nacional sobre el Abuso de Alcohol y Alcoholismo (o *NIAAA*, por sus siglas en inglés). El habitante normal de los Estados Unidos bebe cerca de 2,5 galones de alcohol (casi 9,5 litros) cada año. Eso es aproximadamente el equivalente a una lata y media de 12 onzas (360 ml) de cerveza por día. Eso está dentro de los límites de una a dos bebidas al día que los doctores creen que puede reducir su riesgo de enfermedades del corazón. Una bebida alcohólica estándar es una cerveza de 12 onzas, una copa de vino de 5 onzas (148 ml) o un cóctel hecho con 1,5 onzas (44 ml, o un trago) de licor.

Casi la mitad de las mujeres entre los 30 y los 44 años de edad se abstienen de beber alcohol y la mayoría de las que sí beben lo hacen más moderadamente que los hombres, según el NIAAA. Pero en un estudio subvencionado por el gobierno federal, una en cada 20 mujeres reportaron un problema significativo relacionado con el alcohol o un síntoma de dependencia alcohólica en los 12 meses previos a ese estudio, dice la doctora Sheila Blume, directora médica de los programas de alcoholismo, dependencia química y de jugar compulsivo en el Hospital South Oaks, en Amityville, Nueva York.

El problema de beber puede causar dificultades tales como ausentismo en el trabajo y descuido de los niños, para nombrar a dos. Pero cuánto y qué tan seguido una mujer bebe no es una prueba concluyente de que ella se encuentre entre los cinco millones de mujeres con problemas serios de beber que viven en los Estados Unidos, dice el doctor Damstra. Ese número, sin embargo, está probablemente subestimado porque las mujeres suelen de esconder sus problemas de bebida. Por ello, nos toma más tiempo buscar ayuda, dice el doctor Damstra. (Como comparación, se considera que 12 millones de hombres tienen un problema serio de alcohol.)

Una medida clave, dice él, es determinar si el beber es más importante que otros aspectos en la vida de una mujer, incluyendo a su familia, su salud y su trabajo.

¿Se encuentra usted en las garras del alcohol?

Entonces, ¿cómo sabe usted si tiene un problema de alcohol? El doctor Melvin L. Selzer, profesor clínico de siquiatría en la Universidad de California, San Diego, y autor de la Prueba de Revisión de Alcoholismo de Michigan, sugiere que usted misma se haga las siguientes preguntas. Responda a las preguntas con sí o no, después vea el puntaje al final de la prueba.

1. ¿ Usted siente que es una bebedora normal?
2. ¿Ha despertado alguna vez en la mañana después de beber la noche anterior y encontrado que no recuerda parte de esa noche?
3. ¿Se preocupa o queja su compañero (o padres) acerca de que usted bebe?
4. ¿Puede usted dejar de beber después de una o dos bebidas sin que le cueste trabajo?
5. ¿Alguna vez se siente usted mal porque bebe?
6. ¿Creen sus amistades y parientes que usted es una bebedora normal?
7. ¿Le es siempre posible dejar de beber cuando quiere?
8. ¿Ha asistido alguna vez a una sesión de Alcohólicos Anónimos?
9. ¿Se ha visto usted involucrada en peleas cuando está bebiendo?
10. ¿El que usted beba ha creado alguna vez problemas entre usted y su compañero?
11. ¿Alguna vez su compañero (u otro miembro de su familia) ha buscado a alguien para que lo ayude debido a que usted bebe?
12. ¿Ha perdido usted alguna vez amigos o amigas debido a que bebe?
13. ¿Ha tenido dificultades alguna vez en su trabajo porque bebe?
14. ¿Ha perdido alguna vez un trabajo debido al alcohol?

"Hay muchas bebedoras fuertes que no son adictas al alcohol. Estas son las mujeres que dejan de beber cuando sus doctores les dicen que tienen úlceras u otras razones convincentes para parar. Pero si usted es adicta al alcohol, le dirá al doctor 'extirpe la úlcera, doctor, porque yo tengo que seguir bebiendo' ", dice el doctor Damstra. "Cuando el beber es causa de serias consecuencias negativas, sin importar si son físicas, sicológicas, sociales, económicas o espirituales, y la mujer continúa bebiendo, entonces su problema está fuera de control y se considera alcoholismo."

15. ¿Ha faltado alguna vez a sus obligaciones, su familia o su trabajo por dos días o más a la vez porque estaba bebiendo?
16. ¿Bebe usted a veces antes del mediodía?
17. ¿Le han dicho alguna vez que tiene problemas con el hígado? ¿Cirrosis?
18. ¿Ha tenido alguna vez *delirium tremens* (DTs) o sacudidas violentas, oído voces o visto cosas que no estaban ahí, después de beber mucho?
19. ¿Ha acudido usted a alguien para que la ayude con el alcohol?
20. ¿Ha estado alguna vez en el hospital debido a beber?
21. ¿Ha sido alguna vez paciente en un hospital siquiátrico cuando beber era parte del problema?
22. ¿La han visto en una clínica siquiátrica o mental, o ha ido a un médico, trabajador social o clérigo para que la ayuden con un problema del cual beber era una parte?
23. ¿La han arrestado alguna vez, aunque sea por unas cuantas horas, por comportamiento de embriaguez?
24. ¿La han arrestado alguna vez por conducir en estado de embriaguez o por conducir después de beber?

Puntuación

Si usted contestó no a las preguntas 1, 4, 6 y 7 anótese dos puntos por cada una. Si contestó sí a las preguntas 3, 5, 9 y 16 anótese un punto por cada una. Respuestas afirmativas a las preguntas 8, 19 y 20 valen cinco puntos cada una. Respuestas afirmativas a todas las otras preguntas excepto 1, 4, 6 y 7 valen dos puntos cada una. Si usted tiene una puntación de cinco o más puntos, podría tener un problema de bebida y debería considerar buscar orientación.

Todavía se está tratando de aclarar por qué algunas mujeres tienen problemas con el alcohol y otras no. Los investigadores creen en una predisposición genética, ya que las mujeres con historias familiares de alcoholismo tienen más probabilidades de volverse alcohólicas. Pero predisposición no significa que una mujer está condenada a volverse alcohólica, tampoco las mujeres sin historias familiares están inmunes a problemas con el alcohol, dice el doctor Norman Miller, profesor asociado de siquiatría en el Colegio de Medicina de la Universidad de Illinois, en Chicago. Aunque el proceso es complejo, algunos investigadores especulan que el riesgo de alcoholismo en una mujer depende de una combinación de factores añadidos a la predisposición genética, incluyendo actitudes religiosas y morales, amor propio, depresión y presión que ejercen las compañeras. Pero cualquiera que sea la causa, el resultado es una adicción que la envejecerá prematuramente en forma trágica e innecesaria.

El genio de la botella

Cuando usted saborea un cóctel después de un largo día de trabajo, está bebiendo una de las substancias más insólitas sobre la tierra. El alcohol actúa como una fuente de calorías vacías y es una droga que afecta su juicio y sus emociones.

Beber moderadamente —una bebida al día para las mujeres, dos bebidas al día para los hombres— tiene algunos beneficios, incluyendo el de reducir su riesgo de enfermedades del corazón. Pero en grandes cantidades, el alcohol es un veneno que afecta cada célula en su cuerpo, dice la doctora Blume.

"El alcohol es una molécula muy pequeña acarreada por su torrente sanguíneo, y a diferencia de otras drogas, es tan pequeña que se mete completamente dentro de cada célula. Por ello, su capacidad para causar daño y averías no tiene fin", explica la doctora Blume.

De hecho, las mujeres pueden ser afectadas por el alcohol antes que los hombres porque nosotras normalmente pesamos menos y tenemos menos de una enzima clave que metaboliza el alcohol en nuestros estómagos. Y por lo mismo terminamos con una concentración de alcohol más alta en nuestra sangre después de beber.

"Todas las complicaciones físicas progresan mucho más rápidamente una vez que el alcoholismo comienza en las mujeres", dice la doctora Blume. "Las mujeres alcanzan un punto de daño serio con menos tragos por día y en menos años que los hombres."

Por ejemplo, el alcohol puede reprimir momentáneamente la producción de la hormona del crecimiento, la cual conserva nuestras células vigorosas y activas a medida que envejecemos, dice la doctora Mary Ann Emanuele, profesora de endocrinología en el Centro Médico de la Universidad Loyola, en Chicago. "Los niveles de sangre en la hormona de crecimiento en adultos normales descienden después de beber, y eso puede ser perjudicial", dice la doctora Emanuele. "Los estudios muestran que esos cambios se invierten después de varias horas. Sin embargo, no sabemos si continuar bebiendo mucho puede causar una supresión permanente de la hormona."

El consumo excesivo de alcohol también genera radicales libres, moléculas de oxígeno químicamente inestables que pueden dañar a su corazón e hígado y acelerar el proceso de envejecimiento en todo el cuerpo, dice Eric Rimm, Sc.D., un epidemiólogo nutricional en la Escuela de Salubridad Pública de la Universidad de Harvard, en Boston.

Beber fuertemente, por ejemplo, daña seriamente el cutis de una mujer. "Causa rinofima, la célebre nariz grande y roja, como la que tenía W.C. Fields. También causa manchas, hinchazón y un tono aminorado del cutis, por lo que una mujer que bebe mucho se verá vieja prematuramente", dice la doctora Blume.

Además, los estudios muestran que la gente que consume tres o más tragos al día tiene el 40 por ciento más de riesgo de desarrollar alta presión arterial, la cual está vinculada con enfermedades del corazón y derrame cerebral.

El uso excesivo del alcohol puede conducir a la cirrosis, una enfermedad incurable que estimula la formación de tejido de cicatrización que destruye el hígado. Pero si una mujer deja de beber, el progreso de la enfermedad se hace más lento, y su vida se puede prolongar. Beber mucho también aumenta el riesgo de cáncer del hígado.

"El alcohol está asociado con algunos tipos de cáncer, particularmente en esas partes del cuerpo que entran en contacto directo con el alcohol, como son el esófago, la garganta y el hígado", dice el doctor Rimm. "Estos tipos de cáncer generalmente son raros, pero entre las personas que beben cinco o seis tragos por día, se vuelven menos raros."

Algunos investigadores creen que estos cánceres son más comunes en bebedores fuertes porque la adicción al alcohol inhibe el sistema inmune y baja las defensas del cuerpo contra enfermedades tales como cáncer y SIDA.

Así afecta a su vida sexual
(… y a la de los demás)

Como si no fuera suficiente, el alcohol también afecta el juicio y disminuye las inhibiciones, por lo que usted tendrá más probabilidades de mezclarse en prácticas sexuales peligrosas y con ello tiene una mayor posibilidad de contraer una infección de SIDA u otras enfermedades transmitidas sexualmente. Además, dice Ronald R. Watson, Ph.D., director del Centro de Investigación sobre el Alcohol de la Universidad de Arizona, en Tucson, la evidencia resultante de estudios a animales sugiere que si usted tiene SIDA y continúa bebiendo, el daño a su sistema inmune aumenta, se reducen los niveles de vitaminas y minerales en su cuerpo y se acelera el progreso de la enfermedad.

Pero si usted bebe demasiado, probablemente no tendrá una gran vida sexual. Beber demasiado puede reprimir los orgasmos y reducir su libido. Puede

Es difícil hablar —pero puede ayudar

No es fácil decirle a una amistad o a alguien querido que usted está preocupada porque bebe. Pero esta puede ser una de las conversaciones más vitales y gratificantes que usted podría tener en su vida.

"Si usted va a compartir sus observaciones y pensamientos acerca de su consumo de bebidas alcohólicas, debe esperar que va a ser una discusión penosa. Pero penosa no significa perjudicial", dice el doctor William Clark, director médico del Centro de Recursos para la Adicción, en el Hospital MidCoast-Bath en Bath, Maine. "Es como la cirugía. Es dolorosa cuando se hace, pero salva vidas."

No le "ponga una etiqueta" a la persona diciendo, "Yo creo que tú eres una alcohólica" o "Tú tienes un problema de beber", sugiere el doctor Clark. Este tipo de afirmación logrará aumentar los sentimientos de irritabilidad, vergüenza e ira en la persona.

En lugar de eso use los mensajes que empiezan con "Yo" para simplemente expresar sus preocupaciones y observaciones, dice la doctora Sheila Blume, directora médica de los programas de alcoholismo, dependencia química y jugar compulsivo en el Hospital South Oaks, en Amityville, Nueva York. Diga algo como, "yo estoy aterrada porque sé que últimamente has estado conduciendo mucho bajo la influencia del alcohol. Eso me asusta. Yo no quiero que te pase nade; a lo mejor te puedes sentar con alguien que sepa más de estas cosas que nosotras."

"Si usted empieza la conversación con respeto y consideración, le escucharán", dice el doctor Clark.

---

también reducir su fertilidad y causar defectos en los niños que están por nacer, dice la doctora Blume.

"Un solo trago probablemente no va a causar daño al cerebro o defectos de nacimiento", dice la doctora Blume. "La razón por la que se aconseja a las mujeres no beber si están planeando embarazarse o están embarazadas es que no se conoce la cantidad mínima real de alcohol que es inofensiva y puede variar de mujer a mujer. Lo que puede no causar daño en el bebé de una mujer puede causar serios daños en el de otra. Por lo tanto, ya que el alcohol no es un nutriente necesario, el recurso más seguro es no beber en lo absoluto."

El alcohol puede interrumpir los ciclos menstruales y causar el comienzo prematuro de la menopausia, agrega Judith S. Gavaler, Ph.D., jefa de investigación de mujeres en el Centro Médico Bautista y miembro de la Fundación de Investigación Médica de Oklahoma, ambos en la ciudad de Oklahoma.

Hay poca duda de que el abuso de alcohol pueda causar desvanecimientos, ataques, alucinaciones y daños al cerebro. Hasta el 70 por ciento de las personas que ingresan a los programas de tratamientos del alcohol tienen dificultades de memoria, de resolución de problemas y de pensamiento claro. Beber demasiado puede causar confusión, tiempo de reacción más lento, vista nublada y pérdida de discernimiento y coordinación muscular, todo lo cual conduce a lesiones y accidentes fatales.

Las mujeres y los hombres que beben más de cinco tragos en una sentada tienen dos veces más probabilidades de morir de lesiones que aquellos que no beben tanto, según los investigadores de los Centros para el Control y la Prevención de las Enfermedades, en Atlanta. De hecho, la Administración Nacional de Seguridad en Tráfico de Carreteras estima que entre el 45 y el 50 por ciento de los accidentes fatales de tráfico en los Estados Unidos cada año están relacionados con el alcohol. Y otras estadísticas sugieren que un estimado 22 por ciento de todas las muertes por enfermedades, accidentes y homicidios están relacionadas con el alcohol.

"Los bebedores empedernidos mueren jóvenes —no hay duda acerca de eso", dice el doctor Michael Criqui, profesor de epidemiología en la Escuela de Medicina de la Universidad de California, en San Diego.

Pero aun cuando usted ha estado bebiendo fuertemente por años, todavía hay esperanzas de que pueda vivir una vida larga y saludable si lo deja, dice el doctor Damstra.

En busca de la sobriedad

El reconocer que usted tiene un problema es un primer paso importante en la lucha para permanecer sobria. "Mientras más pronto se reconoce y se trata el alcoholismo, menos probable será que este padecimiento cause daño permanente", dice el doctor Damstra. "La mayoría de los alcohólicos empiezan a sentirse mejor rápidamente después de haber dejado de beber. Muchas de las complicaciones físicas causadas por el consumo excesivo empiezan a curarse dentro de un lapso de dos a tres semanas."

La alta presión arterial, por ejemplo, a menudo regresa a lo normal en una semana o dos, mientras que la irritación del estómago y otros tipos de daños al hígado son reversibles dentro del transcurso de un mes. Pero recuperarse de algunos de los efectos de tantos años consumiendo alcohol puede llevar más de un año, por ejemplo la memoria y concentración deterioradas. Otras condiciones, tales como la cirrosis del hígado y las lesiones al páncreas, pueden ser irreversibles. Aquí hay algunos consejos para que usted pueda hacer borrón y cuenta nueva, sin alcohol.

Pida ayuda. Si usted cree que el alcohol está controlando su vida, pida a su doctor que la ayude o póngase en contacto con un programa de tratamiento de alcohol en su área. O para obtener información confidencial, escriba a *Women for Sobriety* (Mujeres por la sobriedad), Box 618, Quakertown, PA 18951 (incluya un sobre rotulado con su dirección y estampillado), o a *Alcoholics Anonymous* (Alcohólicos anónimos), P.O. Box 459, Grand Central Station, New York, NY 10163.

Dígaselo a una amiga. Algunos estudios sugieren que si la persona con un problema de alcohol lo hace público, le será más fácil dejarlo, dice el doctor Blow. Si usted le dice a las personas que son importantes para usted —compañeros de trabajo, familiares— que usted ya no va a beber más, logra dos cosas. Primero, reduce el grado de presión que sus compañeros pueden ejercer sobre usted para que beba. Segundo, le será más fácil no apartarse de su compromiso, ya que usted se lo dijo a todo el mundo.

Acuérdese que la sobriedad empieza en casa. En la primera fase de la recuperación, pídale a sus amistades y familiares que no beban cuando se encuentren a su alrededor. Pídale a su compañero que participe en su recuperación al asistir a las sesiones de terapia con usted, dice el doctor Damstra. Si él se rehusa, puede también tener un problema, y usted tendrá que decidir si vale la pena continuar con la relación y poner en peligro su recuperación.

Diga las tres palabras mágicas. Si decide ir a una fiesta u otra reunión y le ofrecen una bebida alcohólica, simplemente diga "yo no tomo" o pida un refresco, dice la doctora Blume. Ninguna otra explicación debería ser necesaria. Si la gente a su alrededor continúa presionándola para que tome, váyase.

Encuentre nuevas amistades. Frecuentar a sus antiguas compañeras de bebida, aun cuando usted jure que no va a beber, tarde o temprano va a terminar en un desastre, dice el doctor Damstra. Primero, usted debe participar en un programa de recuperación de 12 pasos. Después, encuentre en su grupo de recuperación, iglesia o gimnasio a las personas que estén interesadas en permanecer sobrias.

Invierta en diversión. Ofrézcase como voluntaria en una escuela de su comunidad o participe en un grupo de teatro, dice el doctor Damstra. Mientras más actividades tenga, más se dará usted cuenta de que estar sobria es más divertido y gratificante que beber.

Aléjese de los substitutos. Manténgase alejada de las cervezas y los vinos sin alcohol. "Le recordarán el sabor de los productos reales y, por asociación, la harán desear el alcohol", dice la doctora Blume.

Problemas de la Vejiga

Cómo domar una molestia desagradable

Su vejiga, por años tan fiel como una amiga de confianza, la está traicionando. Actualmente, siempre que usted va a algún lado, tiene el temor de que las compuertas se van a abrir, avergonzándola en forma increíble.

Su vida social se está marchitando. Usted se siente frustrada, enojada y humillada. Usted es demasiado joven para ese tipo de problemas, se dice a sí misma. Sin embargo, usted tiene vergüenza de pedirle ayuda a alguien, incluso a su doctor.

"El impacto sicológico de un problema con la vejiga, es tremendo. Si una mujer entre los 30 y los 50 años de edad empieza a orinar más frecuentemente, se orina encima o tiene otros problemas con la vejiga que ella asocia con envejecer, estoy seguro que ella debe pensar 'esto no solía pasarme. Dios mío, debo estar haciéndome vieja. Esto es lo primero que le pasó a la tía Millie cuando empezó a declinar' ", dice el doctor Alan J. Wein, presidente de la División de Urología en la Escuela de Medicina de la Universidad de Pennsylvania, en Filadelfia.

Pero en realidad, la mayoría de las dificultades con la vejiga no son una señal inevitable de envejecimiento. De hecho, las infecciones del tracto urinario y la incontinencia, las dos causas más comunes de problemas con la vejiga, pueden afectar a las mujeres a cualquier edad y usualmente pueden ser tratadas efectivamente o curadas, dice el doctor Wein.

A continuación estudiaremos más de cerca las causas y los remedios para estas dos molestias.

La invasión de las bacterias

Puede comenzar con un dolor fuerte cada vez que usted orina. Pronto usted sentirá el deseo inequívoco que tiene que ir otra vez, a pesar de que fue hace apenas unos minutos. Y cuando usted va, sale una cantidad muy pequeña de orina. Algunas veces su orina despide un fuerte olor y usted pasa sangre. En casos graves, usted también puede desarrollar dolor de espalda, escalofríos, fiebre, náusea y vómito.

Lo más probable es que usted tenga una infección del tracto urinario (o *UTI* por sus siglas en inglés), el más común de los problemas de la vejiga en las mujeres que se encuentran entre los 30 y los 50 años de edad, dice el doctor Wein. Por lo menos el 25 al 35 por ciento de las mujeres entre las edades de 20 y 40 han tenido por lo menos una UTI. De estas, casi el 20 por ciento tendrá por lo menos una recurrencia, dice la doctora Penny Wise Budoff, profesora asociada clínica de medicina familiar de la Universidad Estatal de Nueva York, en la Escuela de Medicina del Centro Stony Brook de Ciencias de la Salud. En general, las mujeres tienen 50 veces más probabilidades de desarrollar UTI que los hombres.

Eso se debe a que la uretra de las mujeres, el tubo que lleva la orina fuera de la vejiga, mide menos de dos pulgadas de largo. Ya que es tan corta, la uretra es vulnerable a la invasión de bacterias que habitan naturalmente en la vagina y el recto. El acto sexual puede empujar las bacterias hacia arriba al tracto urinario, donde estos microorganismos pueden causar inflamación de la uretra, vejiga o riñones.

Esperar demasiado para orinar es otra causa común de UTI. Si usted se pasa horas sin orinar, puede expandir el músculo de la vejiga y debilitarlo hasta el punto en que no puede expulsar la orina. Este residuo de orina aumenta su riesgo de infección.

Una vez que la infección ataca, su doctor le recetará antibióticos, dice el doctor Jonathan Vapnek, profesor asociado de urología en la Escuela de Medicina Monte Sinaí, en la ciudad de Nueva York.

Mientras que su médico familiar puede tratar una UTI, usted debería ver a un urólogo o ginecólogo si es que tiene sangre en la orina, UTIs recurrentes o una historia de infecciones o cálculos en los riñones, dice el doctor Vapnek.

En algunos casos, las mujeres con UTI pueden desarrollar cistitis intersticial, una enfermedad crónica que causa inflamación de la vejiga. Las mujeres que sufren esto sienten a menudo la urgencia de orinar hasta 60 veces diarias. No existe una causa o cura conocida, pero sus síntomas se alivian a menudo con drogas tales como esteroides o antihistamínicos.

Aunque las infecciones de la vejiga deben darse a conocer a su doctor, hay muchas formas de prevenirlas en primer lugar. Aquí le decimos cómo.

Llénela. Tomando por lo menos seis vasos de 8 onzas (237 ml) de agua y otras bebidas sin cafeína por día diluirá la orina en su vejiga, lo cual hace más difícil que las bacterias se desarrollen, dice la doctora Budoff.

Orine a menudo. Trate de vaciar su vejiga por lo menos cuatro a seis veces diarias, dice la doctora Budoff. Eso ayudará a su vejiga a mantenerse libre de bacterias. Ir al baño así de seguido no debe ser un problema si usted toma suficientes líquidos.

Beba jugo de arándanos rojos. Este antiguo remedio recibió una validación científica de investigadores de la Escuela de Medicina de Harvard, quienes dividieron a 153 mujeres entre bebedoras y no bebedoras de jugo de arándanos rojos (*cranberry*). Aquellas que bebían cerca de 10 onzas (300 ml) al día de esta bebida ácida experimentaron infecciones de la vejiga sólo 42 por ciento tan a menudo como aquellas que no lo tomaban. Los investigadores especulan que el jugo de arándanos rojos posiblemente inhiba la capacidad de las bacterias para adherirse a las paredes de la vejiga.

Orine después del sexo. Orine enseguida después de haber tenido contacto sexual, sugiere la doctora Deborah Erickson, una uróloga y profesora asistente de cirugía en el colegio de Medicina de la Universidad Estatal de Pennsylvania, en Hershey. Orinar expulsará cualquier bacteria que hubiera sido empujada en la vejiga durante el sexo. Si usted tiene infecciones recurrentes, pregunte a su médico acerca de la posibilidad de tomar un antibiótico después del sexo.

Observe con más detenimiento su control de natalidad. Investigadores en la Universidad de Washington encontraron una conexión entre las UTIs recurrentes y las mujeres que usan diafragmas en combinación con espermicidas. Las mujeres que usan este método anticonceptivo tienen un mayor riesgo de tener bacterias *Eschericia coli*, el culpable más probable de causar UTI, en su orina. Si usted usa un diafragma con espermicida y frecuentemente sufre de UTI, considere cambiar a otra forma de control de natalidad, dice la doctora Seth Lerner, profesora asistente de urología en el Colegio Baylor de Medicina, en Houston. Consulte con su médico.

Practique una buena higiene. Lavándose las manos antes y después de orinar puede reducir las posibilidades de UTI, dice la doctora Budoff. Cuando se limpia por debajo, hágalo del frente hacia atrás. Esto mantendrá las bacterias potencialmente dañinas lejos de su uretra. Para limpieza adicional, la doctora Budoff sugiere usar una bola grande de algodón humedecida para limpiarse del frente hacia atrás.

Dúchese, no se bañe. Remojarse en una tina llena de agua jabonosa o un baño de burbujas puede irritar el revestimiento del tracto urinario, particularmente si usted tiene una historia de infecciones recurrentes de la vejiga, dice el doctor David Rivas, un urólogo en el Hospital de la Universidad Thomas Jefferson, en Filadelfia.

Quédese con el algodón. Los calzones de nylon ajustados pueden restringir el flujo de aire, conservar la humedad y promover el desarrollo de bacteria alrededor de la uretra, dice el doctor Rivas. En su lugar use ropa interior suelta de algodón que permite una mejor circulación del aire. Si usa pantimedias (*pantyhose*), asegúrese de que tenga la entrepierna de algodón.

El terror de perder el control

Cuando su hijo avienta una pelota de béisbol por la ventana o su esposo estrella su carro en un montón de nieve, usted se encoge de hombros porque sabe que los accidentes pasan. Pero los accidentes que la han asediado últimamente no son tan fáciles de desechar. Usted puede tener dificultad en llegar a un baño a tiempo o sufrir un goteo embarazoso cuando tose, estornuda o aun cuando levanta pesas en el gimnasio.

"La incontinencia hace que algunas mujeres se sientan más viejas porque piensan que es un signo seguro de que se están volviendo decrépitas. Significa una falta de control y sugiere que otras cualidades valiosas de la vida, tales como ejercitar, viajar y aun vivir independientemente, están en peligro", dice Katherine Jeter, Ed. D., directora ejecutiva de Ayuda para Personas Incontinentes, en Union, Carolina del Sur.

Pero la incontinencia no es necesariamente una señal de envejecimiento, dice la doctora Lerner. De hecho, los estudios indican que cerca de una en cada cuatro mujeres entre los 30 y 59 los años de edad ha tenido por lo menos un suceso de incontinencia en su vida adulta. Esa es aproximadamente la misma proporción para mujeres mayores de 60 años de edad.

"La incontinencia no es como tener canas. No es inevitable", dice la doctora Lerner. "Usualmente tienen una causa fisiológica subyacente que puede ser tratable."

Las mujeres mayores tienden a sufrir de incontinencia por razones diferentes a las de las mujeres más jóvenes, dice la doctora Tamara Bavendam, profesora asistente de urología y directora de la Clínica de Urología Femenina en el Centro Médico de la Universidad de Washington, en Seattle. La artritis, por ejemplo, puede hacer que sea más difícil para una mujer mayor caminar rápidamente al baño. Las mujeres mayores tienen más probabilidades de tomar medicamentos, y algunas drogas —tales como aquellas para tratar enfermedades del corazón— pueden causar una producción excesiva de orina que abruma la capacidad de la vejiga.

Entre las formas más notables de escapes de la vejiga, la incontinencia por esfuerzo y la incontinencia por urgencia (urgencia miccional) son las más comunes para las mujeres entre los 30 y los 50 años de edad, dice la doctora Lerner. La incontinencia por esfuerzo puede resultar cuando los músculos del fondo de la pelvis se han debilitado o dañado. Esto puede ocurrir debido a embarazarse y dar a luz, peso excesivo o una producción hormonal disminuida. La vejiga y la uretra cuelgan, y el músculo del esfínter ya no puede cerrar completamente. Por lo tanto, cualquier presión abdominal como es reírse, o estornudar o levantar un objeto pesado, puede provocar un escape.

La incontinencia por urgencia, la cual puede ser causada por las UTI o inflamación de la vejiga, ocurre cuando los músculos irritados o hiperactivos de la vejiga se contraen incontrolablemente. Como resultado, una mujer puede sentir una necesidad imperiosa de orinar. Si vacila, ella puede dejar escapar orina antes de llegar a un baño, dice la doctora Bavendam. A veces una mujer puede tener una combinación de incontinencia por esfuerzo y por urgencia.

En otro tipo de incontinencia llamada incontinencia por rebosamiento, una mujer no siente ganas de orinar, así que la vejiga se llena hasta el borde y causa tanta presión que un exceso de orina se derrama. La diabetes es una de las causas principales de este tipo de escape de la vejiga. Pero las mujeres que habitualmente contienen su orina por más de cinco o seis horas a la vez pueden dañar sus músculos de la vejiga y desarrollar incontinencia por rebosamiento, dice la doctora Bavendam. Un derrame cerebral, lesiones en la médula espinal, múltiple esclerosis y otros desórdenes neurológicos también pueden causar incontinencia por rebosamiento.

Es importante recordar que la incontinencia no es una enfermedad sino un síntoma de un padecimiento subyacente, dice la doctora Erickson. Por lo tanto, si usted tiene una vejiga que gotea, no asuma que necesitará usar pañales para adultos por el resto de sus días. Lo más probable es que su doctor la pueda ayudar. A veces, eso puede significar tomar drogas para contraer el músculo del esfínter o relajar el músculo de la vejiga para suprimir contracciones impropias de la vejiga. En última instancia, la cirugía puede volver a colocar una vejiga colgante en su posición natural o contraer la uretra. Pero en la mayoría de los casos, los remedios sencillos como hacer ejercicios con el músculo de la pelvis o cambiando los hábitos en su dieta o cómo usted va al baño alivian el problema. Aquí hay algunos consejos para mantenerla seca.

Lleve la cuenta. Lleve un diario urinario por una semana o dos antes de ver a un médico, sugiere el doctor Vapnek. Anote lo que usted come y bebe, cuándo va al baño y cuándo y dónde sufre escapes. ¿Estaba tosiendo, o sintió usted ganas y no llegó al baño a tiempo? El diario le ayudará a usted y a su médico a determinar su problema.

Conozca sus drogas. Algunos medicamentos, incluyendo diuréticos, antihistamínicos, sedantes, anticlorigénicos como son las drogas contra la enfermedad del movimiento (cinetosis) y remedios que se compran sin receta para el resfriado (catarro), pueden debilitar el control de la vejiga, dice el doctor Wein. Si usted está tomando alguna droga, pregunte a su doctor o farmacéutico si podrían estar contribuyendo a su problema.

Controle su dieta. Algunas mujeres reportan que consumir café, té, refrescos carbonados, endulzantes artificiales, chocolate, tomates, especias picantes y otros alimentos y bebidas empeoran su incontinencia, dice la doctora Bavendam. Si usted sospecha que un alimento está contribuyendo a su problema, trate de eliminarlo de su dieta por una semana y observe qué pasa. Si sus síntomas mejoran, continúe evitando ese alimento ya que puede haber estado irritando su vejiga.

Deje de echar humo. Las mujeres que fuman tienen 2,5 veces más probabilidades de desarrollar incontinencia que las mujeres que no encienden un cigarrillo, dice el doctor Richard Bump, profesor asociado y jefe de la División de Especialidades Ginecológicas en el Centro Médico de la Universidad Duke, en Durham, Carolina del Norte, quien estudió incontinencia en 606 mujeres fumadoras y no fumadoras. Él sospecha que el toser excesivo, común entre los fumadores, debilita los músculos del fondo de la pelvis y causa incontinencia por esfuerzo. Fumar puede también irritar los músculos de la vejiga, por lo que estos se contraen más seguido y causan escapes. Por lo tanto si usted fuma, déjelo.

Siga bebiendo. "Muchas mujeres reducirán lo que beben con la esperanza de que cuanto menos ingrese menos saldrá", dice la doctora Jeter. Pero si usted hace eso, puede resultar en que usted tenga más, no menos, probabilidades de tener problemas, porque una orina altamente concentrada irrita a la vejiga y causa que se contraiga para deshacerse de esa orina tan pronto como sea posible. Restringir líquidos también puede llevar a la deshidratación, estreñimiento, las UTI y cálculos renales. Beba por lo menos seis a ocho vasos de agua, jugos u otros líquidos por día, dice la doctora Erickson.

Use laxantes naturales. El estreñimiento puede contribuir a la incontinencia. Cuando su recto está lleno de materia fecal, puede provocar presión sobre la vejiga y aumentar el riesgo de incontinencia por urgencia. Por lo tanto asegúrese de comer una dieta con mucha fibra que incluya frutas, verduras, y panes y cereales de grano integral.

La doctora Jeter recomienda una receta de una taza de salsa de manzana, una taza de salvado de avena y un cuarto de taza de jugo de ciruelas en un bol. Agregue especias tales como canela o nuez moscada para darle sabor, y después refrigere. Introduzca esta mezcla en su dieta lentamente, aumentando a dos cucharadas cada noche según sea necesario, seguidas por un vaso de 8 onzas (237 ml) de agua. El agua es esencial, dice la doctora Jeter; sin ella, el añadir fibra puede de hecho empeorar las cosas.

Haga un doblete. Si usted siente que su vejiga no se está vaciando completamente, trate de orinar doble. Para hacerlo, permanezca sobre la taza hasta que su vejiga se sienta vacía. Entonces párese por 10 a 20 segundos, siéntese, inclínese ligeramente hacia adelante sobre sus rodillas, relájese, y espere a que su vejiga se vacíe completamente, dice la doctora Jeter.

Deshágase de unas cuantas libras. El peso excesivo ejerce presión sobre los músculos del fondo de la pelvis y aumenta el riesgo de incontinencia, dice el doctor Vapnek. "Las mujeres que tienen un sobrepeso moderado nos dicen que una diferencia de sólo cinco a siete libras (dos a tres kilos) significa la diferencia entre estar húmeda o estar seca", dice la doctora Jeter. Pregunte a su médico si perder unas pocas libras podría ayudarla.

Evite los tragos. El alcohol es un diurético que la hará producir mucha orina muy rápidamente. Así que si usted tiene un problema de incontinencia, beber alcohol puede empeorarlo, dice el doctor Rivas.

Use esos músculos. Los ejercicios *Kegel* pueden reforzar los músculos del fondo de la pelvis y reducir las posibilidades de un escape, dice la doctora Erickson. Para hacer Kegels contraiga los músculos en su recto como si usted estuviera tratando de evitar que salga el gas. Esto también hará más tensos los músculos del fondo de la pelvis. Sienta la sensación de los músculos tirando hacia arriba. Esa es la sensación que usted quiere lograr cuando hace estos ejercicios. Contraiga los músculos, manténgalos así mientras cuenta lentamente hasta cuatro, entonces relájese por otra cuenta hasta cuatro. Trate de hacer diez series de *Kegels* diariamente. A medida que estos músculos se fortalecen, aumente gradualmente el tiempo en que usted contrae hasta que pueda mantener la posición por 25 a 30 series de diez segundos cada una. El control de su vejiga debería mejorar dentro del transcurso de tres a cuatro semanas.

Como una alternativa, considere usar conos vaginales con peso. Estos conos, que son más o menos del tamaño de un tampón, están disponibles en juegos de cinco pesas que van desde tres cuartos de onza hasta tres onzas (21 g hasta 85 g). Cuando usted inserta un cono en su vagina, debe contraer los músculos del fondo de la pelvis para mantenerlo adentro. Cuando los músculos se cansan, el cono se desliza hacia afuera.

"Si usted puede mantener el cono adentro, sabe que está haciendo sus *Kegels* correctamente", dice la doctora Erickson. "Usted probablemente sea capaz de mantener el cono adentro por sólo un par de minutos al principio, pero a medida que sus músculos se hacen más fuertes, usted lo podrá mantener adentro por más y más tiempo. Yo le digo a mis pacientes que cuando ellas pueden mantener un cono adentro por 15 minutos, entonces es el momento de pasar a la pesa siguiente."

Balancee sus necesidades. El control de la vejiga a menudo es un asunto de equilibrio, dice la doctora Bavendam. Las mujeres en promedio pueden estar tres a cuatro horas sin orinar. Pero si usted orina cada hora, por ejemplo, no está expandiendo su vejiga a su capacidad máxima. Por otro lado, si usted espera más de cuatro horas, usted está poniendo una presión sobre los músculos de su vejiga a tal punto que llega un momento en que no pueden contener más la orina.

Si usted tiende a contener la orina demasiado, no vaya en contra de la naturaleza, dice la doctora Erickson. Cuando usted siente ganas de orinar, hágalo, aunque tenga que excusarse en una junta importante de negocios. Puede evitar un bochorno después.

Si usted orina más de lo que usted quisiera, trate de entrenar a su vejiga. Para hacerlo, orine al momento que se levanta por primera vez en la mañana. Entonces ponga una alarma para que suene en una hora. Cuando la alarma suene, vaya al baño, aunque no tenga ganas. Vuelva a poner la alarma para que suene en una hora. Haga esto durante cada hora en que usted está despierta durante una semana. Entonces cada semana subsecuente, agregue 30 minutos al tiempo entre visitas al baño hasta la semana siete, en que usted debería estar yendo cada cuatro horas. Si usted siente ganas de orinar antes que sea el tiempo, haga ejercicios *Kegel* o concéntrese en una tarea que la distraiga —tal como recordar el número de teléfono de diez amigas o parientes— hasta que las ganas pasen.

PROBLEMAS DE LOS PIES

Cómo arreglar su andar paso a paso

La mujer común da hasta 10.000 pasos cada día. En el transcurso de su vida, si suma esa cantidad de pasos diarios tendrá suficiente como para dar la vuelta al mundo varias veces. Desafortunadamente, mucho de ese trotar por el mundo se realiza en calzado diseñado más para ficción que para función.

Los mismos zapatos que le dan forma a nuestras piernas, nos dan estatura y nos hacen sentir jóvenes y a la moda pueden ser un talón de Aquiles para nuestros pies, causando problemas numerosos que nos acosan con dolor y envejecen nuestro espíritu. Según un estudio de 15 años realizado por el doctor Michael J. Coughlin, un cirujano ortopédico en práctica privada en Boise, Idaho, el 80 por ciento de los pacientes de cirugía en los pies son mujeres, y la mayoría de los problemas provienen de nuestros zapatos.

"No hay duda que muchos de los estilos de calzado que usan las mujeres pueden contribuir a problemas debilitantes en los pies", dice Glenn Gastwirth, D.P.M., director ejecutivo adjunto de la Asociación Médica de Podología de los Estados Unidos. "Y esos extenuantes problemas de los pies la hacen sentirse más vieja al robarle el vigor y la energía que usted tenía antes. Cuando sus pies le duelen, usted no puede llevar a cabo sus tareas diarias por lo tanto se siente mal con usted misma."

Estos problemas causan daños no solamente a nuestros pies y psiquis. "Los pies en mal estado pueden arruinar su postura, haciéndola más propensa a posibles dolores de rodillas, de caderas, de espalda y de cuello" dice Marc A.

Brenner, D.P.M., un doctor en medicina podológica en práctica privada, en Glendale, Nueva York.

Apretado no es apropiado

Así que, ¿qué tienen de malo nuestros zapatos? Mucho, dicen los expertos. "Los tacones altos pueden ser terribles para sus pies", dice Philip Sanfilippo, D.P.M., un podólogo en práctica privada en San Francisco. "Pueden causar que sus pies se deslicen hacia adelante, haciéndola propensa a juanetes y otros problemas. Y al usar tacones por demasiado tiempo, muchas mujeres desarrollan un acortamiento en sus tendones de Aquiles. Después de un tiempo, esto puede resultar en una rigidez del tendón y la incapacidad de usar zapatos de piso o andar descalza sin sentir dolor."

Los zapatos terminados en punta —sin importar la altura del tacón— son igual de malos, agrega el doctor Sanfilippo. "Estos comprimen sus dedos, lo cual puede causar callos y ampollas y agravar los juanetes." Los zapatos terminados en punta también pueden causar neuromas, nervios pellizcados rodeados por tejido fibroso que pueden volverse muy dolorosos.

Pero el problema más serio —que resulta en una cantidad estimada de $2.000 millones al año en asistencia médica, según el estudio del doctor Coughlin— es que los zapatos de las mujeres simplemente son demasiado apretados. Un estudio encontró que la mayoría de las mujeres con dolores significantes de pies usan zapatos que son dos tamaños más angostos. No es que nosotras a sabiendas tratemos de encoger nuestros zapatos tamaño B en tamaño AA. Aunque, según una encuesta de la Asociación Médica de Podología de los Estados Unidos, casi la mitad de las mujeres a quienes se les preguntó admitieron que usan zapatos incómodos a propósito por razones de apariencia, comparado con sólo el 20 por ciento de los hombres.

"Lo que pasa es que cuando envejecemos, nuestros pies se hacen más largos y anchos, un proceso llamado extendimiento", dice el doctor Sanfilippo. "Esto ocurre cuando los ligamentos en nuestros pies comienzan a distenderse y los arcos se vencen debido a la gravedad y al desgaste por uso. Esto aplana nuestros pies. Desafortunadamente, muchas personas no están conscientes de este proceso —que puede ocurrir cuando se encuentran entre los 30 y los 50 años de edad— y continúan usando el mismo tamaño de zapatos que siempre han usado. Y eso causa el problema."

El embarazo puede causar que este extendimiento ocurra antes y sea más grave. "Cuando una mujer está embarazada, ella secreta hormonas que preparan el tejido conectivo alrededor del canal del parto para dar a luz", dice el doctor Gastwirth. "Lo que esto hace es debilitar parte del tejido conectivo en otros lugares del cuerpo. Así que si usted no usa zapatos que sostengan o camina mucho descalza durante el embarazo, este extendimiento del pie puede hacerse aún más pronunciado."

Otros sospechosos comunes

Pero los zapatos no son la única razón para el dolor de pies. Además de causar que nuestros pies se extiendan, el proceso natural del envejecimiento también desgasta las almohadillas de grasa en nuestros antepies, las cuales acolchonan nuestros pasos y absorben el impacto. "Al envejecer, estas almohadillas de grasa tienden a desgastarse, exactamente como el acolchonado de una alfombra. Cuando lo instalan, es agradable y cómodo. Pero después de 20 años, ese acolchonado puede estar bastante deteriorado", dice el doctor Gastwirth. "Lo mismo sucede con sus pies: en el momento en que usted empieza a caminar, comienza el proceso de desgaste por uso que puede conducir a problemas futuros con los pies."

Otro problema común: pérdida de humedad en la piel de sus pies, lo cual ocurre frecuentemente después de los 30 años de edad y puede resultar en picazón en los pies y en hacerlos más susceptible al pie de atleta y otros tipos de hongos. Algunas mujeres, especialmente fumadoras y aquellas con la enfermedad de Raynaud, tienen problemas circulatorios que afectan a sus pies causando pérdida de sensación, particularmente en clima frío. Suzanne M. Levine, D.P.M., instructora clínica adjunta en el Colegio de Medicina Podológica de Nueva York, en la ciudad de Nueva York y autora de *My Feet Are Killing Me* (Mis pies me están matando), dice: "Cualquier pie con más de 25 años es un pie envejecido".

Pero no tiene que ser así. Con un poco de conocimiento, usted puede vencer muchos de los problemas e inyectarles nueva vida a sus cansados piececitos.

Dolor en el pie y talón: dónde buscar apoyo

Hay varias causas para esos dolores "inexplicables" en su piel o talón, y la mayoría son el resultado del uso de sus pies a largo plazo. Esto incluye arcos vencidos, rigidez en el tendón de Aquiles, fascitis plantar, lo cual es una inflamación en la planta de sus pies, y espolones en los talones, que son pequeños crecimientos de hueso que se pueden formar por el constante estiramiento de los ligamentos al saltar, caminar o correr. "Usualmente, estos problemas resultan de un abuso de sus pies", dice Richard Braver, D.P.M., médico podólogo de deportes para los equipos de la Universidad de Seton Hall, en South Orange, New Jersey, de la Universidad de Fairleigh Dickinson en Rutherford, New Jersey, y del Colegio Estatal de Montclair, en Upper Montclair, New Jersey. No importa cuál sea la causa, aquí están las soluciones.

Sosténgase. No hay forma de evitar el deterioro de las almohadillas de grasa en sus pies, pero sí puede hacer algo con el dolor que éste causa en las plantas de sus pies. "El usar plantillas (*insoles*) en sus zapatos que sean de buena calidad, que apoyen y acolchen, puede con seguridad aliviar algo de la molestia", dice el doctor Sanfilippo. Estas plantillas se encuentran disponibles en boticas y tiendas de artículos deportivos. Si el dolor se concentra en su talón, un soporte para el talón, también disponible en estas tiendas, puede ayudar a prevenir el movimiento excesivo del talón y aliviar el dolor. Pero quizás más importante que las plantillas y soporte para los talones es usar zapatos que sostengan.

Estire su pantorrilla. Para el dolor en los talones, muchas mujeres encuentran alivio al estirar el cordón del talón, o tendón de Aquiles, en la parte de atrás de su pie, dice el doctor Gilbert Wright, un cirujano ortopédico en práctica privada en Sacramento, California. Párese a unos tres pies (casi un metro)de distancia de una pared y coloque las manos sobre la pared. Inclínese hacia la pared, moviendo una pierna hacia adelante y flexionando sus codos. Su pierna trasera debe permanecer derecha, con el talón sobre el piso para que sienta un estiramiento ligero.

Dígale adiós al dolor masajeándolo. Para los espolones en los talones y la fascitis plantar, pruebe un masaje de las plantas de los pies. "Haga rodar su pie desde el talón hasta los dedos sobre un rodillo, una pelota de golf o hasta una lata de sopa", aconseja el doctor Braver. "Esto alivia el dolor al estirar los ligamentos."

Caliente sus pies por la mañana. "Si siente rigidez en su pie cuando se despierta, caliéntelo para estimular el flujo de la sangre", dice el doctor Braver. Él recomienda colocar una compresa caliente o una bolsa de agua caliente en la plantas de sus pies por unos 20 minutos.

Congélelos por la noche. A la noche, use hielo. La doctora Suzanne M. Tanner, profesora asistente en el Departamento de Ortopedia del Centro de Medicina Deportiva en la Universidad de Colorado, en Denver, sugiere colocar un paquete con hielo sobre su pie por 20 minutos, quitándolo por 20 minutos y volviéndolo a aplicar de nuevo por otros 20 minutos. Asegúrese de envolver el hielo en una toalla para prevenir una quemadura o congelación por el hielo.

Neuromas: apriete el paso

Este es exclusivamente un problema de las mujeres debido a nuestros estilos de zapatos apretados y estrechos. "Lo que pasa es que el zapato aprieta su pie aún más y pellizca un nervio", dice el doctor Braver. "Entonces, el tejido crece alrededor de este nervio pellizcado causando un dolor tremendo." Los neuromas ocurren por lo general entre el tercer y el cuarto dedo o a lo largo de la planta del pie. En casos extremos se puede necesitar la cirugía. Pero antes de que el dolor llegue tan lejos, aquí está lo que sugiere el doctor Braver.

Acolchónelos. "Cualquier cosa que se pueda hacer para sostener el arco ayudará a las mujeres con neuromas", dice el doctor Braver. "Una de las mejores cosas que usted puede hacer es comprar una almohadilla para soportar el arco (*arch support pads*), disponible en boticas, y colóquela en su zapato. Esto reduce la presión sobre el nervio."

Enfríelos. Una aplicación nocturna de un paquete con hielo reduce la hinchazón y adormece el dolor, agrega el doctor Braver. Recuerde envolver una toalla alrededor del hielo y siga la rutina de 20 minutos sí y 20 minutos no (descrita en la sección anterior sobre el dolor en el pie y talón).

Pruebe con la terapia física. "El masaje básico no ayudará, pero estimular eléctricamente el nervio y las terapias que reducen la inflamación sí lo harán", dice el doctor Braver. Usted va a necesitar la ayuda de un terapeuta físico para esto. Otra cosa que también puede aliviar el dolor son las inyecciones de esteroides aplicadas por un doctor.

Para callos: algunos remedios sin fallo

Los callos se forman de la piel muerta que se acumula en los pies a través del tiempo. Hay dos tipos de callos. El primero se forma en las áreas huesudas de sus pies, como los dedos. La fricción crea este tipo de callo a resultado de uno ponerse zapatos demasiado apretados. El segundo tipo de callo se forma en las áreas no huesudas de sus pies. Ambos tipos de callos pueden hacer que se sienta como si estuviera caminando sobre guijarros. A menos que usted sufra un dolor fuerte y constante, en cuyo caso necesita la atención de un doctor, por lo general puede remediar estos problemas por usted misma. Y aquí le decimos cómo.

Si no le viene, no lo use. "Si usted usa zapatos que le quedan bien, normalmente no tendrá callos", dice la doctora Jan P. Silfverskiold, una cirujana ortopédica en práctica privada en Wheat Ridge, Colorado, quien se especializa en problemas de los pies.

Para asegurarse de que su calzado le quede, haga que le midan ambos pies a lo largo y a lo ancho cada vez que compra zapatos, aconseja el doctor Gastwirth. Esté consciente de que la forma de su pie influye sobre cuál estilo de zapato es el mejor para comprar. Por lo general, los mejores estilos para la persona propensa a callos incluyen las sandalias y los zapatos para correr y caminar, los cuales cuentan con amplio espacio para los dedos. "Si usted necesita usar tacones", agrega el doctor Gastwirth, "compre zapatos con tacones anchos y sólidos que no excedan dos pulgadas y busque zapatos finos de un estilo cómodo que le proporcionen mayor acolchonamiento para absorber el impacto".

Aplique un humectante. Ya que los callos son el resultado de una fricción excesiva, es mejor mantener la piel suave y bastante húmeda. La doctora Levine recomienda ponerse un humectante de piel sobre los pies inmediatamente después de su baño o ducha. Si su piel ya se endureció con los callos, ráspelos con una lima de esmeril o una piedra pómez desde dos veces por semana hasta una vez al día, agrega la doctora Silfverskiold.

Tenga cuidado con los químicos. Las soluciones de venta sin receta para quitar callos (como la del *Dr. Scholl*) contienen ácido salicílico, el cual desgastará las lesiones protuberantes en sus pies. Pero tenga cuidado: estos medicamentos deben aplicarse sólo sobre el área afectada, ya que pueden quemar la piel saludable, dice la doctora Levine. Pero no use productos que contienen ácido salicílico si tiene diabetes o mala circulación, advierte la doctora Levine. Hay unas almohadillas sin medicamento disponibles (tales como los *Advanced Pain Relief Corn Cushions* del *Dr. Scholl*) que usted puede usar para proteger sus callos.

Juanetes y ampollas: burbujas dolorosas

Las ampollas son rasgones dolorosos en la piel, como una burbuja que generalmente se llena con líquido debido a una fricción excesiva. Los juanetes son protuberancias de hueso y piel engrosada en los lados de su pie justo abajo de sus dedos gordos o pequeños. Pueden ser acompañados por extendimiento del pie y desviación del dedo gordo hacia el dedo pequeño. Los zapatos apretados, la artritis y la herencia pueden todos conducir a juanetes. Como en el caso de los callos, el usar zapatos que sostengan y que le queden bien puede prevenir las ampollas y los juanetes. Pero si usted ya tiene alguno de los dos problemas, aquí está como arreglarlo.

Mímelos o reviéntelos. Las plantillas, el molesquín (tela especie de fustán) o aun pequeñas bolas de algodón metidas entre los dedos del pie pueden aliviar el martirio inmediato de las ampollas y evitar que recurran. Sin embargo, cuando las ampollas se vuelven demasiado grandes para las almohadillas, reviéntelas empujando el líquido hacia un extremo de la "burbuja" y pinchando esa área con una aguja que haya sido esterilizada con una llama o alcohol. Después de vaciar el líquido, repita el procedimiento 12 horas más tarde, y otra vez 12 horas después, para asegurarse de que ha vaciado todo el líquido, aconseja el doctor Rodney Basler, un dermatólogo y profesor asistente de medicina interna de la Universidad de Nebraska, en Omaha. No desprenda la piel, pero si ésta se ha desprendido, lave la llaga con agua oxigenada o jabón y agua, y aplique un ungüento antibiótico.

Pruebe el entablillado. El dolor de los juanetes puede aliviarse con una tablilla para enderezar los dedos que se puede obtener sin necesidad de receta en la mayoría de las farmacias. La versión más común es un tapón de caucho que "jala" el dedo gordo separándolo del segundo dedo y aliviando el dolor. A pesar de que las almohadillas de molesquín son usadas a menudo por los que sufren de juanetes, no son tan efectivas como estas tablillas.

Pie de atleta: combata los hongos

Este hongo, que deja a los pies escamosos, con picazón, agrietados y enrojecidos, puede contraerse prácticamente en cualquier parte —especialmente en las áreas templadas y húmedas como son los vestuarios deportivos (de ahí el nombre). Una vez que usted lo contrae, es difícil deshacerse del pie de atleta porque medra en sus zapatos, pero los medicamentos sin receta suelen ser el recurso preferido. Las lociones son mejores que las cremas, ya que las cremas pueden atrapar la humedad. De todos modos, la mejor forma de tratar con el pie de atleta es evitándolo. Y aquí está cómo.

Seque la humedad. Cuando se quite los calcetines (medias), frote la piel que se encuentra en el espacio entre los dedos con uno de los calcetines moviéndolo de arriba hacia abajo, aconseja el doctor Basler. Esto ayuda a mantener sus pies bien secos. Si frotar con los calcetines no es su estilo, puede usar un secador de pelo puesto en la graduación baja para secar esas zonas problemáticas. Y si usted tiene problema con el sudor después de que se secó los pies, puede rodar un antiperspirante por los pies después de la ducha, agrega él.

Cambie a menudo de zapatos. Trate de usar diferentes pares de zapatos tan a menudo como le sea posible, dice el doctor Basler. Eso es porque los zapatos están llenos de humedad después de usarlos todo un día y necesitan por lo menos un día de "descanso" para secarse. Si no tiene muchos pares de zapatos, rocíelos con *Lysol* al final del día para ayudar a desinfectarlos y a prevenir el pie de atleta.

Use bicarbonato de soda. Hay muchos polvos de venta sin receta para prevenir el pie de atleta, pero el bicarbonato de soda cumple la misma función por mucho menos dinero, dice la doctora Levine. Simplemente espolvoréelo en seco diariamente para absorber la humedad excesiva.

Uñas encarnadas: un dolor punzante

Sólo se necesita un pequeño pedazo de uña para causar un dolor muy fuerte. Una vez más, los zapatos apretados pueden contribuir a este problema al forzar la uña hacia abajo. Si la uña se le ha encarnado al punto de que usted se encuentra con un dolor constante, puede ser que necesite a un médico para que se la extirpe. Pero aquí está cómo evitar esa angustia y mantener a sus uñas sin problemas.

Córtese las uñas rectas. Olvídese de las medias lunas. La mejor forma de curar una uña encarnada y evitar que se forme una nueva es cortar la uña en línea recta no ligeramente curvada o en forma de media luna como lo hacen la mayoría de las personas, dice William Van Pelt, D.P.M., un podólogo de Houston y presidente anterior de la Academia Americana de Medicina Podológica Deportiva. Y no se la corte demasiado corta; debería cortársela un poco más arriba de la línea en donde termina su dedo. Asegúrese de remojar sus pies primero en agua templada para que las uñas se puedan cortar más fácilmente.

Vea qué encuentra en el mercado. Hay muchos productos de venta sin receta que pueden ablandar una uña encarnada y la piel a su alrededor, aliviando así el dolor. La doctora Levine recomienda el alivio para uñas encarnadas del *Dr. Scholl* y la solución *Outgrow* como dos de las marcas más comunes. Esté segura de seguir las instrucciones cuidadosamente. No use estos productos si usted tiene diabetes o problemas con su circulación porque contienen ácidos fuertes que pueden ser peligrosos para las mujeres con sensación limitada en sus pies.

Hongo de las uñas: evitarlo es lo mejor

El hongo de las uñas no duele. No dañará su salud. De hecho, nadie ni siquiera notará estas uñas de los pies gruesas y ásperas si usted no se quita los zapatos. Pero el hongo de las uñas es difícil de curar. "Hay una competencia acelerada entre las compañías farmacéuticas para encontrar una cura para el hongo de las uñas, y hasta la fecha, nadie la ha ganado", dice el doctor Braver, quien prueba productos para los pies para una de las compañías más dominantes. "Si yo supiera la solución para curar el hongo de las uñas, sería un hombre muy rico."

Algunos expertos creen que el hongo de las uñas a menudo es causado por un problema del sistema inmune y agravado por la humedad. Por ello, mantener sus pies limpios y secos es esencial para contener el hongo de las uñas. Mientras que curarlo es difícil y requiere de la atención de un médico, especialmente si sus pies tienden a sudar, aquí está cómo evitarlo en primer lugar.

Déjelos respirar. "Una forma de prevenir el hongo de las uñas es asegurándose de que sus zapatos sean lo suficientemente grandes como para que sus dedos tengan espacio para respirar", dice el doctor Braver. "Los corredores, bailarines y otros atletas contraen a menudo hongo de las uñas porque ocasionan un microtrauma en los dedos de sus pies al golpearlos contra el frente de sus zapatos. Si puede, use zapatos más sueltos."

Póngase un antiperspirante. El sudor empeora las cosas, así que prevenga un problema potencial tratando a sus pies como axilas —use una cantidad pequeña de desodorante de esfera todos los días, dice el doctor Braver. "Hay un producto bajo receta llamado *Drysol* hecho especialmente para este fin. Es como usar un antiperspirante para las axilas mucho más fuerte."

Olor de pies: cómo vencerlo

Si usted se lava los pies y cambia los calcetines (medias) diariamente y sus pies todavía huelen, usted no es la única. Aquí está qué hacer con el olor de pies.

Tenga pies saludables. "El olor de pies está relacionado por lo general con una infección fungosa; los pies sudorosos y la piel llena de granos o pelándose son las señales usuales de advertencia", dice el doctor Braver. "Trate entonces el olor de pies como lo haría con cualquier problema de hongos, con una loción fungicida como *Lotrimin*, que está disponible sin receta."

Pulverice el olor. Las otras maneras para matar el olor son aplicar *Lysol* a sus zapatos y un antiperspirante a sus pies, agrega el doctor Braver.

Verrugas plantares: un golpe bajo

Como otras verrugas, estas cosas desagradables de un cuarto de pulgada que se forman en las plantas de sus pies están causadas por un virus, que probablemente se contrae al caminar descalza. El problema con las verrugas plantares sin embargo, es que la presión al caminar las aplana hasta que se cubren de callos. Cuando los callos se endurecen, usted podrá sentir el golpe bajo de la verruga planteres, que es similar a caminar sobre un guijarro. "Cerca del 13 por ciento de todas las verrugas plantares desaparecen por sí solas, sin tratamiento alguno", dice el doctor Braver. "Sin embargo, se ha visto que varias cepas del virus de las verrugas se extienden rápidamente." Él aconseja un tratamiento agresivo para deshacerse de estas verrugas antes de que esto suceda. Pruebe estas medidas.

Cómase sus verduras. "Hay evidencia considerable de que la vitamina A ayuda a proteger contra las verrugas", dice el doctor Braver. Mientras que la vitamina A en forma de suplemento puede ser tóxica, usted puede obtener esta protección adicional comiendo más verduras y frutas amarillas o anaranjadas tales como las zanahorias, las calabazas, *sweet potatoes* (camotes, boniatos), el cantaloup, los albaricoques y los nectarinos, así como las verduras verdes hojosas como la espinaca.

Liquídelas. El usar un líquido para quitar verrugas o callos (tal como *Occlusal*) puede deshacerse de sus verrugas plantares, dice el doctor Braver. Estos productos están disponibles en boticas y no se necesita receta.

No ande descalza. La mejor forma de evitar verrugas plantares es usando zapatos o sandalias, dice el doctor Braver. "Es importante mantener las plantas de sus pies cubiertas, especialmente si anda usted alrededor de piscinas u otras áreas húmedas que atraen a los virus." Si un miembro de su familia tiene una verruga plantar, evite que se extienda al mantener los pisos y las duchas limpias y desinfectadas.

Vea a un doctor. Si usted ya ha tratado con las medidas anteriores por seis semanas y nota poca mejoría, o si los problemas se empeoran, vea a su podólogo para que la atienda. El tratamiento profesional puede incluir el congelamiento o quemadura de las verrugas o los métodos quirúrgicos de extirpación tradicionales o por láser.

PROBLEMAS DENTALES

Los dientes pueden durar para siempre

La cámara hace clic en una fiesta familiar, y sus labios se cierran de un golpe como platillos musicales. ¿Por qué está usted saludando al mundo con una pequeña sonrisa de Mona Lisa cuando realmente tiene ganas de mostrar una sonrisa de oreja a oreja?

Pocas cosas pueden avejentar la apariencia de una mujer como los dientes en malas condiciones. Cuando usted era joven, un poco de negligencia dental pudo haber significado una tapadura ocasional. Pero a medida que usted envejece, ignorar sus dientes puede traerle problemas más serios, como por ejemplo la enfermedad periodontal. Y si no la detiene pronto, un abandono a largo plazo puede eventualmente causar que usted pierda completamente sus dientes.

Pero, ¿y si usted siempre ha estado consciente acerca del cuidado dental? Aun así, la edad trae consigo cambios en la apariencia y salud de su sonrisa. Años de masticar desgastan la superficie de sus dientes y de hecho los acortan. Las encías se retraen con la edad y el uso. Y aun el cepillar cuidadoso tiene sus desventajas si usted usó la técnica incorrecta por décadas. El frotar con fuerza desgasta el recubrimiento de esmalte traslúcido de tal manera que el material amarillento debajo, llamado dentina, empieza a dejarse ver. Muchas mujeres por lo demás preciosas y tan jóvenes como de 40 años de edad están frustradas debido a sus dientes de aspecto manchado.

A medida que usted envejece, sus dientes también van a mostrar las señales reveladoras de años de indulgencia. El café, el vino tinto, el tabaco y las tinturas de alimentos pueden penetrar en las grietas microscópicas en el esmalte de los dientes, resultando en manchas cafés o amarillentas.

Los enemigos de su sonrisa

Cuando usted era una adolescente, la temida cuenta de caries debe haber estado presente en su mente cuando iba al dentista. Pero ahora, su dentista le dirá

313

Enfrentando el miedo

Si usted prefiere enfrentarse con Drácula que con el dentista, no se crea la única que piensa así —muchas mujeres, aunque sean adultas hechas y derechas, temen estar sentadas en esa silla bajo esa luz fuerte.

Temores absurdos acerca de la odontología abundan, dice Mark Slovin, D.D.S., director de la Clínica de Fobia Dental en la Universidad Estatal de Nueva York, en Stony Brook. Pero muchos de estos temores son infundados, añade. La odontología moderna, aunque no siempre completamente indolora, no es razón para pánico. Si a usted le entra el pánico, aquí le decimos cómo calmarse.

Comunique su miedo. Si usted le tiene miedo al taladro, comparta sus temores. "Un buen dentista es capaz de entender los sentimientos y pensamientos de un paciente", dice Arthur A. Weiner, D.M.D., profesor clínico asociado en la Escuela de Medicina Dental de la Universidad Tufts, en Boston. No sea tímida con respecto a probar y comparar entre varios dentistas hasta encontrar a aquél con quien se siente cómoda.

Pida una demostración. Pida a su dentista que le explique paso por paso los procedimientos desconocidos y que le muestre como usaría él los instrumentos. Pregúntele qué tipo de sensaciones puede esperar mientras le están haciendo el trabajo.

Planee comunicarse. Pídale a su dentista que la ponga en alerta antes de un pinchazo o una presión para que entretanto pueda relajarse, dice el doctor Weiner. Y pónganse de acuerdo respecto a las señales con la mano que usará para avisarle cuando quiera usted sentarse por un minuto, descansar o enjuagarse.

Use técnicas de relajamiento. Trate de respirar profundamente, concentrarse en una imagen agradable como por ejemplo un día en la playa, o escuchar sus melodías favoritas en unos audífonos para tranquilizar su estadía en el sillón, dice el doctor Slovin.

Pida más alivio para el dolor. Si usted necesita anestesia adicional, pídala. Los sedantes no son una solución permanente, pero pueden hacer que le permitan pasar por un procedimiento que necesita.

Busque ayuda profesional. Si su temor es abrumador llame a la sociedad dental de su estado para que le ayuden a encontrar una clínica de fobia dental cerca suyo. O pídale a su dentista que le recomiende un consejero sicológico que esté familiarizado con fobias dentales.

que el mayor enemigo de su boca no son las caries sino la enfermedad de las encías.

Hay un pequeño foso alrededor de cada diente que forma un pequeño resquicio entre el diente y la encía. Cuando las bacterias entran y permanecen allí causan inflamación la cual, al paso del tiempo, profundiza los resquicios y los hace bolsas. Cuando la inflamación fermenta, los huesos, las encías y el tejido conector pueden carcomerse, dejándola con menos base para sostener a los dientes en su lugar. Toda esa fermentación también puede ser causa de dolor y sangre así como de mal aliento.

El otro enemigo son las caries (sí, todavía cuentan). Las caries empiezan cuando una capa pegajosa llamada sarro (placa) se forma en sus dientes, atrapando bacterias y ocasionando descomposición. Aunque usted a lo mejor no tuvo muchas caries nuevas en sus primeros años adultos, no suelte ese cepillo. Muchas mujeres acercándose a la madurez empiezan a tener caries junto con la enfermedad en las encías. Eso es porque al retraerse las encías con la edad, la raíz (que no tiene el esmalte protector) queda expuesta a la descomposición.

Un plan diario a pedir de boca

Si usted quiere conservar una sonrisa deslumbrante y saludable a medida que envejece, va a requerir un nuevo compromiso de su parte a un cuidado preventivo diario. Eso puede significar gastar más tiempo que el acostumbrado cepillándose y usando el hilo dental —y volverse más consciente de los alimentos que ingiere. El primer paso es ponerse al corriente con los últimos métodos de limpieza y mantener una visión informada sobre lo que está metiendo en su boca.

Cepíllese bien y a menudo. El cepillarse es su defensa número uno contra los problemas dentales a medida que usted envejece. "Como mínimo, asegúrese de cepillarse después del desayuno y antes de irse a la cama en la noche", dice Hazel Harper, D.D.S., profesora asociada de odontología comunitaria en la Universidad Howard, en Washington, D.C., y vicepresidenta de la Asociación Dental Nacional. Por supuesto, es mejor cepillarse después de cada comida —con la técnica correcta.

Si usted lo hace correctamente, cepillarse remueve las bacterias y sarro responsables de tantas aflicciones dentales. Cepillarse correctamente, dice la doctora Harper, quiere decir sostener el cepillo con el mango en la palma de su mano y su pulgar extendido actuando como una abrazadera. Esta forma de sostener con la palma y el pulgar inclina el cepillo a un ángulo, de tal manera que las cerdas alcanzan las encías y justo abajo de las encías así como las superficies de los dientes. Haga vibrar el cepillo suavemente con un movimiento corto de ida y vuelta, cubriendo sólo tres dientes a la vez. Entonces, con un giro de la muñeca, pase el cepillo sobre los lados de los dientes para arrastrar los desperdicios y bacterias lejos de la línea de las encías. Termine cepillándose la lengua —el mejor antídoto contra el mal aliento, dice la doctora Harper.

Use el cepillo correcto. Deshágase de esa cosa con copete duro y raída en su portacepillos, dice la doctora Harper. Usted necesita usar un cepillo de cerdas

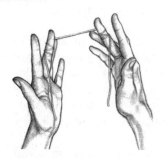 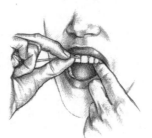 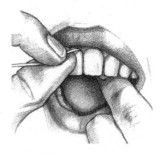

Corte cerca de 18 pulgadas (46 cm) de hilo dental y enrede la mayor parte alrededor de un dedo medio. Enrede el resto alrededor del dedo medio de su otra mano.

Usando sus pulgares y dedos índices, deslice cerca de una pulgada de hilo dental tenso entre sus dientes. Curve con cuidado el hilo dental en forma de C alrededor del diente al nivel de la línea de la encía.

Deslice con cuidado el hilo dental para arriba y para abajo entre los dientes y la encía, asegurándose que llegue abajo de la línea de la encía. Repita con el resto de sus dientes usando secciones limpias de hilo dental.

suaves, y debería reponerlo cada tres meses —antes, si las cerdas empiezan a desgastarse, dice ella.

Escoja el dentífrico apropiado. Cualquier dentífrico con el sello de aprobación de la Asociación Dental de los Estados Unidos servirá con el mínimo de abrasión. Si usted tiene tendencia a que se le forme sarro, trate con un dentífrico para controlar el sarro. El sarro se endurece y se siente como un recubrimiento áspero sobre los dientes, dice Richard Price, D.D.S., instructor clínico de odontología en la Escuela de Odontología Henry Goldman de la Universidad de Boston. "Estos dentífricos reducen la cantidad de sarro que se le forma, y el sarro que se forme se suavizará y será más fácil de remover", dice él.

Mueva los hilos. Use el hilo dental diariamente para estar segura de una limpieza completa y de encías saludables, dice el doctor Price. Las cerdas del cepillo simplemente no pueden meterse en las hendiduras alrededor de los dientes. No importa qué clase de hilo dental usa usted —encerado, sin encerar, con sabor; simplemente escoja con el que usted sienta más cómoda, dice él.

Si usted tiene un poco de artritis en sus dedos, una boca pequeña o un problema de destreza, trate de usar el hilo dental con una sola mano. Envuelva el hilo dental alrededor de los dedos pulgar e índice de una mano, como si usted estuviera formando una pequeña honda, dice el doctor Price. O pregúntele a su dentista acerca de dispositivos para usar el hilo dental.

No se pegue a ciertas comidas. Los alimentos que se adhieren a sus dientes son los alimentos que causan caries, dicen los expertos. Pero es difícil estar seguro de qué comestibles en las parejas siguientes son más pegajosos: ¿caramelos o galletas? ¿Helados de crema con *fudge* o pan? ¿Higos secos o cereal de avena inflada? Créalo o no, galletas, pan y cereal son los más posibles de adherirse por períodos largos. Su mejor defensa es cepillarse después de cada bocadillo (merienda o *snack*), azucarado o no. Pero si no puede usted llegar pronto a un cepillo, lo mejor es evitar los alimentos pegajosos.

Confórmese con el queso. Es una vieja costumbre en algunas culturas servir queso a la hora del postre, y esto puede ayudar a eliminar caries cuando usted no se puede cepillar los dientes inmediatamente después de una comida. Unos cuantos estudios indican que con ciertos quesos, especialmente los duros y añejos como es el *cheddar* y el *Monterey Jack*, pueden reducirse las bacterias causantes de caries. Sólo una pequeña rebanada servirá —y no agregará mucha grasa o colesterol a su dieta.

Enjuáguelos. Independientemente de lo que usted comió, si no se puede cepillar enseguida, lo mejor que puede hacer en su lugar es encontrar un lavabo y enjuagarse los dientes con un trago de agua, dice Andrew M. Lewis, D.D.S., un dentista en práctica privada en Beverly Hills. Al enjuagar los dientes con agua se removerá la mayor parte de los desperdicios y también diluirá los ácidos formados por las partículas de alimentos.

Cómo cuidar sus dientes en casa

Si su dentista ha notado caries nuevas o indicios de enfermedad en las encías, no pierda las esperanzas con sus dientes —hágase cargo. Hay muchas cosas que usted puede hacer para cambiar la dirección de la marea a cualquier edad. Pruebe estos tratamientos en casa, bajo la guía de su dentista.

Use un enjuague de fluoruro. "Si usted es propensa a las caries, use un enjuague de fluoruro sin receta cada noche", dice el doctor Lewis. "Lo que usted quiere hacer es enjuagarse y escupirlo para que éste sea lo último en su boca antes de irse a dormir." El fluoruro de hecho remineraliza los dientes, haciéndolos más fuertes y menos propensos a caries y sensibilidad de las raíces.

Enchufe su cepillo de dientes. Trate un cepillo eléctrico si tiene problemas para cepillarse manualmente a conciencia o si tiene problemas con las encías, dice la doctora Harper. La vibración suave de la cabeza del cepillo da un masaje a las encías al mismo tiempo que limpia los dientes, dice ella. Y la investigación en la Escuela de Odontología de la Universidad de Alabama, en Birmingham ha comprobado que los cepillos de dientes eléctricos pueden reducir significativamente la gingivitis. Antes de irse de compras, consulte con su dentista. Muchos profesionales recomiendan la nueva generación de cepillos de dientes eléctricos, con cerdas que giran en lugar de vibrar. Hay varias marcas a la venta incluyendo *Interplak* y el *Braun Oral-B Plaque Remover* (removedor de sarro).

Pruebe un irrigador. Un irrigador oral como es el *Water Pik* puede ayudar a limpiar los desperdicios entre los dientes y debajo de las encías, pero úselo con cuidado, dice la doctora Harper. "Algunos irrigadores no están ajustados correctamente, y el flujo de agua es lo suficientemente fuerte como para causar daño en el tejido de sus encías", dice. Haga más lento el flujo si siente sus encías lastimadas o irritadas después de usar su irrigador.

La verdad sobre las tapaduras

Su dentista le dice que tiene unas cuantas caries. "¿Cómo?", le dice usted. "Qué, ¿está usted bromeando? Yo ya estoy muy vieja para tener caries."

Lo siento mucho, mi amiga, pero usted nunca está muy vieja para tener caries.

Muchas mujeres tienen caries en una edad bien avanzada, dice Richard Price, D.D.S., instructor clínico de odontología en la Escuela de Odontología Henry Goldman de la Universidad de Boston. Una razón es que los empastes o tapaduras antiguos se desgastan. Aunque algunos de ellos pueden durar décadas, la vida promedio de una tapadura de plata es de nueve años. Después de allí, tienden a desportillarse, resquebrajarse y desgastarse.

"Son solamente partes de repuesto", dice el doctor Price. "Cada vez que a usted le taladran y tapan un diente, éste tendrá que ser taladrado y tapado por el resto de su vida. Es como cuando una garantía caduca."

Algunas veces las mujeres adultas, aun las campeonas en cepillarse y usar hilo dental, también pueden tener caries nuevas. El lugar más común para estos agujeros negros es en la base de los dientes, donde las encías se han retraído con la edad exponiendo las raíces sensibles a la descomposición, dice el doctor Price. Si usted necesita una tapadura —ya sea un repuesto o una nueva— alístese para escoger entre un

Ayuda de los profesionales

No hay fervor alguno en el lavabo de su baño que pueda substituir los exámenes dentales regulares, dice la doctora Harper. Para hacer que sus dientes se vean más jóvenes, vea a un higienista dental dos veces al año para limpieza y a su dentista por lo menos una vez al año para un examen.

Su primera parada es la silla del higienista para una limpieza profesional que quite el sarro, dice el doctor Lewis. Una vez que sus dientes estén super limpios, su dentista examinará su boca. Si le están apareciendo más caries de lo acostumbrado, es posible que usted reciba un tratamiento de fluoruro en el consultorio y un enjuague o jalea de fluoruro para usar en la casa. Pero antes, su dentista tapará las caries.

Y más rápidamente de lo que usted podría esperar. Con los taladros nuevos y más rápidos, su dentista usualmente puede tapar una carie en unos 15 minutos, un procedimiento que tomaba una hora hace 20 años, dice la doctora Harper. ¿Y qué tal el dolor? Si está volviendo a pasar por su mente la escena de tortura número de materiales alternos. La plata es por lejos la más común, porque es durable y asequible. La plata está mezclada con el mercurio lo que hace que sea más fácil para darle forma. De vez en cuando ha surgido la pregunta de que si este mercurio, un metal venenoso, podría filtrarse al cuerpo. Algunas mujeres incluso han hecho que les quiten tapaduras en buenas condiciones debido a ese miedo al mercurio.

Eso es una lastima.

Sí, algo de mercurio se desprende de las tapaduras cuando usted mastica pero son cantidades minúsculas. Todavía menos es lo que realmente absorbe su cuerpo. "No hay nada de qué preocuparse", dice Joel M. Boriskin, D.D.S., jefe de la División de Odontología en el Centro Médico del Condado de Alameda, en Oakland, California. Un número de estudios midieron el desprendimiento de mercurio de las tapaduras de plata y llegaron a la misma conclusión: no hay razón para preocuparse a menos que usted tenga 1.000 tapaduras en su boca.

Pero solamente porque la plata es segura, no quiere decir que siempre sea lo mejor. El oro, aunque caro, es extremadamente fuerte y especialmente bueno para caries muy grandes. Las tapaduras hechas de porcelana, cuarzo o acrílico, aunque no tan durables como las de metal, pueden ser preferibles para tapaduras más visibles, ya que se les puede dar color para hacer juego con sus propios dientes.

dental en la película *Marathon Man* (Hombre de la maratón) no se preocupe, no necesitará usted volver a vivir algo tan horrible. Los procedimientos dentales modernos están años luz adelante de sus peores recuerdos dentales.

En raras ocasiones, usted necesitará un tratamiento de conducto para extirpar la pulpa dental o nervio de un diente cariado y llenar el agujero. A pesar de su reputación dolorosa, un tratamiento de conducto hecho correctamente no puede ser más incómodo que cualquier otro procedimiento dental, dice el doctor Lewis.

Para una enfermedad avanzada de las encías, su dentista puede mandarla con un periodontólogo o un especialista en enfermedades de las encías. El tratamiento puede incluir antibióticos orales, ungüentos antibacteriales para exprimirse en las bolsas de las encías o, en casos graves, extirpación quirúrgica de la parte de la encía infectada o hueso enfermo.

Y si las manchas o dientes torcidos son su mayor problema dental, un dentista cosmético puede ayudarla. Blanquear manchas y una variedad de otras técnicas pueden restaurar la juventud y belleza de su sonrisa.

PROBLEMAS DIGESTIVOS

Cómo calmar el dolor y los rugidos

Como si las barras de chocolate y los chicharrones no nos hubieran causado suficientes problemas en todo este tiempo, ya que nos engordan, ahora estamos teniendo dudas acerca de los alimentos comunes como las cebollas, los tomates y aun las fresas. ¿Dónde está el problema?

Aparentemente, donde menos pensaba —su tracto digestivo.

Usted puede entender por qué los hombres tienen problemas digestivos; todo lo que tiene que hacer es verlos comer. Pero últimamente, usted se sorprendió a sí misma agarrando el *Di-Gel* o el *Pepto-Bismol* un poco más seguido. ¿Por qué? Por el gas. O por la acidez. O por sentirse hinchada. O por diarrea o estreñimiento. O varios de estos problemas.

Bueno, usted está en buena compañía.

"Al igual que toma más tiempo recuperarse de un resfriado (catarro) o de una lesión cuando usted envejece, lo mismo sucede con su sistema digestivo. Todo parece como que va más despacio, y los mecanismos de reparación ya no son los mismos que solían ser antes", dice el doctor William B. Ruderman, presidente del Departamento de Gastroenterología en la Clínica Cleveland de Florida, en Fort Lauderdale. "Usted no puede tolerar ciertos alimentos o los efectos del alcohol tan bien como antes. Esto ciertamente le hace sentir su propia mortalidad."

Todos esos eructos, rugidos y otros movimientos internos no pasan solamente en su tracto digestivo. "Es posible que vacile en tomar un autobús o salir afuera, ya que puede ser que tenga que ir al baño. A lo mejor ya no va a ciertos restaurantes porque no puede comer ciertos alimentos", dice el doctor Devendra Mehta, un gastroenterólogo y profesor asistente de pediatría en el Hospital Universitario de Hahnemann, en Filadelfia. "Esto puede ser muy penoso en cualquier edad. Pero cuando usted está joven y tiene estos problemas, le perturba su vida."

Solo porque sus entrañas están estropeadas, no significa que tienen que permanecer así. Cualquiera que sea el problema, aquí está cómo arreglarlo.

Estreñimiento: póngase en movimiento

Si el estreñimiento nunca le ha dado molestias, espere unos cuantos años. "El estreñimiento se vuelve más común a medida que usted envejece", dice el doctor Jorge Herrera, profesor asociado de medicina en el Colegio de Medicina de la Universidad de Alabama del Sur, en Mobile. "Por una parte, al envejecer, la mayoría de las personas tienden a comer menos y se vuelven menos activas." Y muchas de las medicinas que la gente tiende a tomar cuando envejece para condiciones tales como enfermedad del corazón y diabetes, también causan estreñimiento, dice el doctor Herrera.

Sin embargo, a cualquier edad, el estreñimiento la puede hacer sentirse más vieja. Sea que usted tenga que hacer esfuerzos para mover sus intestinos o que simplemente no tenga ganas, el estreñimiento ocupa su mente con pensamientos de lo que usted no puede hacer, y debido a eso su cuerpo puede no sentirse con ganas de hacer mucho. La mayoría de las mujeres mayores de los 30 años de edad pueden esperar por lo menos un encuentro ocasional con el estreñimiento —y más al hacerse mayores. Pero aquí está cómo mantener los problemas al mínimo, no importa cuál sea su edad.

Cuide lo que come. "Si usted come la típica dieta occidental con muchos alimentos procesados, ésta la llevará al estreñimiento", dice el doctor Mehta. "Pero una dieta con mucha fibra que se concentre en bastantes frutas frescas y verduras es lo más importante que usted puede hacer para evitar el estreñimiento, especialmente al hacerse mayor."

Los expertos dicen que usted necesita por lo menos cinco porciones al día para alcanzar el mínimo recomendado de 25 gramos de fibra —cerca del doble de lo que el típico estadounidense consume. Además de las verduras y frutas frescas, las buenas fuentes de fibra dietética incluyen panes y cereales de grano integral, pastas, arroz integral, frijoles (habichuelas) y salvado.

Haga ejercicio. Cualquier tipo de ejercicio acelera el tiempo de tránsito gastrointestinal, el tiempo que toman los alimentos para ir de su boca a través del estómago e intestinos. Pero los investigadores en la Universidad de Maryland College Park encontraron que las personas que se someten a programas de entrenamiento de fuerza pueden mejorar el tiempo de tránsito de su deposición en un 56 por ciento en comparación con sus días antes de levantar pesas. Parece ser que la contracción de los músculos abdominales que ocurre al levantar pesas "exprime" los desperdicios más rápidamente a través de los intestinos. Los investigadores creen que cualquier tipo de ejercicio tiene un efecto en la motilina, una hormona gastrointestinal que está relacionada con el tiempo de tránsito más rápido. El ejercicio también mejora el flujo de la sangre a los intestinos, lo cual mejora también la evacuación.

Tome agua. "Una razón por la cual el estreñimiento es más común al envejecerse, es que generalmente, mientras mayor se hace una persona, menos bebe", dice el doctor Mehta. "Y mientras menos bebe usted, más duro y menos frecuente es su materia fecal." Aun cuando no tenga un problema de estreñimiento, usted se mantendrá sin problemas si bebe por lo menos seis vasos de agua o alguna otra bebida no alcohólica cada día.

Mientras tanto, trate de limitar su consumo de café, té y alcohol. Aun cuando las bebidas cafeinadas de hecho hacen más rápido el tiempo de tránsito de su evacuación (el alcohol no tiene ningún efecto), estás bebidas son diuréticas y pueden deshidratarla, y usted necesita líquido en su sistema para ayudar a mover el intestino. Y aquellas con estreñimiento frecuente deberían evitar la leche, el queso y otros productos lácteos, los cuales contienen caseína, una proteína insoluble que tiende a atorar su tracto intestinal.

Acidez: apague el fuego

Usted probablemente ya sabe cómo se siente cuando tiene acidez: pésima. Parece que nada le puede quitar su alegría —por no mencionar su apetito— más rápidamente que tener que descansar después de cada comida hasta que el dolor mengua, o tener que supervisar casi cada mordida que da para prevenir el dolor.

La acidez ocurre cuando los ácidos estomacales, en un proceso llamado reflujo, salpican hacia arriba dentro del esófago, dice Sheila Rodríguez, Ph.D., directora del laboratorio gastrointestinal de la Fundación para Investigación Digestiva de Oklahoma, en la ciudad de Oklahoma. Comer muy rápidamente o demasiado es una causa común, pero hartarse no es la única razón de este padecimiento tan común que se produce después de comer. La acidez también puede ser el primer síntoma de otras condiciones, como por ejemplo la gastritis, una inflamación en el revestimiento del estómago.

"No es que el proceso natural de envejecer contribuya por sí a la acidez, pero la condición parece ser un problema mayor al hacerse usted más vieja", dice el doctor Mehta. Una razón es que hay una asociación clara entre la acidez y el sobrepeso —y la mayoría de nosotras hemos puesto algunas cuantas libras durante los últimos años.

Pero otra razón, menos obvia, es las bacterias. Las mismas bacterias —*Helicobacter pylori*— que causan úlceras se han vinculado con síntomas de acidez en muchas mujeres, dice el doctor Mehta. También, después de los 40 años de edad nuestros músculos esofágicos empiezan a debilitarse, lo cual puede contribuir al reflujo. Pero no importa la razón, aquí está cómo apagar el fuego de la acidez.

Coma cantidades más pequeñas. Muchas mujeres con problemas de acidez encuentran que comer menos más veces ayuda a extinguir el incendio interno. Cuando usted come cuatro o cinco comidas más pequeñas en lugar de tres comidas grandes al día, su estómago produce menos ácido, dice el doctor Frank Hamilton, director del Programa de Enfermedades Gastrointestinales en los Institutos Nacionales de Salud, en Bethesda, Maryland.

Pásesela con agua. Beber grandes cantidades de agua —especialmente con las comidas— ayuda a lavar los ácidos del estómago de la superficie del esófago mandándolos de vuelta a su estómago, dice el doctor Ronald L. Hoffman, un médico en la ciudad de Nueva York y autor de *Seven Weeks to a Settled Stomach* (Siete semanas para un estómago estable).

Conozca a los infractores. Ciertos alimentos tienen mayores probabilidades que otros de despertar los síntomas de la acidez. De acuerdo con la doctora Rodríguez, las cebollas, el chocolate y las mentas relajan el esfínter esofágico inferior, el cual permite que los ácidos de su estómago se suban. Las frutas cítricas como son las naranjas y toronjas, así como los productos de tomate, café y alimentos fritos o grasosos, también pueden causar dificultades porque pueden irritar el revestimiento esofágico, agrega el doctor Hamilton.

Duerma inclinada. Si seguido tiene problemas de acidez, coloque bloques de madera o concreto bajo la cabecera de su cama para dormir inclinada, aconseja el doctor William Lipshultz, jefe de gastroenterología del Hospital de Pennsylvania, en Filadelfia. Al elevar la cabecera de su cama 6 pulgadas (15 cm), es difícil para los ácidos estomacales fluir. Eso es porque tendrían que ir cuesta arriba.

Si usted debe acostarse derecha, descansar sobre su lado izquierdo produce menos acidez, dice el doctor Leo Katz, un gastroenterólogo en el Colegio Médico Jefferson de la Universidad Thomas Jefferson, en Filadelfia. Al hacer pruebas, él encontró que las personas que comían las mismas comidas que producen la acidez, usualmente tienen más acidez cuando descansan sobre su lado derecho comparado con su lado izquierdo. "Pensamos que esto tienen algo que ver con la anatomía del estómago y la gravedad", dice.

Intolerancia a la lactosa: cómo vencerla

¿Se atreve a tomar lácteos? Quizás no. Tanto como el 70 por ciento de la población mundial tiene algún síntoma de intolerancia a la lactosa, lo que significa que estas personas experimentan efectos adversos a la leche, helados de crema y otros productos lácteos. Los síntomas incluyen hincharse, gas, retortijones de estómago y diarrea, los cuales pueden restringir sus actividades y dificultar su estilo de vida. Además de hacerla sentirse más vieja, los síntomas a menudo empeoran con la edad.

Pero aproximadamente a los ocho años de edad, muchas de nosotras empezamos a perder una enzima llamada lactasa, que nos ayuda a digerir la lactosa, el azúcar que hace que la leche sepa dulce. Sin la lactasa, gran parte de la lactosa pasa por su sistema digestivo sin digerir, causando posiblemente que su colon tenga espasmos y produzca gas. "Para los 20 años de edad, las personas con intolerancia a la lactosa prácticamente pierden la capacidad de digerir la leche, dice el doctor Herrera.

La intolerancia a la lactosa varía de persona a persona. Algunas mujeres pueden sufrir una incomodidad ligera después de muchos lácteos, mientras que otras pueden tener problemas mayores con sólo un sorbo o dos de leche. Por ello, controlar su tolerancia individual y mantenerse dentro de esos límites es la mejor manera de evitar problemas. Mientras que hay muchos productos libres de lactosa —usted los encontrará en la sección de lácteos de su supermercado— aquí está cómo usted puede tomar sus lácteos (reales) y disfrutarlos.

Arrebate el chocolate. Cierta investigación sugiere que el cacao hace más lento el vaciamiento del estómago, lo cual reduce el ritmo al que la lactosa llega al colon, dice Dennis A. Savaiano, Ph.D., profesor de ciencia de alimentos y nutrición y decano asociado en el Colegio de Ecología Humana de la Universidad de Minnesota, en St. Paul. Así que si toma leche de chocolate o come helado de crema de chocolate usted puede evitar, si no disminuir, los síntomas. Si usted prepara su propia leche de chocolate, use leche baja en grasa y cacao en polvo, los cuales no tienen grasa; trate de no usar almíbar (sirope) de chocolate, porque éste contiene mucha grasa.

Combine las comidas con los lácteos. Algunas personas encuentran que pueden estar libres de los síntomas si toman sus productos lácteos con las comidas. Eso es debido a que teniendo algún alimento en su estómago hace más lenta la liberación de lactosa en sus intestinos, dice el doctor Douglas B. McGill, profesor de medicina en la Escuela Médica Mayo de la Clínica Mayo, en Rochester, Minnesota. Aun así, no es aconsejable llenarse de varios productos lácteos en una sola comida.

Escoja el yogur correcto. El yogur puede ser un producto de la leche que usted puede comer sin preocuparse. Pero no asuma que todos los productos de yogur son iguales. "Algunas marcas comerciales agregan productos de leche, que pueden causar problemas", dice el doctor Mehta. "Lo mejor es hacer su propio yogur." Usted puede encontrar máquinas de hacer yogur en las tiendas de artículos para cocinar.

Si está comprando yogur, asegúrese de que escoge una marca cuya etiqueta dice que contiene culturas vivas activas. "Tan pronto como las culturas del yogur pasan al intestino, se vuelven activas y empiezan a descomponer la lactosa", dice el doctor McGill. Lo sentimos, pero el yogur helado no ayuda, ya que tiene muy pocas bacterias para ser de utilidad.

La enfermedad diverticular: evítele las molestias a su colon

Está bien que actúe refinadamente en la mesa, pero cuando usted está comiendo así, no cuente con que su colon va a mantener sus buenos modales. Después de décadas de vivir de alimentos refinados y procesados y otros comestibles con poca fibra, y tratando de pasar la materia fecal dura y seca que estos producen, las paredes del colon se debilitan y a menudo causan la creación de pequeños sacos llamados divertículos. Aunque esta condición, llamada diverticulosis, no va causar ningún síntoma para mucha gente, algunas personas pueden desarrollar gas, calambres, indigestión grave o aun estreñimiento o diarrea.

Ya que la diverticulosis es el resultado de descuidar por años las necesidades de su colon, usualmente nos ataca después de los 40 años de edad —pero puede hacer que se sienta décadas más vieja. Algunas mujeres cambian sus dietas para evitar alimentos como palomitas de maíz (*popcorn*), semillas y nueces, ya que éstas pueden quedar atrapadas en los sacos y causar dolor. Otras mujeres, impedidas por el dolor abdominal, reducen sus actividades físicas o hacen otros cambios en su estilo de vida.

Cerca del 5 por ciento de los casos se convierten en la peor de las situaciones, cuando los divertículos se rompen y causan infecciones serias o cuando sangran, lo cual puede resultar en una hemorragia significativa. Sin embargo, la mayoría de las que tenemos diverticulosis podemos controlar el problema por nosotras mismas y mantenernos tan jóvenes como deberíamos sentirnos. Aquí está cómo.

Coma a granel. Coma más verduras, más frutas frescas, más granos integrales. Si usted no come mucha fibra vaya aumentando la cantidad de a poco. "Comer demasiada fibra muy pronto puede hacer que los síntomas empeoren", dice el doctor Alex Aslan, un gastroenterólogo en práctica privada en Fairfield, California. Comience por agregar unas cuantas porciones pequeñas de alimentos ricos en fibra —frutas, verduras, pastas, arroz integral, frijoles (habichuelas), salvado o cereales y panes de grano integral— a su dieta, y gradualmente incluya más cada día por aproximadamente seis semanas hasta que esté consumiendo por lo menos 25 gramos de fibra diariamente. Si usted no puede comer toda esa cantidad de fibra, considere tomar un concentrado de fibra sin receta (como el *Metamucil*).

No fume. Además de ser lo peor para su salud en general, el fumar es terrible para aquellas personas con diverticulosis, dice el doctor Stephen B. Hanauer, profesor de medicina en la Sección de Gastroenterología del Centro Médico de la Universidad de Chicago. Fumar puede aumentar el movimiento de sus intestinos, pero la nicotina disminuye el abastecimiento de sangre, lo cual causa o aumenta los calambres.

Ejercítese. Cualquier tipo de ejercicio ayuda al aumentar la actividad en sus intestinos, lo cual a su vez mejora la función de su intestino grueso, dice el doctor Aslan. Póngase como objetivo por lo menos 20 minutos de ejercicio continuo no menos de tres veces por semana.

Intestino irritable: apláquelo

Aquí hay una enfermedad que algunos expertos dicen que podría estar tan extendida como el resfriado (catarro) común —y eso causa aún más sufrimiento. Los médicos no están seguros de qué es lo que específicamente causa el síndrome de intestino irritable (o *IBS*, por sus siglos en inglés) o aun, cómo tratarlo. Pero IBS —algunas veces llamado colon espástico— es el diagnóstico para las personas que regularmente están acosadas por el estreñimiento, la diarrea, la hinchazón, las naúseas o los calambres abdominales, ya sea por sí solos o en alguna combinación, y usualmente con dolor abdominal.

La buena noticia (si es que existe) es que a medida que usted envejece, probablemente tendrá menos problemas con esta enfermedad. "IBS es más un problema para aquellos entre los 20 y los 50 años de edad", dice el doctor Mehta. "Pero a cualquier edad tiene algunos efectos envejecedores significativos." Muchas pacientes se encuentran planificando sus vidas alrededor de estos síntomas, dice. "Usted no sabe si súbitamente necesitará correr al baño, por lo tanto planea día a día sus actividades con esto en mente."

Pero tener un intestino irritable no debe ponerla a usted en ese estado mental. Aunque usted debería ver a su médico si sospecha que tiene IBS, hay muchas otras cosas que usted puede hacer para disminuir sus síntomas.

Controle su antojo de dulces. El limitar la cantidad de azúcar que usted consume es una clave para cerrar la puerta a la diarrea provocada por el IBS. Eso es porque los azúcares —especialmente la fructosa y el endulzante artificial sorbitol— no se digieren fácilmente y eso puede causar las carreras al baño, dice el doctor Hanauer. Esos endulzantes existen mayormente en dulces y chicles libres de azúcar y bajos en calorías, así como en jugos de frutas comprados en la tienda. Así que si a usted le gusta el jugo, hágalo usted misma con un exprimidor.

Tranquilícese. Estar bajo estrés empeora los síntomas de IBS, y a la inversa, no estar estresada puede ayudarle, agrega el doctor Hanauer. Él sugiere que las mujeres muy presionadas manejen su estrés con la ayuda de técnicas de terapia de relajamiento tales como la meditación, autohipnosis, *biofeedback* y ejercicio regular. También puede llevar un "diario de estrés" que le ayude a determinar el origen de sus dificultades.

Caliéntese. Los calambres abdominales pueden aliviarse con una almohadilla de calor colocada directamente sobre la zona dolorida, dice el doctor Arvey I. Rogers, jefe de gastroenterología en el Centro Médico de la Administración de Veteranos, en Miami. Solamente esté segura de colocarla en una graduación baja para evitar que le queme la piel.

Los calambres de un intestino irritable pueden no reaccionar al calor. Vea a un médico si sus síntomas son persistentes.

Cuide lo que bebe. El café y otras bebidas cafeinadas pueden agravar el IBS al acelerar su movilidad, el paso al cual se mueve la materia fecal por sus intestinos —mala noticia si usted es propensa a la diarrea. Además de eso, hay un químico en el café que causa calambres, dice el doctor Aslan. Mientras tanto, la leche puede no ser mucho mejor, porque algunas personas con IBS también tienen intolerancia a la lactosa.

Consuma más fibra. Una dieta alta en fibra tiende a calmar a ese colon inquieto. La fibra aumenta la producción de materia fecal y reduce la presión en el intestino, lo cual puede beneficiar a aquellos con estreñimiento o diarrea (o ambos), dice el doctor Hanauer. Se les aconseja a las personas con IBS que coman de 35 a 50 gramos de fibra por día. Empiece agregando unas tres cucharadas de salvado puro a su cereal de cada mañana y comiendo por lo menos cuatro porciones de frutas y verduras diariamente. Los granos y los frijoles (habichuelas) son grandes fuentes de fibra. Póngase como meta comer una taza de frijoles u otras legumbres por día. Otros alimentos ricos en fibra incluyen los panes y cereales de grano integral, pastas y arroz integral. Pero agregue fibra a su dieta gradualmente para ayudar a evitar los efectos secundarios gaseosos.

Elimine la grasa. Los alimentos grasosos pueden hacer que su estómago se vacíe mas lentamente, causándole nausea e hinchazón, dice el doctor Aslan. Por lo tanto, evite los quesos, los helados de crema, los postres muy ricos, los alimentos fritos y las carnes grasosas como son los perros calientes, las salchichas y el tocino.

Intestino inflamatorio: tómelo con calma

La enfermedad de intestino inflamatorio (*inflammatory bowel disease* o *IBD*, por sus siglas en inglés) es un nombre de esos que abarcan muchas cosas y que se usa para dos condiciones similares: enfermedad de *Crohn*, una inflamación crónica del tracto intestinal; y colitis ulcerativa, en la cual el intestino grueso se inflama y se llena de úlceras. En cada uno de los casos, las quejas principales consisten de alguna combinación de dolor abdominal, sangrado del recto, calambres, pérdida de peso, diarrea y algunas veces fiebre junto con síndrome de malabsorción, o la incapacidad para tomar y usar los nutrientes de los alimentos. Esto, por supuesto, la puede hacer sentir débil y fatigada, especialmente cuando usted considera que un encuentro con la enfermedad del intestino inflamatorio (IBD) puede durar de dos a tres semanas o más.

Así que, ¿qué causa la IBD? La mayor parte de la investigación señala un problema técnico en el sistema inmune, o un defecto genético heredado o debilidad en el intestino, ya que la IBD viene de familia. Pero la IBD no debe costarle a usted su vitalidad juvenil. Tomando las medidas apropiadas, usted todavía puede seguir en el juego. Aquí está cómo.

Coma liviano. "Evite las grandes comilonas", aconseja el doctor Sidney Phillips, director de la unidad de investigación de gastroenterología en la Clínica Mayo. Mientras más coma, más duramente tendrán que trabajar sus intestinos ya de por sí inflamados.

Cierre los ojos. Nunca deje pasar una oportunidad de hacer una siesta. Mientras sus síntomas le están molestando, es importante dormir tanto como sea posible para evitar que usted se canse excesivamente, mental o físicamente, dice el doctor Phillips.

Sepa cómo llevarla. Si sus síntomas son leves, una dieta alta en fibra es importante. Comer muchas frutas, verduras y panes de grano integral y pastas, pueden ayudarla a controlar el estreñimiento y la diarrea absorbiendo el agua extra en sus intestinos, dice el doctor Samuel Meyers, profesor clínico de medicina en la Escuela de Medicina Monte Sinaí, de la Universidad de la Ciudad de Nueva York. Pero cuando los síntomas se vuelven graves, aplace el tomar fibra hasta que las cosas mejoren. Demasiada fibra durante un encuentro con IBD puede de hecho empeorar las cosas.

Calme los síntomas con medicamentos sin receta. Muchos síntomas de IBD pueden mantenerse bajo control con los antiácidos y medicamentos sin receta para la diarrea, dice el doctor Phillips. Por supuesto, la mayoría de las mujeres con IBD también necesitan medicamentos con receta para ayudarlas en sus peores días.

PROBLEMAS SEXUALES Y LAS *STD*

La mayoría se pueden prevenir y curar

Usted ha tratado por años de tener un orgasmo pero sin éxito. Usted ha combatido las dolorosas infecciones de las vías urinarias y la sequedad vaginal.

Ahora está preocupada por perder su atracción sexual en una sociedad que codicia la belleza y el encanto de la juventud. Y todo este hablar acerca del SIDA la está haciendo pensar, por primera vez, si sus prácticas sexuales podrían conducir a una enfermedad transmitida sexualmente.

Y usted pensaba que el sexo era supuestamente algo divertido.

Lo es, y lo puede ser. Pero la realidad es que las dificultades sexuales y las enfermedades transmitidas sexualmente pueden poner tensión en sus relaciones íntimas, destruir su autoestima y, en el caso del SIDA, matarla. Como mínimo, los problemas sexuales pueden hacerla sentir como si la edad finalmente la estuviera alcanzando —minando su atracción sexual y haciendo las relaciones sexuales tan excitantes como ver crecer el césped.

"En nuestra cultura, el sexo se ve como algo muy importante y dentro del territorio de los jóvenes. Así que cuando una mujer empieza a verse a sí misma como menos atractiva sexualmente o siente que algo anda mal en sus relaciones sexuales, puede socavar su sentido de sí misma y hacerla sentir como que se está haciendo vieja", dice la doctora Beth Alexander, consejera sexual y presidenta asociada del Departamento de Práctica Familiar en el Colegio de Medicina Humana de la Universidad Estatal de Michigan, en East Lansing.

Todos los años, cerca de seis millones de mujeres estadounidenses contraen enfermedades transmitidas sexualmente. Si no se las trata, estas enfermedades pueden reducir el libido, provocar artritis grave y algunas enfermedades crónicas y perturbar el sistema nervioso central. Algunas enfermedades causan demencia y hasta la muerte.

"Cuando una mujer descubre que tiene una enfermedad transmitida sexualmente, se puede sentir sicológicamente sucia. Afecta su sexualidad, a menudo hasta el punto de que ella pierde todo interés en las relaciones sexuales", dice el doctor Michael Brodman, profesor de obstetricia y ginecología en la Escuela de Medicina Monte Sinaí de la Universidad de la Ciudad de Nueva York.

Pero afortunadamente, dicen los doctores, hay muchas formas en que usted puede prevenir que los problemas sexuales y las enfermedades transmitidas sexualmente lleguen a desarrollarse en primer lugar. Aun así, la mayoría de las dificultades sexuales y enfermedades pueden ser curadas, lo que significa que usted puede aspirar a toda una vida de relaciones sexuales activas y satisfactorias.

Cómo prevenirlos

Muchas mujeres tienen o tendrán problemas sexuales alguna vez durante sus vidas, incluyendo coito doloroso, infecciones de las vías urinarias y deseo sexual inhibido, dice la doctora Domeena Renshaw, directora de la Clínica de Disfunción Sexual en la Escuela de Medicina Stritch de la Universidad Loyola de Chicago.

Algunos de estos problemas están causados o complicados por padecimientos como la diabetes o enfermedad del corazón y requieren atención médica. Pero los médicos dicen que la mayoría de nosotras podemos cortar por lo sano con los trastornos sexuales angustiantes y mejorar nuestras posibilidades de tener vidas sexuales vigorosas si seguimos estás guías básicas.

Aplaste sus cigarrillos. "Si usted está entre los 30 y los 50 años de edad y quiere seguir disfrutando de una vida sexual maravillosa hasta que tenga 70 ó 80 años de edad, mejor deje de fumar ahora", aconseja la doctora Alexander. Fumar estrecha el flujo de sangre a los órganos sexuales e inhibe la excitación en las mujeres.

Despídase de la bebida. Seguro, un vaso o dos de vino o cerveza puede liberarla de sus inhibiciones sexuales, pero más que eso puede dificultar su capacidad de tener un orgasmo, dice la doctora Alexander. El alcohol también puede provocar cambios hormonales que harán disminuir su deseo sexual.

Pregunte acerca de los medicamentos. "Muchas drogas pueden afectar su reacción sexual", dice la doctora Alexander. Las medicinas para la presión arterial alta, los antidepresivos como el *fluoxetine hydrochloride* (*Prozac*) y el litio (por ejemplo *Lithotabs*), los esteroides, las drogas para las úlceras y los bloqueadores beta como el *timolol* (por ejemplo *Timoptic*) están entre las múltiples drogas que pueden afectar negativamente su reacción sexual. Si usted sospecha que un medicamento está interfiriendo con su vida sexual, pregunte a su médico si se puede cambiar la droga o se puede reducir la dosis.

Afloje el paso un poco. Si usted está apresurándose constantemente y trabajando 50 horas o más a la semana, puede estar en camino a un problema sexual, dice la doctora Alexander. "Si puede cambiar las cosas que son estresantes para usted, hágalo, porque el reducir el estrés y tomar más tiempo para usted misma mejorará su desempeño sexual", dice ella. Encuentre formas de asegurar que usted se relaje regularmente; dé un paseo nocturno por el vecindario o relájese leyendo una buena novela antes de meterse a la cama para dormir.

Si está cansada, no lo haga. Evite el sexo cuando está cansada; es menos probable que sufra una frustración sexual si lo hace. "Usted no debe sentirse como que va a gastar su última reserva de energía para tener relaciones sexuales al final de un día muy largo" dice Shirley Zussman, Ed.D., una terapeuta sexual y matrimonial y codirectora de la Asociación de la Disfunción Sexual Masculina, en la Ciudad de Nueva York. "Yo le recomiendo que reserve un tiempo especial para el sexo. Eso suena poco espontáneo, pero a la larga agrega algo a su relación. No solo puede el sexo ocurrir de esa forma sino que usted puede hacerlo con un cierto entusiasmo."

Ya no se agobie. Cada mujer, sin importar qué tan experimentada sea en la cama, ocasionalmente tendrá una frustración sexual. Cuando ocurre, usted no debe pensar demasiado en ella. De lo contrario, usted se está preparando para un trastorno sexual crónico, dice Marty Klein, Ph.D., un consejero matrimonial licenciado y terapeuta sexual, en Palo Alto, California, y autor de *Ask Me Anything: A Sex Therapist Asnwers the Most Important Questions for the '90s* (Pregúnteme cualquier cosa: un terapeuta sexual contesta las preguntas más importantes de la década de los años 90).

"Si usted cree que le va a pasar en algún momento, cuando sí le pasa no representa mayor problema", dice él. "Es como tener un sarpullido. Todos tienen sarpullidos alguna vez en sus vidas. Pero si usted cree que nunca lo va a tener y un día lo tiene, usted se desconcierta completamente. Esto incluso puede preparar el terreno para que esto pase una y otra vez bajo las mismas circunstancias."

Dificultad para alcanzar el orgasmo

La naturaleza puede tener la habilidad de escoger el momento más inoportuno para hacer de las suyas. Tome por ejemplo los orgasmos. A las mujeres les toma hasta cuatro veces más tiempo alcanzar el orgasmo que a los hombres, dice el doctor Renshaw. No es de asombrarse entonces, que solamente un 20 a 30 por ciento de las mujeres tengan orgasmos regularmente y hasta un 10 por ciento diga que nunca ha alcanzado el clímax durante el coito. Aquí hay algunas sugerencias que pueden ayudar.

Haga ejercicios *Kegel*. Estos pueden ayudar a las mujeres a alcanzar el orgasmo al aumentar el conocimiento de las sensaciones sexuales de su cuerpo, dice la doctora Cynthia Mervis Watson, una doctora familiar, en Santa Mónica, California, y autora de *Love Potions* (Brebajes de amor). Los ejercicios *Kegel* hacen más fuertes los músculos pubococcígeos (o *PC*, por sus siglas en inglés) alrededor del área genital. Para localizar estos músculos, trate de detener el flujo de su orina. Separe las piernas de manera tal que sus muslos no se toquen. Al tratar de retener el flujo de su orina, usted sentirá como que está jalando hacia arriba con la pelvis y sentirá una tensión alrededor del ano. Así es como se hacen los ejercicios *Kegel*. Una vez que usted haya llegado a dominar la técnica, apriete esos músculos, manténgase así, después suéltelos por tres segundos a la vez. Practique hasta llegar a series de 30.

No piense demasiado en eso. Simplemente dígale a su compañero que no va a tratar de alcanzar un orgasmo por las próximas dos semanas. Al hacer eso se librará de cualquier presión que usted pudiera sentir para alcanzar el clímax y le permitirá disfrutar más al sexo, dice el doctor Klein. Por supuesto, mientras más relajada usted esté, más probable es que tenga un orgasmo.

Infecciones de las vías urinarias: cómo prevenirlas

Durante el coito, el pene puede empujar bacterias dentro de la vejiga y causar una infección de las vías urinarias (o *UTI*, por sus siglas en inglés). Una en cada cinco mujeres tiene al menos un encuentro con este trastorno desagradable que causa ganas frecuentes de orinar, una sensación ardiente al orinar, dolor arriba del hueso pélvico y ocasionalmente sangre en la orina. Aquí hay algunas cosas que usted puede hacer para prevenirla.

Orine después del sexo. Orinar después del coito reducirá su riesgo de una UTI, dice el doctor Thomas Hooton, profesor asociado de medicina en la División de Enfermedades Infecciosas en la Escuela de Medicina de la Universidad de Washington, en Seattle. "Si usted orina inmediatamente después de haber tenido relaciones sexuales, hará salir para afuera cualquier bacteria que podría causar una infección en la vejiga", dice él.

Límpiese con cuidado. "Después de orinar, límpiese desde adelante hacia atrás, hacia su recto", dice el doctor Brodman. Si usted se limpia en sentido contrario puede arrastrar las bacterias de su recto hacia la uretra y aumentar sus probabilidades de contraer una UTI.

Reexamine su método de control de natalidad. Si usted tiene UTIs frecuentes y recurrentes y usa un diafragma con espermicida, piense en cambiar a un método anticonceptivo diferente. En estudios hechos en la Universidad de Washington, las muestras de orina tomadas después del sexo revelaron que las mujeres que usaron diafragmas con espermicida tenían un mayor riesgo de tener la bacteria *Escherichia coli* que causa la UTI. La combinación de espermicida y diafragma aparentemente mata las bacterias buenas que protegen de infección a la vagina y las vías urinarias y estimula el crecimiento de la bacteria *E. coli*.

Deseo sexual disminuido: cómo reavivar la llama

Cuando estuvieron juntos por primera vez, usted y su compañero contaban las horas entre sus intervalos sexuales. Pero gradualmente, al enfriarse la pasión, las horas se convirtieron en días, y después en semanas, y ahora usted se encuentra en realidad tratando de evitar el sexo.

En un momento u otro, hasta un 48 por ciento de los adultos en los Estados Unidos pierden interés en el sexo por lo menos temporalmente, según lo estiman los investigadores. Cerca del 70 por ciento de la gente que solicita tratamiento para un deseo sexual disminuido son mujeres. La depresión, el alcoholismo y las enfermedades crónicas como la enfermedad del hígado son algunas de las causas físicas que pueden acelerar el proceso, dice la doctora Alexander. Pero los problemas físicos raramente inhiben el deseo sexual en las mujeres menores de 55 años de edad.

"El problema no es necesariamente que una persona sea infeliz o esté incómoda con su propio deseo de relaciones sexuales. El problema es que normalmente ella quiere más o menos veces las relaciones sexuales que su compañero", dice Michael Seiler, Ph.D., director asistente del Instituto Phoenix en Chicago, y autor de *Inhibited Sexual Desire* (El deseo sexual inhibido). "Si usted quiere tener relaciones sexuales menos veces que su compañero, usted puede sentirse extraña, anormal y seguramente más vieja."

Por lo tanto, aquí tenemos un par de ideas para reavivar la pasión en sus relaciones.

Hable al respecto. Si su amante quiere tener relaciones sexuales cuatro veces a la semana y usted sólo quiere cuatro veces al mes, deberían hablar acerca de sus necesidades y llegar a un acuerdo. De lo contrario, el problema se intensificará. "Una pareja necesita hablar acerca de sus sentimientos," dice el doctor Seiler. "Si no pueden conectarse emocionalmente, la posibilidad de que lleguen a juntarse de otra manera es remota."

Si usted siente que su compañero está perdiendo interés en el sexo, evite decir cosas como: "este es un problema serio" o "tú tienes esta mala costumbre", sugiere el doctor Anthony Pietropinto, un siquiatra en la ciudad de Nueva York y autor de *Not Tonight, Dear: How to Reawaken Your Sexual Desires* (No esta noche, querido: cómo volver a despertar sus deseos sexuales). En lugar de eso trate de decir: "He notado que tú no pareces estar interesado en tener relaciones sexuales últimamente, ¿hay algo que yo puedo hacer?" Lo importante es quitar la presión de su compañero.

Sueñe con eso. "Aprender a tener fantasías y jugar sexualmente en su mente puede reavivar su deseo sexual", dice el doctor Seiler. Para lograrlo, tome cinco minutos todos los días para traer a la memoria cualquier imagen sexual que la excite. Puede ser una estrella de cine, su esposo o incluso un amante antiguo. Haga una nota mental de esto. Entonces, cuando se encuentre en una situación sexual, evoque esta memoria y vea si la excita.

Dolores de cabeza antes y después

Un buen retozo en la cama ocasionalmente cura un dolor de cabeza, pero más a menudo el sexo realmente provoca uno, dice el doctor George H. Sands, profesor asistente de neurología en la Escuela de Medicina Monte Sinaí. Los más comunes son los dolores de cabeza tipo explosivos que se sienten como si una granada hubiera estallado dentro de su cabeza cuando se acerca al orgasmo. Cualquier dolor de cabeza que ocurre durante el coito debería ser controlado por un doctor ya que puede ser síntoma de una condición seria, como un aneurisma cerebral.

Cómo hacer frente a la sequedad vaginal

Va desde un achaque ocasional sin importancia hasta un dolor serio frecuente que hace al sexo prácticamente imposible. Aunque una relación sexual doloroso puede ser causado por los herpes genitales, el síndrome premenstrual, las infecciones pélvicas o vaginales, la endometriosis, el embarazo o parto reciente, a menudo el culpable es la sequedad vaginal. Y la sequedad vaginal es una queja común entre las mujeres que están atravesando por la menopausia. Aquí está como combatirla.

Tómelo con calma. Pida a su compañero que vaya más despacio y que tome más tiempo en la estimulación erótica. Tenga en mente que a medida que las mujeres envejecen, hay frecuentemente menos lubricación.

Ayude un poco. Es posible que usted quiera considerar el uso de un lubricante vaginal soluble en agua sin receta como *Astroglide*, dice Lonnie Barbach, Ph.D., una terapeuta sexual y sicóloga en San Francisco y autora de *The Pause: Positive Approaches to Menopause* (La pausa: enfoques positivos a la menopausia). Algunas mujeres prefieren jaleas a base de petróleo, pero recuerde, usted no debe usar estos productos con condones de látex porque los aceites pueden debilitar el látex y aumentar las posibilidades de un escape.

Cuando no se puede tener sexo

Tome su dedo y muévalo lentamente hacia el ojo. Justo cuando parece que está a punto de tocar el globo ocular, el párpado se cierra con rapidez para protegerlo.

Ese es básicamente el mismo reflejo que causa el vaginismo, un cierre involuntario de los músculos rodeando la vagina que hace el acto sexual imposible.

Cerca de 2 en cada 100 mujeres padecen de esta condición, la cual está provocada por las relaciones sexuales dolorosas, el temor extremo al embarazo, los sentimientos de culpa o vergüenza acerca del sexo u otras causas sicológicas.

Para vencer el vaginismo a menudo se requiere de la ayuda de un terapeuta sexual o de un siquiatra.

Cómo vivir sin las *STD*

Si cada persona que vive en los Estados Unidos que tiene una enfermedad transmitida sexualmente se mudara al Canadá aumentaría a más del doble la población de nuestro vecino en el norte. Cerca de 40 millones de estadounidenses tienen enfermedades transmitidas sexualmente, o *STD* (por sus siglas en inglés). Cada año hay 12 millones de casos nuevos y 6 millones de estos son mujeres.

SIDA: cómo combatir la plaga

Muchas de nosotras conocemos por lo menos a una persona que tiene SIDA o que ha muerto a causa de esta. Pero detrás de los números nefastos que nos dicen que más de un millón de personas que viven en los Estados Unidos tienen esta fatal enfermedad viral, existe un rayito de esperanza.

"Al principio, las personas se morían a los pocos meses de su diagnóstico. Pero hemos aprendido mucho más acerca de esta enfermedad desde entonces, y ahora tenemos sobrevivientes a largo plazo que se mantienen saludables por un buen período de tiempo", dice Peggy Clarke, presidenta de la Asociación de la Salud Social de los Estados Unidos, en Research Triangle Park, Carolina del Norte.

Las drogas antivirales como la *zidovudine* (*AZT*), *didanosine* (*Videx*) y *zalcitabine* (*Hivid*) pueden hacer más lento el progreso de la enfermedad, la cual gradualmente destruye el sistema inmune, haciendo posible que las infecciones que ponen en peligro la vida y los cánceres invadan el cuerpo a voluntad.

Pero no hay una cura para esta enfermedad mortal. Por ello, la mejor manera de combatir el SIDA es no contraerlo en primer lugar. Eso significa usar condones de látex o tener relaciones sexuales monógamas en las cuales ambas partes hayan sido examinadas encontrándose libres del virus de inmunodeficiencia humano o VIH, que causa el SIDA. Si usted usa drogas intravenosas, no comparta las agujas con otros, ya que el VIH puede ser transmitido a través de los líquidos del cuerpo que quedan en la aguja.

"Tenemos una epidemia enorme en nuestras manos", dice Peggy Clarke, presidenta de la Asociación de Salud Social de los Estados Unidos, en Research Triangle Park, Carolina del Norte.

La mayoría de las STD se pueden curar, aunque mientras más tiempo pase usted sin tratamiento, más probable es que tenga incapacidades físicas y mentales persistentes y posiblemente permanentes como resultado de estas enfermedades. Usted también debería estar consciente de que las STD a menudo no muestran síntomas y pueden esconderse dentro del cuerpo por años mientras la persona involuntariamente está infectando a otros.

Fuera de la abstinencia, su mejor póliza de seguro para no contraer una STD es hacer que su compañero use condones de látex, dice Clarke. Si usted tiene o ha tenido una lesión, descarga o erupción en el área genital, vea a su médico.

Los Centros para el Control y la Prevención de Enfermedades del gobierno federal, en Atlanta han identificado más de 50 organismos y síndromes transmitidos sexualmente. Aquí le echamos una mirada a los más comunes.

Herpes genitales. Casi 31 millones de personas —uno en cada seis estadounidenses— tienen herpes genitales. El herpes, causado por el virus herpes simple tipo 2, es una infección que dura de por vida la cual produce llagas genitales tan a menudo como una vez al mes en algunas mujeres. Otras mujeres nunca desarrollan síntomas, aunque sí son infecciosas. El *acyclovir* (*Zovirax*), una droga oral con receta, puede aliviar los síntomas pero no va a curar la enfermedad. Las llagas del herpes o alguna otra STD también aumentan su riesgo de contraer SIDA, ya que los virus pueden entrar en el cuerpo a través de las llagas abiertas.

Gonorrea. Conocida desde los tiempos antiguos, hoy en día la gonorrea ataca a cerca de 1,5 millones de estadounidenses anualmente. Esta amenaza bacterial puede causar que el orinar sea doloroso y la secreción de fluido de la vagina dentro de los dos a diez días de la infección. Si no se trata, puede llevar a la esterilidad, artritis, las llagas de la piel, e infecciones en el corazón y el cerebro. La gonorrea se puede pasar a un bebé durante el embarazo. Los antibióticos pueden curarla.

Chlamydia. Esta condición tiene síntomas similares a los de la gonorrea, aunque también puede no tener ningún síntoma. La más curable de las STD en los Estados Unidos, la chlamydia infecta a cerca de cuatro millones de personas anualmente. Es una de las causas principales de esterilidad en las mujeres; puede dañar permanentemente las trompas de Falopio. También se puede curar con antibióticos.

Verrugas genitales. Cada año se reportan casi un millón de casos nuevos. Esta STD es causada por el papilomavirus humano, algunos tipos del cual se han vinculado con el cáncer cervical. No tiene cura, aunque las verrugas se pueden extirpar quirúrgicamente, quemar o congelar. La reaparición es común.

Hepatis B. Esta enfermedad puede llevar a la cirrosis del hígado o cáncer del hígado. Hasta 200.000 casos se reportan anualmente, a pesar del hecho de que hay una vacuna que puede evitarla.

Para mayor información sobre las STD o recomendaciones a los grupos de autoayuda en su área, hable con los Centros de Control de Enfermedades a su línea telefónica nacional para las STD la cual es 1-800-227-8922. En ese número de teléfono hablan sólo inglés, pero hay un número para hispanohablantes de los Centros de Control de Enfermedades, el cual es 1-800-344-7432. Los representantes que contestan en esa línea principalmente están entrenados para responder a preguntas sobre la SIDA, sin embargo ofrecen alguna información básica sobre las otras STD. En Puerto Rico la línea de información sobre VIH/SIDA y las STD es (787) 765-1010.

SÍNDROME PREMENSTRUAL

La vida sigue adelante

Cuántas veces hemos dicho en conversación con nuestras amigas, "fulana de tal siempre se pone imposible cuando le va a dar la regla". "Imposible" muchas veces significa que fulana (o tal vez usted) se siente nerviosa, de mal humor, o está temperamental. También puede significar que se siente fea, gorda y que no puede hacer nada con su cabello. También significa que se siente menos joven de lo que acostumbraba. Se siente vieja, cansada, dolorida, irritable, hinchada, deprimida y retraída. Tiene dificultad para concentrarse. Su espalda le duele. No se siente con muchas ganas de hacer algo o de ver a alguien.

Su gusto por la vida ha desaparecido.

Cómo definir el PMS

El término PMS se ha convertido en parte del habla estadounidense; las mujeres aquí dicen *"I have PMS"* (Tengo síndrome premenstrual) para referirse a los síntomas que experimentan cuando les va a dar la regla. Y muchas sí experimentan síntomas premenstruales que son molestos, alarmantes y difíciles. Pero no todas las mujeres que dicen o piensan que tienen PMS necesariamente lo tienen.

Hay bastante desacuerdo entre los expertos sobre cómo debería definirse el PMS, pero la mayoría están de acuerdo en que para que una mujer oficialmente tenga PMS sus síntomas deben recurrir en dos de cada tres ciclos menstruales. Y el período de síntomas premenstruales debe ser seguido por un período libre de síntomas. Los síntomas —y hay más de 150 que las mujeres pueden experimentar— también interfieren con su capacidad de funcionar.

Aproximadamente del 20 al 95 por ciento de todas las mujeres en sus años de fertilidad experimentan síntomas premenstruales. La condición varía de mujer a mujer y aun de un mes al otro. Pero se dice que sólo un 3 a 5 por ciento sufre en forma suficientemente severa como para que interfiera con su vida cotidiana.

"Las mujeres que tienen PMS se describen como que se sienten diferentes, no como ellas mismas", dice Kathleen Hubbs Ulman, Ph.D., una instructora en la Escuela de Medicina de Harvard, en Boston. "Para algunas, estos cambios llegan lentamente, en el transcurso de un día o unas cuantas horas. Otras dicen que al despertarse en la mañana se sienten como una persona diferente." Algunas mujeres dicen que sienten ganas de salirse de sus propios cuerpos. Otras están excepcionalmente tristes, más lentas, cansadas y deprimidas. También se "sienten muy irritables", dice la doctora Ulman. "Es difícil para ellas morderse la lengua. Son capaces de empezar una pelea con sus esposos o de criticar a sus hijos más rápidamente. Pero esos son sentimientos. Las mujeres que se sienten así no tienen que actuar impulsadas por esos sentimientos." Con un diagnóstico y orientación adecuada, las mujeres pueden hacer algo para encontrar las maneras de expresar los sentimientos sin actuar de manera impulsiva y destructiva, dice ella.

La condición polémica

La controversia rodea al PMS. Mientras que los expertos coinciden en los elementos esenciales de la condición, la definición completa es una cuestión de opinión. Algunos prefieren ver al PMS como que consiste de varios diferentes subtipos organizados alrededor de los síntomas que sufren las mujeres. Las mujeres *PMS-H* son aquellas cuyos síntomas predominantes son el aumento de peso, la inflamación de las manos, los pies y tobillos, la sensibilidad en los senos y la hinchazón abdominal. Las mujeres *PMS-A* son aquellas que tienden a sufrir mayormente de tensión nerviosa, irritabilidad y cambios súbitos en el estado de ánimo. Otros determinan los niveles de PMS basándose en la intensidad y el patrón de los síntomas. Las mujeres con síntomas más leves que no cambian a lo largo del ciclo están en una categoría de síntomas bajos (o *LS*, por sus siglas en inglés). Aquellas que sufren consistentemente síntomas severos, tales como un estado de ánimo deprimido crónico o irritabilidad, que se empeoran aun antes de la menstruación tienen un patrón conocido como magnificación premenstrual (o *PMM*, por sus siglas en inglés). Las mujeres con un PMS típico tienen síntomas que son leves o imperceptibles después de sus períodos pero empeoran notablemente al acercarse sus próximos períodos.

Otro asunto en discusión es si el PMS debe clasificarse oficialmente como un padecimiento siquiátrico. El PMS leve no está incluido en el manual de la Asociación de Siquiatría de los Estados Unidos sobre los trastornos mentales. Sin embargo, el trastorno disfórico premenstrual (o *PMDD*, por sus siglas en inglés), distinguido por una depresión lo suficientemente fuerte como para interferir con su vida cotidiana, sí está incluido en el apéndice del manual.

Según la Asociación de Siquiatría de los Estados Unidos, esto no designa oficialmente al PMDD como un trastorno mental. Las opiniones respecto a esto están divididas; algunos piensan que aunque esta clasificación puede ayudar a las mujeres que sufren fuertes síntomas premenstruales a obtener la asistencia médica que necesitan, otros piensan que el vincular los trastornos mentales con el proceso biológico de la menstruación puede estigmatizar a las mujeres.

También hay desacuerdo sobre qué causa el PMS. Las teorías varían entre los niveles hormonales, los factores nutritivos como es la falta de Vitamina B_6 o magnesio, el impacto de los niveles fluctuantes de las hormonas en los neurotransmisores del cerebro como son la serotonina o la dopamina y los factores sicológicos como el estrés.

¿Por qué las mujeres en la década de sus 30 años de edad?

El PMS tiende a aparecer menos seguido durante la adolescencia y al principio de la década de los 20 años de edad de una mujer. "Yo veo más mujeres en su década de los 30 años de edad, definitivamente. Incluso muchas están entre los 40 y los 45 años de edad", dice la doctora Marcia Szewczyk, directora de la Clínica de PMS en la escuela de Medicina Bowman Gray de la Universidad Wake Forest, en Winston-Salem, Carolina del Norte.

Y los investigadores tienen sus teorías de por qué sucede eso.

Una es que el PMS es el resultado de un desequilibrio hormonal —específicamente, una disminución en la relación entre la progesterona y el estrógeno. Se cree que la progesterona tiene un efecto tranquilizante. Por lo tanto, la creencia es que si la relación de progesterona a estrógeno es demasiada baja, puede resultar en un aumento de la tensión, ansiedad e irritabilidad.

Además de esto, una de las razones fundamentales por qué las mujeres entre los 30 y los 40 años de edad sufren de PMS es que tienen un número de oportunidades para tener cambios hormonales, tales como el embarazo, el aborto o al tomar y dejar de tomar la píldora anticonceptiva, dice Stephanie DeGraff Bender, directora clínica de la clínica de PMS en Boulder, Colorado, y autora de *PMS: A Positive Program to Gain Control* (PMS: un programa positivo para adquirir control) y *PMS: Questions and Answers* (PMS: preguntas y respuestas).

Otros investigadores, incluyendo a Nancy Fugate Woods, Ph.D., del Centro para la Investigación de la Salud Femenina, en la Escuela de Enfermería de la Universidad de Washington, en Seattle, dicen que el estrés desempeña un papel importante en el desarrollo del PMS y que la razón por la cual podemos ver más al PMS en las mujeres en sus décadas de los 30 y los 40 años de edad es que las vidas de las mujeres tienden a hacerse más complejas al ir envejeciendo, dice la doctora Fugate Woods. Para las mujeres que hoy están entre los 30 y los 45 años de edad, hay expectativas increíbles, dice ella. Ellas pueden tener niños, mantener a sus padres, trabajar en dos o tres empleos o ser madres solteras, dice ella. "Si uno se enfoca solamente en la biología de las mujeres no se les está haciendo justicia. Necesitamos empezar a basar la investigación sobre la vida de las mujeres", dice ella.

Cómo prevenir el PMS

Lo que sea que lo cause, si usted cree que tiene PMS y está preocupada acerca de la forma en que está afectando su juventud —tanto en mente como en cuerpo— hay algunas cosas que usted puede hacer para tratar de mantener los síntomas a un mínimo. Aquí hay algunas sugerencias.

Levántese y camine. "Las mujeres que hacen ejercicio en forma regular encuentran que realmente ayuda a su PMS", dice la doctora Szewczyk. El tipo de ejercicio que las mujeres escogen depende de sus preferencias y los niveles de condición en que se encuentran, dice ella. Caminar, trotar y jugar tenis son sólo algunas posibilidades. El ejercicio ayuda a estimular las endorfinas, los analgésicos naturales del cuerpo, así que pueden ayudar a evitar los calambres y a mejorar el estado de ánimo. También puede darles a las mujeres una sensación de control, dice la doctora Szewczyk. Hay muchas oportunidades de ejercicio que a menudo pasamos por alto, agrega Bender. Las actividades sencillas como es caminar, andar en bicicleta o poner un cassette y bailar rápido durante dos o tres canciones pueden servir para el caso, dice ella.

Reduzca los dulces. Evite el azúcar en su dieta, dice la doctora Szewczyk. Eso quiere decir cosas como galletitas, dulces y chocolate, dice ella. Si mantiene su consumo de azúcar bajo evitará que su nivel de azúcar en la sangre fluctúe desordenadamente. Sus niveles de energía serán más estables y usted será capaz de hacer frente mejor a cualquier molestia que tenga.

Controle la cafeína. "Yo le digo a las personas que eviten la cafeína", dice la doctora Szewczyk. La cafeína estimula al sistema nervioso, conduciendo a la ansiedad y a los cambios de estado de ánimo. Las mujeres deberían reducir ésta despacio, básicamente quitándose la costumbre del café con cafeína, dice ella. Un truco que a veces funciona es mezclar proporciones de cafés con y sin cafeína hasta que usted esté tomando solamente café descafeinado, dice ella.

Sacuda la sal. Reducir su consumo de sal también puede ayudarle a reducir los síntomas de hinchazón y retención de agua. Lea las etiquetas de los alimentos cuidadosamente. Cualquier cosa que empiece o termine con *sodio* es una sal, así que si hay más de tres ingredientes con ese término, la probabilidad es que el alimento sea alto en sal, dice Bender. Y cuídese de las fuentes escondidas de sodio, como el aliño (aderezo) para las ensaladas, dice ella. Si tiene que comer afuera, opte por el vinagre y el aceite en lugar de los aliños cuyos contenidos usted no puede descubrir.

Aumente el calcio. Al aumentar su consumo de calcio por encima de la Asignación Dietética Recomendada de 800 miligramos (para las mujeres mayores de 24 años de edad) puede ayudarle a disminuir sus síntomas premenstruales, dicen los investigadores. En un estudio breve de las mujeres con PMS, aumentar el calcio ayudó a reducir los problemas de estado de ánimo y concentración deficiente, dice James G. Penland, Ph.D., un sicólogo investigador en el Centro

Grand Forks de Investigación sobre Nutrición, del Departamento de Agricultura de los Estados Unidos, en Grand Forks, Dakota del Norte, donde se llevó a cabo el estudio. Otros estudios de mujeres con PMS encontró efectos similares al aumentar el calcio, dice él.

Se piensa que el calcio desempeña un papel en la regulación de algunos tipos de músculos y también afecta a los neurotransmisores, químicos en el cerebro que pueden influir sobre el estado de ánimo. La mayoría de las mujeres consumen unos 600 miligramos de calcio al día, dice el doctor Penland. Todo lo que tienen que hacer es agregar un vaso de 8 onzas (24 ml) de leche descremada al 1 ó 2 por ciento y una taza de yogur, e impulsarán su consumo de calcio a cerca de 1.200 miligramos, dice él. "La información sugiere que si alguien experimenta síntomas desagradables premenstruales, puede haber un beneficio inmediato al aumentar el consumo de calcio", dice él.

Preste atención a sus síntomas. Muchas mujeres dicen que llevar un diario de los síntomas las ayuda, dice Ellen Freeman, Ph.D., directora del Programa de PMS en el Centro Médico de la Universidad de Pensilvania, en Filadelfia. Esto ayuda a las mujeres a observar la pauta de sus síntomas mensuales, dice ella, lo cual puede ayudarles para aprender a anticipar cuándo se van a sentir mal. Las mujeres "pueden ser las mejores expertas con sus propios cuerpos —ellas pueden ser las mejores expertas en hacer diagnósticos", asiente la doctora Fugate Woods.

Tome tiempo para relajarse. Las mujeres con PMS pueden aprovechar los múltiples métodos de relajación, dice la doctora Freeman. "Estos incluyen cosas desde escuchar música, practicar yoga y meditar hasta retirarse para leer un libro", dice ella. "Cualquier cosa que funcione para usted está bien." Busque libros que la ayuden a empezar, o tome una clase en técnicas de relajamiento.

Pruebe la reflexología. El aplicar presión manual a puntos específicos en sus orejas, manos y pies puede aliviar algunos de los síntomas que las mujeres experimentan con el PMS, dice Terry Oleson, Ph.D., presidente del Departamento de Medicina de la Conducta en el Instituto de Graduados de California, en Los Ángeles quien completó el primer estudio controlado sobre el uso de la reflexología. Las mujeres pueden practicar la reflexología en ellas mismas, dice él. Oprima los diferentes puntos en sus orejas en medio de dos dedos hasta que encuentre los que son sensibles, dice él. Una vez que los localice, aplique una presión firme pero ligera durante 30 segundos a un minuto, después suelte. Repita hasta tres veces si lo desea.

Enfréntese al PMS con anticipación. Hable con su compañero acerca de sufrir PMS, cómo la hace sentir, cómo usted puede actuar, qué es lo que está haciendo al respecto y qué es lo que él puede hacer para ayudar, dice Bender. Haga esto durante el momento del mes cuando está libre de síntomas, dice ella. La comunicación acerca del PMS "necesita llevarse a cabo durante el tiempo sin PMS", dice Bender.

Comuníquese con sus hijos. Es importante decirle a sus hijos que usted tiene un problema de salud pero que está haciendo algo al respecto, dice Bender. Ella sugiere que usted le diga a su hijo "Yo tengo un desequilibrio en mi cuerpo, y estoy haciendo algo para arreglarlo. Pero cuando lo tengo, puede ser que no vaya a jugar tanto contigo, y puede ser que no vaya a hablar mucho contigo tampoco. Y aunque yo me veo igual, puedo no comportarme igual que siempre".

Proporcione las señales a su hijo para indicarle en qué días su PMS es un problema. Para los niños más pequeños, ponga imanes de caras sonrientes en el refrigerador; en los días que usted tiene PMS, voltee las caras sonrientes boca abajo. Eso le hace saber a su hijo que no se siente bien. Para los niños más grandes, marque en un calendario los días en que usted espera que no se va a sentir muy bien. Bender también recomienda decirle a los niños que ellos pueden ayudar. Ofrézcales dejarlos que ayuden a encontrar los alimentos bajos en azúcar, por ejemplo.

Obtenga un diagnóstico. A pesar de que usted puede pensar que tiene PMS, es necesario ver a un doctor para que lo diagnostique oficialmente. Le harán una evaluación de su historia clínica, un examen físico y una evaluación sicológica y se le pedirá que complete un diario de síntomas durante tres meses. Muchas mujeres que piensan que tienen PMS descubren que no es así cuando siguen la trayectoria de sus propios síntomas, dice la doctora Fugate Woods. A menudo las mujeres encuentran que los síntomas corresponden a factores que no tienen nada que ver con sus ciclos menstruales, tales como sucesos o relaciones en sus vidas, dice ella.

SOBREPESO

Cómo volver al peso ideal

¿**V**e a esa mujer esbelta dirigiendo la clase de aeróbicos? Pues antes —con su estatura de cinco pies cinco pulgadas (1.65m)— pesaba 200 libras (90 kg). ¿Puede creerlo?

Esa fue una época en que la vida le pesaba a Karen Faye, una enfermera en su década de los 40 años de edad quien eventualmente se puso en forma y es ahora la propietaria de *Body Basics Aerobics Workout* (Gimnasia de aeróbicos para lo básico del cuerpo), en Tyngsboro, Massachusetts.

"Yo estaba mental y físicamente extenuada todo el tiempo, lo cual era una preocupación adicional al hecho de tener sobrepeso", recuerda ella. Como muchas otras mujeres, ella luchó con su peso desde la adolescencia. "Yo recuerdo que cuando tenía 16 años de edad y fui a la playa con mi mamá, los muchachos le silbaban a mi madre, no a mí. Yo no me sentía como la mujer joven que se suponía que era."

Ese sentimiento de ser más vieja que su edad permaneció con ella hasta bien avanzada en su edad adulta, mientras tenía sobrepeso, Faye dice. "Mentalmente, yo era una mujer joven —tenía tres niños y un esposo delgado que todavía cabía en su uniforme de infante de marina. Pero físicamente, me sentía como mi propia abuela, y no podía creer lo que me estaba pasando a mí. Yo sentía que mi verdadera persona estaba atrapada en el cuerpo de una mujer mayor."

Por años, Faye pensó que su problema de la glándula tiroides era la causa de su peso. Pero cuando llegó a las 200 libras, dice ella, "yo vi mis días contados, especialmente debido a mis arterias". Por esta razón, se puso en un régimen de comidas bajas en grasa y ejercicio. En el lapso de ocho meses, ella había perdido 80 libras (36 kg), y estaba en forma por primera vez en su vida y ha mantenido su peso por once años.

Después de tener su peso bajo control, se volvió una consultora en cómo ponerse en buena forma y abrió *Body Basics Aerobics Workout*. En agosto de 1993, ganó el premio de buena forma física en el concurso de Mrs. United States (Señora Estados Unidos) compitiendo con algunas mujeres que estaban entre los 20 y los 30 años de edad.

Como Faye lo sabe, el sobrepeso es una carga para el cuerpo y para el espíritu. Usted siente que ha perdido su juventud y vitalidad. Además de abrirle la puerta a los padecimientos del envejecimiento tales como las enfermedades del corazón, la presión arterial alta, diabetes, artritis y el colesterol alto —ya no se diga los dolores de espalda y otros dolores causados por estar cargando por todas partes más peso de lo que debería.

Hay también una conexión con el cáncer. "Cuando usted tiene sobrepeso, también está aumentando su riesgo a diferentes cánceres, incluyendo cáncer del endometrio, del útero, del cuello uterino, de los ovarios y de la vesícula biliar", dice John Foreyt, Ph.D., director de la Clínica de Investigación de la Nutrición del Colegio de Medicina de Baylor, en Houston.

Más grande no es mejor

La mayoría de los estudios sobre la conexión entre el sobrepeso y las enfermedades del corazón se han limitado a los hombres. Pero esto está empezando a cambiar. En un estudio a 116.000 mujeres, los investigadores de la Universidad de Harvard, en Cambridge, Massachusetts, encontraron que la relación entre el sobrepeso y las enfermedades del corazón es tan fuerte para las mujeres como para los hombres. Tener sobrepeso fue la causa de las enfermedades del corazón en el 70 por ciento de las mujeres obesas en el estudio y en el 40 por ciento de otras mujeres que estaban arriba de su peso ideal.

La presión arterial alta tiene un vínculo estrecho con el sobrepeso. Cuando un corazón tiene que trabajar tiempo de más para cargar libras adicionales, la presión arterial se va por las nubes.

La diabetes tipo II también está vinculada con el tener sobrepeso. Cargar con esas libras adicionales directamente afecta la capacidad del cuerpo para utilizar el azúcar en la sangre. Muchas personas con peso de más y con diabetes, que necesitan medicación regular, encuentran que una vez que reducen 20 o más libras pueden dejar de tomar sus medicamentos.

La conexión entre el sobrepeso y la artritis es relativamente obvia: mientras más libras carga usted, más presión está poniendo sobre sus articulaciones. El Estudio Framingham sobre la Osteoartritis en las Rodillas, que usó información recolectada de más de 5.200 residentes en Framingham, Massachusetts, en un estudio del corazón que marcó un hito, mostró que las mujeres con sobrepeso que simplemente perdieron 11 libras (5 kilos) redujeron su riesgo de desarrollar artritis en las rodillas en casi un 50 por ciento.

Y cuando se trata del cáncer, en especial del cáncer de mama, perder esas libras extras puede darle una protección adicional. La investigación de los Centros Federales para el Control y la Prevención de Enfermedades, en Atlanta muestra un peligro en particular para las mujeres que tienen un 25 por ciento o

¿Después de todo, cuál es su peso saludable?

Usted no necesita ser una esclava de la balanza (pesa). "Su peso saludable es aquel que es producto de comer y hacer ejercicio saludables", dice John Foreyt, Ph.D., director de la Clínica de Investigación de la Nutrición del Colegio de Medicina de Baylor, en Houston. "Ese es su objetivo, y punto."

Pero probablemente usted se sentiría mejor si tuviera un nivel medio de peso como objetivo a fijarse. Si tal es el caso, la tabla del gobierno federal a continuación, le dará una idea general sobre dónde usted podría estar. Estas guías fueron preparadas tanto para hombres como para mujeres; generalmente las mujeres quedarían en el extremo inferior de cada escala.

Estatura	Peso (en libras)	
	Edad 19 a 34	Edad 35 y mayor
5'0"	97–128	108–138
5'1"	101–132	111–143
5'2"	104–137	115–148
5'3"	107–141	119–152
5'4"	111–146	122–157
5'5"	114–150	126–162
5'6"	118–155	130–167
5'7"	121–160	134–172
5'8"	125–164	138–178
5'9"	129–169	142–183
5'10"	132–174	146–188
5'11"	136–179	151–194
6'0"	140–184	155–199
6'1"	144–189	159–205
6'2"	148–195	164–210
6'3"	152–200	168–216
6'4"	156–205	173–222
6'5"	160–211	177–228
6'6"	164–216	182–234

más de peso por arriba de su peso óptimo en el momento en que el cáncer de mama les fue diagnosticado. Estas mujeres se enfrentan a un riesgo del 42 por ciento mayor de que el cáncer regrese.

El tener sobrepeso también puede aumentar el riesgo de una mujer para desarrollar cáncer de mama, dice el doctor Foreyt. "Una dieta alta en grasas conduje a la obesidad y la grasa en la dieta está asociada con un aumento en el riesgo de cáncer de mama", dice él.

Envejecer agrava la situación

La mayoría de nosotras ya nos hemos dado cuenta de que cada vez se hace más difícil perder peso. Eso es porque nuestro metabolismo, el proceso por el cual nuestros cuerpos queman calorías, se hace más lento al pasar el tiempo. El doctor Reubin Andres, director clínico del Instituto Nacional sobre el Envejecimiento, en Bethesda, Maryland, cree que es inofensivo aumentar 5 libras (2,3 kilos) por cada década después de los 20 años de edad, pero solamente si para empezar usted se encuentra en buen estado de salud y permanece libre de padecimientos tales como la diabetes y las enfermedades del corazón. Sin embargo muchos expertos dicen que debería evitarse cualquier aumento de peso a través de los años.

Pero es mejor no subir de peso. Después de seguir a un grupo de alumnos de la Universidad de Harvard por 27 años, los investigadores encontraron el índice más bajo de mortalidad entre los hombres que estaban un 20 por ciento debajo del peso normal para los hombres en edades y estaturas similares. Estas conclusiones se mantuvieron firmes aun cuando los investigadores tomaron en cuenta el peso menor al normal debido a fumar o a enfermedades, lo cual ellos creen puede haber distorsionado los resultados de los estudios anteriores.

El estudio también mostró que los hombres que sólo tenían un sobrepeso ligero —2 a 6 por ciento sobre sus pesos ideales— aún tenían grandes posibilidades de morir de una enfermedad del corazón, y que los hombres que pesaban 20 por ciento más de sus pesos deseables de hecho duplicaban su riesgo.

Pero independientemente de dónde usted encaja en las gráficas, si usted siente que está luchando con más que unas cuantas libras adicionales y no tiene problemas con la glándula tiroides u otros problemas de salud, puede ser que esté comiendo demasiado —especialmente comidas grasosas— y haciendo muy poco ejercicio.

¿Qué hacer al respecto? Bueno, usted podría ponerse en un régimen drástico. Pero con eso probablemente no va a lograr nada excepto frustración. "Las dietas no funcionan", dice Janet Polivy, Ph.D., profesora de sicología en la Facultad de Medicina de la Universidad de Toronto. "Las dietas se popularizan porque funcionan por una semana o dos y todos le dicen 'tienes que probarla'. Bueno, hable con esas personas dentro de un año o dos y descubrirá que fracasaron." Cuando usted se deja convencer por uno de esos programas veloces de perder 5 libras a la semana, usted las pierde, sí, pero pierde libras de líquido no de grasa. Y tan pronto como usted abandona la dieta, el peso regresa otra vez al lugar donde estaba antes.

A la larga, lo que mejor resulta para lograr un peso saludable es modificar sus hábitos de comida y hacer más ejercicio.

Funcionó para Karen Faye. "Ahora tengo 45 años de edad y realmente soy una abuela", dice Faye. "Pero desde que perdí peso, cuando la gente me ve con mi hijo de 25 años de edad, ¡piensan que es mi novio! Si yo lo puedo hacer, usted también puede."

Usted dicte los resultados

El primer paso hacia una pérdida de peso exitosa es aceptarse a sí misma, tal y como está ahora, dice Thomas A. Wadden, Ph.D., profesor asociado de sicología y director del Programa de Trastornos de Peso y Alimentación de la Universidad de Pensilvania, en Filadelfia. Entonces, usted tiene que desarrollar una estrategia para tomar el control de su peso. Aquí está cómo.

Haga un compromiso a largo plazo. La clave para una pérdida de peso exitosa a cualquier edad, dicen los expertos, es hacer los cambios gradualmente. Perder media libra a la semana es lo ideal, dice el doctor George Blackburn, Ph.D., profesor asociado de cirugía en la Escuela de Medicina de Harvard y jefe del Laboratorio de Nutrición y Metabolismo en el Hospital Deaconess de Nueva Inglaterra, ambos en Boston. Así que fíjese como objetivo alcanzar un peso saludable en un año a partir de ahora, no de la semana entrante, dice él.

No trate de volverse una modelo. No importa que las modelos profesionales a menudo están tan flacas como un palo. Muchas de ellas son adolescentes con bastante maquillaje. "Usted tiene que reconocer que no puede verse como esas modelos flacas de las revistas y cuando llega a una edad madura es un buen momento para hacerlo", dice el doctor Wadden. Una vez que usted se desprende de las fantasías poco realistas y acepta la premisa que no es justo que usted se compare con una adolescente, entonces puede continuar con un plan de pérdida de peso saludable y alcanzable, dice él.

Rodéese de apoyo. Un buen sistema de apoyo es una clave para una pérdida de peso exitosa, dice el doctor Foreyt. Pida a sus familiares y amistades que la animen. A lo mejor pueden unirse a usted en comer alimentos saludables y bajos en grasa.

"Forme un grupo de vecinos que caminen juntos, o busque en la Asociación Cristiana de Jóvenes (o *YMCA*, por sus siglas en inglés) o en el Jewish Community Center (Centro Judío de la Comunidad), o en su iglesia o escuela local, grupos de apoyo para pérdida de peso", dice el doctor Foreyt. "Y los grupos como *Weight Watchers*, que enseñan el mantenimiento por sí mismo pueden ser muy, muy útiles." Si usted tiende a perder el control y come de más en forma compulsiva, o entra en rachas de comer sin control seguidas por un sentimiento de vergüenza, un grupo de *Overeaters Anonymous* (Comedores en Exceso Anónimos) u orientación profesional puede ser de tremenda ayuda, dice él.

Ponga atención a sus necesidades emocionales. Algunas veces usted puede confundir el hambre con otros sentimientos, especialmente si se siente deprimida o estresada o simplemente está reaccionando a una fotografía tentadora en una revista sobre platillos sabrosos. Si no es su estómago el que está hablando, usted necesita descubrir qué clase de emociones o inquietudes están

Vacíe el almacén de grasa

Aunque usted esté cuidando su peso diligentemente, todavía puede tener un estómago obstinadamente prominente. A menudo esto es una consecuencia natural del envejecimiento tanto para los hombres como para las mujeres, según muestra la investigación. En el caso de las mujeres es a menudo debido a ponerse repetidamente a dieta —el peso que se recupera tiende a depositarse en la barriga, dicen los investigadores. O puede ser un recuerdo persistente del embarazo. Sin embargo usted puede aplanar su estómago sin necesidad de aparatitos y artilugios complicados. Aquí está cómo.

No la conserve en alcohol. Sí, realmente existe lo que se conoce como una barriga de bebedor de cerveza, y dejar de consumir alcohol puede ser la clave para aplanarla. En un amplio estudio, las mujeres y los hombres que bebieron más de dos bebidas alcohólicas al día tenían los índices de relación entre cintura y cadera más altos, que es como los doctores cuantifican las barrigas.

Pisotee los cigarrillos. En el mismo estudio, los investigadores de la Escuela de Medicina de la Universidad de Stanford, California y de la Universidad de California, en San Diego detectaron un efecto similar debido al fumar. Hubo el doble de abdómenes gordos entre aquellos que fumaban que entre aquellos que no fumaban. Vea a su doctor para que le ayude a dejarlo.

Actívese ahora. Posiblemente la danza del medioriente es justamente lo que esa barriga necesita. Para quemar una barriga, el ejercicio

provocando sus ganas de comer, dice el doctor Foreyt. Desarrolle entonces un enfoque para resolver el problema. "¿Cómo puede usted satisfacer esa necesidad sin comer? Camine alrededor de la manzana, llámele a una amiga, medite, dese un baño, cepíllese los dientes o haga gárgaras con un enjuague bucal", dice él. "Esto rompe la cadena y desarrolla un patrón alterno de conducta."

Apague la caja de la gordura. Si usted mira televisión más de tres horas por día, está duplicando su riesgo de agregar libras extras, dice Larry A. Tucker, Ph.D., profesor y director del programa de promoción de salud de la Universidad Brigham Young, en Provo, Utah. Al estar tirada en un sillón usted no está quemando muchas calorías, y probablemente está aumentando algunas al comer bocadillos (meriendas o *snacks*) que engordan. Así que apague el televisor (y debe hacer dos cosas, dice Bryant Stamford, Ph.D., director del Centro de Promoción de Salud de la Universidad de Louisville, en Kentucky. Primero, debe comenzar vigorosamente para provocar una secreción fuerte de adrenalina, la cual libera a la grasa que se va usar como combustible. Usted puede lograr este efecto si camina vigorosamente, dice él. Después, la actividad vigorosa debe ser seguida por un ejercicio aeróbico prolongado que va a quemar la grasa liberada. Caminar a un paso cómodo logrará esto. También podría lograrlo unas torrientes de quehaceres pesados seguidos por un rastrillado prolongado en el jardín. "Sólo tiene que aumentar el paso de vez en cuando para impulsar la secreción de la adrenalina", dice él.

Endurézcala. Una vez que la grasa se ha ido reduciendo debido a comer poca grasa y al ejercicio aeróbico, los ejercicios diarios abdominales pueden realmente ayudar a mejorar su forma, dice el doctor Stamford. Empiece con apretones isométricos: tensione sus músculos abdominales al máximo y mantenga la posición por seis a diez segundos. Descanse, después repita varias veces. Más tarde, dice él, usted puede pasar a las contracciones: acuéstese boca arriba con las piernas separadas y las rodillas flexionadas. Cruce los brazos sobre su pecho. Levante la cabeza hacia el techo. Siga levantándose hasta que pueda levantar los omóplatos ligeramente del piso. Mantenga la posición por dos segundos y entonces recuéstese otra vez. Vaya aumentando gradualmente hasta llegar a diez repeticiones por serie.

suspenda el hábito de ingerir comida basura que usualmente acompaña al hecho de mirar televisión) para estimular su campaña de pérdida de peso.

Cómo perder peso sin hambre

La última investigación sobre la nutrición muestra que realmente hay una manera totalmente nueva de perder peso —sin ponerse a dieta y sin pasar hambre. Está basada en el conocimiento de cuáles son los tipos de alimentos que la vigorizan y le dan energía real y cuáles son los alimentos que se van directamente a sus muslos. Usted se sorprenderá de encontrar que los cambios más cruciales no requieren que coma menos —sólo en forma diferente. Aquí está cómo.

Absténgase de la grasa en exceso. La grasa dietética nos hace aumentar de peso porque se almacena en el cuerpo mucho más fácilmente que los carbohidratos o las proteínas, dice el doctor Peter D. Vash, profesor clínico asistente de medicina en la Universidad de California, en Los Ángeles. El cuerpo quema carbohidratos y proteínas como combustible casi inmediatamente, mientras que la grasa, la cual es más densa en calorías, se quema más despacio y hay más probabilidad de que sobrará —y se quedará— en el cuerpo.

Empiece por cortar la grasa en los lugares obvios: coma menos carnes grasosas, alimentos fritos, lácteos altos en grasa y postres. También, tenga cuidado con las ensaladas embadurnadas de aceite u otros aliños (aderezos) grasosos. Se recomienda que usted mantenga su total de calorías provenientes de la grasa en un 25 por ciento o menos de su dieta diaria.

"La dieta alta en grasa se ha vinculado con la obesidad, la cual a su vez se asocia con un riesgo en aumento de contraer varios tipos de cánceres. La prudencia indica que una dieta alta en grasa es un factor causante de tantas enfermedades que sólo tiene sentido común comer los alimentos bajos en grasa en su lugar", dice el doctor Foreyt.

Ahóguelo. "Tomar cantidades generosas de agua es indudablemente la mejor manera de reducir el apetito", dice el doctor Blackburn. El agua no solamente hace que su estómago continúe sintiéndose lleno, sino que también mucha gente piensa que tiene ganas de comer cuando en realidad está sedienta, dice él. Así que póngase como objetivo tomar ocho tazas de líquidos al día, sorbiendo media taza a la vez durante el día.

Mientras está sorbiendo durante el transcurso del día, tenga en mente que la cafeína —en colas, café o té— tiene sus desventajas. La cafeína es un diurético, el cual extrae agua de su cuerpo. Por esta razón, la mayoría de los doctores recomiendan a la gente que se encuentra en programas para perder peso que no beban más de tres bebidas cafeinadas al día.

Cuente con los carbohidratos. No pase hambre. Cuando usted reemplaza las calorías de la grasa excesiva que ha estado comiendo con alimentos tales como los carbohidratos, usted realmente puede comer más y todavía perder peso. En un estudio de la Universidad de Illinois en Chicago, se les pidió a las personas en dietas con contenido de grasa moderadamente alto que mantuvieran su peso por 20 semanas mientras cambiaban a dietas bajas en grasa y altas en carbohidratos. Estas personas comieron todo lo que quisieron y a pesar de eso perdieron más del 11 por ciento de la grasa en su cuerpo y el 2 por ciento de su peso. Así que para satisfacerse mientras está perdiendo peso, disfrute de abundante pasta rica en carbohidratos (sin salsa grasosa), cereales bajos en grasa, panes, frijoles (habichuelas), verduras y frutas frescas y crujientes.

Dese un gusto de vez en cuando. Si usted siente que todo lo que se está diciendo a sí misma con respecto a los alimentos es no, no, no, eventualmente usted va a dejar que los deslices se conviertan en una avalancha, dice Susan Kayman, R.D., Dr.P.H., una dietista y consultora con el grupo médico Kaiser Permanente, en Oakland, California. Por eso es que ella aboga seguir la regla

El problema de las alas de murciélago

Un precioso vestido de playa le llama la atención. Pero... espere un poco. No tiene mangas. Usted se da un apretón en la parte superior de sus brazos regordetes, y desafortunadamente, siguen ahí.

Llamados en forma encantadora por los doctores, "alas de murciélago", estos trozos gruesos de piel y grasa tienen tres causas principales, dice el doctor Alan Matarasso, un cirujano plástico en el Hospital de Ojos, Oídos y Garganta de Manhattan, en la ciudad de Nueva York. Primero, usted puede haber heredado una tendencia a depositar grasa abajo de la parte superior de sus brazos. Segundo, si usted ha aumentado y perdido peso repetidamente a lo largo de los años, su piel se ha estirado y contraído tantas veces que ha perdido algo de su elasticidad. Tercero, es piel floja y delgada la que está allí debajo. Es tan sensible como la piel delicada en la parte interior de sus muslos, dice el doctor Matarasso. "Es más delgada y más floja que la piel en la parte exterior de sus brazos o del abdomen", dice él.

¿Cómo cortarse sus alas? Cualquier ejercicio que refuerce su músculo tríceps —el que corre a lo largo del dorso de su brazo desde la axila hasta el codo— ayudará, dice el doctor Matarasso. Cualquier entrenador puede mostrarle varios, dice él, pero aquí hay uno que usted puede probar.

Mientras está parada, sostenga con ambas manos verticalmente enfrente suyo y con los codos flexionados ligeramente (derecha) una pesa de tres a cinco libras. Levante lentamente la pesa en línea recta por encima de la cabeza (derecha extrema). Esa es su posición para empezar. Flexionando sus codos, baje la pesa hacia la parte de atrás de su cuello, entonces levántela nuevamente a la posición para empezar por encima de su cabeza. Continúe levantando y bajando la pesa despacio, aumentando hasta llegar a series de diez repeticiones.

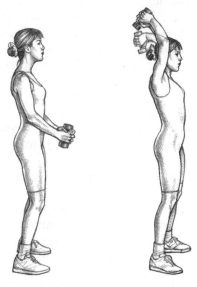

80/20. Si usted come poca grasa el 80 por ciento del tiempo entonces, cuando está comiendo con las amistades, se va de fiesta o visita a los suegros, ocasionalmente se puede dar el gusto de comer algo con un contenido de grasa más alto sin tener que sentirse culpable, dice ella.

Separe al dúo fatal. Este es las grasas y los dulces. Cuando el cuerpo recibe una sacudida de azúcar, secreta una grande cantidad de insulina como reacción. Debido a que la insulina es una hormona propensa al almacenamiento, ésta abre las células grasosas y las prepara para almacenar grasa. Así que cuando tome azúcar, mantenga baja su ingestión de grasa. También, cuando toma la grasa y el azúcar juntos pueden despertar su apetito a niveles incontrolables. Comer dulces conduce a un aumento del azúcar en la sangre, el cual, debido a una cadena de reacciones en el cuerpo, aumenta su apetito, dice el doctor Wadden. Así que calme su antojo de dulces con una fruta fresca y jugosa o un bol de cereal azucarado bajo en grasa, en lugar de *donuts* o barras de confitura.

Sea persistente. Aquí hay un consejo para luchar contra la grasa que merece atención: si usted persiste en ello, después de un tiempo, usted en realidad va a perder su gusto por los alimentos altos en grasa. Un estudio de cuatro años a más de 2.000 mujeres en el Centro Fred Hutchinson para Investigación del Cáncer en la Universidad de Washington, en Seattle mostró que las mujeres que limitan su consumo de grasa pierden su gusto por la grasa en seis meses o menos, eventualmente encontrando desagradables los alimentos grasosos.

Coma a menudo. Algunos investigadores apoyan la idea de "picotear" — en el sentido de ingerir varias pequeñas comidas a lo largo del día en lugar de tres comidas grandes— para controlar el apetito y evitar el atiborramiento. "Pero usted no puede 'picotear' con dulces *M&M*, papas fritas y (helado de crema) *Häagen-Dazs*", dice James Kenney, R.D., Ph.D. un especialista en investigación de nutrición en el Centro Pritikin de Longevidad, en Santa Mónica, California. "Pero si usted 'picotea' con alimentos bajos en grasa y altos en fibra que no están rellenos de calorías, como son las zanahorias, manzanas, los melocotones (duraznos), las naranjas y los pimientos rojos, va a mantener su apetito controlado."

Prenda el calor. Sea generosa con las especias picantes como la pimienta de Cayena y el rábano picante para impulsar su ritmo metabólico, los cuales pueden ayudar a su cuerpo a quemar más calorías, dice el doctor Kenney. "Cuando la gente come alimentos picantes, a menudo suda, una señal inequívoca del aumento del ritmo metabólico. Y mientras más rápido sea el ritmo metabólico, más calor producirá su cuerpo. Recuerde, cualquier cosa que suba su temperatura hará a su vez que usted adelgace", dice él. Pero asegúrese de evitar los platillos altos en grasa, aunque estén cargados de condimentos.

Empiece por la sopa. Varios estudios sugieren que una sopa como primer plato tiende a reducir la cantidad que usted come en una comida. En un estudio de la Universidad Johns Hopkins, en Baltimore, las personas que tomaron sopa al empezar la comida consumieron el 25 por ciento menos de las calorías del plato principal que aquellos que empezaron la comida con queso y galletas.

Puede ser el volumen de espacio que la sopa ocupa en el estómago o el hecho de que la mayoría de las calorías en la sopa vienen de los carbohidratos en lugar de la grasa, dicen los investigadores. O, puede ser que un elemento sicológico tome parte en esto, dice el doctor Kenney. "La sopa caliente es muy relajante si usted tiene un apetito nervioso y persistente."

Aguántese las ganas. Cuando le atacan las ganas de un pastel relleno de crema de chocolate, no confunda el antojo con una orden, dice Linda Crawford, una especialista en la conducta de comer, en *Green Mountain at Fox Run*, un centro residencial del manejo de peso y salud, en Ludlow, Vermont. No obstante que muchas personas piensan que los antojos van haciéndose más fuertes hasta que son irresistibles, la investigación muestra que los antojos de alimentos de hecho empiezan y en efecto aumentan, pero después llegan al pico máximo y disminuyen. Distráigase con una caminata o alguna otra cosa que sea incompatible con el hecho de comer, dice Crawford, y aguántese el antojo. "Exactamente igual que con el *surfing*", dice ella, "mientras más practique dejar pasar una ola de antojo, más fácil se hará". Pero si usted todavía tiene el antojo después de 20 minutos, satisfágalo y coma una pequeña porción —y disfrútela, aconseja ella.

Actividades para la mujer que quiere perder

Si adopta una dieta más saludable le ayudará a perder peso, pero si combina sus nuevos hábitos de comer más saludables con el ejercicio usted adquirirá una figura más firme más pronto —y la conservará.

El ejercicio también fortalece su corazón y sus arterias, y estimula su confianza en sí misma —en resumen, contrarrestará muchos de los efectos dañinos del sobrepeso. El ejercicio incluso puede ayudarle a frenar su apetito.

Si usted no está acostumbrada a hacer ejercicio, vea a su médico antes de empezar. Una vez que tenga su autorización, está lista. Aquí hay algunos consejos para que empiece.

Repítalo. "El mejor presagio de un manejo del peso a largo plazo es la actividad aeróbica regular, la cual impulsa el ritmo de su corazón", dice el doctor Foreyt. "Caminar vigorosamente es una buena elección porque para la mayoría de la gente es muy fácil de hacer regularmente. Pero la efectividad de cualquier actividad aeróbica para el control de peso se ha probado repetidamente." Cualquier tipo de ejercicio diario ayuda. Treinta minutos de ejercicio aeróbico quema gordura y tonifica los músculos —siempre y cuando lo haga regularmente.

Queme grasa al formar músculo. El ejercicio aeróbico siempre debería formar parte de su plan de pérdida de peso, pero cuando usted agrega entrenamiento de resistencia como es levantar pesas, usted mantendrá su peso bajo con la ayuda de "músculos hambrientos. El tejido muscular necesita más calorías", dice Janet Walberg-Rankin, Ph.D., profesora asociada en el Programa de Ciencia del Ejercicio de la División de Salud y Educación Física en el Instituto Politécnico y Universidad Estatal de Virginia, en Blacksburg. "Por lo tanto si usted aumenta la masa muscular mientras está perdiendo grasa, usted estimula su capacidad de quemar combustible." Después durante el día, cuando usted está en una reunión o haciendo cola en el banco, es cuando sus músculos nuevos y hambrientos están pulverizando sus calorías, dice ella.

"El entrenamiento de resistencia no es simplemente levantar barras con pesas", agrega el doctor Foreyt, a pesar de que es excelente para hacer sus brazos más firmes. Para realmente trabajar los diferentes grupos de músculos, lo mejor que usted puede hacer es ir a un gimnasio y pedir a un entrenador allí que le muestre cómo hacer una tabla de gimnasia (*circuit-train*), dice él. Usted usa una serie de máquinas diferentes con pesas para presionar las pesas contra los músculos del cuello, de los brazos, del pecho y de las piernas. Usted puede lograr lo mismo usando pesas sueltas en la casa, dice él. "Presionar sus músculos contra algo que no cede —eso es resistencia."

TELEVISIÓN

La caja electrónica de Pandora

La vida social de Karen Dykeman estaba confinada a una caja de 19 pulgadas en su sala. Se desayunaba con Regis Philbin, almorzaba con Phil Donahue, cenaba con Dan Rather y comía un bocadillo (merienda o *snack*) a medianoche con Johnny Carson.

"Mi vida giraba alrededor de la televisión virtualmente desde las primeras horas de la mañana hasta las últimas horas de la noche", dice la operadora de teléfonos de 35 años de edad en Seven Lakes, Carolina del Norte. "Gracias a Dios, me he podido separar de eso. En los dos años desde que dejé de ver televisión, he perdido 60 libras (27 kilos), me he involucrado con un grupo teatral de la comunidad, volví a la universidad, empecé a salir con amigos y en general me estoy divirtiendo mucho. Ahora tengo una vida real. Definitivamente me siento más vigorosa y siento que puedo pensar más claramente."

El estilo de vida energético de Karen desde que abandonó el hábito de la televisión no sorprende a los médicos quienes sospechan desde hace tiempo que el atractivo magnético de la televisión nos roba nuestra juventud de muchas maneras.

"No existe en absoluto duda alguna de que ver la televisión por mucho tiempo la puede hacer sentir vieja y fatigada antes de tiempo", dice el doctor Kurt V. Gold, un médico especializado en medicina física y rehabilitación en el Centro Médico Immanuel, en Omaha, Nebraska, quien ha estudiado los efectos que ver televisión tiene en los niños. "Nada más piense qué pasa cuando usted ve televisión. Usted está sentada pasivamente, no está usando mucho sus músculos. Después de ver un programa largo, se siente tiesa, cansada y mentalmente vacía."

"A la larga, esto puede reducir su capacidad de pensar y de desempeñar tareas físicas. Si usted ve mucha televisión, simplemente no está haciendo algo que podría renovar su cuerpo. Como resultado, sus músculos cuelgan y su mente se estanca. Es sentido común. Si no lo usa, lo pierde."

Mire cómo puede engordar

Pero el peligro de la televisión no está limitado a perder el tono muscular o a abusar de sus células cerebrales. Algunos investigadores también creen que hay un vínculo definitivo entre ver mucha televisión y esa temida gordura de los años maduros. En un estudio a 4.771 mujeres cuya edad promedio era de 35 años, Larry A. Tucker, Ph.D., profesor y director de promoción de salud en la Universidad Brigham Young, en Provo, Utah, descubrió que aquellas que se pasaban más de tres a cuatro horas al día viendo la televisión tenían el doble de riesgo de hacerse obesas que las mujeres que veían menos de una hora diaria.

Un estudio de 800 adultos publicado en la revista *American Dietetic Association* (Asociación Dietética de los Estados Unidos), encontró que el riesgo de la obesidad puede ser mayor que eso. En este estudio, la incidencia de obesidad entre aquellas que veían una hora o menos de televisión al día era del 4,5 por ciento, pero la frecuencia subió al 19,2 por ciento entre aquellos que veían cuatro horas o más al día.

Una evidencia adicional de la conexión entre ver televisión y la desaparición de una buena forma física proviene de otro estudio de la Universidad de Brigham Young. En este estudio de 9.000 adultos, los investigadores concluyeron que las personas que veían televisión por menos de una hora al día eran las que estaban en mejor forma. En comparación con ellas, las que tenían hábitos de ver tres a cuatro horas estaban un 41 por ciento en peor forma y aquellas que hacían maratones regulares de ver televisión por cuatro o más horas estaban un 50 por ciento en peor forma.

"Ver televisión en forma excesiva puede no ser el principio de la decadencia física, pero puede ser parte de ella", dice el doctor Tucker. "Las personas que ven mucha televisión tienden a ser menos activas físicamente, a comer más bocadillos (meriendas o *snacks*) altos en grasa y a ser más obesas. Otras investigaciones han demostrado que las personas que ven mucha televisión probablemente tienen mayor probabilidad de ser fumadoras. Así que hay bastantes consecuencias negativas para la salud que pueden estar asociadas con ver mucha televisión."

En un estudio a 11.947 adultos, el doctor Tucker encontró que las personas que veían de tres a cuatro horas de televisión al día tenían el doble de riesgo de desarrollar altos niveles de colesterol que las personas que veían menos de una hora diaria. Aun aquellos que veían de dos a tres horas al día tenían 1,5 más probabilidades de tener colesterol alto. Colesterol excesivo en la sangre es un factor de riesgo para una enfermedad cardiovascular.

Evite el "telenvejecimiento"

¿Pero cuántas personas tienen el tiempo de ver tanta televisión diariamente? Muchas. De hecho, según la compañía de mercadeo *Strategic Research Corporation* (Corporación de Investigación y Estrategia) en Miami, Florida, los latinos que viven en los Estados Unidos ven un promedio de más de cuatro horas de televisión diarias. Esto significa que muchos de ellos pueden estar corriendo un

¿Es usted una víctima de la televisión?

Marque cada pregunta a la que usted conteste sí.

1. ¿Ve usted más de dos horas de televisión por día?

2. ¿Deja usted de hablar con otros cuando está viendo televisión?

3. ¿Se siente usted infeliz o irritada si tiene que apagar el televisor para hacer alguna otra cosa?

4. ¿Se siente usted ocasionalmente muy cansada durante el programa de actividades de un día regular?

5. ¿Come usted frecuentemente comida basura o bocadillos (meriendas o *snacks*) poco saludables cuando se sienta a ver televisión?

6. ¿Experimenta usted frecuentemente insomnio y usa la televisión como un medio para distraerse durante sus horas sin sueño?

7. En un día agradable, ¿es más probable que usted se quede en casa a ver televisión que salir a hacer algo afuera?

8. ¿Es difícil para usted compartir o comunicar sus sentimientos y experiencias con otros?

9. ¿Está usted involucrada activamente en menos de dos pasatiempos, clubes o deportes por lo menos cuatro horas por semana?

10. ¿Prende usted el televisor frecuentemente y recorre las estaciones sin estar buscando un programa específico para ver?

Cómo sumar su puntuación

Por cada pregunta con número impar a la que usted contestó sí, anótese dos puntos. Estos factores están determinados por expertos como indicadores de ver demasiada televisión.

Por cada pregunta con un número par que usted contesto sí, anótese un punto. Estos factores, en combinación con los hábitos malos de ver televisión, son una señal de dificultades potenciales.

Sume su puntuación y use la siguiente escala para determinar su calificación.

3 o menos. No hay problema

4 a 6. Dificultad potencial avecinándose.

7 a 9. Sí, usted probablemente está viendo demasiada televisión.

10 o más. ¡Ay, ay, ay! Su cerebro se está fusionando con los circuitos del televisor.

riesgo alto de desarrollar las llamadas pancitas, enfermedades del corazón y otros padecimientos crónicos normalmente asociados con el envejecimiento.

Ver televisión también puede embotar su mente. Los investigadores encontraron que dos años después que la televisión se introdujo en una aldea canadiense, en 1973, el tiempo que un residente típico se pasaba frente al televisor aumentó de 0 a 22 horas a la semana. Ese aumento redujo drásticamente la participación de los habitantes en las actividades sociales y deportivas de la comunidad. Los investigadores también encontraron que los habitantes que veían mucha televisión no resolvían los problemas de rompecabezas tan bien como los habitantes que veían menos televisión. Además, después de que la televisión llegó a la aldea, los habitantes renunciaban a tratar de resolver esos problemas mucho más rápidamente que antes de la llegada de la televisión, dice Tannis MacBeth Williams, Ph.D., profesor de sicología en la Universidad de Columbia Británica, en Vancouver.

Tampoco cuente con la televisión para animarse. De hecho, la investigación ha demostrado que ver televisión por períodos prolongados deja a las personas con peor humor de lo que estaban antes de empezar a verla. La irritabilidad, la dificultad para relacionarse con otros o el aburrimiento también pueden vincularse con ver televisión en forma excesiva.

"Yo no diría que la televisión es un desperdicio total del tiempo libre de uno. Hay algunos buenos programas que nos informan y entretienen", dice el doctor Tucker. "Sin embargo, hay una tendencia a excederse con la televisión, y eso es un derroche y hasta cierto punto, es poco saludable."

Aquí hay algunas sugerencias para que usted pueda controlar la televisión en lugar de dejar que ésta la controle a usted.

Ponga límites. Establezca un límite a la cantidad de tiempo que usted va a ver por semana y manténgase firme. "Usted necesita poner límites o el tiempo que pase viendo televisión puede fácilmente volverse incontrolable", dice el doctor Tucker.

Tenga una noche libre. Prohíbase ver televisión una noche a la semana. Vea qué cosas creativas puede encontrar para que usted y su familia hagan juntos, dice el doctor Tucker.

Sea su propia guía. Estudie el programa de televisión y marque uno o dos programas por noche que usted quisiera ver. Prenda el televisor cuando el programa empieza y apáguelo enseguida que el programa termina, dice el doctor Tucker. Esto la desalentará de quedarse a ver el programa siguiente.

Use la imaginación. Antes de prender el televisor para ver un programa, tome un momento para imaginarse caminando hacia el aparato y apagándolo cuando el programa termina. "Eso programará en su mente que el televisor se va a apagar realmente en ese momento y usted encontrará alguna otra cosa que hacer", dice Jane M. Healy, Ph.D., una sicóloga educacional en Vail, Colorado y autora de *Endangered Minds: Why Our Children Don't Think and What We Can Do About It* (Mentes en peligro: por qué nuestros niños no piensan y qué podemos hacer al respecto).

Recompénsese por no verla. Por cada hora que no ve la televisión cuando usted normalmente la vería, dese un punto. Después de que junte 10 ó 20 puntos, regálese boletos para ir al teatro, o para pasar una noche en un club de comedia o salga a comer con su familia o amistades, sugiere Leonard Jason,

Ph.D., profesor de sicología clínica y comunitaria en la Universidad DePaul, en Chicago.

Sintonícese sin sonido. Pruebe prender el televisor pero sin sonido, dice la doctora Healy. Más que seguro, usted va a encontrar alguna otra cosa que hacer con su tiempo. "Mucho del atractivo de la televisión viene de la banda de sonido", dice la doctora Healy.

Muévalo a algún lugar fuera de la vista. Pruebe poniendo el televisor en un lugar poco común, como por ejemplo a un cuarto lleno de cosas sin sillas, así usted tendría que hacer un esfuerzo para ver televisión. "Yo he estado remodelando mi casa, y puse un montón de muebles enfrente del aparato, así que no puedo llegar a éste fácilmente", dice el doctor Gold. "¿Sabe lo bueno de esto? He estado trabajando en el jardín y pasando tiempo con mi familia en lugar de con el televisor."

Salga de la casa. Dé un paseo, o vaya a la piscina (alberca) y póngase a nadar por placer. Salga a ver el mundo real. "Si usted ve tres horas de televisión, ¿se siente usted llena de energía? Probablemente no. Si usted sale a caminar 15 minutos, tendrá usted la oportunidad de hablar con sus vecinos y tomar algo de aire fresco. Le apuesto a que usted regresaría a la casa sintiéndose vigorizada y lista para hacer cualquier cosa menos ver televisión", dice el doctor C. Noel Bairey Merz, director médico del Centro Preventivo y de Rehabilitación Cardiaca del Centro Médico Cedars-Sinai, en Los Ángeles.

Llámame. "Arregle con una amiga para que la llame por teléfono a la hora que se termina su programa favorito. Eso puede ser todo el incentivo que usted necesita para romper con su hábito, ya que una vez que la separan del televisor, le va ser más fácil no regresar a éste", dice la doctora Healy.

Busque un pasatiempo. "Encuentre algo que le interese, ya sea el dibujo, la fotografía, el cuidado de mascotas o el estudio", dice Karen Dykeman. "Yo me involucré en cosas tales como el teatro que me hizo sentir importante, necesitada y útil. Si usted encuentra algo útil en su vida, puede romper el hábito de la televisión realmente rápido."

No ponga cable. Mientras menos opciones usted tenga para ver, más probable es que usted encuentre alguna otra cosa que hacer con su tiempo, dice el doctor Gold.

TRASTORNOS
DE LA TIROIDES

Cómo mantener
a su regulador en forma

Durante la mayor parte de nuestras vidas, la glándula tiroides actúa como el socio secreto en una compañía, trabajando entre los bastidores para mantener a nuestros cuerpos en funcionamiento. Pequeña y con forma de mariposa, descansa sin pretensiones en la base de la garganta, produciendo las hormonas que regulan el metabolismo del cuerpo, la temperatura y el ritmo del corazón. Cuando está funcionando correctamente, difícilmente nos enteramos que está ahí.

Pero esta glándula sencilla a menudo hace notar su presencia en forma espectacular. Al igual que el dispositivo para hacer hielo en su refrigerador, éste puede descomponerse, ya sea bombeando hormonas a un ritmo enloquecido o reduciendo su producción a escasamente un hilito.

Cuando esto sucede, la glándula tiroides poco activa o muy activa puede acelerar o hacer más lenta la actividad metabólica de su cuerpo en forma dramática. Al mismo tiempo, estos cambios metabólicos pueden producir una amplia gama de síntomas desagradables que afectarán de manera devastadora la forma en que usted se ve y se siente. Y si no se trata, una glándula tiroides que está funcionando mal puede provocar problemas del corazón —y puede incluso llevar a un estado de coma o a la muerte.

A pesar de lo mal que todo esto suena, en realidad no es para tanto. "Con una detección precoz y tratamiento apropiado, casi todos los problemas de una glándula tiroides anormal pueden corregirse y los síntomas invertirse", dice el doctor Brian Tulloch, profesor clínico asociado en la Escuela de Medicina de la Universidad de Texas, en Houston. "Y la mayoría de los pacientes pueden llegar a vivir una vida normal, funcional y productiva."

La tiroides poco activa

Cuando su glándula tiroides pierde energía y reduce su producción de hormonas, su cuerpo gradualmente muestra toda clase de señales de que está funcionando al mínimo: fatiga, escalofríos, piel seca, cabello áspero, flujo menstrual abundante, inflamación e hinchazón alrededor de la cara y los ojos, para mencionar algunas de ellas. También puede afectar su funcionamiento mental, conduciendo a una concentración deficiente, olvido y depresión. Su libido y su fertilidad pueden vacilar y detenerse. Esta condición se llama hipotiroidismo.

El problema con el hipotiroidismo es que muchos de los síntomas asociados con éste son tan comunes que usted difícilmente podría sospechar que la culpable es su glándula enferma. "Es fácil pasar por alto una glándula tiroides poco activa, porque los síntomas son similares a aquellos asociados con otras enfermedades comunes y simulan muchos de los cambios físicos asociados con el envejecimiento normal", dice el doctor Lawrence Wood, presidente y director médico de la Fundación de la Tiroides de los Estados Unidos y un especialista en la glándula tiroides en el Hospital General de Massachusetts, en Boston. "Muchos pacientes —e incluso algunos médicos— piensan que estos síntomas simplemente significan que el cuerpo se está haciendo viejo y, muy a menudo, el problema no se reporta o no se diagnostica."

Generaciones atrás, el engrosamiento de la glándula tiroides, o bocio, era común en los Estados Unidos debido a una falta de yodo en la dieta. Hoy en día, sin embargo, la deficiencia de yodo no es un problema en la dieta típica de los Estados Unidos; la causa más común de hipotiroidismo es la enfermedad de Hashimoto, un trastorno del sistema autoinmune del cuerpo.

Debido a que el hipotiroidismo hace más lenta la forma en que el cuerpo quema las calorías, muchas mujeres con peso de más tratan anhelosamente de echarle la culpa de sus aumentos de peso a una glándula tiroides lenta. Pero no se la puede culpar. "La obesidad y los aumentos mayores de peso raramente están relacionados con una glándula tiroides poco activa", dice el doctor Tulloch. "La mayoría de los aumentos de peso relacionados con la glándula tiroides son sólo de unas cuantas libras y eso se debe principalmente a la retención de agua."

Mientras que por lo general los médicos no pueden hacer que una glándula tiroides poco activa se vuelva otra vez activa, sí fácilmente pueden tratarla y controlarla. "Todo lo que necesitamos hacer es restablecer el equilibrio correcto de las hormonas tiroideas en el sistema por medio del reemplazo de lo que no se está produciendo", dice el doctor Martin I. Surks, jefe de la División de Endocrinología y Metabolismo en el Centro Médico Montefiore, de la Ciudad de Nueva York. Las mujeres con la glándula tiroides lenta toman pastillas pequeñas que contienen una versión sintética de la hormona tiroxina. La desventaja es que tienen que tomarla diariamente por el resto de sus vidas.

La tiroides muy activa

Ahora imagínese a la glándula tiroides actuando en reversa, bombeando demasiadas hormonas. Estas hormonas en exceso empujan el metabolismo del cuerpo a trabajar a toda marcha, produciendo una combinación única de hiper-síntomas que incluyen latido rápido del corazón, pérdida de peso, debilidad, nerviosismo, irritabilidad y estremecimientos.

No es de sorprenderse que a esto se le llama hipertiroidismo. La causa más común es la enfermedad de Grave, el trastorno autoinmune que atacó a ambos, el ex presidente George Bush y a Barbara Bush. La ex primera dama, —usted podrá recordar— sufrió una pérdida rápida de peso, los globos de los ojos saltones y problemas de la vista, clásicos síntomas de Grave. Su esposo tomó consciencia de su enfermedad de Grave después del susto que se dio por un latido irregular del corazón.

Cuando se trata una glándula tiroides muy activa, los médicos tienen varias opciones. La más simple y más recetada es usar yodo radioactivo para reducir el número de células en la glándula tiroides que están produciendo de más. Los médicos también pueden recetar drogas que bloquean la producción de la hormona tiroidea o que bloquean los efectos de la hormona en el cuerpo. Y como último recurso, los doctores pueden extirpar quirúrgicamente toda o parte de una glándula tiroides muy activa. Pero ya que la cirugía y el yodo radioactivo pueden hacer que las mujeres más adelante desarrollen hipotiroidismo, a menudo es necesario tomar pastillas de tiroxina durante toda la vida.

Quién corre el riesgo

Varios factores claves pueden poner a una mujer en riesgo de desarrollar trastornos de la glándula tiroides. El más importante es simplemente el ser una mujer. "Las mujeres tienen cinco veces más probabilidades que los hombres de desarrollar problemas con sus glándulas tiroides", dice el doctor Surks. "Muchos trastornos de la glándula tiroides también se manifiestan durante o después del embarazo o después de la menopausia."

La enfermedad de Grave y otras causas de glándula tiroides muy activa son más comunes en el grupo de personas entre los 20 y los 40 años de edad, pero también pueden ocurrir en las personas mayores. Para los 50 años de edad, al menos una mujer en cada diez tiene señales de una glándula tiroides poco activa. Y el 17 por ciento de las mujeres mayores de los 60 años de edad sufren de alguna forma de hipotiroidismo.

La genética también desempeña un papel. Si en su familia hay una historia de enfermedad de la glándula tiroides o enfermedades autoinmunes como la diabetes o artritis reumatoide, usted es una candidata a los problemas de la glándula tiroides a medida que se vaya haciendo mayor. Otro factor a considerar: de acuerdo con un estudio holandés, el fumar cigarrillos parece ser un factor significante que produce la enfermedad de Grave en las personas propensas. Estos resultados implican que dejando el hábito puede evitar el desarrollo de la enfermedad si es que viene de familia.

Otros factores de riesgo: haber recibido tratamientos de radiación alrededor de la cabeza y cuello cuando era niña, el uso de ciertos medicamentos tales como litio o haber pasado por una experiencia especialmente impresionante como es el perder a un ser querido.

Lo que las mujeres deberían hacer

Con la excepción de comer una dieta balanceada y no fumar, no hay mucho que usted pueda hacer para prevenir la enfermedad de la glándula tiroides. "Es importante detectar la enfermedad de la glándula tiroides temprano, antes de que eche a perder su cuerpo, sus emociones y su vida", dice el doctor Wood.

Haga que su doctor revise cualquier síntoma o anormalidad que pudiera sugerir hipo o hipertiroidismo. Según el doctor Wood, cualquier mujer mayor de los 50 años de edad, especialmente si se encuentra en uno de los grupos con riesgo, debería hacer una prueba de la glándula tiroides parte de su examen físico anual. "Los exámenes regulares se vuelven cada vez más importantes a medida que usted envejece, porque muchos de los síntomas de la enfermedad de la glándula tiroides se hacen menos obvios y más difíciles de que usted los detecte por sí misma", dice él.

Revisar la función de la glándula tiroides normalmente requiere sólo una prueba de sangre. Si aparece un abultamiento o un nódulo, puede ser que el médico tome una muestra del tejido de la glándula tiroides para examinarlo en un procedimiento relativamente indoloro llamado biopsia con aguja delgada.

Aunque los tratamientos con hormonas tiroideas casi siempre son seguros, los estudios han mostrado que cuando se reemplaza la hormona tiroidea puede aumentar el riesgo de una mujer a la osteoporosis, el trastorno en el cual los huesos se debilitan y puede llevar a las fracturas de la cadera y de las vértebras. Por eso es importante hacerse un examen anual que incluya una prueba de la hormona estimulante de la secreción tiroidea, tomar la dosis de la hormona tiroidea adecuada para usted y mantener un programa apropiado de nutrición y ejercicio.

ÚLCERAS

Cómo dominar al fuego interior

Si usted tiene una úlcera, piense dos veces antes de echarle la culpa a los sospechosos de costumbre. Una en cada diez personas que tiene o que tendrá úlceras piensa que son el resultado de demasiada presión en el trabajo o demasiada comida muy condimentada.

Pero en realidad, dicen los investigadores, esas teorías son inválidas. La investigación muestra que las úlceras son más comunes entre los desempleados. Y no hay pruebas de que las comidas condimentadas desempeñan un papel en su formación.

"A menudo no es lo que la gente piensa, pero hay muchas causas para las úlceras y la edad parece que desempeña un papel en la mayoría de ellas", dice el doctor Jorge Herrera, profesor asociado de medicina en el Colegio de Medicina de la Universidad de Alabama del Sur, en Mobile. Esto es aparentemente apropiado, ya que las úlceras parece que envejecen a una mujer antes de tiempo, causando un dolor que puede obstaculizar la actividad física y requerir bastante atención. La mayoría de las mujeres parece que controlan las úlceras al tratar a sus trabajos y presiones con mucho tacto y al adoptar la dieta de las viejitas de salsa de manzana, requesón y otros alimentos insípidos.

Cómo nos las buscamos

Las úlceras se forman cuando los jugos digestivos —ácidos, realmente— empiezan a quemar a través del delicado revestimiento color rosa de sus órganos digestivos. Esto es por lo general el resultado de un deterioro en la capa protectora que cubre el revestimiento del estómago y el duodeno, el extremo superior del intestino delgado.

Hay dos tipos principales: úlceras gástricas, las cuales aparecen más frecuentemente en las mujeres y usualmente después de los 50 años de edad; ocurren en el estómago y los síntomas incluyen una sensación de ardor o de "hambre" en el estómago o abajo del esternón, una ansiedad indefinida del estómago y aun náusea crónica. Las úlceras duodenales, que son más comunes entre los hombres y tienden a aparecer entre los 20 y los 40 años de edad, atacan más abajo, en el extremo superior del intestino delgado. Con las úlceras duodenales, a menudo el dolor se alivia después de comer; con las úlceras gástricas, ese no es el caso. Cualquier tipo de úlcera puede causar que la deposición sea de color negro o castaño y con olor muy desagradable y el vomitar de lo que parece ser un material como granos de café.

"La causa principal de las úlceras gástricas es tomar ciertos medicamentos", dice el doctor Herrera. "Estas úlceras son más comunes en las mujeres, particularmente al envejecer, porque muchos de estos medicamentos son para trastornos que por lo general ocurren cuando usted envejece, tales como las drogas para la artritis y otros analgésicos."

Pero aun las mujeres jóvenes pueden estar buscándose las úlceras gástricas. "Posiblemente los peores infractores, simplemente porque son los que se usan más frecuentemente, son las aspirinas y las drogas antiinflamatorias no esteroidales disponibles sin receta", dice el doctor Herrera. "Si usted toma algunas de estas drogas por más de tres meses seguidos, como muchas mujeres lo hacen, aumenta significativamente su riesgo de úlceras."

Estas drogas hacen su trabajo sucio al inhibir la producción de mucosidad y agentes protectores neutralizadores de ácido; la aspirina también puede debilitar el revestimiento estomacal y causar sangramiento. "De hecho, muchos pacientes ni siquiera saben que tienen úlceras debido a los analgésicos en la drogas que toman", agrega. "Algunas veces vienen al consultorio por problemas de sangre o con su deposición, y sólo entonces se dan cuenta de que tienen úlceras."

A menudo las úlceras duodenales son producidas por fumar, lo cual causa la producción de cantidades excesivas de ácidos digestivos. Pero los estudios muestran que por lo menos el 95 por ciento de los pacientes con úlceras duodenales también albergan bacterias comunes llamadas *Helicobacter pylori*, dice el doctor William R. Ruderman, presidente del Departamento de Gastroenterología en la Clínica Cleveland Florida, en Fort Lauderdale. Las bacterias pasan de persona a persona, como cualquier otra enfermedad infecciosa, y se pueden curar con antibióticos. "Estas bacterias son más comunes al envejecer", dice el doctor Ruderman. "Por principio, la exposición a estas bacterias aumenta al pasar el tiempo. Y las defensas de su cuerpo también pueden verse afectadas al pasar el tiempo." De hecho, una de cada cinco personas con estas bacterias se enferma de úlceras duodenales.

Cómo nos podemos escapar de la trampa

Si usted piensa que tiene una úlcera, vea a su médico. Un médico puede recetar los medicamentos para reducir las secreciones de ácido y aliviar el dolor así como los antibióticos para *H. pylori*. Entretanto, aquí está lo que usted puede hacer para prevenir las úlceras o para reducir su gravedad.

Escoja *Tylenol*. Para los dolores de cabeza y otros achaques y dolores menores tome acetaminófeno —el cual viene en productos como *Tylenol*— en lugar de ibuprofen, vendido comúnmente como *Advil* y *Nuprin*. El ibuprofen es un antiinflamatorio, y los productos que lo contienen pueden causar úlceras, dice el doctor Herrera. "Cierto, tienen ingredientes para matar el dolor, pero también los tienen otros productos que no conducen a las úlceras. Así que si usted tiene un dolor de cabeza u otro problema menor que requiere un analgésico, tome *Tylenol*." Y aléjese de la aspirina, ya que ésta puede causar aún más daño que el ibuprofen. La aspirina puede debilitar el revestimiento del estómago y causar sangramientos.

Extinga el cigarrillo. Los cigarrillos producen el doble de daño a las personas propensas a las úlceras. "Fumar puede conducir a las úlceras porque aumenta multiformemente la producción de ácido. Especialmente si usted fuma después de la cena o antes de irse a la cama", dice el doctor Herrera. "Eso es debido a que normalmente la producción de ácido es peor durante la noche."

Una vez que usted tiene úlceras, el ácido creado al fumar dificulta deshacerse de éstas. "Eso evita que las úlceras sanen y hace más probable que regresen", agrega el doctor Mark H. Ebell, profesor asistente en el Departamento de Medicina Familiar de la Universidad Estatal de Wayne, en Detroit.

Aprenda a calmarse. Las personas que ven su vida como muy estresante tienen hasta tres veces más probabilidades de desarrollar úlceras que aquellas que aprenden a aceptar los golpes de la vida, dice el doctor Robert Anda, del Centro Nacional de Prevención de Enfermedades Crónicas y Promoción de la Salud, en Atlanta. Pero ya que todas estamos bajo estrés, ¿por qué algunas de nosotras tenemos úlceras y otras no?

"Es cuestión de cómo usted interpreta el estrés", dice el doctor Anda. Si usted siente el peso del mundo sobre sus espaldas y percibe los eventos estresantes como negativos, es una candidata segura para las úlceras, porque esta percepción resulta en la producción de más ácidos estomacales. Por otro lado, las mujeres que reconocen que tienen estrés pero lo ven como un hecho de la vida cotidiana y no dejan que las abrume, tienen menos probabilidades de tener úlceras.

Muchas mujeres que reaccionan negativamente al estrés encuentran que les ayuda cuando hablan acerca de sus problemas con buenos amigos, meditan o hacen ejercicios para relajarse en forma regular, o aun comienzan programas regulares de ejercicio, dice el doctor Howard Mertz, profesor asistente de medicina en la Escuela de Medicina UCLA de la Universidad de California, Los Ángeles.

Reevalúe su dieta insípida. Aunque no hay prueba de que comer una dieta insípida va a ayudar, hay evidencia de que beber una puede perjudicarla. De hecho, el antiguo remedio de tomar leche para una úlcera puede hacer más daño que bien, dice el doctor Richard W. McCallum, profesor de medicina y jefe de gastroenterología en la Escuela de Medicina de la Universidad de Virginia, en Charlottesville. Eso es porque mientras que la leche inicialmente puede tener un efecto neutralizante sobre estos ácidos, después de unos 30 minutos, usted sufre un "efecto de rebote" en el cual el calcio y la proteína de la leche realmente estimulan la producción de ácidos.

VELLO INDESEADO

Pelusa, pelusa, no se luzca

Puede ser que usted no lo haya notado cuando era joven, cuando una pelusa de durazno apenas perceptible sobre un cutis suave de niña no importaba en lo más mínimo. Pero ahora que es mayor, usted puede encontrar que el vello es más profuso o de repente más oscuro. Posiblemente usted recuerde a una tía cariñosa cuya sonrisa mostraba una sombra pronunciada, pero, ¡seguramente usted no ha llegado a esa edad todavía!

Quizás sí. O a lo mejor el vello indeseado simplemente ha llegado más temprano. De cualquier manera, esto la hace sentirse envejecida y poco atractiva, como si su cuerpo estuviera saboteando a su belleza. Es un problema común para muchas mujeres, a pesar de que muchas de nosotras preferiríamos morir antes que admitirlo.

A menudo se basa en la genética, dicen los médicos. Si el árbol genealógico de su familia tiene raíces mediterráneas, usted puede desarrollar un crecimiento oscuro y aterciopelado en su labio superior o bajo la línea donde terminan las "patillas". Algunas veces sólo aparecerán unos cuantos vellos testarudos parecidos a los de una barba, a menudo en la barbilla.

Pero la causa más común del crecimiento de vello excesivo cuando las mujeres envejecen son los cambios hormonales de la menopausia, dice el doctor Victor Newcomer, profesor de dermatología en la Escuela de Medicina UCLA de la Universidad de California, Los Ángeles. "La mayoría de las mujeres tienen un poco de bozo en el labio superior después de la pubertad, y en las personas con cabello oscuro, puede ser muy acentuado. Pero después de la menopausia, realmente se agrava con la aparición de vellos gruesos y fibrosos." Eso es debido a que los efectos de la hormona masculina andrógeno (que todas las mujeres tienen) se vuelven más pronunciados cuando los niveles de la hormona femenina estrógeno disminuyen. El andrógeno queda entonces en libertad para estimular más el crecimiento del vello, dice él.

Si el vello en exceso, facial o en el cuerpo, no es común entre las mujeres de su familia, usted puede preguntarle a su doctor si es que alguna medicina que

Electrólisis: la solución permanente —eventualmente

Hay una forma de eliminar el vello permanentemente y es a través de la electrólisis profesional. Este método es apropiado para el vello en cualquier parte del cuerpo, desde el labio superior y el área del pezón hasta los dedos de los pies —con excepción de las pestañas, la nariz y las orejas— aunque es doloroso y lleva tiempo. Esto es lo que usted experimentará en el consultorio de un electrolizador con licencia a tarifas que oscilan entre $15 y $100, según la duración de la sesión.

La electrolisista limpia su piel con alcohol, guía una aguja eléctrica estéril dentro del folículo del vello y prende la corriente. La corriente destruirá el folículo del vello, pero algunas veces se requieren sesiones múltiples. Y algunas mujeres encuentran los tratamientos simplemente demasiado dolorosos para tolerar. Lo que motiva a muchas de ellas a soportar el proceso es que si se persiste con los tratamientos, eventualmente el vello no volverá a crecer.

Para un área pequeña de vello indeseado, puede valer la pena, dice el doctor Seth L. Matarasso, profesor asistente de dermatología en la Escuela de Medicina de la Universidad de California, San Francisco. Pero hay riesgos involucrados. Existe la posibilidad de un cambio en la pigmentación de su piel, de cicatrices leves o de foliculitis, una inflamación de los folículos de los vellos, dice él. Y aunque es muy poco probable con las técnicas de esterilización usadas por la mayoría de los

---

está tomando podría estar causando el problema, dice el doctor Seth L. Matarasso, profesor asistente de dermatología en la escuela de Medicina de la Universidad de California, San Francisco. Algunas veces la medicina para la presión arterial, los esteroides para la artritis, los diuréticos (píldoras de agua) o las píldoras anticonceptivas pueden estimular el crecimiento del vello, dice él.

Si nota que aparecen más que unos cuantos vellos súbitamente, dice el doctor Matarasso, vea a su médico para que le hagan pruebas endocrinológicas. Aunque es muy raro, el crecimiento del vello fuera de lo común en las mujeres puede indicar un problema con la glándula tiroides u hormonal.

Y, aunque el vello en las piernas y los brazos es normal, es poco usual tener algún crecimiento sobre las mejillas o la frente. El vello en esas áreas podría ser el resultado de varias causas, incluyendo una enfermedad de los ovarios o de las glándulas pituitaria o adrenal, dice el doctor Newcomer. Algunas enfermedades raras del hígado también pueden estimular el crecimiento del vello en las mejillas o en la frente, dice él.

electrolisistas profesionales, existe el potencial de la propagación de enfermedades incluyendo la hepatitis, dice.

Su mejor protección contra la infección es estar segura de que su electrolisista usa una aguja nueva todas las veces y pedirle a ella que use guantes de látex, dice el doctor Victor Newcomer, profesor de dermatología en la Escuela de Medicina UCLA de la Universidad de California, Los Ángeles.

Si usted se pregunta si las máquinas para hacerse la electrólisis en casa que usted ve en los catálogos para ordenar por correo funcionan tan bien como los equipos de salón, los expertos son escépticos.

"Algunas de estas máquinas se supone que van a funcionar sin dolor usando ondas de radio para destruir los folículos del vello en su base", dice Carole Walderman, una cosmetóloga y esteta y presidenta de la Escuela de Estética y Maquillaje Von Lee International, en Baltimore. "Pero el pelo no es un conductor de electricidad, así que ¿cómo puede este método destruir la raíz del vello?"

Aun cuando la corriente galvánica de las máquinas normales de electrólisis cauterizan el folículo directamente, dice Walderman, usted todavía tiene hasta el 90 por ciento de crecimiento nuevo, razón por la cual se necesitan tratamientos repetidos para eliminar el vello permanentemente.

O su problema puede simplemente ser que usted está molesta por el vello persistente en la cara o en el cuerpo que ha tenido desde la pubertad. Ya sea que el vello esté relacionado con la edad o no, hay varias maneras de abordar esto.

Métodos delicados y no tan delicados

Por lo tanto, ¿cómo hace usted para que todo ese vello se vaya? Aquí hay algunas sugerencias.

Blanquéelo. Con el vello que es oscuro y no muy grueso, pruebe usar un blanqueador de vello facial que usted puede comprar en su farmacia, dice el doctor Newcomer. Al blanquearlo, el vello puede notarse menos así que no hay necesidad de quitárselo.

Pero si el crecimiento del vello la pone incómoda o usted siente que se vería mejor y con el cutis más terso sin éste, aquí hay algunas otras soluciones temporales.

Rasúrese el vello. Es uno de los primeros mitos sobre el acicalamiento que las mujeres pasan de una a la otra, pero el rasurar no hace que el vello crezca de nuevo más grueso, dice el doctor Matarasso. Es fácil confundirse, porque los vellos que están creciendo pueden verse más oscuros, dice. Todos los vellos empiezan su ciclo al mismo tiempo, y cuando todos llegan a la superficie de la piel a la vez, los vellos que están saliendo se ven gruesos y se sienten ásperos, dice él. Pero en realidad el vello que está creciendo de nuevo ni es más grueso ni sale en mayor cantidad.

Usar una rasuradora eléctrica o una navaja queda a su elección; lo que se sienta mejor, dice el doctor Matarasso. Ambas rasuran igual, aunque una rasuradora eléctrica se usa sobre el cutis seco. Si usa una navaja, remójela en agua primero, entonces deje que su crema o jalea de rasurar favorita permanezca sobre la piel por un momento o dos antes de rasurarse, dice él. Esto suavizará el vello y le dará resultados más tersos. Y si usted está pensando en rasurar una parte de su cara, no hay ningún problema en hacerlo. Pero si el crecimiento facial es profuso, verifique primero con su médico para descartar razones médicas.

Use pinzas. Cuando sólo se trata de unos cuantos vellos recurrentes, uno de los métodos más sencillos para eliminar el vello es usar pinzas —con la ayuda de un espejo que amplifique si lo necesita— dice el doctor Newcomer. Algunos beneficios de este método son que es efectivo y usted lo puede hacer en privado. Pero aunque las pinzas han extirpado los folículos de los vellos, pueden pasar muchos años para que se logre un resultado permanente de quitar el vello, dice él.

Pruebe un depilatorio. Las lociones químicas como *Neet* y *Nair* son perfectamente adecuadas para usar, dice el doctor Matarasso, siempre y cuando usted haga primero una prueba sobre un área pequeña para asegurarse de que no es alérgica al producto. "Los químicos no son malos pero pueden ser abrasivos", dice él. Estos funcionan al disolver el vello en o ligeramente debajo de la capa de la piel, así que los resultados duran por hasta dos semanas, dice el doctor Matarasso.

Los depilatorios son sencillos e indoloros para usar, pero algunos tienen olores desagradables. Usted aplica la loción espesa a la piel, espera hasta 15 minutos y después la quita enjuagándola con agua templada. Debería evitar usarla cerca de los ojos o el área púbica.

Si usted usa depilatorios sobre su rostro, al principio aplique sólo un poco. No los deje puestos por mucho tiempo, o usted va a terminar con una erupción, dice el doctor Newcomer. "Si usted es morena con cutis graso, lo va a poder tolerar más tiempo. Pero las rubias con cutis delgado tienen menos tolerancia a los químicos," dice él. La textura del vello también establece una diferencia en cómo los depilatorios funcionan. Los vellos grandes y gruesos tardan más tiempo en disolverse, y el vello fino se remueve más fácilmente, dice.

Considere usar cera... por lo menos una vez. Usted probablemente ha oído la comparación entre eliminar el vello con cera y eliminarlo tipo curita, pero la cera es un poco más desafiante que eso. La parte más agradable de usar cera (y la razón por la que muchas mujeres se la aguantan) es que usted va a tener una piel libre de vello por una seis semanas después del procedimiento. Y al principio el nuevo crecimiento es suave y sedoso.

Usar cera es apropiado para cualquier parte del cuerpo —la cara, los brazos, las piernas y aun el área del bikini. Pero tenga mucho cuidado cerca de la ingle, dice el doctor Newcomer. "La cera se puede enredar en el área púbica y usted no se la va a poder quitar", dice él.

¿Cómo funciona? En un salón, se aplica la cera caliente a su piel con una espátula de madera. Cuando la cera se endurece, la persona técnica le da un buen jalón a las tiras levantando el vello con estas. Después se le pondrá una loción calmante, pero algunas mujeres encuentran el proceso muy doloroso. Usted puede comprar juegos para hacérselo usted misma para la cara o el cuerpo en la farmacia, pero, como dice el doctor Newcomer, "se requiere de un espíritu muy valeroso para levantar esas tiras."

¿Es el dolor de jalar del vello demasiado intenso? "Vaya a ver a su dermatólogo una hora antes de aplicarse la cera y haga que le adormezca la piel con una anestesia local", dice el doctor Matarasso. "Usted no sentirá casi nada."

Si usted quisiera probar con la cera y resulta que está usando la crema contra las arrugas *tretinoin* (*Retin-A*) o cualquier loción para el cutis que contiene ácido glicólico, asegúrese de suspender el uso de estos productos unos cuantos días antes de depilarse con cera, dice el doctor Matarasso. Estos preparados son exfoliantes y realmente remueven las dos capas exteriores de la piel, haciendo que esta se vuelva mucho más sensible, dice él. "Si se aplica la cera sobre la piel despojada después de usar estos preparados, usted se va a ocasionar una herida tremenda", dice él. "Usted puede arrancar una cantidad significante de piel."

Tenga también en mente que usted tiene que esperar hasta que el vello haya crecido otra vez a un cuarto de pulgada (6mm) de largo antes de aplicarse cera otra vez. Esto puede ser un problema en el verano, cuando a usted le gustaría andar con las piernas descubiertas.

Evite los guantes y las espirales eléctricas. No use los guantes con una especie de pómez para quitar el vello que se venden en muchos salones y farmacias, dice el doctor Matarasso. "Realmente son muy abrasivos y pueden lastimar su piel", dice él. Los guantes "solamente cortan mecánicamente el vello, como si fueran una rasuradora tosca", dice el doctor Newcomer.

Las espirales vibratorias funcionan levantando varios vellos a la vez y desprendiéndolos de la raíz. A diferencia de la cera que jala el vello rápidamente en el sentido contrario al crecimiento, la espiral jala de los vellos en todas las direcciones. "Es como usar pinzas mecánicas para depilar en grupo", dice el doctor Matarasso. "Algunas mujeres que las usan son muy estoicas. La mayoría de las personas encuentran a este método demasiado doloroso, además de que no la deja libre de vello por más tiempo que el rasurarse o el usar un depilatorio."

VENAS VARICOSAS

Usted no tiene que vivir con ellas

¿Qué mujer no odia las venas varicosas, ya sean las pequeñas en forma de arañas o las de cuerdas azules protuberantes? Después de los 40 años de edad, las venas varicosas se trepan sigilosamente por las piernas de más de la mitad de nosotras, y son un poderoso recordatorio del envejecimiento. De repente, usar pantalones cortos (*shorts*) o un traje de baño ya no es una opción automática.

Lo que nosotras llamamos venas de araña los médicos llaman telangiectasia venosa. Se trata en realidad de venas dilatadas, que se encuentran a menudo en la parte superior de las pantorrillas y los muslos. Tanto las venas de araña como las venas varicosas, las cuales por lo general se encuentran en las piernas, son venas más grandes de lo que deberían ser.

Aunque muchas de las mujeres encuentran a la venas de araña tan sólo como una molestia cosmética, las venas varicosas grandes verdaderamente pueden ser muy incómodas. Algunas veces causan una sensación de pesadez, cansancio y dolor crónico en las pantorrillas. Estas pueden provocar calambres nocturnos y piernas inquietas que perturban el sueño y la dejan a usted arrastrándose y muy extenuada. Las venas inflamadas a menudo se vuelven dolorosas y con picazón. Y aunque es raro, las venas varicosas pueden indicar un coágulo en una vena más profunda de la pierna.

Principalmente para las mujeres

¿De dónde vienen? De sus genes, para empezar. Usted puede heredar de ambos lados de la familia la tendencia a formar venas varicosas.

Pero el hecho es que las venas varicosas son hasta seis veces más comunes en las mujeres que en los hombres, lo que lleva a los científicos a pensar que las hormonas femeninas desempeñan un papel importante en su formación.

Una teoría sugiere que cuando una mujer está embarazada, su mayor volumen de sangre aumenta la presión sobre las venas. Al mismo tiempo, sus niveles más altos de la hormona progesterona pueden ayudar a dilatar las venas. Agregue a esto el peso del útero que presiona sobre las venas pélvicas, las cuales, a su vez, transmiten más presión sobre las venas de las piernas. Ese es el plano que las venas varicosas siguen.

La menstruación también puede causar presión en sus venas debido al aumento en el volumen de sangre antes de que usted menstrúe. Esa es la razón por la cual sus piernas pueden sentirse doloridas justo antes de su período.

Los factores del estilo de vida también pueden agravar el problema de las venas. Si usted fuma, las venas varicosas tienen más probabilidad de atacarla sigilosamente, debido a que fumar afecta el flujo de la sangre al interferir con la regulación de la fibrina, una proteína coagulante de sangre. Aunque tener peso de más no causa directamente las venas varicosas, tener más de un 20 por ciento sobre su peso ideal puede hacer aparecer las venas varicosas en aquellas mujeres que tienen la tendencia hereditaria a estas. Levantar objetos muy pesados y correr sobre superficies duras también pueden apresurar la aparición de las venas varicosas.

Algunas veces el problema subyacente es fisiológico. Las personas con venas varicosas tienen una debilidad heredada en las válvulas dentro de las venas de las piernas. Cuando la sangre fluye para arriba en dirección al corazón, estas venas normalmente evitan que la sangre corra otra vez hacia abajo. Si una válvula tiene un escape, la fuerza de gravedad manda la sangre hacia las venas inferiores cuando usted se para. Una vez que este proceso se repite suficientes veces, las paredes de las venas pueden quedar estiradas permanentemente.

"Siempre que usted esté parada o sentada con sus piernas debajo del corazón, la gravedad está actuando en su contra", explica el doctor Malcolm O. Perry, profesor y jefe de cirugía vascular en el Centro de Ciencias de la Salud de la Universidad Texas Tech, en Lubbock.

Resultados de una dieta baja en fibra

Hay una cosa que los médicos saben con seguridad acerca de las venas varicosas: no son una parte natural del envejecimiento. De hecho, el doctor Gleen Geelhoed, profesor de cirugía y educación médica internacional en el Centro Médico de la Universidad George Washington, en Washington, D.C., ha estudiado las venas varicosas en poblaciones alrededor del mundo y ha encontrado que en algunas culturas del Tercer Mundo, las venas varicosas prácticamente son inexistentes, aun en las mujeres que han tenido niños. Él también ha descubierto que cuando estas personas emigran a los países como los Estados Unidos y aprenden ciertas costumbres, principalmente las de comer alimentos bajos en fibra y llevar un estilo de vida sedentario, empiezan a tener venas varicosas.

Muy poca fibra produce estreñimiento y esfuerzo excesivo en el excusado, y allí puede ser donde la dieta afecta más a la salud de sus venas. Las poblaciones occidentales con dietas bajas en fibra evacuan feces más pequeñas

Deshágase de las telarañas

Algunas mujeres las llaman venas de araña —esas líneas rojas visibles que usualmente trepan por las piernas, especialmente en los muslos, y se asemejan a los diseños delicados de una tela de araña.

¿Cómo se deshace usted de éstas? Si son lo suficientemente grandes, por lo general la escleroterapia convencional es la mejor opción, dice el doctor Arthur Bertolino, profesor clínico asociado de dermatología en el Centro Médico de la Universidad de Nueva York, en la Ciudad de Nueva York, y un dermatólogo en Ridgewood, New Jersey.

"El tamaño óptimo para el tratamiento es de por lo menos el tamaño de la línea que usted dibujaría en un pedazo de papel con un bolígrafo normal", dice él. "Si son demasiado pequeñas, no se puede insertar una aguja."

Si usted sólo tiene unas cuantas arañas diminutas, para ocultarlas considere maquillaje con una base verdosa la cual oculta los tonos rojos, sugiere el doctor Bertolino.

Pero cuando hay más de unas cuantas sobre la cara o las piernas, la escleroterapia es usualmente muy exitosa, dice él. Una aguja minúscula se inserta dentro de la vena y se inyecta una solución. Realmente se puede ver la red roja desaparecer al entrar la solución transparente en la vena, dice él.

y más duras que la gente del Tercer Mundo, quienes tienen menos venas varicosas, hace notar el doctor Geelhoed. Y cuando hace esfuerzo excesivo en vano, eso aumenta la presión en las venas rectales, las cuales a su vez pasan más presión a las venas de las piernas.

En realidad, el conocido Estudio Framingham del Corazón, que observó por más de 40 años los estilos de vida de residentes en esa ciudad de Massachusetts, encontró que el factor de riesgo de las venas varicosas es el mismo que para las enfermedades del corazón —particularmente si se tiene sobrepeso y se es sedentario. El estudio Framingham también mostró que comparadas con las mujeres sin venas varicosas, aquellas con problemas de venas eran más a menudo obesas, menos activas, tenían presión arterial alta y eran más mayores cuando empezó su menopausia.

No son inevitables

Si las venas varicosas le vienen de familia pero todavía no le han aparecido, hay muchas cosas que usted puede hacer para ayudar a prevenirlas.

¿Efectos secundarios? Ocasionalmente, la solución causará un calambre muscular temporal cerca del tobillo o en la parte de atrás de la pantorrilla inferior, el cual su médico puede hacer desaparecer con un masaje en un minuto o dos. Raramente, puede resultar una úlcera en la piel debido a que el líquido escapa de una vena, o se pueden formar nuevas venas de araña llamadas *mats*, dice él. También puede haber unas decoloraciones color café en la piel, las cuales casi siempre se desvanecen completamente por sí solas aunque pueden quitarse usando láser de vapor de cobre.

El láser *pulsed-dye* también es usado por algunos médicos para extirpar los capilares faciales dilatados, dice el doctor David Green, un dermatólogo en el Centro de Venas Varicosas en Bethesda, Maryland. Los ondas de luz que emite el láser son absorbidas por las moléculas de hemoglobina en la sangre. "Esto vaporiza la hemoglobina, la cual convierte la energía de la luz en energía de calor y 'esfuma' la pared del vaso", dice él.

Los láseres actuales no son tan efectivos sobre las venas o los capilares de la cintura para abajo" dice el doctor Green. "Pero son fantásticos en aquellos arriba del cuello, particularmente en la nariz y en las mejillas."

Quítese ese exceso de peso. Si usted está significativamente excedida de peso, un plan saludable y gradual de pérdida de peso puede ser el mayor aliado de sus venas, dice el doctor Alan Kanter, director médico del Centro de Venas del Condado de Orange, en Irvine, California. Las libras adicionales ponen una presión innecesaria en sus piernas.

Ponga fibra en su dieta. Asegúrese de que su dieta sea alta en fibra para mantener a sus intestinos saludables y su defecación suave. Esto evitará el esfuerzo excesivo debido al estreñimiento, dice el doctor Kanter. La fibra se encuentra en abundancia en las frutas, las verduras y los granos integrales.

Beba agua. Otra forma de suavizar su defecación es asegurándose de que está bien hidratada bebiendo por lo menos ocho vasos de agua diariamente, dice el doctor Kanter.

No empiece a fumar. O, si lo hace, déjelo, dice el doctor Geelhoed. Fumar aumenta su riesgo de desarrollar una enfermedad de las venas subyacente, la cual puede contribuir a las venas varicosas.

Levante pesas prudentemente. Los ejercicios de levantar pesas le ayudarán a controlar su peso, pero usted necesita hacerlo correctamente para evitar provocar un problema con las venas, dice el doctor Kanter. Use pesas pequeñas y haga más repeticiones en lugar de esforzarse con pesas más pesadas, dice él. Pida a un entrenador que diseñe un programa para usted.

Trote en piso suave. Planee su ruta para correr en superficies suaves como la tierra, el césped o la pista de toba volcánica (*cinder track*) siempre que sea posible, sugiere el doctor Kanter. El impacto al correr sobre el pavimento puede agravar la hinchazón de las venas.

Manténgase en movimiento en el trabajo. No permanezca sentada por dos o tres horas ininterrumpidamente mientras está trabajando, dice el doctor Perry. Asegúrese de levantarse y caminar a menudo para mantener la sangre circulando. El estudio Framingham encontró que las mujeres que se pasaban ocho horas o más al día en actividades sedentarias, sentadas o paradas, tenían una mayor incidencia de venas varicosas.

Tratamientos caseros para las que ya tiene

Si a usted ya le están apareciendo unas cuantas venas varicosas, aquí está como mantenerlas bajo control.

Duerma sobre algo inclinado. Coloque bloques de seis por seis pulgadas (15 x 15cm) bajo el pie de su cama y déjelos allí, dice el doctor Perry. Esto evita que la sangre se acumule en sus piernas durante la noche. Usted puede adaptarse fácilmente a la inclinación.

Use medias elásticas. Para unas cuantas venas pequeñas, compre medias elásticas de buena calidad en una buena tienda de ropa y úselas regularmente, dice el doctor Perry. Las medias elásticas están disponibles en estilos que llegan a la rodilla, hasta los muslos y pantimedias. La compresión leve ayudará a mantener a sus venas bajas, dice él. Cuando hay una mayor cantidad de venas o son más grandes, usted puede necesitar usar medias de compresión gradiente, disponibles sin receta en la mayoría de las farmacias.

Pruebe las medias gradientes. Si sus venas son relativamente grandes, aun las medias elásticas de buena calidad no van a ser suficientes, dice el doctor Perry. En lugar de estas, pídale a su doctor que le recete medias de compresión gradientes hechas a medida. (En inglés, éstas se llaman *gradient compression stockings*.) "Son calientes y pesadas pero sí ayudan", dice él. La mayoría de las mujeres optan por usarlas en el trabajo debajo de los pantalones y guardan las medias elásticas más finas para ocasiones especiales.

Opciones médicas para desvanecer esas venas

Hay dos tratamientos médicos básicos disponibles para las venas varicosas: la escleroterapia (inyección) y la extirpación quirúrgica (*stripping*).

El último avance tanto en la escleroterapia como en la cirugía de venas es el uso de la tecnología de ondas de sonido, llamada imaginología dúplex de ultrasonido. El equipo de ultrasonido se usa para localizar las venas profundas con problemas y para guiar las inyecciones con precisión, dice el doctor Kanter. Y el ultrasonido es tanto indoloro como seguro.

La escleroterapia consiste en inyectar una solución dentro de la vena, causando que las paredes de la vena sean absorbidas por el cuerpo. No se necesita anestesia y "usted puede estar caminando y atendiendo sus asuntos inmediatamente después", dice el doctor David Green, un dermatólogo en el Centro de Venas Varicosas en Bethesda, Maryland. Unas cuantas semanas o meses después, la vena se seca y se vuelve un hilo invisible de tejido de cicatriz bajo la piel.

Si usted ha tenido venas varicosas grandes tratadas por escleroterapia, necesitará usar medias de compresión gradientes por hasta seis semanas después, dice el doctor Green.

El costo oscila por lo general entre $100 y varios cientos de dólares, dependiendo del número de inyecciones que se necesiten. Pueden requerirse tratamientos múltiples si usted tiene varias venas afectadas.

¿Quién es candidata? Prácticamente cualquiera, siempre y cuando usted no esté embarazada y no tenga una historia de trastornos de obstrucción en la sangre, dice el doctor Green. Pero aunque el procedimiento es sencillo y efectivo, hay efectos secundarios potenciales. Si la solución se escapa de la vena, puede causar una úlcera en la piel. Y en hasta un 20 por ciento de los pacientes, aparece una línea color café sobre la piel, siguiendo el curso de la vena. En más del 90 por ciento de estos pacientes, la decoloración se desvanece completamente al pasar los meses o en un año o dos, dice el doctor Green.

Los láseres pueden remover la decoloración cuando son manejados por un médico experto en usar el láser de vapor de cobre. Un estudio australiano mostró que 11 de 16 pacientes tratadas con la terapia de láser con vapor de cobre para la decoloración causada por la escleroterapia mejoraron significativamente después de tres meses.

La extirpación quirúrgica (*stripping*) se recomienda algunas veces para venas varicosas graves. Aunque algunas pacientes pueden someterse a la operación con anestesia local, la mayoría de los cirujanos prefieren una anestesia general ligera, dice el doctor Perry. Muchas pacientes se someten a la operación como pacientes ambulantes, regresando a sus casas más tarde el mismo día. Las medias de compresión se usan por varias semanas a meses después de la operación.

A pesar de que las venas afectadas se extirpan completamente, no existe ningún riesgo para su circulación, porque otros vasos pueden fácilmente compensar la pérdida de las venas superficiales, dice el doctor Perry.

Aunque usualmente quedan algunas cicatrices como resultado de la cirugía, a menudo se pueden extirpar grandes longitudes de vena a través de varias incisiones minúsculas.

¿Cuáles son las ventajas de la cirugía? Muchos especialistas en venas dicen que aun las venas varicosas grandes se pueden tratar efectivamente con escleroterapia. Pero algunos cirujanos vasculares hacen notar que hay un índice alto de recurrencia con el tratamiento por inyecciones, y a menudo se requieren visitas múltiples si usted tiene muchas venas afectadas. Sin embargo, cuando se usa la imaginología de ultrasonido para ayudar a guiar la cirugía, los resultados preliminares muestran un índice de éxito más alto en menos visitas.

Tercera Parte

Recupere su juventud

AERÓBICOS

Beba de la fuente de la juventud

¿Qué piensa usted cuando oye la palabra "aeróbicos"? Lo más probable es que piense en las clases de aeróbicos, a las que usted asiste fielmente dos o tres días a la semana —siempre que tiene tiempo.

Hoy en día las clases de aeróbicos son una de las actividades más populares en los gimnasios, especialmente entre las mujeres. Tanto es así que la palabra "aeróbicos" se ha convertido en una especie de palabra de moda para estar en buena condición física.

Y eso es apropiado. Las clases de aeróbicos aceleran a su corazón, por lo general duran de 20 minutos a una hora y hacen trabajar a sus grupos de músculos más importantes, mejorando su sistema cardiovascular y poniéndola a usted en forma.

Pero el término *aeróbicos* va más allá de sus clases en el gimnasio. Toda una gama de ejercicios —andar en bicicleta, correr, caminar y nadar, por ejemplo— son aeróbicos. Y estos pueden lograr más que sólo hacerla sentirse en buena forma. Pueden hacer que se sienta más joven, tanto ahora como en los años por venir. De hecho, cuando se trata de rejuvenecedores, el ejercicio aeróbico está allí justo a la cabeza de la lista. Sus beneficios son a largo plazo.

Los ejercicios aeróbicos ayudan a combatir el envejecimiento al prevenir las enfermedades del corazón, mantener la fuerza en los músculos y huesos y conservar su mente aguda. Es posible que también desempeñe un papel en evitar la diabetes y ciertas formas de cáncer. Además puede ayudar a quitar fuerza al estrés diario estimulando su estado de ánimo y nivel de energía. A menudo el síndrome premenstrual (o *PMS*, por sus siglas en inglés) y los síntomas de la menopausia se reducen con el ejercicio.

"El cliché es que si alguna vez hubo una Fuente de la Juventud, es esta", dice el doctor William Simpson, profesor de medicina familiar en el Departamento de Medicina Familiar en la Universidad Médica de Carolina del Sur, en Charleston. La persona que se involucra regularmente en el ejercicio aeróbico junto con un entrenamiento de resistencia tiene la preparación física óptima para envejecer, dice él.

Un amigo de su corazón

Un mayor beneficio del ejercicio aeróbico es su efecto en el corazón y sistema cardiovascular. La evidencia existente muestra que el ejercicio aeróbico ayuda a disminuir el riesgo de enfermedades cardiovasculares, el asesino número uno tanto de los hombres como de las mujeres en los Estados Unidos, dice Alan Mikesky, Ph.D., un fisiólogo en ejercicio y profesor en la Escuela de Educación Física de la Universidad de Indiana, en Indianápolis. Y esa es la razón principal por la cual el ejercicio aeróbico debería ser una prioridad, dice Mikesky.

La cantidad de protección que el ejercicio aeróbico ofrece a las mujeres contra las enfermedades del corazón no se conoce, dice el doctor Simpson. Eso es debido a que los estudios de las últimas dos décadas se han concentrado en los hombres. "Realmente todavía no ha habido estudios amplios con las mujeres", dice él. Pero los investigadores sospechan que las mujeres obtienen los mismos beneficios que los hombres.

La investigación muestra que el ejercicio aeróbico puede reducir el riesgo del primer ataque al corazón en los hombres. En un estudio a 16.936 ex alumnos de Harvard entre los 35 y los 74 años de edad, los hombres que eran menos activos tenían un riesgo de más del 64 por ciento de un ataque al corazón que los hombres más activos.

Los datos precisos también indican que los hombres sedentarios tienen un riesgo de más del 30 al 40 por ciento de morir de una enfermedad coronaria del corazón que los hombres que queman arriba de 1.000 calorías a la semana haciendo ejercicio —el equivalente a caminar 10 millas/16 km (cerca de 40 minutos al día, tres a cuatro veces por semana).

Bombear para circular, quemar y bajar

El ejercicio aeróbico puede ayudar a reducir su riesgo de una enfermedad del corazón al fortalecer a su corazón y hacerlo más eficiente. Cuando usted hace ejercicio, sus músculos requieren más combustible, es decir, oxígeno. Por lo tanto su corazón bombea más enérgicamente a fin de empujar más sangre — el vehículo que transporta al oxígeno— a los músculos distantes. Cuando el corazón trabaja más enérgicamente de esta manera en forma regular, se vuelve más fuerte y más eficiente, dice el doctor Simpson.

El ejercicio también ayuda a mejorar la calidad de la circulación. "El ejercicio tiende a dilatar los vasos para que el corazón pueda bombear más fácilmente y abastecer de sangre al resto del cuerpo", dice el doctor Simpson. El resultado es que cuando usted está reposando la presión de la sangre disminuye. "El corazón no necesita trabajar tan enérgicamente contra la resistencia."

El ejercicio aeróbico también ayuda a aumentar su ritmo metabólico, el ritmo al cual su cuerpo quema calorías. A los niveles de bombeo del corazón, el ejercicio quema suficientes calorías como para reducir la grasa en el cuerpo, lo cual resulta en una pérdida de peso.

Mantenerse en forma no solamente la ayuda a sentirse mejor pero también puede ayudar a mantener la presión arterial baja, un riesgo importante para las enfermedades del corazón. Los estudios indican que la presión arterial también se puede reducir haciendo ejercicio por lo menos tres veces a la semana. Y en un estudio a 641 mujeres entre los 50 y los 89 años de edad realizado en la Universidad de California, San Diego, la presión arterial era notablemente más baja en las mujeres activas en comparación con las mujeres sedentarias.

Dele una paliza al colesterol

El ejercicio puede también ayudar a reducir su riesgo de enfermedades del corazón al mantener a su colesterol bajo control. Los estudios muestran que el ejercicio aumenta el colesterol tipo lipoproteína de alta densidad (o *HDL*, por sus siglas en inglés), el colesterol bueno que ayuda a barrer de sus arterias el colesterol tipo lipoproteína de baja densidad (o *LDL*, por sus siglas en inglés), el colesterol malo. Se ha demostrado que el ejercicio de alta intensidad aumenta los niveles de HDL de un 5 a un 15 por ciento.

La investigación indica que el ejercicio aeróbico aumenta los niveles de colesterol HDL en las mujeres así como en los hombres. Cuando las mujeres participan en hacer ejercicio regularmente —digamos, los 30 minutos recomendados de ejercicio tres veces a la semana a un mínimo del 50 por ciento del ritmo máximo cardíaco (220 menos su edad)— los niveles elevados de colesterol tienden a disminuir.

La buena noticia para las mujeres es que ellas no tienen que ejercitar tan duro como los hombres para obtener los mismos resultados. Para las mujeres, los niveles moderados de ejercicio parecen ser efectivos para levantar el HDL. Los hombres, por otro lado, parece que requieren ejercicios más extenuantes.

Una buena manera de ayudar a los huesos

El ejercicio aeróbico también es efectivo para ayudar a mantener la fuerza de los huesos. Los ejercicios de cargar el propio peso provocan tensión en el hueso, y esa tensión ayuda a mantener o aumentar la fuerza de éste. Esto es especialmente importante en las mujeres que han pasado la menopausia, las cuales experimentan una rápida pérdida de hueso a un paso de 2 a 4 por ciento cada año.

La disminución en la densidad ósea que ocurre con el envejecimiento, conocida como osteoporosis, es responsable de 1,3 millones de fracturas de huesos por año. Un tercio de las mujeres mayores de 65 años de edad sufren fracturas de la espina vertebral y un 15 por ciento se fracturan las caderas.

Los ejercicios aeróbicos que son especialmente efectivos son los de cargar el propio peso tales como caminar y correr. Aun andar en bicicleta, ya sea estacionaria o moviéndose, puede ser efectivo. Simplemente aumente la resistencia contra la cual usted pedalea, dice la doctora Sydney Bonnick, directora de servicios de osteoporosis en la Universidad para Mujeres de Texas, en Denton. "Eso fortalece los músculos de la parte superior de las caderas y los muslos para que jalen del hueso, lo cual es un buen estímulo para el crecimiento óseo", dice ella. Desafortunadamente, un ejercicio popular para las mujeres mayores, el nadar, no es de cargar el propio peso y parece ser menos efectivo.

Una cuestión de cómo conservar la memoria

¿Sabía usted que el ejercicio puede conservarla joven al prevenir la disminución de su bienestar mental? Pues sí puede, según Joanne Stevenson, R.N., Ph.D., profesora de enfermería en el Colegio de Enfermería de la Universidad Estatal de Ohio, en Columbus, quien se especializa en cómo el ejercicio afecta la memoria en los ancianos.

La memoria de largo plazo —la capacidad de recordar sucesos distantes— generalmente no se deteriora al envejecer. Pero la memoria de corto plazo —la capacidad de recordar sucesos recientes— sí. Parte de la razón para esto, dice la doctora Stevenson, es que al hacernos viejas, las células del cerebro no reciben la misma cantidad de nutrientes y oxígeno que solían recibir antes. El ejercicio aeróbico puede desacelerar eso. También ayuda a aumentar el número de químicos cerebrales llamados neurotransmisores para que los mensajes se puedan llevar más rápidamente a través de las células cerebrales, dice ella. "El ejercicio, al mantener un alto nivel de nutrientes y alto nivel de oxigenación, previene el proceso de envejecer en cierta forma."

El envejecer también puede afectar lo que los investigadores llaman inteligencia fluida —su capacidad para conceptualizar. Este tipo de memoria requiere más oxígeno al cerebro que cualquier otra tarea mental. "Pensar y adquirir ideas realmente rápido —obtener el gestaltismo en su totalidad— se hace más lento cuando llega a la edad madura y al entrar a la edad avanzada", dice la doctora Stevenson. "El ejercicio aeróbico haría mas lento este proceso del envejecimiento de la mente", dice ella, y le permitiría a la gente conservar la flexibilidad y rapidez mental por un período más largo de tiempo.

Resistencia a las enfermedades

El ejercicio puede desempeñar un papel importante en eludir la diabetes y el cáncer.

La diabetes tipo II, una enfermedad en la cual el cuerpo produce menos insulina y se vuelve resistente a la insulina, afecta a entre 10 y 12 millones de adultos de 20 años de edad o mayores. La evidencia preliminar sugiere que el ejercicio ayuda a aumentar la sensibilidad a la insulina y la resistencia a la enfermedad.

En un estudio a 87.253 mujeres entre los 34 y los 59 años de edad llevado a cabo en el Laboratorio Channing de la Escuela de Medicina de Harvard y en el Hospital Brigham y de Mujeres, ambos en Boston, las mujeres que hacían ejercicio vigorosamente por lo menos una vez por semana redujeron su riesgo a la diabetes.

En otro estudio a 5.990 ex alumnos masculinos de la Universidad de Pensilvania, en Filadelfia, la incidencia de diabetes disminuyó al aumentar la actividad física. Por cada 500 calorías adicionales que se quemaban a través de la actividad, el riesgo de diabetes bajó en un 6 por ciento. El estudio indicó que la actividad física creciente puede ayudar a prevenir o retrasar la diabetes, y que las actividades vigorosas pueden tener un impacto mayor que las más moderadas.

La actividad física puede desempeñar un papel en disuadir al cáncer, particularmente el cáncer del colon. En un estudio a 17.148 ex alumnos de Harvard, aquellos que eran altamente activos redujeron su riesgo de cáncer del colon en un 15 por ciento en comparación con los ex alumnos inactivos. Los investigadores sospechan que el ejercicio puede proteger contra el cáncer del colon probablemente reduciendo la cantidad de tiempo que los agentes potenciales causantes del cáncer toman para moverse a través del sistema intestinal.

El rendimiento inmediato

El ejercicio aeróbico puede hacer que se sienta más joven hoy estimulando su autoestima y mejorando su actitud mental. El ejercicio regular produce varias recompensas —fuerza muscular, beneficios en su nivel de condición aeróbica, sensación de control sobre su entorno y reacciones positivas de las amistades con quienes usted hace ejercicio— que la pueden hacer sentir mejor con usted misma.

Un estudio a 26 atletas universitarios encontró que una sesión de 30 minutos de andar en una bicicleta especial de ejercicio redujo la ansiedad significativamente y el efecto duró por hasta una hora después de la sesión de ejercicio.

El ejercicio aeróbico también puede ayudar a combatir la fatiga. "A pesar de lo que la gente siente a veces, un programa de ejercicio tiende a aumentar los niveles de energía más que a reducirlos", dice el doctor Simpson. Si las personas se detuvieran y prestaran atención a cómo se sienten después del ejercicio, reconocerían que se sienten más alertas y más vigorosas, y que esas sensaciones pueden durar por varias horas después de la sesión de ejercicio, dice él.

El ejercicio probablemente ayuda a reducir la ansiedad y la fatiga al estimular los niveles de las endorfinas, los elevadores naturales del estado de ánimo del cuerpo. Las mujeres que hacen ejercicio regularmente también encuentran que el ejercicio ayuda a disminuir los síntomas del síndrome premenstrual (*PMS*, por sus siglas en inglés) como son la ansiedad, irritabilidad y depresión así como los sentimientos de depresión que acompañan a la menopausia.

Baile al son que toca su corazón

Digamos que usted no ha estado haciendo ejercicio y apenas empieza un programa. ¿Cómo sabe si está ejercitando lo suficiente? Una forma de saberlo es tomándose el pulso.

Empiece por ponerse como objetivo el 50 a 65 por ciento del ritmo máximo de su corazón. Tome su edad y réstela de 220. El resultado es su ritmo máximo del corazón. Tome el 50 por ciento y el 65 por ciento de eso para obtener el alcance objetivo del ritmo de su corazón.

Por lo tanto si usted tiene 40 años de edad, aquí está cómo determinar su alcance del corazón: 220 menos 40 es 180; el 50 por ciento de 180 es 90, y el 65 por ciento de 180 es 117. Eso quiere decir que su objetivo debe estar entre 90 y 117 pulsaciones por minuto. Para evaluar si usted está haciendo ejercicio a ese ritmo, se puede tomar el pulso por 15 segundos y multiplicar el número de pulsaciones por 4.

Si el número que obtiene como resultado es menor que su ritmo objetivo del corazón, en este caso 90, usted necesita ejercitar un poco más enérgicamente. Si su número es superior a 117, vaya un poco más despacio; lo más probable es que está ejercitando a un paso que es demasiado rápido para su nivel de condición física, y probablemente no será capaz de mantener esa intensidad por los 30 minutos designados. También podría elevar su presión arterial demasiado alta.

Otra forma de medir si está ejercitando lo suficiente es la escala para la clasificación de esfuerzo percibido (o *RPE*, por sus siglas en inglés). Esta es una escala de 10 puntos que va desde 0 hasta 10. Si usted estaba haciendo ejercicio a una intensidad que se sentía muy ligera para usted, usted estaría en el 1 de la escala, mientras que si estaba haciendo ejercicio a un nivel que es muy enérgico, usted se daría un 10. Si siente que su nivel de ejercicio es moderado, su clasificación sería de 3.

Las endorfinas también pueden servir como los analgésicos naturales del cuerpo. Esa podría ser la razón por la cual la actividad física regular, que provoca la secreción de las endorfinas, puede ayudar a reducir los calambres premenstruales.

Con todos estos beneficios no debería sorprenderle que el ejercicio aeróbico pueda ayudarle a vivir más tiempo. En un estudio a 3.120 mujeres adultas realizado por el Instituto Cooper para la Investigación de Aeróbicos, en Dallas, cuanto más alto era su nivel de estar en forma, más bajo era su índice de fallecimientos.

Un seguimiento a un estudio de Harvard encontró que para cuando tenían 80 años de edad, los hombres que habían hecho el ejercicio adecuado entre los 35 y los 79 años de edad vivieron uno a dos años más que los hombres que no habían hecho ejercicio regular.

Lo que los médicos recomiendan

Las pautas generales para los ejercicios aeróbicos han sido hacer 30 minutos de ejercicios aeróbicos continuos que eleven el ritmo de su corazón entre el 50 y 90 por ciento de su ritmo máximo, al menos tres veces por semana. Qué tan alto necesita usted elevar el ritmo de su corazón para obtener los beneficios rejuvenecedores depende de su edad, sexo y nivel actual de condición física. Por lo general, las mujeres que están en un nivel bajo de condición física deberían tratar de alcanzar una intensidad de ejercicio entre el 50 y 65 por ciento de su ritmo máximo del corazón. Las mujeres en un estado normal de condición física deberían tratar de llegar entre el 70 y 75 por ciento de su ritmo máximo del corazón, y las mujeres en forma excelente deberían tratar de llegar entre el 80 y 90 por ciento de su ritmo máximo del corazón.

Las estadísticas muestran que sólo el 22 por ciento de los estadounidenses hacen los 30 minutos recomendados tres veces por semana. Por ello, si hacer esa cantidad de ejercicio está fuera de sus posibilidades, entonces trate de acumular 30 minutos de ejercicio durante el transcurso del día —digamos caminando 10 minutos antes del trabajo, 10 minutos a la hora del almuerzo y 10 minutos después de que llega usted a la casa. Hay evidencia creciente para sugerir que es la cantidad acumulada de actividad, no la cantidad hecha en una sola vez, la que puede rendir los beneficios de salud a largo plazo.

Manos a la obra

Una cosa es saber que usted debería hacer ejercicio, y otra es llevarlo a la práctica y mantenerse en ello. Aquí hay algunos consejos para ayudarla.

Antes de todo, hágase revisar. Eso quiere decir un examen físico. Si usted apenas está empezando con un programa de ejercicios, vea a su doctora. Ella la revisará para ver si usted fumó alguna vez o si tiene una historia familiar de enfermedades del corazón, presión arterial alta, colesterol alto, muerte prematura o ataques al corazón, dice el doctor Simpson. Durante el examen físico su doctora le examinará la presión arterial y verificará si tiene alguna lesión previa en sus músculos o huesos que pudiera agravarse con el ejercicio, dice él. Si usted no ha hecho ejercicio en el pasado, tiene más de 35 años de edad y tiene factores de riesgo a una enfermedad del corazón, su doctora puede recomendar un electrocardiograma de estrés o una prueba sobre una estera mecánica (*treadmill*).

Obtenga asesoramiento. Cuando usted empieza con su programa de ejercicios por primera vez, es muy importante obtener la supervisión de alguien que sepa acerca de ejercicio, dice Janet P. Wallace, Ph.D., profesora asociada de cinesiología de la Universidad de Indiana, en Bloomington. Si lo hace sola usted tenderá a excederse, así que encuentre a un entrenador que la mantenga en el camino correcto. Pregunte a los candidatos si han sido certificados por el Colegio de Medicina Deportiva de los Estados Unidos, el Consejo sobre Ejercicio de los Estados Unidos, la Asociación de Aeróbicos y Condición Física de los Estados Unidos, o la Asociación Nacional de Fuerza y Acondicionamiento. Trabajar con un entrenador puede hacer que usted se mantenga en el programa, dice la doctora Stevenson. Eso se debe a que si usted hace una cita para hacer ejercicio, existen menos probabilidades de que usted haga a un lado el ejercicio por unas cuantas horas en el sofá de la casa.

Hágalo una cita fija. En lugar de ver al ejercicio como una actividad para hacer durante su tiempo libre, véalo como una necesidad, dice el doctor Mikesky. En otras palabras, haga una cita con usted misma para hacer ejercicio, y decida que no puede cancelarse, posponerse o volverse a programar. Respete esa cita tal cual lo haría con cualquier otra.

Haga ejercicios de calentamiento. Es importante hacer ejercicios de calentamiento y estirarse antes de tirarse de cabeza en su sesión de ejercicio. Esto aumenta la circulación en los músculos, los hace más flexibles y ayuda a prevenir una lesión, dice Mark Taranta, un terapeuta físico y director de Práctica de Terapia Física, en Filadelfia. Pruebe caminar, trotar despacio o andar en una bicicleta a paso despacio por unos cuantos minutos, hasta que empieza a sudar ligeramente. Luego estírese por ocho a diez minutos.

Disfrútelo. Las personas tienen más éxito poniéndose en un programa regular de ejercicios cuando escogen una actividad que disfrutan, dice la doctora Wallace. Si es aburrido o demasiado duro, no va a mantenerse con este, así que pruebe diferentes cosas hasta que encuentre el tipo de ejercicio que a usted realmente le gusta.

Combínelas. "Las actividades aeróbicas no son las actividades más divertidas", dice la doctora Wallace, por ello trate de combinarlas con alguna otra actividad que a usted le guste. Si a usted le gusta el racquetball o el tenis (actividades anaeróbicas), trate de caminar durante 15 minutos antes o después. O combine diferentes tipos de actividades aeróbicas. "Si usted está en el gimnasio con muchos equipos aeróbicos, muévase de uno al otro", dice ella. Pasar diez minutos en cada uno va a ser menos aburrido. Por lo tanto pruebe la máquina escaladora (*stair climber*), después la bicicleta y después la estera mecánica (*treadmill*).

Vaya en pareja. Considere ir al gimnasio con su compañero, dice la doctora Wallace. Un estudio de 16 parejas casadas en su institución encontró que el índice de abandono por parte de los individuos que iban al gimnasio con sus cónyuges era mucho más bajo (6 por ciento) que el de aquellos que iban solos (42 por ciento). Ustedes no necesariamente tienen que hacer ejercicios juntos, nada más planeen ir juntos, dice la doctora Wallace.

Métase en un grupo. Si realmente tiene dificultades para hacer ejercicio por sí sola, considere la actividad en grupo. Participe en una clase de aeróbicos o en un grupo que corre. Empiece su propio club para caminar con compañeros del trabajo. Hacer ejercicio con otros le ayudará a perseverar en esto, dice la doctora Stevenson, porque va a tener que responder por usted misma. Si usted pierde una clase una semana, la próxima semana alguien le va a preguntar dónde estuvo, dice ella.

Sea floja de vez en cuando. Ponerse en una rutina regular de ejercicio puede tomar algo de tiempo, así que permítase usted un desliz de vez en cuando. Tome una semana a la vez, dice la doctora Wallace. "Si usted no lo hace un día o una semana, todavía tiene la próxima semana", dice ella.

Afirmaciones

Honores que usted merece

Algunos días, todas las personas son muy criticonas. Como nuestros maridos ("Ese vestido te queda horrible"). Y nuestras hijas ("Mami, ¡el arroz quedó malísimo!"). Por no mencionar a nuestros jefes ("Esa idea es atroz"). ¡Caramba! ¿Sería mucho pedir que se nos hiciera un elogio de vez en cuando?

Bueno, en lugar de esperar que otra persona lo haga, ¿por qué no decir algo agradable acerca de usted a si misma —una afirmación? Estas son frases cortas, positivas acerca de usted, su vida y su mundo. Y los expertos dicen que el repetirlas diariamente puede desarrollar la autoestima, darle una impulsión estimulante de vitalidad y ayudarla a ver las cosas de una manera más optimista.

"Hay tanto negatividad alrededor que después de un tiempo tiende a hundirla", dice Susan Jeffers, Ph.D., una sicóloga en Tesuque, Nuevo México y autora de *Feel the Fear and Do It Anyway* (Sienta el temor y hágalo de todos modos). "Las afirmaciones pueden ayudarla a vivir una vida más feliz y a disminuir el desorden negativo que empaña su propósito en la vida. Son unos estimulantes extraordinariamente potentes."

El poder de hablar positivamente

Deténgase y escuche sus pensamientos por unos cuantos minutos. Si usted es como la mayoría de las mujeres, la charla dentro de su cabeza es abrumadoramente negativo. "Cada vez que alguien le hace un elogio, usted lo ahuyenta con un coro de abucheos", dice la doctora Jeffers. "Por alguna razón, la "cotorra" que tenemos en nuestras mentes simplemente no quiere aceptar el hecho de que nosotras tenemos puntos positivos."

Las afirmaciones pueden contrarrestar esa potente voz interna negativa y reducirla eventualmente a un susurro. Mientras más cosas positivas digamos —acerca de nuestros éxitos, nuestros sentimientos y nuestras ambiciones—

Palabras de éxito

¿Quiere ser fuerte, agresiva y exitosa? ¡Empiece a hablar como si lo fuera! "Mucho de lo que decimos a otras personas está lleno de palabras de dolor —frases como 'no puedo' o 'yo debería' dice Susan Jeffers, Ph.D., una sicóloga en Tesuque, Nuevo México, y autora de *Feel the Fear and Do It Anyway* (Sienta el temor y hágalo de todos modos). "Si nosotras reemplazamos estas palabras de dolor con palabras de fuerza, realmente cambia nuestra actitud y punto de vista. Las palabras de fuerza son como afirmaciones que usted puede incluir dentro del hablar cotidiano, y usarlas todo el tiempo."

Ponga atención a lo que usted dice por unos cuantos días, dice la doctora Jeffers. Si se oye a usted misma repitiendo frases de dolor como las que aparecen en la columna de la izquierda, trate de reemplazarlas con las frases de poder a la derecha.

Frases de dolor	Frases de poder
No puedo.	No lo haré.
Yo debería.	Yo podría.
Yo espero.	Yo lo sé.
Si acaso.	La próxima vez.
No es mi culpa.	Soy responsable.
Es un problema.	Es una oportunidad.
¿Qué haré?	Yo lo puedo manejar.
La vida es una lucha.	La vida es una aventura.

menos tiempo tendremos para los pensamientos negativos. Aun cuando usted al principio no crea lo que está diciendo, la doctora Jeffers dice que tarde o temprano los mensajes optimistas se filtrarán dentro de nuestro subconsciente y se volverán exactamente tan poderosos como alguna vez lo fueron los pensamientos negativos.

Seguro, suena un poco exagerado. ¿Cómo puede ser que repitiendo una frase como "yo tengo éxito en todo lo que hago" realmente haga que usted tenga éxito?

"El poder de la sugestión es muy fuerte", dice Douglas Bloch, un consejero con base en Portland, Oregon, conferencista y autor de *Words That Heal: Affirmations and Meditations for Daily Living* (Palabras que curan: afirmaciones y meditaciones para el vivir cotidiano). "Cuando usted dice algo en voz alta y lo repite, hace que ese pensamiento sea concreto. Usted empieza a creerlo y comienza a tomar acción de acuerdo con ello." En otras palabras, si usted dice que es una empresaria exitosa, probablemente empezará a actuar con mayor confianza, ímpetu y deseo. Y el éxito es probable que la siga.

A menos que usted dude de la fuerza del optimismo, considere este estudio. Los investigadores de la Universidad de Pensilvania, en Filadelfia revisaron los discursos de la campaña de todos los candidatos importantes para Presidente de los Estados Unidos, entre 1948 y 1984. ¿El resultado? Los políticos que consistentemente dieron los discursos más positivos, basados en acción, durante la campaña ganaron nueve de las diez elecciones. Los candidatos que se restregaban las manos y rumiaban los temas —¿está escuchando, Jimmy Carter?— fueron derrotados.

"Es la actitud", dice la doctora Jeffers. "Cuando nos decimos a nosotras mismas que vamos a fracasar, que va a ser una lucha, nos estamos preparando para el fracaso. Pero cuando nos decimos que vamos a resolver cualquier cosa que pase en nuestras vidas, ganamos fuerza interna. Y nos preparamos para el éxito."

Las afirmaciones también son eliminadores de estrés infalibles. "Usted debería tener una lista de afirmaciones a la mano que pueda empezar a repetir cuando se sienta estresada", sugiere el doctor Emmett Miller, un experto en estrés reconocido nacionalmente y director médico del Centro de Apoyo y

---

Decir sí a sí misma

Por lo regular las afirmaciones funcionan mejor si las adapta a sus necesidades. Pero si usted recién empieza, los expertos sugieren que primero pruebe algunas de estas frases:

Yo estoy llena de potencial.
Yo puedo manejarlo.
Yo siento que me estoy haciendo más fuerte.
Todo está sucediendo perfectamente bien.
No hay nada que temer.
Yo tengo confianza y estoy segura de mi misma.
Yo merezco ser feliz.
Yo me perdono a mi misma y a otros.
Me acepto como soy.
Mis oraciones siempre encuentran una respuesta.

Educación del Cáncer, en Menlo Park, California. "No tienen que ser complicadas. Solamente pensar para usted misma 'yo puedo manejar esto' o 'yo sé más acerca de esto que nadie más aquí' funcionará. Esto la aleja del reflejo instintivo al estrés —el respirar rápido, las manos frías— y la lleva hacia la reacción razonada, el intelecto, la parte de usted que realmente puede manejarlo."

Dese una palmadita en la espalda

Antes de empezar a usar las afirmaciones, debe tener dos cosas. La primera es paciencia. "Puede tomar algo de tiempo superar todo la negatividad que usted ha formado", dice la doctora Jeffers. "Algunos de los efectos de las afirmaciones son inmediatos; se empezará a sentir un poco más optimista enseguida. Pero solamente con la repetición usted puede construir un sistema de pensamientos internos que le durará toda la vida."

La segunda cosa que usted necesita, por supuesto, son las afirmaciones. Aquí hay algunas sugerencias sobre cómo crearlas y usarlas.

Guárdelas como cosa personal. Las afirmaciones son para usted y para usted solamente. Así que examine su vida en búsqueda de las áreas que podrían mejorarse. ¿Quiere tener más confianza en sí misma?, ¿quisiera estar menos enojada?, ¿quiere llevarse mejor con sus compañeros de trabajo? Escoja una o dos metas para empezar, dice la doctora Jeffers, y anote el resto para tratar después.

Hágalas cortas y positivas. Probablemente decidió que una de sus metas es dejar de preocuparse tanto. Ponga sus pensamientos en forma positiva, manifieste su afirmación en una frase y fórmela siempre en el tiempo presente para hacerla más inmediata. "Yo lo dejo pasar y confío" o "todo está funcionando perfectamente bien" pueden funcionar para usted. Trate de decir sus afirmaciones unas cuantas veces para ver si funcionan. "Si funcionan, usted puede sentir cómo la tensión se escapa inmediatamente", dice la doctora Jeffers.

Escoja afirmaciones que manifiestan lo positivo, dice la doctora Jeffers. Estas son mejores que las frases que niegan algo negativo. Por ejemplo, diga "yo estoy creando una carrera exitosa" en lugar de "yo no voy a arruinar mi carrera."

Sea realista. Las afirmaciones son herramientas para ayudarla a alcanzar sus metas. No son encantos mágicos, así que no pida mucho muy rápido. "Hay una diferencia mínima entre el pensamiento positivo y el pensamiento anhelante", dice Bloch. Usted probablemente tendrá el mayor éxito si escoge afirmaciones que tienen que ver con las emociones, la confianza y la autoestima. Trate de evitar las afirmaciones que tienen que ver solamente con los bienes materiales. "Probablemente no va a funcionar si usted sigue repitiendo 'ahora estoy conduciendo un precioso carro deportivo rojo' ", dice Bloch.

Eso no quiere decir que eventualmente no tendrá su carro soñado. Si usted usa las afirmaciones correctamente, Bloch dice que pueden ayudar. Una afirmación como "yo tengo confianza en mi misma y soy exitosa" puede llevar a otra como "yo estoy lista para encontrar un empleo importante" y, a lo mejor, a una conversación real como por ejemplo "me llevaré ese carro deportivo ahora, señor vendedor, y que sea rojo."

Repita, repita, repita. Diga sus afirmaciones diariamente. La doctora Jeffers sugiere por lo menos 20 a 30 repeticiones por día. Y asegúrese de que las dice en voz alta. "Hay algo con respecto a oírlas que las hace más poderosas", dice la doctora Jeffers. Es una buena idea apartar regularmente ciertas horas del día para decirlas, y entonces agregue más cuando sea necesario.

Si siente la necesidad de decir afirmaciones en un lugar público, está bien decírselas mentalmente a si misma, según la doctora Jeffers.

Póngalas una y otra vez. Además de sus repeticiones orales diarias, pruebe grabar sus afirmaciones en un cassette. La doctora Jeffers sugiere ponerlas cuando se deja llevar por el sueño y otra vez enseguida después que se despierta. "Esos son momentos cuando existe una mayor probabilidad de que usted absorba el mensaje", dice ella. Otros momentos buenos: cuando está haciendo ejercicio, cuando está paseando al perro y mientras está preparando la cena. Si a usted no le gusta el sonido de su voz sin acompañamiento, ponga alguna música relajante de fondo cuando esté grabando sus afirmaciones.

Sorpréndase a usted misma. Esconda recordatorios en los lugares más inesperados. Escriba sus afirmaciones en días elegidos al azar en su agenda de citas. Póngalas en un marcador para libros dentro de una novela favorita. Péguelas abajo del lavabo en el baño para que las encuentre cuando esté limpiando. "Ver sus afirmaciones en lugares extraños en momentos inesperados es una forma excelente de reforzar el mensaje", dice la doctora Jeffers. "Es una sacudida de energía positiva."

Explore lo espiritual. Las afirmaciones funcionan mejor cuando usted menciona un poder superior, dice Bloch. "Nosotros obtenemos energía de la sensación que no estamos solos. Es confortante y liberador pedir guía espiritual", dice él.

Pruebe una afirmación como "yo soy verdaderamente afortunada" o "donde yo estoy está Dios". Incluso usted puede usar versos de la Biblia como afirmaciones: "El Señor es mi pastor; yo no careceré". Si las referencias religiosas la ponen incómoda, pruebe mirar hacia dentro, hacia lo que la doctora Jeffers llama su yo superior. Ella sugiere afirmaciones como "yo confío en mi misma" o "yo soy parte del universo". Ella explica "usted no tiene que creer que existe un dios. Sólo tiene que creer que puede alcanzar un punto más alto en su vida a través de la reflexión y la confianza."

Persevere. Las afirmaciones son un compromiso a largo plazo. Siga usándolas aunque las cosas vayan bien. "De lo contrario, se encontrará que cae en hábitos que la hunden", dice la doctora Jeffers. "Puede haber mucha negatividad en el mundo, pero el uso apropiado de las afirmaciones nos ayuda a ver la oportunidad de crecimiento en todas las cosas."

ALIMENTOS
BAJOS EN GRASA

Coma mejor sin perder el sabor

Usted ha recorrido incontables veces anteriormente el sendero del bajo contenido de grasa. Usted sabe que el secreto para verse bien y vivir más tiempo es organizarse y sacar toda esa grasa, manteca y aceite fuera de su dieta. Por lo tanto usted corta la grasa por lo sano, gasta su presupuesto de comestibles en "comida saludable" de color verde y finge estar contenta.

No toma mucho tiempo para que sus papilas gustativas empiecen a cosquillear, su estómago empiece a gruñir y su imaginación se vuelva loca con las imágenes extrañas de helados de crema gigantes, bistecs jugosos y baldes de papas fritas doradas. Antes de que se dé cuenta, usted está cargando su carrito lleno de golosinas con suficientes chicharrones de harina, galletas y caramelos como para llenar un almacén. Y otro intento de hacer dieta se va al tacho.

Comer alimentos bajos en grasa solía ser una experiencia solitaria y miserable: casi nada de sabor y muy rara vez quedaba uno satisfecho. Pero en la actualidad, no tenemos que morirnos de hambre, sufrir o sacrificar el sabor por reducir el exceso de grasa en nuestras dietas. Hoy en día, los supermercados ofrecen tal surtido de frutas y verduras frescas y pasillo tras pasillo de productos que nos satisfacen, de buen sabor y bajos en grasa o de grasa reducida, que controlar el consumo de grasa es pan comido.

"Es una idea falsa que cortar la grasa significa renunciar a todos los alimentos que nos gustan", dice Judy Dodd, R.D., ex presidenta de la Asociación Dietética de los Estados Unidos y una consejera en alimentos y nutrición. "No hay alimentos malos, sólo los hábitos de comer son malos, los cuales se pueden cambiar fácilmente si usted toma las cosas paso a paso." Aquí esta cómo.

Una dieta para una vida más larga

¿Qué tal si una dieta especial baja en grasa la llevara más lejos de lo que usted se imagina —incluso a décadas adicionales de vida? Algunos científicos dicen que si usted reduce notablemente el número de calorías que come, podría vivir más años y aun décadas. ¿La trampa? Esta dieta debe ser para siempre —y requiere bastante autodenegación.

La Dieta Muy Baja en Calorías (o *VLCD*, por sus siglas en inglés) es también llamada un ayuno modificado. Algunos investigadores definen a las VLCDs como dietas que contienen 800 calorías o menos por día. Pero otros consideran que una dieta baja en grasa, llena de nutrientes de hasta 1.800 calorías por día para mujeres u hombres, es un ayuno razonablemente modificado.

Y funciona, dice el doctor Roy Walford, profesor de patología en la Universidad de California, Los Ángeles, y autor de *The 120-Year Diet* (La dieta de los 120 años). El doctor Walford sirvió como funcionario médico en jefe para *Biosphere 2* —un ecosistema cerrado en Arizona donde por dos años los científicos residentes experimentaron una escasez inesperada de alimento. En raciones estrictas diarias de aproximadamente 1.800 y 2.200 calorías (en lugar de las normales 2.500 que ellos esperaban dados sus altos niveles de actividad física), todos perdieron peso y mostraron reducciones marcadas en la presión arterial y el colesterol.

Estos resultados son consistentes con la restricción de alimento a roedores, la cual aumentó la duración de vida e hizo más lentos casi todos los cambios y enfermedades asociados con la edad, dice Edward J. Masoro, Ph.D., un fisiólogo y director del Centro de Investigación y Educación sobre el Envejecimiento, en el Centro de Ciencias de la Salud de la Universidad de Texas, en San Antonio. Pero el doctor Masoro piensa que un ayuno

Hágale un favor a su cuerpo

Supóngase que por años usted no ha tenido ningún problema con sus alimentos favoritos de costumbre. O usted realmente no está excedida de peso. ¿Necesita realmente tomarse la molestia de cambiar a un estilo de vida bajo en grasa a medida que envejece? La respuesta es un sí rotundo. La mayoría de los expertos concuerdan en que una dieta alta en grasa es una causante importante de toda clase de asesinos incluyendo la enfermedad cardiovascular, la presión arterial alta, la diabetes, el derrame cerebral y algunos tipos de cáncer.

modificado a largo plazo está "inexplorado" en los humanos y duda que mucha gente vaya a adoptar tal dieta estricta por la mayor parte de su vida.

Pero si usted es un espartano en secreto, aquí está como hacer una VLCD en forma segura.

Pídale ayuda a su médico. Nadie debería embarcarse en una dieta de ayuno a largo plazo sin supervisión médica, dicen los expertos.

Conozca su historia. Si usted es propensa a los cálculos biliares, aléjese de las VLCDs, dice el doctor James E. Everhart, de la División de Enfermedades Digestivas y Nutrición en el Instituto Nacional de Diabetes y Enfermedades Digestivas y del Riñón. Los estudios han mostrado que hasta un 25 por ciento de las personas en VLCDs desarrollan cálculos biliares, dice él.

Coma sanamente. "Un ayuno modificado saludable tiene que ser muy alto en nutrientes, sin comida basura", dice el doctor Walford. Simplemente no hay lugar para los alimentos altos en grasa o calorías desperdiciadas.

Lea Pritikin. Junto a la Dieta de los 120 Años, la más cercana a la del equipo de la *Biosphere* es el plan del Centro Pritikin de Longevidad —mayormente vegetariano, alto en fibra y con sólo 10 por ciento de sus calorías provenientes de la grasa, dice el doctor Walford.

Libérese del alcohol. Los resultados de la *Biosphere* provinieron de un ayuno modificado libre de alcohol, dice el doctor Walford.

Tome un suplemento de vitaminas y minerales. "Tome un complejo multivitamínico que contenga por lo menos la Asignación Dietética Recomendada para evitar deficiencias", dice el doctor Walford. Además, el equipo de la *Biosphere* tomó diariamente 400 UI de vitamina E y 500 miligramos de vitamina C.

Si una vida larga y libre de enfermedades no es una buena razón para optar por el bajo contenido de grasa, aquí hay otras tres que usted no puede ignorar: sus caderas, sus muslos y su barriga. "La grasa que usted come tiene mucha más probabilidad de ser la grasa que usted cargue", dice el doctor Robert Kushner, director de la Clínica de Nutrición y Control de Peso, en la Universidad de Chicago. "La grasa contiene cerca de nueve calorías por gramo, lo cual es cerca del doble de calorías que las proteínas y los carbohidratos. Y a diferencia de las proteínas y los carbohidratos, que fácilmente se queman y se metabolizan en el cuerpo, los alimentos grasos se queman despacio y tienen más probabilidades de almacenarse en las partes adiposas del cuerpo."

El problema, dice el doctor Kushner, es que nuestros cuerpos almacenan las calorías excesivas como células de grasa. Si nosotras comiéramos 100 calorías de grasa, casi todo se almacenaría como células de grasa en nuestras cinturas y caderas. Pero al convertir la misma cantidad de carbohidratos o proteína en grasa almacenada, su cuerpo en realidad quemaría cerca del 20 por ciento de ese total. En otras palabras, menos calorías se convierten en grasa en el cuerpo cuando comemos carbohidratos y proteínas que cuando comemos grasa sola.

De hecho, bastantes investigaciones científicas indican que sólo un poco menos de grasa en su dieta puede resultar en que usted se vea más delgada y en forma. Según un estudio de la Universidad de Cornell, en Ithaca, Nueva York, las personas en dietas bajas en grasa pierden peso aun cuando no tratan de restringir el total de calorías o la cantidad de alimentos que comen. Por once semanas, los trece participantes en este estudio simplemente redujeron su consumo de grasa entre un 20 y 25 por ciento del total de las calorías y en el proceso, perdieron peso al ritmo de cerca de media libra (225 g) por semana. Lo mejor de todo, estas personas no experimentaron retortijones de hambre, antojos o depresión.

Los estudios también muestran que una dieta baja en grasa reduce su riesgo de desarrollar enfermedades crónicas. El doctor James W. Anderson e investigadores de la Universidad de Kentucky, mostraron que adultos de 30 a 50 años de edad con niveles moderadamente altos de colesterol sérico (la substancia obstructora de las arterias que causa la presión arterial alta, la enfermedad del corazón y el derrame cerebral) pueden reducir sus niveles de colesterol en hasta un 9 por ciento con sólo recortar su consumo de grasa a un 25 por ciento de las calorías totales. Lo que es más, cuando esa dieta baja en grasa se combina con un consumo alto de fibra soluble (la substancia libre de la grasa que se encuentra en los productos de salvado de avena y de grano integral), el colesterol sérico se puede reducir aún más, hasta en un 13 por ciento.

En resumen: si la salud y la longevidad están entre sus metas, los alimentos bajos en grasa pueden llevarla hasta allí.

La verdad sobre la grasa

¿Así que todo esto significa que la grasa es una cosa mala, correcto? ¡Falso! En realidad es un nutriente esencial que actúa como una fuente de energía para el cuerpo y proporciona compuestos vitales a las células de nuestro cuerpo para que éstas pueden realizar sus funciones diarias.

Es solamente cuando comemos demasiada grasa —lo cual hacen la mayoría de las mujeres— que la grasa tiene el potencial de empezar problemas. "La típica mujer estadounidense obtiene tanto como el 40 por ciento de sus calorías de la grasa, lo cual es demasiado", dice Diane Grabowski, R.D., educadora de nutrición en el Centro Pritikin de Longevidad, en Santa Mónica, California.

LA CUENTA DE GRASA

Esta tabla enumera los porcentajes de grasa saturada e insaturada en los aceites y las grasas usados comúnmente para cocinar. (Los porcentajes pueden no sumar a un 100 por ciento ya que muchas de estas grasas tienen pequeñas cantidades de otras substancias grasosas).

Aceite/Grasa	(%) Grasa Saturada	(%) Grasa Monoinsaturada	(%) Grasa Poliinsaturada
11 MAGNÍFICOS ACEITES Y GRASAS PARA COCINAR . . .			
Aceite de *canola*	7	60	30
Aceite de cártamo	9	13	76
Aceite de nuez (nogal)	9	23	65
Aceite de girasol	11	20	67
Aceite de maíz	13	25	59
Aceite de oliva	14	76	9
Aceite de soja	15	24	59
Aceite de cacahuate (maní)	17	47	32
Aceite de arroz	19	42	38
Aceite de germen de trigo	19	15	63
Margarina	20	48	32
. . . MÁS 7 PARA EVITAR			
Aceite de coco	89	6	2
Mantequilla	64	29	4
Aceite de palma	50	36	9
Manteca	39	45	11
Grasa de pollo	30	45	20
Aceite de semilla de algodón	26	18	53
Manteca vegetal	25	45	20

"Eso es mucho, mucho más alto que las dietas de otras culturas. No es coincidencia que los Estados Unidos tenga una incidencia mucho más alta de enfermedades del corazón y obesidad que otras naciones del mundo."

(continúa en la página 408)

UNA LETANÍA DE ALIMENTOS BAJOS EN GRASA

Esta guía práctica le dará una buena idea de las clases de alimentos que usted debería hacer parte de su programa de comer menos grasa y cuántos gramos de grasa contiene cada uno.

Alimento	Porción	Grasa (g.)
PAN Y PRODUCTOS DE PAN		
Italiano	1 rebanada	0,0
Tortita de arroz (*Rice cake*)	1	0,3
Pita	1	0,6
Grano mixto	1 rebanada	0,9
Centeno	1 rebanada	0,9
Blanco	1 rebanada	1,0
Inglés	1	1,1
Integral de centeno (*Pumpernickel*)	1 rebanada	1,1
Tortilla, maíz	1	1,1
Trigo integral	1 rebanada	1,1
Salvado de avena	1 rebanada	1,2
Bagel	1	1,4
Francés	1 rebanada	1,4
Tortilla para taco	1	2,2
CEREALES		
Hojuelas de trigo	1 taza	0,0
Hojuelas de maíz	1 taza	0,1
Cuadrados de maíz	1 taza	0,1
Arroz inflado	1 taza	0,1
Trigo inflado	1 taza	0,1
Trigo desmenuzado (*Shredded wheat*)	1 *biscuit*	0,3
Hojuelas de salvado	1 taza	0,7
Germen de trigo, tostado	1 cucharada	0,8
Salvado con pasas	1 taza	1,0
Cuadrados de salvado	1 taza	1,4
Anillos de avena	1 taza	1,5
Harina de avena, instantánea	1 paquete	1,7
Harina de avena, cocinada	½ taza	2,4
QUESOS		
Queso de yogur	1 onza (28 g)	0,6
Requesón, 1% de grasa	½ taza	1,2

Alimento	Porción	Grasa (g.)
Parmesano, molido	1 cucharada	1,5
Suizo, de dieta	1 onza	2,0
Mozzarella, leche descremada	1 onza	4,5
Requesón, 4% de grasa	½ taza	4,7
Ricotta, parcialmente descremado	¼ taza	4,9
Monterey Jack, bajo en grasa	1 onza	6,0
Feta	1 onza	6,1
Queso azul	1 onza	8,1
Americano	1 onza	8,9

POLLO

Pechuga, sin piel, asada al horno	3½ onza (99 g)	3,5
Muslo, sin piel, asado al horno	1 pequeño	5,7
Enrollado de pollo, carne blanca	3½ onza	7,3
Pechuga, con piel, asada al horno	3½ onza	7,8
Pierna, sin piel, asada al horno	3½ onza	8,0
Pierna, sin piel, estofada	3½ onza	8,1
Pechuga, frita, enharinada	3½ onza	8,8
Muslo, frito, enharinado	1 pequeño	9,2

CONDIMENTOS

Rábano picante, preparado	1 cucharada	0,0
Salsa de soja, bajo sodio	1 cucharada	0,0
Salsa *Teriyaki*	1 cucharada	0,0
Salsa *Worcestershire*	1 cucharada	0,0
Salsa de arándanos rojos (*cranberry*)	¼ taza	0,1
Catsup	1 cucharada	0,1
Encurtido de pepino dulce (*Relish*)	1 cucharada	0,1
Mostaza amarilla	1 cucharada	0,3
Mostaza café	1 cucharada	1,0

GALLETAS

Obleas de centeno	1	0,0
Trigo integral, bajo sodio	1	0,0

(continúa)

UNA LETANÍA DE ALIMENTOS BAJOS EN GRASA —CONTINUADO

Alimento	Porción	Grasa (g.)
GALLETAS —CONTINUADO		
Bocadillos (meriendas o *snacks*) de centeno	1	0,4
Bocadillos de trigo	1	0,4
Graham	1	0,5
POSTRES		
Gelatina	½ taza	0,0
Torta blanca esponjosa	1 rebanada	0,1
Barra de higo	1	1,0
Yogur helado sabor a fruta	½ taza	1,0
Pudín (budín) de vainilla, sin azúcar, leche 2%	½ taza	1,2
Pudín de chocolate, sin azúcar, leche 2%	½ taza	1,9
Sorbete de naranja	½ taza	1,9
Galletita con pedacitos de chocolate	1	2,7
Vainilla, leche helada	½ taza	2,8
Magdalena (*cupcake*), sin glaseado	1	3,0
Bizcochuelo (*sponge cake*)	1 rebanada	3,1
Pudín de chocolate	½ taza	4,0
Pudín de tapioca	½ taza	4,0
Pudín de arroz con pasas	½ taza	4,1
Empanadilla de manzana	1 onza	4,7
Brownie, glaseado de chocolate	1	5,0
Magdalena, glaseado de chocolate	1	5,0
Donut sencilla	1	5,8
Vainilla, helado de crema	½ taza	7,2
Tarta de fresa	1	8,9
HUEVOS		
Clara solamente, cruda	1 grande	0,0
Entero, crudo	1 grande	5,0
PESCADO		
Anchoa, filete, enlatado	1	0,4
Atún, claro, enlatado en agua	3½ onzas (99 g)	0,5

Alimento	Porción	Grasa (g.)
Bacalao, cocido	3½ onzas	0,9
Abadejo (*haddock*), cocido	3½ onzas	0,9
Platija (*flounder*), asado a la parrilla	3½ onzas	1,5
Lenguado, asado a la parrilla	3½ onzas	1,5
Hipogloso (halibut), asado a la parrilla	3½ onzas	2,9
Trucha arcoiris, cocida	3½ onzas	4,3
Pez espada, cocido	3½ onzas	5,1

FRUTAS

Ciruelos (*plums*)	2 pequeñas	0,0
Toronja	½ mediana	0,1
Melocotón (durazno)	1 mediano	0,1
Melón casaba, en cubos	1 taza	0,2
Melón *honeydew*, en cubos	1 taza	0,2
Naranja	1 mediana	0,2
Papaya (fruta bomba), rebanada	1 taza	0,2
Albaricoque	2 pequeños	0,3
Uvas	12	0,3
Kiwi	1 mediano	0,3
Cantaloup, en cubos	1 taza	0,4
Dátiles	½ taza	0,4
Ciruelas (*prunes*)	½ taza	0,4
Pasas	½ taza	0,4
Manzana, sin pelar	1 mediana	0,5
Plátano (guineo) amarillo	1 mediano	0,6
Arándanos (*blueberries*)	1 taza	0,6
Mango	1 mediano	0,6
Nectarina	1 mediana	0,6
Fresas	1 taza	0,6
Pera *Bartlett*	1 mediana	0,7
Piña, en trozos	1 taza	0,7
Sandía, en trozos	1 taza	0,7
Cerezas, dulces	12	0,8

SALSAS Y *GRAVIES* (JUGOS DE CARNE)

Salsa de chile	¼ taza	0,0
Salsa de tomate, enlatada	¼ taza	0,1

(continúa)

UNA LETANÍA DE ALIMENTOS BAJOS EN GRASA —CONTINUADO

Alimento	Porción	Grasa (g.)
SALSAS Y *GRAVIES* **(JUGOS DE CARNE) —**CONTINUADO		
Salsa de barbacoa	¼ taza	1,2
Gravy de res, enlatada	¼ taza	1,2
Gravy de pavo, enlatada	¼ taza	1,2
Salsa para tacos	¼ taza	1,4
Gravy de champiñones (hongos), enlatada	¼ taza	1,6
Salsa *Marinara*, enlatada	¼ taza	2,1
Salsa para espaguetis, enlatada	¼ taza	3,0
Gravy de pollo, enlatada	¼ taza	3,6
JUGOS		
Ciruela	1 taza	0,1
Arándano rojo (*Cranberry*)	1 taza	0,1
Uvas	1 taza	0,2
Manzana	1 taza	0,3
Naranja	1 taza	0,5
LEGUMBRES Y FRIJOLES (HABICHUELAS)		
Frijoles *Mung*, brotes	1 taza	0,2
Habas blancas (*Lima beans*)	1 taza	0,5
Lentejas, hervidas	1 taza	0,7
Frijoles *navy*, cocidos	1 taza	1,0
Frijoles colorados, enlatados	1 taza	1,0
Chícharos (guisantes) partidos, secos, cocidos	1 taza	1,0
Frijoles pintos, hervidos	1 taza	1,2
Frijoles blancos, hervidos	1 taza	1,2
Frijoles refritos	1 taza	2,7
Garbanzos, enlatados	1 taza	4,6
CARNES		
Tocino canadiense	1 rebanada	2,0
Lomo de puerco para asar, magro	3½ onzas (99 g)	4,8
Jamón, extra magro	3½ onzas	5,5
Ternera para asar, hombros y brazo, magros	3½ onzas	5,8

Alimento	Porción	Grasa (g.)
Chuleta de carnero, costilla, magra, asada a la parrilla	1	7,4
Pierna de carnero, magra, asada al horno	3$\frac{1}{2}$ onzas	7,7
Ternera, costilla, magra, dorada a fuego moderado (*braised*)	3$\frac{1}{2}$ onzas	7,8
Jamón, para asar, magro	3$\frac{1}{2}$ onzas	8,9
Rosbif, nalga, magro	3$\frac{1}{2}$ onzas	9,6
Res para estofado, brazo	3$\frac{1}{2}$ onzas	9,9

PRODUCTOS LACTEOS

Alimento	Porción	Grasa (g.)
Leche evaporada, descremada	$\frac{1}{2}$ taza	0,3
Leche descremada	1 taza	0,4
Sustituto de crema (*nondairy*)	1 cucharada	1,0
Sustituto de crema para batir, helada (*nondairy whipped topping*)	1 cucharada	1,2
Mitad crema y mitad leche (*half-and-half*)	1 cucharada	1,7
Suero de leche (*buttermilk*)	1 taza	2,2
Leche baja en grasa, 1%	1 taza	2,6
Crema agria, imitación	1 cucharada	2,6
Crema, baja en grasa	1 cucharada	2,9
Crema agria, cultivada	1 cucharada	3,0
Leche baja en grasa, 2%	1 taza	4,7
Crema, espesa, para batir	1 cucharada	5,5
Leche entera	1 taza	8,2

MUFFINS

Alimento	Porción	Grasa (g.)
Avena de salvado con pasas	1 pequeño	3,0
Arándano azul (*blueberry*)	1 pequeño	4,0
Maíz	1 pequeño	4,0
Salvado	1 pequeño	5,1

NUECES Y SEMILLAS

Alimento	Porción	Grasa (g.)
Castañas, asadas	$\frac{1}{2}$ taza	0,9
Semillas de sésamo, tostadas	1 cucharada	4,3
Semillas de calabaza *squash/pumpkin*, tostadas	$\frac{1}{2}$ taza	6,2

(continúa)

UNA LETANÍA DE ALIMENTOS BAJOS EN GRASA —CONTINUADO

Alimento	Porción	Grasa (g.)
ACEITES Y GRASAS		
Mayonesa baja en calorías	1 cucharadita	1,3
Margarina, de dieta, maíz	1 cucharadita	1,9
Mantequilla batida	1 cucharadita	2,4
Margarina batida	1 cucharadita	2,7
Mayonesa regular	1 cucharadita	3,7
Mantequilla regular	1 cucharadita	3,8
Margarina suave, maíz o cártamo	1 cucharadita	3,8
Margarina en barra, maíz	1 cucharadita	3,8
Aceite de oliva	1 cucharadita	4,5
Aceite vegetal	1 cucharadita	4,5
PASTAS Y GRANOS		
Arroz blanco, cocido	1 taza	0,0
Pasta *Bulgur*, cocida	1 taza	0,4
Macarrones, trigo integral, cocidos	1 taza	0,8
Espaguetis, cocidos	1 taza	1,0
Pasta de espinaca, cocida	1 taza	1,3
Arroz integral, cocido	1 taza	1,8
Fideos de huevo, cocidos	1 taza	2,0
Arroz español	1 taza	4,2
PANECILLOS Y *BISCUITS*		
Panecillos listos para hornear, *Brown 'n' serve*	1	2,0
Panecillos duros	1	2,0
Bollos para hamburguesas/ perros calientes	1	2,1
Biscuit	1 pequeño	5,1
MARISCOS		
Camarón, cocido	3½ onzas	1,1
Escalopes (vieiras), al vapor	3½ onzas	1,4
Almejas, cocidas	3½ onzas	5,8

Alimento	Porción	Grasa (g.)
PAVO		
Pechuga, sin piel, asada al horno	3½ onzas	0,7
Pastel de carne, de la pechuga	3½ onzas	1,6
Ahumado	3½ onzas	3,9
Jamón de pavo, del muslo	3½ onzas	5,0
Carne oscura, sin piel	3 onzas	7,2
Pastrami de pavo	3½ onzas	7,2
Rollo de pavo, carne blanca	3½ onzas	7,2
VERDURAS		
Zanahoria, cruda	1 mediana	0,1
Apio	1 tallo	0,1
Lechuga romana, cortada en tiras	1 taza	0,1
Sweet potato (camote, boniato), horneado	1 mediano	0,1
Acelga suiza, hervida	1 taza	0,1
Calabacín, hervido	1 taza	0,1
Butternut squash, horneada	1 taza	0,2
Coliflor, cruda	1 taza	0,2
Papa, asada, pelada	1 mediana	0,2
Espinaca, cruda, picada	1 taza	0,2
Acorn squash, horneada	1 taza	0,3
Champiñones (hongos), crudos	1 taza	0,3
Pimienta dulce, cruda	1 small	0,3
Tomate	1 medium	0,3
Brócoli, hervido	1 taza	0,4
Repollo, hervido	1 taza	0,4
Frijoles verdes o encerados, hervidos	1 taza	0,4
Espárragos, hervidos	1 taza	0,6
Summer squash, hervida	1 taza	0,6
Brussels sprouts, hervidos	1 taza	0,8
Maíz, fresco, hervido	1 mazorca pequeña	1,0
Anillo de cebolla, frito	1	2,7
Papas fritas, congeladas	10	4,4

La mayoría de los alimentos contienen algo de grasa en una cantidad u otra. Algunas veces es visible, como un trozo de bistec; otras veces está cuidadosamente escondida. Y la composición de la grasa puede variar de un alimento a otro. Cuando usted la ve bajo un microscopio, la grasa realmente consiste de compuestos llamados ácidos grasos. Los especialistas en nutrición han identificado tres ácidos grasos primarios basados en su composición química: saturados, monoinsaturados y poliinsaturados.

Cada alimento graso contiene estos tres ácidos grasos en distintas combinaciones. Por ejemplo, las grasas animales, la mantequilla y los aceites tropicales (como los aceites de palma o de coco) tienen concentraciones de grasas saturadas extremadamente altas. La margarina, el pescado y ciertos aceites para cocinar (como los aceites de cártamo y de maíz) contienen principalmente grasa poliinsaturada. Y los otros aceites (como los de *canola* y de oliva) así como los aguacates (paltas) y ciertas nueces, consisten principalmente de grasa monoinsaturada.

Cada uno de estos tres tipos engordan por igual nuestras cinturas, así que si usted está vigilando su consumo de grasa, lo mejor es cortar los tres. Pero los expertos piensan que deberíamos poner más énfasis en comer menos alimentos que son altos en grasas saturadas. "Las grasas saturadas tienden a elevar el nivel de colesterol en la sangre, lo cual aumenta el riesgo de la enfermedad del corazón", dice Grabowski.

Las grasas monoinsaturadas, por otro lado, parece que no producen este aumento en los niveles de colesterol de la sangre, mientras que los estudios muestran que las grasas poliinsaturadas en realidad pueden bajar su cuenta de colesterol. Esa es la razón por la cual si usted va a usar aceites en su cocina o va a comer alimentos que contienen grasa, sería mucho mejor para usted si esos alimentos o aceites contienen principalmente grasas monoinsaturadas o poliinsaturadas.

Los generales de la guerra contra la grasa

Cortar la grasa no debería ser una cuestión de todo o nada. De hecho, muchos de los alimentos que a usted le gustan ya son bajos en grasa. Y otros, no son tan malos —siempre y cuando usted no los coma todos los días. Aquí hay algunas opciones que Grabowski recomienda para que las incluya en su menú bajo en grasa.

Papas y sweet potatoes (*camotes*, *boniatos*). Las papas —del tipo para hornear— son una fuente de energía ligera y satisfaciente. Solamente no las cubra de mantequilla, crema agria o la salsa hecha de jugo de carne con harina.(*gravy*).

Legumbres. Los frijoles (habichuelas), los chícharos (guisantes) y las lentejas ofrecen las mismas vitaminas, minerales y proteínas esenciales que se encuentran en las carnes pero virtualmente sin nada de la grasa.

Frutas y verduras. Aunque hay un puñado de frutas y verduras altas en grasa (como los aguacates / paltas y los cocos), la mayoría contienen muy poca o nada de grasa. Y la poca que usted encuentra es por lo general monoinsaturada o poliinsaturada. Las frutas y las verduras también son excelentes fuentes de nutrientes tales como la fibra, las vitaminas, los minerales y los carbohidratos.

Panes y cereales de grano integral, pastas y arroz integral. Estos alimentos prácticamente no tienen grasa, a menos que los sobrecargue con mantequilla y salsas. También son nuestras mejores fuentes de carbohidratos complejos —los nutrientes que proporcionan a nuestros cuerpos la forma de energía más confiable y duradera— y fibra, la cual combate las enfermedades y ayuda en la digestión.

Pescado y aves. Una dieta baja en grasa no significa que debe pasársela sin carne. Si usted hace que el pescado, los mariscos y las aves sean sus principales fuentes de carne, obtendrá todas las proteínas y minerales de las carnes rojas, pero ni por cerca con tanta grasa.

Consejos para cortar la grasa

Usted no necesita parar en seco para reducir su consumo de grasa. Todo lo que se necesita son algunos cambios sencillos y graduales en sus hábitos de comer, para lograr algunas reducciones significativas. "Mire lo que usted ya está comiendo y cómo podría comer los mismos alimentos con menos grasa", aconseja Susan Kayman, R.D., Dr.P.H., una dietista y consultora con el Grupo Médico Kaiser Permanente, en Oakland, California. Aquí hay algunas sugerencias.

Evite ingredientes extras. Muchos de los alimentos que comemos son naturalmente bajos en grasa hasta que nosotras les agregamos esos extras como la mantequilla, los aliños (aderezos) y las cremas. Su programa de reducción de grasas puede comenzar al usar menos condimentos y adiciones grasosas. Por ejemplo, si usa sólo una cucharada de mermelada en su pan tostado de la mañana en lugar de mantequilla se ahorrará 100 calorías de grasa. O pruebe usar mostaza en sus sándwiches en lugar de mayonesa. "En el transcurso de un año, eso hará una gran diferencia", dice la doctora Kayman.

Póngale sazón. Añada hierbas, especias, o jugo de tomate o limón para reavivar a los alimentos que contienen poco sabor sin agregar grasa, dice Grabowski.

Opte por el queso bajo en grasa. El queso es uno de los estimulantes de la grasa más comunes en la dieta de una mujer, dice el investigador Wayne Miller, Ph.D., director de la Clínica de Pérdida de Peso en la Universidad de Indiana, en Bloomington. La mayoría de los quesos tienen un promedio de 66 por ciento de calorías de la grasa, pero algunos alcanzan incluso hasta el 80 por ciento. Generalmente usted puede distinguir las variedades altas y bajas en grasa por su color, dice el doctor Miller; los quesos blancos como el *mozarella*, el suizo, el *ricotta*, y el parmesano son más bajos en grasa que los quesos amarillos como el *cheddar* y el americano.

Redúzcala en la leche. Cambiar de leche entera a la de 1 por ciento puede reducir substancialmente su consumo de grasa: la leche de 1 por ciento obtiene el 23 por ciento de sus calorías de la grasa mientras que la leche entera obtiene el

48 por ciento. Para lograr los mejores resultados, opte por la leche descremada; prácticamente no tiene grasa. Si usted tiene problemas en acostumbrarse al sabor de la leche descremada o de la leche baja en grasa, el doctor Miller sugiere que haga la transición lentamente, combinándola con leche entera normal y aumentando gradualmente la cantidad de leche descremada o de 1 por ciento en la mezcla.

Pruebe las versiones bajas en grasa de sus favoritos. "Es más difícil resolverse a abandonar completamente la costumbre del helado de crema que simplemente cambiarlo por las variedades bajas en grasa o por el yogur helado bajo en grasa", dice la doctora Kayman. Hoy en día, con todos los productos especiales bajos en grasa y sin grasa disponibles, encontrar alternativas saludables a sus alimentos favoritos es más fácil de lo que jamás lo ha sido. Sólo tiene que buscar en su tienda de víveres los productos que dicen "*low fat*". Un estudio encontró que substituir los productos sin grasa en sólo siete categorías (queso crema, crema agria, aliño (aderezo) para ensaladas, postres congelados, queso procesado, dulces horneados y requesón) reduce el consumo diario de grasa en un 14 por ciento.

Consuma carnes más magras. Hay un lugar para la carne roja en una dieta baja en grasa si usted escoge correctamente y la come sólo dos o tres veces por semana, dice Dodd. Sus mejores opciones incluyen cortes como el *London broil* (bistec asado y cortado en lascas finas), *eye of round steak* (bistec de tapa) y sirloin tip (bistec de lomo), los cuales obtienen menos del 40 por ciento de sus calorías de la grasa. Mantenga sus porciones en aproximadamente 3 a 4 onzas (85 a 115 g) —el tamaño de un mazo de naipes. Recórteles la grasa visible antes de cocinarlas y prepárelas para asar a la parrilla o al horno.

Evite freír para reducir. Al consumir menos alimentos fritos va a cortar un montón de grasa de su dieta. Cocinar cualquier cosa en aceite, aun carne magra de aves, aumenta su contenido de grasa considerablemente, dice el doctor Miller. Según el Departamento de Agricultura de los Estados Unidos, el típico sándwich de pollo frito empanado tiene 15 gramos más de grasa que una hamburguesa de un cuarto de libra (113 g). En su lugar, opte por los alimentos asados u horneados, sugiere él.

Despelleje las aves. El pollo y el pavo ya son alternativas más magras a las carnes de res y de puerco, dice Grabowski, pero usted puede hacerlas aún más magras si les quita la piel antes de comerlas.

Refrigere y desnate. Grabowski recomienda una forma sencilla de hacer las salsas tipo *gravy* (hechas de jugo de carne con harina) y los caldos menos grasosos: después de cocinarlos, simplemente métalos en el refrigerador por varias horas. Mucha de la grasa se congelará y se elevará, entonces todo lo que tiene que hacer es quitar la capa de grasa con una cuchara o un colador. Cuando está lista para servirlos, simplemente recaliéntelos o métalos en el horno de microondas.

Llene su tanque cuando ataca el hambre. Si reemplaza la grasa por otros alimentos más satisfactorios y densos en nutrientes, en realidad usted puede comer más y todavía perder libras o mantener un peso saludable, dice Annette

Natow, R.D., Ph.D., de N.R.H. Nutrition Consultants, una compañía que asesora a las personas sobre temas de nutrición, en Valley Stream, Nueva York, y coautora de *The Fat Attack Plan* (El plan de ataque a la gordura). Dependa de los carbohidratos —pasta, cereales, panes, frijoles (habichuelas) y la mayoría de las verduras y frutas frescas— para llenarse sin la grasa. La mayoría de estos alimentos en su forma integral o sin procesar también están llenos de fibra, la cual se junta con la grasa y la hace salir con rapidez de su sistema.

Deje de ser golosa. Muchos alimentos azucarados también son altos en grasa. Una barra de chocolate, por ejemplo, obtiene la mayoría de sus calorías de la grasa, dice la doctora Natow. A menudo los antojos de dulces son realmente antojos de grasa disfrazados. Si usted quiere algo dulce, trate de comer alguna fruta fresca o un bol de cereal azucarado para desayunar con leche baja en grasa, dice ella. O cuando esté cocinando, use cocoa que tiene mucha menos grasa que el chocolate para cocinar.

Cómo controlar su consumo de grasa

Al seguir las normas anteriores, usted debería ser capaz de reducir su consumo de grasa a cerca del 30 por ciento del total de las calorías, que es la recomendación oficial del gobierno.

SUS METAS PERSONALES

Esta tabla le muestra el número máximo de gramos de grasa que debería consumir por día tanto para asegurarse de que no está consumiendo más del 20 por ciento de sus calorías totales de la grasa como para mantener su peso actual. Si usted está tratando de perder peso, concéntrese en el límite de grasa para su peso meta.

Su peso (lb.)/(kg)	Consumo de calorías	Límite de grasa (g)
110/50 kg.	1,300	29
120/55 kg.	1,400	31
130/59 kg.	1,600	35
140/64 kg.	1,700	38
150/68 kg.	1,800	40
160/73 kg.	1,900	42
170/77 kg.	2,000	44
180/82 kg.	2,200	48

Sin embargo, muchos expertos dicen que la meta del 30 por ciento no es suficiente. Por ejemplo, según Grabowski, el régimen para combatir la grasa del Centro Pritikin pide que se reduzca su consumo de grasa al 10 por ciento del total de las calorías.

Pero a menos que su médico recomiende específicamente que usted reduzca su consumo tanto así, una meta más realista es alrededor del 20 al 25 por ciento. Para lograr eso, usted necesita controlar muy de cerca la cantidad de grasa que come. "No es suficiente saber que las hojuelas de papa frita son malas", dice Ron Goor, Ph.D., ex coordinador del Programa Nacional de Educación sobre el Colesterol y coautor de *Choose to Lose Diet: a Food Lover's Guide to Permanent Weight Loss* (Dieta de optar por perder: una guía de pérdida permanente de peso para los amantes de la comida). "Necesita saber qué tan malas." Aquí está lo que usted debería hacer.

Haga un presupuesto de la grasa. Saber cuánta grasa puede comer por día es como recibir un salario, dice el doctor Goor. "Una vez que usted sabe cuánta grasa se puede permitir, si quiere usted puede despilfarrar su presupuesto en una doble hamburguesa con queso, siempre y cuando coma menos grasa por el resto del día." Su presupuesto está basado en su consumo total de calorías al día.

Lleve un diario de los alimentos. Consígase una guía para contar la grasa y las calorías (disponible en las librerías y supermercados) y lleve un registro de toda la comida que come durante unos tres días, dice el doctor Goor. Esto le dará una buena idea de cómo su dieta normal toma forma. Esto mejorará su conciencia más sobre lo que pone dentro de su boca, y aumentará la probabilidad de que piense en alternativas bajas en grasa. Y en unos meses, le dará una manera de medir su progreso.

Lea las etiquetas. La mayoría de los alimentos empaquetados enumeran sus contenidos de grasa por porción. A lo largo del día, usted necesita llevar una cuenta de estos números y mantener un ojo avizor en los tamaños de las porciones, que a menudo son tan pequeñas que no son realistas. Por ejemplo, la lista de grasa en una caja de *Oreos* es para una galletita. Si usted se come seis en una sentada, asegúrese de multiplicar por el número correspondiente.

AMISTADES

Son buenas para toda la vida

Linda estaba tan contenta de escaparse de la ciudad por una semana con su amiga Teresa que la abrazó cuando se encontró con ella en la parada del autobús. Empezaron a platicar durante el viaje de dos horas a la playa, y pareció que nunca pararon en todas las vacaciones.

Mientras que caminaban hacia el mercado de agricultores para comprar verduras, hablaron de sus matrimonios. Cuando salieron a correr, Linda habló acerca de cómo ella y Pedro habían hecho últimamente un esfuerzo para mejorar su vida sexual.

Acostada en la playa, Teresa le mencionó que ya no se sentía útil en su trabajo —y Linda sabía exactamente lo que ella quería decir. Los sentimientos fluían ininterrumpidamente de ambas. De alguna manera, cuando Linda y Teresa se reunían siempre existía esta fuente renovadora de emociones.

Pedro estaba en la casa cuando Linda regresó. Él acababa de pasar una semana con Roberto, el marido de Teresa pescando en un lago remoto.

"¿Cómo estuvo la pesca?", preguntó Linda.

"Maravillosa", dijo él. "Y tú y Teresa, ¿se divirtieron?"

"Cielos, hablamos por horas y horas. Parecía que nunca íbamos a parar. Le conté todos mis secretos. Ella es una amiga maravillosa. ¿Y qué tal tú y Roberto, hablaron de cosas personales?"

Pedro tuvo que detenerse a pensar por un momento. "No, realmente", dijo.

Esta historia refleja el hecho de que los hombres tienden a "hacer" cosas juntos mientras que las mujeres tienden a "compartir" cosas, notablemente sus sentimientos y necesidades. Pero aun cuando pueden tener distintas maneras de hacerlo, los hombres y las mujeres obtienen lo mismo de sus amistades: vidas más largas y saludables.

Hágase simpática

El ser simpática es un talento. Y como cualquier talento, usted puede cultivarlo, dice Arthur Wassmer, Ph.D., un sicólogo en práctica privada en Kirkland, Washington, y autor de *Making Contact* (Haga contacto). Aquí hay varios consejos para que usted le caiga simpática a todos, con la excepción de la gente más miserable, cuando los conozca.

- Rompa el hielo con preguntas como "¿De dónde es usted?" o "¿Está usted disfrutando de la fiesta?"
- Preste atención.
- Haga preguntas.
- Revele sus sentimientos y experiencias.
- Haga un cumplido.

Lo que hacen por usted

"La amistad tiene un profundo efecto en su bienestar físico", dice Eugene Kennedy, Ph.D., profesor de sicología en la Universidad de Loyola de Chicago. "Tener buenas relaciones mejora la salud y disipa las depresiones. Usted no necesita necesariamente de las drogas o de un tratamiento médico para lograr esto —solamente los amigos", dice el doctor Kennedy.

Y quizás uno de los beneficios más grandes para la salud que proviene de la amistad es el vigor juvenil de una vida prolongada, de años extras de goce y satisfacción.

Uno de los primeros estudios que vinculan las relaciones sociales con la longevidad se efectuó en el Condado de Alameda, California. Allí, los investigadores encontraron que durante un período de nueve años, las personas con los vínculos sociales y comunitarios más fuertes tenían las probabilidades de morir más bajas. No sorprendentemente, las personas más aisladas tenían el índice de muerte más alto.

Tres estudios más recientes duplicaron estas conclusiones: en cada estudio, las personas que estaban aisladas tenían probabilidades de tres a cinco veces mayores de morir que las personas que tenían relaciones íntimas.

El doctor Redford B. Williams, director del Centro de Investigación de Medicina de la Conducta y un profesor de siquiatría en el Centro Médico de la Universidad de Duke, en Durham, Carolina del Norte, observa una conexión definitiva entre la amistad y longevidad. Su equipo estudió a 1.368 pacientes de enfermedad del corazón por nueve años. Ellos descubrieron que el solo hecho de estar casado (aun cuando fuera un mal matrimonio) o tener un buen amigo era un pronóstico de quién vivía y quién moría después de un ataque al corazón.

"Lo que encontramos", dice el doctor Williams, "fue que aquellos pacientes sin un cónyuge o un amigo tenían una probabilidad tres veces mayor de morir que aquellos involucrados en una relación afectuosa."

Como mujer, usted tenderá a tener más amistades íntimas que los hombres. "Las mujeres son más emocionales y más dispuestas a expresar necesidades emocionales. Cuando sienten la necesidad de conocer nuevas personas o sólo platicar, es más probable que se acerquen a alguien. Esa es una buena cualidad", dice Michael Cunningham, Ph.D., profesor de sicología en la Universidad de Louisville, en Kentucky.

Pero el sólo hecho de estar dispuesto a expresar emociones no es siempre suficiente cuando se trata de formar amistades. Muchas mujeres tienen dificultad para desarrollar relaciones porque les faltan ciertas habilidades para formar relaciones. Afortunadamente, nunca es demasiado tarde para empezar a aprenderlas.

Cómo cultivar la amistad

Las amistades no surgen como si fueran flores silvestres. Tienen que ser cultivados como las rosas. Y, como las rosas, se mantendrán floreciendo y creciendo mientras que usted las alimente. Aquí hay algunos consejos para hacer crecer un jardín de amistades y cosechar los beneficios rejuvenecedores del amor y la amistad.

Sea una amiga de por vida. Las amistades no suceden de la noche a la mañana. Requieren de un intercambio de confianza y sinceridad que sólo se puede desarrollar con el paso del tiempo, dice el doctor Cunningham. Usted tiene que mantener y alimentar a sus amistades a través de una muestra de interés genuino y continuo en ellas. No diga tan sólo "¿cómo estás?". Dígalo pero realmente escuche la respuesta. Y entonces dígales cómo está usted.

Intente nuevas actividades. A menudo usted atrae amigos por estar haciendo cosas en que ellos están interesados, dice el doctor Cunningham. El mensaje es: "esté dispuesta a intentar actividades nuevas que la pongan en contacto con personas que podrían volverse buenos amigos", dice él.

Sea receptiva y sea real. "La amistad depende de compartir y responder el uno con el otro", dice el doctor Kennedy. "No hay una fórmula para formar amistades. El requisito real es ser uno mismo y mostrarle a la otra persona quién es usted."

Muchas mujeres tienen la idea de que revelarse tal como son es un riesgo tremendo, y que ellas pueden ser ridiculizadas, dice Arthur Wassmer, Ph.D., un sicólogo en práctica privada en Kirkland, Washington, y autor de *Making Contact* (Haga contacto). Este sentimiento viene por lo general de una baja autoestima y hace que las mujeres crean que no son merecedoras de compartir sus sentimientos con otra persona, dice él. En realidad, él agrega, usted casi nunca va a tener una mala respuesta de alguien cuando trata de ser genuina y abierta con algo personal.

Pida lo que usted necesita. Sólo porque le cuente a alguien sus problemas no quiere decir que va a tener el apoyo emocional que necesita, según el doctor Cunningham. Usted tiene que pedir el tipo de apoyo que necesita. Si quiere consejos, dígalo. Si quiere aceptación y compasión, también hágaselo saber a su amiga.

Encuentre un grupo de personas comprensivas. Es un círculo vicioso, pero las personas solitarias y necesitadas son las que tienen más dificultad para formar amistades. Sus estados de necesidad asustan a los demás. El doctor Cunningham dice que la gente desarrolla "alergias sociales" a las personas necesitadas y se cansa e irrita con ellas. Por eso es que ayuda buscar amistades entre las personas que entienden por lo que usted está atravesando. Si usted es una viuda acongojada o una adicta en recuperación, o si usted sufre de un número de problemas alienantes, busque los grupos de autoayuda o de 12 pasos en su área. Tiene que haber uno para usted. Estos grupos pueden ayudar a una persona aislada a enfrentarse con sus problemas y eventualmente a que sea menos necesitada y por consiguiente más atractiva para los demás.

Tenga amistades del sexo opuesto. Trate de tener una amistad platónica con los hombres que a usted le agraden. A veces las mujeres aprecian a sus amistades del sexo opuesto porque ellos proporcionan el punto de vista masculino, y puede ser útil escuchar el ángulo masculino una vez en cuando. El hombre puede ofrecer orientación fraternal que proporcione a la mujer una perspectiva diferente de la que podría obtener de sus amistades femeninas.

Manténgase en contacto. En estos días, las personas están tan ocupadas que puede ser difícil encontrar tiempo para los amigos. Pero siempre hay teléfonos, faxes y las cartas. Usted no tiene que tener contacto directo constante para mantener una buena amistad.

Cuente con varias. Puede ser peligroso depender de una sola persona para todo su apoyo emocional, sea que ésta sea una amiga o su esposo. ¿Qué pasa si su única amiga se cansa de escucharla hablar acerca de sus problemas? ¿O, qué pasa si usted enviuda súbitamente y se queda sin alguien a quien acudir? De repente usted estará sola y aislada, y probablemente se sentirá mucho más vieja en un período de tiempo corto. Es más prudente repartir sus necesidades emocionales entre varias personas.

ANTIOXIDANTES

La mejor defensa es un buen ataque

Usted compra una encantadora casa de dos pisos. La pinta, la decora y la hace especial. Pero justo abajo de sus narices, o más específicamente, abajo de la estructura de madera, se ha mudado una colonia de termitas.

Así que mientras usted está gozando de su dicha doméstica, estos invasores furtivos en forma lenta pero segura, están destruyendo su hogar feliz. Cuando usted finalmente se da cuenta, el daño ya está hecho. Las tablas del piso se están rajando, los cimientos se están desmoronando y su casa se está inclinando como la Torre de Pisa. Es hora de llamar a un exterminador —y a un contratista.

En la vida real, su cuerpo que está envejeciendo es asediado no por insectos voraces y repulsivos sino por moléculas dañinas y desequilibradas llamadas radicales libres. Estas substancias merodeadoras deambulan por su cuerpo buscando células saludables. Una vez que encuentran algo a lo que pueden adherirse y destruir, se multiplican, causando un efecto destructivo como fichas de dominó.

Así que, ¿dónde está el exterminador de su cuerpo? Podría estar en su refrigerador. O en su botiquín de medicinas. Ciertos nutrientes han mostrado su capacidad de parar en seco a estos radicales libres. A estos nutrientes rejuvenecedores —vitaminas C y E y betacaroteno— se les llama antioxidantes.

Oxígeno: la raíz del problema

Es una de las ironías más grandes. El oxígeno —ese elemento glorioso que llena nuestros pulmones y nos mantiene vivos— está involucrado en un proceso que nos puede perjudicar seriamente.

Para obtener la energía que necesitan, las células del cuerpo usan el oxígeno para quemar combustibles tales como la glucosa (azúcar en la sangre) y, en el

417

proceso, algunas moléculas de oxígeno pueden perder un electrón. Tal molécula es ahora un radical libre, completamente decidido a reemplazar el electrón perdido al asaltar otras moléculas que forman la célula.

Al robarle un electrón, este radical libre ladrón transforma a la molécula desprevenida en un nuevo radical libre. "Pronto, una reacción en cadena de robo de electrones empieza, la cual puede producir un daño difundido a la composición química y función de la célula", dice el doctor Denham Harman, Ph.D., profesor emérito de medicina y bioquímica en el Colegio de Medicina de la Universidad de Nebraska, en Omaha. "Este proceso de oxidación bioquímica no es muy diferente al proceso por medio del cual una pieza de metal brillante se convierte en herrumbre."

La piel arrugada, los músculos escogidos y los huesos débiles —algunas de las señales de volverse vieja que una mujer más teme— podrían ser debido en parte a este proceso destructivo de oxidación, la suma de millones de reacciones continuas de los radicales libres. Pero aun de mayor preocupación para los investigadores es la idea que estos radicales libres están causando algunas de las enfermedades más insidiosas del envejecimiento.

Por ejemplo, la arteriosclerosis (endurecimiento de las arterias), la causa principal de las enfermedades del corazón y el derrame cerebral, está causada por la acumulación de colesterol tipo de lipoproteína de baja densidad (o *LDL*, por sus siglas en inglés), el así llamado colesterol malo. Pero probablemente no es sino hasta que los radicales libres oxidan el colesterol LDL que éste asume su forma potencialmente mortal, según Balz Frei, Ph.D., profesor asociado de medicina y bioquímica en el Centro Médico de la Universidad de Boston.

Si pudiéramos parar o hacer más lenta la reacción en cadena antes de que comience, entonces podría ser que el colesterol LDL nunca se volviera "malo" en primer lugar, dice el doctor Frei. O, podría ser que el ADN, el material genético dentro de nuestras células, nunca se transformara para llevar a la formación de cáncer. O, también podría ser que los tejidos en los ojos se volvieran más resistentes a las cataratas. En otras palabras, sería posible hacer más lento el proceso del envejecimiento, prolongar las expectativas de vida y mejorar la calidad de la vida.

Antioxidantes al rescate

Su cuerpo no está completamente indefenso cuando los radicales libres se ponen en pie de guerra. De hecho, su cuerpo empieza a producir ciertas enzimas para combatir a los invasores radicales libres. El problema es que simplemente no produce suficiente como para detenerlos a todos. Necesita ayuda exterior, rápidamente.

Entran los antioxidantes dietéticos, los "barrenderos" nutritivos que patrullan nuestros cuerpos buscando radicales libres, atacando a las partículas ofensivas. "Debido a sus estructuras moleculares únicas, los antioxidantes pueden ceder uno o más de sus electrones a los radicales libres sin volverse dañinos ellos mismos", dice el doctor Frei. "Estos, en realidad, vuelven indefensos a los

Una palabra acerca de la vitamina A

Además de ser un protector antioxidante, el betacaroteno es una gran fuente de otro nutriente importante, la vitamina A. El cuerpo convierte el betacaroteno en vitamina A a medida que la va necesitando.

Pero usted debe saber que el betacaroteno y la vitamina A no son la misma cosa. La vitamina A no le dará la misma protección antioxidante que el betacaroteno, y demasiada vitamina A puede ser altamente tóxica.

Por esta razón, los especialistas en nutrición recomiendan que usted no exceda la Asignación Dietética Recomendada (o *RDAs*, por sus siglas en inglés) para la vitamina A (800 microgramos equivalentes de retinol o 4.000 UI) y a menos que el doctor se los recete, evite los suplementos con sólo vitamina A o los suplementos que contienen más de 100 por ciento de la RDA para vitamina A. "Nosotros obtenemos toda la vitamina A que necesitamos de las carnes y verduras o de los alimentos que contienen betacaroteno", dice Jeffrey Blumberg, Ph.D., profesor de nutrición y director asociado del Centro de Nutrición Humana sobre el Envejecimiento, del Departamento de Agricultura de los Estados Unidos, en la Universidad Tufts, en Boston.

Las dosis excesivas de betacaroteno no son ni cerca tan peligrosas como las de vitamina A, dice el doctor Blumberg. Él dice que es casi imposible consumir niveles tóxicos de betacaroteno, pero demasiado puede producir un efecto secundario raro: puede hacer que su piel se vuelva anaranjada.

---

radicales libres y atajan la reacción en cadena destructiva antes de que el daño ocurra o se propague."

La mayoría de los investigadores han enfocado su atención en tres nutrientes antioxidantes: vitamina C, vitamina E y betacaroteno, una substancia que el cuerpo convierte en vitamina A. Estudio tras estudio ha mostrado que altas dosis de cada uno de estos nutrientes resulta en menos ocurrencias de muchas de las enfermedades crónicas.

En su investigación, el doctor Frei ha encontrado que las vitaminas C y E pueden proteger a los LDLs de daño por oxidación. "Estos estudios sugieren que los nutrientes antioxidantes, en particular la vitamina C, son capaces de prevenir las enfermedades del corazón o pueden hacer más lento su sucesión", dice él.

Los científicos también han notado una relación entre los antioxidantes y la incidencia de cataratas. Un estudio conducido por los investigadores canadienses sugiere que con la suplementación dietética de las vitaminas C y E se puede reducir el riesgo de cataratas por al menos un 50 por ciento.

Paul F. Jacques, Sc.D., un epidemiólogo en el Centro de Nutrición Humana sobre el Envejecimiento, del Departamento de Agricultura de los Estados Unidos (o *USDA*, por sus siglas en inglés), en la Universidad Tufts, en Boston, observó que el riesgo de desarrollar cataratas era cinco veces más alto en aquellos con "niveles bajos de todo tipo de caroteno, incluyendo el betacaroteno" en su sangre.

El doctor Jacques también ha estudiado el papel del antioxidante vitamina C en combatir la presión arterial alta. Según su investigación, los índices de presión arterial alta son aproximadamente dos veces más altos en aquellos con un consumo bajo de vitamina C en sus dietas (menos que la Asignación Dietética Recomendada, o *RDA*, por sus siglas en inglés, de 60 miligramos).

También existe evidencia creciente de que los antioxidantes pueden ser asimismo nuestra mejor fuente de protección contra el cáncer. Los investigadores en la Escuela de Medicina Dental de Harvard han demostrado en un experimento reciente con hámsters que una mezcla de betacaroteno, vitamina E y vitamina C produce una protección significativa contra el cáncer oral.

Y la investigación no para ahí. La epidemióloga de cáncer Gladys Block, Ph.D., profesora de nutrición de la salud pública en la Universidad de California, Berkeley, ha revisado 180 estudios que comparan los efectos de frutas y verduras y sus nutrientes antioxidantes en varios cánceres. "Ciento cincuenta y seis de estos estudios han demostrado una reducción estadísticamente significante del riesgo de cáncer en virtualmente todos los lugares donde había cáncer", dice ella.

Entre las conclusiones de la doctora Block se incluye que un consumo bajo de vitamina C dobla su riesgo de desarrollar cáncer oral, del esófago y del estómago. La vitamina E y el betacaroteno pueden proteger contra los cánceres de los pulmones y del estómago. Ella también nota que la vitamina C dietética presente en frutas y verduras puede ser tan potente como factor de protección contra el cáncer de mama así como la grasa saturada es dañina, y que hay pruebas que las vitaminas C y E y betacaroteno pueden tener un efecto protector contra el cáncer cervical.

¿Cuánto necesita una mujer?

La junta de Alimento y Nutrición del Consejo Nacional de Investigación ha establecido los RDAs como normas para cuánto de cada nutriente necesitamos consumir diariamente para satisfacer nuestras necesidades básicas de salud, y para prevenir las enfermedades por deficiencia. Para las mujeres entre los 25 y los 50 años de edad, las cantidades diarias son 60 miligramos de vitamina C, 8 miligramos de equivalentes *alpha-tocopherol* (o 12 UI) de vitamina E, y 800 microgramos de equivalentes retinol (o 4.000 UI) de vitamina A o 4,8 miligramos de betacaroteno.

UN JARDÍN LLENO DE DELEITES

Mucha de la protección antioxidante puede venir de los alimentos que a usted ya le gustan y come. "Una buena regla basada en la experiencia es comer una variedad colorida de frutas y verduras", dice Diane Grabowski, R.D., educadora en nutrición en el Centro de Longevidad Pritikin, en Santa Mónica, California. "En general, las de color verde oscuro o frutas y verduras con colores más vibrantes tienen el contenido más alto de antioxidantes."

Aquí están algunas de las mejores fuentes disponibles.

Fuentes de vitamina C

Alimento	Porción	Vitamina C (mg.)
Jugo de naranja, fresco	1 taza	124
Brócoli, fresco, hervido	1 taza	116
Brussels sprouts, frescos, cocidos	1 taza	97
Pimientos (ajíes) rojos, crudos	½ taza	95
Cóctel de jugo de arándanos rojos (*cranberry*)	1 taza	90
Cantaloup, en cubitos	1 taza	68

Fuentes de vitamina E

Alimento	Porción	Vitamina E (UI)
Semillas de girasol, secas	¼ taza	26,8
Sweet potatoes, (camote, boniato), hervido	1 taza	22,3
Col rizada, fresca, hervida	1 taza	14,9
Ñame (*yam*), hervido o asado	1 taza	8,9
Espinaca, hervida	1 taza	5,9

Fuentes de betacaroteno

Alimento	Porción	Betacaroteno (mg.)
Sweet potato, (camote, boniato), asado	1	14,9
Zanahoria, cruda	1	12,2
Espinaca, hervida	½ taza	4,4
Butternut squash, asada	½ taza	4,3
Atún fresco, cocido, al calor seco	3 onzas (85 g)	3,9
Cantaloup, en cubos	1 taza	3,1
Hojas de la remolacha, hervida	½ taza	2,2

Una dieta balanceada que consista de una amplia variedad de frutas y verduras es la mejor forma de garantizar que usted satisfaga diariamente la RDA de antioxidantes. "Cuatro a cinco porciones de frutas y verduras por día deberían proporcionar fácilmente la mayoría, si no es que todos, los antioxidantes de la RDA así como otras vitaminas y minerales importantes", dice Diane Grabowski, R.D., educadora en nutrición en el Centro de Longevidad Pritikin, en Santa Mónica, California.

Eso está bien para la salud básica, pero para poder lograr el tipo de resultados para combatir enfermedades que se han visto en los estudios científicos, usted necesita sobrepasar las RDAs actuales. Aun la más saludable de las dietas no alcanza a proporcionar la misma cantidad de antioxidantes usados en los experimentos de laboratorio.

Allí es donde los suplementos vitamínicos pueden desempeñar un papel. Un suplemento puede asegurarle la máxima protección antioxidante así como corregir cualquier deficiencia en su dieta. Pero tragarse una tableta de vitaminas por sí sola no es la respuesta. "Estos nutrientes no son 'balas mágicas' y funcionan mejor en combinación con otras prácticas saludables nutritivas tales como comer alimentos bajos en grasa y altos en fibra", dice Jeffrey Blumberg, Ph.D., profesor de nutrición y director asociado del Centro de Nutrición Humana sobre el Envejecimiento del Departamento de Agricultura de los Estados Unidos (o *USDA* por sus siglas en inglés), en la Universidad Tufts.

Se está llevando a cabo más investigación para determinar la forma y cantidad exacta de los antioxidantes necesarios para la salud óptima y para protección contra las enfermedades. Por el momento, la mayoría de los investigadores creen que podemos protegernos mejor por nosotras mismas con una combinación de dieta y suplementos. El doctor Blumberg sugiere que usted trate de obtener todas o tantas como sea posible de las RDAs para cada antioxidante, en los alimentos que usted come. Para protección adicional, él sugiere tomar suplementos diarios que contengan entre 100 y 400 UI de vitamina E, entre 500 y 1.000 miligramos de vitamina C, y entre 6 y 30 miligramos de betacaroteno.

Cómo derrotar este ejército molecular

Aquí está la manera en que las mujeres pueden hacer que los antioxidantes funcionen mejor y prevengan los efectos dañinos de los radicales libres.

Coma menos calorías. La digestión requiere oxígeno, y mucho. Mientras más calorías consumimos, más oxígeno se requiere y mayores serán las oportunidades para la formación de radicales libres. Al reducir las cantidades que comemos podemos disminuir nuestro riesgo de daño por oxidación, dice el doctor Harman. Eso no quiere decir que usted debería pasar hambre o hacer algo para reducir su consumo de nutrientes esenciales, advierte él. En su lugar, concéntrese en reducir esas calorías no esenciales de su dieta, como postres, dulces y refrescos de *soda*.

Viva del aire. Los radicales libres también se generan en el medio ambiente por los químicos industriales, metales pesados, gases, escape de los carros, aire acondicionado y otros contaminantes del aire. Mientras que nosotros no podemos escaparnos de todos estos contaminantes producidos por el hombre, cualquier cosa que limite nuestra exposición a ellos es benéfica, dice el doctor Harman. Por ejemplo, si usted trabaja en una fábrica o en una oficina, puede salir a caminar a la hora del almuerzo para escapar brevemente de las impurezas que pueden estar circulando alrededor de su lugar de trabajo. Abra las ventanas. O use un dispositivo comercial para purificar el aire.

Ahogue al pitillo. El humo de los cigarrillos aporta cantidades enormes de radicales libres con cada fumada. Los antioxidantes pueden prevenir mucho del daño oxidante causado por fumar, dice el doctor Frei. Pero si usted evita el hábito en primer lugar, esos antioxidantes estarán disponibles para combatir los radicales libres en otros lugares del cuerpo.

Tranquila con los tragos. El cóctel ocasional no va a causar ningún daño y en realidad puede reducir su riesgo de enfermedad del corazón, pero el consumo frecuente de alcohol puede aumentar el número de radicales libres en el cuerpo, dice el doctor Frei. No solamente eso, sino que las personas con alcoholismo muestran niveles bajos de antioxidantes en sus sistemas. De acuerdo con un estudio de la Escuela de Medicina y Odontología del Colegio del Rey, en Londres, los pacientes alcohólicos mostraron niveles notablemente más bajos de vitamina E y betacaroteno, que coincidieron respectivamente con las incidencias más altas de cirrosis y daño al hígado.

Ejercítese sin exceso. Cuando se trata de ejercicio, acuérdese de que hay que "entrenarse sin lastimarse". Tan benéfico como es el ejercicio para nuestra salud, el oxígeno adicional que inhalamos siempre que hacemos ejercicio somete a los músculos y otros tejidos a un daño adicional de oxidación. El forzar al cuerpo más allá de sus límites puede llevar a una sobreproducción de radicales libres y eso puede tener un efecto devastador en la forma en que usted se ve y se siente. "Esa puede ser la razón por la cual los atletas que se sobreentrenan encuentran que su desempeño sufre o se enferman", dice Robert R. Jenkins, Ph.D., profesor de biología en el Colegio Ithaca en Nueva York.

¿Significa esto que usted no debería hacer ejercicio? ¡No! La mayoría de los médicos y científicos creen que cualquier daño oxidante causado por el ejercicio normal es mínimo y éste se compensa con los beneficios adicionales que el ejercicio proporciona. Según un estudio británico a corredores de resistencia, el ejercicio regular que no agota aumenta los niveles de algunas enzimas antioxidantes en la sangre. Y un estudio realizado en la Escuela de Medicina de la Universidad de Washington, en St. Louis encontró que las dosis altas de vitamina C, vitamina E y betacaroteno, aunque no evitan que el cuerpo sufra un estrés oxidante inducido por el ejercicio, sí parece que reducen las señales de daño por oxidación en el cuerpo.

Parece que el ejercicio regular y moderado consigue el equilibrio perfecto, dice el doctor Harman. Y no importa qué, siga con su consumo de vitaminas antioxidantes.

APRENDIZAJE

Sálgase con la suya

Seguro que usted se acuerda de su lucha con las matemáticas, o la historia, u otra materia que le costaba trabajo aprender en su infancia —pero ya usted es adulta, y todo eso ha "pasado a la historia". Ahora, usted puede escoger y estudiar la materia que quiera dondequiera, comoquiera, y además, sentirse realizada por lo que ha logrado mientras se entretiene.

"Es una de las mejores cosas acerca de ser adulto", dice Ronald Gross, presidente del Seminario Universitario sobre Innovación en la Educación, en la Universidad Columbia, en la Ciudad de Nueva York y autor de *Peak Learning: a Master Course in Learning How to Learn* (Aprendizaje máximo: un curso maestro en aprender cómo aprender). "Cuando usted estaba en la escuela realmente le imponían lo que debía aprender. Ahora, usted puede escoger sus propias materias y cambiar cuando se siente con ganas. Esto le proporciona una gran sensación de libertad."

Y una sensación de juventud, también. Cuando era una niña el mundo le parecía un lugar sin límites, lleno de potencial y esperanza. Aprender puede hacer que esa sensación vuelva. Por ello, lea a los grandes filósofos. Programe una computadora. Aprenda a arreglar su cortadora de césped. Es como ser una niña otra vez, descubriendo por qué llueve o qué hace que el cielo sea azul. Y su vida no está reglamentada por los exámenes finales, los pases para andar por los corredores o las pruebas repentinas.

Ejercite su cerebro

Vamos a empezar por demoler uno de los mitos más grandes del envejecimiento. Sí, en efecto, usted está perdiendo 50.000 a 100.000 células cerebrales irreemplazables por día. Pero eso no tiene el menor significado porque usted empezó con más de 100.000 mil millones. Para cuando llega a los 70 años de edad, todavía tiene el 99 por ciento de su total original.

De cualquier manera, los expertos dicen que no es el número de células lo que cuenta. Es lo que usted hace con ellas. "El refrán 'úselo o piérdalo' se refiere tanto a la mente como a los músculos", dice Marian Diamond, Ph.D., profesora de neurociencias en el Departamento de Biología Integrada de la Universidad de California, Berkeley. El ejercicio físico hace crecer los músculos y el ejercicio mental hace que las conexiones entre las células cerebrales crezcan.

"Los estudios muestran que el área en el cerebro dedicada a la comprensión de la palabra es significativamente mayor en el graduado típico de una universidad que en el graduado de una escuela secundaria", dice la doctora Diamond. "¿Por qué? Porque los graduados de universidad pasan más tiempo haciendo uso de las palabras."

Así que no hay razón por la cual los adultos no puedan aprender tan bien como los niños. De hecho, ser un adulto a menudo facilita el aprendizaje. "Usted puede poner las cosas en contexto", dice Gross. "Cuando está aprendiendo algo, como filosofía, usted cuenta con los años de experiencia para ayudarle a ver cómo las cosas encajan. Usted nunca tuvo esa ventaja cuando era joven", dice él.

Incluso los expertos dicen que las mujeres mayores pueden soportar los rigores de la vida universitaria mejor que las mujeres más jóvenes. Un estudio a 85 mujeres estudiantes en la Universidad Estatal de Pensilvania, en University Park encontró que aquellas de 26 años de edad en adelante sentían menos estrés en la escuela que las estudiantes en la edad típica para la universidad. La experiencia vivida al criar sus hijos y tener carreras puede amortiguarlas contra el estrés.

Un manual para las mujeres

La clave para aprender es superar la idea de que todo el proceso es aburrido, o temeroso. No tiene que ser ninguna de las dos cosas. "Aprender puede ser el placer más grande de la vida", dice Gross. "Es lo que hace humanos a los seres humanos". ¿Y con respecto al temor? "¿Para qué preocuparse si lo está haciendo por usted misma?", pregunta Gross. "Fracasar no es la cuestión. No va a haber una prueba. Aprenda por aprender y usted verá qué bien se siente."

¿Lista para empezar? Los expertos ofrecen estos consejos.

Siga a su corazón. ¿Qué quiso aprender usted siempre? ¿Jardinería? ¿Inglés? ¿Soldadura de arco? Gross dice que usted debería hacer una lista —y no se preocupe si los puntos parecen no ser lo suficientemente "importantes". Recuerde, usted está aprendiendo para usted misma.

Escoja uno o dos temas, guarde los otros para después y empiece a partir de allí.

Hágalo a su manera. En la escuela todo el mundo aprendía de la misma manera: estar callada, escuchar al maestro, ir a la casa y estudiar. Algunas personas tenían éxito y otras no.

(continúa en la página 428)

¿Usted generaliza o detalla?

¿Cuál es la mejor manera de aprender? A su manera. Si usted prefiere leer el final de un libro primero, magnífico. Si a usted le gusta hacer malabares con diez temas al mismo tiempo, fantástico. Los expertos están de acuerdo en que seguir su propio estilo es la clave para aprender.

Para ver cómo usted puede aprender mejor, haga esta prueba desarrollada por David Lewis y James Greene del Grupo de Estudio del Potencial de la Mente, en Londres. Haga un círculo alrededor de *a* o *b* después de cada pregunta.

1. Cuando estudia un tema poco familiar, usted:
   a. prefiere reunir información sobre temas variados.
   b. prefiere enfocarse en un tema.
2. Usted preferiría:
   a. saber un poco acerca de una gran cantidad de temas.
   b. volverse una experta en un solo tema.
3. Cuando estudia de un libro de texto, usted:
   a. salta hacia adelante y lee capítulos de interés especial fuera de secuencia.
   b. va sistemáticamente de un capítulo al siguiente, sin seguir hacia adelante hasta que ha entendido el material anterior.
4. Cuando le pide información a la gente acerca de algún tema de interés, usted:
   a. tiende a hacer preguntas amplias que piden respuestas mas bien generales.
   b. tiende a hacer preguntas precisas que exigen respuestas específicas.
5. Cuando está curioseando en una biblioteca o una librería, usted:
   a. da vueltas por todo el lugar mirando libros sobre muchos temas variados.
   b. permanece más o menos en un mismo lugar mirando libros sobre sólo un par de temas.
6. Usted recuerda mejor los:
   a. principios generales.
   b. hechos específicos.
7. Cuando está por desempeñar algunas tareas, a usted:
   a. le gusta tener antecedentes no relacionados estrictamente con el trabajo.
   b. prefiere concentrarse únicamente en la información estrictamente pertinente.

8. Usted piensa que los educadores deberían:
a. hacer que los estudiantes se expongan a una amplia gama de temas en la universidad.
b. asegurarse de que los estudiantes adquieran principalmente un conocimiento profundo relacionado con sus especialidades.
9. Cuando está de vacaciones, usted preferiría:
a. pasar un tiempo corto en varios lugares.
b. permanecer en un solo lugar todo el tiempo y llegar a conocerlo bien.
10. Cuando está aprendiendo algo, usted preferiría:
a. seguir las guías generales.
b. trabajar con un plan de acción detallado.
11. ¿Está de acuerdo en que, además del conocimiento especializado, una persona debería saber algo de matemáticas, arte, física, literatura, sicología, política, idiomas, biología, historia y medicina? Si usted piensa que las personas deberían estudiar cuatro o más de estas materias, anote una a en esta pregunta.

Sume las respuestas *a* y *b*. Si usted marcó seis o más de las preguntas con una *a*, usted es una "generalizadora". Si usted contestó seis o más con una *b*, usted es una "detallista".

¿Qué quiere decir esto? Las generalizadoras son personas de "cuadro completo" quienes necesitan aprender de una forma no estructurada, según Ronald Gross, presidente del Seminario Universitario sobre Innovación en la Educación, en la Universidad Columbia , en la Ciudad de Nueva York y autor de *Peak Learning: a Master Course in Learning How to Learn* (Aprendizaje máximo: un curso maestro en aprender cómo aprender). Usted debería escoger un tema al azar, leer manuales empezando por el final y terminando por el principio si así lo prefiere y nunca tener temor de emprender varias tareas al mismo tiempo. Y no se preocupe acerca de los detalles al principio. Usted los irá adquiriendo a medida que los necesite.

Las detallistas están más orientadas al detalle. A ellas les gusta seguir un plan, o estructura que las guiará lógicamente por un tema. Gross sugiere leer los índices en varios libros buenos en la materia de elección. Desarrolle un plan de ataque. Y asegúrese de haber absorbido el material antes de seguir adelante. Usted disfrutará más aprender si en el camino obtiene una sensación de maestría.

Eso es porque las personas aprenden de distintas maneras. Algunas lo hacen mejor en grupos grandes. Otras prefieren hacerlo por sí solas. A otras les gusta interactuar con una o dos amigas, para compartir las ideas.

¿Y a usted? ¿Le gustan los seminarios con mucha gente o las sesiones individuales? ¿Se siente usted más lúcida por las mañanas o por las noches? ¿Se concentra mejor cuando hay música de fondo tocando suavemente?

"Cómo usted aprende es una parte importante de lo que usted aprende", dice Gross. "Encuentre su propio estilo y póngase cómoda."

Poco a poco. Una cosa es aprender a tocar las Chapanecas. Otra es tocar la Quinta Sinfonía de Beethoven. Y todavía otra es tocar la Quinta de Beethoven mientras que prepara un flan à la Chef Pepín y escribe una novela como Isabel Allende.

En otras palabras, tómese su tiempo. De lo contrario, usted puede agotarse al aprender. "Demasiado estímulo pierde su valor", dice la doctora Diamond. "Sin lugar a dudas, enriquezca su vida mental y mantenga a su cerebro activo pero dese el tiempo adecuado para asimilar la nueva información."

¡Abandone el barco! Así que usted siempre quiso aprender a navegar. Y allí está usted, navegando sola, orientando el foque y arriando la vela mayor. Pero no es tan divertido como usted se lo imaginaba.

Diríjase a los botes salvavidas e intente alguna otra cosa. "No tiene sentido continuar con algo que no es lo que usted realmente quiere hacer", dice Gross. "Y, ciertamente no hay nada de qué avergonzarse. Simplemente intente otra cosa en su lugar."

Hay una excepción. Antes de tirarlo todo por la borda, asegúrese de que sea por la razón correcta. ¿Está dejándolo porque no es interesante? ¿O tiene usted problemas con ello porque todavía está aprendiendo los fundamentos? Para llegar a dominar una tarea nueva se necesita navegar a través de aguas agitadas. Pero vencer el temporal tiene sus recompensas.

Desafíese a usted misma. ¿Le gustan a usted solamente los crucigramas que puede resolver? Entonces no se está desafiando a sí misma. Aunque poner demasiada presión inhibe el aprendizaje, no poner nada de presión también puede ser sofocante. Gross dice que usted siempre debería dejar un puente por cruzar. "Progrese a su propio paso, pero progrese siempre", dice él. Si usted logra una meta, deléitese con la victoria. Entonces establezca otra meta y trate de alcanzarla.

Pregunte sin temor. Si está tomando una clase de tejido y usted no sabe la diferencia entre un punto y un revés, suelte las agujas y levante la mano. Si usted no sabe cuánto debe ajustar un filtro de aceite, llame a un taller y pregúnteles. O consulte en la biblioteca más cercana (una tarjeta de biblioteca es una de las herramientas de aprendizaje más poderosas). "Parte de aprender es saber cuándo hacer preguntas", dice Gross. "Trate de solucionar las cosas usted sola. Pero no se está haciendo ningún beneficio si llega a un callejón sin salida y allí se queda."

ASPIRINA

Está disponible, es versátil y funciona

Todas las semanas usted ve los mismos encabezados sensacionales de esos tabloides en los supermercados: "¡Asombrosa Nueva Píldora Restaura la Juventud y la Vitalidad!", "¡Droga Maravillosa Vence al Cáncer!", "¡Potente Pastilla Previene los Ataques al Corazón!"

Desafortunadamente, borrar las señales del envejecimiento no es tan fácil como tragarse una píldora. No importa lo que los periódicos digan, no hay un substituto para una dieta saludable, ejercicio moderado y una vida libre de estrés y libre de humo.

Pero si usted está buscando una droga en la vida real que pudiera ayudarla a mantenerse joven al actuar en la prevención de ataques al corazón, cáncer, cálculos biliares, migrañas y otros padecimientos, puede ser que ya la tenga en su botiquín de las medicinas.

Es la aspirina, la superpastilla más modesta del mundo.

Sus poderes de prevención

Los médicos han respaldado a la aspirina por casi 2.000 años. Hipócrates mismo les dijo a sus amistades griegas que mascaran la corteza de un árbol sauce cuando tuvieran dolor o fiebre. Resulta ser que la corteza contiene ácido salicílico, una forma sin refinar de la aspirina.

Usted probablemente ya sabe que la aspirina puede aliviar el dolor leve, el dolor de cabeza común, los síntomas de la artritis y las fiebres bajas. Ésta funciona al inhibir la producción del cuerpo de prostaglandinas, químicos que ayudan a llevar los mensajes de dolor desde el lugar de una lesión al cerebro.

Pero también hay un efecto secundario importante. Las prostaglandinas ayudan en la coagulación de la sangre, por lo tanto el uso de la aspirina reduce la coagulación. Y aunque eso puede ser un problema en algunos casos, las pruebas van aumentando con respecto a que esto puede ayudar a prevenir los ataques al corazón al reducir las obstrucciones en las arterias coronarias que alimentan al corazón.

Un Estudio de la Salud de Enfermeras de Harvard que observó a más de 121.000 enfermeras por 15 años, encontró que las mujeres que tomaron de una a seis pastillas de aspirina por semana redujeron su riesgo de ataque al corazón en un 30 por ciento.

La aspirina no es para todos, dice una de las investigadoras principales del componente cardiovascular del estudio, la doctora JoAnn E. Manson, profesora asociada de medicina en la Escuela de Medicina de Harvard, y directora adjunta de salud femenina en el Hospital Brigham y de Mujeres, ambos en Boston. "Puede ser que la aspirina beneficie a las mujeres postmenopáusicas con un riesgo alto de una enfermedad cardiovascular." Pero para el resto de nosotras, dice ella, la imagen no está tan clara.

"Bajo cualquier circunstancia, la terapia de aspirinas debería seguirse solamente bajo la supervisión médica", dice la doctora Manson.

Los poderes antienvejecedores de la aspirina pueden llegar aún más allá de su corazón. La aspirina podría ayudarla a protegerse contra algunas de las formas de derrame cerebral al reducir los coágulos de sangre. Sin embargo, los expertos advierten que la terapia con aspirinas podría ponerla a usted en un riesgo ligeramente más alto de derrames cerebrales hemorrágicos, los cuales son causados cuando se revientan los vasos sanguíneos. Vea a su doctor antes de empezar a tomar aspirina para prevenir el derrame cerebral. El histórico Estudio de la Salud de Médicos mostró que los hombres que tomaban aspirina un día sí y un día no, tenían una necesidad significativamente reducida de cirugía para reparar otros vasos sanguíneos bloqueados en el cuerpo.

Y la aspirina podría estimular sus posibilidades de evitar el cáncer de colon. En un estudio a más de 600.000 personas, aquellas que tomaron aspirina 16 o más veces por mes tenían un 50 por ciento menos de riesgo de desarrollar tal cáncer. El doctor Clark W. Heath, Jr., vicepresidente de epidemiología y estadísticas en la Sociedad del Cáncer de los Estados Unidos, dice que eso es debido a que aparentemente la aspirina hace más lento el desarrollo de los adenomas —pólipos que son probablemente los precursores del cáncer de colon.

Y con respecto a los dolores de cabeza: el Estudio de la Salud de Médicos, también encontró que aquellos que tomaron aspirina un día sí y un día no desarrollaron un 20 por ciento menos de migrañas. Ahora los investigadores están tratando de ver si los mismos resultados son válidos para las mujeres, según el doctor Seymour Diamond, director de la Clínica Diamond para Dolores de Cabeza, en Chicago, y director ejecutivo de la Fundación Nacional de Dolores

Analgésicos: escoja su arma prudentemente

La aspirina ya no es la única opción para los achaques y dolores leves, y puede ser que no sea la mejor. Otros medicamentos sin receta pueden manejar muchas de las tareas pequeñas de la aspirina sin causar los efectos secundarios como el estómago descompuesto o los oídos que zumban.

Todos los analgésicos sin receta se basan en una o más de tres drogas: aspirina; ibuprofen, el cual se encuentra en marcas como *Advil*, *Nuprin* y *Motrin*; y acetaminófeno, encontrado en *Tylenol*, *Panadol* y algunos productos *Anacin*. Escoger entre estos no es tan difícil cuando usted sabe qué es lo que cada uno hace mejor.

Dolores de cabeza. Para los dolores de cabeza por tensión cotidianos, cualquiera de los tres calmantes para el dolor puede funcionar, dice Frederick Freitag, D.O., un miembro del consejo de la Fundación Nacional para Dolores de Cabeza.

Achaques leves y fiebre. Cualquiera de los tres puede hacerse cargo de estos, pero puede que en este caso usted prefiriera el acetaminófeno ya que es más suave para el recubrimiento de su estómago que los otros.

Dolores de dientes. Aquí, su mejor opción es el ibuprofen. Éste sobrepasó en su desempeño a la aspirina y al acetaminófeno en un estudio reportado en *American Pharmacy* (Farmacia norteamericana).

Músculos doloridos. El ibuprofen y la aspirina llevan aquí la ventaja porque son agentes antiinflamatorios que ayudan a reducir la inflamación de los músculos doloridos o lastimados. El ibuprofen es menos irritante que la aspirina en los estómagos de la mayoría de las personas.

Torceduras y tendonitis. De nuevo, la aspirina y el ibuprofen llevan la ventaja porque ayudan a reducir el hinchazón.

Calambres menstruales. El ibuprofen es la droga a escoger. Obtendrá los mejores resultados si empieza tres días antes de la menstruación.

de Cabeza. Sin embargo, él también hace notar que la aspirina ayuda poco para suprimir las migrañas que ya están en camino.

Las personas con riesgo de desarrollar cálculos biliares también pueden beneficiarse de la aspirina. Un estudio británico a 75 pacientes predispuestos a la formación de cálculos encontró que los 12 usuarios regulares de aspirina en el grupo no tuvieron cálculos, mientras que 20 de los 63 que no la usaban, sí los tuvieron.

Útil, pero no inofensiva

Así que ¿dónde está la trampa? Bueno, la aspirina es una droga, y como la mayoría de las drogas, para algunas mujeres tiene efectos secundarios que pueden ser mayores que sus beneficios.

Para empezar, la aspirina puede irritar el recubrimiento del estómago. Si tal cosa sucede, usted puede sentir una sensación de ardor, aunque por lo general el daño no es serio. En casos poco comunes, el uso de la aspirina puede provocar dolor abdominal intenso, úlceras o aun hemorragia gastrointestinal.

También existe la posibilidad que la aspirina pudiera aumentar su riesgo de derrame cerebral provocado por una hemorragia dentro del cerebro, dice Julie Buring, Sc.D., investigadora principal del Estudio de Salud de Mujeres y profesora asociada de cuidado ambulatorio y prevención en la Escuela de Medicina de Harvard. Por otro lado, la aspirina puede reducir el riesgo a la forma más común de derrame cerebral, el cual es causado no por una hemorragia sino por coágulos de sangre en la cabeza.

La aspirina también puede causar tinnitus, o zumbido en los oídos. La condición por lo general es temporal, y la aspirina no causará ningún daño permanente a sus oídos. Si la aspirina hace zumbar sus oídos, los médicos sugieren usar un producto que contenga acetaminófeno.

Tips para la toma de tabletas

Si usted piensa que la aspirina podría estimular sus posibilidades de evitar la enfermedad del corazón u otros problemas, nada más recuerde:

Pregúnteselo al médico. La terapia de aspirinas tiene sus riesgos. Hable con su médico sobre si es apropiada o no para usted. "Usted debería consultar con su doctor antes de tomar aspirina por un período prolongado de tiempo", dice el doctor James E. Muller, director adjunto del Instituto para la Prevención de Enfermedades Cardiovasculares, en el Hospital Deaconess de Nueva Inglaterra, en Boston.

Dosifíquese con calma. Si una aspirina hace maravillas, ¿por qué no tomar muchas? Sencillo: los resultados de las pruebas muestran que tomar dosis enormes de aspirina no hace mejor que tomar dosis más pequeñas.

La mayor parte de la investigación se ha enfocado en aquellos que toman una pastilla de 325 miligramos —el tamaño de una aspirina de concentración normal— un día sí y un día no. El histórico Estudio de la Salud de Médicos encontró que una aspirina un día sí y un día no ayudaba a reducir el riesgo de un ataque al corazón.

Un estudio holandés mostró que las dosis más pequeñas —quizás un décimo del tamaño de una pastilla normal— pueden proporcionar básicamente los mismos resultados. "Este estudio agrega más peso al punto de vista que las dosis de aspirina actualmente usadas para prevención pueden ser más altas de lo necesario", dice el doctor Muller.

Su doctor debería ser capaz de determinar una dosis apropiada para usted, dice el doctor Muller. Él también advierte no disminuir la dosis si un doctor ya le ha recetado la aspirina.

Sírvala con acompañantes. Trate de tomar aspirina con la comida porque así tendrá menos probabilidades de sentir dolor de estómago o náusea. Si usted está entre comidas, pruebe tragar la aspirina con un vaso lleno de 8 onzas (24 ml) de agua.

Asegúrese de que le caiga bien. Algunas aspirinas de concentraciones regular o baja tienen un recubrimiento especial que les permiten pasar a través de su estómago y en vez ser digeridas en el intestino delgado, lo cual es un poco más fácil para su sistema digestivo. Busque marcas que están *buffered* (amortiguadas) o *"enteric-coated"* (con cubierta entérica).

Enfóquese en vivir saludablemente. No importa qué tan potente resulte ser la aspirina, no va a resolver todos sus problemas. Puede ser que ayude a prevenir los ataques al corazón, pero una dieta saludable y ejercicio regular también logran esto.

"Usted debería hacer todo lo que pueda para reducir los factores de riesgo tales como el colesterol alto, fumar, sobrepeso y falta de ejercicio", dice el doctor Alexander Leaf, fundador del Centro de Salud Cardiovascular en el Hospital General de Massachusetts, en Boston.

BEBIDAS ALCOHÓLICAS

Una al día puede mantenerla joven

Usted rara vez se ha excedido, casi nunca ha sufrido una resaca (cruda) y nunca usó una pantalla de lámpara como sombrero. Pero usted sí bebe una relajante copa de vino al final de cada día, y a pesar de todo lo que ha escuchado acerca de los beneficios de beber con moderación, se pregunta si lo que está haciendo está bien.

Pues, brindémonos —con moderación, como recomiendan los doctores— porque una copa de alcohol al día puede ser justo el tónico para aliviar el estrés, ayudarle a pensar más claramente, prevenir las enfermedades del corazón y estimular la longevidad.

"Si usted observa los estudios sobre la mortalidad, las personas que viven más son las que beben una copa o dos de alcohol al día. Así que si una mujer puede controlar su consumo de alcohol, entonces una copa de vino, una lata de cerveza o una bebida mezclada al día puede prolongar su vida", dice Eric Rimm, Sc.D., un epidemiólogo en nutrición en la Escuela de Salubridad Pública de la Universidad de Harvard, en Boston.

De hecho, los índices de muerte para las mujeres que saborean un trago al día son un 16 por ciento más bajos que para aquellas mujeres que beben más o nada en absoluto, dice el doctor Rimm.

¡Salud!

La mayoría de nosotras hemos escuchado acerca de los estudios franceses que concluyeron que beber cantidades moderadas de vino tinto reduce el riesgo de una enfermedad del corazón. Pero otros estudios han mostrado que una cerveza de 12 onzas (35 ml), un cóctel hecho con 1,5 onzas (4 ml) o una medida de licor, o una copa de vino de 5 onzas (15 ml) protegen igualmente al corazón.

En Oakland, California, por ejemplo, los investigadores del Centro Médico Kaiser Permanente siguieron a 72.008 mujeres por siete años. Aunque concluyeron que los vinos blanco y tinto eran los que más protegían —redujeron la enfermedad del corazón en un 30 por ciento— los investigadores encontraron que la cerveza y el licor también protegían pero sólo un poco menos.

"No importa lo que usted bebe. Si usted ve los estudios, estos muestran que podría ser licor fuerte, vino o cerveza", dice el doctor William P. Castelli, director del Estudio Framingham del Corazón, en Massachusetts, el cual ha seguido a más de 5.200 personas desde 1948.

El efecto en la enfermedad del corazón

Por lo general, los estudios mundiales han encontrado consistentemente un 20 a 40 por ciento de disminución del riesgo de enfermedad del corazón entre los bebedores moderados. Esa es más o menos la misma reducción en riesgo que si baja el colesterol, la presión arterial o hace ejercicio aeróbico regular, dice el doctor Michael Criqui, profesor de epidemiología en la Escuela de Medicina de la Universidad de California, San Diego.

Las mujeres, por ejemplo, en un estudio a 87.526 enfermeras entre los 34 y los 59 años de edad realizado por la Escuela de Medicina de Harvard, en Boston, quienes bebieron tres a nueve tragos por semana tenían un 40 por ciento menos de probabilidades de desarrollar enfermedad del corazón que las no bebedoras.

Otro estudio grande del Centro Nacional de Estadísticas de la Salud siguió a 3.718 mujeres por 13 años. Las mujeres que reportaron beber hasta dos tragos diariamente tenían casi un 40 por ciento menos de probabilidades de desarrollar enfermedad del corazón.

Pequeñas cantidades de alcohol pueden combatir la enfermedad del corazón al aumentar las cantidades del colesterol tipo lipoproteína de alta densidad (o *HDL*, por sus siglas en inglés) en su torrente sanguíneo, dice el doctor Criqui. El colesterol bueno, o HDL, ayuda a arrastrar del torrente sanguíneo al colesterol tipo lipoproteína de baja densidad (o *LDL*, por sus siglas en inglés), el tipo malo que puede obstruir y dañar las arterias que van al corazón. El doctor Criqui también sospecha que el alcohol puede ayudar a prevenir los coágulos de sangre que pueden conducir a un ataque al corazón y a algunos tipos de derrames cerebrales.

En un estudio británico que comparó a 172 mujeres quienes habían sufrido derrames cerebrales con 172 mujeres que no lo habían sufrido, los investigadores encontraron que las mujeres que se abstuvieron del alcohol tenían casi 2,5 veces más probabilidades de sufrir un derrame cerebral que las bebedoras moderadas. Pero moderación es la clave. Otros estudios han encontrado que las personas que beben fuertemente tienen un riesgo mayor de tener un derrame cerebral.

El alcohol también puede elevar los niveles de estrógeno en las mujeres postmenopáusicas, dice Judith S. Gavaler, Ph.D., jefa de la investigación de mujeres en el Centro Médico Bautista y miembro de la Fundación de Investigación

Médica de Oklahoma, ambos en la Ciudad de Oklahoma. En un estudio a 128 mujeres, la doctora Gavaler encontró que aquellas que habían bebido tres a seis tragos en una semana tenían niveles de estrógeno que eran un 10 a 20 por ciento más altos que las mujeres que no habían bebido. Los niveles más altos de estrógeno pueden ayudar a prevenir las enfermedades del corazón y la osteoporosis en las mujeres que han pasado la menopausia.

En cantidades moderadas, el alcohol ayuda a disipar las inhibiciones y hacer que la tensión se esfume, dice Frederic C. Blow, Ph.D., director de investigación del Centro de Investigación del Alcohol en la Universidad de Michigan, en Ann Arbor. Al disminuir las inhibiciones sexuales, el alcohol puede ayudar a que las personas se relajen, logrando de esa manera que las relaciones sexuales sean más placenteras.

Lo que la bebida hace por su mente

Adicionalmente, un trago puede ayudar a mantener su mente aguda, dice el doctor Joe Christian, Ph.D., presidente del Departamento de Genéticas Médica y Molecular en la Escuela de Medicina de la Universidad de Indiana, en Indianápolis.

En un estudio de 20 años a 4.000 gemelos masculinos, el doctor Christian encontró que los hombres que continuaron bebiendo una o dos bebidas al día tenían mejores habilidades de aprendizaje y razonamiento en sus décadas de los 60 y 70 años de edad que aquellos que bebieron menos o más. Aunque este estudio no incluyó a mujeres, él sospecha que las cantidades moderadas de alcohol mejoran la circulación de la sangre al cerebro y probablemente tienen el mismo efecto en las mujeres.

Pero si un trago al día es bueno, ¿por qué cuatro al día no son mejores? "El alcohol es indudablemente algo muy polémico ya que tiene tantos pros y contras", dice el doctor Criqui. "Al tomar uno o dos tragos al día, no vemos la mayoría de las complicaciones del alcohol. Sin embargo, los problemas médicos así como los personales y sociales de beber en exceso son bien conocidos. Hay problemas familiares terribles, hogares destruidos y abuso a los cónyuges y a los niños. Todo esto está asociado con el uso excesivo del alcohol."

Además, el peligro de derrame cerebral, enfermedad del corazón, del hígado y alcoholismo todo aumenta con más de un par de tragos al día. Y el riesgo de cáncer de mama puede aumentar con más de uno. Un estudio a 34 mujeres entre los 21 y los 44 años de edad por el Instituto Nacional del Cáncer encontró que solamente dos bebidas al día entre los días 12 y 15 del ciclo menstrual de una mujer pueden elevar los niveles de estrógeno entre un 21 y 31 por ciento. Se piensa que los niveles elevados de estrógeno aumentan el riesgo de cáncer de mama. Los científicos no están seguros de cuánto estrógeno adicional es suficiente para provocar una enfermedad, así que prefieren errar hacia lo seguro: no beba más de uno al día.

Si usted bebe, aquí hay algunas formas de moderar su consumo del alcohol.

Tome poco a poco. Un trago al día quiere decir precisamente eso. "La mejor prueba es que el beber tiene que hacerse en pequeñas cantidades repartidas durante varios días", dice el doctor Criqui. "Beber siete tragos el viernes en la noche y siete más el sábado puede aumentar dramáticamente su presión arterial y en efecto aumentar la posibilidad de coágulos en la sangre."

Saque bien la cuenta. Si usted sabe cuánto va a beber antes de dar su primer sorbo, le será más fácil atenerse a ese límite, aun cuando las amistades la presionen para que beba más, dice William R. Miller, Ph.D., director de investigación en el Centro de Alcoholismo, Abuso de Substancias y Adicción de la Universidad de Nuevo México, en Albuquerque.

Las mujeres no deberían beber más de uno al día, aconseja la doctora Sheila Blume, directora médica de los programas sobre alcoholismo, dependencia química y jugar compulsivo en el Hospital South Oaks, en Amityville, Nueva York. Las mujeres se emborrachan con menos alcohol que los hombres porque pesan menos, tienen menos agua en el cuerpo para diluir el alcohol y tienen menos cantidad de un tipo de enzima en sus estómagos que ayuda a metabolizar las bebidas.

Hágalo durar. Si usted bebe lentamente, usted le dará a su hígado la oportunidad de metabolizar el alcohol para que no se acumule en su cuerpo. Haga que su trago diario dure más de una hora, dice la doctora Blume.

Cómase algo con la bebida. El comer hará más lento el paso al cual el alcohol se absorbe en su torrente sanguíneo. Pero evite los alimentos salados como los cacahuates (maníes) o *pretzels* que la harán más sedienta y la tentarán a beber más, dice el doctor Miller.

Haga algo. Baile, juegue al billar o juegos de vídeo o hable con alguien, sugiere el doctor Miller. Usted probablemente beberá menos si lo hace.

Diluya su bebida. Empiece con una bebida pura, pero cuando haya bebido la mitad agréguele agua o *club soda*. Cada vez que la mitad de su copa se vacíe, agregue más agua o agua tónica (*club soda*), dice la doctora Blume.

Tome agua. "Si usted tiene sed, su cuerpo quiere agua, no alcohol", dice el doctor Miller. "Todas esas tonterías de que el alcohol quita la sed no son verdad. En realidad, la hace más sedienta. Por ello, si usted toma un vaso grande de agua primero, es más probable que beba alcohol con moderación."

Pruebe jugo de uva. El jugo de uva, como los vinos tintos, contiene *resveratrol*, un químico que se produce en la piel de las uvas para combatir los hongos. Los investigadores sospechan que este químico reduce el riesgo de arteriosclerosis. Así que en lugar de sorber vino después de que su trago del día se acabó, pruebe beber jugo de uva.

Proteja a su bebé. Los defectos de nacimiento son más comunes si una mujer embarazada continúa bebiendo, dice la doctora Blume. "Un trago durante el transcurso de nueve meses no va a dañar al bebé, pero debido a que no sabemos cuál es un nivel seguro de consumo de alcohol para las mujeres embarazadas

—probablemente es diferente para cada individuo— el camino más seguro es no beber", dice ella.

Llame un taxi. El alcohol está involucrado en casi la mitad de todos los accidentes fatales automovilísticos en los Estados Unidos. Por ejemplo, si usted pesa 150 libras (68 kg) y toma cuatro tragos antes de colocarse detrás del volante, tiene 4 veces más probabilidades de estar envuelta en un accidente que si estuviera sobria, dice Steve Creel, un funcionario de Asuntos Públicos en la Patrulla de Carreteras de California. Si toma diez tragos, su riesgo es 65 veces mayor. Aun cuando usted no beba lo suficiente como para estar legalmente en estado de embriaguez, se le puede arrestar por conducir embriagada si la policía cree que está poniéndose en peligro o poniendo en peligro a otros automovilistas, dice Creel. Así que si bebe, designe a un conductor o pida un taxi para que la lleve a casa.

CALCIO

Un fortalecedor crucial
de los huesos, y más

Muchas mujeres desafían a la edad invirtiendo tiempo y energía en formar sus cuerpos —rebajando una curva aquí, formando un músculo allá. ¿Pero qué pasa con los huesos debajo de esos músculos y curvas? Sus huesos le dan estatura y sostén. Son órganos vivientes llenos de vasos sanguíneos, que fabrican constantemente células nuevas para dar fuerza a su cuerpo.

Si usted quiere un cuerpo recto y robusto para los años venideros, es importante entender que sus huesos necesitan alimento. El nutriente que le da juventud y fuerza a sus huesos, y lo que es más importante, evita los efectos del desgaste de los huesos causados por la osteoporosis, es el calcio. Y si sus huesos pudieran hablar, probablemente pedirían más.

Si usted es como la mayoría de las mujeres, ya sabe que la forma más fácil de obtener su calcio es tomando leche y comiendo otros productos lácteos. Pero, si usted es como la mayoría de las mujeres, no está consumiendo lo suficiente. Puede ser que usted tome leche pero sólo una gotita en su café. O quizás resolvió abandonar los productos lácteos como el queso porque está controlando su consumo de grasa.

Si está dependiendo del calcio de las verduras, puede estar consumiendo menos de lo que cree. El calcio en las verduras frondosas oscuras como la espinaca y la col rizada no siempre encuentran el camino a sus huesos, dice el doctor Clifford Rosen, director del Centro de Maine para Investigación y Educación sobre la Osteoporosis, en Bangor. "Debido a que las personas absorben el calcio de las verduras en varias formas, usted no sabrá si lo está absorbiendo eficientemente, aunque lo esté tomando en cantidades generosas", dice él.

Algunas veces el estrés de las vidas ocupadas y una cultura que presiona a las mujeres a ser delgadas nos incita a comer esporádicamente o a hacer dieta repetidamente a lo largo de los años. Ese tipo de nutrición sobre la marcha puede dejarla con una deficiencia de calcio seria.

Usted no puede vivir sin él

El calcio es un mineral que usted necesita para sobrevivir. Cuando su cuerpo pide su dosis diaria de calcio y no puede encontrarla en el alimento, la arranca de sus huesos. A medida que usted envejece, esta manera de alimentar a los huesos finalmente causa que estos se vuelvan porosos y quebradizos. Desafortunadamente, sus huesos no se lo pueden hacer saber hasta que sea demasiado tarde —cuando se cae y se fractura uno. Esta pérdida de hueso se llama osteoporosis, y es especialmente cruel con las mujeres mayores.

La hormona femenina estrógeno ayuda en una buena medida a proteger sus huesos del robo de calcio. Pero una vez que llega a la menopausia y el estrógeno mengua, sus huesos se vuelven vulnerables. Combine esta pérdida con un consumo bajo de calcio, y la reducción de los huesos se acelera.

El calcio también ayuda a bajar su colesterol. En un estudio, los investigadores encontraron que cuando la gente con niveles de colesterol en el rango alto de 240 a 260 tomaron 1.800 miligramos adicionales de calcio por día, redujeron el total de su colesterol en un 6 por ciento, según informa quien condujo el estudio, la doctora Margo Denke, profesora asistente de medicina en el Centro para Nutrición Humana del Centro Médico de la Universidad de Texas Sudoeste, en Dallas, y miembro del comité de nutrición en la Asociación del Corazón de los Estados Unidos. Aún mejor, el colesterol tipo lipoproteína de baja densidad (o *LDL*, por sus siglas en inglés) —el colesterol malo que causa todo el daño a las arterias coronarias— se redujo en un 11 por ciento. Aunque el estudio se condujo en hombres, la doctora Denke piensa que el resultado sería similar en las mujeres.

Cómo consumir más

Debido a que el calcio es tan importante, nuestra necesidad de éste cambia a lo largo de la vida. Un niño con huesos en crecimiento tiene una Asignación Dietética Recomendada (o *RDA*, por sus siglas en inglés) de 1.200 miligramos. Después de los 24 años de edad, cuando el crecimiento de los huesos se ha detenido, la RDA es sólo de 800 miligramos.

Pero muchos doctores creen que las mujeres deberían consumir mucho más. Muchos investigadores dicen que 1.000 a 1.500 miligramos diariamente es el nivel seguro y óptimo para la protección de los huesos. Y algunos, incluyendo a la doctora Denke, dicen que se necesitan 2.000 miligramos diarios para lograr un efecto que reduzca el colesterol.

Los estudios muestran que el 85 por ciento de todas las mujeres ni siquiera consumen la RDA para el calcio. Se estima que el consumo promedio de calcio

SUS MEJORES FUENTES DE CALCIO

El calcio está disponible en muchos alimentos, pero los productos lácteos son los líderes del grupo. Aquí hay un resumen de algunas de las fuentes alimenticias excelentes.

Alimento	Porción	Calcio (mg.)
Yogur sin grasa	1 taza	452
Yogur bajo en grasa	1 taza	414
Leche descremada	8 onzas (24 ml)	351
Queso *ricotta* parcialmente descremado	½ taza	337
Yogur bajo en grasa con sabor de frutas	1 taza	314
Leche baja en grasa 1%	8 onzas	300
Leche baja en grasa 2%	8 onzas	296
Leche entera	8 onzas	290
Suero de leche	8 onzas	285
Leche de chocolate	8 onzas	280
Yogur con leche entera	1 taza	274
Queso suizo	1 onza (28 g)	269
Queso *ricotta* de leche entera	½ taza	256
Queso *Provolone*	1 onza	211
Queso *Monterey Jack*	1 onza	209
Brócoli, cocido	3½ onzas (99 g)	205
Queso *Cheddar*	1 onza	202
Queso *Muenster*	1 onza	200
Salmón rosado, enlatado, con espinas	3 onzas (85 g)	181
Sardinas, drenadas, con espinas	2 sardinas (aprox. 1 onza en total)	92

para las mujeres que viven en los Estados Unidos, entre los 35 y los 50 años de edad, es de 530 miligramos al día. Aquí está lo que usted puede hacer para aumentar ese número.

Vaya con la vaca. ¿Qué tan importante son los lácteos? "El calcio está más disponible para su cuerpo cuando proviene de la leche y sus productos derivados", dice Richard J. Wood, Ph.D., jefe del Laboratorio de Biodisponibilidad Mineral, en el Centro de Investigación de la Nutrición Humana sobre la Vejez del Departamento de Agricultura de los Estados Unidos en la Universidad de Tufts, en Boston.

Para evitar la grasa y las calorías, escoja sólo las opciones bajas en grasa. Su supermercado favorito ofrece versiones bajas en grasa de una selección amplia de productos lácteos: leche, quesos, crema agria, queso crema y yogur, para mencionar algunos. Y no haga muecas hasta que los haya probado.

Los productos lácteos también le dan a usted la mayor cantidad de calcio por cucharada. Una taza de 8 onzas (227 g) de yogur bajo en grasa sin sabor le ofrece 414 miligramos. La leche descremada se jacta de contener 351 miligramos por una porción de 8 onzas (24 ml). Una media taza de queso *ricotta* parcialmente descremado, que usted puede encontrar en una porción considerable de lasaña, tiene 337 miligramos.

Experimente con otras fuentes. Si usted tiene dificultad para digerir los productos lácteos o simplemente no los disfruta, el brócoli es una buena opción como fuente de calcio. Sólo 3,5 onzas (99 g) de brócoli cocido le darán 205 miligramos de calcio, mucho más que otras verduras.

Pruebe también tofu, un producto de soja ligero y versátil que usted encontrará en la sección de productos agrícolas de su tienda de comestibles. Está cargado de calcio. Pero algunas marcas de tofu tienen más calcio que otras, todo depende de los ingredientes usados para formar la cuajada. Una media taza de tofu hecha con *nigari* (cloruro de magnesio) contiene 258 miligramos de calcio. Pero la misma cantidad de tofu hecho con sulfato de calcio contiene en total unos 860 miligramos de calcio. Busque en la etiqueta el agente usado para cuajar.

Pesque lo que necesita. Ya que el calcio reside en sus huesos, tiene sentido pensar que los pescados con muchas espinas son una buena fuente de calcio. El salmón rosa enlatado, con huesos contiene 181 miligramos de calcio en una porción de 3 onzas (85 g), y dos sardinas (cerca de 1 onza / 28 g en total) contienen 92 miligramos.

Dele con la D. "No importa cuánto calcio usted incluye en su dieta, sus huesos no podrán recuperarlo sin la ayuda de la vitamina D", dice el doctor Michael F. Holick, Ph.D., director del Laboratorio de Investigación de Vitamina D, Piel y Hueso en el Centro Médico de la Universidad de Boston. Afortunadamente, para la mayoría de las mujeres, el obtener suficiente vitamina D no es un problema. La exposición casual diaria a la luz solar —15 minutos serán suficientes— satisfarán los requisitos diarios de vitamina D del cuerpo, dice el doctor Holick. ¿Cómo? La luz solar provoca la producción de vitamina D en su piel, dice él.

También, la vitamina D viene en un surtido de alimentos fortificados que comemos diariamente, como la leche, los cereales y panes. Sin embargo, los médicos no aconsejan tomar suplementos de vitamina D porque demasiada puede ser tóxica.

Deje la dieta de Popeye. La espinaca contiene bastante calcio pero también contiene compuestos llamados oxalatos, los cuales se unen con los minerales y hacen que la mayor parte de éste no esté disponible para su cuerpo. Aunque usted debería disfrutar la espinaca por los otros nutrientes que le ofrece, no se exceda, dice Paul R. Thomas, Ed.D., R.D., científico en el equipo del Consejo de Nutrición de la Academia Nacional de Ciencias, en Washington, D.C. "Comer ensalada de espinaca cuatro a cinco veces por semana está bien; solo que no dependa de esta como fuente importante de calcio", dice él.

Suplemente su dieta

La mayoría de los médicos le dirán que una dieta completa que consiste de carnes magras y pescado y bastantes frutas, granos integrales, verduras y productos lácteos bajos en grasa le proporcionarán a usted todas las vitaminas y minerales que necesita para mantener una buena salud. Pero ellos también pueden decirle que comer una dieta completa no es garantía de que usted está obteniendo todo el calcio que necesita, especialmente si usted es una mujer que tiene más de 30 años de edad. Así que su mejor protección pueden ser los suplementos de calcio.

"Si usted prefiere obtener su calcio de suplementos, escoja aquellos hechos con citrato de calcio", dice la doctora Denke. En algunas ocasiones, todas las formas de calcio pueden interferir con la absorción de hierro o causar cálculos renales. El citrato de calcio es el suplemento que tiene menos probabilidad de promover la formación de cálculos renales.

Si usted escoge carbonato de calcio, es mejor tomarlo con las comidas, dice el doctor Rosen. El ácido que su cuerpo produce cuando usted come descompondrá el carbonato de calcio y hará posible su absorción.

El carbonato de calcio se encuentra en las tabletas antiácidas, y muchas mujeres optan por masticarlas como una fuente de calcio. Pero usted debe tener cuidado. Algunas marcas de antiácidos, tales como *Gelusil*, *Maalox* y *Mylanta* no se recomiendan como fuentes de calcio porque también contienen aluminio, el cual puede evitar la mineralización adecuada en el hueso. Sus mejores opciones, dice el doctor Rosen, son *Tums* y *Rolaids* —ambos son libres de aluminio.

¿Cuánto debería usted tomar? "Si usted se toma tres vasos de 8 onzas (24 ml) de leche al día, entonces un suplemento de 500 miligramos de calcio debería ser suficiente", dice el doctor Rosen. "Si usted puede llegar a 1.500 miligramos ya sea a través de dieta o una combinación de dieta y suplementos, entonces usted está bien."

CONFIANZA EN SÍ MISMA Y AUTOESTIMA

Sea su mejor amiga

Cuando usted se imagina a usted misma, ¿qué es lo que ve? Quizás usted ve a una persona enérgica, inteligente y exitosa, alguien a quien usted quisiera como su mejor amiga. O a lo mejor ve a una mujer un poco maltratada por los años, una mujer cuyos atributos más notables son las arrugas pequeñas alrededor de sus ojos y los hoyuelos en sus muslos.

Es asombroso como unas cuantas arrugas o un poco de celulitis pueden hacer añicos la autoestima (el aprecio y aceptación de nuestro valor interior) de una mujer. Unas cuantas señales leves de envejecimiento también pueden destruir la confianza en sí misma de una mujer, y la fe que tiene en sus capacidades y talentos. "Nuestra cultura pone un precio extremadamente alto a la juventud", dice Bonnie Jacobson, Ph.D., directora del Instituto para Cambio Sicológico en la Ciudad de Nueva York. "Si usted ve la juventud como el único punto de referencia de cuán valiosa es, inevitablemente va a experimentar sentimientos de falta de valor y duda a medida que aparecen más señales de envejecimiento."

Pero esto no tiene que sucederle a usted. La confianza en sí misma y la autoestima no son realmente cuestiones de edad o de apariencia sino de actitud. Para algunas mujeres, la confianza en sí misma y la autoestima de hecho se vuelven más fuertes al envejecer, independientemente de unas cuantas arrugas, canas o una talla de vestidos que ha ido aumentando con los años. Y qué afortunadas son estas mujeres.

La confianza en sí misma y la autoestima producen algunos resultados engendrantes de juventud. Una mujer confiada y segura de sí misma —a pesar de cualquier señal de envejecimiento que pueda mostrar— se ve, se siente y se comporta como una mujer mucho más joven. Casi que ella irradia fuerza interna y energía, dice Thomas Tutko, Ph.D., profesor de sicología en la Universidad Estatal de San José, en California. También, es más probable que la mujer segura de sí misma respete a su cuerpo comiendo bien, haciendo ejercicio y evitando cosas dañinas como los cigarrillos, las drogas y el alcohol.

¿Por qué odiamos las matemáticas?

Por años usted ha sentido que simplemente no es buena para las matemáticas. No vaya a pensar que usted es la única que se encuentra atacada por la aritmética y confundida por las cálculos, ya que muchas mujeres sienten lo mismo, dice Sylvia Beyer, Ph.D., profesora asistente de sicología en la Universidad de Wisconsin-Parkside, en Kenosha.

¿Son las mujeres genéticamente inferiores como matemáticas? No realmente, dice la doctora Beyer. Pero a lo largo de los años las mujeres han sido condicionadas, dice ella, a subestimar sus capacidades y a tener expectativas bajas para ellas mismas en matemáticas y otros campos tradicionalmente orientados a los hombres.

En su investigación, la doctora Beyer ha revisado los resultados en pruebas de matemáticas y las expectativas de desempeño tanto de los hombres como de las mujeres. Ella ha encontrado que al ir a presentar una prueba de matemáticas las mujeres tienden a tener expectativas más bajas que los hombres. Y después, las mujeres tienen más probabilidad de pensar que tuvieron resultados peores de los que realmente tuvieron.

Estas conclusiones pueden aclarar por qué pocas mujeres tratan de dedicarse a carreras o materias tradicionalmente dominadas por los hombres, aunque tengan las habilidades para triunfar. "Debido a que ellas han sido educadas para pensar que no deben ser buenas en materias como matemáticas, muchas mujeres reducirán al mínimo sus logros aunque tengan éxito en ellos", dice la doctora Beyer. "Dirán que su desempeño fue pura suerte o inventarán alguna otra excusa. El peligro de esta manera de pensar es que a algunas mujeres muy talentosas podría impedirles que se dediquen a un interés o una carrera en un área donde puede haber un gran potencial o donde podrían encontrar bastante felicidad."

¿La respuesta? Dese cuenta que todos estos años usted ha estado bajando sus expectativas innecesariamente y entérese que probablemente no hay razón para que usted no sobresalga en matemáticas, ingeniería, mecánica automotriz —o lo que sea que a usted le guste.

La confianza en sí misma y la autoestima también hacen maravillas en su mente. Le proporcionan un amortiguador contra la ansiedad. Alivian los sentimientos de culpa, desesperación e insuficiencia. Nos dan el valor de realizar nuestros sueños. Y nos dan una buena disposición para intentar cosas nuevas, enfrentar desafíos nuevos y ampliar nuestros mundos, dice el doctor Tutko.

Y lo mejor de todo es que la confianza en sí misma y la autoestima se autoperpetúan; los beneficios que obtenemos de éstas tienden a regresar a nosotras y reforzar lo que tenemos. Generalmente, mientras más fuertes son nuestros sentimientos de autoestima y confianza en nosotras mismas, más satisfechas estaremos con la vida. Y eso no solamente nos da la fuerza de sobrevivir sino también de aceptar a la vida.

Mensajes sutiles de nuestra niñez

Es difícil hablar de confianza en sí misma y autoestima a menos que sea como un conjunto. "Una persona con autoestima alta tiene una buena imagen de su persona, y eso invariablemente inspira confianza en sí misma", dice el doctor Tutko. "Asimismo, una fuerte creencia en su capacidad, y la actitud positiva que viene con ésta, van a estimular sus sentimientos de autoestima."

¿De dónde vienen estos sentimientos?

Según un estudio hecho por Robert A. Josephs, Ph.D., y sus asociados en la Universidad de Texas, en Austin, los hombres y las mujeres obtienen su autoestima y confianza en sí mismos de distintos lugares. Mientras que los sentimientos que un hombre tiene acerca de su valor están más vinculados con sus logros, los de una mujer probablemente están vinculados con los papeles interpersonales que desempeña, o sea cómo se ve a sí misma como esposa, madre, hija y amiga.

Todo se remonta a nuestros años de la niñez. A los niños se les alienta mucho más a adquirir aptitudes y saber cómo hacer cosas. A las niñas, por otro lado, se les anima por lo general a desarrollar personalidades agradables y a ser bonitas", dice el sicólogo Nathaniel Branden, Ph.D., presidente del Instituto Branden para Autoestima, en Beverly Hills, y autor de *Six Pillars of Self-Esteem* (Seis pilares de la autoestima). "El problema es que ni la belleza ni la personalidad sugieren alguna forma de competencia o proporcionan realización personal y por lo tanto no producen ningún sentido perdurable de confianza en sí misma o autoestima."

Mantenga la cabeza en alto

Si usted siente que su confianza en usted misma y autoestima podrían necesitar un estímulo, probablemente eso es una señal de que es así. Aquí está lo que los expertos recomiendan.

Póngase en forma. ¿El hacer ejercicio podría mejorar su autoestima? Sí, seguramente. En un estudio en la Universidad Estatal del Colegio de Nueva York, en Brockport, se dividió a 57 personas en dos grupos: un grupo levantó pesas por 16 semanas, mientras que el otro grupo completó un curso teórico en educación física. ¿Adivine cuál fue el grupo que terminó con los espíritus en alto? Merrill J. Melnick, Ph.D., el sociólogo en deportes que condujo el estudio, explica por qué el grupo de ejercicio resultó tanto mejor: "Usted se puede ver como inferior si no está feliz con su propio físico". Al formar un poco de músculo y perder un poco de grasa, dice él, usted puede mejorar sus sentimientos acerca de su cuerpo y acerca de sí misma.

Amordace a su crítico interno. Las mujeres con autoestima baja tienden a oír una pequeña voz en sus cabezas que les dice: "no puedes", "eres débil" y "no vales nada". Cuando su voz crítica interna empieza a menospreciarla, hágala callar de inmediato, dice la doctora Jacobson. Esté consciente de los momentos en que hay más probabilidad de que aparezca, como por ejemplo cuando se siente deprimida. Reconozca que está tratando de herirla. Entonces contrarreste sus argumentos con afirmaciones en contra. Dígase a usted misma una y otra vez que usted es fuerte, capaz y valiosa hasta sentir que la voz desaparece. La misma regla también se aplica a los críticos externos. "Usted tiene que quitarle la fuerza a las otras personas al aprender a aceptarse a sí misma desde su punto de vista", dice ella.

Haga un inventario personal. "En lugar de pensar demasiado en sus deficiencias, necesitamos obtener satisfacción de las cosas que tenemos y podemos hacer bien", dice Stanley Teitelbaum, Ph.D., un sicólogo clínico en práctica privada en la Ciudad de Nueva York. Para hacer esto, enumere en un lado de un pedazo de papel sus logros, actividades, rasgos positivos y virtudes. Luego enumere en el otro lado sus debilidades, rasgos negativos y aspectos de su persona que usted desearía cambiar. Le sorprenderá darse cuenta de cuántas ventajas tiene a su favor. Y eso por sí solo puede lograr que se sienta extraordinariamente bien acerca de usted misma. Entonces, para confianza en sí misma y autoestima a largo plazo, acentúe lo positivo y elimine lo negativo.

Establezca una jerarquía de metas. Fijarse metas poco realistas seguramente conducirá al fracaso, lo cual puede afectar su autoestima. "Tratar de alcanzar una meta está muy bien, pero usted debe aprender a gatear antes de poder caminar", dice el doctor Tutko. Suponga que tiene una meta de alcanzar una puntuación de 300 en un juego de bolos. Una meta respetable, pero poco realista si su promedio es, digamos, 58. En lugar de aspirar desde el principio a su meta final, concéntrese en alcanzar diferentes etapas: 100, 150, 200, 250 y entonces 300. "Primero alcance el éxito en un nivel, luego trate de alcanzarlo en el siguiente", dice él.

Especialícese en algo. ¿Es usted una aprendiz de todo y oficial de nada? ¿Está usted envuelta en tantas tareas que no puede prestar la atención adecuada a ninguna? Tratar de abarcar demasiado sólo la preparará para una decepción, dice el doctor Tutko. Encuentre dos o tres cosas en la vida que realmente disfrute —sea tocar el clarinete, trabajar con una computadora o esquiar a campo traviesa— y concentre la mayor parte de sus energías en esto. Es mejor tener éxito en unas cuantas cosas que fallar en muchas.

¿Cuánta confianza tiene usted en sí misma?

¿Piensa usted muy favorablemente de su persona, o se ve a usted misma como que está en el ocaso y que le están pesando los años? Parece ser una pregunta sencilla, pero no lo es, dice Thomas Tutko, Ph.D., profesor de sicología en la Universidad Estatal de San José, en California. Muchas mujeres están vagamente conscientes de que tienen un cierto tipo de problema en sus vidas, pero no saben realmente de qué se trata.

Aquí hay algunas señales que le dirán si usted tiene un problema de autoestima.

- Está obsesionada con sus defectos, flaquezas y errores y se critica por estos.
- Usted permite a menudo que otros la menosprecien.
- Frecuentemente prueba nuevos peinados, ropa, dietas o artimañas para verse más atractiva o ser aceptada por los demás.
- Usted valora las decisiones y opiniones de otros más que las propias.
- Frecuentemente se compara usted misma y sus logros con otros.
- Se siente destrozada por la crítica negativa.
- Se desilusiona fácilmente.

Aquí están las señales de advertencia para una confianza baja en usted misma.

- Su rutina diaria raramente cambia.
- Usted escapa de los desafíos nuevos y de las situaciones incómodas.
- Rara vez intenta las cosas más de una vez.
- Siempre escoge lo seguro a lo riesgoso.
- Usted mide el éxito solamente en relación a ganar o adquirir.
- No puede expresar sus necesidades y deseos íntimos.
- Inventa excusas para no hacer cosas o para razonar por qué las cosas son de la forma que son.

Persevere en lo que a usted le gusta. La forma más fácil de perder la fe en usted misma es quedar atrapada en hacer algo que a usted le disgusta o que otros le dicen que tiene que hacer, dice el doctor Tutko. Antes de sumirse en una carrera o actividad que la hace sentirse miserable o que usted hace con poco entusiasmo, busque esas cosas que realmente la atraen y dedíquese a ellas con gusto. Tendrá una mayor probabilidad de hacerlas bien, lo cual ocasionará un efecto positivo en su psiquis.

Sea servicial. El brindar su tiempo y talentos para ayudar a su comunidad o a las personas que necesitan ayuda, estimula su autoestima y confianza en usted misma de varias formas, dice la doctora Jacobson. Sobre todo, le proporciona un sentimiento maravilloso de logro y refuerza la convicción de ser útil y valiosa.

Busque personas positivas. Lo menos que usted necesita en su vida cuando su confianza en usted misma está flaqueando son personas que la critican o encuentran fallas en usted. En su lugar, debería rodearse de personas que buscan lo bueno en usted. Invariablemente, estas son personas que disfrutan de niveles altos de confianza en sí mismas y autoestima. "Las personas con alta autoestima y confianza en sí mismas no se apresuran a juzgar o rebajar a otras", dice la doctora Jacobson. "Tienen mucho amor y aliento para brindar, y sus actitudes con respecto a la vida pueden contagiársele a usted."

Recompénsese a usted misma. Aumente su confianza en usted misma y autoestima haciendo algo agradable por usted misma cada vez que haga algo bien, dice el doctor Tutko. Felicítese a usted misma o regálese algo. Esto refuerza su fe en sí misma y pone más énfasis en el valor de su logro.

Actúe según su edad. "Algunas personas erróneamente creen que si compran todos los adornos externos de la juventud, esto mejorará la forma en que se sienten acerca de sí mismas", dice el doctor Teitelbaum. La verdad es que usted no se convertirá otra vez en una jovencita por meterse a presión en un bikini del tamaño de una servilleta. Lo más probable es que se vea ridícula.

Sea *lo* mejor, no *la* mejor. Los deportes competitivos son una gran forma de mejorar su confianza en usted misma y su autoestima. Pero si usted considera que vencer a los oponentes y ganar trofeos es la única forma de medir el éxito, su confianza en sí misma y autoestima ya están en terreno inseguro. "Practicar deportes puede ser fantástico, pero sólo si lo hace porque le gustan y por averiguar qué tan buena puede ser en ellos", dice el doctor Tutko.

Sepa que puede fracasar. Vea al fracaso no como un mal sino como una oportunidad para un éxito nuevo, dice Daniel Wegner, Ph.D., profesor de sicología en la Universidad de Virginia, en Charlottesville. "La vida es un proceso a base de tanteos, y no progresamos si no nos arriesgamos ante la posibilidad de fracasar", dice él. "En el orden del universo, muchos de los 'fracasos' reales que vamos a experimentar no son ni tan perjudiciales como el daño que nos hacemos cuando nos obsesionamos y preocupamos acerca de los fracasos que todavía están por venir."

Prográmese para preocuparse. Hacer callar a su crítica interna no siempre es tan fácil. Algunas veces usted puede simplemente cerrarle la puerta en las narices; en otras ocasiones ella se va a defender. Algunas veces, mientras más trata usted de suprimir los pensamientos y las ansiedades no deseados, más probable es que se obsesione con ellos, dice el doctor Wegner. En lugar de gastar energía suprimiendo los pensamientos poco felices, trate de ceder ante ellos un poco. Programe 30 minutos diarios para "sesiones de preocupación" para desahogarse; entonces siga hacia adelante y disfrute de la vida.

Patalee un poco. ¿ Alguna vez consideró usted aprender un arte marcial? Como profesor de sicología y director del programa de artes marciales de la Universidad de Wake Forest, en Winston-Salem, Carolina del Norte, Charles L. Richman, Ph.D., apoya enfáticamente los efectos de mejora en actitud por parte de las artes marciales. Como otros deportes, la harán más fuerte y acrecentarán la imagen de su cuerpo, lo cual por sí solo puede mejorar su autoestima, dice él. Las artes marciales también tienden a enfatizar la disciplina y el control. "Cuando usted combina este pensamiento disciplinado con la maestría de nuevas habilidades y la realización de que se puede defender por usted misma de un ataque físico, experimenta una transformación asombrosa en ambas, confianza en sí misma y autoestima", dice el doctor Richman. Busque en las páginas amarillas de su directorio telefónico o en su periódico las escuelas en su área.

CREATIVIDAD

Mantiene la mente y el cuerpo en armonía

Pintar a la acuarela es creativo. También lo es componer una sinfonía, dirigir una obra de teatro o esculpir una fuente.

Pero la creatividad no está limitada a las artes. Plantar un jardín es creativo, como también lo es diseñar un programa de computación, crear una receta nueva, planear una comida, mapear genes o construir una casa de pan de jengibre con un montón de niños.

En otras palabras, la creatividad se define como el acto de hacer, inventar o producir. Y eso es algo que todas hacemos.

"Yo le llamo conciencia de creatividad diaria —cuando nos enfocamos en el proceso de inventar en lugar de en el resultado. Esta creatividad diaria o tener conciencia de algo, es en realidad bueno para la salud y el bienestar de uno", explica Ellen J. Langer, Ph.D., profesora de sicología de la Universidad de Harvard, en Cambridge, Massachusetts, y autora de *Mindfulness* (Conciencia).

Es tan esencial para nuestra existencia que la novedad, sorpresa y variedad proporcionada por nuestra creatividad realmente le proporciona combustible a nuestras ganas de vivir. La investigación con los ancianos de la doctora Langer ha mostrado que cuando se les alienta a ser creativos o conscientes, como ella dice, ellos realmente viven vidas más largas y felices. "Cuando no mantenemos activas a nuestras mentes, la mente y el cuerpo gradualmente se van apagando por sí solos", dice la doctora Langer.

En otras palabras, cuando dejamos de crear, dejamos de vivir.

Afortunadamente, la capacidad de crear permanece intacta en nuestras vidas, aunque el número real de ciertos productos que podemos crear —las pinturas, los jardines o las esculturas— pueda declinar al hacernos mayores.

"La productividad creativa para la matemáticas, la ciencia, la poesía y cualquier cosa que requiere del pensamiento abstracto generalmente llega a su

Los asesinos del espíritu creativo

Algunos días la creatividad fluye a través de nuestro cuerpo y sale hacia el mundo sin esfuerzo. Otros días es como si el flujo estuviera bloqueado por una pared impenetrable.

"La creatividad es un producto frágil que puede ser suprimido o afectado mucho más fácilmente de lo que puede ser encendido", dice Teresa Amabile, Ph.D., profesora de sicología de la Universidad Brandeis, en Waltham, Massachusetts.

Pero, dice ella, usted puede prevenir la interferencia de su flujo al evitar a estos asesinos de la creatividad.

• Los que dicen que no. Los críticos y los escépticos pueden limitar su ámbito de pensamiento y despedazar su progreso creativo.

• Motivación material. La mayor parte de la motivación creativa viene de adentro, pero los motivadores extrínsecos —como el dinero, la fama, los premios y la aceptación— pueden disminuir severamente sus poderes creativos.

• Llevar la cuenta. La presión de tener que ganar puntos, cumplir con ciertas normas o satisfacer las expectativas de otros pueden reprimir seriamente su capacidad creativa.

• Crear con muchos a su alrededor. ¿Qué tan creativa podría usted ser si supiera que su maestro, jefe o el mundo entero están mirando por encima de sus hombros cada minuto? La investigación de la doctora Amabile ha mostrado que tales entornos pueden reprimir sus habilidades creativas. Trate de trabajar en un lugar que ponga alguna distancia entre usted y un par de ojos penetrantes.

• Muy poco tiempo. Los relojes, programas y plazos pueden dificultar la evolución de una gran idea. Trate de trabajar a un paso cómodo y regular.

• Drogas y alcohol. No hay ninguna buena prueba científica de que la creatividad pueda mejorarse químicamente. A la larga, estas substancias tienen el potencial de destruir su capacidad creativa mucho más de lo que pueden mejorarla.

ápice a los 30 años de edad", dice Carolyn Adams-Price, Ph.D., profesora asistente de sicología de la Universidad Estatal de Misisipí, en Starkville. "En el caso de la historia, la filosofía, el escribir y cualquier cosa que requiera mucho conocimiento, generalmente llega a su ápice a los 60 años de edad."

Pero lo que declina es solamente el número de productos creativos, no la capacidad de crear o la calidad de lo que se produce, enfatiza la doctora Adams-Price.

Una historia de supresión

Hasta la última mitad del siglo veinte, la educación y el entrenamiento que permitiría a las mujeres expresar su creatividad era a menudo desalentado por los estereotipos culturales que definían y limitaban el papel de una mujer en el mundo.

La escritora Virginia Woolf, por ejemplo, imaginaba que William Shakespeare había tenido una hermana igualmente creativa, Judith, a quien se le mandó a remendar medias o preparar la comida mientras que a William se le envió a la escuela a estudiar literatura y drama.

Históricamente, los hombres han tenido una ventaja notoria sobre las mujeres cuando se trata de obtener ayuda para desarrollar su creatividad.

Los estudios muestran que, la mayoría de las veces, la sociedad se ha apresurado a proporcionar a los hombres posibilidades de educación y admisión a sociedades profesionales y otro entrenamiento especializado para estimular su creatividad. Los estudios muestran también, que los maestros tendían a reforzar la conducta creativa en los muchachos al mismo tiempo que esperaban que las muchachas se comportaran bien y estuvieran listas a seguir las reglas. Los expertos también han sugerido que el estímulo que nuestra sociedad brinda a los muchachos en cuanto a la agresividad natural, el dominio, el ego y la voluntad de tomar riesgos —en todo, desde el fútbol hasta la física— ayuda a los hombres jóvenes a desarrollar el empuje, la determinación y la persistencia necesarios para seguir sus propias visiones creativas en una cultura a veces hostil a la creatividad.

Dele rienda suelta

Hoy en día, las mujeres están bien representadas en las galerías de arte, los teatros, los conjuntos de danza, las escuelas médicas, los negocios y otras instituciones. De hecho, el número de mujeres en las escuelas de arte y ballet ahora excede el número de hombres.

¿Cómo puede liberar la creatividad escondida dentro de usted? Ya sea que esté decidida a crear una obra de arte pública o una expresión privada de su yo interno, todo lo que necesita para empezar es una idea y un deseo de explorarla. Aquí está cómo empezar.

Identifique un problema. Pregúntese a usted misma: "¿Qué podría usar realmente el mundo ahora?" "¿Alternativas creativas a los asilos para ancianos?" "¿Formas de aprovechar el talento de individuos jubilados?" A menudo, el primer paso solamente requiere identificar un problema, dice la doctora Langer. De allí, sus ideas pueden bifurcarse en cientos de direcciones diferentes.

La creatividad y la locura

Isadora Duncan bailó a la luz de la luna con hadas. Vincent van Gogh se amputó su propia oreja. Sylvia Plath se suicidó. ¿Significa esto que las personas sumamente creativas tienen más probabilidad de enloquecer que el resto de nosotras? Es una pregunta intrigante. Pero a pesar de los mejores esfuerzos de la ciencia, la respuesta todavía no es clara.

En un estudio a más de 1.000 hombres y mujeres realizado en la Universidad de Kentucky, en Lexington, el investigador doctor Arnold M. Ludwig, encontró que los poetas, los escritores, los artistas, los músicos y otros en profesiones creativas acusaban una mayor probabilidad de exhibir una tendencia hacia la locura que otros en profesiones supuestamente menos creativas —personas que eran funcionarios públicos, en negocios y oficiales militares.

Aquellos en el teatro demostraron índices más altos de abuso de alcohol y drogas, episodios maníacos, trastornos de ansiedad e intentos de suicidio. Los escritores se inclinaban más hacia la depresión y el alcohol. Los artistas tenían más problemas relacionados con el alcohol, la depresión, la ansiedad y las dificultades de adaptación. Los músicos y los compositores tenían más probabilidad de deprimirse. Los poetas eran más propensos al abuso del alcohol y las drogas, la depresión, las manías, el suicidio y la sicosis en general.

La tendencia hacia la locura en las personas creativas parece clara hasta que usted considera un par de puntos, como el doctor Ludwig lo hace en su estudio. Primero, las exigencias de aquellos en las profesiones más creativas pueden tener mayor probabilidad de agravar los problemas ya existentes. Si por ejemplo usted estuviera predispuesta genéticamente a la depresión, una carrera en el teatro podría empujarla completamente hacia la depresión, mientras que una carrera como banquera podría no hacerlo.

Un segundo punto es que ya que nuestra cultura espera que sus escritores y artistas sean extraños y sus oficiales militares y banqueros sean estables, las profesiones tales como la música y el arte simplemente pueden atraer a las personas que están predispuestas al exceso, mientras que las profesiones como la banca y la milicia atraen a las personas que tienen más probabilidad de ser estables.

Una forma excelente de hacer que se le ocurran a uno buenas ideas es tener muchas y no juzgarlas. Luego simplemente escoja las mejores, dice la doctora Langer.

Anote ideas en una hoja de papel. Entonces, usando la inspiración de la primera idea, escriba tantas ideas relacionadas con ésta como sea posible. Recopile una lista de ideas, estúdiela cuidadosamente y saque las que le gusten más. Deseche las otras.

"Algunas veces una gran idea es sencillamente tomar una idea antigua y darle vuelta", dice Gabriele Rico, Ph.D., profesora de inglés y artes creativos de la Universidad Estatal de San José, en California, y autora de *Pain and Possibility* (Dolor y posibilidad). Por ejemplo, en una ocasión se sirvió un helado de crema sobre un *waffle* plano. Entonces algún pensador innovador decidió doblar ese *waffle* en forma de embudo, y ¡*voilà*! El mundo tuvo su primer cono de *waffle*.

Anote sus ideas y sueños. Las grandes ideas pueden materializarse y desvanecerse en un instante, por lo cual muchas mujeres creativas llevan un diario para anotar las ideas que se les ocurren a lo largo del día, dice la doctora Rico. Todo lo que usted necesita es un pequeño cuaderno que quepa en su bolsillo o cartera o aun debajo de su almohada, ya que los sueños también pueden ser abundantes en creatividad.

"La mente hace algunas de sus conexiones y asociaciones más originales mientras que usted duerme", dice la doctora Rico. Así que empiece el día escribiendo en un cuaderno de notas lo que usted recuerda de sus sueños.

Recapacite sobre los fracasos. Los errores y los resultados inesperados pueden resultar en las mayores recompensas, dice la doctora Langer. Por ejemplo, se pensó que una nueva goma de pegar desarrollada por la compañía 3M se creía que era un fracaso porque no era lo suficientemente pegajosa. Pero cuando esa goma de pegar se aplicó a una hoja de papel, se convirtió en uno de los productos para oficina más innovadores de todos los tiempos: los pequeños papelitos adhesivos *Post-it Notes*. Así que la próxima vez que usted tenga un "fracaso" aparente en sus manos, no se apresure a condenarlo. En su lugar, dele la vuelta y estúdiela desde otra perspectiva.

Desafíe el pensamiento ortodoxo. "Una de las desventajas de nuestra sociedad es que alienta la inhibición y la conformidad ciega", dice la doctora Langer. "Nos volvemos temerosas de mirar al mundo desde perspectivas diferentes para desafiar las ideas establecidas." Para aumentar nuestra creatividad, debemos estar dispuestas a desaprender muchas de las convenciones que nos pasamos aprendiendo toda la vida.

Una persona creativa no debería tener temor a desafiar ideas o a pensar en direcciones que para otros podrían considerarse poco ortodoxas.

Aprenda. Si usted ha decidido expresar su creatividad en un medio específico como la pintura o el canto, aprenda tanto como sea posible acerca de ese medio, dice la doctora Rico. Empiece despacio, practique en su medio regularmente e identifique sus puntos fuertes y débiles. A medida que su familiaridad y habilidad aumenten, su capacidad de manipular el medio escogido para expresar su creatividad va a ampliarse.

Encuentre un modelo de conducta. Usted puede obtener una gran cantidad de inspiración emulando el trabajo y la técnica de algunos de los gigantes creativos en su área de interés, dice la doctora Rico. Pero no sea una copiona. La imitación no es creatividad. En lugar de eso, observe a su modelo de conducta para que la haga pensar en formas que usted nunca había considerado. O, tome temas que ellos han explorado y enfóquelos desde otro ángulo.

Explórese usted misma. La mujer creativa debe estar dispuesta a explorar una amplia gama de emociones, experiencias y memorias profundamente arraigadas. "Las personas mayores a menudo usan sus experiencias personales como una fuente de creatividad", dice la doctora Adams-Price.

Explore el mundo. La mayoría de nosotras obtenemos la inspiración y la energía creativa de las cosas a nuestro alrededor: la vista de una puesta de sol, el aroma de una flor, el sonido de un silbato de tren, el tacto del musgo. "Mientras más cosas sabemos, sentimos y experimentamos acerca de nuestro mundo, mas creativas seremos", dice la doctora Rico.

CUIDADO DEL CUTIS

Pautas para piel perfectamente joven

Su vida está tan ocupada que usted apenas tiene tiempo de dormir o comer o ir al supermercado. Usted definitivamente no tiene tiempo para cuidarse el cutis, ¿o sí lo tiene?

La verdad es, que proteger su cutis no necesita llevarle tanto tiempo. Y, a pesar de todo el bombo y platillo que rodea a los productos de renombre y a las rutinas confusas de pasos múltiples, en realidad no tiene que ser complicado o caro.

Solamente tiene que limpiar, humectar y proteger su cutis del fotoenvejecimiento —las arrugas, los surcos y las manchas por pasar demasiado tiempo en el sol.

Si usted usa una protección contra el sol diariamente, los médicos dicen que después de un tiempo usted encontrará que su cutis reparará por sí solo algo del daño, haciendo que usted se vea más joven y fresca y se sienta bien como consecuencia.

Algunos productos, tal como la *Neutrogena Moisturizer*, que combinan los humectantes con las lociones antisolares y los tintes le ahorrarán tiempo.

Por lo tanto consideremos una rutina realista que va a dejar a su cutis en su mejor apariencia juvenil, sin echar a perder su programa diario.

Trátelo con ternura

No importa si su cutis es normal, grasoso, seco o está dañado por el sol, la consigna para su limpieza es "suave", dicen los dermatólogos. Los limpiadores suaves y el manejo suave. ¿Por qué? Cada vez que usted frota, jala, refriega o de alguna manera tira de su cutis, puede aflojar las fibras minúsculas abajo de la superficie las cuales promueven la firmeza y el aspecto juvenil.

"Cualquier cosa que le haga a su cara agrega algo de daño de edad", dice el doctor Albert M. Kligman, un profesor de dermatología en la Escuela de Medicina de la Universidad de Pensilvania, en Filadelfia.

Escoja productos suaves. Olvídese de los astringentes y limpiadores ásperos, aconseja el doctor Seth L. Matarasso, profesor asistente de dermatología en la Escuela de Medicina de la Universidad de California, San Francisco. Todo lo que usted necesita son jabones suaves baratos como Purpose, *Basis*, *Neutrogena* y *Dove*.

Si su cutis está muy seco, aun un enjuague completo por la mañana con un substituto de jabón como *Cetaphil* o nada de jabón está bien, dice el doctor Matarasso. Simplemente experimente para ver cuál es el mejor para usted.

Evite la erupción. Lavarse con esas friegas de nueces molidas y esponjas abrasivas es como usar limpiadores de la cocina para su cutis, dice Carole Walderman, una cosmetóloga y esteticista y presidenta de la Von Lee International School of Aesthetics and Makeup, una escuela de maquillaje y belleza, en Baltimore. Los pequeños rasguños que estos dejan inflaman su cutis y juntan bacterias, por lo tanto pueden promover una erupción cuando usted pensaba que había dejado el acné atrás para siempre.

Mantenga el agua a una temperatura moderada. Use agua tibia, no caliente, para enjuagar su limpiador, dice Leila Cohoon, una cosmetóloga y esteticista y dueña de Leila's Skin Care, una compañía que se especializa en el cuidado del cutis, en Independence, Misuri. Y no se moleste en darse una salpicada de agua fría después para "cerrar los poros". Los poros no se abren y cierran como se piensa comúnmente.

Séquese con palmaditas. Dese palmaditas en la cara no completamente seca con una toalla tan suavemente como si fuera el toque de un bebé, dice el doctor Matarasso. "Deje solamente una telilla húmeda en el cutis, como un rocío."

Pruebe tónicos suaves. Para una optativa sensación de estar extra limpia, use un agua de flores calmante, tal como *Rosewater*, y tónico después de que se limpia y se enjuaga, dice Walderman. "Cuando llegamos a la década de los 30 años de edad nuestros poros pueden empezar a verse más grandes, porque la gravedad empieza a jalar hacia abajo alrededor de los folículos de los vellos, haciendo que se vean más profundos", dice ella. "Los tónicos cerrarán temporalmente los poros, posiblemente por cerca de 45 minutos, dejando una buena base para aplicar el maquillaje". Apliquese el tónico con una almohadilla de algodón que primeramente haya sido saturada con agua y luego exprimida, dando pasadas suaves hacia arriba.

Adelante con los humectantes

Los humectantes no agregan humedad al cutis, no importa lo que los redactores de publicidad dicen. No obstante, sí ayudan a retener el agua que usted dejó sobre la cara y el cuerpo después de lavarse, lo cual esponja las arrugas finas y hace más tersa la superficie, dice el doctor Matarasso. Si usted usa la

Faciales rápidos en la casa

Si usted tiene un paquete de frijoles (habichuelas) rojos secos, un procesador de alimentos y unos cuantos ingredientes sencillos, fácilmente puede darse el gusto de un facial casero de lujo de vez en cuando. Marina Valmy, una cosmetóloga en la Christine Valmy Skin Care School, una escuela que se especializa en el cuidado del cutis, en la Ciudad de Nueva York, ofrece estas recetas para refrescar su cutis para usar dos veces por semana.

Para cutis normal a seco:

Empiece con una máscara limpiadora. Ponga 2 tazas de frijoles rojos secos en su procesador de alimentos y muélalos hasta hacerlos polvo. Mezcle entonces ½ taza con un poco de agua para formar una pasta y distribúyala por todo su rostro (excepto en el área de los ojos), como una máscara. Deje la máscara por unos cinco minutos, entonces enjuáguela completamente con agua. Guarde el resto del polvo de frijoles en un frasco cerrado herméticamente para otra ocasión.

Siga con una máscara para hidratar. Mezcle 1 cucharadita de miel, 1 yema de huevo, ½ cucharadita de aceite de oliva y ½ cucharadita de mitad crema y mitad leche (*half and half*) o crema pesada. Aplique a su rostro, incluyendo el área de sus ojos, y déjela por 15 a 20 minutos mientras descansa. Enjuague después con agua.

Para cutis grasoso:

Límpiese con la máscara de frijoles rojos secos (arriba), después siga con la máscara tonificante. Mezcle 1 cucharadita de yogur bajo en grasa simple, ½ clara de huevo, ¼ de cucharadita de aceite de aguacate (palta) y 1 cucharadita de perejil fresco molido. Déjela puesta por 15 a 20 minutos y enjuague después con agua.

---

toalla hasta que está seca como un hueso, cualquier humectante —no importa qué tan caro sea— permanecerá solamente en la superficie y se sentirá grasoso. Pero si usted deja una telilla húmeda después de enjuagarse, el humectante ayudará al agua a meterse dentro de los poros y a hundirse más profundamente dentro del cutis. Si su cutis es graso, posiblemente no necesite un humectante, el cual podría agravar el acné.

Aquí está lo que debe saber acerca de los humectantes.

Pregunte acerca de los AHAs. Los ácidos alfahidróxidos (o *AHAs*, por sus siglas en inglés) se derivan de las fuentes alimenticias tales como el vino tinto, la leche agria y la fruta. Algunos estudios muestran que estos ácidos pueden aumentar la renovación de las células del cutis quemadas por el sol, al hacer tersa y firme su textura. Aunque son temas actuales en las revistas de belleza, los investigadores difieren en si los AHAs en muchos humectantes pueden en realidad reducir las arrugas finas.

Las concentraciones bajas que se encuentran en los productos comerciales pueden ser el problema, dice el doctor Matarasso. La mayoría de los humectantes cosméticos usan muy pequeñas cantidades de AHAs, dice él. Si usted quisiera ver lo que los AHAs pueden hacer por usted, su mejor opción es hablar con su dermatólogo acerca de los humectantes con alta concentración de AHAs.

Escoja las lociones que no tapen. Si usted solamente quiere un buen humectante para todos los días, pero tiene la tendencia a tener erupción de vez en cuando, escoja un humectante que diga en la etiqueta *"noncomedogenic"* (no comedogénico), dice el doctor Thomas Griffin, un dermatólogo con el Hospital de Graduados y profesor asistente clínico de dermatología en la Escuela de Medicina de la Universidad de Pensilvania, ambos en Filadelfia. Estos productos no taparán los poros.

Chequee el pH. Si su cutis es sensible, use un producto que tenga la misma proporción ácida (pH) del cutis normal, la cual se encuentra en un pH de 4,5 a 5,5, dice Cohoon. Muchas etiquetas dicen *'pH-balanced'* (pH balanceado) pero eso no significa nada", dice ella. "Podría significar ácido con pH balanceado o alcalino con pH balanceado, el cual no es bueno para su cutis. Lo que usted quiere es que sea ácido con pH balanceado para el cuidado del cutis."

¿Cómo estar segura? "Compre papeles pH (tales como *pHydrion*) en su salón de cuidado del cutis y sumérjalos en el producto", dice Cohoon. "El papel cambiará de color y usted lo compara a la tabla adjunta, la cual le mostrará qué pH tiene el humectante."

Vaya con cuidado en el área de los ojos. Durante el día use solamente una crema para los ojos liviana en el área de los ojos, dice Walderman. Algunas mujeres usan cremas espesas para los ojos las cuales tienden a hacer que el maquillaje se vea grueso y pastoso.

Cómo conservar su cara y cuerpo

De cualquier forma que usted la use, la loción antisolar es el paso rejuvenecedor más importante para el cuidado del cutis. Aun si en el pasado usted no lo haya hecho muy fielmente, el empezar a usar una loción antisolar ahora mismo le pagará dividendos de juventud en las décadas venideras.

Simplifique el proceso. A menos que usted disfrute aplicándose capa tras capa de pociones y lociones, la forma más fácil de agregar la loción antisolar a su rutina es usar una loción antisolar con base de crema como su humectante, dice el doctor Matarasso.

Asegúrese de que sea una protección real. Escoja una loción antisolar o una combinación humectante-loción antisolar con un factor de protección solar (o *SPF*, por sus siglas en inglés) de por lo menos 15, dice el doctor Kligman. Y las lociones antisolares (a menudo llamadas lociones antisolares de espectro completo) las cuales bloquean los dos tipos de rayos ultravioletas, *UVA* y *UVB* (por sus siglas en inglés) le ofrecerán a usted la mejor protección contra la quemadura superficial y contra el daño más profundo a los tejidos que causan las arrugas y bolsas, dice él. Muchos humectantes cosméticos pregonan a los cuatro vientos sus capacidades de protección solar, pero la mayoría contienen lociones antisolares con SPF muy bajos.

Cómo mejorar su cutis mientras duerme

En la noche usted se limpia otra vez. Si su cutis tiende hacia la sequedad, agregue un humectante para pasar la noche o a lo mejor *tretinoin* (*Retin-A*) si usted quiere combatir el daño del sol activamente. Y entonces, a dormir, lo cual de por sí le da un aspecto juvenil a su cutis al borrarle el estrés de su tez.

Trate de agregar estos consejos a su rutina de limpieza nocturna.

Quítese el maquillaje. Es verdad lo que dicen: nunca debería irse a dormir con éste puesto. Para una limpieza a fondo, use un limpiador con petrolado para quitar el maquillaje, dice Marina Valmy, una cosmetóloga en la Christine Valmy Skin Care School, una escuela que se especializa en el cuidado del cutis, en la Ciudad de Nueva York. Pero solamente por la noche —el petrolado es muy pesado para limpiarse o humectarse durante el día, dice ella. Otra opción es su jabón suave favorito; solamente limpie y enjuague por completo.

Pruebe un limpiador profundo de poros. Tres veces a la semana, use un limpiador profundo de poros y un cepillo facial suave para una limpieza más a fondo de su cutis, dice Walderman.

Duerma con un combatiente de arrugas. Si el daño del sol ha grabado su cutis con líneas finas, pídale a su doctor una receta para la crema *Retin-A*, dice el doctor Jonathan Weiss, profesor clínico asistente de dermatología en la Escuela de Medicina de la Universidad de Emory, en Atlanta. "La *Retin-A* es un producto maravilloso para el daño causado por el sol", dice él. "Puede mejorar la apariencia amarillenta del cutis y hacerla más rosada. Pero su mejoría más notable es en las arrugas y las manchas de edad." El doctor Weiss hace notar que la Administración de Alimentos y Drogas todavía no aprueba la *Retin-A* para el tratamiento del cutis dañado por el sol y arrugado, aunque la crema parece ser efectiva.

Con la ayuda de su dermatólogo, usted puede adaptar a la concentración de *Retin-A* según las necesidades de su cutis. "Después de limpiarse con un jabón suave, deje secar su cutis completamente por unos 10 a 20 minutos", dice el doctor Matarasso. "Luego aplíquese una cantidad del tamaño de un chícharo (guisante) por todos lados, alrededor de sus ojos (dejando sin crema aproximadamente 0,5 pulgada/1,25 cm abajo de los ojos), la boca, el pecho, los antebrazos y el dorso de las manos. Si usted usa *Retin-A*, no necesitará un humectante por la noche a menos que la *Retin-A* cause un poco de enrojecimiento y escamado. Si eso sucede, use un humectante esa noche y altérnelo con *Retin-A*". Usted también puede usar vaselina alrededor del área de los ojos. (Para mayor información sobre la *Retin-A*, vea Arrugas en la página 32)

Use humectante si lo desea. Si a usted le gusta la sensación del humectante por la noche y su cutis se ha secado un poco con el tiempo, aplique una crema nocturna sustanciosa, sugiere Walderman. Y este es el momento de usar cremas para los ojos más pesadas sobre todo en el cutis alrededor de los ojos. Estos productos muy pesados para el uso durante el día o bajo el maquillaje, son buenos para conservar la humedad natural mientras usted duerme, dice ella.

Cuídese los labios. En la noche, póngase vaselina en los labios, dice Valmy. Debido a que la piel de los labios es muy delgada, la circulación de la sangre está muy cerca de la superficie y puede hacer que los labios se sequen. La vaselina no permitirá que la humedad se evapore, y evita que usted se despierte con los labios agrietados.

CUIDADO DE LOS SENOS

Conserve sus senos firmes y saludables

Usted se voltea hacia la derecha y mira sus senos de lado en el espejo. Después se voltea otra vez hacia el frente, levanta los brazos sobre la cabeza y los observa de nuevo. Entonces se voltea hacia la izquierda y mira otra vez.

¿Qué está buscando?

Dos cosas: lo caído y las estrías que sugieren que usted está empezando a envejecer —y lo cual usted tiene la intención de combatir con cada truco imaginable— y cualquier bulto, protuberancia, hoyuelo, secreción, caída, arruga o diferencia en tamaño, forma o color que pudieran señalar la presencia de cáncer.

Aunque ninguna de nosotras queremos ver las señales del envejecimiento, lo que más tememos es el cáncer de mama. Y con buena razón —es el tipo de cáncer más común que sufren las mujeres.

La mayoría de los cánceres de mama son descubiertos por las mujeres mismas, no por el médico o un mamograma. Ellas notan que algo no se ve o se siente bien. Y a pesar de ello, el 80 por ciento de las mujeres dicen que ellas no se hacen autoexámenes de los senos (o *BSEs*, por sus siglas en inglés) en forma regular. Algunas dicen que se sienten incómodas tocándose a sí mismas y otras simplemente no pueden encarar la posibilidad de que el cáncer de mama pudiera pasarles a ellas.

Estos sentimientos reflejan el hecho de que nuestros senos actúan como marcadores físicos para nuestra transición de una etapa de la vida a la otra: los senos emergen cuando empezamos a menstruar, florecen al comenzar nuestra vida sexual activa, llegan a su plenitud cuando nos preparamos a dar a luz, y eventualmente se marchitan o se caen.

Sin embargo las mismas razones que nos hacen renuentes a examinarnos los senos también son las más convincentes de que deberíamos hacerlo.

El cáncer de mama es una amenaza importante a la salud de cualquier mujer que haya pasado su trigésimo cumpleaños, dice la doctora Sondra Lynne Carter, una ginecóloga en práctica privada en la ciudad de Nueva York quien trata a pacientes con problemas en los senos. Y la amenaza aumenta con cada año que pasa.

A los 25 años de edad, usted tenía 1 en 21.441 probabilidades de tener cáncer de mama, a los 30 años es 1 en 2.426. A los 35 años es 1 en 622. A los 45 años es 1 en 96, y a los 80 años es 1 en 10.

Ya que la mayoría de los cánceres de mama realmente ocurren después de los 45 años de edad, muchas mujeres tienden a pensar en el cáncer de mama y en los senos caídos de la misma forma: "es algo de qué preocuparme cuando esté vieja". Eso es incorrecto. Ambas cosas tienen más probabilidad de ocurrir después de los 45 años de edad, asienten los expertos. Pero para prevenir ambos se necesita empezar con un buen cuidado de los senos en las décadas anteriores.

El autoexamen de los senos

El buen cuidado de los senos empieza con el aprendizaje de cuándo y cómo hacerse un autoexamen de los senos.

Los médicos están de acuerdo en que el autoexamen debería hacerse la primera semana después de su período todos los meses. Su meta se divide en dos: una, familiarizarse con los contornos normales, los bultos y las protuberancias en sus senos que cualquier cosa fuera de lo común será muy aparente y, dos, detectar cualquier bulto (de 0,5 pulgada /1,3 cm, por ejemplo) que aparezca súbitamente, esté en el mismo lugar y dure por uno o dos ciclos.

¿Cuál es la mejor manera de hacerse un autoexamen? De cualquier manera que usted se sienta cómoda, dicen los doctores. Algunas mujeres prefieren hacérselo paradas en la ducha cuando sus senos están resbalosos por el jabón. Otras prefieren hacérselos paradas enfrente de un espejo. Mientras que otras prefieren hacérselo acostadas boca arriba.

Aquí está cómo los médicos sugieren examinarse los senos de la manera más correcta posible.

Estírese primero. Es importante que antes de empezar, usted estire los brazos por encima de la cabeza y se mire en el espejo para ver si nota algún cambio obvio en sus senos. Busque algo importante: un hoyuelo en la piel que no había notado antes, o un pezón de repente se ha invertido, ha desarrollado eczema o tiene una secreción que no es resultado de habérselo apretado. Ponga las manos sobre las caderas, empuje los hombros hacia atrás y busque cambios de nuevo. Luego empuje sus hombros hacia adelante, mientras contrae sus músculos pectorales. Cualquier hoyuelo debería ser obvio en esta posición.

Escoja una estrategia de búsqueda. Hay diferentes maneras de hacer el mismo autoexamen: puede usar el pezón como punto focal y ver si siente bultos a lo largo de las líneas imaginarias que salen de su pezón hasta llegar a la clavícula y hacia abajo hasta la línea del sostén; usted puede usar el pezón como el

Ponga los brazos por encima de su cabeza y busque algún hoyuelo en la piel, secreción (de fluido) del pezón u otros cambios en apariencia.

Ponga las manos sobre las caderas, primero empuje sus hombros hacia atrás, después hacia adelante, y busque algún cambio en sus senos que haya ocurrido desde su último autoexamen.

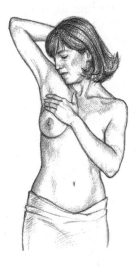

Coloque su mano derecha detrás de la cabeza. Con las yemas de los dedos de su mano izquierda, examine su seno derecho completamente desde la clavícula hasta la línea del sostén y dentro de su axila. Repita el proceso en su seno izquierdo con la mano izquierda detrás de la cabeza. Vea en la página opuesta la descripción de las diferentes estrategias para la búsqueda.

centro y seguir haciendo círculos alrededor con sus dedos en círculos cada vez más amplios; o simplemente puede imaginarse una cuadrícula colocada sobre su seno y examinarlo en franjas que vayan desde arriba hacia abajo entre la clavícula y la parte de abajo de la línea del sostén.

Cualquiera sea el método que escoja, ponga la mano del lado que usted quiere examinar detrás de la cabeza antes de empezar. Esto traslada cualquier tejido del seno que está abajo de su axila hacia arriba de la pared torácica donde usted lo puede examinar detenidamente.

El estilo de vida anticáncer

El buen cuidado de los senos también significa adoptar un estilo de vida que reduzca su riesgo de cáncer. Nadie ha descubierto exactamente por qué, pero las mujeres que adoptan estilos de vida que reducen la cantidad de estrógeno que circula a través de sus cuerpos, pueden reducir significativamente su riesgo de desarrollar cáncer de mama. Y eso incluye a las mujeres que tienen una historia familiar de la enfermedad.

¿Cuáles son las mejores estrategias? Aquí está lo que los médicos sugieren.

Reduzca la grasa. Un estudio de la Escuela de Medicina en la Universidad de Tufts, en Boston, comparó los niveles de estrógeno en un grupo de mujeres que siguió una dieta que obtenía el 40 por ciento de sus calorías de la grasa, con un grupo de mujeres que obtenían sólo el 21 por ciento de sus calorías de la grasa.

¿El resultado? Las mujeres premenopaúsicas en el grupo de alta grasa tenían niveles de estrógeno en la sangre que eran un 30 a 75 por ciento más altos que sus hermanas que comían menos grasa. En el grupo postmenopáusico, las mujeres que comían la dieta más alta en grasa tenían niveles de estrógeno que eran un 300 por ciento más altos.

Coma fibra de plantas. Los estudios a animales indican que las substancias en las plantas —fitoestrógenos— pueden ser capaces de evitar que el estrógeno que circula en su cuerpo cause cáncer de mama. Las buenas fuentes de fitoestrógeno incluyen los productos de soja, los brotes de alfalfa, las manzanas, la cebada, la avena y los chícharos (guisantes).

Sea una comilona de verduras. En un Estudio de la Salud de Enfermeras de Harvard, el cual estudió a cerca de 90.000 mujeres en Boston, los investigadores encontraron que aquellas que reportaban comer dos o tres porciones de verduras al día tenían un 17 por ciento de reducción en el riesgo de cáncer de mama en comparación con aquellas que comían menos de una porción completa por día.

Nadie está dispuesto a apostar mucho en una explicación, pero muchos científicos sospechan que podría tener algo que ver con la presencia de las vitaminas A y C, antioxidantes que se creen bloquean a las substancias causantes del cáncer producidas por el proceso metabólico normal del cuerpo.

Evite el brindis en el medio del ciclo. Un estudio del Instituto Nacional del Cáncer encontró que solamente dos bebidas mezcladas al día entre los días 12 y 15 del ciclo menstrual de una mujer elevarán los niveles de estrógeno entre el 21 y 31 por ciento.

Cómo contrarrestar la caída

Aunque el buen cuidado de los senos primordialmente significa mantener a sus senos sanos, para algunas mujeres también significa mantener a sus senos tersos y firmes.

Cómo desafiar a la gravedad

Usted se para derecha y echa los hombros hacia atrás, y se caen. Usted se para derecha, echa sus hombros hacia atrás y mete la barriga, y todavía se caen.

Lo que se está cayendo son sus senos. El resultado es: mujer 1, gravedad 2.

¿Pero significa eso que está lista para tener un levantamiento de senos? Sólo usted puede contestar esa pregunta basada en discusiones con su médico. Pero aquí hay algo de información sobre sus opciones.

"Básicamente hay dos tipos de procedimientos de levantamiento que hacemos en este país", dice el doctor Robert L. Cucin, instructor clínico de cirugía plástica en el Colegio de Medicina de la Universidad de Cornell, en la Ciudad de Nueva York.

"Para grados menores de caída, podemos hacer lo que se llama *mastopexy* (mastopexía) de *donut*. Se quita un poco de piel de alrededor de la aréola del pezón, luego se mete esa piel abajo donde le da un grado modesto de levantamiento y ajuste."

Cuando la caída es más severa, los cirujanos estadounidenses tienden a usar la *mastopexy* (mastopexía) con forma de T invertida o de ancla, dice el doctor Cucin. El cirujano corta alrededor del pezón, en forma recta hacia abajo del pezón hasta la línea del sostén, luego a lo largo de la línea del sostén en ambas direcciones por varias pulgadas. Se quita la piel en exceso y la grasa, el pezón se vuelve a colocar y la piel restante se tensa apretadamente para sostener el seno. Las cicatrices serán de unas 9 pulgadas (23 cm) de largo, y cuánta sensación quede en su pezón depende de cuánto se le mueve durante el procedimiento.

Hay dos formas en que se pueden caer cuando pasamos nuestra década de los 30 años de edad, dicen los doctores: cuando los senos grandes se caen, los pezones se van de cabeza hacia su cintura; cuando los senos pequeños se caen, los pezones se hunden elegantemente hacia su pecho.

De una manera usted se ve como una vaca que necesita ser ordeñada. De la otra manera usted se ve como un muchacho. Eso tal vez no sea lo que Dios, la naturaleza y *Victoria's Secret* tenían pensado, pero la caída puede ser la realidad de los senos pasando los 30 años de edad.

"En algún momento entre los 30 y los 40 años de edad, el tejido elástico en el seno empieza a degenerarse", explica el doctor Albert M. Kligman, profesor de dermatología en la Escuela de Medicina de la Universidad de Pensilvania, en Filadelfia. Las fibras de los senos, que actúan como ligas elásticas y proporcionan ese rebote flexible cuando usted camina, todavía se estirarán. Pero ya no se repercutan tan bien como antes. El resultado es senos caídos, con algunas estrías como para complementar.

Como si eso fuera poco, los cambios hormonales —tanto durante el embarazo como cuando usted llega a la menopausia— hacen que los senos se caigan todavía más.

Durante el embarazo, las hormonas estrógeno y progesterona, que los ovarios y la placenta secretan, estimulan el desarrollo de los 15 a 20 lóbulos de glándulas secretantes de leche incrustadas en el tejido grasoso de los senos. Estos cambios son permanentes. Y aunque las glándulas pueden estar vacías después de que no necesitan producir más leche, todavía añaden bulto y firmeza al seno.

Una vez que la menopausia llega, sin embargo, la reducción en el estrógeno y la progesterona indica al seno que sus conductos y lóbulos de leche se pueden jubilar. Como resultado, el seno se encoge, añade grasa y empieza a caerse más allá de lo que demanda la gravedad.

Afortunadamente hay formas de prevenir, y algunas veces invertir, tanto la caída como las estrías.

Considere levantar pesas. "No hay forma que yo conozca de fortalecer el tejido grasoso del seno", dice la doctora Carter. "Pero usted sí puede fortalecer los músculos pectorales bajo los tejidos grasosos para obtener el mismo efecto."

Para prevenir o reducir la caída, consígase un par de pesas de 2 libras (900 g) cada una —no más pesadas— y haga trabajar a esos músculos cinco veces a la semana, dice la doctora Carter.

Con una pesa en cada mano, extienda sus brazos hacia los lados y haga 15 círculos pequeños hacia atrás de aproximadamente 1 pie (30 cm) de diámetro. Ensanche los círculos ligeramente y haga otros 15; ensanche de nuevo otra vez y repita. Vaya aumentando lentamente hasta hacer 50 círculos para cada repetición.

Gire sus hombros. Deje las pesas de lado y con sus brazos colgando a los lados, haga girar sus hombros hacia atrás, hacia abajo y hacia adelante en un movimiento circular 15 a 20 veces, dice la doctora Carter. Haga esto cinco días por semana.

Tírese al piso. "Empiece tratando de hacer 10 planchas (lagartijas) y vaya aumentando hasta llegar a las 20", dice la doctora Carter. Esto le puede llevar hasta seis meses, agrega ella. Pero usted tendrá más probabilidad de hacerlas regularmente si agrega una plancha por vez. Simplemente póngase sobre sus manos y rodillas, levante los pies 6 pulgadas (15 cm) del piso, y baje la parte superior de su cuerpo hasta 1 pulgada (2,5 cm) del piso. También haga esto cinco días por semana.

Sosténgase. Usar un sostén es una buena forma de prevenir la caída, dice el doctor Kligman. De hecho, él sugiere que cualquier mujer mayor de 15 años de edad use uno.

Adquiera un estilo que proporcione mucho soporte y permita un rebote mínimo, dice el doctor Kligman. Y úselo todo el día, no solamente cuando está haciendo ejercicio.

Encoja las estrías. Si usted acaba de tener un bebé y las estrías en la parte de arriba y a los lados de sus senos están rojas e inflamadas, puede tratarlas con aplicaciones diarias de *tretinoin* (*Retin-A*), dice el doctor Kligman. Hable con su doctor acerca de obtener una receta para la droga. La *Retin-A* no sólo tensa la piel estirada pero existen algunas pruebas de que también forma una superestructura nueva debajo de la piel para ayudar a afirmarla.

Hable con su médico acerca de *HRT*. La terapia de reposición hormonal o *HRT* (por sus siglas en inglés), puede detener la caída de los senos que ocurre después de la menopausia, al ayudar a evitar que las fibras de los senos sigan degenerándose, dicen los médicos. No podrá atrasar el tiempo para volver a su década de los 20 años, pero evitará que sus senos se caigan aún más.

DESAYUNO

Nos beneficia por dentro y por fuera

Quién le hubiera dicho a Ponce de León que La Fuente de la Juventud no estaba en la Florida, sino en su cocina. ¿Qué no? Claro que sí, a lo menos en parte —si usted desayuna. Aparentemente el desayuno sirve como "despertador" para su metabolismo, y la estimula para que queme más calorías.

En un estudio que condujo el doctor Wayne Callaway, profesor asociado de medicina en la Universidad George Washington, en Washington, D.C., encontró que los que se desayunan tienen índices metabólicos de un 3 a 4 por ciento arriba del promedio, mientras que los que omiten el desayuno tienen índices lentos, un 4 a 5 por ciento abajo del promedio. Eso significa que en el transcurso de un año, los que omiten el desayuno van a "conservar" 10 a 15 libras (4,5 a 7 kg) de grasa en el cuerpo, explica el doctor Callaway.

Desayunar también puede ayudarla a controlar el hambre, y cuando sí sienten hambre, le ayuda a escoger los alimentos correctos bajos en grasa. Un estudio de la Universidad Vanderbilt, en Nashville, dirigido por David Schlundt, Ph.D., sicólogo clínico y profesor asistente de sicología, encontró que los que se desayunaban escogieron menos alimentos altos en grasa y alimentos más saludables altos en carbohidratos, además de que combatieron con más éxito su antojo al final del día de bocadillos poco saludables, en comparación con los que no se desayunaban.

Los cambios en la composición química del cerebro a través del día hacen más probable que tengamos antojo de grasas al hacerse más tarde en el día, explica el doctor Callaway. La mayoría de nosotros nos despertamos deseando carbohidratos más que grasas. "Es como si estuviéramos biológicamente programados para tomar un desayuno saludable", dice él.

Un desayuno saludable, alto en carbohidratos y bajo en grasa va a tratar algo más que su lucha contra la gordura. También puede tratar otro asunto relacionado con el peso: la enfermedad circulatoria —la epidemia nacional de arterias obstruidas que lleva a millones de personas a ataques al corazón y derrames cerebrales, los cuales matan o las dejan incapacitadas.

Los coágulos de sangre son una causa de la enfermedad circulatoria; estos son tapones pegajosos que bloquean las arterias. Los coágulos están formados de plaquetas, las diminutas partes de la sangre en forma de discos que son responsables de la coagulación normal (como cuando usted se corta) pero pueden ponerse más bien como ColaLoca que como cinta *Scotch*.

Los investigadores en la Universidad Memorial de Newfoundland, en St. John observaron los efectos del desayuno en las plaquetas. Ellos encontraron que los niveles en la mañana del factor que hace pegajosas a las plaquetas eran mucho más altos en las personas que no se desayunaban. Los científicos ya saben que la mayoría de los ataques al corazón y derrames cerebrales ocurren en la mañana. ¿Significa esto que si usted salta el desayuno puede hacer que su corazón se salte algo más que un latido?

"Es definitivamente prudente e importante desayunarse todas las mañanas", dice el doctor George Fodor quien guió el estudio, un profesor de epidemiología clínica en la Universidad Memorial.

El desayuno también podría ayudar a su corazón a reducir el colesterol. Los investigadores en la Universidad de St. Joseph, en Filadelfia estudiaron los hábitos de desayuno de 12.000 personas y encontraron que aquellas que comían cereal —cualquier cereal— en el desayuno tenían los niveles más bajos de colesterol. Adivine quién tenía los más altos. Aquellos que no desayunaban.

"Nosotros sabemos que una de las peores cosas que usted puede hacer para un consumo apropiado de nutrientes es omitir el desayuno. Pero ahora tenemos nueva evidencia que las personas que desayunan incluyendo cereal tienen un colesterol más bajo", dice John Stanton, Ph.D., el autor del estudio y director del Instituto de Investigación de Alimento, Nutrición y Salud, en St. Joseph.

El desayuno también puede protegerla a usted contra el desarrollo cálculos biliares, dice el doctor James E. Everhart, un investigador con la División de Enfermedades Digestivas y Nutrición en el Instituto Nacional de Diabetes y Enfermedades Digestivas y del Riñón. Las personas que no se desayunan en esencia están haciendo un ayuno a corto plazo, y se ha comprobado que los ayunos aumentan el riesgo de la enfermedad de la vesícula biliar.

Acostúmbrese a desayunar

Muy bien, usted ya está convencida: desayunar puede tonificar su cuerpo, por dentro y por fuera. A lo mejor usted simplemente no se puede acostumbrar a la idea de una comida abundante tan temprano en el día. O, a lo mejor, a usted le gusta el desayuno... la versión de huevos y tocino que convierten a sus arterias en un depósito de chatarra de colesterol. Bueno, aquí tiene algunas formas fáciles y saludables para decirse buenos días.

Simplemente hágalo. Usted puede acostumbrar a su cuerpo a tomar un desayuno saludable aunque no lo hubiera comido nunca antes en su vida, dice John Foreyt, Ph.D., director de la Clínica de Investigación de Nutrición del

CÓMO ESCOGER EL CEREAL CORRECTO

No es tan difícil escoger el cereal más nutritivo. Usted quiere un cereal con bastantes vitaminas, minerales y fibra, pero sin tanta grasa, calorías, azúcar o sodio. Busque las selecciones para adultos en el estante superior de la mayoría de los pasillos de cereales en los supermercados y estudie las opciones saludables abajo. Los niveles de nutrientes son para porciones sencillas. Vea al lado de la caja cuánto cereal constituye una porción.

Cereales	Fibra (g.)	Calorías	Grasa (g.)	Azúcar (g.)	Sodio (mg.)
All-Bran (original)	10	80	1	5	280
Cheerios (original)	3	110	2	1	280
Common Sense Oat Bran	4	110	1	6	270
Cracklin' Oat Bran	6	230	8	18	180
Fiber One	14	60	1	0	140
Frosted Mini-Wheats	6	190	1	12	0
Grape-Nuts	5	200	0	7	350
Healthy Valley Organic Amaranth Flakes	4	100	0	8	10

Colegio de Medicina Baylor, en Houston. "Desayune, almuerce y cene por una semana aunque no tenga apetito", dice él. Dentro de una semana o algo así usted empezará a sentir como si fuera un hábito antiguo.

Olvídese de los bocadillos por las noches. Comer bocadillos (meriendas o *snacks*) por la noche la hará sentirse con menos hambre en la mañana, dice Robert Klesges, Ph.D., profesor de sicología y medicina preventiva en la Universidad Estatal de Memphis. Y eso, dice él, empieza un círculo vicioso: usted no tiene apetito para desayunar, lo cual la hace tener más hambre por la noche, lo cual a su vez la hace comer más bocadillos por las noches.

Haga del cereal un hábito. No importa lo que usted coma en el desayuno, haga que el cereal sea parte de esa comida, dice el doctor Stanton. Escoja una marca que sea baja en grasa y alta en fibra y agregue algo de fruta rebanada para sabor y nutriente adicionales.

Cereales	Fibra (g.)	Calorías	Grasa (g.)	Azúcar (g.)	Sodio (mg.)
Kellogg's Complete Bran Flakes	5	100	0,5	6	230
Kellogg's Corn Flakes	1	110	0	2	330
Kenmei Rice Bran	1	110	1	4	250
Multi Bran Chex	7	220	2	11	320
Nabisco 100% Bran	8	80	0,5	7	120
Nut & Honey Crunch	0	120	2	10	200
Oat Bran O's	3	110	0	7	10
Product 19	1	110	0	3	330
Quaker Oat Bran High Oat Fiber	6	150	3	1	0
Raisin Nut Bran	5	210	4,5	15	260
Rice Chex	0	120	0	2	230
Rice Krispies	1	110	0	3	360
Special K	1	110	0	3	250
Total (original)	3	100	0,5	5	200
100% Whole Grain Wheat Chex	5	190	1	5	390
Wheaties	3	110	1	4	210

Coma queques en el desayuno. Es decir, coma panqueques (*pancakes*). "Los panqueques tienen un alto contenido de carbohidratos que estimulan la energía y son bajos en grasa si usted los prepara sin mucho aceite", dice el doctor Schlundt.

Usted puede hacer suficientes para una semana y congelar una capa singular en una bandeja recubierta con papel de aluminio. Luego apílelos y envuélvalos apretadamente con papel encerado o de plástico. En una de esas mañanas apresuradas durante la semana, simplemente meta dos en un horno tostador; eso es todo lo que se necesita para un gran desayuno.

Empiece con un licuado en la mañana. Los licuados (batidos, *smoothies*) son bebidas deliciosas y supernutritivas para el desayuno que se preparan en minutos. Tome un pedazo ya cortado de alguna fruta, una taza de yogur sin grasa (cualquier sabor), un cuarto de taza de jugo de naranja y unos cuantos cubos de hielo. Eche todo eso en una licuadora, bátalo y viértalo en un vaso —o en su taza de café para el carro.

Guarde la carne para más tarde. "Nadie necesita comer carne en el desayuno", dice el doctor Schlundt. "Coma pan, cereal, jugo o fruta, más leche descremada o yogur bajo en grasa", sugiere él. "Con estos alimentos, es realmente fácil sentirse satisfecho en la mañana, y sus carbohidratos son una gran fuente de energía."

ENTRENAMIENTO
DE RESISTENCIA

Sea más joven a la fuerza

Usted ha visto a su abuela luchar para hacer las tareas más sencillas. Simplemente levantarse de la silla, requiere de toda la energía que puede reunir. Y caminar por el pasillo le toma una eternidad. Está logrando hacer todo por sí sola, pero sólo apenas.

Usted se jura que nunca llegará a estar así.

Por eso, usted hace muchos ejercicios aeróbicos, come bien y trata de dormir lo suficiente. Hace directamente lo que dice la receta de la publicidad de *Geritol*.

Pero, ¿no se está olvidando de algo?

Se llama entrenamiento de resistencia, conocido de otra manera como levantar pesas. Y puede ayudarle a mantener, sino a mejorar, su calidad de vida.

El entrenamiento de resistencia mejora la fuerza muscular y el aguante, cualidades que la capacitarán para hacer las actividades que le gustan bien hasta una edad bien avanzada. También puede mejorar su nivel de colesterol, aumentar la fuerza de sus huesos, mantener o perder peso y mejorar la imagen de su cuerpo y su autoestima.

"Si las personas perseveran con esto, siguen siendo activas y hacen actividades que ponen presión en los músculos, pueden combatir algunos de los efectos de la vejez", dice Alan Mikesky, Ph.D., un fisiólogo de ejercicios y profesor en la Escuela de Educación Física de la Universidad de Indiana, en Indianápolis. "Las personas pueden continuar haciendo las cosas que disfrutan en la vida por más tiempo. Y no sólo eso, sino también pueden mantener su índice de rendimiento en lo que están haciendo", dice el doctor Mikesky.

Apodérese de las pesas

Uno de los beneficios más importantes —y más obvios— del entrenamiento de resistencia es su efecto en la fuerza de los músculos. Mantener y aumentar la fuerza muscular es crucial para mantener nuestra independencia al envejecer, dice Miriam E. Nelson, Ph.D., una científica de investigación y fisióloga de ejercicio en el Centro de Investigación de la Nutrición Humana Sobre la Vejez del Departamento de Agricultura de los Estados Unidos en la Universidad de Tufts, en Boston. La fuerza muscular adecuada es lo que la hace capaz de hacer cosas como llevar su propio equipaje, subir escaleras y entrar y salir de la cama.

El entrenamiento de resistencia aumenta la fuerza muscular al poner más presión en un músculo de lo que éste está acostumbrado. Esta carga aumentada estimula el crecimiento de proteínas pequeñas dentro de las células de cada músculo que desempeñan un papel central en la capacidad de generar fuerza. "Cuando usted levanta pesas, pone presión o desafía a las células musculares, y éstas se adaptan al producir más proteínas generadoras de fuerza", dice el doctor Mikesky.

El entrenamiento de pesas también ayuda a mejorar el aguante de los músculos, dice el doctor Mikesky. Así que además de darle a usted la fuerza para levantar una maleta, le da el aguante necesario para cargar esa maleta por más tiempo.

No se necesita mucho tiempo para mejorar su fuerza muscular, dice el doctor Mikesky. "Usted puede aumentar la fuerza muy rápidamente, en tan poco como dos a tres semanas", dice él. Los aumentos notables en el tamaño de los músculos toman más tiempo, aproximadamente de seis a ocho semanas. Algunos estudios han mostrado aumentos de fuerza del 100 por ciento o más en 12 semanas, dice él. La mala noticia es que usted puede perder los aumentos de fuerza igual de rápido. "Si se pierde una semana de sesiones de ejercicio y regresa y pone las mismas pesas, le va a costar más trabajo levantarlas", explica el doctor Mikesky.

Hay varios distintos métodos para el entrenamiento de resistencia incluyendo pesas libres, máquinas con pesas, calistenia y entubado (*tubing*) de resistencia. Las pesas libres incluyen el uso de pesas de mano (mancuernas, *dumbells*) y barras con discos de pesas apilados; el que levanta es responsable tanto de levantar el peso como de determinar y controlar la posición del cuerpo a través de todo el ámbito del movimiento. Las máquinas de pesas, por otro lado, le permiten a usted levantar placas, pero la máquina impone el movimiento que usted efectúa. La calistenia, como en el caso de alzar el cuerpo con las manos hasta la barbilla, las planchas (lagartijas) y los abdominales, utiliza el peso de su propio cuerpo como la fuerza de resistencia. El entubado de resistencia involucra el uso de una banda elástica que proporciona resistencia a los músculos activos. En un estudio en la Universidad de Indiana-Universidad de Purdue, en Indianápolis, 62 adultos mayores fueron puestos en un programa de entrenamiento de 12 semanas con entubado elástico. Los participantes mostraron un aumento de fuerza en un promedio de 82 por ciento, según se midió por el aumento del nivel de resistencia en el entubado.

"La diferencia entre las pesas libres y las máquinas es que las máquinas son más fáciles de usar", dice Mark Taranta, un terapeuta físico y director de *The Physical Therapy Practice* (La práctica de terapia física), en Filadelfia. Entrenar con máquinas no requiere mucha habilidad o coordinación. "Con pesas libres, se requiere más equilibrio y se necesitan también más técnicas de aprendizaje", dice él.

Hay diferentes teorías sobre cuál es el mejor tipo de programa de entrenamiento de resistencia para seguir. Mucho depende de sus metas individuales. En general, levantar una pesa pesada en tres series de 8 a 12 repeticiones es la mejor forma de desarrollar fuerza. Y levantar una pesa más liviana para hacer más repeticiones ayuda a desarrollar el aguante y el tono.

Puede llegarle al corazón

El entrenamiento con pesas también puede mejorar su salud cardiovascular, dicen los expertos. Los estudios sobre el efecto de entrenar con pesas en los perfiles del colesterol son discutibles, dice el doctor Mikesky, pero algunos estudios sugieren una mejoría en los niveles de colesterol similar a la del entrenamiento de resistencia, dice él.

En un estudio, seis hombres y ocho mujeres usaron entrenamiento de resistencia tres días a la semana por 45 a 60 minutos cada sesión. Como resultado mostraron cambios significantes en sus niveles de colesterol. Para las mujeres, la relación del colesterol total al bueno, o colesterol tipo lipoproteína de alta densidad (o *HDL*, por sus siglas en inglés) cayó en un 14,3 por ciento. Esta medida es el mejor pronosticador de enfermedad del corazón debido a que ayuda a estimar cuánto colesterol malo tipo lipoproteína de baja densidad (o *LDL*, por sus siglas en inglés) tiene usted.

En los hombres, la relación de colesterol total a HDL se redujo en un 21,6 por ciento. Idealmente, usted quiere que su relación de colesterol total a HDL sea baja; una relación de menos de 3,5 es lo deseable. Una relación entre 3,5 y 6,9 indica riesgo moderado y arriba de 7,0 indica riesgo alto.

En otro estudio a 88 mujeres saludables, de ascendencia europea y premenopáusicas, 46 de ellas fueron puestas en un programa de entrenamiento de resistencia que incluía ejercicios de levantar pesas para los grupos de músculos más importantes en los brazos, las piernas, el tronco y la parte baja de la espalda, y las mujeres restantes formaron un grupo de control. El grupo de entrenamiento de resistencia levantó un 70 por ciento de su peso máximo en tres series de ocho repeticiones tres días por semana. Cinco meses de entrenamiento de resistencia llevó a reducciones significantes en el colesterol total y en el colesterol LDL. No se observó ningún efecto significativo en el HDL o los triglicéridos.

Existe algún indicio de que el entrenamiento con pesas en gran cantidad —el que involucra levantar pesas más livianas para hacer más repeticiones—

puede tener un mayor efecto en los niveles de colesterol que el entrenamiento con pesas que involucra levantar pesas más pesadas para hacer menos repeticiones, según Janet Walberg-Rankin, Ph.D., profesora asociada en el Programa de la Ciencia del Ejercicio en la División de Salud y Educación Física en el Instituto Politécnico de Virginia y Universidad Estatal, en Blacksburg.

Mientras que los investigadores no entienden completamente cómo el levantar pesas disminuye el colesterol, un instrumento podría ser su efecto en la composición y peso del cuerpo, dice la doctora Walberg-Rankin. El entrenamiento con pesas algunas veces lleva a la pérdida de peso y a la reducción de grasa en el cuerpo, lo cual puede causar que el colesterol disminuya, dice ella.

Peso para los huesos

El entrenamiento de resistencia con seguridad puede tener un efecto en la composición de su cuerpo. Los músculos queman más calorías que grasa, así que al aumentar la masa muscular, usted aumenta su ritmo metabólico y puede quemar las calorías y reducir el tejido grasoso.

Un estudio de mujeres cuyo consumo de calorías se restringió modestamente encontró que cuando las mujeres usan entrenamiento con pesas además de hacer dieta, hubo un aumento en la masa cenceña del cuerpo aunque estaban perdiendo peso.

El entrenamiento de resistencia pone presión en los huesos así como en los músculos y de esa manera ayuda a aumentar la masa mineral de los huesos y a prevenir la osteoporosis, dicen los expertos. Mientras que el ejercicio aeróbico de cargar el propio peso, como caminar y correr, ayuda a mantener la fuerza de los huesos en las piernas y caderas, es menos efectivo para la columna vertebral y la parte superior del cuerpo. El entrenamiento de resistencia ayuda a mantener la fuerza de los huesos en esas áreas, dice la doctora Walberg-Rankin.

Un estudio a 40 mujeres entre los 17 y los 38 años de edad quienes todavía menstruaban realizado en la Universidad de Arizona, en Tucson, encontró que levantar pesas proporcionó un mayor estímulo para aumentar la densidad de los huesos que los ejercicios de aguante. Las mujeres que levantaron pesas tenían una mayor densidad de hueso en sus muñecas, columna vertebral y caderas.

Véase mejor

El entrenamiento de resistencia es una buena manera de sentirse mejor con respecto a la forma en que se ve. Un estudio a 60 mujeres sedentarias entre los 35 y los 59 años de edad llevado a cabo en la Universidad Brigham Young, en Provo, Utah, encontró que las mujeres que entrenaron para resistencia mejoraron las imágenes que tenían de su cuerpo 2,4 veces más que las mujeres que participaron en un programa de caminar. Los investigadores encontraron que la imagen del cuerpo mejoró más en las mujeres que entrenaron fuerte y consistentemente.

Una razón por la cual el entrenamiento con pesas puede ser tan efectivo en estimular la autoestima es que la reacción es inmediata. Además de poder ver el crecimiento de los músculos y el mejor tono muscular, es fácil detectar el progreso. "Uno sabrá dentro de dos semanas cuándo podrá levantar más peso en una máquina", dice la doctora Walberg-Rankin. Eso es un poco más fácil de detectar que una mejoría en su buena forma aeróbica, dice ella.

Cómo comenzar a entrenarse con pesas

¿Por qué esperar si ya podría estar levantando pesas? Aquí hay algunos consejos para empezar.

Examínela. Nos referimos a su salud. Si usted va a empezar un programa de entrenamiento de resistencia, debería ver a su doctor primero para un examen general, dice la doctora Walberg-Rankin. Su doctor le hará un examen físico y obtendrá una historia de su salud. Si usted tiene una historia de osteoporosis, enfermedad del corazón o presión arterial alta, esté segura de mencionárselo.

Obtenga instrucción. Si usted va a comenzar un entrenamiento de resistencia, debe recibir instrucciones de una persona experimentada, dice la doctora Walberg-Rankin. Si usted pertenece a un club de gimnasia, haga que un instructor calificado la ayude. Vea si el instructor tiene una certificación del Colegio de medicina deportiva de los Estados Unidos o de la Asociación Nacional de Fuerza y Acondicionamiento. Su instructor puede ayudarle a decidir cuál es el mejor método de entrenamiento de resistencia para usted y empezarla en un programa. Si está haciendo un programa en la casa con una máquina de gimnasia o pesas de mano (mancuernas, *dumbells*), consulte un video para aprender las técnicas apropiadas de levantar pesas, dice ella. Si está interesada en usar entubado (*tubing*) de resistencia, consulte con un terapeuta físico o con un fisiólogo de ejercicio.

Asegúrese de respirar. Mientras está levantando pesas, no aguante la respiración, dice la doctora Walberg-Rankin. Respire hacia afuera o hacia adentro mientras que las levanta, dice ella. Realmente no importa cuándo respira hacia adentro o hacia afuera, dice ella; sólo asegúrese de hacerlo durante todo el ejercicio. Si aguanta la respiración puede hacer que su presión arterial suba como un cohete lo cual puede ser muy peligroso.

Empiece livianito. "Empiece con poco peso y progrese lentamente", dice el doctor Mikesky. Eso significa empezar con un peso que usted pueda levantar entre 10 a 15 veces y entonces progrese despacio durante las próximas semanas para levantar pesas más pesadas.

Sea persistente. Si usted es persistente y consistente acerca de levantar pesas, su fuerza debería aumentar gradualmente en un número de meses. Usted puede llegar a un punto, donde se quede, dice Taranta, pero es importante seguir levantando pesas aun a ese nivel donde se quedó para mantener la fuerza.

Levante como a usted le gusta. Hay muchos distintos ejercicios para cada grupo de músculos. "Si a usted no le gusta algún ejercicio, no lo siga haciendo. Encuentre uno que le agrade", dice el doctor Mikesky.

Baje lentamente. Concéntrese en bajar las pesas despacio. Esa mitad del movimiento, llamada contracción negativa o excéntrica, en realidad estimula el crecimiento de los músculos, dice la doctora Nelson. Un método es tomar más tiempo al bajar la pesa que al levantarla. Pruebe levantar la pesa a la cuenta de tres y bajarla a la cuenta de cuatro.

Empiece. Nunca es demasiado tarde para empezar con el entrenamiento de pesas, dice el doctor Mikesky. El músculo puede adaptarse y aumentar en fuerza hasta bien avanzada en sus años de vejez, dice él. La investigación en la Universidad de Tufts ha mostrado aumentos de fuerza entre el 100 y 200 por ciento en individuos bien avanzados en su década de los noventa años de edad.

EXÁMENES
MÉDICOS GENERALES

Una visita que bien vale la pena

Nadie se siente muy entusiasmada con la idea de tener que acostarse medio desnuda en una mesa fría para que casi un desconocido le examine su cuerpo. Sin embargo lo hacemos, porque sabemos que los exámenes médicos generales son buenos para nosotras.

De hecho, cada año las mujeres que viven en los Estados Unidos hacen aproximadamente 130 millones más de visitas al consultorio del doctor que los hombres. Y nosotras también vivimos en promedio siete años más que los hombres. Algunos expertos dicen que estas dos estadísticas de ninguna manera están desconectadas. Al recibir un examen médico general regularmente, usted y su médico pueden observar los problemas que empiezan a desarrollarse y tal vez detenerlos. Igual de importante, reunirse con su médico puede darles a ambos la oportunidad de discutir ciertos factores de estilo de vida que pueden ser la diferencia entre una vida larga y vigorosa y una vida corta plagada de problemas que usted no debería de tener antes de los 85 años de edad.

Cómo escoger al doctor adecuado

Tener un examen médico general parece ser algo muy sencillo, sin embargo puede transformarse rápidamente en la búsqueda del Santo Grial cuando usted empieza a buscar un doctor. ¿Quién está capacitado? ¿Qué debería usted, como consumidora inteligente, buscar?

"Básicamente, cualquiera que se presenta por su entrenamiento y práctica como un médico de cuidado primario del paciente debe estar capacitado completamente para hacerse cargo de un examen médico general a adultos

¿Qué tan a menudo debería ir usted?

El examen físico anual. Cuando la mayoría de la gente piensa en un examen médico general, tienden a imaginarse en un aluvión anual de metidas, aguijonazos y pinchazos de agujas que se aplican en forma sistemática sean o no necesarios. Eso tiene mucho que ver con la tradición.

Por el año 1922, la Asociación Médica de los Estados Unidos (o *AMA*, por sus siglas en inglés), patrocinó por primera vez el examen anual de las personas saludables, y por muchos años después fue una práctica estándar. "Fue solo en 1983 que la AMA retiró su apoyo a este concepto", dice Douglas Kamerow, director del Equipo de Servicios Preventivos Clínicos para la Oficina de Prevención de Enfermedades y Fomento de la Salud en el Servicio de Salubridad Pública de los Estados Unidos.

Actualmente, la opinión médica ortodoxa es que un programa de servicios preventivos adaptado a nuestras necesidades personales puede ser efectivo. En términos laicos, esto significa que menos exámenes médicos generales serán tan útiles como el examen físico anual consagrado por la tradición.

Si usted no tiene padecimientos serios que requieran observación, la mayoría de los expertos aconsejan que se ponga en contacto con su médico de cuidado primario cada tres a cinco años desde los 30 a los 39 años de edad, cada dos años de los 40 a los 49 años de edad y, anualmente pasados los 50 años de edad.

Pero, agrega el doctor Kamerow, una prueba de Papanicolau (*Pap smear*) todavía se recomienda anualmente sin tomar en cuenta su edad si usted ha mostrado alguna señal potencial de problemas en la cérvix o si usted tiene compañeros múltiples en sus relaciones sexuales.

normales y saludables", dice el doctor Douglas Kamerow, director del Equipo de Servicios Preventivos Clínicos para la Oficina de Prevención de Enfermedades y Fomento de la Salud en el Servicio de Salubridad Pública de los Estados Unidos. "Pero, en mi opinión, realmente hay sólo dos grupos capacitados por su entrenamiento para hacerlo: los internistas generales y los médicos familiares."

Algunos expertos en la salud de las mujeres, sin embargo, harían la lista aún más corta y añadirían unas cuantas condiciones. "Mi opción número uno sería un internista general", dice la doctora Lila Wallis, profesora clínica del Colegio Médico de la Universidad de Cornell, ex presidenta de la Asociación Médica de Mujeres de los Estados Unidos y fundadora del Consejo Nacional de Salud de las Mujeres, en la Ciudad de Nueva York. "Y no sólo cualquier internista general, sino uno que haya tenido entrenamiento especial en ginecología de consultorio y en las necesidades sicológicas de las pacientes femeninas."

Según la doctora Wallis, un médico familiar podría llenar los requisitos si no hay un internista disponible. "La única razón por la cual él o ella no sería mi primera opción es que el médico familiar tiene que aprender tanto más acerca de los niños que ello podría reducir la cantidad de tiempo necesario para mantenerse al corriente de los desarrollos de la salud femenina."

Y los ginecólogos, a quienes muchas mujeres escogen en primer lugar, de hecho vienen en tercer lugar. "Mientras que los internistas y médicos familiares ya tienen un firme conocimiento del resto del cuerpo, los ginecólogos se especializan específicamente en los órganos sexuales de las mujeres y en el tracto reproductivo", señala la doctora Wallis. "Esto hace que tengan mucho más para aprender que los otros dos para convertirse en un médico de cuidado primario del paciente."

La especialización no es algo que usted quiera pasar por alto, agrega la doctora Wallis. "Muchos internistas tienen áreas de especialización tales como la cardiología o hematología. Pero usted debe tener cuidado de que ellos no estén descuidando los cursos de educación continua en temas de la salud femenina en favor de sus otros intereses."

Cómo prepararse
para su examen médico general

El detective ficticio Sherlock Holmes pudo haber sido capaz de llegar a la verdad basándose en las pistas más insignificantes, pero en la vida real, su médico necesita información más sólida. Usted puede proporcionar esa información mejor si se prepara un poco antes de su visita al médico.

Lleve un diario de alimentos. Cuando se trata de hábitos de salud, la información más turbia tiende a rodear a la dieta. ¿Qué tan a menudo usted realmente presta atención a lo que come durante del día? Tal vez a media mañana usted disfruta una barra de chocolate, luego una bolsa de chicharrones por la tarde y finalmente un sándwich tipo medianoche al ver el noticiero de las once. Todo esto la va afectando a través del tiempo, pero usted se olvida fácilmente de estos pecados veniales de la nutrición en el momento de informar al doctor acerca de sus hábitos de comer. Por consiguiente, lo que en realidad no son hábitos de comer de los más saludables de repente se pueden volver perfectos en el consultorio del doctor.

"Si usted sabe que va a un examen médico general y planea discutir la dieta, no es una mala idea llevar un diario de alimentos durante una semana antes del examen médico general", sugiere el doctor Kamerow. "No cambie sus hábitos de comer, simplemente sígalas con atención. Son las pequeñas cosas que se olvidan tales como los bocadillos (meriendas o _snacks_) los que suman una gran cantidad de grasa dietética, y éstas son las cosas en que usted necesitará concentrarse cuando hable con su doctor."

Trépese al árbol genealógico. Producir una historia familiar de enfermedades completa también va a requerir un poco de atención y, según sea lo que usted descubra, puede afectar el tipo de pruebas que va a necesitar. "Las personas con una historia familiar de ciertos problemas de salud pueden estar en un mayor riesgo de desarrollarlos, y es razonable examinar a estas personas más regular o prematuramente por estas enfermedades", dice el doctor Kamerow.

Aunque muy bien puede haber cientos de enfermedades que pueden transmitirse genéticamente, en realidad, sólo hay unas cuantas de las que usted debe preocuparse.

"El cáncer de mama es una preocupación principal", dice el doctor Kamerow. "El Equipo de Trabajo de Servicios Preventivos de los Estados Unidos no recomienda mamogramas antes de cumplir los 50 años de edad. Pero tal vez se pueda hacer una excepción con las mujeres que están en mayor riesgo debido a la evidencia de que su madre o su hermana lo tuvo, especialmente si el cáncer fue anterior a la menopausia."

La osteoporosis es otra preocupación para las mujeres. "Una historia familiar de osteoporosis podría predisponerme para sugerir un estudio de densidad mineral de los huesos en la menopausia, el cual normalmente yo no usaría rutinariamente", dice la doctora Wallis. Una historia familiar de enfermedad del corazón o cualquier cáncer incluyendo el de los ovarios, del colon, de mama, uterino y pancreático también debería platicarse con su doctor.

Prepare sus expedientes. Usted querrá asegurarse de que su médico tenga los antecedentes de otros médicos a los que usted haya visitado. También querrá informarle a ella acerca de los medicamentos que está tomando y de cualquier problema que usted siente que está experimentando debido a estos. También sería conveniente preparar una lista de todas las dolencias actuales completa con los síntomas y las fechas si es posible.

Cómo sacarle la mayor ventaja

Usted ha escogido al doctor, preparó su información sobre su alimentación, historia familiar y medicamentos, y ahora está aguardando en la sala de espera mientras que escucha música por el altavoz del consultorio. ¿Qué le espera a usted detrás de la sonrisa de la enfermera? O más específicamente, ¿qué debería ocurrir en el cuarto de exámenes para que éste sea un examen médico general perfecto?

"Uno de los componentes más importantes del examen médico general es el examen de los senos", dice la doctora JoAnn E. Manson, una de las investigadoras principales del componente cardiovascular del Estudio a la Salud de Enfermeras, profesora asociada de medicina en la Escuela Médica de Harvard y directora adjunta de salud femenina en el Hospital Brigham y de Mujeres, ambos en Boston. "Después de eso y, por supuesto, un examen pélvico y una prueba de Papanicolau (*Pap smear*), hay una lista completa de opciones que pueden llevarse a cabo, algunas más importantes que otras."

La doctora Manson sugiere enfáticamente que su doctor haga lo siguiente:

• Medir su presión arterial, peso y altura.

• Revisar su lengua y encías por cualquier señal de cáncer bucal o necesidad de cuidado dental.

• Revisar el pulso de la arteria en su cuello y escuchar si hay rumoreos — sonidos anormales que pueden indicar una arteria obstruida.

• Inspeccionar el área del cuello para ver el tamaño de la tiroides y los nódulos por si existe la posibilidad de cáncer.

• Examinar su piel, especialmente en las áreas expuestas al sol, por cualquier señal de cáncer de la piel.

• Escuchar los sonidos del corazón y la congestión pulmonar, las crepitaciones o la respiración jadeante en su pecho.

"En algunas personas, especialmente en aquellas que son jóvenes y saludables, puede ser menos importante revisar el hígado, los riñones, el bazo y los reflejos, y hacer pruebas para ver si hay señales de daños a los nervios", dice la doctora Manson. "La necesidad para muchas de estas pruebas depende de la edad, historia médica previa y factores de riesgo. Así que no todas las mujeres deben esperar que se les hagan todas estas pruebas en cada examen médico general." ¿Qué más podría esperar usted?

"También no es una mala idea que le hagan una revisión total sin ayuno del colesterol en la sangre, y eso es especialmente importante si hay una historia de enfermedad del corazón en la familia", dice el doctor Kamerow.

Las pruebas de Papanicolau (*Pap smear*) también son tema estándar. La mayoría de los expertos recomiendan una prueba de Papanicolau anual. Las pruebas de Papanicolau regulares son especialmente importantes para las mujeres activas sexualmente fuera de las relaciones monógamas, porque muchos médicos piensan que el virus humano de la papiloma —una enfermedad transmitida sexualmente— es un causante principal del cáncer cérvico. Si su actividad sexual no se dirige hacia una sola persona, el doctor Kamerow sugiere que usted también se haga revisiones rutinarias para otras enfermedades transmitidas sexualmente, como la *chlamydia*.

Cuando se trata de las pruebas más exóticas de sangre y de orina, electrocardiogramas y radiografías, el Equipo de Trabajo de Servicios Preventivos de los Estados Unidos no las recomienda rutinariamente para las pacientes saludables.

Después de la menopausia

Cuando llegamos a la menopausia, se puede agregar una prueba más a su examen médico general rutinario. "No hay mejor forma de determinar cómo le irá a los huesos de una mujer más adelante que con un estudio de densidad mineral de los huesos en la menopausia", dice la doctora Wallis. "Si la paciente muestra cualquier factor de riesgo, tal como una historia familiar de osteoporosis, tez pálida, cabello rojo o rubio, origen del norte de Europa, poca exposición al sol, falta de ejercicio o de consumo de calcio, yo definitivamente sugeriría que la recibiera."

Tardándose entre cinco minutos a media hora (según sea la tecnología que se use), un estudio de la densidad mineral de los huesos es un escán indoloro, no invasivo, realizado por máquinas que usan una radiación de baja dosis para medir la masa ósea.

El otro cambio en la rutina del examen médico general ocurre a los 40 años de edad. A esa edad la mayoría de los doctores recomiendan mamogramas regulares para las mujeres. "Algunos también recomendarían una prueba de sangre oculta en la materia fecal y una sigmoidoscopía para revisar si hay cáncer colorrectal", dice el doctor Kamerow.

De las tres pruebas, la prueba de sangre oculta en la materia fecal ofrece la menor incomodidad para la paciente, requiriendo solamente una muestra de la defecación que se trae de la casa para que el médico pueda verificar si hay sangre como un síntoma posible de cáncer colorrectal. Los mamogramas, aunque simplemente son una radiografía baja en dosis de los senos, pueden causar molestias cuando el seno se comprime firmemente entre dos placas. Finalmente, la sigmoidoscopía. No es agradable. Un tubo delgado, hueco y con luz se inserta en el recto y parte inferior del colon para buscar pólipos precancerosos.

Llevarse el consejo del doctor a la casa

Bueno, ya se puede relajar un poco. Las metidas de cosas ajenas y los aguijonazos se han quedado atrás. Ahora es tiempo de enfocar la poderosa luz de la ciencia sobre su estilo de vida. "Fuera de unas cuantas pruebas e inyecciones que usted debería recibir, lo más importante que se puede hacer en un examen médico general es unirse con su doctor y evaluar la situación de sus hábitos de salud", declara el doctor Kamerow. Los cuatro grandes temas de discusión deberían ser el ejercicio, la dieta, las prácticas sexuales y los vicios tales como fumar y beber, dice él. "Los hábitos malos en esas áreas contribuyen tremendamente a las causas principales de enfermedad y muerte en este país, y sin embargo esas son precisamente las cosas que no podemos examinar o arreglar con la medicina."

Si usted fuma, hable con su doctor acerca de las formas para dejarlo. Lo mismo es aplicable a las drogas "recreativas", al uso excesivo de medicamentos tales como los sedantes, las píldoras para dietas, y al abuso de alcohol. Si usted es propensa a las relaciones sexuales arriesgadas, tenga una conversación seria sobre las relaciones sexuales seguras así como también sobre los peligros potenciales involucrados en acostarse con uno y con otro. ¿Dieta? Saque ese diario de alimentos y revíselo en detalle. Y en lo que a ejercicio se refiere, pídale consejos a su doctor para incorporar más actividad física en su vida. No se preocupe por estar tomando mucho tiempo de su doctor. "Lo más importante que sucede en un examen médico general es la orientación y lo que la paciente hace luego debido a esa orientación", dice el doctor Kamerow. "Los doctores están empezando a darse cuenta de que lo más curativo que ellos pueden hacer es proporcionar información y motivación."

FIBRA

Integral para nuestro interior y exterior

Cuando usted era jovencita, posiblemente le caían mal los consejos de Mamá. Por ejemplo, ella siempre la obligaba a ponerse los vestidos más fuera de moda del mundo entero, o no la dejaba maquillarse para las fiestas. Sin embargo, en algunas cosas ella estaba clara. Por ejemplo, si la obligaba a comer cereal de salvado o insistía en que comiera un pedazo de fruta en vez de flan, hacía bien. Hoy en día la ciencia ha confirmado lo que decía Mamá: hay algo especial acerca de las frutas, las verduras y los granos que realmente le hace bien al cuerpo de las mujeres. Los especialistas en nutrición le llaman fibra dietética, y es una de las armas más sencillas y potentes que tenemos en nuestro arsenal de rejuvenecedores.

La fibra es un guerrero de primera línea en la batalla contra la enfermedad del corazón, cáncer de mama y otros cánceres, arteriosclerosis, colesterol alto, presión arterial alta, estreñimiento, problemas digestivos, diabetes e incluso sobrepeso. Consuma suficiente fibra y su cuerpo será más saludable y funcionará como una máquina bien aceitada.

Pero la mayoría de las mujeres no consumen suficiente fibra. El consumo recomendado es de 25 gramos de fibra por día. "Sin embargo, la mayoría de las personas que viven en los Estados Unidos solamente consumen aproximadamente un tercio de ese total", dice Diane Grabowski, R.D., educadora de nutrición en el Centro de Longevidad Pritikin, en Santa Mónica, California.

La cura natural

La fibra es una mezcla compleja de substancias indigeribles que forman el material estructural de las plantas. Tiene muy pocas calorías y proporciona poca energía alimenticia al cuerpo. Cuando la consumimos, pasa a través de nuestro sistema sin descomponerse.

La fibra ejerce su magia al llevarse los elementos malos —como el colesterol, los ácidos biliares y otras toxinas— fuera de nuestro sistema. Y viene en dos formas básicas: soluble, que se disuelve en agua, e insoluble, que no se disuelve. La mayoría de los alimentos de las plantas contienen ambos tipos de fibra, aunque algunos alimentos son más ricos en una que en la otra.

Las fibras insolubles, más gruesas, "literalmente la depuran", dice el doctor David Jenkins, Ph.D., director de la Clínica de Nutrición y Centro de Modificación del Factor de Riesgo, en el Hospital St. Michael de la Universidad de Toronto. "Una vez dentro del cuerpo, éstas absorben agua, haciendo la defecación más suave, con más cuerpo y más fácil de pasar. Esto mantiene al alimento moviéndose a través del tracto intestinal."

También sirven como un remedio natural para tales padecimientos como el estreñimiento, el síndrome de intestino irritable, la diverticulosis y los hemorroides.

Las fibras solubles actúan en forma diferente. Dentro del cuerpo se vuelven gomosas y pegajosas. Al moverse a través del tracto intestinal, recogen ácidos biliares y otras toxinas y entonces las arrastran fuera del cuerpo.

Al rescate

La fibra desempeña un papel vital en la ofensiva contra la enfermedad del corazón y la arteriosclerosis. Los estudios han mostrado que una dieta alta en fibra soluble reduce los niveles del colesterol lipoproteína de baja densidad (o *LDL*, por sus siglas en inglés) en la sangre, conocido como el colesterol malo. Un estudio hecho por el doctor Jenkins encontró que los consumos altos de fibra soluble continuaron bajando el colesterol aun después de que se habían logrado las reducciones dietéticas de grasa y colesterol.

"El colesterol se acumula en nuestra sangre y obstruye las arterias si no se excreta de nuestro tracto digestivo en forma de ácidos biliares", dice el doctor Jenkins. "Cuando la fibra soluble lleva estas substancias fuera del cuerpo, extrae colesterol fuera de nuestro torrente sanguíneo para ser convertido en más bilis, la cual nosotros continuamos sacando fuera del cuerpo, siempre y cuando consumamos fibra soluble regularmente."

Otros estudios han mostrado que la fibra es efectiva en reducir la presión arterial, de esa forma disminuyendo su riesgo a un ataque al corazón o derrame cerebral.

Y eso no es todo lo que la fibra puede hacer. Los médicos creen que la fibra insoluble es la clave para la prevención del cáncer de mama, el cáncer más común entre las mujeres. ¿Cómo? Reduciendo los niveles de estrógeno. Los niveles altos de estrógeno aumentan su riesgo de cáncer de mama.

Una dieta alta en fibra parece que también reduce su riesgo de cáncer del colon y del recto. Logra esto al diluir la concentración de ácidos biliares y otros carcinógenos y al hacer que la defecación se mueva rápidamente a través de los intestinos, disminuyendo el tiempo que las paredes del colon están en contacto con los carcinógenos. Asimismo, la fibra aumenta la acidez del colon, haciéndolo menos hospitalario con las toxinas causantes de cáncer.

La fibra también puede ayudarle a manejar mejor la diabetes al controlar el azúcar en la sangre reduciendo así la necesidad de insulina. La fibra retrasa el vaciamiento del estómago, permitiendo que el azúcar en sus alimentos se absorba más gradualmente.

Una dieta llena de fibra también facilita la pérdida de peso debido a que la hace sentir llena —lo cual significa que va a comer mucho menos de esos alimentos cargados de grasa que la aumentan de peso. Los alimentos fibrosos proporcionan bocados fuertes que deben masticarse completamente, haciendo más lento su tiempo de comida. Y estos también tienden a tener menos calorías en cada bocado.

Estar a salvo por el salvado

Un método infalible de agregar a un montón de fibra en su dieta es comiendo salvado, el recubrimiento áspero de las avenas, el trigo, el arroz y el maíz los cuales contienen la concentración de fibra más alta.

Considere el salvado de avena, el salvado que ha recibido la mayor atención del público en los últimos años. "Lo que distingue al salvado de avena de los otros salvados es que es extremadamente alto en una fibra llamada *beta-glucan*", dice el investigador de salvado doctor Michael H. Davidson, director médico del Centro de Chicago de Investigación Clínica en el Hospital Rush Presbyterian-St. Luke. "La *beta-glucan* parece ser bastante más efectiva en reducir los niveles de colesterol en la sangre que otras fibras solubles."

¿Qué tan efectiva? Sólo 2 onzas (57 g) de salvado de avena por día (un bol mediano) son suficientes para disminuir su colesterol LDL de 10 a 15 por ciento. La trampa está en que usted tiene que comer el salvado de avena diariamente; de lo contrario sus niveles de colesterol subirán otra vez.

El salvado de trigo está atiborrado de fibra insoluble, por lo tanto es el salvado que escogen las personas con problemas digestivos. Éste es probablemente el salvado más común, y se encuentra en la mayoría de los cereales de salvado para el desayuno y en todos los productos de grano integral.

Los salvados de arroz, avena y maíz son altos tanto en fibra soluble como insoluble.

A menos que su médico le indique otra cosa, el mejor plan de salvado para la mayoría de las mujeres es consumir una cantidad pequeña de cada uno. De esta manera usted tendrá una dosis saludable de fibras soluble e insoluble, por no mencionar algo de variedad en su dieta.

Para saciarse de salvado sólo necesita comer en el desayuno un cereal de salvado, un *muffin* de salvado o un pan de grano integral. Pero asegúrese de obtener lo bueno del salvado. "A los productos refinados de grano como el arroz

(continúa en la página 492)

OBTENER LO SUFICIENTE: ES MÁS FÁCIL DE LO QUE USTED CREE

¿Le parece que consumir 25 gramos de fibra al día es imposible? No si usted sabe dónde obtenerla. Aquí hay alguna ayuda.

Alimento	Porción	Fibra (g.)
PANES Y PRODUCTOS DE PAN		
Trigo integral	1 rebanada	2,1
Pan negro de centeno	1 rebanada	1,9
Muffin inglés	1	1,6
Centeno	1 rebanada	1,6
Bagel	1	1,2
Blanco	1 rebanada	0,5
FRUTAS		
Fresas, frescas	1 taza	3,9
Dátiles	5 medianos	3,5
Naranja	1	3,1
Manzana, sin pelar	1	3,0
Salsa de manzana	½ taza	1,9
Piña, enlatada	1 taza	1,9
Plátano (guineo) amarillo	1	1,8
Ciruelas	3 medianas	1,8
Cantaloup, cortado en cubos	1 taza	1,3
Uvas	1 taza	1,1
Jugo de naranja	½ taza	0,1
VERDURAS		
Brussels sprouts, cocidas	½ taza	3,4
Chícharos (guisantes), congelados	½ taza	2,4
Zanahoria, cruda, 7½-pulgada (19 cm)	1	2,3
Brócoli, cocido	½ taza	2,0
Habichuelas verdes (ejotes, *green beans*), congeladas	½ taza	1,8
Champiñones (hongos), cocinados	½ taza	1,7
Tomate	1 mediano	1,6
Remolacha (betarraga), enlatada	½ taza	1,4

Alimento	Porción	Fibra (g.)
Lechuga con repollo, cortada en tiras	1 taza	1,4
Maíz, enlatado	½ taza	1,2
Apio, picado	½ taza	1,0

FRIJOLES (HABICHUELAS) Y LEGUMBRES

Frijoles de caritas, hervidos	½ taza	8,3
Frijoles colorados, enlatados	½ taza	7,9
Garbanzos, enlatados	½ taza	7,0
Frijoles con puerco, enlatados	½ taza	6,9
Lentejas, secas, cocidas	½ taza	5,2
Frijoles pintos, hervidos	½ taza	3,4

CEREALES PARA DESAYUNAR

All-Bran with Extra Fiber	½ taza	15,0
Fiber One	½ taza	14,0
Bran Buds	⅓ taza	11,0
All-Bran (original)	½ taza	10,0
Raisin Bran	1 taza	7,0
Fiberwise	⅔ taza	5,0
Grape-Nuts	½ taza	5,0
Common Sense Oat Bran	¾ taza	4,0
Cheerios (original)	1 taza	3,0
Frosted Bran	⅔ taza	3,0
Nutri-Grain Wheat	⅔ taza	3,0
Spoon Size Shredded Wheat	⅔ taza	3,0
Total (original)	¾ taza	3,0
Wheaties	1 taza	3,0
Puffed Rice	1 taza	1,2
Product 19	1 taza	1,0
Special K	1 taza	1,0
Rice Krispies	1¼ taza	1,0

blanco, el pan blanco y la mayoría de las harinas se les quitó el salvado rico en fibra durante el proceso de molienda", dice Grabowski. "La avena instantánea, por ejemplo, tiene mucha menos fibra que las avenas integrales o el salvado de avena puro."

Cómo agregar fibra a su dieta

Comprometerse a seguir una dieta alta en fibra es relativamente fácil. Aquí hay algunos consejos.

Hágalo lentamente. A pesar de lo buena que es la fibra, mucha cantidad muy rápido puede ocasionar efectos secundarios desagradables incluyendo gas, hinchazón, diarrea y calambres, dice el doctor Jenkins. Comience su primera semana aumentando su consumo en unos cinco gramos al día. Tómese entonces cerca de un mes para llegar al nivel recomendado. De ahí en más, si su médico lo aprueba y usted no siente efectos molestos, puede aumentar su consumo aun más.

Agua que *has* de beber —déjela correr. Todas sabemos que una dieta alta en fibra ayuda al estreñimiento, pero si usted no toma bastante agua, de hecho puede tener el efecto contrario y taparla, dice el doctor Jenkins. Beba de ocho a diez vasos de agua al día para prevenir el estreñimiento.

Varíe sus fuentes. Los doctores no saben con exactitud qué relación de soluble a insoluble usted debería usar cuando escoge sus 25 gramos de fibra diarios, dice el doctor Jenkins, así que probablemente lo más prudente es consumir dosis iguales de ambas. La mejor forma de hacer esto es comer una amplia variedad de alimentos ricos en fibra a lo largo del día.

Póngase verde. Los salvados y los granos no son sus únicas fuentes de fibra. "No se olvide de sus frutas y verduras frescas", aconseja Grabowski. Las legumbres, los frijoles (habichuelas), los chícharos (guisantes), las ensaladas y las frutas pueden agregar a su dieta una gran cantidad de la tan necesaria fibra. Para algo de fibra adicional, escoja las frutas que tienen semillas comestibles, como las fresas y los *kiwis*, sugiere Grabowski.

Espolvoree algo encima. "Es fácil obtener la fibra para su dieta si usted incluye alimentos integrales como son el pan de trigo integral, los frijoles, los chícharos y las frutas y verduras frescas", dice Grabowski. Pero para tener algo de fibra adicional, compre una caja de salvado de avena en su tienda de comestibles y espolvoréelo sobre yogur, helado de crema, fruta, cereal para el desayuno y ensaladas. Úselo en lugar del pan rallado en la comida empanizada o en rellenos o como espesante para sopas, guisos y salsas. O substituya la harina blanca por salvado de avena en los productos horneados.

Lea las etiquetas cuidadosamente. No asuma que los productos con las palabras "*fiber*" (fibra), "*bran*" (salvado), o "*oat*" (avena) en el título necesariamente tienen el contenido de fibra que usted está buscando. Siempre verifique la información nutritiva en la caja o bolsa para ver exactamente cuánta fibra contiene cada porción. "Fíjese si está la palabra '*whole*' (integral) antecediendo a la palabra '*grain*' (grano) en la lista de ingredientes", sugiere Grabowski. "De esa manera usted sabe que no se ha quitado nada y está segura de que obtendrá el beneficio completo del salvado."

Evite las píldoras de fibra. Las píldoras de fibra y las mezclas para beber son una forma rápida de obtener más fibra, pero la mayoría de los profesionales no las recomiendan, dice Grabowski. Son caras y necesita tomar muchas píldoras y bebidas para igualar la fibra contenida en una fruta. Su mejor opción es satisfacer sus requisitos de fibra comiendo alimentos que son naturalmente ricos en ésta.

Integre lo integral. Los cambios mínimos en la manera de comer pueden llenar de fibra a su dieta, dice Grabowski. En lugar de su vaso de jugo de naranja en la mañana, pruebe comer una fruta entera ya que casi toda la fibra de la naranja se pierde en el proceso de hacer el jugo. Sirva arroz integral en lugar de arroz blanco. Y si a usted le gustan la carne y las papas, substituya el puré de papas por una papa asada con la cáscara.

Siga comiendo saludablemente. Usted podría pensar que comer fibra significa que puede comer más grasa ya que la fibra se llevará los materiales malos fuera de su cuerpo. No es así. "Una dieta alta en fibra no neutraliza de manera alguna o compensa otros hábitos de comida poco saludables", dice el doctor Davidson. "Si come una barra de confitura o hamburguesa de más solo le hace más difícil a la fibra hacer su trabajo. La fibra sólo funcionará cuando se usa en combinación con una dieta baja en grasas y en colesterol, y bastante ejercicio."

HUMOR

Bromas aparte
—el humor es saludable

"Si nunca quiere volver a ver a un hombre, dígale: "Te amo. Quiero casarme contigo. Quiero tener niños. Se van tan rápido que rompen la barrera del sonido."
—Rita Rudner

Hay un viejo refrán que dice: el que ríe último ríe mejor. Pero según los estudios, parece también que la mujer que se ríe vive mejor, y además, al reír, se mantiene joven. Esto sucede porque el humor relaja su cuerpo y su mente, alivia el estrés, y aumenta su creatividad.

"Un sentido del humor no es algo que todo lo cura o que acaba con todo para vivir saludablemente", dice Joel Goodman, Ed.D., director del Proyecto Humor, en Saratoga Springs, Nueva York. "Pero es una gran forma de vencer el estrés y la preocupación, además que realmente puede hacerla sentir mejor acerca de la vida. Y la mejor parte de todo es que usted lo puede hacer por usted misma."

Mente feliz, cuerpo feliz

Cuando algo le parece chistoso, usted se ríe. Y cuando usted se ríe, su cuerpo reacciona, dice el doctor siquiatra William F. Fry, profesor clínico asociado emérito en la Escuela de Medicina de la Universidad de Stanford, en Palo Alto, California. Usted flexiona, y luego relaja los 15 músculos faciales más docenas de otros por todo su cuerpo. Su pulso y su respiración aumentan brevemente, oxigenando su sangre. Y su cerebro experimenta una disminución en la percepción del dolor, posiblemente asociada con la producción de las endorfinas que matan el dolor y le ocasionan placer.

Hay pruebas de que la risa puede estimular a su sistema inmune, al aumentar la actividad de los linfocitos y otros "asesinos de células" (anticuerpos) y posiblemente al aumentar los niveles de la inmunoglobulina A conocida como la combatiente de las enfermedades en su torrente sanguíneo, según Kathleen Dillon, Ph.D., una sicóloga y profesora en el Colegio de Nueva Inglaterra del Oeste, en Springfield, Massachusetts. Incluso un estudio mostró que la inmunoglobulina A puede pasar a través de la leche materna a los niños y que las mamás graciosas y los bebés felices sufren menos infecciones respiratorias.

Para cuando ha dejado de reírse, su cuerpo está más relajado, su cerebro más claro y hasta puede darse cuenta de que su dolor de cabeza o cuello tieso ha desaparecido. La investigación muestra que usted podría ser más capaz de resolver problemas, los cuales parecían imposibles unos cuantos malhumorados minutos antes. No está mal para medio minuto de trabajo —si se le puede llamar trabajo al reírse.

Tómeselo a broma

"Mis antepasados judíos deambularon perdidos en el desierto durante 40 años porque aun en los tiempos bíblicos, los hombres no se detenían para pedir direcciones."

—Elayne Boosler

Los efectos del humor a largo plazo son difíciles de medir. El autor ya fallecido Norman Cousins le daba crédito a la risa por haberle ayudado a vencer una enfermedad potencialmente mortal del tejido conectivo. Después de su diagnóstico, Cousins se mudó a un cuarto de hotel, vio videocintas y películas chistosas, leyó libros y revistas chistosos —y se rehabilitó en forma espectacular.

A pesar de la historia del éxito de Cousins, los expertos dicen que el humor por sí solo no cura enfermedades o hace que usted viva más tiempo. Sin embargo, muchos doctores han empezado a incluir el humor en los tratamientos para todos, desde pacientes de cáncer hasta personas que reciben sicoterapia. "Cuando se usa sensatamente, yo creo que sí puede ayudar con la recuperación", dice el doctor Fry. "Aunque no logre otra cosa, hace que el paciente se sienta mejor por períodos cortos de tiempo."

Aun cuando usted esté perfectamente sana, un sentido del humor afinado propiciamente puede elevar su autoestima, y quizás puede hacerla más popular. "El humor puede ayudarla a enfrentarse a circunstancias desagradables o difíciles", dice el doctor Goodman. "Si es capaz de reírse de usted misma o de una situación difícil, probablemente va a poder sobrellevarla mejor y a la larga también sentirse mejor."

Ah, y otra cosa: no se preocupe acerca de que se le hagan líneas por reírse en su rostro. Le van a salir arrugas no importa lo que haga, sea fruncir el entrecejo, entrecerrar los ojos o reír. Y los especialistas como la doctora Karen Burke, Ph.D., una dermatóloga en práctica privada en la Ciudad de Nueva York, dice que las arrugas "positivas" como las líneas por reírse le dan a su cara algo de personalidad —así como las mujeres que fruncen el entrecejo pueden desarrollar arrugas que hacen que se vean perpetuamente tristes.

Cómo afinar su sentido del humor

"Las mujeres deberían tratar de aumentar su talla en lugar de reducirla, porque yo creo que mientras más volumen tengamos, más espacio ocuparemos y más se nos tomará en cuenta. Yo creo que todas las mujeres deberían ser gordas como yo."
—*Roseanne Arnold*

La querida Señorita Enojosa. Usted se acuerda de ella, la maestra de cuarto grado cuya idea de lo gracioso era pasarse media hora después de la clase sacudiendo los borradores. Bueno, el doctor Goodman dice que aun ella podría haber desarrollado un sentido del humor funcional.

"Todos se pueden reír, aunque usted piense que eso es difícil de creer", dice el doctor Goodman. "El 'chiste' es trabajar sobre su sentido del humor, afinarlo propiciamente, para que usted pueda usarlo para su propio beneficio."

Así que, ¿cómo puede usted hacer su vida un poco más divertida? Los expertos ofrecen estos consejos.

Enfóquese en las cosas graciosas. Trate de buscar el humor en la vida cotidiana. Podría ayudar, dice el doctor Goodman, si usted hace cuenta que es uno de los presentadores de *Lente Loco* por unos cuantos minutos todos los días. "Actúe como si tuviera con usted una cámara de vídeo", dice él. "Busque personas que están haciendo cosas graciosas, o animales o niños o cualquier cosa que pudiera hacerla reír. Mientras más busque usted el humor, más lo encontrará."

Tome el punto de vista de un niño. ¿Está enterrada bajo una montaña de papeleo? Si a usted le parece alta, piense qué tan elevada le parecería a un niño de siete años. El doctor Goodman dice que usted debería tratar de imaginarse cómo las situaciones más estresantes para un adulto le parecerían a un niño. ¿El jefe gruñón? ¿El vendedor fanfarrón? ¿La fastidiosa tía Lola? Todos ellos son menos amenazadores cuando se les ve desde la perspectiva de un niño.

Tómese su pulso de humor. Cuando se trata de la risa, se necesitan chistes diferentes para personas diferentes. El doctor Fry sugiere que se tome una semana o algo así para medir su propio sentido del humor. ¿Qué tiras cómicas la hacen reír?, ¿cuáles películas?, ¿cuáles amigos o compañeros de trabajo? ¿Se encuentra a sí misma riéndose de las payasadas de su hijo? Una vez que descubra la respuesta a esto, empiece una biblioteca de bromas. Recorte tiras cómicas y péguelas en la puerta de su refrigerador. Alquile o compre películas cómicas o rutinas de comediantes. Filme videocintas en su casa de su perro chiflado o de Roberto, su vecino torpe.

"Es algo sencillo de hacer, dice el doctor Fry. "Sin embargo, muchas mujeres aún no piensan en agregar un poco de risa a sus vidas, y es bastante triste, porque realmente la puede hacer que se sienta mejor."

Cumpla con su cuota de risas. El doctor Goodman sugiere tratar de reírse 15 veces al día, aun cuando usted tenga que buscar el humor. "No hay nada mágico en el número", dice él. "Sencillamente me pareció como un número adecuado. Si usted logra alcanzar su cuota de humor, probablemente se siente bastante bien con respecto a la vida."

Aun cuando no se sienta necesariamente con ganas de reírse, de todas maneras trate de hacerlo de vez en cuando. Los reflejos, la sonrisa y los cambios fisiológicos por los que atraviesa su cuerpo, simplemente pueden hacer que se sienta mejor. Usted hasta puede encontrarse introduciendo humor en las situaciones tensas —una gran herramienta en todas partes desde el salón de juntas hasta la recámara.

Escoja prudentemente. La risa puede ser contagiosa, pero también lo puede ser la peste. Si usted empieza a hacer chistes racistas o acerca de las minorías étnicas, la gente va a empezar a evitarla. "Escoja temas en los que las personas se sientan unidas por el buen humor", dice el doctor Fry. "Y nunca señale a alguien en particular. Eso hará que esa persona se retire —y puede darle el incentivo para desquitarse cuando usted sea más vulnerable", dice él.

Ponga un límite. No todo es gracioso. Y el humor no va a resolver todos los problemas. "Hay ocasiones en que usted debe tomar las cosas en serio", dice el doctor Goodman. "Reírse de todo puede ser una forma de eludir. Sí le ayuda a tener una buena actitud, pero hay ciertos momentos en que necesitamos ser sensatos —como en los funerales o en la corte o en las reuniones importantes de negocios— y necesitamos considerar si el humor va a funcionar en nuestro favor o en nuestra contra.

INMUNIDAD

Una defensa poderosa contra el envejecimiento

En alguna parte de su cuerpo, en este mismo momento, su sistema inmune está bailando un vals mortal con los virus, las bacterias, los hongos y otros intrusos indeseados.

Al igual que un grupo profesional de baile, un sistema inmune saludable parece tener un ritmo y una sincronización perfecta. En su mejor momento, es un combatiente agresivo de la edad que la mantiene sintiéndose y viéndose bien, y rebosante de energía, dice Terry Phillips, Ph.D., director de los laboratorios de inmunogenética e inmunoquímica del Centro Médico de la Universidad George Washington, en Washington, D.C.

"Si el sistema inmune está haciendo su trabajo y usted goza de buena salud, ni siquiera piensa acerca de esto", dice el doctor Phillips. "La mejor manera de conservarlo así es hacer todas las cosas que la van a mantener naturalmente fuerte tales como hacer ejercicio, comer bien y sobrellevar el estrés como mejor pueda."

Pero al envejecer, nuestro sistema inmune, como un bailarín que envejece, pierde algo de su destreza. Este sistema defensivo extremadamente complejo gradualmente se debilita y es menos capaz de abalanzarse sobre los organismos invasores y destruirlos.

"El sistema inmune se envejece ciertamente y es claro que funciona menos óptimamente al envejecer. Nosotros creemos que la pérdida de la función del sistema inmune está relacionada con la aparición de cáncer, enfermedades autoinmunes como la artritis reumatoidea, y la frecuencia y gravedad de las enfermedades infecciosas. A los 27 años de edad, por ejemplo, la pulmonía es una molestia, pero a los 70 puede poner en peligro su vida", dice el doctor Michael Osband, profesor adjunto en la Escuela de Medicina de la Universidad de Boston.

Una mirada al elenco de las estrellas

El sistema inmune en realidad consiste de millones de células que tienen una variedad de papeles especializados. Algunas desempeñan papeles estelares, mientras que a las otras se las estimula a actuar sólo en situaciones específicas. Entre los actores claves están las células B y las células T que son tipos de glóbulos blancos de la sangre. Las células B se alojan en el bazo y los ganglios linfáticos esperando la llegada de los invasores específicos, también conocidos como antígenos. Una vez que una célula B identifica a un invasor, emite anticuerpos en el torrente sanguíneo. Estas proteínas en forma de Y se agarran del antígeno y lo marcan para que varias células lo destruyan.

Las células T maduran en el timo —una glándula pequeña en la garganta— y son unas de las partes del sistema inmune más importantes. Son unas de las pocas células en el cuerpo que pueden distinguir entre las células normales y las enemigas como las células del cáncer, virus, hongos y bacterias, dice John Marchalonis, Ph.D., profesor y presidente del Departamento de Microbiología e Inmunología en el Colegio de Medicina de la Universidad de Arizona, en Tucson. Cómo aprenden las células T a hacer eso es algo complicado. Pero básicamente, en la superficie de cada célula T hay un receptor, una molécula química que reconoce uno de los diez millones de antígenos conocidos. Entonces, cuando una célula T detecta a un antígeno, no solamente busca y trata de destruir a ese intruso, sino que también manda señales a las otras partes del sistema inmune que determinan qué tan agresivamente el cuerpo va a atacar al invasor.

Las células T, por ejemplo, pueden activar macrófagos, células tipo amebas que literalmente se devoran al intruso o indican a las células B para que activen su producción de anticuerpos.

Una disminución lenta

El sistema inmune alcanza su apogeo justamente cuando usted entra a la pubertad. El timo entonces empieza a marchitarse, y su producción y función de células T decaen considerablemente. Aunque usted continúe produciendo células T por el resto de su vida, estas células no identifican a los invasores ni hacen la coreografía del esfuerzo defensivo del sistema inmune tan bien como las producidas cuando el timo estaba en su apogeo, dice el doctor Osband. Por qué el timo se encoge sigue siendo un misterio, pero algunos investigadores sospechan que las hormonas que provocan la pubertad también pueden interrumpir el funcionamiento del timo.

"Por lo general usted no produce muchas células T después de que el timo deja de funcionar. El timo es importante porque es allí donde las células T aprenden a reconocer a los antígenos", dice el doctor Osband. "Es obvio que ese proceso de aprendizaje no se detiene cuando el timo deja de funcionar, pero a partir de allí sus células T se ven obligadas a aprender por sí solas. Es como si

Cómo ganarle a la gripa

Su sistema inmune es resistente, pero cada año usted parece que atrae la atención de la última versión del virus de la gripa. Sin embargo, todo lo que se necesita para proteger a la gente contra la enfermedad es una inyección. De hecho, una vacuna anual contra la gripa es probablemente una de las mejores gangas para su salud que usted podrá conseguir, dice el doctor William H. Adler, jefe de inmunología clínica en el Instituto Nacional sobre el Envejecimiento, en Baltimore.

No se espere a inmunizarse hasta que todos a su alrededor estén estornudando y tosiendo. Eso puede ser demasiado tarde, ya que toma por lo menos dos semanas para que la inyección haga efecto completamente. Si es posible, hágase inyectar a principios de octubre. Cerca de un tercio de las personas que fueron vacunadas de todas maneras contraerán la gripa, aunque, por lo general, en una forma mucho más ligera que si no se hubieran protegido en lo absoluto. Espere pagar entre \$10 y \$15. En los consultorios de algunos médicos ni siquiera necesita usted una cita previa; usted puede nada más entrar y una enfermera le pondrá la vacuna enseguida.

usted tratara de educarse leyendo una enciclopedia en lugar de ir a la universidad."

La genética y los radicales libres —moléculas de oxígeno químicamente inestables que causan estragos a través del cuerpo— también contribuyen al decaimiento del sistema inmune, dice la doctora Marguerite Kay, profesora de microbiología e inmunología en el Colegio de Medicina de la Universidad de Arizona.

Además, algunos invasores como el VIH (virus de inmunodeficiencia humano), el virus que causa el SIDA, atacan directamente al sistema inmune y lo destruyen.

Cómo mantener fuerte a su inmunidad

Mientras que algunas de las disminuciones en la fuerza inmune pueden ser una parte natural de envejecer, los investigadores incluyendo al doctor Phillips dicen que hacer solamente unos cuantos cambios en el estilo de vida usted puede mantener su inmunidad alerta hasta bien avanzada en su vida. "Al final", dice el doctor Phillips, "qué tan bien nuestro sistema inmune cuidará de nosotras depende de qué tan bien cuidamos de nosotras mismas". Aquí hay algunas formas de estimular las defensas naturales de su cuerpo.

Elimine el estrés. Los investigadores han sospechado desde hace mucho tiempo que el estrés reprime al sistema inmune, y la evidencia emergente apoya esa teoría.

Los investigadores en la Universidad Carnegie Mellon, en Pittsburgh, por ejemplo, dieron virus de resfriado (catarro) en forma de gotas nasales a 400 voluntarios. Se les dieron gotas de placebo a 26 sujetos. Los investigadores entonces identificaron los niveles de estrés en ambos grupos y observaron si había nuevas infecciones. Los voluntarios altamente estresados terminaron teniendo el doble de probabilidad de desarrollar resfriados que los voluntarios con estrés bajo. Ninguna de las 26 personas que recibieron el placebo tuvo un resfriado.

Los científicos creen que los esteroides producidos por las glándulas adrenales se liberan durante el estrés y reprimen la actividad de las células del sistema inmune, dice el doctor Phillips.

Cómo reduce usted el estrés es una opción individual, pero para empezar usted podría jugar con sus niños o una mascota, practicar un pasatiempo como la jardinería o carpintería, meditar o practicar yoga, ver una película cómica o un programa de televisión, o simplemente leer un libro agradable.

Váyase a dormir. "Dormir es el taller de reparación para el sistema inmune", dice el doctor Phillips. Durante el sueño, su cerebro y su cuerpo descansan pero su sistema inmune no. Por ello, cuando usted está haciendo una siesta, su sistema inmune tiene menos competencia en cuanto a los nutrientes que se necesitan para reforzar sus mecanismos que combaten las enfermedades. Sin suficiente descanso, su sistema inmune va a sufrir. En un estudio a 23 personas, por ejemplo, los investigadores de la Escuela de Medicina de la Universidad de California en San Diego encontraron una disminución del 30 por ciento en la reacción inmune después que a estas personas les faltaron tres o más horas de sueño en una noche.

Trate de dormir de seis a ocho horas por noche, sugiere el doctor Phillips.

Deshágase del humo. El humo del tabaco contiene formaldehído, un químico que puede paralizar los macrófagos en los pulmones y hacerla a usted más susceptible a los padecimientos respiratorios, incluyendo los resfriados y las gripas, dice el doctor Phillips. Así que si usted fuma, déjelo.

Salga y sude. El ejercicio moderado ayuda a impedir que las bacterias se acumulen en los pulmones y refuerza la vigilancia del sistema inmune al aumentar la circulación de los anticuerpos en la sangre, dice el doctor William H. Adler, jefe de inmunología clínica en el Instituto Nacional sobre el Envejecimiento, en Baltimore.

Después de un estudio de 15 semanas a 18 mujeres en su década de los 30 años de edad, a quienes se les pidió caminar 45 minutos al día, cinco días a la semana, los investigadores en la Universidad Estatal Appalachian, en Boon, Carolina del Norte, encontraron que las caminantes tuvieron la mitad de los resfriados y las gripas que un grupo de mujeres sedentarias.

Para mantener a su sistema inmune en forma óptima, haga ejercicio aeróbico como caminar, trotar, nadar o andar en bicicleta por lo menos 20 minutos al día tan seguido como sea posible.

Vitaminas que aumentan la inmunidad

"El papel de la dieta en la inmunidad es muy directo", dice Jeffrey Blumberg, Ph.D., director asociado en el Centro de Investigación sobre el Envejecimiento del Departamento de Agricultura de los Estados Unidos, en la Universidad de Tufts, en Boston. "Nutrientes específicos desempeñan papeles específicos en empujar la inmunidad para arriba y para abajo."

Aquí hay una guía para algunas vitaminas y minerales que podrían ayudar a mantener su inmunidad en condición óptima.

Vaya "A" la batalla. La vitamina A fortifica la capa superior de la piel contra las grietas a través de las cuales los invasores pueden entrar, y combate los tumores de cáncer, posiblemente al estimular la actividad de los glóbulos blancos de la sangre. Pero ya que demasiada vitamina A puede ser tóxica, probablemente es una buena idea obtener sus requerimientos diarios de los alimentos en lugar de los suplementos con dosis altas, dice el doctor Ranjit Chandra, profesor investigador en la Universidad Memorial de Newfoundland, en St. John y director del Centro de Inmunología Nutritiva de la Organización Mundial de la Salud. La Asignación Dietética Recomendada (o *RDA*, por sus siglas en inglés) es de 800 microgramos de equivalentes de retinol (o 4.000 UI). Un *sweet potato* (camote, boniato) mediano tiene más del doble de su requerimiento diario de vitamina A. Otros alimentos ricos en vitamina A son el hígado, las zanahorias, la espinaca, el brócoli, la lechuga, los albaricoques y la sandía.

Además, batalle con betacaroteno. Un antioxidante, el betacaroteno, el cual se convierte en vitamina A en el cuerpo, también combate los radicales libres y puede reforzar la capacidad del sistema inmune para prevenir el cáncer. Como la vitamina A, el betacaroteno se encuentra en alimentos como las zanahorias, la espinaca, el brócoli y la lechuga. Pero, a diferencia de la vitamina A, el betacaroteno no es tóxico y puede tomarse con poco peligro como suplemento. El doctor Osband sugiere tomar de seis a nueve miligramos por día.

Acuérdese de la B$_6$. "Cuando las personas mayores recibieron dietas deficientes en vitamina B$_6$, su inmunidad se redujo substancialmente", dice el doctor Blumberg. "Cuando su consumo se aumentó de a poco, la inmunidad regresó gradualmente a la normalidad —pero sólo después de que se les proporcionó una dosis de más de 1,6 miligramos (la RDA)."

Usted puede obtener la RDA de 1,6 miligramos de vitamina B$_6$ comiendo dos plátanos (guineos) amarillos grandes. Otras buenas fuentes dietéticas son el pollo, el pescado, el hígado, el arroz, los aguacates (paltas), las nueces, el germen de trigo y las semillas de girasol. La vitamina B$_6$ puede ser tóxica en dosis muy altas (1.000 a 2.000 miligramos por día), dice el doctor Blumberg.

Cargue su sistema con la C. Desde evitar que los virus se multipliquen hasta estimular las células que atacan a los tumores, la vitamina C proporciona un estímulo a casi todas las partes del sistema inmune, dice el doctor Blumberg. Las frutas y verduras como las naranjas, las fresas, el brócoli y los pimientos rojos son buenas fuentes de este nutriente. Aparentemente, las dosis óptimas van de 500 a 1.000 miligramos por día, dice el doctor Blumberg.

Dese sólo un poco de la D. Aunque algunos científicos saben que la vitamina D es un estímulo para la inmunidad, están desconcertados con su papel. Ellos saben que la vitamina D es necesaria para los huesos fuertes, lo cual es significante porque las células del sistema inmune se forman en la médula ósea. Afortunadamente, la mayoría de las personas obtienen la parte que les corresponde de vitamina D. (La RDA para la vitamina D es 5 microgramos o 200 UI al día). Un vaso de 8 onzas (24 ml) de leche fortificada tiene cerca de 100 UI. También es abundante en los quesos y pescados aceitosos como el arenque, atún y salmón. También puede obtener vitamina D de la luz del sol, ya que la radiación ultravioleta produce una substancia productora de vitamina D en la piel. En el verano, aproximadamente 10 a 15 minutos de sol al día le darán toda la vitamina D que usted necesita. La vitamina D es tóxica en cantidades grandes, por eso los médicos dicen que nunca se debe tomar en suplementos.

Estimúlelo con la E. Una verdadera fuente de fuerza, la vitamina E puede fomentar su inmunidad en general. En particular, impide el daño de los radicales libres a las células, mejora la actividad de los glóbulos blancos de la sangre y aumenta la *interleukin-2*, una substancia que fomenta el crecimiento de las células T. También interrumpe el funcionamiento de la prostaglandina E2, una substancia que ocurre naturalmente la cual reprime el sistema inmune.

La vitamina E — también considerada un antioxidante— puede encontrarse en los aceites, las nueces y las semillas, pero es difícil obtener una dosis fomentadora de la salud o estimulante de la inmunidad a través de los alimentos solamente, dice el doctor Blumberg. Generalmente las dietas saludables proporcionan sólo 20 UI diarias. Las dosis óptimas parecen estar entre las 100 y 400 UI por día, dice él.

Recorte la grasa. En estudios a animales, la dieta que derivaba el 40 por ciento de sus calorías de la grasa —la dieta típica de los Estados Unidos— tenía una influencia perjudicial en el sistema inmune, dice el doctor Chandra. Así que trate de reducir su consumo de grasa para que usted sólo derive el 25 por ciento de sus calorías diarias de la grasa.

Para hacerlo, use productos lácteos bajos en grasa o sin grasa, recorte la piel o la grasa visible de las carnes y no coma más de una porción de 3 onzas (85 g) — aproximadamente el tamaño de un mazo de naipes— de aves, pescado o carne roja al día. Asegúrese de consumir diariamente por lo menos seis porciones de productos de grano como los panes, los frijoles (habichuelas) y el arroz, y por lo menos cinco porciones de frutas y verduras como las manzanas, las peras, el brócoli y la espinaca.

Sea una mujer de hierro. El hierro es un catalizador vital que ayuda a su sistema inmune a atrapar a los intrusos y a acorralar a las células renegadas como las del cáncer. La mayoría de las mujeres necesitan cerca de 15 miligramos de hierro al día. Una comida que incluya un bistec magro asado de 3 onzas, una papa asada de tamaño mediano y media taza de chícharos (guisantes) proporciona más de siete miligramos. Otros alimentos ricos en hierro son las almejas y las ostras, el puerco, la carne oscura de pollo, los albaricoques secos y los vegetales verdes frondosos. Pero no dependa de los suplementos de hierro a menos que el médico se los recete. Demasiado hierro puede causar problemas en su salud como estreñimiento, decoloración de la piel, cirrosis del hígado y diabetes.

Mejórelo con magnesio. Algunos estudios sugieren que la deficiencia de magnesio puede hacer que el sistema inmune se comporte como enajenado, ataque las células normales en el cuerpo y provoque enfermedades autoinmunes tales como la artritis reumatoidea, dice el doctor Phillips. Tomar un suplemento de magnesio puede ser una buena idea para las mujeres que toman píldoras de agua (diuréticos) o drogas para la presión arterial alta. Ambas hacen que usted pierda este mineral, al igual que lo hace el beber cantidades excesivas de alcohol. El resto de nosotras puede tomar la RDA de 280 miligramos sin suplementos al comer regularmente vegetales frondosos, papas, granos enteros, leche y mariscos.

Suminístrese suficiente selenio. Este nutriente, un antioxidante conocido como un combatiente del cáncer, puede ser necesario para infundirle entusiasmo al equipo de su sistema inmune que lucha contra las enfermedades. Usted debería obtener suficiente selenio en su dieta normal. La RDA de selenio para las mujeres es de 55 microgramos, y usted obtendrá 138 microgramos sólo en un sandwich de atún. Todos los pescados, los mariscos y los cereales y panes de grano integral son ricos en selenio. Sin embargo las dosis muy altas, pueden perjudicar las respuestas inmunes así que los suplementos no deben exceder los 200 microgramos por día, dice el doctor Chandra.

Zámpese el cinc. "De todos los minerales, el cinc es probablemente el más importante para mantener la inmunidad", dice el doctor Phillips. La escasez puede causar una caída en la producción de los glóbulos blancos de la sangre que rodean y destruyen a los invasores microscópicos. El cinc también ayuda al cuerpo a procesar la vitamina D, otro nutriente importante para estimular la inmunidad. Para obtener de su dieta la RDA de 12 miligramos, coma carne magra roja, ostras, leche, avenas, granos enteros, huevos y aves. Evite los suplementos que proporcionan más de 40 miligramos, advierte el doctor Blumberg. Por encima de esos niveles, el cinc puede en realidad hacer más lento al sistema inmune.

LÍQUIDOS

Sígales la corriente

Allí están. Una cena íntima para dos a la luz de las velas. La voz de Luis Miguel sirve de fondo para esta noche romántica. Él mete la mano en el balde del hielo, saca una garrafa y vierte en su copa de pie largo... agua.

¿Qué es esto? Sólo un líquido incoloro, sin calorías con una fuerza poderosa para rejuvenecer. El agua es una parte nuestra. Presente en todas las células y los tejidos, desempeña un papel vital en casi todos los procesos biológicos incluyendo la digestión, respiración y circulación. Transporta los nutrientes a través del cuerpo, y se lleva las toxinas perjudiciales y los productos de desperdicio fuera de nuestro cuerpo. Regula la temperatura del cuerpo. Y lubrica nuestras articulaciones y órganos.

Debido a que el agua hace tanto, el cuerpo necesita un abastecimiento fresco y constante. "El agua necesita fluir continuamente, dentro, a través y fuera del cuerpo", dice Diane Grabowski, R.D., una educadora de nutrición en el Centro de Longevidad Pritikin, en Santa Mónica, California. "Eliminamos un mínimo de dos a tres cuartos de galón (aproximadamente dos a tres litros) diarios en nuestra orina, sudor y respiración, todo lo cual debe reponerse."

Y eso es solamente para satisfacer nuestras necesidades mínimas de salud. Tomar bastante agua es esencial para una mujer a fin de mantener todo desde la piel juvenil hasta los músculos fuertes. "Al satisfacer consistentemente sus necesidades de líquido diarias logra que todos los órganos en su cuerpo funcionen mejor", dice Grabowski. "Es un ingrediente clave si usted quiere verse, sentirse y desempeñarse en su nivel óptimo."

A secas sin saberlo

A menos que usted sea un camello, su cuerpo sólo puede aguantar cerca de tres días sin agua antes de abandonar la partida. Pero no crea que la deshidratación ocurre sólo cuando está tan seca como un hueso. Técnicamente usted puede estar deshidratada aun cuando sus niveles internos de líquido sólo bajan un poco más de lo normal.

Ordinariamente, esto no es un problema porque su sentido de sed va a gritar, "¡yo necesito algo de agua... AHORA!". Pero a veces sus poderes detectores de sed no pueden seguirle el ritmo a los otros factores, tales como el clima cálido, la gran altitud, el ejercicio, o la edad. Y sí, nuestra sensibilidad a la sed empieza a disminuir al envejecer.

Cuando usted se deshidrata, pierde agua y electrolitos valiosos —minerales esenciales en el agua como el potasio y el sodio. Esto la puede hacer sentirse sumamente vacía. "Cuando empiezan a faltarle los líquidos a nuestro cuerpo, el rendimiento físico y la fuerza cerebral empiezan a irse cuesta abajo", dice Miriam E. Nelson, Ph.D., una científica investigadora y fisióloga de ejercicio en el Laboratorio de Fisiología Humana, en el Centro de Nutrición Humana sobre Envejecimiento, del Departamento de Agricultura de los Estados Unidos, en la Universidad de Tufts, en Boston. "Mucho antes de que usted experimente la sensación de sed, su cuerpo puede presentar síntomas tales como la fatiga, el

Aviso de alerta para la deshidratación

La deshidratación puede aparecer de repente. Usted podría estar con un nivel de líquidos peligrosamente bajo y ni siquiera saberlo. Vigile estas señales de peligro.

Señales tempranas

- Mareo, fatiga
- Debilidad, dolor de cabeza
- Piel enrojecida
- Boca seca
- Pérdida de apetito

Señales avanzadas

- Vista borrosa, pérdida de la audición
- Dificultad para tragar
- Piel seca, caliente
- Pulso rápido, respiración corta
- Andar inestable
- Urinación extremadamente frecuente (especialmente si usted no ha estado tomando líquidos y la orina es turbia y de color amarillo intenso)

mareo, el dolor de cabeza y la piel enrojecida. Todas estas condiciones son causadas por un aumento en la temperatura del cuerpo."

La deshidratación frecuente o a largo plazo puede darle una sensación general de sequedad, causando un latido irregular del corazón, andar inestable, dificultad para tragar y respiración entrecortada. Los casos extremos de deshidratación pueden causar que la piel y los labios se arruguen.

Llene el tanque

La llave del agua no es su única fuente de agua. Los expertos recomiendan que necesitamos consumir de seis a ocho vasos de 8 onzas (24 ml) de líquido al día. Eso quiere decir seis a ocho vasos de agua, jugo, caldo u otras bebidas.

"Las personas con más peso requieren más, así que una buena regla es tratar de beber aproximadamente media onza (1,5 ml) por cada libra (454 g) de peso en el cuerpo", dice Grabowski. Si usted pesa 160 libras (73 kilos), eso quiere decir que debería tomar diez vasos de 8 onzas por día. Usted también necesitará más si está a dieta, si vive en un clima cálido o seco, o está enferma con fiebre, vomitando o con diarrea, todo lo cual puede robarle líquidos a su cuerpo.

El agua está por todos lados, así que es relativamente fácil mantener su consumo adecuado de líquidos. Aquí hay algunos consejos para que empiece.

Amanezca con un vaso. Mientras usted dormía, su pobre cuerpo estuvo por horas sin agua. Así que al despertar sírvase un vaso, dice Grabowski. No dependa de su café de la mañana. Aunque éste estimula, puede deshidratarla ya que es un diurético.

Bébalo poco a poco. No trate de tragar todo su consumo diario de una sola vez. Se va a sentir como que va a reventar y, debido a que su cuerpo no puede soportar esa sobrecarga de líquido, usted excretará más, dice Grabowski. En lugar de eso, tome agua varias veces durante el día —aproximadamente un vaso cada una o dos horas— para que esté constantemente hidratada. Tome más si hace calor o está húmedo o si sus ojos, boca o piel se sienten secos.

Coma regularmente. Gran parte de nuestro consumo diario de líquido proviene de las comidas. Consuma muchos alimentos ricos en agua como las frutas y verduras y siempre tome agua u otra bebida con su comida, dice Grabowski.

Descarte el alcohol y la cafeína. Los tragos, la cerveza, el café, el té y las colas son diuréticos —en otras palabras, estimulan la excreción de líquido. Estas bebidas pueden apagar su sed al principio, pero a la larga extraen líquidos de su cuerpo, dice Grabowski.

Evite los alimentos que la vacían. Los alimentos salados pueden secarla, dice Grabowski. Si tiene que comerlos, limite al mínimo su consumo y asegúrese de tomar bastante líquido.

Vigile esos laxantes. Usar laxantes frecuentemente puede extraer una cantidad enorme de agua de su cuerpo e interrumpir las funciones normales de

su sistema digestivo y de eliminación. Los laxantes no deben tomarse regularmente a menos que se encuentre bajo cuidado médico, dice Grabowski.

Póngale pulpa. Los aparatos hogareños para hacer jugo proporcionan un
excelente medio para obtener sus líquidos diarios, dice Grabowski. Pero algunos
de estos dispositivos separan completamente el jugo de la pulpa de las frutas o
verduras, la parte que contiene la concentración de fibra más alta así como los
nutrientes adicionales y agua. Ponga algo de esa pulpa dentro de su vaso.

Cómo controlar el ejercicio y los líquidos

Una mujer puede sudar dos cuartos de galón (dos litros) por hora cuando
está haciendo ejercicio o practicando algún deporte, especialmente si hay
mucho calor y humedad, dice la doctora Nelson. Por eso es que las mujeres
activas necesitan prestar atención a sus necesidades de líquido. Tenga estos
consejos en mente.

Beba antes, durante y después. Tome 8 a 20 onzas (24 a 60 ml) de agua
una hora antes de empezar a hacer ejercicio, dice la doctora Nelson. "El tamaño
del cuerpo y la temperatura en donde va a hacer ejercicio afectan la cantidad de
agua que usted debería tomar. Mientras más grande sea su cuerpo y más calor
haga, más agua necesitará", dice la doctora Nelson. Sin embargo no se sobrepase
con el agua; esto resultará en un rendimiento pobre, advierte la doctora Nelson.
Los síntomas de tomar demasiada agua incluyen una sensación incomoda de
estómago hinchado y retortijones en el estómago. Mientras que esté haciendo
ejercicio trate de tomar de media taza a tres cuartos de taza de agua cada diez
minutos. Después, beba tanto como necesite para calmar su sed.

Pésese. ¿Cuánto debería tomar después del ejercicio? Si usted se pesa antes
y después del ejercicio, podrá descubrir cuánta agua pierde. Por cada media
libra (227 g) que usted pierda, beba 8 onzas (24 ml), dice la doctora Nelson.

Vaya más allá de la sed. Aunque su sed inmediata se sienta calmada, sus
reservas de líquido en el cuerpo pueden no estar adecuadamente repuestas,
dice la doctora Nelson. Vaya a lo seguro y tome unos cuantos sorbos más. Unos
cuantos minutos más tarde tome otro poco más, y así sucesivamente hasta cerca
de una hora después.

Quédese fría. El agua fría bajará la temperatura de su cuerpo más rápidamente que el agua templada. También se dispersa mucho más rápidamente a
los tejidos resecos del cuerpo, dice la doctora Nelson.

Adáptese a su medio ambiente. Si usted sale de un edificio con aire
acondicionado en un día cálido e inmediatamente trata de trotar cinco millas
(ocho km), el choque a su sistema sacará más agua de su cuerpo que si usted se
acostumbra despacio al calor de afuera, dice la doctora Nelson.

Bloquee el sol. La luz solar directa en un día cálido de verano la secará
como una ciruela pasa, dice la doctora Nelson. Si hace ejercicio en el calor bajo
el sol, use un sombrero y ropa liviana y holgada que respira y deja entrar el aire

fresco. "Si se siente mareada o desorientada, suspenda el ejercicio inmediatamente", advierte la doctora Nelson. Encuentre algo de sombra y líquidos para ayudarle a enfriar la temperatura de su cuerpo.

Empiece con prudencia. Si no ha estado haciendo ejercicio, no trate de empezar con un programa avanzado de ejercicio. Debido a que usted va a hacer un mayor esfuerzo, va a sudar más que alguien que está en mejor forma. Para evitar el riesgo de la deshidratación, comience su programa de ejercicios lentamente, acostúmbrese a hacer ejercicio y gradualmente aumente la intensidad. Esto contribuirá bastante en ayudar a su cuerpo a regular sus líquidos y temperatura, dice la doctora Nelson.

Use las bebidas para deportistas con moderación. Las bebidas para deportistas, las cuales son ricas en los electrolitos que perdemos cuando hacemos ejercicio, a menudo se promocionan por sus capacidades de reabastecimiento, y muchas de ellas realmente son excelentes fuentes de líquido. Pero usted realmente no necesita bebidas para deportistas en cada sesión de ejercicio. "Después de una sesión de ejercicio o si usted necesita un estímulo durante el juego, pueden ser de gran ayuda, pero no son más efectivas que el agua, y es ésta la que su cuerpo realmente está pidiendo", dice la doctora Nelson. La única ocasión en que estas bebidas tienen una ventaja sobre el agua es cuando usted acaba de salir de una sesión de ejercicio extremadamente agotadora, como una maratón o dos horas de tenis bajo el sol quemante. Entonces usted puede necesitar un estímulo inmediato de electrolitos.

MAQUILLAJE

Aproveche su poder para rejuvenecer

¿**R**ecuerda aquellos viejos tiempos en el mostrador de maquillaje de la botica? ¿La vez que usted y sus amigas compraron lápiz de labios de color anaranjado brillante, rímel verde y sombra iridiscente para los ojos en cuatro tonos pastel, por no mencionar el rubor destellante, el esmalte negro para las uñas y las estrellas pequeñas para pegarse en la cara y las orejas?

¡Madre mía! ¿De veras hicimos eso?

Claro que sí. Pero ya no más.

Para verse joven, fresca y llena de vida —en vez de como un letrero de neón muy gastado— use el maquillaje a su favor. Aquí está cómo, empezando por el principio con su base.

Use una base más oscura. Una de las primeras señales de que el tiempo está avanzando son las líneas finas que aparecen en nuestros rostros. Para suavizarlas, pruebe usar una base ligeramente más oscura que la que ha estado usando, dice Marina Valmy, una cosmetóloga en la Christine Valmy Skin Care School, una escuela para el cuidado de la piel en la Ciudad de Nueva York.

"Si su cabello se está volviendo canoso o le gusta usar ropa negra, escoja una base con un tono ligeramente rosado o póngase una pequeña cantidad de rubor rosado sobre las mejillas, la frente, la nariz y el mentón", dice Carole Walderman, una cosmetóloga, esteticista y presidenta de la Von Lee International School of Aesthetics and Makeup, una escuela de maquillaje y belleza, en Baltimore.

La base correcta también equilibrará el tono de su cutis.

Barra con la bacteria. En lugar de usar sus dedos, use un depresor de madera para la lengua o un palito de naranjo, disponibles en su farmacia, para sacar base de la botella, dice Leila Cohoon, una cosmetóloga, esteticista y propietaria de Leila's Skin Care (Cuidado de la piel de Leila), en Independence,

Misuri. Esto evitará que la bacteria entre en su maquillaje y destruya su potencia o cause un sarpullido en su cutis.

"Ponga un poco de la base con un aplicador limpio sobre una esponja para maquillaje que haya sido humedecida con agua limpia", dice Walderman.

Aplique suavemente. "Aplique la base muy gentilmente, sin frotarla", dice Walderman. Frotarla con fuerza puede rasgar los tejidos delicados debajo del cutis. Cerca de sus ojos, use solamente su dedo anular, el cual ejerce menos presión que una esponja, y aplique desde el ángulo exterior del ojo hacia la nariz con pasadas cortas y suaves, dice ella.

Esconda y realce. Destaque sus mejores rasgos, como esos pómulos fantásticos, y oculte los defectos insignificantes, como esas pequeñas bolsas bajo los ojos, con un toque de disimulador (*concealer*) bien untado, dice Walderman. El disimulador se encuentra disponible en una amplia variedad de tonos, y uno ligeramente más claro que su base es el mejor para usted, añade ella.

Para disimular las ojeras, aplique el disimulador solamente sobre la parte oscura con un cepillo pequeño. Si usted cubre el área por completo, a la luz del día puede hacer que los círculos se vean hinchados, dice Walderman.

Si tiene un área problemática grande que ocultar, como por ejemplo una mancha oscura de pigmentación, pruebe con un maquillaje especial, sugiere Cohoon. "Es pigmento puro, no está hecho con aceites pesados o una base de cera, y cubre muy naturalmente", dice ella.

Use polvo sólo si lo necesita. Use un polvo translúcido para dar un terminado "muy suave, sólo para quitar el brillo en las áreas grasosas como la nariz, la frente y el mentón, pero no lo amontone sobre la cara", dice Walderman. "Eso sólo acentuará cualquier línea o arruga."

Y evite los colores de polvo llamados "*pearlized*" (aperlados) o "*frosted*" (iridiscentes). ¿Por qué? Estos contienen partículas de reflexión de luz que actúan como un realzador. Si usted realza las colinas (la superficie de su cutis), los valles (las arrugas o los poros grandes) se ven más profundos, dice Walderman.

Úntesela bien. No debería notarse dónde termina su cara y empieza su cuello, así que asegúrese de que su base no termina en una línea a través de su mandíbula.

Termine con un rocío. Si a usted le gusta tener una apariencia fresca, después de su base y polvo rocíese ligeramente con un tónico o agua destilada, dice Walderman. Éste humedece y fija su maquillaje sin que se vea terroso o pastoso.

Ponga sonrojo a sus mejillas

Usted tal vez no se ruborice tanto como cuando era una niña, pero aún es agradable dar una apariencia cálida a su cutis con un toque de color en las mejillas.

Aplíquelo sutilmente. Tenga como objetivo un sonrojo natural que apenas se note y no aplique el rubor muy cerca de la nariz, lo cual haría aparecer su

Siete trampas que evitar

Algunas de las técnicas de maquillaje que usted ha estado usando por años pueden hacer que se vea más vieja de lo que es. Para conservar su apariencia joven y natural, tenga cuidado con estos hábitos.

Sombras azules escandalosas. La sombra para ojos color turquesa, o cualquier azul brillante, ha seguido el mismo camino que el de la moda del delineador de charol, dice Leila Cohoon, una cosmetóloga, esteticista y propietaria de Leila's Skin Care, una compañía que se especializa en el cuidado del cutis, en Independence, Misuri.

Bases enceradas. El maquillaje anticuado a base de cera es algo que usan las presentadoras de televisión sobre la cara pero que podría perjudicar su cutis, dice Cohoon.

Perfil tenebroso. El polvo oscuro para perfilar usado a lo largo de las mejillas para fingir que están hundidas es demasiado obvio, dice Carole Walderman, una cosmetóloga, esteticista y presidenta de la Von Lee International School of Aesthetics and Makeup, una escuela de maquillaje y belleza, en Baltimore.

Mejillas de payasa. De vez en cuando usted todavía verá mujeres con pequeñas manchas rojizas de rubor en las mejillas. Eso ni es sutil ni le favorece, dice Cohoon.

Mandíbulas rojas. El rubor se debe poner en la parte de arriba y a lo largo de los pómulos, no hacia abajo y a lo largo de la línea de la mandíbula, lo cual le da una apariencia de tener una cara larga, dice Cohoon.

Cejas oscuras y pobladas. Usted no querrá sobreenfatizar las cejas cuando envejece, dice Walderman. Puede verse chillón y duro.

La máscara mate. Los expertos dicen, ¡manténgalo ligero, ligero, ligero! Un toque ligero de maquillaje puede darle un cutis natural de aspecto juvenil. Al recargarlose agregan años.

---

nariz más ancha, dice Walderman. Aplique apenas una pizca de rubor en un ángulo de 45 grados sobre la mejilla a fin de "destacar" la cara para un aspecto más juvenil, dice ella. Nunca aplique el rubor más abajo de la base de su nariz o más arriba del ángulo exterior de sus ojos.

Hágalo desaparecer. Haga que el rubor se combine con el color de las mejillas completamente con un cepillo suave para maquillaje, haciéndolo desaparecer levemente apenas pase el ángulo exterior de sus ojos hacia las sienes, dice Walderman.

Consulte con un profesional. Si usted no puede decidir qué tono de rubor es el que mejor le va, pida ayuda en el mostrador de maquillaje. Por lo general las especialistas en maquillaje pueden decirle qué colores de rubor le quedan bien, dice Valmy. Las consultoras profesionales de color son otra opción, pero usted tendrá que pagar por sus servicios.

Los secretos de la sombra para ojos

Nuestros ojos todavía pueden ser las ventanas de nuestras almas, pero las sombras pueden empezar a verse un poco arrugadas con surcos y líneas. El maquillaje puede ocultar el cambio.

Úsela apenitas. Use menos sombra que la que estaba acostumbrada, dice Valmy. Las dosis cargadas de sombra para los ojos pueden hacer que los pliegues y las líneas se noten más.

Corrija con color. Si sus ojos se ven demasiado juntos, demasiado separados o les falta profundidad, o usted empieza a notar los párpados caídos, la sombra viene al rescate, dice Cohoon. "Si sus ojos están demasiado juntos, ponga sombra más oscura en la parte exterior del párpado superior", dice ella. "Si están demasiado separados, aplique la sombra oscura más hacia el centro."

Los ojos muy hundidos darán la impresión de venirse hacia adelante con los tonos más claros de sombra y usted puede darle más profundidad a sus ojos con maquillaje más oscuro de ojos. Sin embargo, recuerde usar un toque suave, agrega ella.

Si los párpados caídos son un problema, la mejor solución es una combinación suave de tres colores que estén relacionados, usando el más pálido bajo el hueso de la ceja. Eso disminuye el aspecto de piel en exceso, dice Cohoon. Pero no use sombra iridiscente, brillante o muy oscura.

Coordine las combinaciones. Si usted tiene ojos oscuros, use una sombra para ojos de un color café suave con una base rojiza, no verdosa, dice Valmy. Si sus ojos son claros, use una sombra café o gris con una base verdosa en lugar de azulada. La base verdosa toma los reflejos de los ojos claros, explica ella.

Evite ver doble. Si usted encuentra que a menudo tiene círculos oscuros bajo los ojos, evite sombras con un tinte ciruela o café. Estas acentuarán los círculos, dice Walderman.

Aproveche los ángulos. Contrarreste la tendencia de sus ojos a caer en los ángulos al aplicar sutilmente sombra en un ángulo de 45 grados para arriba hacia la ceja en el ángulo exterior del ojo, dice Walderman.

El arte del delineador

Usted no tiene que abandonar el delineador, pero sí quiere una definición de los ojos más suave y sutil, dice Cohoon.

Cuidado con el color. A menos que usted tenga el tono de tez muy moreno, si usa un delineador negro se verá muy chillón. Las demás deberían escoger cafés suaves, marrón topo y grises en lugar de ése, sugiere Walderman.

Maquíllese con mesura. Use delineador con moderación y tan cerca de sus pestañas como sea posible para darle más cuerpo a las pestañas ralas, dice Valmy.

Suavecito, suavecito. Afile sus lápices delineadores antes de cada uso, dice Walderman. ¿La razón? La punta más afilada facilita hacer la línea sin jalar la piel delicada de sus párpados. Si usted usa un delineador líquido, nunca lo aplique en una línea recta y plana. Siempre tizne su delineador para que tenga un aspecto más suave, ahumado, dice ella. Sumerja un aplicador limpio de algodón bajo el agua corriente y exprímalo primero antes de hacer que la línea se tizne.

Mantenga las líneas a raya. No deje que las líneas del delineador en los párpados superior e inferior se junten en el ángulo de sus ojos. Si hace eso sus ojos se verán más pequeños, explica Walderman.

Cómo cuidar las pestañas y las cejas

Sus pestañas y cejas se hacen más ralas con la edad, pero hay diferentes maneras de aumentar la ilusión de estar más llenas y sedosas.

Revitalícese con el rímel. El rímel todavía es el mejor amigo de las pestañas. Para evitar esos irritantes manchones y círculos de mapache bajo sus ojos, después de aplicarse el rímel dese un toquecito de polvo para la cara, con un cepillo pequeño, justamente debajo de sus pestañas inferiores, dice Valmy.

Haga la prueba con las postizas. En la actualidad, hay disponibles pestañas artificiales de aspecto muy natural tanto en tiras como en grupos individuales, dice Walderman. Usted se aplica las tiras justo en la base de sus propias pestañas adhiriéndolas en su lugar sobre el párpado. Con la práctica, parecerá como si las pestañas crecieran de su propio párpado, dice ella.

Sin embargo, si usted usa las tiras de pestañas postizas, aplique primero el rímel solamente a sus propias pestañas y déjelo secar, o de lo contrario va a perder pestañas cuando desprenda la tira, dice Valmy.

Colocar un juego completo de pestañas individuales puede tomar hasta 45 minutos, dice Walderman. Pero estas pueden permanecer en su lugar durante seis semanas hasta que sus propias pestañas completen su ciclo de crecimiento. Y permanecerán en su lugar cuando se duche y nade porque se adhieren con un pegamento permanente. Las pestañas individuales vienen en juegos de unas cuatro pestañas por raíz, y usted se coloca cada juego sobre una de sus propias pestañas. Evite los limpiadores a base de aceite alrededor de los ojos cuando las tenga puestas, porque estos desprenderán las pestañas, dice Walderman.

Acicale sus cejas. Una buena guía de color para las cejas es que una tonalidad más clara que su cabello hace que se vean más naturales, dice Walderman. Si su cabello es castaño claro, canoso o blanco, el marrón topo es el que más la favorece, dice ella.

Si sus cejas son muy claras, puede usar un lápiz de grafito para escribir Nº 2 —ya no se hacen de plomo, así que no existe riesgo para su salud, dice Valmy. "Usted puede rellenar los lugares ralos, y se verá muy bien y natural, dice ella.

Cómo hacer lucir a sus labios

Sus labios también son parte de su cutis y a medida que envejece, pueden contribuir dando un toque encantador de color a su rostro.

Busque los corales. Los tonos coral son los mejores para los labios más mayores, dice Walderman. Si los tonos de su cutis son frescos, busque un coral rosado. Si son cálidos, un tono anaranjado le quedaría bien. Pero asegúrese de no abusar del anaranjado, ya que puede acentuar lo amarillento natural de sus dientes conforme envejece.

Pare el aspecto sangriento. Cuando el lápiz labial se corre en forma desagradable por las líneas delgadas de su labio superior le da un aspecto sangriento a los labios. Un lápiz delineador para labios parará esto en seco, dice Valmy. Para hacer que el color de los labios se adhiera mejor y dure más, aplique el delineador de los labios alrededor de las orillas de sus labios. Aplique entonces el lápiz labial, empañe el exceso y póngase otra capa, dice ella.

Evite el encerado. Si las arrugas labiales y el lápiz labial sangriento son unos verdaderos problemas y usted normalmente se pone cera sobre el bozo en el labio superior, en lugar de eso pruebe la decoloración, dice Walderman. "El bozo sobre el labio absorbe la humedad que de otro modo haría que el lápiz labial se derritiera y promoviera que se metiera en las arrugas", dice ella.

Equilibre la forma de su boca. Algunas veces el labio superior se adelgaza un poco al envejecer, dice Cohoon. Si éste es el caso, dibuje la línea de su labio ligeramente fuera del borde de su labio superior y rellene con el lápiz labial.

MASAJE

¡Qué alivio!

Usted ha estado esperando esta hora de éxtasis durante toda la semana. Ansiedad en el trabajo —frotar, frotar. Tensión en la casa —friccionar, friccionar. Esos músculos y articulaciones que duelen —tápiti, tápiti, tap. Todo esto va desapareciendo gracias a cada pasada que recibe de las manos de su masajista.

Después de 45 minutos esa magia rejuvenecedora funcionó otra vez. Nada de espalda dolorida. Nada de cuello tieso. Usted se levanta refrescada y relajada, dejando allí en la mesa de masaje lo que se siente como 20 años de dolores y preocupaciones.

"No hay nada que la haga sentir tan rejuvenecida como un masaje", dice Madeline P. Rudy, una terapeuta licenciada en masaje con Massage Therapy, un centro de terapia de masaje, en West Reading, Pensilvania. "Si usted está buscando una forma de sentirse otra vez en sincronía y más joven, no hay nada mejor."

Estudios sobre el relajamiento

Cualquier mujer le dirá que un masaje viene de maravillas. Sin embargo la ciencia médica todavía no sabe exactamente por qué.

"No existe mucha investigación todavía", dice Tiffany Field, Ph.D., directora del Instituto de Investigación sobre el Toque en la Escuela de Medicina de la Universidad de Miami. Este instituto es la primera organización en el país dedicada a estudiar los beneficios médicos del masaje.

La doctora Field dice que sin embargo hemos obtenido algunas ideas sobre cómo funciona el masaje. Por un lado, parece que restringe la secreción de cortisol por parte del cuerpo, una hormona que desempeña un papel importante en provocar reacciones de estrés. Mientras menos cortisol usted produce, menos estrés puede sentir, dice la doctora Field. El masaje también ha mostrado mejorar la etapa profunda y tranquilizante del sueño. Y puede impulsar su producción de serotonina, una hormona vinculada con los cambios positivos del estado de ánimo y una inmunidad mejorada, dice la doctora Field.

En un estudio realizado al cuerpo docente y personal médico del Instituto de Investigación sobre el Toque, parece que 15 minutos de masaje diario logran disminuir la ansiedad, hacen a las personas más alertas y aumentan la velocidad a la cual pueden completar los problemas de matemáticas. "La clave para una mejor mano de obra", dice la doctora Field, "podría ser un masaje regular".

El instituto está trabajando en una serie de 34 estudios, con cientos de participantes, para observar los efectos de la terapia de masaje en todo desde la depresión y el embarazo hasta la presión arterial alta y las migrañas. Los estudios también observaron cómo la terapia de masajes podría ayudar a los hombres que tienen resultados positivos de VIH (el virus de inmunodeficiencia humano que causa el SIDA) a mejorar su funcionamiento de inmunidad.

Por ahora, algunos médicos dicen que necesitan saber más acerca de lo que el masaje puede hacer antes de empezar a recetarlo como terapia.

"Nadie está dispuesto a aceptar una explicación confusa que involucre las metáforas de energía, toxinas, buenas vibraciones o cualquier otro verso poético", dice el doctor Larry Dossey, presidente adjunto en el panel sobre Intervenciones Mente/Cuerpo, Oficina de Medicina Alternativa en los Institutos Nacionales de Salud, en Bethesda, Maryland, y ex jefe del personal en el Hospital Ciudad Médica Dallas.

Pero esa actitud puede estar cambiando. Muchas compañías de seguros cubren ahora el masaje si el médico lo ordena. Y algunos terapeutas de masaje señalan que algunos de sus mejores y más leales clientes son médicos.

Algunos consejos prácticos

Si usted está pensando en probar la terapia de masaje, Rudy dice que debe estar preparada para gastar entre $25 y $65 por sesión; la duración típica de una sesión es de aproximadamente 50 a 55 minutos. Vaya tan a menudo como quiera o como lo pueda afrontar económicamente. Para estar mejor asesorada, pruebe estos consejos.

Escoja cuidadosamente. El último lugar al que usted quiere ir es a un "salón" de masaje, con su clientela grimosa y algunas veces prácticas dudosas. Para encontrar un terapeuta de masaje respetable y calificado, haga preguntas antes de ir. "Busque en el directorio telefónico", dice Rudy. "Asegúrese de que son miembros de la Asociación de Terapia de Masaje de los Estados Unidos (o *AMTA*, por sus siglas en inglés). Pregúnteles si fueron a escuelas reconocidas para aprender masaje. Y siempre evite lugares que ofrecen 'facturación discreta'. Eso es señal de que no son de fiar."

(continúa en la página 520)

Lo puede hacer usted misma

Algunas veces, ese masaje de los viernes en la tarde se ve como si estuviera a semanas de distancia. Usted sabe que se va a sentir bien cuando vaya, ¿pero mientras tanto qué?

Pruebe el automasaje. Estos pequeños estimulantes pueden hacer maravillas por usted. Y no requieren nada más que un par de pelotas de tenis, un rincón tranquilo y sus dos manos.

Cabeza

Los puntos de presión en su cráneo pueden relajar todo su cuerpo.

"Hay dos puntos de digitopuntura muy significantes en la base de su cráneo en lo que se llama el borde occipital", dice Robert DeIulio, Ed.D., un sicólogo licenciado y terapeuta de músculos, en práctica privada en Wellesley Hills, Massachusetts. "Si usted aplica presión constante sobre estos, puede lograr un relajamiento total."

¿Cómo lo hace? Ponga dos pelotas de tenis en un calcetín y amarre el extremo. Recuéstese sobre la espalda en el suelo y coloque el calcetín detrás de la parte superior del cuello, para que las dos pelotas toquen el borde del cráneo justo arriba del lugar hueco. Permanezca así por 20 minutos. Escuche música sedante, si lo desea. "Esos puntos de digito puntura mandan mensajes hacia abajo por la columna vertebral para relajar todos los músculos", dice el doctor DeIulio.

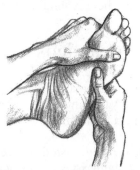

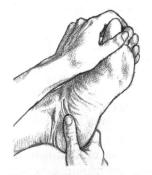

Siéntese en una silla y coloque un pie sobre el muslo opuesto. Frote un aceite para masaje o loción sobre su pie si así lo desea. Aplique presión con sus pulgares sobre la planta del pie, vaya desde el fondo del arco hacia la parte de arriba cerca de su dedo gordo. Repita cinco veces.

Masajee cada dedo mientras que lo sostiene firmemente y lo mueve de un lado al otro. Extienda cada dedo suavemente hacia afuera y lejos de la parte anterior de la planta del pie. Entonces aplique presión a las áreas entre sus dedos.

Cara

Solamente tóquese la cara. No hay necesidad de masajearla. En forma muy ligera, toque sus mejillas y sienes con las manos ahuecadas no usando más presión que el peso de una moneda de cinco centavos. Mantenga sus manos allí por un minuto. "El calor de las manos relaja los músculos y el tejido conectivo, ocasionando una sensación de alivio total", dice el doctor DeIulio.

Mandíbula

Jale suavemente los lados de sus orejas derecho hacia afuera, luego derecho hacia arriba y después derecho hacia abajo. O, usando el dedo índice presione el lugar sensible junto a su lóbulo donde se junta con la cabeza. Oprima y suelte, alternando las orejas, de 10 a 15 veces.

Torso

Obtenga un estímulo rápido al frotar el área arriba de sus riñones. Eso está al nivel de la cintura donde el tejido aún es suave. Frote vigorosamente con sus puños en un movimiento circular. "Es una forma agradable de vigorizar el cuerpo", dice el doctor DeIulio.

Pies

Pocas cosas en el mundo son tan ricas como un masaje en los pies. Aquí hay algunas técnicas efectivas. Después de que usted las prueba en un pie, cambie de pie y repítalas.

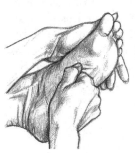

Presione y haga girar sus pulgares entre los huesos de la parte anterior de la planta del pie.

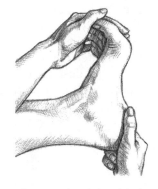

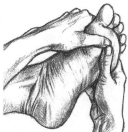

Haga un puño y presione a la planta de su pie con sus nudillos, moviéndose del talón a los dedos. Repita cinco veces.

Sostenga los dedos del pie con una mano y dóblelos hacia atrás, sosténgalos así por cinco a diez segundos. Entonces dóblelos en la dirección opuesta y sosténgalos así por cinco a diez segundos. Repita tres veces.

Escoja lo que le gusta. Cuando se trata de masajes, realmente hay diferentes tipos para diferentes personas. El masaje sueco —con su masajear, frotar y uso de aceites— es el método en que la mayoría de las personas piensan. Pero también está el *shiatsu* o masaje oriental, en el cual una terapeuta trabaja sobre los puntos de presión a lo largo de los senderos de nervios para aliviar el dolor y el estrés (Rudy dice que algunas personas pueden sentirse incómodas con este método). Existe el masaje deportivo especializado que se concentra en aliviar los músculos y las articulaciones demasiado trabajadas. Y hay una cantidad de técnicas y subtécnicas como *Rolfing*, Feldenkrais, *Trager, Alexander* y *Astos-Patterning*, que promueven todo desde el alargamiento del cuerpo hasta el realineamiento de la columna vertebral y el mejoramiento de la postura.

"La clave es hablar con los terapeutas primero", dice Rudy. "Usted tiene que buscar a alguien cuya especialidad coincida con sus necesidades. Y usted necesita estar segura de que son legítimos."

Respete sus límites. El masaje es relajamiento. Y seamos francas: algunas mujeres no se sienten cómodas desnudándose para un masaje sueco. "Sólo vaya tan lejos como sus sentimientos le permitan", dice Rudy. "Tal vez necesite más tiempo hasta llegar a ese punto. Este es su tiempo especial. Disfrútelo."

Los terapeutas deben estar conscientes de sus sentimientos. Deben cubrir las partes de su cuerpo en las que no están trabajando y no deben tocar sus senos o las áreas genitales. No deben preguntarle detalles íntimos de su vida o darle detalles de las de las suyas. Se supone que deben respetar sus deseos. Si no lo hacen, encuentre a otro terapeuta de masaje.

"Lo importante", dice Rudy, "es su salud y bienestar y el sentirse mejor. Si hay tensión o presión en una relación, vaya a otra parte."

Sepa cuándo decir que no. El masaje no es para todos. Las normas de AMTA dicen que las personas con flebitis u otros padecimientos circulatorios, algunas formas de cáncer o enfermedad del corazón, infecciones o fiebres no deberían usar la terapia de masaje. En la mayoría de los casos, evite el masaje por unos tres días después de sufrir una fractura o una torcedura seria. Si tiene alguna duda, consulte con su médico.

MATRIMONIO

Mejora la salud
y mantiene la juventud

Casarse puede ser una de las cosas que inspire más miedo que usted jamás vaya a hacer en su vida. Pero lo que la lleva a caminar por ese pasillo es la esperanza de que la vida será mejor cuando esté casada de lo que era cuando estaba soltera. ¿Será? Probablemente.

Si usted está felizmente casada, probablemente bebe menos, come menos comida basura y hace ejercicio más regularmente. Parecerá más relajada y optimista y se enfermará menos.

"Por supuesto que un matrimonio satisfactorio puede ayudarla a sentirse más joven y más llena de vida. Es bueno para su salud, y puede ayudarla a vivir una vida más productiva y feliz", dice Howard Markman, Ph.D., un sicólogo de la Universidad de Denver y coautor de *We Can Work It Out: Making Sense of Marital Conflict* (Podemos resolverlo: encuentre el sentido en el conflicto matrimonial).

¿Qué tiene de bueno?

Si usted le pregunta a una docena de científicos si estar casada la va a ayudar a vivir más tiempo, podría recibir doce respuestas diferentes. Los investigadores en el Centro Nacional de Estadísticas de la Salud, por ejemplo, estiman que las mujeres casadas viven cerca de diez años más que las mujeres solteras. Muchos estudios muestran que las mujeres solteras o divorciadas son más propensas a enfermedades, lesiones y suicidio que las mujeres felizmente casadas.

En una encuesta a 47.000 hogares, el Centro Nacional de Estadísticas de la Salud encontró que las mujeres casadas tenían más probabilidad de decir que su salud era buena o excelente que las mujeres solteras, divorciadas o viudas. Las mujeres casadas también tenían menos probabilidad de sufrir enfermedades crónicas, reportaron seis días menos de enfermedad por año que las mujeres divorciadas, y se recuperaron más rápidamente de los resfriados (catarros), las gripas y las lesiones que las mujeres solteras o divorciadas. Y las mujeres divorciadas reportaron el doble de lesiones.

Otros estudios indican que la duración de la vida de las mujeres solteras y casadas es aproximadamente la misma. Pero también existe investigación que sugiere que las mujeres solteras sobreviven a sus amigas casadas, dice Estelle Ramey, Ph.D., fisióloga y profesora emérita en el Centro Médico de la Universidad de Georgetown, en Washington, D.C.

¿Por qué estas estadísticas contradictorias? Porque, dicen los expertos, no es el matrimonio en sí sino la felicidad en el matrimonio lo que contribuye a la longevidad de una mujer.

"La salud de una mujer parece que sigue al bienestar de una relación", dice Robert W. Levenson, Ph.D., un sicólogo en la Universidad de California, Berkeley. "Si el matrimonio es satisfactorio, entonces su salud parece ser buena. Si su matrimonio no es satisfactorio, su salud sufre."

Sin embargo no es lo mismo para los hombres, quienes se benefician de cualquier tipo de matrimonio. Para los hombres, la calidad de la vida de casado no parece importar. Su salud parece mejorar aun cuando están en un matrimonio desdichado.

Los investigadores están desconcertados por esta diferencia. Algunos sospechan que las mujeres solteras comen mejor, hacen más ejercicio y en general cuidan más de su persona que los hombres solteros. Así que cuando una pareja se casa —y por lo general un hombre casado adopta el estilo de vida de su esposa— hay pocos cambios que podrían tener una influencia positiva en la salud de una mujer. Al mismo tiempo, ella por lo regular pasa más tiempo haciendo los quehaceres del hogar y en la cocina.

Otros, como el doctor Levenson, especulan que cuando los hombres tienen matrimonios infelices tratan de alejarse de la relación, las mujeres trabajan más y más duro para curar las heridas. Ese esfuerzo afecta la salud de una mujer.

"En un matrimonio infeliz, hay mucha ira, recriminación y otras emociones en el ambiente, pero por alguna razón no afecta a los hombres como afecta a las mujeres. Los hombres se desentienden de esto", dice el doctor Levenson. "Hay menos probabilidad de que las mujeres se alejen. A menudo se quedan allí tratando de resolver los problemas hasta el último momento amargo. Eso produce una gran cantidad de estrés que es potencialmente malo para su salud", dice él.

Puede ayudar en una crisis

Aun cuando una mujer casada contraiga una enfermedad que ponga en peligro su vida, es más probable que ella busque tratamiento antes y tenga una mejor oportunidad de sobrevivencia que su hermana soltera. De hecho, después de estudiar 27.779 casos de cáncer, el doctor James Goodwin, director del Centro

---

Parece que están felices

Cuando usted mira a su esposo hoy en día, ¿parece como si estuviera viéndose en el espejo? Es una buena posibilidad, especialmente si ustedes han tenido una relación larga y duradera.

Después de examinar las fotografías de 12 parejas que habían estado casadas por lo menos 25 años, un panel de observadores de la Universidad de Michigan en Ann Arbor concluyó que los rasgos faciales de las parejas se vuelven más similares después de años de vivir juntos.

¿Por qué? Las parejas tienden a imitarse inconscientemente las expresiones faciales entre sí, dice Robert Zajonc, Ph.D., profesor de sicología en la Universidad de Michigan en Ann Arbor. Al pasar el tiempo, esta imitación reforma los músculos faciales y las arrugas de tal forma que sus rostros adquieren muchos de los mismos rasgos. Las parejas también tienden a adoptar los mismos gestos con las manos, la postura del cuerpo y la forma de andar, dice el doctor Zajonc.

---

sobre el Envejecimiento en la División Médica de la Universidad de Texas, en Galveston, concluyó que las mujeres casadas tenían índices de sobrevivencia comparables a los de las mujeres solteras diez años más jóvenes.

"Esa fue una conclusión bastante asombrosa", dice el doctor Goodwin. "Los tratamientos para el cáncer —quimioterapia y radiación— pueden hacerlas sentir muy enfermas. Por lo tanto tiene sentido que al tener un compañero que las apoye sea más fácil para las pacientes sobrellevar la situación."

Un matrimonio feliz también puede ayudarla a restablecerse de otras enfermedades serias. En un pequeño estudio preliminar, las mujeres que sufrieron ataques al corazón y que fueron capaces de hablar con sus esposos abierta y honestamente acerca de eso, reportaron una mejor salud y fueron menos propensas a tener dolores en el pecho o a volver a ser internadas en un hospital dentro del lapso de un año después de sufrir el ataque, según Vicki Helgeson, Ph.D., una sicóloga en la Universidad de Carnegie Mellon, en Pittsburgh.

Las mujeres satisfechas con sus matrimonios también tienen menos probabilidad de sufrir de depresión fuerte que las mujeres quienes están en uniones problemáticas, dice James Coyne, Ph.D., profesor de sicología en el Departamento de Práctica Familiar y Siquiatría de la Escuela de Medicina en la Universidad de Michigan, en Ann Arbor.

Además, los investigadores en la Universidad Estatal de Ohio encontraron que mientras más desaires, sarcasmo y otras palabras y gestos hostiles usaron las parejas de recién casados cuando discutían los conflictos matrimoniales, más

Darse por vencida

Su relación está más fría que un cubo de hielo. Su pasión ha faltado por tanto tiempo que usted ha pensado en llamar al equipo de búsqueda y rescate. Pero, ¿es tiempo de separarse?

"Terminar un matrimonio es el equivalente sicológico a cortarse su propio brazo o pierna. Va a doler", dice John Mirowsky, Ph.D., profesor de sociología en la Universidad Estatal de Ohio, en Columbus.

Pero hay algunas indicaciones claras de que puede ser tiempo de terminar a su matrimonio. Y estas varían entre problemas de alcohol o drogas, hasta abuso emocional o físico o la simple incapacidad de comunicarse más.

"Mis pacientes siempre me preguntan cuándo deberían irse. Yo les digo 'usted sabrá cuándo es el momento' ", dice Sherelynn Lehman, una terapeuta licenciada en familia, matrimonio y relaciones sexuales en práctica privada en Cleveland. "Es cuando su alma muere, cuando su espíritu es pisoteado. Yo digo que 'hasta que la muerte nos separe' significa la muerte del espíritu. Si usted se está muriendo por dentro, entonces quizás es el momento de tomar otro camino."

---

probable era que tuvieran presión arterial alta y sistemas inmunes debilitados. No, una discusión matrimonial el martes no quiere decir que usted va a tener un resfriado el miércoles. Pero los investigadores concluyeron que las parejas que a menudo tienen discusiones desagradables pueden ser más susceptibles a la infección y la enfermedad.

Cómo mantener la chispa encendida

Usted tiene sus disputas, su pasión flaquea y algunas veces la sofoca el aburrimiento. A pesar de todo eso, valora mucho al hombre de su vida. Pero aun las mejores relaciones necesitan afinaciones ocasionales. Aquí hay algunas sugerencias para mantener a su matrimonio funcionando.

Haga que el momento ocurra. Si ustedes no programan tiempo juntos, puede ser que nunca suceda. Traten de pasar por lo menos 20 minutos al día conversando. "Usted hace ejercicio diariamente por ese tiempo para mantener su cuerpo en forma; usted también necesita pasar por lo menos el mismo tiempo para mantener su matrimonio en forma", dice Sherelynn Lehman, una terapeuta licenciada en familia, matrimonio y sexo, en práctica privada en Cleveland.

Escuche hasta que lo oiga. Si su esposo le dice que se siente frustrado porque le parece que usted lo está ignorando, deténgase, reconozca que él puede tener razón y tome su tiempo para realmente escucharlo, dice el doctor Dennis Gersten, un siquiatra en práctica privada en San Diego. Hágale saber que usted oyó lo que dijo repitiéndole lo que le preocupaba: "Sé que debes estar disgustado porque trabajé hasta tarde y no te hablé por teléfono para avisarte". Si esa no es la razón por la que él está molesto, pídale entonces que lo repita hasta que usted entienda. "Diga 'estoy tratando de entender tu preocupación, pero parece

Volver a casarse

Más de la mitad de todos los matrimonios terminan en divorcio. Usted se sintió devastada cuando su unión se desbarató. Pero aquí está, pensando en encaminarse otra vez al altar.

En cierta forma eso es bueno, porque las mujeres divorciadas que se vuelven a casar probablemente recuperan muchas de las ventajas de salud de las mujeres felizmente casadas, dice Patrick McKenry, Ph.D., un profesor de Relaciones Familiares y Desarrollo Humano en la Universidad Estatal de Ohio, en Columbus.

Pero antes de que usted entre a la capilla del amor, debería reflexionar sobre algunas cosas que pueden aumentar sus probabilidades de tener en esta ocasión un matrimonio feliz y perdurable.

Primero, no se apresure a un matrimonio nuevo. "La forma en que algunas mujeres tratan de adaptarse al divorcio es volviéndose a casar, dice el doctor McKenry. Él dice que una mujer necesita uno a dos años antes de continuar con otra relación seria.

Pregúntese a sí misma qué espera del matrimonio, sugiere el doctor Joel Kahan, un siquiatra en el Colegio Médico de la Escuela de Medicina de Georgia, en Augusta quien ha estudiado los matrimonios múltiples. "Si una mujer no quiere o espera una relación fuerte e íntima, entonces quizás no debería casarse", dice el doctor Kahan. "Ella tendrá que resolver ese asunto antes de sumergirse en otra relación."

Piense detenidamente qué no funcionó en su último matrimonio y pregúntese si problemas similares se avecinan en su nueva relación. "Un número enorme de mujeres se vuelven a casar con hombres que se parecen mucho a sus esposos anteriores. Esa es una de las cosas más importantes que hay que evitar", dice Sol Gordon, Ph.D., sicólogo, profesor emérito en la Universidad de Syracuse, en Nueva York, y autor de *Why Love Is Not Enough* (Por qué el amor no es suficiente). Si su nuevo amor tiene características molestas que le recuerdan a su exesposo, pregúntese si va a poder sobrellevarlas mejor esta vez. Si no, no se case.

que no lo logro. ¿Podrías decirlo en forma diferente para que pueda ser más claro para mí?' ", sugiere el doctor Gersten.

Sorpréndalo. "Para mantener la chispa viva en su matrimonio, usted necesita ser creativa", dice Ruth Rice, Ph.D., una sicóloga en práctica privada en Dallas. Organice sorpresas ocasionales como un fin de semana en uno de esos hoteles que incluyen el desayuno o una caminata a la luz de la luna alrededor de un lago o simplemente ponga una tarjeta romántica debajo de su almohada.

En la diversión está la unión. Los intereses y los pasatiempos comunes alivian el aburrimiento y son el pegamento que mantiene juntos a muchos buenos matrimonios. "La pareja que realmente disfruta haciendo cosas juntos como viajar, jugar al golf o al tenis va a tener una ventaja al entrar en sus últimos años de matrimonio cuando tienen más tiempo disponible", dice el doctor Martin Goldberg, un siquiatra y director del Consejo de Matrimonio de Filadelfia, un servicio de orientación.

Ríanse juntos. "Tener la capacidad de ser infantiles y reírse juntos es importante porque eso significa que ustedes se sienten lo suficientemente

---

Cómo sobrellevar una infidelidad

Su mejor amiga es el tema de conversación en la oficina ahora que su aventura amorosa destruyó su matrimonio. Afortunadamente, nada de eso puede suceder en su relación, ¿correcto?

"Usted nunca puede estar 100 por ciento segura de que su matrimonio estará inmune de aventuras", dice Sherelynn Lehman, una terapeuta licenciada en familia, matrimonio y relaciones sexuales en práctica privada en Cleveland y autora de *Love Me, Love Me Not: How to Survive Infidelity* (Ámame, no me ames: cómo sobrevivir la infidelidad). "Usted debe cortejar a su compañero todos los días. Nunca puede bajar la guardia." Allá afuera, dice ella, hay alguien que piensa que su esposo es un buen partido.

Las mujeres y los hombres a menudo se ven atraídos a las aventuras por aburrimiento o soledad, dice Lehman. El mantener una buena comunicación y conservar el entusiasmo en su vida sexual están entre los factores claves para evitar una aventura. Pero una aventura no quiere decir que todo está perdido.

"Un matrimonio sacudido por una aventura es como un huevo que se casca. Aunque la cascadura estará siempre allí, usted puede seguir adelante. El matrimonio no necesita destrozarse, pero el buscar orientación es esencial", dice Lehman.

cómodos para permitirse ser vulnerables el uno con el otro", dice Arlene Goldman, Ph.D., una sicóloga y terapeuta en relaciones sexuales de la facultad del Instituto Familiar, en Filadelfia.

Enfóquese en sus sentimientos. La manera más segura de empezar una pelea, según la doctora Goldman, es decir cosas como "tú estás equivocado" o "yo creo que estás portándote como un tonto". Ella agrega, "las declaraciones que empiezan con 'tú' son siempre pensamientos y por lo regular son hirientes". En lugar de eso trate de decir, "yo me preocupo cuando no sé dónde estás. Una manera en que me puedes ayudar a sobrellevar esa sensación es mandándome a decir para que yo sepa dónde me puedo comunicar contigo". Eso es menos provocativo que decir "tú siempre llegas tarde".

Mírese primero a usted misma. Enfóquese en sus propios defectos en vez de las de su compañero, sugiere el doctor Markman. Usted tiene más control sobre su propio comportamiento que sobre las acciones de su compañero, y a menudo, cuando una persona en una relación empieza a hacer cambios, la otra la seguirá.

Haga cambios pequeños. "Hacer cambios grandes en una relación es realmente el resultado de hacer una serie de cambios pequeños", dice el doctor Markman. "Si usted puede decir aunque sea una cosa crítica menos a su esposo todos los días, puede estar en camino a un cambio significante."

Muérdase la lengua. Decir algo sarcástico en el medio de una discusión puede hacer que se sienta bien, pero lo hiriente de esa frase puede borrar sus últimos 20 actos de amabilidad de la memoria de su esposo, dice el doctor Markman. Es mejor morderse la lengua que abrir innecesariamente una nueva herida.

Reconozca su culpabilidad también. Culpar a su esposo en lugar de reconocer que usted comparte algo de la responsabilidad de un problema en el matrimonio aumenta la probabilidad de que ustedes acaben en una corte de divorcio, dice el doctor Markman. Para salir de ese patrón, trate diciéndole a su esposo "sé que últimamente hemos estado atrapados en este patrón de criticarnos el uno al otro por la menor causa, así que yo voy a tratar de criticarte menos y de verte desde una perspectiva más positiva".

Dividan los quehaceres más justamente. Si usted o su esposo está haciendo más de lo que le corresponde de los quehaceres, eso puede causar resentimiento, dice la doctora Rice. Haga una lista de todo lo que necesita hacer: limpiar, lavar, hacer las compras, trabajar en el jardín, pagar las cuentas, reparar la casa. Negocien entonces una división justa que incluya un número igual de cosas que cada uno de ustedes disfruten hacer y cosas que ustedes consideren fastidiosas. Si su presupuesto se los permite, consideren contratar personas para que los ayuden.

Déjelo en manos de los aparatos. Si la televisión es importante para uno de ustedes pero no para el otro, verla puede quitarles tiempo valioso juntos, dice la doctora Rice. Hágase de una videograbadora, grabe el programa y véalo después. Si el teléfono está sonando todo el tiempo, compre una máquina contestadora y filtre sus mensajes para poder pasar más tiempo con su esposo.

METAS

Un mapa del camino a la vitalidad

Después de su primer paso, usted quería correr. Después de su primera voltereta, usted quería dar un salto mortal hacia atrás. Después de haber conseguido su primer empleo, usted quería uno mejor.

Usted ha tenido metas toda su vida. Cada vez que logra una tarea significativa usted siente una oleada de orgullo y exuberancia. Como para la mayoría de las mujeres, las metas son una parte esencial de su vida. Le dan vitalidad y energía; la mantienen en movimiento.

"Las metas hacen suponer que existe un futuro que vale la pena vivir", dice Marilee C. Goldberg, Ph.D., una sicoterapeuta en práctica privada, en Lambertville, New Jersey, quien se especializa en terapia cognitiva y de conducta. "Éstas la pueden alentar a seguir adelante, lo cual la mantiene optimista, y tener algo que esperar puede hacerla sentir más joven."

"Las metas sustentan en una mujer la sensación de bienestar y propósito. Simplemente es natural sentirse mejor con usted misma y valiosa si está siendo productiva de alguna manera", dice el doctor Barry Rovner, un siquiatra geriátrico en el Centro Médico Thomas Jefferson, en Filadelfia. "Es así de simple: así como su corazón necesita sangre, su mente necesita tener un punto central o una meta", dice él. "Las personas sin metas se sienten perdidas y a la deriva."

Le hacen bien al cuerpo

Todas nosotras tenemos metas, incluyendo las mundanas como es pagar las cuentas a tiempo. De hecho, durante cualquier semana la mujer típica satisface docenas de metas que pueden incluir alcanzar una cuota de ventas en el trabajo, llegar a la casa a tiempo para ver el partido de fútbol de su hija, o dar un paseo por la tarde con su esposo, dice Phil Karoly, Ph.D., profesor de sicología en la Universidad Estatal de Arizona, en Tempe.

"Todos tenemos el mismo deseo general en la vida, y éste es ir del punto 'A' al punto 'B' ", dice el doctor Karoly. "En esencia, eso significa tener metas y aprender a navegar hacia ellas. Los estudios indican que las personas que tienen metas razonables están más satisfechas de la vida y se sienten mejor acerca de sí mismas."

Las metas también pueden ayudarla a mantener su mente y su cuerpo en condición óptima, dice el doctor Dennis Gersten, un siquiatra en práctica privada en San Diego y editor de *Atlantis: the Imagery Newsletter* (Atlántida: el boletín informativo de imaginería). "Si usted no tiene metas, ¿qué pasa? No tendrá motivación para conservar su salud y mantener su cuerpo", dice él. "Su vida no tendrá sentido y no se sentirá completa. Por lo tanto, tener metas la hace sentir completa en lo espiritual, lo físico y lo emocional. Y el estar completa puede hacerla sentir más saludable y aliviar el estrés."

Las metas impiden el aburrimiento, y eso es importante porque el aburrimiento puede ponerla en un riesgo más alto de enfermedades, dice Howard Friedman, Ph.D., profesor de sicología y medicina comunitaria en la Universidad de California, Riverside, y autor de *The Self-Healing Personality* (La personalidad autocurativa).

"Algo está ocurriendo por ahí, pero realmente no sabemos cómo todo encaja en su lugar", dice el doctor Friedman. "Puede ser que cuando usted se siente desafiada por una meta, ocasiona un proceso sicofisiológico en el cuerpo. O podría ser que las personas que tienen metas hacen otras cosas positivas como comer bien y hacer más ejercicio."

Además, las metas difíciles pero alcanzables pueden ser más vigorizadoras que las metas que se perciben como fáciles o imposibles, especula el doctor Karoly.

"Si usted ve la tarea como fácil o imposible, entonces no tiene motivación", dice el doctor Karoly. "Si usted la ve como razonablemente posible, entonces vale la pena tratar. Cuando lo hace, el ritmo de su corazón puede aumentar y usted puede sentirse más energética."

¿Es su meta realmente un sueño?

Imagine que usted quiere conducir de Nueva York a Los Ángeles. Pero cuando se sube al carro, no hay un mapa de caminos y la carretera no tiene señales. Usted no tendría forma de saber qué tan lejos ha viajado o si está yendo en la dirección correcta. Eso es como tener un sueño o una visión sin metas.

Las metas son mapas de caminos, las señales en la carretera, que le ayudan a seguir en su curso para que pueda realizar sus sueños, dice la doctora Goldberg. A menudo los sueños o las visiones son difíciles de cumplir simplemente porque son vagas. Las metas son específicas.

"Las personas se confunden acerca de la distinción entre metas y visiones, y eso las prepara para el fracaso", dice la doctora Goldberg. "Decir 'yo quiero ser popular' es una visión, no una meta. Esa declaración no tiene criterios que puedan medir si usted está progresando y es imposible de cumplir. Una meta sería 'voy a hablar por teléfono con diez personas y las voy a invitar a tomar un café conmigo, y no voy a parar hasta que una de ellas me diga que sí'. Usted puede medir eso. Usted definitivamente sabrá si hizo las llamadas y si alguien dijo que sí."

Cómo planear su estrategia

Sus metas no necesitan ser grandiosas o espectaculares para vigorizarla, dice el doctor Gersten. Pero ya sea que usted esté tratando de pasar más tiempo con su familia, organizar una venta en el jardín de su casa, o recaudar un millón de dólares para construir un nuevo centro comunitario, mientras más cuidadosamente usted defina sus metas, más probable será que sus sueños se conviertan en realidad. Aquí está cómo.

Escríbalas. Poner sus metas por escrito en un papel hará que sean más tangibles para usted, dice el doctor Friedman. Conserve su lista en un lugar conspicuo y marque las metas a medida que las realice. Asegúrese de incluir una mezcla de metas sencillas que la estimulen, tal como leer el periódico diariamente, y varias más difíciles que la desafíen, como aumentar su productividad en el trabajo en un 10 por ciento.

Logre las más importantes primero. Después de enumerar sus metas, decida cuáles son las más importantes para usted y empiece a trabajar sobre éstas. "A menudo las personas hacen las metas menos importantes primero, y las cosas que son realmente importantes para ellas nunca se realizan", dice el doctor Friedman.

Sea selectiva. Como dice el refrán, quien mucho abarca poco aprieta. Si tiene más metas de las que usted puede lograr de manera realista, agotará su energía y se sentirá desanimada y deprimida. Es mejor tener una o dos metas bien definidas que sean significativas para usted que una docena de metas menos importantes, dice el doctor Friedman.

Enamórese de ellas. Escoja metas que la apasionen, y habrá más probabilidad de que continúe con éstas, dice el doctor Gersten. Así que si usted empieza a coleccionar cucharas de plata, pero su corazón no está realmente en eso, lo más probable es que no vaya a continuar. Pero si usted es una admiradora del tenis, las probabilidades son que usted va a tener más éxito si colecciona autógrafos u otros objetos de interés relacionados con el tenis.

Vaya por lo positivo. "En lugar de concentrarse en lo que no quiere, invente una meta que exprese lo que usted sí quiere", dice el doctor Gersten. Las metas positivas son más placenteras y más efectivas que las negativas. Si dice por ejemplo "no voy a comer pasteles de crema", está enfocando su atención en una meta negativa. Eso puede hacer más tentadores a los pasteles de crema. Una meta mejor sería "voy a comer una dieta más balanceada que incluya más verduras, frutas y granos. Entonces, si quiero un pastel de crema ocasional para darme un gusto, puedo comerlo sin sentirme culpable."

Sea realista. Las metas no sólo necesitan ser específicas, deben ser realistas, dice la doctora Goldberg. Si usted dice que nunca más va a ver la televisión, eso probablemente no es realista porque las metas que incluyen las palabras absolutas "siempre" o "nunca" rara vez son realizables. Una meta más específica y razonable podría ser limitar el tiempo a no más de dos horas cada noche para ver la televisión.

Hágalo por su bien. Una meta que es un tormento alcanzarla o pone en peligro su salud no vale la pena. "Algunas mujeres dirán 'me mataré para hacer esto' ", dice la doctora Goldberg. "Usted tiene que tomar en cuenta su bienestar sin importar cuál es su meta. Así que si quiere plantar un jardín pero le duele la espalda, el forzarse a arrodillarse y hacerlo es una mala idea. Si realmente es tan importante para usted, pídale a una amistad o páguele a alguien para que lo haga."

Establezca plazos. Sin fechas límites para empujarnos un poquito, muchas de nosotras nunca alcanzaríamos nuestras metas. "Establecer un plazo no quiere decir que si no lo logra algo anda mal con usted", dice la doctora Goldberg. "Pero un límite de tiempo marca un punto de referencia para tener como objetivo. Entonces, si no ha logrado hacer todo lo que había planeado cuando el plazo se cumple, perdónese, vuelva a evaluar su plan y ponga un plazo nuevo."

Divida y conquiste. Si divide su meta en varias etapas intermedias su meta parecerá menos abrumadora y más realizable, dice la doctora Goldberg. Si usted quiere separar $2.500 durante los próximos dos años para un viaje a Inglaterra, probablemente le será más difícil ahorrar el dinero si trata de reunir la cantidad entera en vez de encontrar la forma de separar $3.50 diarios o $24 por semana.

Incluya a sus amistades. Si le cuenta a una amiga acerca de su meta, o mejor aun, hace que la ayude en alcanzarla, tendrá más motivación para continuar con esto, dice el doctor Friedman.

Inspírese por alguien. Si alguien a quien usted admira ha alcanzado una meta similar a la suya, use a esa persona como inspiración, dice el doctor Gersten. Ponga su fotografía o sus citas en un lugar tal como su escritorio o el refrigerador. Aparte un momento todos los días para imaginarse la emoción de alcanzar lo que ella logró.

Aprenda de los demás. Usted debería aprender del éxito de los otros, pero no debería tratar de superarlos. Si escribe canciones por ejemplo, debería estudiar el trabajo de los grandes artistas populares, pero no debería sentir que necesita vender más discos que Ana Gabriel para ser exitosa. "Se estresará menos y será más creativa si trata de ser lo mejor que pueda, en lugar de tratar de ser la mejor del mundo", dice el doctor Gersten.

Despréndase de su ego. Prepárese para el rechazo y la crítica. De hecho, debería darle la bienvenida ya que la crítica puede ayudarla a enfocar su meta. "Cuando empieza a trabajar en una meta que es importante para usted, debería poner a su ego a un lado y dejar que la gente haga pedazos su trabajo", dice el doctor Gersten. "Por ejemplo, yo estoy escribiendo un libro, por consiguiente se lo di a seis amistades y les pedí que lo despedazaran. Luego pague a un editor para que hiciera lo mismo. Como resultado, tuve que reorganizar completamente el manuscrito. Pero si usted quiere alcanzar su meta con éxito, tiene que estar dispuesta a recibir crítica como esa."

Olvídese de la perfección. Si cree que tiene que hacer algo perfectamente, probablemente nunca va a alcanzar sus metas. Recuerde, no tiene que hacer algo perfectamente. "Usted quiere hacer lo mejor posible, pero su meta no debe ser la perfección", dice el doctor Gersten.

Conserve su perspectiva. Las metas están bien, pero si interfieren con su familia o su vida social, usted puede estar buscándose un problema, según Brian Little, Ph.D., un profesor de sicología en la Universidad de Carleton, en Ottawa, Ontario. "Su meta podría ser perder 20 libras (9 kilos), por lo tanto empieza a trotar una hora todas las mañanas", dice él. "Pero a menos que hable con su esposo, podría ser que no se dé cuenta de que a él le gusta platicar con usted durante esa hora porque es la única hora en el día cuando pueden estar juntos a solas antes de que los niños se levanten. Así que sus metas no sólo tienen que acomodarse a sus necesidades, también tienen que ser oportunas, justas y tomar en cuenta las necesidades sociales de las otras personas por las que usted siente afecto." En este caso, en lugar de trotar por una hora, quizás podría llegar a un arreglo y hacerlo por 30 minutos dos veces al día.

Visualice el éxito. Imagine que ya logró su meta y la gente está alabando su esfuerzo. Esto puede motivarla a alcanzar la meta y a hacerlo bien. "Yo imagino que el libro que estoy escribiendo está a la cabeza de la lista de bestséllers del periódico *New York Times*, y eso me hace sentir con ganas de crear el mejor libro que pueda", dice el doctor Gersten.

Dispárese un gusto. Recompénsese a usted misma, por ejemplo con un cassette nuevo de su artista favorita, una manicura o un yogur helado sin grasa cuando complete una meta, no importa que tan pequeña, sugiere la doctora Goldberg. Esto sirve como un incentivo para establecer y lograr nuevas tareas. Y no se olvide de darse una palmadita en la espalda.

Actualice sus metas. "Es importante volver a evaluar sus metas cada seis meses ya que las circunstancias pueden haber cambiado, y algunas metas quizás ya no se acomoden a sus necesidades actuales", dice la doctora Goldberg. Si tal es el caso, no se aferre a esto. Deje que se desvanezca y entonces escoja alguna otra cosa que sea importante para usted *ahora*.

OPTIMISMO

El poder del pensamiento positivo

A veces piensa si a la vecina alegre y jovial de enfrente le falta un tornillo. Aun cuando ella atraviesa épocas difíciles, parece que siempre le encuentra el lado positivo a las cosas. Y usted se pregunta, "¿no se siente deprimida a veces, como el resto de nosotras?, ¿es que las optimistas hacen caso omiso del lado oscuro de la vida?"

Absolutamente no. El optimismo no se trata de ignorar lo que es real, sino de estar consciente de sus pensamientos acerca de por qué pasan las cosas, dice Martin Seligman, Ph.D., profesor de sicología y director de entrenamiento clínico en la Universidad de Pensilvania, en Filadelfia, y autor de *Learned Optimism* (Optimismo aprendido). "Y hay una buena posibilidad de que el optimismo pueda ayudarla a conservarse más saludable a lo largo de la edad madura y la edad avanzada."

Lo que realmente está en el centro del optimismo, dice el doctor Seligman, es cómo usted se explica a sí misma las experiencias negativas. Cuando algo malo le ocurre a una pesimista, es probable que entre en un rezongo mental sombrío y desesperado que le hace pensar cosas como "todo es mi culpa, es permanente y todo se ha arruinado."

¿La explicación del optimista? Fue mala suerte, pasará y la próxima vez lo haré en forma diferente porque yo aprendo de mis experiencias. Con este tipo de razonamiento, una optimista tiene una sensación de mayor control sobre su futuro, y su salud.

El poder del retorno

El optimismo puede darle una resiliencia real a medida que envejece. "La investigación ha mostrado que las actitudes y creencias optimistas están asociadas con menos enfermedades y más rápida recuperación de ellas", dice

Christopher Peterson, Ph.D., profesor de sicología en la Universidad de Michigan, en Ann Arbor y autor de *Health and Optimism* (Salud y optimismo).

"Usted no va a encontrar a alguien de 85 años de edad con un botón puesto que tiene un dibujo de una carita sonriente que se vea como si tuviera 20 años", dice el doctor Peterson. Pero debido a que es más probable que las optimistas sientan que ellas pueden hacerse cargo de su salud y no sólo deslizarse pasivamente hacia la vejez, tienden a cuidarse mejor de ellas mismas. "Duermen mejor, no beben o fuman tanto, hacen ejercicio regularmente y están más libres de depresión", dice él.

Entonces, ¿quién tiene probabilidad de vivir más y de envejecer despacio? Si usted es fatalista y cree que no hay nada que pueda hacer para hacer más lento el proceso del envejecimiento, puede estar menos motivada para alejarse de los hábitos aceleradores de la edad, dice el doctor Peterson. Las optimistas, en cambio, tienden a tomar decisiones más saludables.

"Y cuando las optimistas realmente se enferman", dice el doctor Peterson, "ellas van al doctor, paran y descansan, convencidas de que eso dará resultado. Se quedan en casa, toman líquidos y siguen las indicaciones del doctor. Se dan la oportunidad de sanar."

Pesimismo peligroso

El hermano negativo del optimismo, el pesimismo, puede reducir su resistencia a las enfermedades, aumentar las probabilidades de enfermedad del corazón e incluso acortar su vida, dicen los investigadores.

El pesimismo puede debilitar al sistema inmune. Esa es la conclusión de los investigadores de la Universidad de Yale, la Universidad de Pensilvania y el Hospital Príncipe de Gales, en Sydney, Australia. Ellos entrevistaron a 26 mujeres y hombres para averiguar qué tipo de explicaciones daban ellos para sus problemas de salud y luego examinaron su actividad de células inmunes. Los investigadores encontraron que los pesimistas tenían niveles más altos de células supresoras T, las cuales interfieren con la actividad de las células que estimulan la inmunidad. Los investigadores no conocen la mecánica exacta de cómo el pesimismo inhibe la inmunidad, pero sí piensan que podría ser un factor de riesgo importante en las enfermedades relacionadas con ésta.

Su sistema inmune no es la única parte de su cuerpo que se reprime por el pesimismo. El doctor Seligman describió al pesimismo como un tipo de depresión, y un estudio muestra que un corazón abatido hace que tenga una mayor tendencia a las enfermedades del corazón, al menos en los hombres. Los investigadores en los Centros para el Control y la Prevención de Enfermedades, en Atlanta, siguieron la salud y actitudes de 2.832 adultos por 12 años. Encontraron que aquellos con las actitudes más negativas y desesperadas estaban en mayor riesgo de desarrollar enfermedades del corazón. Aunque el estudio incluía sólo a los hombres, puede ser que las mujeres deprimidas también sean vulnerables, dice el doctor Seligman.

Muchos estudios han indicado que a las mujeres se les diagnostica con depresión más a menudo que a los hombres. Las razones ofrecidas varían mucho

—desde diferencias genéticas, niveles de estrés y salarios desiguales, hasta el hecho que las mujeres tienen una mayor disposición para reconocer su depresión y buscar ayuda.

Pero la sicóloga Susan Nolen-Hoeksema, Ph.D., de la Universidad de Stanford, en California ha revisado cientos de estudios sobre la depresión y el sexo y concluye que la mayoría de estas razones no están apoyadas por evidencia convincente. En lugar de eso, ella ofrece otra explicación de por qué hay más mujeres deprimidas que hombres.

Una clave importante puede estar en las distintas formas en que las mujeres y los hombres responden a los pensamientos y las situaciones depresivas, sugiere la doctora Nolen-Hoeksema. Los estudios también han mostrado que los hombres tienden a tomar medidas para distraerse cuando están deprimidos. Pero las mujeres más a menudo analizan y le dan vueltas al asunto —un proceso ruminante que puede hacer más profundos los sentimientos pesimistas.

Y existen muchas razones para cultivar las actitudes optimistas ahora, antes de que tengamos que enfrentarnos con los retos de la vejez. Algunos investigadores especulan que el pesimismo empieza a tener un efecto negativo sobre la salud al llegar a la edad madura, alrededor de los 35 a los 50 años de edad. Y otros estudios muestran que si usted se siente desconsolada, incluso podría esperar la visita temprana y fatal de la Parca.

Los investigadores en el Centro para Gerontología e Investigación del Cuidado de la Salud, en la Universidad Brown, en Providence, Rhode Island, estudiaron las respuestas de 1.390 mujeres y hombres mayores a preguntas sobre sus vidas cotidianas y los problemas de la edad. Aquellos que creyeron que sus problemas eran el inevitable resultado del envejecimiento tenían un índice de muerte del 16 por ciento más alto en los próximos cuatro años que aquellos que creían que sus problemas eran debidos a condiciones específicas y tratables.

"Las personas que dicen que sus problemas se deben a la edad están diciendo 'yo tengo algo que realmente no es tratable' ", dice William Rakowski, Ph.D., el gerontólogo que es uno de los autores del estudio en Brown. "Mientras que los optimistas —las personas que dicen que se trata de una condición específica y tratable— están diciendo 'yo puedo hacer algo al respecto.' "

Cómo aprender a tener esperanza

¿Qué sucede si escarbar en el jardín de la negatividad ha sido su hábito de toda la vida? Usted puede aprender a cultivar una actitud más optimista, y nunca es demasiado tarde para empezar, dice el doctor Seligman. "Yo nací pesimista, así que he tenido que aprender estas técnicas y las uso todos los días", dice él.

Observe cómo se sienten sus amigas. Vea la actitud de sus amigas, dice el doctor Peterson. "El optimismo y el pesimismo son ambos estados contagiosos", dice él. "Así que para 'contraer' optimismo, asóciese tanto como le sea posible con personas positivas."

A veces el pesimismo vale la pena

Aunque el pesimismo extremo nunca le hace bien a nadie, algunos trabajos demandan una dosis constante de realismo. Y en estos campos el pesimismo moderado puede significar éxito, dice Martin Seligman, Ph.D., profesor de sicología y director de entrenamiento clínico en la Universidad de Pensilvania, en Filadelfia, y autor de *Learned Optimism* (Optimismo aprendido).

Según el doctor Seligman, las pesimistas moderadas tienen éxito en estas áreas:

- Ingeniería de diseño y seguridad
- Estimación de técnica y costo
- Negociación de contratos
- Control financiero y contabilidad
- Leyes (pero no litigio)
- Administración de negocios
- Estadística
- Redacción técnica
- Control de calidad
- Administración de personal y relaciones industriales

¿Cuándo necesita usted ser una optimista acérrima? Un punto de vista optimista es una necesidad en ventas, corretaje, relaciones públicas, actuación, recaudación de fondos, trabajos creativos, trabajos altamente competitivos y trabajos de alto agotamiento, dice él.

Negocie con los negativos. De la misma forma, usted no puede ser la única optimista en una familia de pesimistas, dice el doctor Peterson. Usted tiene la probabilidad de caer, quedar entumecida por la embestida y volverse usted misma una pesimista. Por lo tanto, si es uno de los miembros de la familia el que suelta negatividad todo el día, trate de decirle: "realmente me vuelvo loca cuando tú hablas así, ¿en su lugar, no podemos ser negativos solamente una vez a la semana?"

Saboree sus éxitos. Estamos entrenados para ser modestos, dice el doctor Peterson, pero no hay necesidad de menospreciar sus propios triunfos diciendo "fue suerte nada más". En lugar de eso puede decirse a sí misma "yo realmente hice un esfuerzo, hice un buen trabajo y estoy muy orgullosa de mi misma", dice él. Esa es la forma de pensar del optimista acerca de los sucesos buenos que usted consiguió por sus propios méritos.

Sea realista sin ser pesimista. El optimismo no quiere decir que usted no está consciente de los hechos concretos, dice el doctor Rakowski. "Sea realista acerca de lo que ha sucedido en su vida: 'sí, ha sido duro'; 'yo fui una víctima de las circunstancias en esa ocasión'; 'esa fue mi culpa'; 'esa no fue'; 'yo hice eso bien' ". Y entonces use el optimismo para resolver eso, a pesar de todo. Dígase: "con esfuerzo, iniciativa y buena suerte, yo todavía tengo cosas buenas que esperar", dice él.

Si del cielo le caen limones, aprenda cómo hacer limonada. Algunas personas se enfrentan a una serie de adversidades y todavía se llaman optimistas, dice el doctor Rakowski. ¿Por qué? "Cuando usted es optimista, usted también cree: 'yo puedo sacar el mejor partido de lo que tengo' ", dice él. "Algunas veces necesita redefinir sus objetivos y dejar ir una expectativa inicial. Entonces, su objetivo básico todavía es sacar el mejor partido de lo que tiene."

Aléjese de sus creencias. Es esencial darse cuenta de que sus creencias son sólo eso, creencias, no hechos, dice el doctor Seligman. Si una rival envidiosa en el trabajo le dice a usted: "tú eres una administradora muy mala y nunca vas a llegar a nada en este negocio", usted sabe que debería ignorar sus insultos. ¿Pero qué pasa con las cosas maliciosas que nos decimos a nosotras mismas? ("No puedo reconciliar la libreta de cheques. Soy tan estúpida.") Estas pueden ser justamente tan infundadas como los insultos de envidia, pero solamente es una manera de pensar equivocada—un reflejo mental que usted no tiene que encontrar convincente. "Verifique la exactitud de sus creencias reflexivas y discuta con usted misma", dice él.

Cambie las consecuencias. Cuando usted se enfrenta a una situación difícil, suceden tres cosas. El doctor Seligman dice que estas cosas siguen este patrón: usted le responde a una *adversidad* con una *creencia*, la cual determina la *consecuencia*. Por ejemplo, supongamos que mañana usted empiece un programa de ejercicios por primera vez en su vida. Ya que es novata, seguro que se cansará fácilmente. Ese cansancio es la adversidad, y si usted responde a éste con una creencia optimista —"Bueno, con el tiempo seguro que me pondré en mejor forma"— la consecuencia es que se sentirá mejor, podrá continuar con los ejercicios y con el tiempo, estará en mejor forma. Pero si hubiera reaccionado ante esa adversidad con una creencia negativa —"Para que seguir con esto, me va a tomar una eternidad para ponerme en forma"—, esto hubiera producido la consecuencia igualmente negativa de que usted piense que está condenada a ser fofa y nunca hará más ejercicios.

Pare en seco los pensamientos negativos. Cuando usted está consciente de sus pensamientos negativos, puede aprender a detener el pensamiento pesimista. Cuando un pensamiento negativo persistente pasa repetidamente por su mente, intente técnicas como estas: dé una palmada fuerte sobre el escritorio y diga, en voz alta: "¡Alto!". O póngase una liga elástica alrededor de su muñeca y cada vez que tenga el pensamiento jálela y suéltela. (Esto le ayudará despabilarse). O escriba el pensamiento y separe un tiempo para después pensar en él. Estas técnicas pueden detener una racha de pesimismo antes de que empiece.

Haga el bien sin mirar a quién. Si circunstancias penosas la han hecho infeliz, hacer lo que pueda para ayudar a otros puede darle a usted un punto de vista más optimista, dice el doctor Rakowski. Ya sea que haga trabajo voluntario o simplemente ofrezca a una amiga escuchar sus problemas, usted puede encontrar una manera de dar, dice él. Hay una verdadera sensación de realización al dar que puede sacarla de su pena, dice él.

Pida ayuda para la depresión. "Si usted es una pesimista de verdad, las probabilidades son que está bastante deprimida", dice el doctor Peterson. "Hay una buena probabilidad de que si usted recibe una terapia para la depresión la hará sentirse más saludable y mejorará su vida." La terapia de conducta cognitiva, durante la cual usted aprende a desafiar las formas derrotistas de pensar, es particularmente útil para lograr que la depresión dé una vuelta, dice él. Las personas crónicamente infelices hacen un comentario negativo continuo sobre sus vidas de lo cual, a menudo, no están conscientes, dice él. Un terapeuta puede enseñarle maneras de distraerse cuando usted está en ese estado de ánimo. Estas técnicas no reducirán la frecuencia de los episodios de depresión que usted tenga, pero sí los hará más cortos, dice él. Y en algunos casos, una receta para medicamentos antidepresivos puede ayudar.

PERDÓN

Buena terapia para el cuerpo y el alma

Todas hemos sido víctimas de las injusticias de la vida. Por ejemplo, está el novio quien destroza su corazón. El jefe que la despide. El ladrón que le roba su bolso. Usted se enoja, y la mayoría de las veces, se repone.

Pero cuando usted no se puede deshacer del rencor, es posible que pierda más que la compostura. Su dolor e ira pueden atormentarla, echando a perder su productividad y desempeño en el trabajo, sus relaciones e incluso su felicidad. Si no tiene cuidado, puede causarse un daño serio.

"No hay duda que el aferrarse a agravios y a pensamientos implacables puede envejecerla", dice el doctor Gerald G. Jampolsky, fundador del Centro de Curación de la Actitud, en Tiburón, California, y autor de nueve libros sobre relaciones incluyendo *Love is Letting Go of Fear* (Amor es dejar ir el temor) y *Good-Bye to Guilt: Releasing Fear through Forgiveness* (Adiós a la culpa: liberando el temor a través del perdón). "Además de la depresión y la ansiedad que causa, también puede conducir a arrugas, enfermedad del corazón, depresión y una cantidad de otros problemas físicos que se llevan la vitalidad y el entusiasmo de su vida. La buena noticia es que cuando usted perdona puede empezar de nuevo, y algunas veces hasta invertir algo del daño hecho."

Usted no tiene que poner la otra mejilla

Pero para hacer eso, tiene que darse cuenta de lo que el perdón no es. No es volverse un felpudo para que la pisoteen, o poner la otra mejilla para que le den una cachetada. Usted no tiene que aparentar ser amable con la persona que causó su furia o aun dejar que la gente que la hizo enojar forme parte de su vida nuevamente.

"Perdonar no significa fingir que la situación no sucedió", dice Robert Enright, Ph.D., sicólogo educacional y profesor de desarrollo humano en la Universidad de Wisconsin-Madison. "Significa que usted está aceptando lo que sucedió, al tratar de aceptar al que la hirió y al reconocer su dolor, pero tomando la decisión de *no* permitir que eso destruya su vida."

El doctor Redford B. Williams, director del Centro de Investigación de Medicina de la Conducta y un profesor de siquiatría en el Centro Médico de la Universidad de Duke, en Durham, Carolina del Norte agrega: "No quiere decir que usted debe perdonar y olvidar. Está bien recordar; solamente que ello no debe controlar sus pensamientos. Una vez que usted abandona la idea de venganza, toma una decisión consciente de evitar pensar acerca de su dolor todo el tiempo. Y cuando usted hace eso, se sentirá mejor emocional y físicamente."

El riesgo de guardar rencor

En una investigación con S.T. Tina Huang, Ph.D., profesor asociado de sicología en la Universidad Nacional Chung-Cheng, en Chia-i, Taiwan, el doctor Enright encontró que cuanto más tiempo las personas se aferran a sus resentimientos, más tiende a afectar sus lecturas de presión arterial. "Encontramos en las personas que estudiamos, que cuando recordaban historias de dolor profundo aquellas que no tenían esa efusión de perdón, mostraban aumentos notables en la presión arterial", dice el doctor Enright.

Pero aquellas otras que sí aprendieron a perdonar, mostraron un descenso en su presión arterial. Y eso es significativo, ya que los expertos creen que un rencor a largo plazo puede causar el mismo daño en el corazón de una mujer que el que causa en el de un hombre. Los hombres, por cierto, tienen índices más altos de enfermedad del corazón y, por coincidencia, tienen mayor dificultad para aprender a perdonar.

"Todo lo malo que el enojo sin resolver causa en los hombres, también lo causa en las mujeres", dice el doctor Williams, autor de *Anger Kills* (La ira mata). "Y lo 'malo' ocurre en las mujeres en la misma proporción que en los hombres. Pero el daño no es solamente a su corazón. Las personas propensas a características asociadas con una falta de voluntad para perdonar están en un riesgo más alto de muerte por todas las causas."

Incluyendo el cáncer. La investigación muestra que una tendencia a aferrarse al resentimiento y una incapacidad marcada para perdonar se han vinculado con un mayor riesgo de cáncer, dice el doctor O. Carl Simonton, director del Centro Simon de Orientación sobre Cáncer, en Pacific Palisades, California, y uno de los autores de *Getting Well Again* (Mejorarse de nuevo). Otros investigadores dicen que el estrés asociado con guardar un rencor también está vinculado con los índices altos de dolor de cabeza, dolor de espalda, úlceras y arrugas, e incluso resfriados (catarros), gripa y otras enfermedades infecciosas.

Las consecuencias emocionales que produce el dejar de perdonar también pueden envejecerla. "Encontramos que aquellos con la tolerancia al perdón más baja también tenían los niveles más bajos de autoestima y los más altos de ansiedad y depresión", dice el doctor Enright. "Pero cuando aprenden a perdonar, su autoestima aumenta mientras que su depresión y ansiedad disminuyen. Y yo me imagino que podría decir que las personas con autoestima alta tienden a cuidar más de ellas mismas, por lo tanto se sienten mejor", dice él. Es aun posible que usted se vea y actúe más joven.

Cómo fomentar el perdón

Así que, ¿cómo aprende usted a perdonar? Después de todo, ¿no es cómo mandar un mensaje que usted ya se repuso de su dolor o, aun, que está aprobando la conducta? ¿No está diciendo al perdonar que usted es una imbécil?

"No, si usted se da cuenta de que hay una diferencia entre el perdón y la reconciliación", dice el doctor Enright. "Digamos que cuando estaba creciendo, uno de sus padres estaba un poco distanciado de usted emocionalmente. Quizás su padre estaba trabajando todo el tiempo o no pasaba mucho tiempo con usted. Con el perdón, usted trata de comprender la situación desde el punto de vista de su padre: quizás él trabajaba tan duro para ser un buen proveedor. En el perdón, *usted* hace lo que puede para fomentar esa relación. En la reconciliación, ustedes, *ambos*, tratan de construir esa relación. Incluso, usted puede no hablar de sus sentimientos sino que en su lugar trata de reparar la relación y construir ahora de ahí en más."

Y afortunadamente, ambos se vuelven más fáciles a medida que maduramos. "En un estudio, los estudiantes universitarios en particular tenían menos probabilidades de perdonar que sus padres y sufrían de más ansiedad relativa a su problema que sus padres", dice el doctor Enright. En la edad adulta, estadísticamente estamos más dispuestas a perdonar. Los expertos dicen que si usted ahora practica a perdonar independientemente de su edad, podría mantener su salud y punto de vista juvenil hasta bien entrada en sus años dorados. Y aquí está cómo.

Piense en hoy. Los niños viven el presente, no viven en el pasado ni se preocupan del futuro. Y eso es un buen consejo para las mujeres que están tratando de enfrentarse con su dolor. "Cuando usted tiene cuatro años de edad y un amigo le quita su juguete usted jura que va a odiar a ese niño para siempre y nunca volverá a jugar con él. Sin embargo, diez minutos más tarde, están jugando juntos como si nada hubiera pasado", dice el doctor Jampolsky.

"Es importante tener a la tranquilidad de espíritu como nuestra única meta y reconocer que obstinarse con el enojo realmente no aporta paz", dice el doctor Jampolsky. "Las personas que se sienten menos preocupadas por la edad son aquellas que se encuentran en sus décadas de los 80 y los 90 años de edad pasando por lo que yo llamo amnesia celestial; viven el presente."

Escoja ser feliz, no tener la razón. Es importante preguntarnos si queremos ser felices o tener la razón, y es importante no hacer que otros estén equivocados y nosotras en lo cierto. "El primer paso para el perdón es nuestra buena disposición a perdonar", dice el doctor Jampolsky. "Cuando nosotras reconocemos que aferrarnos a pensamientos implacables es realmente estar decidida a sufrir, es más fácil sentir el deseo de perdonar, dejar pasar y cicatrizar el pasado. Cuando nosotras perdonamos, la otra persona no tiene que cambiar en lo absoluto. Es sólo una cuestión de cambiar nuestra forma de pensar y actitud. Perdonar no significa tener que estar de acuerdo con la conducta", dice él.

Guárdelo para usted. ¿Se avergüenza usted o se siente tonta diciendo "te perdono"? Entonces guárdeselo para usted. No tiene que ofrecer perdón directamente a las personas que la han herido, dice Sidney B. Simon, Ed.D., un consejero y profesor emérito de educación sicológica en la Universidad de Massachusetts-Amherts, quien con su esposa, Suzanne Simon, escribió un libro llamado *Forgiveness: How to Make Peace with Your Past and Get On with Your Life* (Perdón: cómo estar en paz con su pasado y continuar con su vida). Usted puede simplemente tratar de ver las cosas desde la perspectiva de ellos.

Pregúntese qué es lo que realmente la molesta. Algunas veces el origen de su resentimiento puede estar en la profundidad de su fuente emocional, escondida aun de usted —hasta que se rompe las pantimedias con el filo de una mesa y la bomba estalla. "Cuando nos ponemos tensas acerca de las cosas pequeñas que pasan diariamente, realmente nos sentimos molestas acerca de algo más profundo que posiblemente nunca hemos perdonado", dice el doctor Simon. Así que pregúntese cuál es la raíz de su ira y trate de abordarla. Si no puede hacer eso por sí sola, probablemente una terapeuta puede ayudarla.

No sea una víctima otra vez. A menudo el resentimiento resulta a veces de haber sido una víctima —de un crimen, corazón destrozado o alguna otra situación donde usted se sintió indefensa. Muchas veces la incapacidad de perdonarnos proviene del sentimiento de que no hicimos lo suficiente para evitar el terrible hecho. Pero al hacer algo después del suceso, muchas mujeres encuentran más fácil perdonarse. Tome medidas con respecto al tratamiento injusto: si su mecánico de carros la trata en forma condescendiente, dígale que no lo haga o va a perder el negocio que usted le trae. Si su esposo le está siendo infiel, hágale saber cómo se siente. Si ha sido víctima de un crimen, entable una acusación.

Póngalo por escrito. Probablemente usted siente ira y resentimiento pero no sabe por qué. O, a lo mejor sí sabe por qué pero no puede hacerse a la idea de perdonar al canalla. De cualquier manera, póngalo por escrito, dice James Pennebaker, Ph.D., profesor de sicología en la Universidad Metodista del Sur, en Dallas y autor de *Opening Up: the Healing Power of Confiding in Others* (Abriéndose: el poder curativo de confiar en otros). Simplemente escriba sus sentimientos —*cómo* se siente en lugar de sólo informar que se siente mal. Al hacer esto diariamente, por cerca de 20 minutos al día, llevando un diario de "lamentos" puede ayudarle a desahogar sus sentimientos mientras que enfoca su resentimiento, por lo tanto será más capaz de perdonar.

RELAJAMIENTO

El secreto natural de la juventud

En sus sueños, usted está recostada en una silla reclinable en una playa tranquila y agradable junto a un mar sereno color turquesa. En la realidad, no puede recordar cuándo fue la última vez que estuvo en la playa o que simplemente tuvo un momento en que no necesitaba ir a algún lado o hacer algo.

Pero el relajamiento es algo de lo que usted no se puede privar hasta sus próximas vacaciones, cuando quiera que estas vayan a ser. De hecho, tomar unos cuantos minutos cada día para relajarse y dejar que las tensiones de la vida pasen de largo no es un lujo; es una necesidad si usted quiere permanecer vigorosa, productiva y saludable.

"Hay tres cosas principales que usted puede hacer para prolongar su vida. Una es hacer ejercicio, otra es mantener una nutrición correcta y la última es relajarse. El relajamiento definitivamente puede ayudarla a envejecer mejor. Es importante para prevenir una amplia variedad de trastornos y para aumentar su efectividad y eficiencia en la vida", dice Frank J. McGuigan, Ph.D., director del Instituto de Manejo de Estrés en la Universidad Internacional de los Estados Unidos, en San Diego. "Yo no creo que haya duda alguna de que el relajamiento puede tener un efecto positivo en las fobias, la depresión, la ansiedad, la presión arterial alta, las úlceras, la colitis, los dolores de cabeza y el dolor en la parte baja de la espalda."

Un requisito para relajarse

Para muchas de nosotras, relajarse significa ir de compras, hablar con una amiga o ver nuestra telenovela favorita.

Pero aunque estas actividades pueden aliviar el estrés, también pueden provocar competencia y frustración, dos cosas que en realidad hacen más difícil relajarse, dice Richard Friedman, Ph.D., profesor asociado de sicología en la Universidad Estatal de Nueva York, en Stony Brook.

"Sabemos a través de los experimentos conducidos cuidadosamente que la mayoría de las personas realmente no entran en un estado fisiológico relajado cuando están haciendo cosas que por lo general la sociedad considera relajantes, como leer un periódico, practicar algún deporte o ver televisión", dice el doctor Friedman. "La forma verdadera de entrar en un estado fisiológico relajado es esencialmente dejar que su mente se ponga en punto neutral."

Poniendo a su mente en neutral la libera momentáneamente, por lo tanto no está juzgando a nada o reflexionando sobre decisiones importantes. Por unos cuantos segundos o minutos, usted no está pensando en lo que hubiera podido hacer ayer o lo que podría pasar mañana. El tomar varias de estas paradas de descanso mental cada día reduce la ansiedad y la ayuda a deshacerse del estrés y la tensión, dice el doctor Friedman. Este estado fisiológico, llamado la reacción al relajamiento, ha mostrado disminuir el ritmo del corazón, el metabolismo, la presión arterial y el ritmo de respiración, hacer más lentas las ondas del cerebro y provocar sensaciones de paz y tranquilidad, dice el doctor Herbert Benson, profesor asociado de medicina en la Escuela Médica de Harvard, jefe de la División de Medicina de la Conducta, en el Hospital Deaconess de Nueva Inglaterra, ambos en Boston, y autor de *The Relaxation Response* (La reacción al relajamiento).

Algunas veces el relajamiento o un sentimiento de alivio y bienestar surgen naturalmente, como por ejemplo después de una carrera larga y agradable o una conversación íntima con una buena amiga cercana. Pero si alguna vez alguien le ha dicho que se "relaje" cuando estaba estresada, además de hacerla sentir más frustrada o molesta, usted sabe lo difícil que es permitirse conscientemente recuperar una sensación de estabilidad y calma.

"Para relajarse usted realmente no debe esforzarse demasiado. Esto es similar a tratar de dormirse. A menudo el esfuerzo involucrado en tratar de dormirse probablemente la va a tener despierta toda la noche", dice Saki Santorelli, Ed.D., director asociado de la Clínica de Reducción de Estrés en el Centro Médico de la Universidad de Massachusetts, en Worcester.

Para realmente relajarse, dice el doctor Santorelli, usted en efecto necesita concentrarse o enfocar su atención en su respiración o alguna otra sensación que le permita a su mente colocarse en una sensación inherente de quietud. Hay muchas maneras de relajarse, pero antes de que hablemos de estas, vamos a averiguar un poco más acerca de los beneficios físicos y sicológicos del relajamiento.

El relajamiento y la salud

Cuando está atascada en el tráfico, luchando para cumplir con un plazo o enfrentándose a cualquier otra situación estresante, sus músculos se tensan, usted respira más rápida y profundamente, su corazón late más rápidamente, los vasos sanguíneos se contraen y la presión arterial se eleva, el tracto digestivo se cierra y el sudor aumenta. Al pasar el tiempo, el estrés constante eleva la presión arterial, los recuentos totales del colesterol y de las plaquetas en la sangre, todo esto puede conducir a la arteriosclerosis (el endurecimiento de las arterias) y los ataques al corazón. Agregue a esto los otros riesgos del estilo de vida moderno, tales como una dieta alta en grasa y muy poco ejercicio, y usted es una bomba a punto de estallar.

En un estudio de monos, cuyos sistemas cardiovasculares son similares a los nuestros, los investigadores en la Escuela de Medicina Bowman Gray, de la Universidad de Wake Forest, en Winston-Salem, Carolina del Norte, encontraron que el estrés emocional (causado por la interrupción de los vínculos sociales de los animales) aumentó significativamente las obstrucciones coronarias. Y estas obstrucciones ocurrieron a pesar de la dieta o los niveles de colesterol en la sangre, dos de los factores de riesgo más importantes para la enfermedad del corazón. Cuando a los monos se les alimentó con una dieta típica alta en grasa, el estrés emocional magnificó el proceso de la arteriosclerosis 30 veces.

El estrés también está vinculado con las úlceras y la colitis y puede provocar dolores de espalda, dolores de cabeza, dolores de piernas, fatiga crónica, depresión, ansiedad e insomnio. También puede agravar la artritis y la diabetes, dice el doctor McGuigan.

De hecho, ocho de diez personas examinadas por los doctores de cuidado primario tienen síntomas relacionados con el estrés, dice el doctor Robert S. Eliot, director del Instituto de Medicina de Estrés, en Jackson Hole, Wyoming, y autor de From *Stress to Strength: How to Lighten Your Load and Save Your Life* (Del estrés a la fortaleza: cómo aliviar su carga y salvar su vida).

Afortunadamente, el practicar las técnicas de relajamiento puede aliviar o prevenir casi todos los efectos dañinos del estrés crónico, dice el doctor Benson.

El entrenamiento para relajamiento, por ejemplo, es un elemento esencial en un programa exitoso para abrir las arterias tapadas y revertir la enfermedad del corazón sin cirugía, aplicado por primera vez por el doctor Dean Ornish, presidente y director del Instituto de Investigación de Medicina Preventiva, en Sausalito, California. Aunque el doctor Ornish cree que todos los componentes de su programa son importantes —incluyendo el ejercicio regular y una dieta vegetariana casi libre de grasa— él dice que el entrenamiento de relajamiento es probablemente uno de sus componentes más poderosos.

"Hemos mostrado, con el uso de escáners *PET* (por sus siglas en inglés) y angiogramas, que las personas quienes practican alguna forma de relajamiento como yoga o meditación y quienes se reúnen regularmente con un grupo de apoyo experimentan un grado de cambio mayor en la dirección contraria a las enfermedades del corazón que si estos sólo atacaran el problema a nivel físico, digamos nada más con una dieta o drogas para bajar el colesterol", dice el doctor Ornish. Un escán PET es una *positron emission tomography* (tomografía con emisión de positrón), una técnica de imágenes tridimensionales que mide el flujo de la sangre al corazón.

Los estudios realizados por el doctor Benson y otros investigadores también han mostrado consistentemente que las técnicas de relajamiento alivian significativamente la presión arterial alta, otro factor de riesgo para la enfermedad del corazón.

Además, las técnicas de relajamiento pueden aliviar hasta los síntomas más severos del síndrome premenstrual (o *PMS*, por sus siglas en inglés), según los investigadores de la Escuela Médica de Harvard. En un estudio de cinco meses a 46 mujeres, los investigadores encontraron, que las mujeres que meditaban por 15 a 20 minutos dos veces al día redujeron sus síntomas de PMS en un 58 por ciento. Eso es más del doble de la mejoría percibida por mujeres que leían dos veces al día y casi 3 veces y media mejor que las mujeres que simplemente llevaban un diario de sus síntomas.

El relajamiento también puede hacer que los dolores de la parte baja de la espalda y de la cabeza hagan un corto. El relajamiento de los músculos, por ejemplo, ayudó a 21 personas cuyos fuertes dolores de cabeza por tensión crónica no fueron aliviados con las drogas, a reducir el número y la intensidad de sus dolores de cabeza en un 42 por ciento, según los investigadores del Centro para Trastornos de Estrés y Ansiedad, en la Universidad Estatal de Nueva York, en Albany. Otro grupo de personas quienes simplemente siguieron con atención la actividad de sus dolores de cabeza no mostraron ninguna mejoría en absoluto.

Fundamentos del relajamiento

Usted probablemente experimentó por primera vez las sensaciones de luchar o huir, las dos reacciones básicas al estrés, en su juventud—especialmente si la pescaron usando el vestido favorito de su hermana sin su permiso. Pero el doctor Eliot sugiere que estaríamos mejor si aprendiéramos otro enfoque.

"Si usted no puede luchar y no puede huir, entonces déjese llevar por la corriente", dice él.

Aunque aprender a estar más relajada y calmada requiere de tiempo y atención, sí se puede hacer. "Yo veo el relajamiento como estar cómodo dentro de su propia piel", dice el doctor Santorelli. "A veces eso es difícil para todos nosotros, pero es posible empezar a cultivar esa habilidad a cualquier edad."

Aquí hay algunas prácticas fundamentales para ayudarle a calmase.

Despachurre los cigarrillos. "Nuestros estudios muestran que fumar causa que los vasos sanguíneos se cierren y restrinjan el flujo de sangre", dice el doctor Eliot. "Eso es como tratar de conducir mientras que aprieta el pedal del freno con el pie. Si hay una sola cosa que las personas pueden hacer para sentirse menos estresadas y más relajadas, esta es librarse del hábito."

Quítese unos kilos. "Es difícil sentirse relajada si está cargando peso de más por todas partes", dice el doctor Eliot. "Su ropa no se siente cómoda y la imagen de su cuerpo sufre." Tener sobrepeso también contribuye a la presión arterial alta, la enfermedad del corazón y la diabetes. Pregunte a su doctor si perder peso podría ayudarla.

Cálmese con los carbohidratos. "Parece que la proteína aumenta los niveles de energía y la mantiene alerta", dice el doctor Eliot. "Por lo tanto si come una hamburguesa tarde a la noche, usted probablemente seguirá pensando en la junta de ventas de ayer hasta el amanecer." Los carbohidratos, por otro lado, provocan la emisión de las hormonas que la van a relajar. Así que si usted quiere relajarse por la noche, coma un plato de espaguetis, frijoles (habichuelas) asados u otros carbohidratos complejos en la cena.

Apúntelos. Más de una docena de estudios han mostrado que si usted escribe acerca de sus problemas puede aliviar el estrés, mejorar su inmunidad, hacer menos visitas al doctor y tener una perspectiva más optimista de la vida, dice James Pennebaker, Ph.D., profesor de sicología en la Universidad Metodista del Sur, en Dallas. Cada día pase 20 minutos todos los días escribiendo acerca de sus pensamientos y sentimientos más profundos, sugiere el doctor Pennebaker. No se preocupe acerca de la gramática y el estilo; simplemente escriba cómo se siente acerca de las cosas que realmente la molestan. Entonces, cuando haya terminado, tire el papel a la basura. Usted puede sentir una sensación de alivio cuando haya terminado.

Ponga al tiempo a su favor. "Después de cada vez que mira el reloj durante el día, respire profundamente mientras que conscientemente levanta y baja los hombros o baja la mandíbula", dice el doctor Santorelli. "Eso probablemente le llevará diez segundos y servirá como un recordatorio de que usted puede estar tranquila mientras lleva a cabo su rutina diaria."

Relájese riéndose. El humor es una técnica potente de relajamiento, dice el doctor Eliot. La risa dispara endorfinas, químicos en el cerebro que producen los sentimientos de euforia. También restringe la producción de cortisol, una hormona emitida cuando usted está bajo estrés que indirectamente eleva la presión arterial al causar que el cuerpo retenga sal. Así que ríase con una amiga o mantenga a la mano un archivo de anécdotas humorosas y dibujos en un cajón que usted pueda sacar rápidamente.

Haga tiempo para los demás. "Tómese un momento para practicar la amabilidad básica", dice el doctor Santorelli. "Sonría y salude a una compañera de trabajo, juegue con una mascota o hable con una buena amiga cercana. Si lo hace, podría sentirse mejor y más relajada y posiblemente ser más productiva."

Duerma a pata ancha. Obtenga suficiente sueño ininterrumpido, aconseja el doctor Eliot. Si usted duerme menos de lo que necesita, podría despertar sintiéndose tensa e incapaz de enfrentarse a las complicaciones básicas de la vida. Trate de conseguir por lo menos de seis a ocho horas de sueño todas las noches. Evite el alcohol o las píldoras para dormir. Aunque estos pueden ayudarla a dormirse, también pueden interferir con sus patrones naturales de sueño y de hecho causarle tener una noche menos descansada, dice el doctor Eliot.

Tips para tranquilizarse

Bien. Usted no fuma, se ríe bastante, duerme bien y hace todas las demás cosas mencionadas en la sección anterior. No obstante, todavía le cuesta trabajo relajarse. Bueno, tranquila —hay muchos métodos disponibles para la estabilidad y el desarrollo de la calma. No hay un método único que sea apropiado para todos. La clave es encontrar uno con el cual usted se sienta cómoda. "Yo siento que es importante separar un poco de tiempo cada día para practicar estos métodos y después incorporarlos en su vida cotidiana. A menudo estos pueden ser tan discretos que la mayoría de las personas no sabrán que usted está haciendo algo especial", dice el doctor Santorelli. Aquí hay algunas ideas.

Hágale caso. Prestar atención a su propia respiración es una forma sencilla de meditación que puede ser muy relajante, dice el doctor Santorelli. Siéntese en una silla cómoda o en el piso para que su espalda, cuello y cabeza estén derechos pero no rígidos. Exhalando profundamente, permita que la inhalación ocurra naturalmente. Simplemente preste atención a la elevación y caída ligera de su abdomen, el movimiento de sus costillas o la sensación de su respiración al pasar a través de sus fosas nasales. No hay necesidad de tratar de "relajarse". Enfoque su mente sólo en la respiración. Si su mente empieza a vagar, condúzcala despacio para que se enfoque nuevamente en su respiración.

Como una alternativa, acuéstese en el piso, ponga un libro sobre su abdomen y respire varias veces en forma lenta y profunda, sugiere el doctor Eliot. Concéntrese en el libro moviéndose para arriba y para abajo sobre su barriga. Al inhalar, piense dentro de sí misma "mente fresca, clara". Entonces, al exhalar, piense "cuerpo calmado, relajado."

Concéntrese en la comida. Otra forma de cultivar la consciencia de momento a momento es al enfocar su atención en un alimento, dice el doctor Santorelli. Tome una tajada sencilla de naranja o manzana, o una almendra o una pasa o cualquier otro alimento que quiera. Mírelo cuidadosamente. Pase sus dedos por la superficie. Concentre la mente en su color, textura o fragancia. Luego, después de unos minutos, decida conscientemente darle una pequeña mordida. Mastíquela lentamente, poniendo atención en su sabor y lo que pasa con esta en su boca. Sienta como su lengua la rodea. Entonces lenta y conscientemente tráguesela.

Como una alternativa, trate de concentrarse intensamente en una actividad diaria como ducharse o lavar los platos. "Algunas personas dicen que se sienten mucho más cómodas después de practicarlo de esta manera", dice el doctor Santorelli.

Escale una montaña mentalmente. Las visualizaciones y las imágenes pueden alentar el bienestar y el desarrollo de la calma, dice el doctor Santorelli. Con los ojos cerrados, una vez mas tome consciencia de su respiración y recuerde una montaña favorita en su vida. Puede ser una que usted haya escalado o que anhela visitar. Permita que su cuerpo se vuelva el fundamento sólido, los lados inclinados y la cima. Siéntase usted estable, sólida, cimentada. Al aumentar su sensación de estabilidad y firmeza, permita que el clima varíe: algunos días la montaña estará bañada por la luz del sol, otros días por la lluvia, la nieve, el aguanieve o el granizo. Aunque el clima cambia, note que la montaña permanece firme y solemne. "Esta imagen la ayuda a darse cuenta de que se puede sentir estable y segura y puede soportar cualquier tormenta que la vida le depare, como verse atascada en un embotellamiento de tráfico, enfrentarse a un plazo o vivir con la muerte de un ser querido" dice el doctor Santorelli.

¡Muévalo! El ejercicio dispara endorfinas, pero ejercitar la mente y el cuerpo simultáneamente podría producir aún mejores resultados, según los investigadores en el Centro Médico de la Universidad de Massachusetts, en Worcester. Ellos les pidieron a 40 personas sedentarias que empezaran a caminar 35 a 40 minutos cada día, tres veces a la semana mientras escuchaban cintas de relajación. Las cintas guiaron a los caminantes a través de la meditación que los ayudó a seguir el ritmo de "uno-dos" con sus pasos. Los investigadores concluyeron que esta rutina provocó más sensaciones de euforia y redujo más la ansiedad en comparación con un grupo similar que hizo ejercicio en la misma intensidad pero no escuchó las cintas.

"Si usted enfoca su mente en un ritmo invariable y repetitivo como el ejercicio, la mente tiende a quedarse en blanco. Esa condición es la que usted está buscando", dice el doctor Friedman. "Le da al cerebro la oportunidad de restaurarse y calmarse."

Para intentar esto, escoja un ejercicio (tal como caminar, correr, nadar, subir escaleras o saltar la cuerda) que tenga un ritmo natural. Enfoque su atención en ese ritmo, hasta el punto de repetir las palabras "uno, dos" en su cabeza en cadencia con el ejercicio. Trate de mantenerse en ese ritmo. Al igual que con la respiración u otro tipo de meditación, su mente puede empezar a vagar después de un par de minutos. Si eso pasa, vuelva a enfocar su atención en los movimientos repetitivos del ejercicio, dice el doctor Benson.

Trate de hacer esto 20 minutos al día, tres veces por semana, siguiere el doctor Benson.

Muestre sus músculos. Hay cerca de 1.030 músculos esqueléticos en el cuerpo. Cuando usted se siente estresada, estos músculos se contraen naturalmente y crean tensión, dice el doctor McGuigan. Una forma de contrarrestar eso es el relajamiento progresivo. Al flexionar y descansar los músculos sistemáticamente, el relajamiento progresivo puede sacudir esa tensión fuera de su cuerpo.

"Es una buena técnica para los principiantes porque es práctica y no depende de la imaginación", dice Martha Davis, Ph.D., una sicóloga en el Centro Médico Kaiser Permanente, en Santa Clara, California, y coautora de *The Relaxation and Stress Reduction Workbook* (El libro de trabajo para el relajamiento y la reducción del estrés). "Funciona porque exagera la tensión en el músculo para que usted se vuelva más consciente de cómo se siente la tensión. En segundo término, usted fatiga al músculo para que cuando lo suelte, el músculo esté más que listo para relajarse", dice ella.

Aunque hay muchas variaciones, la doctora Davis sugiere este enfoque: haga un puño con su mano derecha tan apretado como pueda. Manténgalo apretado por cerca de diez segundos y entonces afloje. Sienta la flojedad en su mano derecha y note cuánto más relajado se siente ahora que cuando la tenía apretada. Haga lo mismo con la mano izquierda, después haga los dos puños al mismo tiempo. Flexione los codos y tense los brazos. Afloje y deje que los brazos cuelguen a los lados. Continúe este proceso al tensar y relajar sus hombros y cuello, arrugar y después descansar su frente y entrecejo. Luego, cierre los ojos y apriete la mandíbula antes de pasar a tensar y después relajar su estómago, parte baja de la espalda, muslos, asentaderas, pantorrillas y pies. Debería tomar cerca de diez minutos para completar toda la secuencia. Trate de hacer estos ejercicios dos veces al día.

Estírelos también. A diferencia del relajamiento progresivo, el cual contrae los músculos, el estiramiento suave permite a los músculos estirarse y relajarse. Eso es mejor para algunas personas, especialmente aquellas con dolor crónico muscular, dice Charles Carlson, Ph.D., profesor de sicología en la Universidad de Kentucky, en Lexington.

"Si usted tensa un músculo que ya le duele, lo más probable es que se ocasione más dolor. Eso no le ayuda a usted a relajarse", dice el doctor Carlson. "El estiramiento suave hace dos cosas. Primero, si usted estira suavemente un músculo y lo descansa, por lo general se relajará. Pero, segundo, cuando usted enfoca su atención en el estiramiento, también ayuda a la mente a descansar. El estiramiento de los músculos siempre debería hacerse despacio y sin dolor. No debería haber estiramiento de más o rebote de los músculos."

Como un ejemplo del relajamiento basado en el estiramiento, empiece por empujar sus cejas hacia arriba usando los dedos índices y empujar las mejillas hacia abajo con los pulgares. (Mientras está haciendo cualquiera de estos ejercicios de estiramiento, note cómo se siente la tensión para que usted aprenda a controlar su tensión muscular, aconseja el doctor Carlson). Mantenga esa posición por unos diez segundos, entonces suelte y deje que los músculos alrededor de sus ojos se relajen. Después de un minuto de relajar sus músculos, deje colgar la cabeza lentamente hacia su hombro derecho por unos diez segundos, entonces lentamente deje colgar la cabeza hacia el hombro izquierdo por otros diez segundos.

A continuación, a la altura del pecho, coloque sus manos juntas como si estuviera rezando. Entonces, mantenga las puntas de los dedos y las palmas juntas, extienda los dedos como si estuviera creando un abanico. Mueva sus pulgares para abajo a lo largo de la línea media de su cuerpo hasta que sienta un estiramiento ligero en la parte baja de los brazos. Mantenga esta posición por diez segundos. Entonces descanse.

A continuación, entrelace los dedos y levante las manos sobre la cabeza. Enderece los codos y haga girar las palmas hacia afuera. Deje que sus brazos caigan sobre su cabeza hasta que sienta resistencia. Mantenga esta posición por diez segundos, entonces suelte rápidamente y deje que sus brazos descansen a sus lados por un minuto.

Haga estos ejercicios por lo menos una vez al día o cada vez que se sienta tensa.

RELIGIÓN Y ESPIRITUALIDAD

La fuerza de un alma eternamente joven

Cuando el espíritu susurra, todas oímos distintas cosas.

Muchas mujeres oyen el sonido de lo sagrado en un libro santo o un himno favorito. Otras encuentran la elevación de sus espíritus en la meditación. Algunas encuentran su espiritualidad en comunión con el mundo natural. Algunas, en una teología nueva que evita exclusivamente los términos masculinos. Las fuentes de nuestra fe y creencia —y las formas de manifestarlas— son tan variadas como nosotras mismas. Pero los beneficios son los mismos, dice Mark Gerzon, autor de *Coming Into Our Own: Understanding the Adult Metamorphosis* (Comprensión propia: entender la metamórfosis adulta).

Las expresiones de la espiritualidad privadas y públicas —desde meditar y orar hasta asistir a servicios religiosos— aumentan la realización emocional al mismo tiempo de que ayudan a aliviar el estrés y la depresión. También reducen su riesgo a la enfermedad del corazón y el cáncer. Los investigadores dicen que incluso pueden ayudar a evitar el alcoholismo, el uso de las drogas y el suicidio.

Lo más importante al obtener estos beneficios es experimentar su propia espiritualidad a su manera, dice Gerzon. "El aspecto clave acerca de la espiritualidad en la segunda mitad de la vida es que hemos vivido bastante y visto a bastante gente irse de este mundo como para sentir una urgencia", dice él. "Empezamos a escuchar a nuestras voces internas. Y cuando lo hacemos, es imprevisible saber adonde nos llevan. Nos pueden llevar de regreso a la iglesia de nuestra niñez, pero también pueden llevarnos a lugares nunca esperados", dice él.

"Por ello es necesario ampliar nuestro punto de vista respecto al significado de lo espiritual. Para algunas podría ser ocuparse de las flores en el jardín y para otras rezar Avemarías en la misa de la mañana", dice Gerzon.

Quizás su sentido de lo sagrado tiene más que ver con caminatas en la naturaleza o con relaciones afectuosas que participar públicamente en los ritos religiosos. Muchas personas encuentran sentido y fortaleza en tal espiritualidad privada, dice Gerzon.

Una forma de buscar el sentido del todo es a través de la meditación o la oración, las cuales han mostrado disminuir el ritmo del corazón y la presión arterial, y ayudarle a sobrellevar mejor el estrés.

El poder curativo de la comunidad

La mayoría de las conclusiones científicas acerca de la religión y la salud se han sacado de la religión organizada porque las organizaciones religiosas proporcionan a los investigadores grupos medibles de sujetos involucrados en conductas específicas, tales como asistir a las ceremonias religiosas o participar juntos en los servicios de la comunidad. Pero quizás hay algo acerca de la comunidad religiosa en sí —además de ser un sistema de creencia compartida— que la hace más saludable para usted.

Cuando usted se une a la vida social de una comunidad religiosa, se vuelve parte de una red humanitaria con la que puede contar en las situaciones difíciles, dice el doctor Dave Larson, profesor asociado adjunto de siquiatría en el Centro Médico de la Universidad de Duke, en Durham, Carolina del Norte, presidente del Instituto Nacional para Investigación del Cuidado de la Salud, en Rockville, Maryland y ex siquiatra sénior de investigación en la Oficina de los Institutos Nacionales de Salubridad de Medicina Alternativa.

Y las mujeres son especialmente efectivas para crear estas redes de amistad y apoyo, dice el doctor Larson, ya que han crecido valorando la comunicación, la educación y el trabajo en conjunto.

Otros investigadores también han reconocido los beneficios curativos de una comunidad espiritual. "Cuando las personas se enferman se visitan y traen comida entre sí, le avisan a los familiares y se llevan una a la otra al doctor", dice Lawrence Calhoun, Ph.D., un sicólogo en la Universidad de Carolina del Norte, en Charlotte. "Cuando usted es parte importante de una comunidad como esa, se puede suavizar el golpe de envejecer."

Desde hace años los expertos en salud saben que el estrés contribuye a muchos problemas físicos que incluyen la náusea, la diarrea, el estreñimiento, la presión arterial alta y las anormalidades en el ritmo del corazón.

Los estudios han mostrado que las creencias religiosas profundas son muy eficaces para curar el estrés, aun cuando usted mantenga esas creencias privadas. Pero los efectos curativos de la fe para el estrés son los más poderosos, dicen los expertos, cuando usted está involucrada regularmente en una comunidad religiosa.

La forma fácil de meditación

Para las mujeres ocupadas y estresadas, los momentos de tranquilidad y quietud son preciosos y raros. Pero hay una manera de elevar al máximo los beneficios de la oración y contemplación, dice Herbert Benson, profesor asociado de medicina en la Escuela Médica de Harvard, jefe de la División de Medicina de la Conducta, en el Hospital Deaconess de Nueva Inglaterra, ambos en Boston, y autor de *The Relaxation Response* (La reacción al relajamiento).

El doctor Benson condujo algunos de los primeros estudios científicos sobre los efectos de la oración y la fe en la reducción del estrés. Para ayudar a los pacientes a aprender a relajarse, él enseñó el método más sencillo de meditación: siéntese callada en una posición cómoda y repita una palabra o una frase en silencio mientras ignora pasivamente otros pensamientos.

Cuando a los pacientes se les ofreció que eligieran una palabra, sonido o frase para repetir, el 80 por ciento de ellos escogió una palabra u oración de su fe. Y eso llevó a un descubrimiento, dice el doctor Benson. Las personas que usaron palabras de su propia religión en lugar de palabras neutrales (como "uno" o "ten calma") se mantuvieron mejor en el programa. Y su salud mejoró como resultado de la "reacción al relajamiento", que se caracteriza por un ritmo reducido del corazón y sentimientos de tranquilidad.

Las palabras pueden variar, dice el doctor Benson, pero no los beneficios. "En todos los distintos contextos religiosos, parece haber un potencial similar para mejorar la salud", dice él. Aquí está cómo traer estos beneficios a su vida cada día.

Escoja una palabra o frase corta que sea fácil de pronunciar y suficientemente corta para decirla en silencio al exhalar. Cuando los pensamientos surjan, como seguramente sucederá, regrese despacio a la palabra en que se está enfocando. Practique esta clase de meditación por 20 minutos dos veces al día.

Los investigadores en la Universidad Ben Gurion del Negev y el Centro Médico Soroka, en Beersheba, Israel, estudiaron cómo 230 miembros de una comunidad religiosa en un kibutz se enfrentaron a los sucesos estresantes de la vida. Las personas dentro de la comunidad encontraron cómo su fe individual y sus habilidades para sobrellevar fueron reforzadas por el apoyo que la comunidad ofrecía. Y eso resultó en una recuperación más rápida del estrés, incluyendo el estrés asociado con envejecer.

Una vida más larga y completa

Otro estudio destaca la amplia gama de beneficios para la salud provenientes de asistir a los servicios religiosos y de la participación activa en la vida social de la congregación. Los sicólogos Stanislav Kasl, de la Universidad de Yale y Ellen Idler, de la Universidad de Rutgers estudiaron a 2.812 mujeres y hombres ancianos en New Haven, Connecticut. Ellos encontraron que los católicos, protestantes y judíos aparentemente religiosos tenían menos probabilidad de volverse médicamente incapacitados que aquellos que consideraban poco importante asistir a una iglesia o sinagoga. Estas personas también permanecieron físicamente más independientes al hacerse más viejos, debido mayormente a su entorno religioso público.

Hanukkah, Pascua, Navidad y otras fiestas religiosas pueden tener aún más significado para usted con el pasar de los años. El estudio de New Haven también encontró que las personas muy religiosas tenían menos probabilidad de morir durante los meses antes y después de las fiestas religiosas significativas. Pero una conclusión en particular puede inspirarla a desempeñar un papel más activo en las celebraciones importantes de su fe. Aunque los índices de muerte tanto para los hombres como para las mujeres judíos disminuyeron durante la Pascua judía, las mujeres estaban menos protegidas. Los investigadores creen que eso probablemente se debe a que las mujeres están excluidas de cualquier papel en los aspectos más importantes de los rituales de la Pascua judía.

La religión en su vida también puede ser una protección poderosa contra el cáncer. Eso puede ser porque algunos grupos de creyentes tales como los mormones y los testigos de Jehová alientan estilos saludables de vida, como comer una dieta vegetariana o evitar fumar. Los analistas del Centro para la Investigación de la Política de Salud de la Universidad de Florida, en Gainesville revisaron la información sobre los fallecimientos por cáncer en los Estados Unidos y encontraron que los condados con el mayor número de personas religiosas también tenían los índices más bajos de cáncer.

Aun las fes que no recomiendan hábitos dietéticos o de salud específicos de todas maneras tienen un efecto protector, los investigadores creen, simplemente porque fomentan la moderación, al advertir a sus miembros sobre los excesos nocivos de cualquier tipo.

A veces le llega al corazón

La espiritualidad ofrece una protección particularmente fuerte contra un asesino mayor: la enfermedad del corazón, dice el doctor Larson.

Un estudio a 85 mujeres y 454 hombres en Jerusalén encontró que las personas que se definen como "seculares" (no religiosas) tienen un mayor riesgo de enfermedad del corazón que aquellas que siguen el camino del judaísmo ortodoxo. Aún después de que los investigadores tomaron en cuenta sus hábitos de fumar y sus niveles de colesterol y de presión arterial, se mantuvo una asociación fuerte entre un riesgo menor de enfermedad del corazón y las prácticas religiosas para ambos sexos.

Aunque los investigadores no están seguros qué aspectos de la creencia son los responsables, especulan que el fuerte sistema de apoyo social de las comunidades tradicionales ortodoxas, como aquellos presentes en muchos otros tipos de congregaciones, desempeña un papel protector del corazón, probablemente al reducir el aislamiento y el estrés.

En otro estudio de la religión y del corazón, el doctor Larson y sus colegas estudiaron los datos sobre presión arterial en más de 400 hombres en el Condado de Evans, Georgia. Ellos encontraron que una creencia personal en Dios o asistir a los servicios religiosos (aun sin creer) tendían a disminuir la presión arterial, aunque las personas que asistían además de ser creyentes tenían las lecturas más bajas.

Sus beneficios emocionales

Una vida espiritual o religiosa activa no sólo mantiene muchas de las formas de estrés y enfermedad a raya, sino que también ayuda a protegerla a usted de las enfermedades mentales y emocionales.

El doctor Larson y su equipo de investigadores revisaron más de 200 estudios sobre los compromisos religiosos y la salud mental. Ellos encontraron que las personas religiosas tienen índices más bajos de depresión, alcoholismo, suicidio y uso de drogas que las personas menos religiosas. Las personas jóvenes que son religiosas se desempeñan mejor en la escuela y tienen menos probabilidad de ser delincuentes o sexualmente activas. Las personas casadas que asisten a la iglesia regularmente reportan una mayor felicidad matrimonial, están más satisfechas con sus vidas sexuales y experimentan índices más bajos de divorcio.

Los estudios también muestran que la fe religiosa está conectada directamente con una sensación de satisfacción superior con la vida en general y con una mayor capacidad para sobrellevar las situaciones estresantes y los problemas de la vida, dice el doctor Larson. Los investigadores examinaron las conductas específicas de "la vida real", como asistir a los servicios religiosos, en lugar de intentar medir las actitudes o creencias.

Tácticas para el desarrollo espiritual

Usted puede sentir un anhelo creciente de encontrar un sentido más profundo del significado en su vida. Aquí está cómo volverse a conectar con su lado espiritual.

Empiece por el principio. Antes de volver a comprometerse con la religión de su niñez o adoptar otra fe, examínela, dice Alan Berger, Ph.D., director de estudios judíos en el Departamento de Religión de la Universidad de Syracuse, en Nueva York. "Pregúntese '¿qué enseña mi religión?' ", dice él. "No sienta que tiene que aceptarla, pero sí sépala."

Vaya más allá de los 'no se debe hacer'. Si la religión parecer ser solamente una serie de reglas o 'tú no debes', dice el doctor Berger, "usted necesita reenfocar su punto de vista. Búsquese un mejor maestro, una nueva comunidad. Lea los textos usted misma o con un compañero y descubra los varios niveles de significado. Entienda que la vida es una experiencia fluida y dinámica con la cual la gente necesita ayuda. La religión es un intento de buscar el significado en un universo por lo demás caótico."

Acéptese a usted misma. "Está muy bien decir 'yo realmente no sé lo que soy espiritualmente' ", dice el Hermano Guerric Plante, un monje en la Abadía de Gethsemane, en New Haven, Connecticut. "La honestidad tiene todo que ver con el desarrollo espiritual." Cuando usted es sincera con usted misma respecto a cualquier confusión que experimenta, el camino se volverá más claro.

Busque con otros. Lea los anuncios de religión y grupos de apoyo en su periódico para encontrar un grupo u organización que pueda ofrecer ayuda en su búsqueda espiritual, dice el Hermano Plante. "La fe puede venir a través de otros, sus ejemplos, sus pláticas, su interés en los demás. La terapia de grupo, los servicios religiosos o aun los grupos de 12 pasos para la adicción pueden reavivar una vida espiritual si usted sinceramente la está buscando."

Medite o rece. Separe algo de tiempo de su programa para sentarse en contemplación callada y trate de ponerse en contacto con la calma interior que todos tenemos, dice Gerzon. "Si nosotros obtenemos significado y propósito en la vida solamente de las cosas que logramos, estamos en problema", dice él. Necesitamos encontrarlo también en nuestro existir, y la meditación es una buena forma de empezar a aprender cómo, simplemente, existir.

Amplíe su perspectiva. Algunas veces el sólo hecho de alentar a su sentido de la curiosidad y especulación acerca de la vida lo conducirá a usted a la verdad espiritual. Cuando reflexiona sobre las antiquísimas preguntas tales como "¿Por qué estoy aquí?" o "¿Cuál es el significado de la vida?" usted alienta a su perspicacia espiritual a desplegarse, dice Gerzon. "Es posible encontrar la dimensión espiritual en las respuestas, pero hay más probabilidad de que la encontremos en las preguntas mismas", dice él. "Cuando realmente estamos movidos por el espíritu de la vida, es porque estamos tocando lo que no sabemos y no lo que sabemos."

Vaya en contra de su naturaleza. Es más probable que usted crezca espiritualmente si busca actividades diferentes de las que suele hacer durante todo el día, dice John Buehrens, un ministro por más de 20 años y presidente de la Asociación Unitaria Universalista, en Boston. Si usted se pasa el día separada de los demás en una oficina corporativa, entonces, servir una comida a personas necesitadas podría ser justo lo que necesita. Pero si usted es una abogada en una clínica gratis o una trabajadora social, puede beneficiarse más de un grupo de discusión religioso, dice él.

¿Cuál es la disciplina espiritual de Buehrens? Ya que confiesa que es un intelectual que tiene "un cuerpo con forma de pera", él dice que "una de mis disciplinas espirituales es hacer más ejercicio regularmente. Ese es para mí realmente un tiempo de meditación y oración."

Preocúpese de los demás. Usted necesita salir de usted misma para sentirse espiritualmente saludable, dice Buehrens. "Esa es la razón por la cual la comunidad es tan importante para el crecimiento espiritual real, porque tenemos que salir de nuestro caparazón. Nunca encontraremos la paz a través de las líneas religiosas, raciales o étnicas a menos que hagamos eso." ¿Su consejo para los buscadores aislados? "Vaya a ayudar en un comedor de beneficencia, vaya a visitar un hogar de ancianos y en general, vaya a meter su cuchara", dice él.

Lleve un diario espiritual. Escribir en un diario acerca de sus preguntas espirituales, dudas, creencias y experiencias puede iluminar el significado y valor en su vida, dice Buehrens. "Puede encontrar que su subconsciente está tratando de llegar a usted con más métodos responsablemente creativos para mejorar la vida."

Pregunte sin tener temor. "Todas las tradiciones espirituales tratan de enseñar una conciencia mejorada de ser alguien, mayor vitalidad espiritual y compasión más profunda por otras personas", dice Buehrens. Pero cualquier comunidad espiritual que no respeta el preguntar o la importancia de su conciencia individual puede ser una comunidad poco saludable, dice él. ¿Su consejo? Siga su propia conciencia hacia el camino espiritual que es el correcto para usted.

SEXO

Parte integral de nuestro bienestar

Por años, usted y sus amigas se han preguntado acerca de la "luminosidad" que una mujer supuestamente adquiere después de tener buen sexo. ¿Pero, cuántas de ustedes realmente la han visto?

La próxima vez que usted se sienta bien después de tener sexo, levántese y mírese en el espejo: usted es bonita, segura de sí misma, vigorosa y viva, ¿lo ve? Realmente hay una luminosidad.

Usted sabe por qué se siente tan bien. Pero esa luminosidad es más que una sensación. Los científicos la atribuyen a las endorfinas, químicos que se secretan en el cerebro después de tener sexo. Estos químicos crean una sensación de euforia y alivian su estrés, dice la doctora Helen S. Kaplan, Ph.D., directora del Programa de Enseñanza de la Sexualidad Humana, en el Centro Médico Cornell del Hospital de Nueva York, en la Ciudad de Nueva York.

Los investigadores médicos dicen que las dosis regulares de sexo también pueden aliviar los achaques y dolores, estimular la creatividad, revolucionar su energía y hacer que se sienta joven.

"Cualquier cosa que la haga sentirse bien, viva y excitada físicamente la hará sentirse joven. Todas esas cosas están asociadas con el sexo", dice Lonnie Barbach, Ph.D., una terapeuta sexual y sicóloga en San Francisco y escritora del vídeo *Sex after Fifty* (El sexo después de los cincuenta). La intimidad también puede estimular su sistema inmune y protegerla contra las enfermedades, dice la doctora Kaplan.

Por ejemplo, el sexo ha ayudado a las mujeres a sobrellevar el dolor de las enfermedades crónicas tales como la artritis, dice el doctor Sanford Roth, un reumatólogo y director del Centro para la Artritis, en Phoenix. Las endorfinas alivian el dolor, pero el doctor Roth cree que el sexo también tiene un impacto sicológico vital. "Muchas veces, cuando los pacientes vienen a verme, el dolor no es el tema número uno. Ellos están más preocupados acerca de cómo la enfermedad está afectando la calidad de sus vidas, y la sexualidad es una parte importante de eso", dice el doctor Roth. "Por ello, mantener la función sexual ante la presencia de la enfermedad ayuda a las personas a sentirse mejor acerca de ellas mismas y sus vidas."

El sexo también podría poner fin al dolor que dio origen a la vieja excusa "esta noche no, querido, me duele la cabeza". Aunque el sexo no es una cura segura, los investigadores han encontrado que realmente puede ayudar a aliviar algunos dolores de cabeza. En un estudio pequeño, el 47 por ciento de las personas con migrañas dijeron que el sexo había aliviado su dolor, según el doctor George H. Sands, profesor asistente de neurología en la Escuela de Medicina Monte Sinaí, en la Ciudad de Nueva York. Una posible razón es que los orgasmos provocan un corto circuito en la actividad del sistema nervioso que es causante del dolor. (Por otro lado, a veces el sexo puede *causar* dolores de cabeza. Si eso sucede, discútalo con su doctor.)

El sexo puede ser para siempre

Usted probablemente fue estimulada sexualmente en el vientre antes de nacer, y puede permanecer sexualmente activa hasta que se muera, dice el doctor William Masters, del Instituto Masters y Johnson, en St. Louis. De hecho, siete de cada diez mujeres mayores de 70 años de edad quienes tienen compañeros, practican el sexo por lo menos una vez a la semana.

"Las relaciones sexuales son una función natural a lo largo de su vida si usted tiene un compañero interesante y se mantiene saludable. No va a desa- parecer", dice la doctora Kaplan. "Es anormal que el sexo desaparezca. La persona normal tiene relaciones sexuales hasta el fin de su vida."

El sexo también puede ser autoafirmante. "El sexo puede ayudarla a que se sienta más competente. Es una forma de conectarse con alguna otra persona. Puede ayudar a que se sienta en control de su propio destino", dice Marty Klein, Ph.D., un consejero matrimonial licenciado, terapeuta sexual en Palo Alto, California, y autor de *Ask Me Anything: A Sex Therapist Answers the Most Important Questions for the '90s* (Pregúnteme cualquier cosa: un terapeuta sexual contesta las preguntas más importantes para los años 90). "El sexo es un lugar donde usted puede ir sin encontrarse limitada por las reglas comunes de la vida."

"El sexo se hace más —no menos— importante a medida que enveje- cemos", dice la doctora Kaplan. "Es uno de los últimos procesos que se ven afectados por el envejecimiento. Primero se van la piel y la vista, luego usted adquiere artritis y enfermedad del corazón. Pero usted todavía puede tener relaciones sexuales. Es uno de los placeres perdurables de la vida."

Cómo hacer una buena relación aún mejor

Para las buenas relaciones sexuales, mantenga su cuerpo saludable al evitar los cigarrillos y los alimentos grasosos que pueden obstruir los vasos sanguíneos

Cómo elegir el mejor anticonceptivo para usted

Aunque ningún control de la natalidad tiene un éxito del 100 por ciento, un anticonceptivo puede ser una protección poderosa contra el embarazo y las enfermedades transmitidas sexualmente (o *STD*, por sus siglas en inglés) si se usa correctamente, dice el doctor Michael Brodman, profesor de obstetricia y ginecología en la Escuela de Medicina Monte Sinaí de la Universidad de la Ciudad de Nueva York.

Hay muchas clases de control de la natalidad disponibles para las mujeres que incluyen la píldora anticonceptiva, los dispositivos intrauterinos (o *IUDs*, por sus siglas en inglés), los diafragmas, los condones femeninos, las esponjas, los espermicidas, las inyecciones hormonales y una varilla conceptiva para implantarse quirúrgicamente que funciona por cinco años.

Escoger el método de control de la natalidad correcto para usted podría requerir el consejo de su doctor. Pero unas cuantas guías generales podrán ayudarla a hacer su elección, dice el doctor Brodman.

Primero, si está usando el método anticonceptivo para evitar las STD, use un anticonceptivo de barrera como un condón femenino, esponja o diafragma o haga que su compañero use un condón. Tanto con el diafragma como con el condón masculino se debe usar un espermicida que contenga *nonoxynol 9* porque éste es efectivo contra el virus que causa el SIDA.

Si está usando anticonceptivos para el control de la natalidad y usted no puede correr absolutamente ningún riesgo use la píldora anticonceptiva, un implante o inyecciones hormonales debido a que estos tienen los índices más altos de éxito, sugiere el doctor Brodman.

Si su elección es el condón masculino, debe usar espermicida ya que los condones son solamente un 80 por ciento efectivos en evitar el embarazo cuando se usan solos. También se deben usar los espermicidas con los diafragmas, ya que estos pueden moverse fuera de lugar durante el coito lo cual permitir que el semen entre en el útero, aumentando la posibilidad de embarazo.

y hacer la excitación y el orgasmo difíciles. Aquí hay algunos consejos para agregarle chispa a su vida sexual.

Estimule el esqueleto. Los ejercicios aeróbicos tres veces por semana, 20 a 30 minutos por sesión, pueden mejorar su apetito y desempeño sexuales, dice el

Lo que quieren de nosotras

Usted quiere platicar, él quiere tener sexo. Usted quiere acurrucarse, él quiere tener sexo. Usted quiere un compromiso más serio, él dice ay, ay, ay, me tengo que ir. ¿Perpleja? Usted no es la única.

"Muchas veces, los hombres son más capaces de separar las relaciones sexuales de las relaciones emocionales. A diferencia de la mayoría de las mujeres, ellos pueden tener relaciones puramente físicas", dice Lonnie Barbach, Ph.D., una terapeuta sexual y sicóloga en San Francisco. "Muchos hombres tienen dificultad para conseguir la intimidad. El sexo es para ellos una forma de hacerlo. Así que a menudo empiezan sus relaciones con el sexo y agregan los sentimientos después."

"Los hombres son tóxicos a demasiada proximidad", asiente el doctor Anthony Pietropinto, un siquiatra en la Ciudad de Nueva York y autor de *Not Tonight Dear: How to Reawaken Your Sexual Desire* (Esta noche no, querido: cómo volver a despertar su deseo sexual). "A muchos hombres no les gustan las mujeres que quieren que ellos hablen acerca de sus emociones más profundas."

A los hombres les gusta la novedad en su vida sexual, dice el doctor Pietropinto. Tienen más probabilidad de sugerirle que use ropa provocativa o buscar lugares exóticos para tener relaciones sexuales.

Cuando ustedes hacen el amor, el hombre probablemente se preocupa más acerca de su desempeño que usted. "Una mujer quiere saber si al hombre le gusta estar cerca de ella y si la encuentra atractiva. El hombre está interesado en averiguar qué tal lo hizo", dice el doctor Pietropinto.

La parte positiva, muchas de estas características desaparecen cuando el hombre envejece y su apetito sexual declina. Después de los 45 años de edad, los hombres necesitan más estimulación sicológica y como resultado a menudo se vuelven más sensibles, cariñosos y receptivos a las necesidades emocionales de una mujer, dice la doctora Helen S. Kaplan, Ph.D., directora del Programa de Enseñanza de la Sexualidad Humana, en el Centro Médico Cornell del Hospital de Nueva York, en la Ciudad de Nueva York.

doctor Roger Crenshaw, un siquiatra y terapeuta sexual en práctica privada en la Jolla, California. Los investigadores en el Colegio Bentley, en Waltham, Massachusets, encontraron por ejemplo, que las mujeres en su década de los cuarenta años de edad que nadaban con regularidad tenían sexo cerca de siete

La opción del celibato

"El matrimonio tiene muchos dolores, pero el celibato no ofrece placeres", según expresó Samuel Johnson, un individuo ingenioso del siglo dieciocho. Pero esa declaración está muy lejos de dar en el blanco, dicen los expertos. Muchas parejas y más de unas cuantas mujeres solteras encuentran el celibato gratificante y de hecho dicen que refuerza sus relaciones y autoestima.

Aproximadamente uno en cada diez matrimonios se abstiene de las relaciones sexuales, según Michael S. Broder, Ph.D., un sicólogo clínico en Filadelfia y autor de *The Art of Staying Together* (El arte de permanecer juntos). Algunas personas se abstienen debido a las convicciones religiosas, los efectos secundarios de medicamentos o las enfermedades crónicas. Pero en realidad un número creciente de parejas se abstienen porque quieren reforzar su lazo de otras maneras.

Muchos solteros escogen la abstinencia en parte para protegerse del SIDA y otras enfermedades transmitidas sexualmente o incluso para terminar su maestría en administración de empresas, dice Shirley Zussman, Ed.D., una terapeuta sexual y de matrimonio y directora adjunta de la Association for Male Sexual Dysfunction (Asociación para la disfunción sexual masculina), en la Ciudad de Nueva York. Algunas mujeres solteras simplemente dicen que están esperando a alguien realmente especial.

"Una gran ventaja de escoger el celibato por algún período de su vida es que le da a usted la oportunidad de entender completamente el lugar del sexo en su vida o relaciones", dice Harrison Voigt, Ph.D., sicólogo clínico, terapeuta sexual y profesor del Instituto California de Estudios Integrales, en San Francisco. "Le ofrece a usted la oportunidad de ver qué tan bien realmente se puede relacionar con otros fuera del contexto sexual."

Aquí hay algunas guías para escoger el celibato.

• Dese cuenta de que va a continuar teniendo impulsos sexuales pero no tiene que hacer nada al respecto.

• Considere a el celibato como unas vacaciones —un tiempo para descansar o intentar nuevas experiencias. En lugar de pensar en eso como una privación, considérelo una opción. Véalo como una oportunidad para encontrar un significado más profundo en su vida.

• Recuerde, no tiene que ser para siempre. Usted puede dejar de ser célibe en el momento que quiera. Y cuando así sea, el sexo puede ser más excitante y gratificante que nunca.

veces por mes y lo disfrutaban más que sus colegas sedentarias, quienes solamente tenían sexo tres veces por mes. En otras palabras, las nadadoras eran tan sexualmente activas como las mujeres 10 a 20 años más jóvenes.

Hable al respecto. Hablar con su compañero ayuda para que ambos puedan explicar lo que cada uno quiere sexualmente. Si usted no le dice a él lo que realmente quiere, no espere que él la complazca, dice Shirley Zussman, Ed.D., una terapeuta sexual y de matrimonio y directora adjunta de la Asociación para la Disfunción Sexual Masculina, en la Ciudad de Nueva York. Evite decir cosas negativas como: "eso no se siente bien", o "tú sabes que eso no me gusta". En su lugar dígalo en forma positiva: "yo disfruto el tener relaciones sexuales contigo, pero tengo algunas ideas para hacerlo aún mejor."

Demuéstrele lo que le gusta. Aunque hablar ayuda, a menudo enseñar a su compañero lo que a usted le complace es igual de útil. Si él, por ejemplo, le está agarrando los senos y frotándola demasiado fuerte tome sus manos suavemente y muéstrele como usted prefiere que la acaricie, sugiere el doctor Klein.

Amplíe sus horizontes. "El coito se enfatiza demasiado como una actividad sexual", dice el doctor Klein. "La mayoría de las parejas se beneficiarían al ver las relaciones sexuales como una serie de experiencias más amplias." Por lo tanto tome el tiempo suficiente para besar, abrazar, acariciar, tomar de las manos, hablar o hacer otras actividades sexuales placenteras tales como masturbarse mutuamente que la hacen sentir cerca de su compañero, sugiere él.

Haga tiempo para la diversión. "Yo se que suena cómico, pero algunas parejas dicen que simplemente no tienen tiempo para el sexo", dice Carol Lassen, Ph.D., una sicóloga y profesora clínica de sicología en la Escuela de Medicina de la Universidad de Colorado, en Denver. "¿Por qué? Todas las otras cosas vienen primero. No pueden tener relaciones sexuales porque tienen que lavar la ropa o ver un partido de fútbol o simplemente dormir. Les queda muy poco tiempo para estar el uno con el otro."

En lugar de dejar que el sexo se pierda en la monotonía diaria, programe tiempo para éste, dice Michael Seiler, Ph.D., autor de *Inhibited Sexual Desire* (El deseo sexual inhibido) y director asistente del Instituto Phoenix, en Chicago. "Usted haría reservaciones en un restaurante elegante para las siete de la noche el sábado. ¿Por qué no decir que se reunirán en la recámara el martes a las nueve de la noche?", dice él. "¿Cómo sabe si se va a sentir con ganas? No lo sabe. Pero tampoco sabe si va tener hambre el sábado por la noche."

Deje sus complejos afuera. "Deje el trabajo, la religión y sus expectativas de desempeño fuera de la recámara", sugiere la doctora Barbach. "Simplemente entre a la recámara con su cuerpo y sus sentimientos. Concéntrese en la conexión emocional que usted tiene con su compañero y el placer que le espera a su cuerpo."

Manténgalo divertido. "¿Sabe usted cómo le llaman los esquimales al sexo? Hora de reírse", dice la doctora Zussman. "El sexo puede ser divertido, frívolo y relajante. Nuestra sociedad está muy lejos de eso. Pensamos que debemos tener sexo fantástico cada vez que lo hacemos." Olvídese del desempeño, dice la doctora Zussman. Concéntrese solamente en pasar un momento agradable con su

El significado de soñar con otro

Usted sueña que está desnuda en una fiesta elegante. Avergonzada, trata de esconderse detrás de su esposo, pero Antonio Banderas la ve desde el otro lado del cuarto, camina hacia usted y la invita a bailar.

¿Qué significa esto? Nada, excepto que usted es una mujer normal.

"Para las mujeres, los sueños sexuales por lo general son románticos y, bastante a menudo, acerca de un hombre que conocen o alguien como un novio, estrella de cine o músico de *rock* quien es emocionalmente significativo para ella", dice Robert Van de Castle, Ph.D., profesor emérito de medicina de la conducta en el Centro Médico de la Universidad de Virginia y ex presidente de la Asociación para el estudio de los sueños.

Las mujeres con sueños sexuales probablemente tienen mejores vidas sexuales que aquellas que no sueñan mucho acerca del sexo, dice él. Eso es porque las mujeres que se sienten cómodas con su sexualidad en el mundo real tienen más probabilidades de soñar acerca de esto.

Si usted tiene un problema sexual, puede aparecer en sus sueños. "Si una mujer no puede alcanzar el orgasmo, puede soñar que está hecha de nieve, lo cual simboliza que se siente fría y frígida", dice el doctor Van De Castle.

Pero algunos sueños sexuales pueden no ser en lo absoluto acerca de las relaciones sexuales, dice Gayle Delaney, Ph.D., una sicóloga en San Francisco y autora de *Sexual Dreams* (Sueños sexuales). "Por ejemplo, si usted sueña acerca de tener relaciones sexuales con un compañero de trabajo, raramente significa que usted tiene un deseo no reconocido de tener relaciones sexuales con esa persona", dice ella. "Si ese compañero de trabajo es increíblemente egoísta, su sueño puede representar algún aspecto egoísta de su propio carácter o del carácter de alguien con quien usted tiene intimidad."

Usted ni siquiera puede escapar del envejecimiento en sus sueños. "Generalmente, tendemos a soñar acerca de compañeros sexuales que son de nuestra misma edad", dice el doctor Van de Castle. "La vasta mayoría de las personas que usted ve en sus sueños están dentro de los 20 años de su propia edad."

compañero y el sexo será más un momento de reírse que de trabajar horas de más.

Enamórense igual que antes. "Las parejas dejan de hacer las cosas que las unieron en primer lugar", dice el doctor Seiler. "Ya no se escriben pequeñas notas ni se mandan flores. Ya no se masajean la espalda ni salen juntos. Usted realmente tiene que esforzarse por conservar la alegría y la diversión en la relación. Sin eso, no habrá ninguna alegría y diversión en la recámara."

Entonces prepare una cena a la luz de las velas y pídale a él que salga con usted a dar una vuelta a la manzana a la noche tomados de la mano. Tal vez se sienta complacida en lo que puede terminar esto.

Hágase de un buen libro de recetas sexuales. Si su vida sexual, como una soda sin gas ha perdido la mayor parte de las burbujas, trate hojear manuales sexuales o ver videos eróticos juntos para obtener nuevas ideas, dice la doctora Domeena Renshaw, directora de la Clínica de Disfunción Sexual de la Escuela Stritch de Medicina de la Universidad de Chicago, en Maywood.

Mírelo profundamente. "El mantener contacto visual durante el sexo engendra intimidad. A menudo, es más íntimo que besarse y tomarse de las manos", dice Harrison Voigt, Ph.D., sicólogo clínico, terapeuta sexual y profesor del Instituto California de Estudios Integrales, en San Francisco. "Es una manera de poner a las personas en contacto con una forma poderosa de unión que no es física."

Cree un ritual. Encender una vela, masajearse el uno al otro los pies o colaborar en el intercambio de algunas intimidades especiales puede convertirse en parte de un ritual único que puede llevar a algunas parejas a conectarse emocionalmente antes del sexo, dice el doctor Voigt. "Un ritual es básicamente un acuerdo mutuo que el sexo debe ser algo único para la pareja. No necesita ser complicado, pero debería cambiar el contexto del sexo para hacerlo algo que es especial en lugar de simplemente tirarse en la cama y decir 'hey, vamos a hacerlo.' "

Concéntrese en la calidad, no en la cantidad. Si ustedes tuvieron relaciones sexuales cuatro veces la semana pasada y usted tuvo un orgasmo todas las veces, pero esta semana tuvieron relaciones sexuales una vez y no llegó a un orgasmo, no se presione para "anotar" la misma cantidad o más que la semana pasada. "La frecuencia no es tan importante como disfrutar verdaderamente las relaciones sexuales que tienen", dice la doctora Zussman.

Haga de la recámara un lugar de tranquilidad. La recámara debería ser un lugar donde usted y su compañero pueden retirarse para interludios íntimos. Si está llena de computadoras, la televisión, una máquina de escribir y archiveros, se parece más a una oficina. "Hay algo con respecto al desorden que distrae del romanticismo. La recámara debería tener una cierta tranquilidad", dice la doctora Zussman.

SUEÑO

Nos convierte en Bellas (y Jóvenes) Durmientes

¿Qué haría usted si le dijeran que podría verse y sentirse más joven, y estimular su nivel de energía sin gastar un solo centavo e incluso sin dejar su casa?

Para la mayoría de nosotras, la reacción sería simple: ¿qué tengo que hacer?

¿La respuesta? Duerma un poco.

No es una exageración que los beneficios del sueño pueden añadir muchísimo a la calidad de su vida. Sin embargo, el sueño a menudo es la primera cosa que se va cuando usted trabaja o se altera de más y se queda levantada sólo una hora más, o dos o tres, para terminar con un proyecto, terminar de planchar, leer un informe, fregar el piso del baño...

"Usted no puede engañar al sueño sin de alguna manera engañarse a sí misma", dice el doctor Mark Mahowald, director del Centro Regional de Trastornos del Sueño de Minnesota, en el Centro Médico del Condado de Hennepin, en Minneapolis.

El rejuvenecedor secreto

Todas podemos reconocer a una persona privada de sueño cuando la vemos: ojos caídos con círculos oscuros; una expresión aturdida, sombría, como un zombi; una postura pobre, caminar despacio, hablar lento. No precisamente la imagen de la juventud. ¿Pero qué pasa si empezamos a practicar buenos hábitos de sueño regularmente? ¿Podemos realmente agregar vitalidad e invertir algunas de esas señales del envejecimiento?

A menos que haya otros problemas médicos, la respuesta es sí. "El sueño es una parte de una constelación de conductas que elevan al máximo la calidad de nuestras vidas", dice Michael Vitiello, Ph.D., director asociado del Programa de

Hacer siesta o no

"Muchos individuos que no logran todo el sueño que necesitan durante la noche se benefician de una siesta corta en la tarde", dice Timothy Monk, Ph.D., director del Programa de Investigación de la Cronobiología Humana en la Escuela de Medicina de la Universidad de Pittsburgh. "Hay un descenso natural de agudeza a media tarde, parte de nuestros ritmos circadianos. Muchas de aquellas privadas de sueño o con fuertes instintos de tomar siestas, a menudo se revigorizan con una siesta de 30 minutos en este período."

Pero no todas tienen tiempo para una siesta, y la siesta no es para todas. "Si usted tiene insomnio, puede tener un deseo fuerte de tomarse una siesta en la tarde, pero eso puede empeorar su insomnio a la noche", dice el doctor Karl Doghramji, director del Centro de Trastornos del Sueño en el Hospital de la Universidad Thomas Jefferson, en Filadelfia. "Además, muchas personas no están hechas para las siestas. En realidad, se sienten peor después de una siesta debido a lo que llamamos inercia del sueño, la sensación de aturdimiento que puede permanecer por horas."

¿Qué debe hacer usted? Los doctores Monk y Doghramji dicen que experimente. Si tomar una siesta hace que se sienta bien por el resto del día y no interfiere con su sueño en la noche, y si su horario lo permite, por supuesto tome la siesta cuando le ataca esa baja repentina de la tarde. Por lo general unos 20 a 45 minutos después del almuerzo es el mejor momento.

Investigación sobre Sueño y Envejecimiento en la Universidad de Washington, en Seattle. "Cuando usted duerme mejor, se siente mejor. Hay más probabilidad de que rinda en sus niveles óptimos y mantenga las conductas de estilo de vida saludables como hacer ejercicio y comer saludablemente. Combine el sueño con estas otras conductas y todas esas cosas que asociamos con la juventud —apariencia, energía y actitud— mejorarán finalmente."

¿Por qué es tan importante?

Los científicos saben que el cuerpo emite su concentración más grande de la hormona del crecimiento —la substancia que ayuda a nuestros cuerpos a reparar los tejidos dañados— cuando duerme. Los animales de laboratorio privados de sueño sufren un colapso completo en sus funciones vitales. Y los estudios recientes muestran que los individuos privados de sueño aparentemente experimentan una disminución en la actividad de sus células asesinas naturales y otros amigos del sistema inmune que mantienen al cuerpo libre de infecciones.

La mayoría de los especialistas en el sueño creen que la mente se beneficia igualmente de una buena noche de sueño.

"La falta de sueño nos pone de mal humor e irritables", dice el doctor Mahowald. También limita nuestra capacidad para concentrarnos, formar opiniones y desempeñar tareas mentales. Como resultado, puede afectar nuestro rendimiento de trabajo o, aún peor, llevar a accidentes fatales en el trabajo o en el tráfico."

El sueño, según resulta, realmente es un estado muy activo compuesto de una serie de ciclos regulares. Hay etapas para cada ciclo: la primera y tercer etapa ocurren durante el sueño ligero y la cuarta etapa (también llamada el sueño delta) representa nuestro sueño más profundo. Una quinta etapa de sueño (llamada movimiento rápido de ojos o *REM*, por sus siglas en inglés) ocurre cuando soñamos. Una cantidad adecuada de sueños delta y REM es esencial, creen los expertos. Sin alguno de ellos, nos sentimos pésimamente y nuestra capacidad de aprender, memorizar y razonar se afectan tremendamente.

Sus patrones de sueño variables

¿Espera usted correr tan rápido o jugar al tenis tan bien cuando esté en sus décadas de los cuarenta, cincuenta o sesenta años de edad que como cuando estaba en su adolescencia o década de los veinte o treinta años? Por supuesto que no. Pero, ¿y qué pasa con el sueño? Usted probablemente piensa que no le llevará ningún esfuerzo o incluso será más fácil. Pero para la mayoría de nosotras, una buena noche de sueño podría ser más difícil de conseguir.

Cuando llegamos a la edad madura y al entrar a nuestros años dorados, a muchas de nosotras nos tomará más tiempo para dormirnos. Nos despertaremos frecuentemente y pasaremos menos tiempo en las valiosas etapas delta y REM. Pasaremos menos tiempo durmiendo, y punto.

"Al envejecer, nuestros relojes internos se perturban mucho más fácilmente", dice Timothy Monk, Ph.D., director del Programa de Investigación de la Cronobiología Humana en la Escuela de Medicina de la Universidad de Pittsburgh. "El efecto principal puede ser que no podamos dormir tan bien y entremos en un estado de malestar y depresión, como un caso crónico de desfase horario (*jet lag*)."

Cómo dormir mejor

¿Cuánto necesita usted dormir? Eso depende del individuo. Algunas de nosotras podemos funcionar perfectamente con sólo cuatro horas de sueño por noche; otras necesitan tantas como diez para sentirse renovadas. Para la mayoría de las mujeres, siete a ocho horas son suficientes, pero solamente usted sabe lo que necesita. "No hay un número mágico. Usted debería dormir tanto como necesite para sentirse descansada y capaz de funcionar al máximo el próximo día", dice el doctor Mahowald.

¿Cómo puede elevar al máximo la calidad y cantidad de su sueño? Aquí hay algo de ayuda.

Manténgase en un programa regular. Irse a la cama y despertarse a la misma hora todos los días (incluyendo los fines de semana) ayuda a mantener un ritmo circadiano consistente, el reloj natural de su cuerpo, dice el doctor Monk. Esto acondicionará a su reloj interno para que pueda dormirse más fácilmente, dormir más profundamente y despertar sintiéndose renovada.

Coma tres comidas regulares a horas regulares. "Nuestros ritmos diarios pueden perturbarse fácilmente por factores externos", dice el doctor Monk. "Usted necesita ciertas indicaciones externas para mantener a su reloj interno funcionando correctamente. Mantener las horas de comida consistentes le ayudará."

Tome tiempo para relajarse. Usted no puede saltar directamente del ajetreo a la cama. Dese dos horas antes de irse a la cama para relajarse y desconectarse del mundo; lea, vea la televisión, escuche música o realice alguna otra actividad que encuentre relajante. Encárguese de los negocios, las cuentas o de los demás fabricantes del estrés durante el día o temprano en la noche.

Establezca una rutina. Muchas personas no pueden dormir bien porque sus estilos de vida son demasiado caóticos antes de que se vayan a la cama. Es decir, se la pasan en distintas actividades noche tras noche sin tener una rutina fija. Si usted puede desarrollar un patrón *regular* de actividades y conductas que hará todas las noches un poco antes de irse a la cama, dormir será una experiencia más amable. Por ejemplo, suponga que todas las noches usted sacara al perro a dar una vuelta, leyera el periódico, tomara una ducha, se cepillara los dientes y se fuera a la cama. Usted estaría relajada y entraría en un buen ritmo previo al sueño.

Mantenga el entorno apropiado. Mejorar su alrededor puede hacer del sueño una mejor experiencia. La mayoría de la gente encuentra la luz y el ruido molestos, por lo tanto apague la radio y baje la persiana. También revise el termostato, la mayoría de la gente duerme mejor con una temperatura un poco más fría de lo normal.

Váyase a dormir sólo cuando está cansada. No se quede en la cama tratando de que le venga el sueño, dice el doctor Vitiello. Sólo se acondicionará a no dormirse mientras permanezca allí. En lugar de eso, levántese y lea un libro o haga algo constructivo hasta que se sienta cansada.

Siga con lo normal. Si necesita despertarse temprano o tiene un día activo por delante, irse a la cama más temprano probablemente no la ayudará, dice el doctor Vitiello. La mayoría de la gente solamente se pasa este tiempo adicional en la cama despierta, sólo para después tener problemas durmiéndose. "Aunque es fácil acumular una deuda de sueño, no es posible ahorrar sueño", dice él.

Evite las comidas y los bocadillos tarde. Un pequeño bocadillo (merienda o *snack*) antes de irse a la cama está bien, pero no coma una comida completa, alimentos picantes o un sándwich tipo medianoche por lo menos tres horas antes de la hora de dormir, dice el doctor Karl Doghramji, director del Centro de Trastornos del Sueño en el Hospital de la Universidad Thomas Jefferson, en

Filadelfia. El ruido de sus tripas puede hacer que se la pase despierta por horas o hacer que su sueño sea menos renovador.

Corte la cafeína. Guarde su café, té, colas, chocolates y otros alimentos que contienen cafeína para la mañana o temprano en la tarde, dice el doctor Doghramji. La cafeína es un inhibidor poderoso del sueño que permanece en el torrente sanguíneo por hasta seis horas.

Limite los líquidos después de las 8 de la noche. Por razones obvias: los viajes frecuentes al baño pueden tenerla despierta toda la noche.

Olvídese del alcohol por la noche. Todas sabemos que el alcohol la puede amodorrar en un abrir y cerrar de ojos. Pero también la puede hacer dar vueltas en la cama mientras duerme y cambiar el patrón de los sueños REM y no-REM. Además, tiene una mayor probabilidad de despertarse por breves períodos durante la noche. Aunque logre dormir varias horas, probablemente no serán buenas horas y se sentirá malísima por la mañana.

Evite los medicamentos. Las píldoras para dormir y otros sedantes, aunque a veces útiles, también pueden perturbar sus patrones de sueño, dice el doctor Doghramji. Además, es fácil volverse adicta, especialmente si no los usa correctamente. Su mejor opción es tratar de dormirse sin ninguna asistencia química. Si debe tomar píldoras para dormir, hágalo solamente bajo el control médico.

Úsela para dormir y para tener relaciones nada más. La cama se diseñó para dos propósitos solamente, dice el doctor Vitiello. "Si usted introduce actividades como pagar cuentas, comer pizza y ver la televisión, el cuerpo se confunde y puede no querer dormirse en la cama."

Tenga relaciones sexuales... o no. Algunas mujeres encuentran que el sexo antes de dormir es relajante; otras sienten que las mantiene despiertas por horas, dice el doctor Mahowald. Si tener relaciones sexuales le provoca sueño, adelante. Si no, guarde su pasión para otra hora del día.

Cambie su turno. "Fuimos hechas para trabajar durante el día y dormir por la noche", dice el doctor Monk. "Al envejecer, la trabajadora de turnos debería considerar seriamente cambiarse a una posición u horario de trabajo que no le requiera horas extrañas en lugar de luchar contra las inclinaciones naturales del cuerpo."

Sea prudente con el ejercicio. Es un mito que el ejercicio pesado la agotará y la hará sentirse soñolienta, dice el doctor Mahowald. Pero las personas que se encuentran físicamente activas y en buena forma duermen mejor, así que haga del ejercicio parte de su régimen diario. Una caminata moderada antes de irse a la cama está bien si la relaja, pero reserve sus sesiones fuertes de ejercicio para más temprano en el día; la mantendrán despierta por bastante rato.

Separe tiempo para preocuparse. "Usted nunca dormirá bien si se acuesta en la cama obsesionada con sus preocupaciones", dice el doctor Vitiello. "Separe 30 minutos, o algo así, lejos de la recámara antes de la hora de acostarse como tiempo para preocuparse y saque las dificultades fuera de su sistema. No use la cama como un escenario para la ansiedad."

TERAPIA DE REPOSICIÓN DE HORMONAS

Una opción para la edad madura

Usted ha tomado bastantes decisiones con respecto a su salud en su vida: qué tipo de control de la natalidad usar, cómo y cuándo hacer ejercicio, a qué doctor ir.

Ahora, con la menopausia por delante, usted se enfrenta a otra. Y esta vez, siente que realmente es una muy significativa. Usted continúa meditando sobre la pregunta: "¿debería yo tomar la terapia de reposición de hormonas?"

Millones de mujeres nacidas inmediatamente después de la segunda guerra mundial se están preguntando lo mismo. Se estima que más mujeres que nunca —de 40 a 50 millones— entrarán en la menopausia durante las próximas dos décadas.

Todas hemos oído acerca de las posibles dificultades de la menopausia: sofocos y sudor por las noches, sequedad vaginal y cambios en la piel, y un mayor riesgo de enfermedad del corazón y osteoporosis una vez que la menopausia ha pasado. También hemos oído acerca de la terapia de reposición de hormonas como un medio para combatir estos efectos envejecedores.

De hecho, una de las primeras preguntas que las mujeres hacen a menudo acerca de la menopausia es si tomar o no la terapia de reposición de hormonas, dice Joan Borton, una consejera licenciada en salud mental, en práctica privada en Rockport, Massachusetts, y autora de *Drawing from the Women's Well:*

Reflections on the Life Passage of Menopause (Extraiga de la fuente femenina: las reflexiones sobre el paso de la menopausia por la vida). "Todavía es una decisión muy difícil de tomar. Yo veo muchas mujeres que son muy precavidas y tratan de obtener la mayor cantidad de información posible", dice ella.

La decisión es difícil, debido a que hay beneficios y riesgos al tomar la terapia de reposición de hormonas (o *HRT*, por sus siglas en inglés). Las mujeres a menudo se encuentran tratando de balancear los pros —la HRT puede aliviar los sofocos y la sequedad vaginal, proteger contra la enfermedad del corazón y la osteoporosis y mantener la piel y el cabello juvenil— y las contras: las mujeres se preocupan que pueda aumentar su riesgo de cáncer de mama, cáncer uterino y cálculos biliares. La HRT también puede causar que las mujeres empiecen otra vez a tener sus períodos, lo cual muchas lo ven como un inconveniente. La mayoría de los expertos están de acuerdo que la decisión es personal y en gran parte depende de la historia de salud de una mujer y su propia experiencia con la menopausia.

Las hormonas de la HRT

La HRT es una formulación de hormonas creada para reponer los niveles naturales de hormonas de una mujer. En los años que anteceden a la menopausia, llamados perimenopausia, los niveles de estrógeno de una mujer disminuyen a un ritmo constante. Entonces, después de que ella deja de ovular y tiene su último período (cuando la menopausia realmente comienza), sus niveles de estrógeno disminuyen aún más. La edad promedio para la menopausia es los 51 años de edad, pero puede ocurrir antes; cerca de un 1 por ciento de las mujeres experimentan la menopausia antes de los 40 años de edad.

El estrógeno desempeña un papel vital en mantener los tejidos y órganos por todo el cuerpo de una mujer, incluyendo su piel, tejido vaginal, senos y huesos. Así que cuando los niveles de estrógeno se reducen durante la menopausia, puede haber sequedad vaginal, arrugas en la piel y deterioro en la masa y fuerza ósea. El estrógeno también afecta a un número de funciones del cuerpo, tales como el metabolismo y la regulación de la temperatura del cuerpo. Por lo tanto, cuando los niveles de estrógeno declinan, el colesterol de una mujer puede elevarse, poniéndola en un riesgo mayor de enfermedad del corazón. Su termómetro interno del cuerpo también puede estropearse —de allí los sofocos y los sudores nocturnos.

Años atrás, las formulaciones de hormonas creadas para las mujeres menopáusicas contenían sólo estrógeno y se llamaban terapia de reposición de estrógeno (o *ERT*, por sus siglas en inglés). Pero esas formulaciones contenían niveles de estrógeno que probaron ser demasiado altos; se encontró que las píldoras contribuían a la formación de coágulos de sangre. Y dar estrógeno solo probó ser peligroso: los estudios mostraron que promovía el cáncer uterino.

Por consiguiente, los investigadores rediseñaron las fórmulas, bajando el contenido de estrógeno y agregando una forma sintética de la hormona progesterona llamada progestina. Además de regular el estrógeno, la progesterona provoca el desprendimiento gradual del recubrimiento uterino. La combinación de estrógeno y progestina es lo que se conoce como la HRT. Las dosis bajas de estrógeno son suficientemente altas para remplazar lo que está faltando y para proporcionar protección del corazón pero lo suficientemente bajas para no promover los coágulos. Y la progestina ofrece protección contra el cáncer uterino porque provoca que el recubrimiento uterino se desprenda gradualmente, de esa manera impidiendo la acumulación peligrosa que puede terminar en cáncer si no se revisa. Así que en la actualidad, si una mujer menopáusica decide que quiere tomar hormonas y todavía tiene su útero, la recomendación de la mayoría de los médicos es una dosis baja de estrógeno más progestina.

Pero algunas mujeres tienen dificultad para tolerar la progestina, dicen los expertos. Ésta puede causar síntomas insoportables similares al síndrome premenstrual (o *PMS*, por sus siglas en inglés). Estas mujeres pueden recibir dosis bajas sólo de estrógeno, pero si lo hacen, tienen que hacerse biopsias del útero regularmente para verificar que no hay cáncer. Si una mujer ya no tiene su útero, está en condición de recibir una dosis baja de estrógeno solo, aunque en estos casos algunos médicos recomiendan estrógeno y progestina.

La HRT que contiene ambos estrógeno y progestina puede tomarse en varias distintas formas. El componente progestina de la terapia está disponible sólo en forma de píldora, la cual las mujeres pueden tomar ya sea en dosis más altas por 10 a 12 días al final de sus ciclos menstruales o en dosis más bajas todos los días del mes.

El estrógeno, sin embargo, está disponible en un número de distintas formas, incluyendo cremas, parches y píldoras, y se toma todos los días del mes o por las tres primeras semanas del ciclo menstrual.

Las cremas de estrógeno se insertan en la vagina con aplicadores y tienen su mayor impacto en el tejido vaginal; esta forma de estrógeno es más efectiva para la sequedad vaginal y los problemas de las vías urinarias. Los parches de estrógeno son del tamaño de un pequeño vendaje y se colocan sobre el abdomen; el estrógeno se emite del parche en secuencias de duración determinada y pasa directamente al torrente sanguíneo. Esta forma es apropiada para las mujeres con condiciones médicas que les prohiben tomar estrógeno en forma oral, tales como la enfermedad de la vesícula biliar o presión arterial alta.

Debido a que tanto el estrógeno en forma de crema como en forma de parche va directamente al torrente sanguíneo, no pasa a través del tracto digestivo y del hígado, donde normalmente tendría su mayor efecto en reducir el colesterol. Por lo tanto, se piensa que las formas de estrógeno en crema y parche son menos efectivas para proteger contra la enfermedad del corazón.

El estrógeno en forma de píldora se toma por la boca y se considera el mejor método para combatir la enfermedad del corazón. La píldora más común de estrógeno, llamada *Premarin*, está hecha de fuentes naturales —estrógeno de yeguas— mientras que las otras píldoras están hechas de fuentes sintéticas.

Preocupaciones inmediatas

Los sofocos y la sequedad vaginal son los dos síntomas principales que hacen que una mujer vaya a ver a su doctor acerca de la menopausia y la HRT, dice el doctor Brian Walsh, director de la Clínica de Menopausia en el Hospital Brigham y de Mujeres, en Boston.

Se estima que los sofocos afectan a un 75 a 85 por ciento de las mujeres menopáusicas. El 80 por ciento de las mujeres que tienen sofocos los experimentan por más de un año, y el 25 al 50 por ciento se quejan de ellos por más de cinco años. Los sofocos pueden variar de una sensación de calor leve a una moderada que dura entre 1 y 5 minutos, hasta una sensación de calor extrema que dura hasta 12 minutos e incluye sudor y sonrojo intensos.

Los sofocos pueden ocurrir durante el día o la noche, que es cuando se los conoce como sudores nocturnos. Las mujeres pueden despertarse con calor y sudando, dice el doctor Walsh. A menudo están tan empapadas que tienen que cambiarse la ropa de dormir, interrumpiendo aún más su sueño y dejándolas exhaustas e irritables durante el día. La HRT es altamente efectiva contra los sofocos, dicen los expertos.

La sequedad vaginal también responde a la HRT, dicen los expertos. El tejido de la vagina tiene receptores de estrógeno. Cuando el estrógeno disminuye con la menopausia, el recubrimiento de la vagina y del útero se adelgaza, y resulta en la sequedad vaginal.

La piel de una mujer también puede tener receptores de estrógeno, por ello cuando llega la menopausia, la piel puede empezar a arrugarse. La HRT es efectiva para mantener la piel suave, con aspecto juvenil, dicen los expertos.

Ayudante del corazón

Una preocupación grande para las mujeres que atraviesan la menopausia es la enfermedad del corazón, ya que el riesgo a ésta aumenta de una en nueve para las mujeres antes de los 65 años de edad a una en tres para las mujeres después de los 65 años de edad, según la Asociación del Corazón de los Estados Unidos.

La razón por la cual el riesgo de una mujer aumenta es que el estrógeno ayuda a mantener altos los niveles de colesterol tipo lipoproteína de alta densidad (o *HDL*, por sus siglas en inglés), el tipo bueno, y bajos los niveles de colesterol tipo lipoproteína de baja densidad (o *LDL*, por sus siglas en inglés), el tipo malo. También ayuda a impedir que las paredes de los vasos sanguíneos atraigan al colesterol. Cuando los niveles naturales de estrógeno en una mujer disminuyen con la menopausia, esta protección contra la enfermedad del corazón se termina.

¿Se podrá restablecer la protección al tomar la HRT? Algunos estudios indican que sí se puede.

El problema con los estudios existentes es que en su mayoría están basados en las formulaciones antiguas de la ERT —aquellas que contenían estrógeno solo. La mayoría de estos estudios indican que el tomar estrógeno sin progestina disminuirá el riesgo de una mujer a la enfermedad del corazón en un 50 por ciento en comparación con lo que podría ser si no la tomara, dice la doctora

Cynthia A. Stuenkel, profesora clínica asociada en el Departamento de Medicina y Medicina Reproductora de la Universidad de California, San Diego.

¿Pero qué pasa con la HRT, la cual usa tanto el estrógeno como la progestina? Bueno, no se ha efectuado tanta investigación en estas formulaciones. Y existen algunas dudas entre los investigadores sobre si la progestina reduce el efecto protector del estrógeno.

Sin embargo, un estudio publicado en el *New England Journal of Medicine* (Revista de Medicina de Nueva Inglaterra) observó los efectos tanto de la HRT como de la ERT sobre la enfermedad del corazón. El informe analizó datos del Estudio de Riesgo de Arteriosclerosis en las Comunidades, un estudio grande a 15.800 personas de cuatro zonas del país. Basándose en sus hallazgos, los investigadores informaron que los niveles de colesterol bueno eran similares tanto para las usuarias de estrógeno solo como para las usuarias de estrógeno más progestina. Y ambos grupos tenían niveles más altos de colesterol bueno que las mujeres que no usaban estrógeno. Los investigadores también estimaron que las mujeres que tomaron estrógeno solo redujeron su riesgo a una enfermedad del corazón en un 42 por ciento en comparación con las que no lo usaban, y que las mujeres que usaron estrógeno con progestina se hubieran beneficiado aún más, aunque no se especificó cuánto más.

La lucha contra la osteoporosis

Otra preocupación para las mujeres menopáusicas es la osteoporosis, una enfermedad en la cual la densidad y fuerza de los huesos, particularmente en las caderas y muñecas, disminuye. Los expertos dicen que cuatro en cada diez mujeres desarrollan esta enfermedad. Las consecuencias pueden ser devastadoras —cada año una cantidad estimada de 1,5 millones de estadounidenses sufren de fracturas relacionadas con la osteoporosis. Después de la menopausia, entre el 25 y el 44 por ciento de las mujeres experimentan fracturas de la cadera debido a la osteoporosis. Y para cuando cumplen los 90 años de edad, las mujeres tienen el doble de probabilidades que los hombres de fracturarse las caderas.

La investigación sugiere que al usar la HRT el riesgo se reducirá en un 50 por ciento de que una mujer sufra fracturas relacionadas con la osteoporosis. Y para las mujeres que ya tienen osteoporosis, se cree que la HRT aún es efectiva y puede aumentar en un 5 por ciento la densidad mineral del hueso, una medida de la fuerza del hueso.

¿Por cuánto tiempo necesita una mujer tomar la HRT para proteger sus huesos? En Boston, el Estudio Framingham de Osteoporosis analizó la densidad mineral de los huesos de 670 mujeres de ascendencia europea del Estudio Framingham del Corazón. (El Estudio Framingham del Corazón comenzó en 1948 y siguió a los participantes del estudio a lo largo de sus vidas para evaluar los factores de riesgo a la enfermedad del corazón). El Estudio Framingham de Osteoporosis concluyó que las mujeres necesitaban tomar la terapia de hormonas por más de siete años para que la densidad mineral de sus huesos aumentara. Las mujeres que la tomaron solamente por tres a cuatro años tenían densidades minerales de los huesos similares a las mujeres que nunca la habían tomado. Por lo tanto, según este estudio, las mujeres pueden tener que continuar con la HRT por lo menos siete años para que la densidad mineral de sus huesos aumente significativamente.

Los investigadores también encontraron que cuando las mujeres tomaron la HRT durante siete a diez años y después pararon, el efecto protector de la HRT contra la disminución de la densidad ósea sólo duró hasta los 75 años de edad. De ahí en más, cualquier efecto de una terapia prolongada pareció ser leve. Eso es importante, dado que el riesgo a la osteoporosis de una mujer es mayor en sus décadas de los 80 y los 90 años de edad.

Los hallazgos de este estudio han provocado discusión en la comunidad médica sobre por cuánto tiempo una mujer necesita tomar la HRT para conservar la densidad de los huesos hasta entrar en las últimas décadas de su vida. Algunos médicos están debatiendo la idea de mantener a las mujeres tomando la HRT indefinidamente, esto es, empezarían después de la menopausia y se mantendrían con ésta hasta sus décadas de los 80 y los 90 años de edad. Otros médicos están considerando la posibilidad de esperar más tiempo después de la menopausia para empezar con la HRT.

Riesgos de la HRT

Hay otros riesgos y temas tocante a la salud para las mujeres que toman hormonas. Primero, existe el riesgo del cáncer uterino, el cual afecta a 1 en cada 1.000 mujeres por año, dice el doctor Walsh. Tomar estrógeno solo aumenta el riesgo de una mujer al cáncer endometrial cerca de cuatro veces, dice el doctor Walsh. Esa es la razón por la cual los doctores hoy en día no recomiendan estrógeno solo a una mujer que aún tiene su útero. Pero las mujeres que toman estrógeno y progestina de hecho pueden tener un riesgo menor que si no tomaran hormonas en lo absoluto, dice el doctor Walsh. Su riesgo es posiblemente un 30 a 40 por ciento más bajo, dice él.

Tomar la HRT pone a una mujer en riesgo de cálculos biliares, particularmente durante el primer año, dice el doctor Walsh. Además, para algunas mujeres no es apropiada la HRT ni la ERT. Ninguna de éstas se recomienda a las mujeres que saben o sospechan que tienen cáncer del útero o de mama, que han tenido problemas con coágulos de sangre llamados émbolos pulmonares o que tienen una enfermedad activa del hígado, dice el doctor Walsh.

La cuestión del cáncer de mama

Una preocupación importante para la mayoría de las mujeres que están considerando la HRT es si ésta aumentará su riesgo al cáncer de mama. Los senos contienen receptores de estrógeno, y el administrar estrógeno a los animales promueve el cáncer. Por lo tanto, hay alguna razón para sospechar que el tomar la HRT o la ERT podría promover el cáncer de mama en las mujeres.

La relación entre la HRT y el cáncer de mama es discutible; varios estudios sobre el tema han resultado en distintas conclusiones y a veces contradictorias. Pero un estudio realizado por los investigadores de los Centros para el Control y la Prevención de las Enfermedades, en Atlanta, recopiló los resultados de un número de distintos estudios y llegó a las siguientes conclusiones: las usuarias actuales pueden estar en un riesgo mayor, pero parece que el riesgo es relativo a la duración de tiempo que una mujer toma la ERT. No parece haber una asociación entre el uso de la ERT y el cáncer de mama en las mujeres que la han tomado por menos de 5 años, pero las mujeres que la han usado por más de 15 años pueden tener un riesgo mayor del 30 por ciento. Las mujeres que usaron la ERT en el pasado pero no la están tomando actualmente no parecen estar en un riesgo mayor de cáncer de mama.

Lo que usted puede hacer

Por consiguiente, ¿cómo decide una mujer? No es fácil. Pero aquí está lo que usted puede hacer.

Encuentre al médico correcto. Los médicos pueden variar en sus enfoques con respecto a la HRT, así que es importante encontrar uno con el cual usted se sienta cómoda y que respete sus sentimientos y opiniones, dice Borton. No tenga miedo de salir a la búsqueda de un médico, y pregúntele a sus amigas acerca de los de ellas.

Conozca su historia familiar. Al decidir acerca de la HRT, es importante conocer su historia familiar, dice el doctor Walsh. Descubra si alguien en su familia tiene una historia de enfermedad del corazón, osteoporosis, cáncer de mama o cáncer endometrial. Dígaselo a su médico.

Sopese sus riesgos. Tomar una decisión con respecto a la HRT a menudo es una cuestión de balancear su riesgo a una enfermedad contra su riesgo a otra. Una solución es tratar "de decidir como mujer a qué está usted en riesgo y cuál es su perfil de riesgo, y tomar una decisión inteligente acerca de cuáles son las enfermedades a las que usted está predispuesta y por lo tanto debería prevenir", dice el doctor David Felson, del Centro de Artritis en la Universidad de Boston.

Lleve un registro menstrual. Cuando las mujeres empiezan con la HRT, a menudo vuelven a tener sus períodos, particularmente si están tomando progestina con estrógeno. Las preparaciones de hormonas pueden afectar su flujo. Así que registre sus patrones de sangramiento, dice el doctor Walsh. Tome un calendario, marque los días en que usted sangra y muéstreselo a su doctora, para que ella puede determinar si el tiempo y la cantidad de flujo son apropiados, dice él.

Anticipe un tiempo de adaptación. Puede tomar de cuatro a seis semanas para que las hormonas empiecen a actuar y para que usted sienta un efecto, dice el doctor Walsh. Y una vez que usted las está tomando, puede llevar varios meses para adaptar su terapia de tal manera que sus períodos se hagan regulares.

Hágase autoexámenes de senos. Todas las preguntas acerca de la conexión entre la HRT y el cáncer de mama no están definitivamente contestadas. Así que protéjase y hágase los autoexámenes mensuales de sus senos; estos le permitirán detectar el cáncer de mama temprano si lo desarrolla. Una de las cosas más importantes que una mujer puede hacer es llevar a cabo autoexámenes mensuales de sus senos, dice el doctor Walsh. "La mayoría de los cánceres de mama son descubiertos por la mujer misma, por eso es que tiene sentido que ella se examine sus senos una vez al mes", dice él. "Eso significa once veces más probabilidad de la que su doctor tiene de encontrar una masa en el seno."

Hágase su mamograma. Un mamograma es otra forma de descubrir el cáncer de mama. La mayoría de los doctores recomiendan que las mujeres tengan sus primeros mamogramas entre los 35 y los 40 años de edad. Es importante hacerse mamogramas regularmente para las mujeres que toman la HRT, dice el doctor Walsh. "La gente discute sobre qué tan a menudo y a qué edad empezar, pero para cuando las mujeres cumplen los 50 años de edad, deberían estar haciéndose los mamogramas por lo menos una vez al año", dice él. Los mamogramas "permiten descubrir el cáncer de mama cuando es pequeño y potencialmente curable", dice el doctor Walsh.

Examínese para el cáncer. Otro tipo de prueba de seguimiento que las mujeres pueden tener se llama biopsia endometrial. Esta revisa el recubrimiento del útero o endometrio, para ver si hay cáncer. Algunos doctores hacen una biopsia de base al empezar con la HRT y luego hacen una biopsia como un examen anual, aunque no todos los doctores hacen esto con las mujeres que están recibiendo tanto estrógeno como progestina. La prueba es más importante cuando la mujer está tomando sólo estrógeno, porque el efecto protector de la progestina está ausente. Pregunte a su doctora cuál es su enfoque.

Busque quien la apoye. Otras mujeres que atraviesan por la menopausia pueden ser una tremenda fuente de apoyo, dice Borton. Hable con otras mujeres de su edad —sean mujeres que usted ya conoce o aquellas que conozca en un grupo de apoyo— acerca de cómo piensan, sus decisiones y experiencias alrededor de la HRT, dice ella. El escuchar las experiencias de otras mujeres puede ayudar frecuentemente. Llame a su hospital local para que le informen sobre los grupos de apoyo en su área. O bien, usted empiece uno propio.

TIEMPO LIBRE

A ninguna mujer le debe faltar

Desde que suena el despertador por la mañana, usted está en movimiento. Hay que hacer café, bañarse, levantar a los niños, hacer el desayuno para todo el mundo, vestirse, y después trabajar duro por ocho horas. Luego llegar a casa, cocinar, limpiar, ayudar a los niños con sus tareas, arbitrarles sus pleitos sobre los juguetes y quién le pegó a quién, coser la camisa de su esposo, planchar la ropa, prepararle el almuerzo a los niños para el próximo día, etc., etc., etc.

Cómo dicen en México, "¡Híjole!" ¡Qué clase de ajetreo! Igual que a los futbolistas, a usted le hace falta un *time out*, un tiempo para descansar. Y, según los médicos, el tiempo libre no es un lujo, sino una necesidad si se quiere sentir joven.

El tiempo libre desempeña un papel importante en su salud y bienestar en general, dice la doctora Leslie Hartley Gise, profesora asociada de siquiatría en el Centro Médico Monte Sinaí, en la Ciudad de Nueva York. Si usted no tiene suficiente de éste, puede empezar a sentirse malhumorada, fatigada y deprimida. Al pasar el tiempo, la vida sin el tiempo libre puede conducir a úlceras, migrañas, enfermedad cardiovascular, presión arterial alta y otros padecimientos físicos, dice ella.

"Las actividades de tiempo libre ciertamente pueden ayudarla a sentirse más satisfecha con su vida. ¿Podría eso hacer que algunas personas se sientan más jóvenes? Supongo que sí", dice Howard Tinsley, Ph.D., profesor de sicología en la Universidad de Illinois del Sur, en Carbondale. "Algunas podrían pensar en esto como literalmente sentirse más joven, mientras que otras podrían sentir que simplemente tienen más entusiasmo por la vida. Pueden sentirse mas vigorizadas y entusiasmadas al despertar por la mañana."

Aumenta sus reservas

Una forma de ver la importancia del tiempo libre es imaginándose que su cuerpo es un gran campo de petróleo con dos tipos de energía. Un tipo de petróleo, llamado energía superficial, es como la gasolina. Proporciona las explosiones rápidas de energía que necesitamos para vivir día a día. Pero el otro tipo, llamado energía profunda, es como un aceite que se quema lentamente para sostenernos cuando estamos enfermas y durante otros períodos extensos de estrés. Su energía es irreemplazable y está calculada para que dure toda la vida, dice Walt Schafer, Ph.D., profesor de sociología en la Universidad Estatal de California, Chico, y director del Instituto de Buena Salud del Pacífico, en Chico.

"Con el sueño adecuado, la diversión adecuada y el tiempo adecuado lejos de las presiones, podemos reponer esas reservas superficiales de energía", dice el doctor Schafer. "Pero si no lo hacemos, entonces comenzamos a sacar de esas reservas profundas de energía, y eso acelera el proceso de envejecimiento."

Aprenda a divertirse

Desafortunadamente, muchas mujeres simplemente no han aprendido cómo crear el tiempo libre o a usarlo debidamente. Para ellas, la diversión es sólo otra tarea más.

"Algunas mujeres tratan su tiempo libre como si fuera un trabajo", dice el doctor Schafer. "Su tiempo libre es orientado a las tareas, orientado a las exigencias y atestado de presión para lograr un buen rendimiento. En lugar de experimentar el placer y la alegría del tiempo libre, se ponen en riesgo de drenar sus reservas de energía aún más."

Irónicamente, la presión de ese enfoque a la diversión puede crear estrés, precisamente lo que el tiempo libre trata de aliviar. Y los expertos sospechan que el estrés chupa la juventud de su cuerpo como un vampiro.

"Todas queremos sentirnos útiles. Todas queremos sentir como si estuviéramos contribuyendo. Pero si eso es todo lo que usted hace, no está siendo justa consigo misma", dice Jeanne Murrone, Ph.D., una sicóloga clínica en el Centro para la Salud Mental, una clínica afiliada al Distrito Hospitalario Charlotte-Mecklenburg, en Charlotte, Carolina del Norte. "El tiempo libre es un tiempo para renovarse. Sin ese tiempo para renovarse, usted se agotará. Así que el tiempo libre —ese tiempo cuando usted no tiene que hacer nada perfectamente, sino solamente por el placer de hacerlo— es probablemente tan necesario para nosotras como dormir, hacer ejercicio y comer correctamente."

Aquí hay algunas formas de crear más tiempo libre en su vida.

Planificar para gozar. El tiempo libre no sucede así porque sí. Se requiere esfuerzo y planificación para introducir las actividades divertidas en su vida. Lea el periódico, revise los tableros de avisos en los supermercados de su vecindad. Llame por teléfono a su departamento local de parques y recreación y pregúnteles acerca de paseos al aire libre, ligas deportivas y clases de artesanía, sugiere Patsy B. Edwards, una consejera de tiempo libre en práctica privada en Los

Ángeles. Usted también puede explorar su biblioteca, colegio comunitario e iglesia para las actividades nuevas.

Separe algo de tiempo todos los días para una actividad de tiempo libre que usted disfrute, aun cuando sólo sea una caminata de diez minutos alrededor de la manzana, dice el doctor Schafer.

Que su motivo tenga sentido. Encuentre una razón para dejar espacio en su vida para el tiempo libre, dice Carol Lassen, Ph.D., profesora clínica de sicología en la Escuela de Medicina de la Universidad de Colorado, en Denver. Esto puede ser tan sencillo como decirse que quiere vivir más tiempo o tener una mejor relación con su esposo, niños o amistades. Pero cualquier cosa que sea, debe ser algo que es más importante para usted que el trabajo. Si no lo es, hay menos probabilidad que persevere con eso.

Cómo aprovechar bien su tiempo

La mayoría de nosotras realmente tenemos más tiempo libre de lo que pensamos. El problema es cómo lo usamos, dicen los expertos.

¡Ni lo piense!

Al final del día su jefe quiere que a usted invente una manera innovadora de resolver un problema que ha estado acosando a su compañía por meses. Pero parece que mientras usted más piensa en el problema, más difícil es tener ideas deslumbrantes.

Entonces deje de pensar tanto, dice Jeanne Murrone, Ph.D., una sicóloga clínica en el Centro para la Salud Mental, una clínica afiliada al Distrito Hospitalario Charlotte-Mecklenburg, en Charlotte, Carolina del Norte. Salga a caminar, haga un crucigrama o alguna otra actividad de tiempo libre. Lo milagroso del tiempo libre es que no sólo puede mantenerla joven, sino que también puede darle una ventaja creativa sobre sus compañeros de trabajo más intensos.

"Algunos de sus momentos más creativos pueden ocurrir cuando no está pensando acerca del trabajo," dice la doctora Murrone. "Es como hacer pan. Usted puede juntar todos los ingredientes, pero a menos que lo ponga a un lado por un rato y permita que la masa se levante y descanse, no va a ser un muy buen pan. El tiempo libre bien tiene el mismo propósito. Si usted deja un espacio en su vida para el tiempo libre, puede darse cuenta de que es más productiva y creativa."

En promedio, las mujeres tienen aproximadamente 41 horas de tiempo libre a la semana cuando no están trabajando, durmiendo o haciendo las tareas de la casa, dice William Danner de Leisure Trends, una compañía en Glastonbury, Connecticut que analiza cómo las personas que viven en los Estados Unidos utilizan su tiempo libre. Pero debido a que el número de actividades de tiempo libre —incluyendo los deportes como hacer *surf* a vela, pasatiempos como fabricar joyas y entretenimientos como la música *country*— están extendiéndose rápidamente, la cantidad de tiempo que podemos dedicar a una sola actividad va en disminución.

Pero una actividad —ver la televisión— está haciendo más estragos con nuestro tiempo libre de lo que usted podría sospechar. De hecho, una encuesta de Leisure Trends a más de 5.000 personas encontró que el 30 por ciento de nuestro tiempo libre —casi una de cada tres horas de nuestro tiempo libre— se gasta anclada enfrente de la pantalla. En comparación, alternar con otra gente y leer —la segunda y tercera actividades más populares— tomaron sólo el 8 y 6 por ciento respectivamente, del tiempo libre disponible todos los días.

Si usted quiere gastar su juventud haciendo cosas mejores, los expertos recomiendan el siguiente enfoque.

Apúntelo en su diario. Durante una semana, escriba lo que está haciendo cada 30 minutos incluyendo cosas como ducharse, preparar la comida y trabajar, dice Roger Mannell, Ph.D., un sicólogo y presidente del Departamento de Recreación y Estudios de Tiempo Libre en la Universidad de Waterloo, en Waterloo, Ontario. Al final de la semana échele una mirada a su diario y vea cuánto tiempo se gastó trabajando y cuánto tiempo libre tuvo.

Todos los días mida su satisfacción con cada actividad de tiempo libre. ¿Fue el tenis el martes más divertido que la fiesta el viernes? Si está llenando su tiempo con obligaciones que no encuentra gratificantes, debería hacer cambios.

Define la frontera. Es importante establecer líneas divisorias entre su trabajo y su vida hogareña. Por ejemplo, evite llevar trabajo a la casa en la noche. "Al hacer eso, le está haciendo saber tanto a su empleador como a su familia que su tiempo libre es tan importante para usted como llegar al trabajo a tiempo, cumplir con sus plazos y lo que sea que haga en su trabajo", dice la doctora Murrone.

Aprenda a cambiar de velocidad. Cree un espacio al final de su día —aunque sólo sea de 10 a 15 minutos— para estar sola con sus pensamientos y para que pueda hacer la transición entre el trabajo y la casa. Caminar, leer el periódico o escuchar música puede funcionar para usted. Para algunas personas, es sólo una cuestión de cambiarse de ropa, dice la doctora Lassen.

Cree su propia diversión. Lo que para una persona es tiempo libre para otra es trabajo. Conózcase a sí misma y lo que usted piensa que es diversión. Haga una lista de todos sus puntos fuertes y sus puntos débiles, de lo que usted disfruta y lo que usted detesta. Entonces haga su selección de tiempo libre basándose en esta lista. "La jardinería, por ejemplo, es diversión para algunas personas, pero para otras es un trabajo aburrido", dice el doctor Schafer. "Yo hago piragüismo en aguas rápidas y pienso que es alegre y muy divertido, pero para otros podría ser aterrador."

Sea imperfecta. Algunas personas evitan hacer ciertos tipos de actividades de tiempo libre porque no se sienten como que las pueden dominar. "Es importante reconocer que usted no necesita hacer todo bien", dice la doctora Murrone. "Escriba una historia pero no la edite, haga un dibujo pero no se lo enseñe a nadie así puede ser tan descuidada como quiera. Usted no tiene que ganar el torneo de golf, ni tiene que ganar la carrera, ni tiene que crear una pintura que es una obra de arte. No se trata de qué tan bien usted lo hace, sino si disfrutó haciéndolo."

VEGETARIANISMO

Vaya por lo verde

La comida latina sí que es tentadora. No importa de qué país sea, nuestros platillos realmente son riquísimos: ropa vieja, chuletas de puerco con plátanos (guineos) fritos, yuca con mojito, tamales, tortillas, frijoles refritos —la lista es extensa. Pero como todo en la vida, nuestra comida no es perfecta. Desafortunadamente, tiene una cantidad enorme de grasa —y si usted quiere mantenerse joven, un exceso de grasa en su dieta puede ser un desastre. Las dietas con alto contenido de grasa producen niveles altos de colesterol, presión arterial alta y problemas con el tracto digestivo. Y luego hay otros problemas como los muslos flácidos y las caderas crecientes de los cuales usted no tenía que preocuparse tan solo unos cuantos años atrás.

Si usted está buscando una forma de recuperar un poco de energía, perder peso y prevenir los problemas de salud serios en el futuro, a lo mejor le interesaría echarle un vistazo a un estilo de vida sin carne.

"Muy sencillamente, los vegetarianos tienden a ser personas más saludables", dice Reed Mangels, R.D., Ph.D., una consejera en nutrición en el Grupo de recursos vegetarianos, en Baltimore. "Uno obtiene la mayor parte de su grasa a través de los productos animales y mientras menos productos animales coma, probablemente se sentirá mejor."

Más delgada, más ligera, más animada

Estudio tras estudio muestra que las vegetarianas están mejor que sus hermanas las carnívoras. Los investigadores en Alemania, por ejemplo, encontraron que un grupo de 1.904 vegetarianos tenía aproximadamente la mitad del índice total de mortalidad de los comedores de carne a lo largo de un período de 11 años. El estudio alemán mostró cómo las mujeres vegetarianas sufrieron cerca de un 25 por ciento menos de casos de cáncer del tracto digestivo que los

584

que se podrían haber esperado de la gente que come dietas normales. También tenían menos de la mitad de la cantidad prevista de enfermedades del corazón.

Otros estudios realizados en budistas, adventistas del séptimo día, personas en países en desarrollo y en occidentales mostró que los vegetarianos generalmente tienen presión arterial más baja que los comedores de carne. Los vegetarianos también tienen menos riesgo de desarrollar diabetes.

Los vegetarianos también reportan menos problemas de estreñimiento y cálculos biliares. Y las personas que se cambian a las dietas vegetarianas dicen que simplemente se sienten mejor —con más energía y vigor— después de haber quitado la carne de sus dietas.

¿Qué es lo que está detrás de todos estos resultados mágicos? En primer lugar, los vegetarianos tienden a pesar menos, en parte porque comen menos grasa, dice la doctora Mangels, y en parte porque tienden a llevar estilos de vida más activos. Los vegetarianos también fuman menos. "Muchos de ellos han hecho un compromiso serio a largo plazo con su salud", dice la doctora Mangels. "Se refleja en sus estilos de vida, no solamente en la comida que comen."

La mayoría de los vegetarianos también tienen dietas que son mucho más bajas en grasa que la típica dieta norteamericana. En promedio, las personas que viven en los Estados Unidos consumen el 36 por ciento de sus calorías en forma de grasa.

Menos grasa, menos peso, más ejercicio y menos cigarrillos pueden tener un efecto beneficioso prolongado para su salud, dice la doctora Mangels. "Todo va en armonía", dice ella. "Usted come mejor, se siente mejor, su corazón puede estar más fuerte, por lo tanto se siente con ganas de hacer más. El resultado final es una mejor salud en general."

Incluso existe cierta evidencia de que las dietas vegetarianas pueden ayudar a combatir el dolor de la artritis. Los síntomas de la forma más común de artritis, osteoartritis, pueden aliviarse porque las personas con menos peso no ponen tanta presión en sus articulaciones como sus rodillas, dice la doctora Mangels.

Y las personas con artritis reumatoide pueden obtener alivio de una dieta vegetariana hecha a la medida de sus necesidades, informan investigadores en Noruega. Ellos pusieron a 27 personas con artritis reumatoide en un ayuno, luego introdujeron lentamente los alimentos vegetarianos en sus dietas, rechazando los alimentos que causaban un empeoramiento del dolor. Después de un año, aquellos en el estudio dijeron sentir menos sensibilidad en sus articulaciones, menos rigidez por la mañana y mayor fuerza cuando agarraban.

Cómo reducir su consumo de carne

¿Suena bien, eh? ¿Pero dejar la carne? ¿Para siempre?

Probablemente no por completo. Usted no tiene que dejar la carne completamente para cosechar la mayoría de los beneficios de salud del vegetarianismo. "Si puede limitar su consumo de carne a una pequeña porción, como un platillo

Un mundo sin carne

Cuando usted era una niña, aprendió todo acerca de los cuatro grupos básicos de alimentos: la carne, los lácteos, las verduras y el pan.

Al crecer, cambió a nuevos grupos: los bistecs, los licuados (batidos), las hojuelas de papa frita y el pastel de queso.

Puede ser el momento de reagrupar.

"No necesita comer carne para ser saludable", dice Suzanne Havala, R.D., una consejera en nutrición para el Grupo de recursos para vegetarianos y una dietista quien fue una de las redactoras del documento aclarando la posición de la Asociación dietética de los Estados Unidos con respecto al vegetarianismo.

Aquí hay un manual vegetariano rápido, cortesía de Havala. Y estos grupos de alimentos son:

Panes, cereales y pasta. Ocho o más porciones por día. Los ejemplos del tamaño de las porciones incluyen una rebanada de pan de grano entero, medio panecillo o *bagel*, media taza de cereal cocido, arroz o pasta y 1 onza (28 g) de cereal seco.

Verduras. Cuatro o más porciones por día. Los tamaños de las porciones son media taza de verduras cocidas o una taza crudas. Asegúrese de incluir una porción cruda rica en beta caroteno como las zanahorias.

Legumbres y sustitutos de carne. Dos o tres porciones por día. Los ejemplos del tamaño de las porciones incluyen media taza de frijoles (habichuelas) cocidos, 4 onzas (113 g) de tofu y 2 cucharadas de nueces o semillas.

Frutas. Tres o más porciones por día. Los tamaños de las porciones son un pedazo de fruta fresca, tres cuartos de taza de jugo y media taza de fruta cocida o enlatada.

Lácteos o alternativas. Opcional, dos a tres porciones por día. Los ejemplos del tamaño de las porciones son una taza de leche baja en grasa o descremada, una taza de yogur bajo en grasa o sin grasa, 1,5 onza (43 g) de queso bajo en grasa y una taza de leche de soja fortificada con calcio.

Huevos. Opcional, tres a cuatro yemas por la semana. Esto incluye los huevos en los alimentos horneados. Nota: los vegetarianos estrictos o vegetalistas no comen huevos. Los sustitutos de huevos funcionan bien en la mayoría de las recetas.

acompañante, probablemente estaría bien", dice Suzanne Havala, R.D., una consejera en nutrición para el Grupo de Recursos para Vegetarianos y una dietista quien fue una de las redactoras del documento aclarando la posición de la Asociación Dietética de los Estados Unidos con respecto al vegetarianismo.

Además, dice Havala, para cuando usted descubre la variedad que las comidas vegetarianas pueden ofrecer, posiblemente extrañará la carne menos y menos. "Por experiencia propia, la gente encuentra las comidas vegetarianas tan deliciosas que con gusto podrían olvidarse de la carne por completo."

Aquí hay algunos consejos para que usted empiece.

Tómese su tiempo. Usted no tiene que eliminar la carne roja de una sola vez, dice Havala. "Para algunas personas es más fácil de esa forma. Pero muchas otras prefieren reducir gradualmente hasta que dejan de comer carne después de unas pocas semanas o meses", dice ella.

Trate de empezar con un día sin carne por semana. ¿Qué tan difícil es eso? Tan difícil, dice Havala, como comer cereal y un pedazo de fruta para el desayuno, un sándwich de mantequilla de cacahuate (maní) y jalea con un pedazo de fruta para el almuerzo, y pasta mezclada con verduras cocidas al vapor y una ensalada para la cena.

Vaya aumentando a dos, después a tres o más días sin carne por semana. Al llegar a ese punto, usted puede fácilmente dar el salto al vegetarianismo total, si así lo desea.

Sírvase unos substitutos. Las tiendas de alimentos saludables y algunos supermercados venden productos llamados análogos de carne. Usted probablemente ha oído hablar de estos —las hamburguesas de tofu y los perros calientes sin carne son los más comunes. "Algunas personas necesitan ver algo que a primera vista parezca como un platillo de carne", dice la doctora Mangels. "Pruebe estos por un tiempo. Podrían ayudarla a hacer la transición."

No calcule sus comidas. La gente solía pensar que los vegetarianos necesitaban planear sus comidas hasta el último gramo para obtener la nutrición adecuada. "Si se asegura solamente de obtener las suficientes calorías para satisfacer sus necesidades de energía al comer una variedad de frutas, vegetales, granos y legumbres, debería estar bien", dice Havala.

Una cosa a evitar: escoger una comida favorita y comerla cinco veces por día. "El equilibrio es la clave", dice la doctora Mangels. "No coma solamente toronja por dos semanas sin interrupción, y después cambie a papas asadas al horno por medio mes."

Busque la B. Los vegetalistas —los vegetarianos estrictos que no comen productos animales incluyendo huevos o leche— deben estar seguros de tener suficiente B_{12}, una vitamina auxiliar en las funciones del sistema nervioso. La vitamina se encuentra principalmente en los productos animales y en suplementos. La Asignación Dietética Recomendada es de dos microgramos.

Si usted bebe leche baja en grasa, come queso bajo en grasa o se cocina una tortilla de huevos ya obtuvo todo lo que necesita. Pero si no hace esto, pruebe un cereal de grano entero o leche de soja.

Tire a la basura la comida basura. Ninguna dieta, sin carne o cualquier otra, necesita incluir mucha comida basura. "Para cosechar el mayor beneficio de la dieta vegetariana, limite o elimine los alimentos llenos de azúcar o grasa", dice Havala.

Deshágase de la grasa. La carne está cargada de grasa. Pero no es el único lugar donde usted encontrará esa diablita que viene en tres variedades: saturada, monoinsaturada y poliinsaturada. Para reducir su consumo de grasa, la doctora Mangels sugiere cocinar al vapor los alimentos, salteándolos en agua, caldo, jugo o vino y teniendo cuidado con el queso y la mayonesa. "Tampoco son una mala idea los aliños (aderezos) bajos en grasa", dice ella.

No se preocupe por las proteínas. La carne no es el único alimento lleno de proteínas. Usted obtendrá más que suficiente con una dieta vegetariana balanceada. "Hay bastante proteína en los granos, verduras y legumbres. Los platillos comunes sin carne como los burritos de frijoles (habichuelas), el chile vegetariano y las verduras fritas en poco aceite (estilo oriental) con arroz también están llenas de proteínas", dice Havala.

Ayúdese con la C. De nuevo, una dieta vegetariana balanceada proporciona la cantidad de hierro suficiente. Aunque la mejor fuente de hierro absorbible todavía se encuentra en la carne. Usted puede aumentar la absorción del hierro en las verduras tomando vitamina C. Havala sugiere comer una fuente de vitamina C en todas las comidas. Los alimentos altos en vitamina C incluyen los tomates, el brócoli, los melones, los pimientos y las frutas cítricas y los jugos.

No se acompleje por el calcio. Usted obtendrá suficiente calcio en una dieta vegetariana balanceada, dice la doctora Mangels. Si bebe leche y come quesos bajos en grasa, obtendrá lo que necesita. El calcio también se puede encontrar en las verduras rizadas, las semillas y nueces, la col rizada y el brócoli.

Salga sin miedo. "Usted no tiene que quedarse en casa para comer sus alimentos tan solo porque es una vegetariana", dice la doctora Mangels. "Puede comer afuera todas las veces que quiera. Solamente encuentre un lugar con un buena mesa de ensaladas y está lista." La mayoría de los restaurantes también, le servirán un plato de verduras cocidas al vapor si las pide.

"O pruebe un restaurante chino. Allí puede comer comida tras comida y ni siquiera pensar en extrañar la carne", agrega la doctora Mangels.

VITAMINAS
Y MINERALES

Las necesidades básicas de la vida

Sin fallar, usted come tres comidas completas al día. Empieza con el desayuno; tal vez usted se comerá unos huevos con chorizo y pan o una tortilla, después un almuerzo completo, y además una merienda por la tarde. Luego viene la cena: puede ser un bistec fino, arroz con gandules, tamales, carne de puerco, o algo no típico, como una pizza o hamburguesas de McDonald's. Lo cierto es que su dieta lleva todos los nutrientes necesarios, ¿no? No. Aunque usted coma esas tres comidas completas de carnes y vegetales y también meriendas o bocadillos, a su cuerpo le hacen falta complementos nutritivos, materiales esenciales para mantenerla joven y saludable, y vital.

Esos materiales esenciales son las vitaminas y los minerales, las herramientas que su cuerpo debe tener para satisfacer sus demandas diarias de trabajo y actividad. Esas maravillas microscópicas rejuvenecen y dan energía a sus células y hacen posible cada uno de los procesos del cuerpo.

Cuando están presentes, todo funciona como sobre ruedas. Pero cuando no lo están prepárese para un aterrizaje forzoso. Llevadas al extremo, las deficiencias en vitaminas y minerales pueden conducir a enfermedades desagradables como el escorbuto, la pelagra y el raquitismo —enfermedades temidas que causan los dientes flojos y las encías sangrantes, los huesos débiles y quebradizos, la piel y el cabello poco saludable e incluso la muerte.

Afortunadamente, las mujeres que viven en los Estados Unidos tienen una dieta lo suficientemente nutritivo como para mantener a esas enfermedades a

(continúa en la página 592)

LAS 13 VITAMINAS ESENCIALES

Aquí hay una tabla de requerimientos de vitaminas para las mujeres de 25 a 50 años de edad.

Vitamina	Consumo diario
Vitamina A	800 mcg. RE o 4.000 UI (1.300 mcg. RE o 6.500 UI si está embarazada o amamantando)
Vitaminas B	
Thiamin	1,1 mg. (1,5 mg. si está embarazada; 1,6 mg. si está amamantando)
Riboflabina	1,3 mg. (1,6 mg. si está embarazada; 1,8 mg. si está amamantando)
Niacina	15 mg. (17 mg. si está embarazada; 20 mg. si está amamantando)
Vitamina B_6	1,6 mg. (2,2 mg. si está embarazada; 2,1 mg. si está amamantando)
Folato	180 mcg. (400 mcg. si está embarazada; 280 mcg. si está amamantando)
Vitamina B_{12}	2 mcg. (2,2 mcg. si está embarazada; 2,6 mcg. si está amamantando)
Biotina	30 a 100 mcg.*
Ácido pantoténico	4 a 7 mg.*
Vitamina C	60 mg. (70 mg. si está embarazada; 95 mg. si está amamantando)
Vitamina D	200 UI o 5 mcg. (10 mcg. si está embarazada o amamantando)
Vitamina E	12 UI o 8 mg. alfa-TE (15 UI o 10 mg. alfa-TE si está embarazada; 18 UI o 12 mg. alfa-TE si está amamantando)
Vitamina K	65 mcg.

NOTA: Los valores diarios de consumo son las Asignaciones Dietéticas Recomendadas (RDAs, por sus siglas en inglés) a menos que se indique de otra manera.
*Valor es el consumo diario estimado como seguro y adecuado. No hay RDA para esta vitamina.

Beneficio rejuvenecedor	Fuentes alimenticias
Necesaria para la visión normal en luz tenue; mantiene la estructura normal y las funciones de las membranas mucosas; ayuda al crecimiento de los huesos, los dientes y la piel	Frutas y verduras amarillas-anaranjadas; verduras frondosas verde oscuro; leche fortificada; huevos
Metabolismo de carbohidratos; mantiene saludable al sistema nervioso	Carne de puerco; productos de grano integral y enriquecido; frijoles (habichuelas); nueces
Metabolismo de grasa, proteínas y carbohidratos; piel saludable	Productos lácteos; productos de grano integral y enriquecido
Metabolismo de grasa, proteínas y carbohidratos; función del sistema nervioso; necesario para el uso de oxígeno por las células	Carnes; aves; leche; huevos; productos de grano integral y enriquecido
Metabolismo de proteínas; necesario para el crecimiento normal	Carnes; aves; pescado; frijoles; granos; verduras frondosas verde oscuro
Desarrollo de los glóbulos rojos; crecimiento y reparación de los tejidos	Verduras frondosas verdes; naranjas; frijoles
Necesaria para el crecimiento de los tejidos, los glóbulos rojos, el sistema nervioso y la piel nuevos	Carne; aves; pescado; productos lácteos
Metabolismo de grasa, proteínas y carbohidratos	Se encuentra en cantidades pequeñas en muchos alimentos
Metabolismo de grasa, proteínas y carbohidratos	Productos de grano integral y enriquecido; verduras; carnes
Forma el colágeno; conserva las encías, los dientes y los vasos sanguíneos saludables	Frutas cítricas; pimientos; repollo; fresas; tomates
Absorción de calcio; crecimiento de los huesos y dientes	Luz del sol; leche fortificada; huevos; pescado
Protege a las células del daño	Aceites vegetales; verduras frondosas verdes; germen de trigo; productos de grano integral
Coagulación de la sangre	Repollo; verduras frondosas verdes

raya —en parte debido al hecho de que muchos de los alimentos que comemos, como los cereales, los panes y la leche, están fortificados con vitaminas y minerales. Pero aún es posible que usted no esté obteniendo todas las vitaminas que necesita especialmente si, como muchas mujeres, está tratando de perder unas cuantas libras o está demasiado ocupada y apenas puede comer algo a la carrera.

"A medida que envejecemos, nuestros requerimientos de ciertas vitaminas y minerales en realidad aumentan", dice Jeffrey Blumberg, Ph.D., director asociado del Centro de Investigación de la Nutrición Humana sobre el Envejecimiento del Departamento de Agricultura de los Estados Unidos, en la Universidad de Tufts, en Boston. "En general tendemos a comer menos alimentos en una base diaria. Así que si a su dieta ya le está faltando algo de ciertos nutrientes, al envejecer, existe la posibilidad de que esa deficiencia aumente, y de alguna manera su cuerpo pagará el precio por esto."

Los niveles bajos de vitaminas y minerales pueden conducir a una mayor susceptibilidad a la infección, a una curación más lenta, una capacidad mental disminuida y fatiga crónica, dicen los especialistas en nutrición. La conclusión es obvia: para verse, sentirse y desempeñarse en su nivel óptimo, usted no puede hacer que el escatimar sus vitaminas y minerales se transforme en un hábito.

Las vitaminas son vitales

Dentro de nuestros cuerpos, se llevan a cabo cientos de reacciones bioquímicas las 24 horas del día. Y al igual que las reacciones químicas en un laboratorio, estas reacciones químicas internas necesitan de catalizadores para facilitarlas y regularlas. Las vitaminas son compuestos químicos orgánicos que actúan como catalizadores. Cada una tiene su función específica —desde ayudar al crecimiento de los huesos y mantener saludable a la piel, hasta ayudar a las células en el procesamiento de la energía. Al carecer de sólo una vitamina, se puede poner en peligro cualquiera de las funciones vitales que dependan de esa vitamina.

Los especialistas en nutrición dividen las 13 vitaminas esenciales en dos grupos basándose en su conducta dentro del cuerpo. Vitaminas solubles en agua —vitamina C y las ocho vitaminas B (tiamina, riboflavina, niacina, B_6, ácido pantoténico, B_{12}, biotina y folato)— son compuestos de vida corta y actuación rápida que se almacenan en las partes acuosas de las células del cuerpo. Pero no por mucho tiempo. El cuerpo pone a estas vitaminas rápidamente a trabajar asistiendo a las células en las reacciones químicas y en el procesamiento de energía, y por lo general excretan cualquier exceso.

Las vitaminas solubles en grasa —A, D, E y K— se encuentran en las partes grasosas de las células y regulan una amplia variedad de procesos metabólicos. Estas tienden a ser almacenadas a largo plazo y el cuerpo las extrae a medida que las necesita.

Aunque muchos estudios reconocen al consumo de las vitaminas como un factor para disminuir el riesgo de las enfermedades crónicas, se han seleccionado a varias vitaminas por su capacidad para hacer más lenta o aun prevenir la aparición de las enfermedades relacionadas con la edad, como la enfermedad del corazón y el cáncer, y potencialmente hacer más lento el proceso mismo del envejecimiento. Estas vitaminas, C y E y betacaroteno (una substancia que el cuerpo convierte en vitamina A), se conocen como antioxidantes por su capacidad para neutralizar las partículas destructivas derivadas del oxígeno, las que se cree que inician muchos de los procesos de las enfermedades.

Los minerales son esenciales

Venimos originalmente de la tierra, y de la tierra extraemos una variedad de nutrientes para mantenernos en buenas condiciones de funcionamiento.

Al igual que las vitaminas, los minerales ayudan a mantener al cuerpo funcionando. Pero a diferencia de las vitaminas, estos son inorgánicos y el cuerpo no los metaboliza. En lugar de eso, actúan más como cubos de construcción, proveyendo estructura a los huesos y dientes, sirviendo como componentes importantes de la sangre, la piel y los tejidos y manteniendo equilibrados a los fluidos de nuestro cuerpo.

Hay dos categorías de minerales. Los minerales mayores —calcio, cloruro, magnesio, fósforo, potasio y sodio— se encuentran en cantidades grandes en el cuerpo y abundan en las fuentes alimenticias. Nosotras necesitamos grandes cantidades de estos minerales.

Los microminerales —cromo, cobre, fluoruro, yodo, hierro, manganeso, molibdeno, selenio y cinc— se encuentran en una cantidad mucho más pequeña en nuestros cuerpos y en nuestros alimentos y por ello, nuestra necesidad de ellos es más baja.

Algunos minerales se almacenan en el cuerpo, en reserva para reponer aquellos que perdemos a través de la orina y el sudor. Si no reponemos nuestras provisiones de minerales tan pronto como se reducen, corremos el riesgo de desarrollar tales enfermedades como la anemia por deficiencia de hierro y la osteoporosis, dos problemas serios de salud que afectan a millones de mujeres.

Las necesidades nutritivas de la mujer

Obtener las cantidades correctas de estos nutrientes esenciales requiere de planificación, y para facilitar la tarea, la Junta de Alimento y Nutrición del Consejo Nacional de Investigación estableció guías para el consumo de vitaminas y minerales. Se conocen con el nombre de Asignaciones Dietéticas Recomendadas (o *RDAs*, por sus siglas en inglés).

Las RDAs son la cantidad de nutrientes considerados como adecuados para la típica persona saludable. "Debido a que los niveles exceden las necesidades reales de la mayoría de las personas usted puede estar por debajo de las RDAs para un nutriente pero estar aún bien por encima del nivel de deficiencia", dice Paul R. Thomas, R.D., Ed.D, científico parte del personal con la Junta de

(continúa en la página 596)

LOS 15 MINERALES ESENCIALES

Aquí hay una tabla útil acerca de requerimientos de minerales importantes y microminerales para las mujeres de 25 a 50 años de edad.

Mineral	Consumo diario
Calcio	800 mg. (1.200 mg. si está embarazada o amamantando)
Cinc	12 mg. (15 mg. si está embarazada; 19 mg. si está amamantando)
Cloruro	750 mg.*
Cobre	1,5 a 3,0 mg.†
Cromo	50 a 200 mcg.†
Fluoruro	1,5 a 4,0 mg.†
Fósforo	800 mg. (1.200 mg. si está embarazada o amamantando)
Hierro	15 mg. (30 mg. si está embarazada; 15 mg. si está amamantando)
Magnesio	280 mg. (300 mg. si está embarazada; 355 mg. si está amamantando)
Manganeso	2,0 a 5,0 mg.†
Molibdeno	75 a 250 mcg.†
Potasio	2,000 mg.*
Selenio	55 mcg. (65 mcg. si está embarazada; 75 mcg. si está amamantando)
Sodio	500 mg.*
Yodo	150 mcg. (175 mcg. si está embarazada; 200 mcg. si está amamantando)

NOTA: Los valores diarios de consumo son las Asignaciones Dietéticas Recomendadas (RDAs, por sus siglas en inglés) a menos que se indique de otra manera.

Beneficio rejuvenecedor	Fuentes alimenticias
Huesos y dientes fuertes; función de los músculos y nervios; coagulación de la sangre	Productos lácteos; verduras frondosas verdes; sardinas con espinas; tofu
Curación de las heridas; crecimiento; apetito	Mariscos; carnes; nueces; legumbres
Ayuda a la digestión; funciona con sodio para mantener el equilibrio de los fluidos	Alimentos con sal
Formación de las células sanguíneas y el tejido conectivo	Granos; legumbres; mariscos
Metabolismo de carbohidratos	Verduras; granos integrales; levadura de cerveza
Refuerza el esmalte de los dientes	Agua fluorizada; pescado; té
Metabolismo de energía; se junta con el calcio para huesos y dientes más fuertes	Carne; aves; pescado; leche; frijoles
Lleva el oxígeno en la sangre; metabolismo de energía	Carne roja; pescado; aves; granos integrales; verduras frondosas verde oscuro; legumbres
Ayuda en el funcionamiento de los nervios y músculos; huesos fuertes	Frijoles (habichuelas); nueces; cocoa; granos; verduras verdes
Formación de los huesos y el tejido conectivo; metabolismo de grasa y carbohidratos	Espinaca; nueces; calabaza; té; legumbres
Metabolismo de nitrógeno	Granos y verduras sin procesar
Controla el equilibrio de los ácidos en el cuerpo; funciona con el sodio para mantener el equilibrio de los fluidos	Verduras; frutas; carnes; leche
Ayuda a la vitamina E a proteger las células y el tejido del cuerpo	Granos; carne; pescado; aves
Equilibrio de los fluidos; función del sistema nervioso	Sal; alimentos procesados; salsa de soja; condimentos
Mantiene el funcionamiento adecuado de la tiroides	Leche; granos; sal yodada

*Valor es el requerimiento mínimo estimado. No hay RDA para este mineral.
†Valor es el consumo diario estimado como seguro y adecuado. No hay RDA para este mineral.

Alimento y Nutrición de la Academia Nacional de Ciencias en Washington, D.C. "Generalmente caer por debajo de las RDAs no es peligroso, pero si su consumo es rutinariamente de 20 a 30 por ciento por debajo de las RDAs, con el tiempo se pueden desarrollar problemas de deficiencia."

Eso está muy bien para las mujeres que quieren evitar la anemia. ¿Pero y qué si usted quiere una salud superior? "Una cantidad de pruebas crecientes indican un vínculo directo entre la longevidad en aumento y la salud mejorada en general cuando ciertos consumos de vitaminas y minerales exceden las RDAs", dice el doctor Blumberg. "Esto sugiere que quizás las RDAs son inadecuadas para las necesidades cambiantes del adulto a medida que envejece."

Pero aun todo en exceso puede ser malo. "Las vitaminas y los minerales tomados en dosis extremadamente altas pueden ser tóxicos", advierte Diane Grabowski, R.D., educadora en nutrición en el Centro Pritikin de Longevidad, en Santa Mónica, California. "Pueden interferir con el funcionamiento de los órganos vitales como el corazón, el hígado o los riñones. O pueden producir cualquier cantidad de efectos secundarios inofensivos pero molestos como la acidez, la náusea o la urinación frecuente."

Hay una investigación en proceso para determinar los niveles exactos de cada vitamina y mineral necesarios para una salud óptima. Hasta que no se llegue a tales resultados, los médicos dicen que su meta debería ser alcanzar por lo menos el 100 por ciento de las RDAs para cada mineral y vitamina esenciales, especialmente si usted lleva una vida activa.

Los alimentos: nuestra mejor fuente

Actualmente, con la gama disponible de alimentos frescos y saludables, la mayoría de las mujeres no deberían tener ninguna dificultad para llegar al 100 por ciento de sus RDAs. "Una dieta bien balanceada que consista de una variedad de alimentos ricos en nutrientes fácilmente proporcionará todas las vitaminas y minerales que usted necesita, probablemente hasta más", dice Grabowski.

Aquí hay algunos consejos para obtener el contenido máximo de las vitaminas y los minerales de los alimentos que usted come, y por la mínima cantidad de calorías.

Vaya a lo básico. "Concéntrese en comer de los cinco grupos básicos de alimentos: frutas, verduras, carnes magras y legumbres, granos y cereales, y productos lácteos bajos en grasa o sin grasa", dice Grabowski. "Si usted come mucha comida basura o bocadillos (meriendas o *snacks*) que son inferiores nutritivamente, solamente le está dando a su cuerpo calorías vacías carentes de vitaminas y minerales."

Enfóquese en las frutas y las verduras. "Usted debería comer un mínimo de cinco porciones abundantes de frutas y verduras todos los días", dice Grabowski. "En la mayoría de los casos, mientras más oscuros y más vibrantes son los colores de las frutas y verduras mayor es su contenido de vitaminas y minerales." Dele color a su dieta con los favoritos de siempre tales como el cantaloup, las naranjas, los melocotones (duraznos), los tomates, la espinaca, los camotes (batatas dulces, *yams*) y las zanahorias. También pregúntele a su verdulero acerca de algunas de las frutas y verduras más exóticas para tener variedad. La mayoría de las frutas tropicales son ricas en vitaminas.

Cómaselas crudas o apenas cocidas. Al cocer los alimentos se les extraen o se destruyen muchas de las vitaminas y minerales, así que siempre que pueda, trate de comer las frutas, las verduras y los granos en su estado natural crudo o sin procesar o cocidos al mínimo.

Absténgase de hervirlas. Hervir tiende a extraer más vitaminas y minerales de los alimentos que otros métodos para cocinar, dice Grabowski. "Mientras menos tiempo se pasen en el horno, en la estufa o rodeados de agua caliente mejor." Ella recomienda cocinar al vapor o con el horno de microondas.

Atrape a los nutrientes. La exposición al aire puede robar las vitaminas y minerales del alimento. Lo mismo puede hacer la luz del sol cuando penetra en las botellas de vidrio o las envolturas de celofán. Grabowski recomienda usar envases herméticos y opacos. Para almacenar alimentos o jugos por largo tiempo, pruebe congelarlos. Esto conserva intactos a los nutrientes por un tiempo prolongado.

Cuídese de los medicamentos. Ciertas drogas y medicamentos sin receta pueden interferir con los depósitos de vitaminas y minerales en el cuerpo. La aspirina, los laxantes, los diuréticos, los antibióticos, los antidepresivos y los antiácidos pueden acelerar la excreción de algunas vitaminas y minerales o impedir su absorción. Si usted está tomando cualquier de estos medicamentos, consulte con su médico antes de dejarlos o probar con alternativas.

La verdad acerca de los suplementos

Si usted cree que se está quedando corta con sus RDAs, busque a un profesional en salud o nutrición quien pueda evaluar su dieta y decirle cuáles son los nutrientes que más puede necesitar. Pero no espere que los suplementos compensen completamente sus malos hábitos de comer; no será así. Si usted prueba los suplementos, el tomar niveles que excedan las RDAs debería hacerse sólo bajo la consulta de un médico.

Aquí hay algunas guías para seleccionar y usar los suplementos.

Vaya por las multi. Un suplemento seguro y benéfico sería el tipo de multivitaminas con minerales para tomar una diaria, dice Grabowski. Un suplemento así debería contener una mezcla de todos o la mayoría de las vitaminas y los minerales esenciales y contener el 100 por ciento de las RDAs en cada uno.

Cuidado con los suplementos individuales. En la mayoría de los casos, usted probablemente no necesita dosis adicionales de vitaminas y minerales específicos si ya está tomando una multivitamina y comiendo correctamente.

Las excepciones podrían ser si se encuentra bajo tratamiento médico por una deficiencia o si está buscando protección antioxidante al tomar vitaminas C, E y betacaroteno adicionales. De otra manera, evite los suplementos individuales, especialmente la vitamina A, la vitamina D y el hierro, dice el doctor Thomas. Estos nutrientes son tóxicos en dosis altas y pueden resultar en efectos secundarios tales como el vómito, la pérdida de cabello, las anormalidades en los huesos, la anemia, el daño cardiovascular, y las insuficiencias del hígado y renal.

Consuma bastante calcio. El calcio es vital para la fuerza de los huesos y para evitar la osteoporosis —la enfermedad del desgaste de los huesos que se les acerca sigilosamente a muchas mujeres después de la menopausia. Sin embargo, muchos estudios muestran que la mayoría de las mujeres no consumen lo suficiente —los 800 miligramos al día recomendados antes de la menopausia y los 1.000 miligramos al día de ahí en adelante. Esa es la razón por la cual el suplemento de calcio se le recomienda a las mujeres como una protección adicional contra la pérdida de los huesos.

Los suplementos de calcio de más fácil absorción son aquellos hechos con citrato de calcio, dice la doctora Margo Denke, profesora asistente de medicina en el Centro Médico de la Universidad de Texas Sudoeste, en el Centro de Dallas para la Nutrición Humana y miembro del comité de nutrición de la Asociación del Corazón de los Estados Unidos. Estos se absorben más fácilmente por el cuerpo que los suplementos hechos con carbonato de calcio, dice ella. El citrato de calcio se puede encontrar en algunos suplementos sin receta o en los jugos de naranja fortificados con calcio. Sólo revise las etiquetas.

Pero usted tal vez prefiere obtener su calcio de las pastillas antiácidas baratas sin receta hechas de carbonato de calcio. Es mejor tomarlas con las comidas, dice el doctor Clifford Rosen, director del Centro Maine para Investigación y Educación de la Osteoporosis, en Bangor. El ácido producido por su cuerpo cuando usted come descompone el carbonato de calcio y permite su absorción, dice él.

Algunas marcas de antiácidos como *Gelusil*, *Maalox* y *Mylanta*, no se recomiendan para usarse como suplementos regulares debido a que también contienen aluminio. Sus mejores opciones son *Tums* o *Rolaids*, ambos sin aluminio.

Pruebe los genéricos. Las marcas genéricas y las de las tiendas típicamente son comparables en calidad a las marcas reconocidas, dice el doctor Thomas. De hecho, los genéricos a veces están hechos por los mismos fabricantes de las marcas más conocidas pero cuestan bastante menos. Su farmacéutico debería poder decirle si un genérico vale la pena.

Olvídese de los "super suplementos". Usted puede ver "*high potency*" (alta potencia) o "*extra strength*" (fuerza extra) en las etiquetas. Estos productos por lo regular contienen niveles de vitaminas y minerales que exceden por mucho las RDA y pueden ser peligrosos, dice el doctor Thomas. O usted puede terminar simplemente por excretar el exceso en cuyo caso está desperdiciando su dinero.

Dígale no a las artimañas. Las frases tales como *"antistress formula"* (fórmula antiestrés) son falaces, dice el doctor Thomas, y aunque *"time-released"* (liberadas con el tiempo) y *"effervescent"* (efervescente) son descripciones legítimas, en algunos suplementos estas cualidades pueden no ser importantes. Por ejemplo, efervescente en el calcio puede ser útil pero no se necesita en la vitamina C. Verifique con su médico o profesional en nutrición.

Acuérdese que una vitamina es una vitamina. También ignore los argumentos acerca de los ingredientes naturales u orgánicos, dice el doctor Thomas. No hay una definición estándar de *natural*. De hecho algunos suplementos "naturales", pueden contener principalmente nutrientes sintéticos.

Evite las dosis múltiples. Si la etiqueta le dice que tome más de una diaria, verifique la cantidad total para ver cómo se compara con las RDAs. Si las excede demasiado, puede ser una estratagema para hacerle gastar a usted más dinero, dice el doctor Thomas.

Tráguelas con las comidas. Como regla general, los suplementos serán absorbidos por el cuerpo más eficientemente si se toman durante una comida en vez de con el estómago vacío, dice el doctor Thomas. También se descompondrán mejor si se toman con agua o alguna otra bebida.

Verifique la fecha de expiración. Cuando compre los suplementos, asegúrese de que la fecha de expiración esté en la etiqueta. Si la fecha ya pasó o está muy cercana, encuentre una botella con una vida más larga en el estante.

Guárdelos en un lugar fresco y seco. La luz, el calor y la humedad pueden quitarle potencia a los suplementos. Debido a esto, probablemente el mejor lugar para guardar sus suplementos es un gabinete en la cocina, lejos del calor de la estufa, en lugar de sobre el alféizar de la ventana o el botiquín de medicinas en el baño. Otro buen lugar para guardarlos es el refrigerador. Trate de usar un envase no transparente. Y siempre cierre la tapa apretadamente.

YOGA

Encuentre paz en el caos

Usted busca un oasis, un lugar tranquilo donde se pueda restablecer después de un día de plazos imposibles, personas imposibles y sueños imposibles.

Para muchas mujeres la respuesta es yoga. Si usted busca algo que la dejará sintiéndose relajada, ágil, con confianza en usted misma y más juvenil, el yoga podría ser lo ideal para usted también.

"Son tantas las cosas que usted hace en la vida las cuales usan energía", dice Alice Christensen, fundadora y directora ejecutiva de la Asociación de yoga de los Estados Unidos, en Sarasota, Florida. "Pero el yoga proporciona una constante fuente de energía. Cuando usted practica yoga, realmente tiene más vitalidad y vigor. De esa manera, yo realmente creo que la puede ayudar a sentirse más joven."

Salud nueva derivada de un arte antiguo

El yoga existe desde hace miles de años. Traducido literalmente significa "unión". Quienes abogan por el yoga creen que la mente, el espíritu y el cuerpo son inseparables. Asimismo, creen que los ejercicios llamados *asanas*, o poses, pueden ayudar en la flexibilidad, el relajamiento, la fuerza creciente y la paz interior.

Aunque hay tantas como ocho ramas diferentes de yoga, la mayoría de las mujeres occidentales se enfocan en el *hatha yoga*. Este yoga destaca el relajamiento a través de asanas y técnicas de respiración y a menudo se enseña en clases en sus *YMCA*s (Asociaciones Cristianas para Hombres Jóvenes) o *YWCA*s (Asociaciones Cristianas para Mujeres Jóvenes) locales, o en clubes de gimnasia.

El hatha yoga no es un ejercicio aeróbico. Sin embargo, los estudios muestran que puede ayudarle a calmar su cuerpo y mente de muchas maneras.

Los beneficios más obvios parece que se logran al reducir el estrés y mejorar el estado de ánimo. Un estudio a 170 estudiantes universitarios mostró que aquellos que toman clases de yoga para principiantes, después de la clase tenían de menos tensión, depresión, ira, fatiga y confusión que antes. Los sentimientos reportados por los estudiantes fueron similares a los de otros que habían comenzado actividades más extenuantes como nadar. Según el estudio, los estudiantes empezaron a notar una reducción del estrés después de tomar su primera clase.

Las técnicas de respiración del yoga también pueden ayudar a las personas con asma. Un estudio británico a 18 pacientes mostró que la respiración del yoga podía reducir los síntomas del asma, aunque no eliminarlos. Algunos médicos ahora recetan yoga como parte de la terapia para ayudar a sus pacientes asmáticos a lograr mayor autocontrol sobre sus dificultades respiratorias.

Christensen dice que el yoga puede ser tremendamente útil para las personas con dolor de espalda, siempre y cuando sigan los principios del yoga de estirarse lentamente y sólo tanto como el cuerpo quiere. Y ella dice que también puede ayudar a las personas con artritis. Aunque hay pocos estudios que vinculan el yoga con la artritis, Christensen dice que muchos de sus estudiantes, con la artritis común relacionada con el envejecimiento, reportan sentirse más flexibles y con menos dolor después de comenzar una clase de yoga. Christensen advierte, no obstante, que las personas con artritis reumatoide del tipo que inutiliza los huesos no deberían intentar los ejercicios de yoga cuando sus articulaciones están inflamadas y doloridas.

Además de las ventajas físicas del yoga, hay un aspecto meditativo difícil de medir con un estetoscopio. "El yoga hace callar la plática continua en su mente", dice Christensen. "Usted se enfrenta constantemente con los pensamientos dispersos, las voces de otras personas, las emociones, los deseos. Y después de un tiempo ya ni siquiera los nota."

El yoga puede despejar eso de su mente. "Le ayuda a mejorar su concentración y le permite hacerse más observadora de sus pensamientos, sentimientos y reacciones", dice Christensen. "Una buena parte del tiempo andamos por el mundo como la bola de acero en un flípper, rebotando de una cosa a la otra. La meditación yoga aumenta la conciencia de las cosas para que usted pueda tomar decisiones más conscientes en su vida."

Cómo empezar a practicar yoga

Suena bien, ¿no cree? Aquí hay algunos consejos para ayudarla a cosechar los considerables beneficios del yoga.

Respire profundamente. El yoga comienza con respirar, algo en lo que rara vez pensamos. La mayoría de nosotras aspiramos desde nuestro pecho respirando rápida y poco profundamente. Los practicantes de yoga, sin embargo, respiran desde sus diafragmas, el músculo grande en forma de domo que se arquea a través de la base de los pulmones. Cuando una persona aspira profundamente, el diafragma se expande, permitiendo más aire en los lóbulos inferiores de los pulmones.

Para comenzar, siéntese cómodamente en el piso, apoyando sus caderas en un cojín firme. O se puede sentar en la orilla de una silla. Coloque las manos en su barriga, un poco más abajo del ombligo. Esta es el área, no su pecho, que

Venza el estrés con el escáner

Ay, ¡qué día! Todo desde se levantó esta mañana le ha ido mal. Ahora usted tiene un dolor de cabeza por la tensión, el cuello que palpita y los dolores punzantes en la espalda y los hombros.

Pero tranquila, no está todo perdido. Un método de meditación efectivo para hacerse cargo del dolor es un ejercicio tipo yoga llamado el escáner del cuerpo. Puede ayudarla a concentrarse en esos dolores y hacer que lentamente desaparezcan de su cuerpo. Enseñado a las pacientes del Centro Médico de la Universidad de Massachusetts, el escáner del cuerpo es una manera excelente de identificar y aliviar los puntos de su propio estrés.

Aquí está cómo hacerlo.

Recuéstese boca arriba, cierre los ojos y simplemente respire. Después de unos cuantos minutos empiece a concentrarse en los dedos de su pie izquierdo. Note las sensaciones: ¿están calientes, fríos, cansados o acalambrados? Después de un minuto o algo así imagine soltar el peso de sus dedos, sintiendo que se derriten en el piso.

Ahora concéntrese en su pierna izquierda, al practicar la misma rutina con su pie, tobillo, pantorrilla, rodilla, muslo y cadera. Luego haga lo mismo con su pierna derecha. Muévase hacia arriba por su torso haciendo una pausa en la pelvis, la parte baja de la espalda, la barriga, la parte de arriba de la espalda, el pecho y los hombros. En sus brazos, muévase hacia los dedos de ambas manos, el dorso de las manos, las palmas, las muñecas, los antebrazos, los codos, la parte de arriba de los brazos y los hombros. Finalmente, muévase hacia el cuello, luego a su cabeza, prestando atención en su mentón, boca, nariz, ojos y cejas, frente, orejas y cuero cabelludo.

La Asociación de Yoga de los Estados Unidos, en Sarasota, Florida recomienda un ejercicio parecido de relajamiento completo, ejercicio que se introduce justo antes de la meditación, aunque cuyo plan va desde la cabeza hacia abajo y después hacia arriba de la parte de atrás del cuerpo.

"El beneficio sutil de practicar este tipo de ejercicio es que usted se volverá más consciente de su cuerpo en una base diaria", dice Alice Christensen, fundadora y directora ejecutiva de la Asociación de Yoga de los Estados Unidos. "Entonces, aun cuando usted esté sentada en su escritorio en el trabajo, notará '¡Ah!, mi estómago está tenso' o 'estoy apretando los dientes.'"

"El simple acto de tomar conciencia del área tensa la ayudará a aflojar la tensión."

debería expandirse cuando usted inhala. Recuerde siempre respirar hacia afuera y hacia adentro por la nariz. Cuando inhale, sienta como sus manos se elevan. Cuando exhala, contraiga su barriga. Respire suave y regularmente. Después de unas cuantas respiraciones, coloque sus manos en las piernas y continúe respirando con los ojos cerrados, concentrándose en el sonido de su respiración.

Idealmente, usted siempre debería respirar desde su diafragma todo el tiempo —en el trabajo, en la casa, en el carro, donde sea. Christensen dice que esto la ayuda a tener más oxígeno en su sistema, haciéndola más alerta. También se encontrará respirando a un paso más relajado de aproximadamente 10 a 14 veces por minuto en lugar de las típicas 16 a 18 veces. Recuerde, siempre respire por la nariz.

Encuentre una buena clase. Muchos lugares ofrecen clases de yoga, pero no todas las clases son iguales. Christensen sugiere buscar una instructora que practique yoga diariamente y quien ve a su propia instructora de yoga regularmente. Pídale recomendaciones a la instructora. Tome una clase de prueba antes de invertir un tiempo prolongado o dinero. Y si usted tiene problemas específicos, como problemas de la espalda o artritis, asegúrese de encontrar una instructora que individualice la instrucción para usted.

Establezca su propio paso. El yoga no es una competencia. No se supone que usted deba estirarse más, meditar más o respirar más que sus amigas o las otras personas en la clase que practican yoga.

"Por lo menos, usted debe saber que no debería competir", dice Martin Pierce, director del Programa Pierce, un estudio de yoga en Atlanta. "Si usted voltea para ver a las demás mientras que piensa que lo debería hacer tan bien como ellas lo hacen, va a crearse más estrés." Dirija su atención hacia adentro, dice Christensen. "Preste atención en sus propias experiencias y logrará los resultados más perdurables."

Póngase a posar. Muchos de los estiramientos del yoga, o asanas, son fáciles para los principiantes, dice Christensen.

Recuerde: no presione a su cuerpo. Estírese lenta y acompasadamente. No rebote. Y haga solamente tanto como su cuerpo le permita. "Ir muy lejos puede lesionarla. Sea amiga de su cuerpo", dice Christensen.

Siempre consulte con su médico antes de empezar a practicar yoga o cualquier programa de ejercicios.

Persevere en esto. Usted puede empezar a sentirse mejor después de una sola sesión de yoga, pero no se quede allí. "Las personas no pueden esperar beneficiarse mucho con el yoga sin comprometerse con éste", dice Jon Kabat-Zinn, Ph.D., director de la Clínica de Reducción de Estrés en el Centro Médico de la Universidad de Massachusetts, en Worcester.

"La práctica de yoga debería ser regular, diariamente si es posible", dice Christensen. "Por lo menos, si usted quiere ver los resultados, requiere tres ejercicios y unos cuantos minutos de respiración y meditación. Esto puede tomarle tan poco como 15 minutos. Si se encuentra con ganas de practicar más, le bastará con una hora al día. Lo importante es disfrutar lo que hace.

(continúa en la página 606)

Yoga para principiantes

Si usted está interesada en intentar el yoga, estas cuatro poses son una buena manera de empezar. Recuerde: vaya a su propio paso y no se estire más allá del punto que le sea cómodo.

La Pose del Árbol. *Esta es una pose de equilibrio para mejorar el porte, la postura y la concentración. Párese con los pies paralelos. Cambie el peso a su pierna derecha y coloque el talón de su pie izquierdo contra el tobillo derecho. Sosténgase de una pared o silla para apoyo si lo necesita. Levante despacio el pie izquierdo hacia arriba, ayudándose con su mano libre, hasta que el pie alcance la parte interior de su muslo derecho. Coloque los brazos a los lados, entonces levántelos lentamente sobre la cabeza tan rectos como sea posible con las palmas juntas. Relaje su estómago y la respiración. Mire fijamente a un punto para equilibrio. Mantenga la posición por varios segundos o tanto como pueda cómodamente. Luego baje despacio y repita en el lado opuesto.*

El Triángulo que Gira. *Este ejercicio hace más flexibles la espalda, las caderas y las piernas y puede ayudar a aliviar la depresión. Párese con sus pies apuntando hacia adelante y tan separados como pueda pararse cómodamente. Aspire y levante los brazos hacia afuera y hacia los lados, entonces suelte la respiración y gire hacia la izquierda. Agarre la parte exterior de su tobillo izquierdo con la mano derecha, extienda el brazo izquierdo recto hacia arriba con los dedos flexionados ligeramente y mire su pulgar izquierdo. Mantenga la posición por sólo un momento, luego aspire y regrese a estar parada con los brazos extendidos. Exhale y repita con la pierna derecha. Estírese tres veces con cada pierna.*

Pose del Sol Sentado. *Este ejercicio hace más flexibles la espalda y las piernas, masajea los órganos internos y mejora la circulación. Siéntese en el piso con las piernas extendidas y los dedos de los pies hacia su cara (arriba). Aspire y levante los brazos a los lados y por encima de la cabeza. Estírese y mire hacia arriba (abajo).*

Luego meta la cabeza, empiece a exhalar y lentamente inclínese hacia adelante tanto como pueda sin esforzarse (arriba). Agárrese bien las piernas hasta donde alcance, flexione los codos y jale suavemente la parte superior de su cuerpo para abajo hacia las piernas (abajo). Use los brazos para jalar, no los músculos de la espalda. Mantenga la posición por unos cuantos segundos. Aspire y alce los brazos otra vez por encima de la cabeza. Entonces exhale y baje sus brazos a los lados. Repita dos veces más.

(continúa)

Yoga para principiantes —continuado

La Pose del Bote. *Este es un ejercicio excelente para fortalecer la espalda y mejorar la postura. Acuéstese boca abajo con sus brazos extendidos hacia adelante y su frente sobre el piso (arriba). Exhale completamente, luego aspire al levantar las piernas, los brazos y la cabeza todo al mismo tiempo, mirando hacia arriba (abajo). Exhale y baje el cuerpo. Repita dos veces más.*

Siga con sus sesiones de ejercicio. El yoga para principiantes no es un ejercicio aeróbico. Christensen recomienda que usted continúe andando en bicicleta, caminando, corriendo o haciendo alguna otra actividad que le proporcione a su corazón una sesión de ejercicio. "Piense en el yoga como una dimensión agregada a su programa de estar en buena condición física", dice ella. "Nunca es aburrido porque además de ofrecer los beneficios físicos de agilidad, salud y fuerza, agrega significado a su vida."

FUENTES Y CRÉDITOS

"¿Cuánto vivirá usted?" en la página 12 está adaptado del libro *Health Risks* (Riesgos de la salud) por el doctor Elliot J. Howard. Copyright © 1986 por el doctor Elliot J. Howard y Susan A. Roth. Reimpreso con autorización.

"¿Está usted en riesgo de glaucoma?" en la página 72 está adaptado de *How's Your Vision? Family Home Eye Test* (¿Cómo tiene la vista? La prueba casera de vista para la familia) por Prevent Blindness America. Copyright © 1991 por Prevent Blindness America. Reimpreso por autorización.

"¿Se está acumulando el estrés?" en la página 180 esta adaptado de *Is It Worth Dying For?* (¿Vale la pena morir por eso?) por el doctor Robert S. Eliot y Dennis L. Breo. Copyright © 1984 por el doctor Robert S. Eliot y Dennis L. Breo. Utilizado con la autorización de Bantam Books, una división de la casa editorial Bantam Doubleday Dell Publishing Group, Inc.

"¿La está desgastando el trabajo?" en la página 182 es del Instituto del Estrés de los Estados Unidos.

"Una solución a la mano" en página 185 está reimpreso con la autorización del Putnam Berkley Group del libro *The 15-Minute Executive Stress Relief Program* (El programa ejecutivo de 15 minutos para aliviar el estrés) por Greg Herzog y Craig Masback. Copyright © 1992 por Herzog Body Tech, Inc. Reimpreso con el permiso de Greg Herzog y Craig Masback.

"¿Se encuentra usted entre las garras del alcohol?" en la página 290 se adaptó de la *American Journal of Psychiatry*, (La Revista Norteamericana de Siquiatría), volumen 127, N° 12, 1655, junio de 1971. Copyright © 1971 por la Asociación Siquiátrica de los Estados Unidos. Reimpreso con autorización.

La tabla en "¿Después de todo, cuál es su peso saludable?" en la página 345 es del Departamento de Agricultura de los EE.UU. y del Departamento de Salud y Servicios Humanos de los Estados Unidos.

"¿Usted generaliza o detalla?" en la página 426 está reimpreso con la autorización de Rawson Associates, una editorial de la casa editorial Macmillan Publishing Company de *Thinking Better* (Pensar mejor) por David Lewis, Ph.D., y James Greene, M.A. Esta reimpresión está hecha a base de un acuerdo con David Lewis, a cargo de la Joan Daves Agency como agente del autor.

RECURSOS DE LA SALUD

A continuación brindamos una lista de organizaciones que proveen información en español sobre varios temas de la salud, organizado por tema. Algunas dan información por el teléfono, otras mandan folletos gratis en español por la correspondencia si les escriben.

Cáncer

National Cancer Institute
(Instituto Nacional de Cáncer)
Cancer Information Service
31 Center Drive, Room 10A-16
Bethesda, MD 20892
Horas: Lunes a viernes, 9 a.m. hasta 4:30 p.m., EST (hora oficial del este de los EE.UU.)
Provee folletos gratis, recomendaciones para mamografías y otra información general.

YM-E National Breast Cancer Organization,
212 West Van Buren Street, Fifth floor
Chicago, IL 60607
Ofrece folletos gratis en español con información general sobre el cáncer de mama, y también da recomendaciones nacionales para mamografías.

Cuidado Prenatal

National Hispanic Prenatal Care Hotline
(Línea Directa Hispana para el Cuidado Prenatal), 1-800-504-7081
Horas: Lunes a viernes 9 a.m. hasta 6 p.m., EST (hora oficial del este de los EE.UU.)
Representantes contestan preguntas acerca del cuidado prenatal.

Diabetes

American Diabetes Association (Asociación de la Diabetes de los Estados Unidos)
Attn: Customer Service
1660 Duke Street
Alexandria, VA 22314
Ofrece folletos gratis en español sobre la diabetes tipo I y tipo II e información sobre la nutrición.

Drogodependencia
National Clearinghouse for Alcohol and Drug Information
P.O. Box 2345
Rockville, MD 20847-2345
Esta organización provee información general sobre el abuso de drogas y del alcohol.

Envejecimiento
National Institute on Aging Information Center
(El Centro de Información del Instituto Nacional sobre el Envejecimiento)
P.O. Box 8057
Gaithersburg, MD 20898-8057
Envía folletos gratis sobre el proceso del envejecimiento.

Osteoporosis
Osteoporosis and Related Bone Diseases, National Resource Center
(Centro Nacional de Recursos de Osteoporosis y Enfermedades
de los Huesos Relacionadas)
1150 17th Street, NW, Suite 500
Washington, DC 20036-4603
Envía folletos sobre la osteoporosis y otras enfermedades de los huesos.

Salud Cardiovascular (Del Corazón)
American Heart Association
(La Asociación del Corazón de los Estados Unidos)
7272 Greenville Avenue
Dallas, TX 75231-4596
*Brinda folletos gratuitos en español sobre nutrición, ejercicio, fumar, derrames cerebrales
y ataques al corazón.*

Salud Femenina (General)
National Latina Institute for Reproductive Health
(Instituto Nacional Latina para la Salud Reproductora)
1200 New York Avenue NW, Suite 300
Washington, DC 20005
*Ofrece información sobre temas generales de la salud femenina y un boletín bilingüe de la
salud que se publica cada tres meses.*

American College of Obstetricians and Gynecologists Resource Center
(Centro de Recursos del Colegio Norteamericano de Obstetras y Ginecólogos)
P.O. Box 96920
Washington, DC 20090-6920
Provee folletos gratis sobre temas de salud femenina como embarazos y anticonceptivos.

Salud Mental y Emocional
National Mental Health Consumers' Self-Help Clearinghouse
1211 Chestnut Street
Suite 1000
Philadelphia, PA 19107
Provee información sobre trastornos mentales.

Office of Scientific Information, National Institute of Mental Heath
(Oficina de Información Científica, Instituto Nacional de Salud Mental)
5600 Fishers Lane, Room 7C-02, MSC 8030
Bethesda, MD 20832
Envía folletos gratis sobre los siguientes temas: depresión, ataques de pánico, esquizofrenia, y otros trastornos mentales y emocionales.

Temas Generales de Salud
National Coalition of Hispanic Health and Human Services Organizations
(COSSHMO)
1501 Sixteenth Street NW
Washington, DC 20036
Brinda información gratis sobre varios temas de salud, entre ellos VIH/SIDA, cáncer cervical, y cáncer de mama.

Amigas Latinas en Acción Pro-Salud
240 A Elm Street Third Floor
Somerville MA 02144
Ofrece información sobre los anticonceptivos, el SIDA, el uso de condones, nutrición, y temas de salud femenina.

SIDA y VIH
CDC National AIDS Hotline
(Línea Directa Nacional del SIDA del Centro para el Control
de las Enfermedades)
1-800-344-7432
Horas: 8 a.m. hasta 2 a.m. todos los días
Representantes contestan preguntas sobre el SIDA.

American Red Cross, Hispanic HIV/AIDS Education Program
(Programa de Educación sobre VIH/SIDA para los Hispanos)
8111 Gatehouse Road
Falls Church, VA 22042
Provee información sobre la comunicación entre familia sobre el SIDA y el VIH.

ÍNDICE DE TÉRMINOS

Los números de páginas subrayados indican que el texto se ubica dentro de los cuadros. Las referencias presentadas en **negrilla** indican las ilustraciones. Se indican los nombres de los medicamentos debidamente recetados por un médico a través del símbolo "Rx".

GUÍA MÉDICA DE REMEDIOS CASEROS

Tapa dura $29.95
739 páginas

El famoso bestséller, traducido en 6 idiomas y con más de 10 millones de ejemplares vendidos en el mundo entero. Contiene más de 2.000 remedios caseros para 138 malestares y problemas comunes de la salud, todos comprobados por médicos.

LAS HIERBAS QUE CURAN

Tapa dura $29.95
559 páginas

La guía esencial del poder curativo de las medicinas naturales. Aprenda cómo usar las 100 hierbas medicinales más potentes del mundo para tratar a más de 200 malestares y enfermedades. También encontrará instrucciones para la preparación de infusiones, herbarios, decocciones y mucho más.

LOS ALIMENTOS QUE CURAN

Tapa dura $29.95
511 páginas

Descubra cuáles comidas pueden contrarrestar y hasta curar 30 enfermedades comunes. Este libro brinda una plétora de recetas ricas y nutritivas más información importante sobre vitaminas y minerales.

GUÍA MÉDICA DE REMEDIOS CASEROS II

Tapa dura $29.95
622 páginas

La continuación del bestséller *Guía médica de remedios caseros*, con más de 1.200 NUEVOS consejos para mejorar y tratar cientos de problemas de la salud.

Si le interesa inspeccionar uno de estos libros gratis por 21 días, favor de llamar al 1-800-424-5152.

ENCICLOPEDIA DE LA SALUD Y EL BIENESTAR EMOCIONAL DE LA MUJER

Tapa dura $29.95
639 páginas

Combina las historias personales y emocionantes de cientos de mujeres con remedios caseros y consejos brindados por doctoras y expertas en la salud. Desde la autoestima hasta las venas varicosas, este libro inspirador abarca todos los temas claves de salud que afectan a la mujer moderna con un toque tanto práctico como personal.

GUÍA COMPLETA DE MEDICAMENTOS Y REMEDIOS NATURALES

Tapa dura $29.95
745 páginas

Elija los tratamientos más eficaces para su familia. Contiene más de 2.000 asombrosos secretos curativos de los médicos. Infórmese sobre hierbas, alimentos, vitaminas y medicamentos para conocer sus efectos secundarios y su interacción; además, encuentre las curas para más de 300 enfermedades con el exclusivo localizador de remedios.

EL ABC DE LOS SÍNTOMAS: SUS CAUSAS Y CURAS

Tapa dura $29.95
741 páginas

Aprenda fácilmente a interpretar las señales que su cuerpo le envía, y también 1.490 maneras de responder a esas señales ANTES de que necesite un médico. Además, aproveche de los cientos de consejos prácticos para prevenir y curar enfermedades.

VIVIR BIEN CON POCA GRASA

Tapa dura $29.95
502 páginas

El primer libro en español que explica cómo podemos eliminar la grasa de nuestra dieta y nuestros cuerpos para perder peso y mejorar tanto nuestra salud como la de nuestra familia. Brinda consejos prácticos, ejercicios y 100 recetas deliciosas bajas en grasa en un programa completo y comprobado científicamente.